Third Edition

D0927722

INTERNATIONAL
F I N A N C I A L
MANAGEMENT

C A N A D I A N   P E R S P E C T I V E S

Donald J.S. Brean
Rotman School of Management
University of Toronto

Cheol S. Eun
Georgia Institute of Technology

Bruce G. Resnick
Wake Forest University

McGraw-Hill
Ryerson

International Financial Management
Third Edition

Copyright © 2014, 2008, 2005 by McGraw-Hill Ryerson Limited. Copyright © 2012, 2009, 2007, 2004, 2001, 1998 by McGraw-Hill Education LLC. All rights reserved. No part of this publication may be reproduced or transmitted in any form or by any means, or stored in a data base or retrieval system, without the prior written permission of McGraw-Hill Ryerson Limited, or in the case of photocopying or other reprographic copying, a licence from The Canadian Copyright Licensing Agency (Access Copyright). For an Access Copyright licence, visit www.accesscopyright.ca or call toll free to 1-800-893-5777.

Statistics Canada information is used with the permission of Statistics Canada. Users are forbidden to copy the data and redisseminate them, in an original or modified form, for commercial purposes, without permission from Statistics Canada. Information on the availability of the wide range of data from Statistics Canada can be obtained from Statistics Canada's Regional Offices, its World Wide Web site at www.statcan.gc.ca, and its toll-free access number 1-800-263-1136.

The Internet addresses listed in the text were accurate at the time of publication. The inclusion of a Web site does not indicate an endorsement by the authors or McGraw-Hill Ryerson, and McGraw-Hill Ryerson does not guarantee the accuracy of the information presented at these sites.

ISBN-13: 978-1-25-907543-8
ISBN-10: 1-25-907543-5

3 4 5 6 7 8 9 WEB 1 9 8 7 6

Printed and bound in Canada.

Care has been taken to trace ownership of copyright material contained in this text; however, the publisher will welcome any information that enables them to rectify any reference or credit for subsequent editions.

Director of Product Management: Rhondda McNabb
Senior Product Manager: Kimberley Veevers
Marketing Manager: Jeremy Guimond
Product Developer: Erin Catto
Product Team Associate: Amelia Chester
Supervising Editor: Jessica Barnoski
Photo/Permissions Researcher: Derek Capitaine
Copy Editor: Rodney Rawlings
Proofreader: Laurel Sparrow
Plant Production Coordinator: Sheryl MacAdam
Manufacturing Production Coordinator: Lena Keating
Cover Design: Peter Papayanakis
Cover Image: © Alison Derry
Interior Design: Peter Papayanakis
Page Layout: Aptara®, Inc.
Printer: Webcom Inc.

Library and Archives Canada Cataloguing in Publication

Eun, Cheol S., author
    International financial management : Canadian perspectives / Donald J.S. Brean, Rotman School of Management, University of Toronto, Cheol S. Eun, Georgia Institute of Technology, Bruce G. Resnick, Wake Forest University. — Third edition. Revision of: International financial management : Canadian perspectives / Cheol S. Eun, Bruce G. Resnick, Donald J.S. Brean. — 2nd ed. — Toronto : McGraw-Hill Ryerson, c2008.

Includes bibliographical references and index.
ISBN 978-1-25-907543-8 (bound)

    1. International finance—Textbooks.   2. International business enterprises—Finance—Textbooks.
3. Foreign exchange—Textbooks.   4. Financial institutions, International—Textbooks.   I. Brean, Donald J. S., 1945-, author   II. Resnick, Bruce G., author   III. Title.

HG3881.E95 2014   658.15'99   C2014-900681-0

ABOUT THE AUTHORS

DONALD J. S. BREAN

Rotman School of Management
University of Toronto

To Mary

D.J.S.B.

Donald J. S. Brean is Professor of Finance and Economics in the Rotman School of Management at the University of Toronto and former Associate Dean. He has held academic appointments at leading universities in Europe, Asia and Africa including Cambridge University, École Supérieure de Commerce Paris, University of Siena, Johannes Kepler University in Austria, University of Nairobi, Nankai University (China) and Chulalongkorn University in Bangkok. He has published extensively in taxation, international finance, risk management, industrial organization, corporate governance and economic policy.

Professor Brean advises numerous international agencies and governments including the Canadian Federal Department of Finance, the United Nations Development Program, the World Bank and the International Monetary Fund. He is the editor of the highly acclaimed *Taxation in Modern China,* a research volume dealing with fiscal reform and financial development in China, and *Bank Reform in China: What It Means for the World.* He is co-editor of *Global Summitry,* a journal dedicated to the study of how nations coordinate, among other things, international financial regulation.

CHEOL S. EUN

Georgia Institute of Technology

To Elizabeth

C.S.E.

Cheol S. Eun (Ph.D., NYU, 1981) is the Thomas R. Williams Chair and Professor of Finance at the College of Management, Georgia Institute of Technology. Before joining Georgia Tech, he taught at the University of Minnesota and the University of Maryland. He also taught at the Wharton School of the University of Pennsylvania, the Korea Advanced Institute of Science and Technology (KAIST), Singapore Management University and the Esslingen University of Technology (Germany) as a visiting professor. He has published extensively on international finance issues in such major journals as *Journal of Finance, JFQA, Journal of Banking and Finance, Journal of International Money and Finance, Management Science* and *Oxford Economic Papers.* Also, he has served on the editorial boards of *Journal of Banking and Finance, Journal of Financial Research, Journal of International Business Studies* and *European Financial Management.*

His research is widely quoted and referenced in various scholarly articles and textbooks in the United States and abroad. Dr. Eun is the founding chair of the Fortis/Georgia Tech Conference on International Finance, the key objectives of which are to promote research on international finance and provide a forum for interactions among academics, practitioners and regulators interested in vital current issues of international finance.

Dr. Eun has taught a variety of courses at the undergraduate, graduate and executive levels, and was the winner of the Krowe Teaching Excellence Award at the University of Maryland. He also has served as a consultant to many national and international organizations, including the World Bank, Apex Capital and the Korean Development Institute, advising on issues relating to capital market liberalization, global capital raising, international investment and exchange risk management. In addition, he has been a frequent speaker at academic and professional meetings held throughout the world.

BRUCE G. RESNICK

Wake Forest University

To Donna

B.G.R.

Bruce G. Resnick is the Joseph M. Bran Jr. Professor of Banking and Finance at the Wake Forest University School of Business in Winston-Salem, North Carolina. He has a D.B.A. (1979) in finance from Indiana University. Additionally, he has an M.B.A. from the University of Colorado and a B.B.A. from the University of Wisconsin at Oshkosh. Prior to coming to Wake Forest, he taught at Indiana University for ten years, the University of Minnesota for five years and California State University for two years. He has also taught as a visiting professor at Bond University, Gold Coast, Queensland, Australia, and at the Helsinki School of Economics and Business Administration in Finland. Additionally, he served as the Indiana University resident director at the Center for European Studies at the University of Limburg, Maastricht, the Netherlands. He also served as an external examiner to the Business Administration Department of Singapore Polytechnic and as the faculty advisor on Wake Forest University study trips to China, Japan and Hong Kong.

Dr. Resnick teaches M.B.A. courses at Wake Forest University. He specializes in the areas of investments, portfolio management and international financial management. Dr. Resnick's research interests include market efficiency studies of options and financial futures markets and empirical tests of asset pricing models. A major interest has been the optimal design of internationally diversified portfolios constructed to control for parameter uncertainty and exchange rate risk. In recent years, he has focused on information transmission in the world money markets and yield spread comparisons of domestic and international bonds. His research articles have been published in most of the major academic journals in finance. His research is widely referenced by other researchers and textbook authors. He is an associate editor for *Emerging Markets Review, Journal of Economics and Business* and *Journal of Multinational Financial Management.*

CONTENTS IN BRIEF

CONTENTS

PART THREE
Foreign Exchange Exposure and Management   307

UNIQUELY CANADIAN PERSPECTIVES AND CONTENT

Here is a sampling of uniquely Canadian perspectives and content found throughout the text:

Chapter 1: Globalization, illustrated with numerous examples of Canadian corporations successfully engaged in international business

Chapter 2: The history of Canada's exchange rate systems including a note on Canadian-born Robert Mundell, Nobel Laureate in Economics for his work on exchange rates

Chapter 3: The Canadian balance of payments, its relation to our exchange rate and a note on the Bank of Canada's policy on exchange rate intervention

Chapter 4: The market for foreign exchange with extensive examples involving the Canadian dollar

Chapter 5: The international parity conditions—with Canadian empirical content

Chapter 6: Canadian banks in global financial markets; extensive discussion of international bank regulatory reform—the Basel Accords

Chapter 7: The international bond market—how Canadians borrow from and lend to foreigners; extensive detail on international bond rating protocols

Chapter 8: An overview of international equity markets with a section on Canadian cross-listed shares

Chapter 9: Currency options and futures with a focus on calls and puts on the Canadian dollar, illustrated through contracts involving Canadian companies; clearly focused, step-by-step presentations of risk management strategies

Chapter 10: Currency and interest rate swaps; extensive illustrations in the context of Canadian firms such as Manulife, CN, and Magna

Chapter 11: International portfolio investment with data on returns and risks from the Canadian perspective which underlie optimal international portfolios from the Canadian perspective

Chapter 12: How appreciation or depreciation of the Canadian dollar affect the international competitiveness of Canadian firms and how such effects depend on specific business characteristics

Chapter 13: Transaction exposure from a Canadian perspective with illustrations including a hedge designed for Bombardier to hedge the risk of a sale of aircraft to Austrian Airways

Chapter 14: Translation exposure from a Canadian managerial perspective—applying CICA Section 1650; corporate illustrations including Four Seasons Hotels and Resorts, Shell Canada, and consolidation of the international accounts of Maple Corporation

Chapter 15: Foreign direct investment and cross-border acquisition, illustrated by Reebok's takeover of CCM

Chapter 16: How Canadian firms determine their cost of capital for risky foreign investments, illustrated by Agrium of Calgary's calculation of the cost of capital for its investment in South America

Chapter 17: Capital budgeting techniques, illustrated by Canada's BlackBerry's investment in Europe; clear, step-by-step approach to adjusted present value

Chapter 18: Multinational cash management, illustrated in the context of a multinational corporation with a Canadian affiliate

Chapter 19: Techniques of financing international trade, with an extensive example based on Black's Photography importing lenses from Germany

Chapter 20: An account of Canada's unique approach to international taxation, with reference to Canadian rules, rates, and regulations

Chapter 21: An overview of corporate governance highlighting issues of concern to Canadian businesses, along with an account of alternative approaches to corporate governance around the world

COMPREHENSIVE TEACHING AND LEARNING PACKAGE

 McGraw-Hill Connect™ is a web-based assignment and assessment platform that gives students the means to better connect with their coursework, with their instructors and with the important concepts they will need to know for success now and in the future.

With Connect, instructors can deliver assignments, quizzes and tests online; edit existing questions and author entirely new problems; track individual student performance—by question, assignment or in relation to the class overall—with detailed grade reports; integrate grade reports easily with Learning Management Systems (LMS); and much more.

By choosing Connect, instructors are providing their students with a powerful tool for improving academic performance and truly mastering course material. Connect allows students to practise important skills at their own pace and on their own schedule. Importantly, students' assessment results and instructors' feedback are all saved online—so students can continually review their progress and plot their course to success.

Connect also provides 24/7 online access to an eBook.

INSTRUCTOR RESOURCES

- Instructor's Solutions Manual created by our author **Don Brean.** Includes detailed suggested answers and solutions to the problems.
- Computerized Test Bank prepared by **Anna Dodonova,** University of Ottawa. Contains multiple-choice test questions for each chapter.
- Microsoft® PowerPoint® Lecture Slides. For use in classroom lecture settings, adapted by **Charles Schell,** VIU.

ACKNOWLEDGMENTS

We are indebted to the many colleagues who provided insight and guidance throughout the development process. Their careful work enabled us to create a text that is current, accurate and modern in its approach. Among those who helped in this endeavor are:

Keith C. K. Cheung	University of Windsor
Anna Dodonova	University of Ottawa
Zaidong Dong	University of Northern British Columbia
Hoshiar Gosal	Langara College
Shahriar Hasan	Thompson Rivers University
Jeremy Jarvis	Kwantlen Polytechnic University
Harmeet Kohli	George Brown College
Peter Miu	McMaster University
Olexandr Pasyeka	University of Manitoba
Dr. Yogendra Prasad Acharya	York University
Dr. Jacques Schnabel	Wilfrid Laurier University
Kamal Smimou	University of Ontario Institute of Technology
Hari K. Thakur	McGill University
H. Semih Yildirim	York University

In the development of *International Financial Management: Canadian Perspectives,* Third Edition, many people were generous with time and thoughtful comments that genuinely enhance the volume. A special word of gratitude for assistance on specific issues goes out to Professors Laurence Booth, Craig Doidge, Walid Hejazi, John Hull, Chris Kobrak, Tom McCurdy, Gordon Richardson and Alan White, all of the Rotman School of Management, University of Toronto. Ambrus Kecskes and Yiyi Yang provided valuable comments from an informed reader's perspective. Bo Xu and Kevin Kim skillfully put extensive illustrations into the current empirical setting of exchange rates, interest rates and various financial instruments that are priced in the light of those rates.

The wise counsel and guidance of the professional staff of McGraw-Hill Ryerson are very much appreciated. Lynn Fisher originally proposed the project and passed the mantle to Senior Product Manager Kimberley Veevers. Along with Kimberley, Product Developer Erin Catto, Group Product Development Manager Kelly Dickson and Supervising Editor Jessica Barnoski ensured that it all came together in the current edition with professional skill and remarkable patience. Finally, the careful text editing by Rodney Rawlings and proofreading by Laurel Sparrow polished the product. My sincere thanks to all.

DJSB

Part 1

Foundations of International Financial Management

Part One lays the macroeconomic foundation for the topics to follow. A thorough understanding of this material is essential for understanding the advanced topics covered in the remaining sections.

1 Globalization and the Multinational Firm

Chapter 1 provides an introduction to International Financial Management. The chapter outlines the importance of studying international finance and distinguishes international finance from domestic finance.

2 International Monetary System

Chapter 2 introduces the various types of international monetary systems under which the world economy can function and has functioned at various times. The chapter traces the historical development of the world's international monetary systems from the early 1800s to the present. Additionally, a detailed discussion of the European Monetary System of the European Union is presented.

3 Balance of Payments

Chapter 3 presents balance-of-payment concepts and accounting. The chapter shows that even a country must keep its "economic house in order" or else it will experience current account deficits that undermine the value of its currency.

4 The Market for Foreign Exchange

Chapter 4 provides an introduction to the organization and operation of the spot-and-forward foreign exchange market. This chapter describes institutional arrangements of the foreign exchange market and details of how foreign exchange is quoted and traded worldwide.

5 International Parity Relationships and Forecasting Foreign Exchange Rates

Chapter 5 presents the fundamental international parity relationships among exchange rates, interest rates and inflation rates. An understanding of these parity relationships is essential for practising financial management in a global setting.

Chapter  1

Globalization and the Multinational Firm

CHAPTER OUTLINE

MORE THAN MOST, Canadians realize that virtually all business is *international* business and, likewise, that all finance is ultimately *international* finance.

A quick run across the country illustrates how economically integrated Canada is with the rest of the world. Electricity originating in Newfoundland keeps the lights on in New England. New Brunswick is home to McCain Foods, one of the largest food processing companies on the globe. Oysters from Prince Edward Island are world-famous. Nova Scotia's universities export quality education. Bombardier of Quebec ranks among the top three aircraft manufacturers in the world. Cross-border trade between Ontario and Michigan exceeds the total value of trade between the United States and Japan. Manitoba and Saskatchewan are among the world's most efficient agriculture producers, with much of the output sold abroad. Alberta is the reason that Canada is a major energy exporter. Beautiful British Columbia, Canada's gateway to Asia, is a major world supplier of wood products and minerals.

Canada exports a great deal and imports even more. Canadian business is forced to be outward-looking. As exporters, Canadian businesses compete directly with businesses abroad. Imports, on the other hand, expose domestic Canadian business to the cold winds of competition. We are a very open economy.

Business requires finance. International business deals with *international* finance. Exports generate receipts in foreign currencies. Imports require payments in foreign currencies. Not just goods and services but capital, too, can be exported or imported. Canadian companies and governments borrow substantial amounts of money from foreign sources. Those funds represent capital imports. On the other hand, when Canadian firms invest abroad, capital moves out of Canada. Agrium, Bombardier, CN and Domtar or, moving further along the alphabet, Linamar, Manulife and Teck Resources—these are prominent firms that operate globally from a Canadian base.

This book deals with international finance—focusing on markets, players, decisions and strategies. We deal with international financial issues from a Canadian perspective. The Canadian point of view is crucial. Opportunities and challenges that confront Canadians in international financial matters are often distinctly Canadian. Foreign exchange risk involving the Canadian dollar, for example, is a uniquely Canadian concern. The laws and regulations that govern how Canadian financial markets connect to the world—such as our bond markets, stock markets and even our system of taxation—have Canadian characteristics that shape transactions within these markets.

A special characteristic of Canada and Canadian business is our close commercial ties to the United States. Ninety percent of Canadians live within 100 kilometres of the American border. Canada and the United States generate the largest bilateral volume of trade in the world. Seventy-five percent of Canadian exports are shipped to the United States. Seventy percent of our imports come from the United States. The Canada–United States Free Trade Agreement, signed in 1988 and broadened to the **North American Free Trade Agreement (NAFTA)** in 1994, represents the most comprehensive trade agreement in the world, governing not just trade but also cross-border investment and legal procedures to deal with disputes. Money and capital flows freely back and forth across the Canada–United States border with the result that our bond and stock markets are highly integrated. Indeed, one of the most important influences on Canadian interest rates is US interest rates. In this respect, Canada enjoys the economic advantages—and risks—of being a close neighbour to the world's largest economy.

On international financial matters, then, Canadian concerns are naturally tilted toward the United States. Nevertheless, Canada has a significant degree of financial independence from the United States and from all other nations as well. This is where the Canadian perspective on international finance comes strongly to the fore. In Canada, we have our own currency, our own central bank—The Bank of Canada—and our own capital markets and financial institutions. Above all, Canada maintains a *flexible* exchange rate. Throughout much of this book, the flexibility of our exchange rate, which suggests exchange rate volatility as well as exchange rate uncertainty, emerges as the central factor that distinguishes international finance from its purely domestic counterpart. Canada has a specific exchange rate with each of the many currencies of the world, including the US dollar, of course, but also the euro, the British pound, the Japanese yen, the Mexican peso and more than one hundred others.

In a world of business in which borders are becoming less of a barrier, it is essential for managers and corporate decision makers to fully understand vital international aspects of financial management.

1.1 WHAT IS SPECIAL ABOUT INTERNATIONAL FINANCE?

While we may be convinced of the importance of studying international finance, we must still ask ourselves, "What is special about international finance?" Put another way, how is international finance different from purely domestic finance (if such a thing exists)? Three major dimensions set international finance apart from domestic finance:

1. Foreign exchange risk and political risk
2. Differences in regulations, tax law and government policies
3. The greater set of business opportunities for production and investment

As we will see, these major dimensions of international finance reflect the fact that sovereign nations have the right and the power to issue their own currencies, to formulate their own economic policies, to impose taxes, and to regulate the movement of goods, services and capital across their borders. Before moving on, it is useful to briefly illustrate each of these key dimensions of international financial management.

Foreign Exchange and Political Risk

An important Canadian export to Mexico is canola, a genetically engineered oil-seed produced in the prairie provinces. Canadian exporters of canola, such as Advanta Seeds of Winnipeg, are vulnerable to changes in the exchange rate between the Canadian dollar and the currency of the nation to which they are exporting, in this case Mexico. If the Mexican peso were to depreciate sharply against the Canadian dollar, as it did in the famous "Tequila crisis" of 1994, the peso price of canola would immediately rise. Advanta Seeds would see sales of the product drop as it becomes more costly for Mexicans.

There would be lost sales and lower profits, all due to an unexpected change in the Canadian dollar–Mexican peso exchange rate. The risk of such losses is **foreign exchange risk**.

Advanta and other Canadian exports faced similar difficulty in the wake of the Asian financial crises of 1997 when the value of the Thai baht, the Korean won and the Malaysian ringgit all fell sharply against other currencies, including the Canadian dollar. When firms are involved in foreign sales, they are potentially exposed to foreign exchange risk of a sort not normally encountered in purely domestic transactions.

In our modern world of flexible exchange rates, the rates fluctuate continuously in unpredictable ways. This has been the case since the early 1970s, when a regime of fixed exchange rates among the major currencies—including the US dollar, the British pound, the Japanese yen and the German deutschemark—was abandoned. Canada, prior to that move, was unique among nations for allowing the Canadian dollar to "float" against the US dollar, although in a very narrow range.

Exhibit 1.1 illustrates that our exchange rate volatility increased dramatically after 1973. Note in particular the relatively low volatility between 1962 and 1970 followed by substantial volatility thereafter. At the far right-hand side of the graph, the extraordinary spikes of the monthly changes—downward spikes are appreciation of the Canadian dollar, while upward spikes are depreciation—graphically depict the heightened exchange rate volatility over the past dozen years. The extreme upward spike occurred in October 2008, the frenzied start of the continuing international financial turmoil. In that month, the Canadian dollar depreciated 12 percent against the US dollar.

Exchange rate volatility creates a bumpy road for international business. There are ways to address the ups and downs, and this book will illustrate effective techniques and strategies.

Another form of risk that firms encounter in an international setting is **political risk**. Political risk ranges from unexpected changes in tax rules to outright expropriation of

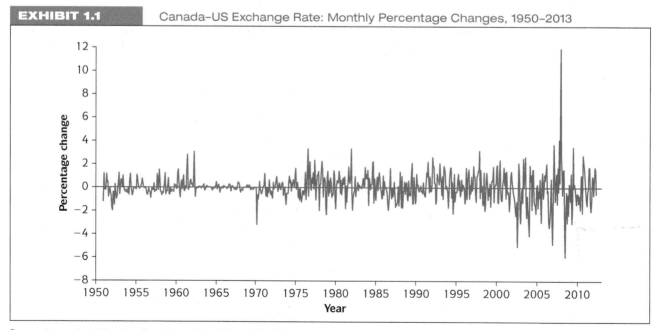

EXHIBIT 1.1   Canada–US Exchange Rate: Monthly Percentage Changes, 1950–2013

Source: International Monetary Fund, *International Financial Statistics*, various issues (Washington, DC).

assets held by foreigners. Political risk arises from the fact that a sovereign nation can change the "rules of the game" and the affected parties may not have effective recourse. We can continue with the example of Canadian exports of canola to illustrate political risk. As a genetically engineered agricultural product, canola is suspect in some countries. In 2002, China banned the import of canola, wiping out a $200 million market for Canadian producers.

Canada in 1997 passed legislation banning the gasoline additive MMT from importation into Canada, offering another illustrative case of political action that penalized a multinational enterprise. The Ethyl Corporation, a US-owned importer of MMT into Canada, challenged the legislation under NAFTA Chapter 11, the section that defines the limits of government action that adversely affects foreign firms. The Government of Canada settled the claim out of court, paying $13 million to Ethyl, including the firm's costs and lost profits. Ethyl dropped its claims against the Government of Canada. The case illustrates how international agreements, such as NAFTA, can mitigate political risk by providing a means by which foreign companies can seek recourse. However, the Ethyl case also caused alarm over whether the provisions of NAFTA could be used to limit sovereign powers of regulation in the fields of environment and public health.

Market Imperfections

Although the world economy is more integrated today than it was 10 or 20 years ago, a variety of barriers still hamper free movements of goods, services and capital across national boundaries. These barriers include trade restrictions, transportation costs and discriminatory taxation. World markets are thus imperfect. As we will discuss later, **market imperfections** represent frictions that prevent markets from functioning effectively, and they play a role in motivating multinational corporations (MNCs) to locate production abroad. Honda, the Japanese automobile company, for instance, established production facilities in Alliston, Ontario, mainly to circumvent a 6.1-percent tax imposed by Canada on imported finished vehicles. In such cases, foreign investment is a product of market imperfections.

Imperfections in world financial markets tend to restrict the extent to which investors can diversify their portfolios. An interesting example involves the Nestlé Corporation, the well-known Swiss MNC. Nestlé used to issue two different classes of common shares—bearer shares and registered shares. Foreigners were allowed to hold only bearer shares. As Exhibit 1.2 shows, prior to 1988 bearer shares traded for about twice the price of registered shares, which were exclusively reserved for Swiss residents.[1] The price disparity is a uniquely international phenomenon attributable to a market intervention.

On 18 November 1988, however, Nestlé lifted restrictions imposed on foreigners, allowing them to hold registered as well as bearer shares. After this announcement, the price spread between the two types of Nestlé shares narrowed dramatically. The price of bearer shares declined sharply whereas registered shares rose sharply. The result was a transfer of wealth from foreign shareholders to Swiss shareholders. Foreigners holding Nestlé bearer shares were exposed to political risk in a country that is widely viewed as a haven from such risk. The Nestlé episode illustrates both the importance of considering market imperfections in international finance and the peril of political risk.

About the same time as the Nestlé case, studies on the international integration of Canada's financial markets made a compelling argument that Canadian tax policies and restrictions on foreign investment were segmenting Canada from the rest of the world, financially speaking. Titles such as "The Wedge of the Withholding Tax" (Brean 1984), "Taxes, Funds Positioning and the Cost of Capital" (Booth 1987), and "The Foreign Property Rule: A Cost–Benefit Analysis" (Burgess 2005) illustrate the efforts of policy

---

[1]Bearer and registered shares of Nestlé had the same claims on dividends but differential voting rights. Chapter 16 provides a detailed discussion of the Nestlé case.

EXHIBIT 1.2

Daily Prices of Nestlé's Bearer and Registered Shares

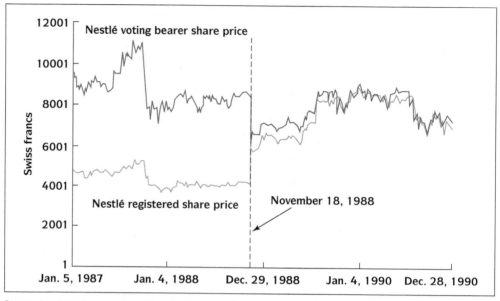

Source: Reprinted from *Journal of Financial Economics,* Volume 37, Issue 3, Claudio Loderer and Andreas Jacobs, "The Nestlé Crash," pp. 315–339, 1995, with kind permission from Elsevier Science S.A., P.O. Box 564, 1001 Lausanne, Switzerland.

analysts to identify how interventions distort international incentives, set the stage for shadowy arbitrage and are generally costly to Canada due to the investment and financial inefficiencies that they cause. Fortunately, these sorts of studies eventually had impact. It is accurate to say that with various barriers removed, Canada's capital markets are more internationally integrated today than ever before.

Expanded Opportunity Set

When firms engage in business beyond their own national borders, when they become transnational or multinational, they benefit from an **expanded opportunity set**. When firms locate production abroad, when they penetrate foreign markets or tap the capital markets of other countries, they are operating in a global context. Firms with a global perspective scan the world for investment opportunities, for low-cost resources and for foreign markets to develop.

Four Seasons Hotels, a world leader in the high-end hospitality sector, began life in Toronto. It later expanded to Paris, New York and Milan among other cities as Four Seasons grew to global prominence. Similarly, McCain Foods of New Brunswick now operates in more than 30 countries. While McCain is primarily associated with French fries—producing one-third of all frozen French fries in the world—McCain is actually exporting its technology and managerial skill. When CN, formerly Canadian National, was developing a strategy for growth, it bought two Midwestern American railway companies and restructured CN from an east-west Canadian railway to a continental logistics system. When Barrick, the Toronto-based mining company, looks for exploration and production opportunities, it looks to Australia, Peru, Chile and Tanzania. When Barrick raises capital for these capital-intensive activities, it issues shares simultaneously in Toronto, New York, London, Paris and Zurich.

These well-known Canadian companies illustrate the successful identification and pursuit of expanded opportunities in each of their respective industries. However, their roots are in Canada, just as the roots of Roots Canada are in Canada, but its business perspective and growth prospects are global.

Individual investors can also benefit if they invest internationally, rather than domestically. Suppose you have a given amount of money to invest in shares. You may invest the entire amount in Canadian (domestic) shares. Alternatively, you may allocate the funds across domestic and foreign shares. If you diversify internationally, the resulting international portfolio may have a lower risk or a higher return (or both) than a purely domestic portfolio. This can happen mainly because share returns tend to covary much less across countries than within a given country. Once you are aware of overseas investment opportunities and are willing to diversify internationally, you face an expanded opportunity set. It makes no sense to play in only one corner of the sandbox.

1.2 GOALS FOR INTERNATIONAL FINANCIAL MANAGEMENT

Understanding and managing foreign exchange and political risks while coping with market imperfections are important parts of the financial manager's job. This text, *International Financial Management*, provides today's financial managers with an appreciation of the fundamental concepts and the tools necessary to be effective global managers. Throughout, we emphasize how to deal with exchange risk and market imperfections through various instruments while maximizing the benefits from an expanded global opportunity set.

Effective financial management is more than the application of the newest business techniques. There must be an underlying goal. The goal of sound financial management is **shareholder wealth maximization**. The firm makes investments and business decisions with an eye toward making the owners of the firm—the shareholders—better off financially, or wealthier, than they were before.

Shareholder wealth maximization is generally accepted as the ultimate goal of financial management in "Anglo-Saxon" countries, such as Australia, Canada, the United Kingdom and the United States. However, it is not widely embraced as a goal in other parts of the world. In France and Germany, for example, shareholders are viewed as one among several "stakeholders" of the firm. The others include employees, customers, suppliers, banks and so forth. European managers tend to consider the promotion of the firm's stakeholders' overall welfare as the most important corporate goal.

In Japan, many companies form interlocking business groups called *keiretsu*, such as Mitsubishi, Mitsui and Sumitomo, which arose from the consolidation of family-owned business empires. Japanese managers tend to regard the prosperity and growth of their *keiretsu* as the critical goal; for instance, they often strive to maximize market share rather than shareholder wealth.

As capital markets become more internationally integrated, even managers in France, Germany, Japan and other non-Anglo-Saxon countries have come to pay serious attention to shareholder wealth maximization. In Germany, for example, companies are now allowed to repurchase shares, if necessary, for the benefit of shareholders. In accepting an unprecedented $183 billion takeover offer by Vodafone AirTouch, a leading British wireless phone company, Klaus Esser, CEO of Mannesmann of Germany, cited shareholder interests: "The shareholders clearly think that this company, Mannesmann, a great company, would be better together with Vodafone AirTouch. . . . The final decision belongs to shareholders."[2]

While managers are hired to run the company for the interests of shareholders, there is no guarantee that they will actually do so. As shown by a series of recent corporate scandals at some companies, such as Enron and Parmalat, managers that are not closely monitored may pursue their own private interests at the expense of shareholders. Corporate malfeasance and accounting manipulations at these companies eventually drove them into financial distress and bankruptcy, devastating shareholders and employees alike. Regrettably, some senior managers enriched themselves enormously in the process. Clearly, the boards of directors, the ultimate guardians of the interests of shareholders, failed to perform their duties at these companies. In the wake of these corporate calamities that have undermined the credibility of the free market system, society has painfully learned the importance of **corporate governance**, the financial and legal framework for regulating the relationship

---

[2]Quoted in *The New York Times*, 4 February 2000, p. C9.

between a company's management and its shareholders. Needless to say, the corporate governance problem is not confined to advanced industrial nations. In fact, it can be a much more serious problem in many other parts of the world, especially emerging and transition economies, such as Indonesia, Korea, China and Russia, where legal protection of shareholders is weak.

As we will discuss in Chapter 21 in detail, corporate governance structure varies greatly across countries, reflecting different cultural, legal, economic, and political environments in different countries. In many countries where shareholders do not have strong legal rights, corporate ownership tends to be concentrated. The concentrated ownership of the firm, in turn, may give rise to the conflicts of interest between dominant shareholders (often the founding family) and small outside shareholders. The collapse of Parmalat, a family-controlled Italian company, after decades of accounting frauds provides an example of corporate governance risk. The company allegedly hid debts, "invented" assets and diverted funds to bail out failing ventures of the family members. Because only the Tanzi (founding) family and close associates knew how the company was run, it was possible to hide the questionable practices for decades. Outside shareholders who collectively control a 49 percent stake did not know how Parmalat was operating. Franco Ferrarotti, professor of sociology at the University of Rome, was quoted as saying, "The government is weak, there is no sense of state, public services are bad and social services are weak. The family is so strong because it is the only institution that doesn't let you down."

Shareholders own the business. Their capital is at risk. Shareholders demand and deserve a fair return on their investment. Private capital may not be forthcoming for the business firm if it intends to pursue any other objective. As we will discuss shortly, the massive privatization currently taking place in the developing and formerly socialist countries, which will eventually enhance the standard of living in these countries, depends on private investment. Thus, it is vitally important to strengthen corporate governance so that shareholders receive fair returns on their investments.

In what follows, we discuss in detail: (1) the globalization of the world economy, (2) the growing role of MNCs in the world economy and (3) the organization of this text.

1.3   GLOBALIZATION OF THE WORLD ECONOMY: RECENT TRENDS

"Globalization" has become a popular buzzword for describing business practices in the last few decades. In this section, we review key trends in the world economy: (1) the emergence of globalized financial markets, (2) the advent of the euro, (3) the European sovereign debt crisis, (4) trade liberalization and economic integration and (5) large-scale privatization of state-owned enterprises.

Emergence of Globalized Financial Markets

The 1980s and 1990s saw a rapid integration of international capital and financial markets. The impetus for globalized financial markets initially came from the governments of major countries that had begun to deregulate their foreign exchange and capital markets. For example, in 1980, Japan deregulated its foreign exchange market, and in 1985, the Tokyo Stock Exchange admitted as members a limited number of foreign brokerage firms. The London Stock Exchange (LSE) began admitting foreign firms as full members in February 1986.

Perhaps the most celebrated deregulation, however, occurred in London on 27 October 1986, and is known as the "Big Bang." On that date, as on "May Day" in 1975 in the United States, the London Stock Exchange eliminated fixed brokerage commissions. In Europe, financial institutions are allowed to perform both investment banking and commercial banking functions. Hence, the London affiliates of foreign commercial banks were eligible for membership on the LSE. These changes gave London the most open and competitive capital markets in the world. It worked. Today, the competition to be in London is especially fierce among the world's major financial firms.

Canada, too, is actively involved in financial sector deregulation. In a significant break from the past, Canadian chartered banks are now allowed to own and operate brokerage houses—such as TD Canada Trust's TD Waterhouse. Canadian banks are also major players in corporate and investment banking with offices in the world's major financial centres.

The United States in 1999 repealed the *Glass-Steagall Act*, which had restricted commercial banks from investment banking activities (such as underwriting corporate securities), further promoting competition among financial institutions. Even developing countries such as Chile, Mexico and Korea began to liberalize by allowing foreigners to invest directly in their financial markets.

Deregulated financial markets and heightened competition in financial services provide a natural environment for financial innovations and the introduction of novel financial instruments. Examples of innovation include currency futures and options, multicurrency bonds, international mutual funds, country funds and foreign stock index futures. Corporations also play an active role in integrating the world financial markets by listing their shares across borders. Such well-known companies as Microsoft, Sony and Virgin list and trade on several stock exchanges throughout the world. IBM and GM are listed on the Brussels, Frankfurt, London and Paris stock exchanges. Stocks of Canadian companies are traded on US stock exchanges. Such cross-border listings of shares allow investors to buy and sell foreign shares as if they were domestic shares, facilitating international investments.[3]

Last but not least, advances in computer and telecommunications technologies contribute substantially to the integration of global financial markets. These technological advancements, especially the internet-based information technologies, give investors around the world immediate access to news and information affecting their investments, sharply reducing information costs. Also, computerized order-processing and settlement procedures reduce the costs of international transactions. The relative cost index of computing power declined from a level of 100 in 1960 to 16 in 1970, 3 in 1980, and only 0.1 in 2013. As a result of these technological developments and the liberalization of financial markets, cross-border financial transactions have increased dramatically over the past 25 years.

www.imf.org

Offers an overview of globalization and ways that countries gain from the process.

The Euro

The advent of the euro in 1999 represents a momentous event in the history of the world financial system. As shown in Exhibit 1.3, more than 300 million Europeans in 17 countries (Austria, Belgium, Cyprus, Estonia, Finland, France, Germany, Greece, Ireland, Italy, Latvia, Luxembourg, Malta, the Netherlands, Portugal, Slovenia and Spain) now have common currency. No single currency has circulated so widely since the days of the Roman Empire. Ten more countries, including the Czech Republic, Hungary and Poland, joined the European Union (EU) in 2004, and most will adopt the euro relatively soon. The **transaction domain** of the euro will become larger than that of the US dollar in the near future.

Once a country adopts the common currency it forgoes its own monetary policy. The common monetary policy for the eurozone is now the responsibility of the **European Central Bank (ECB)** located in Frankfurt. The ECB oversees price stability for the eurozone. Considering the sheer size of the eurozone in terms of population, economic output and world trade, the euro has emerged as a global currency, rivalling the US dollar for dominance in international trade and finance. Reflecting the significance of the euro's introduction, Professor Robert Mundell, often referred to as the intellectual father of the euro, remarked: "The creation of the euro area will eventually, but inevitably, lead to competition with the dollar area, both from the standpoint of excellence in monetary policy and in the

---

[3]Various studies indicate that the liberalization of capital markets tends to lower the cost of capital. See, for example, Peter Henry, "Stock Market Liberalization, Economic Reform, and Emerging Market Equity Prices," *Journal Finance* 2000, pp. 529–64.

EXHIBIT 1.3

Eurozone (EZ)
Member States:
Date of Eurozone
Entry, Absolute and
Relative GDP Size

	GDP, Euro, 2012	% Share of EZ GDP	Entry Date
Germany	2,570,000	27.3	1999
France	1,987,699	21.1	1999
Italy	1,586,209	16.8	1999
Spain	1,074,941	11.4	1999
Netherlands	607,435	6.4	1999
Belgium	370,436	3.9	1999
Austria	300,891	3.2	1999
Greece	217,829	2.3	2001
Finland	190,257	2.0	1999
Portugal	171,632	1.8	1999
Ireland	156,109	1.7	1999
Slovakia	69,945	0.7	2009
Luxembourg	41,778	0.4	1999
Slovenia	36,446	0.4	2007
Cyprus	17,929	0.2	2008
Estonia	16,012	0.2	2011
Malta	6,440	0.1	2008
Eurozone GDP, 2012/Euro	*9,421,989*		
EU Member States Not in the Eurozone			
United Kingdom	1,747,316		
Poland	369,318		
Sweden	386,202		
Denmark	241,148		
Czech Republic	157,538		
Romania	131,528		
Hungary	99,286		
Bulgaria	38,990		
Latvia	19,606		
Lithuania	30,807		
Total GDP, 2012/Euro	*3,221,738*		

Sources: EU and Eurozone Membership: *Eurozone Portal,* www.eurozone.europa.eu; GDP data: World Bank.

enlistment of other currencies."[4] The world, thus, faces the prospect of a bipolar international monetary system.

Since its inception, the euro has brought about revolutionary changes in European finance. For instance, by redenominating corporate and government bonds and shares from 17 different currencies into the common currency, the euro has precipitated the emergence of continent-wide capital markets in Europe characterized by depth and liquidity. Companies all over the world benefit from this development by raising capital more easily and on favourable terms in Europe. In addition, the recent surge in European merger and acquisition (M&A) activities, cross-border alliances among financial exchanges and lessening dependence on the banking sectors for capital raising are all manifestations of the profound effects of the euro. The International Finance in Practice box "Why We Believe in the Euro" presents an upbeat view of the euro expressed by Jürgen Schrempp, CEO of DaimlerChrysler.

Since the end of World War I, the US dollar has been the dominant global currency, having displaced the British pound. As a result, foreign exchange rates of currencies are quoted against the dollar and the majority of currency trading involves the dollar on either the buy or the sell side. Similarly, international trade in primary commodities, such as petroleum, coffee, wheat and gold, is conducted using the US dollar as the invoice currency. Reflecting the dominant position of the dollar in the world economy, central banks of the world hold a major portion of their external reserves in dollars. The ascendance of the dollar reflects several key factors such as the substantial size of the US economy, its mature and open capital markets and the international influence of the United States. The dominant global currency status of the dollar confers upon the United States unique privileges such as the ability to run trade deficits without having to hold foreign exchange reserves, that is, "deficits without tears." US firms conduct a large portion of international transactions in dollars without bearing exchange risks. However, once economic agents start to use the euro in earnest as an invoice, vehicle and reserve currency, the dollar may have to share the aforementioned privileges with the euro.[5]

Europe's Sovereign Debt Crisis

Recently, the euro's emergence as a global currency was dealt a serious setback in the midst of Europe's sovereign debt crisis. The crisis started in December 2009 when the new Greek government revealed that its budget deficit for the year would be 12.7 percent of GDP, not the 3.7 percent previously forecast. The previous government had falsified the national account data. Unbeknownst to the outside world, Greece was in a serious violation of Europe's stability pact, which limits the annual budget deficit of a eurozone country to a maximum of 3 percent of GDP. This news surprised financial markets and prompted investors, who became worried about sovereign default, to sell off Greek government bonds. The Greek predicament is attributable to excessive borrowing and spending, with wages and prices rising faster than productivity. With the adoption of the euro, Greece can no longer use the traditional means of restoring competitiveness, that is, depreciation of the national currency.

The panic spread to other weak European economies, especially Ireland, Portugal and Spain. In the spring of 2010, both Standard & Poor's and Moody's, credit rating agencies, downgraded the government bonds of the affected countries, making borrowing and

---

[4]Robert Mundell, "Currency Area, Volatility and Intervention," *Journal of Policy Modeling* 22 (2000), pp. 281–99.

[5]A recent study by Eun and Lai, 2002, "The Power Contest in FX Markets: The Euro vs. the Dollar," indicates that within three years since its inception the euro succeeded in establishing its own currency bloc in Europe, comprising the currencies of Croatia, Czech Republic, Hungary, Norway, Slovakia, Slovenia, Sweden and Switzerland. The study, however, shows that the US dollar remains the dominant global currency. In contrast, the Japanese yen does not have its own currency bloc in Asia.

INTERNATIONAL FINANCE *in Practice*

Why We Believe in the Euro

By Jürgen Schrempp, CEO of DaimlerChrysler

In our company, we don't mean to waste even a day in putting the euro to work. On Jan. 1, 1999—day one for the new currency—our company will switch over completely to the euro as the internal and external unit of account. We expect to be one of the first German-based companies—perhaps *the* first—to make such a complete change. We'll also encourage our suppliers within Euroland to invoice us in euros from the very beginning. Our Euroland customers, of course, will have the option of paying in either euros or their domestic currency until 2001.

Nearly all major European companies are in favor of the single currency. But having recently agreed on a historic, transatlantic merger with Chrysler Corp. of the United States, we feel especially attuned to the forces of global competition that make the euro so essential. For our new company, DaimlerChrysler AG, and for Germany and Europe as a whole, economic and monetary union will bring substantial and lasting benefits as we take our place in the interdependent world of the 21st century.

Those benefits will take shape—indeed, are already occurring—in several realms at once. First and most fundamental is the political. The single currency will push the countries of Europe into cooperating more and more in seeking solutions to common economic problems. As they do so, they'll grow increasingly intertwined politically.

At the same time, the euro will unleash powerful market forces certain to transform the way Europeans live and work. The years ahead will bring increased efficiency, greater productivity, higher overall living standards and lower unemployment. For businesses, a common currency will reduce transaction costs—eliminating, among other things, the unnecessary waste of resources involved in dealing with several European currencies. At present, doing business across borders means having to buy and sell foreign currencies—and taking the risk that sudden changes in their relative value could upend an otherwise sound business strategy. The risks can be hedged, of course, but only at a cost that must ultimately be borne by customers.

The market forces unleashed by the euro will be felt not just by corporate managers but also by political leaders. Business executives are already working to rationalize their companies, enhancing productivity and improving labor flexibility. Elected officials, facing competition as they try to attract the investments that create jobs, will eventually lower corporate tax rates and streamline regulation. In so doing, governments will give corporations a boost, like the reduction in the cost of capital that came about as countries tightened their fiscal and monetary policies in preparation for EMU.

These changes are mutually reinforcing. And as they take hold, Euroland companies will grow more confident about committing resources to long-term projects. A look

refinancing more costly. In particular, the Greek government bond was downgraded to "junk," ineligible for institutional investment. The unfolding "Greek drama" is illustrated in Exhibit 1.4, which plots the two-year government bond yields for Greece and

EXHIBIT 1.4

The Greek Drama

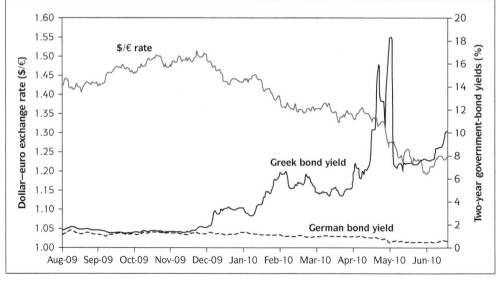

Source: Bloomberg.

at the level of corporate mergers in recent years shows that managers have already stepped up their strategic decision making. Europe saw 237 such deals last year, worth $250 billion, of which 25 percent were European cross-border transactions. In 1995, by contrast, there were just 100 deals, worth $168 billion—and only 17 percent were European cross-border transactions.

Euroland will be a strong base for companies striving to compete globally. In 1997 its combined population numbered 290 million, compared with 268 million for the United States and 126 million for Japan. Its combined GDP was $6.3 trillion, versus $7.8 trillion for the United States and $4.2 trillion for Japan. Euroland already trades with the rest of the world as much as the United States does, and the picture will change in favor of Europe as soon as the United Kingdom, and others who have stayed out of the first wave, join the currency union. Such a development—the sooner the better—is something we would very much welcome.

Launching the new euro is one thing; successfully managing the EMU process in the years ahead is quite another. Implementation poses major challenges. Some will be technical; others will have to do with maintaining a unity of purpose among a diverse group of nations, regions, peoples and cultures. I believe, however, that Europe possesses the unshakable political will and financial expertise needed to keep this endeavor on track.

It will help that—as we at DaimlerChrysler well know—some of the payoffs are immediate and obvious. Currently, one third of our group's revenues are earned in Deutsche marks, but nearly three quarters of our costs are incurred in that currency. That makes planning harder and running the company more complex. But with the coming of the euro, the disparity between our DM costs and DM revenues will diminish. As of January, 50 percent of our revenues will be in euros, with 80 percent of our costs incurred in the same currency.

How will the euro affect our ability to compete in the United States, our main export market outside the EU? In a word, positively. Higher productivity and a stable "home" currency will allow us to maintain a competitive pricing structure. Such long-term consistency in our business practices is something our U.S. customers have come to appreciate.

One final point. Thanks to the single market and the pending introduction of a single currency, Europe has matured both politically and economically. As a major transatlantic player, DaimlerChrysler is now in a position to communicate an important message to its business partners in that other great single-currency market, the United States. Working through the World Trade Organization and other groups, the globe has made great progress toward free and fair trade over the years. Now let us together examine opportunities for removing some of the remaining obstacles to trade between Europe and the United States. The beneficiaries will be consumers on both sides of the Atlantic.

Source: *Newsweek*, Special Issue, Winter 1998, p. 38. Reprinted with permission.

Germany, as well as the dollar–euro exchange rate. As can be seen from the exhibit, Greece paid a minimal or practically nonexistent premium above the German interest rate until December 2009. This was possible owing to Greece's membership in the euro club. However, the Greek interest rate began to rise sharply thereafter, reaching 18.3 percent on 7 May 2010, before it fell following the announcement of the bailout package on 9 May. Also, the specter of chaotic sovereign defaults led to a sharp fall of the euro's exchange value in currency markets.

The sovereign debt crisis in Greece, which accounts for only about 2.5 percent of eurozone GDP, quickly escalated to a Europe-wide debt crisis, threatening the nascent recovery of the world economy from the severe global financial crisis of 2008–2009. Facing the spreading crisis, the European Union (EU) countries, led by France and Germany jointly with the International Monetary Fund (IMF), put together a massive €750 billion package to bail out Greece and other weak economies. It is noted that Europe's lack of political union and fragmented decision-making structure made it slow and contentious for EU countries to reach agreement on the bailout plan, making the rescue more expensive than it might otherwise have been.

Europe's sovereign-debt crisis reveals a profound weakness of the euro as the common currency: Eurozone countries have achieved monetary integration by adopting the euro, but without fiscal integration. While eurozone countries share the common monetary policy, fiscal policies governing taxation, spending and borrowing remain firmly under the control of national governments. Hence, a lack of fiscal discipline in a eurozone country can always become a Europe-wide crisis, threatening the value and credibility of the common currency. The long-term viability of the euro and its potential as a global currency thus critically depend on how this disparity between monetary and fiscal integration will be addressed. Regarding this challenge, Jean-Claude Trichet, then president of the European Central Bank (ECB), in 2011 called for a "quantum leap" in the eurozone's economic governance and urged Europe to form a "fiscal confederation." Indeed, constructive steps—if not a leap—are being taken, including the call for a pan-European "banking union" to address the pernicious relationships between national banks and their sovereigns.

Trade Liberalization and Economic Integration

International trade, which has been the traditional link between national economies, continues to expand. As Exhibit 1.5 shows, the ratio of exports to GDP for the world increased from 7 percent in 1950 to 30 percent in 2012. Over the same time period, international trade increased three times as fast as world GDP. For some countries, international trade grew much faster; for Germany, the ratio rose from 6.2 percent to 50 percent, while for Taiwan it grew from 2.5 percent to 46.4 percent over the same time period. Latin American countries, such as Argentina and Brazil, have relatively low export-to-GDP ratios. This reflects the inward-looking, protectionist economic policies these countries pursued in the past. Even these once-protectionist countries are now increasingly embracing free market and open economy policies because of the gains from international trade.

The fundamental argument for international trade is **comparative advantage** advanced by David Ricardo in his seminal book, *Principles of Political Economy* (1817). According to Ricardo, it is mutually beneficial for countries to specialize in production of those goods they can produce most efficiently and trade such goods among them.

Suppose England produces textiles efficiently, whereas France produces wine efficiently. It then makes sense for England to specialize in textiles and France in wine, and for the two countries to then trade their products. By doing so, the two countries can increase their combined production of textiles and wine, which in turn allows both countries to consume more of both goods. This argument remains valid even if one country can produce both goods more efficiently than the other country.[6] Ricardo's theory has a clear policy implication: *Liberalization of international trade will enhance the welfare of the world's citizens.* In other words, international trade is not a "zero-sum" game in which one country benefits at the expense of another country—the view held by the "mercantilists." Rather, international trade is an "increasing-sum" game in which all players win.

The concept of comparative advantage provides a powerful rationale for free trade. Currently, international trade is being liberalized at both the global and regional levels. At the global level, the **General Agreement on Tariffs and Trade (GATT)**, a multilateral agreement among member countries, played a key role in dismantling barriers to trade. Since it was established in 1947, GATT was successful in gradually eliminating and reducing tariffs, subsidies, quotas, and other barriers to trade. Through various rounds of talks, the GATT worked to (1) reduce import tariffs worldwide by an average of 38 percent, (2) increase the proportion of duty-free products from 20 percent to 54 percent for industrialized countries and (3) extend the rules of world trade to cover agriculture, such services as banking and insurance, and intellectual property rights. It also created a permanent **World Trade Organization (WTO)** to replace GATT. The WTO has more power to enforce the rules of international trade. China joined the WTO in 2001. China's WTO membership further legitimizes the idea of free trade.

On the regional level, formal arrangements among countries promote economic integration. The **European Union (EU)** is a prime example. The European Union is the direct descendant of the European Community (formerly the European Economic Community), which was established to foster economic integration among the countries of Western Europe. Today, the EU includes 28 member states that have eliminated barriers to the free flow of goods, capital and people.

www.wto.org

The World Trade Organization website covers news and data about international trade development.

europa.eu

This is the official website of the European Union.

---

[6]Readers are referred to Appendix 1A for a detailed discussion of the theory of comparative advantage.

EXHIBIT 1.5

Economic Openness
in Long-Term
Perspective
(Exports/GDP, %)

Country	1870	1913	1929	1950	1973	2001	2003	2006	2012
Canada	12.0	12.2	15.8	13.0	19.9	44.0	44.2	42.8	31.0
United States	2.5	3.7	3.6	3.0	5.0	10.0	8.9	10.0	14.0
Australia	7.4	12.8	11.2	9.1	11.2	17.6	19.1	20.2	21.0
United Kingdom	12.0	17.7	13.3	11.4	14.0	19.0	22.4	27.0	32.0
Germany	9.5	15.6	12.8	6.2	23.8	31.1	34.2	36.0	50.0
France	4.9	8.2	8.6	7.7	15.4	24.7	25.1	25.2	27.1
Spain	3.8	8.1	5.0	1.6	5.0	29.0	23.6	27.4	30.0
Japan	0.2	2.4	3.5	2.3	7.9	10.7	10.7	16.0	15.0
China	1.2	2.0	5.1	1.1	0.3	23.0	23.3	39.0	31.0
Korea	0.0	1.0	4.5	1.0	8.2	36.0	39.4	40.2	56.0
Taiwan	0.0	2.5	5.2	2.5	10.2	45.2	47.3	47.5	46.4
Thailand	2.1	6.7	6.6	7.0	4.5	59.4	62.6	61.5	77.0
Argentina	9.4	6.8	6.1	2.4	2.1	12.0	13.1	15.2	22.0
Brazil	11.8	9.5	7.1	4.0	2.6	10.3	11.3	15.4	12.0
Mexico	3.7	10.8	14.8	3.5	2.2	28.7	33.6	36.0	32.0
World	5.0	8.7	9.0	7.0	11.2	24.0	24.9	27.4	30.0

Note: Exports of goods and services represent the value of all goods and other market services provided to the rest of the world. They include the value of merchandise, freight, insurance transport, travel, royalties, licence fees and other services such as communication, construction, financial, Information, business, personal and government services. They exclude compensation of employees and investment income (formerly called factor services) and transfer payments.
Source: World Bank national accounts data and OECD National Accounts data files.

Whereas the economic and monetary union formed by the EU is one of the most advanced forms of economic integration, a free trade area is the most basic. In 1994, Canada, the United States and Mexico entered into the North American Free Trade Agreement (NAFTA). Canada is the United States' largest trading partner and Mexico is the third-largest. In a free trade area, impediments to trade such as tariffs and import quotas are eliminated among members. The terms of NAFTA call for phasing out tariffs. Many observers believe that NAFTA will foster increased trade among its members, resulting in an increase in the number of jobs and the standard of living in all member countries. Exhibit 1.5 shows that for Canada, the ratio of exports to GDP increased dramatically from 20 percent in 1973 to 43 percent in 2006. The weak US and European economies following 2007 caused Canada's exports/GDP ratio to decline.

Privatization

The economic integration and globalization that began in the 1980s picked up speed in the 1990s via privatization. Through **privatization**, a country divests itself of the ownership and operation of a business venture by turning it over to the free market system. Privatization did not begin with the fall of the Berlin Wall; nevertheless, its pace has accelerated since the collapse of communism in the Eastern Bloc countries. It is ironic that the very political and economic system that only a short while ago extolled the virtues of state ownership should so dramatically be shifting toward market economics by shedding state-operated businesses.

Privatization can be viewed in many ways. In one sense, it is a denationalization process. When a national government divests itself of a state-run business, it gives up part of its national identity. Moreover, if the new owners are foreign, the country may simultaneously be importing a cultural influence that did not previously exist. Privatization is frequently viewed as a means to an end. One benefit of privatization for many less-developed countries is that the sale of state-owned businesses brings to the national treasury hard-currency foreign reserves. The sale proceeds are often used to pay down sovereign debt that has weighed heavily on the economy. Additionally, privatization is often seen as a cure for bureaucratic inefficiency and waste; some economists estimate that privatization improves efficiency and reduces operating costs by as much as 20 percent.

There is no one single way to privatize state-owned operations. The objectives of the country seem to be the prevailing guide. For the Czech Republic, speed was the overriding factor. To accomplish privatization en masse, the Czech government essentially gave away its businesses to the Czech people. For a nominal fee, vouchers were sold that allowed Czech citizens to bid on businesses as they went on the auction block. From 1991 to 1995, more than 1,700 companies were turned over to private hands. Moreover, three-quarters of the Czech citizens became shareholders in these newly privatized firms.

In Russia, there has been an "irreversible" shift to private ownership. More than 80 percent of the country's nonfarm workers are now employed in the private sector. Eleven million apartment units have been privatized, as have half of the country's 240,000 other business firms. Via a Czech-style voucher system, 40 million Russians now own shares in over 15,000 medium- to large-size corporations that recently became privatized through mass auctions of state-owned enterprises.

1.4 MULTINATIONAL CORPORATIONS

In addition to international trade, foreign direct investment by multinational corporations (MNCs) is a major force driving globalization of the world economy. There are about 75,000 MNCs in the world with over 600,000 foreign affiliates.[7] As indicated in the International Finance in Practice box that follows, MNCs are reshaping the structure of the world economy.

A **multinational corporation** is a business firm incorporated in one country that has production and sales operations in several other countries. The term suggests a firm obtaining raw materials from one national market and financial capital from another, producing goods with labour and capital equipment in a third country and selling the finished product in yet other national markets. Indeed, some MNCs have operations in dozens of different countries. MNCs obtain financing from major money centres around the world in many different currencies to finance their operations. Global operations require the treasurer's office to establish international banking relationships, to handle short-term funds in several currency denominations and to effectively manage foreign exchange risk.

unctad.org/wir/

This UNCTAD website provides a broad coverage of cross-border investment activities by multinational corporations.

Exhibit 1.6 lists the top 40 largest MNCs ranked by the size of foreign assets as of 2011. The list was compiled by the United Nations Conference on Trade and Development (UNCTAD). Many firms on the full list of the largest MNCs are well-known household names because of their presence in consumer product markets. For example, General Motors, Exxon, Royal Dutch Shell, Toyota, British Petroleum, Unilever, Procter & Gamble, Nestlé, Sony and Siemens are company names recognized by most people. By country of origin, American MNCs, with 27 of the top 100, represent the largest group. France ranks second with 15, followed by Germany with 13, the United Kingdom with 12 and Japan with 9. It is interesting to note that some firms from smaller countries can be extremely multinational. Nestlé of Switzerland, for example, derives about 98 percent of its sales from foreign markets.

---

[7]*World Investment Report 2012.*

Multinationals More Efficient

Foreign-owned manufacturing companies in the world's most highly developed countries are generally more productive and pay their workers more than comparable locally-owned businesses, according to the Organisation for Economic Co-operation and Development.

The Paris-based organisation also says that the proportion of manufacturing under foreign ownership in European Union countries rose substantially during the 1990s, a sign of increasing economic integration.

In a report on the global role of multinationals, the OECD points out that for some countries, the level of production abroad by foreign subsidiaries of national businesses was comparable to total exports from these countries.

The finding underlines the increasing importance in the world economy of large companies with bases scattered across the globe.

Gross output per employee, a measure of productivity, in most OECD nations tends to be greater in multinationals than in locally-owned companies, the report says.

This is partly a factor of the multinationals being bigger and more geared to operating according to world-class levels of efficiency. But it also reflects their ability to transfer new thinking in production technologies through an international factory network.

Reflecting the greater efficiencies, workers in foreign-owned plants tend to earn more money than those in locally-owned ones.

In Turkey, employees of multinationals earn double the wages of their counterparts. The equivalent figure in the UK is 23 per cent and in the US it is 9 per cent.

In the EU in 1998, a quarter of total manufacturing production was controlled by a foreign subsidiary of a

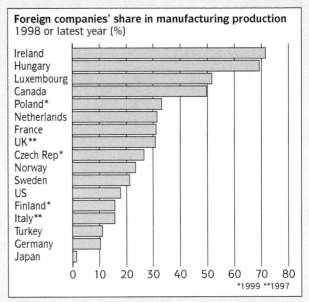

Source: Organization for Economic Cooperation and Development (OECD), Activities of Foreign Affiliates database.

bigger company compared to 17 per cent in 1990. The figure has probably increased since then, and is expected to climb further as the impact of the euro tightens the link between member countries' economies.

Measuring Globalisation: The Role of Multinationals in OECD Economies. For details see www.oecd.org.

Source: Peter Marsh, *Financial Times*, 20 March 2002, p. 6. Reprinted with permission.

In the *World Investment Report*'s ranking of the top 100 nonfinancial multinational corporations in 2011, Canada is represented only by Barrick Gold at number 62.

MNCs gain from their global presence in a variety of ways. First of all, foreign direct investment often involves moving production closer to the market. Many Canadian firms such as CN, IPSCO (the steel pipe producer), Couche-Tard, McCain Foods or Four Seasons Hotels set up affiliates in the United States or even farther away to serve those large and lucrative foreign markets. Other firms such as Barrick Gold must simply go to where the gold is, including Peru and Papua New Guinea.

In terms of motives to become international, MNCs can benefit from economies of scale by (1) spreading research and development (R&D) expenditures and advertising costs over their global sales, (2) pooling global purchasing power over suppliers, (3) utilizing their technological and managerial know-how globally with minimum additional costs and so forth. Furthermore, MNCs can use their global presence to take advantage of low-cost labour available in certain developing countries while gaining access to special R&D capabilities in advanced nations. MNCs can, indeed, leverage their global presence to boost their profit margins and create shareholder value.

EXHIBIT 1.6 The World's Top 40 Nonfinancial MNCs Ranked by Foreign Assets, 2011ᵃ (millions of US dollars and number of employees)

Ranking By: Foreign Assets	TNIᵇ	Corporation	Home Economy	Industryᶜ	Assets Foreign	Assets Total	Sales Foreign	Sales Total	Employment Foreignᵈ	Employment Total	TNIᵇ (%)
1	67	General Electric	United States	Electrical & electronic equipment	502,612	717,242	77,480	147,300	170,000	301,000	59.7
2	31	Royal Dutch Shell	Netherlands/UK	Petroleum expl./ref./distr.	296,449	345,257	282,673	470,171	75,000	90,000	76.4
3	21	British Petroleum	United Kingdom	Petroleum expl./ref./distr.	263,577	293,068	308,437	386,463	68,005	83,433	83.8
4	51	Exxon Mobil	United States	Petroleum expl./ref./distr.	214,231	331,052	316,686	433,526	49,496	82,100	66.0
5	86	Toyota Motor	Japan	Motor vehicles	214,117	372,566	142,888	235,200	123,655	325,905	52.1
6	29	Total	France	Petroleum expl./ref./distr.	211,314	228,036	197,480	256,732	61,067	96,104	77.7
7	63	GDF Suez	France	Electricity, gas & water	194,422	296,650	82,731	126,040	110,554	218,873	60.6
8	10	Vodafone	United Kingdom	Telecommunications	171,941	186,176	65,448	74,089	75,476	83,862ᵉ	90.2
9	73	Enel	Italy	Electricity, gas & water	153,665	236,037	66,817	110,528	36,656	75,360	58.1
10	27	Telefonica	Spain	Telecommunications	147,903	180,186	63,014	87,346	231,066	286,145	78.3
11	70	Chevron	United States	Petroleum expl./ref./distr.	139,816	209,474	139,344	236,286	31,000	61,000	58.8
12	71	E.ON	Germany	Electricity, gas & water	133,006	212,499	90,958	157,011	43,756	78,889	58.7
13	58	Eni	Italy	Petroleum expl./ref./distr.	122,081	198,700	106,240	153,631	45,516	78,686	62.8
14	8	ArcelorMittal	Luxembourg	Metal & metal products	117,023	121,880	93,679	93,973	197,149	260,523	90.5
15	1	Nestlé	Switzerland	Food, beverages & tobacco	116,130	121,257	92,166	94,191	318,301	328,000	96.9
16	60	Volkswagen	Germany	Motor vehicles	115,081	221,486	173,390	221,486	277,105	501,956	61.8
17	30	Siemens	Germany	Electrical & electronic equipment	112,356	141,750	87,418	102,488	244,000	360,000	77.4
18	4	Anheuser-Busch InBev	Belgium	Food, beverages and tobacco	106,336	112,427	34,944	39,046	108,446	116,278	92.4
19	41	Honda	Japan	Motor vehicles	105,151	143,196	78,134	100,594	109,400	179,060ᵇ	70.7
20	83	Deutsche Telekom	Germany	Telecommunications	102,047	170,339	44,887	81,530	113,568	235,132	54.4
21	72	Pfizer	United States	Pharmaceuticals	100,394	188,002	40,492	67,425	64,420	103,700	58.5
22	95	Mitsubishi	Japan	Wholesale trade	98,171	153,015	47,157	254,725	17,615	58,723	37.6
23	98	EDF SA	France	Electricity, gas & water	95,001	322,084	35,486	90,780	28,902	156,168	29.0
24	81	Daimler	Germany	Motor vehicles	94,157	205,910	120,638	148,096	103,686	271,370	55.1
25	69	Iberdrola	Spain	Electricity, gas & water	88,048	134,702	23,211	44,896	19,436	31,885	59.3
26	49	Sanofi	France	Pharmaceuticals	85,768	139,234	42,095	46,412	55,380	113,719	67.0
27	32	Fiat	Italy	Motor vehicles	85,238	111,247	69,921	82,790	134,438	197,021	76.4
28	94	ConocoPhillips	United States	Petroleum expl./ref./distr.	82,683	153,230	85,684	230,859	8,529	29,600	39.9
29	50	BMW	Germany	Motor vehicles	79,351	171,572	77,790	95,664	73,324	100,306	66.9
30	38	EADS	France	Aircraft	77,793	122,986	61,671	68,290	84,721	133,115	72.4
31	23	Hutchison Whampoa	Hong Kong, China	Diversified	77,291	92,788	23,477	30,023	206,986	250,000	81.4
32	88	General Motors	United States	Motor vehicles	77,092	144,603	69,045	150,276	106,000	207,000	50.2
33	89	Ford Motor	United States	Motor vehicles	76,998	179,248	65,099	136,264	85,000	164,000	47.5
34	97	Walmart	United States	Retail & Trade	74,660	180,663	109,232	421,849	800,000	2,100,000	35.1
35	68	Sony	Japan	Electrical & electronic equipment	73,839	161,610	55,543	82,180	109,200	168,200ᵉ	59.4
36	92	France Telecom	France	Telecommunications	73,082	133,560	23,818	62,937	66,699	171,949	43.8
37	62	Nissan Motor	Japan	Motor vehicles	71,912	134,582	90,879	119,084	82,223	155,099ᵉ	60.9
38	3	Xstrata	Switzerland	Mining & quarrying	71,771	74,832	30,425	33,877	38,248	40,391	93.5
39	64	Procter & Gamble	United States	Diversified	68,077	138,354	48,710	82,559	94,618	129,000	60.5
40	2	Anglo American	United Kingdom	Mining & quarrying	68,036	72,442	28,640	30,580	94,000	100,000	93.9

ᵃPreliminary results based on data from the companies' financial reporting; corresponds to the financial year from 1 April 2011 to 31 March 2012.
ᵇTNI, the Transnationality Index, is calculated as the average of the following three ratios: foreign assets to total assets, foreign sales to total sales and foreign employment to total employment.
ᶜIndustry classification for companies follows the United States Standard Industrial Classification as used by the United States Securities and Exchange Commission (SEC).
ᵈIn a number of cases foreign employment data were calculated by applying the share of foreign employment in total employment of the previous year to total employment of 2011.
ᵉEmployment data refers to revised 2010 figures, as data was not yet available.

Source: UNCTAD, *World Investment Report 2012.*

Being "multinational" is both a source of value and a reflection of industrial strength. Our list of the "top 40" includes very large and influential firms. The vast majority of the world's largest MNCs are based in large countries such as the United States, France, Germany, the UK and Japan. In the "top 100," there are only seven MNCs from countries with a smaller population than Canada—Nestlé and Novartis of Switzerland, Phillips and Inbev of the Netherlands, Nokia of Finland, Volvo of Sweden and Hutchison Whampoa of Hong Kong.

For smaller countries such as Canada with few large companies that rank among the largest, another perspective emerges that is useful for the broader picture of international investment that is our primary concern. The Toronto-based Institute for Competitiveness and Prosperity annually releases a list of Canadian nonfinancial companies that rank in the international top five (by revenue) of their respective industries. In 2012 the Institute identified 60 such Canadian companies which we report in Exhibit 1.7. Without exception, there is a significant international dimension for each of these companies whether it be MacDonald Dettwiler designing and manufacturing the Canadarm for NASA's space program, Cinram exporting its CDs around the globe or TLC Vision importing sophisticated laser surgery machines from Europe. All of these modern Canadian companies are engaged commercially and financially with the world.

One ought to keep in mind these sorts of Canadian companies, as well as our traditional firms involved in energy, forestry, mining, manufacturing, finance and telecommunications, as we consider the challenges of international financial management.

1.5   ORGANIZATION OF THIS TEXT

International Financial Management consists of 21 chapters divided into four parts. Part One, Foundations of International Financial Management, contains five chapters on the fundamentals of international finance. This section lays the macroeconomic foundation for all topics to follow. A thorough understanding of this material is essential for understanding the advanced topics covered in the remaining sections.

Chapter 2 introduces various types of international monetary systems under which the world economy has functioned at various times. Extensive treatment is given to the differences between fixed and flexible exchange rate regimes. The chapter traces the historical development of the world's international monetary systems from the early 1800s to the present. A detailed discussion of the European Monetary System is presented. Chapter 3 outlines balance-of-payment concepts and accounting. The chapter is designed to show that even a national government must keep its "economic house in order" or else it will suffer current account deficits that undermine the value of its currency. This chapter also shows how the balance of payments reveals the sources of demand for and supply of a country's currency. It concludes by surveying the balance-of-payments trends in major countries.

Chapter 4 provides an introduction to the organization and operation of the spot-and-forward foreign exchange market. It describes institutional arrangements of the foreign exchange markets and details of how foreign exchange is quoted and traded worldwide. Chapter 5, in turn, presents some of the fundamental international parity relationships among exchange rates, interest rates and inflation rates. An understanding of these parity relationships, which are manifestations of market equilibrium, is essential for astute financial management in a global setting.

Chapter 5 begins with the derivation of *interest rate parity*, showing the interrelationship between the interest rates of two countries and the spot and forward exchange rates between the same two countries. Similarly, *purchasing power parity (PPP)* deals with the relationship between a change in exchange rate between two countries and the relative values of their inflation rates. The chapter concludes with a discussion of forecasting exchange rates using parity relationships and other fundamental and technical forecasting techniques.

EXHIBIT 1.7

Canada's Global Leaders

The Institute for Competitiveness and Prosperity identified companies that are "Canada's Global Leaders." The criterion for inclusion is that the company be a public or private Canadian-controlled company on *Report on Business Top 1000* or *Financial Post 500* with revenues greater than $100 million in 2012. This list is drawn from the Institute's list.

Company	Head Office City	Niche Industry	Revenue ($000s)
Automobile, Aerospace & Defence Technology			
Magna International	Aurora, ON	Parts and Accessories for Motor Vehicles	28,431,772
Linamar	Guelph, ON	Camshafts, Scissor-Type Elevating Work Platforms	2,861,445
CAE	St-Laurent, QC	Flight Simulators	1,629,000
Chemicals			
Agrium	Calgary, AB	Fertilizer	15,299,830
Potash of Saskatchewan	Saskatoon, SK	Fertilizer	8,128,591
Methanex	Vancouver, BC	Methanol Supplier	2,579,348
Chemtrade Logistics Income Fund	Toronto, ON	Sulphuric Acid and Other Sulphur Chemicals	880,592
Neo Material Technologies	Toronto, ON	Specialty Chemicals	791,244
Engineering and Construction			
Enbridge	Calgary, AB	Pipeline Transportation	19,402,000
ATCO	Calgary, AB	Acoustical Consulting and Noise Abatement Technology	3,991,000
Héroux-Devtek	Longueuil, PQ	Aircraft Landing Gear	357,572
Farming Products			
Viterra	Calgary, AB	Support Activities For Crop Production	11,790,458
Alliance Grain Traders	Regina, SK	Split Pea and Lentil Producers	759,974
Financial Services			
Royal Bank of Canada	Toronto, ON	Banking	35,750,000
Fairfax Financial Holdings	Toronto, ON	Insurance Brokering	7,392,775
MFC Industrial	Vancouver, BC	Commodity Contracts Dealing	509,134
Food and Beverage			
Alimentation Couche-Tard	Laval, PQ	Retail Sales	19,231,422
McCain Foods	Florenceville, NB	Frozen Food Products	6,093,105
Cott	Mississauga, ON	Retailer Brand Beverage	2,308,919
High Liner Foods Incorporated	Lunenburg, NS	Seafood Processing	668,589
Forestry, Logging, Pulp and Paper			
West Fraser Timber	Vancouver, BC	Integrated Forest Products	2,762,100
Canfor	Vancouver, BC	Softwood Pulp and Bleached Paper	2,421,400
Tembec	Montreal, PQ	Specialty Cellulose Pulp and High Yield Pulp	1,743,000
Catalyst Paper	Richmond, BC	Paper for Directories and Catalogues	1,261,500
Norbord	Toronto, ON	Oriented Strand Board	954,385
Goodfellow	Delson, PQ	Wood and Wood By-Products	466,809
Information Technology			
Research In Motion	Waterloo, ON	Mobile Communications Technology	18,287,520
Open Text	Waterloo, ON	Enterprise Content Management Software	1,035,369
Mitel Networks	Kanata, ON	Communications Solutions	658,146
Sierra Wireless	Richmond, BC	Wireless Solutions for Mobile Broadband	571,824

EXHIBIT 1.7

(continued)

Company	Head Office City	Niche Industry	Revenue ($000s)
Machinery and Heavy Industries			
Finning International	Vancouver, BC	Construction Equipment Rental	5,894,910
ShawCor	Toronto, ON	Pre-Eminent Pipe Coating	1,157,265
Husky Injection Molding Systems	Bolton, ON	Plastics Injection Equipment	1,127,000
ATS Automation Tooling Systems	Cambridge, ON	High-Precision Micro-Manufacturing Systems	704,599
GLV	Montreal, PQ	Paper Industry Machinery	672,380
Ritchie Bros. Auctioneers Incorporated	Burnaby, BC	Industrial Assets Auctions	391,741
Velan	St-Laurent, PQ	Industrial Valve Manufacturing	388,466
Media Communication and Entertainment			
Harlequin (Torstar)	Toronto, ON	Romance Fiction	1,548,757
Mining and Metals			
Barrick Gold	Toronto, ON	Silver/Gold Ore Mining	13,823,253
Teck Resources	Vancouver, BC	Diversified Metals & Mining	11,514,000
Goldcorp	Vancouver, BC	Gold Ore Mining	5,303,018
Cameco	Saskatoon, SK	Uranium	2,384,404
Pan American Silver	Vancouver, BC	Silver/Gold Ore Mining	824,078
Silver Wheaton	Vancouver, BC	Silver/Gold Ore Mining	721,967
Harry Winston Diamond	Toronto, ON	Precious Gems	695,724
Major Drilling Group International	Moncton, NB	Drilling Services	482,276
Oil and Gas Equipment and Services			
Keyera	Calgary, AB	Midstream Operators	2,569,158
Retail and Consumer Goods/Services			
Dorel Industries	Westmount, PQ	Manufacturing and Upholstered Products	2,338,222
Gildan Activewear	Montreal, PQ	Clothing	1,703,602
CCL Industries	Toronto, ON	Pressure Sensitive and Film Materials	1,268,477
Garda World Security	Montreal, PQ	Security and Alarm Services	1,224,887
Cirque du Soleil	Montreal, PQ	Live Entertainment	850,000
Liquor Stores N.A.	Edmonton, AB	Beer, Wine & Liquor Stores	591,502
Transport Services			
Bombardier	Montreal, PQ	Rail Equipment Manufacturing	18,145,184
Canadian National Railway	Montreal, PQ	North American Rail Services	9,028,000
Travel Services and Real Estate			
Brookfield Asset Management	Toronto, ON	Real Estate Transactions	15,745,869
Transat A.T.	Montreal, PQ	Travel Agencies	3,658,164
FirstService	Toronto, ON	Residential and Commercial Property Manager	2,199,705
Utility			
Bruce Power Partnership	Tiverton, ON	Nuclear Power	2,166,000
Wholesalers			
Richelieu Hardware	St-Laurent, PQ	Hardware Merchant Wholesalers	523,786

Source: © Institute for Competitiveness and Prosperity.

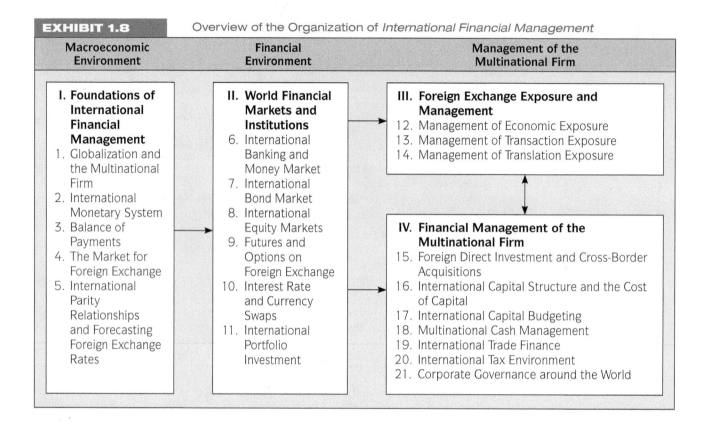

EXHIBIT 1.8   Overview of the Organization of *International Financial Management*

The chapters in Part One lay the macroeconomic foundation for *International Financial Management.* Exhibit 1.8 provides a diagram that shows the text layout. The diagram shows discussion moving from a study of macroeconomic foundations to a study of the financial environment in which the firm and the financial manager must function. Financial strategy and decision making can be discussed intelligently only after one has an appreciation of the financial environment.

Part Two, World Financial Markets and Institutions, provides a thorough discussion of international financial institutions, financial assets, and marketplaces and develops the tools necessary to manage exchange rate uncertainty. Chapter 6, International Banking and Money Market, begins the section. The chapter differentiates between international and domestic bank operations and examines the institutional differences between various types of international banking offices. International banks and their clients make up the Eurocurrency market and form the core of the international money market. The chapter examines the features of the major international money market instruments: forward rate agreements, Euronotes, Euro-medium-term notes and Eurocommercial paper. The chapter concludes with discussion of the international debt crises that have occasionally brought turbulence to global financial markets.

Chapter 7 distinguishes foreign bonds and Eurobonds, which together make up the international bond market. It discusses the advantages to the issuer of sourcing funds from the international bond market as opposed to raising funds domestically. It describes both the underwriting procedure for issuing new Eurobonds and the procedure for trading existing international bonds in the secondary market. A discussion of the major types of international bonds is included in the chapter. The chapter concludes with a discussion of international bond ratings.

Chapter 8 covers international equity markets. There is no separate international equity market that operates parallel to domestic equity markets. Instead, the equity shares of certain corporations have broad appeal to international investors, rather than just investors from the country in which the corporation is incorporated. Chapter 8 documents the size of equity markets in both the developed and the developing countries. Various methods of trading equity shares in the secondary markets are discussed. The chapter discusses the advantages to the firm of cross-listing equity shares in more than one country.

Chapter 9 provides an extensive treatment of exchange-traded currency futures and options contracts. The chapter covers the institutional details of trading these derivative securities and also develops basic valuation models for pricing them. We believe that derivative securities are best understood if one also understands what drives their value. How to use derivative securities is saved for Chapters 13 and 14, which examine the topics of transaction exposure and translation exposure.

Approximately 50 percent of bonds issued in the world end up being involved in an interest rate or currency swap. Chapter 10 provides an extensive treatment of both types of swaps. The chapter provides detailed examples and real-life illustrations of swap arrangements that highlight the cash flows between counterparties while delineating the risks inherent in swap transactions. Swap pricing is also covered.

Chapter 11 covers international portfolio investment. The chapter begins by examining the benefits to the investor from diversifying his or her portfolio internationally rather than just domestically. It shows that the gains from international diversification come from the lower correlations that typically exist among international assets in comparison with those existing among domestic assets. The chapter documents the potential benefits from international diversification that are available to all national investors. An appendix shows how the rewards from international diversification can be further enhanced by using derivative contracts to hedge the exchange rate risk in the portfolio.

Part Three, Foreign Exchange Exposure and Management, comprises three chapters, one each devoted to the topics of economic, transaction and translation exposure management. Chapter 12 covers economic exposure, that is, the extent to which the value of the firm will be affected by unexpected changes in exchange rates. The chapter provides a way to measure economic exposure, discusses its determinants and presents methods for managing and hedging economic exposure. Several real-life illustrations are provided.

Chapter 13 covers the management of transaction exposure that arises from contractual obligations denominated in a foreign currency. Several methods for hedging this exposure are compared and contrasted: the forward hedge, the futures hedge, the money market hedge and the options hedge. The chapter also discusses why an MNC should hedge, a debatable subject in the minds of both academics and practitioners.

Chapter 14 covers translation exposure or, as it is sometimes called, accounting exposure. Translation exposure refers to the effect that an unanticipated change in exchange rates will have on the consolidated financial reports of an MNC. The chapter discusses, compares and contrasts the various methods for translating financial statements denominated in foreign currencies. The chapter includes a discussion of managing translation exposure using funds adjustment and the pros and cons of using balance sheet and derivatives hedges.

Part Four, Financial Management of the Multinational Firm, covers topics on financial management practices for the MNC. The section begins with Chapter 15 on foreign direct investment, explaining why MNCs make capital expenditures in productive capacity in foreign lands rather than just produce domestically and then export to overseas markets. The chapter also deals with an increasingly popular form of foreign investment, cross-border mergers and acquisitions. The chapter includes a full treatment of the political risk associated with foreign investment.

Chapter 16 deals with the international capital structure and the cost of capital of an MNC. An analytical argument is presented showing that the firm's cost of equity capital is lower when its shares trade internationally rather than just in the home country. Moreover, the cost of debt can be reduced if debt capital is sourced internationally. The result of international trading of equity and sourcing debt in the international bond market is a lower weighted average cost of capital, which increases the net present value of capital expenditures as well as the value of the firm.

Chapter 17 presents the adjusted present value (APV) framework, which is useful for analyzing capital expenditures in foreign operations. The APV framework is a value additivity model that determines the present value of each relevant cash flow of a capital project by discounting at a rate of discount consistent with the risk inherent in the cash flow.

Chapter 18 covers issues in cash management for the MNC. The chapter begins with an illustration of a cash management system for an MNC. It is shown that if a centralized cash depository is established and if the parent firm and its foreign affiliates employ a multinational netting system, the number of foreign cash flows can be reduced, thus saving the firm money and giving the MNC better control of its cash. It is also shown that managing cash transactions through a centralized depository that administers a precautionary cash balance portfolio reduces the systemwide investment in cash. Transfer pricing strategies are explored as a means for reducing an MNC's worldwide tax liability. Further, transfer pricing strategies and other methods are considered as means for removing blocked funds from a host country.

Chapter 19 provides a brief introduction to trade financing and countertrade. Through the use of an example, a typical foreign trade transaction is traced from beginning to end. The example shows the three primary documents used in trade financing: letter of credit, time draft and bill of lading. The example also shows how a time draft can become a negotiable money market instrument, called a banker's acceptance. The chapter concludes with a discussion of countertrade transactions, which are reciprocal promises between a buyer and a seller to purchase goods or services from one another.

Chapter 20 examines the international tax environment. The chapter opens with a discussion on the theory of taxation, exploring the issues of tax neutrality and tax equity. Different methods of taxation—income tax, withholding tax, value-added tax—are considered. Income tax rates in select countries are compared, as are the withholding tax rates that exist through tax treaties between Canada and various countries. The chapter concludes with a treatment of the organizational structures MNCs use for reducing tax liabilities.

The text concludes with Chapter 21, which deals with the important issue of corporate governance. Among other things, the chapter explains how separation of ownership and control in modern corporations gives rise to agency problems—conflict of interest between agents (managers) and principals (shareholders)—and how different countries deal with the problem using different corporate governance frameworks. The chapter also discusses the practical issue of how to improve corporate governance practices so that the interests of managers and shareholders can be better aligned.

SUMMARY

This chapter provides an introduction to *International Financial Management.*

1. It is essential to study "international" financial management because we live in a highly globalized and integrated world economy. Owing to continuous liberalization of international trade and investment along with rapid advances in telecommunications and transportation technologies, the world economy will become even more integrated.

2. Three major dimensions distinguish international finance from domestic finance. They are foreign exchange and political risks, market imperfections and an expanded opportunity set.

3. Financial managers of MNCs must learn to manage foreign exchange and political risks using proper tools and instruments, deal with (and take advantage of) market imperfections and benefit from the expanded investment and financing opportunities. Financial managers contribute to shareholder wealth maximization, which is the ultimate goal of international financial management.

4. The theory of comparative advantage states that prosperity is enhanced when countries produce goods for which they have comparative advantage and then trade those goods. Comparative advantage provides a powerful rationale for free trade. Currently, international trade is being liberalized at both the global and the regional levels. At the global level, the WTO plays a key role in promoting free trade. At the regional level, the European Union and NAFTA play a vital role in dismantling trade barriers within regions.

5. A major economic trend of the present decade is the rapid pace with which former state-owned businesses are being privatized. With the fall of communism, many Eastern Bloc countries began stripping themselves of inefficient business operations formerly run by the state. Privatization has placed a new demand on international capital markets to finance the purchase of the former state enterprises, and it has also

brought about a demand for new managers with international business skills.

6. In modern times, corporate capital and control of industrial technology are at the heart of one country's comparative advantage over another country. These controllers of capital and know-how are multinational corporations (MNCs). Today, it is not uncommon for an MNC to produce merchandise in one country on capital equipment financed by funds raised in a number of different currencies through issuing securities to investors in many countries and then selling the finished product to customers in yet other countries.

QUESTIONS

1. Why is it important to study international financial management?

2. How is international financial management different from domestic financial management?

3. Discuss the major trends that have prevailed in international business during the last two decades.

4. How is Canada's economic well being enhanced through free international trade in goods and services?

5. What is Canada's comparative advantage?

6. What Canadian companies—and their products—reflect Canada's comparative advantage?

7. What considerations might limit the extent to which the theory of comparative advantage is realistic?

8. What are multinational corporations (MNCs), and what economic roles do they play?

9. Critics of the North American Free Trade Agreement (NAFTA) in both the United States and Canada feared the loss of jobs to Mexico where labour is cheaper to hire workers. What are the merits and demerits of this position on NAFTA? Considering recent economic developments in North America, how would you assess the success of NAFTA?

10. In 1995, a working group of French chief executive officers set up by the Confederation of French Industry (CNPF) and the French Association of Private Companies (AFEP) examined French corporate governance. The group reported the following: "The board of directors should not simply aim at maximizing share values as in the U.K. and the U.S. Rather, its goal should be to serve the company, whose interests should be clearly distinguished from those of its shareholders, employees, creditors, suppliers and clients but still equated with their general common interest, which is to safeguard the prosperity and continuity of the company." Evaluate the recommendation.[8]

11. Emphasizing the importance of voluntary compliance, as opposed to enforcement, in the aftermath of such corporate scandals as those involving Enron and World-Com, US President Bush stated that while tougher laws might help, "ultimately, the ethics of business depends on the conscience of business leaders." Describe your view on this statement.

12. Suppose you are interested in investing in the shares of Nokia Corporation of Finland, which is a world leader in wireless communication. But before you make your investment decision, you would like to learn about the company. Visit the website of CNN Financial Network (www.cnnfn.com) and collect information about Nokia, including the recent share price history and analysts' views of the company. Discuss what you learn about the company. Also discuss how the instantaneous access to information via the internet would affect the nature and workings of financial markets.

INTERNET EXERCISE

1. Visit the corporate websites of Nestlé, one of the biggest multinational companies in the world, and study the scope of geographical diversification of its sales and revenues. Also, gather and evaluate the company's financial information from the related websites. You may use such internet search engines as Netscape, Microsoft Internet Explorer and Yahoo.

2. Go to the website for McCain Foods. Get a sense of the corporate history and its global presence. Since McCain is not a public company, you will not find publicly available financial information.

---

[8]This question draws on the article by François Degeorge, "French Boardrooms Wake Up Slowly to the Need for Reform," in the Complete MBA Companion in Global Business, *Financial Times,* 1999, pp. 156–60.

MINI CASE

Nike's Decision

Nike, an American-based company with a globally recognized brand name, manufactures athletic shoes in such Asian developing countries as China, Indonesia and Vietnam using subcontractors and sells the products in the United States and foreign markets. The company has no production facilities in the United States. In each of those Asian countries where Nike has production facilities, the rates of unemployment and underemployment are quite high. The wage rate is very low in those countries by US standards; the hourly wage rate in the manufacturing sector is less than one dollar in each of those countries, compared with about $18 in the United States.

In addition, workers in those countries often operate in poor and unhealthy environments, and their rights are not well protected. Understandably, the Asian host countries are eager to attract foreign investments, such as Nike's, to develop their economies and raise the living standards of their citizens. Recently, however, Nike came under worldwide criticism for its practice of hiring workers for such a low pay—"next to nothing" in the words of critics—and condoning the poor working conditions in the host countries.

Evaluate and discuss various ethical as well as economic ramifications of Nike's decision to invest in those Asian countries.

REFERENCES & SUGGESTED READINGS

Basic Finance References

Bodie, Zvi, A. Kane, P. Ryan, A. Marcus and S. Perrakis. *Investments*, 7th Canadian ed. Toronto; McGraw-Hill Ryerson, 2011.

Ross, Stephen A., W. Westerfield, F. Jaffee, and G. Roberts. *Corporate Finance*, 6th Canadian edition. Toronto: McGraw-Hill Ryerson, 2013.

International Accounting References

Radebaugh, Lee, and Sidney Gray. *International Accounting and Multinational Enterprises*, 5th ed. (Hoboken, NJ: Wiley, 2005).

Meuller, Gerhard G., Helen Gernon, and Gary Meek. *Accounting: An International Perspective*, 5th ed. Burr Ridge, IL: Richard D. Irwin, 2000.

International Economics References

Krugman, Paul R., Maurice Obstfeld, and Marc Meltz. *International Economics: Theory and Policy*, 9th ed. Reading, MA: Addison-Wesley, 2012.

Appendix 1A

Gains from Trade: The Theory of Comparative Advantage

The theory of comparative advantage was originally advanced by the nineteenth-century economist David Ricardo as an explanation for why nations trade with one another. The theory claims that economic well being is enhanced if each country's citizens produce that which they have a comparative advantage in producing relative to the citizens of other countries and then trade products. Underlying the theory are the assumptions of free trade between nations and that the factors of production (land, buildings, labour, technology and capital) are relatively immobile. Consider the example described in Exhibit A.1 as a vehicle for explaining the theory.

Exhibit A.1 assumes two countries, A and B, which each produce only food and textiles, but they do not trade with one another. Country A and B each have 60,000,000 units of input. Each country presently allocates 40,000,000 units to the production of food and 20,000,000 units to the production of textiles. The exhibit shows that Country A can produce five kilograms of food with one unit of production or three metres of textiles. Country B has an absolute advantage over Country A in production of both food and textiles. Country B can produce 15 kilograms of food or four metres of textiles with one unit of production. When all units of production are employed, Country A can produce 200,000,000 kilograms of food and 60,000,000 metres of textiles. Country B can produce 600,000,000 kilograms of food and 80,000,000 metres of textiles. Total output is 800,000,000 kilograms of food and 140,000,000 metres of textiles. Without trade, each nation's citizens can consume only what they produce.

While it is clear from Exhibit A.1 that Country B has an absolute advantage in the production of food and textiles, it is not so clear that Country A (B) has a relative advantage over Country B (A) in producing textiles (food). In using units of production, Country A can "trade off" one unit of production needed to produce five kilograms of food for three metres of textiles. Thus, a metre of textiles has an *opportunity cost* of $5/3 = 1.67$ kilograms of food, or a kilogram of food has an opportunity cost of $3/5 = 0.60$ metres of textiles. Analogously, Country B has an opportunity cost of $15/4 = 3.75$ kilograms of food per metre of textiles, or $4/15 = 0.27$ metres of textiles per kilogram of food. When viewed in terms of opportunity costs, it is clear that Country A is relatively more efficient in producing textiles and Country B is relatively more efficient in producing food. That is, Country A's (B's) opportunity cost for producing textiles (food) is less than Country B's (A's). A *relative efficiency* that shows up via a lower opportunity cost is referred to as a comparative advantage.

Exhibit A.2 shows that when there are no restrictions or impediments to free trade, such as import quotas, import tariffs or costly transportation, the economic well being of both countries is enhanced through trade. Exhibit A.2 shows that Country A has shifted 20,000,000 units from the production of food to the production of textiles where it has a comparative advantage and that Country B has shifted 10,000,000 units from the production of textiles to the production of food where it has a comparative advantage. Total output is now 850,000,000 kilograms of food and 160,000,000 metres of textiles. Suppose that Country A and Country B agree on a price of 2.50 kilograms of food for one metre of textiles, and that Country A sells Country B 50,000,000 metres of textiles for 125,000,000 kilograms of food. With free trade, Exhibit A.2 makes it clear that the citizens of each country have increased their consumption of food by 25,000,000 kilograms and textiles by 10,000,000 metres.

EXHIBIT A.1

Input/Output without Trade

	Country		
	A	B	Total
I. Units of input (000,000)			
Food	40	40	
Textiles	20	20	
II. Output per unit of input (kilograms or metres)			
Food	5	15	
Textiles	3	4	
III. Total output (kilograms or metres) (000,000)			
Food	200	600	800
Textiles	60	80	140
IV. Consumption (kilograms or metres) (000,000)			
Food	200	600	800
Textiles	60	80	140

EXHIBIT A.2

Input/Output with Free Trade

	Country		
	A	B	Total
I. Units of input (000,000)			
Food	20	50	
Textiles	40	10	
II. Output per unit of input (kilograms or metres)			
Food	5	15	
Textiles	3	4	
III. Total output (kilograms or metres) (000,000)			
Food	100	750	850
Textiles	120	40	160
IV. Consumption (kilograms or metres) (000,000)			
Food	225	625	850
Textiles	70	90	160

PROBLEMS

1. Country C can produce seven kilograms of food or four metres of textiles per unit of input. Compute the opportunity cost of producing food instead of textiles. Similarly, compute the opportunity cost of producing textiles instead of food.

2. Consider the no-trade input/output situation presented in the following table for Countries X and Y. Assuming that free trade is allowed, develop a scenario that will benefit the citizens of both countries.

Input/Output without Trade

	Country		
	X	Y	Total
I. Units of input (000,000)			
Food	70	60	
Textiles	40	30	
II. Output per unit of input (kilograms or metres)			
Food	17	5	
Textiles	5	2	
III. Total output (kilograms or metres) (000,000)			
Food	1,190	300	1,490
Textiles	200	60	260
IV. Consumption (kilograms or metres) (000,000)			
Food	1,190	300	1,490
Textiles	200	60	260

Chapter 2

International Monetary System

CHAPTER OUTLINE

THIS CHAPTER EXAMINES the international monetary system that defines the financial environment in which multinational corporations and international investors operate. The international monetary system includes the foreign exchange markets where values of exchange rates are determined. As mentioned in Chapter 1, exchange rates among major currencies such as the US dollar, the British pound and the Japanese yen have been floating since the fixed exchange rate regime—known as the Bretton Woods Agreement—was abandoned in 1973.

Earlier, from 1950 to 1962, when most other nations in the world were on fixed rates, Canada maintained a flexible exchange rate. Canada's concern was that a fixed exchange rate would contribute to inflation in Canada as Canadian exports at the time were strong—especially to Europe, which was rebuilding following the war. Capital was also flowing into Canada. Canada intended the "managed float" to be temporary and to be kept within a small range, plus or minus 1 percent of US$0.91, but this proved to be much too restrictive. In fact, in 1957, the Canadian dollar touched US$1.06. In 1962, Canada fixed the exchange rate at US$0.925, again with a commitment to keep it within plus or minus 1 percent of that figure. In 1970, following several episodes of sharp swings in the Current Account Balance, Canada announced that our exchange rate would float. Since then, the external value of the Canadian dollar—the exchange rate—has been determined in the markets for foreign exchange.

Floating exchange rates are a fact of modern life and a source of concern for all businesses. Exchange rate changes can present opportunities as well as pleasant or unpleasant surprises. It is crucial for firms to carefully measure and manage their exchange rate risk and exposure. The complex international monetary arrangements imply that for adroit financial decision making, it is essential for managers to appreciate the arrangements and workings of the international monetary system.

The **international monetary system** is the *institutional framework within which international payments are made, movements of capital are accommodated,* and *exchange rates among currencies are determined*. It is a complex set of institutions, rules and policies regarding exchange rates, international payments and the international flow of capital. The international monetary system has evolved over time and will continue to do so in the future as fundamental economic and political conditions underlying the world economy continue to shift.

In this chapter, we review the history of the international monetary system and contemplate its future prospects. In addition, we compare and contrast the alternative exchange rate systems, that is, fixed versus flexible exchange rates.

2.1 EVOLUTION OF THE INTERNATIONAL MONETARY SYSTEM

The international monetary system has gone through several distinct stages of evolution. These stages are summarized as follows:

1. Bimetallism: Before 1875.
2. Classical gold standard: 1875–1914.
3. Interwar period: 1915–1944.
4. Bretton Woods system: 1945–1972.
5. Flexible exchange rate regime: Since 1973.

We now examine each of the five stages in some detail.

2.2 BIMETALLISM: BEFORE 1875

Prior to the 1870s, many countries had **bimetallism**, a monetary system based on precious metals with coinage maintained for both gold and silver. In Great Britain, for example, bimetallism was maintained until 1816 (after the conclusion of the Napoleonic Wars), when Parliament passed a law maintaining coinage of gold only, abolishing coinage of silver. In the United States, bimetallism was adopted by the *Coinage Act* of 1792 and remained a legal standard until 1873 when Congress dropped the silver dollar from the list of coins to be minted. France, on the other hand, introduced and maintained its bimetallism from the French Revolution to 1878. Some other countries, such as China, India, Germany and Holland, were on the silver standard.

The international monetary system before the 1870s can be characterized as "bimetallism" in the sense that both gold and silver were used as international means of payment. Exchange rates among currencies were determined by either their gold or silver contents.[1] Around 1870, for example, the exchange rate between the British pound, which was fully on a gold standard, and the French franc, which was officially on a bimetallic standard, was determined by the gold content of the two currencies. On the other hand, the exchange rate between the franc and the German mark, which was on a silver standard, was determined by the silver content of the currencies. The exchange rate between the pound and the mark was determined by their exchange rates against the franc.

Due to various wars and political upheavals, some major countries, such as the United States, Russia and Austria-Hungary, had irredeemable currencies at one time or another during the period 1848–1879. One might say that the international monetary system was less than fully *systematic* up until the 1870s.

Countries on the bimetallic standard often experienced a phenomenon referred to as **Gresham's law**. Since the exchange ratio between the two metals was fixed officially, only the abundant metal was used as money, driving more scarce metal out of circulation. According to Gresham's law, "bad" (abundant) money drives out "good" (scarce) money. For example, when gold from newly discovered mines in California and Australia poured into the market in the 1850s, the value of gold became depressed, causing overvaluation of gold under the French official ratio, which equated a gold franc to a silver franc 15½ times as heavy. As a result, the franc effectively became a gold currency.

---

[1]This does not imply that each individual country was on a bimetallic standard. In fact, many countries were on either a gold standard or a silver standard by 1870.

2.3 CLASSICAL GOLD STANDARD: 1875–1914

Mankind's fondness for gold as a storage of wealth and means of exchange dates back to antiquity and was shared widely by diverse civilizations. Christopher Columbus once said, "Gold constitutes treasure, and he who possesses it has all he needs in this world." The first full-fledged monetary **gold standard**, however, was not established until 1821 in Great Britain, when notes from the Bank of England were made fully redeemable for gold. As previously mentioned, France was effectively on the gold standard beginning in the 1850s and formally adopted the standard in 1878. The newly emergent German empire, which was to receive a sizable war indemnity from France, converted to the gold standard in 1875 and discontinued coinage of silver. The United States adopted the gold standard in 1879 and Russia and Japan in 1897.

One can say roughly that the *international* gold standard existed as a historical reality during the period 1875–1914. The majority of countries got off gold in 1914, when World War I broke out. The classical gold standard as an international monetary system thus lasted for about 40 years. During this period, London became the centre of the international financial system, reflecting Britain's advanced economy and its preeminent position in international trade.

An *international* gold standard can be said to exist when, in most major countries, (1) gold alone is assured of unrestricted coinage, (2) there is two-way convertibility between gold and national currencies at a stable ratio and (3) gold may be freely exported or imported. In order to support unrestricted convertibility into gold, banknotes need to be backed by a gold reserve of a minimum stated ratio. In addition, the domestic money stock should rise and fall as gold flows into and out of the country. The above conditions were roughly met between 1875 and 1914.

Under the gold standard, the exchange rate between any two currencies is determined by their gold content. For example, suppose that the pound is pegged to gold at six pounds per ounce, whereas one ounce of gold is worth 12 francs. The exchange rate between the pound and the franc should then be two francs per pound. To the extent that the pound and the franc remain pegged to gold at given prices, the exchange rate between the two currencies will remain stable. There were, indeed, no significant changes in exchange rates among the currencies of such major countries as Great Britain, France, Germany and the United States during the entire period. The dollar–sterling exchange rate remained within a narrow range of $4.84 and $4.90 per pound. Highly stable exchange rates under the classical gold standard provided an environment conducive to international trade and investment.

Under the gold standard, misalignment of the exchange rate is automatically corrected by cross-border flows of gold. In the above example, suppose that one pound is trading for 1.80 francs at the moment. Since the pound is undervalued in the exchange market, people will buy pounds with francs but not francs with pounds. For people who need francs, it would be cheaper first to buy gold from the Bank of England and ship it to France and sell it for francs. To illustrate, suppose you need to buy 1,000 francs using pounds. If you buy 1,000 francs in the exchange market, it will cost you £555.56 at the exchange rate of Fr1.80/£. Alternatively, you can buy 83.33 = 1,000/12 ounces of gold from the Bank of England for £500:

$$£500 = (1,000/12) \times 6$$

Then you could ship the gold to France and sell it to the Bank of France for 1,000 francs. This way, you can save about £55.56.[2] Since people only want to buy, not sell, pounds at the exchange rate of Fr1.80/£, the pound will eventually appreciate to its fair value, namely, Fr2/£.

---

[2]In this example, we ignored shipping costs. But as long as the shipping costs do not exceed £55.56, it is still more advantageous to buy francs via "gold export" than via the foreign exchange market.

Under the gold standard, international imbalances of payments are corrected automatically. Suppose Great Britain exported more to France than it imported from France. This trade imbalance would not persist under the gold standard. Net exports from Great Britain to France would trigger a net flow of gold in the opposite direction. This flow of gold leads to a lower price level in France and, at the same time, a higher price level in Great Britain. (Recall that under the gold standard, the domestic money stock rises or falls as the country experiences an inflow or outflow of gold.) The resultant change in the relative price level, in turn, would slow exports from Great Britain and encourage exports from France. As a result, the initial net export from Great Britain would eventually disappear. This adjustment mechanism is referred to as the **price-specie-flow mechanism**, which is attributed to David Hume, a Scottish philosopher.[3]

Despite its demise a long time ago, the gold standard still has ardent supporters in academic, business and political circles, who view it as an ultimate hedge against price inflation. Gold has a natural scarcity, and no one can increase its quantity at will. Therefore, if gold serves as the sole base for domestic money creation, the money supply cannot get out of control and cause inflation. In addition, if gold is used as the sole international means of payment, then countries' balance of payments is regulated automatically via the movements of gold.[4]

The gold standard, however, has a few serious shortcomings. First of all, the supply of newly minted gold is so restricted that the growth of world trade and investment can be seriously hampered for the lack of sufficient monetary reserves. The world economy can face deflationary pressures. Second, whenever government finds it politically necessary to pursue national objectives that are inconsistent with maintaining the gold standard, it may abandon the gold standard. In other words, the international gold standard *per se* has no mechanism to compel each individual country to abide by the rules of the game.[5] For such reasons, it is not very likely that the classical gold standard will be restored in the foreseeable future.

2.4   INTERWAR PERIOD: 1915–1944

World War I ended the classical gold standard in August 1914 as major countries such as Great Britain, France, Germany and Russia suspended redemption of banknotes in gold and imposed embargoes on gold exports. After the war, many countries, especially Germany, Austria, Hungary, Poland and Russia, suffered hyperinflation. The German experience provides a classic example of hyperinflation: by the end of 1923, the wholesale price index in Germany was more than one trillion times as high as its prewar level. Freed from wartime pegging, exchange rates among currencies fluctuated in the early 1920s.

As major countries began to recover from the war and stabilize their economies, they attempted to restore the gold standard. The United States, which replaced Great Britain as the dominant financial power, spearheaded efforts to restore the gold standard. With only mild inflation, the United States was able to lift restrictions on gold exports and return to a gold standard in 1919. In Great Britain, Winston Churchill, the British Chancellor of the Exchequer, played a key role in restoring the gold standard in 1925. Besides Great Britain, such countries as Switzerland, France and the Scandinavian countries restored the gold standard by 1928.

---

[3]The price-specie-flow mechanism will work only if governments are willing to abide by the rules of the game by letting the money stock rise and fall as gold flows in and out. Once government demonetizes (neutralizes) gold, the mechanism will break down. In addition, the effectiveness of the mechanism depends on the price elasticity of the demand for imports.

[4]The balance of payments will be discussed in detail in Chapter 3.

[5]This point need not be viewed as a weakness of the gold standard *per se*, but it casts doubt on the long-term feasibility of the gold standard.

The international gold standard of the late 1920s, however, was little more than a façade. Most major countries gave priority to the stabilization of domestic economies and systematically followed a policy of **sterilization of gold** by matching inflows and outflows of gold, respectively, with reductions and increases in domestic money and credit. The Federal Reserve of the United States, for example, kept some gold outside the credit base by circulating it as gold certificates. The Bank of England kept domestic credit stable by neutralizing the effects of gold flows. In short, since countries lacked the political will to abide by the "rules of the game," the automatic adjustment mechanism of the gold standard was unable to work.

Even the façade of the restored gold standard was destroyed in the wake of the Great Depression and the accompanying financial crises. Following the stock market crash and the onset of the Great Depression in 1929, many banks, especially in Austria, Germany and the United States, suffered sharp declines in their portfolio values touching off runs on the banks. Against this backdrop, Britain experienced a massive outflow of gold, due to chronic balance-of-payment deficits and lack of confidence in the pound sterling. Despite coordinated international efforts to rescue the pound, British gold reserves continued to fall to the point where it was impossible to maintain the gold standard. In September 1931, the British government suspended gold payments and let the pound float. As Great Britain got off gold, Canada, Sweden, Austria and Japan followed suit by the end of 1931. The United States got off gold in April 1933 after experiencing a spate of bank failures and outflows of gold. Lastly, France abandoned the gold standard in 1936 because of the flight from the franc, which, in turn, reflected the economic and political instability following the inception of the socialist Popular Front government led by Leon Blum. Paper standards came into being when the gold standard was abandoned.

In sum, the interwar period was characterized by economic nationalism, half-hearted attempts and failure to restore the gold standard, economic and political instabilities, bank failures and panicky flights of capital across borders. No coherent international monetary system prevailed during this period, with profoundly detrimental effects on international trade and investment.

2.5 BRETTON WOODS SYSTEM: 1945–1972

In July 1944, representatives of 44 nations gathered at Bretton Woods, New Hampshire, to discuss and design the postwar international monetary system. After lengthy discussions and bargaining, representatives succeeded in drafting and signing the Articles of Agreement of the International Monetary Fund (IMF), which constitutes the core of the **Bretton Woods system**. The agreement was subsequently ratified by the majority of countries to launch the IMF in 1945. The IMF embodied an explicit set of rules about the conduct of international monetary policies and was responsible for enforcing these rules. Delegates also created a sister institution, the International Bank for Reconstruction and Development (IBRD), better known as the World Bank, that was chiefly responsible for financing individual development projects.

In designing the Bretton Woods system, representatives were concerned with how to prevent the recurrence of economic nationalism with destructive "beggar-thy-neighbour" policies and how to address the lack of clear rules of the game plaguing the interwar years. The British delegates led by John Maynard Keynes proposed an international clearing union that would create an international reserve asset called "bancor." Countries would accept payments in bancor to settle international transactions, without limit. They would also be allowed to acquire bancor by using overdraft facilities with the clearing union. On the other hand, the American delegates, headed by Harry Dexter White, proposed a currency pool to which member countries would make contributions and from which they might borrow to tide themselves over during short-term balance-of-payments deficits. Both delegates desired exchange rate stability without restoring an international gold standard. The American proposal was largely incorporated into the Articles of Agreement of the IMF.

Under the Bretton Woods system, each country established a **par value** in relation to the US dollar, which was pegged to gold at $35 per ounce. This point is illustrated in Exhibit 2.1. Each country was responsible for maintaining its exchange rate within ±1 percent of the adopted par value by buying or selling foreign exchanges, as necessary. However, a member country with a "fundamental disequilibrium" may be allowed to make a change in the par value of its currency. Under the Bretton Woods system, the US dollar was the only currency that was fully convertible to gold; other currencies were not directly convertible to gold. Countries held US dollars, as well as gold, for use as an international means of payment. Because of these arrangements, the Bretton Woods system can be described as a dollar-based **gold-exchange standard**. A country on the gold-exchange standard holds most of its reserves in the form of currency of a country that is *really* on the gold standard.

Advocates of the gold-exchange system argue that the system economizes on gold because countries can use not only gold but also foreign exchanges as an international means of payment. Foreign exchange reserves offset the deflationary effects of limited addition to the world's monetary gold stock. Another advantage of the gold-exchange system is that individual countries can earn interest on their foreign exchange holdings, whereas gold holdings yield no returns. In addition, countries save on transaction costs associated with transporting gold across countries under the gold-exchange system. An ample supply of international monetary reserves coupled with stable exchange rates provided an environment highly conducive to the growth of international trade and investment throughout the 1950s and 1960s.

Professor Robert Triffin warned, however, that the gold-exchange system was programmed to collapse in the long run. To satisfy the growing need for reserves, the United States had to run balance-of-payments deficits continuously. Yet, if the United States ran perennial balance-of-payments deficits, it would eventually impair the public confidence in the dollar, triggering a run on the dollar. Under the gold-exchange system, the reserve-currency country should run balance-of-payments deficits to supply reserves, but if such deficits are large and persistent, they can lead to a crisis of confidence in the reserve currency itself, causing the downfall of the system. This dilemma, known as the **Triffin paradox**, was indeed responsible for the eventual collapse of the dollar-based gold-exchange system in the early 1970s.

The United States began to experience trade deficits with the rest of the world in the late 1950s, and the problem persisted into the 1960s. By the early 1960s, the total value of the US gold stock, when valued at $35 per ounce, fell short of foreign dollar holdings. This naturally created concern about the viability of the dollar-based system. Against this backdrop, President Charles de Gaulle prodded the Bank of France to buy gold from the US Treasury, unloading its dollar holdings. Efforts to remedy the problem centred on (1) a series of dollar defence measures taken by the US government and (2) the creation of a new reserve asset, **special drawing rights (SDRs)**, by the IMF.

EXHIBIT 2.1

The Design of the Gold-Exchange System

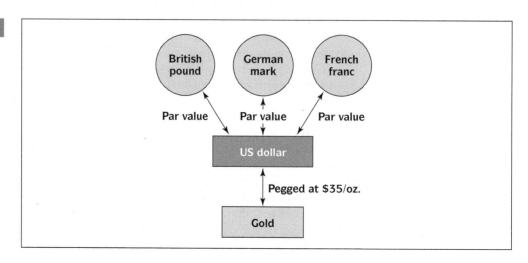

In 1963, President John Kennedy imposed the Interest Equalization Tax (IET) on purchases of foreign securities in order to stem the outflow of dollars. The IET was designed to increase the cost of foreign borrowing in the US bond market. In 1965, the US Federal Reserve introduced the voluntary Foreign Credit Restraint Program (FCRP), which regulated the amount of dollars US banks could lend to US multinational companies engaged in foreign direct investments. In 1968, these regulations became legally binding. Such measures as IET and FCRP gave a strong impetus to the growth of the Eurodollar market, which is a transnational, unregulated fund market.

To partially alleviate the pressure on the dollar as the central reserve currency, the IMF created an artificial international reserve called the SDR in 1970. The SDR, which stands for "Special Drawing Rights," is a basket currency comprising major individual currencies allotted to the members of the IMF, who could then use SDRs for transactions among themselves or with the IMF. In addition to gold and foreign exchange, countries could use the SDR to make international payments.

Initially, the SDR was designed as the weighted average of 16 currencies of those countries whose shares in world exports exceeded more than 1 percent. The percentage share of each currency in the SDR was about the same as the country's share in world exports. In 1981, however, the SDR was greatly simplified to comprise only five major currencies: US dollar, German mark, Japanese yen, British pound and French franc. As Exhibit 2.2 shows, the weight for each currency is updated periodically, reflecting the relative importance of each country in the world trade of goods and services and the amount of the currencies held as reserves by the members of the IMF. Currently, the SDR comprises four major currencies—US dollar (42 percent weight), euro (37 percent), Japanese yen (9 percent) and British pound (11 percent).

The SDR is used not only as a reserve asset but also as a denomination currency for international transactions. Since the SDR is a "portfolio" of currencies, its value tends to be more stable than the value of any individual currency included in the SDR. The portfolio nature of the SDR makes it an attractive denomination currency for international commercial and financial contracts under exchange rate uncertainty.

The efforts to support the dollar-based gold-exchange standard, however, turned out to be ineffective in the face of expansionary monetary policy and rising inflation in the United States related to the financing of the Vietnam War. In the early 1970s, it became clear that the dollar was overvalued, especially relative to the mark and the yen. As a result, the German and Japanese central banks had to make massive interventions in the foreign exchange market to maintain their par values. Given the unwillingness of the United States to control its monetary expansion, the repeated central bank interventions could not solve the underlying disparities. In August 1971, US President Nixon suspended the convertibility of the dollar into gold and imposed a 10-percent import surcharge. The foundation of the Bretton Woods system cracked under the strain.

EXHIBIT 2.2	The Composition of the Special Drawing Right (SDR)[a]						
Currencies	1981–85	1986–90	1991–95	1996–2000	2001–2005	2006–2010	2011–
U.S. dollar	42%	42%	40%	39%	45%	44%	41.9%
Euro	—	—	—	—	29	34	37.4
German mark	19	19	21	21	—	—	—
Japanese yen	13	15	17	18	15	11	9.4
British pound	13	12	11	11	11	11	11.3
French franc	13	12	11	11	—	—	—

[a]The composition of the SDR changes every five years.
Source: IMF.

In an attempt to save the Bretton Woods system, 10 major countries, known as the Group of Ten, met at the Smithsonian Institution in Washington, D.C., in December 1971. They reached the **Smithsonian Agreement**, according to which (1) the price of gold was raised to $38 per ounce, (2) each of the other countries revalued its currency against the US dollar by up to 10 percent and (3) the band within which the exchange rates were allowed to move was expanded from 1 percent to 2.25 percent in either direction.

The Smithsonian Agreement lasted for little more than a year before it came under attack again. Clearly, the devaluation of the US dollar was not sufficient to stabilize the situation. In February 1973, the dollar came under heavy selling pressure, again prompting central banks around the world to buy dollars. The price of gold was further raised from $38 to $42 per ounce. By March 1973, European and Japanese currencies were allowed to float, completing the decline and fall of the Bretton Woods system. Since then, exchange rates among major currencies such as the dollar, the pound and the yen have been fluctuating against each other.

2.6   THE FLEXIBLE EXCHANGE RATE REGIME: 1973–PRESENT

The flexible exchange rate regime that followed the demise of the Bretton Woods system was ratified after the fact in January 1976 when the IMF members met in Jamaica and agreed to a new set of rules for the international monetary system. The key elements of the **Jamaica Agreement** include the following:

1. Flexible exchange rates were declared acceptable to the IMF members, and central banks were allowed to intervene in the exchange markets to iron out unwarranted volatilities.

2. Gold was officially abandoned (i.e., demonetized) as an international reserve asset. Half of the IMF's gold holdings was returned to the members and the other half was sold, with the proceeds to be used to help poor nations.

3. Non-oil-exporting countries and less-developed countries were given greater access to IMF funds.

The IMF continued to provide assistance to countries facing balance-of-payments and exchange rate difficulties. The IMF, however, extended assistance and loans to the member countries on the condition that those countries follow the IMF's macroeconomic policy prescriptions. This "conditionality," which often involves deflationary macroeconomic policies and elimination of various subsidy programs, provoked resentment among the people of the developing countries receiving the IMF's balance-of-payments loans.

As can be expected, exchange rates have become substantially more volatile since 1973 than they previously were under the Bretton Woods system. Exhibit 2.3 summarizes the behaviour of the US dollar exchange rate since 1960. The exhibit shows the exchange rate between the US dollar and a weighted basket of 21 other major currencies. The decline of the dollar between 1970 and 1973 represents the transition from the Bretton Woods to the flexible exchange rate system. The most conspicuous phenomena shown in Exhibit 2.3 are the dollar's spectacular rise between 1980 and 1984 and its equally spectacular decline between 1985 and 1988. These unusual episodes merit some discussion.

Following the American presidential election of 1980, the Reagan administration ushered in a period of growing US budget deficits and balance-of-payments deficits. The US dollar, however, experienced a major appreciation throughout the first half of the 1980s because of large-scale inflows of foreign capital caused by unusually high real interest rates available in the US. To attract foreign investment to finance the budget deficit, the United States had to offer high real interest rates. The heavy demand for dollars by foreign investors pushed up the value of the US dollar in the exchange market.

The value of the dollar reached its peak in February 1985 and then began a persistent downward drift until it stabilized in 1988. The reversal in the exchange rate trend partially reflected the effect of the record-high US trade deficit, about $160 billion in 1985, brought about by the

http://fx.sauder.ubc.ca

Provides a list of all the currencies of the world with information on each country's exchange rate regime. Also provides current and historical exchange rates.

EXHIBIT 2.3   The External Value of the US Dollar since 1960[a]

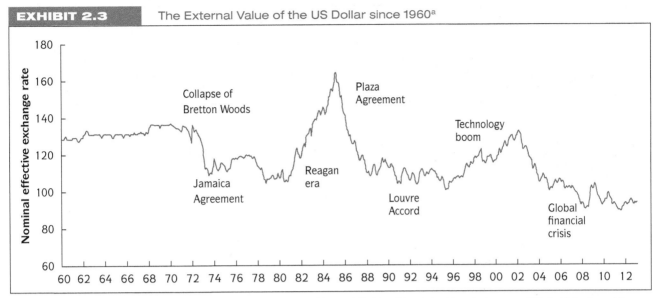

[a]The value of the U.S. dollar represents the nominal exchange rate index (2005 = 100) with weights derived from trade among 21 industrialized countries.
Source: IMF, *International Financial Statistics*, various issues (Washington, DC).

soaring dollar. The downward trend was also reinforced by concerted government interventions. In September 1985, the so-called G-5 countries (France, Japan, Germany, the United Kingdom and the United States) met at the Plaza Hotel in New York and reached what became known as the **Plaza Accord**. They agreed that it would be desirable for the dollar to depreciate against most major currencies to solve the US trade deficit problem and expressed their willingness to intervene in the exchange market to realize this objective. The slide of the dollar that had begun in February was further precipitated by the Plaza Accord.

As the dollar continued its decline, the governments of the major industrial countries began to worry that the dollar might fall too far. To address the problem of exchange rate volatility and other related issues, the G-7 economic summit meeting was convened in Paris in 1987.[6] The meeting produced the **Louvre Accord**, according to which:

1. The G-7 countries would cooperate to achieve greater exchange rate stability.
2. The G-7 countries agreed to more closely consult and coordinate their macroeconomic policies.

The Louvre Accord marked the inception of the **managed-float system**, under which the G-7 countries would jointly intervene in the exchange market to correct over- or undervaluation of currencies. Since the Louvre Accord, exchange rates became relatively more stable for a while. During the period 1996–2001, however, the US dollar generally appreciated, reflecting a robust performance of the US economy fuelled by the technology boom. During this period, foreigners invested heavily in the United States to participate in the booming US economy and stock markets. This helped the dollar to appreciate.

2.7   THE CURRENT EXCHANGE RATE ARRANGEMENTS

Although the most actively traded currencies of the world, such as the dollar, the yen, the pound and the euro, fluctuate against each other, a significant number of the world's smaller currencies are pegged to single currencies, particularly the US dollar and the euro, or baskets of currencies such as the SDR. The current exchange rate arrangements as classified by the IMF are provided in Exhibit 2.4.

---

[6]The G-7 is composed of Canada, France, Japan, Germany, Italy, the United Kingdom and the United States.

Exchange Rate Arrangement (number of countries)	Monetary Policy Framework						
	Exchange Rate Anchor				Monetary Aggregate Target (29)	Inflation-Targeting Framework (32)	Other[1] (38)
	U.S. dollar (43)	Euro (27)	Composite (13)	Other (8)			
No separate legal tender (13)	Ecuador El Salvador Marshall Islands Micronesia Palau Panama Timor-Leste Zimbabwe	Kosovo Montenegro San Marino		Kiribati Tuvalu			
Currency board (12)	ECCU Antigua and Barbuda Dominica Grenada St. Kitts and Nevis St. Lucia St. Vincent and the Grenadines Djibouti Hong Kong SAR	Bosnia and Herzegovina Bulgaria Lithuania[2]		Brunei Darussalam			
Conventional peg (43)	Aruba Bahamas, The Bahrain Barbados Belize Curacao and Sint Eritrea Jordan Netherlands Antilles Oman Qatar Saudi Arabia Turkmenistan United Arab Emirates Venezuela	Cape Verde Comoros Denmark[2] Latvia[2] Sao Tome and Principe **WAEMU** Benin Burkina Faso Côte d'Ivoire Guinea-Bissau Mali Niger Senegal Togo **CAEMC** Cameroon Central African Rep. Chad Congo, Rep. of Equatorial Guinea Gabon	Fiji Kuwait Libya Morocco Samoa	Bhutan Lesotho Namibia Nepal Swaziland			

(Continued)

Stabilized arrangement (16)	Cambodia Guyana Iraq	Lebanon Maldives (04/11) Suriname Trinidad and Tobago	Macedonia, FYR	Vietnam[5]	Tajikistan[4,5] (09/11) Ukraine[5]	Guatemala[5] (6/11)	Angola[4,5] (11/10) Azerbaijan[5] Egypt[4,6] (04/11) Lao P.D.R.[5]
Crawling peg (3)	Nicaragua			Botswana			Bolivia[4,5] (11/10)
Crawl-like arrangement (12)	Ethiopia Honduras (07/11)	Jamaica (06/11) Kazakhstan	Croatia		Argentina[5] China[5] Rwanda[5] Uzbekistan[5,7] (04/08)	Dominican Rep.[5]	Haiti[5] Tunisia[6] (09/11)
Pegged exchange rate within horizontal bands (1)				Tonga			
Other managed arrangement (24)	Liberia[4] (11/11)			Algeria Iran Singapore[4] (09/11) Syria[4] (04/11) Vanuatu	Bangladesh (12/11) Burundi (07/11) Congo, Dem. Rep. (11/11) Guinea Kyrgyz Malawi (08/11) Nigeria Paraguay Yemen		Belarus (05/11) Costa Rica Malaysia Mauritania Myanmar Russia Solomon Islands (02/11) Sudan Switzerland (09/11)
Floating (35)					Afghanistan Gambia Guinea Kenya Madagascar Mongolia Mozambique Pakistan[4] Papua New Guinea Paraguay Seychelles Sierra Leone Sri Lanka (02/13) Tanzania Uganda Zambia	Albania Armenia[8] Brazil Colombia Georgia[8] Ghana Hungary Iceland Indonesia (02/11) Korea Moldova Peru (04/11) Philippines Romania Serbia South Africa Thailand Turkey (10/08) Uruguay	India Mauritius

EXHIBIT 2.4 Exchange Rate Regimes and Anchors of Monetary Policy (as of 2012)

Exchange Rate Arrangement (number of countries)	Monetary Policy Framework						
	Exchange Rate Anchor				Monetary Aggregate Target	Inflation-Targeting Framework	Other[1]
	U.S. dollar (43)	Euro (27)	Composite (13)	Other (8)	(29)	(32)	(38)
Free-floating (31)						Australia Canada Chile Czech Rep. Israel (08/11) Mexico (11/11) New Zealand Norway Poland (12/11) Sweden United Kingdom	Japan Somalia United States **EMU** Austria Belgium Cyprus Estonia (01/11) Finland France Germany Greece Ireland Italy Luxembourg Malta Netherlands Portugal Slovak Rep. Slovenia Spain

Note: If the member country's *de facto* exchange rate arrangement has been reclassified during the reporting period, the date of change is indicated in parentheses.

[1]Includes countries that have no explicitly stated nominal anchor, but rather monitor various indicators in conducting monetary policy.

[2]The member participates in the European Exchange Rate Mechanism (ERM II).

[3]Within the framework of an exchange rate fixed to a currency composite, the Bank Al-Maghrib (BAM) adopted a monetary policy framework in 2006 based on various inflation indicators with the overnight interest rate as its operational target to pursue its main objective of price stability. Since March 2009, the BAM reference interest rate has been set at 3.25 percent.

[4]The exchange rate arrangement was reclassified retroactively, overriding a previously published classification.

[5]The *de facto* monetary policy framework is an exchange rate anchored to the dollar.

[6] The *de facto* monetary policy framework is an exchange rate anchored to a composite.

[7]This reclassification reflects only a methodological correction and does not imply a judgment that there was an alteration in the exchange arrangement or other policies. The change is applied retroactively to 30 April 2008, the date on which the Revised System for the Classification of Exchange Rate Arrangement became effective.

[8]The central bank has taken preliminary steps toward inflation targeting and is preparing for the transition to full-fledged inflation targeting.

Source: IMF, *Annual Report.*

As can be seen from the exhibit, the IMF currently classifies exchange rate arrangements into eight separate regimes:[7]

Exchange arrangements with no separate legal tender: The currency of another country circulates as the sole legal tender or the country belongs to a monetary or currency union in which the same legal tender is shared by the members of the union. Examples include Ecuador, El Salvador and Panama using the US dollar and the 17 Eurozone member countries (such as France, Germany and Italy) sharing the common currency, the euro.

Currency board arrangements: A monetary regime based on an explicit legislative commitment to exchange domestic currency for a specified foreign currency at a fixed exchange rate, combined with restrictions on the issuing authority to ensure the fulfillment of its legal obligation. Examples include Hong Kong fixed to the US dollar and Estonia fixed to the euro.

Other conventional fixed peg arrangement: The country pegs its currency (formally or *de facto*) at a fixed rate to a major currency or a basket of currencies where the exchange rate fluctuates within a narrow margin of less than 1 percent, plus or minus, around a central rate. Examples include Lebanon, Malaysia and Saudi Arabia.

Pegged exchange rates within horizontal bands: The value of the currency is maintained within margins of fluctuation around a formal or *de facto* fixed peg that are wider than at least 1 percent, plus or minus, around a central rate. Tonga is the only example.

Crawling pegs: The currency is adjusted periodically in small amounts at a fixed, preannounced rate or in response to changes in selective quantitative indicators. Examples are Bolivia and Costa Rica.

Exchange rates within crawling bands: The currency is maintained within certain fluctuation margins around a central rate that is adjusted periodically at a fixed preannounced rate or in response to changes in selective quantitative indicators. Examples are Israel, Romania and Venezuela.

Managed floating with no preannounced path for the exchange rate: The monetary authority influences the movements of the exchange rate through active intervention in the foreign exchange market without specifying, or precommitting to, a preannounced path for the exchange rate. Examples include Algeria, Singapore and Thailand.

Independent floating: The exchange rate is market determined, with any foreign exchange intervention aimed at moderating the rate of change and preventing undue fluctuations in the exchange rate, rather than at establishing a level for it. Examples include Australia, Brazil, Canada, Korea, Mexico, the United Kingdom, Japan, Switzerland and the United States.

As of 2013, a large number of countries, including Australia, Canada, Japan, the United Kingdom and the United States, allow their currencies to float independently against other currencies; the exchange rates of these countries are essentially determined by market forces. Fifty countries, including India, Russia and Singapore, have some form of "managed floating" system that combines market forces and government intervention in setting the exchange rates. In contrast, approximately 40 countries do not have their own national currencies. For example, 14 central and western African countries jointly use the CFA-franc, which is fixed to the euro. Seven countries, including Hong Kong and Estonia, on the other hand, maintain national currencies that are permanently fixed to such hard currencies as the US dollar or euro. The remaining countries adopt a mixture of fixed and

---

[7]We draw on IMF classifications provided in *International Financial Statistics.*

floating exchange rate regimes. As is well known, the European Union pursued Europe-wide monetary integration by first establishing the European Monetary System and then the European Monetary Union. These topics deserve a detailed discussion.

2.8 EUROPEAN MONETARY SYSTEM

According to the Smithsonian Agreement signed in 1971, the band of exchange rate movements was expanded from the original plus or minus 1 percent to plus or minus 2.25 percent. Members of the European Economic Community (EEC), however, decided on a narrower band of ±1.125 percent for their currencies. This scaled-down European version of the fixed exchange rate system that arose concurrently with the decline of the Bretton Woods system was called the **snake**. The name "snake" was derived from the way the EEC currencies moved closely together within the wider band allowed for other currencies like the dollar.

The EEC countries adopted the snake because they felt that stable exchange rates among the EEC countries were essential for promoting intra-EEC trade and deepening economic integration. The snake arrangement was replaced by the **European Monetary System (EMS)**, which was formally launched in 1979. Among its chief objectives are:

1. To establish a "zone of monetary stability" in Europe.
2. To coordinate exchange rate policies *vis-à-vis* the non-EMS currencies.
3. To pave the way for the eventual European monetary union.

At the political level, the EMS represented an initiative to accelerate the movement toward European economic and political unification. All EEC member countries except the United Kingdom and Greece joined the EMS. The two main instruments of the EMS are the European Currency Unit and the Exchange Rate Mechanism.

The **European Currency Unit (ECU)** was a "basket" currency constructed as a weighted average of the currencies of member countries of the European Union (EU). The weights were based on each currency's relative GNP and shares in intra-EU trade. The ECU served as the accounting unit of the EMS and played an important role in the workings of the exchange rate mechanism.

The **Exchange Rate Mechanism (ERM)** refers to the procedure by which EMS member countries collectively manage their exchange rates. The ERM was based on a "parity grid" system, which was a system of par values among ERM currencies. The par values in the parity grid were computed by first defining the par values of EMS currencies in terms of the ECU. These par values are called the ECU central rates. The ECU central rates of the German mark and the French franc were DM1.949 per ECU and Fr6.538 per ECU. This implied that the parity between the two member currencies Fr6.538/DM1.949 = Fr3.353/DM. The parity grid was computed by referring to the ECU central rates set by the European Commission.

When the EMS was launched in 1979, a currency was allowed to deviate from the parities with other currencies by a maximum of plus or minus 2.25 percent, with the exception of the Italian lira, for which a maximum deviation of plus or minus 6 percent was allowed. In 1993, however, the band was widened to a maximum of plus or minus 15 percent. When a currency was at the lower or upper bound, the central banks of both countries were required to intervene in the foreign exchange markets to keep the market exchange rate within the band. To intervene in the exchange markets, the central banks could borrow from a credit fund to which member countries contributed gold and foreign reserves.

Since the EMS members were less than fully committed to coordinating their economic policies, the EMS went through a series of realignments. The Italian lira, for instance, was devalued by 6 percent in 1985 and again by 3.7 percent in 1990. In 1992, Italy and the United Kingdom pulled out of the ERM as high German interest rates were inducing massive capital flows into Germany. Following German reunification in 1990, the German government experienced substantial budget deficits that were not accommodated by monetary policy. Germany would not lower its interest rates for fear of inflation, and the

United Kingdom and Italy were not willing to raise their interest rates (which was necessary to maintain their exchange rates) for fear of higher unemployment. Italy, however, rejoined the ERM in 1996 in an effort to participate in the European monetary union.

Despite the recurrent turbulence in the EMS, European Union members met at Maastricht (the Netherlands) in 1991 and signed the **Maastricht Treaty**. According to the treaty, the member states of the European Union committed irrevocably to fix exchange rates by 1 January 1999, and subsequently to introduce a common European currency that would replace individual national currencies. The European Central Bank, to be located in Frankfurt, Germany, would be solely responsible for the issuance of common currency and conducting monetary policy in the European Union. National central banks of individual countries would then function as regional member banks of the European system. Exhibit 2.5 provides a chronology of the European Union.

EXHIBIT 2.5

Chronology of the European Union

1951	The treaty establishing the European Coal and Steel Community (ECSC), which was inspired by French Foreign Minister Robert Schuman, was signed in Paris by six countries: France, Germany, Italy, the Netherlands, Belgium and Luxembourg.
1957	The treaty establishing the European Economic Community (EEC) was signed in Rome.
1968	The Custom Union became fully operational; trade restrictions among the EEC member countries were abolished and a common external tariff system was established.
1973	The United Kingdom, Ireland and Denmark became EEC members.
1978	The EEC became the European Community (EC).
1979	The European Monetary System (EMS) was established for the purpose of promoting exchange rate stability among the EC member countries.
1980	Greece became an EC member.
1986	Portugal and Spain became EC members.
1987	The *Single European Act* was adopted to provide a framework within which the common internal market could be achieved by the end of 1992.
1991	The Maastricht Treaty was signed and subsequently ratified by 12 member states. The treaty establishes a timetable for fulfilling the European Monetary Union (EMU). The treaty also commits the EC to political union.
1994	The European Community was renamed the European Union (EU).
1995	Austria, Finland and Sweden became EU members.
1999	A common European currency, the euro, was adopted by 11 EU member countries.
2001	Greece adopted the euro on January 1.
2002	Euro notes and coins were introduced; national currencies were withdrawn from circulation.
2004	EU expanded by admitting 10 new member countries: Cyprus, Czech Republic, Estonia, Hungary, Latvia, Lithuania, Malta, Poland, Slovak Republic, and Slovenia.
2007	Bulgaria and Romania were admitted to the EU. Slovenia adopted the euro.
2008	Cyprus and Malta adopted the euro.
2009	Slovakia adopted the euro.
2010	Europe's sovereign debt crisis occurred.
2011	Estonia adopted the euro.

To pave the way for the European Monetary Union (EMU), the member states of the European Union agreed to closely coordinate their fiscal, monetary and exchange rate policies and achieve a *convergence* of their economies. Specifically, each member country shall strive to: (1) keep the ratio of government budget deficits to gross domestic product (GDP) below 3 percent, (2) keep gross public debts below 60 percent of GDP, (3) achieve a high degree of price stability and (4) maintain its currency within the prescribed exchange rate ranges of the ERM.

2.9   THE EURO AND THE EUROPEAN MONETARY UNION

On 1 January 1999, an epochal event took place in the arena of international finance: Eleven of 15 EU countries adopted a common currency called the **euro**, voluntarily giving up their monetary sovereignty. The original euro-11 included Austria, Belgium, Finland, France, Germany, Ireland, Italy, Luxembourg, the Netherlands, Portugal and Spain. Four member countries of the European Union—Denmark, Greece, Sweden and the United Kingdom—did not join the first wave. Greece, however, joined the euro club in 2001 when it could satisfy the convergence criteria. There are now 17 member nations in the Eurozone.

The advent of a European single currency, which may potentially rival the US dollar as a global currency, has profound implications for various aspects of international finance. In this section, we (1) describe briefly the historical background for the euro and its implementation process, (2) discuss the potential benefits and costs of the euro from the perspective of the member countries and (3) investigate the broad impacts of the euro on international finance in general.

A Brief History of the Euro

Considering that no European currency has been in circulation since the fall of the Roman Empire, the advent of the euro in January 1999, indeed, qualifies as a historic event. The launch of the euro marks the first time that sovereign countries voluntarily have given up their monetary independence to foster economic integration. The euro thus represents a historically unprecedented experiment, the outcome of which will have far-reaching implications. If the experiment succeeds, for example, both the euro and the dollar will dominate the world of international finance.

The euro represents a step toward the ever-deepening integration of Europe that had begun with the formation of the European Economic Community in 1958. As discussed previously, the European Monetary System (EMS) was created in 1979 to establish a European zone of monetary stability; members were required to restrict fluctuations of their currencies. In 1991, the Maastricht European Council reached agreement on a draft Treaty on the European Union, which called for the introduction of a single European currency by 1999. The European Monetary System merged into the **European Monetary Union (EMU)** on 1 January 1999. The euro became the common currency. For a three-year transition period, each member of the EMU continued to keep its own currency in circulation—the German mark, the French franc and the Dutch guilder, for example. Meanwhile, financial statements, public accounts and contracts were expressed in both the new euro values and the old domestic currency values. The European Central Bank formally took on new authority and responsibility for monetary policy within the EMU.

As the euro was introduced, each national currency of the euro-11 countries was *irrevocably* fixed to the euro at a conversion rate as of 1 January 1999. The conversion rates are provided in Exhibit 2.6. National currencies, such as the French franc, German mark and Italian lira, are no longer independent currencies. Rather, they are just different denominations of the same currency, the euro. On 1 January 2002, euro notes and coins were introduced in circulation, while national bills and coins were gradually withdrawn.

www.ecb.int

Website of the European Central Bank; offers a comprehensive coverage of the euro and links to EU central banks.

EXHIBIT 2.6

Euro Conversion
Rates

1 Euro Is Equal To:	
Austrian schilling	13.7603
Belgian franc	40.3399
Dutch guilder	2.20371
Finnish markka	5.94573
French franc	6.55957
German mark	1.95583
Greek drachma	340.750
Irish punt	0.78756
Italian lira	1936.27
Luxembourg franc	40.3399
Portuguese escudo	200.482
Spanish peseta	166.386

Source: *The Wall Street Journal.*

Once the changeover was completed by 1 July 2002, the legal-tender status of national currencies was cancelled, leaving the euro as the sole legal tender in the euro-12 countries. (As Greece joined the Eurozone in 2001, the euro-11 became the euro-12.)

Monetary policy for the euro-12 countries is conducted by the European Central Bank (ECB) headquartered in Frankfurt, Germany. The primary purpose of the ECB is to maintain price stability. The independence of the ECB is legally guaranteed so that in conducting its monetary policy, it will not be unduly subjected to political pressure from any member country or institution. By and large, the ECB is modelled after the German Bundesbank, which was highly successful in achieving price stability in Germany.

The national central banks of the euro-12 countries have not disappeared. Together with the European Central Bank, they form the **European System of Central Banks (ESCB)**. The responsibilities of the ESCB are threefold: (1) to define and implement the common monetary policy of the Union; (2) to conduct foreign exchange operations; and (3) to hold and manage the official foreign reserves of the euro member states. In addition, governors of national central banks sit on the Governing Council of the ECB. Although national central banks must follow the policies of the ECB, they continue to perform important functions in their jurisdiction such as distributing credit, collecting resources and managing payment systems.

From the perspective of those outside of Europe, bilateral exchange rates *vis-à-vis* the euro are important indicators of the strength and stability of Europe's new common currency. Exhibit 2.7 presents data since euro-inception until June 2013 for the Canadian dollar–euro exchange rate along with the US dollar–euro rate. At the launch of the euro, the Canadian dollar–euro rate was 1.79 Canadian dollars per euro, while the initial US dollar–euro rate was 1.18 US dollars per euro. Immediately thereafter, the euro started a downward slide against both North American dollars, reaching a low of 1.25 Canadian dollars in October 2000 and 0.825 US dollars in the same month. Canadian and US dollars tend to be highly correlated in their movements *vis-à-vis* the euro.

With the early decline of the euro, it appeared that the new currency was more fragile than first anticipated. However, by April 2002, the euro began to recapture the value that it had lost against other currencies, including both the Canadian and the US dollars. By January 2004, the euro had strengthened to 1.29 US dollars per euro, substantially above its "launch" value five years earlier. Meanwhile, against the Canadian dollar—which had

EXHIBIT 2.7

Exchange Rates
since the Euro's
Inception for
Canadian Dollar and
US Dollar

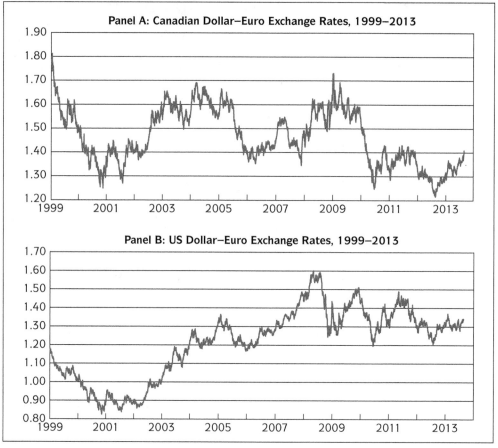

Source: Rotman Finance Centre.

gained strength against the American dollar—the euro rose to 1.65 Canadian dollars per
euro which compares with its "launch value" of 1.79.

What Are the Benefits of the Monetary Union?

The original euro-11 countries decided to form a monetary union with a common currency
because they believed the benefits from such a union would outweigh the associated
costs—in contrast to those eligible countries that chose not to adopt the single currency. It
is thus important to understand the potential benefits and costs of monetary union.

What are the main benefits from adopting a common currency? The most direct and
immediate benefits are reduced transaction costs and the elimination of exchange rate
uncertainty. There was a popular saying in Europe that if one travelled through all 15 EU
countries, changing money in each country into its currency but not actually spending it,
one would return home with only half the original amount. However, when countries use
the same currency, such transactions costs are reduced substantially. These savings accrue
to practically all economic agents, benefiting individuals, companies and governments.
Although it is difficult to estimate accurately the magnitude of foreign exchange transaction costs, a consensus estimation is around 0.4 percent of Europe's GDP.

Economic agents also benefit from the elimination of exchange rate uncertainty.
Companies no longer suffer currency loss from intra-Eurozone transactions. Companies
that used to hedge exchange risk now save hedging costs. As price comparison becomes
easier because of the common currency, consumers can benefit from comparison shopping.
Increased price transparency promotes Europe-wide competition, exerting downward
pressure on prices. Reduced transaction costs and the elimination of currency risk together

have the net effect of promoting cross-border investment and trade within the eurozone. By furthering economic integration of Europe, the single currency promotes corporate restructuring via mergers and acquisitions, encourages optimal business location decisions and ultimately strengthens the international competitive position of European companies. Thus, the enhanced efficiency and competitiveness of the European economy can be regarded as the third major benefit of the monetary union.

The advent of the common European currency also helps create conditions conducive to the development of continental capital markets. In the past, national currencies and local-ized legal/regulatory frameworks resulted in largely illiquid, fragmented capital markets in Europe, which prevented European companies from raising capital on competitive terms. The common currency and the integration of European financial markets pave the way for a European capital market in which both European and non-European companies can raise money at favourable rates.

Last but not least, sharing a common currency promotes political cooperation and peace in Europe. The founding fathers of the European Union, including Jean Monnet, Paul-Henri Spaak, Robert Schuman and their successors, took a series of economic measures designed to link the European countries together. They envisioned a new Europe in which economic interdependence and cooperation among regions and countries would replace nationalistic rivalries which so often led to calamitous wars in the past. In this context, Helmut Kohl, a former German chancellor, said that the European Monetary Union was a "matter of war and peace." A stable, continentally accepted euro advances the political integration of Europe.

Costs of Monetary Union

The main cost of monetary union is the loss of national monetary and exchange rate policy independence. Suppose Finland, a country heavily dependent on the paper and pulp indus-tries, faces a sudden drop in world paper and pulp prices. This price drop could severely hurt the Finnish economy, causing unemployment and income decline while scarcely affecting other Eurozone countries. Finland, thus, faces an "asymmetric shock." Generally speaking, a country is more prone to asymmetric shocks when its economy is less diversi-fied and more trade-dependent.

www.columbia.
edu/~ram15

This homepage of Professor Robert Mundell provides a synopsis of his academic works, Nobel lecture, etc.

If Finland maintained monetary independence, the country could consider lowering domestic interest rates to stimulate the weak economy as well as letting its currency depre-ciate to boost foreigners' demand for Finnish products. But because Finland has joined the EMU, the country no longer has these policy options at its disposal. Further, with the rest of the Eurozone unaffected by Finland's particular problem, the ECB is not likely to tune its monetary policy to address a local Finnish shock. In other words, a common monetary policy dictated in Frankfurt cannot address asymmetric economic shocks that affect only a particular country or subregion; it can only deal with Eurozone-wide shocks.

If, however, wage and price levels in Finland are flexible, then the country may still be able to deal with an asymmetric shock; lower wage and price levels in Finland would have economic effects similar to those of a depreciation of the Finnish currency. Furthermore, if capital flows freely across the Eurozone and workers are willing to relocate to where jobs are, then again much of the asymmetric shock can be absorbed without monetary adjust-ments. If these conditions are not met, however, the asymmetric shock could cause a reces-sion in the affected country. In this case, monetary union could become a costly venture. The concept of an **optimum currency area**, originally conceived by Robert Mundell in 1961, suggests that the relevant criterion for identifying and designing a common currency zone is the degree of factor (i.e., capital and labour) mobility within the zone. A high degree of factor mobility provides an adjustment mechanism as an alternative to country-specific monetary/currency adjustments.

Considering the high degree of capital and labour mobility in Canada, one might argue that Canada approximates an optimum currency area. It would be suboptimal for each

Mundell Wins Nobel Prize for Economics

Robert A. Mundell, one of the intellectual fathers of both the new European common currency and Reagan-era supply-side economics, won the Nobel Memorial Prize for Economic Science.

Mr. Mundell conducted innovative research into common currencies when the idea of the euro, Europe's new currency, was still a fantasy. The 66-year-old Columbia University professor, a native of Canada, also examined the implications of cross-border capital flows and flexible foreign-exchange rates when capital flows were still restricted and currencies still fixed to each other.

"Mundell chose his problems with uncommon—almost prophetic—accuracy in terms of predicting the future development of international monetary arrangements and capital markets," the selection committee said in announcing the prize.

An eccentric, white-haired figure who once bought an abandoned Italian castle as a hedge against inflation, Mr. Mundell later became a hero of the economic Right with his dogged defense of the gold standard and early advocacy of the controversial tax-cutting, supply-side economics that became the hallmark of the Reagan administration.

While the Nobel committee sidestepped his political impact in awarding Mr. Mundell the $975,000 prize for his work in the 1960s, his conservative fans celebrated the award as an endorsement of supply-side thinking.

"I know it will take a little longer, but history eventually will note that it was Mundell who made it possible for Ronald Reagan to be elected president," by providing the intellectual backing for the Reagan tax cuts, wrote conservative economist Jude Wanniski on his Web site.

Mundell's View

Great currencies and great powers according to Robert Mundell:

Country	Period
Greece	7th–3rd C. B.C.
Persia	6th–4th C. B.C.
Macedonia	4th–2nd C. B.C.
Rome	2nd C. B.C.–4th C.
Byzantium	5th–13th C.
Franks	8th–11th C.
Italian city states	13th–6th C.
France	13th–18th C.
Holland	17th–18th C.
Germany (thaler)	14th–19th C.
France (franc)	1803–1870
Britain (pound)	1820–1914
U.S. (dollar)	1915–present
E.U. (euro)	1999

Source: "The Euro and the Stability of the International Monetary System," Robert Mundell, Columbia University.

Mr. Mundell's advocacy of supply-side economics sprang from his work in the 1960s examining what fiscal and monetary policies are appropriate if exchange rates are either fixed—as they were prior to the collapse of the gold-based Bretton Woods system in the early 1970s—or floating, as they are in the U.S. and many other countries today.

One major finding has since become conventional wisdom: When money can move freely across borders, policy makers must choose between exchange-rate

province to issue its own currency. Canadian workers are highly mobile within Canada, moving to wherever job opportunities are. In contrast, unemployed workers in Helsinki, for example, are not very likely to move to Milan or Stuttgart for job opportunities because of cultural, religious, linguistic and other barriers. The stability pact of EMU, designed to discourage irresponsible fiscal behaviour in the post-EMU era, also constrains the Finnish government to restrict its budget deficit to 3 percent of GDP at most. At the same time, Finland cannot expect to receive transfer payments from Brussels because of a rather low degree of fiscal integration among the EU countries. These considerations taken together suggest that the European Monetary Union could involve significant economic costs. An empirical study by von Hagen and Neumann (1994) identified Austria, Belgium, France, Luxembourg, the Netherlands and Germany as nations that satisfy the conditions for an optimum currency area. However, Denmark, Italy and the United Kingdom do not. It is interesting to note that Denmark and the United Kingdom actually chose to stay out of the EMU. Von Hagen and Neumann's study suggests that Italy joined the EMU prematurely.

The International Finance in Practice box "Mundell Wins Nobel Prize for Economics" explains Professor Mundell's view on the monetary union. Professor Mundell contends that as an economist with Canadian roots, he was naturally more attuned to international financial stability and an independent monetary policy. They can't have both.

Mr. Mundell's work has long had an impact on policy makers. In 1962, he wrote a paper addressing the Kennedy administration's predicament of how to spur the economy while facing a balance-of-payments deficit. "The only correct way to do it was to have a tax cut and then protect the balance of payments by tight money," he recalled in a 1996 interview. The Kennedy administration eventually came around to the same way of thinking.

Mr. Mundell traces the supply-side movement to a 1971 meeting of distinguished economists, including Paul Volcker and Paul Samuelson, at the Treasury Department. At the time, most economists were stumped by the onset of stagflation—a combination of inflationary pressures, a troubled dollar, a worsening balance of payments and persistent unemployment. They thought any tightening of monetary or fiscal policy would bolster the dollar and improve the balance of payments, but worsen unemployment. An easing of monetary or fiscal policy might generate jobs, but weaken the dollar, lift prices and expand the balance-of-payments deficit.

Mr. Mundell suggested a heretical solution: Raise interest rates to protect the dollar, but cut taxes to spur the economy. Most others in the room were aghast at the idea, fearing tax cuts would lead to a swelling budget deficit—something many nonsupply-siders believe was exactly what happened during the Reagan years.

"I knew I was in the minority," he said in an 1988 interview. "But I thought my vote should count much more than the others because I understood the subject."

While in Chicago, he found himself constantly at odds with Milton Friedman, who advocated monetary rules and floating exchange rates. Mr. Mundell joined Columbia in 1974, two years before Mr. Friedman won the economics Nobel.

Ever the maverick, Mr. Mundell remains a fan of the gold standard and fixed exchange rates at a time when they're out of favor with most other economists. "You have fixed rates between New York and California, and it works perfectly," he said.

The Nobel committee also praised Mr. Mundell's research into common currency zones, which laid the intellectual foundation for the 11-country euro. In 1961, when European countries still clung to their national currencies, he described the circumstances in which nations could share a common currency.

"At the time, it just seemed like such a wacko thing to work on, and that's why it's so visionary," said Kenneth Rogoff, a Harvard economist.

In particular, Mr. Mundell argued that in any successful currency zone, workers must be able to move freely from areas that are slowing to areas that are booming. Some critics suggest the euro nations don't fit his description.

But Mr. Mundell believes the new currency will eventually challenge the dollar for global dominance. "The benefits will derive from transparency of pricing, stability of expectations and lower transactions costs, as well as a common monetary policy run by the best minds that Europe can muster," Mr. Mundell wrote last year. He began working on the euro project as a consultant to European monetary authorities in 1969.

Source: Michael M. Phillips, *The Wall Street Journal*, 14 October 1999, p. A2. © 1999 Dow Jones & Company, Inc. All rights reserved worldwide.

issues, including capital flows, exchange rates and the like, which piqued his interest in common currency areas and his work that was ultimately recognized with the Nobel Prize.

Prospects of the Euro: Some Critical Questions

Will the euro succeed? The first real test of the euro will come when the Eurozone experiences major asymmetric shocks. A successful response to these shocks will require wage, price and fiscal flexibility. A cautionary note is in order: Asymmetric shocks can occur even within a country. In Canada, for example, when oil prices jump as they did in the 1970s and, more recently, in 2005–2006, oil-consuming regions such as the eastern provinces suffer adverse effects whereas Alberta, a major oil-producing province, experiences a boom. Likewise in Italy, the highly industrialized Genoa–Milan region and the southern Mezzogiorno, an underdeveloped region, can be in very different phases of the business cycle. Canada and Italy cannot manage *internal* asymmetric shocks with national monetary policy. Italy is precluded from doing so because it gave up its national monetary policy when it joined the Eurozone. Canada knows that it cannot effectively have regionally targeted monetary policy.

The Canadian Dollar in Historical Perspective

The monetary history of Canada has been admirably recorded by James Powell (2005). Powell demonstrates that our monetary history is more than a story of money. Canada's currency provides a unique optic through which to examine our rich economic and political history and, above all, our relationship with other countries. Through this monetary lens, we witness the clash of empires in the eighteenth century, the building of a continent-spanning nation during the nineteenth century and development of a sophisticated structure of trade and international investment in the late twentieth century.

Through history we see economic pressures brought to bear on Canada and the ingenuity of Canadians in dealing with them. Born of necessity, de Meulles's card money in 1685 is believed to be the first issue of paper money by a Western government. The Great Depression and deflation of the 1930s also challenged the orthodox monetary wisdom of the time, leading once again to monetary experimentation and to the creation of the Bank of Canada.

The following paragraphs, drawn from the conclusion to Powell's fascinating history of the Canadian dollar, offer a number of pertinent ties to the issues that we have addressed in this chapter dealing with the international monetary system.

Canada's monetary history illustrates the strong economic attraction of the United States, as well as the weakening economic and political ties with the United Kingdom. North–south economic linkages were the reason why Canada, over imperial opposition, chose the dollar instead of the pound as its monetary standard in the 1850s. However, in a typical Canadian compromise, both U.S. and British coins remained legal tender in Canada, alongside distinctive Canadian notes and coins, into the 1930s.

A similar tension can be found in Canada's choice of exchange rate regime. Through much of the nineteenth and early twentieth centuries, a fixed one-for-one exchange rate was maintained between Canada and the United States, supported by both countries' adherence to the gold standard. Such a relationship seemed natural in light of the close commercial and financial links between the two countries.

On the other hand, the Canadian economy, a major exporter of commodities, was, and remains, very different from that of the United States, a major supplier of manufactured goods. This distinction, as well as a desire in Canada to direct macroeconomic policy towards achieving domestic policy objectives, argues for a flexible exchange rate. These factors were the reason why Canada adopted a floating exchange rate in 1950 and again in 1970. Canada's history has shown, however, that no exchange rate regime is perfect. The choice of regime involves trade-offs that may change with the passage of time and with differing circumstances.

Dissatisfaction with the severe policy limitations of the gold standard led Canada and other countries to break the link between their currencies and gold during the 1930s. Dissatisfaction with the competitive devaluations and "beggar-thy-neighbour" policies of the Depression years led to the Bretton Woods system

Although asymmetric shocks are no doubt serious, one should be careful not to exaggerate their significance as an impediment to monetary union. Since the advent of the EMS in 1979, the EMU member countries have restricted their monetary policies in order to maintain exchange rate stability in Europe. Considering that intra-Eurozone trade accounts for about 60 percent of foreign trade of the euro-12 countries, benefits from the EMU are likely to exceed substantially the associated costs. Leaders in political and business circles in Europe have invested substantial political capital in the success of the euro. It seems safe to predict that the euro will be a success.

Will the euro become a global currency to rival the US dollar? The US dollar has been the dominant global currency since the end of World War I, replacing the British pound as the currency of choice in international commercial and financial transactions. Even after the US dollar went off the gold standard, it retained its dominant position in the world economy. This dominance was possible because the dollar was backed by the sheer size of the US economy and the relatively sound monetary policy of the Federal Reserve. Now, as can be seen from Exhibit 2.8, the Eurozone is comparable with the United States in terms of population size, GDP and international trade share. Exhibit 2.8 also shows that the euro is as important a denomination currency as the dollar in international bond markets. In contrast, the Japanese yen plays an insignificant role in international bond markets. As previously discussed, there is little doubt that the ECB will pursue a sound monetary policy. Considering both the size of the Eurozone economy and the mandate of

of fixed, but adjustable, exchange rates after the Second World War. Dissatisfaction with pegged exchange rates in an environment of global inflationary pressures and rising capital mobility led to the floating of all major currencies in 1973.

The launch of the euro on 1 January 1999 and the collapse of fixed exchange rate regimes in many emerging-market economies led to a renewed debate in Canada and abroad on appropriate exchange rate regimes. The debate in Canada was also fuelled by the persistent weakness of the Canadian dollar and a view held by some economists that a common North American currency was appropriate and, possibly, inevitable. But the weight of economic analysis and opinion continue to favour Canada maintaining its flexible exchange rate and retaining its monetary policy independence.

Until relatively recently, however, it was not clear that Canada and other countries with floating exchange rates had used their monetary independence to their best advantage. Immediately prior to the floating of the Canadian dollar in 1970, Harry Johnson, the great Canadian monetary economist, noted that

> . . . a flexible exchange rate is not, of course, a pana-cea; it simply provides an extra degree of freedom, by removing the balance-of-payments constraint on pol-icy formulation. (Johnson 1972)

This observation was prophetic. Through the following decades, exchange rates, liberated from the constraints imposed by the Bretton Woods system, moved in a wide range, reflecting both real and monetary shocks in the domestic economy and in the anchor country, i.e.,

the United States. The Canadian dollar was no exception. While countries were now free to direct policy at achiev-ing domestic objectives, the "extra degree of freedom" was often squandered. In Canada, the rationale behind floating the Canadian dollar in 1970 was to avoid import-ing U.S. inflation. In the event, Canada's inflation perfor-mance was very similar to that of the United States.

David Laidler, a noted monetary economist and eco-nomic historian at the University of Western Ontario, has argued that a flexible exchange rate, unlike a fixed rate, is not a coherent monetary order, since a flexible rate does not "define a policy goal, but merely permits some other goal . . . to be pursued" (Laidler 2002). For a country with a flexible rate to have a coherent mone-tary order, other elements are required—a clear goal for monetary policy (and a broader supportive policy framework that includes sustainable fiscal policy), cred-ibility and public accountability.

Laidler contends that such a coherent monetary order was not firmly in place in Canada until about 1995. This was four years after inflation targets were introduced and 25 years after Canada last floated the dollar. It was only when a coherent monetary order was established that the Bank of Canada was in a position to use its policy independence to its best advantage by focusing on pre-serving the domestic purchasing power of the Canadian dollar through low inflation, while at the same time allow-ing the external value of the currency to adjust to shocks.

Source: Excerpt from Powell, James (2005). *A History of the Canadian Dollar,* Ottawa: Bank of Canada (Publications Division), pp. 85–87.

the ECB, the euro is likely to emerge as the second global currency, ending the dollar's sole dominance. The Japanese yen is likely to be a junior partner in the dollar–euro conundrum. However, the emergence of the euro as another global currency may prompt Japan and other Asian countries to explore cooperative monetary arrangements for the region.

EXHIBIT 2.8

Macroeconomic Data for Major Economies[a]

Economy	Population (millions)	GDP ($ trillions)	Annual Inflation, %/yr.	World Trade Share, %	International Bonds Outstanding ($ billions)
United States	315	15.6	2.4	10.2	7,183
Canada	34	1.8	1.6	3.2	695
Euro-17	333	16.4	2.2	14.1	7,637
Japan	128	5.9	−0.3	4.6	471
United Kingdom	63	2.4	2.9	3.1	1,187

[a]The inflation rate is the annual average from 1999 to 2012. International bonds outstanding refer to international bonds and notes outstanding by December 2012 by currency of issue. The remaining data are 2012 figures.
Source: IMF, International Financial Statistics, European Commission Economic and Financial Affairs.

2.10   FIXED VERSUS FLEXIBLE EXCHANGE RATE REGIMES

Since some countries, including Canada, prefer flexible exchange rates, while others, notably the members of the EMU and many developing countries, prefer to maintain fixed exchange rates, it is worthwhile to examine some of the arguments advanced in favour of fixed versus flexible exchange rates.

The key arguments for flexible exchange rates rest on (1) easier external adjustments and (2) national policy autonomy. Suppose a country is experiencing a balance-of-payments deficit at the moment. This means that there is an excess supply of the country's currency at the prevailing exchange rate in the foreign exchange market. Under a flexible exchange rate regime, the external value of the country's currency will simply depreciate to the level at which there is no excess supply of the country's currency. At the new exchange rate level, the balance-of-payments disequilibrium will disappear.

As long as the exchange rate is allowed to be determined according to market forces, external balance will be achieved automatically. Consequently, the government does not have to take policy actions to correct the balance-of-payments disequilibrium. With flexible exchange rates, therefore, the government can use its monetary and fiscal policies to pursue whatever economic goals it chooses. Under a fixed rate regime, however, the government may have to take contractionary (expansionary) monetary and fiscal policies to correct the balance-of-payments deficit (surplus) at the existing exchange rate. Since policy tools need to be committed to maintaining the exchange rate, the government cannot use the same policy tools to pursue other economic objectives. As a result, the government loses its policy autonomy under a fixed exchange rate regime.

Using the British pound as the representative foreign exchange, Exhibit 2.9 illustrates the preceding discussion on how the balance-of-payment disequilibrium between Britain and the United States is corrected under alternative exchange rate regimes. As is the case with most other commodities, the demand for British pounds would be downward-sloping, whereas the supply of British pounds would be upward-sloping. Suppose that the exchange rate for US dollars is initially $1.40/£. As can be seen from the exhibit, the demand for British pounds far exceeds the supply (i.e., the supply of dollars far exceeds the demand) at this exchange rate. The United States experiences trade (or balance-of-payment) deficits. Under the flexible exchange rate regime, the dollar will simply depreciate to a new level of exchange rate, $1.60/£, at which the excess demand for British pounds (and thus the trade deficit) will disappear. Now, suppose that the exchange rate is "fixed" at $1.40/£ and, consequently, the excess demand for British pounds cannot be eliminated by the exchange rate

EXHIBIT 2.9

External Adjustment Mechanism: Fixed versus Flexible Exchange Rates

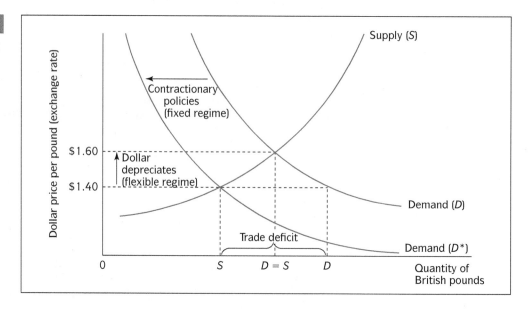

adjustment. Facing this situation, the US Federal Reserve Bank may initially draw on its foreign exchange reserve holdings to satisfy the excess demand for British pounds. If the excess demand persists, however, the US government may have to resort to contractionary monetary and fiscal policies so that the demand curve can shift to the left (from D to D^* in the exhibit) until the excess demand for British pounds can be eliminated at the fixed exchange rate, $1.40/£. In other words, it is necessary for the government to take policy actions to maintain the fixed exchange rate.

A possible drawback of the flexible exchange rate regime is that exchange rate uncertainty may hamper international trade and investment. Proponents of fixed exchange rates argue that when exchange rates are uncertain, businesses tend to shun foreign trade. Since countries cannot fully benefit from international trade under exchange rate uncertainty, resources will be allocated suboptimally on a global basis. Proponents of fixed exchange rates argue that fixed exchange rates eliminate such uncertainty and thus promote international trade. However, to the extent that firms can hedge exchange risk by means of currency forward or options contracts, uncertain exchange rates do not necessarily hamper international trade.

As the above discussion suggests, the choice between the alternative exchange rate regimes is likely to involve a trade-off between national policy independence and international economic integration. If countries are intent on aggressively pursuing domestic economic goals, they are likely to pursue divergent macroeconomic policies, rendering fixed exchange rates infeasible. On the other hand, if countries are committed to promoting international economic integration (as is the case with the core members of the European Union), the benefits of fixed exchange rates are likely to outweigh the associated costs.

A "good" (or ideal) international monetary system should provide (1) liquidity, (2) adjustment and (3) confidence. In other words, a good IMS should be able to provide the world economy with sufficient monetary reserves to support the growth of international trade and investment. It should also provide an effective mechanism that restores the balance-of-payments equilibrium whenever it is disturbed. Lastly, it should offer a safeguard to prevent crises of confidence in the system that result in panicked flights from one reserve asset to another. Politicians and economists should keep these three criteria in mind when they design and evaluate the international monetary system.

SUMMARY

This chapter provides an overview of the international monetary system, which defines an environment in which multinational corporations operate.

1. The international monetary system can be defined as the institutional framework within which international payments are made, the movements of capital are accommodated and exchange rates among currencies are determined.

2. The international monetary system went through five stages of evolution: (a) bimetallism, (b) classical gold standard, (c) interwar period, (d) Bretton Woods system and (e) flexible exchange rate regime.

3. The classical gold standard spanned 1875 to 1914. Under the gold standard, the exchange rate between two currencies is determined by the gold contents of the currencies. Balance-of-payments disequilibrium is automatically corrected through the price-specie-flow mechanism. The gold standard still has ardent supporters who believe that it provides an effective hedge against price inflation. Under the gold standard, however, the world economy can be subject to

deflationary pressure due to the limited supply of monetary gold.

4. To prevent the recurrence of economic nationalism with no clear "rules of the game" witnessed during the interwar period, representatives of 44 nations met at Bretton Woods, New Hampshire, in 1944 and adopted a new international monetary system. Under the Bretton Woods system, each country established a par value in relation to the US dollar, which was fully convertible to gold. Countries used foreign exchanges, especially the US dollar, as well as gold as international means of payments. The system was designed to maintain stable exchange rates and economize on gold. Bretton Woods eventually collapsed in 1973 mainly because of US domestic inflation and the persistent balance-of-payments deficits.

5. The flexible exchange rate regime that replaced the Bretton Woods system was ratified by the Jamaica

Agreement. Following a spectacular rise and fall of the US dollar in the 1980s, major industrial countries agreed to cooperate to achieve greater exchange rate stability. The Louvre Accord of 1987 marked the inception of the managed-float system under which the G-7 countries would jointly intervene in the foreign exchange market to correct over- or undervaluation of currencies.

6. In 1979, the EEC countries launched the European Monetary System (EMS) to establish a "zone of monetary stability" in Europe. The two main instruments of the EMS are the European Currency Unit (ECU) and the Exchange Rate Mechanism (ERM). The ECU is a basket currency comprising the currencies of the EMS members and serves as the accounting unit of the EMS. The ERM refers to the procedure by which EMS members collectively manage their exchange rates. The ERM is based on a parity grid that the member countries are required to maintain.

7. On 1 January 1999, eleven European countries including France and Germany adopted a common currency called the euro. Greece adopted the euro in 2001. The advent of a single European currency, which may eventually rival the US dollar as a global vehicle currency, will have major implications for the European as well as world economy. The euro-12 countries will benefit from reduced transaction costs and the elimination of exchange rate uncertainty. The advent of the euro will also help develop continent-wide capital markets where companies can raise capital at favourable rates.

8. Under the European Monetary Union (EMU), the common monetary policy for the euro-12 countries is formulated by the European Central Bank (ECB) located in Frankfurt. The ECB is legally mandated to maintain price stability in Europe. Together with the ECB, the national central banks of the euro-12 countries form the European System of Central Banks (ESBC), which is responsible for defining and implementing the common monetary policy for the EMU.

9. While the core EMU members, including France and Germany, apparently prefer the fixed exchange rate regime, other major countries, such as the United States and Japan, are willing to live with flexible exchange rates. Under the flexible exchange rate regime, governments retain policy independence because the external balance will be achieved by the exchange rate adjustments rather than by policy intervention. Exchange rate uncertainty, however, can potentially hamper international trade and investment. The choice between the alternative exchange rate regimes is likely to involve a trade-off between national policy autonomy and international economic integration.

QUESTIONS

1. Explain Gresham's law.

2. Explain the mechanism that restores the balance-of-payments equilibrium when it is disturbed under the gold standard.

3. Suppose that the pound is pegged to gold at 6 pounds per ounce, whereas the franc is pegged to gold at 12 francs per ounce. This, of course, implies that the equilibrium exchange rate should be 2 francs per pound. If the current market exchange rate is 2.2 francs per pound, how would you take advantage of this situation? What would be the effect of shipping costs?

4. Discuss the advantages and disadvantages of the gold standard.

5. What were the main objectives of the Bretton Woods system?

6. Comment on the proposition that the Bretton Woods system was programmed to an eventual demise.

7. How are special drawing rights (SDR) constructed? Discuss the circumstances under which the SDR was created.

8. Explain the arrangements and workings of the European Monetary System (EMS).

9. There are arguments for and against the alternative exchange rate regimes.

   a. List the advantages of flexible exchange rates.

   b. Criticize flexible exchange rates from the viewpoint of the proponents of fixed exchange rates.

   c. Rebut the above criticism from the viewpoint of the proponents of flexible exchange rates.

10. Discuss the criteria for a "good" international monetary system.

11. Once capital markets are integrated, it is difficult for a country to maintain a fixed exchange rate. Explain why this may be so.

12. Assess the possibility for the euro to become another global currency rivalling the US dollar. If the euro really becomes a global currency, what impact will it have on the US dollar and the world economy?

13. What are the basic characteristics of a *bona fide* common currency area? Is Canada a common currency area?

INTERNET EXERCISE

1. Using the data from http://fx.sauder.ubc.ca, first plot the daily exchange rate between the euro and the US dollar since 1 January 2002, and try to explain why the exchange rate behaved the way it did.

2. Repeat the exercise with the Canadian dollar and the euro.

MINI CASE

Will the United Kingdom Join the Euro Club?

When the euro was introduced in January 1999, the United Kingdom was conspicuously absent from the list of European countries adopting the common currency. Although the Labour government led by Prime Minister Tony Blair appeared to be in favour of joining the euro club, it did not happen. The opposition Tory party was not in favour of adopting the euro and thus giving up monetary sovereignty of the country. Public opinion was also divided on the issue and still is.

Whether the United Kingdom will eventually join the euro club is a matter of considerable importance for the future of the European Union as well as that of the United Kingdom. If the United Kingdom, with its sophisticated finance industry, joins, it will most certainly propel the euro into a global currency status rivalling the US dollar. The United Kingdom, for its part, will firmly join the process of economic and political unionization of Europe, abandoning its traditional balancing role.

Investigate the political, economic, and historical situations surrounding British participation in the European economic and monetary integration, and write your own assessment of the prospect of the United Kingdom joining the euro club. In doing so, assess from the British perspective, among other things, (1) potential benefits and costs of adopting the euro, (2) economic and political constraints facing the country and (3) the potential impact of British adoption of the euro on the international financial system, including the role of the US dollar.

REFERENCES & SUGGESTED READINGS

Brean, Donald J. S. "Financial Liberalization in Canada: Historical, Institutional and Economic Perspectives," in *International Financial Reform,* Albert Berry and Gustavo Indart, eds. London: Transaction Publishers, 2003.

Courchene, Thomas J., and Richard G. Harris. "North American Monetary Union: Analytical Principles and Operational Guidelines." *The North American Journal of Economics and Finance,* Volume 11, Issue 1 (August 2000), pp. 3–18.

Eichengreen, Barry. *The Gold Standard in Theory and History.* Methuen: London, 1985, pp. 39–48.

Grubel, Herbert G. "The Merit of a Canada–US Monetary Union." *The North American Journal of Economics and Finance.* Volume 11, Issue 1 (August 2000), pp. 19–40.

Johnson, Harry G. (1972). *Further Essays in Monetary Economics.* London: George Allen & Unwin.

Laidler, David E. W. (2002). "Inflation Targets versus International Monetary Integration: A Canadian Perspective." University of Western Ontario, EPRI Working Paper Series No. 2002–3.

Mundell, Robert. "A Theory of Optimum Currency Areas." *American Economic Review* 51 (1961), pp. 657–65.

———. "Currency Areas, Volatility and Intervention." *Journal of Policy Modeling* 22 (2000), pp. 281–99.

Murray, John. "Why Canada Needs a Flexible Exchange Rate." *The North American Journal of Economics and Finance,* Volume 11, Issue 1 (August 2000), pp. 41–60.

Powell, James. *A History of The Canadian Dollar.* Ottawa: The Bank of Canada (2005). Available in PDF from *www.bankofcanada.ca.*

Robson, William B. P., and David Laidler. *The Awkward Economics and Politics of North American Monetary Integration.* Toronto: C. D. Howe Institute, July 2002.

Stiglitz, Joseph. "Reforming the Global Economic Architecture: Lessons from Recent Crisis." *Journal of Finance* 54 (1999), pp. 1508–21.

TD Economics. *Loonie Tunes: Understanding the Rally in the Canadian Dollar and Its Consequences.* A Special Report on the Canadian Dollar by the Economics Department of TD CanadaTrust (2004). Available in PDF from *www.td.com/economics.*

von Hagen, Jürgen, and M. J. M. Neumann. "Real Exchange Rates within and between Currency Areas—How Far Away Is EMU?" *The Review of Economics and Statistics* 76, June 1994, 236–44.

 **For more information on the resources available from McGraw-Hill Ryerson, go to www.mcgrawhill.ca/he/solutions.**

Chapter 3

Balance of Payments

CHAPTER OUTLINE

3.1 CANADA'S BALANCE OF PAYMENTS

Canada is one of the most economically "open" nations in the world. Canada's trade—our exports plus imports—amounts to more than a trillion dollars per year. Much of that trade, close to 75 percent, is with the United States. Canada's financial markets are highly integrated with world financial markets, again predominantly with markets in the United States. Vast volumes of finance flow back and forth across the border. Over the past 25 years, spurred by the Canada–United States Free Trade Agreement of 1988 and NAFTA of 1994, the external side of Canada's economy has grown at impressive rates.

Exhibit 3.1 uses a conventional measure of "openness" to illustrate the ever-expanding share of international trade in Canada's Gross Domestic Product (GDP). The measure simply involves adding Canada's Current Account Receipts and Current Account Payments and dividing by GDP. The Receipts and Payments figures from the Current Account represent the most direct measures of Canada's commerce with the rest of the world. Exhibit 3.2 shows the equally impressive growth in international financial flows to and from Canada. In this case we take the sum of cross-border financial payments—such as interest and dividends paid to or received from foreigners—and divide by GDP.

Canada's commerce with other nations is recorded in the accounts that make up the **Balance of Payments**. In this chapter, we look at these accounts in some detail. The numbers highlight the importance of international trade and foreign investment. Moreover, since Canada's trade and cross-border investment involve some form of exchange of Canadian dollars for foreign currency, we will see how developments in the Balance of Payments influence the exchange rate—the "external value" of the Canadian dollar.

The word "payments" in the Balance of Payments refers to payments to foreigners for things that Canadians buy from abroad—imported cars or clothing, trips to Europe, or a US government bond—as well as payments to Canadians for Canadian products and services that foreigners want—for example, oil or natural gas, insurance services from Manulife or shares in Bombardier. All such payments involving international transactions, whether they are inbound or outbound from Canada, are recorded in Canadian dollars.

When Canadians want to buy foreign goods, services or financial assets, Canadian dollars must be sold in order to buy foreign currency for those transactions. Likewise, Canadian dollars must be purchased by foreigners in order to buy the Canadian currency to buy Canadian goods, services or financial assets.

EXHIBIT 3.1

Canada's "Economic Openness": 1980–2012

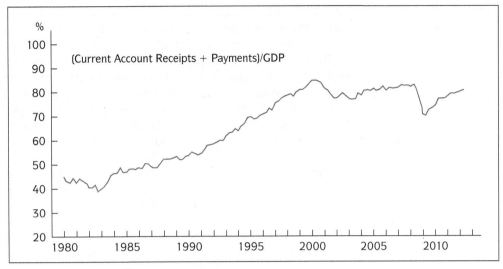

Source: CANSIM on CHASS at the University of Toronto.

EXHIBIT 3.2

Canada's "Financial Openness": 1980–2012

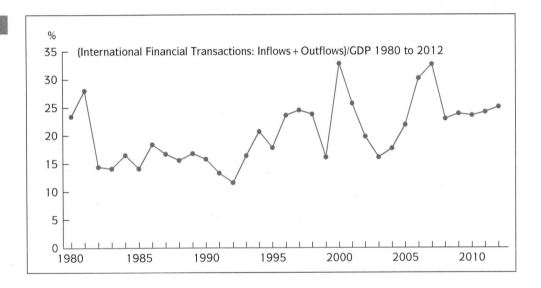

As we shall soon see, the Balance of Payments must "balance." However, within that balance, there are pressures that can cause the Canadian exchange rate to strengthen or weaken. In view of our keen focus on the Canadian exchange rate—what determines its value and, above all, what causes it to change—a solid grasp of the Balance of Payments is the appropriate first step toward understanding the forces that determine the exchange rate.

3.2 BALANCE-OF-PAYMENTS ACCOUNTS

Canada's international transactions are grouped into three accounts that make up the Balance of Payments:

1. The Current Account

2. The Capital and Financial Account

3. The Reserve Account

The **Current Account** records—on a quarterly or annual basis—flows of exports, imports, investment income and international financial transfers. Transactions that involve foreign purchases of Canadian dollars (to buy Canadian goods or services or to travel in

Canada) are recorded as "credits." Transactions that involve Canadian purchases of foreign currencies (when Canadians import goods or services, when Canadians travel abroad or when Canada pays interest or dividends to foreigners) are recorded as "debits."

The **Capital and Financial Account** records—on a quarterly or annual basis—flows of capital that move into or out of Canada within the period. For example, if an American buys a bond issued by a Canadian government or corporation, this represents an inflow of capital to Canada. Such transactions are recorded in the Capital and Financial Account as "credits." On the other hand, if a Canadian buys a bond issued by a foreign government or corporation, this represents an outflow of Canadian capital. Such transactions enter the Capital and Financial Account as "debits."

The **Reserve Account** of the Balance of Payments records changes in the amount of "official" foreign exchange reserves held by the Bank of Canada. In Canada and most industrial nations, such changes tend to be small relative to the total foreign exchange for commercial and international investment purposes.

Exhibit 3.3 provides a variety of specific examples of transactions that enter the Current Account and the Capital and Financial Account of the Canadian Balance of Payments. Exhibit 3.4 shows selected entries in the Current Account of the Canadian Balance of Payments for the years 2001–2012. Exhibit 3.6 presents entries in the Capital and Financial Account for the same years.

EXHIBIT 3.3

Examples of Entries in Canada's Balance-of-Payments Accounts

Credits	Debits
Current Account	*Current Account*
a. The Alberta Natural Gas Company exports natural gas to California.	a. Ford (Canada) buys automobile transmissions from a supplier in Michigan.
b. Bombardier of Montreal sells aircraft to Australia.	b. The LCBO buys wine from Italy.
c. Corel of Ottawa sells a licence to a Mexican software producer.	c. The CN Tower pays an insurance premium to Lloyds of London.
d. Nickelback gives a concert in New York and deposits the receipts in a Toronto Bank.	d. Tom McNeil of Charlottetown goes to the London School of Economics and takes $20,000 to pay tuition and expenses.
e. Canada hosts the G20 Summit in Toronto, and 1,000 foreign press visit the city for five days.	e. Canada Drugs pays a patent royalty to Novo of Sweden.
f. The Ontario Teachers Pension Fund receives $100,000 in dividends on its holdings of Microsoft (USA) shares.	f. Hydro Quebec pays interest on its bonds to bondholders in Switzerland.
Capital and Financial Account	*Capital and Financial Account*
g. Fidelity Mutual Fund of New York buys 10,000 shares of Rogers Communications (Toronto).	g. Altamira Investments (Toronto) buys shares in Xerox (USA).
h. Société Générale of Paris buys Province of Nova Scotia bonds.	h. Saskatchewan Teachers Superannuation Commission buys State of Montana bonds.
i. Professor Jones moves from Harvard to McGill and transfers his personal assets from Boston to Montreal.	i. Barrick buys a gold mine in Peru.
	j. Irving Oil of New Brunswick buys gas stations in Maine.

EXHIBIT 3.4 Canada's International Balance of Payments Current Account, 2001–2012, Canadian Dollars, Millions

	2001	2002	2003	2004	2005	2006	2007	2008	2009	2010	2011	2012
Total receipts	**513,754**	**514,913**	**496,899**	**539,637**	**573,774**	**595,156**	**611,294**	**648,105**	**511,855**	**555,594**	**619,460**	**629,007**
Goods and services	480,795	477,522	460,903	494,387	517,281	520,960	530,332	567,337	445,692	483,213	540,658	546,614
Goods	420,730	414,039	399,122	429,006	450,150	453,732	463,051	487,262	367,211	403,967	456,807	462,528
Services	60,065	63,483	61,781	65,381	67,131	67,227	67,280	80,075	78,481	79,247	83,850	84,086
Travel	16,437	16,741	14,776	16,980	16,674	16,610	16,634	16,544	15,547	16,320	16,624	17,388
Transportation	10,625	11,060	9,942	11,040	11,730	11,879	12,157	13,246	11,624	12,757	13,588	13,508
Other services	33,003	35,681	37,063	37,361	38,727	38,738	38,490	50,285	51,310	50,170	53,639	53,190
Investment income	25,990	30,502	29,253	38,095	48,317	64,497	71,417	68,399	54,904	61,637	68,174	71,441
Direct investments	6,391	13,766	13,706	21,179	26,118	34,978	37,139	35,771	29,030	38,612	44,030	45,390
Portfolio investments	8,070	8,859	8,654	10,070	12,383	17,387	21,683	22,272	19,888	17,940	18,946	20,574
Other investments	11,529	7,877	6,893	6,846	9,816	12,131	12,595	10,356	5,986	5,084	5,198	5,478
Transfers	6,968	6,890	6,743	7,155	8,176	9,700	9,545	11,099	9,937	9,485	9,475	9,747
Total payments	**488,649**	**495,135**	**482,250**	**509,800**	**547,321**	**574,925**	**597,686**	**646,197**	**557,605**	**614,013**	**667,926**	**691,222**
Goods and services	417,945	427,434	416,011	439,575	467,077	486,245	501,474	538,871	468,702	514,817	562,523	582,835
Goods	350,071	356,727	342,710	363,158	387,804	404,253	415,006	443,592	373,984	413,670	456,055	474,544
Services	67,874	70,707	73,302	76,417	79,273	81,992	86,468	95,279	94,717	101,147	106,468	108,291
Travel	18,487	18,401	18,727	20,237	21,865	23,402	26,663	28,645	27,544	30,638	32,974	35,030
Transportation	13,970	14,438	14,509	15,919	17,586	18,695	20,032	22,682	20,076	22,209	23,674	23,697
Other services	35,417	37,868	40,065	40,261	39,822	39,895	39,773	43,952	47,097	48,300	49,820	49,563
Investment income	65,320	60,799	59,284	62,399	70,735	77,872	85,611	92,614	73,499	83,417	89,329	91,852
Direct investments	22,266	21,529	23,765	27,673	34,432	34,354	38,444	43,998	30,442	40,940	44,828	45,129
Portfolio investments	30,668	30,804	28,816	27,964	28,051	29,270	30,809	32,802	34,036	36,331	38,215	39,745
Other investments	12,386	8,466	6,702	6,762	8,251	14,247	16,358	15,814	9,021	6,146	6,286	6,977
Transfers	5,384	6,902	6,955	7,825	9,509	10,809	10,601	11,712	12,526	12,802	12,958	13,293
Total balance on Current Account	**25,104**	**19,778**	**14,649**	**29,837**	**26,453**	**20,231**	**13,607**	**1,908**	**−45,750**	**−58,419**	**−48,466**	**−62,215**
Goods and services	62,850	50,088	44,892	54,811	50,204	34,715	28,858	28,466	−23,010	−31,604	−21,866	−36,221
Goods	70,659	57,311	56,413	65,848	62,346	49,480	48,046	43,670	−6,773	−9,703	753	−12,016
Services	−7,809	−7,224	−11,521	−11,037	−12,141	−14,765	−19,188	−15,204	−16,237	−21,900	−22,618	−24,205
Travel	−2,050	−1,659	−3,951	−3,257	−5,191	−6,792	−10,029	−12,101	−11,998	−14,317	−16,351	−17,643
Transportation	−3,345	−3,378	−4,567	−4,879	−5,856	−6,816	−7,875	−9,436	−8,452	−9,452	−10,086	−10,188
Other services	−2,414	−2,187	−3,002	−2,900	−1,094	−1,157	−1,283	6,333	4,213	1,869	3,819	3,626
Investment income	−39,330	−30,297	−30,031	−24,304	−22,418	−13,375	−14,194	−24,215	−18,595	−21,780	−21,155	−20,411
Direct investments	−15,875	−7,763	−10,059	−6,494	−8,315	623	−1,305	−8,227	−1,412	−2,328	−798	260
Portfolio investments	−22,598	−21,945	−20,163	−17,894	−15,668	−11,883	−9,126	−10,530	−14,148	−18,391	−19,269	−19,172
Other investments	−857	−589	191	84	1,565	−2,115	−3,763	−5,458	−3,035	−1,061	−1,088	−1,500
Transfers	1,584	−12	−212	−670	−1,333	−1,109	−1,056	−613	−2,589	−3,316	−3,483	−3,546

Source: Statistics Canada, CANSIM, Tables 376-0001 and 376-0002. Reproduced and distributed on an "as is" basis with the permission of Statistics Canada.

The **balance-of-payments identity** is an accounting relationship that in principle (that is, aside from statistical errors) must hold. The Balance-of-Payments Identity is:

BCA + BKA + BRA = 0

where

BCA = Balance on Current Account
BKA = Balance on Capital and Financial Account
BRA = Balance on Reserves Account

The Balance on Reserves Account serves as a foreign exchange buffer managed by the government or the central bank—the Bank of Canada, for example. In countries with governments or central banks that actively intervene in the foreign market to "fix" their exchange rate against one of the world's major currencies, such as the US dollar or the euro, the Reserves Account is drawn down to buy one's own currency in order to raise its "external" value or to resist a fall in value. Most industrial nations tend to do very little exchange rate fixing. Consequently, changes in the Balance on Reserves Account tend to be small and random, and hence for all practical purposes the key Balance-of-Payments relationship is that the Balance on Current Account equals the Balance on Capital and Financial Account.

Canada's policy on intervention in the foreign exchange market is outlined in the International Finance in Practice box on page 68. The policy is *not* to intervene, or to do so only in extraordinary circumstances.

The Current Account

Exhibit 3.4 highlights a number of points that characterize Canada as a trading nation. On the Current Account, the value of our exports and investment income receipts from abroad exceeds the value of our imports and investment income payments paid to foreigners. For business-minded people who think in terms of cash flow, this suggests that Canada enjoys a positive operating cash flow in its business dealings with the rest of the world. It is interesting to look a little more closely at the composition of these cash flows.

Canada enjoys a highly favourable balance of merchandise trade. In practical terms, the total value of Canadian exports of such items as forest products, minerals, energy, agricultural products, airplanes and automobiles exceeds the value of our imported merchandise—such as electronics, clothing and food products from warmer climates. A graphical summary of Canada's merchandise trade over the past 35 years is presented in Exhibit 3.5.

In respect of services, the so-called **invisible trade**, Canada generally runs a small deficit. Patent royalties, fees for movies, travel, insurance, consultants and engineering are the sorts of "invisible" import items in this category.

EXHIBIT 3.5

Canada's Trade in Goods and Services: 1980–2012

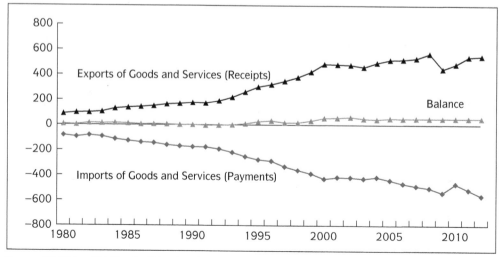

Source: CANSIM on CHASS at the University of Toronto.

EXHIBIT 3.6 Canada's Balance of International Payments Capital and Financial Account, 2001–2012 Canadian Dollars, millions

	2001	2002	2003	2004	2005	2006	2007	2008	2009	2010	2011	2012
Total Capital and Financial Accounts, net flow	**−15,623**	**−17,208**	**−15,711**	**−32,809**	**−23,350**	**−22,768**	**−14,673**	**−1,971**	**45,750**	**49,707**	**55,843**	**−54,014**
Capital Account, net flow	**5,752**	**4,936**	**4,171**	**4,449**	**5,932**	**4,202**	**4,233**	**4,579**	**3,830**	**4,758**	**4,818**	**−74**
Financial Account, net flow[1]	**−21,375**	**−22,144**	**−19,868**	**−36,956**	**−35,109**	**−26,969**	**−18,906**	**−6,550**	**41,920**	**44,949**	**51,025**	**−53,940**
Canadian Assets, net flow[2]	**−113,930**	**−83,631**	**−66,287**	**−87,065**	**−110,460**	**−166,967**	**−177,021**	**−112,995**	**−106,918**	**−106,482**	**−110,485**	**98,818**
Canadian Direct Investment Abroad	−55,800	−42,015	−32,118	−56,395	−33,370	−52,423	−62,003	−85,143	−43,627	−39,749	−49,050	26,445
Canadian Portfolio Investment	−37,573	−29,319	−19,054	−24,369	−53,455	−78,669	−48,426	11,653	−8,727	−14,535	−18,331	53,008
Loans and Deposits	−10,223	−2,743	−11,672	−7,217	−8,492	−20,821	−53,058	−39,500	−36,688	−28,185	−43,734	21,249
Official International Reserves	−3,353	298	4,693	3,427	−1,653	−1,013	−4,644	−1,711	−11,618	−3,989	−8,061	20,761
Canadian Liabilities, net flow	**92,555**	**61,487**	**47,789**	**49,818**	**81,205**	**139,998**	**158,115**	**106,445**	**148,838**	**151,431**	**161,510**	**152,758**
Foreign Direct Investment in Canada	42,844	34,769	10,483	−579	31,132	68,395	123,148	61,010	24,469	24,119	40,503	17,462
Foreign Portfolio Investment	37,779	18,599	19,362	54,267	8,472	21,325	9,876	33,487	44,654	58,021	45,634	63,842
Loans and Deposits	17,775	14,965	20,496	−2,563	34,943	40,024	61,183	15,511	42,190	34,231	21,386	29,875

[1] A minus sign denotes an outflow of capital resulting from an increase in claims on non-residents or a decrease in liabilities to non-residents.

[2] The total "Canadian Assets, net flow" is not equal to the sum of the sub-categories in the table. Likewise for total "Canadian Liabilities, net flow." Only four major sub-categories for Assets and three major sub-categories for Liabilities are shown.

Source: Statistics Canada, "Balance of payments and international investment position" (CANSIM Tables 376-0101 and 376-0102). Reproduced and distributed on an "as is" basis with the permission of Statistics Canada.

A large gap between debits and credits on Current Account involves the line items, Investment Income Receipts and Investment Income Payments. The Canadian outflow of these financial payments far exceeds the inflow of receipts from abroad. This imbalance reflects Canada's heritage as a small country that over the years has imported vast amounts of capital for nation building and industry. Canadian industry ranks among the most capital-intensive in the world. Capital is used intensively in mining, energy, forestry, fishing and manufacturing. The federal and provincial governments have also imported capital to build the national infrastructure—including roads, bridges and telecommunication networks. The foreign capital that has been drawn to Canada is paid for through interest and dividends.

The Balance on Current Account was negative in 2012, as well as in each of the three previous years. That is to say, in recent years, Canada generated less in receipts through exports and income on foreign investments than it paid out for imports and the payments to foreign investors. Without judging the economic merits of a positive or negative balance, one should note that a negative Balance on Current Account is a phenomenon that Canada has experienced before. Through virtually all of the 1980s and 1990s, Canada had a negative Balance on Current Account due, in large measure, to the high interest burden of foreign debt paid for the most part by corporations and provinces that had sold bonds to foreign investors.

Before turning to the Capital and Financial Account, it is useful to draw a crucial link between the Current Account and the Capital and Financial Account. A negative Balance on Current Account can be interpreted as Canada and Canadians earning less foreign exchange—US dollars, euros, Mexican pesos and so on—than was needed to purchase things with those currencies. The "deficiency in foreign exchange" on the Current Account had to be financed somehow and so Canada borrowed a similar amount from foreigners. As a result, the overall Balance of Payments balances, which means that the surplus (or deficit) on the Current Account corresponds to the deficit (or surplus) on the Capital and Financial Account.

The Current Account balance, especially the trade balance, tends to be sensitive to changes in the exchange rate. When the Canadian dollar appreciates relative to the US dollar, for example, then Canadian-produced goods become more expensive in the export market. Meanwhile, the stronger Canadian dollar makes imports cheaper. As Canadian exports fall and imports rise, the trade balance deteriorates.

One would predict that the **trade balance**, exports minus imports, would improve if a country's currency depreciated against the currency of its major trading partners. Indeed so, but adjustments generally require time to work themselves through. The length of time required to adjust production plans and contracts with foreign customers results in lags that result in a predictable pattern in the trade balance following a change in the exchange rate.

The classic reaction pattern of the trade balance to a currency depreciation is referred to as the **J-curve effect**, illustrated in Exhibit 3.7. The J-curve depicts an initial deterioration and eventual improvement of the trade balance following currency depreciation. The pattern is due to the difficulty and costliness of adjustment in production and marketing in international trade. One observes short-term inelasticity or lack of price-responsiveness of exports and imports to the change in the exchange rate. Following a currency depreciation, some importers continue to import at the higher import price before they find alternative domestic sources. Likewise, exporters require time before they fully exploit the new opportunities in their markets abroad. In the transition immediately following a currency depreciation, the country's import bill tends to rise, while export receipts tend not to respond immediately. The net effect is deterioration of the trade balance. In the longer run, adjustments take place, imports fall, exports rise and the trade balance improves.

The Capital and Financial Account

The Capital and Financial Account records sales to foreigners of Canadian financial assets and Canadian purchases of foreign financial assets. The Balance on Capital and Financial

EXHIBIT 3.7

A Currency
Depreciation and
the Time-Path of
the Trade Balance:
The J-Curve Effect

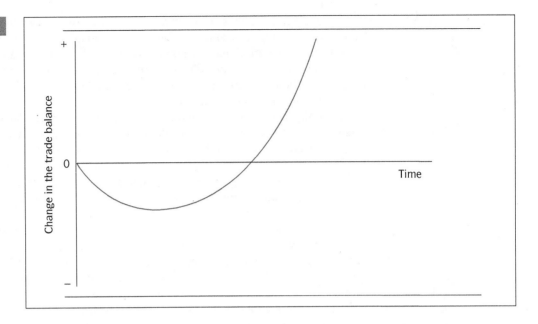

Account is simply the difference between the value of foreign purchases of Canadian financial assets and Canadian purchases of foreign financial assets.

There are two main categories of financial assets recorded in the Capital and Financial Account—direct investment and portfolio investment. The economic and industrial characters of these two categories of cross-border investment are significantly different, and that difference is especially pertinent to the types of issues that arise in international financial management.

Foreign direct investment (FDI) is what multinational enterprises do. When McCain Foods of New Brunswick sets up a food processing plant in France, when the Bank of Montreal expands operations of its wholly owned Harris Bank of Chicago or when media giant Quebecor doubles its printing facilities in New Delhi, these corporate investments represent Canadian outbound foreign direct investment.

The distinguishing features of foreign direct investment are corporate ownership and control. For instance, McCain Foods, the Bank of Montreal and Quebecor directly own, control and manage their operations abroad. These Canadian-based multinational companies assign their corporate names and transfer technology, trademarks, marketing and strategy to their subsidiaries abroad.

In the Capital and Financial Account of the Balance of Payments for a particular year, McCain's contribution to outbound foreign direct investment would consist of the new direct investment—in the form of corporate equity—made in that year. So, when McCain sets up a food processing plant in France with equity injections of $10 million per year in 2011 and 2012, $10 million is recorded as a debit in the Capital and Financial Account in each of those years. Reinvested earnings and non-arm's-length (intrafirm) debt are also recorded in the Capital and Financial Account.

While foreign direct investment is recorded in the Capital and Financial Account, the subsequent flow of earnings on that capital is recorded as investment income in the Current Account. Since the difference between the Current Account and the Capital and Financial Account hinges on the difference between foreign-source income and foreign investment, if McCain earns $1 million on its operations in France and then immediately reinvests those earnings in the French subsidiary, the Current Account would record $1 million of foreign investment income (a credit) while the Capital and Financial Account would record $1 million of foreign direct investment (a debit).

Portfolio investment refers to (1) changes in Canadian holdings of noncontrolling equity in foreign companies, (2) foreign holdings of noncontrolling equity in Canadian companies, (3) Canadian holdings of debt issued by foreigners and (4) foreign holdings of debt issued by Canadians. Canadian purchases of shares of foreign companies, foreign purchases of shares in Canadian companies, Canadian purchases of foreign bonds and foreign purchases of Canadian bonds are the main transaction categories for portfolio investment. The Capital and Financial Account records net changes under each of these categories. The principal purpose is to report the totals and the composition of Canadian lending to foreigners and foreign lending to Canada.

To put the foregoing points into specific numbers, in 2012 Canada sent $55.4 billion of foreign direct investment abroad, while foreigners directly invested somewhat less, $43 billion, in Canada. Outbound portfolio investment—Canada lending to foreigners—amounted to $35.1 billion, while inbound portfolio investment was substantially more at $83.2 billion.

The motives for foreign direct investment are the conventional motives of business in an international setting. Firms "go abroad" to expand their markets or to take advantage of more profitable sites of production. For example, Molson finds the Latin American market tantalizing and a good strategic move. In 2000, Molson entered this market by acquiring Bavaria, a leading beer brand in Brazil. On the other hand, foreign firms find Canada an attractive destination for investment, either for market access or for resources. For instance, Stora Enso of Finland or Weyerhaeuser of the State of Washington have been aggressive investors in the Canadian forest industry by buying Canadian companies. We will look into such decisions in greater detail in Chapters 15 to 17.

The $118 billion in net cross-border portfolio investment is driven by somewhat different concerns. Portfolio capital seeks out attractive bond interest, noncontrolling equity returns, diversification and tax advantages. As we shall see in Chapter 8 (on international equity markets) and Chapter 11 (on bond portfolio investment), the world's capital markets offer a wide array of investment opportunities in risk categories, industries and currencies that are otherwise unavailable if money is kept exclusively at home.

External Balance and the Exchange Rate

In principle, the Current Account and the Capital and Financial Account should balance each other out. If Canada buys more goods, services and the like than it sells (i.e., if Canada runs a Current Account deficit), it must finance that deficit. A Current Account deficit is financed by means of a Capital and Financial Account surplus. In theory, therefore, since the balance of payments is the sum of the Current Account and the Capital and Financial Account, the balance of payments is always zero.

To a rough approximation, a Current Account deficit indicates that a nation has spent more than it has earned. In that case, other nations lend money to the nation in Current Account deficit to finance the difference between its income and spending. The nation as a whole borrows money from the rest of the world by means of the net sale of financial assets. Of course, the net sale of financial assets to the rest of the world is that nation's Capital and Financial Account surplus. Again, we see that a deficit on Current Account is mirrored by a surplus on Capital and Financial Account such that the balance of payments "balances."

Current Account surpluses or deficits may or may not be a matter of economic or policy concern, depending on specific circumstances. Surpluses or deficits in either account are not necessarily problematic. For example, as a relatively new and rapidly growing country in the twentieth century, Canada often experienced strong inflows of both direct investment and portfolio investment. These inflows helped Canada grow and prosper. In contrast and more recently, Canadians have substantially increased their investment abroad as reflected in our Capital and Financial Account deficit balanced by our Current Account surplus.

In view of our focus on international financial management at the corporate level, impatient managers may find the macroeconomic perspective on external balance—the relation between the Current Account and the Capital and Financial Account—to be somewhat distant from their immediate concerns about exchange rates and exchange rate risk. As we shall see in later chapters that deal directly with the management of foreign exchange risk—Chapters 12, 13 and 14—foreign exchange *risk* and exchange rate *volatility* are, for all practical purposes, the same thing. Exchange rate volatility is a macroeconomic phenomenon with microeconomic (corporate-level) implications.

Short-term volatility in the exchange rate is perplexing for international financial management. If the Current Account deficit or surplus is always offset by the Capital and Financial Account surplus or deficit, what sort of "imbalance" causes the exchange rate to change, especially in the short run, say day to day, week to week or within six months? To answer this question in a way that managers and business students have a unique advantage in understanding, it helps to view the surplus on the Capital and Financial Account as "loans" from financiers in the rest of the world to the country in Current Account deficit. Such loans are attracted to capital importing nations by interest rates. The interest rate is an important mechanism for "balancing" the Capital and Financial Account and the Current Account. The point can be illustrated by the case of the United States over the past 30 years.

Exhibit 3.8b shows that since 1982 the United States has had continuous deficits on Current Account and surpluses on Capital Account. The size of US Current Account deficits is greater than for any other country over this period (see Canada's in Exhibit 3.8a). In more recent years—through the 1990s and onward—the US Current Account deficit has grown steadily owing in large part to the investment boom driven by the impressive increases in US industrial productivity, especially in high-end manufacturing such as electronics and information technology. The fact that these Current Account deficits were financed through Capital Account surpluses reflects the enormous capacity of the United States to borrow from the rest of the world, that is, the capacity of the United States to sell financial assets to foreigners.

By 2006, the US Current Account deficit had swollen to more than $800 billion. Meanwhile the investment boom had subsided, the United States teetered on the verge of recession and interest rates had fallen to historic lows. The question for American "external balance" was whether the rest of the world would continue to buy and hold the American financial assets that had underwritten past Current Account deficits and that were also necessary for further deficits.

If the rest of the world becomes uncomfortable with mounting loans to the United States, and if they reduce the flow of capital to the United States, that is, reduce the Capital Account surpluses, then one of two things (or a combination of the two) will occur. Either US interest rates must rise to attract new capital inflows or the US dollar will fall against other currencies as foreign financiers' willingness to buy US dollars (to buy American financial assets) subsides. In either case, the US Current Account will shrink to match the reduced capital inflows. For example, if the US dollar falls, imports become more costly for Americans and American exports become cheaper on world markets, and hence the US trade balance improves. On the other hand, if US interest rates rise, the American economy is negatively affected and imports fall, likewise improving the US trade balance and reducing the overall need for capital imports.

Looking at the persistent positive balance on the US Capital Account, it seems that the world has an insatiable appetite for US "paper." The world is awash in US Treasury bills. China, for example, now holds more than US$3 trillion in foreign exchange reserves, of which US$2 billion is in the form of US securities. China, and the other countries that continue to accumulate US securities, are financing the voracious US appetite for consumption and investment. Patterns of Current Account and Capital Account imbalances can ultimately be traced to nations' saving rates. China's saving rate is in the range of 45 percent of income. The US saving rate is less than 1 percent!

The US Current Account imbalances are offset by other nations' willingness to extend finance to the US. These are macroeconomic phenomena. To address shorter-term movements in the exchange rate, we assume that the exchange rate between two countries is initially in equilibrium, a concept to be explored in more detail in Chapter 5.

News of an *unexpected* boost to a macroeconomic factor—news that points to greater economic strength or higher interest rates, for example—is likely to trigger a strengthening

EXHIBIT 3.8a   Canada's Balance of Payments: 1982–2012

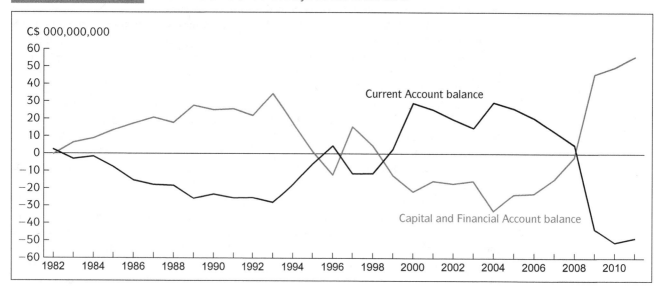

EXHIBIT 3.8b   US Balance of Payments: 1982–2012

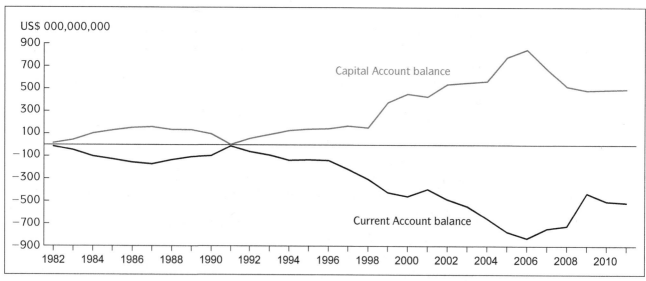

Source: IMF, *International Financial Statistics,* various issues.

of that country's currency. For instance, the Canadian dollar is likely to rise relative to the US dollar on news of the following sorts:

Statistics Canada Reports Surprise Jump in Canadian Output

The Bank of Canada Announces Higher-Than-Expected Interest Rate Hike

Industrial Unemployment well below Forecast Values

Exports Up Sharply above Trend

Oil and Energy Prices Jump 10 Percent

These headlines suggest an element of surprise in terms of macroeconomic forces that play on the exchange rate. News that the economy is stronger or more vibrant than was previously thought will generally strengthen the exchange rate, whereas unexpected negative news—concerning economic growth, investment, employment or exports—will generally cause a nation's currency to weaken. In terms of exchange rate volatility, "news" is by definition new and equally likely to be good or bad. Therefore, in the short term at least, movement of the exchange rate is random. Consequently, the best estimate of tomorrow's exchange rate is today's exchange rate.

3.3   BALANCE-OF-PAYMENTS TRENDS IN MAJOR COUNTRIES

Considering the significant attention that balance-of-payments data receive in the news media, it is useful to closely examine balance-of-payments trends in some of the major countries. Exhibit 3.9 provides the balance on Current Account (BCA) as well as the balance on the Capital Account (BKA) for each of six key countries—China, Japan, Germany, the United Kingdom, the United States, and Canada during the period 1982–2011.

The exhibit shows first that the United States has experienced continuous deficits on the Current Account since 1982 and continuous surpluses on the Capital Account. Clearly, the magnitude of US Current Account deficits is far greater than any that other countries ever experienced during the 21-year sample period. This growing imbalance has led some politicians and commentators to lament that Americans are living far beyond their means. As a matter of fact, the net international investment position of the United States turned negative in 1987 for the first time in decades and continued to deteriorate. The overseas debt burden of the

EXHIBIT 3.9   Balances on Current (BCA) and Capital (BKA) Accounts of Six Major Countries: 1982–2011 (US$ billions)

Year	China BCA	China BKA	Japan BCA	Japan BKA	Germany BCA	Germany BKA	UK BCA	UK BKA	US BCA	US BKA	Canada BCA	Canada BKA
1982	5.7	0.6	6.9	−11.6	4.9	2.0	8.0	−10.6	−11.6	−16.6	2.3	0.0
1983	4.2	−0.1	20.8	−19.3	4.6	6.6	5.3	−7.1	−44.2	−45.4	−3.1	6.5
1984	2.0	−1.9	35.0	−32.9	9.6	−9.9	1.8	−2.8	−99	−102.1	−1.7	9.0
1985	−11.4	9.0	51.1	−51.6	17.6	−15.4	3.3	−0.7	−124.5	−128.3	−7.8	13.7
1986	−7.0	5.0	85.9	−70.7	40.9	−35.5	−1.3	5.0	−150.5	−150.2	−15.5	17.4
1987	0.3	4.5	84.4	−46.3	46.4	−24.9	−8.1	28.2	−166.5	−157.3	−17.8	20.9
1988	−3.8	6.2	79.2	−61.7	50.4	−66.0	−29.3	33.9	−127.7	−131.6	−18.3	17.8
1989	−4.3	3.8	63.2	−76.3	57.0	−54.1	−36.7	28.6	−104.3	−129.5	−25.8	27.6
1990	12.0	0.1	44.1	−53.2	48.3	−41.1	−32.5	32.5	−94.3	−96.5	−23.1	25.2
1991	13.3	1.3	68.2	−76.6	−17.7	11.5	−14.3	19.0	−9.3	−3.5	−25.6	25.8
1992	6.4	−8.5	112.6	−112.0	−19.1	56.3	−18.4	11.7	−61.4	57.4	−25.4	21.9
1993	−11.6	13.4	131.6	−104.2	−13.9	−0.3	−15.5	21.0	−90.6	91.9	−28.1	34.5
1994	6.9	23.5	130.3	−105.0	−20.9	18.9	−2.3	3.8	−132.9	127.6	−17.7	17.8
1995	1.6	20.9	111.0	−52.4	−22.6	29.8	−5.9	5.0	−129.2	138.9	−6.1	1.3
1996	7.2	24.5	65.9	−30.7	−13.8	12.6	−3.7	3.2	−148.7	142.1	4.6	−12.2
1997	29.7	6.1	94.4	−87.8	−1.2	−2.6	6.8	−11.0	−166.8	167.8	−11.4	15.8
1998	31.5	−6.3	120.7	−116.8	−6.4	17.6	−8.0	0.2	−217.4	151.6	−11.4	4.5
1999	21.1	5.2	106.9	−31.1	−18.0	−40.5	−31.9	31.0	−324.4	367.9	2.6	−12.5
2000	20.5	2.0	116.9	−75.5	−18.7	13.2	−28.8	26.2	−444.7	443.6	29.3	−21.8
2001	17.4	34.8	87.8	−51.0	1.7	−24.1	−32.1	31.5	−385.7	419.9	25.1	−15.6
2002	35.4	32.3	112.5	−66.7	43.4	−70.4	−26.2	17.3	−473.9	572.7	19.8	−17.2
2003	45.9	52.7	136.2	67.9	54.9	−79.3	−24.5	24.8	−530.7	541.2	14.6	−15.7
2004	68.7	110.7	172.1	22.5	120.3	−146.9	−35.2	10.4	−640.2	553.9	29.8	0.5
2005	160.8	58.9	165.8	−122.7	131.8	−151.2	−55.0	73.8	−754.9	763.3	26.4	−4.6
2006	249.9	6.0	170.5	−102.3	150.8	−179.8	−77.6	49.0	−811.5	830.8	20.2	−6.3
2007	371.8	70.4	210.5	−187.2	263.1	−325.3	−74.7	66.2	−726.6	663.7	13.6	15.4
2008	426.1	18.9	156.6	−172.6	243.9	−300.8	−39.9	21.5	−706.1	509.9	1.9	−4.7
2009	297.1	144.8	142.2	−130.2	168.0	−185.9	−28.7	38.1	−419.8	474.9	−45.8	−54.6
2010	237.8	229.2	203.9	−155.1	200.7	−194.8	−75.2	79.5	−470.9	472.8	−58.4	−95.1
2011	201.7	180.6	119.1	57.1	204.3	−201.7	−46.0	51.2	−473.4	489.5	−48.5	−61.0

Source: IMF, *International Financial Statistics,* various issues.

Bank of Canada's Policy on Intervention in the Foreign Exchange Market

The Bank of Canada occasionally releases informal statements concerning the Bank's approach to policy on various matters. The following statement, released in October 2003, outlines the Bank's policy in regard to intervention in the foreign exchange market to influence the external value of the Canadian dollar. The policy is not to intervene or to do so only in extraordinary circumstances.

The Canadian dollar, like the currencies of most industrialized nations, operates on the basis of a floating exchange rate, which means that the price of a Canadian dollar fluctuates according to market conditions. A floating currency is a key component of Canada's monetary policy framework, helping the economy to adjust to shocks and playing an important part in the transmission of monetary policy.

Neither the government nor the Bank of Canada target any particular level for the currency, believing that this should be determined by the market. Over time, the value of the Canadian dollar is determined by economic forces (fundamentals), such as the rate of inflation and the level of interest rates in Canada, which depend on the conduct of Canada's monetary policy, the growth of the Canadian economy and the competitiveness of goods produced.

Policy on Foreign Exchange Intervention

Currency markets can be volatile, and the Bank of Canada may intervene in the foreign exchange markets on behalf of the federal government to counter disruptive short-term movements in the Canadian dollar. Any intervention is governed by an intervention policy, which is established by the government in close consultation with the Bank of Canada.

Prior to September 1998, Canada's policy was to intervene systematically in the foreign exchange market to resist, in an automatic fashion, significant upward or downward pressure on the Canadian dollar.[1,2] In September 1998, the policy was changed because of the ineffectiveness of intervening to resist movements in the exchange rate caused by changes in fundamental factors. Canada's current policy is to intervene in foreign exchange markets on a discretionary, rather than a systematic, basis and only in the most exceptional of circumstances.

Intervention might be considered if there were signs of a serious near-term market breakdown (e.g., extreme price volatility with both buyers and sellers increasingly unwilling to transact), indicating a severe lack of liquidity in the Canadian-dollar market. It might also be considered if extreme currency movements seriously threatened the conditions that support sustainable long-term growth of the Canadian economy; and the goal would be to help stabilize the currency and to signal a commitment to back up the intervention with further policy actions, as necessary.

The Mechanics of Foreign Exchange Intervention

Foreign exchange market intervention is conducted by the Bank of Canada, acting as agent for the federal government, using the government's holdings of foreign currencies in the Exchange Fund Account.[3]

If the government and the Bank want to moderate a decline in the relative price of the Canadian dollar, the Bank will buy Canadian dollars in foreign exchange markets in exchange for other currencies, mainly US dollars, which come from the Exchange Fund Account. This boosts demand for Canadian dollars and helps support the dollar's value. To make sure that the Bank's purchases do not take money out of circulation and create a shortage of Canadian dollars, which could put upward pressure on Canadian interest rates, the Bank "sterilizes" its purchases by redepositing the same amount of Canadian-dollar balances in the financial system.

Conversely, if the government and the Bank want to slow the currency's rate of appreciation, the Bank could sell Canadian dollars from its Canadian-dollar cash balances and purchase other currencies. By selling Canadian dollars, the Bank increases the supply of Canadian dollars in foreign exchange markets, and this provides some resistance to the upward movement in the currency. To "sterilize" the effect of the Bank's sales of Canadian dollars (and prevent downward pressure on Canadian interest rates), the same amount of Canadian-dollar balances are withdrawn from the financial system. The foreign currencies purchased when Canadian dollars are sold are added to the Exchange Fund Account.

When an intervention occurs, an announcement indicating the intervention is made on the Bank's Web site. The amount of the intervention undertaken is publicly available in the government's monthly official press release on international reserves.

---

[1] The last time the Bank intervened in foreign exchange markets to affect movements in the Canadian dollar was in September, 1998 [to deal with the extraordinary pressures following the Asian financial crisis].

[2] From time to time, Canada participates with other countries in coordinated intervention. For example, on 22 September 2000, the Bank of Canada joined the European Central Bank, the Federal Reserve Bank of New York, the Bank of Japan and the Bank of England in a concerted intervention to support the euro. This backgrounder deals exclusively with intervention directed at affecting movements in the Canadian dollar.

[3] The Fund holds foreign reserves, such as US dollars, Japanese yen, European euros, as well as other assets like Special Drawing Rights (SDRs) with the International Monetary Fund (IMF) and gold.

Copyright © Bank of Canada. Reprinted with permission. http://www.bankofcanada.ca/about/educational-resources/backgrounders.

United States—the difference between the value of foreign-owned assets in the United States and the value of American-owned assets abroad—reached about $4 trillion at the end of 2012, when valued by the replacement cost of the investments made abroad and at home. As recently as 1986, the United States was a net creditor nation, with about $35 billion more in assets overseas than foreigners owned in the United States.

Second, Exhibit 3.9 reveals that Japan has had an unbroken string of Current Account surpluses since 1982 despite the fact that the value of the yen rose steadily until the mid-1990s. As might be expected, during this period Japan realized continuous Capital Account deficits; Japan invested heavily in foreign shares and bonds, businesses, real estate, art objects and the like to recycle its huge, persistent Current Account surpluses. Consequently, Japan emerged as the world's largest creditor nation whereas the United States became the largest debtor nation. The persistent Current Account disequilibrium has been a major source of friction between Japan and its key trading partners. In fact, Japan has often been criticized for pursuing **mercantilism** to ensure continuous trade surpluses.[1]

Third, like the United States, the United Kingdom recently experienced continuous Current Account deficits, coupled with Capital Account surpluses. The magnitude, however, is far less than that of the United States. Germany, on the other hand, traditionally had Current Account surpluses. Since 1991, however, Germany has been experiencing Current Account deficits. This is largely due to German reunification and the resultant need to absorb more output domestically to rebuild the East German region. This has left less output available for exports.

Fourth, like Japan, China tends to have a surplus on Current Account. Unlike Japan, however, China tends to realize a surplus on Capital Account as well. In 2011, for instance, China had a $202 billion surplus on Current Account and, at the same time, a $181 billion surplus on the Capital Account. This implies that China's official reserve holdings must have gone up for the year. In fact, China's official reserves have increased sharply in recent years, reaching more than $3 trillion in 2013.

While perennial balance-of-payments deficits or surpluses can be a problem, each country need not achieve balance-of-payments equilibrium every year. Suppose a country is currently experiencing a trade deficit because of the import demand for capital goods that are necessary for economic development projects. In this case, the trade deficit can be self-correcting in the long run, because once the projects are completed, the country may be able to export more or import less by substituting domestic products for foreign imports. In contrast, if the trade deficit is the result of importing consumption goods, the situation will not correct by itself. Thus, what matters is the nature and causes of the disequilibrium.

SUMMARY

1. The Balance of Payments can be defined as the statistical record of a country's international transactions over a certain period of time presented in the form of double-entry bookkeeping.

2. In the Balance of Payments, any transaction resulting in a receipt from foreigners is recorded as a credit, with a positive sign, whereas any transaction resulting in a payment to foreigners is recorded as a debit, with a minus sign.

3. Canada's international transactions can be grouped into three main categories: the Current Account, the Capital and Financial Account and the official Reserve Account. The Current Account includes exports and imports of goods and services, whereas the Capital and Financial Account includes all purchases and sales of assets such as shares, bonds, bank accounts, real estate and businesses. The official Reserve Account covers all purchases and sales

---

[1]Mercantilism, which originated in Europe during the period of absolute monarchies, holds that precious metals like gold and silver are the key components of national wealth and that a continuing trade surplus should be a major policy goal as it ensures a continuing inflow of precious metals and, thus, continuous increases in national wealth. Mercantilists, therefore, abhor trade deficits and argue for imposing various restrictions on imports. Mercantilist ideas were criticized by such British thinkers as David Hume and Adam Smith. Both argued that the main source of wealth of a country is its productive capacity, not precious metals.

of international reserve assets, such as dollars, foreign exchanges, gold and SDRs.

4. The Current Account is divided into four subcategories: merchandise trade, services, factor income and transfers. Merchandise trade represents exports and imports of tangible goods, whereas trade in services includes payments and receipts for legal, engineering, consulting and other performed services and tourist expenditures. Factor income consists of payments and receipts of interest, dividends and other income on previously made foreign investments. Lastly, transfers involve unrequited payments, such as gifts, foreign aid and reparations.

5. The Capital and Financial Account is divided into three subcategories: direct investment, portfolio investment and other investment. Direct investment involves acquisitions of controlling interests in foreign businesses. Portfolio investment represents investments in foreign shares and bonds that do not involve acquisitions of control. Other investment includes bank deposits, currency investment, trade credit and the like.

6. When we compute Canada's cumulative Balance of Payments including the Current Account, the Capital and Financial Account and the statistical discrepancies, we obtain the overall balance or official settlement balance. The overall balance is indicative of a country's balance-of-payments gap that must be accommodated by official reserve transactions. If a country must make a net payment to foreigners because of a balance-of-payments deficit, the country should either run down its official reserve assets, such as gold, foreign exchanges, and SDRs, or borrow anew from foreigners.

7. A country can run a balance-of-payments surplus or deficit by increasing or decreasing its official reserves. Under the fixed-exchange-rate regime, the combined balance on the Current and Capital Accounts will be equal in size, but opposite in sign, to the change in the official reserves. Under the flexible exchange rate regime where the central bank does not maintain any official reserves, a Current Account surplus or deficit must be matched by a Capital Account deficit or surplus.

QUESTIONS

1. Define *Balance of Payments*.

2. Why would it be useful to examine a country's balance-of-payments data?

3. The United States has run current account deficits continuously since the early 1980s. What do you think are the main causes for the deficits? What are the global consequences of continuous US current account deficits?

4. In contrast to the United States, Japan has realized continuous Current Account surpluses. What could be the main causes for these surpluses? Is it desirable to have continuous Current Account surpluses?

5. Comment on the following statement: "When Canada imports more than it exports, it is necessary for Canada to import capital from foreign countries to finance its Current Account deficits."

6. Explain how a country can run an overall balance-of-payments deficit or surplus.

7. Explain *official reserve assets* and its major components.

8. Explain how to compute the overall balance, and discuss its significance.

9. Since the early 1980s, foreign portfolio investors have purchased a significant portion of US Treasury bond issues. Discuss the short-term and long-term effects of foreigners' portfolio investment on the US Balance of Payments.

10. Describe the *balance-of-payments identity,* and discuss its implications under the fixed and flexible exchange rate regimes.

11. Occasionally, a country will have a Current Account deficit and a Capital Account deficit at the same time. Explain how this can happen.

12. Explain how each of the following transactions will be classified and recorded in the debit and credit of the Canadian Balance of Payments:

a. A Japanese insurance company purchases Government of Ontario bonds and pays out of its bank account kept in Toronto.

b. A Canadian citizen has a meal at a restaurant in Paris and pays with her Royal Bank Visa card.

c. An Indian immigrant living in Halifax sends a cheque drawn on his Halifax bank account as a gift to his parents living in New Delhi.

d. A Canadian computer programmer is hired by a British company for consulting and gets paid from a Canadian bank account maintained by the British company.

13. Construct the balance-of-payments table for Japan for the year 2012, which is comparable in format to Exhibit 3.4, and interpret the numerical data. You may consult *International Financial Statistics* published by the IMF or search for useful websites for the data yourself.

INTERNET EXERCISE

Study the website of the International Monetary Fund (IMF), www.imf.org/external, and discuss the role of the IMF in dealing with balance-of-payments and currency crises.

MINI CASE

Mexico's Balance-of-Payments Problem

Balance-of-payments crises arise when a nation—typically a smaller, poorer, trade-dependent nation—attempts to manage its economic growth and stability by pegging the exchange rate, usually to the US dollar. If the exchange rate is pegged too high, the nation tends to run a Current Account deficit. Meanwhile, foreign exchange reserves are depleted as the central bank exchanges its reserves into foreign currencies at the overvalued exchange rate.

In the mid-1990s Mexico experienced large-scale trade deficits, depletion of foreign reserve holdings and a major currency devaluation in December 1994. The IMF, the Bank for International Settlements (BIS), the US Treasury and Canada intervened in this "peso crisis" with substantial loans to bolster Mexico's reserves. This intervention was followed by Mexico's decision to freely float the peso. All told, these events also brought about a severe recession and high unemployment in Mexico. Since the devaluation, however, Mexico's trade balance has improved.

Investigate the Mexico experiences in detail, and write a report on the subject. In the report, you may:

1. Document the trend in Mexico's key economic indicators, such as the Balance of Payments, the exchange rate and foreign reserve holdings during the period 1994 through 1996.

2. Investigate the causes of Mexico's balance-of-payments difficulties prior to the peso devaluation. Discuss alternative policy actions that might have prevented or mitigated the problem and the subsequent collapse of the peso.

3. Mexican industry involved in exports and import-competing goods generally fared better following these difficult times than those industries (and their employees) involved in nontraded goods. Why might this be so?

4. Key question: What lessons from the Mexican experience might be useful for other developing countries? Are flexible exchange rates preferred to fixed exchange rates. Why? Or why not?

In your report, you are expected to identify and address any other relevant issues concerning Mexico's balance-of-payments problem. International Financial Statistics published by the IMF provide basic macroeconomic data on Mexico.

A useful account is Ian Vásquez, "Retrospective on the Mexican Bailout," *Cato Journal,* Volume 21, Issue 3 (Winter 2002), http://www.cato.org/pubs/journal/cj21n3/cj21n3-12.pdf.

Mexican Holdings of SDRs (from the first quarter of 1993 until the last quarter of 1996):							
1993Q1	469	1994Q1	165	1995Q1	331	1996Q1	1,176
1993Q2	379	1994Q2	113	1995Q2	457	1996Q2	754
1993Q3	301	1994Q3	135	1995Q3	1,677	1996Q3	476
1993Q4	223	1994Q4	176	1995Q4	1,596	1996Q4	256

REFERENCES & SUGGESTED READINGS

Edwards, Sebastian. *Real Exchange Rates, Devaluation and Adjustment: Exchange Rate Policy in Developing Countries.* Cambridge, MA.: MIT Press, 1989.

Ohmae, Kenichi. "Lies, Damned Lies and Statistics: Why the Trade Deficit Doesn't Matter in a Borderless World." *Journal of Applied Corporate World* (Winter, 1991), pp. 98–106.

Salop, Joan, and Erich Spitaller. "Why Does the Current Account Matter?" International Monetary Fund, *Staff Papers* (March 1980), pp. 101–34.

 For more information on the resources available from McGraw-Hill Ryerson, go to www.mcgrawhill.ca/he/solutions.

Appendix 3A

The Relationship between Balance of Payments and National Income Accounting

This section is designed to explore the relationship between balance-of-payments accounting and national income accounting and to discuss the implications of this relationship. National income (Y), or gross national product (GNP), is identically equal to the sum of nominal consumption (C) of goods and services, private investment expenditures (I), government expenditures (G), and the difference between exports (X) and imports (M) of goods and services:

$$\text{GNP} \equiv Y \equiv C + I + G + X - M \tag{3A.1}$$

Private savings (S) is defined as the amount left from national income after consumption and taxes (T) are paid:

$$S \equiv Y - C - T, \text{ or} \tag{3A.2}$$

$$S \equiv C + I + G + X - M - C - T \tag{3A.3}$$

Noting that the BCA $\equiv X - M$, Equation (3A.3) can be rearranged as

$$(S - I) + (T - G) \equiv X - M \equiv \text{BCA} \tag{3A.4}$$

Equation (3A.4) shows that there is an intimate relationship between a country's BCA and how the country finances its domestic investment and pays for government expenditures. In Equation (3A.4), ($S - I$) is the difference between a country's savings and investment. If ($S - I$) is negative, it implies that a country's domestic savings are insufficient to finance domestic investment. Similarly, ($T - G$) is the difference between tax revenue and government expenditures. If ($T - G$) is negative, it implies that tax revenue is insufficient to cover government spending and a government budget deficit exists. This deficit must be financed by the government issuing debt securities.

Equation (3A.4) also shows that when a country imports more than it exports, its BCA will be negative, because through trade foreigners obtain a larger claim to domestic assets than the claim the country's citizens obtain to foreign assets. Consequently, when BCA is negative, it implies that government budget deficits and/or part of domestic investment are being financed with foreign-controlled capital. In order for a country to reduce a BCA deficit, one of the following must occur:

1. For a given level of S and I, the government budget deficit ($T - G$) must be reduced.
2. For a given level of I and ($T - G$), S must be increased.
3. For a given level of S and ($T - G$), I must fall.

Chapter 4

The Market for Foreign Exchange

CALPERS, THE CALIFORNIA pension fund, purchases one million Canadian dollars in order to buy shares in BlackBerry (formerly Research In Motion) of Waterloo. Deutsche Bank of Frankfurt arranges to buy 10 million Canadian dollars for a German customer who is purchasing real estate in Nova Scotia. WisconsinAir of Milwaukee needs 200 million Canadian dollars to acquire a fleet of commuter airplanes from Bombardier of Montreal. A construction firm in Tokyo buys 15 million Canadian dollars to pay for a shipment of softwood lumber from British Columbia.

These sorts of transactions—industrial firms and financial institutions buying Canadian dollars with foreign currency—take place every day in the world of international trade and cross-border investment. The purchase of Canadian dollars with foreign currency is a crucial step taken by foreigners to pay for Canadian exports or to invest in Canadian financial assets.

Likewise, Canadians and non-Canadians alike use their Canadian dollars to buy foreign currencies—for example, US dollars, euro, yen or Swedish kronor. The Manitoba Treasury might buy 10 million US dollars to retire a bond denominated in US dollars that the province had issued five years ago. Or Magna, the giant auto parts manufacturer in Ontario, might go to its bank to buy 15 million euro to pay for machinery imported from Germany. Perhaps Volvo (Canada) of Halifax buys five million Swedish kronor to pay management fees to the Volvo head office in Sweden. Calpers of California, mentioned above, would be selling Canadian dollars if it decided to unwind its position in BlackBerry.

Firms, governments, financial institutions and ordinary citizens are frequently involved—indeed they are constantly involved, if we look at it at a reasonable level of aggregation—in purchases of foreign currencies to buy foreign things (imports) from foreign suppliers. Foreign currencies are also required by those who want to make financial investments in foreign assets or to retire outstanding foreign debt.

The purchase of Canadian dollars with foreign currencies and the purchase of foreign currencies with Canadian dollars are typical transactions in the global market for foreign exchange. The purpose of this chapter is to describe this fascinating market in some detail, outlining its functions and operations as well as its institutional makeup. Our concerns are Canadian, but our perspective is global.

The market for foreign exchange is the largest financial market in the world by virtually any standard. It is open somewhere in the world every day, 24 hours a day. The market is involved in financial products—currencies and contracts related to currencies—that are liquid, costless to store and transportable at the speed of light. In 2010, the Bank of International Settlements (BIS) estimated the worldwide daily volume of trading in the spot and forward foreign exchange at US$3.73 trillion. This is equivalent to US$540 per day for every person on earth. Exhibit 4.1 presents a pie chart showing the shares of global foreign exchange turnover.

Broadly defined, the **foreign exchange (FX or FOREX)** market encompasses the conversion of purchasing power from one country into another—as when US purchasing power comes to Canada to buy Bombardier aircraft. In addition the FX market involves bank deposits of foreign currency, credit denominated in foreign currency, foreign trade financing, trading in foreign currency options and futures contracts and currency swaps. One chapter cannot adequately cover all these topics. At this point we confine our discussion to the spot and forward markets for foreign exchange. Later, in Chapter 9, we examine currency futures and options contracts. In Chapter 10, we look at swaps.

This chapter begins with an overview of the function and structure of the foreign exchange market and the major players who trade in this market. We then turn to a discussion of the spot market for foreign exchange. "Spot" simply means "now" or today. This section will show you how to read spot quotes and how to derive **cross-rates**. We outline the concept of triangular arbitrage as a means of ensuring market efficiency.

The chapter concludes with discussion of the forward market for foreign exchange. A forward contract is an agreement to exchange foreign currencies at a particular point in the future at a specifically agreed rate of exchange. We show how to read forward market quotes. We illustrate the purpose of the forward market and we describe the closely allied concept of swap rate quotes.

This chapter lays the foundation for much of the discussion throughout the remainder of the text. Without a solid understanding of how the foreign exchange market works, international finance cannot be studied in an informed and effective way. As authors, we urge you to read this chapter carefully and thoughtfully.

www.ny.frb.org

This is the website of the Federal Reserve Bank of New York. An especially useful article is "The Basics of Foreign Trade and Exchange."

EXHIBIT 4.1

Shares of Reported Global Foreign Exchange Turnover by Country, 2010

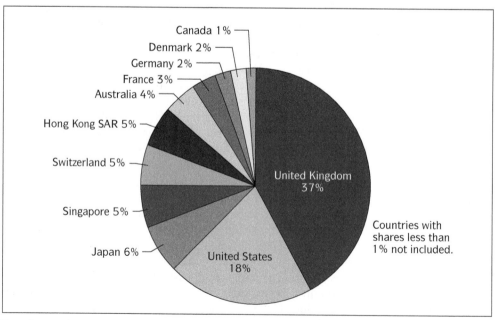

Note: Percent of total reporting foreign exchange turnover, adjusted for local inter-dealer double-counting.
Source: Tabulated from data in Table 5 in the *Triennial Central Bank Survey, Preliminary Results*. Bank for International Settlements, Basle, Switzerland, September 2010.

4.1 FUNCTION AND STRUCTURE OF THE FOREX MARKET

The foreign exchange market is an outgrowth of commercial banking: the twist is that two or more currencies are involved. For example, when Canadian Tire Corp imports merchandise from Mexico, Canadian Tire needs a source for foreign exchange, in this case Mexican *pesos,* to settle invoices from its Mexican suppliers. On the other hand, SNC Lavalin, the Canadian engineering consulting firm based in Montreal, might need to convert Brazilian *reals* that SNC Lavalin receives for its consulting work in Brazil into Canadian dollars. Assisting in foreign exchange transactions of this sort is a service that commercial banks provide for their clients. Bank customers expect dependable service from their bank.

www.about.reuters.com/ productinfo/index.aspx

This website explains the various Reuters spot and forward FX electronic trading systems.

The foreign exchange market is an **over-the-counter (OTC)** market; that is, currency trading does not take place in a central marketplace where buyers and sellers carry out transactions face to face. Rather, the foreign exchange market is a worldwide linkage of bank currency traders, nonbank dealers and FX brokers who are connected to one another via a network of telephones, computer terminals and automated dealing systems. Reuters and EBS are the largest vendors of quote screen monitors used in trading currencies. The communications systems that serve the foreign exchange market are extraordinarily sophisticated, surpassing in speed and efficiency the communications systems of nonfinancial industry, governments or the military.

www.ebs.org

This website explains the EBS Spot electronic dealing system.

Twenty-four-hour-a-day currency trading follows the sun around the globe. Three major market segments can be identified: Australasia, Europe and North America. Australasia includes the trading centres of Sydney, Tokyo, Hong Kong, Singapore and Bahrain; Europe includes Zurich, Frankfurt, Paris, Brussels, Amsterdam and London; and North America includes New York, Montreal, Toronto, Chicago, San Francisco and Los Angeles. Most trading rooms operate over a 9-to-12-hour working day, although some banks have experimented with operating three 8-hour shifts in order to trade around the clock. Especially active trading takes place when the trading hours of the Australasia centres and the European centres overlap and when the European and North American centres overlap. More than half of the trading in North America occurs between 8:00 A.M. and noon eastern standard time (1:00 P.M. and 5:00 P.M. Greenwich Mean Time [London]), when the European markets are still open. Certain trading centres have a more dominant effect on the market than others. For example, trading diminishes dramatically in the Australasian market segment when the Tokyo traders are taking their lunch break! Exhibit 4.2 provides a general indication of the participation level in the global FX market by showing electronic trades per hour.

EXHIBIT 4.2

The Circadian Rhythms of the FX Market

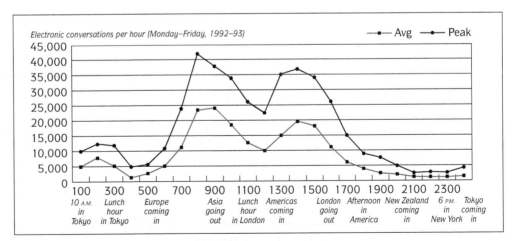

Note: Time (0100–2400 hours, Greenwich Mean Time).

Source: Sam Y. Cross, *All about the Foreign Exchange Market in the United States,* Federal Reserve Bank of New York, www.ny.frb.org.

The Mouse Takes Over the Floor

When electronic trading first began to make a significant dent in the foreign exchange market, traders, reportedly concerned about the loss of the human factor in dealing, were heard to grumble that a computer wasn't going to buy them a beer.

Ten years ago a deal was still done when somebody yelled "done" into one of their telephones amid the background noise of other traders doing the same while voice broker prices were constantly being pumped out via a Tannoy system known as the squawkbox or the "hoot 'n holler."

"It was bloody noisy and bloody good fun," reminisced one ex-dealer, who felt the advent of technology had robbed the market of much of its personality.

Today, that roar is more of a steady hum as traders face banks of screens and hold electronic conversations while the "hoot 'n holler" is used to spread analyst assessments of the latest economic data. The old noise level has been transplanted to bars where, it seems, plenty of beers are still being bought.

Reuters' first screen-based trading system was launched in 1982 for the interbank market, where the majority of foreign exchange dealing takes place. The company launched a conversational dealing product in 1989 and an anonymous "matching" platform in 1992, but faced its first stiff competition only in 1993 with the launch of Electronic Broking Services (EBS), a platform owned by a number of the big banks and designed with the express purpose of preventing Reuters gaining a monopoly position. Now, both platforms still dominate the interbank market but face competition from the internet, where a number of web-based portals are encouraging new participants to trade directly.

In simple volume terms the online platforms look like minnows. EBS reports average daily volumes worth about $100bn whereas the larger internet platforms have average volumes between $15bn–$20bn. But Justyn Trenner of ClientKnowledge calculates the combined value of all online trading is now worth $100bn a day and highlights the rapid growth in the sector.

Platforms such as FXAll, Hotspot FXi and e-Speed are quick to dismiss suggestions of direct competition with the giants. Instead, they say they offer different parties, such as corporate treasurers or fund managers, the opportunity to participate directly and trade outside their usual banking relationships.

If electronic technology in the interbank market helped smaller banks access price transparency in the interbank market, the latest generation of internet platforms is doing the same for those banks' clients.

"We're not going for the interbank market; we live in the space where banks face out to clients," says John Eley, chief executive of Hotspot foreign exchange, who says bank clients, who would previously call three or four dealers for quotes, can get the same range in seconds off a web-based platform, and then deal themselves.

"Multibank portals lower the barriers for third-party foreign exchange trades by cutting costs and reducing risk," adds Mark Warms, chief marketing officer at FXAll, who says the volumes traded by hedge funds have tripled on the platform.

Rick Sears, head of foreign exchange at the Chicago Mercantile Exchange, says volumes in its foreign

FX Market Participants

The market for foreign exchange can be viewed as a two-tier market. One tier is the **wholesale** or **interbank market** and the other tier is the **retail** or **client market**. FX market participants can be categorized into five groups: international banks, bank customers, nonbank dealers, FX brokers and central banks.

International banks provide the core of the FX market. Approximately 100 to 200 banks worldwide actively "make a market" in foreign exchange, that is, they stand willing to buy or sell foreign currency for their own account. These international banks serve their retail clients, the *bank customers*, in conducting foreign commerce or making international investment in financial assets that require foreign exchange. Bank customers broadly include multinational corporations (MNCs), money managers and private speculators. According to 2010 BIS statistics, retail or bank client transactions account for approximately 14 percent of FX trading volume. The other 86 percent of trading volume is from interbank trades between international banks or nonbank dealers. *Nonbank dealers* are large nonbank financial institutions such as investment banks whose size and frequency of trades make it cost-effective to establish their own dealing rooms to trade directly in the interbank market for their foreign exchange needs. Nonbank dealers account for approximately 47 percent of interbank trading volume.

Part of the interbank trading among international banks involves adjusting the inventory positions they hold in various foreign currencies. However, most interbank trades are

exchange products had risen sharply since its electronic Globex platform allowed investors to trade its futures contracts 24 hours a day. Between 40 and 45 percent of CME's foreign exchange participants are commodity trading accounts (CTAs) and hedge funds.

"These groups are a lot more comfortable dealing electronically than before. They used to worry about execution risk but e-trading is increasingly popular," he says.

The considerable growth of online platforms, and the survival of a number of different models has surpassed most observers' expectations. Early predictions were that multibank portals such as FXAll, which offer prices from a wide range of banks, would surpass proprietary platforms owned by a single bank. Instead, both are growing rapidly. A recent survey by Greenwich Associates, the US consultancy group, listed both FXAll and UBS's proprietary platforms as leading online trading volumes.

There were also initial fears that the sudden surge in trading outlets could fragment liquidity, hampering trading, but this does not yet appear to have happened. "Instead, it is more channels for the same market—a price on one platform or another is virtually the same," says Fabian Shey, global head of foreign exchange distribution at UBS.

Mr. Trenner suggested that overall, the shrinking of foreign exchange trading into a few global centers—Tokyo, London and New York—and banks' reorganization to follow suit had instead consolidated liquidity.

When EBS was first launched, dealers raised concerns about the demise of voice brokers' and dealers' marketmaking role, warning that removing the obligation to quote two-way prices could weaken liquidity in times of crisis with dealers happy to take prices and less prepared to quote them.

But 11 years on, the market has not suffered a significant problem and very little evidence of prices lurching through "grapping"—when the new bid-offer spread does not overlap with the last price posted.

The relative smoothness of price moves is proof, says Jack Jeffery, chief executive of EBS, that the marketplace has evolved with the development of trading technologies.

"The market is so liquid with so many diverse views and flows that marketmaking has changed," he said. "It is now about participation. If you participate, you are contributing to liquidity, not just taking it out."

Some still fret, however, that the market's current dependence on technology leaves it at the mercy of computer servers.

Outages are extremely rare, however, and long-time participants are sanguine about the risks posed.

"Yes, there's a risk, but the market is very adaptable," says Nick Beecroft, head of foreign exchange trading at Standard Chartered.

"In the event of a serious IT meltdown, there are plenty of lines from broking houses to dealing floors and it would just be a question of pulling all the ex–spot brokers back on to the phones, from other products. FX is a highly resilient marketplace."

It seems fears about the loss of the human factor are as yet groundless.

Source: Jennifer Hughes, *Financial Times,* Special Report: Foreign Exchange, May 27, 2004, p. 1.

speculative or *arbitrage* transactions, where market participants attempt to correctly judge the future direction of price movements in one currency versus another or attempt to profit from temporary price discrepancies in currencies between competing dealers. Market psychology is a key ingredient in currency trading, and a dealer can often infer another's trading intention from the currency position being accumulated.

FX brokers match dealer orders to buy and sell currencies for a fee, but brokers seldom take a position themselves. Brokers have knowledge of the quotes offered by many dealers in the market. Today, however, only a few specialized broking firms exist. The vast majority of interbank trades of currencies flow through Reuters and EBS platforms. The International Finance in Practice box "Where Money Talks Very Loudly" explains how FX trading has changed in the past 10 years and how nonbank dealers using electronic trading platforms can compete with bank trades and other nonbank dealers.

Since the exchange *rate* is determined in the market for foreign exchange and since the exchange rate is of crucial concern to government and policy makers, there is a question of the extent to which governments—through their central banks—should intervene in the foreign exchange market in order to push the exchange rate up or down. A lower exchange rate, for example, encourages exports and discourages imports. Such matters are of particular concern in Canada where 60 percent of our GDP is touched by trade and more than 65 percent of our trade involves just one country, the United States. On the specific issue of *exchange rate intervention* by the Bank of Canada, the key point is that the Bank does not

Where Money Talks Very Loudly

Foreign exchange is the largest, most dynamic market in the world. About $1.88 trillion worth of currency is traded daily in a market that literally does not sleep. Centered in Tokyo, London and New York, traders deal smoothly across borders and time-zones, often in multiples of $1bn, in transactions that take less than a second.

The market's development into its current form has left it virtually unrecognizable from 10 years ago.

Then, banks dealt currencies on behalf of their clients via traders holding multiple telephone conversations or perhaps using the relatively new electronic systems offered by Reuters and Electronic Broking Services (EBS). Today, clients can deal alongside banks on a number of platforms and the quiet hum of computers has done much to reduce the noise level on trading floors.

Old timers complain that a lot of the "personality" has been drained from trading by the rise of faceless systems. But the marketplace itself is, if anything, more vigorous now than then. Many banks and trading platforms are reporting stiff rises in recent volumes traded and, allowing for some growth in market share, most believe overall trading activity has risen as the transparency of the market, and access to it, has improved.

EBS recently said that half of its top 35 busiest trading days since the launch of the company 10 years ago had been in the first two months of 2004. Reuters said it saw growth of 35 percent year-on-year in 2003 in spot market transactions and that year-to-date, it estimated spot volumes to be 50 percent higher from a year ago.

"FX has come of age as an asset class over the last five years," says Nick Beecroft, head of foreign exchange trading at Standard Chartered. "There is much more activity, from active hedgers and from asset managers in other classes who tend to worry about FX much more than they did five, let alone 10 years ago."

Then, the market largely consisted of deals between banks and the technologies being introduced were designed to replicate that. Roughly 50 percent of foreign exchange deals were conducted by conversations between two counterparties and a further 35 percent were conducted through voice brokers, who "matched" bids and offers without either side knowing who the counterparty was.

Reuters had launched its first screen-based system in 1982, and in 1989 followed it up with a conversational platform designed to mimic dealers' telephone trades. In 1992 it went live with a matching system aimed at reproducing the role played by voice brokers. EBS's matching platform was launched in 1993 in a bid by banks to curb Reuters' development of a monopoly position.

The advent of electronic broking for the interbank market gave smaller banks, which previously had little access to the best prices, the opportunity to deal alongside the bigger banks on an even basis because of the transparency afforded by electronic price provision.

Today, only a few specialist voice-broking firms still operate and the bulk of interbank business flows over Reuters and EBS's platforms.

Since then however, there has been another seismic shift in the foreign exchange (FX) marketplace; the extension of price transparency to clients outside the banking world.

Foreign Exchange Survey 2010					
Overall		**Nonfinancial Corporations**		**Banks**	
Company	Market Share %	Company	Market Share %	Company	Market Share %
Deutsche Bank	18.06	Citi	10.07	Deutsche Bank	20.22
UBS	11.30	HSBC	9.13	UBS	15.54
Barclays Capital	11.08	Deutsche Bank	7.80	Barclays Capital	11.97
Citi	7.69	RBS	7.65	Citi	6.53
RBS	6.50	BNP Paribas	6.84	RBS	6.21
JPMorgan	6.35	Barclays Capital	5.74	JPMorgan	5.35
HSBC	4.55	Société Générale	5.60	Credit Suisse	4.68
Credit Suisse	4.44	JPMorgan	5.17	HSBC	4.31
Goldman Sachs	4.28	UBS	4.93	Goldman Sachs	3.35
Morgan Stanley	2.91	Bank of America Merrill Lynch	3.31	BNP Paribas	2.53

Source: *Euromoney,* May 2010.

Through an array of web-based platforms fund managers and hedge funds, for example, can rapidly view a series of quotes for a particular currency pair, and conduct the deal themselves. On some platforms, the counterparty could as easily be another fund manager as a bank.

"The market has changed more in the last three years than the previous seven," says John Nelson, global head of FX markets at ABN Amro. "One stroke of a key will send a trade from the back office of one counterparty and settle in the back of the other almost instantly."

Rapid price dissemination has, to a great extent, now levelled the playing field and extended the reach of FX trading well beyond the core investment bank market.

"What differentiated banks from customers then was that banks could see the real market prices and customers couldn't. Fast-forward to now, and I can see real-time market prices streaming over my desktop," says Justyn Trenner, chief executive of ClientKnowledge, an independent research firm. "This greatly facilitates the more sophisticated fund managers in actively trading FX as an asset class." The near instant dissemination of news, data and price information has led to what market theorists call "efficiency"—an accurate price at any given time. But it has affected the way in which currency pairs move.

"You get more zigs and zags within a trend than you used to see because everybody reacts to every piece of news at the same time," says Chris Furness, senior currencies strategist at 4Cast economic consultancy, who likened today's behaviour to a school of fish that all change direction at the same time. The upshot of more dramatic intraday price movement, particularly over the past two years, is greater overall volatility.

"Having absorbed the uncertainties around the launch of the euro and despite a contraction in the number of traders, this is a very healthy time for the market," says Mark Robson, head of treasury and fixed income at Reuters.

But although there are new direct players as a result of new trading opportunities and as the price playing field has been levelled, many of the smaller banks have been relegated to the sidelines.

Once more they may specialise in their regional currency but they are more usually clients of the bigger banks because of the expense of the new wave of trading technology.

The few banks with the deepest pockets have developed and operate successful e-trading platforms of their own that add to the volumes they trade and their profits. In turn, they can afford to offer clients the tailormade products that are becoming the norm.

"The intense competition in this space means everyone is trying to distinguish themselves through customisation," says Joe Noviello, chief information officer at e-speed, Cantor Fitzgerald's online platform, which expanded to offer FX trading last year.

Source: Excerpted from Jennifer Hughes, *Financial Times*, Special Report: Foreign Exchange, May 27, 2004, p. 2.

Leveraged Funds		E-trading, Proprietary Platforms		E-trading, Multibank and Independent Platforms	
Company	Market Share %	Company	Market Share %	Company	Market Share %
Deutsche Bank	24.29	Deutsche Bank	26.41	FXall	27.63
Barclays Capital	14.63	Barclays Capital	19.40	Reuters Dealing 3000 Direct	21.15
UBS	7.92	UBS	11.84	Currenex	19.02
Citi	6.86	Citi	10.46	FX Connect	15.96
JPMorgan	6.52	JPMorgan	3.56	360 Treasury Systems	6.26
Credit Suisse	6.45	Credit Suisse	3.50	FX Trading on Bloomberg	3.85
Goldman Sachs	5.89	Goldman Sachs	3.21	Integral—FX Inside	1.64
Morgan Stanley	5.82	HSBC	2.65	HotspotFXi	1.23
RBS	5.76	Morgan Stanley	2.27	Chicago Mercantile Exchange	1.15
Bank of America Merrill Lynch	2.79	RBS	1.97	LavaFX	0.94

do much of it. First of all, large as it is, the Bank of Canada is still a very small player in the foreign exchange market, even for the Canadian dollar. The main policy instrument that the Bank uses to influence the exchange rate (and also inflation) is the interest rate. The Bank is in a position to influence Canadian short-term interest rates. A bump-up in Canadian short-term interest rates attracts foreign capital to Canada and, in the process, this raises demand for Canadian dollars, which, in turn, puts upward pressure on the exchange rate. Lowering Canadian short-term interest rates has the opposite effect.

In fact, the central banks of most industrial countries remain largely neutral in the international markets for foreign exchange. They are involved to the extent that they deal in foreign exchange for operational purposes, for example, as they manage their nations' foreign exchange reserves. However, central banks of industrialized nations seldom intervene actively to achieve a specific value for their exchange rate. They, at most, serve a stabilizing function, dampening some of the volatility in the exchange in times of particular stress, such as during the political uncertainty that gripped Canada during the 1995 Quebec Referendum on Separation or amid the global chaos of the Asian Financial Crisis of 1997. Other, less dramatic episodes call for a regular steadying influence of the central bank.

There is little evidence that industrialized countries can effectively intervene in the foreign exchange market to influence the value of their exchange rate for any length of time. Perhaps the best-known recent cases that illustrate the limits to central banks' power to resist the relentless forces of foreign exchange markets occurred in the early 1990s when both the United Kingdom and Italy lost huge volumes of foreign exchange reserves as well as the battle to maintain the value of their currencies—the pound and the lira—at exchange rates to which they made commitments to the European Monetary System.

Japan is somewhat of an exception to the passivity of central banks. Japan has been more willing than most industrialized nations to intervene in the foreign exchange market for extended periods. It has proven to be a costly exercise.

Correspondent Banking Relationships

The interbank market is a network of **correspondent banking relationships**, with large commercial banks maintaining demand deposit accounts with one another, called *correspondent banking accounts*. The correspondent bank account network allows for the efficient functioning of the foreign exchange market.

Example 4.1 *Correspondent Banking Relationship*

As an example of how the network of correspondent bank accounts facilitates international foreign exchange transactions, consider Ottawa Importer arranging the finance of an order of merchandise from Dutch Exporter of Amsterdam. The order is invoiced in euros at €200,000. Ottawa Importer will contact his local bank, CIBC, and inquire about the €/$ exchange rate. The quote is €1 = $1.30. If Ottawa Importer accepts this exchange rate, then CIBC will debit Ottawa Importer's demand deposit account for $260,000, which equals €200,000 times $1.30. CIBC will instruct its correspondent bank in Amsterdam, ING, to debit CIBC's correspondent bank account €200,000 and to credit that amount to Dutch Exporter. CIBC will then debit its books €200,000 as an offset to the $260,000 debit to Ottawa Importer's account, to reflect the decrease in its correspondent bank account with ING.

This rather contrived example assumes that CIBC and Dutch Exporter both have bank accounts with ING. A more realistic interpretation is to recognize that within Europe, the sophistication of the banking system is such that Ottawa Importer can directly contact its correspondent bank in Holland, say ING, confident that ING will have relationships with Dutch Importer's bank and will hold funds and release funds for Ottawa Importer appropriate to the shipment.

The *Society for Worldwide Interbank Financial Telecommunications (SWIFT)* allows international commercial banks to communicate instructions of the type in this example to one another. SWIFT is a private nonprofit message transfer system with headquarters in Brussels with intercontinental switching centres in the Netherlands and in the United States (which serves Canada). The *Clearing House Interbank Payments System (CHIPS)* provides a clearinghouse for the interbank settlements (primarily in US dollars) between intenational banks. Returning to our example, suppose CIBC first needed to purchase euros in order to have them for transfer to Dutch Exporter. CIBC can use CHIPS for settling the purchase of euros from Canadian dollars from, say, Barclays, with instructions via SWIFT to Barclays to deposit the euros in its account with ING and to ING to transfer ownership to Dutch Exporter. The transfer between Barclays and ING would, in turn, be executed through correspondent bank accounts or through the European clearinghouse.

In 1995, *Exchange Clearing House Limited (ECHO)*, the first global clearinghouse for settling interbank FOREX transactions, began operation. ECHO is a multilateral netting system that on each settlement date netted a client's payments and receipts in each currency, regardless of whether they are due to or from multiple counterparties. Multilateral netting eliminates the risk and inefficiency of individual settlement. In 1997, CLS Services Limited merged with ECHO. Within the new CLS Group, 17 currencies are eligible for settlement among 64 members.

4.2 THE SPOT MARKET

The **spot market** involves almost the immediate purchase or sale of foreign exchange. Typically, cash settlement is made two business days (excluding holidays of either the buyer or the seller) after the transaction for trades between the US dollar and a non–North American currency. For regular spot trades between the US dollar and the Canadian dollar, settlement takes only one business day. According to BIS statistics, spot foreign exchange trading accounted for 40 percent of FX trades. Exhibit 4.3 provides a detailed analysis of daily foreign exchange turnover by instrument and counterparty for 2010.

Spot Rate Quotations

Spot rate currency quotations can be stated in direct or indirect terms. To understand the difference, let us refer to Exhibit 4.4. The exhibit shows currency quotations for 10 May 2013.

EXHIBIT 4.3

Average Daily Foreign Exchange Turnover by Instrument and Counterparty, 2010

Instrument/Counterparty	Turnover in USD (billion)	Percent
Spot	*$1,490*	*40*
With reporting dealers	518	14
With other financial institutions	755	20
With nonfinancial customers	217	6
Outright Forwards	*475*	*13*
With reporting dealers	113	3
With other financial institutions	254	7
With nonfinancial customers	108	3
Foreign Exchange Swaps	*1,765*	*47*
With reporting dealers	837	22
With other financial institutions	258	20
With nonfinancial customers	170	5
Total	$3,730	100

Note: Turnover is net of local and cross-border interdealer double-counting.

Source: Tabulated from data in Table 2 in the *Triennial Central Bank Survey, Preliminary Results,* Bank for International Settlements, Basle, Switzerland, September 2010.

EXHIBIT 4.4

Exchange Rates

	US$ Equivalent	Local Currency per US$	C$ Equivalent	Local Currency per C$

The foreign exchange mid-range rates below apply to trading among banks in amounts of US$1 million or more as quoted on 10 May 2013 Bloomberg Terminal.

Retail transactions provide fewer units of foreign currency per dollar.

	US$ Equivalent	Local Currency per US$	C$ Equivalent	Local Currency per C$
Argentina (peso)	0.1913	5.2284	0.1932	5.1767
Australia (dollar)	1.0025	0.9975	1.0125	0.9877
Bahrain (dinar)	2.6525	0.3770	2.6790	0.3733
Brazil (real)	0.4950	2.0204	0.4999	2.0004
Canada (dollar)	0.9901	1.0100	—	—
1 month forward	0.9894	1.0107	—	—
3 months forward	0.9880	1.0121	—	—
6 months forward	0.9859	1.0143	—	—
Chile (peso)	0.0021	474	0.0021	469
China (renminbi)	0.1628	6.1418	0.1644	6.0811
Colombia (peso)	0.0005	1834	0.0006	1816
Czech Republic (koruna)	0.0504	19.86	0.0509	19.6647
Denmark (krone)	0.1742	5.7395	0.1760	5.6828
Ecuador (US dollar)	1.0000	1.0000	1.0100	0.9901
Egypt (pound)	0.1438	6.9565	0.1452	6.8878
Hong Kong (dollar)	0.1289	7.7610	0.1301	7.6843
Hungary (forint)	0.0044	226.7	0.0045	225
India (rupee)	0.0182	54.8847	0.0184	54.3425
Indonesia (rupiah)	0.0001	9737	0.0001	9640
Israel (shekel)	0.2800	3.5710	0.2828	3.5358
Japan (yen)	0.0098	101.62	0.0099	100.6220
1 month forward	0.0098	101.62	0.0099	100.6220
3 months forward	0.0099	101.52	0.0099	100.5198
6 months forward	0.0099	101.52	0.0099	100.5198
Jordan (dinar)	1.4131	0.7077	1.4272	0.7007
Kuwait (dinar)	3.5059	0.2852	3.5409	0.2824
Lebanon (pound)	0.0007	1514	0.0007	1499
Malaysia (ringgit)	0.3341	2.9930	0.3374	2.9635
Malta (lira)	3.0261	0.3305	3.0563	0.3272
Mexico (peso)	0.0828	12.0846	0.0836	11.9652
New Zealand (dollar)	0.8302	1.2045	0.8385	1.1926
Norway (krone)	0.1727	5.7921	0.1744	5.7348
Pakistan (rupee)	0.0102	98.42	0.0103	97.4476
Peru (new sol)	0.3844	2.6015	0.3882	2.5758
Philippines (peso)	0.0243	41.1184	0.0246	40.7122
Poland (zloty)	0.3135	3.1894	0.3167	3.1579
Russia (ruble)	0.0318	31.4169	0.0321	31.1065
Saudi Arabia (riyal)	0.2666	3.7509	0.2693	3.7139
Singapore (dollar)	0.8076	1.2383	0.8156	1.2260
Slovak Republic (koruna)	0.0431	23	0.0436	22.96
South Africa (rand)	0.1096	9.1216	0.1107	9.0315
South Korea (won)	0.0009	1106	0.0009	1096
Sweden (krona)	0.1515	6.5994	0.1530	6.5342
Switzerland (franc)	1.0451	0.9568	1.0555	0.9474
1 month forward	1.0454	0.9566	1.0558	0.9471
3 months forward	1.0461	0.9559	1.0565	0.9465
6 months forward	1.0472	0.9549	1.0576	0.9455
Taiwan (dollar)	0.0337	29.64	0.0341	29.3456
Thailand (baht)	0.0336	29.78	0.0339	29.4854
Turkey (lira)	0.5552	1.8010	0.5608	1.7832
United Kingdom (pound)	1.5358	0.6511	1.5511	0.6447
1 month forward	1.5354	0.6513	1.5507	0.6449
3 months forward	1.5349	0.6515	1.5502	0.6451
6 months forward	1.5342	0.6518	1.5495	0.6454
United Arab (dirham)	0.2722	3.6738	0.2749	3.6375
United States (dollar)	—	—	1.0100	0.9901
Uruguay (peso)	0.0528	18.950	0.0533	18.76
Venezuela (bolivar)	0.1589	6.2921	0.1605	6.2299
SDR (IMF)	1.4999	0.6667	1.5148	0.6601
Euro	1.2989	0.7699	1.3119	0.7623

Notes: Special drawing rights (SDR) are based on a weighted sum of exchange rates for the US dollar, euro, British pound and Japanese yen. Canadian dollar figures are this book's authors' calculations from the US dollar data.

Source: Financial Research and Trading Lab, Rotman School of Management.

The first numerical column provides **direct quotes** from the American perspective, that is, the price of one unit of the foreign currency priced in US dollars. For example, the spot quote for one British pound is $1.5358. (Forward quotes for one-, three-, and six-month contracts, which will be discussed in a following section, appear directly under the spot quotes for four currencies.) The second column provides **indirect quotes** from the American perspective, that is, the price of one US dollar in the foreign currency. For example, in the second column, we see that the Monday spot quote for one US dollar in British pounds sterling is £0.6511. The third and fourth columns present direct and indirect foreign exchange quotes in terms of our Canadian dollar.

It is common practice among currency traders worldwide to both price and trade currencies against the US dollar. For example, BIS statistics indicate that in 2010, 85 percent of currency trading in the world involved the US dollar on one side of the transaction. In recent years, however, the use of other currencies has been increasing, especially in dealing done by smaller regional banks. For example, in Europe many European currencies were traded against the deutschemark. Overall, in 2010, 39 percent of all currency trading worldwide involved the euro on one side of the transaction. With respect to other major currencies, 19 percent involved the Japanese yen, 12 percent the British pound, 6 percent the Swiss franc, and 5 percent the Canadian dollar. Exhibit 4.5 provides a detailed analysis of foreign exchange turnover by currency.

Most currencies in the interbank market are quoted in **European terms**, that is, the US dollar is priced in terms of the foreign currency (an indirect quote from the American perspective). By convention, however, it is standard practice to price certain currencies in terms of the US dollar, or in what is referred to as **American terms** (a direct quote from the American perspective). Prior to 1971, the British pound was a nondecimal currency; that is, a pound was not naturally divisible into 10 subcurrency units. Thus it was cumbersome to price decimal currencies in terms of the pound. By necessity, the practice developed of pricing the British pound as well as the Australian dollar and New Zealand dollar in terms of decimal currencies. This convention continues today. When the common euro currency was introduced, it was decided that it also would be quoted in American terms. To the uninitiated, this can be confusing, and it is something to bear in mind when examining currency quotations.

EXHIBIT 4.5

Average Daily Foreign Exchange Turnover by Currency against All Other Currencies, 2010

Currency	Turnover Stated in US$ (billions)	Percent
US dollar	$3,378	85
Euro	1,556	39
Japanese yen	756	19
Pound sterling	469	12
Australian dollar	285	7
Swiss franc	240	6
Canadian dollar	196	5
Other currencies	1,082	27
Total—double-counted	$7,962	200
Total—not double-counted	$3,981	100

Note: Since there are two sides to each transaction, each currency is reported twice. Turnover is net of local and cross-border interdealer double-counting. The total of $3,981 billion includes $250 billion of foreign exchange trading in currency swaps, options and other products.

Source: Tabulated from data in Table 4 in the *Triennial Central Bank Survey, Preliminary Results*, Bank for International Settlements, Basle, Switzerland, September 2010.

In this textbook, we will use the following notation for spot rate quotations. In general, $S(j/k)$ will refer to the price of one unit of currency k in terms of currency j. Thus, the American-term quote for a US dollar in exchange for British pounds on 10 May 2013, is $S(\$/£) = 1.5358$. The corresponding European quote is $S(£/\$) = 0.6511$. When the context is clear as to what terms the quotation is in, the less-cumbersome S will be used to denote the spot rate.

Since "American terms" and "European terms" are standard expressions in the world of currency exchange, it is useful to stick with those working expressions even though one may be primarily interested in currencies from a *Canadian* perspective. For convenience, Exhibit 4.4 reports exchange rates in "Canadian dollar equivalent" and in "local currency in Canadian dollars" (columns 3 and 4). However, when we turn to a more technical discussion of spot FX trading, cross-rate quotes and triangular arbitrage, as we do in the following pages, we focus on *US dollar exchange rates* for other major currencies such as the euro or the British pound. And for good reason. As we shall see, an exchange rate—either spot or forward—between the Canadian dollar and any non-US currency, say the Canadian dollar–Swiss franc exchange rate, is not determined or priced *directly* between the two. Rather the Canadian dollar–Swiss franc exchange rate is determined *indirectly* in a triangular fashion through the US dollar. To be specific, the Canadian dollar–Swiss franc exchange rate is determined (and priced) as (US\$/SF)/(US\$/C\$) = C\$/SF.

It should be intuitive that American and European quotes are reciprocals of one another. That is,

$$S(\$/£) = \frac{1}{S(£/\$)}$$

$$1.5358 = \frac{1}{0.6511} \tag{4.1}$$

and

$$S(£/\$) = \frac{1}{S(\$/£)}$$

$$0.6511 = \frac{1}{1.5358} \tag{4.2}$$

The Bid-Ask Spread

Up to this point in our discussion, we have ignored the bid-ask spread in FX transactions. Interbank FX traders buy currency for inventory at the **bid price** and sell from inventory at the higher **offer** or **ask price**. Consider the Bloomberg quotes from Exhibit 4.4. What are they, bid or ask? In a manner of speaking, the answer is both, depending on whether one is referring to the American- or European-term quotes. Note the wording directly under the *Exchange Rates* title. The key to our inquiry is the sentence that reads: "Retail transactions provide fewer units of foreign currency per dollar." The word "provide" implies that the quotes in the second column under the "Currency per US\$" heading are buying, or bid quotes. Thus European-term quotes are interbank bid prices.

To be more specific about the £/\$ quote we have been using as an example, we can specify that it is a bid quote by writing $S^b(£/\$) = 0.6511$, meaning the bank dealer will bid, or pay, £0.6511 for one dollar. However, if the bank dealer is buying dollars for British pounds sterling, it must be selling British pounds for dollars. This implies that the \$/£ quote we have been using as an example is an ask quote, which we can designate as $S^a(\$/£) = 1.5358$. That is, the bank dealer will sell one British pound for \$1.5358.

Returning to the reciprocal relationship between European- and American-term quotes, the recognition of the bid-ask spread implies:

$$S^a(\$/\pounds) = \frac{1}{S^b(\pounds/\$)} \qquad (4.3)$$

In American terms, the bank dealer is asking \$1.5358 for one British pound; that means the bank dealer is willing to pay, or bid, less. Interbank bid-ask spreads are quite small. Let us assume the bid price is \$0.0005 less than the ask; thus, $S^b(\$/\pounds) = 1.5353$. Similarly, the bank dealer will want an ask price in European terms greater than its bid price. The reciprocal relationship between European- and American-term quotes implies:

$$S^a(\pounds/\$) = \frac{1}{S^b(\$/\pounds)} \qquad (4.4)$$

$$= \frac{1}{1.5353}$$

$$= 0.6513$$

Thus, the bank dealer's ask price of £0.6513 per dollar is, indeed, greater than its bid price of £0.6511.

The following template summarizes the reciprocal relationship between American/European (or direct/indirect) bid and ask quotes:

	Bid	**Ask**
$S(\$/\pounds)$	1.5353	1.5358
	reciprocal equals	reciprocal equals
$S(\pounds/\$)$	0.6511	0.6513

Spot FX Trading

Exhibit 4.4 indicates that for most currencies, quotations are carried out to four decimal places in both American and European terms. However, for some currencies (e.g., the Japanese yen) quotations in European terms are carried out only to two or three decimal places, but in American terms, the quotations may be carried out to as many as eight decimal places.

In the interbank market, the standard-size trade among large banks in the major currencies is for the dollar equivalent of \$10,000,000, or "ten dollars" in trader jargon. Dealers quote both the bid and the ask, willing to either buy or sell up to \$10,000,000 at the quoted prices. Spot quotations are good for only a few seconds. If a trader cannot immediately make up his mind whether to buy or sell at the proffered prices, the quotes are likely to be withdrawn.

In conversation, interbank FX traders use a shorthand abbreviation in expressing spot currency quotations. Consider the \$/£ bid-ask quotes from above, \$1.5353–\$1.5358. The "1.53" is known as the *big figure,* and it is assumed to be known by all traders. The third and fourth digits to the right of the decimal place are referred to as the *small figure.* Since spot bid-ask spreads are typically around 5 "points," it is unambiguous for a trader to respond with "53–58" when asked what is his quote for British pounds sterling.

The bid-ask spread mechanism facilitates acquiring or disposing of inventory. Suppose most \$/£ dealers are trading at \$1.5353–\$1.5358. A trader believing the pound will soon appreciate substantially against the dollar will want to acquire a larger inventory of British pounds. A quote of "55–60" will encourage some traders to sell at the higher than market bid price but also dissuade other traders from purchasing at the higher offer price.

Analogously, a quote of "51–56" will allow a dealer to lower his pound inventory if he thinks the pound is ready to depreciate.

The retail bid-ask spread is wider than the interbank spread; that is, lower bid and higher ask prices apply to the smaller sums traded at the retail level. This is necessary to cover the fixed costs of a transaction that exist regardless of which tier the trade is made in.

Interbank trading rooms are typically organized with individual traders dealing in a particular currency. The dealing rooms of large banks are set up with traders dealing against the US dollar in all the major currencies: Japanese yen, euro, Canadian dollar, Swiss franc and British pound, plus the local currency if it is not one of the majors. Individual banks may also specialize by making a market in regional currencies or in the currencies of less-developed countries, again all versus the US dollar. Banks will usually also have a cross-rate desk where trades between two currencies not involving the US dollar are handled. It is not uncommon for a trader of an active currency pair to make as many as 1,500 quotes and 400 trades in a day. In smaller European banks accustomed to more regional trading, dealers will frequently quote and trade versus the euro.

Cross-Exchange Rate Quotations

Let us ignore the transaction costs of trading temporarily while we develop the concept of a cross-rate. A **cross-exchange rate** is an exchange rate between a currency pair where neither currency is the US dollar. It is useful to bear in mind that in 90 percent of foreign currency transactions, regardless of where they occur, the US dollar is on one side of the transaction. The cross-exchange rate can be calculated from the US dollar exchange rates for the two currencies, using either European- or American-term quotations. For example, the €/£ cross-rate can be calculated from American-term quotations as follows:

$$S(€/£) = \frac{S(\$/£)}{S(\$/€)} \qquad (4.5)$$

where from Exhibit 4.4,

$$S(€/£) = \frac{1.5358}{1.2989} = 1.1824$$

That is, if £1 cost $1.5358 and €1 cost $1.2989, the cost of £1 in euros is €1.1824. In European terms, the calculation is

$$S(€/£) = \frac{S(€/\$)}{S(£/\$)} \qquad (4.6)$$

$$= \frac{0.7699}{0.6511}$$

$$= 1.1825 \text{ where the difference from 1.1824 is due to rounding.}$$

Analogously,

$$S(£/€) = \frac{S(\$/€)}{S(\$/£)} \qquad (4.7)$$

$$= \frac{1.2989}{1.5358}$$

$$= 0.8457$$

http://money.cnn.com/tq/currconv

This subsite at the CNN and *Money* magazine website provides a currency converter. As an example, use the converter to calculate the current $S(€/£)$ and $S(£/€)$ cross-exchange rates.

and

$$S(\text{£}/\text{€}) = \frac{S(\text{£}/\$)}{S(\text{€}/\$)}$$

(4.8)

$$= \frac{0.6511}{0.7699}$$

$$= 0.8457$$

Equations 4.5 to 4.8 imply that given *N* currencies, one can calculate a triangular matrix of the $(N \times (N - 1))/2$ cross-exchange rates. Daily in the *Financial Times* appear the 36 cross-exchange rates for all pair combinations of nine currencies and stated as $S(j/k)$ and $S(k/j)$. Exhibit 4.6 presents an example of the table for 10 May 2013. Reading across a row for a country, say Canada, each cell in the row indicates the number of units of the respective foreign currency designated in the column headings, say the Danish kroner, that can be purchased with one Canadian dollar. Reading down a column indicates the number of units of the column-currency, again say the Canadian dollar, that are required to purchase a unit of the respective foreign currency. Looking at the extreme upper-right and lower-left cells in the table, in the first instance, we see that one Canadian dollar will buy 0.9901 US dollars and then, correspondingly, that 1.0100 Canadian dollars are required to purchase one US dollar.

Alternative Expressions for the Cross-Exchange Rate

For some purposes, it is easier to think of cross-exchange rates calculated as the product of an American-term and a European-exchange rate, rather than as the quotient of two American-term or two European-term exchange rates. For example, substituting $S(\text{€}/\$)$ for $1/S(\$/\text{€})$ allows Equation 4.5 to be rewritten as:

$$S(\text{€}/\text{£}) = S(\$/\text{£}) \times S(\text{€}/\$)$$

(4.9)

$$= 1.5358 \times 0.7699$$

$$= 1.1824$$

In general terms,

$$S(j/k) = S(\$/k) \times S(j/\$)$$

(4.10)

and taking reciprocals of both sides of Equation 4.10 yields

$$S(k/j) = S(k/\$) \times S(\$/j)$$

(4.11)

The Cross-Rate Trading Desk

Most interbank trading goes through the US dollar. Suppose a bank customer wants to trade out of British pounds sterling into Swiss francs. In dealer jargon, a nondollar trade such as this is referred to as a **currency against currency** trade. The bank will frequently (or effectively) handle this trade for its customer by selling British pounds for US dollars and then selling US dollars for Swiss francs. At first blush, this might seem ridiculous. Why not just sell the British pounds directly for Swiss francs? To answer this question, let us return to Exhibit 4.6 of the cross-exchange rates. Suppose a bank's home currency was one of the nine currencies in the exhibit and that it made markets in the other eight currencies. The bank's trading room would typically be organized with eight trading desks, each for trading one of the nondollar currencies against the US dollar. A dealer needs only to be concerned with making a market in his nondollar currency against the dollar. However, if each of the nine currencies was traded directly with the others, the dealing room would

EXHIBIT 4.6   Exchange Cross-Rates, 10 May 2013

		C$	DKr	€	Y	NKr	SKr	SFr	£	US$
Canada	C$	1.000	5.683	0.762	100.620	5.735	6.534	0.947	0.645	0.990
Denmark	DKr	0.176	1.000	0.134	17.706	1.009	1.150	0.167	0.113	0.174
Euro	€	1.312	7.455	1.000	131.990	7.523	8.572	1.243	0.846	1.299
Japan	Y*	0.994	5.648	0.758	100.000	5.700	6.494	0.942	0.641	0.984
Norway	NKr	0.174	0.991	0.133	17.544	1.000	1.139	0.165	0.112	0.173
Sweden	SKr	0.153	0.870	0.117	15.399	0.878	1.000	0.145	0.099	0.152
Switzerland	SFr	1.056	5.998	0.805	106.157	6.053	6.898	1.000	0.681	1.045
United Kingdom	£	1.551	8.814	1.182	156.006	8.895	10.135	1.469	1.000	1.536
United States	US$	1.010	5.740	0.770	101.626	5.792	6.599	0.957	0.651	1.000

*Per 100 Y; e.g., 100 Yen = C$0.994 = 5.648 DKr.

Source: Financial Research and Trading Lab, Rotman School of Management.

need to accommodate 36 trading desks. Or worse, individual traders would be responsible for making a market in several currency pairs, say, the €/$, €/£, and €/SF, instead of just the €/$. This would entail an informational complexity that would be virtually impossible to handle.

Banks handle currency against currency trades, such as for the bank customer who wants to trade out of British pounds into Swiss francs, at the cross-rate desk. Recall from Equation 4.10 that a $S(\text{SF}/\pounds)$ quote can be obtained from the product of $S(\$/\pounds)$ and $S(\text{SF}/\$)$. Recognizing transaction costs implies the following restatement of Equation 4.10:

$$S^b(\text{SF}/\pounds) = S^b(\$/\pounds) \times S^b(\text{SF}/\$) \tag{4.12}$$

The bank will quote its customer a selling (bid) price for the British pounds in terms of Swiss francs determined by multiplying its American-term bid price for British pounds and its European-term bid price (for US dollars) stated in Swiss francs.

Taking reciprocals of Equation 4.12 yields

$$S^a(\pounds/\text{SF}) = S^a(\pounds/\$) \times S^a(\$/\text{SF}) \tag{4.13}$$

which is analogous to Equation 4.11. In terms of our example, Equation 4.13 says the bank could alternatively quote its customer an offer (ask) price for Swiss francs in terms of British pounds determined by multiplying its European-term ask price (for US dollars) stated in British pounds by its American-term ask price for Swiss francs.

Triangular Arbitrage

Certain banks specialize in making a direct market between nondollar currencies, pricing at a narrower bid-ask spread than the cross-rate spread. Nevertheless, the implied cross-rate bid-ask quotations impose a discipline on the nondollar market makers. If their direct quotes are not consistent with cross-exchange rates, a triangular arbitrage profit is possible. **Triangular arbitrage** is the process of trading out of the US dollar into a second currency, then trading it for a third currency, which is, in turn, traded for US dollars. The purpose is to earn an arbitrage profit via trading from the second to the third currency when the direct exchange rate between the two is not in alignment with the cross-exchange rate.

Example **4.2** *Calculating the Cross-Exchange Rate Bid-Ask Spread*

Let us assume (as we did earlier) that the $/£ bid-ask prices are 1.5353–1.5358 and the £/$ bid-ask prices are 0.6511–0.6513.

Let us also assume the $/€ bid-ask prices are 1.2989–1.2995 and the €/$ bid-ask prices are 0.7695–0.7699.

These bid and ask prices and Equation 4.12 imply that $S^b(\text{€/£}) = 1.5353 \times 0.7695 = 1.1814$. The reciprocal of $S^b(\text{€/£})$, or Equation 4.13, implies that $S^a(\text{£/€}) = 1.2995 \times 0.6513 = 0.8464$.

Analogously, Equation 4.13 suggests that $S^a(\text{€/£}) = 1.5358 \times 0.7699 = 1.1824$, and its reciprocal implies that $S^b(\text{£/€}) = 0.8457$.

That is, the €/£ bid-ask prices are 1.1814–1.1824 and the £/€ bid-ask prices are 0.8457–0.8464.

Note that the cross-rate bid-ask spreads are much larger than the American or European bid-ask spreads. For example, the €/£ bid-ask spread is 0.0010 versus the €/$ spread of 0.0004. The £/€ bid-ask spread is 0.0007 versus the $/€ spread of 0.0006, which is a sizable difference.

The implication is that cross-exchange rates implicitly incorporate the bid-ask spreads of the two transactions that are necessary for trading out of one nondollar currency and into another. Hence, even when a bank makes a direct market in one nondollar currency versus another, the trade is effectively going through the dollar because the "currency against currency" exchange rate is consistent with a cross-exchange rate calculated from the dollar exchange rates of the two currencies. Exhibit 4.7 provides a more detailed presentation of cross-rate foreign exchange translations.

Example **4.3** *Taking Advantage of Triangular Arbitrage Opportunities*

To illustrate triangular arbitrage, assume the cross-rate trader at Deutsche Bank notices that Crédit Lyonnais is buying dollars at $S^b(\text{€/\$}) = 0.7695$, the same as Deutsche Bank's bid price. Similarly, he notices that Barclays Bank is offering dollars for pounds at $S^b(\text{\$/£}) = 1.5353$, also the same as Deutsche Bank. Next, he finds that BNP Paribas is making a direct market between the euro and the pound with a current ask price of $S^a(\text{€/£}) = 1.1810$.

The cross-rate formula and the American and European quotes, as we saw above, imply that the €/£ bid price should be no lower than $S^b(\text{€/£}) = 1.5353 \times 0.7695 = 1.1814$. Yet, BNP Paribas is offering to sell British pounds at a rate of only 1.1810!

A triangular arbitrage profit is available if Deutsche Bank traders are quick enough.

A sale of $5,000,000 to Crédit Lyonnais for euros will yield $5,000,000 × 0.7695 which equals €3,847,500. The €3,847,500 will be immediately resold to BNP Paribas for British pounds, that is, €3,847,500/1.1810 which amounts to £3,257,832. Then, to complete the triangle, the British pounds are sold for dollars at £3,257,832 × 1.5353 or $5,001,750.

The result is an arbitrage profit of $1,750.

BNP Paribas obviously must raise its asking price above €1.1810/£1. The cross-exchange rates (from Exhibit 4.7) indicate €/£ bid-ask prices of 1.1814–1.1818. These prices imply that BNP Paribas can deal inside the spread and sell for less than €1.1818 but not less than €1.1814. An ask price of €1.1815 would eliminate the arbitrage profit. At that price, the €3,847,500 would be resold into pounds for £3,256,454, which, in turn, would yield only £3,256,454 × 1.5353 or $4,999,633. An attempt at the triangular trip would result in a loss of $367.

In today's technology-intensive FX market, many FX trading rooms around the world have developed in-house software that receives a digital feed of real-time FX prices from the EBS Spot electronic brokering system to continuously scan for triangular arbitrage opportunities. Opportunities are exploited almost instantaneously through programmed trades in the relevant configuration. Exhibit 4.8 presents a diagram and a summary of our triangular arbitrage example.

EXHIBIT 4.7

Cross-Rate Foreign
Exchange
Transactions

Bank Quotations	American Terms		European Terms	
	Bid	Ask	Bid	Ask
British pounds	1.5353	1.5358	0.6511	0.6513
Euros	1.2989	1.2995	0.7695	0.7699

a. Bank Customer wants to sell £1,000,000 for euros. The Bank will sell US dollars (buy British pounds) for $1.5353. The sale yields Bank Customer

£1,000,000 × $1.5353 = $1,535,300

The Bank will buy dollars (sell euros) for €0.7695. The sale of dollars yields Bank Customer

$1,535,300 × €0.7695 = €1,181,413

Bank Customer has effectively sold British pounds at a €/£ bid price of

€1,181,413/£1,000,000 = €1.1814/£1.00.

b. Bank Customer wants to sell €1,000,000 for British pounds. The Bank will sell US dollars (buy euros) for €0.7695. The sale yields Bank Customer

€1,000,000/0.7695 = $1,299,545

The Bank will buy dollars (sell British pounds) for $1.5358. The sale of dollars yields Bank Customer

$1,299,545/1.5358 = £846,168

Bank customer has effectively bought British pounds at a €/£ ask price of

€1,000,000/£846,168 = €1.1818/£1.00

From parts (a) and (b), we see the currency-against-currency bid-ask spread for British pounds is €1.1814–€1.1818.

EXHIBIT 4.8

Triangular Arbitrage
Example

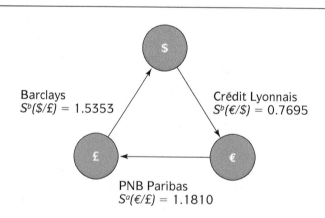

Barclays
$S^b(\$/£) = 1.5353$

Crédit Lyonnais
$S^b(€/\$) = 0.7695$

PNB Paribas
$S^a(€/£) = 1.1810$

Deutsche Bank arbitrage strategy

$	5,000,000	
×	0.7695	
€	3,847,500	Sell US dollars for euros
÷	1.1810	
£	3,257,832	Sell euros for British pounds
×	1.5353	
$	5,001,750	Sell British pounds for US dollars
−$	5,000,000	
$	1,750	Arbitrage profit

Spot Foreign Exchange Market Microstructure

Market microstructure refers to the basic mechanics of how a marketplace operates. Five empirical studies on FX market microstructure shed light on the operation of the spot FX marketplace. Huang and Masulis (1999) study spot FX rates on DM/$ trades over the period October 1992 to September 1993. They find that bid-ask spreads in the spot FX market increase with FX exchange rate volatility and decrease with dealer competition. These results are consistent with models of market microstructure. They also find that the bid-ask spread decreases when the percentage of large dealers in the marketplace increases. They conclude that dealer competition is a fundamental determinant of the spot FX bid-ask spread.

Lyons (1998) tracks the trading activity of a DM/$ trader at a large New York bank over a period of five trading days. The dealer was extremely profitable over the study period, averaging profits of $100,000 per day on volume of $1 billion. Lyons is able to disentangle total trades into those that are speculative and those that are nonspeculative, or where the dealer acts as a financial intermediary for a retail client. He determines that the dealer's profits come primarily from the dealer's role as an intermediary. This makes sense, since speculative trading is a zero-sum game among all speculators, and in the long run, it is unlikely that any one trader has a unique advantage. Interestingly, Lyons finds that the half-life of the dealer's position in nonspeculative trades is only 10 minutes! That is, the dealer typically trades or swaps out of a nonspeculative position within 20 minutes.

Ito, Lyons and Melvin (1998) study the role of private information in the spot FX market. They examine ¥/$ and DM/$ between September 1994 and March 1995. Their study provides evidence against the common view that private information is irrelevant, since all market participants are assumed to possess the same set of public information. Their evidence comes from the Tokyo foreign exchange market, which prior to December 1994, closed for lunch between noon and 1:30 P.M. After 21 December 1994, the variance in spot exchange rates increased during the lunch period relative to the period of closed trading. This was true for both ¥/$ and DM/$ trades, but more so for the ¥/$ data, which is to be expected since ¥/$ trading is more intensive in the Tokyo FX market. Ito, Lyons and Melvin attribute these results to a greater revelation of private information in trades being allocated to the lunch hour. This suggests that private information is indeed an important determinant of spot exchange rates.

Cheung and Chinn (2001) conducted a survey of foreign exchange traders in order to explore several aspects of exchange rate dynamics not typically observable in trading data. In particular, they are interested in traders' perceptions of news events—innovations in macroeconomic variables—that cause movements in exchange rates. The traders they survey respond that the bulk of the adjustment to economic announcements regarding unemployment, trade deficits, inflation, GDP and the Federal Reserve funds rate takes place within one minute. In fact, "about one-third of the respondents claim that full price adjustment takes place in less than 10 seconds"! They also find that central bank intervention does not appear to have a substantial impact on exchange rates, but intervention does increase market volatility. Dominguez (1998) confirms this latter finding.

4.3 THE FORWARD MARKET

In conjunction with spot trading, there is also a forward foreign exchange market. The **forward market** involves contracting today for the future purchase or sale of foreign exchange. The forward price may be the same as the spot price, but usually it is higher (at a premium) or lower (at a discount) than the spot price. Forward exchange rates are quoted on most major currencies for a variety of maturities. Bank quotes for maturities of 1, 3, 6, 9 and 12 months are readily available. Quotations on nonstandard, or broken-term, maturities are also available. Maturities extending beyond one year are becoming more frequent, and for good bank customers, a maturity extending out to five, and even as long as 10 years, is possible.

Forward Rate Quotations

To learn how to read **forward exchange rate** quotations, let us go back to Exhibit 4.4. Note that forward rate quotations appear directly under the spot rate quotations for four major currencies—British pound, Canadian dollar, Japanese yen and Swiss franc—in one-, three- and six-month maturities. The settlement date of, for example, a three-month forward transaction is three calendar months from the spot settlement date for the currency. That is, if today is 10 May 2013 and spot settlement is 12 May, then the forward settlement date would be 12 August 2013, a period of 94 days from 10 May.

In this textbook, we use the following notation for forward rate quotations. In general $F_N(j/k)$ refers to the price of one unit of currency k in terms of currency j for delivery in N months. N equal to 1 denotes a one-month maturity based on a 360-day banker's year. Thus, N equal to 3 denotes three-month maturity. When the context is clear, the simpler notation F is used to denote a forward exchange rate. Forward quotes are either direct or indirect, one being the reciprocal of the other. From the American perspective, reflecting the quotes in Exhibit 4.4, a direct forward quote is in US dollar terms.

From the Canadian point of view, a *direct* quote for a US dollar—spot or forward—is expressed in Canadian dollar terms, such as "1.0100," indicating 1.0100 Canadian dollars for one US dollar. On the other hand, an *indirect* quote, from the Canadian perspective, of the exchange rate would be "0.9901," indicating 99.01 US cents per Canadian dollar.

As an example, let us consider the direct quotes (from the Canadian perspective) of forward rates involving the Canadian dollar and the US dollar. For convenience and clarity, the spot rate is defined as $S(C/US)$ and similarly as $F_N(C/US)$ for forward rates. We see that

$$S(C/US) = 1.0100$$
$$F_1(C/US) = 1.0107$$
$$F_3(C/US) = 1.0121$$
$$F_6(C/US) = 1.0143$$

From these quotes, we can see that from the Canadian perspective, the US dollar is trading at a forward *premium* to the Canadian dollar and that the premium increases out to six months. In other words, the forward premium is greater the further the forward contract settlement date is from 10 May. The forward market is "pricing in" a weakening of the Canadian dollar *vis-à-vis* the US dollar. The forward market demands more and more Canadian dollars per US dollar the further out in time we go. A significant element of implicit forecasting or "market thinking" about currency depreciation or appreciation is built into the structure of forward foreign exchange rates.

Indirect quotes are reciprocals of direct quotes. In indirect terms from the Canadian perspective, the spot and forward quotes, $S(US/C)$ and $F_N(US/C)$, involving the Canadian dollar and the US dollar are

$$S(US/C) = 0.9901$$
$$F_1(US/C) = 0.9894$$
$$F_3(US/C) = 0.9880$$
$$F_6(US/C) = 0.9859$$

We see that in indirect terms the Canadian dollar is trading at a forward discount to the US dollar and that the discount increases out to six months. This is exactly what we would expect, since *indirect* quotations are reciprocals of *direct* quotations. The "pricing in" of a weakening of the Canadian dollar *vis-à-vis* the US dollar is reflected in the fewer and fewer US dollars per Canadian dollar in the forward rates the further out in time one goes.

EXHIBIT 4.9

Graph of Long
and Short Position
in Three-Month
Forward Contract
to Deliver US
Dollars

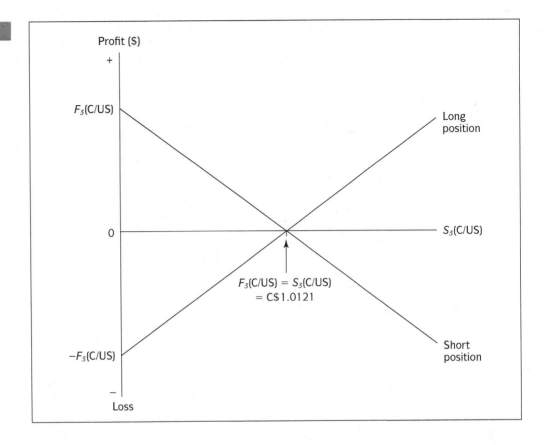

One can buy (take a long position) or sell (take a short position) in a foreign currency forward contract. Bank customers can contact the foreign exchange desk of their bank to buy or sell a specific sum of FX for delivery on a certain date. Likewise interbank traders, who do the vast bulk of forward foreign currency trading, can establish long or short positions with traders from other banks.

Exhibit 4.9 graphs both the long and short positions for a three-month forward contract to buy US dollars with Canadian dollars. The contract is expressed in direct Canadian dollar terms, F_3(C/US). F_3(C/US) is 1.0121 Canadian dollars per US dollar.

The long position in this contract commits the party to *buy* the contract amount of US dollars at a rate of C$1.0121 on the contract maturity date of 10 August 2013 with settlement two days later. The short position in the contract commits the party to *deliver* the contract amount of US dollars at a rate of C$1.0121 on the settlement date.

The graph in Exhibit 4.9 measures profits or losses (per unit of the contract currency) on the vertical axis. The horizontal axis shows the spot price of foreign exchange on the maturity date of 10 August 2013. Since neither the long position nor the short position has a pay-off if the spot rate on 10 August is identical to the F_3(C/US) of 1.0121, the line of pay-off for the long position and the line of pay-off for the short position intersect at F_3(C/US) at zero pay-off.

The line of pay-off for the long position is upward-sloping, indicating that if the spot rate is above 1.0121 on 10 August, the holder of the long position makes a profit. If the spot rate on 10 August is above 1.0121, then the holder of the long position pays C$1.0121 for US dollars that are worth somewhat more than C$1.0121. In other words, the long position on a US dollar forward contract pays off in Canadian dollar terms if the Canadian dollar weakens.

On the other hand, the line of pay-off for the short position is downward-sloping, indicating that if the spot rate is above 1.0121 on 10 August, the holder of the short position incurs a loss. If the spot rate on 10 August is above 1.0121, then the holder of the short position must deliver US dollars for C$1.0121 per US dollar at a time when US funds cost somewhat more than that in Canadian dollar terms. In other words, a short position on a US dollar forward contract is a losing proposition if the Canadian dollar weakens (or even if it does not strengthen as much as is implied in the forward rate).

Example 4.4 *A Speculative Forward Position*

It is 10 May 2013. The US dollar/Swiss franc trader at Citibank in New York has just received a memo from his bank's economic forecasting unit that the forecasters believe the US dollar is likely to appreciate against the Swiss franc. In other words, Citibank is "bullish" on the US dollar versus the Swiss franc. With the three-month forward rate (in American terms) at 1.0461 above the spot rate at 1.0451, the currency market in fact is pricing in some US-dollar *depreciation* against the Swiss franc. How can the dollar/Swiss franc trader at Citibank act on the contrarian information from his bank's economic forecasting unit?

If the trader decides to act on this information, he will take a short position in a three-month $/SF forward contract. Let's say that he does act. He will be speculating. He phones the $/SF trader at Chemical Bank, another bank that trades US dollars for Swiss francs. He sells SF5,000,000 forward against US dollars at $1.0461 with delivery on 10 August 2013. Citibank is committed to deliver SF5,000,000 to Chemical Bank on 10 August 2013.

Suppose Citibank's forecast proves to be correct and on 10 August 2013, the spot $/SF is $1.0445. The trader can buy Swiss francs spot at $1.0445 and deliver the funds to Chemical Bank under the forward contract where he receives $1.0461 per Swiss franc. The trader has made a speculative profit of ($1.0461 − $1.0445) = $0.0016 per unit. This is illustrated in Figure 4.10. The total profit from the trade is $8,000 = (5,000,000 × $0.0016).

If, on the other hand, the US dollar depreciates against the Swiss franc and the spot rate turns out to be, say, $1.0481 on 10 August 2013, then Citibank's $/SF trader would have lost ($1.0461 − $1.0481) = $0.002 per unit, for a loss of $10,000 on his speculative position.

EXHIBIT 4.10

Graph of Long and Short Position in the Three-Month Swiss Franc Contract

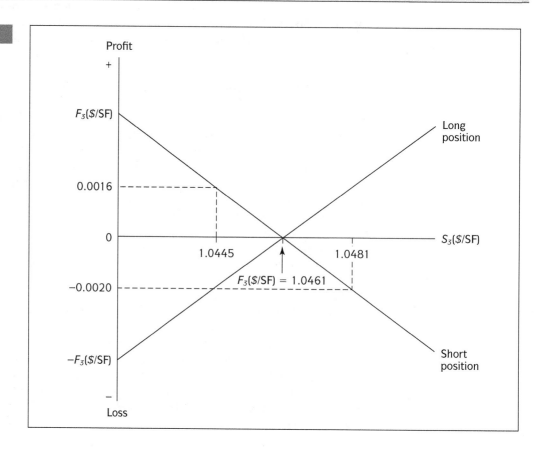

Forward Cross-Exchange Rates

Forward cross-exchange rate quotations are calculated in a manner analogous to spot cross-rates, and so it is not necessary to provide detailed examples. In generic terms,

$$F_N(j/k) = \frac{F_N(\$/k)}{F_N(\$/j)} \tag{4.14}$$

or

$$F_N(j/k) = \frac{F_N(j/\$)}{F_N(k/\$)} \tag{4.15}$$

and

$$F_N(k/j) = \frac{F_N(\$/j)}{F_N(\$/k)} \tag{4.16}$$

or

$$F_N(k/j) = \frac{F_N(k/\$)}{F_N(j/\$)} \tag{4.17}$$

Swap Transactions

Forward trades can be classified as outright or swap transactions. In conducting their trading, bank dealers do take speculative positions in the currencies they trade, but more often, traders offset the currency exposure inherent in a trade. From the bank's standpoint, an **outright forward transaction** is an uncovered speculative position in a currency, even though it might be part of a currency hedge to the bank customer on the other side of the transaction. Swap transactions provide a means for the bank to mitigate the currency exposure in a forward trade. A **swap transaction** is the simultaneous sale (or purchase) of spot foreign exchange against a forward purchase (or sale) of approximately an equal amount of the foreign currency.

Swap transactions account for approximately 47 percent of interbank FX trading, whereas outright forward trades are 13 percent. (See Exhibit 4.3.) Because interbank forward transactions are most frequently made as part of a swap transaction, bank dealers in conversation among themselves use a shorthand notation to quote bid and ask forward prices in terms of *forward points* that are either added to or subtracted from the spot bid and ask quotations.

Example 4.5 *Forward Point Quotations*

Recall the $/£ spot bid-ask rates of $1.5353–$1.5358 developed previously. With reference to these spot rates, forward rates might be displayed thus:

Spot	1.5353–1.5358
One-month	39–37
Three-month	57–53
Six-month	145–138

When the second number in a forward point pair is smaller than the first, the dealer understands that the forward points are *subtracted* from the spot bid and ask prices to obtain the outright forward rates. For example, the spot bid price of $1.5353 minus 0.0039 (or 39 points) equals $1.5314, the one-month bid price. The spot ask price of $1.5358 minus 0.0037 (or 37 points) equals $1.5321, the one-month ask price. Similarly, the three-month outright forward bid-ask rates are $1.5296–$1.5305 and the six-month outright forward bid-ask rates are $1.5208–$1.5220. The following table summarizes the calculations:

Spot	Forward Point Quotations	1.5353–1.5358 Outright Forward Quotations
One-month	39–37	1.5314–1.5321
Three-month	57–53	1.5296–1.5305
Six-month	145–138	1.5208–1.5220

Three things are notable about the outright forward prices. First, the British pound is trading at a forward discount to the US dollar. Second, all bid prices are less than the corresponding ask prices, as they must be for a trader to be willing to make a market. Third, the bid-ask spread increases in time to maturity, as is typical. These three conditions prevail only because the forward points are *subtracted* from the spot prices. As a check, note that in points the spot bid-ask spread is 5 points, the one-month forward spread is 7 points, the three-month spread is 9 points, and the six-month spread is 12 points.

If the British pound was trading at a forward premium to the dollar, the second number in each forward pair would be larger than the first number in the pair. The trader would know to *add* the points to the spot bid and ask prices to obtain the outright forward bid and ask rates. For example, if the three-month and six-month point-pairs were 54–57 and 138–145, the corresponding three-month and six-month bid-ask spreads would be $1.5407–$1.5415 and $1.5491–$1.5503, that is, increasing in term to maturity.

Quoting forward rates in terms of forward points is convenient for two reasons. First, forward points may remain constant for long periods of time, even if the spot rate fluctuates frequently. Second, in swap transactions where the trader is attempting to minimize currency exposure, the actual spot and outright forward rates are often of no consequence. What is important is the premium or discount differential measured in forward points. To illustrate, suppose a bank customer wants to sell dollars three months forward against British sterling. The bank can handle this trade for its customer and simultaneously neutralize the exchange rate risk in the trade by selling (borrowed) dollars spot against British pounds. The bank will lend sterling for three months until pounds are needed to deliver against the dollars it has purchased forward. The dollars received will be used to liquidate the dollar loan. Implicit in this transaction is the interest rate differential between the dollar borrowing rate and the pound sterling lending rate. The interest rate differential is captured by the forward premium or discount measured in forward points. As a rule, when the interest rate of the foreign currency is greater than the interest rate of the quoting currency, the outright forward rate is less than the spot exchange rate, and *vice versa*. This will become clear in the following chapter on international parity relationships.

Forward Premium

It is common to express the premium or discount of a forward rate as an annualized percentage deviation from the spot rate. The forward premium (or discount) is useful for comparing against the interest rate differential between two countries, as we will see more clearly in Chapter 5 on international parity relationships. The **forward premium** or **discount** can be expressed in direct or indirect terms. If a currency is trading at a premium (discount), the market expects the currency to appreciate (depreciate) in the future.

Example 4.6 *Calculating the Forward Position*

The formula for the forward premium or discount in *direct* terms for, say, the Canadian dollar versus the US dollar is

$$f_{N,(C\$/US\$)} = \frac{F_{N,(C\$/US\$)} - S_{C\$/US\$} \times 360/N}{S_{C\$/US\$}}$$

$S_{C\$/US\$}$ is the spot exchange rate in Canadian dollars per US dollar. $F_{N,(C\$/US\$)}$ is the N-days forward rate, similarly expressed in Canadian dollar per US dollar. N is the number of days until the forward contract is settled.

When the context is clear, the forward premium (or discount) can be stated simply as f. By convention, the premium (or discount) is expressed as an annualized percent. Without subscripts, we have this easier-on-the-eyes expression for a three-month forward contract:

$$f_N = \frac{F_N - S \times 360/N}{S}$$

Let's use the 10 May 2013 quotes from Exhibit 4.4 for the three-month forward to calculate the premium (or discount) for the Canadian dollar (C\$) versus the US dollar (US\$). In direct Canadian terms (C\$/US\$), the Canadian dollar is at a forward premium to the US dollar. The annualized percentage forward premium is

$$f_{94,(C\$/US\$)} = \frac{1.0121 - 1.0100}{1.0100} \times 360/94 = 0.0080$$

The forward premium is 0.0080 or 0.80 percent. We say the US dollar is trading at a 0.80 percent premium against the Canadian dollar for delivery in three months. The forward premium indicates that the currency market is pricing in a strengthening US dollar. The market is calling for more Canadian dollars per US dollar in the days ahead.

Turning to the *indirect* quote, the annualized percentage forward discount is

$$f_{94,(US\$/C\$)} = \frac{0.9880 - 0.9901}{0.9901} \times 360/94$$

$$= -0.0081$$

The three-month forward discount is −0.0081 or −0.81 percent. In words, the Canadian dollar is trading at a 0.81 percent annualized discount against the US dollar for delivery in three months. In these *indirect* terms (US\$/C\$), the forward discount of the Canadian dollar again indicates that the currency market is pricing in a weakening of the Canadian dollar. The forward structure calls for fewer US dollars per Canadian dollar in the days ahead.

SUMMARY

This chapter presents an introduction to the market for foreign exchange. Broadly defined, the foreign exchange market encompasses the conversion of purchasing power from one currency into another, bank deposits of foreign currency, the extension of credit denominated in a foreign currency, foreign trade financing and trading in foreign currency options and futures contracts. This chapter limits the discussion to the spot and forward markets for foreign exchange. The other topics are covered in later chapters.

1. The FX market is the largest and most active financial market in the world. It is open somewhere in the world 24 hours a day, 365 days a year.
2. The FX market is divided into two tiers: the retail or client market and the wholesale or interbank market. The retail market is where international banks service their customers who need foreign exchange to conduct international commerce or trade in international financial assets. The great majority of FX trading takes place in the interbank market among international banks that are adjusting inventory positions or conducting speculative and arbitrage trades.

3. The FX market participants include international banks, bank customers, nonbank FX dealers, FX brokers and central banks.

4. In the spot market for FX, nearly immediate purchases and sales of currencies take place. In the chapter, notation for defining a spot rate quotation was developed. Additionally, the concept of a cross-exchange rate was developed. It was determined that nondollar currency transactions must satisfy the bid-ask spread determined from the cross-rate formula or a triangular arbitrage opportunity exists.

5. In the forward market, buyers and sellers can transact today at the forward price for the future purchase and sale of foreign exchange. Notation for forward exchange rate quotations was developed. The use of forward points as a shorthand method for expressing forward quotes from spot rate quotations was presented. Additionally, the concept of a forward premium was developed.

QUESTIONS

1. Give a full definition of the market for foreign exchange.

2. What is the difference between the retail or client market and the wholesale or interbank market for foreign exchange?

3. Who are the market participants in the foreign exchange market?

4. How are foreign exchange transactions between international banks settled?

5. What is meant by a currency trading at a discount or at a premium in the forward market?

6. Why does most interbank currency trading worldwide involve the US dollar?

7. Banks find it necessary to accommodate their clients' needs to buy or sell FX forward, in many instances for hedging purposes. How can the bank eliminate the currency exposure it has created for itself by accommodating a client's forward transaction?

8. A \$/€ bank trader is currently quoting a *small figure* bid-ask of 83–88, when the rest of the market is trading at \$1.2989–\$1.2995. What is implied about the trader's beliefs by his prices?

PROBLEMS

1. Using Exhibit 4.4, construct a "Latin America" cross-rate matrix for the currencies of Argentina, Brazil, Colombia and Mexico. Present "indirect" quotes (units of foreign currency per one unit of domestic currency) above the matrix diagonal and "direct" quotes (units of domestic per one unit of foreign currency) below the diagonal, as was done in Exhibit 4.6.

2. Using US dollar data in Exhibit 4.4 (the first two data columns) for forward cross-exchange rates for the Canadian dollar and the Swiss franc, calculate the one-, three- and six-month forward rates between the Canadian dollar and the Swiss franc. State the cross-rates in Canadian-direct terms.

3. Restate the following one-, three-, and six-month outright forward European-term bid-ask quotes in forward points.

Spot	1.3431–1.3436
One-month	1.3432–1.3442
Three-month	1.3448–1.3463
Six-month	1.3488–1.3508

4. Using the spot and outright forward quotes in problem 3, determine the corresponding bid-ask spreads in points.

5. Using Exhibit 4.4, calculate the one-, three-, and six-month forward premium or discount for the Canadian dollar in European terms. For simplicity, assume each month has 30 days.

6. Using Exhibit 4.4, calculate the one-, three-, and six-month forward premium or discount for the British pound in US terms using the most current quotations. For simplicity, assume each month has 30 days.

7. Given the following information, what are the NZD/SGD currency against currency bid-ask quotations?

	US Terms		European Terms	
Bank Quotations	**Bid**	**Ask**	**Bid**	**Ask**
New Zealand dollar (NZ\$)	0.7265	0.7272	1.3751	1.3765
Singapore dollar (SG\$)	0.6135	0.6140	1.6287	1.6300

8. Assume you are a trader with Deutsche Bank. From the quote screen on your computer terminal, you notice that Dresdner Bank is quoting €0.7627/\$1 and Credit Suisse is offering SF1.1806/\$1. You learn that UBS is making a direct market between the Swiss franc and the euro, with a current €/SF quote of 0.6395. Show how you can make a triangular arbitrage

profit by trading at these prices. (Ignore bid-ask spreads for this problem.) Assume you have $5,000,000 with which to conduct the arbitrage. What happens if you initially sell dollars for Swiss francs? What €/SF price will eliminate triangular arbitrage?

9. The current spot exchange rate is $1.95/£ and the three-month forward rate is $1.90/£. On the basis of your analysis of the exchange rate, you are pretty confident that the spot exchange rate will be $1.92/£ in three months. Assume that you would like to buy or sell £1,000,000.

 a. What actions do you need to take to speculate in the forward market? What is the expected dollar profit from speculation?

 b. What would be your speculative profit in dollar terms if the spot exchange rate actually turns out to be $1.86/£ in three months?

10. Omni Advisors, an international pension fund manager, plans to sell equities denominated in Swiss francs (CHF) and purchase an equivalent amount of equities denominated in South African rands (ZAR).

 Omni will realize net proceeds of three million CHF at the end of 30 days and wants to eliminate the risk that the ZAR will appreciate relative to the CHF during this 30-day period. The following exhibit shows current exchange rates between the ZAR, the CHF, and US dollar (USD).

Currency Exchange Rates

Maturity	ZAR/US$ Bid	Ask	CHF/US$ Bid	Ask
Spot	6.2681	6.2789	1.5282	1.5343
30-day	6.2538	6.2641	1.5226	1.5285
90-day	6.2104	6.2200	1.5058	1.5115

 a. Describe the currency transaction that Omni should undertake to eliminate currency risk over the 30-day period.

 b. Calculate the following:
 • The CHF/ZAR cross-currency rate Omni would use in valuing the Swiss equity portfolio.
 • The current value of Omni's Swiss equity portfolio in ZAR.
 • The annualized forward premium or discount at which the ZAR is trading versus the CHF.

11. In Exhibit 4.4, look at the forward rates for the US dollar against the Japanese yen.

 a. Does the forward rate structure imply that the Japanese yen will depreciate or appreciate against the US dollar over the next six months? Explain.

Indicate whether you are using forward rates expressed in "American terms" (US$ per yen) or in "European terms" (yen per US$).

 b. What is the implied rate of appreciation/depreciation of the yen against the US dollar over the next six months?

 c. Now, say the one-year forward rate for the US dollar against the Japanese yen, which is not given in Exhibit 4.4, is US$0.0110/¥ (or ¥ 90.9091/ US$). What is the implied annual rate of appreciation/depreciation of the yen against the US dollar over the next year?

 d. What is the implied annualized rate of appreciation/ depreciation of the yen against the US dollar through the second half of the year?

12. In Exhibit 4.4, look at the forward rates for the Canadian dollar against the Japanese yen.

 a. Does the forward rate structure imply that the Japanese yen will depreciate or appreciate against the Canadian dollar over the next six months? Explain.

 b. What is the implied rate of appreciation/depreciation of the yen against the Canadian dollar over the next six months?

 c. Now, say the 1-year forward rate in Canadian dollars against the yen, which is not given in Exhibit 4.4, is C$0.01030/¥ (or ¥97.0874/C$). What is the implied average annual rate of appreciation/depreciation of the yen against the Canadian dollar over the next year?

 d. What is the implied annualized rate of appreciation/ depreciation of the yen against the Canadian dollar through the second half of the year?

13. In Canadian dollar terms, what is the implied rate of appreciation/depreciation of the US dollar against the Canadian dollar over the next six months?

 Look back at your calculations for the implied six-month rates of appreciation/depreciation of the yen against the US dollar and against the Canadian dollar. Is your estimate of the implied rate of appreciation/depreciation of the US dollar against the Canadian dollar over the next six months consistent with the *difference* (if any) between the implied six-month rates of depreciation/appreciation of the Japanese yen against the US dollar and the Japanese yen against the Canadian dollar? Explain.

14. Look at Example 4.4. Calculate the gain or loss that would result if the Citibank trader speculates as described in the example but it turns out that on 10 August 2013 the US dollar–Swiss franc exchange rate has not changed at all from the spot rate on 10 May 2013.

INTERNET EXERCISE

1. A currency trader makes a market in a currency and attempts to generate speculative profits from dealing against other currency traders. Today, electronic dealing systems are frequently used by currency traders. Go to www.fxcm.com/getting-started.jsp, the website of FOREX Capital Market. Register for and test-drive FXCM's free practice account for trading foreign currencies.

2. In addition to the historic currency symbols, such as $, ¥, £, and €, there is an official three-letter symbol for each currency that is recognized worldwide. These symbols can be found at the Bloomberg website: www.bloomberg.com/markets/wcvl.html. Go to this site. What is the currency symbol for the Congo franc? The Guyana dollar?

MINI CASE

Shrewsbury Herbal Products, Ltd.

Shrewsbury Herbal Products, located in central England close to the Welsh border, is an old-line producer of herbal teas, seasonings and medicines. Their products are marketed all over the United Kingdom and in many parts of continental Europe as well.

Shrewsbury Herbal generally invoices in British pounds sterling when it sells to foreign customers in order to guard against adverse exchange rate changes. Nevertheless, it has just received an order from a large wholesaler in central France for £320,000 of its products, conditional upon delivery being made in three months' time and the order invoiced in euros.

Shrewsbury's controller, Elton Peters, is concerned with whether the pound will appreciate versus the euro over the next three months, thus eliminating all or most of the profit when the euro receivable is paid. He thinks this an unlikely possibility, but he decides to contact the firm's banker for suggestions about hedging the exchange rate exposure.

Mr. Peters learns from the banker that the current spot exchange rate in €/£ is €1.5641; thus, the invoice amount should be €500,512. Mr. Peters also learns that the three-month forward rates for the pound and the euro versus the US dollar are $1.5188/£1 and $0.9727/€1, respectively. The banker offers to set up a forward hedge for selling the franc receivable for pound sterling based on the €/£ cross-forward exchange rate implicit in the forward rates against the US dollar.

What would you do if you were Mr. Peters?

REFERENCES & SUGGESTED READINGS

Bank for International Settlements. *Triennial Central Bank Survey.* Basle, Switzerland: Bank for International Settlements, March 2005.

Cheung, Yin-Wong, and Menzie David Chinn. "Currency Traders and Exchange Rate Dynamics: A Survey of the US Market." *Journal of International Money and Finance* 20 (2001), pp. 439–71.

Dominguez, Kathryn M. "Central Bank Intervention and Exchange Rate Volatility." *Journal of International Money and Finance* 17 (1998), pp. 161–90.

D'Souza, Chris. *A Market Microstructure Analysis of Foreign Exchange Intervention in Canada.* Bank of Canada Working Paper 2002–16 (Financial Markets Department). Ottawa: Bank of Canada, 2002.

Federal Reserve Bank of New York. *The Foreign Exchange and Interest Rate Derivatives Markets Survey: Turnover in the United States.* New York: Federal Reserve Bank of New York, 2001.

Grabbe, J. Orlin. *International Financial Markets*, 3rd ed. Upper Saddle River, NJ: Prentice Hall, 1996.

Huang, Roger D., and Ronald W. Masulis. "FX Spreads and Dealer Competition across the 24-Hour Trading Day." *Review of Financial Studies* 12 (1999), pp. 61–93.

Ito, Takatoshi, Richard K. Lyons, and Michael T. Melvin. "Is There Private Information in the FX Market? The Tokyo Experiment." *Journal of Finance* 53 (1998), pp. 1111–30.

Lyons, Richard K. "Profits and Position Control: A Week of FX Dealing." *Journal of International Money and Finance* 17 (1998), pp. 97–115.

McCallum, John. "Seven Issues in the Choice of an Exchange Rate Regime for Canada." *Current Analysis*, Economics Department, Royal Bank of Canada (1999).

Murray, John, Lawrence Schembri, and Pierre St-Amant. "Revisiting the Case for Flexible Exchange Rates in North America." *The North American Journal of Economics and Finance.* Volume 14, Issue 2 (2000), pp. 207–400.

For more information on the resources available from McGraw-Hill Ryerson, go to www.mcgrawhill.ca/he/solutions.

Chapter 5

International Parity Relationships and Forecasting Foreign Exchange Rates

CHAPTER OUTLINE

THIS CHAPTER EXAMINES the international *parity conditions* that govern the exchange rate between pairs of currencies. The parity conditions offer the economic explanation for the value of the exchange rate and also for the rate of change of the exchange rate. The parity conditions are the foundation of most models of forecasting exchange rates.

The parity conditions reflect the international Law of One Price, the fundamental idea that two things that are identical ought to sell for the same price. Whereas the Law of One Price, sometimes called Purchasing Power Parity, is crucial in international trade—essentially the idea that traded goods tend to have the same price everywhere—we will focus on the financial aspect of the Law of One Price and deal with financial assets, capital flows and interest rates.

Since *arbitrage* plays a crucial role in the following discussion, we will define it at the outset. **Arbitrage** is *the simultaneous purchase and sale of equivalent assets for the purpose of generating a certain and riskless profit.* An arbitrager sells an overpriced asset and buys an identical underpriced asset.

As long as profitable arbitrage opportunities exist, the market cannot be in equilibrium. Conversely and usefully, a market is said to be in equilibrium when no profitable arbitrage opportunities exist. In international finance, *interest rate parity* is an important zero-arbitrage relationship.

5.1   INTEREST RATE PARITY

Interest rate parity (IRP) is a zero-arbitrage condition that must hold when international financial markets are in equilibrium. Interest rate parity, in effect, means that financial assets of similar risk in two countries yield the same rate of return, regardless of the currency in which the assets are denominated.

Consider two alternative ways of investing 100 dollars. You could invest the $100 in Canada in a one-year Government of Canada bond. The Canadian bond pays the Canadian interest rate, $i_\$$. Alternatively, you could invest in a one-year British government bond that pays the British interest rate, $i_£$.

Note that the example is constructed with Canadian and British bonds that are both considered riskless and have one-year maturity. In other words, they are in the same (zero) risk class, and they have the same maturity.

The investment in Canada will result in cash at maturity of $100(1 + i_\$)$. This is a certain amount of Canadian dollars.

To invest in the United Kingdom, on the other hand, you must carry out the following three-step procedure:

1. Pay $100 to buy British pounds at the prevailing spot exchange rate (S). This will provide you with £$100(1/S)$. The spot rate is defined in direct terms, that is, $/£.

2. Invest the pounds at the British interest rate. This will result in cash at maturity of £$100(1/S)(1 + i_£)$. This is a certain amount of British pounds.

3. Sell the maturity value of the British investment *forward* at the forward exchange rate (F). This will result in cash at maturity of £$100(1/S)(1 + i_£)F$. This is a certain amount of Canadian dollars.

The investment in the United Kingdom begins with Canadian dollars and ends with Canadian dollars. Canadian dollars are sold (spot) for pounds at the beginning, and pounds are sold (forward) to result in Canadian dollars at the end. From your point of view as a Canadian investor, your investment in British bonds is *hedged*. At the outset, you know the British interest rate, the spot exchange rate and the forward exchange rate. Hence you know for certain the number of Canadian dollars that you will end up with at the maturity of the British investment.

The "effective" dollar interest rate from the British investment is $(F/S)(1 + i_£) - 1$.

Zero-arbitrage equilibrium dictates that the future dollar proceeds (or, equivalently, the dollar interest rate) from investing in Canada or in the United Kingdom are the same, that is,

$$\$100(1 + i_\$) = \$100(F/S)(1 + i_£)$$

or

$$(1 + i_\$) = (F/S)(1 + i_£) \tag{5.1}$$

This is a formal statement of interest rate parity. It represents the Law of One Price applied to cross-currency borrowing or lending.

If IRP in fact holds, the immediate implication is that it makes no difference where the Canadian investor invests. The dollar return will be the same whether the investment is in Canadian bonds or British bonds. In other words, arbitrage opportunities do not exist. The *net cash flow* from investing in British bonds versus Canadian bonds is zero.

Exhibit 5.1 traces the transactions of a Canadian investor's purchase of British bonds in the situation in which IRP holds. The slight difference from the previous example is that

EXHIBIT 5.1			
Cash Flows in Arbitrage Transactions	**Transactions**	**CF₀**	**CF₁**
	1. Borrow in Canada	$1	
	2. Exchange to pounds, spot	£$(1/S)$	
	3. Lend pounds in Britain	$-$£$(1/S)$	
	4. Recover proceeds from pound-loan		£$(1/S) \times (1 + i_£)$
	5. Exchange to dollars at previously contracted forward rate (F)		$F(1/S) \times (1 + i_£)$
	6. Repay Canadian dollar loan		$-(1 + i_\$)$
	Net arbitrage profit (in dollars)		$(F/S) \times (1 + i_£) - (1 + i_\$)$

Note: Arbitrage profit is *zero* if: $(F/S)(1 + i_£) - (1 + i_\$) = 0$, in which case $F = S\left[\dfrac{1 + i_\$}{1 + i_£}\right]$, which defines interest rate parity.

the Canadian investor borrows in Canada to finance the investment. The Canadian investor borrows $1, converts that dollar to British pounds at the spot rate (S), and sells the pound-proceeds forward at the forward rate (F). Once the proceeds from the British investment are exchanged back into Canadian dollars, the Canadian dollar loan is retired. If the net cash flow from the full set of transactions is zero, there is no arbitrage gain.

Interest rate parity is often approximated as[1]

$$(i_\$ - i_£) = (F - S)/S \tag{5.2}$$

Equation 5.2 indicates that interest rate parity implies an explicit linkage between the interest rates in two countries. The "linkage" is explicit in the relationship between the spot rate of exchange and the forward rate. Specifically, the interest rate will be higher in Canada than in Britain when the Canadian dollar is at a forward discount, that is, $F > S$.

Recall that the exchange rates, S and F, represent the dollar prices of one unit of foreign currency. When the dollar is at a forward discount, the implication is that the dollar is expected to depreciate against the British pound. If so, the Canadian interest rate (in equilibrium) must be higher than the British interest rate to compensate for the expected depreciation of the dollar. Otherwise, investors would shy away from dollar-denominated securities. On the other hand, the Canadian interest rate will be lower than the British interest rate when the dollar is at a forward premium, that is, when $F < S$. In general, Equation 5.2 indicates that under interest rate parity the forward exchange rate will deviate from the spot exchange rate whenever the interest rates in the two countries are not the same.

When IRP holds, you will be indifferent to investing your money in Canada or Britain with forward hedging. However, if IRP does not hold, you will prefer one country to the other. You will be better off investing in Canada if $(1 + i_\$)$ is greater than $(F/S)(1 + i_£)$. You will be better off investing in Britain if $(1 + i_\$)$ is less than $(F/S)(1 + i_£)$.

When you need to borrow, you will choose to borrow where the dollar interest is lower. It is better to borrow in Canada when $(1 + i_\$)$ is less than $(F/S)(1 + i_£)$.

When IRP does not hold, the situation gives rise to **covered interest arbitrage (CIA)** opportunities. To explain the covered interest arbitrage process, it is convenient to work with a numerical example.

Example (5.1) *The Adjustment Process*

Suppose that the annual interest rate is 5 percent in Canada and 7 percent in Britain. The spot exchange rate is $2.20/£. The forward exchange rate is $2.18/£. In terms of our notation,

$i_\$ = 5\%$, $i_£ = 7\%$, $S = \$2.20$ and $F = \$2.18$

Assume that an arbitrager can borrow up to $1,000,000 or £454,545. The latter figure (in pounds) is equivalent to $1,000,000 at the spot exchange rate.

Let us check to see if IRP is holding under current market conditions. Substituting the given data, we find

$(F/S)(1 + i_£) = (2.18/2.20)(1.07) = 1.0603$

which is not equal to $(1 + i_\$) = 1.05$. Specifically, we find that the current market conditions are characterized by

$$(1 + i_\$) < (F/S)(1 + i_£) \tag{5.3}$$

Interest rate parity is not holding, implying that a profitable arbitrage opportunity exists. Since the interest rate in Canada is lower than the effective dollar interest rate on a British investment, arbitrage transactions involve borrowing in Canada and lending in Britain.

---

[1]Equation 5.2 is an approximate version. The exact version is $(i_\$ - i_£) = [(F - S)/S](1 + i_£)$. To determine if an arbitage opportunity exists, one should use the exact version of IRP.

The arbitrager can carry out the following transactions:

1. In Canada, borrow $1,000,000. Repayment in one year will be $1,050,000 = $1,000,000 × 1.05.
2. Buy £454,545 spot using the $1,000,000.
3. Invest £454,545 in British securities. The maturity value will be £486,364 = £454,545 × 1.07.
4. Sell £486,364 forward in exchange for $1,060,273 = £486,364 ($2.18/£).

In one year, when everything matures, the arbitrager will receive the full maturity value of the British investment, that is, £486,364. The arbitrager will deliver the pound amount to the counterparty of the forward contract and will receive $1,060,273 in return. Out of this dollar amount, the initial loan plus interest, $1,050,000, will be repaid. The arbitrager still has $10,273 (= $1,060,273 − $1,050,000) left in his account. This is the arbitrage profit. In making this certain profit, the arbitrager neither invested any money out of his own pocket nor bore any risk. He, indeed, carried out "covered interest arbitrage," which means that he borrowed at one interest rate and simultaneously loaned the funds at another interest rate, all the while with the exchange risk fully covered via forward hedging. Exhibit 5.2 provides a summary of the covered interest arbitrage transactions.

How long will this arbitrage opportunity last? A simple answer is: only for a short while. As soon as deviations from IRP are detected, informed traders will immediately carry out CIA transactions. As a result of these arbitrage activities, IRP will be restored quite quickly. To see this, let us get back to our numerical example, which induced covered interest arbitrage activities. Since every trader will (1) borrow in Canada as much as possible, (2) lend in Britain, (3) buy the pound spot and, at the same time, (4) sell the pound forward, the following adjustments will occur to the initial market condition described in Equation 5.3:

1. The interest rate will rise in Canada ($i_\$\uparrow$).
2. The interest rate will fall in the United Kingdom ($i_£\downarrow$).
3. The ($/£) spot rate will rise ($S\uparrow$).
4. The ($/£) forward rate will fall ($F\downarrow$).

These adjustments will raise the left-hand side of Equation 5.3 and, at the same time, lower the right-hand side until both sides are equalized, restoring IRP.

The adjustment process is depicted in Exhibit 5.3. The initial market condition described by Equation 5.3 is represented by point A in the exhibit, substantially off the IRP line. CIA activities will increase the interest rate differential (as indicated by the horizontal arrow, $i_\$ - i_£$ becomes less negative) and, at the same time, lower the forward premium/discount (as indicated by the vertical arrow). Since the foreign exchange and money markets share

EXHIBIT 5.2

Covered Interest Arbitrage: Cash Flow Analysis

Transactions	CF₀	CF₁
1. Borrow $1,000,000	$1,000,000	−$1,050,000
2. Buy £ spot	−$1,000,000 £454.545	
3. Lend £454.545	−£454.545	£486,364
4. Sell £486,364 forward		−£486,364 $1,060,273
Net cash flow	0	$10,273

EXHIBIT 5.3

The Interest Rate
Parity Diagram

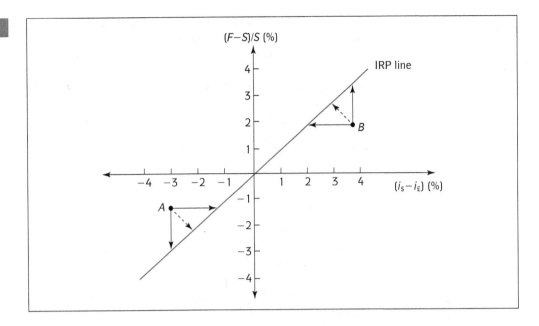

the burden of adjustments, the actual path of adjustment to IRP can be depicted by the dotted arrow. When the initial market condition is located at point *B,* IRP will be restored partly by an increase in the forward premium, $(F - S)/S$, and partly by a decrease in the interest rate differential, $i_\$ - i_£$.

Interest Rate Parity and Exchange Rate Determination

As a zero-arbitrage equilibrium condition involving the (spot) exchange rate, IRP has an immediate implication for exchange rate determination. To see why, let us reformulate the IRP relationship in terms of the spot exchange rate:

$$S = \left[\frac{1 + i_£}{1 + i_\$}\right]F \tag{5.4}$$

Equation 5.4 indicates that given the forward exchange rate, the spot exchange rate depends on relative interest rates. All else equal, an increase in the Canadian interest rate will lead to a higher foreign exchange value of the dollar.[2] This is so because a higher Canadian interest rate will attract capital to Canada, increasing the demand for dollars. In contrast, a decrease in the Canadian interest rate will lower the foreign exchange value of the dollar.

In addition to relative interest rates, the forward exchange rate is an important factor in spot exchange rate determination. Under certain conditions the forward exchange rate can be viewed as the expected future spot exchange rate conditional on all relevant information being available now, that is,

$$F = E(S_{t+1}|I_t) \tag{5.5}$$

where S_{t+1} is the future spot rate when the forward contract matures, and I_t denotes the set of information currently available.[3] When Equations 5.4 and 5.5 are combined, we obtain

$$S = \left[\frac{1 + i_£}{1 + i_\$}\right]E(S_{t+1}|I_t) \tag{5.6}$$

---

[2] A higher Canadian interest rate ($i_\$\uparrow$) will lead to a lower spot exchange rate ($S\downarrow$), which means a stronger dollar. *S* represents the number of Canadian dollars per pound.

[3] The set of relevant information includes money supplies, interest rates, trade balances and so on that influences exchange rates.

Two things are noteworthy from Equation 5.6. First, "expectation" plays a key role in exchange rate determination. Specifically, the expected future exchange rate is shown to be a major determinant of the current exchange rate; when people "expect" the exchange rate to go up in the future, it goes up now. People's expectations thus become self-fulfilling. Second, exchange rate behaviour is driven by news events. People form expectations based on the information (I_t) they possess. As they receive news continuously, they update their expectations continuously. As a result, the exchange rate tends to exhibit *dynamic* and *volatile* short-term behaviour responding to various news events. By definition, news events are unpredictable, making forecasting future exchange rates an arduous task.

When the forward exchange rate F is replaced by the expected future spot exchange rate, $E(S_{t+1})$ in Equation 5.2, we obtain

$$(i_\$ - i_£) = E(e) \tag{5.7}$$

where $E(e)$ is the expected rate of change in the exchange rate, that is, $[E(S_{t+1}) - S_t]/S_t$. Equation 5.7 states that the interest rate differential between a pair of countries is (approximately) equal to the expected rate of change in the exchange rate. This relationship is known as the **uncovered interest rate parity**. If, for instance, the annual interest rate is 5 percent in Canada and 7 percent in Britain, as assumed in our numerical example, uncovered IRP suggests that the pound will depreciate against the dollar by about 2 percent, that is, $E(e) = -2\%$.

Reasons for Deviations from Interest Rate Parity

Although IRP tends to hold quite well, it may not hold precisely all the time for at least two reasons: transaction costs and capital controls.

In our previous examples of CIA transactions, we implicitly assumed, among other things, no transaction costs. In that case, for each dollar borrowed at the Canadian interest rate ($i_\$$) the arbitrager could realize the following amount of positive profit:

$$(F/S)(1 + i_£) - (1 + i_\$) > 0 \tag{5.8}$$

In reality, transaction costs do exist. The interest rate at which the arbitrager borrows, i^a, tends to be higher than the rate at which he lends, i^b, reflecting the bid-ask spread. Likewise, there are bid-ask spreads in the foreign exchange market as well. The arbitrager has to buy foreign exchange at the higher ask price and sell it at the lower bid price. Each of the four variables in Equation 5.8 can be regarded as representing the midpoint of the spread.

Because of spreads, arbitrage profit from each dollar borrowed may become non-positive:

$$(F^b/S^a)(1 + i_£^b) - (1 + i_\$^a) \le 0 \tag{5.9}$$

where the superscripts a and b to the exchange rates and interest rates denote the ask and bid prices, respectively. This is so because

$$(F^b/S^a) < (F/S)$$
$$(1 + i_£^b) < (1 + i_£)$$
$$(1 + i_\$^a) > (1 + i_\$)$$

If the arbitrage profit turns negative because of transaction costs, the current deviation from IRP does not represent a profitable arbitrage opportunity. Thus, the IRP line in Exhibit 5.4 can be viewed within a band around it. Only IRP deviations outside the band, such as point C, represent profitable arbitrage opportunities. IRP deviations within the band, such as point D, would not represent profitable arbitrage opportunities. The width of this band will depend on the size of transaction costs.

Another potential reason for deviations from IRP is capital controls imposed by governments. For various macroeconomic reasons, governments sometimes restrict capital flows, inbound and/or outbound. Instruments to restrict capital inflow or outflow

EXHIBIT 5.4

Interest Rate Parity
with Transaction
Costs

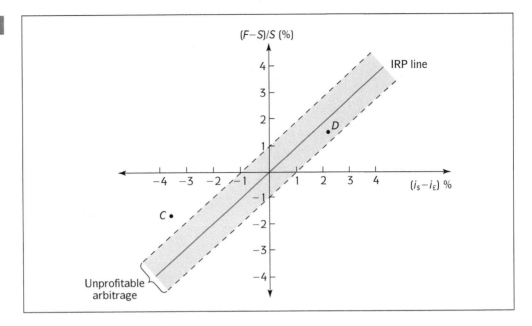

include taxes or explicit controls. Capital controls were often imposed by governments in an effort to improve the balance-of-payments situations and to keep the exchange rate at a desirable level.

An interesting historical example is provided by Japan, where capital controls were imposed on and off until December 1980, when the Japanese government liberalized international capital flows. Otani and Tiwari (1981) investigated the effect of capital controls on IRP deviations during the period 1978–81. They computed deviations from interest rate parity (DIRP) as follows:[4]

$$\text{DIRP} = [(1 + i_\yen)S/(1 + i_\$)F] - 1 \qquad (5.10)$$

where

$i_\yen$ = interest rate on three-month Gensaki bonds[5]

$i_\$$ = interest rate on three-month euro-dollar deposits

S = yen/dollar spot exchange rate in Tokyo

F = yen/dollar three-month forward exchange rate in Tokyo

Deviations from IRP computed as above are plotted in Exhibit 5.5. If IRP holds strictly, deviations from it would be randomly distributed, with the expected value of zero.

Exhibit 5.5, however, shows that deviations from IRP hardly hover around zero. The deviations were quite significant at times until near the end of 1980. They were the greatest during 1978. This can be attributed to various measures the Japanese government took to discourage capital inflows, which was done to keep the yen from appreciating. As these measures were removed in 1979, the deviations were reduced. They increased again considerably in 1980, however, reflecting an introduction of capital control; Japanese financial institutions were asked to discourage foreign currency deposits.

In December 1980, Japan adopted the new *Foreign Exchange and Foreign Trade Control Law,* which generally liberalized foreign exchange transactions. Not surprisingly, the deviations hover around zero in the first quarter of 1981. The empirical evidence presented in Exhibit 5.5 closely reflects changes in capital controls during the study period. This implies that deviations

---

[4]Readers can convince themselves that DIRP in Equation 5.10 will be zero if IRP holds exactly.

[5]Gensaki bonds, issued in the Tokyo money market, are sold with a repurchase agreement. While interest rates on Gensaki bonds are determined by market forces, they can still be affected by various market imperfections.

EXHIBIT 5.5

Deviations from
Interest Rate Parity:
Japan, 1978–1981
(in percent)

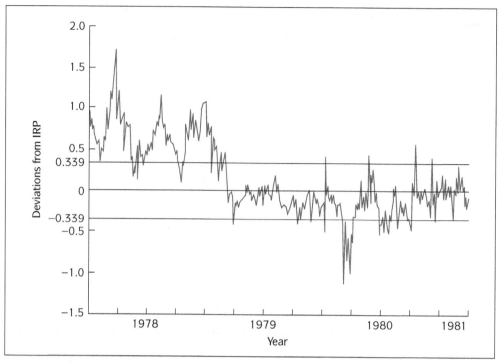

Note: Daily data were used in computing the deviations. The zone bounded by +0.339 and −0.339 represents the average width of the band around the IRP for the sample period.

Source: I. Otani and S. Tiwari, "Capital Controls and Interest Rate Parity: The Japanese Experience, 1978–81," *IMF Staff Papers* 28 (1981), pp. 793–815.

from IRP, especially in 1978 and 1980, do not represent unexploited profit opportunities; rather, they reflect the existence of significant barriers to cross-border arbitrage.

Currency Carry Trade

Unlike IRP, the uncovered interest rate parity often doesn't hold, giving rise to uncovered interest arbitrage opportunities. A popular example of such trade is provided by **currency carry trade**. Currency carry trade involves buying a high-yielding currency and funding it with a low-yielding currency, without any hedging. Since the interest rate in Japan has been near zero since the mid-1990s, the yen has been the most popular funding currency for carry trade, followed by the Swiss franc. Due to the low-interest-rate policy of the Federal Reserve to combat the Great Recession, the US dollar has also become a popular funding currency in recent years. Popular investment currencies, on the other hand, include the Australian dollar, New Zealand dollar and British pound, due to relatively high interest rates prevalent in these countries. Suppose you borrow in Japanese yen and invest in the Australian dollar. Your carry trade then will be profitable as long as the interest rate spread between the Australian dollar and Japanese yen, $i_{A\$} - i_{¥}$, is greater than the rate of appreciation ($e_{A\$,¥}$) of the yen against the Australian dollar during the carry period, that is, $i_{A\$} - i_{¥} > e_{A\$,¥}$.

   If many investors carry out the preceding trade on a massive scale, the yen may even depreciate, at least in the short run, against the Australian dollar, which is contrary to the prediction of the uncovered interest rate parity. The yen may depreciate in the short run as investors are selling the yen for the Australian dollar. If the yen depreciates against the Australian dollar by more than the Japanese interest rate, the funding cost for this carry trade would be effectively negative, making the carry trade more profitable.[6] However, if the Japanese yen appreciates against the Australian dollar by more than the interest rate

---

[6]Suppose you borrowed in Japanese yen at a 0.50% interest rate and the yen depreciated by 1.25% during the carry period. Then, the effective funding cost for the carry trade would become negative, −0.75% (= 0.50% − 1.25%).

EXHIBIT 5.6

Interest Rate
Spreads and
Exchange Rate
Changes: Six-Month
Carry Periods
for Australian
Dollar–Japanese
Yen Pair

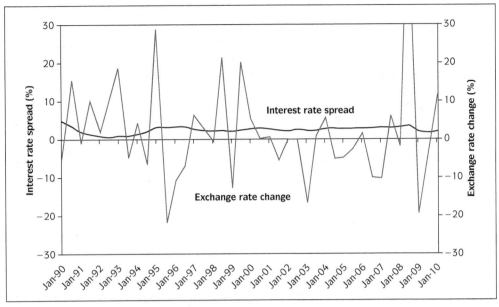

Note: Interest rates and exchange rates are obtained from Datastream. For interest rates, interbank six-month rates are used for both countries. The interest rate spread and the rate of change in the exchange rate are plotted at the start of each six-month carry period.

spread, you would lose money from the carry trade. Clearly, currency carry trade is a risky investment, especially when the exchange rate is volatile.

Exhibit 5.6 plots the six-month interest rate spread between the yen and Australian dollar, $i_{A\$} - i_{¥}$, and the rate of change in the exchange rate between the two currencies, $e_{A\$,¥}$, during the same six-month period. The exhibit shows that for (nonoverlapping) six-month periods examined, this carry trade was mostly profitable during the period 2000–2007, when the yen often depreciated against the Australian dollar. At other times, the carry trade was often unprofitable due to intermittent, sharp appreciations of the yen. Note that the yen appreciated very sharply in the second half of 2008, reflecting the surging demand for Japanese yen as a safe-haven asset during the recent global financial crisis, generating significant loss for the carry trade.

5.2 PURCHASING POWER PARITY

When the Law of One Price is applied internationally to a *standard commodity basket,* we have the concept of **purchasing power parity (PPP)**: the exchange rate between currencies of two countries should be equal to the ratio of the countries' price levels.

Let $P_\$$ be the dollar price of the standard commodity basket in Canada and $P_£$ the pound price of the same basket in Britain. Formally, PPP states that the exchange rate between the dollar and the pound should be

$$S = P_\$/P_£ \qquad (5.11)$$

where S is the dollar price of one pound. PPP implies that if the standard commodity basket costs \$200 in Canada and £100 in the United Kingdom, then the exchange rate should be \$2.00 per pound:

$$\$2/£ = \$200/£100$$

If the price of the commodity basket is higher in Canada, say \$300, then PPP dictates that the exchange rate should be higher, that is, \$3/£.

To give an alternative interpretation to PPP, let us rewrite Equation 5.11 as follows:

$$P_\$ = S \times P_£$$

McCurrencies

When our economics editor invented the Big Mac index in 1986 as a light-hearted introduction to exchange-rate theory, little did she think that 20 years later she would still be munching her way, a little less sylph-like, around the world. As burgernomics enters its third decade, the Big Mac index is widely used and abused around the globe. It is time to take stock of what burgers do and do not tell you about exchange rates.

The Economist's Big Mac index is based on one of the oldest concepts in international economics: the theory of purchasing-power parity (PPP), which argues that in the long run, exchange rates should move towards levels that would equalise the prices of an identical basket of goods and services in any two countries. Our "basket" is a McDonald's Big Mac, produced in around 120 countries. The Big Mac PPP is the exchange rate that would leave burgers costing the same in America as elsewhere. Thus a Big Mac in China costs 15.65 yuan, against an average price in four American cities of $4.33. To make the two prices equal would require an exchange rate of 3.62 yuan to the dollar, compared with a market rate of 6.39. In other words, the yuan is 43% "undervalued" against the dollar. To put it another way, converted into dollars at market rates the Chinese burger is among the cheapest in the table.

In contrast, using the same method, the Australian dollar is overvalued against the dollar, by 8%; the Swiss and Swedish currencies are even more overvalued. On the other hand, despite its recent climb, the yen appears to be 5% undervalued, with a PPP of only ¥74 to the dollar. Note that most emerging-market currencies also look too cheap.

The index was never intended to be a precise predictor of currency movements, simply a take-away guide to whether currencies are at their "correct" long-run level. Curiously, however, burgernomics has an impressive record in predicting exchange rates: currencies that show up as overvalued often tend to weaken in later years. But you must always remember the Big Mac's limitations. Burgers cannot sensibly be traded across borders and prices are distorted by differences in taxes and the cost of non-tradable inputs, such as rents.

Despite our frequent health warnings, some American politicians are fond of citing the Big Mac index rather too freely when it suits their cause—most

notably in their demands for a big appreciation of the Chinese currency in order to reduce America's huge trade deficit. But the cheapness of a Big Mac in China does not really prove that the yuan is being held far below its fair-market value. Purchasing-power parity is a long-run concept. It signals where exchange rates are eventually heading, but it says little about today's market-equilibrium exchange rate that would make the prices of tradable goods equal. A burger is a product of both traded and non-traded inputs.

It is quite natural for average prices to be lower in poorer countries than in developed ones. Although the prices of tradable things should be similar, non-tradable services will be cheaper because of lower wages. PPPs are therefore a more reliable way to convert GDP per head into dollars than market exchange rates, because cheaper prices mean that money goes further. This is also why every poor country has an implied PPP exchange rate that is higher than today's market rate, making them all appear undervalued. Both theory and practice show that as countries get richer and their productivity rises, their real exchange rates appreciate. But this does not mean that a currency needs to rise massively today. Jonathan Anderson, chief economist at UBS in Hong Kong, reckons that the yuan is now only 10–15% below its fair-market value.

Even over the long run, adjustment towards PPP need not come from a shift in exchange rates; relative prices can change instead. For example, since 1995, when the yen was overvalued by 100% according to the Big Mac index, the local price of Japanese burgers has dropped by one-third. In the same period, American burgers have become one-third dearer. Similarly, the yuan's future real appreciation could come through faster inflation in China than in the United States.

The Big Mac index is most useful for assessing the exchange rates of countries with similar incomes per head. Thus, among emerging markets, the yuan does indeed look undervalued, while the currencies of Brazil and Turkey look overvalued. Economists would be unwise to exclude Big Macs from their diet, but Super Size servings would equally be a mistake.

Source: "McCurrencies," *The Economist*, May 25, 2006, values updated as of July 25, 2012.

This equation states that the dollar price of the commodity basket in Canada, $P_\$$, must be the same as the dollar price of the basket in Britain, that is, $P_£$ multiplied by S. In other words, PPP requires that the price of the standard commodity basket be the same across countries when measured in a common currency. Clearly, PPP is the manifestation of the Law of One Price applied to the standard consumption baskets. As the International Finance in Practice box "McCurrencies" shows, PPP is a way of illustrating the equilibrium exchange rate.

The Hamburger Standard

	Big Mac Prices		Implied PPP[a] of the dollar[a]	Actual dollar exchange rate 7/13/2012	Under (−)/over (+) valuation against the dollar, %
	In local currency	In dollars			
United States[b]	$4.33	4.33	—	1.00	—
Argentina	Peso 19	4.16	4.39	4.57	−4
Australia	A$4.56	4.68	1.05	0.97	8
Brazil	Real 10.08	4.94	2.33	2.04	14
Britain	£2.69	4.16	1.61[c]	1.55[c]	−4
Canada	C$3.89	3.82	0.90	1.02	−12
Chile	Peso 2050	4.16	473.71	493.05	−4
China	Yuan 15.65	2.45	3.62	6.39	−43
Czech Republic	Koruna 70.33	4.77	16.25	21.05	−23
Denmark	DK 28.5	4.65	6.59	6.14	7
Egypt	Pound 16	2.64	3.70	6.07	−39
Euro area[d]	€3.58	4.34	1.21[e]	1.21[e]	0
Hong Kong	HK$16.5	2.13	3.81	7.76	−51
Hungary	Forint 830	3.48	191.69	238.22	−19
Indonesia	Rupiah 24200	2.55	5592.00	9482.50	−41
Japan	Yen 320	4.09	73.95	78.22	−5
Malaysia	Ringgit 7.4	2.33	1.71	3.17	−46
Mexico	Peso 37	2.70	8.55	13.69	−38
New Zealand	NZ$5.1	4.02	1.18	1.27	−7
Peru	New Sol 8.932	3.15	2.75	3.45	−30
Philippines	Peso 118	2.80	27.27	42.20	−35
Poland	Zloty 9.1	2.63	2.10	3.46	−39
Russia	Ruble 75	2.29	17.33	32.77	−47
Singapore	S$4.4	3.49	1.02	1.26	−19
South Africa	Rand 19.95	2.36	4.61	8.47	−46
South Korea	Won 3700	3.21	855.00	1151.00	−26
Sweden	SKr 48.4	6.94	11.18	6.98	60
Switzerland	SFr 6.5	6.56	1.52	0.99	52
Taiwan	NT$75	2.48	17.33	30.20	−43
Thailand	Baht 82	2.59	18.95	31.70	−40
Turkey	Lire 8.25	4.52	1.91	1.83	4

[a]Purchasing power parity: local price divided by price in United States.
[b]Average of New York, Chicago, Atlanta, and San Francisco
[c]Dollars per pound
[d]Weighted average of prices in euro area
[e]Dollars per euro

Source: McDonald's; *The Economist*, 25 July 2012.

www.economist.com/content/big-mac-index

Offers a discussion of exchange rate theory using Big Mac Index.

As a light-hearted guide to the "correct" level of exchange rate, *The Economist* each year compiles local prices of Big Macs around the world and computes the so-called "Big Mac PPP," the exchange rate that would equalize the hamburger prices between America and elsewhere. To compare this PPP and the actual exchange rate, a currency may be judged to be either undervalued or overvalued. In July 2012, a Big Mac cost (on average) $4.33 in the United States and 19 pesos in Argentina. Thus, the Big Mac PPP would be about 19/4.33 = 4.39 pesos per dollar. The actual exchange rate, however, is 4.57 pesos per dollar, implying that the peso is undervalued. In contrast, the Big Mac PPP for Switzerland is 1.52 Swiss francs per dollar, compared with the actual exchange rate of 0.99 francs per dollar. This implies that the Swiss franc is overvalued.

The PPP relationship of Equation 5.11 is called the *absolute* version of PPP. When the PPP relationship is presented in the "rate of change" form, we obtain the *relative* version:

$$e = (\pi_\$ - \pi_£)/(1 + \pi_£) \approx \pi_\$ - \pi_£ \tag{5.12}$$

where e is the rate of change in the exchange rate and $\pi_\$$ and $\pi_£$ are the inflation rates in Canada and Britain, respectively. For example, if the inflation rate is 6 percent per year in Canada and 4 percent in Britain, then the pound should appreciate against the dollar by about 2 percent, that is, $e = 2$ percent per year. Note that even if absolute PPP does not hold, relative PPP may hold.[7]

PPP Deviations and the Real Exchange Rate

Whether PPP holds or not has important implications for international trade. If PPP holds and thus the differential inflation rates between countries are exactly offset by exchange rate changes, countries' competitive positions in world export markets will not be systematically affected by exchange rate changes. However, if there are deviations from PPP, changes in nominal exchange rates cause changes in the **real exchange rates**, affecting the international competitive positions of countries. This, in turn, would affect countries' trade balances.

The real exchange rate, q, which measures deviations from PPP, can be defined as follows:[8]

$$q = \frac{1 + \pi_\$}{(1 + e)(1 + \pi_£)} \tag{5.13}$$

First, note that if PPP holds, that is, $(1 + e) = (1 + \pi_\$)/(1 + \pi_£)$, the real exchange rate will be unity, $q = 1$. When PPP is violated, however, the real exchange rate will deviate from unity. Suppose, for example, the annual inflation rate is 5 percent in Canada and 3.5 percent in Britain, and the dollar depreciated against the pound by 4.5 percent. Then, the real exchange rate is 0.97:

$$q = (1.05)/(1.045)(1.035) = 0.97$$

In the above example, the dollar depreciated by more than is warranted by PPP, strengthening the competitiveness of Canadian industries in the world market. If the dollar depreciates by less than the inflation rate differential, the real exchange rate will be greater than unity, weakening the competitiveness of Canadian industries. To summarize,

$q = 1$: Competitiveness of the domestic country unaltered.

$q < 1$: Competitiveness of the domestic country improves.

$q > 1$: Competitiveness of the domestic country deteriorates.

Exhibit 5.7 plots the real "effective" exchange rates for the currencies of the United States, Canada, China, Japan, Germany, and the United Kingdom since 1980. The rates plotted are, however, the real effective exchange rate "indexes" computed using 2005 rates as the base, that is, 2005 = 100. The real effective exchange rate is a weighted average of bilateral real exchange rates, with the weight for each foreign currency determined by the country's share in the domestic country's international trade. The real effective exchange rate rises if domestic inflation exceeds inflation abroad and the nominal exchange rate fails to depreciate to

---

[7]From Equation 5.12, we obtain $(1 + e) = (1 + \pi_\$)/(1 + \pi_£)$. Rearranging the above expression we obtain $e = (\pi_\$ - \pi_£)/(1 + \pi_£)$, which is approximated by $e = \pi_\$ - \pi_£$ as in Equation 5.11.

[8]The real exchange rate measures the degree of deviations from PPP over a certain period of time, assuming that PPP held roughly at a starting point. If PPP holds continuously, the real exchange rate will remain unity.

EXHIBIT 5.7   Real Effective Exchange Rates for Selected Currencies

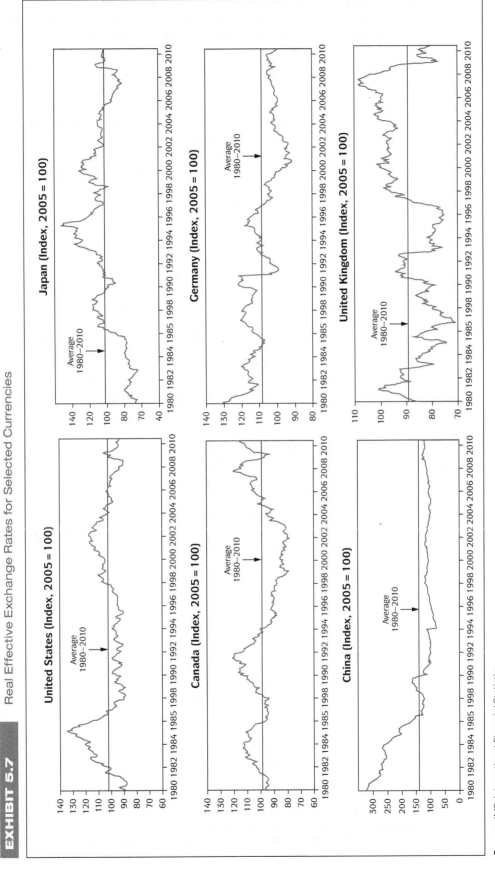

Source: IMF, *International Financial Statistics.*

compensate for the higher domestic inflation rate. Thus, if the real effective exchange rate rises (falls), the domestic country's competitiveness declines (improves). The history of the real effective exchange rate of the Mexican peso reveals several sharp declines that correspond to devaluations of the peso.

Real versus Nominal Exchange Rates—A Closer Look

If purchasing power parity—the "international Law of One Price"—held at all times, which it certainly does not, the exchange rate between two currencies would continuously adjust to reflect the difference in inflation between the two countries. On the other hand, if the exchange rate does not adjust to fully reflect the difference between the two countries' inflation rates, the *real* exchange rate is altered. This result underlies the distinction between the *nominal* exchange rate (the exchange rate that you "see") and the *real* exchange rate. The latter takes explicit account of purchasing power parity or deviations from it.

The *nominal–real* distinction is important for understanding the influence of exchange rates on a nation's competitiveness. We will briefly examine the *nominal–real* distinction in two specific contexts:

1. the nominal exchange rate changes despite no inflation differential between two countries
2. the nominal exchange rate is steady despite an inflation differential between two countries

Let us make the first context even more specific. Say, we have zero inflation in both Canada and the United States. Now, let us also say that the Canadian dollar appreciates against the US dollar, from $1.20/US$ to $1.10/US$. With Canadian dollar appreciation, Canadian goods become more expensive for Americans while American goods become cheaper for Canadians. The *real* value of the Canadian dollar has risen. Canada experiences a rise in the *real* exchange rate.

> *In general, if an exchange rate appreciates more than the difference between the rates of inflation in the two countries, then the country that experiences the nominal exchange rate appreciation also experiences a rise in its real exchange rate. The other country experiences a fall in its real exchange rate.*

Now, to deal with the second context, where the nominal exchange rate is steady despite an inflation differential between two countries, let us be specific and say that the Canada–United States exchange rate is slow to adjust to a Canada–United States inflation differential. Let us also say that American inflation exceeds Canadian inflation. In other words, the nominal price of goods in the United States rises faster than the price of goods in Canada. Since the exchange rate does not fully adjust for the inflation differential, American consumers will soon discover that goods imported from Canada are cheaper than American goods. Canadians will discover that American goods have become more expensive. Canada experiences a fall in the *real* exchange rate.

> *In general, if an international inflation differential is not reflected in depreciation of the currency of the country with higher inflation, then the country with higher inflation experiences a rise in its real exchange rate while the country with lower inflation experiences a reduction in the real value of its exchange rate.*[9]

---

[9]This type of effect led to the 1971–1973 collapse of the Bretton Woods fixed exchange rate regime that had been in place since 1944. The main strain was between the United States and Germany. By 1971, the United States had experienced several years of substantial inflation. Germany had relatively low inflation. The inevitable rise in the real exchange rate (from the American perspective) resulted in a large and widening American trade deficit. Germany, on the other hand, had a substantial trade surplus that put "demand pressure" on the German economy, largely from the United States. The fixed exchange regime in effect meant that the United States was "exporting" its inflation to Germany and, to a lesser extent, Japan. Meanwhile, the United States was bleeding foreign exchange reserves via capital outflows. When the stable exchange rate regime finally collapsed, the American dollar depreciated sharply against all other major currencies, first by 9 percent in 1971 and then by 11 percent in 1973.

EXHIBIT 5.8   Canada–United States Exchange Rates, Inflation and the Canadian Dollar Real Exchange Rate Index, 1987–2013

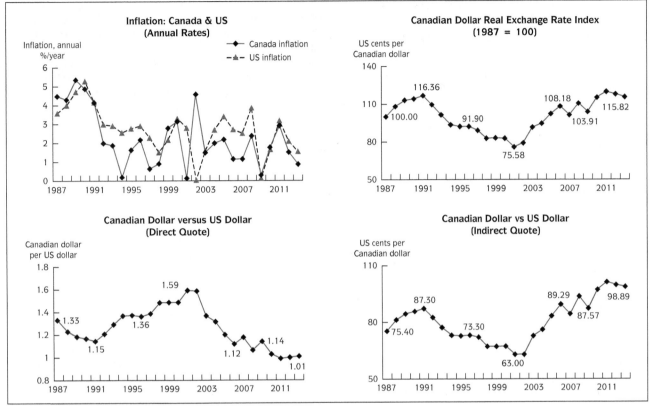

Source: Bank of Canada Review Banking and Financial Statistics, Table 11 (Exchange Rates) and Table 48 (Price Indexes).

Exhibit 5.8 illustrates the recent 25-year history of the nominal and real values of the Canadian exchange rate *vis-à-vis* the US dollar. The top chart presents the values of the exchange rate with a *direct* quote—the number of Canadian dollars required to purchase one US dollar. The second chart graphs the values of the exchange rate using the *indirect* quote—the value of the Canadian dollar expressed in terms of US dollars.

The third chart in Exhibit 5.8 presents rates of inflation in Canada and in the United States in each year of the 25-year period. In most years since 1990 (with 2002 being a striking exception), Canadian inflation has been below inflation in the United States.

Finally, the bottom chart on the right in Exhibit 5.8 integrates data on the nominal exchange rate and inflation differentials into a Real Exchange Rate Index for the period 1987 to 2013.[10] A year-over-year rise in the index indicates a rise in the Canadian real exchange rate. A year-over-year fall in the index indicates a fall in the Canadian real exchange rate. We see that the index rose sharply from 1987 to 1991, a period in which the Bank of Canada committed to austere monetary policy and high interest rates in an effort to rid the country of inflation. In 1991, Canada's merchandise trade balance touched its lowest level in the entire 1980–2013 period, in large part due to the exceptionally high real value of the Canadian exchange rate (but also in part due to the 1991–1992 recession in the

---

[10]The Real Exchange Rate Index equals the nominal exchange rate (indirect quote) in year t divided by the ratio of the American Price Index to the Canadian Price Index in the same year t. The two price indexes are normalized to the same base value in the year t_0. The Real Exchange Rate Index is normalized to a value of 100 for the year 1987. This computational approach is consistent with Equation 5.13.

INTERNATIONAL FINANCE *in Practice*

Exchange Rates and International Industrial Competitiveness: An Illustration

Canada and Germany both produce "ice wine." We will assume that the quality of ice wine out of the two countries is the same. Assume that

A case of German ice wine sells in Germany for €1,000

A case of Canadian ice wine sells in Canada for $1,300

The spot rate of exchange, $S(\$/€) = 1.300$

Thus, ignoring transportation costs, absolute PPP— or the International Law of One Price—for ice wine seems to hold between Germany and Canada. At the prevailing spot rate of exchange, $S(\$/€) = 1.300$, Europeans and Canadians are indifferent on a price basis between German and Canadian ice wine.

Absolute (or "Real") PPP, Inflation Rates and the Rate of Change of the Spot Rate

Now, assume that

Ice wine price inflation in Canada, $\pi^\$$, is 2 percent per annum

Ice wine price inflation in Germany, $\pi^€$, is 4 percent per annum

What must the $/€ spot exchange rate be one year from now in order to maintain the international Law of One Price, that is, such that Europeans and Canadians one year from now remain indifferent on a price-per-case basis between German and Canadian ice wine?

Think of it this way:

Price of a case of Canadian ice wine one year from now will be $1,300 \times (1 + \pi^\$) = \$1,326$

Price of a case of German ice wine one year from now will be €1,000 $\times (1 + \pi^€) = €1,040$

$1,326/€1,040 = 1.275$

This spot rate, 1.275, if it occurs this time next year, would allow Europeans and Canadians to remain indifferent on a price-per-case basis between German and Canadian ice wine.

Formally, the relation that must hold to maintain absolute PPP is

$S_1/S_0 = (1 + \pi^\$)/(1 + \pi^€)$
$S_1 = S_0 \times [(1 + \pi^\$)/(1 + \pi^€)]$
$S_1 = 1.300 \times [(1.02)/(1.04)]$
$S_1 = 1.275 (\$/€)$

The annualized rate of change of the spot exchange rate retains PPP at

$(S_1 - S_0)/S_0 = (1.275 - 1.300)/1.300$
$\qquad\qquad = -1.923$ percent per annum

Here is the intuition. The spot rate is expressed as $S(\$/€)$ or "dollars per euro." Euro inflation exceeds Canadian inflation. The value of the euro is eroding (via its 4 percent inflation) more rapidly than the erosion of the value of the Canadian dollar (at its 2 percent inflation). Therefore, to maintain PPP, the number of dollars required to purchase one euro must fall from 1.300 to 1.275. This rate of euro depreciation (or Canadian dollar appreciation) is approximately 4% − 2%, or 2 percent, that is, the difference between the respective inflation rates.

The axiom: For absolute (or "real") PPP to hold over time, the spot exchange rate must change at a rate (approximately) equal to the difference in the respective domestic rates of inflation.

For absolute (or "real") PPP to hold over time,

$$\%\Delta S = \pi^\$ - \pi^€$$

The currency of the nation with the relatively lower rate of inflation appreciates; the currency of the nation with the relatively higher rate of inflation depreciates.

Inflation Rates, the Rate of Change of the Spot Rate and International Competitiveness

This focus helps us understand the interaction of inflation differentials, the spot rate of exchange and the international competitive position of companies or industries.

As above, say

Ice wine price inflation in Canada, $\pi^\$$, is 2 percent per annum

Ice wine price inflation in Germany, $\pi^€$, is 4 percent per annum

However, now let's say that the spot $(\$/€)$ exchange rate this time next year turns out to be 1.285 rather than the PPP-maintaining value that we solved for as 1.275.

At $S(\$/€) = 1.285$, an ice wine merchant in Canada can purchase a case this time next year for

$1,300 \times (1.020) = \$1,326$ in Canada

or for

€1,000 $\times (1.040) \times (1.285) = \$1,336$ from a German supplier

Canadian producers of ice wine would move to an exchange-rate-induced international competitive *advantage* with respect to their German competitors. The reason? While the Canadian dollar indeed appreciated (from $S(\$/€) = 1.300$ to 1.285) in the face of the 2 percent German–Canadian inflation differential, the 0.77% Canadian dollar appreciation (or approximately 0.77% euro depreciation) is less than the inflation differential itself. By this time next year, Canadian ice wine producers will come to enjoy a *real* exchange rate *depreciation* of the Canadian dollar with respect to the euro. (Note that the 0.77% Canadian dollar appreciation is expressed here as a percentage change in the spot rate and not as an annualized rate, which we return to below.)

Let's summarize. Call the real exchange rate "Q."

$$Q = (1 + \pi^{\$})(1 + \Delta S)(1 + \pi^{€})$$

For the real exchange rate (Q) to hold constant, that is, for real PPP to hold over time,

$$(1 + \Delta S) = (1 + \pi^{\$})/(1 + \pi^{€}) \Rightarrow Q = 1$$

From our commentary above, we know that for given values of $\pi^{\$}$ and $\pi^{€}$ of 0.02 and 0.04 respectively, the one-year ΔS necessary to hold PPP is an annualized rate of -1.923 percent.

$$1 + (-0.01923) = 1.02/1.04$$

If $Q < 1$, Canada's international competitiveness improves. In our example, this is the case where the Canadian dollar appreciates (a *negative* ΔS) by only 1.154%, an amount that is *less* than the 1.923% dollar appreciation required to hold (absolute) PPP.

If $Q > 1$, Canada's international competitiveness deteriorates. In our example, this would have been the case of the Canadian dollar appreciating by more than 1.923 percent.

Bilateral PPP versus Trilateral PPP

Let's go back to the original data where we had German ice wine selling for €1,000 a case, Canadian ice wine selling for $1,300 and the spot rate of exchange $S(\$/€) = 1.300$. Can we unequivocally say ice wine lovers in a third country, say Japan, are indifferent (on a price basis) between German and Canadian ice wine? Again, we ignore perceived quality differences and transportation costs.

First, look at the $S(\$/¥)$ and the $S(€/¥)$ exchange rates, that is, the current spot rate of the Canadian dollar for yen and the current spot rate of euro for yen. Assume that

$S(\$/¥) = 0.0130$ (One yen equals 1.3 Canadian cents)

$S(€/¥) = 0.0100$ (One yen equals one euro cent)

A Japanese ice wine importer can import a case of ice wine from Germany for €1,000/0.0100, which equals ¥100,000, and can import a case of ice wine from Canada for $1,300/0.0130, which equals ¥100,000. In this alignment of bilateral exchange rates, $S(\$/¥)$ and $S(€/¥)$, we have trilateral PPP. Neither Germany nor Canada has an advantage in serving the Japanese market for ice wine.

However, what if

$S(\$/¥) = 0.0140$ (One yen equals 1.4 Canadian cents)

$S(€/¥) = 0.0100$ (One yen equals one euro cent)

A Japanese ice wine importer can import a case of ice wine from Germany for €1,000/0.0100, which equals ¥100,000, but, on the other hand, can import a case of ice wine from Canada for $1,300/0.0140, which equals ¥92,857.

$S(\$/¥) = 0.0140$ represents a cheaper Canadian dollar for the Japanese importer. As a result, Canadian ice wine makers have an advantage *vis-à-vis* their German competitors in the Japanese market for ice wine.

United States). From 1992 to 2001, the Real Exchange Rate Index fell 35 percent, from 116 to 76, puzzling most economists who deal with these issues. Since then the index has bounced back approximately 50 percent (May 2013).

Evidence on Purchasing Power Parity

As is clear from the above discussions, whether PPP holds in reality is a question of considerable importance. In view of the fact that PPP is the manifestation of the Law of One Price applied to a standard commodity basket, it will hold only if the prices of constituent commodities are equalized across countries in a given currency and if the composition of the consumption basket is the same across countries.

The PPP has been the subject of a series of tests, yielding generally negative results. For example, in his study of disaggregated commodity arbitrage between Canada and the United States, Richardson (1978) was unable to detect commodity arbitrage for a majority of commodity classes. Richardson reported: "The presence of commodity arbitrage could be rejected with 95 percent confidence for at least 13 out of the 22 commodity groups" (p. 346). Although Richardson did not directly test PPP, his findings can be viewed as highly negative news for PPP. If commodity arbitrage is imperfect between neighbouring countries, such as the United States and Canada, that have relatively few trade restrictions, PPP is not likely to hold much better for other pairs of countries.

Exhibit 5.9 also provides evidence against commodity price parity. The price of aspirin (20 units) ranges from $0.77 in Mexico City to $6.25 in Tokyo. Likewise, the cost of a man's haircut ranges from $18.34 in Mexico City to $81.49 in Copenhagen. It is more than four times as expensive to have a haircut in Copenhagen than in Mexico City. That price differential, moreover, is likely to persist, because haircuts are simply not tradable. In comparison, the global price disparity for memory sticks is substantially less. A memory stick is a highly standardized commodity actively traded across national borders.

Generally unfavourable evidence about PPP suggests substantial barriers to international commodity arbitrage. Obviously, commodity prices can diverge between countries up to the transportation costs without triggering arbitrage. If it costs $50 to ship a tonne of rice from Thailand to Korea, the price of rice can diverge by up to $50 in either direction between the two countries without violating PPP. Likewise, deviations from PPP can result from tariffs and quotas imposed on international trade.

As is well recognized, some commodities never enter into international trade. Examples of such **nontradables** include haircuts, medical services, housing and the like. These items

EXHIBIT 5.9				

A Guide to World Prices: 2012

Location	Hamburger (1 unit)	Aspirin (20 units)	Man's Haircut (1 unit)	Memory Stick (4GB)
Athens	$4.32	$0.93	$51.01	$15.48
Copenhagen	$5.35	$4.07	$81.49	$33.15
Hong Kong	$2.09	$5.24	$72.38	$11.41
London	$3.51	$3.36	$55.21	$19.92
Los Angeles	$3.79	$2.79	$23.75	$16.99
Madrid	$4.73	$4.61	$18.38	$28.11
Mexico City	$2.61	$0.77	$18.34	$21.14
Munich	$4.72	$4.78	$23.42	$19.11
Paris	$4.66	$3.77	$49.32	$32.26
Rio de Janeiro	$4.69	$4.43	$28.11	$19.29
Rome	$5.68	$5.70	$34.46	$21.21
Sydney	$4.12	$3.52	$39.81	$30.88
Tokyo	$3.45	$6.25	$66.23	$12.54
Toronto	$4.95	$2.10	$38.28	$19.83
Vienna	$4.04	$5.77	$41.89	$20.26
Average	$4.18	$3.87	$42.81	$21.44
Standard deviation	$0.94	$1.62	$19.03	$6.53
Coefficient of variation[b]	0.23	0.42	0.44	0.30

[a]Prices include sales tax and value added tax except in the United States location.
[b]The coefficient of variation is obtained from dividing the standard deviation by the average. It thus provides a measure of dispersion adjusted for the magnitude of the variable.
Source: AIRINC.

are either immovable or inseparable from the providers of these services. Suppose a quality haircut costs $60 in Toronto but the comparable haircut costs only $20 in Mexico City. Obviously, you cannot import haircuts from Mexico. Either you have to travel to Mexico or a Mexican barber must travel to Toronto, both of which, of course, are impractical in view of travel costs and immigration laws. Consequently, the Canadian–Mexican price differential for haircuts will persist. As long as there are nontradables, PPP will not hold in its absolute version. If PPP holds for tradables and the relative prices between tradables and nontradables are maintained, then PPP can hold in its relative version. These conditions, however, are not likely to hold.

Even if PPP may not hold in reality, it can still play a useful role in economic analysis. First, one can use the PPP-determined exchange rate as a benchmark in deciding if a country's currency is undervalued or overvalued against other currencies. Second, one can often make more meaningful international comparisons of economic data using PPP-determined, rather than market-determined, exchange rates. This point is highlighted in Exhibit 5.10, "How Large Is India's Economy?"

Suppose you want to rank countries in terms of gross domestic product (GDP). If you use market exchange rates, you can either underestimate or overestimate the true GDP values. The exhibit provides the GDP values of the major economies in 2012 computed using both PPP and market exchange rates. A country's ranking in terms of GDP value is quite sensitive to which exchange rate is used. India provides a striking example. When the market exchange rate is used, India ranks 11th, lagging behind such countries as France,

EXHIBIT 5.10

How Large Is India's Economy? Comparative GDP at Market Exchange Rates and PPP, 2012 ($US, trillions)

GDP at PPP Exchange Rate	Rank	GDP at Market Exchange Rate
16.07 — EU	1	EU — 16.58
15.65 — U.S	2	U.S. — 15.65
12.38 — China	3	China — 8.23
4.71 — India	4	Japan — 5.96
4.62 — Japan	5	Germany — 3.40
3.19 — Germany	6	France — 2.61
2.51 — Russia	7	U.K — 2.44
2.37 — UK	8	Brazil — 2.40
2.32 — Brazil	9	Russia — 2.02
2.25 — France	10	Italy — 2.01
1.83 — Italy	11	India — 1.82
1.76 — Mexico	12	Canada — 1.82
1.62 — Korea,Rep	13	Australia — 1.54
1.45 — Canada	14	Spain — 1.35
1.41 — Spain	15	Mexico — 1.18
1.21 — Indonesia	16	Korea, Rep — 1.16
1.13 — Turkey	17	Indonesia — 0.88
1.01 — Iran	18	Turkey — 0.79
0.96 — Australia	19	Iran — 0.55
0.90 — Taiwan	20	Poland — 0.49
0.80 — Poland	21	Taiwan — 0.47

Source: IMF, World Economic Outlook database, October 2012.

the United Kingdom and Germany. However, when the PPP exchange rate is used, India moves up to fourth after China, but ahead of Germany, France and the United Kingdom. In contrast, Canada moves down in the GDP ranking when PPP exchange rates are used.

5.3 FISHER EFFECT

Another parity condition we often encounter in the literature is the **Fisher effect**. The Fisher effect holds that *an increase (decrease) in the expected inflation rate will cause a proportionate increase (decrease) in the nominal interest rate.* Formally, the Fisher effect can be written as follows:

$$i_\$ = \rho_\$ + E(\pi_\$) + \rho_\$ E(\pi_\$) \approx \rho_\$ + E(\pi_\$) \tag{5.14}$$

where $\rho_\$$ denotes the equilibrium expected "real" interest rate in Canada.[11]

For example, suppose the expected real interest rate is 2 percent per year in Canada. Given this, the Canadian (nominal) interest rate will be entirely determined by expected inflation. If, for instance, the expected inflation rate is 4 percent per year, the nominal interest rate will then be about 6 percent. With a 6 percent interest rate, the lender will be compensated for the expected erosion of the purchasing power of money while still expecting to realize a 2 percent real return. The Fisher effect should hold in each country. The expected inflation rate is the difference between the nominal and real interest rates in each country, that is,

$$E(\pi_\$) = (i_\$ - \rho_\$)/(1 + \rho_\$) \approx i_\$ - \rho_\$$$
$$E(\pi_£) = (i_£ - \rho_£)/(1 + \rho_£) \approx i_£ - \rho_£$$

Now, let us assume that the real interest rate is the same between countries, that is, $\rho_\$ = \rho_£$, because of unrestricted capital flows. When we substitute the above results into the relative PPP in its expectational form in Equation 5.13, we obtain

$$E(e) = (i_\$ - i_£)/(1 + i_£) \approx i_\$ - i_£ \tag{5.15}$$

which is known as the **international Fisher effect (IFE)**.[12] IFE suggests that the nominal interest rate differential reflects the expected change in exchange rate. For instance, if the interest rate is 5 percent per year in Canada and 7 percent in the United Kingdom, the Canadian dollar is expected to appreciate against the British pound by about 2 percent per year.

Lastly, when the international Fisher effect is combined with IRP, that is,

$$(F - S)/S = (i_\$ - i_£)/(1 + i_£), \text{ we obtain}$$
$$(F - S)/S = E(e) \tag{5.16}$$

which is referred to as **forward expectations parity (FEP)**. Forward parity states that any forward premium or discount is equal to the expected change in the exchange rate. When investors are risk-neutral, forward parity will hold as long as the foreign exchange market is informationally efficient. Otherwise, it need not hold even if the market is efficient. Exhibit 5.11 summarizes the parity relationships discussed so far.[13]

---

[11] It is noted that Equation 5.15 obtains from the relationship $(1 + i_\$) = (1 + \rho_\$)(1 + E(\pi_\$))$.

[12] The international Fisher effect is the same as the uncovered IRP previously discussed. While the Fisher effect should hold in an efficient market, the international Fisher effect need not hold even in an efficient market unless investors are risk-neutral. Generally speaking, the interest rate differential may reflect not only the expected change in the exchange rate but also a risk premium.

[13] Suppose that the Fisher effect holds both in Canada and in the United Kingdom and that the real interest rate is the same in both the countries. As shown in Exhibit 5.11, the Fisher effect (FE) then implies that the interest rate differential should be equal to the expected inflation differential. Furthermore, when forward parity and PPP are combined, we obtain what might be called "forward-PPP" (FPPP), that is, the forward premium/discount is equal to the expected inflation differential.

EXHIBIT 5.11

International Parity
Relationships among
Exchange Rates,
Interest Rates and
Inflation Rates

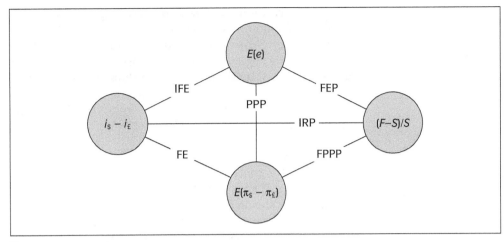

Notes:
1. With the assumption of the same real interest rate, the Fisher effect (FE) implies that the interest rate differential is equal to the expected inflation rate differential.
2. If both purchasing power parity (PPP) and forward expectations parity (FEP) hold, then the forward exchange premium or discount will be equal to the expected inflation rate differential. The latter relationship is denoted by the forward-PPP that is, FPPP, in the exhibit.
3. IFE stands for the international Fisher effect.

5.4   FORECASTING EXCHANGE RATES

http://fx.sauder.ubc.ca

Provides historical time
series of exchange rates.

In our world of flexible exchange rates, many business decisions must take account of forecasts of exchange rates. Understandably, forecasting exchange rates as accurately as possible is a matter of vital importance for currency traders who are actively engaged in speculating, hedging and arbitrage in the foreign exchange markets. It is also a vital concern for multinational corporations that are formulating international sourcing, production, financing and marketing strategies. The quality of these corporate decisions depends on the accuracy of exchange rate forecasts.

Some corporations generate their own forecasts, while others subscribe to outside services for a fee. While forecasters use a wide variety of forecasting techniques, most can be classified into three distinct approaches:

- Efficient market approach
- Fundamental approach
- Technical approach

Let us briefly examine each of these approaches.

Efficient Market Approach

Financial markets are said to be efficient if the current asset prices fully reflect all the available and relevant information. The **efficient market hypothesis (EMH)** has strong implications for forecasting.

If foreign exchange markets are efficient, the current exchange rate reflects all relevant information pertinent to the value of the exchange rate, such as money supplies, inflation rates, trade balances and output growth. The exchange rate will then change only when the market receives new information. Since news, by definition, is unpredictable, the exchange rate will change randomly over time. In other words, incremental changes in the exchange rate are independent of the past history of the exchange rate. If the exchange rate indeed follows a random walk, the future exchange rate is expected to be the same as the current exchange rate, that is,

$$S_t = E(S_{t+1})$$

In a sense, the **random walk hypothesis** suggests that today's exchange rate is the best predictor of tomorrow's exchange rate.

While researchers found it difficult to reject the random walk hypothesis for exchange rates on empirical grounds, there is no theoretical reason why exchange rates should follow a pure random walk. The parity relationships we discussed previously indicate that the current forward exchange rate can be viewed as the market's consensus forecast of the future exchange rate based on the available information (I_t) if the foreign exchange markets are efficient, that is,

$$F_t = E(S_{t+1} | I_t)$$

To the extent that interest rates are different between two countries, the forward exchange rate will be different from the current spot exchange rate. This means that the future exchange rate should be expected to be different from the current spot exchange rate.

Those who subscribe to the efficient market hypothesis may predict the future exchange rate using either the current spot exchange rate or the current forward exchange rate. But which one is better? Agmon and Amihud (1981) compared the performance of the forward exchange rate with that of the random walk model as a predictor of the future spot exchange rate. The forward exchange rate failed to outperform the random walk model in predicting the future exchange rate. The two prediction models based on the efficient market hypothesis registered largely comparable performances.

Predicting exchange rates using the efficient market approach has two advantages. First, since the efficient market approach is based on market-determined prices, it is costless to generate forecasts. Both the current spot and forward exchange rates are public information. As such, everyone has free access to it. Second, given the efficiency of foreign exchange markets, it is difficult to outperform the market-based forecasts unless the forecaster has access to private information that is not yet reflected in the current exchange rate.

Fundamental Approach

www.oecd.org

Provides macroeconomic data useful for fundamental analysis.

The "fundamental approach" to exchange rate forecasting is a much more complex and data-intensive exercise. Analysis of this type is typically done by large financial institutions, such as the Bank of Canada, or the research divisions of the commercial banks.

While there are many models of exchange rate behaviour, we will briefly outline one typical structure that reflects the idea that exchange rates are driven by monetary conditions and expectations of economic growth, as we outlined in Chapter 3.

The "model" takes the following form:

$$s = \alpha + \beta_1(m - m^*) + \beta_2(y - y^*) + u \qquad (5.17)$$

where

s = the rate of change of the spot exchange rate

m = the expected rate of growth of domestic money

m^* = the expected rate of growth of money in the foreign country

y = the expected rate of real economic growth in the domestic economy

y^* = the expected rate of real economic growth in the foreign economy

u = an error term

The theory underlying this model is twofold. First, the country that expands its money supply relatively faster will incur relatively more inflation and can expect to see its exchange rate fall. Second, the country that experiences relatively greater economic growth can expect its exchange rate to rise on that account. This latter effect indirectly works through a higher real interest in the more rapidly growing country, which attracts capital inflows and boosts the exchange rate.

The exchange rate is defined as units of domestic currency required to purchase one unit of the foreign currency. For example, if it takes \$1.20 to purchase one US dollar, the exchange rate is 1.20. With this "direct" quote, a higher exchange rate is simply a lower numerical value of the quote, say from \$1.20 to \$1.15 per US dollar. As a result, we would expect β_1 to be positive and β_2 to be negative. The model parameters β_1 and β_2 are estimated from the past history of the relationship between the rate of change of the exchange rate(s) and the explanatory variables, $(m - m^*)$ and $(y - y^*)$.

The application of the exchange rate forecasting model is a three-step process:

Step 1: Estimation of the structural model (Equation 5.17) to determine empirical values for the parameters, α, β_1 and β_2

Step 2: Estimation of future values of the independent explanatory variables m, m^*, y, and y^*

Step 3: Substitution of the estimated (forecast) values of the independent variables into the estimated structural model to generate the exchange rate forecast

If, for example, the forecaster wants to predict the rate of change of the exchange rate over the next year, he would estimate the values of the independent variables over the next year and substitute these explanatory variables into the structural model.

The fundamental approach to exchange rate forecasting has three main difficulties. First, one must forecast a set of independent variables to forecast exchange rates. Forecasting the former will certainly be subject to error. Second, the parameter values, that is, α and βs, that are estimated using historical data may change over time because of changes in government policies and/or the underlying structure of the economy. Either difficulty can diminish the accuracy of forecasts even if the model is correct. Third, the model itself can be wrong. For example, the model described by Equation 5.17 may be wrong. The forecast generated by a wrong model cannot be reliably accurate.

Not surprisingly, researchers found that the fundamental models failed to more accurately forecast exchange rates than either the forward rate or the random walk model. Meese and Rogoff (1983), for example, found that the fundamental models developed on the basis of the monetary approach did worse than the random walk even if realized (true) values were used for the independent variables. They also confirmed that the forward rate did not do better than a random walk. In the words of Meese and Rogoff:

> Ignoring for the present the fact that the spot rate does no worse than the forward rate, the striking feature . . . is that none of the models achieves lower, much less significantly lower, RMSE than the random walk model at any horizon. . . . The structural models in particular fail to improve on the random walk model in spite of the fact that their forecasts are based on realized values of the explanatory variables.[14] (p. 12)

Technical Approach

www.forexe.com

Provides information about technical analysis and currency charts.

The technical approach to exchange rate forecasting analyzes the past behaviour of exchange rates in a search for "patterns" and then projects these patterns into the future to generate forecasts. Clearly, the technical approach is based on the premise that *history repeats itself.* The technical approach, thus, is at odds with the efficient market approach. At the same time, it differs from the fundamental approach in that it does not use the key economic variables, such as money supplies or trade balances, for the purpose of forecasting. However, technical analysts sometimes consider various transaction data, such as trading volume, outstanding interests and bid-ask spreads, to aid their analyses.

---

[14]RMSE, which stands for root mean squared error, is the criterion that Meese and Rogoff used in evaluating the accuracy of forecasts.

EXHIBIT 5.12

Moving Average
Cross-over Rule:
A Technical
Analysis

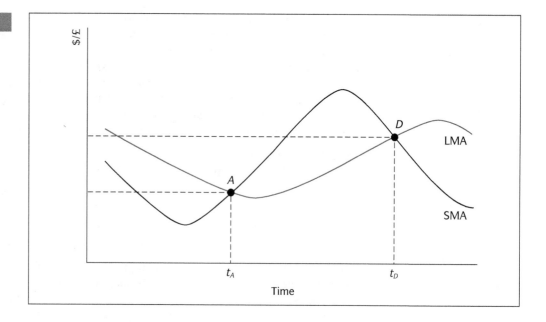

An example of technical analysis is provided by the moving average cross-over rule illustrated in Exhibit 5.12. Many technical analysts or chartists compute moving averages as a way of separating short- and long-term trends from the vicissitudes of daily exchange rates. The exhibit illustrates how exchange rates may be forecast on the basis of the movements of short- and long-term moving averages. Since the short-term moving average (SMA) weighs recent exchange rate changes more heavily than the long-term moving average (LMA), the SMA will lie below (above) the LMA when the British pound is falling (rising) against the dollar. This implies that one can forecast exchange rate movements on the basis of the cross-over of the moving averages. According to this rule, a cross-over of the SMA above the LMA at point A signals that the British pound is appreciating. On the other hand, a cross-over of the SMA below the LMA at point D signals that the British pound is depreciating.

While academic studies tend to discredit the validity of **technical analysis**, many traders depend on technical analyses for their trading strategies. If a trader knows that other traders use technical analysis, it can be rational for the trader to use technical analysis, too. If enough traders use technical analysis, the predictions based on it can become self-fulfilling to some extent, at least in the short run.

Performance of the Forecasters

Because predicting exchange rates is difficult, many firms and investors subscribe to professional forecasting services for a fee. Since an alternative to subscribing to professional forecasting services is to use a market-determined price, such as the forward exchange rate, it is relevant to ask: *Can professional forecasters outperform the market?*

An answer to the above question was provided by Richard Levich, who evaluated the performances of 13 forecasting services using the forward exchange rate as a benchmark. Under certain conditions, the forward exchange rate can be viewed as the market's consensus forecast of the future exchange rate.[15] These services use different methods of

---

[15]These conditions are: (a) the foreign exchange markets are efficient and (b) the forward exchange rate does not contain a significant risk premium.

forecasting, such as econometric, technical and judgmental. In evaluating the performance of forecasters, Levich computed the following ratio:

$$R = \text{MAE}(S)/\text{MAE}(F) \tag{5.18}$$

where

MAE(S) = mean absolute forecast error of a forecasting service

MAE(F) = mean absolute forecast error of the forward exchange rate as a predictor[16]

If a professional forecasting service provides more accurate forecasts than the forward exchange rate, that is, MAE(S) < MAE(F), then the ratio R will be less than unity for the service. If the service fails to outperform the forward exchange rate, the ratio R will be greater than unity.

Exhibit 5.13 provides the R ratios for each service for the US dollar exchange rates of nine major foreign currencies for a three-month forecasting horizon. The most striking finding presented in the exhibit is that only 24 percent of the entries, 25 out of 104, are less than unity. This, of course, means that the professional services as a whole clearly failed to outperform the forward exchange rate.[17] In other words, they failed to beat the market.

However, there are substantial variations in the performance records across individual services. In the cases of services 4 and 11, for instance, every entry is greater than unity.

EXHIBIT 5.13 Performance of Exchange Rate Forecasting Services

Currency	\multicolumn{13}{c}{Forecasting Services}
	1	2	3	4	5	6	7	8	9	10	11	12	13
Canadian dollar	1.29	1.13	1.00	1.59	0.99	1.08	n.a.	1.47	1.17	1.03	1.47	1.74	0.80
British pound	1.11	1.24	0.91	1.44	1.09	0.98	1.05	1.09	1.27	1.69	1.03	1.22	1.01
Belgian franc	0.95	1.07	n.a.	1.33	1.17	n.a.	n.a.	0.99	1.21	n.a.	1.06	1.01	0.77
French franc	0.91	0.98	1.02	1.43	1.27	n.a.	0.98	0.92	1.00	0.96	1.03	1.16	0.70
German mark	1.08	1.13	1.07	1.28	1.19	1.35	1.06	0.83	1.19	1.07	1.13	1.04	0.76
Italian lira	1.07	0.91	1.09	1.45	1.14	n.a.	1.12	1.12	1.00	1.17	1.64	1.54	0.93
Dutch guilder	0.80	1.10	n.a.	1.41	1.06	n.a.	n.a.	0.91	1.26	1.26	1.10	1.01	0.81
Swiss franc	1.01	n.a.	1.08	1.21	1.32	n.a.	n.a.	0.86	1.06	1.04	1.04	0.94	0.63
Japanese yen	1.42	1.05	1.02	1.23	1.08	1.45	1.09	1.24	0.94	0.47	1.31	1.30	1.79

Note: Each entry represents the R ratio defined in Equation 5.18. If a forecasting service outperforms (underperforms) the forward exchange rate, the R ratio will be less (greater) than unity.

Source: Richard Levich, "Evaluating the Performance of the Forecasters," in Richard Ensor, ed., *The Management of Foreign Exchange Risk,* 2nd ed. (London, UK: Euromoney Publications, 1982).

[16]The mean absolute forecast error (MAE) is computed as follows:

MAE = $\Sigma_i |P_i - A_i|/n$

where P is the predicted exchange rate, A is the actual (realized) exchange rate, and n is the number of forecasts made. The MAE criterion penalizes the over- and underestimation equally. If a forecaster has perfect foresight so that $P = A$ always, then MAE will be zero.

[17]Levich found that the same qualitative result holds for different horizons like 1 month, 6 months and 12 months.

In contrast, for service 13, which is Wharton Econometric Forecasting Associates, the majority of entries, seven out of nine, are less than unity. It is also clear from the exhibit that the performance record of each service varies substantially across currencies. The R ratio for Wharton, for example, ranges from 0.63 for the Swiss franc to 1.79 for the Japanese yen. Wharton Associates clearly has difficulty in forecasting the dollar/yen exchange rate. Service 10, on the other hand, convincingly beat the market in forecasting the yen exchange rate, with an R ratio of 0.47! This suggests that consumers need to discriminate among forecasting services depending on what currencies they are interested in. Lastly, note that service 12, which is known to use technical analysis, outperformed neither the forward rate nor other services. This result certainly does not add credence to the technical approach to exchange rate forecasting.

In a more recent study, Eun and Sabherwal (2002) evaluated the forecasting performances of 10 major commercial banks from around the world. They used the data from *Risk*, a London-based monthly publication dealing with practical issues related to derivative securities and risk management. During the period April 1989 to February 1993, *Risk* published forecasts provided by the banks for exchange rates 3, 6, 9 and 12 months ahead. These forecasts were made for the American dollar exchange rates of the British pound, German mark, Swiss franc and Japanese yen on the same day of the month by all the banks. This is a rare case where banks' exchange rate forecasts were made available to the public. Since commercial banks are the market makers as well as key players in foreign exchange markets, they should be in a position to observe the order flows and the market sentiments closely. It is thus interesting to check how these banks perform.

In evaluating the performance of the banks, Eun and Sabherwal used the spot exchange rate as the benchmark. Recall that if you believe the exchange rate follows a random walk, today's spot exchange rate can be taken as the prediction of the future spot exchange rate. They thus computed the forecasting accuracy of each bank and compared it with that of the current spot exchange rate, that is, the rate prevailing on the day when forecast is made. In evaluating the performance of banks, they computed the following ratio:

$$R = MSE(B)/MSE(S)$$

where

MSE(B) = mean squared forecast error of a bank

MSE(S) = mean squared forecast error of the spot exchange rate

If a bank provides more accurate forecasts than the spot exchange rate, that is, MSE(B) < MSE(S), then the ratio R will be less than unity, that is, $R < 1$.

Exhibit 5.14 provides the computed R ratios for each of the 10 sample banks as well as the forward exchange rate. Overall, the majority of entries in the exhibit exceed unity, implying that these banks as a whole could not outperform the random walk model. However, some banks significantly outperformed the random walk model, especially in the longer run. For example, in forecasting the British pound exchange rate 12 months into the future, Barclays Bank ($R = 0.60$), Commerz Bank ($R = 0.72$) and Industrial Bank of Japan ($R = 0.68$) provided more accurate forecasts, on average, than the random walk model. Likewise, Commerz Bank outperformed the random walk model in forecasting the German mark and Swiss franc rates 12 months into the future. But these are more exceptional cases. It is noted that no bank, including the Japanese bank, could beat the random walk model in forecasting the Japanese yen rate at any lead. The last column of Exhibit 5.14 shows that the R-ratio for the forward exchange rate is about unity, implying that the performance of the forward rate is comparable with that of the spot rate.

EXHIBIT 5.14 Forecasting Exchange Rates: Do Banks Know Better?

Currency	Forecast Lead (months)	ANZ Bank (Australia)	Banque-Paribas (France)	Barclays Bank (United Kingdom)	Chemical Bank (US)	Commerz Bank (Germany)	Generale Bank (France)	Harris Bank (U.S)	Ind. Bank of Japan (Japan)	Midland-Montagu (United Kingdom)	Union Bank (Switzerland)	Forward Rate
British pound	3	2.09	1.31	1.08	1.33	1.31	1.41	1.95	1.10	1.10	0.98	1.02
	6	1.60	1.12	0.92	0.96	1.01	1.17	1.97	0.94	1.11	0.96	1.04
	9	1.42	1.04	0.81	0.88	0.78	0.97	1.65	0.81	0.99	1.09	0.83
	12	**1.06**	**0.84**	**0.60**	**1.07**	**0.72**	**0.77**	**1.69**	**0.68**	**0.95**	**1.16**	**1.02**
German mark	3	1.98	1.39	1.09	1.19	1.59	1.39	1.95	1.14	1.26	1.00	1.01
	6	1.15	1.53	1.16	1.03	1.21	1.21	1.97	1.07	1.27	1.05	1.00
	9	0.92	1.45	1.33	0.99	0.85	0.96	1.71	1.00	1.09	0.93	1.06
	12	**0.80**	**1.19**	**1.14**	**1.16**	**0.62**	**0.97**	**1.51**	**1.00**	**0.87**	**1.16**	**0.96**
Swiss franc	3	2.15	1.47	1.13	1.26	1.66	1.32	1.98	1.05	1.19	1.03	1.02
	6	1.18	1.58	1.30	0.98	1.29	1.35	1.88	1.04	1.24	1.05	1.00
	9	0.88	1.46	1.38	0.84	0.96	1.10	1.66	0.96	1.13	0.87	0.99
	12	**0.67**	**1.16**	**1.15**	**0.88**	**0.74**	**1.01**	**1.40**	**0.91**	**0.98**	**1.01**	**0.94**
Japanese yen	3	3.52	2.31	1.46	1.44	1.73	2.19	2.51	1.52	2.16	1.80	1.08
	6	2.32	2.43	1.55	1.39	1.59	1.62	2.31	1.62	1.68	1.70	1.06
	9	2.54	2.73	1.80	1.57	1.60	1.85	2.22	1.90	1.74	1.97	0.99
	12	**2.70**	**2.61**	**1.83**	**1.79**	**1.44**	**1.97**	**1.89**	**1.93**	**1.68**	**2.00**	**1.10**

Source: Cheol Eun and Sanjiv Sabherwal, "Forecasting Exchange Rates: Do Banks Know Better?" *Global Finance Journal* (2002), pp. 195–215.

SUMMARY

This chapter provides a systematic discussion of the key international parity relationships and two related issues, exchange rate determination and prediction. A thorough understanding of parity relationships is essential for astute financial management.

1. Interest rate parity (IRP) holds that the forward premium or discount should be equal to the interest rate differential between two countries. IRP represents a zero-arbitrage equilibrium condition that should hold in the absence of barriers to international capital flows.

2. If IRP is violated, one can lock in guaranteed profit by borrowing in one currency and lending in another, with exchange risk hedged via a forward contract. As a result of this covered interest arbitrage, IRP will be restored.

3. IRP implies that in the short run, the exchange rate depends on (a) the relative interest rates between two countries and (b) the expected future exchange rate. Other things being equal, a higher (lower) domestic interest rate will lead to appreciation (depreciation) of the domestic currency. People's expectations concerning future exchange rates are self-fulfilling.

4. Purchasing power parity (PPP) states that the exchange rate between two countries' currencies should be equal to the ratio of their price levels. PPP is a manifestation of the Law of One Price applied internationally to a standard commodity basket. The relative version of PPP states that the rate of change in the exchange rate should be equal to the inflation rate differential between countries. The existing empirical evidence, however, is generally negative on PPP. This implies that substantial barriers to international commodity arbitrage exist.

5. There are three distinct approaches to exchange rate forecasting: (a) the efficient market approach, (b) the fundamental approach and (c) the technical approach. The efficient market approach uses such market-determined prices as the current exchange rate or the forward exchange rate to forecast the future exchange rate. The fundamental approach uses various formal models of exchange rate determination for forecasting purposes. The technical approach, on the other hand, identifies patterns from the past history of the exchange rate and projects it into the future. Empirical evidence indicates that neither the fundamental nor the technical approach outperforms the efficient market approach.

QUESTIONS

1. Give a full definition of *arbitrage*.
2. Discuss the implications of interest rate parity for exchange rate determination.
3. Explain the conditions under which the forward exchange rate will be an unbiased predictor of the future spot exchange rate.
4. Explain purchasing power parity, both the absolute and relative versions. What causes deviations from purchasing power parity?
5. Discuss the implications of the deviations from purchasing power parity for countries' competitive positions in the world market.
6. Explain and derive the international Fisher effect.
7. Researchers found that it is very difficult to forecast future exchange rates more accurately than the forward exchange rate or the current spot exchange rate. How would you interpret this finding?
8. Explain the random walk model for exchange rate forecasting. Can it be consistent with technical analysis?
9. Derive and explain the monetary approach to exchange rate determination.
10. **CFA® PROBLEMS** Explain the following three concepts of purchasing power parity (PPP):
   a. The Law of One Price
   b. Absolute PPP
   c. Relative PPP
11. **CFA® PROBLEMS** Evaluate the usefulness of relative PPP in predicting movements in foreign exchange rates on a
   a. Short-term basis (e.g., three months)
   b. Long-term basis (e.g., six years)

PROBLEMS

1. Suppose that the treasurer of Weston's has an extra cash reserve of $10 million to invest for six months. The six-month interest rate is 4 percent per annum in Canada and 5 percent per annum in Germany. Currently, the spot exchange rate is €0.65 per dollar and the six-month forward exchange rate is €0.66 per dollar. The treasurer of Weston's does not wish to bear any exchange risk. Where should he invest?

2. While you were visiting Paris, you purchased a Renault for €10,000, payable in three months. You

have enough cash at your bank in Vancouver, which pays 0.35 percent interest per month, compounding monthly, to pay for the car. Currently, the spot exchange rate is $1.45/€ and the three-month forward exchange rate is $1.40/€. In Paris, the money market interest rate is 2 percent for a three-month investment. There are two alternative ways of paying for your Renault.

a. Keep the funds at your bank in Canada and buy €10,000 forward.

b. Buy a certain euro amount spot today and invest the amount in Europe for three months so that the maturity value becomes equal to €10,000. Evaluate each payment method. Which method would you prefer? Why?

3. Currently, the spot exchange rate is $1.50/€ and the three-month forward exchange rate is $1.49/€. The three-month interest rate is 4 percent per annum in Canada and 5 percent per annum in Europe. Assume that you can borrow as much as $1,500,000 or €1,000,000.

a. Determine whether interest rate parity is currently holding.

b. If IRP is not holding, how would you carry out covered interest arbitrage? Show all the steps and determine the arbitrage profit.

c. Explain how IRP will be restored as a result of covered arbitrage activities.

4. Suppose that the current spot exchange rate is €0.65/$ and the three-month forward exchange rate is €0.64/$. The three-month interest rate is 5.6 percent per annum in Canada and 5.40 percent per annum in France. Assume that you can borrow up to $1,000,000 or €1,060,000.

a. Show how to realize a certain profit via covered interest arbitrage, assuming that you want to realize profit in terms of dollars. Also determine the size of your arbitrage profit.

b. Assume that you want to realize profit in terms of euros. Show the covered arbitrage process and determine the arbitrage profit in euros.

5. *The Economist* reports that the interest rate per annum is 5 percent in Canada and 50 percent in Turkey. Why do you think the interest rate is so high in Turkey? On the basis of the reported interest rates, how would you predict the change of the exchange rate between the Canadian dollar and the Turkish lira?

6. As of 1 November 2007, the exchange rate between the Brazilian real and the US dollar was R$2.10/$. The consensus forecast for the US and Brazil inflation rates for the next one-year period was 3 percent and 15 percent, respectively. What would you forecast the exchange rate to have been at around 1 November 2008?

7. Omni Advisors, an international pension fund manager, uses the concepts of purchasing power parity (PPP) and the international Fisher effect (IFE) to forecast spot exchange rates. Omni gathers the financial information as follows:

Base price level	100
Current Canadian price level	105
Current South African price level	111
Base rand spot exchange rate	$0.175
Current rand spot exchange rate	$0.158
Expected annual Canadian inflation	7%
Expected annual South African inflation	5%
Expected Canadian one-year interest rate	10%
Expected South African one-year interest rate	8%

Calculate the following exchange rates (ZAR refers to the South African rand):

a. The current ZAR spot rate in dollars that would have been forecast by PPP

b. Using the IFE, the expected ZAR spot rate in dollars one year from now

c. Using PPP, the expected ZAR spot rate in dollars four years from now

8. Suppose that the current spot exchange rate is €1.50/£ and the one-year forward exchange rate is €1.60/£. The one-year interest rate is 5.4 percent in euros and 5.2 percent in pounds. You can borrow at most €1,000,000 or the equivalent pound amount, that is, £666,667, at the current spot exchange rate.

a. Show how you can realize a guaranteed profit from covered interest arbitrage. Assume that you are a euro-based investor. Also determine the size of the arbitrage profit.

b. Discuss how interest rate parity may be restored as a result of the above transactions.

c. Suppose you are a pound-based investor. Show the covered arbitrage process and determine the pound profit amount.

9. Due to the integrated nature of their capital markets, investors in both Canada and the United Kingdom require the same real interest rate, 2.5 percent, on their lending. There is a consensus in capital markets that the annual inflation rate is likely to be 3.5 percent in Canada and 1.5 percent in the United Kingdom for the next three years. The spot exchange rate is currently $2.30/£.

a. Compute the nominal interest rate per annum in both Canada and the United Kingdom, assuming that the Fisher effect holds.

b. What is your expected future spot dollar–pound exchange rate in three years from now?

c. Can you infer the forward dollar–pound exchange rate for one-year maturity?

	Spot	1 mo.	3 mo.	6 mo.	1 yr.	2 yr.	3 yr.	4 yr.	5 yr.
US$	0.9340	0.9343	0.9350	0.9370	0.9418	0.9501	0.9569	0.9608	0.9603
Euro	1.4411	1.4414	1.4423	1.4435	1.4454	1.4563	1.4646	1.4751	1.4961
Yen	115.42	115.20	114.78	114.18	112.89	109.96	107.04	103.99	100.76
£	2.1382	2.1343	2.1259	2.1131	2.0902	2.0570	2.0339	2.0148	2.0128

10. Spot and forward foreign exchange quotes for the Canadian dollar against four major currencies are recorded above for 26 June 2007.

    US$ and yen are direct quotes—foreign currency units per Canadian dollar.

    Euro and British pound are indirect quotes—Canadian dollars per unit of foreign currency.

    a. According to the forward rate structure, which currencies are expected to appreciate against the Canadian dollar over the next year? Explain briefly.

    b. According to the forward rate structure, which currencies are expected to depreciate against the Canadian dollar over the next year? Explain briefly.

    c. For each case, express the expected currency appreciation (or depreciation) in annual terms.

11. On the same day as mentioned in problem 10, the yield on Canadian six-month Treasury bills (annual terms) was 4.71 percent.

    The corresponding yield on US six-month Treasury bills (in US dollars) was 4.96 percent.

    Does interest rate parity hold between Canada and the US in view of the difference in six-month Treasury bill rates? Explain the difference, if any.

12. Where should an investor invest, Canada or the United States? Explain.

13. Assume that US–Canada six-month interest rate parity holds on a net-of-cost basis. What does your analysis imply about the cost of obtaining forward cover?

14. Record the accuracy of the forward rates on 26 June 2007 as a predictor of the spot rates for the most recent relevant date for the reader today. For instance, if today is 1 July 2008, the (one year) forward rates observed on 26 June 2007 imply the following expected exchange rates on 26 June 2008.

US$	0.9418
Euro	1.4454
Yen	112.89
£	2.0902

Find the spot rates on 26 June 2008 (or closest) and compare to the one-year forward rates observed on 26 June 2007. Compute the errors *vis-à-vis* the (forward rate) forecast implied by the forward rates observed on 26 June 2007.

(The results of this exercise depend on the time-specific data collected to answer the questions.)

15. The one-year Canadian Treasury bill rate is 4.71 percent. In view of the observed spot and one-year forward foreign exchange rates for the euro, British pound and Japanese yen, what are respectively the interest-rate-parity-satisfying one-year Treasury bill rates in Europe, Britain and Japan? Ignore transactions costs.

INTERNET EXERCISE

You provide foreign exchange consulting services based on technical (chartist) analysis. Your client would like to have a good idea about the Canadian dollar and Mexican peso exchange rate six months into the future. First plot the past exchange rates and try to identify patterns that can be projected into the future. What forecast exchange rate would you offer to your client? You may download exchange rate data from http://fx.sauder.ubc.ca/.

MINI CASE

Turkish Lira and Purchasing Power Parity

Veritas Emerging Market Fund specializes in investing in the emerging stock markets of the world. Mr. Henry Mobaus, an experienced hand in international investment and your boss, is currently interested in Turkish stock markets. He thinks that Turkey will eventually be invited to negotiate its membership in the European Union. If this happens, it will boost stock prices in Turkey. But, at the same time, he is quite concerned with the volatile exchange rates of the Turkish currency. He would like to understand what drives Turkish exchange rates. Since the inflation rate is much higher in Turkey than in the United States, he thinks that purchasing power parity may be holding at least to some extent. As a research assistant for him, you are assigned to check this out. In other words, you have to study and prepare a report on the following question: Does purchasing power parity hold for the Turkish lira–US dollar exchange rate? Among other things, Mr. Mobaus would like you to do the following:

1. Plot past exchange rate changes against the differential inflation rates between Turkey and the United States for the last four years

2. Regress the rate of exchange rate changes on the inflation rate differential to estimate the intercept and the slope coefficient, and interpret the regression results

Data sources: You may download consumer price index data for the United States and Turkey from the following website: http://www.oecd.org/. You may download exchange rate data from the website http://fx.sauder. ubc.ca/.

REFERENCES & SUGGESTED READINGS

Abuaf, N., and P. Jorion. "Purchasing Power Parity in the Long Run." *Journal of Finance* 45 (1990), pp. 157–74.

Alexius, A., and J. Nilsson. "Real Exchange Rate Fundamentals: Evidence from 15 OECD Countries." *Open Economies Review* 11 (2000), pp. 383–97.

Aliber, R. "The Interest Rate Parity: A Reinterpretation." *Journal of Political Economy* (1973), pp. 1451–59.

Adler, Michael, and Bruce Lehman. "Deviations from Purchasing Power Parity in the Long Run." *Journal of Finance* 38 (1983), pp. 1471–87.

Agmon, T., and Y. Amihud. "The Forward Exchange Rate and the Prediction of the Future Spot Rate." *Journal of Banking and Finance* 5 (1981), pp. 425–37.

Baillie, Richard T., and Tim Bollerslev. "The Forward Premium Anomaly Is Not as Bad as You Think." *Journal of International Money and Finance* (August 2000), pp. 471–88.

Baxter, M. "Real Exchange Rates and Real Interest Differentials: Have We Missed the Business Cycle Relationship?" *Journal of Monetary Economics* 33 (1994), pp. 5–37.

Brean, D.J.S. "International Portfolio Capital: The Wedge of the Withholding Tax." *National Tax Journal* (June 1984), pp. 239–47.

Chadha, B., and E. Prasad. "Real Exchange Rate Fluctuations and the Business Cycle." *IMF Staff Papers* 44 (1997), pp. 328–55.

Frankel, Jeffrey. "Flexible Exchange Rate: Experience versus Theory." *Journal of Portfolio Management* (Winter 1989), pp. 45–54.

Frenkel, Jacob. "Flexible Exchange Rates, Prices and the Role of News: Lessons from the 1970s." *Journal of Political Economy* 89 (1981), pp. 665–705.

Frenkel, Jacob, and Richard Levich. "Covered Interest Arbitrage: Unexploited Profits?" *Journal of Political Economy* 83 (1975), pp. 325–38.

Froot, Kenneth A., and Richard H. Thaler. "Anomalies: Foreign Exchange." *Journal of Economic Perspectives* (Summer 1990), pp. 179–92.

Gauthier, Céline, and David Tessier. "Supply Shocks and Real Exchange Dynamics: Canadian Evidence." Bank of Canada Working Paper (Monetary and Financial Analysis Department) 2002–31, November 2002.

Keynes, John M. *Monetary Reform.* New York: Harcourt Brace, 1924.

Kravis, I., and R. Lipsey. "Price Behavior in the Light of Balance of Payment Theories." *Journal of International Economics* (1978), pp. 193–246.

Lafrance, Robert, and Pierre St-Amant. "Real Exchange Rate Indexes for the Canadian Dollar." *Bank of Canada Review* (Autumn 1999), pp. 19–28.

Lafrance, Robert, and Pierre St-Amant. "Exchange Rate Fundamentals and the Canadian Dollar." *Bank of Canada Review* (Autumn 1995), pp. 17–33.

Larsen, Glen, and Bruce Resnick. "International Parity Relationships and Tests for Risk Premia in Forward Foreign Exchange Rates." *Journal of International Financial Markets, Institutions and Money* 3 (1993), pp. 33–56.

Levich, Richard. "Evaluating the Performance of the Forecasters," in Richard Ensor, ed., *The Management of Foreign Exchange Risk,* 2nd ed. London, UK: Euromoney Publications, 1982, pp. 121–34.

Lothian, James R., and Mark P. Taylor. "Real Exchange Rate Behavior: The Recent Float from the Perspective of the Past Two Centuries." *Journal of Political Economy* (June 1996).

Meese, Richard, and Kenneth Rogoff. "Empirical Exchange Rate Models of the Seventies: Do They Fit out of Sample?" *Journal of International Economics* 14 (1983), pp. 3–24.

Mishkin, Frederick S. "Are Real Interest Rates Equal across Countries? An International Investigation of Parity Conditions." *Journal of Finance* (December 1984), pp. 1345–57.

Richardson, J. "Some Empirical Evidence on Commodity Arbitrage and the Law of One Price." *Journal of International Economics* 8 (1978), pp. 341–52.

Appendix 5

Purchasing Power Parity and Exchange Rate Determination

Although PPP itself can be viewed as a theory of exchange rate determination, it also serves as a foundation for a more complete theory, namely the **monetary approach**. The monetary approach is based on two basic tenets: purchasing power parity and the quantity theory of money.

From the **quantity theory of money**, we obtain the following identity that must hold in each country:

$$P_\$ = M_\$ V_\$ / y_\$$$
$$P_£ = M_£ V_£ / y_£$$

where M denotes the money supply, V the velocity of money, measuring the speed at which money is being circulated in the economy, y the national aggregate output and P the general price level; the subscripts denote countries. When the above equations are substituted for the price levels in the PPP Equation 5.11, we obtain the following expression for the exchange rate:

$$S = (M_\$/M_£)(V_\$/V_£)(y_£/y_\$)$$

According to the monetary approach, what matters in the exchange rate determination are

1. The relative money supplies
2. The relative velocities of money
3. The relative national outputs

All else equal, an increase in the Canadian money supply will result in a proportionate depreciation of the Canadian dollar against the pound. So will an increase in the velocity of the dollar, which has the same effect as an increased supply of dollars. But an increase in the rate of growth of Canadian GDP output will result in a proportionate appreciation of the dollar.

The monetary approach, which is based on PPP, can be viewed as a long-run theory, not a short-run theory, of exchange rate determination. This is so because the monetary approach does not allow for price rigidities. It assumes that prices adjust fully and completely, which is unrealistic in the short run. Prices of many commodities and services are often fixed over a certain period of time. A good example of short-term price rigidity is the wage rate set by a labour contract. Despite this apparent shortcoming, the monetary approach remains an influential theory and serves as a benchmark in modern exchange rate economics.

Part 2

World Financial Markets and Institutions

Part Two provides a thorough discussion of international financial institutions, assets and marketplaces, and develops the tools necessary to manage exchange rate uncertainty.

6 International Banking and Money Market

Chapter 6 distinguishes international from domestic bank operations and examines the institutional differences of various types of international banking offices. International banks and their clients constitute the Eurocurrency market and form the core of the international money market.

7 International Bond Market

Chapter 7 distinguishes foreign and Eurobonds which together make up the international bond market. The advantages of sourcing funds from the international bond market as opposed to raising funds domestically are discussed. A discussion of the major types of international bonds is included in the chapter.

8 International Equity Markets

Chapter 8 covers international equity markets. The chapter begins with statistical documentation of the size of equity markets in both developed and developing countries. Various methods of trading equity shares in the secondary markets are discussed. The chapter examines the advantages to the firm of cross-listing equity shares in more than one country.

9 Futures and Options on Foreign Exchange

Chapter 9 provides an extensive treatment of exchange-traded currency futures and options contracts. Basic valuation models are developed.

10 Interest Rate and Currency Swaps

Chapter 10 covers currency and interest rate swaps.

11 International Portfolio Investment

Chapter 11 covers international portfolio investment. It documents that the potential benefits from international diversification are available to all national investors.

Chapter 6

International Banking and Money Market

CHAPTER OUTLINE

"WORLD" FINANCIAL MARKETS involve a global network of financial institutions that facilitate the financing of international trade and foreign investment. Banks are the major players. Whenever business crosses borders or whenever one currency is exchanged for another, a bank or a combination of banks is there to facilitate the international financial transactions.

To begin discussion of world financial markets and institutions, we take up two fundamental topics—international banking and international money market operations.

We open this chapter with an outline of the services provided by international banks for their corporate clients. While any bank could be termed "international" if it offers such services as currency exchange or foreign currency deposits, a more substantial criterion of being "international" is whether the bank has a network of branches or subsidiaries abroad. The major Canadian banks, we shall see, easily meet this test. Likewise, many foreign banks maintain permanent operations in Canada.

The second part of the chapter focuses on the Eurocurrency market, the creation of Eurocurrency deposits by international banks and the nature of Eurocurrency loans. We explain Euronotes, Eurocommercial paper and forward rate agreements. The prefix "Euro" in these expressions is no longer literal. It is a carryover from a time when international finance sought out the relatively unregulated financial environment of Europe to avoid domestic banking regulations, especially on the part of US-based international business. "Euro" is now understood to refer to financial instruments that are subject to the financial regulations of no specific country.

Eurofinancial instruments are denominated in major currencies. The distinguishing characteristic is that the financial instrument is issued in a country other than the country from which the currency is derived. For example, if Siemens of Germany issues commercial paper denominated in US dollars and the paper is bought by the Barclays Bank of England, these are US dollar Eurotransactions. It would still be a US dollar Euro issue even if US-owned CitiBank bought some of the Siemens paper.

6.1 INTERNATIONAL BANKING SERVICES

Multinational business is multicurrency business. When Toronto-based Four Seasons receives foreign hotel earnings in US dollars, euros or yen, the "banking" of those foreign funds is done by Canadian banks chosen by Four Seasons. In the evolution of international business—such as Four Seasons but also Barrick's offshore gold mining, McCain Foods operations around the world or CN's major expansion into the United States—domestic banks tend to travel hand in hand internationally with the industrial companies that they serve. Whereas the industrial companies know how to establish hotels or how to operate mines, food processing plants or transportation systems, they turn to banks to provide deposit accounts in various local currencies and to facilitate such transactions as converting foreign earnings into Canadian dollars. Domestic banks that have been involved with non-financial companies for many years generally continue to provide banking services when these companies venture abroad. This, of course, requires the domestic banks to establish their own operating facilities abroad.

The major features that distinguish international banks from strictly domestic banks are the types of deposits that they accept and the currency-denomination of the investments they make. International banks borrow (by accepting deposits), lend and intermediate in a variety of currencies. International banks facilitate their clients' export and import operations by arranging trade finance. When, for example, Inniskillin Wines of Niagara exports a million dollar shipment of ice wine to France, an international bank—perhaps the Bank of Nova Scotia through its branch in Paris—will receive the French importer's payment in euros and convert these funds into Canadian dollars, all the while attending to important legal and contractual matters to secure the wine delivery through its various steps.

In the finance of international trade, banks often assist clients in hedging exchange rate risk in foreign currency receivables and payables through forward and options contracts. The advisory services of international banks to their corporate clients extend to cash management, project financing and a range of risk management services.

With their skills and systems to deal in foreign exchange for clients, international banks also trade currencies and foreign exchange products for their own account. Virtually all international trade finance and payments on international investments ultimately flow through international banks. The global network of banks involved in foreign currency operations gives rise to an enormous volume of interbank foreign currency transactions and the network "makes the market" in foreign currencies. Spot rates, forward rates and the various intercurrency products that are priced off exchange rates and their risks, such as options and futures, are determined in markets in which international banks carry out essentially all the transactions.

International banks frequently form loan syndicates wherein several banks team up to lend large sums to multinational corporations (MNCs) for investment and project financing or to sovereign governments that go to the global markets to issue bonds.

The World's Largest Banks

Exhibit 6.1 lists the world's 30 largest banks ranked by total assets. The exhibit shows total assets, net income, and market value in billions of U.S. dollars. The exhibit indicates that 5 of the world's 30 largest banks are from the United States; 4 are from Australia; 3 each are from Canada, China, Japan, and the United Kingdom; 2 each are from Brazil, France, Italy, and Spain; and, 1 is from Germany.

From Exhibit 6.1, one might correctly surmise that the world's major international finance centres are New York, London, Tokyo, Paris, and increasingly Sydney and Beijing. London, New York, and Tokyo, however, are by far the most important international finance centres because of the relatively liberal banking regulations of their respective countries, the size of their economies, and the importance of their currencies in international transactions. These three financial centres are frequently referred to as *full service centres* because the major banks that operate in them usually provide a full range of services.

One tier below London, New York and Tokyo, we have a larger number of important regional financial centres, including Frankfurt, Paris, Zurich, Singapore, Hong Kong, Johannesburg, Beirut and Buenos Aires. Toronto fits nicely into this second tier given its importance as the financial centre of Canada with strong ties to world markets.

EXHIBIT 6.1

The World's
30 Largest Banks
(in Billions of U.S.
Dollars, as of
April 2012)

Rank	Bank	Country	Total Assets	Net Income	Market Value
1	Deutsche Bank	Germany	2,809.4	5.4	47.3
2	HSBC Holdings	United Kingdom	2,550.0	16.2	164.3
3	BNP Paribas	France	2,539.1	7.9	61.5
4	Mitsubishi UFJ Financial	Japan	2,478.8	7.0	74.5
5	Barclays	United Kingdom	2,425.2	4.7	49.1
6	JPMorgan Chase	USA	2,265.8	19.0	170.1
7	Bank of America	USA	2,129.0	1.4	105.2
8	ICBC	China	2,039.1	25.1	237.4
9	Mizuho Financial	Japan	1,934.4	5.0	40.6
10	Citigroup	USA	1,837.9	11.1	107.5
11	Sumitomo Mitsui Financial	Japan	1,654.9	5.7	47.8
12	Banco Santander	Spain	1,624.7	6.9	75.6
13	Bank of China	China	1,583.7	15.8	129.1
14	Société Générale	France	1,531.1	3.3	25.8
15	Wells Fargo	USA	1,313.9	15.9	178.7
16	UniCredit Group	Italy	1,231.8	1.6	31.8
17	Intesa Sanpaolo	Italy	875.7	3.6	33.9
18	Royal Bank of Canada	Canada	812.7	4.7	84.4
19	TD Bank	Canada	771.5	5.8	76.1
20	BBVA-Banco Bilbao Vizcaya	Spain	767.7	3.9	43.1
21	National Australia Bank	Australia	730.4	5.0	56.3
22	Commonwealth Bank	Australia	713.7	6.9	81.6
23	Westpac Banking Group	Australia	651.7	7.2	67.5
24	Bank of Nova Scotia	Canada	635.2	5.3	62.2
25	Standard Chartered	United Kingdom	598.7	4.7	62.5
26	Bank of Communications	China	598.5	5.9	48.8
27	ANZ	Australia	577.2	5.2	62.6
28	Bando do Brasil	Brazil	516.3	6.5	45.9
29	Itaú Unibanco Holding	Brazil	426.4	7.4	91.2
30	US Bancorp	USA	340.1	4.9	60.5

Source: Compiled from Forbes.com. Global 2000: World's Biggest Public Companies. www.forbes.com/global2000.

6.2   TYPES OF INTERNATIONAL BANKING OFFICES

The services and operations of international banks are a function of the regulatory environment in which the bank operates and the type of banking facility established. Following is a discussion of the major types of international banking offices, detailing the purpose of each and the regulatory rationale for its existence. The discussion moves from correspondent bank relationships, through which minimal service is provided to bank customers, to a description of offices providing a fuller array of services, to a description of those established in order to minimize restrictions on international finance.

Correspondent Bank Relationships

Large banks generally have correspondent relationships with other banks in the major financial centres in which they do not have their own operations. **A correspondent bank relationship** is established when two banks maintain a correspondent bank account with one another. For example, a large Canadian bank could have a correspondent bank in Vienna, and the Viennese bank could maintain a correspondent relationship with the Canadian bank.

The correspondent banking system enables a bank's MNC clients to conduct business worldwide through the firm's local bank or its contacts. Correspondent banking services centre around foreign exchange conversions that arise through the international transactions the MNC makes. However, correspondent bank services also include assistance with trade financing, such as honouring letters of credit and accepting drafts drawn on the correspondent bank. An MNC needing foreign local financing for one of its subsidiaries may rely on its local bank to provide it with a letter of introduction to the correspondent bank in the foreign country.

The correspondent bank relationship is beneficial because it enables a bank to service its MNC clients at low cost and without the need of bank personnel physically located in many countries. A disadvantage is that the bank's clients may not receive the level of service through the correspondent bank that they would if the bank had its own foreign facilities to service its clients.

Representative Offices

A **representative office** is a small service facility staffed by parent bank personnel that is designed to assist MNC clients of the parent bank in dealings with the bank's correspondents. It is a way for the parent bank to provide its MNC clients with a level of service greater than that provided through merely a correspondent relationship. The parent bank may open a representative office in a country in which it has many MNC clients or at least an important client. Representative offices also assist MNC clients with information about local business practices, economic information and credit evaluation of the MNC's foreign customers.

Foreign Branches

A **foreign branch bank** operates much like a local bank, but legally it is a part of the parent bank. As such, a branch bank is subject to the banking regulations of both its home country and the country in which it operates. Canadian branch banks in foreign countries are regulated from Canada under the *Bank Act* and similar legislation that pertains to Canadian banks operating in foreign countries.

There are several reasons why a parent bank might establish a branch bank abroad. The primary one is that the bank organization can provide a much fuller range of services for its MNC customers through a foreign branch office than it can through a representative office. For example, branch bank loan limits are based on the capital of the parent bank, not the branch bank. Consequently, a branch bank will likely be able to extend a larger loan to a customer than a locally chartered subsidiary bank of the parent. The books of a foreign branch are part of the parent bank's books. Thus, a branch bank system allows customers much faster cheque clearing than does a correspondent bank network because the debit and credit procedure is handled internally within one organization.

Another reason a Canadian parent bank may establish a foreign branch bank is to compete on a local level with the banks of the host country. Foreign branches are not subject to Canadian reserve requirements on deposits and are not required to have Canadian

Scotia Capital Named Best Foreign Exchange Bank in Canada for Third Straight Year

TORONTO, December 11, 2006—For the third year in a row, Scotia Capital has been named the "Best Foreign Exchange Bank" in Canada by the international financial magazine *Global Finance*. The annual award recognizes the best Foreign Exchange Banks from 79 countries and regions around the world.

"We are honoured to be recognized globally for the expertise of our foreign exchange operations for the third consecutive year," said Barry Wainstein, Vice-Chairman and Global Head of Foreign Exchange & Precious Metals, Scotia Capital. "This award is a testament to the depth and breadth of knowledge, experience and commitment to client service at Scotia Capital."

With input from industry experts, corporate executives and consultants, *Global Finance* selected winners on the basis of multiple criteria including: transaction volume, market share, scope of global coverage, currencies traded, customer service, competitive pricing, narrow spreads and innovative technologies.

"Scotia Capital was selected because of the reliable and efficient foreign exchange service it provides to major corporations with global business activities," said Joseph D. Giarraputo, publisher and president of *Global Finance*.

Commitment to the foreign exchange business, evidenced by number and size of trading desks and investment in technology, as well as product range and liquidity, were important considerations. *Global Finance* also considered: skill in structuring transactions, advice on market positioning and hedging and efficient execution of trades, including forwards, futures, swaps and options. Financial soundness, profitability and the ability to handle large transactions without moving the market were also taken into account.

Scotia Capital represents the global corporate and investment banking and capital markets platform of the Scotiabank Group, one of North America's premier financial institutions. The Scotiabank Group has combined assets of $379 billion (as at October 31, 2006) and close to 57,000 employees worldwide, including affiliates. It is also Canada's most international bank, serving customers in some 50 countries around the world. For more information, visit www.scotiabank.com.

Source: Scotiabank Global Banking and Markets, Press Release, 11 December 2006. http://www.gbm.scotiabank.com/AboutUs/WhatsNew/BestFXThirdYear.pdf.

Deposit Insurance (CDI) insurance on deposits. Consequently, branch banks are on the same competitive level as local banks in terms of their cost structure in making loans.

Branch banking is the most popular way for Canadian banks to expand operations overseas. The networks of Canadian branch banks are extensive in the United States and Europe. Many branch banks are operated as "shell" branches in offshore banking centres, a topic covered later in this section.

Subsidiary and Affiliate Banks

A **subsidiary bank** is a locally incorporated bank that is either wholly owned or owned in major part by a foreign parent. An **affiliate bank** is one that is only partially owned but not controlled by its foreign parent. Both subsidiary and affiliate banks operate under the banking laws of the country in which they are incorporated. Canadian parent banks find subsidiary and affiliate banking structures desirable because they are allowed to underwrite securities.

Foreign-owned subsidiary banks in Canada tend to locate in major centres of financial and commercial activity such as Vancouver, Toronto and Montreal.

Edge Act Banks

In the United States, international banking by domestic banks has a unique federal regulation that has a bearing on how Canadian banks operate in the United States. **Edge Act banks** are federally chartered subsidiaries of American banks physically located in the United States that are allowed to engage in a full range of international banking activities. Senator Walter E. Edge sponsored the *Edge Act*, a 1919 amendment to the *Federal Reserve Act*, to allow American banks to be competitive with the services foreign banks could supply their customers. *Edge Act* banks accept foreign deposits, extend trade credit, finance foreign projects abroad, trade foreign currencies and engage in investment banking activities with American citizens involving foreign securities. As a result, *Edge Act* banks do not compete directly with the services provided by American commercial banks.

Foreign banks operating in the United States may establish *Edge Act* banks. Thus, both American and foreign *Edge Act* banks operate on an equal competitive basis.

Edge Act banks are not prohibited from owning equity in business corporations, as are domestic commercial banks. Thus, it is *through* the *Edge Act* that American parent banks own foreign banking subsidiaries and have ownership positions in foreign banking affiliates.

Offshore Banking Centres

A significant portion of the external banking activity takes place through offshore banking centres. An **offshore banking centre** is a country whose banking system is organized to permit external accounts beyond the normal economic activity of the country. The International Monetary Fund recognizes the Bahamas, Bahrain, the Cayman Islands, Hong Kong, the Netherlands Antilles, Panama and Singapore as major offshore banking centres.

Offshore banks operate as branches or subsidiaries of the parent bank. The principal features that make a country attractive for establishing an offshore banking operation are virtually total freedom from host-country governmental banking regulations—for example, low reserve requirements and no deposit insurance, low taxes, a favourable time zone that facilitates international banking transactions and, to a minor extent, strict banking secrecy laws. It should not be inferred that offshore host governments tolerate or encourage poor banking practices, as entry is usually confined to reputable international banks.

The primary activities of offshore banks are to seek deposits and grant loans in currencies other than the currency of the host government. The purpose is to allow smaller banks the opportunity to participate in the Eurodollar market without having to bear the expense of setting up operations in a major European money centre. Most offshore banking centres continue to serve as locations for shell branches, but Hong Kong and Singapore have developed into full-service banking centres that now rival London, New York and Tokyo.

6.3 CAPITAL ADEQUACY STANDARDS

A concern of bank regulators worldwide and of bank depositors is the safety of bank deposits. **Bank capital adequacy** refers to the amount of equity capital and other securities a bank holds as reserves against risky assets to reduce the probability of a bank failure. In a 1988 agreement known as the **Basle Accord**, after the Swiss city in which it is headquartered, the Bank for International Settlements (BIS) established a framework for measuring bank capital adequacy for banks in the Group of Ten countries and Luxembourg. The BIS is the central bank for clearing international transactions between national central banks and also serves as a facilitator in reaching international banking agreements among its members.

www.bis.org.

The official website of the Bank for International Settlements. It is quite extensive. One can download papers on international bank policies, and statistics on international banks, capital markets and derivative securities markets. There is also a link to the websites of most central banks in the world.

The Basle Accord called for a minimum bank capital adequacy ratio of 8 percent of risk-weighted assets for banks that engage in cross-border transactions. The accord divides bank capital into two categories: Tier I Core capital, which consists of shareholder equity and retained earnings, and Tier II Supplemental capital, which consists of internationally recognized nonequity items such as preferred shares and subordinated bonds. Supplemental capital is allowed to count for no more than 50 percent of total bank capital or no more than 4 percent of risk-weighted assets. In determining risk-weighted assets, four categories of risky assets are each weighted differently. More risky assets receive a higher weight. Government obligations are weighted at 0 percent, short-term interbank assets at 20 percent, residential mortgages at 50 percent and other assets at 100 percent. Thus, a bank with $100 million in each of the four asset categories would have the equivalent of $170 million in risk-weighted assets. It would need to maintain $13.6 million in capital against these investments, of which no more than one-half of this amount, or $6.8 million, could be Tier II capital.

The 1988 Basle Capital Accord has been widely adopted throughout the world by national bank regulators. Nevertheless, it is not without problems. National banking supervisors

Value at Risk

A bank's portfolio is the monetary value of its on- and off-balance-sheet trading account positions. Estimating the portfolio standard deviation of return allows the bank's value-at-risk to be calculated. **Value-at-risk (VAR)** is the loss that will be exceeded with a specified probability over a specified time horizon. VAR is calculated daily according to the criterion that there be only 1 percent chance that the maximum loss over a 10-day time period will exceed the bank's capital.

VAR is calculated as VAR = Portfolio Value × Daily Standard Deviation of Return × Confidence Interval Factor × √Horizon. The confidence interval factor is the appropriate z-value from the standard normal density function associated with the maximum level of loss that is tolerable. For example, the 1 percent VAR for a portfolio of $400 million with a daily portfolio standard deviation of 0.75 percent for a 10-day planning horizon is $22.07 million = $400 million × 0.0075 × 2.326 × √10,

where 2.326 is the z-value associated with a one-tail 99 percent confidence interval. That is, there is only a 1 percent chance that the loss during a 10-day period will exceed $22.07 million. Assuming accurate inputs into the VAR formula, the bank would be required to maintain an equivalent amount of capital as an explicit cushion against its price-risk exposure.

As an estimate of capital adequacy, VAR is only as good as the accuracy of its inputs. The true portfolio standard deviation is never known and must be estimated. Thus, implementing VAR analysis is subject to the problem of *estimation risk*, or *parameter uncertainty*. The Basle Committee on Banking Supervision is aware of this and other implementation problems. To address them, the capital charge for a bank that uses its own internal proprietary model to estimate VAR is the larger of the previous day's VAR, or three times the average of the daily VAR of the preceding 60 business days.

www.riskmetrics.com

The website of Risk Metrics Group, one of the pioneers in applying value-at-risk techniques. It has a sub-site devoted to educational matters. Students can take an online course on market and credit risk management called "Managing Risk."

criticized the arbitrary nature of the "*rules-based*" Basle Capital Accord, especially the constant 8 percent minimum capital assigned to risk-weighted assets. The argument is that risk is not constant throughout the business cycle. Thus, it may be preferable to require banks to keep more than the 8 percent minimum in the expansionary phase of a business cycle to guard against the more risky operating environment usually associated with an economic downturn. Furthermore, the 8 percent minimum was set with the banks of industrial countries in mind. The Basle Capital Accord has been adopted by many developing countries that experience longer and more severe business cycles than do the developed countries, in which case 8 percent capital on risk-weighted assets is probably not adequate.

An additional problem with the "rules-based" 1988 Basle Capital Accord has to do with the type of business in which banks engage. Bank trading in equity, interest rate and exchange rate derivative products has escalated in recent years. Many of these products did not exist when the Basle Accord was drafted. Notwithstanding the criticisms with respect to traditional credit risk, the capital adequacy standards of the 1988 Basle Accord are not sufficient to safeguard against the market risk from derivatives trading. Barings Bank, for example, which collapsed in 1995 due in part to the activities of a rogue derivatives trader, was considered to be a safe bank by the Basle capital adequacy standards.

A 1996 amendment to the 1988 accord requires commercial banks engaged in significant trading activity to set aside additional capital to cover the market risks inherent in their trading accounts. The amendment allows banks to use internally developed portfolio models to assess adequate capital requirements. Instead of using a "rules-based" approach to determining adequate bank capital, they may apply a "*risk-focused*" approach that relies on modern portfolio theory. See the box on the most important of these models, "Value at Risk."

Recognizing the deficiencies of the 1988 accord, the Basle Committee drafted the New Basel Capital Accord, known as Basel II, and it was implemented in 2006. The new capital adequacy framework incorporates three mutually reinforcing pillars that allow banks and supervisors to evaluate the risks that banks face: minimum capital requirements, a supervisory review process and the effective use of market discipline. With respect to the first pillar, a bank's minimum 8 percent capital ratio is calculated on the sum of the bank's credit, market and operational risks. Operational risks include such threats as computer failure and fraud. In determining the bank's risk-weighted assets, weights for high-quality corporate credits are reduced. Weights in excess of 100 percent are assigned for certain low-quality exposures. In determining adequate capital, banks are allowed to calculate their own market risks, such as VAR analysis. The second pillar is designed to ensure that each bank has a sound internal process in place to properly assess the adequacy of its capital based on a systematic and continuous evaluation of its risks. Implementation of this pillar encourages supervisory intervention at the national level with the authority to require capital in excess of the minimum. The third pillar seeks to enhance bank disclosure standards to bolster the role that market participants have in encouraging banks to hold adequate capital.

6.4 INTERNATIONAL MONEY MARKET

Eurocurrency Market

The core of the international money market is the Eurocurrency market. A **Eurocurrency** is a *time* deposit of money in an international bank located in a country different from the country that issued the currency. For example, Eurodollars are deposits of US dollars in banks located outside of the United States, Eurosterling are deposits of British pound sterling in banks outside of the United Kingdom, and Euroyen are deposits of Japanese yen in banks outside of Japan. The prefix *Euro* is something of a misnomer, since the bank in which the deposit is made does not have to be located in Europe. The depository bank could be located in Europe, the Caribbean or Asia. Indeed, Eurodollar deposits can be made in offshore shell branches or **International Banking Facilities (IBFs)**, where the physical dollar deposits are actually with the US parent bank. An "Asian dollar" market exists, with headquarters in Singapore, but it can be viewed as a major division of the Eurocurrency market.

The origin of the Eurocurrency market can be traced back to the 1950s and early 1960s, when the former Soviet Union and Soviet-bloc countries sold gold and commodities to raise hard currency. Because of anti-Soviet sentiment, these Communist countries were afraid of depositing their US dollars in American banks for fear that the deposits could be frozen or taken. Instead, they deposited their US dollars in a French bank whose telex address was EURO-BANK. Since that time, dollar deposits outside the United States have been called *Eurodollars* and banks accepting Eurocurrency deposits have been called **Eurobanks**.

The Eurocurrency market is an *external* banking system that runs parallel to the *domestic* banking system of the country that issued the currency. Both banking systems seek deposits and make loans to customers from the deposited funds. Euro-deposits are not subject to reserve requirements or deposit insurance; hence, the cost of operations is less. Because of the reduced cost and regulatory structure, the Eurocurrency market has grown spectacularly since its inception.

The Eurocurrency market operates at the *interbank* and/or *wholesale* level. The majority of Eurocurrency transactions are interbank transactions involving sums of $1,000,000 or more. Eurobanks with surplus funds lend to Eurobanks that need loanable funds. The rate charged by banks with excess funds is referred to as the *interbank offered rate*; they accept interbank deposits at the *interbank bid rate*. The spread is generally one-eighth of 1 percent for major Eurocurrencies.

London has historically been, and remains, the major Eurocurrency financial centre. The name of the city gives rise to the **London Interbank Offered Rate (LIBOR)**, the reference rate in London for Eurocurrency deposits. To be clear, there is a LIBOR for Eurodollars, Euro–Canadian dollars, Euroyen and even euros. Exhibit 6.2 presents a brief account of how LIBOR is calculated daily along with LIBOR values on 10 May 2013.

In other financial centres, other reference rates are used. For example, *SIBOR* is the Singapore Interbank Offered Rate, *PIBOR* is the Paris Interbank Offered Rate and *BRIBOR* is the Brussels Interbank Offered Rate. Competition forces the various interbank rates for a particular Eurocurrency to be close to one another.

EXHIBIT 6.2

LIBOR

LIBOR, or the London Interbank Offered Rate, is an indicative average interest rate at which a selection of banks, the so-called "panel banks," are prepared to lend one another unsecured funds on the London money market. Although reference is often made to the LIBOR rate, there are actually 150 different LIBOR interest rates. LIBOR is calculated for 10 different currencies for 15 different maturities. The official LIBOR rates are announced once a day at around 11:45 A.M. London time by Thomson Reuters on behalf of the British Bankers' Association.

The LIBOR rates are not based on actual transactions. On every working day at around 11 A.M. London time, the panel banks inform Thomson Reuters for each maturity at what interest rate they would expect to be able to raise a substantial loan in the interbank money market at that moment. The reason that the measurement is not based on actual transactions is that not every bank borrows substantial amounts for each maturity every day. Once Thomson Reuters has collected the rates from all panel banks, the highest and lowest 25 percent of values are eliminated. An average is calculated of the 50 percent remaining "mid values" in order to produce the official LIBOR rate.

LIBOR is viewed as the most important benchmark in the world for short-term interest rates. It is used as the base rate for a large variety of financial products such as futures, options and swaps. Banks also use these rates as a base for setting the interest rates for loans, savings and mortgages.

LIBOR on Eurocurrencies, 10 May 2013						
	CAD	USD	EUR	GBP	JPY	AUD
Overnight	1.0400	0.1326	0.0279	0.4800	0.0929	2.7560
1 week	1.0420	0.1585	0.0376	0.4863	0.1014	2.7840
2 weeks	1.0440	0.1743	0.0750	0.4878	0.1102	2.8060
1 month	1.0520	0.1924	0.0600	0.4925	0.1201	2.8650
2 months	1.1230	0.2303	0.0921	0.4994	0.1400	2.9070
3 months	1.1735	0.2752	0.1214	0.5058	0.1543	2.9570
4 months	1.2520	0.3175	0.1575	0.5375	0.1859	2.9900
5 months	1.3240	0.3623	0.1875	0.5675	0.2180	3.0250
6 months	1.3850	0.4098	0.2129	0.5913	0.2407	3.0580
7 months	1.4495	0.4561	0.2422	0.6415	0.2724	3.0940
8 months	1.5195	0.5024	0.2814	0.6917	0.3104	3.1480
9 months	1.5850	0.5487	0.3157	0.7419	0.3484	3.1890
10 months	1.6415	0.5950	0.3500	0.7921	0.3864	3.2280
11 months	1.7210	0.6413	0.3843	0.8423	0.4244	3.2900
12 months	1.7865	0.6852	0.4186	0.8925	0.4307	3.3380

www.euribor.org

This website provides a brief history of the Euro common currency and a discussion of EURIBOR.

The 1999 launch of the common euro currency of 12 countries (now 17) that make up the European Economic and Monetary Union created a need for a new interbank offer rate. To dispel the confusion as to whether one is referring to the common euro currency or another Eurocurrency, such as Eurodollars, *international* currencies is replacing "Eurocurrencies" and *prime* banks replace Eurobanks. **EURIBOR** is the rate at which interbank deposits of the euro are offered by one prime bank to another in the eurozone.

In the wholesale money market, Eurobanks accept Eurocurrency fixed time deposits and issue **negotiable certificates of deposit (NCDs)**. In fact, these are the preferred ways for

EXHIBIT 6.3	Eurocurrency Interest Rate Quotes, 10 May 2013*					
10-May	Short-Term	7 Days' Notice	1 Month	3 Months	6 Months	One Year
Euro	0.17 – 0.07	0.20 – 0.15	0.11 – 0.01	0.25 – 0.05	0.33 – 0.18	0.65 – 0.45
Danish krone	0.12 – –0.12	–0.18 – –0.23	–0.12 – –0.15	–0.08 – –0.10	0.13 – –0.07	0.33 – 0.13
Sterling	0.54 – 0.44	0.55 – 0.45	0.55 – 0.45	0.65 – 0.45	0.61 – 0.49	0.93 – 0.83
Swiss franc	–0.03 – –0.23	0.02 – –0.10	0.02 – –0.10	0.10 – 0.08	0.13 – –0.05	0.25 – 0.05
Canadian dollar	1.05 – 0.95	1.10 – 0.95	1.13 – 0.98	1.23 – 1.08	1.39 – 1.24	1.62 – 1.47
US dollar	0.13 – 0.07	0.31 – 0.24	0.30 – 0.20	0.40 – 0.30	0.54 – 0.44	0.96 – 0.71
Japanese yen	0.13 – 0.03	0.15 – 0.05	0.13 – 0.01	0.25 – 0.05	0.20 – 0.08	0.29 – 0.17
Singapore $	0.03 – 0.01	0.31 – 0.06	0.37 – 0.20	0.38 – 0.13	0.44 – 0.19	0.56 – 0.31

*In each pair of interest-rates-by-currency quotes, the first or left-hand entry shows the rate at which banks will lend (to each other), while the right-hand entry is the rate that banks will pay on deposits in the respective currency. In these times (2013–14) of extraordinarily low interest rates, Eurocurrency inter-bank interest rates in some countries are negative, such as for Switzerland (which is attempting to discourage the inflow of short-term foreign funds).
Source: Rotman Finance Centre, May 2013.

Eurobanks to raise loanable funds as the deposits tend to be for a lengthier period and the acquiring rate is often less than the interbank rate. Denominations are at least $500,000, but sizes of $1,000,000 or larger are more typical. Rates on Eurocurrency deposits are quoted for maturities ranging from one day to several years; standard maturities are for 1, 2, 3, 6, 9 and 12 months. Exhibit 6.3 shows sample Eurocurrency interest rates. Appendix 6A illustrates the creation of the Eurocurrency.

Exhibit 6.4 shows the year-end values in billions of US dollars of international bank credit for the years 2000 through 2012. The 2012 column shows that the gross value of international bank credits was $42 trillion and that interbank credits accounted for $30 trillion, or about three-quarters of the total. The major currencies denominating these were the US dollar, the euro and the Japanese yen. Since the source of international bank credits is international deposits, these amounts indicate the size of the Eurocurrency market.

Approximately 95 percent of wholesale Eurobank deposits come from fixed time deposits, with the remainder from NCDs. There is an interest penalty for the early withdrawal of funds from a fixed time deposit. NCDs, on the other hand, being negotiable, can be sold in the secondary market if the depositor suddenly needs funds prior to scheduled maturity. The NCD market began in 1967 in London for Eurodollars. EuroCDs for currencies other than the US dollar are offered by banks in London and in other financial centres, but the secondary market for nondollar NCDs is not very liquid.

Eurocredits

Eurocredits are short-to-medium-term loans of Eurocurrency extended by Eurobanks to corporations, sovereign governments, nonprime banks or international organizations. The

EXHIBIT 6.4	International Bank External Liabilities (at year-end, US$ billions)												
	2000	2001	2002	2003	2004	2005	2006	2007	2008	2009	2010	2011	2012
Type of Liability													
Interbank	7,908	8,330	9,534	11,097	13,090	14,740	17,888	23,109	21,431	20,765	23,803	26,841	29,878
Nonbank	2,513	2,860	3,318	4,265	5,025	5,143	6,590	8,309	7,636	7,310	8,766	9,234	11,677
Total	10,421	11,190	12,852	15,362	18,115	19,883	24,478	31,418	29,067	28,075	32,569	36,075	41,555

Source: Bank for International Settlements, *International Banking and Financial Market Developments,* Table 1, various issues.

EXHIBIT 6.5

Comparison of
U.S. Lending and
Borrowing Rates
with Eurodollar
Rates on 10 May
2013

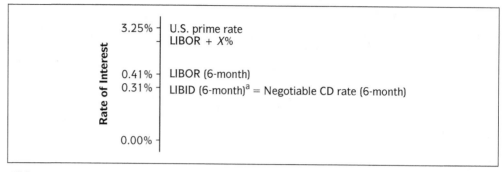

^aLIBID denotes the London Interbank Bid rate.

loans are denominated in currencies other than the home currency of the Eurobank. Because these loans are frequently too large for a single bank to handle, Eurobanks will band together to form a bank lending **syndicate** to share the risk.

The credit risk on these loans is greater than on loans to other banks in the interbank market. Thus, the interest rate on Eurocredits must compensate the bank, or banking syndicate, for the added credit risk. On Eurocredits originating in London, the base lending rate is LIBOR. The lending rate on these credits is stated as LIBOR + X percent, where X is the lending margin charged depending upon the creditworthiness of the borrower. Rollover pricing was created on Eurocredits so that Eurobanks do not end up paying more on Eurocurrency time deposits than they earn from the loans. Thus, a Eurocredit may be viewed as a series of shorter-term loans, where at the end of each time period (generally three or six months), the loan is rolled over and the base lending rate is repriced to current LIBOR over the next time interval of the loan.

Exhibit 6.5 shows the relationship among the various interest rates discussed in this section. On 10 May 2013, US domestic banks paid 0.31 percent for six-month negotiable certificates of deposit. The prime US lending rate, the base rate charged banks' most creditworthy corporate clients, on that day was 3.25 percent. This represents a spread of 2.94 percent for banks to cover operating costs and earn a profit. By comparison, Eurobanks also accept six-month Eurodollar time deposits, say Eurodollar NCDs, at a rate of 0.41 percent. (We use the London Late Eurodollar bid rate reported in Exhibit 6.2 for the Eurodollar quote, the afternoon closing rate on large deposits.) The rate charged for Eurodollar credits is LIBOR + X percent, where any lending margin less than 2.83 percent appears to make the Eurodollar loan more attractive than the prime rate loan ($0.41 + 2.83 = 3.24 < 3.25$).

Since lending margins typically fall in the range of ¼ percent to 3 percent, with the median rate being ½ percent to 1½ percent, Exhibit 6.3 shows the narrow borrowing–lending spreads of Eurobankers in the Eurodollar credit market. This seems to suggest that borrowers can obtain funds more cheaply in the Eurodollar market. However, international competition in recent years has forced commercial banks to lend domestically at subprime rates.

Example 6.1   *Rollover Pricing of a Eurocredit*

Teltrex International can borrow $3,000,000 at LIBOR plus a lending margin of 0.30 percent per annum on a three-month rollover basis from Barclays in London. Suppose that three-month LIBOR is currently 0.5 percent. Further suppose that over the second three-month interval, LIBOR falls to 0.45 percent. How much will Teltrex pay in interest to Barclays over the six-month period for the Eurodollar loan?

Solution: $3,000,000 × (0.00500 + 0.0075)/4 + $3,000,000 ×
(0.00450 + 0.0075)/4 = $6,000 + $5,625
= $11,625

A major risk Eurobanks face in accepting Eurodeposits and in extending Eurocredits is interest rate risk resulting from a mismatch in the maturities of the deposits and credits. For example, if deposit maturities are longer than credit maturities and interest rates fall, the credit rates will be adjusted downward while the bank is still paying a higher rate on deposits. Conversely, if deposit maturities are shorter than credit maturities and interest rates rise, deposit rates will adjust upward while the bank is still receiving a lower rate on credits. Only when deposit and credit maturities are perfectly matched will the rollover feature of Eurocredits allow the bank to earn the desired deposit–loan rate spread.

A **forward rate agreement (FRA)** is an interbank contract that allows the Eurobank to hedge the interest rate risk in mismatched deposits and credits. The size of the market is enormous. At year-end 2012, the notional value of FRAs outstanding was $70,000 billion.

An FRA involves two parties, a buyer and a seller, where

1. the buyer agrees to pay the seller the increased interest cost on a notional amount if interest rates fall below an agreement rate, or

2. the seller agrees to pay the buyer the increased interest cost if interest rates increase above the agreement rate.

FRAs are structured to capture the maturity mismatch in standard-length Eurodeposits and credits. For example, the FRA might be on a six-month interest rate for a six-month period beginning three months from today and ending nine months from today; this would be a "three against nine" FRA. The following time line depicts this FRA example.

| Start | Agreement Period (3 Months) | Cash Settlement | | FRA Period (6 Months) | End |

The payment amount under an FRA is calculated as the absolute value of

$$\frac{\text{Notional Amount} \times (SR - AR) \times \text{days}/360}{1 + (SR \times \text{days}/360)}$$

where SR denotes the settlement rate, AR denotes the agreement rate and *days* denotes the length of the FRA period.

Example **6.2** *Three against Six Forward Rate Agreement*

As an example, consider a bank that has made a three-month Eurodollar loan of US$10,000,000 against an offsetting six-month Eurodollar deposit. The bank's concern is that three-month LIBOR will fall below expectations and the Eurocredit is rolled over at the new lower base rate, making the six-month deposit unprofitable.[1] To protect itself, the bank could sell a $10,000,000 "three against six" FRA. The FRA will be priced such that the agreement rate is the expected three-month dollar LIBOR in three months.

---

[1]Consistently with the Unbiased Expectations Hypothesis (UEH), the agreement rate AR is the expected rate at the beginning of the FRA period. For example, in a "three against six" FRA, the AR can be calculated from the forward rate that ties together current three-month LIBOR and six-month LIBOR:

$$([1 + (\text{6-month LIBOR})(T_2/360)]/[1 + (\text{3-month LIBOR})(T_1/360)] - 1) \times 360/(T_2 - T_1)$$
$$= f \times 360/(T_2 - T_1) = AR$$

where T_2 and T_1 are, respectively, the actual number of days to maturity of the six-month and three-month Eurocurrency periods and f is the forward rate.

Assume *AR* is 6 percent and the actual number of days in the three-month FRA period is 91. Thus, the bank expects to receive $8,847 (= 10,000,000 × 0.00350 × 91/360) as the base amount of interest when the Eurodollar loan is rolled over for a second three-month period. If *SR* (i.e., three-month market LIBOR) is 0.2752 percent, the bank will receive only $6,956.44 in base interest, or a shortfall of $1,890.78. Since *SR* is less than *AR*, the bank will profit from the FRA it sold. It will receive from the buyer in three months a cash settlement at the beginning of the 91-day FRA period equalling the present value of the *absolute* value of $6,956 (= 10,000,000 × (0.002752 − 0.00350) × 91/360). This *absolute* present value is

$$\frac{\$10,000,000 \times (0.002752 - 0.00350) \times 91/360}{1 + (0.002752 \times 91/360)}$$

$$= \frac{\$1,890.78}{1.0006956}$$

$$= \$1,889.46$$

The sum, $1,889.46, equals the present value as of the *beginning* of the 91-day FRA period of the shortfall of $1,890.78 from the expected Eurodollar loan proceeds that are needed to meet the interest on the Eurodollar deposit. Had *SR* been greater than *AR*, the bank would have paid the buyer the present value of the excess amount of interest above what was expected from rolling over the Eurodollar credit. In this event, the bank would have effectively received the agreement rate on its three-month Eurodollar loan, which would have made the loan a profitable transaction.

FRAs can be used for speculative purposes also. If one believes rates will be less than the *AR*, the sale of an FRA is the suitable position. In contrast, the purchase of an FRA is the suitable position if one believes rates will be greater than the *AR*. See Exhibit 6.6 for a forward rate agreement payoff profile.

Euronotes

Euronotes are short-term notes underwritten by a group of international investment or commercial banks called a "facility." A client-borrower makes an agreement with a facility to issue Euronotes in its own name for a period of time, generally three to ten years. Euronotes are sold at a discount from face value and pay back the full face value at maturity. Euronotes typically have maturities of from three to six months. Borrowers find Euronotes attractive because the interest expense is usually slightly less—typically LIBOR plus ⅛ percent—in comparison with syndicated Eurobank loans. The banks find them attractive to issue because they earn a small fee from the underwriting or supply the funds and earn the interest return.

EXHIBIT 6.6

Forward Rate Agreement Payoff Profile

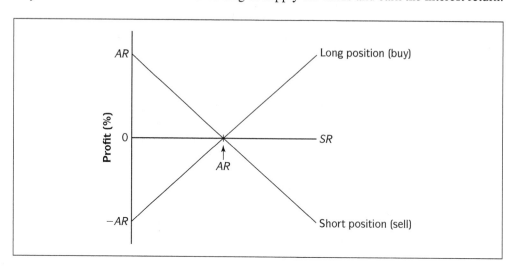

EXHIBIT 6.7		Size of the Euronote and Eurocommercial Paper Market (at year-end, US$ billions)											
Instrument	2000	2001	2002	2003	2004	2005	2006	2007	2008	2009	2010	2011	2012
Euronotes	271	155	146	152	176	181	240	441	423	333	300	266	339
Eurocommercial paper	223	243	292	418	483	470	635	696	709	599	574	548	504
Total	494	398	438	569	659	650	875	1,136	1,132	932	874	814	843

Source: Bank for International Settlements, *International Banking and Financial Market Developments,* Table 13A, various issues.

Eurocommercial Paper

Eurocommercial paper, like domestic commercial paper, is an unsecured short-term promissory note issued by a corporation or a bank and placed directly with the investment public through a dealer. Like Euronotes, Eurocommercial paper is sold at a discount from face value. Maturities typically range from one to six months.

The vast majority of Eurocommercial paper is US-dollar-denominated. There are, however, a number of differences between the US and Eurocommercial paper markets. The maturity of Eurocommercial paper tends to be about twice as long as US commercial paper. For this reason, the secondary market is more active than for US paper. Eurocommercial paper issuers also tend to be of much lower quality than their US counterparts; consequently, yields tend to be higher. The higher quality (lower credit risk) of the Eurocommercial paper is a direct result of the less stringent regulatory environment in the Eurosystem and hence is an illustration of the effects of "self-regulation."

Exhibit 6.7 shows the year-end value of the Euronote and Eurocommercial paper market in billions of US dollars for the years 2000 through 2012.

6.5 INTERNATIONAL FINANCIAL CRISES

Bank operations—holding deposits and lending—are seemingly benign to the real economy. After all, banks do not generate real economic activity in their own right. Banks are merely intermediaries. They facilitate the flow of finance from lenders to borrowers, from savers to investors. It is all other people's money.

Nevertheless, the enormous volume of flow-through in banking and money markets suggests that if things go wrong in the financial system, serious real problems can ensue. Frightened lenders may withdraw their deposits. Liquidity can rapidly dry up. As banks try to recall outstanding loans, borrowers may be unable to pay quickly or to pay at all, adding to the distress of the system. Banks can fail. Industry unable to weather the financial storm will likewise collapse. When banking breaks down, the real economy suffers.

In today's financially integrated world, distress in a specific country's banking and money market often has international causes and consequences. For instance, to the extent that foreigners provide short-term (money market) finance to emerging markets, a rapid withdrawal of such funds results in a credit crunch and loss of liquidity in the stranded nation. Interest rates rise, while the exchange rate falls. After the fact, in the effort to explain the rapid exodus of funds, it often turns out that international lenders acted in concert, triggered by a single piece of threatening news. Such "news" could involve problems with local banks' lending practices or an unexpected deterioration of the country's Current Account.

International banking and money market operations are like the weather. We take notice only when it is stormy and destructive, like the hurricane season.

International financial turbulence can be informative. The following review of the more dramatic international financial "crises" over the past quarter-century illustrates underlying factors in financial turmoil and the sorts of corrective action that follow. Our synopses include the global debt crisis of the 1980s, the Mexico peso problem, the Asian financial meltdown, Argentina's currency board collapse, the Russian default and the recent US subprime lending fiasco.

Global Debt Crisis of the 1980s

In 1982, Mexico asked more than 100 foreign banks to forgive its US$68 billion in loans. Soon Brazil, Argentina and more than 20 other developing countries announced similar problems in meeting the debt service on their bank loans. At the height of the international debt crisis, Third World countries owed US$1.2 *trillion*! Interest obligations alone amounted to 22 percent of the export earnings of these poor nations crippled by debt. To paraphrase an old banking dictum, if a country owes a billion dollars to a bank, that country may be in trouble, but if 20 countries owe $1.2 trillion, the banks are in trouble. Indeed, the international banking community was shaken.

The origin of this international debt crisis was oil. In the mid-1970s, the Organization of Petroleum Exporting Countries (OPEC), a cartel with a major influence on world oil prices, raised oil prices dramatically. As a result of these oil price rises, OPEC nations amassed a tremendous amount of US dollars, the currency of global oil. The OPEC dollars, dubbed *petrodollars*, soon made their way into the international financial system.

OPEC nations—such as Saudi Arabia and the Gulf States—put billions in Eurodollar deposits. The Eurobanks were then faced with the huge challenge of lending those funds. Third World nations, especially their governments, were eager to assist the Eurobankers by accepting Eurodollar loans for economic development *and* to pay for their oil imports.

When governments borrow from foreigners, such debt is known as *sovereign debt* and it is generally secured only by the creditworthiness and good name of the country. In other words, if a country should default on its sovereign borrowings, there is no recourse for the lender.

Of course, there would have been no financial problem if the borrowing nations could have repaid their loans. But before long, they could not. The 1980s were an era of high and volatile inflation and general economic instability throughout the world. To address inflation in particular, monetary authorities, especially the US Federal Reserve, brought in restrictive monetary policy (reduced money supply growth). In due course, interest rates rose and the industrial nations' economies slumped.

The industrial nations' slump reduced developing nations' export earnings. Higher interest rates hurt them even more, since their debt was virtually all in US dollars at floating rates. Major international banks' exposure to these unfolding events is indicated in Exhibit 6.8, which lists the outstanding loans of the 10 largest US banks *just to Mexico*.

EXHIBIT 6.8

Ten Biggest American Bank Lenders to Mexico (billions of American dollars as of 30 September 1987)

Bank	Outstanding to Mexico	Loan Loss Reserves for Developing-Country Loans
Citicorp	$2.900	$3.432
BankAmerica Corp.	2.407	1.808
Manufacturers Hanover Corp.	1.883	1.833*
Chemical New York Corp.	1.733	1.505*
Chase Manhattan Corp.	1.660	1.970
Bankers Trust New York Corp.	1.277	1.000
J. P. Morgan & Co.	1.137	1.317
First Chicago Corp.	0.898	0.930
First Interstate Bancorp.	0.689	0.500
Wells Fargo & Co.	0.587	0.760

*As of 30 June 1987.

Source: *The Wall Street Journal*, 30 December 1987. Reprinted by permission of *The Wall Street Journal*, © 1987 Dow Jones & Company, Inc. All rights reserved worldwide.

Why would international banks make such risky loans to LDC sovereign governments in the first place? One obvious explanation is that they held vast sums of money in Eurodollar deposits that needed to be quickly placed to start producing interest income. In the process, however, the banks were woefully lax in their assessment of the risks involved in lending to unfamiliar, unseasoned borrowers. Many banks, especially US banks, complained of *arm-twisting* from Washington to have banks assist the economic development of Third World countries. Nevertheless, had the bankers and the policy makers been better versed in international financial history, perhaps the international debt crisis of the 1980s could have been avoided or at least mitigated.

The debt distress of the 1980s is especially interesting for the way it ended. A number of innovations emerged to improve the strength, stability and flexibility of global debt markets. A vibrant secondary market developed for LDC debt in which distressed debt was sold at deep discounts. Also, cleverly designed debt-for-equity swaps allowed distressed sovereign debt to be purchased at a discount and presented to the issuer, say the Mexican government, for redemption at a favourable currency exchange rate. For example, Volkswagen bought (face value) $280 million of Mexican debt from Citibank for $170 million and redeemed it with the Mexican authorities for pesos worth $250 million on the understanding that Volkswagen would invest the pesos in the Mexican automotive industry.

Another creative contribution to correcting banks' overextension into Third World debt resulted in Brady bonds, named for the US Treasury Secretary who devised the plan. The Treasury played the role of negotiator between banks and governments, promoting compromise to share losses and restore the debt markets. The solution was to convert sovereign loans into collateralized bonds with a reduced interest rate and extended maturity, out to 25 years. As an opening gesture, banks typically agreed to forgive part of the debt. The key to mobilizing the debt was the collateral. Debtor nations were required to purchase zero-coupon US Treasury bonds with a maturity corresponding to the revised maturity of the sovereign debt. These are the "Brady bonds." With the sovereign debt linked to the collateral of US Treasuries, the debt became marketable.

By 1992, agreements had been negotiated in many countries including Argentina, Brazil, Mexico, Uruguay, Venezuela, Nigeria and the Philippines. Debtor nations refinanced more than 90 percent of their outstanding private debt to international banks. In total, over $100 billion in bank debt was converted to Brady bonds.

Brady bonds and debt-to-equity swaps, while demonstrating creativity and commitment, nevertheless were *ad hoc* adjustments to serious systemic problems in international banking. Eager to recycle petrodollars, banks overextended themselves into sovereign debt while seemingly oblivious to the collective risks involved. More long-lasting corrective action involved improvements in risk assessment techniques, the development of formal rules for capital adequacy (Basel Accords I and II) and a general shift away from lending to countries as opposed to companies.

Mexican Peso Crisis, 1994

On 20 December 1994, President Ernesto Zedillo of Mexico announced that his government would immediately devalue the peso against the US dollar by 14 percent. The surprise set off a stampede sale of Mexican shares and bonds. Within a month, as Exhibit 6.9 shows, the peso lost 40 percent of its value against the US dollar. Mexico was forced to float the peso. Worried international investors reduced their holdings of securities and currencies of *all* emerging markets, not just Mexico, rapidly causing the peso problem to spill over to other Latin American and Asian countries. World financial markets were frantic.

Faced with impending default on Mexican sovereign debt along with the possibility of a global financial meltdown, the US Treasury took action. The Treasury orchestrated an emergency fund, called the Exchange Stabilization Fund, to support (buy) the peso and reduce its volatility. Canada joined the supporting group along with the International Monetary Fund (IMF), the Bank for International Settlements (BIS), and several Latin

EXHIBIT 6.9

American Dollar versus Mexican Peso Exchange Rate (1 November 1994–31 January 1995)

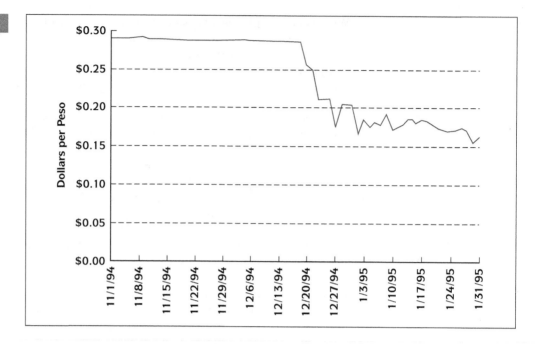

American countries and commercial banks. The $53 billion bailout worked. Almost immediately, the peso began to stabilize.

The Mexican peso crisis is the first financial crisis ignited by a cross-border flight of portfolio capital. International mutual funds had invested $45 billion in Mexican securities in the three years leading up to the peso crisis. As the peso fell, fund managers quickly liquidated their Mexican holdings thus putting pressure on the peso to fall further, precipitating "groupthink." Around the globe, fund managers simultaneously sought safe haven in US-dollar securities.

Two lessons emerge from the peso crisis. First, only multilateral intervention with the combined clout of major industrial nations, through the IMF and the BIS, can contain a peso-type crisis once it has ignited. While critics of such intervention properly point to the "moral hazard" problem that such a safety net creates, the economic and social costs of *not* intervening demand decisive action. A few years later, the G-7 countries endorsed a $50 billion bailout fund for countries in financial distress which would be administered by the IMF. The IMF negotiation also increased disclosure requirements for all countries. Mexican authorities had been reluctant to disclose the true state of the economy, in particular the rapid depletion of foreign exchange reserves. More accurate and timely information could have prompted remedial action to avert the crisis.

Second, Mexico depended excessively on foreign portfolio capital to finance its economic development. Such capital can leave at a moment's notice, as Mexico came to learn. The country should have encouraged domestic savings and sought out longer-term, rather than short-term, foreign investments.

Asian Financial Crisis, 1997

On 2 July 1997, the Thai baht, which had been fixed to the US dollar, was suddenly devalued. What at first appeared to be local financial strains in Thailand quickly escalated into a global financial crisis, spreading to other Asian countries—Indonesia, Korea, Malaysia and the Philippines—then far afield to Russia and Latin America, especially Brazil. At the height of the crisis, the Korean won fell by about 50 percent in its dollar value from its pre-crisis level while the Indonesian rupiah fell an incredible 80 percent.

The Asian crisis was the third major currency crisis of the 1990s. It was preceded by the collapse of the European Monetary System (EMS) in 1992 and the Mexican peso problem of 1994–1995. The Asian crisis, however, turned out to be far more serious than its two predecessors in terms of contagion effects and the severity of subsequent economic and social costs. The currency crisis led to deep recession in East Asia, a region that for more than a decade had enjoyed rapid economic growth. At the same time, lenders and investors from the developed countries suffered large capital losses from their investments in emerging-market securities.

Factors contributing to the Asian currency crisis included highly mobile international capital, weak domestic financial systems and inconsistent economic policies. In the lead-up, firms and financial institutions in Asia eagerly borrowed foreign currencies from US, Japanese and European investors attracted to these fast-growing markets for extra returns. In 1996 alone, five Asian countries—Indonesia, Korea, Malaysia, the Philippines and Thailand—enjoyed a new inflow of private capital of $93 billion.

The large inflows of private capital created an Asian credit boom. However, easy credit together with poor credit supervision is a dangerous mix. Local lending institutions, especially in Thailand, funded speculative investment in real estate and questionable industrial projects. Fixed or stable exchange rates encouraged unhedged international financial borrowing and excessive risk taken by both international lenders and local borrowers. Both sides were seemingly oblivious to the mounting difficulty that the monetary authorities faced in keeping the exchange rate fixed. Meanwhile, the booming economy with a fixed nominal exchange rate inevitably brought about appreciation of the real exchange rate. This in turn led to a marked slowdown in export growth, especially for Thailand and Korea. In addition, a long-lasting recession in Japan and the yen's depreciation against the dollar hurt Japan's neighbours, further worsening trade balances throughout Asia. If Asian currencies had been more flexible and allowed to depreciate in real terms, the catastrophic changes of exchange rates that occurred in 1997 might have been avoided.

In Thailand, as the run on the baht started, the Thai central bank initially injected liquidity to the domestic financial system and tried to defend the exchange rate by drawing on its foreign exchange reserves. With its foreign reserves declining rapidly, the central bank eventually had no choice but to devalue the baht. The sudden collapse of the baht touched off a panicky flight of capital from *all* Asian countries as international lenders acted as if all countries were in the same boat. Year over year, the $93 billion foreign capital inflow mentioned above reversed into a $12 billion outflow. Contagion of the currency crisis was caused, at least in part, by the panicky, indiscriminate flight of capital from the Asian countries for fear of a spreading crisis. Fear, thus, became self-fulfilling.

As foreign lenders withdrew and refused to renew short-term loans, the former credit boom turned into a credit crunch, hurting creditworthy as well as marginal borrowers. The International Monetary Fund (IMF) offered emergency support to the three hardest-hit countries—Thailand, Korea and Indonesia. As a condition for support, however, the IMF demanded austerity measures involving increased domestic interest rates and reduced government expenditures designed to support the exchange rate. Since these policy actions were contractionary at a point when the economies were already experiencing a severe credit crunch, the Asian economies slid into a deep, long-lasting recession. One-year declines in industrial production of 20 percent or more in Thailand and Indonesia are comparable with those in North America and Europe during the Great Depression.

One can thus argue that the IMF initially prescribed the wrong medicine for the afflicted Asian economies. The IMF bailout can also be criticized on another ground: moral hazard. The IMF safety net may breed complacency in the developing countries and encourage excessive risk-taking on the part of international lenders.

It is doubtful whether the international debt crisis of the 1980s or the Asian crisis has taught banks lasting lessons about the risks of lending to sovereign governments or sending large amounts of short-term funds to specific regions of the world. For some reason, bankers always seem willing to lend huge amounts to borrowers with a limited potential to repay. Regardless, there is no excuse for failing to properly evaluate the potential risks of an investment or loan. In lending to a sovereign government or making loans to private parties in distant parts of the world, the risks are unique. Proper analysis of the economic, political and social factors that constitute **political risk** is warranted. While this topic might fit nicely with the current discussion, we leave it instead for the next chapter, on the international bond market, and Chapter 15, on direct foreign investment.

Generally speaking, liberalization of financial markets when combined with a weak domestic financial system creates an environment susceptible to currency and financial crises. Both Mexico and Korea experienced a major currency crisis within a few years after joining the Organization for Economic Cooperation and Development (OECD), which required significant liberalization of financial markets. A more appropriate sequence of reform is to strengthen a country's domestic financial system first and then to liberalize financial markets while leaving capital account liberalization (and exchange rate flexibility) as the last step.

Constructive measures can strengthen a nation's domestic financial system focusing first on financial-sector regulation and supervision. One approach is to sign on to the "Core Principle of Effective Banking Supervision" drafted by the Basle Committee on Banking Supervision. Banks should be encouraged to base lending decisions on economic merit and creditworthiness. Financial institutions and the government should be required to provide reliable financial data in a timely fashion. A higher level of disclosure of financial information and transparency about the state of the economy make it easier for all concerned to monitor the situation and mitigate the destabilizing cycles of investor euphoria and panic otherwise accentuated by the lack of reliable information.

Even if a country chooses to liberalize its financial markets by allowing cross-border capital flows, it should encourage foreign direct investment and long-term bond investments; it should not encourage short-term investments that can be reversed overnight, causing financial turmoil.

In the "trilemma" of open economy macroeconomics, a country can maintain only two of the following three policy stances: (1) a fixed exchange rate, (2) free cross-border capital flows and (3) independent monetary policy. If a country wants independent monetary policy to pursue its own domestic economic goals and if it also prefers to have a fixed exchange rate *vis-à-vis* other currencies, then the country must restrict cross-border capital flows. China and India were noticeably unaffected by the Asian currency crisis because both countries maintain firm capital controls, segmenting their capital markets from the rest of the world. Hong Kong was less affected by the crisis, having fixed its exchange rate to the US dollar via a currency board and allowed free flows of capital. Hong Kong had long ago given up its monetary independence.

Argentina's Currency Board Collapse, 2002

A **currency board** is an extreme form of a fixed exchange rate with local currency fully backed by the US dollar (or another chosen standard currency). Each new dollar in the system is held by the currency board and substituted with units of local currency. A recent episode with the Argentine peso, however, shows that even a currency board is not immune from collapse. Exhibit 6.10 shows how the peso–dollar exchange rate, fixed at parity throughout much of the 1990s, collapsed in January 2002. Short of complete dollarization (as with Panama, for example), a currency board can collapse unless it is backed by political will and economic discipline to defend it. When the peso was first linked to the US dollar in 1991, economic effects were positive: Argentina's chronic inflation fell and foreign investment poured in, leading to an economic boom. Over time, however, the peso appreciated against neighbouring Latin American currencies as the US dollar strengthened in the second half of the 1990s. The strong peso hurt Argentina's exports and caused a protracted economic downturn that eventually led to the abandonment of peso–dollar parity in January 2002. This in turn resulted in severe economic and political distress in the country. In contrast, Hong Kong was able to successfully defend its currency board arrangement during the Asian financial crisis, a major stress test for the arrangement.

EXHIBIT 6.10

Collapse of the
Currency Board
Arrangement in
Argentina

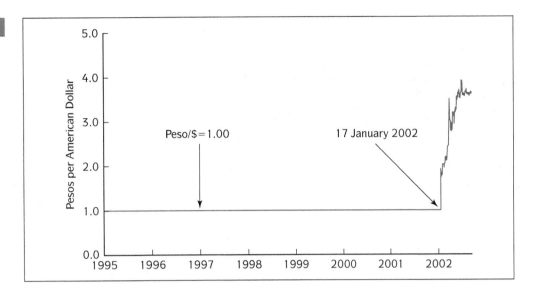

Japanese Banking: A Crisis?

If a financial crisis, like a tsunami, hits unexpectedly, imparts damage quickly and is followed at some reasonable interval by a return to a renewed and stronger state, the Japanese banking problems cannot be called a crisis. Japan's financial problems have been around for too long and they remain deeply embedded in the Japanese politico-industrial system.

In Japan, commercial banks have historically served as the financing arm of a collaborative group of business firms known as *keiretsu*. Keiretsu members have cross-holdings of one another's equity and close ties of trade and credit. Typically, these equity shares are not traded. Japanese banks frequently hold large equity positions in *keiretsu* members, which, in turn, tend to be highly levered in comparison to western business firms. The robust Japanese economy of the late 1980s, fuelled by large trade surpluses, drove rapidly accelerating financial and real asset prices. Japanese banks, flush with cash and a desire to gain worldwide market share, engaged in tremendous lending both at home and abroad. Much was in real estate loans. At the time, Japanese firms had little trouble servicing their bank loans.

The 1989 Japanese stock market collapse was followed by a downward spiral for the entire Japanese economy and, in particular, Japanese banks. By 2007, the Nikkei stock market index stood at less than half its value at the peak.

The Japanese economic downturn and the collapse in real estate values put massive amounts of bank loans to industry in jeopardy. Nonperforming loans mounted to ¥32 trillion (US$245 billion). To defend the industrial side of *keiretsu*, Japanese monetary authorities dramatically reduced interest rates—for an extended period, rates were zero! Even today (2014), the Japanese bank rate is only one-half a percent. At low interest rates it is easier for bank customers to meet periodic interest payments. Moreover, low rates reduce the banks' cost of carrying nonperforming loans on their books. However, it is questionable whether these same customers will be able to make debt service obligations when interest rates turn up or whether they have the incentive or means to eventually pay off the loans. It is unlikely that the Japanese banking structure and performance will improve anytime soon. At least two important factors make this true. First, the Japanese financial system does not have a legal infrastructure that allows for an expedient method to restructure bad bank loans. Second, Japanese bank management have little incentive to change outdated business practices because of the interrelations that exist between bank shareholders and bank customers.

US Subprime Implosion and Credit Crunch, 2007

The most recent major spate of international financial turmoil has its origins firmly in the United States. This ought to shatter any preconception that countries with sophisticated

Contagion without Borders

The lessons taught by the "Tequila Effect" or the "Brazilian Sneeze"

Economists are developing a fascinating body of work around how international markets interact and behave during times of economic crises. The extension of this work could prove seminal to how institutional investors model their portfolios and manage risk.

The phenomenon known as financial contagion is the cross-border financial shock that propagates between countries and cannot be explained by examining standard channels of interaction, such as trade links.

The Contagions

Evidence of contagion and subsequent study is based on the following prominent examples:

- Tequila Effect (1994)—Mexican devaluation of the peso. Economics noticed the shock unduly influenced several Latin American markets, while the rest of the world came away relatively unscathed.
- Asian Flu (1997)—Speculative attacks in Indonesian, Korean, Malaysian and Thai markets. Almost all emerging markets—and even some developed markets—were affected. With the exception of Chile, these countries in Latin America had almost no direct trading relationships with the southeast Asian region.
- Russian Cold (1997)—Russia defaulted on its sovereign bonds and followed with a devaluation of the ruble, leading to a dramatic drop in the Russian stock market. The Russian Cold had a surprisingly large impact on international markets, given its small size relative to global market capitalization.
- Brazilian Sneeze (1999)—Speculative attack on the Brazilian real, which eventually caused the central bank to devalue the currency. The impact was smaller than the Russian or Asian crises, and did not have a consistent effect on other emerging markets.
- The NASDAQ Rash (2000)—Drop in the NASDAQ index and rise in its volatility. The losses sustained from this shock in the majority of the emerging markets were greater than in the U.S. market. As well, the impact was widespread in all developed markets.

Shift Contagion

There are two schools of thought identifying when contagion is taking place: shift contagion and pure contagion. Shift contagion refers to changes in the normal strength of transmission mechanisms, including the fundamental channels of trade links, financial links, monetary policy and common shocks affecting those links. Fundamental channels are the oldest and best understood of all linkages between countries. Bilateral trade relationships, for example, are most often believed responsible for transmitting financial, market and economic shocks across countries.

Pure Contagion

Pure contagion refers to non-fundamental links. The transmission channels relate to investors' expectations and behaviour. The "herding" theory of investor behaviour, for example, focuses on the notion that individuals copy others in their group, acting on the perception that others have better information. The key points here are that imitation may be rewarded and individuals have an intrinsic preference for conformity.

Every country has contagious links both directly and indirectly to other nations. These links are present all the time, not just during the crises. With the integration of global markets, this means that contagion can spread quickly and affect developed and emerging markets, regardless of whether or not there is an apparent disconnect. What's more, many of the linkages cannot be controlled through macroeconomic policy decisions.

Advancements in the study of financial contagion and subsequent application of this learning to the institutional investment arena will result in:

- A better understanding of the stability relationship between international markets and how they move together;
- An improved forecasting ability for these markets;
- More robust Value-at-Risk (VaR) and asset allocation modelling: and,
- Improved buy/sell decisions during times of market distress.

Source: Robert Boston, "Contagion without Borders," *Canadian Investment Review*, Vol. 16, No. 2, Summer 2003, p. 35.

financial markets are immune to financial crises. The 2007 episode was a result of unreasonable optimism together with reckless application of financial engineering applied to home mortgages.

A brief synopsis: In 2002, the US Federal Reserve Board brought in "easy money" to keep interest rates low and boost a lagging post-recession US economy. Once economic growth returned, the Fed steadily raised interest rates—the short-term interest rates that it directly influences. While interest rates had been low, commercial banks were eager to lend money for home mortgages. Some lenders were so eager, in fact, that they willingly made risky loans, often without fully investigating the creditworthiness of the lender or the quality of the real estate that supported the mortgage. Such loans of dubious quality are called "subprime" loans, to reflect the fact that the borrowers do not qualify for the best mortgage rates.

If house prices always rose, then the "subprime" lending would tend to be protected by the appreciation of the collateral. However, in 2007 house prices in certain parts of the US began to fall. Borrowers walked away from their mortgages or, if banks foreclosed on the borrower, the principal of the loan often could not be fully recovered. Banks were under great strain.

Moreover, many banks had aggressively created "asset-backed securities" with their portfolio of mortgages, issuing bonds "backed" by the real estate and the flow of mortgage payments. These asset-backed securities traded in conventional credit markets. When the housing market soured, the credit markets had great difficulty in determining the value of these securities. Whenever a financial asset is difficult to value, buyers become wary and sellers cannot sell. Liquidity dries up. The 2007 US subprime implosion was a classic credit crunch in the new guise of asset-backed securities.

The vast volume of questionable paper and much of US credit tied to real estate meant that the credit crunch was not contained within the United States. Foreign holders of US paper withdrew. Interest rates rose and bond values fell. Many international banks, including some Canadian ones, suffered significant losses.

From Credit Crunch to Financial Crisis As the credit crunch escalated, many CDOs found themselves stuck with various tranches of MBS debt, especially the highest-risk tranches, which they had not yet placed or were unable to place as subprime foreclosure rates around the country escalated. Commercial and investment banks in the US in particular were forced to write down billions of subprime debt, which initially was not expected to exceed $285 billion—a large but manageable sum. But matters only worsened and did not stay limited to the subprime mortgage market for long.

As the global economy slipped into recession, banks around the world started to set aside billions to prepare for a tsunami of defaults. The credit rating firms—Moody's, S&P and Fitch—lowered their ratings on many CDOs after recognizing that the models they had used to evaluate the risk of the various tranches were mis-specified. The credit rating firms downgraded many MBSs, especially those containing subprime mortgages, as foreclosures increased. An unsustainable problem arose for bond insurers who sold **credit default swap (CDS)** contracts and the banks that purchased this credit insurance. As the bond insurers got hit with claims from bank-sponsored SIVs as the MBS debt in their portfolios defaulted, the credit rating agencies required insurers to put up more collateral with the counterparties who held the other side of the CDSs, which put stress on their capital base and prompted credit-rating downgrades, which in turn triggered more margin calls. If big bond insurers such as American International Group (AIG) failed, the banks that relied on the insurance protection would be forced to write down even more mortgage-backed debt, which would further erode their Tier I core capital bases. By September 2008, a worldwide flight to quality investments—primarily short-term US Treasury securities—ensued. On 10 October 2008, the TED spread reached a record level of 543 basis points. Exhibit 6.11 graphs the TED spread from January 2007 through mid-December 2008. The demand for safety was so great that at one point in November 2008 the one-month US Treasury bill was yielding only one basis point. Investors were essentially willing to accept zero return for a safe place to put their funds! They were not willing to buy commercial paper that banks and industrial corporations needed for survival. The modern-day equivalent of a bank run was operating in full force, and many financial institutions could not survive.

Impact of the Financial Crisis

The financial crisis has had a pronounced effect on the world economy. As a result, dramatic changes have taken place in financial markets worldwide. Some of the most significant changes are detailed here.

EXHIBIT 6.11

TED Spread (%)

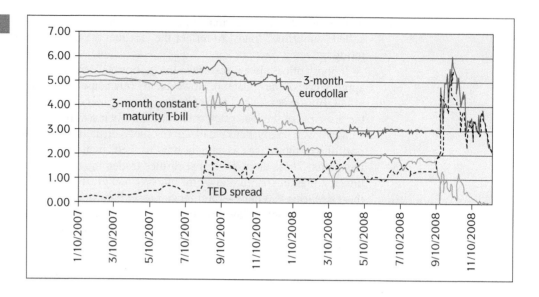

Financial Services Industry

- Northern Rock, a British bank, was nationalized as a result of a liquidity crisis.

- Bear Stearns was sold to J.P. Morgan Chase in a forced sale for $1.2 billion.

- The Federal National Mortgage Association (Fannie Mae) and the Federal Home Loan Mortgage Corporation (Freddie Mac) were placed under conservatorship, where they remain.

- Bank of America acquired Merrill Lynch after it reported large CDO losses.

- Lehman Brothers, a 158-year-old firm, was allowed to fail after suffering unprecedented losses from holdings of subprime mortgage debt and other low-rated tranches of mortgages.

- AIG was rescued by the US Federal Reserve Board in a $150 billion deal, consisting of $60 billion of loans, $40 billion of preferred stock investment and $50 billion of capital, that enabled it to meet collateral and other cash obligations and stay in business.

- Fearing a loss of confidence among counterparties and facing a liquidity crisis, Goldman Sachs and Morgan Stanley, the last two remaining "bulge bracket" investment banking firms, restructured themselves into commercial bank holding companies.[2]

- Washington Mutual, the largest US savings and loan association, was put into receivership and sold to J.P. Morgan Chase by the Federal Reserve after a 10-day bank run.

- Wachovia was acquired by Wells Fargo. Wachovia's problems began with its 2006 purchase of Golden West Financial Corp., a savings and loan association that built its business making adjustable-rate mortgage loans.

- After suffering a liquidity crisis, Citigroup was rescued by the US Treasury and the Federal Reserve, who viewed Citigroup as too big and too important to fail. In December 2010, the Treasury completed the sale of its ownership position in Citigroup, earning $12 billion on its $45 billion cash bailout.

---

[2]"Bulge bracket" is an old Wall Street term that is applied to the former major investment banking firms. It derives from the fact that in print announcements of new security issues, known as "tombstones," the names of the prominent investment banking firms underwriting an issue were printed in bold font that seemed to "bulge" out from the page.

Financial Markets   The financial crisis had a devastating effect on financial markets and on investments that depend on their returns. In the United States, stock prices fell to levels once thought unimaginable. As of December 2010, the Dow Jones Industrial Average was down 18.5 percent and the Standard & Poor's 500 was down 21.0 percent from its peak in October 2007. Over the same time period, the MSCI World Index was down 25.3 percent.

In the fixed-income market, the sovereign debt of countries with big budget deficits has become worrisome to investors and been downgraded by the rating agencies. In particular, in exchange for long-overdue austerity measures, Greece needed a bailout from stronger EMU partners and the IMF when it encountered difficulty rolling over its debt at reasonable interest rates in the second quarter of 2010. (In April, the two-year yield on Greek debt was 14 percent higher than on German debt.) Subsequently, the EU agreed to give $89 billion in bailout loans to Ireland to help it weather the cost of the massive banking crisis that it had fiscally internalized. A flight to quality investments denominated in the US dollar resulted in an appreciation of the dollar. For example, in April 2008 the $/€ spot exchange rate was $1.60/€ and it currently trades at $1.33/€ (June 2013). The corresponding $/£ rate went from $2.00/£ to $1.58/£.

Economic Stimulus

Many new initiatives were taken to spur US and world economic activity:

- On 18 September 2007, the US Federal Reserve Board ("the Fed") began reducing its funds rate from the recent high of 5.25 percent to a range of 0–25 basis points on 16 December 2008.
- Similarly, central banks around the world reduced their short-term rates. A coordinated effort of rate cuts involving the Federal Reserve, European Central Bank, Bank of Canada, Bank of England and People's Bank of China took place on 8 October 2008. And, on 17 December 2008, central banks in Norway, the Czech Republic, Hong Kong, Saudi Arabia, Oman and Kuwait cut interest rates.
- As a result of frozen credit markets, corporations encountered problems obtaining working capital. In an effort to provide credit, the Fed established the Commercial Paper Facility to buy $1.3 trillion in commercial paper directly from US companies.
- The Fed established the $540 billion Money Market Investor Funding Facility to buy commercial paper and certificates of deposit from money market funds to restore the public's confidence in these funds.
- Congress authorized the Federal Deposit Insurance Corporation (FDIC) to increase the level of bank deposit insurance from $100,000 to $250,000.
- The $700 billion Troubled Assets Relief Program (TARP) to purchase poorly performing mortgages and MBSs from financial institutions was signed into law on 3 October 2008. The idea was to get these assets off of banks' books to alleviate the fears of depositors. In a startling change of tactics, one month later the US government announced that it would no longer use TARP funds to buy distressed mortgage-related assets from banks, but instead would concentrate on direct capital injections into banks. In total, $550 billion of the TARP funds were paid out or committed.

The Aftermath

The global economic crisis is ongoing. At this stage, virtually every economic entity has experienced a downturn. Many lessons should be learned from these experiences. One lesson is that bankers seem not to scrutinize credit risk as closely when they serve only as mortgage originators and then pass it on to MBS investors rather than hold the paper themselves. As things have turned out, when the subprime mortgage crisis hit, commercial and investment banks found themselves exposed, in one fashion or another, to more mortgage debt than they realized they held. This outcome is partially a result of the repeal of the *Glass-Steagall Act*, which allowed commercial banks to engage in investment banking functions. As we have seen, the market has spoken with respect to investment banking as a viable business model—the bulge-bracket Wall Street firms no longer exist. It remains doubtful, however, if the subprime credit crunch has taught commercial bankers a lasting lesson. As shown during the international debt crisis in the 1980s or the Asian crisis in the 1990s, for some reason bankers always seem willing to lend huge amounts to borrowers with a limited potential to repay. There is no excuse for bankers not to properly evaluate the potential risks of an investment or loan. In lending to a sovereign government or making loans to private parties in distant parts of the world, the risks are unique, and proper analysis is warranted.

The decision to allow the CDS market to operate without supervision by the CFTC or some other regulatory agency was a serious error. CDSs are a useful vehicle for offsetting credit risk, but the market is in need of more transparency with respect to OTC derivatives, and market makers need to fully understand the extent of the risk of their positions. Another lesson is that credit rating agencies need to refine their models for evaluating esoteric credit risk in securities such as MBSs and CDOs, and borrowers must be more wary of putting complete faith in credit ratings.

As one might expect, more political and regulatory scrutiny of banking operations and the functioning of financial markets was a virtual certainty in the aftermath of the crisis. In this regard, as previously mentioned, the Basel Committee on Banking Supervision finalized a package of proposed enhancements to Basel II to strengthen the regulation and supervision of internationally active banks. A broader program labelled "Basel III" aims to strengthen the regulatory capital framework of international banks. At the country level, in June 2010 the UK unveiled a new system of regulation that, according to the UK's treasury chief, "learns the lessons of the greatest banking crisis in our lifetime." Already responsible for monetary policy, broad new powers were given to the Bank of England to prevent **systemic risks** and include day-to-day supervision of the UK financial sector. The European Monetary Union is proposing its own policies, including new oversight for hedge funds.

In the United States, on 21 July 2010, President Barack Obama signed into law the *Dodd-Frank Wall Street Reform and Consumer Protection Act*. This legislation institutes new broad financial regulations that rewrote the rules covering all aspects of finance and expanded the power of the government over banking and financial markets. Such sweeping new regulation has not been seen since the Great Depression. Specifically, the new financial regulation gives the FDIC power to seize and break up troubled big financial service firms whose collapse would be a systemic risk to the economy—no longer will banks be viewed as too big to fail. The CFTC has been given expansive new power to regulate derivatives that hopefully will prevent the misuse of OTC derivatives, such as CDSs, in the future. Moreover, hedge funds and private equity funds must now register with the SEC. And market makers must maintain an investment stake in MBSs, rather than merely create and sell them to others. The Fed has been given new power to restrict proprietary trading and to ban some types of derivatives trading by banks. A new consumer protection agency will be established to write new consumer finance rules regulating home mortgages and credit cards that require banks to provide more transparent disclosure to borrowers and to ensure that borrowers have the means to repay loans. And a new Office of Credit Ratings will watch over the credit rating agencies. In the area of corporate governance, shareholders will have nonbinding votes on executive compensation and golden parachutes. It should be clear that these new financial regulations have been carefully crafted to address the weaknesses we noted that led to the financial crisis. While some doubt the usefulness of financial regulations, and believe that financial crises cannot be prevented, we believe that financial regulations serve as a useful benchmark to guide financial behaviour and establish what is appropriate. When no rules are present, anything seems to go.

Canada, compared to virtually all other countries, fared relatively well during the great financial crisis of 2007–2010. For example, whereas the United States had 465 bank failures

Mark Carney's Tribute to Canada

Canadians are not in the habit of thinking of their country as similar to the euro zone group of countries, but Mark Carney, in his speech to the Board of Trade of Metropolitan Montreal on Tuesday, presented Canada's monetary union, with "internal real exchange rates," as a much more successful version of the same phenomenon as the euro zone.

Canada's different regions do have different price structures, though Albertans and Quebeckers, for example, do not engage in foreign-exchange transactions. Indeed, according to Mr. Carney, Canadian regions have more volatile exchange rates with each other than the countries of the euro zone—more than between Spain and Germany.

With a degree of simplification, Mr. Carney maintains that a "rising tide" in Alberta lifts "all boats" across Canada. He attributes this happy state of affairs to Canada's having a single financial market, a flexible labour market and fiscal transfers, all of which help to offset economic shocks and to smooth adjustments. In particular, he offered Employment Insurance as a model for Europe; a pan-European employment-insurance, a

means of sharing risks of job loss, could be a building block of fiscal federalism for Europe.

Similarly, he presented Canada's regulatory framework for banking, with such institutions as the Office of the Superintendent of Financial Institutions, as a good template for a euro zone banking union. The financial crisis has shown how unwilling European banks can become to lend across borders even inside the euro zone. In contrast, Canada's large banks, very much present across the whole country, and for all their imperfections and occasional errors—do much to spread risks, rather than letting regions suffer disruptions on their own.

This speech appears to have been Mr. Carney's farewell address, soon before the end of his governorship of the Bank of Canada. It contained very little that might be construed as self-congratulation about his own work at the central bank; it was more of a tribute to Canada, or at least to some of this country's better institutions.

Source: Editorial, *Globe and Mail*, 23 May 2013, http://www.theglobeandmail.com/commentary/editorials/mark-carneys-tribute-to-canada/article12109564, accessed 11 October 2013.

from 2008 to 2010, Canada had none. Canada, of course, has a fundamentally different banking structure from the United States. The Canadian system comprises six large banks, each with a nationwide network of branches, the basis of regional diversification. Canadian laws and regulations, such as no mortgage interest tax deductibility and a cautious attitude toward securitization, lessen the threat of escalating securitized debt and erosion of credit quality. Canadian central banking officials were called on to play key roles in guiding the renewed attention to bank regulation worldwide at the Financial Stability Board in Basel. Then–Bank of Canada Governor Mark Carney, who was drawn to the Governorship of the Bank of England in 2013, was especially recognized for his stewardship of both Canadian and global finance during a particularly difficult era. The box "Mark Carney's Tribute to Canada" presents a *Globe and Mail* editorial praising Mr. Carney.

SUMMARY

This chapter addresses the topics of international banking, the international money market and the Third World debt crisis. It begins the textbook's six-chapter sequence on world financial markets and institutions.

1. International banks can be characterized by the types of services they provide. International banks facilitate the imports and exports of their clients by arranging trade financing. They also arrange foreign currency exchange, assist in hedging exchange rate exposure, trade foreign exchange for their own account and make a market in currency derivative products. Some international banks seek deposits of foreign currencies and make foreign currency loans to nondomestic bank customers. Some international banks may participate in the underwriting of international bonds if banking regulations allow.

2. Various types of international banking offices include correspondent bank relationships, representative offices, foreign branches, subsidiaries and affiliates, *Edge Act* banks, offshore banking centres and International Banking Facilities. The reasons for the various types of international banking offices and the services they provide vary considerably.

3. The core of the international money market is the Eurocurrency market. A Eurocurrency is a time deposit of money in an international bank located in a country different from the country that issued the currency. For example, Eurodollars, which make up the

largest part of the market, are deposits of US dollars in banks outside of the United States. The Eurocurrency market is headquartered in London. Eurobanks are international banks that seek Eurocurrency deposits and make Eurocurrency loans. The chapter illustrates the creation of Eurocurrency and discusses the nature of Eurocredits, or Eurocurrency loans.

4. Other main international money market instruments include forward rate agreements, Euronotes and Eurocommercial paper.

5. Capital adequacy refers to the amount of equity capital and other securities a bank holds as reserves against risky assets to reduce the probability of a bank failure. The BIS 1988 Basle Capital Accord establishes a "rules-based" framework establishing the capital charge to safeguard depositors. This framework has been widely adopted throughout the world by national bank regulators. A 1996 amendment to the accord develops a "risk-focused" approach to capital adequacy for protection against the price risk exposure of its trading accounts. The amendment requires banks to determine their value-at-risk (VAR) according to the criterion that there be only a 1 percent chance that the maximum loss over a 10-day time period will exceed the bank's capital. A New Basle Capital Accord, designed to correct several deficiencies in the 1988 accord, was implemented in 2006.

6. The international debt crisis was caused by international banks lending more to Third World sovereign governments than they should have. The crisis began during the 1970s when OPEC countries flooded banks with huge sums of Eurodollars that needed to be lent to cover the interest being paid on the deposits. Because of a subsequent collapse in oil prices, high unemployment and high inflation, many less-developed countries could not afford to meet the debt service on their loans. The huge sums involved jeopardized some of the world's largest banks, in particular US banks that had lent most of the money. Debt-for-equity swaps were one means by which some banks shed themselves of problem Third World debt. But the main solution was collateralized Brady bonds, which allowed debt-stressed countries to reduce the debt service on their loans and extend the maturities far into the future.

7. The Asian crisis began in mid-1997. The troubles, which began in Thailand, soon affected other countries in the region and also emerging markets in other regions. Not since the LDC debt crisis have international financial markets experienced such widespread turbulence. The crisis followed a period of economic expansion in the region financed by record private capital inflows. Bankers from industrialized countries actively sought to finance the growth opportunities. The risk exposure of the lending banks in East Asia was primarily to local banks and commercial firms, and not to sovereignties, as in the LDC debt crisis. Nevertheless, the political and economic risks were not correctly assessed. The Asian crisis is the most recent example of commercial banks making a multitude of poor loans.

8. The global financial crisis began in the United States in the summer of 2007 as a credit crunch, or the inability of borrowers to easily obtain credit. The origin of the crunch can be traced to three key factors: liberalization of banking and securities regulation, a global savings glut and the low-interest-rate environment created by the Federal Reserve Bank in the earlier part of the decade. Low interest rates created the means for first-time homeowners to afford mortgage financing and for existing homeowners to trade up to more expensive homes. During this time, many banks and mortgage financers lowered their credit standards to attract new home buyers who could afford to make mortgage payments at current low interest rates. These so-called subprime mortgages were typically not held by the originating bank making the loan, but instead were resold for packaging into mortgage-backed securities (MBSs) to be sold to investors. As the economy cooled, many subprime borrowers found it difficult, if not impossible, to make mortgage payments, especially when their adjustable-rate mortgages were reset at higher rates. As matters unfolded, it was discovered that the amount of subprime debt held in exotic investment vehicles, and who exactly held it, was essentially unknown. When subprime debtors began defaulting on their mortgages, liquidity worldwide essentially dried up. Commercial and investment banks suffered huge losses, and many were forced into mergers with stronger banks or had to receive government bailout funds to stay in business. A deep, worldwide recession resulted. At this stage, virtually every economic entity has experienced a downturn. Many lessons should be learned from these experiences. One is that bankers seem not to scrutinize credit risk as closely when they serve only as mortgage originators and then pass it on to MBS investors rather than hold the paper themselves. New banking regulations and financial regulations are currently being implemented to try to prevent or mitigate future financial crises.

9. Canadian banks fared relatively well during the stressful period 2007–2010. This is largely attributed to Canada's concentrated, resilient banking structure and an aggressive bank regulatory and supervisory system.

QUESTIONS

1. Briefly discuss some of the services that international banks provide their customers and the marketplace.

2. Briefly discuss the various types of international banking offices.

3. How does the deposit–loan rate spread in the Eurodollar market compare with the deposit–loan rate spread in the domestic Canadian banking system? Why?

4. What is the difference between the Euronote market and the Eurocommercial paper market?

5. Briefly discuss the cause and the solution(s) to the international bank crisis involving less-developed countries.

PROBLEMS

1. SNC-Lavalin of Montreal borrows US$1,500,000 at LIBOR plus a lending margin of 1.25 percent per annum on a six-month rollover basis from a London bank. If six-month LIBOR is 4½ percent over the first six-month interval and 5⅜ percent over the second six-month interval, how much will SNC-Lavalin pay in interest over the first year of its Eurodollar loan?

2. A bank sells a "three against six" $3,000,000 FRA for a three-month period beginning three months from today and ending six months from today. The purpose of the FRA is to cover the interest rate risk caused by the maturity mismatch from having made a three-month Eurodollar loan and having accepted a six-month Eurodollar deposit. The agreement rate with the buyer is 3.5 percent. There are actually 92 days in the three-month FRA period. Assume that three months from today the settlement rate is 2.88 percent. Determine how much the FRA is worth and who pays whom—the buyer pays the seller or the seller pays the buyer.

3. Assume the settlement rate in problem 2 is 3.88 percent. What is the solution now?

4. A three-against-nine FRA has an agreement rate of 3.75 percent. You believe six-month LIBOR in three months will be 4.125 percent. You decide to take a speculative position in an FRA with a $1,000,000 notional value. There are 183 days in the FRA period. Determine whether you should buy or sell the FRA and what your expected profit will be if your forecast is correct about the six-month LIBOR rate.

5. The Fisher effect (Chapter 5) suggests that nominal interest rates differ between countries because of differences in the respective rates of inflation. According to the Fisher effect and your examination of the one-year Eurocurrency interest rates presented in Exhibit 6.3, order the currencies from the eight countries from highest to lowest in terms of the size of the inflation premium embedded in the nominal interest rates for 10 May 2013.

6. A bank has a $500 million portfolio of investments and bank credits. The daily standard deviation of return on this portfolio is 0.666 percent. Capital adequacy standards require the bank to maintain capital equal to its VAR calculated over a 10-day holding period at a maximum 1 percent loss level. What is the capital charge for the bank?

INTERNET EXERCISE

1. Exhibit 6.5 compares the spread between the prime borrowing rate and dollar LIBOR. Go to the Bloomberg website www.bloomberg.com/markets/rates. html to see the current spread for terms to maturity between one month and one year.

2. In this chapter, we noted that universal banks provide a host of services to corporate clients. Scotiabank, one of the world's largest banks, is one example. Go to its website www.scotiabank.com to view the global services it provides.

MINI CASE

Detroit Motors' Latin American Expansion

It is September 1990, and Detroit Motors of Detroit, Michigan, is considering establishing an assembly plant in Latin America for a new utility vehicle it has just designed. The cost of the capital expenditures has been estimated at $65,000,000. There is not much of a sales market in Latin America, and virtually all output would be exported to the United States for sale. Nevertheless, an assembly plant in Latin America is attractive for at least two reasons. First, labour costs are expected to be half what Detroit Motors would have to pay in the United States to union workers. Since the assembly plant will be a new facility for a newly designed vehicle, Detroit Motors does not expect any hassle from its American union in establishing the plant in Latin America. Secondly, the chief financial officer (CFO) of Detroit Motors believes that a debt-for-equity swap can be arranged with at least one of the Latin American countries that has not been able to meet its debt service on its sovereign debt with some of the major American banks.

The 10 September 1990 issue of *Barron's* indicated the following prices (cents on the dollar) on Latin American bank debt:

Brazil	21.75
Mexico	43.12
Argentina	14.25
Venezuela	46.25
Chile	70.25

The CFO is not comfortable with the level of political risk in Brazil and Argentina and has decided to eliminate them from consideration. After some preliminary discussions with the central banks of Mexico, Venezuela and Chile, the CFO has learned that all three countries would be interested in hearing a detailed presentation about the type of facility Detroit Motors would construct, how long it would take, the number of locals that would be employed and the number of units that would be manufactured per year. Since it is time-consuming to prepare and make these presentations, the CFO would like to approach the most attractive candidate first. He has learned that the central bank of Mexico will redeem its debt at 80 percent of face value in a debt-for-equity swap, Venezuela at 75 percent, and Chile 100 percent.

As a first step, the CFO decides an analysis based purely on financial considerations is necessary to determine which country looks like the most viable candidate. You are asked to assist in the analysis. What do you advise?

REFERENCES & SUGGESTED READINGS

Bank for International Settlements. "Overview of the Amendment to the Capital Accord to Incorporate Market Risks." Basle: Bank for International Settlements, January 1996.

_____ "A New Capital Adequacy Framework." Basle: Bank for International Settlements, June 1999.

_____ "Supervisory Lessons to Be Drawn from the Asian Crisis." Basle: Bank for International Settlements, June 1999.

_____ "The New Basel Capital Accord: An Explanatory Note." Basle: Bank for International Settlements, January 2001.

_____ *72nd Annual Report.* Basle: Bank for International Settlements, July 2002.

Barry, Andrew. "The Lust for Latin Debt: Yield-Seeking Funds Downplay Perils in Brady Bonds." *Barron's* (August 16, 1993).

Beder, Tanya Styblo. "VAR: Seductive but Dangerous." *Financial Analysts Journal* (September/October 1995), pp. 12–24.

Chung, Sam Y. "Portfolio Risk Measurement: A Review of Value at Risk." *Journal of Alternative Investments* (Summer 1999), pp. 34–42.

Eng, Maximo V., Francis A. Lees, and Laurence J. Maurer. *Global Finance,* 2nd ed. Reading, MA.: Addison-Wesley, 1998.

Goldberg, Lawrence G., and Robert Grosse. "Location Choice of Foreign Banks in the United States." *Journal of Economics and Business* 46 (1994), pp. 367–79.

Hartman, Philipp, Michele Manna, and Andrés Manyanares. "The Microstructure of the Euro Money Market." *Journal of International Money and Finance* 20 (2001), pp. 895–948.

Hultman, Charles W. *The Environment of International Banking.* Englewood Cliffs, NJ: Prentice Hall, 1990.

International Monetary Fund. *International Capital Markets: Part I. Exchange Rate Management and International Capital Flows.* Washington, DC: International Monetary Fund, April 1993.

_____ *International Capital Markets: Part II. Systemic Issues in International Finance.* Washington, DC: International Monetary Fund, August 1993.

_____ *International Capital Markets: Developments, Prospects, and Policy Issues.* Washington, DC: International Monetary Fund, annual.

Johansson, Frederik, Michael J. Seiler, and Mikael Tjarnberg. "Measuring Downside Portfolio Risk." *Journal of Portfolio Management* (Fall 1999), pp. 96–107.

Jorion, Phillipe. "Risk: Measuring the Risk in Value at Risk." *Financial Analysts Journal* (November/December 1996), pp. 47–56.

Ju, Xiongwei, and Neil Pearson. "Using Value-at-Risk to Control Risk Taking: How Wrong Can You Be?" *Journal of Risk* 1 (1999), pp. 5–36.

Lopez, Jose. "Regulatory Evaluation of Value-at-Risk." *Journal of Risk* 1 (1999), pp. 37–63.

Rugman, Alan M., and Shyan J. Kamath. "International Diversification and Multinational Banking." In Sarkis J. Khoury and Alo Ghosh, eds., *Recent Developments in International Banking and Finance.* Lexington, MA.: Lexington Books, 1987.

Saunders, Anthony. *Financial Institutions Management,* 3rd ed. New York: Irwin/McGraw-Hill, 2000.

Smith, Roy C., and Ingo Walter. *Global Banking.* New York: Oxford University Press, 1997.

Appendix 6A

Eurocurrency Creation

As an illustration, consider the following simplified example of the creation of Eurodollars. American Importer purchases $100 of merchandise from German Exporter and pays for the purchase by drawing a $100 cheque on his US chequing account (demand deposit). Further assume German Exporter deposits the $100 cheque received as payment in a demand deposit in the US bank (which in actuality represents the entire US commercial banking system). This transaction can be represented by T-accounts, where changes in assets are on the left and changes in liabilities are on the right side of the T, as follows:

US Commercial Bank	
	Demand Deposits
	American Importer −$100
	German Exporter +$100

At this point, all that has changed in the US banking system is that ownership of $100 of demand deposits has been transferred from domestic to foreign control.

German Exporter is not likely to leave his deposit in the form of a demand deposit for long, as no interest is being earned on this type of account. If the funds are not needed for the operation of the business, German Exporter can deposit the $100 in a time deposit in a bank outside the United States and receive a greater rate of interest than if the funds were put in a US time deposit. Assume German Exporter closes out his demand deposit in the US Bank and redeposits the funds in a London Eurobank. The London Eurobank credits German Exporter with a $100 time deposit and deposits the $100 into its correspondent bank account (demand deposit) with the US Bank (banking system). These transactions are represented as follows by T accounts:

US Commercial Bank	
	Demand Deposits
	German Exporter −$100
	London Eurobank +$100

London Eurobank	
Demand Deposits	*Time Deposits*
Amercian Bank +$100	German Exporter +$100

Two points are noteworthy from these transactions. First, ownership of $100 of demand deposits has again been transferred (from German Exporter to the London Eurobank), but the entire $100 still remains on deposit in the US Bank. Second, the $100 time deposit of German Exporter in the London Eurobank represents the creation of Eurodollars. This deposit exists *in addition* to the dollars deposited in the United States. Hence, no dollars have flowed out of the US banking system in the creation of Eurodollars.

The London Eurobank will soon lend out the dollars, as it cannot afford to pay interest on a time deposit on which it is not earning a return. To whom will the London Eurobank lend the dollars? Most obviously, to a party needing dollars for a dollar-denominated business transaction or to an investor desiring to invest in the United States. Let us assume that Dutch Importer borrows $100 from the London Eurobank for the purpose of purchasing from US Exporter merchandise for resale in the Netherlands. The T-accounts representing these transactions are as follows:

London Eurobank

Demand Deposits			
US Bank	−$100		
Loans			
Dutch Importer	+$100		

US Commercial Bank

		Demand Deposits	
		London Eurobank	−$100
		Dutch Importer	+$100

Dutch Importer

Demand Deposits		Loan from	
in US Bank	+$100	London Eurobank	+$100

Note from these transactions that the London Eurobank transfers ownership of $100 of its demand deposits held in the US Commercial Bank to Dutch Importer in exchange for the $100 loan.

Dutch Importer will draw a cheque on his demand deposit in the US Bank to pay US Exporter for the merchandise shipment. US Exporter will deposit the cheque in his US Bank demand deposit. These transactions are represented as follows:

Dutch Importer

Demand Deposit in		
US Bank	−$100	
Inventory	+$100	

US Exporter

Inventory	−$100	
Demand Deposit in		
US Bank	+$100	

US Commercial Bank

		Demand Deposit	
		Dutch Importer	−$100
		US Exporter	+$100

The T-accounts show that $100 of demand deposits in the US Bank have changed ownership, going from the control of Dutch Exporter to US Exporter—or from foreign to American ownership. The original $100, however, never left the US banking system.

The process of Eurocurrency expansion outlined above is the Eurocurrency counterpart of the well-known "domestic money multiplier." An injection of US dollars into the Eurosystem (triggered by the German export to the United States) puts those dollars into circulation of US dollars *outside* the United States. This $100 in the illustration is, in effect, an increase in so-called "high-powered money" in the Eurocurrency system which provides the basis for US dollar credit expansion within the Euro system.

Chapter 7

International Bond Market

CHAPTER OUTLINE

THIS CHAPTER CONTINUES our discussion of international capital markets and institutions, focusing on the international bond market. The chapter should be especially useful for the financial officer of an MNC interested in sourcing new debt capital in the international bond market as well as for the investor interested in fixed-income securities trading in the global bond market.

On the other hand, the typical reader of this chapter is a university student of international finance. In that case, you will be introduced to the fascinating and rapidly expanding field of international bonds and borrowing.

A bond, international or otherwise, is a financial security that is issued—say, by an industrial corporation, a financial institution or a government—as part of large-scale borrowing. To say that a bond is "issued" is simply to say that it is sold. The borrower sells bonds and receives money. The bond is a formal promise to repay the borrowed money. Purchasers of bonds receive regular interest payments while the bond is outstanding. When the bond matures or retires, the issuer pays the "face value" of the bond, i.e., the amount originally borrowed, to whoever is holding the bond at its retirement. Corporations or governments that issue bonds today—say, in 2014—typically plan to retire the bonds 10, 20 or even 30 years from now, all the while paying interest to the bondholders.

Borrowers, of course, look for the "best" or lowest cost of borrowing. If CN Rail of Montreal decides to borrow $100 million to finance the purchase of new locomotives, CN would like to raise the funds at the lowest financial cost. Rather than issuing bonds in Canada, it might be to CN's advantage to issue bonds in the United States or in Europe. Likewise, the Danish pharmaceutical giant Novo Nordisk, perhaps finding the local Danish bond market a bit small for its needs, might issue a "global bond" simultaneously in several financial centres around the world such as New York, London and Toronto. Canadian purchasers of Novo Nordisk bonds are players in the international bond market.

Two features distinguish the international bond market from its national counterpart. First, of course, the international market bond spans international borders wherein issuers of bonds and purchasers of bonds are nationals of different countries. Second, the currency of the bond issue—the currency denomination of its face value and interest payments—may not necessarily be the currency of the issuer. For instance, CN's bond and its interest obligations may well be denominated in US dollars.

The chapter opens with statistics on the size of the world's bond markets and the major currencies in which bonds are denominated. This is followed by a few useful definitions that describe the types of securities issued and traded in the international bond market. We identify market segments and the types of bonds traded in them. Throughout the chapter, the relative importance of these market segments, based on currency as well as the nationality of the bond issuer and the type of borrower, is illustrated with selective statistics. The chapter concludes with a discussion of international bond credit ratings and bond market indexes that are useful for risk analysis.

7.1   THE WORLD'S BOND MARKETS: A STATISTICAL OVERVIEW

Exhibit 7.1 offers an empirical perspective on the world's bond markets. It shows as of 2012 the amounts of domestic and international bonds outstanding categorized by the currency of the bonds.

At the highest level of aggregation, the total volume (in terms of value) of debt in the world exceeds US$92 trillion. Of this, about US$28 trillion or 30 percent of the total is categorized as *international* debt. International debt refers to debt denominated in a particular currency but not issued and/or held within the country of that currency. This was illustrated above by foreign bonds issued by CN and Novo Nordisk.

The share of international debt is growing steadily. Ten years ago the international share of total global debt was less than 15 percent. Today it is 30 percent. The rising share of international debt reflects the global integration of bond markets. It is becoming easier for borrowers to tap global capital markets.

Debt denominated in US dollars, totalling US$38 trillion, represents 41 percent of all debt in the world. Of this, almost US$26 trillion is US *domestic* debt (issued and held within the United States) while almost US$12 trillion circulates within the global bond markets outside the United States.

For debt denominated in British sterling, the international share exceeds domestic debt within the UK. This reflects the importance of London as an international financial centre. Banks and other financial institutions based in London issue vast amounts of debt to foreign corporations and governments—far more than could ever be sold within the UK. Such borrowing is used by corporations and governments outside of England although the debt servicing (interest payments and debt retirement) flows through London.

The Canadian role in global bond finance is relatively small. Of our US$1.96 trillion in total debt (which, incidentally, is remarkably close to the size of Canada's GDP), about 18 percent is international. As we shall explain later in this chapter, however, the

EXHIBIT 7.1	Amounts of Domestic and International Debt Securities Outstanding, June 2012 (by currency of denomination billions of US dollars)					
Currency	Domestic	Percent	International	Percent	Total	Percent
US dollar	26,391	41	11,829	42	38,219	41
Euro*	12,338	19	11,513	41	23,851	26
British sterling	1,823	3	2,119	8	3,942	4
Japanese yen	14,051	22	726	3	14,777	16
Canadian dollar	1,622	3	347	1	1,969	2
Other	8,045	13	1,407	5	9,451	10
Total	64,268	100	27,940	100	92,209	100

Source: Bank for International Settlements, *BIS Quarterly Review*, September 2012, Tables 13B and 16A.

international share of Canadian bonds outstanding has risen sharply of late and, for reasons largely attributable to changes in Canadian taxation, it is likely to continue to rise.

7.2 FOREIGN BONDS AND EUROBONDS

The international bond market encompasses two basic market segments: foreign bonds and Eurobonds. A **foreign bond** is issued outside the issuer's home country and is denominated in a currency other than the issuer's home currency. An example might be a German corporation, say Siemens, issuing US dollar bonds in New York. Siemens would have to meet the regulatory requirements of the US Securities and Exchange Commission (SEC).

A **Eurobond** is issued outside the country in whose currency the bond is denominated.[1] An example is a Dutch borrower, say Phillips, issuing dollar-denominated bonds to investors in London and Tokyo.

Markets for foreign bonds and Eurobonds operate in parallel with domestic national bond markets. All three market groups compete with one another.

Exhibit 7.2 presents the outstanding amounts of international bonds for 1997 through to June 2012 classified by type of issue. Overall, the amounts of international bonds have increased each year. In 1997, $3,323 billion were outstanding; by 2012 the total had increased eightfold to $27,941 billion, or an average rate of almost 15 percent per annum. Most debt is so-called "straight fixed rate," and most of this is issued by investment banks that borrow in order to re-lend to industrial users of funds.

In any given year, roughly 80 percent of new international bonds are likely to be Eurobonds rather than foreign bonds. Eurobonds are known by the currency in which they are denominated, for example Eurodollar, Euroyen and EuroSwiss bonds. Foreign bonds, on the other hand, frequently have colourful names that designate the country of issue. *Yankee* bonds are dollar-denominated foreign bonds originally sold to US investors. *Samurai* bonds are yen-denominated foreign bonds sold in Japan, and *Bulldogs* are sterling-denominated foreign bonds sold in Britain.

For a number of reasons, Canada has been a small player in the Euro- and foreign bond markets, especially on the lending side. Until 2005, Canada's Foreign Property Rules severely restricted the amount of foreign financial assets that Canadian investors could hold. As a result, foreigners had difficulty selling Canadian-dollar-denominated bonds in Canada.

EXHIBIT 7.2 International Bond Amounts Outstanding: Classified by Major Instruments (year-end, except for 2012, billions of US dollars)

	2003	2004	2005	2006	2007	2008	2009	2010	2011	June 2012
Instrument Straight fixed-rate	7,892	8,787	9,682	10,991	14,006	14,428	17,274	18,394	19,399	20,089
Floating-rate notes	2,849	3,404	3,959	4,941	7,169	7,892	8,357	7,871	7,673	7,374
Convertible issues	352	334	315	328	390	392	443	482	485	476
With equity warrants	10	9	7	7	7	5	4	3	2	2
Total	11,103	12,534	13,964	16,267	21,571	22,717	26,079	26,751	27,559	27,941

Source: Bank for International Settlements, *International Banking and Financial Markets Developments*, various issues.

[1] In international finance, reference is made frequently to "Euro-this" and "Euro-that." The terminology dates back to a time, in the 1960s, when the main drivers of the international bond market were American corporations borrowing in Europe. American corporations typically wanted to borrow US dollars and so their bonds were denominated in US dollars. Bonds issued by Americans, denominated in dollars and sold in Europe, were dubbed "Eurodollar" bonds. The "Euro-" prefix became a permanent part of the jargon of international finance in reference to bonds sold to investors outside the country in whose currency the bond is denominated.

Scotia Capital Launches Maple Bond Index

TORONTO, April 3, 2006—Scotia Capital, the leading provider of Canadian fixed income benchmarks, analytics and performance measurement, today announced the launch of a new index for the Canadian fixed income marketplace—the Scotia Capital Maple Bond Index.

The new index was developed following the elimination of Canadian foreign content restrictions and the resulting increase in issuance of foreign names in Canadian dollars. The Scotia Capital Maple Bond Index is the first index to track performance of this growing sector of the Canadian bond market.

The new Scotia Capital Maple Bond Index reflects the performance of foreign domicile issuers of Canadian currency denominated government and corporate bonds in the Canadian market. The index tracks investment grade bonds with a minimum of 10 institutional buyers with a $100-million minimum amount outstanding for each issue. As of March 31, 2006, the index contained 55 government and corporate issues, with a total market value of approximately $20-billion, and a modified duration of 6.749 years. To better address the use of this index in analytics, performance and benchmarking services, Scotia Capital has built and released a history from December 30, 2005.

This new index is similar to all other Scotia Capital fixed income indices in that it utilizes a rules-based published methodology, which has been kept consistent for compiling historical data. Methodologies for all of the indices can be found on Scotia Capital's public website at: www.scotiacapital.com/ResearchCapabilities/RE_Fixed_Income_Research.htm.

The numerous Scotia Capital fixed income indices and data sets are accessible to all interested market participants for license into or for use in third-party systems, derivatives and exchange-traded products. Scotia Capital also licenses the PC-Bond Fixed Income Analytical software, which contains the entire history of Scotia Capital data and indices back to 1947, as well as the ScotiaBond Attribution platform, which provides performance measurement tools for the Canadian fixed income community.

Scotiabank is one of North America's premier financial institutions and Canada's most international bank. With more than 50,000 employees, Scotiabank Group and its affiliates serve about 10 million customers in some 50 countries around the world. Scotiabank offers a diverse range of products and services including personal, commercial, corporate and investment banking. With $325 billion in assets (as at January 31, 2006), Scotiabank trades on the Toronto (BNS) and New York (BNS) Stock Exchanges.

Source: Scotiabank Global Banking and Markets, Press Release, 3 April 2006. http://www.gbm.scotiabank.com/AboutUs/WhatsNew/2006MapleBond.pdf.

Meanwhile, Canadian pension plans and tax-sheltered retirement plans were largely captive to whatever Canadian bonds they could find, which for the most part consisted of government debt. Recently, however, in 2005 the restrictive Foreign Property Rules were scuttled. Soon thereafter, foreigners came knocking at Canada's door looking to issue bonds in Canada. The term "Maple bonds" now applies to Canadian-dollar-denominated debt issued in Canada by foreign governments or corporations. Maple bonds represent the fastest-growing segment of Canada's international loan portfolio.

Bearer Bonds and Registered Bonds

Eurobonds are usually bearer bonds. With a **bearer bond**, possession is evidence of ownership. The issuer does not keep records indicating the current owner of a bond. With **registered bonds**, the owner's name is on the bond and it is recorded by the issuer, or the owner's name is assigned to a bond serial number recorded by the issuer. When a registered bond is sold, a new bond certificate is issued with the new owner's name or the new owner's name is assigned to the bond serial number.

Bearer bonds are attractive to investors interested in privacy and anonymity—attractive features for tax planning. Consequently, investors will generally accept a lower yield on bearer bonds than on registered bonds of comparable terms, making them a less costly source of funds for the issuer to service.

National Security Regulations

Foreign bonds must meet security regulations of the country where they are issued. We will comment briefly on securities regulation concerning international bonds involving the United States and Canada. Securities regulations in the two countries are similar in purpose and design. Because the US market is overwhelmingly larger than its Canadian counterpart, key points are best illustrated in terms of the US.

Recall that *Yankee* bonds are issued by non-Americans, denominated in US dollars and sold in the United States. Yankee bonds must meet the same regulations as US domestic bonds. Securities sold to public investors in the United States must be registered with the Securities and Exchange Commission (SEC). A prospectus that discloses detailed financial information about the issuer must be made available to prospective investors. The expense of the registration process, the time required to bring a new issue to market (four additional weeks) and the mandatory disclosure of information tend to discourage foreign borrowers from issuing Yankee bonds. Alternatively, Eurodollar bonds are often considered to be a more attractive route to raising US dollars. The shorter time to bring a Eurodollar bond issue to market together with lower interest rates on Eurodollar bond financing (compared to Yankee bonds) are major reasons why the Eurobond segment of the international bond market is roughly four times the size of the (US) foreign bond segment. Since Eurobonds are not required to meet national security regulations, name recognition of the issuer is a crucial factor in being able to source funds in the international bond market.

Eurobonds issued in the US may not be sold immediately to American investors. After 90 days, an American can purchase (foreign) bearer bonds in the secondary market which by then are deemed to be "seasoned."

Withholding Taxes

Prior to 1984, the United States required a 30 percent withholding tax on interest paid to nonresidents who held US government or corporate bonds. Moreover, American firms issuing Eurodollar bonds from the United States were required to withhold the tax on interest paid to foreigners. In 1984, the withholding tax law was repealed. American corporations were allowed to issue domestic bearer bonds to nonresidents, but Congress would not grant this privilege to the Treasury.

The repeal of the withholding tax law caused a substantial shift in the relative yields on US government and Eurodollar bonds. Prior to 1984, top-quality Eurodollar bonds sold overseas traded at lower yields than US Treasury bonds of similar maturities that were subject to the withholding tax. Afterward, the situation was reversed; foreign investors found the safety of registered US Treasury bonds without the withholding tax more attractive than higher yields on corporate Eurodollar bond issues.

When it was in effect, the US withholding tax on interest paid to foreigners resulted in a substantial amount of US corporate borrowings from Europe—more than 90 percent—being channelled through the tiny tax haven of the Netherlands Antilles. The Netherlands Antilles had a tax treaty with the United States that stipulated a zero withholding tax rate on American-source interest paid on bonds issued from the Netherlands Antilles. As a result, interest payments from the United States could flow through to European recipients (who, of course, registered their bonds in the Netherlands Antilles) without the burden of the US withholding tax as long as the interest flowed through the Netherlands Antilles. When the withholding tax was repealed, the so-called "Dutch Treat" was no longer sought out by US corporate borrowers.

Canadian corporate borrowers are also familiar with withholding taxes and their potential effect on the after-tax cost of borrowing abroad. For many years, Canada imposed a withholding tax on interest paid to foreigners, in particular, interest paid by a Canadian corporation to a bondholder in, say, the United States. The rate of withholding tax was punitive, ranging from 15 to 25 percent of the interest payment. When it was in effect, the withholding tax forced Canadian corporate borrowers to rely heavily on the relatively small Canadian bond market. It drove a wedge between Canadian borrowing rates and the "world" interest rate, and it discouraged capital from flowing into Canada. When the tax was scrapped in 1975, these adverse effects promptly disappeared.

Today, most industrial nations cooperate through tax treaties to maintain low or zero rates of withholding taxes on interest paid on arm's-length (i.e., *not* intracorporate) borrowing. This enlightened tax policy on international capital is analogous to the elimination of tariffs on traded goods.

Other Regulatory Features

Two other features of securities regulations in the United States and Canada have a significant effect on the international bond market. These are regulations that enhance the flexibility and reduce the regulatory hurdles that issuers otherwise encounter in bringing issues to market. The US SEC Rule 415, instituted in 1982, provides for "shelf registration." **Shelf registration** allows an issuer to preregister a securities issue and then shelve the securities for later sale when financing is actually needed. While shelf registration reduces the time required to bring a foreign bond issue to market in the United States, it does not eliminate the information disclosure that many foreign borrowers find expensive and/or objectionable. To address this problem, US SEC Rule 144A allows qualified institutional investors in the United States to trade in **private placement** issues without the strict disclosure requirements of **publicly traded issues**. The Rule is designed to make US bond markets competitive with the Eurobond market. A large portion of the 144A market consists of Yankee bonds.

Canada has similar securities regulations, including shelf registration for a 25-month period. Canada has also developed the **Prompt Offering Qualification System ("POP")** to expedite the process of bringing issues to market. With POP, Canadian underwriters are more willing to do **bought deals** whereby they purchase the entire issue. Issuers, of course, find that attractive. With bought deals, the underwriters bear the risk of "market deterioration" during the span of time that they (the underwriters) hold the fresh securities in advance of selling them. The ability of the Canadian investment banking community to offer bought deals has created a significant degree of competitiveness in Canadian capital markets. Foreign issuers have taken notice as witnessed by the dramatic increase in interest in Maple bonds—bonds that are issued in Canada by foreigners and are denominated in Canadian dollars.

Global Bonds

A **global bond** issue is an international bond offering by a single borrower that is simultaneously sold in North America, Europe and Asia. Global bonds follow the registration requirements of domestic bonds but have the fee structure of Eurobonds. Global bond offerings enlarge the borrower's opportunities for financing at reduced costs. Purchasers, mainly institutional investors, like the increased liquidity of the issues and have been willing to accept lower yields.

The largest corporate global bond issue, to date, is the $14.6 billion Deutsche Telekom multicurrency offering. The issue includes three US dollar tranches with 5-, 10-, and 30-year maturities totalling $9.5 billion, two euro tranches with 5- and 10-year maturities totalling €3 billion, two British pound sterling tranches with 5- and 30-year maturities totalling £950 million, and one 5-year Japanese yen tranche of ¥90 billion. Another large global bond issue is the AT&T package of $2 billion of 5.625 percent notes that came due in 2004, $3 billion of 6.000 percent notes due 2009, and $3 billion of 6.500 percent notes due 2029 issued in March 1999. The Republic of Italy issued one of the largest sovereign global bond issues in September 1993, a package of $2 billion of 6.000 percent notes that came due in 2003 and $3.5 billion of 6.875 percent debentures due 2023. One of the largest emerging markets global bond issues, to date, is the Republic of Korea package issued April 1998 of $1 billion of 8.750 percent notes that came due in 2003 and $3 billion of 8.875 percent bonds due 2008.

7.3 TYPES OF INSTRUMENTS

The international bond market has been more innovative than the domestic bond market in the types of instruments offered to investors. In this section, we examine the major types of international bonds. We begin with a discussion of the standard types of instruments and conclude with more exotic innovations that have appeared in recent years.

Straight Fixed-Rate Issues

Straight fixed-rate bond issues have a designated maturity date at which the principal of the bond issue is promised to be repaid. During the life of the bond, fixed coupon payments, which are a percentage of the face value, are paid as interest to the bondholders. In contrast to many domestic bonds that make semiannual coupon payments, coupon interest on Eurobonds is typically paid annually. The reason is that Eurobonds are usually bearer bonds, and annual coupon redemption is more convenient for bondholders and less costly for the bond issuer as bondholders are scattered geographically. Exhibit 7.2 shows that the majority of new international bond offerings in any year are straight fixed-rate issues. The US dollar, euro, British pound and Japanese yen have been the most common currencies denominating straight fixed-rate bonds in recent years.

Euro-Medium-Term Notes

Euro-medium-term notes (Euro-MTNs) are fixed-rate notes issued by a corporation with maturities ranging from less than a year to about 10 years. Like fixed-rate bonds, Euro-MTNs have a fixed maturity and pay coupon interest on periodic dates. Unlike a bond issue in which the entire issue is brought to market at once, a Euro-MTN issue is partially sold on a continuous basis through an issuance facility that allows the borrower to obtain funds as needed. This is an attractive feature to issuers. Euro-MTNs have become a popular means of raising medium-term funds since they were first introduced in 1986.

The Euro-MTN market accommodates a cross-section of borrowers, in terms of both the country of origin and the type of borrower, which includes sovereign countries, supranational institutions, financial institutions and industrial companies. Similarly, Euro-MTNs have a diverse international investor base.

The compelling feature of Euro-medium-term notes for the issuer is flexibility for tapping a variety of international sources of finance. Under a single documentation framework, the Euro-MTN offers flexibility in the size, currency denomination and structure of offerings. Farm Credit Canada (FCC), a self-financing federal Crown corporation and the largest provider of financial services to Canada's agricultural industry, borrows approximately $12 billion per year of which $1 billion is in the form of Euro-MTNs denominated in the Canadian dollar, US dollar, euro and yen.

Floating-Rate Notes

Floating-rate notes (FRNs) are medium-term bonds with coupon payments indexed to a reference rate. Common reference rates are three-month or six-month dollar LIBOR. Coupon payments on FRNs are quarterly or semiannual in accord with the reference rate.

For example, consider a five-year FRN with coupons referenced to six-month dollar LIBOR paying coupon interest semiannually. At the beginning of every six-month period, the next semiannual coupon payment is *reset* to be $0.5 \times (\text{LIBOR} + X \text{ percent})$ of face value, where X represents the default risk premium above LIBOR based on the issuer's creditworthiness. The premium is typically no larger than ⅛ percent for top-quality issuers. For example, if X equals ⅛ percent and the current six-month LIBOR is 0.43 percent, the next period's coupon rate on a $1,000 face value FRN will be $0.5 \times (0.0043 + 0.00125) \times \$1,000 = \$2,775$. If on the next reset date six-month LIBOR was 0.5 percent, the following semiannual coupon would be set at $3.125.

Angiotech's Floating Rate Notes

Angiotech Pharmaceuticals is a Vancouver based company that develops and manufactures medical devices and biomaterials. On November 27, 2006, Angiotech announced its intention to offer US$325 million in senior floating rate notes due 2013 in a private placement. The notes were unsecured obligations ranked equally in right of payment with the company's existing and future senior indebtedness. The net proceeds of the offering, plus cash in hand, would terminate Angiotech's existing revolving credit facility. The notes paid interest at LIBOR plus 3.75%.

The notes were offered and sold in the United States to qualified institutional buyers pursuant to the Securities Act and outside the United States to persons in compliance with Regulation S of the Securities Act. The notes were also offered in Canada on a private placement basis to those permitted to purchase notes in accordance with applicable (provincial) securities laws.

Angiotech's 2006 floating rate issue due 2013 was sold successfully.

In 2008, after interest rates fell amidst the global financial crisis, Angiotech offered to buy back the floating rate notes due in 2013. The offer was not successful.

In April 2013 Angiotech's floating rate note issue was retired and rolled over into a 2016 issue.

Source: Angiotech Pharmaceuticals, Inc., "Angiotech Announces Pricing of Senior Floating-Rate Notes Due 2013." Press Release, 30 November 2006.

FRNs have interest rate risk different from that of straight fixed-rate bonds. All bonds experience an inverse price change when the market rate of interest changes. FRNs experience only mild price changes between reset dates which are relatively frequent. On the reset date, the market price will gravitate back close to par value when the next period's coupon payment is reset to the new market value of the reference rate, and subsequent coupon payments are repriced to market expectations of future values of the reference rate. That is to say that FRNs have "short duration" and therefore relatively small interest rate risk.

FRNs make attractive investments for investors with a strong need to preserve the principal value of the investment should they need to liquidate the investment prior to the maturity of the bonds. Exhibit 7.2 shows that FRNs are the second most common type of international bond issue. The American dollar and the euro are the two currencies denominating most outstanding FRNs.

Angiotech Pharmaceuticals, a Vancouver-based firm, in 2006 offered US$325 million in senior floating-rate notes to be retired in 2013. The *International Finance in Practice* box summarizes the main features of Angiotech's FRN issue including the reason for the financing, the basis of the yield (LIBOR plus 3.75%) and the regulatory fact that it is a private placement available to qualified institutional buyers in the United States and Canada.

Equity-Related Bonds

There are two types of **equity-related bonds**: convertible bonds and bonds with equity warrants. A **convertible bond** issue allows the investor to exchange the bond for a predetermined number of equity shares of the issuer. The *floor-value* of a convertible bond is its straight fixed-rate bond value. Convertibles usually sell at a premium above the larger of their straight debt value and their conversion value. Investors are usually willing to accept a lower coupon rate of interest than the comparable straight fixed coupon bond rate because they find the conversion feature attractive. **Bonds with equity warrants** can be viewed as straight fixed-rate bonds with the addition of a call option (or warrant) feature. The warrant entitles the bondholder to purchase a certain number of equity shares in the issuer at a prestated price over a predetermined period of time.

Zero-Coupon Bonds

Zero-coupon bonds are sold at a discount from face value and do not pay any coupon interest over their life. At maturity, the investor receives the full face value. Alternatively, some zero-coupon bonds originally sell for face value and at maturity the investor receives an amount in excess of face value to compensate the investor for the use of the money, but this is really nothing more than a semantic difference as to what constitutes "face value." Zero-coupon bonds have been denominated primarily in the US dollar and the Swiss franc. Japanese investors are particularly attracted to zero-coupon bonds because their tax law treats the difference between face value and the discounted purchase price of the bond as a tax-free capital gain, whereas coupon interest is taxable. More generally, zero-coupon bonds are attractive to investors who want to avoid the reinvestment risk of coupon receipts at lower interest rates.

Another form of zero-coupon bond is the stripped bond. A **stripped bond** is a zero-coupon bond that results from separating the coupons and principal of a coupon bond. The result is a series of zero-coupon bonds consisting of the individual coupons and the principal payment. This practice began in the early 1980s when several investment banks created stripped bonds to satisfy the demand for zero-coupon US Treasury securities with various maturity dates. For example, Salomon Brothers offered CATS, an acronym for Certificates of Accrual for Treasury Securities. The stripped bonds are actually *receipts* representing a portion of the Treasury security held in trust. The US Treasury later introduced its own product called STRIPS, for Separate Trading of Registered Interest and Principal of Securities. Investment firms are allowed under Treasury regulations to sell the stripped bonds in bearer form to non-American citizens, but, as previously mentioned, the Treasury does not have this privilege.

Strip bonds are now available in at least 16 countries around the world, including Canada, the US, Japan, the United Kingdom, France and Germany. Others are working on or considering such services.

Canadian strip bonds are among the most popular in the world. Canada has by far the most strip bond issues (over 7,000), the most underlying bonds (over 400) and strip bonds with the longest term to maturity (93 years). Canada also is the only market that supports the integration of (Canada) Treasury bill and strip bond markets. Strip bonds, of course, are pure discount bonds (since the coupons have been stripped). Treasury bills are exclusively issued on a discount basis. From an investor's point of view, "strip short Canadas" are priced to offer yields comparable to Treasury bills. In other words, short-term stripped Government of Canada bonds provide an additional supply of securities that are identical (in risk and return) to Treasury bills. Treasury bills (or their close substitutes) are crucial for the construction of many financial products.

Canada is the only country that supports the stripping of all bonds in its domestic market as well as Canadian issuer bonds issued in other markets. In terms of the underlying bonds that may be stripped, Canada has the broadest eligibility criteria, processing bonds that are callable, retractable, and inflation-indexed, with structured payments, multiple rates, long and short coupons and many other features.

Investors appear to appreciate the expanded functionality available in Canada. The relatively high fees for the Canadian service seem not to have reduced international demand significantly.

www.stripbonds.info

This Canadian website provides a wealth of historical and institutional information on strip bonds, a market in which Canada is a world leader in innovation.

Dual-Currency Bonds

Dual-currency bonds became popular in the mid-1980s. A **dual-currency bond** is a straight fixed-rate bond issued in one currency, say Swiss francs, that pays coupon interest in that same currency. At maturity, the principal is repaid in another currency, say dollars. Coupon interest is frequently at a higher rate than comparable straight fixed-rate bonds. The amount of the dollar principal repayment at maturity is set at inception; frequently, the amount allows for some appreciation in the exchange rate of the stronger currency.

From the investor's perspective, a dual-currency bond includes a long-term forward contract. If the dollar appreciates over the life of the bond, the principal repayment will be worth more than a return of principal in Swiss francs. The market value of a dual-currency bond in Swiss francs should equal the sum of the present value of the Swiss franc coupon stream discounted at the Swiss market rate of interest plus the dollar principal repayment, converted to Swiss francs at the expected future exchange rate, and discounted at the Swiss market rate of interest.

Japanese firms have been large issuers of dual currency bonds. These bonds are issued and pay coupon interest in yen with the principal reimbursement in US dollars. Yen/dollar dual currency bonds are an attractive financing method for Japanese MNCs wanting to

EXHIBIT 7.3

Typical Characteristics of International Bond Market Instruments

Instrument	Frequency of Interest Payment	Size of Coupon Payment	Pay-off at Maturity
Straight fixed-rate	Annual	Fixed	Currency of issue
Floating-rate note	Quarterly or semiannual	Variable	Currency of issue
Convertible bond	Annual	Fixed	Currency of issue or conversion to equity shares
Straight fixed-rate with equity warrants	Annual	Fixed	Currency of issue plus equity shares from exercised warrants
Zero-coupon	None	Zero	Currency of issue
Dual-currency	Annual	Fixed	Dual currency

establish or expand their foreign subsidiaries. The yen proceeds can be converted to dollars to finance the capital investment. During the early years, the coupon payments can be made by the parent firm in yen. At maturity, the dollar principal repayment can be made from dollar profits earned by the subsidiary.

Exhibit 7.3 summarizes the typical characteristics of the international bond market instruments discussed in this section.

7.4 INTERNATIONAL BONDS AND NOTES: CURRENCY, NATIONALITY AND TYPE OF ISSUER

Exhibit 7.4 presents the distribution of the amounts of international bonds and notes outstanding for the period 2003 to 2012 in each of the major currencies—the US dollar, euro, Japanese yen, British pound sterling, Swiss franc and Canadian dollar.

A number of salient points emerge from this table of the currency distribution of international bonds and notes. First, throughout the most recent time period, say from 2005 to 2012, the growth of international borrowing is striking. Total outstanding issues grew at

EXHIBIT 7.4 International Bonds and Notes: Currency Distribution (2003–2012, billions of US dollars)

Currency	2003	2004	2005	2006	2007	2008	2009	2010	2011	2012
US dollar	4,493	4,868	5,242	5,897	7,535	8,215	9,429	10,499	11,306	7,208
Euro	4,835	5,517	6,200	7,470	10,535	10,874	12,388	11,791	11,722	9,585
Pound sterling	489	770	1,051	1,298	1,704	1,702	2,146	2,072	2,062	1,959
Yen	779	606	433	434	577	747	694	762	758	645
Swiss franc	196	198	200	230	301	332	366	403	389	380
Canadian dollar	79	113	146	174	266	240	307	354	358	287
Other	233	288	343	428	652	608	750	871	977	1,015
Total	11,104	12,359	13,615	15,932	21,571	22,717	26,079	26,751	27,573	21,079

Source: Bank for International Settlements, *BIS Quarterly Review*, Table 13B, various issues. Eurozone currencies prior to 1999.

a compounded annual rate of almost 15 percent per year. Much of this growth is observed in Euro-denominated issues, to such an extent that the value of outstanding Euro issues now exceeds the value of US dollar issues. Euro issues grew at a compounded annual rate of 19 percent. However, the relative growth is somewhat illusory. The statistics in Exhibit 7.4 are denominated in US dollars, which involves converting, say, euro or yen values each year by the respective US dollar exchange rate.

International bonds issued in Canadian dollars represent less than 1 percent of the world total and less than 2 percent of the value of international issues denominated in US dollars. Since this ratio is not at all reflective of the relative size of the Canadian economy to the American economy, approximately 1:10, the relatively large role of the US-dollar-denominated issues reflects the much more accepted and substantial international role of the US dollar in international finance.

The fact that the value of Canadian dollar issues has not grown substantially over this period reflects, in part, the effect of the aggressive reduction of Canadian government debt at both the federal and provincial levels during the past decade.

Exhibit 7.5 is divided into two panels that show the nationality and the type of issuer of international bonds and notes. The top panel indicates that the United States, Germany, the

EXHIBIT 7.5	International Bonds and Notes: Nationality and Type of Issuer (2003–2012, billions of US dollars at year-end)									
	2003	**2004**	**2005**	**2006**	**2007**	**2008**	**2009**	**2010**	**2011**	**2012**
Nationality										
Australia	164	229	262	352	433	440	529	572	581	548
Canada	268	295	311	347	438	464	564	650	694	709
France	723	892	940	1,197	1,457	1,583	1,917	1,876	1,985	1,562
Germany	1,732	2,109	2,071	2,464	2,786	2,739	2,827	2,624	2,607	1,246
Italy	556	709	699	903	1,104	1,177	1,359	1,316	1,326	935
Japan	255	281	261	304	346	385	380	400	389	181
Netherlands	532	651	677	870	1,040	1,036	1,191	1,258	1,325	1,992
United Kingdom	991	1,264	1,422	1,881	2,278	2,540	3,045	3,021	3,013	3,329
United States	2,987	3,262	3,450	4,297	5,439	5,928	6,646	7,075	7,296	2,033
Other developed countries	1,594	2,091	2,322	3,192	4,232	4,398	5,268	5,291	5,327	4,061
Offshore centres	132	152	172	196	217	223	248	257	267	1,664
Developing countries	702	792	841	990	1,160	1,167	1,315	1,532	1,740	1,494
International Institutions	501	549	535	576	642	638	792	882	1,023	1,327
Total	11,135	13,276	13,964	17,569	21,571	22,717	26,079	26,751	27,573	21,079
Type										
Financial institutions	8,015	9,752	10,507	13,538	16,905	17,926	20,030	19,935	20,047	15,722
Governments	1,194	1,413	1,417	1,622	1,844	1,795	2,232	2,389	2,500	1,580
International institutions	502	549	534	576	642	638	792	882	1,023	1,329
Corporate issuers	1,424	1,562	1,506	1,834	2,180	2,359	3,025	3,545	4,004	2,447
Total	11,135	13,276	13,964	17,569	21,571	22,717	26,079	26,751	27,573	21,079

Source: Bank for International Settlements, *BIS Quarterly Review,* Table 13B and 15B, various issues.

Sara Lee Corp. Offers 3-Year Eurobonds at 6%

Sara Lee Corp. is serving up a brand name and a shorter maturity than other recent corporate borrowers to entice buyers to its first-ever dollar Eurobonds.

The U.S. maker of consumer products, from Sara Lee cheesecake to Hanes pantyhose and Hillshire Farm meats, is selling $100 million in bonds with a 6 percent coupon.

These are three-year bonds; other corporate bond sellers including Coca-Cola Co., Unilever NV, and Wal-Mart Stores Inc. have concentrated on five-year maturities.

"It is a well-known name and it is bringing paper to a part of the maturity curve where there is not much there," said Noel Dunn of Goldman Sachs International.

Goldman Sachs expects to find most buyers in the Swiss retail market, where "high-quality American corporate paper is their favorite buy," Dunn said.

These are the first bonds out of a $500 million Eurobond program that Sara Lee announced in August, and the proceeds will be used for general corporate purposes, said Jeffrey Smith, a spokesman for the company.

The bond is fairly priced, according to Bloomberg Fair Value analysis, which compared a bond with similar issues available in the market.

The bond offers investors a yield of 5.881 percent annually or 5.797 percent semiannually. That is 22 basis points more than they can get on the benchmark five-year U.S. Treasury note.

BFV analysis calculates that the bond is worth $100,145 on a $100,000 bond, compared with the re-offer price of $100,320. Anything within a $500 range on a $100,000 bond more or less than its BFV price is deemed fairly priced.

Sara Lee is rated "AA2" by Standard & Poor's Corp. and "A1," one notch lower, by Moody's Investors Service.

Sara Lee's Netherlands division recently sold 200 million Dutch guilders ($127 million) of three-year bonds at 35 basis points over comparable Netherlands government bonds. In January, its Australian division sold 51 million British pounds ($78 million) of bonds maturing in 2008, to yield 6.28 percent.

Source: Excerpted from *Bloomberg News* (2004).

United Kingdom, France and Italy are the major issuers of international debt securities. Since the top panel of Exhibit 7.5 presents the *nationality* of the issuer without reference to the *currency* of the issue, we now see a relation between the size of the national economy and the amount of international issues outstanding. Canada, for example, has approximately one-tenth the amount of international issues of the United States.

The bottom panel of Exhibit 7.5 indicates that financial institutions—banks, in particular—issue, by far, the largest share of international bonds and notes. This reflects the prominent operational role and, indeed, the comparative advantage of banks in international finance. Banks have the global perspective and credit capacity to borrow in a variety of currencies and then to convert those borrowings into currencies according to the specific needs of their industrial and commercial clients.

The International Finance in Practice box "Sara Lee Corp Offers 3-year Eurobonds at 6%" is a financial news report on a routine issue. The report makes specific reference to the fact that the bond is priced to offer a yield to investors that is calculated in reference to a US Treasury note. The yield on the US Treasury is a relevant benchmark since the Sara Lee issue is denominated in US dollars. That, rather than the fact that Sara Lee is an American company, is the pertinent point in determining the initial price of the Eurodollar bond.

7.5 INTERNATIONAL BOND MARKET CREDIT RATINGS

www.fitchibca.com

The website of Fitch IBCA, an international bond rating service. Information about Fitch and its philosophy can be found here.

Fitch Ratings, Moody's Investor Service, and Standard & Poor's (S&P) have for years provided credit ratings on domestic and international bonds and their issuers. These three credit-rating organizations classify bond issues into categories based upon the creditworthiness of the borrower. The ratings are based on an analysis of current information regarding the likelihood of default and the specifics of the debt obligation. The ratings reflect both creditworthiness and exchange rate uncertainty.

Moody's rates bond issues (and issuers) into nine categories, from Aaa, Aa, A, Baa, and Ba down to C. Ratings of Aaa to Baa are known as *investment grade* ratings. These issues are judged not to have any speculative elements; interest payments and principal safety appear adequate at present. The future prospects of lower-rated issues cannot be considered as well

INTERNATIONAL FINANCE *in Practice*

Lafarge Makes Dollar Debut in America

This commentary touches on several topics pertinent to international bond issuance including the use of the funds, the structure of the deal, the attractions of issuing in the US (liquidity and broad range of acceptable maturities), bond ratings, the advantage for a European firm borrowing directly in dollars rather than issuing in euro and then swapping into dollars and the calculation of the cost advantage of that arrangement.

Building materials company Lafarge has become the first French firm to issue an SEC-registered deal for five years. Despite the ease with which Lafarge did this, it seems unlikely many will follow its example.

The Lafarge deal highlights the challenges and advantages of accessing the US bond market. Lafarge sold a $2 billion debut deal split into $600 million, $800 million and $600 million tranches of, respectively, five, 10 and 30 years.

The benefits of US market liquidity are indisputable. Over the past few years, however, heightened US regulatory oversight has reduced its attraction. At the same time the European investor base has deepened. Only the largest European bond issuers cross the Atlantic these days.

"The US market has liquidity and other advantages *vis-à-vis* the Euromarket. It offers an issuer rating (BBB) for maturities that we couldn't find in Europe. As you can see we have issued 5, 10 and 30 years," says Patrice Tourlière, chief treasurer at Lafarge.

Lafarge was refinancing a bank loan following its purchase of minority shares of Lafarge North America for $3.5 billion. It wanted to raise a significant amount of cash but also wanted to go further up the yield curve than it had managed before. Barclays, BNP Paribas, Citigroup and JPMorgan were bookrunners on the Baa2/BBB rated deal.

Tourlière says, "Beyond the competitiveness of the straight dollar which when compared with euro-swapped-to-dollar was worth 5 to 10 basis points depending on maturities, there were many other reasons to go to the US, including high liquidity for a large issue, a new investor base with limited or no exposure to us or to the sector, and long maturities."

Lafarge has issued in the euro or sterling market every year for the past 10. European investors in Lafarge paper view the move to the US as diversifying Lafarge's financial base. That's good.

Exact estimates of the savings are difficult to make. A back-of-the-envelope calculation put the savings on the five-year deal alone at around $3 million. Across three tranches, the $400,000 expenditure in legal, registration and other costs associated with a deal seemed worthwhile, over and above the attractions of international diversification, liquidity and expanded term.

Lafarge took advantage of a streamlined SEC registration process for foreign borrowers classified as a "well-known seasoned issuer" (WKSI).

Tourlière says, "Lafarge has been registered with the SEC since 2001. We comply with all SEC regulations. We use US GAAP. The additional compliance burden for us in the US is small."

In general, WKSI criteria for foreign issuers in the US are onerous. The most important is for securities to be listed on a US exchange or Nasdaq and to be subject to reporting requirements of the *Securities Exchange Act*. A WKSI must also have filed accounts reconciled to US GAAP in the previous 12 months.

Lafarge jumped these hurdles with no problem. However, smaller and less well-known firms looking to issue bonds in the US might have more difficulty. SEC registration alone is a lot of work.

"If we had to do everything from scratch," says Lafarge's Tourlière, "we probably would have issued in the Euromarket and swapped to dollars. Or perhaps a private placement in the US. But those deals are not priced as competitively as the US public market with a registered deal. It was a no-brainer."

Source: *Euromoney,* Volume 37, Issue 448 (August 2006), p. 23; www.euromoney.com.

---

www.moodys.com

The website of Moody's Investor Service. Information about investment services that Moody's provides and their bond ratings can be found here.

www.standardand poors.com

The website of Standard & Poor's, a provider of investment information, such as bond ratings.

assured. Within categories Aa through Caa, Moody's has three numeric modifiers, 1, 2 and 3, to place an issue, respectively, at the upper, middle or lower end of the category.

Standard & Poor's rates bond issues (and issuers) into 10 categories. For bond issuers, the categories are AAA, AA, A, BBB and BB down to CC and R, SD and D. Categories AAA to BBB are investment grade ratings. An obligor rated R is under regulatory supervision owing to its financial condition. An obligor rated SD or D has failed to pay one or more of its financial obligations when due. Ratings for categories AA to CCC may be modified with a plus (+) or minus (−) to reflect the relative standing of an issue to others in the category. Fitch uses ratings symbols and definitions similar to S&P's.

A disproportionate share of Eurobonds have higher credit ratings than domestic and foreign bonds. Claes, DeCeuster and Polfliet (2002) report that approximately 40 percent of Eurobond issues are rated AAA and 30 percent are AA. One explanation is that the issuers receiving low credit ratings invoke their publication rights and have had them withdrawn prior to dissemination. Kim and Stulz (1988) suggest another explanation that we believe seems more

Heineken Refreshes Euromarket with Spectacular Unrated Bonds

Heineken launched the euro market's largest unrated bond this week with a spectacular two tranche Eu1.1bn debut transaction. The deal, in 6- and 10-year tranches, was more than four times oversubscribed and priced well inside price guidance. Heineken's success demonstrates the depth of demand for unrated credits in the Eurobond market, despite the growing prevalence of ratings and well publicized investor calls for borrowers to have at least two ratings. The major factor in Heineken's favour was the global reach of its brand—the brewer has operations in over 170 countries.

The 10 year bond—the first from an unrated corporate—was five times oversubscribed, enabling bookrunners Barclays Capital, Citigroup, Credit Suisse First Boston and JP Morgan to increase it from Eu500m to Eu600m. "There was no clear guidance in the market about what we could achieve for Heineken or where they could be positioned as a credit—we had to convince people," said Chris Tuffey, head of corporate syndicate at CSFB in London. "Unrated issues are typically tough to sell investors on, but the Heineken transaction was exactly the opposite—both tranches were heavily oversubscribed." Although the lead managers looked at brand names such as Louis Vuitton Moet Hennessy, McDonald's and Carlsberg in pricing the transaction, the price was decided by investors' perception of the credit. Heineken was priced as a single-A credit, although it paid a small premium for the absence of a rating.

Rene Hooft Graafland, a member of Heineken's executive board, said the Heineken family retains a controlling interest in the company and maintains a very conservative approach in running it. He said the diversity of the company's cash flows and profit sources made Heineken an attractive credit. Explaining why Heineken is not rated, Hooft Graafland said the bond was a one-off issue to partially finance the Eu1.9bn acquisition of Brau-Beteiligung AG, Austria's largest brewer, which was completed on October 15. Heineken does not intend to become a regular bond issuer. "The decision not to obtain a rating was not taken lightly but there were clear indications that there was demand among investors for the Heineken name on an unrated basis," said Hooft Graafland. "The Heineken business model is relatively straightforward and there is high transparency in the way the company is run."

The acquisition of BBAG makes Heineken the leading regional player in central eastern Europe, with a market share of 27%. Besides its lack of a rating, investors were concerned by the level of subsidiary indebtedness and the possibility that the new bonds would be subordinated to the company's outstanding debt. Both issues were tackled by management on the five-day roadshow—and successfully so, judging by the level of oversubscription.

The reason that Heineken's previous debt had been concentrated in the operating subsidiaries rather than the holding company was simply that it was more cost effective under Dutch tax law, which has changed in the last month. "However, we made it clear that the debt level is modest and is historically concentrated in the three big operating companies," said Hooft Graafland. "In addition to the standard covenant package, the bond has a covenant that limits the level of subsidiary indebtedness at 35% of the total consolidated group assets." The main buyers of the 2010s were investors in Switzerland taking 25%, the UK with 22%, and France and the Benelux each with 17%. There was a large retail bid for the shorter maturity at 38%, while fund managers and insurance companies took 32% and 26% respectively. UK investors were by far the largest players in the 2013s, accounting for 36%, followed by French accounts with 14%, while Switzerland and Austria each took 10%. Fund managers predominated by taking 39% of the book, the retail bid was strong at 31%, and insurance companies followed closely with 28%.

Source: Excerpted from *Euroweek* (London), 26 October 2003, p. 1.

likely. That is, the Eurobond market is accessible only to firms that have good credit ratings and name recognition to begin with; hence, they are rated highly. Regardless, it is beneficial to know about the ratings Fitch, Moody's and S&P assign to international bond issues.

Gande and Parsley (2005) study cross-border financial market linkages by examining changes in foreign US-dollar-denominated sovereign debt yield spreads (i.e., sovereign yield above comparable US Treasury yield) associated with ratings events abroad. They find an asymmetrical relationship. They find that positive ratings events in one country have no impact on sovereign spreads in other countries; however, negative ratings events are associated with a significant increase in spreads. On average, a one-notch downgrade of a sovereign bond is associated with a 12-basis-point increase in spreads of sovereign bonds of other countries. They attribute the spillover among countries to highly positively correlated capital and trade flows.

Exhibit 7.6 presents a guide to S&P's Long-Term Issuer Credit Ratings for sovereigns, municipalities, corporations, utilities and supranationals. As noted in Exhibit 7.5,

EXHIBIT 7.6 — Long-Term Issuer Credit Rating Definitions

A Standard & Poor's issuer credit rating is a forward-looking opinion about an obligor's overall financial capacity (its creditworthiness) to pay its financial obligations. This opinion focuses on the obligor's capacity and willingness to meet its financial commitments as they come due. It does not apply to any specific financial obligation, as it does not take into account the nature of and provisions of the obligation. In addition it does not take into account the creditworthiness of the guarantors, insurers, or other forms of credit enhancement on the obligation.

Counter-party credit ratings, ratings assigned under the Corporate Credit Rating Service (formerly called the Credit Assessment Service), and sovereign credit ratings are all forms of issuer credit ratings.

Issuer credit ratings can be either long term or short term. Short-term issuer credit ratings reflect the obligor's creditworthiness over a short-term horizon.

Long-Term Issuer Credit Ratings

AAA: An obligor rated AAA has extremely strong capacity to meet its financial commitments. AAA is the highest issuer credit rating assigned by Standard & Poor's.

AA: An obligor rated AA has very strong capacity to meet its financial commitments. It differs from the highest-rated obligors only to a small degree.

A: An obligor rated A has strong capacity to meet its financial commitments but is somewhat more susceptible to the adverse effects of changes in circumstances and economic conditions than obligors in higher-rated categories.

BBB: An obligor rated BBB has adequate capacity to meet its financial commitments. However, adverse economic conditions or changing circumstances are more likely to lead to a weakened capacity of the obligor to meet its financial commitments.

BB, B, CCC, and CC: Obligors rated BB, B, CCC, and CC are regarded as having significant speculative characteristics. BB indicates the least degree of speculation and CC the highest. While such obligors will likely have some quality and protective characteristics, these may be outweighed by large uncertainties or major exposures to adverse conditions.

BB: An obligor rated BB is less vulnerable in the near term than other lower-rated obligors. However, it faces major ongoing uncertainties or exposure to adverse business, financial, or economic conditions which could lead to the obligor's inadequate capacity to meet its financial commitments.

B: An obligor rated B is more vulnerable than the obligors rated BB, but the obligor currently has the capacity to meet its financial commitments. Adverse business, financial, or economic conditions will likely impair the obligor's capacity or willingness to meet its financial commitments.

CCC: An obligor rated CCC is currently vulnerable, and is dependent upon favourable business, financial, and economic conditions to meet its financial commitments.

CC: An obligor rated CC is currently highly vulnerable.

Plus (+) or minus (−): The ratings from AA to CCC may be modified by the addition of a plus (+) or minus (−) sign to show relative standing within the major rating categories.

R: An obligor rated R is under regulatory supervision owing to its financial condition. During the pendency of the regulatory supervision, the regulators may have the power to favour one class of obligations over others or pay some obligations and not others. Please see Standard & Poor's issue credit ratings for a more detailed description of the effects of regulatory supervision on specific issues or classes of obligations.

SD and D: An obligor rated SD (selective default) or D has failed to pay one or more of its financial obligations (rated or unrated) when it came due. A D rating is assigned when Standard & Poor's believes that the default will be a general default and that the obligor will fail to pay all or substantially all of its obligations as they come due. An SD rating is assigned when Standard & Poor's believes that the obligor has selectively defaulted on a specific issue or class of obligations, excluding those that qualify as regulatory capital, but it will continue to meet its payment obligations on other issues or classes of obligations in a timely manner. A selective default includes the completion of a distressed exchange offer, whereby one or more financial obligations is either repurchased for an amount of cash or replaced by other instruments having a total value that is less than par.

NR: An issuer designated NR is not rated.

Local Currency and Foreign Currency Rates

Country risk considerations are a standard part of Standard & Poor's analysis for credit ratings on any issuer or issue. Currency of repayment is a key factor in this analysis. An obligor's capacity to repay foreign currency obligations may be lower than its capacity to repay obligations in its local currency due to the sovereign government's own relatively lower capacity to repay external versus domestic debt. These sovereign risk considerations are incorporated in the debt ratings assigned to specific issues. Foreign currency issuer ratings are also distinguished from local currency issuer ratings to identify those instances where sovereign risks make them different for the same issuer.

The ratings and other credit-related opinions of Standard & Poor's and its affiliates are statements of opinion as of the date they are expressed and not statements of fact or recommendations to purchase, hold, or sell any securities or make any investment

(Continued)

EXHIBIT 7.6   (continued)

decisions. Standard & Poor's assumes no obligation to update any information following publication. Users of ratings and credit-related opinions should not rely on them in making any investment decision. Standard & Poor's opinions and analyses do not address the suitability of any security. Standard & Poor's Financial Services LLC does not act as a fiduciary or an investment advisor. While Standard & Poor's has obtained information from sources it believes to be reliable, Standard & Poor's does not perform an audit and undertakes no duty of due diligence or independent verification of any information it receives. Ratings and credit-related opinions may be changed, suspended, or withdrawn at any time.

Source: www.standardandpoors.com, 25 April 2013. Reproduced with permission of Standard & Poor's.

sovereigns issue a sizable portion of all international bonds. In rating a sovereign government, S&P's analysis centres around an examination of 5 "scores" as depicted in Exhibit 7.7. The rating assigned to a sovereign is particularly important because it usually represents the ceiling for ratings S&P will assign to an obligation of an entity resident within that country.

7.6 EUROBOND MARKET STRUCTURE AND PRACTICES

Given that in any year the Eurobond segment of the international bond market accounts for approximately 80 percent of new offerings, it is useful to know something about the Eurobond market structure and practices.

Primary Market

A borrower planning to raise funds by issuing Eurobonds will contact an investment banker to serve as the **lead manager** of an underwriting syndicate that will bring the bonds to market. The **underwriting syndicate** is a group of investment banks, merchant banks and the merchant banking arms of commercial banks that specialize in some phase of a public issuance. The lead manager will sometimes invite comanagers to form a **managing group** to help negotiate terms with the borrower, ascertain market conditions and manage the issuance. Exhibit 7.8 provides the 2011 and 2012 rankings for the top debt arrangers (underwriters) of international bonds and medium-term notes. Separate rankings are provided for the top underwriters of straight bonds and FRNs denominated in dollars and the euro.

The managing group, along with other banks, will serve as **underwriters** for the issue, that is, they will commit their own capital to buy the issue from the borrower at a discount from the issue price. The discount, or **underwriting spread**, is typically in the 2 to 2.5 percent range. By comparison, spreads average about 1 percent for domestic issues. Most of the underwriters, along with other banks, will be part of a **selling group** that sells the bonds to the investing public. The various members of the underwriting syndicate receive a portion of the spread depending on the number and type of functions they perform. The lead manager will obviously receive the full spread, while a bank serving only as a member of the selling group will receive a smaller portion. The time from the decision to issue Eurobonds until the net proceeds are received is typically five to six weeks. Exhibit 7.9 presents a tombstone (announcement) for a dollar-denominated Euro-medium-term note issue and the underwriting syndicate that brought the issue to market.

Secondary Market

Eurobonds initially purchased in the **primary market** from a member of the selling group may be resold to other investors in the secondary market. The **secondary market** for Eurobonds is an over-the-counter market with principal trading in London. However, important

EXHIBIT 7.7   Standard & Poor's Sovereign Rating Framework

The *political score* reflects Standard & Poor's view of how a government's institutions and policy making affect a sovereign's credit fundamentals by delivering sustainable public finances, promoting balanced economic growth and responding to economic or political shocks. It also reflects S&P's view of the transparency and reliability of data and institutions and of potential geopolitical risks.

The three key drivers of a sovereign's *economic score* are S&P's view of its income levels, its growth prospects and its economic diversity and volatility.

Three factors also drive a sovereign's *external score,* namely S&P's view of the status of a sovereign's currency in international transactions; the sovereign's external liquidity; and the sovereign's external indebtedness, which shows residents' assets and liabilities relative to the rest of the world.

The *fiscal score* reflects S&P's view of the sustainability of a sovereign's deficits and its debt burden. This measure considers fiscal flexibility; long-term fiscal trends and vulnerabilities; debt structure and funding access; and potential risks arising from contingent liabilities. Given the many dimensions this score captures, the analysis is divided into two segments, "fiscal performance and flexibility" and "debt burden."

The main drivers of the *monetary score* are S&P's view of the monetary authority's ability to use monetary policy to address domestic economic stresses, particularly through its control of money supply and domestic liquidity conditions; the credibility of monetary policy, as measured by inflation trends; and the effectiveness of mechanisms for transmitting the impact of monetary policy decisions to the real economy, largely a function of the depth and diversification of the domestic financial system and capital markets.

Each of the five scores uses a six-point numerical scale from 1 (strongest) to 6 (weakest). A series of quantitative factors and qualitative considerations form the basis for assigning these forward-looking scores. The criteria then call for those five scores to be combined to form a sovereign's political and economic profile (the average of the political score and the economic score) and its flexibility and performance profile (the average of the external score, the fiscal score and the monetary score).

These two profiles are then used to determine an "indicative rating level." S&P expects that a sovereign foreign-currency rating would, in most cases, fall within one notch of the indicative rating level, on the basis of the sovereign's positioning relative to its peers. For example, for a sovereign viewed as having a "moderately strong" political and economic profile and a "very strong" flexibility and performance profile, Standard & Poor's would most likely assign a rating within one notch of "AA−."

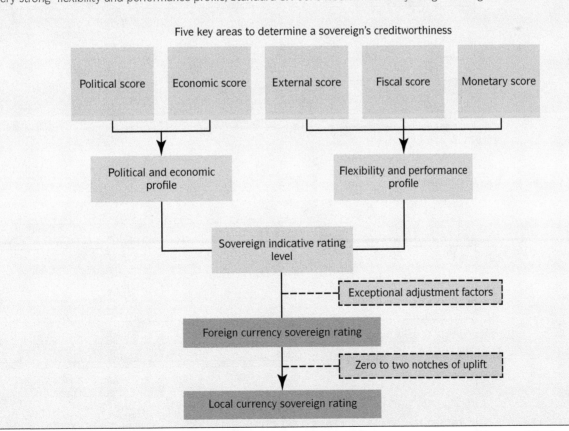

Five key areas to determine a sovereign's creditworthiness

Source: www.standardandpoors.com. From "How We Rate Sovereigns," 13 March 2012. Reproduced with permission of Standard & Poor's.

EXHIBIT 7.8

Ranking of Top
International
Bond and MTN
Underwriters

Bond Issues Overall

2012	2011	Bank
1	5	Barclays
2	4	Deutsche Bank
3	1	HSBC
4	7	Société Générale
5	2	JPMorgan
6	6	RBS
7	3	BNP Paribas
8	9	Citi
9	8	Bank of America Merrill Lynch
10	10	Crédit Agricole CIB
11	13	Morgan Stanley
12	11	Credit Suisse
13	16	UBS
14	12	Goldman Sachs
15	15	Commerzbank
16	14	Natixis
17	19	UniCredit
18	18	Nomura
19	25	ING
20	17	Santander

Benchmark

2012	2011	Bank
1	5	Barclays
2	3	Société Générale
3	4	Deutsche Bank
4	6 =	RBS
5	8	JPMorgan

Structured Products

2012	2011	Bank
1	7	Deutsche Bank
2	4 =	Société Générale
3	16 =	Barclays
4 =	8	JPMorgan
4 =	4 =	Morgan Stanley

USD Issues

2012	2011	Bank
1	1	JPMorgan
2	2	Citi
3	3	Bank of America Merrill Lynch
4	4	HSBC
5	9	Barclays

Sterling Issues

2012	2011	Bank
1	1	RBS
2	2	Barclays
3	3	HSBC
4	6	Deutsche Bank
5	13	JPMorgan

Euro Issues

2012	2011	Bank
1	1	Deutsche Bank
2	3	Société Générale
3	2	BNP Paribas
4	7	Barclays
5	4	HSBC

Source: *Euromoney,* June 2012.

EXHIBIT 7.9

Eurobond
Tombstone

This announcement appears as a matter of record only

Hamburgische Landesbank

Hamburgische Landesbank – Girozentrale –
(incorporated as a credit institution under public law in the Federal Republic of Germany)

Hamburgische Landesbank London Branch
Hamburgische LB Finance (Guernsey) Limited
(incorporated in Guernsey)

U.S.$2,000,000,000

Euro Medium Term Note Programme

Guaranteed in respect of Notes issued by
Hamburgische LB Finance (Guernsey) Limited by
Hamburgische Landesbank – Girozentrale –

The Programme is rated Aa1 by Moody's and AAA by Fitch IBCA

NOW RATED Aa1 BY MOODY'S

Arrangers

Merrill Lynch International

Merrill Lynch Capital Markets Bank Limited,
Frankfurt/Main Branch

Merrill Lynch Finance SA

Dealers

Credit Suisse First Boston
Hamburgische Landesbank – Girozentrale –
Merrill Lynch International
Morgan Stanley Dean Witter
Salomon Smith Barney

Deutsche Morgan Grenfell
Merrill Lynch Finance SA
J.P. Morgan Securities Ltd.
Nomura International
Warburg Dillon Read

Source: *Euromoney,* January 1999, p. 11.

trading is also done in other major European money centres, such as Zurich, Luxembourg, Frankfurt and Amsterdam.

The secondary market comprises market makers and brokers connected by an array of telecommunications equipment. **Market makers** stand ready to buy or sell for their own account by quoting two-way **bid** and **ask** prices. Market makers trade directly with one another, through a broker, or with retail customers. The bid–ask spread represents their only profit; no other commission is charged.

Eurobond market makers and dealers are members of the International Securities Market Association (ISMA), a self-regulatory body based in Zurich. Market makers tend to be the same investment banks, merchant banks and commercial banks that serve as lead managers in the underwriting process. **Brokers**, on the other hand, accept buy or sell orders from market makers and then attempt to find a matching party for the other side of the trade; they may also trade for their own account. Brokers charge a small commission for their services to the market maker that engaged them. They do not deal directly with retail clients.

Clearing Procedures

www.euroclear.com

www.clearstream.com

Eurobond transactions in the secondary market require a system for transferring ownership and payment from one party to another. Two major clearing systems, Euroclear and Clearstream International, handle most Eurobond trades. Euroclear is based in Brussels and is operated by Euroclear Bank. Clearstream, located in Luxembourg, was established in 2000 through a merger of Deutsche Börse Clearing and Cedel International, two other clearing firms.

Both clearing systems operate in a similar manner. Each clearing system has a group of depository banks that physically store bond certificates. Members of either system hold cash and bond accounts. When a transaction is conducted, electronic book entries transfer book ownership of the bond certificates from the seller to the buyer and transfer funds from the purchaser's cash account to the seller's. Physical transfer of the bonds seldom takes place.

Euroclear and Clearstream perform other functions associated with the efficient operation of the Eurobond market. The clearing systems will finance up to 90 percent of the inventory that a Eurobond market maker has deposited within the system. The clearing systems will also assist in the distribution of a new bond issue. The clearing systems will take physical possession of the newly printed bond certificates in the depository, collect subscription payments from the purchasers and record ownership of the bonds. The clearing systems will also distribute coupon payments. The borrower pays to the clearing system the coupon interest due on the portion of the issue held in the depository, which in turn credits the appropriate amounts to the bond owners' cash accounts.

7.7   INTERNATIONAL BOND MARKET INDEXES

There are several international bond market indexes. The best known include the J. P. Morgan Domestic Government Bond Indices and their Global Government Bond Index. J. P. Morgan publishes government bond indexes for 18 individual countries: Australia, Canada, Belgium, Denmark, France, Germany, Italy, Japan, the Netherlands, Spain, Sweden, the United Kingdom, the United States, New Zealand, Ireland, Finland, Portugal and South Africa. Each bond index includes only government bonds in five maturity categories: 1–3 years, 3–5 years, 5–7 years, 7–10 years and 10-plus years. The Global Government Bond Index is a value-weighted representation of the 18 government bond indexes.

www.jpmorgan.com

This is the website of J. P. Morgan and Company, an international investment banking firm. This is an extensive website detailing products and services of the firm.

The J. P. Morgan Domestic and Global Government Bond indexes are widely used benchmarks of international bond performance. The Domestic Government Indices, European Monetary Union Government Bond Index (EMU), the 18-country Global Government Bond Index and an Emerging Market Government Bond Index (EMBI) appear daily in *The Wall Street Journal*. Exhibit 7.10 reports yields on the Domestic and Global Government Bond indexes as reported 10 May 2013.

Every day the financial press also publishes yields for government bonds of various nations and various terms to maturity. These data compare term structures of interest rates across countries. The bottom panel of Exhibit 7.10 presents such "mapping yields" for government bonds of eight industrial countries including Canada. For each country, the

| EXHIBIT 7.10 | International Bond Market Data Provided Daily in *The Wall Street Journal* |

Global Government Bonds

Friday, 10 May 2013
Yields and spreads over or under U.S. Treasuries on benchmark two, five and 10-year government bonds in selected other countries; arrows indicate whether the yield rose (△) or fell (▼) in the latest session.

Coupon (%)	Country/Maturity, in Years		Yield (%) Latest (●)	Previous	Month Ago	Year Ago		Spread Latest	Chg, from Prev	Year Ago
4.300	Austria*	2	0.156▲	0.106	0.098	0.525	−8.5		3.6	25.5
3.200		5	0.645▲	0.551	0.692	1.439	−16.8		2.9	67.1
3.650		10	1.774▲	1.662	1.658	2.548	−12.5		2.9	67.5
4.000	Belgium	2	0.147▲	0.109	0.188	0.917	−9.4		2.5	64.7
4.000		5	0.951▲	0.852	0.996	2.038		13.8	3.4	127.1
4.000		10	2.083▲	1.971	2.105	3.185		18.4	2.9	131.2
3.125	Finland*	2	0.116▲	0.073	0.114	0.217	−12.5		3.1	−5.3
1.875		5	0.503▲	0.414	0.551	0.948	−31.0		2.3	18.1
3.500		10	1.551▲	1.461	1.555	1.893	−34.8		0.7	2.0
2.500	France	2	0.112▲	0.079	0.131	0.453	−12.9		2.0	18.3
1.750		5	0.814▲	0.713	0.829	1.601		0.1	3.6	83.4
3.250		10	1.958▲	1.836	1.871	2.713		5.9	3.9	83.9
0.250	Germany	2	0.050▲	0.009	0.050	0.086	−19.1		2.8	−18.4
0.750		5	0.414▲	0.327	0.364	0.509	−39.9		2.2	−25.9
1.750		10	1.375▲	1.267	1.303	1.520	−52.4		2.5	−35.4
n.a.	Greece	2	n.a.	n.a.	n.a.	n.a.		n.a.	n.a.	n.a.
n.a.		5	n.a.	n.a.	n.a.	n.a.		n.a.	n.a.	n.a.
n.a.		10	n.a.	n.a.	n.a.	n.a.		n.a.	n.a.	n.a.
3.000	Italy	2	1.653▲	1.630	2.122	2.938		141.2	1.0	266.8
4.750		5	2.815▲	2.774	3.116	4.478		200.2	−2.4	371.0
5.000		10	3.872▲	3.842	4.305	5.433		197.3	−5.3	356.0
1.000	Netherlands	2	0.103▲	0.072	0.126	0.277	−13.8		1.8	0.7
4.500		5	0.643▲	0.549	0.700	1.152	−17.0		2.9	38.4
2.250		10	1.700▲	1.593	1.755	2.085	−19.9		2.4	21.2
5.450	Portugal*	2	2.392▲	2.353	2.813	7.371		215.1	2.6	710.1
4.200		5	4.088▲	4.074	4.963	12.299		327.5	−5.1	1153.2
3.850		10	5.412▲	5.409	6.334	10.805		351.3	−8.0	893.2
6.750	Spain	2	1.637▲	1.602	2.069	3.542		139.6	2.2	327.2
3.000		5	2.922▲	2.878	3.355	4.833		210.9	−2.1	406.6
3.500		10	4.213▲	4.185	4.627	5.952		231.4	−5.5	407.9
2.250	U.K.	2	0.317▲	0.292	0.246	0.425		7.6	1.2	15.5
1.750		5	0.764▲	0.702	0.663	1.014	−4.9		−0.3	24.6
4.000		10	1.886▲	1.783	1.787	1.987	−1.3		2.0	11.3
0.250	U.S.	2	0.241▲	0.228	0.238	0.270	—	—	—
0.875		5	0.813▲	0.748	0.737	0.767	—	—	—
2.000		10	1.899▲	1.816	1.807	1.873	—	—	—

Source: *The Wall Street Journal*, 6 June 2013, p. C6. Reprinted by permission of *The Wall Street Journal*, © 2013 Dow Jones & Company, Inc. All rights reserved worldwide.

table identifies the coupon and the yield for a government bond that retires in two, five or ten years.

The graphics in the bottom panel of Exhibit 7.10 allow us to quickly see whether the yields have increased or decreased over the past day, month or year. The panel also identifies the spread between each country's government bonds and the corresponding yield on

US Treasuries, the best known, universally traded and most liquid government security in the world. The yields on US Treasuries are benchmarks for virtually all other government securities around the globe.

Another source of international bond data is the coupon rates, prices and yields to maturity found in the daily "Benchmark Government Bonds" table in the *Financial Times*. Exhibit 7.11 provides an example.

EXHIBIT 7.11

International Government Bond Market Data Provided Daily in the *Financial Times*

	Benchmark Government Bonds			
	Redemption Date	Coupon	Bid Price	Bid Yield
Australia	04/15	6.25	106.79	2.60
	04/23	5.50	118.74	3.28
Austria	07/15	3.50	107.20	0.17
	10/23	1.75	99.76	1.77
Belgium	03/15	3.50	106.22	0.16
	06/23	2.25	101.55	2.08
Canada	05/15	1.00	99.99	1.01
	06/23	1.50	96.40	1.90
Denmark	11/16	2.50	108.07	0.19
	11/23	1.50	100.02	1.50
Finland	07/15	4.25	108.82	0.12
	04/23	1.50	98.75	1.64
France	04/15	3.50	106.54	0.13
	05/18	1.00	100.90	0.82
	10/22	2.25	103.48	1.85
	04/41	4.50	128.84	2.97
Germany	03/15	0.25	100.37	0.05
	04/18	0.25	99.07	0.44
	02/23	1.50	101.09	1.38
	07/44	4.50	104.35	2.30
Greece	02/23	2.00	58.57	9.73
	02/33	2.00	46.95	9.35
Ireland	10/17	5.50	113.75	2.20
	03/23	3.90	103.63	3.46
Italy	03/15	2.50	102.17	1.27
	06/18	3.50	103.27	2.82
	05/23	4.50	105.30	3.89
	09/40	5.00	106.37	4.64
Japan	05/15	0.10	99.97	0.12
	03/18	0.30	100.06	0.29
	03/23	0.60	99.07	0.70
	03/33	1.50	98.84	1.58
Netherlands	01/15	2.75	104.44	0.09
	07/23	1.75	100.47	1.70
New Zealand	04/15	6.00	106.49	2.51
	04/23	5.50	117.74	3.38

(Continued)

EXHIBIT 7.11

(continued)

Benchmark Government Bonds				
	Redemption Date	Coupon	Bid Price	Bid Yield
Norway	05/17	4.25	111.05	1.40
	05/23	2.00	99.30	2.08
Portugal	10/14	3.60	101.53	2.48
	10/23	4.95	99.30	5.50
Spain	03/15	2.75	102.07	1.62
	01/23	5.40	109.09	4.24
Sweden	08/15	4.50	108.11	0.83
	11/23	1.50	97.25	1.79
Switzerland	06/15	3.75	107.84	−0.04
	02/23	4.00	131.99	0.61
United Kingdom	03/14	2.25	101.55	0.35
	03/18	5.00	119.69	0.82
	09/22	1.75	98.72	1.90
	12/42	4.50	124.77	3.20
United States	04/15	0.13	99.77	0.24
	04/18	0.63	99.07	0.82
	05/23	1.75	98.64	1.90
	05/43	2.88	95.59	3.10

London close. New York close. On 10 May 2013. Yields: Local market standard annualized yield basis.
Source: *Financial Times,* 7 June 2013. p. 19.

SUMMARY

This chapter introduces and discusses the international bond market. The chapter presents a statistical perspective of the market, noting its size, an analysis of the market segments, the types of instruments issued, the major currencies used to denominate international bonds and the major borrowers by nationality and type. Trading practices of the Eurobond market are examined, as are credit ratings for international bonds and international bond market indexes.

1. At June 2012, there were nearly $70 trillion in domestic bonds outstanding and $28 trillion in international bonds. The four major currencies that are used to denominate bonds are the US dollar, euro, pound sterling and yen.

2. A foreign bond issue is offered by a foreign borrower to investors in a national capital market and denominated in that nation's currency. A Eurobond issue is denominated in a particular currency but sold to investors in national capital markets other than the country that issues the denominating currency.

3. The Eurobond segment of the international bond market is roughly eight times the size of the foreign bond segment. The two major reasons for this stem from the fact that the US dollar is the currency most frequently sought in international bond financing. First, Eurodollar bonds can be brought to market

more quickly than Yankee bonds because they are not offered to US investors and thus do not have to meet the strict SEC registration requirements. Second, Eurobonds are typically bearer bonds that provide anonymity to the owner and thus allow a means for avoiding taxes on the interest received. Because of this feature, investors are generally willing to accept a lower yield on Eurodollar bonds in comparison to registered Yankee bonds of comparable terms, where ownership is recorded. For borrowers, the lower yield means a lower cost of debt service.

4. Straight fixed-rate bonds are the most frequent type of international bond issue, and floating-rate notes are the second. Other types of issues found in the international bond market are convertible bonds, bonds with equity warrants, zero-coupon bonds, stripped bonds and dual-currency bonds.

5. Fitch Ratings, Moody's Investors Service and Standard & Poor's provide credit ratings on most international bond issues. A disproportionate share of Eurobonds have high credit ratings. Evidence suggests the reason for this is that the Eurobond market is accessible only to firms that have good credit ratings to begin with. An entity's credit rating is usually never higher than the rating assigned the sovereign government of the country in which it resides. S&P's analysis of a sovereign includes an examination of political risk and economic risk.

6. New Eurobond issues are offered in the primary market through an underwriting syndicate hired by the borrower to bring the bonds to market. The secondary market for Eurobonds is an over-the-counter arrangement with principal trading done in London.

7. The investment banking firm of J. P. Morgan provides some of the best international bond market indexes for performance evaluations. J. P. Morgan publishes a Domestic Government Bond Index for 18 countries, a euro zone Government Index, a Global Government Bond Index and an Emerging Market Bond Index.

QUESTIONS

1. Describe the differences between foreign bonds and Eurobonds. Why do Eurobonds make up the lion's share of the international bond market?

2. Briefly define each of the major types of international bond market instruments, noting their distinguishing characteristics.

3. Why do most international bonds have high Moody's or Standard & Poor's credit ratings?

4. What factors does Standard & Poor's analyze in determining the credit rating it assigns to a sovereign government?

5. Discuss the process of bringing a new international bond issue to market.

6. You are an investment banker advising a Eurobank about a new international bond offering it is considering. The proceeds are to be used to fund Eurodollar loans to bank clients. What type of bond instrument would you recommend that the bank consider issuing? Why?

7. What should a borrower consider before issuing dual-currency bonds? What should an investor consider before investing in dual-currency bonds?

8. What explains the dramatic emergence of Maple bonds?

PROBLEMS

1. Your firm has just issued five-year floating-rate notes indexed to six-month US dollar LIBOR plus ¼ percent. What is the amount of the first coupon payment your firm will pay per US$1,000 of face value, if six-month LIBOR is currently 0.43 percent?

2. Two issues of zero-coupon bonds with value of DM300,000,000 were both issued in 2005. The issue due in 2015 sold at 60 percent of face value, and the issue due in 2020 sold at 43⅓ percent of face value. Calculate the implied yield to maturity of each of these two issues.

INTERNET EXERCISE

BondMarkets.com is the website of the Bond Market Association, a trade association representing the world bond market. A newsletter can be found at the website. Go to the website www.bondmarkets.com to see what current events are of concern in the global bond market.

REFERENCES & SUGGESTED READINGS

Claes, A., Marc J. K. DeCeuster, and R. Polfliet. "Anatomy of the Eurobond Market." *European Financial Management* Volume 8, Issue 3 (2002).

Gande, Amar, and David C. Parsley. "News Spillovers in the Soverign Debt Market." *Journal of Financial Economics* 75 (2005), pp. 691–734.

Kim, Yong Cheol, and René M. Stulz. "The Eurobond Market and Corporate Financial Policy: A Test of the Clientele Hypothesis." *Journal of Financial Economics* 22 (1988), pp. 189–205.

Miller, Darius P., and John Puthenpurackal. "Do Multi-market Offerings Lower the Cost of Capital? Evidence from Global Bond Issuance by U.S. Firms." Indiana University, Kelley School of Business working paper, March 2002.

Resnick, Bruce G. "Investor Yield and Gross Underwriting Spread Comparisons among US Dollar, Yankee, Eurodollar and Global Bonds." *Journal of International Money and Finance* 31 (2012), pp. 445–463.

Chapter 8

International Equity Markets

THIS CHAPTER FOCUSES on equity markets, or how shares in publicly owned corporations are created and traded throughout the world. It addresses both the *primary* sale of new corporate shares and the *secondary* market in which previously issued shares are traded among investors.

This chapter is useful for understanding how modern companies raise equity capital. It also provides useful institutional information for investors interested in international portfolio diversification.

We begin with an empirical overview of equity markets around the world. The statistics reveal the comparative size, trading activity and market performance for a cross-section of equities markets in industrial nations—those with well-developed financial markets—as well as for emerging economies where financial systems are not so well developed. Differences in market size and structure explain differences in the efficiency of equity markets, which ultimately reflect differences in technical sophistication, liquidity and transactions volume.

International finance is in a remarkable modern phase. Cross-border barriers are falling. Equities markets that were once a patchwork of unconnected national institutions are now forging integrated operations en route to building a truly global market for corporate equities. Just as trade liberalization creates a global market for goods and services, financial liberalization creates a global market for corporate shares.

We do not lose sight of our readers' concern for financial management. Our discussion of equities markets and institutions is groundwork for understanding corporate opportunities to raise capital in the broad sphere of *international* equities markets. For example, more and more Canadian companies are choosing to list their shares on stock markets in other countries, especially in the United States and Europe. We identify Canadian companies that have done so, we assess their success in achieving a lower cost of capital (which, of course, is their main objective) and we give guidance to the financial strategy of "going abroad" for equity capital.

To begin an informed discussion of international equity markets, it is helpful to recognize where the major markets are located along with information about their relative sizes and trading activity.

8.1 A STATISTICAL PERSPECTIVE

At year-end 2012, global market capitalization, the market value of all corporate equity around the world, stood at $53 trillion. Of this, 75 percent represents equity in 31 developed economies. Exhibit 8.1 reports market capitalization for these countries for each year from 2002 to 2012. Over the decade, the market value of equity capital in the industrial world increased by 135 percent, from 23 to 54 trillion dollars.

Growth in equity capital has not been spread evenly among advanced countries. For example, North America registered an average annual increase of 5.9 percent over the decade. In Europe the value of corporate equity grew at a stronger 6.5 percent. The Far East nations with sophisticated financial markets registered a remarkable 9.6 percent

EXHIBIT 8.1	Market Capitalization of Equity Markets in Developed Economies, 2002–2012 (US$, billions)										
Region or Country	2002	2003	2004	2005	2006	2007	2008	2009	2010	2011	2012
Europe	*6,171*	*8,538*	*10,591*	*11,136*	*14,748*	*16,848*	*8,362*	*10,842*	*11,879*	*10,391*	*11,580*
Austria	32	55	86	124	191	229	72	54	68	82	106
Belgium	128	174	368	289	396	386	167	261	269	230	300
Denmark	77	122	151	178	231	278	132	187	232	180	225
Finland	139	170	184	210	265	369	154	91	118	143	159
France	967	1,356	1,857	1,759	2,429	2,771	1,492	1,972	1,926	1,569	1,823
Germany	691	1,079	1,195	1,221	1,638	2,106	1,108	1,298	1,430	1,184	1,486
Greece	85	120	127	145	208	265	90	55	73	34	45
Ireland	60	85	114	114	163	144	49	30	34	108	109
Italy	480	615	790	798	1,027	1,073	521	317	318	431	480
Luxembourg	25	37	50	51	80	166	68	106	101	68	70
Netherlands	401	489	622	593	780	956	388	543	661	595	651
Norway	67	95	141	191	281	357	126	227	251	219	253
Portugal	43	58	73	67	104	132	69	99	82	62	66
Spain	465	726	941	960	1,323	1,800	946	1,297	1,172	1,031	995
Sweden	179	290	377	404	573	612	253	432	581	470	561
Switzerland	553	727	826	939	1,213	1,275	863	1,071	1,229	932	1,079
United Kingdom	1,864	2,460	2,816	3,058	3,794	3,859	1,852	2,796	3,107	2,903	3,019
Far East	*3,092*	*4,520*	*5,531*	*6,594*	*7,038*	*7,314*	*5,429*	*7,306*	*8,130*	*7,003*	*7,749*
Australia	379	585	776	804	1,096	1,298	676	1,258	1,455	1,198	1,286
Hong Kong	463	715	861	693	895	1,163	1,329	2,292	1,080	890	1,109
Japan	2,126	3,041	3,678	4,737	4,726	4,453	3,220	3,378	4,100	3,541	3,681
Korea	808	888	901	924	944	960	1,180	1,089	1,089	994	1,180
New Zealand	22	33	44	43	45	47	24	67	36	72	80
Singapore	102	146	172	317	279	353	180	311	370	308	414
North America	*11,673*	*15,160*	*17,502*	*18,452*	*21,127*	*22,134*	*12,740*	*16,758*	*19,299*	*17,548*	*20,684*
Canada	575	894	1,178	1,481	2,187	2,187	1,002	1,681	2,160	1,907	2,016
United States	11,098	14,266	16,324	16,971	19,426	19,947	11,738	15,077	17,139	15,641	18,668
Total Developed Markets	*20,936*	*28,218*	*33,624*	*36,183*	*42,917*	*46,301*	*26,534*	*34,907*	*39,310*	*34,943*	*40,016*
World Total	*23,406*	*31,990*	*38,570*	*46,461*	*51,883*	*56,465*	*33,168*	*44,753*	*50,397*	*45,978*	*54,076*
Developed Markets, % of Total	89	88	87	85	83	82	80	78	78	76	75

Source: *Global Stock Market Factbook,* Standard & Poor's, various issues.

average annual increase in corporate equity value despite the fact that Japan, the largest member of that group, had fallen upon hard times.[1]

Exhibit 8.1 illustrates the decline in total equity market capitalization across the globe since 2007. Equity capitalization for all developed markets fell from $46,301 billion in 2007 to $40,016 billion in 2012. In two—North America and Europe—of the three major regions, regional totals are substantially lower in 2012 than five years earlier. Every country in these two regions shows a decline in equity market capitalization. The Far East presents a small departure from the global trend owing to expansion in Korea, New Zealand and Singapore. Overall, the dramatic loss in equity value results from the extreme stress on the world economy brought on by the financial crisis of 2007.

Market Capitalization in Emerging Markets

Exhibit 8.2 presents data on **market capitalization** in 29 **emerging markets**. Standard & Poor's classify a stock market as "emerging" if it meets at least one of two criteria. First, it is located in a low- or middle-income economy and/or second, its market capitalization is low relative to gross domestic product (GDP).

Exhibit 8.2 reports market capitalization each year from 2002 to 2012. Looking first at the summary data at the bottom of the exhibit, we see that corporate equity capitalization in emerging markets exceeds $13.5 trillion or 25 percent of the global total. Average annual growth over the past decade is an astounding 19 percent, the bulk of which is explained by the impressive **BRIC**—Brazil, Russia, India and China—which together make up about 52 percent of total emerging markets capitalization and 25 percent of the average annual growth.[2]

The size, growth and development of equities markets in emerging markets demonstrate that equities markets are no longer restricted to wealthy industrial nations. Important implications for international financial management stem from the rise of emerging economies. A strong, sound, vibrant equities market indicates institutional strength in a country that can be reassuring to multinational enterprises planning operations there. Meanwhile, equities markets of emerging nations command the attention of major international investors such as mutual funds and pension funds. As emerging markets expand their listings, liquidity and trading volumes, the role of emerging markets in international diversification increases.

Measures of Liquidity

A liquid stock market is one in which investors can buy and sell shares quickly at close to the current quoted prices. A measure of **liquidity** for a stock market is the turnover ratio—the ratio of stock market transactions over a period of time divided by the size, or market capitalization, of the stock market. Generally, the higher the turnover ratio, the more liquid the secondary stock market, with correspondingly low bid-ask spreads.

Exhibit 8.3 presents turnover ratio percentages for equity markets of the developed countries for the 10 years beginning with 2002. The turnover ratio varies considerably over time for most national equity markets. The table also indicates that most national equity markets have high turnover ratios, with the majority in excess of 50 percent turnover per year.

[1]A word of caution is in order concerning international comparisons of equity values. Such comparisons are based on conversion to a common currency. Surveys by Standard & Poor's and the World Federation of Exchanges report values in US dollars. As a result, equities values and stock market indexes in non-US currencies rise when the value of the US dollar falls. For example, European equity recorded as 1 million US dollars rises to 1.1 million dollars when the euro appreciates against the US dollar by 10 percent.

[2]BRIC was conceived in a 2003 Goldman Sachs report, "Dreaming with BRICs: The Path to 2050," Global Economics Paper Number 99.

EXHIBIT 8.2	Market Capitalization of Equity Markets in Selected Emerging Markets, 2002–2012 (US$, billions)										
Region/Country	**2002**	**2003**	**2004**	**2005**	**2006**	**2007**	**2008**	**2009**	**2010**	**2011**	**2012**
Latin America											
Argentina	103	39	46	61	51	87	52	49	64	44	34
Brazil	124	235	330	475	711	1,370	589	1,167	1,564	1,229	1,230
Chile	48	86	117	136	174	231	132	209	342	270	313
Colombia	10	14	13	46	56	102	87	133	209	201	262
Mexico	103	123	172	239	348	398	233	341	200	409	525
Peru	13	16	16	36	60	106	56	70	74	79	97
Asia											
China	463	681	640	781	2,426	6,226	2,794	5,008	4,763	3,389	3,697
India	131	279	388	553	819	1,819	645	1,179	1,616	1,015	1,263
Indonesia	30	55	73	81	139	212	99	178	360	390	397
Korea	250	330	429	718	835	1,124	495	836	994	1,180	1,089
Pakistan	10	17	30	46	46	70	23	33	38	33	44
Philippines	19	24	29	40	68	103	52	80	157	165	264
Taiwan	261	379	441	516	655	724	381	696	804	623	712
Thailand	46	119	115	125	141	196	103	138	278	268	383
Europe											
Czech Republic	29	37	71	94	149	207	90	135	190	138	178
Hungary	13	17	26	33	42	48	19	28	28	21	19
Poland	29	37	60	94	149	207	90	135	190	178	138
Russia	124	231	268	549	1,057	1,503	397	861	1,005	796	875
Turkey	34	68	98	162	162	287	118	226	307	202	309
Mideast/Africa											
Egypt	26	27	39	80	93	139	86	90	82	49	58
Iran	na	an	na	39	38	46	49	63	87	107	141
Israel	45	76	96	120	173	236	134	182	218	145	148
Kuwait	31	59	69	130	129	188	107	96	120	101	97
Morocco	9	13	19	27	49	75	66	63	69	60	53
Nigeria	6	9	14	19	33	86	50	33	51	39	56
Qatar	na	na	na	87	62	95	76	88	124	125	126
Saudi Arabia	75	157	306	646	327	515	246	319	353	339	373
South Africa	185	268	456	565	715	834	491	705	1,013	523	612
UAE	na	na	na	226	139	225	98	110	105	71	68
Emerging Markets, Total	2,470	3,772	4,946	7,104	9,037	10,164	6,634	9,846	11,087	11,035	13,519
World Total	23,406	31,990	38,570	46,461	51,883	56,465	33,168	44,753	50,397	45,978	54,076
Developed Markets, % of Total	11	12	13	15	17	18	20	22	22	24	25

Source: *Global Stock Market Factbook*, Standard & Poor's, various issues.

The data also reveal that equity market turnover ratios have declined sharply across the globe since 2007, the year that marks the start of international financial turmoil. From Exhibit 8.3 we see that all except one of the 29 developed nations (Hong Kong) had lower liquidity in 2012 than in 2007.

Exhibit 8.4 presents equity market liquidity data for 26 markets in the "emerging nations" category. The data reveal considerable difference in turnover ratios among the emerging economies. Many of the smaller, less developed equities markets in each region (Argentina, Peru, Philippines, Czech Republic, Morocco, and Nigeria, for instance) have relatively low turnover ratios, indicating poor liquidity at present. Meanwhile, the larger

Region/Country	2002	2003	2004	2005	2006	2007	2008	2009	2010	2011	2012
EXHIBIT 8.3				Turnover Ratio of Equity Markets in Selected Developed Nations, 2002–2012 (annual value of transactions/year-end market capitalization)							
Europe											
Austria	21	25	37	43	50	58	69	41	79	52	50
Belgium	26	25	24	21	49	65	77	60	42	43	39
Denmark	60	65	70	92	86	99	104	93	69	73	52
Finland	107	106	120	139	150	182	149	74	97	134	84
France	88	86	84	83	120	132	153	79	75	84	66
Germany	141	130	135	146	174	180	193	107	103	135	92
Greece	26	44	46	48	61	64	27	71	68	47	38
Iceland	73	94	84	76	98	115	67	12	10	28	28
Ireland	51	61	60	57	58	89	39	33	28	19	11
Italy	109	122	133	141	150	220	84	110	170	237	167
Luxembourg	2	1	1	<1	<1	<1	3	<1	<1	<1	<1
Netherlands	124	104	108	112	160	208	170	130	98	88	71
Norway	68	86	94	117	149	148	152	140	91	89	56
Portugal	52	42	47	55	82	122	82	55	35	50	42
Spain	211	158	160	164	169	190	178	143	110	129	106
Sweden	96	114	116	119	139	147	148	114	87	96	73
Switzerland	101	90	95	100	120	143	141	82	76	86	64
United Kingdom	135	101	124	142	124	270	227	146	102	99	84
Far East											
Australia	77	77	78	78	87	111	103	79	90	94	85
Hong Kong	44	56	54	49	60	89	131	133	160	158	123
Japan	71	88	94	119	132	142	153	127	115	109	100
New Zealand	38	38	40	41	45	47	88	40	26	30	33
Singapore	39	71	68	63	62	122	102	103	83	75	43
North America											
Canada	68	64	66	64	81	85	123	92	71	75	62
United States	203	123	124	129	183	217	232	349	189	188	125

Source: *Global Stock Markets Factbook,* Standard & Poor's, various issues.

emerging equity markets such as China, India, Taiwan, Turkey and Saudi Arabia demonstrate fairly robust liquidity. Overall, the key concern is whether liquidity is improving.

Primary and Secondary Markets

The expression "equity market" has two distinct—but interrelated—meanings. First, the equity market is where business goes to "raise equity" by selling shares. When a firm first "goes public" by selling shares or when it sells additional shares, it is involved in the **primary** market which means that the shares are new to the market. Money flows directly from investors to the firm that issues those shares. That money is then available to the firm to invest in machinery, equipment, buildings and working capital or perhaps to buy another firm or to pay off debt. The first time that a firm sells shares is referred to as an initial public offering or IPO.

A smoothly functioning, efficient, properly regulated equities market—"stock market," if you prefer—is important for industry and economic development since it is a key source of fresh finance for industry.

Once shares are issued by companies and purchased by investors, they are then available to be traded among investors. Outstanding shares traded among investors do not supply fresh funds to firms. Such trading gives rise to the second meaning of "equities market"—the **secondary** market.

EXHIBIT 8.4	Turnover Ratio of Selected Emerging Equity Markets, 2002–2012 (annual transactions/year-end capitalization)										
Region/Country	2002	2003	2004	2005	2006	2007	2008	2009	2010	2011	2012
Latin America											
Argentina	2	6	18	30	6	10	19	5	5	5	4
Brazil	32	32	34	38	43	56	74	74	66	69	68
Chile	6	10	12	15	19	23	21	22	20	19	16
Colombia	2	3	11	18	22	13	13	12	13	13	11
Mexico	24	21	14	26	27	31	34	27	27	26	25
Peru	9	6	7	7	9	9	6	5	5	6	6
Asia											
China	68	83	84	83	102	180	121	230	164	188	164
India	165	139	111	94	93	84	85	119	76	56	55
Indonesia	48	34	44	54	44	64	85	119	48	37	23
Korea*	322	237	240	210	173	202	181	238	169	195	139
Philippines	21	35	28	20	21	34	22	26	23	20	16
Taiwan	226	185	156	133	157	185	171	198	119	121	99
Thailand	114	117	101	75	71	64	78	112	105	85	70
Europe											
Czech Republic	49	35	88	119	76	69	70	41	29	38	27
Hungary	52	58	64	78	84	106	93	111	95	84	55
Poland	22	27	33	36	45	48	46	50	48	58	43
Russia	36	46	44	39	64	59	75	109	86	127	88
Turkey	170	192	161	155	141	135	119	142	158	163	137
Mideast/Africa											
Egypt	10	14	24	43	55	46	62	60	43	34	48
Israel*	45	99	66	56	61	55	59	56	67	65	46
Jordan	20	29	58	85	60	49	73	40	30	14	10
Morocco	7	7	12	16	25	42	31	46	16	10	6
Nigeria	8	11	11	12	14	28	44	36	13	9	9
Oman	16	28	28	30	21	28	44	36	18	13	13
Saudi Arabia	48	137	164	232	288	162	138	119	61	85	144
South Africa	37	50	44	39	49	55	61	57	40	40	55

*Korea and Israel were classified as developed markets in 2010.

Source: *Global Stock Market Factbook,* Standard & Poor's, various issues.

The volume of transactions in the secondary market is vastly greater than the volume of new issues in the primary market. Think of the ratio as 99 to 1.

The primary and secondary markets are related in significant ways. The secondary market provides liquidity for investors. The large variety of shares available in relatively small denominations allows the investor to build a diversified portfolio and to manage risk. Equally important, the secondary market continuously determines prices for all traded equities. Since the prevailing share price is important for the firm that wants to sell additional shares (a firm naturally wants to sell new shares at the highest possible price per share) the secondary market provides price "signals" for firms when they consider raising equity capital—which, of course, takes us back to the primary market.

When equities markets function well—free of distortion, manipulation and inefficiencies—then industrial finance is more readily available and more likely to be channelled to its most productive use. On the other hand, if the equities markets are poorly developed, industry is forced to rely on internal funds or debt that is intermediated by banks. Such capital is generally less flexible and is less inclined to finance riskier investments that are the impetus for growth. *Intermediated debt* (or bank loans) tends to be allocated to industry on a somewhat arbitrary and *ad hoc* basis. These are unfortunate characteristics of financial markets, including equities markets, that are not well developed.

www.nasdaq.com

The official website of the NASDAQ stock exchange. Provides information about the exchange, portfolio-monitoring software, and price quotations.

Equities markets are complex systems that involve not just the stock market itself but also the supporting participation of brokerages, investment banks and regulatory agencies. The efficiency and strength of a nation's equities market depend directly on the integrity of the legal system, regulation and the supporting functions of accounting and communications. In Canada and in other advanced nations, financial institutional development tends to be taken for granted by corporations looking to raise equity capital relatively smoothly and at reasonable cost. A striking feature of international finance, as we shall discuss shortly, is the *integration* of various national equities markets throughout the world as companies *cross-list* their shares on several stock exchanges—in both Toronto and New York, for example—which results in a number of advantages for both firms and investors.

www.nyse.com

The website of the New York Stock Exchange. Information about the NYSE, its operation, membership and listed companies is provided here. US share price quotations are available.

In recent years, most national stock markets have become highly automated. The first was the Toronto Stock Exchange, which introduced the Computer Assisted Trading System (CATS) in 1977. An automated trading system electronically displays public orders on a continuous basis, and allows traders to execute trades from computer terminals. Automated systems allow orders to be filled faster and more efficiently since fewer exchange personnel are needed. Indeed, in some countries, the exchange trading floor has been completely eliminated. The old trading floor at the Toronto Stock Exchange has been turned into a showplace of modern art and design!

www.tsx.com

The website of the Toronto Stock Exchange. Information about the exchange and its operation, membership and listed companies is provided here. Canadian shares, futures, options, and mutual fund prices are available.

Automated, computer-facilitated trading naturally lends itself to **continuous** trading. Continuous trading is desirable for actively traded issues. On the other hand, **call markets** and **crowd trading**—involving traders and **specialists** crying out bids and offers in the noisy "pit" while recording trades on bits of paper—has advantages for thinly traded issues. Person-to-person trading and the buffering role of the specialists smooth the trading process and mitigate the effects of short-term imbalances between bids and offers.

Exhibit 8.5 provides a summary of locations and market trading systems of various major stock markets throughout the world. The exhibit also shows the typical taxes applicable to equity trades and the number of business days required to settle a trade.

8.2   INTERNATIONAL EQUITY MARKET BENCHMARKS

For a benchmark of activity or performance of a given national equity market, an index of shares traded on the secondary exchange (or exchanges) of a country is used. Several national equity indexes are available for use by investors.

Standard & Poor's annual *Stock Market Factbook* is an authoritative source of data on stock markets in both the developed countries and emerging countries.

www.msci.com

The website of Morgan Stanley Capital International. Information about MSCI's international stock market indexes is provided, as is information about index performance. One can download index data.

Morgan Stanley Capital International (MSCI) is another useful source of information on stock market performance around the globe. *Morgan Stanley Capital International Perspective* presents return and market capitalization data for 23 national stock market indexes from the developed countries. These indexes include equity issues that represent at least 60 percent of the market capitalization of each industry within the country. Shares in each country index are market-value-weighted, that is, the proportion of the index a share represents is determined by its proportion of the total market capitalization of all shares in the index. MSCI publishes a market-value-weighted World Index comprising 24 country indexes. The World Index includes approximately 2,600 share issues of major corporations in the world. MSCI also publishes several regional indexes: the European, Australasia, Far East (EAFE) Index comprising approximately 1,000 shares from 22 countries; the North American Index comprising the United States and Canada;

EXHIBIT 8.5	Trading Practices and Costs of Major Equity Markets		
Country	**System**	**Taxes**	**Settlement**
Argentina Buenos Aires	Auction market; automated	.0951% + VAT of 21% on commission	Trade date + 3 days
Australia National market	Automated	Off shore: none domestic: 10% of commission	Trade date + 3 days
Austria Vienna	Automated quote and market-making	None	Trade date + 3 days
Belgium Brussels	Euronext	None	Trade date + 3 days
Brazil Sao Paulo	Automated	Fee: .035%	Trade date + 3 days
Canada Toronto	Automated	None	Trade date + 3 days
Czech Republic Prague	Automated and OTC	.080–.125%; OTC: 0%	Trade date + 3 days
Chile Santiago	Automated and crowd trading	Cumulative schedule from .50%–0%	Trade date + 2 days Trade date + 1 day
China Shenzhen and Shanghai	Automated	Shenzhen: .1841% Shanghai: .18%	B shares: Trade date + 3 days
Colombia National market	Automated	None	Trade date + 3 days
Denmark Copenhagen	Norex	None	Trade date + 3 days
Egypt Cairo, Alexandria	Automated	.025%	Trade date + 1 day (2 days) for sell (buy)
Finland Helsinki	Norex	None	Trade date + 3 days
France Paris	Euronext	VAT on commission None for foreigners	Trade date + 3 days
Germany Frankfurt trading	Automated and floor	None	Trade date + 2 days
Greece Athens	Automated on sales	Fees: .06% +.15%	Trade date + 3 days
Hong Kong Hong Kong	Automated	.112%	Trade date + 2 days
Hungary Budapest	Automated	None	Trade date + 3 days
India National Stock Exchange; Bombay Stock Exchange	Automated	.075% +10.2% of commission	Trade date + 2 days
Indonesia Jakarta	Automated	.111%+VAT on commission	Trade date + 3 days
Ireland Dublin	Automated	1.00% on purchases	Trade date + 3 days
Israel Tel Aviv	Automated	None	Trade date + 0(2) days
Italy Milan	Automated	None	Trade date + 3 days

(Continued)

EXHIBIT 8.5 (continued)

Country		System	Taxes	Settlement
Japan	Tokyo, Osaka,	Automated JASDAQ	None	Trade date + 3 days
Malaysia	Kuala Lumpur	Automated	.04%	Trade date + 3 days
Mexico	Mexico City	Automated	.04%	Trade date + 2 days
Netherlands	Amsterdam	Euronext	None	Trade date + 3 days
New Zealand	Wellington	Automated	None	Trade date + 3 days
Norway	Oslo	Norex	None	Trade date + 3 days
Peru	Lima	Automated	.2356%	Trade date + 3 days
Philippines	Pasig, Makati	Automated	.50%(sales)+VAT on commission	Trade date + 3 days
Poland	Warsaw	Automated	.04%	Trade date + 3 days
Portugal	Lisbon	Euronext	None	Trade date + 3 days
Russia	Moscow	Automated	None	Trade date + 5 to 10 days; depository receipt: Trade date + 3 days
Singapore	Singapore	Automated	.05% (max SGD200) + 5% on commission and fees	Trade date + 3 days
South Africa	Johannesburg	Automated	.25% on buys + VAT on commission	Trade date + 5 days
South Korea	Seoul	Automated	.30% on sales	Trade date + 2 days
Spain	Madrid	Automated and crowd trading(<3%)	None	Trade date + 3 days
Sweden	Stockholm	Norex	None	Trade date + 3 days
Switzerland	Zurich	Automated	.085%	Trade date + 3 days
Taiwan	Taipei	Automated	.30% on sells	Trade date + 1 day
Thailand	Bangkok	Automated	VAT .0175%	Trade date + 3 days
Turkey	Istanbul	Automated	None	Trade date + 2 days
United Kingdom	London	Automated	.50% on purchases	Trade date + 3 days
United States	New York and OTC	Specialist: NYSE and AMEX; automated quotation: NASDAQ OTC	USD 32.90 per USD 1 million sale value	Trade date + 3 days

Note: Euronext is a merger of the Amsterdam, Brussels, Paris and Lisbon stock exchanges where trading is conducted over a single automated platform. Norex is an alliance of Nordic and Baltic stock exchanges where trading is conducted over a common automated trading system.

Source: Excerpted from *Guide to Global Equity Markets,* 14th ed., UBS Investment Bank, February 2005.

the Far East Index (three countries); several Europe Indexes; the Nordic Countries Index (four countries); and the Pacific Index (five countries). The EAFE Index is widely followed, and it is representative of World Index excluding North American stock market performance. Daily values of several of the MSCI country indexes and the World Index can be found in the financial press such as the Report on Business in *The Globe and Mail* and, of course, *The Wall Street Journal.* MSCI also publishes dozens of industry indexes, each of which includes equity issues from the respective industry from the countries it follows.

MSCI also publishes 26 national emerging stock market indexes for the developing countries, covering approximately 1,700 securities. The *Emerging Markets Free* version of these indexes recognizes that some countries impose ownership restrictions on shares by foreigners. In this case, the constituent national indexes are excluded or underweighted to recognize the particular restriction in order to provide an index representative of investments that can be freely made.

The Dow Jones Company (DJ) provides stock market index values for a number of countries. The values and percentage changes of these indexes can be found daily in the financial press. The data are presented in local currency terms and for comparative purposes in US and Canadian dollars. Exhibit 8.6 presents an example of the daily report of these indexes as found in *The Wall Street Journal.*

In addition to their own Dow Jones country stock market indexes, the financial press also reports values and percentage changes in local currency values of the major stock market indexes of the national exchanges or markets from various countries in the world. Many of these are prepared by the stock markets themselves or well-known investment advisory firms. Exhibit 8.7 presents a list of the indexes that appear daily in *The Wall Street Journal.*

EXHIBIT 8.6	Examples of Annual Changes and Rates of Return on Stock Market Indices, 2012–2013

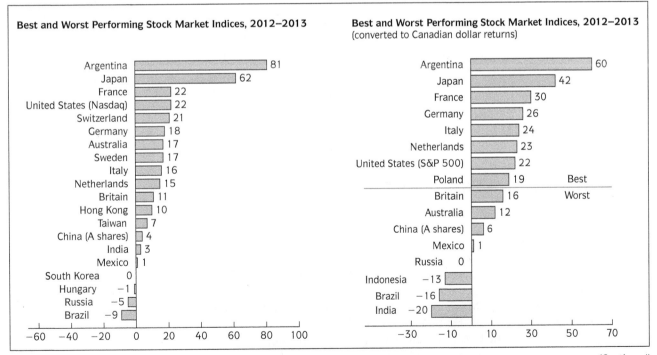

(Continued)

EXHIBIT 8.6　　(continued)

Country Stock Market Indices, 2012–2013

		2013, Oct	2012, Oct	Year/Year Change, %	
				in local currency	in terms of Canadian $
Industrial Nations	Australia	5,215	4,459	17	12
	Britain	6,438	5,826	11	16
	Canada	12,839	12,360	4	4
	France	4,158	3,406	22	30
	Germany	8,629	7,322	18	26
	Italy	18,098	15,535	16	24
	Japan	14,170	8,747	62	42
	Netherlands	376	328	15	23
	Spain	951	788	21	29
	Sweden	1,260	1,080	17	25
	Switzerland	7,964	6,604	21	29
	United States (S&P 500)	1,694	1,451	17	22
	United States (Nasdaq)	3,815	3,135	22	27
	Euro Area (FTSE Euro 100)	956	816	17	22
	World MSCI (US$)	384	333	15	20
Emerging Markets Asia	China (A shares)	2,276	2,185	4	6
	Hong Kong	22,985	20,888	10	15
	India	19,517	18,870	3	−20
	Indonesia	4,388	4,252	3	−13
	Singapore	3,153	3,077	2	2
	South Korea	2,000	1,996	0	0
	Taiwan	8,217	7,685	7	12
Latin America	Argentina	4,870	2,456	81	60
	Brazil	53,100	58,627	−9	−16
	Chile	18,811	20,633	−9	−9
	Mexico	41,301	41,005	1	1
Middle East & Africa	Egypt	5,694	5,656	1	2
	Israel	1,149	1,089	6	12
	Saudi Arabia	8,014	6,887	16	21
	South Africa	43,968	36,121	22	25
Eastern Eurpoe	Czech Republic	969	964	1	7
	Hungary	18,645	18,928	−1	4
	Poland	50,803	44,099	15	19
	Russia	1,422	1,492	−5	0
	Turkey	75,163	66,822	12	16

Source: World Federation of Exchanges.

iShares MSCI

www.ishares.com

This website describes the iShares MSCI created by Barclays Global Investors.

Barclays Global Investors introduced **iShares MSCI** as vehicles to facilitate investment in country funds. iShares MSCI are country-specific baskets of stocks designed to replicate the MSCI country indexes of 31 countries and four regions. They are exchange-traded funds that trade on the American Stock Exchange. The indexed equity system is now run by Blackrock, an international investment management firm.

iShares are subject to US SEC and Internal Revenue Service diversification requirements. These requirements prohibit the investment of more than 50 percent of the fund in five or fewer securities, or 25 percent of the fund in a single security. Thus, for some countries, the

EXHIBIT 8.7   Major National Stock Market Indexes

Country	Index	Country	Index	Country	Index
Argentina	Merval	Israel	Tel Aviv 100	Turkey	ISE 100
Australia	All Ordinaries	Italy	FTSE MIB	UK	FTSE 100
	S&P/ASX 200 Res		FTSE Italia Mid Cap		FT 30
	S&P/ASX 200		FTSE Italia All-Sh		FTSE All Share
Austria	ATX	Japan	Nikkei 225		FTSE techMARK 100
Belgium	BEL 20		Topix		FTSE4Good UK
	BEL Mid		S&P Topix 150	USA	S&P 500
Brazil	Bovespa		2nd Section		FTSE NASDAQ 500
Canada	S&P/TSX Met & Min	Jordan	Amman SE		NASDAQ Cmp
	S&P/TSX 60	Kenya	NSE 20		NASDAQ 100
	S&P/TSX Comp	Latvia	OMX Riga		Russell 2000
Chile	IGPA Gen	Lithuania	OMX Vilnlus		NYSE Comp.
China	Shanghai A	Luxembourg	Luxembourg General		Wilshire 5000
	Shanghai B	Malaysia	FTSE Bursa KLCI		DJ Industrial
	Shanghai Comp	Mexico	IPC		DJ Composite
	Shenzhen A	Morocco	MASI		DJ Transport
	Shenzhen B	Netherlands	AEX		DJ Utilities
	FTSE A200		AEX All Share	Venezuela	IBC
	FTSE B35	New Zealand	NZX 50	Vietnam	VNI
Colombia	CSE Index	Nigeria	SE All Share	CROSS-BORDER	Stoxx 50 €
Croatia	CROBEX	Norway	Oslo All Share		Euro Stoxx 50 €
Cyprus	CSE M&P Gen	Pakistan	KSE 100		DJ Global Titans $
Czech Republic	PX	Philippines	Manila Comp		Euronext 100 ID
Denmark	OMX Copenhagen	Poland	Wig		FTSE Multinatts $
	20	Portugal	PSI General		FTSE Global 100 $
Egypt	EGX 30		PSI 20		FTSE 4Good Glob $
Estonia	OMX Tallinn	Romania	BET Index		FTSE E300
Finland	OMX Helsinki	Russia	RTS		FTSEurofirst 80 €
	General		MICEX Comp.		FTSEurofirst 100 €
France	CAC 40	Singapore	FTSE Straits Times		FTSE Lattbex Top €
	SBF 120	Slovakia	SAX		FTSE Eurotop 100
Germany	M-DAX	Slovenia	SBI TOP		FTSE Gold Min $
	XETRA Dax	South Africa	FTSE/JSE All Share		FTSE All World
	TecDAX		FTSE/JSE Top 40		FTSE World $
Greece	Athens Gen		FTSE/JSE Res 20		MSCI All World $
	FTSE/ASE 20	South Korea	Kospi		MSCI ACWI Fr $
Hong Kong	Hang Seng		Kospi 200		MSCI Europe €
	HS China	Spain	Madrid SE		MSCI Pacific $
	Enterprise		IBEX 35		SAP Global 1200 $
	HSCC Red Chip	Sri Lanka	CSE All Share		SAP Europe 350 €
Hungary	Bux	Sweden	OMX Stockholm 30		SAP Euro €
India	BSE Sens		OMX Stockholm AS		
	S&P CNX 500	Switzerland	SMI Index		
Indonesia	Jakarta Comp	Taiwan	Weighted Pr		
Ireland	ISEQ Overall	Thailand	Bangkok SET		

Source: *Financial Times* April 18, 2012, p. 21.

fund does not perfectly replicate the MSCI country index. Nevertheless, iShares are a low-cost, convenient way for investors to hold diversified investments in several different countries.

The International Finance in Practice box "Foreign Interest in South Africa Takes Off" discusses investing in South Africa via the iShares MSCI South Africa exchange-traded fund.

Foreign Interest in South Africa Takes Off

For the past three years South Africa's equity market has been among the world's strongest performers, with returns to foreign investors boosted substantially by a strengthening currency. For most of this period, however, foreign interest was modest, and it is only during the last quarter of 2004 that this began to change as net foreign purchases of South African shares on the Johannesburg Securities Exchange (JSE) soared to ZAR21 billion ($3.74 billion), the highest quarterly level ever.

Fourth quarter net equity purchases were up from a five-year average of ZAR3.7 billion per quarter, or $5,895 million at the average exchange rate over the period. Andre Roux, Investec's chief economist in South Africa, says: "There appears to be a concerted move by foreign investors to reduce what has been a protracted period of holding an underweight position in South Africa [SA] equity."

Unlike past foreign buying, this time it is not confined to resource stocks. "They are buying into a buoyant domestic economic story and are including banks, local industrials and telecoms in their buying programmes," says Roux. "In a global context, SA shares offer reasonable value and buyers also appear satisfied that the country is in a period of higher growth with more currency and interest rate stability."

Unfortunately, scope is limited for investment in pure South African-asset mutual funds denominated in dollars, euros or sterling. Currently, the two largest investment vehicles are Barclays Global Investor's $127 million iShares MSCI South Africa Index (iShares SA), an exchange-traded fund (ETF) listed on the American Stock Exchange, and Old Mutual's Bermuda-based pound 65 million South Africa Trust (SAT), an investment company listed on the London Stock Exchange.

As an ETF, iShares SA is an index tracking product; SAT is actively managed and has as its benchmark the FTSE/JSE All Share Index. Portfolios of both products are dominated by big-cap, blue-chip stocks, but SAT has a lower exposure to resources at 41.3 percent and to financials at 24.6 percent than does iShares SA (48.1 percent and 27.0 percent, respectively). By contrast, SAT has a considerably higher exposure to industrials at 34.1 percent (versus 24.9 percent).

Lower exposure to resources, which suffered in 2004 as a result of the rand's strength, and a higher industrial content which includes top-performing retailers such as Truworths and Massmart, gave SAT the performance edge in 2004. SAT ended the year with a 49.9 percent gain, while iShares SA advanced 43.6 percent in sterling terms. However, in dollar terms iShares SA was ahead with a gain of 55.4 percent.

Source: Excerpted from *Funds International* (London: January 2005), p.1. Reprinted by kind permission of VRL Publishing, Ltd. 2005. All rights reserved.

8.3 TRADING IN INTERNATIONAL EQUITIES

World capital markets are on a trend toward greater global integration. Several factors account for this movement. First, investors realize the benefits of international portfolio diversification. Today, capital flows readily and in huge volumes across international borders. Second, the institution builders and regulators of capital markets are seriously engaged in reducing the cost of raising capital. In this respect, it is clear that larger markets, often from the integration of several markets, are more efficient than the set of smaller, local markets. Third, advances in communications technology have dramatically enhanced securities trading through rapid order routing and execution followed by clearance and settlement. Fourth, corporations see the value in sourcing new capital internationally.

In this section and the following sections, we explore the impact that global integration has on the world's equity markets and international corporate finance. We begin by examining international cross-listing of corporate shares.

Cross-Listing of Shares

Cross-listing refers to a firm listing its shares on one or more foreign exchanges in addition to its home country stock exchange. Cross-listing is not a new concept. With the increased globalization of world equity markets, however, cross-listing has grown dramatically in recent years.

Exhibit 8.8 reports the number of companies listed on various national stock exchanges throughout the world along with a breakdown into domestic and foreign listings. The exhibit also shows the split between new domestic and foreign listing in 2011. Several exchanges have a large proportion of foreign listings. The Luxembourg Stock Exchange, for example, has more foreign listings than domestic. On the Swiss bourse, foreign listings exceed 15 percent of the total.

EXHIBIT 8.8   Domestic and Foreign Company Listings on Major Stock Exchanges, 2011

	Total Listings			New Listings		
		2011			2011	
Exchange	Total	Domestic	Foreign	Total	Domestic	Foreign
Americas						
Bermuda SE	40	13	27	2	0	2
BM&F BOVESPA	373	366	7	15	15	0
Buenos Aires SE	105	99	6	1	1	0
Colombia SE	83	79	4	4	1	3
Lima SE	254	202	52	11	6	5
Mexican Exchange	476	128	348	63	3	60
NASDAQ OMX	2,680	2,383	297	151	124	27
NYSE Euronext (US)	2,308	1,788	520	144	109	35
Santiago SE	267	229	38	49	9	40
TMX Group	3,945	3,845	100	369	350	19
Total region	**10,531**	**9,132**	**1,399**	**809**	**618**	**191**
Asia Pacific						
Australian Securities Exchange	2,079	1,983	96	121	108	13
Bombay SE	5,112	5,112	0	39	39	0
Bursa Malaysia	940	932	8	28	28	0
Colombo SE	272	272	0	31	31	0
Gre Tai Securities Market	608	607	1	52	51	1
Hong Kong Exchanges	1,496	1,472	24	101	93	8
Indonesia SE	440	440	0	25	25	0
Korea Exchange	1,816	1,799	17	72	70	2
National Stock Exchange India	1,640	1,639	1	107	107	0
Osaka Securities Exchange	1,229	1,228	1	16	16	0
Philippine SE	253	251	2	6	6	0
Shanghai SE	931	931	0	39	39	0
Shenzhen SE	1,411	1,411	0	243	243	0
Singapore Exchange	773	462	311	24	10	14
Taiwan SE Corp	824	772	52	48	27	21
Thailand SE	545	545	0	12	12	0
Tokyo SE Group	2,291	2,280	11	50	50	0
Total region	**22,660**	**22,136**	**524**	**1014**	**955**	**59**
Europe-Africa-Middle East						
Amman SE	247	247	0	2	2	0
Athens Exchange	272	269	3	0	0	0
BME Spanish Exchanges	3,276	3,241	35	88	87	1
Budapest SE	54	52	2	6	6	0
Casablanca SE	76	75	1	3	3	0
Cyprus SE	106	106	0	0	0	0
Deutsche Börse	746	670	76	216	29	187
Egyptian Exchange	233	232	1	9	9	0
Irish SE	55	48	7	2	1	1
IMKB	264	263	1	25	25	0
Johannesburg SE	395	347	48	16	12	4
Ljubljaria SE	66	66	0	1	1	0
London SE Group	2,886	2,288	598	163	120	43
Luxembourg SE	298	27	271	21	2	19
Malta SE	21	21	0	0	0	0
Mauritius SE	64	63	1	1	1	0
MICEX	284	283	1	96	96	0

(Continued)

EXHIBIT 8.8 (continued)

Exchange	Total Listings 2011			New Listings 2011		
	Total	Domestic	Foreign	Total	Domestic	Foreign
NASDAQ OMX Nordic Exchange	773	743	30	26	22	4
NYSE Euronext (Europe)	1,112	969	143	45	40	5
Oslo Børs	238	194	44	13	8	5
RTS Stock Exchange	252	251	1	8	8	0
Saudi Stock Market—Tadawul	150	150	0	4	4	0
SIX Swiss Exchange	280	246	34	0	0	0
Tel-Aviv SE	593	576	17	11	10	1
Warsaw SE	777	757	20	204	198	6
Wiener Börse	105	88	17	4	3	1
Total region	**13,623**	**12,272**	**1,351**	**964**	**687**	**277**
WFE total	**46,814**	**43,540**	**3,274**	**2,787**	**2,260**	**527**

Source: World Federation of Exchanges, *Annual Report and Statistics,* 2011. Table 1.3, p. 94 and Table 1.4, p. 95.

A firm may decide to cross-list its shares for one or a combination of several reasons:

1. International cross-listing expands the investor base for a firm's shares. Access to more investors can potentially increase the demand for the firm's shares. Increased demand may also increase share price and lower the cost of capital. Greater demand and turnover generally improve the share's liquidity.

2. Cross-listing creates name recognition for the company in new capital markets, thus paving the way to a source of equity or debt capital from foreign markets.

3. Companies based in countries with relatively weak financial institutions and poor capital market regulation sometimes decide to list abroad on the larger exchanges of the world in order to subject themselves to the discipline required, for instance, by the New York, London or Toronto Stock Exchanges. By listing their shares on exchanges that demand fuller disclosure, more transparency and a higher standard of corporate governance than is required "at home," such firms signal their strength and credibility. This can result in lower cost of capital and higher valuation.

International cross-listing of shares obligates the firm to adhere to the securities regulations of the (foreign) country in which it cross-lists as well as the regulations of its home country. A company from, say, Mexico that wants to cross-list on a US exchange must meet the accounting and disclosure requirements of the US Securities and Exchange Commission. Reconciliation of a company's financial statements can be a laborious and costly process that some foreign firms are reluctant to do. Moreover, they may have a preference to avoid the glare of public accounting exposure. In such cases, foreign firms can arrange to have their shares traded in a restricted format, limited to only large "knowledgeable" institutions rather than being listed on an exchange. These less rigorous accounting and disclosure requirements are often an arrangement of choice for family-owned companies that for reasons of privacy operate their business with accounting standards that are short of the US or Canadian Generally Accepted Accounting Principles (GAAP).

The cross-listing of Canadian corporate shares in the United States is facilitated by the Multi-jurisdictional Disclosure System (MJDS), a joint initiative of the Canadian Securities Association and the Securities and Exchange Commission in the US. Under the MJDS, Canadian issuers with market capitalization of at least $75 million may use their Canadian disclosure documents rather than carry out the more detailed filing of the US system, except in the case of an initial public offering. In effect, Canadian corporations can list shares in the US under less rigorous disclosure criteria than those that apply to other non-American corporations. Although the MJDS was drawn up jointly by Canadian and

American regulators and put forward as means to a reciprocal recognition system, the fact of the matter is that rigorous disclosure is less of a problem from the Canadian side. The MJDS can be fairly described as a unilateral concession by the US SEC that eases the initial regulatory burden facing Canadian firms as they look to list on US exchanges.

Canadian Cross-Listed Shares

Many of Canada's largest corporations list their shares in New York and other foreign stock exchanges as well as on Canadian exchanges. As of March 2013, 224 Canadian firms listed on exchanges in the United States. Most of the Canadian companies (92 of the 224) are listed on the New York Stock Exchange (see Exhibit 8.9), while 90 were listed on the Nasdaq. The remaining 42 are listed on regional exchanges or on the American Stock Exchange (AMEX). A small number of Canadian firms are listed on the London Stock Exchange.

EXHIBIT 8.9	Canadian Firms Listed on NYSE (2013)

Before a company can begin trading on the New York Stock Exchange, it must meet certain initial requirements or "listing standards" set by the NYSE. For a non-US company, the minimum thresholds include the number of publicly traded shares (2.5 million), the number of shareholders that hold 100 or more shares (5,000 worldwide), global market capitalization ($500 million), annual revenues ($100 million) and pre-tax income ($25 million). The stock exchange also imposes similar standards for "continuous listing."

These high thresholds preclude only the largest Canadian firms from listing on the NYSE. The following is a list of Canadian firms and income trusts listed on the New York Stock Exchange as of March 2013.

Abitibi-Consolidated	ABY	CP	HCH	NOVA Chemicals	NCX
Advantage Energy Income		Domtar	UFS	Novelis	NVL
Fund	AAV	Domtar	UFSWI	Oppenheimer Holdings	OPY
Agnico-Eagle Mines	AEM	Enbridge	ENB	Pengrowth Energy Trust	PGH
Agrium	AGU	Encana	ECA	Penn West Energy Trust	PWE
Alcan	AL	Energy Metals	EMU	Petro-Canada	PCZ
Bank of Nova Scotia	BNS	Enerplus Resources Fund	ERF	Potash Corporation of	
Barrick Gold	ABX	Enterra Energy Trust	ENT	Saskatchewan	POT
Baytex Energy Trust	BTE	Fairfax Financial Holdings	FFH	Precision Drilling Trust	PDS
BCE	BCE	Fording Canadian Coal Trust	FDG	PrimeWest Energy Trust	PWI
Biovail	BVF	Four Seasons Hotels	FS	Provident Energy Trust	PVX
BMO Financial Group	BMO	Gerdau Ameristeel	GNA	Quebecor World,	IQW
Brookfield Asset		Gildan Activewear	GIL	RBC Financial Group	RY
Management	BAM	Goldcorp	GG	Ritchie Bros Auctioneers	RBA
Brookfield Properties	BPO	Goldcorp	GGWS	Rogers Communications	RG
CAE	CGT	Harvest Energy Trust	HTE	Shaw Communications	SJR
Cameco	CCJ	IAMGOLD	IAG	Silver Wheaton	SLW
Canadian Imperial Bank of		Intertape Polymer Group	ITP	Stantec	SXC
Commerce	CM	IPSCO	IPS	Sun Life Financial,	SLF
Canadian National Railway		Ivanhoe Mines	IVN	Suncor Energy	SU
Company	CNI	Kingsway Financial Services	KFS	Talisman Energy	TLM
Canadian Natural Resources	CNQ	Kinross Gold	KGC	Teck Cominco	TCK
Canadian Pacific Railway	CP	Lions Gate Entertainment	LGF	TELUS	TU
Canetic Resources Trust	CNE	Magna International	MGA	Thomson	TOC
CanWest Global		Manulife Financial	MFC	Tim Hortons	THI
Communications	CWG	MDS	MDZ	Toronto-Dominion Bank	TD
Celestica	CLS	Meridian Gold	MDG	TransAlta	TAC
CGI Group	GIB	MI Developments	MIM	TransCanada	TRP
CHC Helicopter	FLI	Nexen	NXY	TransCanada Pipelines	TCAPR
Compton Petroleum	CMZ	Nortel Networks	NT	Yamana Gold	AUY
Corus Entertainment	CJR	North American Energy		Zarlink Semiconductor	ZL
Cott	COT	Partners	NOA		

Source: New York Stock Exchange.

Guide to Raising Capital on the Canadian Equity Markets

The Toronto Stock Exchange (TSX) is Canada's senior equity market. A TSX listing provides a range of benefits, including opportunities to access capital, liquidity, specialized indexes, visibility and analyst coverage. TSX Venture Exchange (TSXV) is Canada's national exchange for venture class securities. Together, TSX and TSX Venture (the "Canadian Exchanges") have become global destinations to finance international businesses. The TSX has prepared a Guide to Raising Capital on the Canadian Equity Markets *that identifies the advantages for a foreign company to list shares in Canada and how to do it. This International Finance in Practice box draws from the TSX Guide.*

Advantages to Listing in Canada

Usually foreign companies consider the Canadian Exchanges because they require equity financing to facilitate further growth. Foreign companies that list in Canada enjoy many advantages. Canadian Exchanges provide foreign companies access to capital through an expansion of their investor base. An initial public offering in Canada sets the stage for future equity financings that can generate additional capital. In Canada, shareholder approval requirements for the issuance of additional shares are less onerous than in many other jurisdictions. Going public in Canada can promote a business's visibility and profile. It also establishes a liquid market for existing shareholders and provides an exit strategy for early stage investors.

Deciding to Go Public

Going public in Canada may subject a company to increased regulation which may alter the way business is conducted and could require enhanced responsibility for the board of directors.

In Canada, public companies must provide timely and continuous reporting, including financial results of the company's operations, executive compensation, share transactions involving insiders, and material corporate changes.

The First Step: Selecting the Team

Foreign companies will need to assemble a team of professional advisors to provide assistance in going public, including an agent, a securities lawyer, an external auditor and an investor relations professional.

The agent is a broker/dealer registered to sell securities in Canada and is a TSX or TSX Venture "Participating Organization." The agent acts as underwriter and investment dealer and in certain cases, as sponsor. The agent/sponsor works with the securities lawyer to evaluate the company's suitability for going public, including assessing the marketability of the company to investors. Companies that apply to list on TSX or TSX Venture and that do not meet certain financial thresholds and other requirements may be required to retain a participating organization to act as a sponsor for the listing.

Securities lawyers work with the external auditors to ensure that listing documents are accurate and meet all regulatory requirements.

External auditors perform various essential tasks during the listing process, including expressing an opinion on how well the listing documents reflect the foreign company's financial position.

An investor relations firm typically carries out communications activities designed to increase public awareness of the company.

Methods of Listing in Canada

Foreign companies generally take one of the following routes to go public in Canada: (i) direct listing; (ii) listing

---

The NYSE list includes the major Canadian banks and financials—the Bank of Montreal (BMO), the Royal Bank of Canada (RBC) Financial, Toronto-Dominion (TD), Scotiabank and Manulife—as well as industrials, such as BCE, CN, Domtar, Encana, Ipsco, Intrawest, Rogers Media, Shaw Communications and Suncor. Canadian (TSX) companies listed on the NYSE and the Nasdaq simultaneously account for more than two-thirds of the current market capitalization of TSX-listed firms. Waterloo-based BlackBerry (formerly Research In Motion (RIM)) reports that two-thirds of the trading in its shares takes place in New York on the Nasdaq.

Only the largest Canadian firms have sufficient size to meet the minimum capitalization requirement of, for instance, the NYSE. When they do, however, international cross-listing offers distinct advantages to both the firm and its investors. The firm has enhanced visibility and access to a substantially larger potential pool of equity for new issues. From the investors' point of view, cross-listed shares are followed up—or monitored—by a larger number of professional analysts which means that investors are generally better informed. Furthermore, the expanded diversification effects as Canadian shares are held together with American shares can lower the risk and the cost of capital of cross-listed firms, which means higher equity value.

concurrently with a prospectus offering; (iii) a reverse take-over; or (iv) a capital pool company transaction.

TSX Venture Exchange (TSXV) lists all companies whether domestic or foreign under the same listing standards. Toronto Stock Exchange (TSX) generally lists companies under one set of standards. Companies that meet the higher "foreign listing standards" may not be required to meet the TSX's Canadian security distribution requirement and may be eligible for exemption from certain TSX policies.

Minimum Listing Requirements/Public Distribution Requirements

The Canadian Exchanges have minimum public distribution requirements to help promote a liquid market.

TSX applicants are generally required to have at the time of listing at least 1 million freely tradable shares with market value of C$4 million. These securities must be held by at least 300 Canadian public security holders, each with 100 shares or more. Where the company is listed and in good standing on another senior exchange and TSX will not be the primary market for the company's securities, the above distribution levels may not be required. However TSX must be satisfied that there will be a sufficient distribution of securities in Canada and a satisfactory plan for a liquid market on the TSX.

An applicant seeking a listing that is able to meet the higher *Foreign Listing Criteria* must have at least 1 million issued shares with a total market value of C$10 million. These shares must be held by at least 3,000 public shareholders. Unless the foreign company is listed on a major stock exchange recognized by TSX, the company must satisfy TSX that there will be a sufficient distribution of securities in Canada and a satisfactory plan for a liquid market on TSX.

Companies applying to list on TSX Venture must satisfy the Exchange that, at the time of listing, they will have at least 10 percent of their issued and outstanding shares freely trading and held by the public. These shares must be held by at least 200 public shareholders, each with 100 shares or more free of resale restrictions. At least 20 percent of issued and outstanding shares must be held by public shareholders. TSX Venture applicants are required to have a minimum distribution of securities consisting of at least 500,000 freely tradable shares with a total market value of C$500,000 held by public shareholders.

The Application Process

Prior to application, foreign companies and/or their advisors should contact TSX for a conference call or advisory meeting. To apply for listing, certain key documents must be submitted:

Disclosure Document: discloses full details on business, strategy, market aspects, prospects, management, financials, et cetera. Must be up-to-date and comprehensive.

Financial Statements: audited financial statements for the most recent fiscal year prepared in accordance with acceptable GAAP and in compliance with securities commission requirements.

Personal Information Forms: background checks for all officers, directors and shareholders with more than 10 percent ownership.

Technical Reports: required for mining and oil and gas companies; prepared by independent qualified people conforming to standards set by CSA.

The *TSX Company Manual* and *TSX Venture Corporate Finance Manual* provide important information about the listing process and are available at www.tmx.com.

A leading Canadian expert on international cross-listing, Usha Mittoo of the University of Manitoba, has carefully examined the performance of Canadian firms that have listed their shares on stock exchanges in the United States. Mittoo finds that before listing in the United States, a typical Canadian firm has enjoyed a dramatic run-up in its value with above-average rate return on equity on a risk-adjusted basis. In other words, Canadian firms that list in the United States show strong performance at home beforehand. That strong stock performance continues for some time after listing in the United States, reflecting a fall in the Canadian companies' cost of equity. The value of trading of Canadian shares, a measure of liquidity, also increases following American listing—by approximately 40 percent in terms of trading value per month.

Now the bad news. A number of empirical studies, including the work by Mittoo, demonstrate that despite the pre- and early post-US-listing rise in equity value (or fall in cost of equity), the long-run performance of US listings of Canadian firms is significantly different from that in the short term. Whereas, on average, the firms that list on US exchanges outperformed the market index by 30 to 40 percent in the year prior to listing, after the listing they underperformed their at-home Canadian peers on average for three years.

The fact that Canadian firms underperform after listing in the United States is puzzling, but there are various explanations. First, it could reflect "selection bias." Firms that enjoy an impressive rise in value in Canada and then opt to list abroad may have misread a one-off boost that is not sustainable. The underperformance following foreign listing may represent performance and values reverting to more normal levels. Alternatively, Canadian firms and their enthusiastic advisors may overlook certain important costs in an international equity issue—such as the "road show"—as well as the risk of being subject to very close scrutiny from a larger number of analysts.

Regardless of the explanation, one implication is clear. Listing in the United States is no guarantee of a lower cost of equity capital in the long run. Each firm must carefully evaluate its foreign-listing decision in light of all factors—earnings growth, risk, liquidity, and transactions costs—that bear on this significant step in the firm's international corporate strategy.

The European Stock Market

Western and Eastern Europe have more than 20 national equity markets, where at least 15 different languages are spoken. Several combinations and trading arrangements have been formed among these national stock exchanges in recent years, but as yet, there is not a single European stock market that comprises all national markets.

www.euronext.com

This is the official website of Euronext.

www.nasdaqeurope.com

This is the official website of Nasdaq Europe.

Euronext N.V. is a pan-European stock exchange based in Paris with subsidiaries in Belgium, France, Netherlands, Portugal and the United Kingdom. In addition to equities and derivatives markets, the Euronext group provides clearing and information services. As of January 2013, markets run by Euronext had a market capitalization of USD$3.8 trillion, making it the fifth-largest exchange on the planet.

Euronext was formed in 2000 through a merger of the Amsterdam Stock Exchange, Brussels Stock Exchange and Paris Bourse. The aim was to take advantage of the harmonization of financial markets in the European Union. Euronext acquired the shares of the London International Financial Futures and Options Exchange (LIFFE), which continues to operate under its own governance. Beginning in 2003, all derivatives products traded on its affiliated exchanges trade on LIFFECONNECT, LIFFE's electronic trading platform.

In December 2006 Euronext merged with NYSE Group to form NYSE Euronext, the first global stock exchange.

Euronext has become a significant force for the consolidation of European financial markets by providing investors with an integrated institutional structure that is broad, liquid and cost-effective. Euronext generates financial synergies by merging the activities of previously unconnected local markets. This business model covers technological integration and the harmonization of market rules and regulatory framework.

Consolidation of Europe's historically fragmented financial market infrastructure began by integrating trading activities on previously separate securities and derivatives exchanges. At the same time, Euronext triggered the development of clearing and settlement services by contributing its clearinghouse to LCH Clearnet, the largest independent central counterparty (CCP) operation in Europe. Euronext also sold most of its settlement and depository activities to Euroclear. Euroclear is now the world's largest settlement system for securities transactions. These are major advances toward the reduction of market fragmentation in Europe and the realization of the so-called horizontal model of independent trading, clearing and settlement organizations.

The first stage of integration focused on the Group's trading platforms, establishing a common platform—a streamlined system that minimizes trading costs through standardization. The single trading platform promotes increases in trading volumes and improved market efficiency through narrower bid-ask spreads and enhanced liquidity.

Standardization and harmonization are key features of the financial integration process, resulting in simplified listing and trading procedures on markets. Euronext introduced modern information technology (IT) for trading and securities clearing along with simplified membership structure to allow easy access to the integrated cross-border market in securities and derivatives. These harmonized arrangements have been achieved with the cooperation of the regulatory authorities in the five Euronext jurisdictions, who work together to design and approve each stage of harmonization. The net result is an innovative market model that provide issuers and investors with access to all Euronext markets, not just their original entry point. Euronext has harmonized its listing structure with Eurolist, a single list of all Euronext markets. For derivatives, contract sizes for equity options have been harmonized in response to customer demand.

Euronext manages two broad-based indexes. The **Euronext 100** is a blue chip index. The **Next 150** is an index of the 150 next largest stocks (based on market capitalization) representing the large- to mid-cap segment of stocks listed on Euronext. The NextEconomy and NextPrime segments each have a price index and a total return index, weighted by market capitalization and excluding the shares listed in the Euronext 100 Index.

Euronext provides users and stakeholders with a range of financial services. Participating groups include financial institutions that require direct access to securities trading; companies whose securities are listed on its markets, enabling them to raise capital; institutional and retail investors who trade securities listed on Euronext markets; other organizations that use Euronext technologies and services; and users of financial information.

Depository Receipts

A Canadian investor can easily purchase stocks listed on US stock exchanges such as the NYSE, AMEX or Nasdaq. Thousands of cross-border transactions of this sort take place every day. Every Canadian brokerage house such as RBCDominion Securities, ScotiaCapital or TDWaterhouse or E*TRADE Canada provides the service. Although for a Canadian, US stocks are foreign securities, the "foreignness" of buying, holding or selling US securities from Canada is simple, fast and efficient. Likewise, American investors can easily purchase Canadian stocks listed on, for example, the TSX, TSX Venture or Montreal Stock Exchange.

On the other hand, a Canadian or an American looking to buy shares traded on more remote stock markets, such as the Paris Bourse, the Hong Kong Stock Exchange or the Johannesburg Stock Exchange, would face special difficulties in making a transaction. The difficulties begin with the need to contact a broker who deals in, say, Hong Kong. Then an account must be set up with payments settled in foreign currency. There may be local taxes and perhaps restrictions. All of this in addition to the nuisance of dealing in different time zones.

www.adr.com

This website sponsored by J. P. Morgan tells you everything there is to know about ADRs. See in particular the online book *The ADR Reference Guide*.

While it is possible for a Canadian investor to purchase foreign shares directly on a national stock market in a foreign country, there is a much easier way of going about it. The mechanism involves *depository receipts*. In the jargon of international finance, depository receipts are often referred to as **American depository receipts**, or ADRs. Indeed the inception of these certificates was an American initiative. However, depository receipts now have names that reflect the cosmopolitan acceptance of this particular form of international investing, names such as European depository receipts, Global depository receipts as well as specifically Dutch, Swedish or Singapore depository receipts. Others will likely follow.

As yet there are no Canadian depository receipts. There is no pressing need. Canadians can conveniently purchase American depository receipts through their Canadian brokers.

A depository receipt is a security that represents a specific number of shares in a foreign country that have been purchased locally and deposited in the vault of a custodian share-issuer's home market. The actual "receipt" is a certificate that gives the holder, in say the United States or Canada, the right to the value of those foreign shares. A depository receipt is an indirect way to hold foreign shares.

The ADR, has been around for a long time. The story of the first American depository receipt provides historical context as well as an illustration of how the arrangement is set up. In 1927, the Guaranty Trust Company of New York, the predecessor of Morgan Guaranty, purchased shares of Selfridges, the British retailer. Guaranty Trust was responding to demand by American and Canadian investors to hold Selfridges stock. However, Britain had recently passed a law that prohibited British companies from registering shares overseas without a British-based transfer agent, and thus UK shares were not allowed physically to leave the United Kingdom. Guaranty Trust's clever plan was to buy Selfridges stock in London, deposit the shares with a reputable custodian in London and then sell "depository receipts" in New York—which were direct claims on the value of the Selfridges shares being held in London. The depository receipts were then traded on the stock exchange in New York, which at that time was called the "curb exchange."

Depository receipts (DR) are a boon to the globalization of equities markets. Today there are 3,700 DR "programs," as they are called, available to investors around the world. The total investment in DRs exceeds $1.5 trillion. In New York alone, there are more than 1,200 DR programs from 82 countries.

To give a specific example, if you were to buy Switzerland's Nestlé ADR, you benefit if the stock rises on the Zurich exchange, plus you share in the foreign currency gain should the Swiss franc rise against the dollar. While trading Nestlé in its home market in Zurich undoubtedly makes sense for European investors, the Nestlé ADR provides easier access for most American and Canadian retail investors. Moreover, there are no withholding taxes and, in most cases, trading costs are usually much lower.

ADRs are certificates issued by a US depository bank, representing foreign shares held by the bank, usually by a branch or correspondent in the country of issue. One ADR may represent a fraction of a foreign share, exactly one share or a bundle of shares of a foreign corporation. If the ADRs are "sponsored," the foreign corporation provides financial information and other assistance to the bank and may subsidize the administration of the ADR. On the other hand, "unsponsored" ADRs do not receive such assistance. ADRs are subject to the same currency, political and economic risks as the underlying foreign share. Arbitrage keeps the prices of ADRs and underlying foreign shares essentially equal. Exhibit 8.10 outlines the four basic types of ADRs and the respective registration and reporting requirements.

EXHIBIT 8.10

Types of ADRs

	Level I	Level II	Level III	Rule 144A
Description	Unlisted program in the US	Listed on a US exchange	Shares offered and listed on a US exchange	Private placement to Qualified Institutional Buyers
Trading	OTC	Nasdaq, AMEX, NYSE	Nasdaq, AMEX, NYSE	US private placement
SEC registration	Form F-6	Form F-6	Forms F-1 and F-6	None
US reporting requirements	Exempt under Rule 12g3-2(b)	Form 20-F*	Form 20-F*	Exempt under Rule 12g3-2(b)

*Financial statements must be partially reconciled to US GAAP.
Level I: The most basic type of ADR program. The issuer is not seeking to raise new equity capital in the US and/or cannot list on the Nasdaq.
Level II: The issuer is not seeking to raise new equity capital in the US and ADRs can be listed on the Nasdaq, AMEX or NYSE.
Level III: The issuer floats a public offering of new equity in the US and lists the ADRs on the Nasdaq, AMEX or NYSE.
Rule 144A: This type of ADR program is a private placement of equity to Qualified Institutional Buyers (QIBs). It can only be traded among QIBs.
Source: Excerpted from J.P. Morgan Chase & Co., www.adr.com.

EXHIBIT 8.11

Mechanics of
Issuance and
Cancellation of
ADRs

A broker-dealer can purchase existing ADRs in the United States or purchase underlying shares in an issuer's home market and have new ADRs created, or issued, by the depositary bank. While the pool of available ADRs is constantly changing, the broker-dealer decides whether to purchase existing ADRs or have new ones issued, depending on such factors as availability, pricing, and market conditions in the United States and the issuer's home market.

To create new ADRs, underlying shares are deposited with a custodian bank in the issuer's home market. The depositary then issues ADRs representing those shares. The process for cancelling ADRs is similar to the issuance process, but the steps are reversed. The following chart and description provide a more detailed explanation, including the parties and steps involved.

The ADR purchase and issuance process: two scenarios

EXISTING ADRS

A1 Investor places order with broker in the United States.

A2 Broker in the United States purchases ADRs in the applicable market.

A3 Settlement and delivery of the ADRs (in book-entry or certificate form).

NEW ADRS

B1 Investor places order with broker in the United States.

B2 Broker in the United States places order with local broker (outside US) for equivalent shares.

B3 Local broker purchases shares in local market.

B4 Local shares are deposited with the depository's custodian.

B5 Depository receives confirmation of share deposit.

B6 Depository issues new ADRs and delivers them to broker in the US.

B7 Settlement and delivery of the ADRs (in book-entry or certificate form).

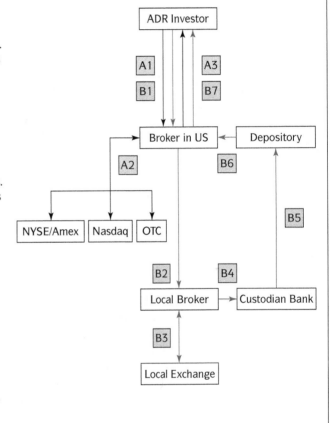

Source: Excerpted from J.P. Morgan Chase & Co., www.adr.com.

Exhibit 8.11 outlines step-by-step the mechanics of issuing or cancelling ADRs.

In short, ADRs are denominated in dollars and trade on US stock exchanges or in the over-the-counter (OTC) market. They can be purchased through the investor's regular broker. ADR trades clear in three business days as do conventional American and Canadian equities, whereas settlement practices for the underlying shares vary in foreign countries, sometimes taking weeks, especially if international delivery is involved.

In December 1990, Citibank introduced the first Global Depository Receipt (GDR). Samsung Corporation, a Korean trading company, wanted to raise equity capital in the United States through a private placement but Samsung also had a strong European investor base that it wanted to include in the offering. The GDRs allowed Samsung to raise capital in the US and Europe through one security issued simultaneously into both markets. Exhibit 8.12 shows a tombstone for a Global Depository Receipt.

Several empirical studies document important findings about the ADR market. Rosenthal (1983), using a time series of weekly, biweekly and monthly rates of return over the time

EXHIBIT 8.12

Global Depository
Receipt Tombstone

CIB

**COMMERCIAL INTERNATIONAL BANK
(EGYPT) S.A.E.**

International Offering of
9,999,000 Global Depository Receipts

corresponding to
999,900 Shares (nominal Value of E£100 per Share)

at an
Offer price of US$11.875 per Global Depository Receipt

Seller
National Bank of Egypt

*Global Co-ordinator
Co Lead Managers*
Robert Fleming & Co. Limited Salomon Brothers International Limited
UBS Limited

Domestic Advisor
Commercial International Investment Company S.A.E.

ING BARINGS

Source: *Euromoney,* October 1998, p. 127.

period of 1974 through 1978 for 54 ADRs, found that the ADR market was weak-form efficient. That is, abnormal trading profits are not likely from studying historical price data.

Park (1990) found that a substantial portion of the variability in (i.e., change in) ADR returns is accounted for by variation in the share price of the underlying security in the home market; however, information observed in the US market is also an important factor in the ADR return-generating process.

Officer and Hoffmeister (1987) and Kao, Wenchi, Wei and Vu (1991) examined ADRs as vehicles for constructing diversified equity portfolios. Officer and Hoffmeister used a sample of 45 ADRs and 45 domestic stocks. For each, they had monthly rates of return for the period 1973 through 1983. They found that as few as four ADRs combined with four domestic stocks allowed the investor to reduce portfolio risk by as much as 25 percent without any reduction in expected return.

Kao, Wenchi, Wei and Vu (1991) used 10 years of monthly return data covering the time period 1979 through 1989 for ADRs with underlying shares from the UK, Australia, Japan, the Netherlands and Sweden. They found that an internationally diversified portfolio of ADRs outperformed both a US stock market and a world stock market benchmark on a risk-adjusted basis. Country ADR portfolios from all countries except Australia also outperformed the US and world benchmarks, but only country ADR portfolios from the UK, Japan and the Netherlands outperformed their home-country stock market benchmark.

Jayaraman, Shastri and Tandon (1993) examined the effect of the listing of ADRs on the risk and return of the underlying stock. They found positive abnormal performance (i.e., return in excess of the expected equilibrium return) of the underlying security on the initial listing date. They interpreted this result as evidence that an ADR listing provides the issuing firm with another market from which to source new equity capital. Additionally, they found an increase in the volatility of (change in) returns of the underlying stock. They interpreted this result as consistent with the theory that traders with proprietary information will attempt to profit from their knowledge by taking advantage of price discrepancies caused by information differentials between the ADR and underlying security markets.

Gagnon and Karolyi (2004) compare synchronous intraday prices of ADRs and other types of cross-listed shares in US markets relative to home-market prices after currency adjustment for 581 companies from 39 countries. They discover that for most stocks, prices of cross-listed shares are within 20 to 85 basis points of the home-market shares, thus limiting arbitrage opportunities after transaction costs. However, when institutional barriers that limit arbitrage exist, prices can deviate by as much as a 66 percent premium and an 87 percent discount. Large deviations seldom exist for more than a day. They also discover that cross-listed shares trading in the US are relatively more (less) correlated with the US market index than with the home market when there is proportionately more (less) trading in the US market.

Global Registered Shares

The merger of Daimler-Benz AG and Chrysler Corporation in 1998 created DaimlerChrysler AG, a German firm. The merger was hailed as a landmark event for global equity markets because it simultaneously created a new type of equity share called *global registered shares (GRS)*. GRS are one share traded globally, unlike ADRs, which are receipts for bank deposits of home-market shares and traded on foreign markets. The primary exchanges for DaimlerChrysler GRS are the Frankfurt Stock Exchange and the NYSE; however, they are traded on a total of 20 exchanges worldwide. The shares are fully fungible—a GRS purchased on one exchange can be sold on another. They trade in both US dollars and euros. A new global share registrar that links the American and German transfer agents and registrars needed to be created to facilitate clearing. The main advantages of GRS over ADRs appear to be that all shareholders have equal status and direct voting rights. The main disadvantage of GRS appears to be the greater expense in establishing the global registrar and clearing facility. GRS have met with limited success; many companies that considered them opted instead for ADRs.[3]

| Example **8.1** | *DaimlerChrysler AG* |

Shares in DaimlerChrysler AG—the result of the merger of Daimler Benz AG, the famous German automobile manufacturer, and Chrysler Corporation—trade on both the Frankfurt Stock Exchange in Germany and the New York Stock Exchange. On the Frankfurt bourse, DaimlerChrysler closed at a price of €41.26 on 11 April 2013. On the same day, DaimlerChrysler closed in New York at $54.13 per share. To prevent arbitrage between trading on the two exchanges, the shares have to trade at the same price when adjusted for the exchange rate. We see that this is true. The $/€ exchange rate on 11 April was $1.3104/€. Thus, €41.26 × $1.3104 = $54.07, an amount very close to the closing price in New York of $54.13. The difference is easily explainable by the fact that the New York market closes several hours after the Frankfurt exchange, and thus market prices had changed slightly.

---

[3]Much of the information in this section is from the 1999 clinical study by G. Andrew Karolyi.

8.4   FACTORS AFFECTING INTERNATIONAL EQUITY RETURNS

Before closing this chapter, it is useful to explore some of the empirical evidence about which factors influence equity returns. After all, to construct an efficiently diversified international portfolio of shares, one must estimate the expected return and the variance of returns for each security in the investment set plus the pairwise correlation structure. It may be easier to accurately estimate these parameters if a common set of factors affect equity returns. Some likely candidates are macroeconomic variables that influence the overall economic environment in which the firm issuing the security conducts its business; exchange rate changes between the currency of the country issuing the shares and the currency of other countries where suppliers, customers and investors of the firm reside; and the industrial structure of the country in which the firm operates.

Macroeconomic Factors

Two landmark studies have tested the significance of various macroeconomic influences on equity returns. Solnik (1984) examined the effect of exchange rate changes, interest rate differentials, the level of the domestic interest rate and changes in domestic inflation expectations. He found that international monetary variables have only weak influence on equity returns in comparison with domestic variables. In another study, Asprem (1989) found that changes in industrial production, employment, imports, interest rates and inflation explained only a small portion of the variability of equity returns for 10 European countries. Substantially more of the variation is explained by an international market index.

Exchange Rates

Adler and Simon (1986) examined the exposure of a sample of foreign equity and bond index returns to exchange rate changes. They found that changes in exchange rates generally explained a larger portion of the variability of foreign bond indexes than foreign equity indexes but that some foreign equity markets were more exposed to exchange rate changes than the respective foreign bond markets. Their results suggest that it would likely be beneficial to hedge (i.e., protect) foreign stock investment against exchange rate uncertainty.

In another study, Eun and Resnick (1988) found cross-correlations among major stock markets and exchange markets to be relatively low but positive. This result implies that the exchange rate changes in a given country reinforce the stock market movements in that country as well as in the other countries examined.

Industrial Structure

Studies examining the influence of industrial structure on foreign equity returns are inconclusive. In a study examining the correlation structure of national equity markets, Roll (1992) concluded that the industrial structure of a country is important in explaining a significant part of the correlation structure of international equity index returns. He also found that industry factors explained a larger portion of stock market variability than did exchange rate changes.

In contrast, Eun and Resnick (1984) found for a sample of 160 shares from eight countries and 12 industries that the pairwise correlation structure of international security returns can be better estimated from models that recognize country factors, rather than industry factors. Similarly, using individual share return data for 829 firms, from 12 countries, and representing seven broad industry groups, Heston and Rouwenhorst (1994) concluded "that industrial structure explains very little of the cross-sectional difference in country return volatility. Low correlation between country indices is almost completely due to country specific sources of variation."

Both Rouwenhorst (1999) and Becker (1999) examined the effect of the European Monetary Union (EMU) on European equity markets and came up with opposite conclusions. Rouwenhorst concluded that country effects in share returns have been larger than industry effects in Western Europe since 1982 and that this situation continued throughout the 1993–1998 period when interest rates were converging and fiscal and monetary policies were being harmonized in the countries entering the EMU. On the other hand, Becker found an increase in correlations between markets and between the same sector in different markets arising from the European integration of fiscal, monetary and economic policies. He concluded that the increase in pairwise correlations in these countries represents a reduction in the diversification benefits from investing in the euro zone.

Griffin and Karolyi (1998) examined the effect of industrial structure on covariances by studying whether a difference exists in the effect between traded-goods industries and non-traded-goods industries. They found cross-country covariances to be larger for firms within a given industry than cross-country covariances across firms in different industries in traded-goods industries. In contrast, for non-traded-goods industries, there is little difference in cross-country covariances between firms in the same industry and those in different industries.

SUMMARY

This chapter provides an overview of international equity markets. The material is designed to provide an understanding of how MNCs source new equity capital outside of their own domestic primary market and to provide useful institutional information to investors interested in diversifying their portfolio internationally.

1. The chapter begins with a statistical perspective of the major equity markets throughout the world.

2. A variety of international equity benchmarks are also presented. Knowledge of where to find comparative equity market performance data is useful. Specifically, Standard & Poor's, Morgan Stanley Capital International and the Dow Jones Country Stock Market indexes are discussed. Also, a list of the major national stock market indexes prepared by the national exchanges or major investment advisory services is presented.

3. A considerable amount of discussion is devoted to differences in secondary equity market structures. Secondary markets have historically been structured as dealer or agency markets. Both of these types of market structure provide for continuous market trading, but noncontinuous markets tended to be agency markets. Over-the-counter trading, specialist markets, and automated markets allow for continuous market trading. Call markets and crowd trading are both types of noncontinuous trading market systems. Trading costs—commissions and taxes—on various national equity markets are summarized in a table comparing market characteristics. Most national stock markets are now automated for at least some of the issues traded on them.

4. Cross-listing of a company's shares on foreign exchanges is extensively discussed. A firm may cross-list its shares to establish a broader investor base for its shares; establish name recognition in foreign capital markets; and pave the way for sourcing new equity and debt capital from investors in these markets.

5. Several empirical studies that test for factors that influence equity returns indicate that domestic factors, such as domestic interest rates and domestic inflation, have the greatest effect on national equity returns. Industrial structure does not appear to be of primary importance. Equity returns are also found to be sensitive to own-currency exchange rate changes.

QUESTIONS

1. Get a current copy of *The Economist*. The Economic and Financial Indicators on the last page report Stock Market Indices for many countries. Examine the 12-month changes for the various national indexes. How do the changes from the most recent issue of *The Economist* compare with the 12-month changes from the sample provided in the textbook as Exhibit 8.6? Are the same national indexes positive and negative in both listings? Discuss your findings.

2. As an investor, what factors would you consider before investing in an emerging stock market?

3. Compare and contrast the various types of secondary market trading structures.

4. Discuss any benefits for a company (a) to cross-list its equity shares on more than one national exchange and (b) to source new equity capital from foreign investors as well as domestic investors.

5. Why might it be easier for an investor to diversify a portfolio internationally by buying depository receipts rather than the actual shares of the company?

6. The empirical studies about factors affecting equity returns basically show that domestic factors are more important than international factors, and that industrial membership of a firm is of little importance in forecasting the international correlation structure of international shares. How do you explain this?

PROBLEMS

1. On the Milan bourse, Fiat shares closed at €11.17 per share on 11 April 2013. Fiat trades as an ADR on the NYSE. One underlying Fiat share equals one ADR. On 11 April the $/€ spot exchange rate was $1.30/€1. At this exchange rate, what is the no-arbitrage dollar price of one ADR?

2. If Fiat ADRs were trading at $15 when the underlying shares were trading in Milan at €11.17, what could you do to earn a trading profit? Use the information in problem 1 to help. Assume transaction costs are negligible.

INTERNET EXERCISE

1. The Bloomberg website provides current values of many of the international stock indexes presented in Exhibit 8.7 at the website www.bloomberg.com. Go to this website and determine what country's stock markets are trading higher and lower today. Is there any current news event that might influence the way different national markets are trading today?

2. The JPMorgan website www.adr.com provides online data on trading in ADRs. Go to this website to view today's total trading volume in ADRs and the year-to-date trading volume. What are the top 10 individual ADRs by trading volume? By dollar value? Does there seem to be a similarity in industry (such as telecom) represented by the top ADRs, or are they from a variety of different industries? Recall from the chapter that the effect of industrial structure on international share returns is an unresolved issue.

MINI CASE

Regional Review—Asia-Pacific

Case Study: New DR Issuer
Mindray Medical International

Chinese medical device manufacturer Mindray Medical International recently successfully completed its IPO and listed DRs on the NYSE. In keeping with recent trends among many mid- and small-capitalization Chinese company IPOs, the deal was structured as a single-listed DR-only offering.

The company saw strong demand for its offering, with bookrunners Goldman Sachs and UBS pricing the deal at $13.50, a price modestly higher than its $10 to $12 offer range, according to Thomson Financial. In total, 23 million DRs were placed, raising $311 million. Mindray DRs promptly rose 30 percent over their offer price on the first day of trading.

Mindray disclosed that it plans to use about $75 million of the proceeds for construction of a new headquarters and an expansion of its manufacturing, assembly and warehouse facilities in Shenzhen.

On the occasion of their NYSE listing, Joyce Hsu, Mindray's chief financial officer, said, "We selected the Bank of New York as depository because of its proven track record. We seek to maximize U.S. investor interest in our program, and we believe the Bank has the resources and expertise necessary to help us achieve that goal."

Mindray closed its year at $23.90, a 77 percent increase from its IPO price. Its DR volume for the year was significant; in total, more than 68 million DRs valued at $1.3 billion changed hands on the NYSE.

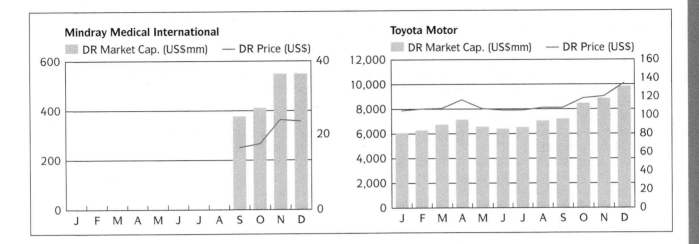

Case Study: Existing DR Issuer
Toyota Motor

Toyota Motor, the Japanese automobile manufacturer, established its sponsored DR program with the Bank of New York when it listed on the NYSE and raised over $135 million in DRs. The sponsored listing allowed the company to take control of a number of "unsponsored" DR programs that had been outstanding and provide its DR holders with more consistent services.

During the years since Toyota's listing, the company's investor relations team has worked closely with advisors including the Bank of New York to build its DR program in the US marketplace so it would reflect the company's stature in the global economy.

Today overall DR investment in Toyota, as measured by DR market capitalization, is growing quickly. Toyota's DR investment grew from $6.1 billion to $9.8 billion during 2006, an increase of 61 percent, making the program one of the world's largest and fastest-growing.

In November 2006, Toyota completed a global follow-on offering valued at $2.5 billion. The deal, which had a 35 percent international tranche, saw the government-backed Banks' Shareholdings Purchase Corporation sell 43.4 million ordinary shares, a 1.2 percent stake in the company. Because of the significant liquidity of Toyota's Tokyo Stock Exchange listed ordinary shares, the DR tranche was relatively small. The company issued more than one million DRs, raising more than $118 million. The transaction was the only DR capital raising in 2006 to come from a Japanese issuer.

You are an international fund manager at Altamira Investment Funds in Toronto with special responsibility for stocks from Asia-Pacific. Comment on the merits of adding Mindray Medical and/or Toyota Motor depository receipts to the portfolio that you manage.

Source: The Bank of New York, *The Depository Receipts Market—The Year in Review, 2006,* p. 17.

REFERENCES & SUGGESTED READINGS

Adler, Michael, and David Simon. "Exchange Rate Surprises in International Portfolios." *The Journal of Portfolio Management* 12 (1986), pp. 44–53.

Asprem, Mads. "Stock Prices, Assets Portfolios and Macroeconomic Variables in Ten European Countries." *Journal of Banking and Finance* 13 (1989), pp. 589–612.

Becker, Stan. "Investment Implications of a Single European Capital Market." *Journal of Portfolio Management* (Spring 1999), pp. 9–17.

Eun, Cheol S., and Bruce G. Resnick. "Exchange Rate Uncertainty, Forward Contracts, and International Portfolio Selection." *Journal of Finance* 43 (1988), pp. 197–215.

Eun, Choel S., and B. G. Resnick, "Estimating the Correlation Structure of International Share Prices." *Journal of Finance* Volume 39, Issue 5 (December 1984), pp. 1311–24.

Eun, Choel S., and S. Sabherwal. "Cross-Border Listings and Price Discovery: Evidence from U.S.-Listed Canadian Stocks." *Journal of Finance* Volume 58, Issue 2 (2003), pp. 549–75.

Foerster, Stephen R., and G. A. Karolyi. "The Effects of Market Segmentation and Investor Recognition on Asset Prices: Evidence from Foreign Stocks Listings in the United States," *Journal of Finance* Volume 54, Issue 2 (1999).

Gagnon, Louis, and G. Andrew Karolyi. "Multi-market Trading and Arbitrage." Ohio State University working paper (July 2004).

Griffin, John M., and G. A. Karolyi. "Another Look at the Role of the Industrial Structure of Markets for International Diversification Strategies." *Journal of Financial Economics* 50 (1998), pp. 351–73.

Heston, Steven L., and K. G. Rouwenhorst. "Does Industrial Structure Explain the Benefits of International Diversification?" *Journal of Financial Economics* 36 (1994), pp. 3–27.

Jayaraman, Narayanan, K. Shastri and K. Tandon. "The Impact of International Cross-Listings on Risk and Return: Evidence from American Depository Receipts." *Journal of Banking and Finance* 17 (1993), pp. 91–103.

Kao, G., K. C. Wenchi, John Wei, and Joseph Vu. "Risk–Return Characteristics of the American Depository Receipts." Unpublished working paper, 1991.

Karolyi, G. Andrew. "DaimlerChrysler AG: The First Truly Global Share." Ohio State University working paper, September 1999.

———. "Why Do Firms List Abroad? A Survey of the Evidence and Its Managerial Implications." *New York University Salomon Bros. Centre Monograph,* Volume 7, Issue 1 (1998).

Miller, Darius P. "The Market Reaction to International Cross-Listings: Evidence from Depository Receipts." *Journal of Financial Economics* 51 (1999), pp. 103–23.

Mittoo, Usha R., "The Value of U.S. Listing." *Canadian Investment Review* Volume 16, Issue 3 (Fall 2003), pp. 31–7.

Officer, Dennis T., and J. Ronald Hoffmeister. "ADRs: A Substitute for the Real Thing?" *Journal of Portfolio Management,* Winter (1987), pp. 61–65.

Park, Jinwoo. *The Impact of Information on ADR Returns and Variances: Some Implications.* Unpublished Ph.D. dissertation from The University of Iowa, 1990.

Roll, Richard, "Industrial Structure and the Comparative Behavior of International Stock Indexes." *Journal of Finance* 47 (1992).

Rosenthal, Leonard. "An Empirical Test of the Efficiency of the ADR Market." *Journal of Banking and Finance* 7 (1983) pp. 17–29.

Rouwenhorst, K. Geert. "European Equity Markets and the EMU." *Financial Analysts Journal* (May/June 1999), pp. 57–64.

Solnik, Bruno. "Capital Markets and International Monetary Variables." *Financial Analysts Journal* 40 (1984), pp. 69–73.

Stulz, Rene, "Globalization, Corporate Finance and the Cost of Capital." *Journal of Applied Corporate Finance* Volume 12, Issue 3 (1999), pp. 8–25.

Wu, Congsheng, and C.Y. Kwok, "Why Do U.S. Firms Choose Global Equity Offerings?" *Financial Management* 31 (2002), pp. 47–65.

Chapter 9

Futures and Options on Foreign Exchange

CHAPTER OUTLINE

ON FEBRUARY 27, 1995, Barings PLC, the oldest merchant bank in the United Kingdom, was placed in "administration" by the Bank of England because of losses that exceeded the bank's entire $860 million in equity capital. The cause of these losses was a breakdown in Barings' risk-management system that allowed a single rogue trader to accumulate and conceal an unhedged $27 billion position in various exchange-traded futures and options contracts, primarily the Nikkei 225 stock index futures contract traded on the Singapore International Monetary Exchange. The losses occurred when the market moved unfavourably against the trader's speculative positions. The trader recently completed a prison term in Singapore for fraudulent trading. Barings was taken over by the ING Group, the Dutch banking and insurance conglomerate.

As this story implies, futures and options contracts can be very risky investments, indeed, when used for speculative purposes. Nevertheless, they are also important risk-management tools. In this chapter, we introduce exchange-traded currency futures contracts, options contracts and **options** on currency futures that are useful for both speculating on foreign exchange price movements and hedging exchange rate uncertainty. These contracts make up part of the foreign exchange market that was introduced in Chapter 4, where we discussed spot and forward exchange rates.

The discussion begins by comparing forward and futures contracts and noting the similarities and differences between the two. We discuss the markets where futures are traded, the currencies on which contracts are written, contract specifications for the various currency contracts, and Eurodollar interest rate futures contracts. These are useful for hedging short-term dollar interest rate risk in much the same way as forward rate agreements, introduced in Chapter 6.

Next, options contracts on foreign exchange are introduced, comparing and contrasting the options and the futures markets. The exchanges where options are traded are identified and contract terms are specified.

This chapter and the knowledge gained about forward contracts in Chapters 4 and 5 set the stage for Chapters 12, 13 and 14 which explain how these vehicles are used for hedging foreign exchange risk.

9.1   FUTURES CONTRACTS: SOME PRELIMINARIES

In Chapter 4, a *forward contract* was defined as a vehicle for buying or selling a stated amount of foreign exchange at a stated price per unit at a specified time in the future. Both forward and futures contracts are classified as **derivative** or **contingent claim securities** because their values are derived from or are contingent upon the value of the underlying asset—foreign currency. A **futures contract** is similar to a forward contract but with a crucial distinction. A forward exchange contract is tailor-made for a client by his international bank; in contrast, a futures contract has **standardized** features and is **exchange-traded**, that is, traded on organized exchanges rather than over the counter.

The main standardized features of future contracts are the **contract size** specifying the amount of the underlying foreign currency for future purchase or sale and the **maturity date** of the contract. A futures contract is written for a specific amount of foreign currency, rather than for a tailor-made sum. Hence, a position in multiple contracts may be necessary to establish a sizable hedge or speculative position. Futures contracts have specific **delivery months** during the year in which contracts mature on a specified day of the month.

To establish a futures position, an **initial margin** must be deposited in a collateral account. The initial margin is generally equal to about 2 percent of the contract value. Either cash or Treasury bills may be used to meet the margin requirement. The account balance will fluctuate through daily settlement, as the following discussion will make clear. The margin put up by the contract holder can be viewed as "good faith" money that he will fulfill his side of the financial obligation.

The major difference between a forward contract and a futures contract is the way the underlying asset is priced for future purchase or sale. A forward contract states a price for the future transaction. By contrast, a futures contract is settled-up, or **marked-to-market**, daily at the settlement price at the close of daily trading on the exchange.

A buyer of a futures contract (one who holds a **long** position) in which the settlement price is higher (lower) than the previous day's settlement price has a positive (negative) settlement for the day. Since a long position entitles the owner to purchase the underlying asset, a higher (lower) settlement price means the futures price of the underlying asset has increased (decreased). Consequently, a long position in the contract is worth more (less). The change in settlement prices from one day to the next determines the settlement amount. That is, the change in settlement price per unit of the underlying asset, multiplied by the amount of the contract, equals the size of the daily settlement to be added to (or subtracted from) the long's margin account.

Analogously, the seller of the futures contract (**short** position) will have his margin account increased (or decreased) by the same amount that the long's margin account is decreased (or increased). Thus, futures trading between the long and the short is a **zero-sum game**; that is, the sum of the long and short's daily settlement is zero.

If the investor's margin account falls below a **maintenance margin** level (roughly equal to 75 percent of the initial margin), **variation margin** must be added to the account to bring it back to the initial margin level in order to keep the position open. An investor who suffers a liquidity crunch and cannot deposit additional margin money will have his position liquidated by his broker.

Marking-to-market of futures accounts means that profits or losses are realized on a day-to-day basis rather than all at once at maturity as with a forward contract. At the end of daily trading, a futures contract is analogous to a new forward contract on the underlying asset at the new settlement price with a one-day-shorter maturity. Because of daily marking-to-market, the futures price will converge through time to the spot price on the last day of trading in the contract. That is, the final settlement price at which any transaction in the underlying asset will transpire is the spot price on the last day of trading. The effective price is, nevertheless, the original futures contract price once the profit or loss in the margin account is included. Exhibit 9.1 summarizes the differences between forward and futures contracts.

EXHIBIT 9.1

Differences between
Futures and Forward
Contracts

Trading Location
Futures: Traded competitively on an organized exchange.
Forward: Traded by bank dealers via a network of telephones and computerized dealing systems.

Contractual Size
Futures: Standardized amount of the underlying asset.
Forward: Tailor-made to the needs of the participant.

Settlement
Futures: Daily settlement, or marking-to-market, by the futures clearinghouse through the participant's margin account.
Forward: Participant buys or sells the contractual amount of the underlying asset from the bank at maturity at the forward (contractual) price.

Expiration Date
Futures: Standardized delivery dates.
Forward: Tailor-made delivery date that meets the need of the investor.

Delivery
Futures: Delivery of the underlying asset is seldom made. Usually, a reversing trade is transacted to exit the market.
Forward: Delivery of the underlying asset is commonly made.

Trading Costs
Futures: Bid-ask spread plus broker's commission.
Forward: Bid-ask spread plus indirect bank charges via compensating balance requirements.

Two types of market participants are necessary for a futures market to operate: **speculators** and **hedgers**. A speculator attempts to profit from a change in the futures price. To do this, the speculator will take a long or short position in a futures contract depending upon his expectations of future price movement. A hedger, on the other hand, wants to avoid price variation by locking in a purchase price of the underlying asset through a long position in the futures contract or locking in a sales price through a short position. In effect, the hedger passes off the risk of price variation to the speculator, who is better able, or at least more willing, to bear this risk.

Both forward and futures markets for foreign exchange are very liquid. A **reversing trade** can be made in either market to close out, or neutralize, a position.[1] In forward markets, approximately 90 percent of all contracts result in the "short" making delivery of the underlying asset to the "long." This is natural given the tailor-made terms of forward contracts. By contrast, only about 1 percent of currency futures contracts result in delivery. While futures contracts are useful for speculation and hedging, their standardized delivery dates are unlikely to correspond to the actual future dates when foreign exchange transactions will transpire. Thus, they are generally closed out in a reversing trade.

The **commission** that buyers and sellers pay to transact in the futures market is a single amount paid upfront that covers the *round-trip* transactions of initiating and closing out the position. These days, through a discount broker, the commission charge can be as little as $15 per currency futures contract.

In futures markets, a **clearinghouse** serves as intermediary to all transactions. The buyer of a futures contract buys from the clearinghouse and the seller sells to the clearinghouse. This facilitates active secondary market trading since the buyer and the seller do not have to evaluate one another's creditworthiness. The clearinghouse is made up of *clearing members*.

---

[1]In the forward market, the investor holds offsetting positions after a reversing trade; in the futures market, the investor actually exits the marketplace.

Individual brokers who are not clearing members must deal through a clearing member to clear a customer's trade. In the event of default of one side of a futures trade, the clearinghouse stands in for the defaulting party and then seeks restitution from that party. The clearinghouse's liability is limited because a contractholder's position is marked-to-market daily. Given this organizational structure, the clearinghouse maintains the futures margin accounts for the clearing members.

Frequently, a futures exchange may have a **daily price limit** on the futures price, that is, a limit as to how much the settlement price can increase or decrease from the previous day's settlement price. Forward markets do not have this. Obviously, when the price limit is hit, trading will halt as a new market-clearing equilibrium price cannot be obtained. Exchange rules expand the daily price limit in an orderly fashion until a market-clearing price is established.

9.2   CURRENCY FUTURES MARKETS

www.cme.com

The Chicago Mercantile Exchange. Provides detailed information about the futures contracts and futures options contracts traded on it.

www.phlx.com

The Philadelphia Stock Exchange and the Philadelphia Board of Trade. Provides detailed information about the shares and derivative products that trade on the exchanges.

www.numa.com/ref/exchange.htm

The Numa Directory provides web addresses of most shares and derivative exchanges in the world.

On 16 May 1972, trading first began at the Chicago Mercantile Exchange (CME) in currency futures contracts. Trading activity in currency futures has expanded rapidly at the CME. In 1978, only two million contracts were traded; this figure stood at over 340 million contracts in 2012. Most CME currency futures trade in a March, June, September and December expiration cycle, with the delivery date being the third Wednesday of the expiration month. The last day of trading is the second business day prior to the delivery date. Additional CME currency futures trading takes place Monday through Thursday on the GLOBEX$_2$ trading system. GLOBEX$_2$ is a worldwide automated order-entry and matching system for futures and options that facilitates trading after the close of regular exchange trading. Exhibit 9.2 summarizes the basic CME currency contract specifications.

The NASDAQ OMX Futures Exchange (NFX) was originally named the Philadelphia Board of Trade (PBOT). It introduced currency futures trading in July 1986, and 17 currencies are available to trade in the Exchange today as illustrated in Exhibit 9.2. The NFX contracts trade in the same expiration cycle as the CME currency futures, plus two additional near-term months.

In addition to the CME and the NFX, currency futures trading takes place on the New York Board of Trade, the MexDer Exchange in Mexico, the BM&F Exchange in Brazil, the Budapest Commodity Exchange and the Korea Futures Exchange.

Canada does not have a currency futures market. However, Canadian foreign currency brokers have direct links to major futures exchanges around the world with, of course, especially active linkage to the Chicago Mercantile Exchange, the Philadelphia Board of Trade and the New York Stock Exchange. A Canadian interested in a futures contract involving, say, the Canadian dollar against the US dollar will find that the futures contracts are expressed in US dollars, including the margin account, marking-to-market and the contract settlement—all these elements are in US dollars. As a result, a Canadian company or individual using currency futures to speculate on or to hedge a Canadian dollar position faces a small overlay of exposure to the US dollar that arises from the fact that the futures contract itself is written and serviced in US dollars.

9.3   BASIC CURRENCY FUTURES RELATIONSHIPS

Exhibit 9.3 shows quotations for CME futures contracts on foreign currencies, including the Canadian dollar against the US dollar.

For each delivery month for each currency, we see the opening price quotation, the high and low quotes for the trading day—in this case Friday 10 May 2013—and the settlement price. Each quotation is presented in direct terms in relation to the US dollar, that is $F(US\$/i)$. (We use the same symbol F for futures prices as well as for forward prices

INTERNATIONAL FINANCE *in Practice*

CME Canadian Dollar Futures

CME® Canadian dollar futures and options on futures contracts offer financial institutions, investment managers, corporations and private investors a means to manage risks associated with currency rate fluctuation and to take advantage of profit opportunities stemming from changes in currency rates.

CME Canadian dollar futures contracts first started trading in 1972 as part of the International Monetary Market, a division of the Exchange. Options contracts began trading in 1988. Currently CME offers a forum for trading Canadian dollars in its FX futures markets on CME Globex® as well as on the trading floor.

Futures contracts are also traded in the CME Australian dollar/Canadian dollar, CME Canadian dollar/Japanese yen and CME Euro FX/Canadian dollar as part of cross-rate currency futures.

CME Canadian dollar futures and options on futures contracts are designed to reflect changes in the US dollar value of the Canadian dollar. Futures contracts are quoted in US dollars per Canadian dollar, and call for physical delivery at expiration, which takes place on the third Wednesday of the contract month in the country of issuance at a bank designated by the Clearing House. Exercised options on futures are settled by the delivery of futures contracts.

The CME Canadian Dollar futures contract trading unit is 100,000 Canadian dollars. The contract moves in 1 point tick increments, which is $0.0001 per Canadian dollar movement equals $10 per contract. Trading may also occur in $0.00005 per Canadian dollar increments, or $5 per contract, for Canadian dollar intra-currency spreads executed on the trading floor and electronically, and for All-or-None transactions.

and we shall explain why shortly.) For each contract, the **open interest** is also reported. This is the total number of long or short contracts outstanding for the particular delivery month. Note that the open interest is greatest for the **nearby** contract, in this case the June 2013 contract. Since few contracts actually result in delivery, the open interest for each different currency decreases as the last day of trading, 15 June 2013, approaches. This reflects increasing activity in *reversing trades*. Open interest in the September 2013 contract increases as trading interest in the soon-to-be nearby contract picks up. Open interest (loosely an indicator of demand) typically decreases with the term to maturity of futures contracts.

EXHIBIT 9.2	Currency	Contract Size	Exchange
Currency Futures Contract Specifications*	*Price Quoted in American Dollars*		
	Australian dollar	AD100,000	CME, NFX
	Brazilian real	BR100,000	CME
	British pound	£62,500	CME, NFX
	Canadian dollar	CD100,000	CME, NFX
	Euro FX	EUR125,000	CME
	Japanese yen	¥12,500,000	CME, NFX
	Mexican peso	MP500,000	CME
	New Zealand dollar	NE100,00	CME
	Russian ruble	RU2,500,000	CME
	South African rand	RA500,000	CME
	Swiss franc	SF125,000	CME, NFX
	Cross-Rate Futures (Underlying Currency/Price Currency)		
	Euro FX/British pound	EUR125,000	CME
	Euro FX/Japanese yen	EUR125,000	CME
	Euro FX/Swiss franc	EUR125,000	CME

*CME denotes Chicago Mercantile Exchange; NFX denotes NASDAQ Futures Exchange.
Sources: Chicago Mercantile Exchange and Philadelphia PBOT Board of Trade.

EXHIBIT 9.3 Currency Futures Quotations (Chicago Mercantile Exchange)

	Open	High	Low	Settle	Change	Lifetime High	Lifetime Low	Open Interest
Canadian dollar	100,000 Canadian dollars; US$ per C$							
SPOT (Close)				0.9901				
June	0.9923	0.9929	0.9842	0.9880	−0.0026	1.0298	0.9518	142,114
September	0.9906	0.9906	0.9822	0.9859	−0.0026	1.0267	0.9545	4,189
December	0.988	0.9885	0.98	0.9838	−0.0026	1.0145	0.9605	2,145
Mar-14	0.98	0.9861	0.9781	0.9818	−0.0026	1.0071	0.9604	299
Jun-14	0	0.9841	0.9765	0.9797	−0.0026	1.0004	0.9598	61
Sep-14	0	0.9816	0.9753	0.9776	−0.0026	0.9863	0.9622	2
Japan yen	12,500,000 Japanese yen; US$ per 100¥							
SPOT (Close)				0.9800				
June	0.994	0.9947	0.9807	0.9850	−0.0094	1.2984	0.9807	222,206
September	0.9938	0.9952	0.9813	0.9855	−0.0094	1.2952	0.9813	2,485
British pound	62,500 British pounds; US$ per £							
SPOT (Close)				1.5358				
June	1.5446	1.5454	1.5309	1.5352	−0.0074	1.6274	1.4823	187,373
September	1.5437	1.5445	1.5305	1.5344	−0.0074	1.6269	1.4827	567
Swiss franc	125,000 Swiss francs; US$ per SF							
SPOT (Close)				1.0451				
June	1.0551	1.0556	1.0389	1.0455	−0.0086	1.1304	1.0148	52,862
September	1.054	1.0561	1.04	1.0465	−0.0087	1.1197	1.0179	36
Australian dollar	100,000 Australian dollars; US$ per A$							
SPOT (Close)				1.0025				
June	1.0064	1.007	0.9935	0.9984	−0.0044	1.0531	0.9438	169,803
September	1.0003	1.0007	0.9874	0.9922	−0.0045	1.0457	0.9874	2,184
Mexican peso	500,000 Mexican peso; US$ per 10 MXN							
SPOT (Close)				0.8280				
June	0.83075	0.83225	0.81925	0.8225	−0.0068	0.83525	0.6773	167,436
September	0	0.826	0.8135	0.8165	−0.0068	0.829	0.6718	288
EURO	125,000 Euro; US$ per €							
SPOT (Close)				1.2989				
June	1.3047	1.3054	1.2938	1.2986	−0.0033	1.3731	1.2116	301,327
September	1.3056	1.306	1.2946	1.2994	−0.0033	1.3716	1.2283	2,436
								304,500

Source: Financial Research and Trading Lab, Rotman School of Management. All quotes are from 10 May 2013.

Example 9.1 Reading Futures Quotations

Learning to read futures quotations is best done through an illustrative example. Let's use the June 2013 Canadian dollar contract traded on the Chicago Mercantile Exchange (CME). All CME futures contract prices are in US dollars. Prices and quotes in US dollars are both conventional and reasonable, as pricing occurs in a market in Chicago. When necessary, we will refer to the Canadian dollar as C$.

From Exhibit 9.3, we see that on 10 May 2013 the Canadian dollar June 2013 futures contract opened for trading at a price of $0.9923/C$. For reference, the table reports the spot rate of exchange for the Canadian dollar on the same day, $0.9901/C$.

Throughout the day, the June 2013 Canadian dollar futures contract traded in a range of $0.9842 (low) to $0.9929 (high). Throughout its lifetime, the contract has traded in the range of $0.9518 (low) to $1.0298 (high). The settlement ("closing") price on 10 May was $0.9880. The open interest, or the number of June 2013 contracts outstanding, was 142,114.

At the settlement price of $0.9880, the holder of a long position in one futures contract commits to paying US$98,800 for C$100,000 on the delivery day, 15 June 2013, if he actually takes delivery. Note that the settlement price decreased $0.0026 from the close of the previous day. That is, it decreased from $0.9906/C$ to $0.9880/C$. Both the buyer and the seller of the contract would have their accounts marked-to-market by the change in the settlement price. That is, one holding a long position from the previous day would have US$260 (= $.0026 × C$100,000) deducted from his margin account while the one with a short position would have US$260 credited (added) to his account.

Marking-to-market is an important institutional difference between the operations of the futures market and the forward market. However, the two markets are similar in their pricing behaviour and, in particular, they are similar in what is referred to as "price discovery" of the spot exchange rate in the days and months ahead. To see this, it is useful to compare the pattern of the Canadian dollar forward exchange rates presented in Exhibit 4.4 of Chapter 4 with the futures prices presented in Exhibit 9.3. Both forward and futures prices are observed on the same day, 10 May 2013. From a spot exchange rate of 0.9901, the forward rate structure is 0.9894 (one month forward), 0.9880 (three months) and 0.9859 (six months). The forward market is pricing in Canadian dollar depreciation in relation to the US dollar over the next six months. A similar pattern is seen in the futures market. The settlement price for the futures contracts is 0.9880 for June settlement, 0.9859 for September and 0.9838 for December. Both the forward market and the futures market are pricing in depreciation of the Canadian dollar.

This, of course, is not surprising. In both markets, participants on both sides of a foreign exchange deal—in the case of a forward contract, the one who purchases the contract versus the seller of that contract (a bank) and, in the case of futures, the one who is long the futures contract versus the one who is short—together reach informed agreement on the exchange rate expected at some point in the future. Buyers and sellers of contracts have different views as to the probabilities of deviations (up or down) from the contract price. If the forward and the futures markets diverge in the exchange rate that they respectively "forecast," a cross-market arbitrage opportunity exists that will quickly eliminate the difference.

Even though marking-to-market is an important operational difference between the futures market and the forward market, both markets are concerned with exchange rates that lie ahead. There are strong market forces that link the pricing of contracts in the two markets. To see this, note the pattern of the spot and forward exchange rates for the US dollar versus the Canadian dollar on 10 May 2013. As before, these are expressed in terms of US dollars per Canadian dollar.

SPOT	0.9901		
1 month forward	0.9894	June futures price	0.9880
3 months forward	0.9880	September futures price	0.9859
6 months forward	0.9859	December futures price	0.9838
12 months forward	0.9818		

To the extent that the forward rates are "predicting" future spot exchange rates, the futures rates are doing so as well. In both series—forward rates and futures rate—we see the respective markets "predicting" depreciation of the Canadian dollar in relation to the US dollar over the next 12 months—hence a strengthening of the US dollar. The forward rate

INTERNATIONAL FINANCE *in Practice*

Arbitrage between the Forward Market and the Futures Market

Say a three-month Canadian dollar futures contract, priced in US dollars, is $0.9900 per Canadian dollar. At the same time, the foreign exchange desk at Acme Bank is offering a three-month forward exchange rate for the Canadian dollar at US$0.9800/C$.

The obvious forward-futures differential presents an arbitrage opportunity. The initial steps to exploit that opportunity are:

1. Enter into a forward contract to buy Canadian dollars in three months at $0.9800. Let's say you contract to buy C$1,000,000 for US$980,000. This step is "buying low."

2. Sell (take a short position in) a three-month Canadian dollar futures contract for C$1,000,000 at $0.9900. This step is "selling high."

The forward contract and the futures contract both expire on the same day three months from now. The forward contract involves no intermediate cash flows. The futures contract is marked-to-market daily.

Let's consider three alternative values of the spot exchange rate on the expiry date. On the day the contracts expire, both the forward contract and the futures contract have settlement balances that are determined in reference to the spot exchange rate on that day. Of course, there is only one spot exchange rate.

Let's say the spot exchange rate turns out to be $0.9900. The balance in the arbitrager's marked-to-market margin account (for the futures contract) is zero. He must deliver C$1,000,000. With his forward contract, he buys C$1,000,000 for US$980,000 and he receives US$990,000 upon delivery to the counterparty to the futures contract. His arbitrage profit is US$10,000.

Let's say the spot exchange rate turns out to be $0.9800. The balance in the arbitrager's marked-to-market margin account (for the futures contract) is US$10,000. With his forward contract, he buys C$1,000,000 for US$980,000 and he receives US$990,000 upon delivery to the counterparty to the futures contract. His arbitrage profit is the US$10,000 in the margin account.

Finally, let's say the spot exchange rate turns out to be $0.9850. The balance in the arbitrager's marked-to-market margin account (for the futures contract) is US$5,000. With his forward contract, he buys C$1,000,000 for US$980,000 and he receives US$985,000 upon delivery to the counterparty to the futures contract. His arbitrage profit is the US$5,000 in the margin account plus the $5,000 gain on the forward contract.

Regardless of the spot exchange rate on the day that the forward and futures contracts expire, the arbitrage profit is US$10,000.

Going back to the beginning, the arbitrage opportunity that stems from the futures: forward pricing differential prompts buying of the three-month forward contract (at $0.9800) and selling (short positions) of the futures contract (at $0.9900). There is pressure for the exchange rate in the forward contract—at least as offered by Acme Bank—to rise and the futures rate to fall.

In our illustration, the driving force is the forward ask-exchange rate offered by Acme Bank, which is lower than alternatives in the market. Arbitragers pounce on such opportunity. Vigilant arbitragers maintain equilibrium between the forward and futures markets with the result that the market-anticipated exchange rate is the same in both.

structure and the futures price structure display a similar chronological pattern. Thus, both the forward market and the futures market are useful and consistent for **price discovery** or obtaining market-based forecasts of the spot exchange rate at different future dates. The International Finance in Practice box "Arbitrage between the Forward Market and the Futures Market" illustrates the market behaviour that maintains the correspondence of forward rates and futures prices.

Example 9.1 implies that futures are priced similarly to forward contracts. In Chapter 5, we developed the interest rate parity (IRP) model which states that the forward price for delivery at time T is

$$F_T(\$/i) = S_0(\$/i)\frac{(1 + r_\$)^T}{(1 + r_i)^T}$$ (9.1)

We will use the same equation to define the futures price. This should work well since the similarities between the forward and the futures markets allow arbitrage opportunities if the prices between the markets are not roughly in accord. (See Example 9.2.)

Example 9.2 *Speculating and Hedging with Currency Futures*

Suppose a trader takes a position on 10 May 2013 in one June Canadian dollar futures contract at US$0.9880. The trader holds the position until the last day of trading, when the spot rate is, say, 0.9780/C$. This will also be the final settlement price because of **price convergence**. The trader's profit or loss depends upon whether he had a long or a short position in the June Canadian dollar contract.

If our trader was a speculator with no underlying position in Canadian dollars, and if he had a long position, he would have suffered a cumulative loss in his margin account of

$$-\$1{,}000 = (\$0.9780 - \$0.9880) \times C\$100{,}000$$

from 10 May through 15 June. This amount would have been subtracted from his margin account through daily marking-to-market. If he takes delivery, he will pay out of pocket US$97,800 for the Canadian $100,000—that is, the spot value. The effective cost, however, is US$98,800 (= US$97,800 + US$1,000), recognizing the amount subtracted from his margin money.

Alternatively, if our trader was a hedger wanting to buy C$100,000 on 15 June for US$0.9880/C$, he would have effectively locked in a purchase price of US$98,800 by taking a long position in the June Canadian dollar futures contract.

If the trader had taken a short position and he was a speculator with no underlying position in Canadian dollars, he would capture a cumulative gain of US$1,000 (= [0.9880 − 0.9780] × C$100,000) from 10 May through 15 June. These gains would have accumulated in his margin account through daily marking-to-market. If he makes delivery of the Canadian dollars, he will receive US$97,800 for the C$100,000—that is, the spot value. The effective amount that he receives, however, is US$98,800 (= US$97,800 + US$1,000), recognizing the amount that has accumulated in his margin account. Alternatively, as a hedger seeking to sell C$100,000 on 15 June for US$0.9880/C$, our trader effectively locked in a price of US$98,800 from a short position in the June Canadian dollar future contract. Exhibit 9.4 graphs these long and short future positions.

EXHIBIT 9.4

Graph of Long and Short Positions in the June 2013 Canadian Dollar Futures Contract

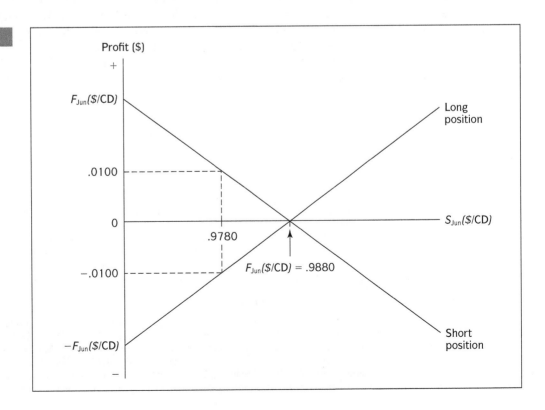

Speculating and Hedging with Currency Futures: Managerial Perspectives

To put our discussion of Canadian dollar futures contract in a *managerial* context, it is useful to consider the sort of Canadian company or organization that might be interested in hedging with Canadian dollar futures. Let us say that Bombardier, the Montreal-based aircraft manufacturer, has sold aircraft to Wisconsin Air and that in the schedule of payments, Bombardier will receive US$1,000,000 on 15 June 2013. (It is now May 2013.) As Bombardier wants certainty in its *Canadian* cash flows, Bombardier would want to hedge its exposure to the foreign exchange risk created by its US dollar receivable. Bombardier would need to take a *long* position in the June Canadian dollar futures contract. There are two practical concerns to keep in mind as we set up a futures hedge for Bombardier. First, Bombardier's receivable is in US dollars but the Canadian dollar futures contract is specified in terms of C$100,000. Second, these contracts are created and traded in the United States and they are settled in US dollars. The following illustration continues as if Bombardier uses the services of a broker who deals in foreign currency futures contracts on the Chicago Mercantile Exchange.

How many June contracts should Bombardier buy? As a starting point, it is useful to think of the *expected* number of Canadian dollars that Bombardier will receive in June if the receivable is not hedged. The price of the June futures contract, at US$0.9880/C$ is a reasonable indicator, indicating that Bombardier can expect to receive $1,000,000 \times (1/0.9880)$ or C$1,012,146 in June. But, of course, this (unhedged) expected figure is subject to risk. Bombardier can address this risk by buying ten June futures contracts at US$0.9880/C$. The figure of 10 is found by dividing the expected receivable in Canadian dollars by the Canadian dollar futures contract size, or $1,012,146/100,000$. Since there are no fractions of contracts, we round to 10.

Bombardier is required to put US$1,265 per contract in a margin account.[2] The total initial margin is (US$1,265 \times 10$) or US$12,650. The direct cost to Bombardier of this margin commitment is the cost of borrowing US$12,650 for one month. Expressed in Canadian dollars, that direct cost is ($[US\$12,650/0.991] \times 0.01 \times [1/12]$) assuming a Canadian interest rate of 1 percent. That direct cost of interest on margin is C$10.64.

The second cost of the hedge is the broker's commission when buying the futures contracts and again when taking delivery of the Canadian dollars in June and closing out the margin account. The commission is US$5 per contract both in and out of the contract, or US$10 per contract on the entire arrangement, which amounts to US$100 for 10 contracts. Converting this to Canadian dollars at the May spot rate (0.991), the commission is C$100.91.

Bombardier's cost of constructing a hedge with ten June Canadian dollar futures contracts is then:

Commission	$ 100.91
Interest on margin	10.64
Total[3]	$111.55

---

[2]The required margin on a foreign currency futures contract is specified by the market on which the contract is traded, for example, the Chicago Mercantile Exchange. The required margin is subject to change. The margin requirement is typically increased as the volatility of the "underlying" increases which in our discussion refers to the volatility of the Canadian dollar–US dollar exchange rate. In May 2013, the required margin on one Canadian dollar futures contract (with a contract amount of C$100,000) is US$1,265 or approximately C$1,271 at the prevailing May 2013 spot rate. This is a bit less than the 2 percent margin requirement that earlier we suggested is typical. The CME's margin requirement for the Canadian dollar futures contract has *not* kept pace with the rather steep run-up of the Canadian dollar from 2003 to 2013. In 2003, when the exchange rate was 0.6750, the margin requirement (at the time) of US$1,350 was exactly C$2,000 or 2 percent of the contract value.

[3]There are two small adjustments to this total cost figure that one might add. First, for simplicity in our illustration we assumed that the full broker's commission—in and out—was paid in May (in US dollars) and hence this amount was converted to Canadian dollars at the May spot rate. In fact, the commission at the close would likely be paid in June and hence perhaps ought to be converted to Canadian dollars at the June futures rate. Second, the margin account is maintained in US dollars. This US dollar exposure has not been hedged. If the US dollar rises (falls) against the Canadian dollar from May to June, the Canadian dollar value of the change in the margin account is a foreign exchange loss (gain).

This cash expense of $111.55 can be viewed as the cost of Bombardier's insurance against a fall in the value of the US dollar in relation to the Canadian dollar over the next month. Of course, since the hedge mechanism is Canadian dollar futures contracts, Bombardier forgoes the "upside," that is a stronger US dollar in relation to the Canadian dollar, while being protected on the "downside."

Our second illustration of the use of Canadian dollar futures looks at a risky situation faced by the treasurer of the Province of Nova Scotia. The treasurer must make a payment of US$1,000,000 on 15 June 2013 to retire Province of Nova Scotia bonds denominated in US dollars. As before, we look at the situation as if it is May 2013. To hedge the foreign exchange risk with Canadian dollar futures contracts, the Nova Scotia treasurer needs to be *short* an appropriate number of contracts. This problem is simply the reverse of Bombardier's situation that we have just outlined. The Nova Scotia treasurer can address the foreign exchange risk by selling ten June futures contracts at US$0.9880/C$. The initial margin, the broker's commissions and the interest on margin are all exactly the same as for Bombardier. For $111.55 the treasurer of Nova Scotia can hedge the foreign exchange risk involved in her bond retirement problem.

9.4   EURODOLLAR INTEREST RATE FUTURES CONTRACTS

To this point, we have considered only futures contracts written on foreign exchange. Nevertheless, futures contracts are traded on many different underlying assets. One particularly important contract is the Eurodollar interest rate futures traded on the Chicago Mercantile Exchange and the Singapore International Monetary Exchange (SIMEX). The Eurodollar contract has become the most widely used futures contract for hedging short-term US dollar interest rate risk. It can be used by Eurobanks as an alternative (see problem 7 at the end of this chapter) to the forward rate agreement (FRA) we considered in Chapter 6 for hedging interest rate risk due to a maturity mismatch between Eurodollar deposits and rollover Eurocredits. Other Eurocurrency futures contracts that trade are the Euroyen, the EuroSwiss and the Euribor, which began trading after the introduction of the euro.

The CME Eurodollar futures contract is written on a hypothetical $1,000,000 90-day deposit of Eurodollars. The contract trades in the March, June, September and December cycle. The hypothetical delivery date is the third Wednesday of the delivery month. The last day of trading is two business days prior to the delivery date. The contract is a cash settlement contract. That is, the delivery of a $1,000,000 Eurodollar deposit is not actually made or received. Instead, final settlement is made through realizing profits or losses on the margin account on the delivery date on the basis of the final settlement price on the last day of trading. Exhibit 9.5 presents an example of CME Eurodollar futures quotations. Note that contracts trade out many years into the future.

www.simex.com.sg

This is the website of the Singapore International Monetary Exchange. It provides detailed information about the derivative products traded on it.

Example 9.3 *Reading Eurodollar Futures Quotations*

Eurodollar futures prices are stated as an index number of three-month LIBOR, calculated as: $F = 100 - \text{LIBOR}$. For example, from Exhibit 9.5 we see that the June 2013 contract (with delivery on 18 June 2013) has a settlement price of 99.685 on 10 May 2013. The implied three-month LIBOR, to be in effect as of 18 June 2013, is thus 0.315 percent (= 100 − 99.685). The minimum price change is one basis point (bp). On $1,000,000 of face value, a one-basis-point change represents $100 on an annual basis. Since the contract is for a 90-day deposit, one basis point in a Eurodollar futures contract corresponds to a $25 price change.

Example **9.4** *Eurodollar Futures Hedge*

Let's construct an illustration of how Eurodollar futures contracts can be used to hedge interest rate risk. Say that on 10 May 2013 the fixed-income manager of Ontario Teachers Pension Fund must decide what to do with $20,000,000 in cash he will receive as US bonds that Teachers holds are retired. The bond retirement will occur on 18 June 2013. The manager at Teachers is reluctant to immediately recommit the funds to bonds. An alternative is to park the funds in a short-term money market instrument, such as a Eurodollar deposit, for 90 days. The problem is that we do not know what the Eurodollar yield will be on 18 June. That uncertainty is "interest rate risk." This is where Eurodollar futures come in.

The manager notes that three-month LIBOR is currently 0.28 percent. The three-month LIBOR rate implied in the June 2013 contract is considerably higher at 0.315 percent. The manager feels that a 90-day rate of return of 0.315 percent is a satisfactory rate to "lock in." So he decides to hedge against lower three-month LIBOR in June 2013. By hedging, the manager locks in a certain return of $15,750 (= $20,000,000 × 0.00315 × 90/360) for the 90-day period following 18 June.

To construct the hedge, the manager will buy, or take a long position, in June 2013 Eurodollar futures contracts. At first, it may seem counterintuitive to take a long position, but remember that a decrease in LIBOR causes Eurodollar futures prices to increase.

To hedge the interest rate risk in a $20,000,000 deposit, the treasurer will need to buy twenty June contracts. (Each futures contract is for $1,000,000.)

Say that on the last day of trading in the June 2013 contract, three-month LIBOR is 0.25 percent. The manager (and Teachers) is indeed fortunate that he chose to hedge. At 0.25 percent, a 90-day Eurodollar deposit of $20,000,000 will generate only $12,500 of interest income, or $3,250 less than at a rate of 0.315 percent. In fact, the manager has no choice but to deposit the bond retirement proceeds at a Eurodollar rate of 0.25 percent. However, the shortfall will be offset by the gain from the long futures position.

At a rate of 0.25 percent, the final settlement price on the June 2013 Eurodollar futures contract is 99.75 (= 100 − 0.25). The gain on the futures position is calculated as

$$(99.75 − 99.685) × 100 \text{ bp} × \$25 × 20 \text{ contracts} = \$3,250$$

This is precisely the amount of the shortfall.

9.5 CURRENCY OPTIONS: SOME PRELIMINARIES

We have seen how forward and futures contracts provide managers with the means to protect their firms against the uncertainty of exchange rate movements. Either a forward contract or futures contracts can lock in a settlement value of one currency exchanged for another at a specific time in the future.

A forward contract is an individually tailored agreement between a bank and one of its retail customers. Say the Potash Corporation of Saskatchewan has a receivable of US$1,000,000 due in six months. A quick call by the treasurer of Potash Corporation to the foreign exchange desk of, say, the Royal Bank will, via a forward contract, turn the US-dollar-denominated receivable into a *certain, specific* number of Canadian dollars to be received in six months.

Futures contracts, as we saw with Bombardier's US dollar receivable or the Nova Scotia Treasurer's bond payment, can similarly lock in the settlement value in Canadian dollars at a specific date in the future. If Potash Corporation wanted to hedge with futures contracts rather than with a forward contract, the Treasurer would call on the services of a broker who deals in futures contracts such as the Friedberg Group in Toronto.

Compared to forwards and futures, currency options provide similar but not identical means to address foreign exchange risk. The important difference is that currency options do not lock in a specific value at some point in the future. Currency options have the attractive feature of being able to provide protection from *adverse* movements of the exchange

EXHIBIT 9.5	Eurodollar Futures Contracts Settlements (Chicago Mercantile Exchange), 10 May 2013

Contract Month		Open	High	Low	Settle	Chg	Yield	Chg	Open Interest
Eurodollar (CME)—$1,000000; pts of 100%									
2013	June	99.690	99.690	99.675	99.685	0.000	0.315	0.000	810,448
	July	99.715	99.715	99.710	99.715	0.000	0.285	0.000	8,188
	August	99.710	99.710	99.705	99.710	−0.005	0.290	0.005	2,058
	September	99.705	99.710	99.695	99.705	−0.005	0.295	0.005	710,251
	October	0.000	0.000	99.690	99.700	−0.005	0.300	0.005	2,556
	November	0.000	0.000	0.000	99.680	0.000	0.320	0.000	0
	December	99.690	99.690	99.675	99.685	−0.005	0.315	0.005	810,448
2014	March	99.670	99.670	99.655	99.660	−0.010	0.340	0.010	737,102
	June	99.640	99.640	99.625	99.630	−0.010	0.370	0.010	735,570
	September	99.605	99.605	99.580	99.590	−0.015	0.410	0.015	650,253
	December	99.550	99.555	99.520	99.530	−0.020	0.470	0.020	750,510
2015	March	99.480	99.485	99.445	99.455	−0.030	0.545	0.030	647,430
	June	99.400	99.400	99.355	99.360	−0.040	0.640	0.040	825,435
	September	99.300	99.300	99.245	99.250	−0.050	0.750	0.050	530,856
	December	99.175	99.180	99.110	99.115	−0.065	0.885	0.065	653,105
2016	March	99.045	99.045	98.960	98.965	−0.080	1.035	0.080	397,014
	June	98.890	98.890	98.795	98.800	−0.095	1.200	0.095	345,617
	September	98.730	98.735	98.620	98.625	−0.110	1.375	0.110	234,749
	December	98.565	98.570	98.435	98.445	−0.125	1.555	0.125	184,660
2017	March	98.400	98.400	98.260	98.270	−0.135	1.730	0.135	185,897
	June	98.225	98.225	98.075	98.090	−0.140	1.910	0.140	120,801
	September	98.060	98.060	97.900	97.920	−0.145	2.080	0.145	88,608
	December	97.885	97.885	97.720	97.745	−0.145	2.255	0.145	127,948

Source: Financial Research and Trading Lab, Rotman School of Management.

rate while still capturing the gain from *favourable* movements of that same exchange rate. With options, one can neutralize the "bad" and still capture the "good." The final result has some uncertainty, but that uncertainty is only among favourable results.

An option gives the holder the *right* but not the *obligation* to buy—in the case of a **call** option—a specific asset at a specific price at a specific time in the future.[4] The asset that

---

[4]A "call" option takes its name from the idea that the option entitles the holder to call the asset from the market; in other words, the option-holder can *buy* the asset at a specific price at a specific time in the future. A "put" option, on the other hand, takes its name from the idea that the option entitles the holder to put the asset on the market; in other words, the put-holder can *sell* the asset at a specific price at a specific time.

concerns us, of course, is foreign currency. Therefore, a foreign currency call option might involve the option to buy 50,000 Canadian dollars at US$1.0000/C$ on 15 June 2013. (It is now 10 May 2013.) This particular option would be of interest to either Bombardier or Potash who plan to have US dollars in hand on 15 June and would like to hedge against adverse movements of the US dollar against the Canadian dollar between now and then. In these cases, an adverse movement of the exchange rate is depreciation of the US dollar against the Canadian dollar. If unhedged, US dollar depreciation results in a smaller number of Canadian dollars received from the US dollar receivable.

A **put** option on currency gives the holder the right but not the obligation to *sell* a currency at a specific exchange rate at a specific time in the future. A foreign currency put option might involve the option to sell 50,000 Canadian dollars at US$1.0000/C$ on 15 June 2013. This particular type of option would interest the Nova Scotia Treasurer who is required to have US dollars in hand on 15 June. In this case an adverse movement of the US–Canadian exchange rate between now and then would take the form of depreciation of the Canadian dollar. That change in the exchange rate would increase the Canadian dollar cost of the US dollar liability.

Like a futures contract, a currency option is a **derivative** or **contingent claim**. The value of the option is derived from a definable relationship with the underlying asset—the foreign currency or some claim on it. The specific price at which the currencies will be exchanged at a specified future date is referred to as the **strike price** or **exercise price**.

In the jargon of options, the buyer of an option is referred to as the "long" whereas the seller of the option is referred to as the "writer" or the "short."

Options have a distinctly **asymmetric pay-off**. The maximum amount that the buyer of an option can lose is limited to the amount that he pays for the option. In contrast, the seller of the option faces potentially much greater losses. There is a close analogy to insurance. Let's say you pay $1,000 to insure your $100,000 house for the year. If your house does not burn down, you have lost $1,000 and the insurance company has gained this $1,000. On the other hand, if your house burns down, you retain the value of the house (the insurance settlement) whereas the insurance company has lost $100,000 as its part of the deal.

Options transfer risk. Since the seller of an option takes on risk, the buyer of the option must pay a **premium**. (To continue the insurance analogy, insurance payments are commonly referred to as "premiums.") When an option is created, and it always has the character of a bet, the buyer of the option pays money to be relieved of risk whereas the seller receives money to bear the risk. The complex issue, of course, is how the amount of the premium is determined. In this chapter, we will keep discussion of the intricacies of option pricing to a minimum and, instead, focus on the role of options in managing currency risk.

First, though, we must provide a sense of where currency options are created and made available. That is the issue of market structure.

There are two types of options: American and European. The names do not refer to the continents where they are traded but, rather, to their exercise characteristics. A **European option** can be exercised only at the maturity or expiration date of the contract, whereas an **American option** can be exercised at any time during the contract. Thus, the American option allows the owner to do everything he can do with a European option, and more.

9.6 MARKET STRUCTURE

Prior to 1982, all currency option contracts were over-the-counter options written by international banks, investment banks, and brokerage houses. Over-the-counter (OTC) options are tailor-made according to the specifications of the buyer in terms of maturity length, exercise price and the amount of the underlying currency. Generally, OTC contracts are written for large amounts, at least $1,000,000 of the currency serving as the underlying asset. Frequently, they are written for US dollars, with the euro, British pound, Japanese yen, Canadian dollar and Swiss franc serving as the underlying currencies. Options are also available on less actively traded currencies. Over-the-counter options are typically European-style.

EXHIBIT 9.6

PHLX World
Currency
Options Product
Specifications

Currency	Contract Size
Australian dollar	AUD10,000
British pound	GBP10,000
Canadian dollar	CAD10,000
Euro	EUR10,000
Japanese yen	JPY10,000,000
Swiss franc	CHF10,000
New Zealand dollar	NZD10,000

Source: Philadelphia Stock Exchange, *Standardized Currency Options*, www.phlx.com.

In December 1982, the Philadelphia Stock Exchange (PHLX) began trading options on foreign currency. In 2008, the PHLX was acquired by the Nasdaq OMX Group. Currently, the PHLX trades World Currency Options on seven currencies against the US dollar, as shown in Exhibit 9.6. Most trading is in *mid-month* options. These options trade in a March, June, September and December expiration cycle with original maturities of 3, 6, 9 and 12 months, plus two near-term months so that there are always options with one-, two- and three-month expirations. These options mature on the Friday before the third Wednesday of the expiration month.

Exhibit 9.6 shows the currencies on which options are traded at the PHLX and the amount, or size, of underlying currency per contract. Note that the size of PHLX option contracts are half the corresponding futures contract size, as noted in Exhibit 9.2. The trading hours of these contracts are 9:30 A.M. to 4:00 P.M. Eastern time.

The volume of OTC currency options trading is much larger than that of organized-exchange option trading. According to the Bank for International Settlements, in 2010 the OTC volume was approximately $207 billion per day. By comparison, exchange-traded currency option volume was negligible. Nevertheless, the market for exchange-traded options is very important, even to the OTC market. International banks and brokerage houses frequently buy or sell standardized exchange-traded options which they then repackage in creating the tailor-made options desired by their clients.

9.7 CURRENCY OPTION-PRICING RELATIONSHIPS AT EXPIRY

To illustrate how currency options transfer risk and provide opportunities for risk management, we use a simple framework to examine the **pay-off structure** for currency options. We deal first with *call* options and then turn to *put* options. In each case we take the perspective of both the purchaser of the option and, in mirror image, the party on the other side—the seller of the option. The illustration is based on options involving the Canadian dollar in exchange for the US dollar as traded on the PHLX on 11 June 2013.

Options contracts necessarily have very specific terms. For purposes of our illustration, the following are the specific terms of a call option as of 11 June 2013 to buy Canadian dollars with US dollars at a strike price of US$0.98 on 20 July 2013.

Currencies involved	US$/C$
Type of option	CALL
Contract size	10,000 Canadian dollars
Strike price (X)	US$0.98 per Canadian dollar
Expiry (T)	20 July 2013
Settlement	in US dollars

On 11 June 2013, a call option with these specific terms traded at a premium of 1.96. That is the number of US cents per C$1 of the options contract. Therefore the price of the option (the call option premium) is US$0.0196 × 10,000, or US$196. The option is fully described as a "Canadian July call at 98."

As we shall see, Canadian dollar call option contracts with expiry in July are available at different strike prices, say US$0.97 or US$0.99. We will concentrate on the 98.

For the price of US$196, a broker in contact with the Philadelphia Stock Exchange will purchase the call option at the instruction of the purchaser. The premium is the upfront money in an options transaction. The money is paid by the purchaser of the option to the seller or **writer** of the option. The broker will also charge a brokerage fee which typically is close to $5 per contract.

If we look at the use of options to hedge currency risk from the point of view of a *Canadian* corporation or agency, then it is pertinent to consider the cost of the call in terms of Canadian dollars. Let's say the spot exchange rate on 11 June is US$0.98 per Canadian dollar. (It would not be unusual for a purchaser of a currency option to choose a strike price equal to the spot rate on the day of the purchase.) Then the Canadian dollar cost of the call option purchased on the Philadelphia Stock Exchange is US$196/0.98, or C$200.

The call option entitles the purchaser of the option to buy Canadian dollars with US dollars on 20 July for US$0.98 per Canadian dollar. The value of that option depends on the (spot) exchange rate on 20 July. If the spot rate (S_T) on 20 July is, say, US$0.97/C$, which means that the US dollar has appreciated against the Canadian dollar, the call option has no value. It would be better to buy Canadian dollars on the spot market at US$0.97 rather than to exercise the option to buy Canadian dollars at US$0.98. Whenever the spot rate is less than the exercise price, the call option is said to be **out-of-the-money**. If the call is out-of-the-money at expiry, it has a value of zero.

The value of a call option for the purchaser stems from the prospect that the spot rate at expiry will be greater than the strike price. If the exchange rate on 20 July is, say, US$0.99/C$, which means that the US dollar has depreciated against the Canadian dollar, the call option entitles the holder to buy Canadian dollars (by exercising the option) for US$0.98/C$. The option is then worth one US cent for each Canadian dollar in the contract. Since the option contract size is 10,000 Canadian dollars, the value of the option at expiry is $100. Whenever the spot rate is greater than the exercise price, the call option is said to be **in-the-money**. If the call option is in-the-money at expiry, the contract has a value of $[S_T - X]10,000$.

Exhibit 9.7 presents the pay-off structure for the Canadian July call at 98. Exhibit 9.8 depicts the same results in the classic "hockey stick" diagram for the Canadian July call at 98. Exhibit 9.7 does not explicitly account for the cost of the option. On the other hand, Exhibit 9.8 shows the loss or gain on the option conditional on the spot exchange rate at expiry *net* of the cost of US$196 (or C$200). The net loss or gain at expiry is presented both in a diagram and a corresponding line of computations.

The net pay-off from holding a call option on a currency is the sum of a negative amount that is certain—the cost of the contract—plus a positive (or zero) uncertain amount that depends on the value of the spot rate at expiry (S_T). At expiry, the call option contract is worth $max[0; S_T - X]10,000$.

The structure of the *net* payoff implies a break-even S_T at the point where $(S_T - X)10,000$ equals the cost of the contract. That particular value of S_T is simply the strike price plus the call price (expressed in cents). In our illustration, the break-even S_T for the purchaser of the option and, likewise, for the writer is 0.98 plus (1.96/100) or 0.9996. The break-even S_T is of interest to someone purchasing or writing options as a speculative position. When we turn to the use of currency options as hedging devices, we will see that the break-even S_T is of no great significance.

A put option on a currency gives the holder the right but not the obligation to *sell* a specific currency at a specific exchange rate at a specific time. For purposes of our illustration,

EXHIBIT 9.7	Exchange Rate at Expiry (S_T) US\$/C\$	$S_T - X_T$	Option Pay-off US\$	Option Pay-off C\$
Call Option Value at Expiry				

	Exchange Rate at Expiry (S_T) US\$/C\$	$S_T - X_T$	Option Pay-off US\$	Option Pay-off C\$
US dollar	0.950	−0.030	0	0
appreciates	0.955	−0.025	0	0
and	0.960	−0.020	0	0
FX option	0.965	−0.015	0	0
expires	0.970	−0.010	0	0
out-of-the-money	0.975	−0.005	0	0
	0.980	0.000	0	0
US dollar	0.985	0.005	50	51
depreciates	0.990	0.010	100	101
and	0.995	0.015	150	151
FX option	1.000	0.020	200	200
expires	1.005	0.025	250	249
in-the-money	1.010	0.030	300	297
Cost of June C\$ CALL option, US\$		196		
Cost of June C\$ CALL option, C\$		200		

the following are the terms of a put option as of 11 June 2013 to sell US dollars for Canadian dollars at a strike price of US\$0.98 on 20 July 2013.

Currencies involved	US\$/C\$
Type of option	PUT
Contract size	10,000 Canadian dollars
Strike price (X)	US\$0.980 per Canadian dollar
Expiry (T)	20 July 2013
Settlement	in US dollars

On 11 June 2013 a put option with these specific terms traded on the Philadelphia Stock Exchange at a premium of 1.00. That is the number of US cents per C\$1 of the options contract. Therefore the price of the option is US\$0.010 times 10,000, or US\$100. The option is fully described as a "Canadian July put at 98."

Put option contracts on the Canadian dollar with expiry in July are available at different strike prices, say US\$0.97 or US\$0.99. We will concentrate on the 98.

For the price of US\$100, a currency broker in contact with the PHLX will purchase the put option at the instruction of the purchaser. As with the call premium, the put premium is the upfront money in an options transaction. The money is paid by the purchaser of the put option to the seller or writer of the option.

The Canadian dollar cost of the put contract is US\$100/0.98, or C\$102.

The value of the put option depends on the spot exchange rate (S_T) on 20 July. If the spot exchange rate on 20 July turns out to be, say, US\$0.99/C\$, which means that the US dollar has depreciated against the Canadian dollar, the put option would expire with no value. It would be better to sell Canadian dollars on the spot market at US\$0.99 rather than to exercise the option to sell Canadian dollars at US\$0.98. Whenever the spot rate is greater than the exercise price, the put option is said to be "out-of-the-money." If the put is out-of-the-money at expiry, it has a value of zero.

The value of a put option for the purchaser stems from the prospect that the spot rate at expiry will be less than the strike price of the put. If the exchange rate on 20 July is, say, US\$0.96/C\$, which means that the US dollar has appreciated against the Canadian dollar, the option entitles the holder to sell Canadian dollars (by exercising the option) for US\$0.98/C\$. The option is then worth two US cents for each Canadian dollar in the contract. Since the option contract size is 10,000 Canadian dollars, the value of the option

EXHIBIT 9.8A

Option Pay-off
Structure: To
Purchaser of
One CALL Option
Contract on
Canadian Dollars
for US Dollars

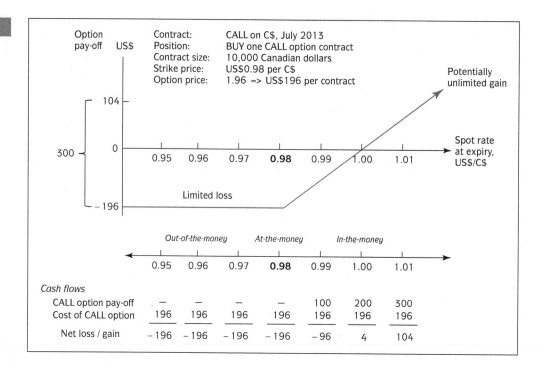

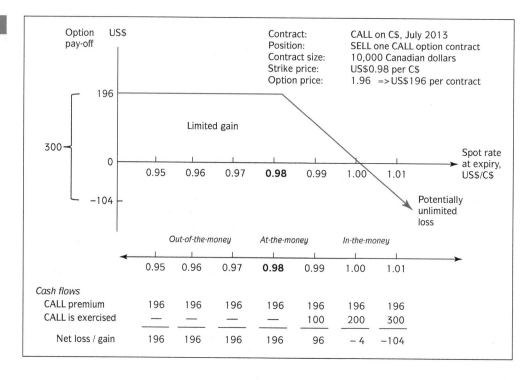

EXHIBIT 9.8B

Option Pay-off
Structure: To
Seller (or "Writer")
of One CALL Option
Contract on
Canadian Dollars
for US Dollars

contract at expiry is $200. Whenever the spot rate is less than the exercise price, the put option is said to be "in-the-money." If the put option is in-the-money at expiry, it has a value equal to $(X - S_T)10,000$.

Exhibit 9.9 shows the loss or gain on the put option conditional on the spot exchange rate at expiry *net* of the cost of US$100 (or C$102). The net loss or gain at expiry is presented both in a diagram and a corresponding line of computations.

EXHIBIT 9.9A

Option Pay-off
Structure: To
Purchaser of Put
Option (to Sell)
Canadian Dollars
for US Dollars

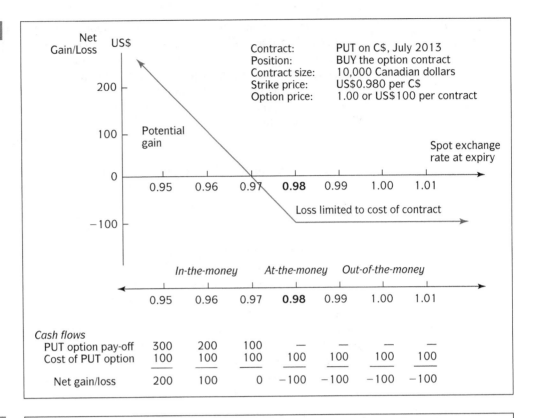

Contract:	PUT on C$, July 2013
Position:	BUY the option contract
Contract size:	10,000 Canadian dollars
Strike price:	US$0.980 per C$
Option price:	1.00 or US$100 per contract

Cash flows

	0.95	0.96	0.97	0.98	0.99	1.00	1.01
PUT option pay-off	300	200	100	—	—	—	—
Cost of PUT option	100	100	100	100	100	100	100
Net gain/loss	200	100	0	−100	−100	−100	−100

EXHIBIT 9.9B

Option Pay-off
Structure: To Writer
of Put Option (to
Sell) Canadian
Dollars for
US Dollars

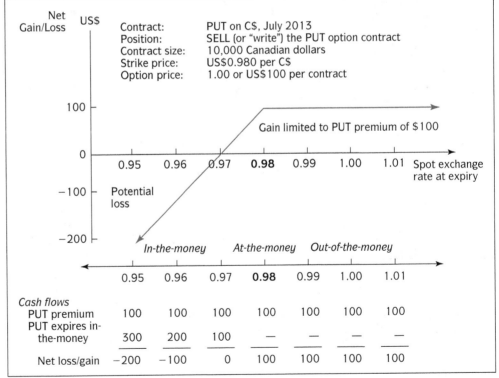

Contract:	PUT on C$, July 2013
Position:	SELL (or "write") the PUT option contract
Contract size:	10,000 Canadian dollars
Strike price:	US$0.980 per C$
Option price:	1.00 or US$100 per contract

Cash flows

	0.95	0.96	0.97	0.98	0.99	1.00	1.01
PUT premium	100	100	100	100	100	100	100
PUT expires in-the-money	300	200	100	—	—	—	—
Net loss/gain	−200	−100	0	100	100	100	100

Hedging with Currency Options

To illustrate the hedging properties of currency options, consider a Canadian corporation or financial institution with a one million US dollar receivable due in one month, say on 20 July. If, between now and then, the US dollar depreciates against the Canadian dollar, the number of Canadian dollars eventually received is correspondingly less. On the other hand, if between now and then the US dollar appreciates against the Canadian dollar, the number of Canadian dollars eventually received is correspondingly greater. A currency call option to buy Canadian dollars with US dollars on 20 July would allow the Canadian corporation to hedge the downside risk (of US dollar depreciation) and capture the potential upside gain (of US dollar appreciation).

The starting point is to have an initial expectation of the spot rate on 20 July knowing that that expectation is only one value within a distribution of possible values for the spot rate on 20 July. A reasonable and observable expectation is the one-month forward rate. Let's say the one-month forward rate is US$0.98/C$.

A call option with a strike price of US$0.98/C$ will hedge the Canadian dollar proceeds from the US dollar receivable against depreciation of the US dollar.

As we saw earlier, the "Canadian July call at 98" is today (11 June) trading on the PHLX at 1.96. The cost of a call contract is US$196.

The spot exchange rate today is US$0.98/C$. (It would not be unusual for the one-month forward rate to equal the spot exchange rate.) Then the Canadian dollar cost of a call option purchased on the PHLX is US$196/0.98, or C$200.

The next issue is how many contracts are required. The number of Canadian dollars that would be received at the "expected" spot rate on 20 July is US$1,000,000/0.98 or C$1,020,408. One Canadian dollar currency option contract involves C$10,000. So 102 contracts is reasonably close, and costs US$19,992 or C$20,400. Brokerage fees are approximately 102 × $5 or C$570. Total outlay is C$20,910.

Exhibit 9.10 presents the detailed results of the conditional pay-off structure resulting from the unhedged and the hedged receivable in both US dollars and, more importantly, Canadian dollars.

EXHIBIT 9.10	US Dollar Receivable Hedged with Currency Options

Receivable (US$)	1,000,000
Option Price (June C$)	1.96
STRIKE (X_T), (US$)	0.980
Contract size (C$)	10,000
Number of contracts	102
Cost of June C$ option, US$(1.09)	19,992
Cost of June C$ option, C$	**20,400**

	(1) Exchange Rate at Expiry (S_T) US$/C$	(2) $S_T - X_T$	(3) Option Pay-off US$	(4) Option Pay-off C$	(5) FX Loss/Gain on Receivable if Unhedged US$	(6) FX Loss/Gain on Receivable if Unhedged C$	(7) Hedge . . . FX Loss/Gain on Receivable Plus Option Pay-off C$
US dollar	0.950	−0.030	0	0	30,000	31,579	**31,579**
appreciates	0.955	−0.025	0	0	25,000	26,178	**26,178**
and	0.960	−0.020	0	0	20,000	20,833	**20,833**
FX option	0.965	−0.015	0	0	15,000	15,544	**15,544**
expires	0.970	−0.010	0	0	10,000	10,309	**10,309**
out-of-the-money	0.975	−0.005	0	0	5,000	5,128	**5,128**
	0.980	0.000	0	0	0	0	**0**
US dollar	0.985	0.005	5,100	5,178	−5,000	−5,076	**102**
depreciates	0.990	0.010	10,200	10,303	−10,000	−10,101	**202**
and	0.995	0.015	15,300	15,377	−15,000	−15,075	**302**
FX option	1.000	0.020	20,400	20,400	−20,000	−20,000	**400**
expires	1.005	0.025	25,500	25,373	−25,000	−24,876	**498**
in-the-money	1.010	0.030	30,600	30,297	−30,000	−29,703	**594**

EXHIBIT 9.11

Call Option Hedge:
With Respect to
US$1 Million to
Be Received in
One Month

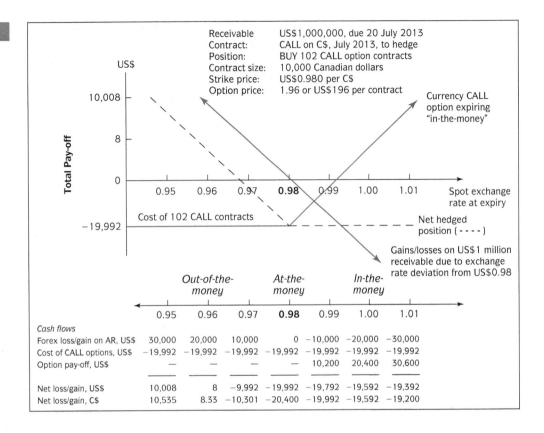

	Out-of-the-money			**At-the-money**		**In-the-money**	
	0.95	0.96	0.97	**0.98**	0.99	1.00	1.01
Cash flows							
Forex loss/gain on AR, US$	30,000	20,000	10,000	0	−10,000	−20,000	−30,000
Cost of CALL options, US$	−19,992	−19,992	−19,992	−19,992	−19,992	−19,992	−19,992
Option pay-off, US$	—	—	—	—	10,200	20,400	30,600
Net loss/gain, US$	10,008	8	−9,992	−19,992	−19,792	−19,592	−19,392
Net loss/gain, C$	10,535	8.33	−10,301	−20,400	−19,992	−19,592	−19,200

The treasurer of a Canadian corporation pondering the wisdom of hedging the US$1,000,000 receivable due in one month must focus on Exhibit 9.10 columns 6 and 7, the unhedged and hedged pay-off structures in Canadian dollars. The treasurer must consider whether the company is willing to pay C$20,910 for currency options to create column 7 as opposed to column 6.

Exhibit 9.11 illustrates the net conditional pay-off structure for the hedged receivable. All figures are in US dollars, since the receivable itself is in US dollars, and the option price and settlement are in US dollars, since the call option is traded on the PHLX. The dashed line depicts the net-of-cost hedged position across the range of (conditional) values of the US$/C$ exchange rate on 20 July. (Brokerage fees are not included in the cost in order to isolate the outlay for 102 option contracts.)

Comparing the Forward, Futures and Options Hedges

We have demonstrated that foreign exchange risk that arises from a one-million-US-dollar receivable due in one month can be addressed with a forward contract, futures contracts, or foreign currency options. The respective hedges are not identical. Above all, the forward contract or futures contracts "lock in" a specific number of Canadian dollars to be received on 20 July, whereas the pay-off to the options depends on the (spot) exchange rate on that final day.

The forward contract, negotiated with a bank, involves no initial cash outlay. On 20 July US dollars are exchanged for Canadian dollars at the agreed rate of exchange (which may or may not equal the spot rate of exchange on 20 July). The "cost" of the forward contract to the retail customer is not explicit. It is embedded in the bid-ask spread offered by the bank at the time the forward contract is negotiated. A rough but reasonable approximation of the cost is found by multiplying one-half of the bid-ask spread by the amount of the contract in Canadian dollars. If the bid-ask spread is, say, 3 basis points, then the cost, essentially the remuneration to the bank, is 0.0015 × C$1,020,408 or C$1,531.

Futures contracts are arranged through a broker. The process requires an initial margin, the account is marked-to-market and setup entails brokerage fees. In the Bombardier example, we computed the all-in cost of the futures contract hedge as C$111.55.

The all-in cost of hedging with currency options is substantially greater at C$20,910. On the other hand, the options hedge comes with the potential reward of foreign currency gains if the US dollar deviates significantly—upward or downward—from the exercise price.

Currency Options Pricing: What a Manager Should Know

In our illustration of the mechanics of using currency options to hedge foreign exchange risk, we focused on the one-month Canadian dollar call with an exercise price of US$0.98 trading on the PHLX. On the day in June that the options were purchased, that option was priced at 1.96 US cents per Canadian dollar in the contract. Since the contract specifies 10,000 Canadian dollars, the cost of the contract was US$0.0196 × 10,000 or US$196. The key figure is 1.96.

Exhibit 9.12 presents a more complete set of prices of call options on the Canadian dollar that traded on 11 June 2013 on the PHLX. Several points are pertinent:

1. Options are available in a range of strike prices, from US$0.960 to US$1.000.
2. Available "expiry dates" range from June through to December. Each of the three near-months is available.
3. In each column, that is for each specific month of expiry, call options prices increase for successively lower values of the strike price. For example, the June 98 call is priced at 0.73 whereas the June 97 is priced at 1.36 and the June 96 is priced at 2.14.
4. Along each row, that is at each specific strike price, option prices increase the longer is the time to expiry. For example, the June 98 call is priced at 0.73 whereas the July 98 is priced at 1.96. The December 98 is 2.78.

The third and fourth points above are worth considering in a bit more depth.

A currency call option with a lower strike price is more valuable (to the purchaser of the option contract) than a call option with the same expiry at a higher strike price. There are essentially two reasons. First, whereas a currency call option has value at expiry only if it

EXHIBIT 9.12

Call Option Prices on the Canadian Dollar

CANADIAN DOLLAR OPTIONS
11 June 2013
SPOT: US$0.9814/C$

Strike Price	Calls		
	June	July	December
960	2.14	3.18	3.91
965	1.73	2.85	3.61
970	1.36	2.54	3.33
975	1.02	2.24	3.05
980	0.73	1.96	2.78
985	0.50	1.69	2.53
990	0.32	1.46	2.30
995	0.20	1.26	2.08
1000	0.12	1.07	1.87

Source: Rotman Finance Centre.

expires in-the-money, that is if $X < S_T$, the likelihood of the option expiring in-the-money is greater the smaller is X. Second, for any in-the-money value of S_T, the lower the strike price the greater is the resulting pay-off. The pay-off is equal to $(S_T - X) \times 10,000$ per contract. If, for example, the spot rate in June turns out to be US$0.98, the June 98 pay-off is zero whereas the June 97.50 pay-off is US$50 and the June 97 pay-off is US$100.

With respect to each row of Exhibit 9.12, the successively higher call option prices for longer expiry dates directly reflect the greater uncertainty of outcomes (for S_T) associated with longer times to expiry. For the purchaser of a currency option, the cost of the option represents a limited downside whereas a positive pay-off is potentially large although not specifically defined. In particular, the option moves deeper in-the-money the more the US dollar depreciates relative to the Canadian dollar by the time expiry arrives. The longer the time to expiry, the greater the likelihood that such a rewarding (to the purchaser) development will occur. Therefore, for a given strike price, the price of currency call options increases with the time to expiry.

Finally, we could add a comment about the relation between the volatility of the underlying asset, in our case the US$/C$ exchange rate, and the price of options on that asset. Options, as mentioned, are designed to transfer risk. The purchaser of the option is relieved of risk while the seller (writer) of the option agrees to bear risk. Greater volatility essentially means greater risk. Therefore sellers of currency options demand larger premiums (higher option prices) the greater the volatility of the exchange rate.

In summary, a manager involved in hedging foreign exchange risk through currency call (put) options ought to realize that the cost of a hedge is greater the lower (higher) the strike price that he chooses, the longer the time to expiry and the more volatile is the exchange rate.

SUMMARY

This chapter introduces currency futures and options on foreign exchange.

1. Forward, futures and options contracts are derivative, or contingent claim, securities. That is, their value is derived or contingent upon the value of the asset that underlies these securities.

2. Forward and futures contracts are similar instruments, but there are important differences. Both are contracts to buy or sell a certain quantity of a specific underlying asset at some specific price in the future. Futures contracts, however, are exchange-traded with standardized features that distinguish futures from the tailor-made terms of forward contracts. The two main standardized features of futures contracts are contract size and maturity date.

3. Futures contracts are marked-to-market on a daily basis at the new settlement price. Hence, the margin account of an individual with a futures position is increased or decreased daily to reflect realized profits or losses resulting from the change in the futures settlement price from the previous day's settlement price.

4. A futures market requires speculators and hedgers to effectively operate. Hedgers attempt to avoid the risk of price change of the underlying asset. Speculators attempt to profit from anticipating the direction of future price changes.

5. The Chicago Mercantile Exchange and the Philadelphia Board of Trade are currency futures exchanges that are readily accessible and widely used by Canadian firms.

6. The pricing equation typically used to price currency futures is the interest parity relationship, which is used also to price currency forward contracts.

7. Eurodollar interest rate futures contracts were introduced as a vehicle for hedging short-term dollar interest rate risk, in much the same way as forward rate agreements, introduced in Chapter 6.

8. A foreign currency option is the right, but not the obligation, to buy or sell the underlying currency for a stated price over a stated time period. Call options give the owner the right to buy, put options the right to sell. American options can be exercised at any time during their life, while European options can only be exercised at maturity.

9. Exchange-traded options with standardized features are traded on two exchanges. Options on spot foreign exchange are traded at the Philadelphia Stock Exchange, and options on currency futures are traded at the Chicago Mercantile Exchange.

10. On the Montreal Exchange, Canadians can take long or short positions in US dollar futures contracts that are denominated, priced, marked-to-market and settled in Canadian dollars.

QUESTIONS

1. Explain the basic differences between the operation of a currency forward market and a futures market.

2. In order for a derivatives market to function, two types of economic agents are needed: hedgers and speculators. Explain.

3. Why are most futures positions closed out through a reversing trade, rather than held to delivery?

4. How can the FX futures market be used for price discovery?

5. What is the major difference in the obligation of one with a long position in a futures (or forward) contract in comparison with an options contract?

6. What is meant by the terminology that an option is in, at, or out of the money?

7. List the arguments (variables) of which an FX call or put option model price is a function. How does the call and put premium change with respect to a change in the arguments?

PROBLEMS

1. Assume today's settlement price on a CME CDN (Canadian dollar) futures contract is US$0.9400/C$. You have a *short* position in one contract. Your margin account currently has a balance of US$1,700. The next three days' settlement prices are US$0.9386, US$0.9393 and US$0.9309. Calculate the changes in the margin account from daily marking-to-market and the balance of the margin account after the third day.

2. Repeat problem 1 assuming you have a *long* position in the futures contract.

3. Using quotations in Exhibit 9.3, calculate the face value of the open interest in the September 2013 euro futures contract.

4. From Exhibit 9.3, the September 2013 Mexican peso futures contract has a price of US$0.8165 per ten Mexican pesos. You believe the spot price in September 2013 will be US$0.8400. Using futures contracts, what speculative position would you enter into to attempt to gain from your beliefs? Calculate your anticipated gains assuming you take a position in three contracts. What is the size of your gain (loss) if the futures price is, indeed, an unbiased predictor of the future spot price and this price materializes? All calculations should be reported in US dollars.

5. Repeat problem 4 assuming you believe the May 2013 spot price will be $0.8000 per ten Mexican pesos. All calculations should be reported in US dollars.

6. For problems 4 and 5, report the cost of the futures contracts and the possible gains or losses in Canadian dollars assuming the US$/C$ exchange rate in May is US$0.9901/C$. What additional risk does a Canadian speculator in Mexican pesos take on through futures contracts (on the CME) that are denominated and settled in US dollars?

7. Barrick Gold of Toronto is considering a possible six-month US$100 million LIBOR-based, floating-rate bank loan to fund a mining project at terms shown in the table below. The chief financial officer (CFO) at Barrick fears a possible rise in the LIBOR rate by December and wants to use the December Eurodollar futures contract to hedge this risk. The contract expires 17 December 2013, and has a contract size of US$ 1 million and an implied LIBOR yield of 0.315 percent.

The CFO will ignore the cash flow implications of marking to market, initial margin requirements and any timing mismatch between exchange-traded futures contract cash flows and the interest payments due in March.

Loan Terms		
17 September 2013	**17 December 2013**	**17 March 2014**
• Borrow $100 million at 17 September LIBOR + 200 basis points (bps)	• Pay interest for first three months	• Pay back principal plus interest
• 17 September LIBOR = 0.295%	• Roll loan over at 17 December LIBOR + 200 bps	

Loan initiated	First loan payment (2.295%) and futures contract expires	Second payment and principal
9/17/13	12/17/13	3/17/14

a. Formulate Barrick's 17 September floating-to-fixed-rate strategy using the Eurodollar future contracts discussed in the text above. Show that this strategy would result in a fixed-rate loan, assuming an increase in the LIBOR rate to 0.515 percent by 17 December, which remains at 0.515 percent through 17 March. Show all calculations.

Hint:

The basis point value (BPV) of a Eurodollar futures contract is found by substituting the contract specifications into the following money market relationship:

$$BPV_{FUT} = \text{Change in Value} = (\text{Face Value}) \times (\text{Days to Maturity}/360) \times (\text{Change in Yield})$$
$$= (\$1 \text{ million}) \times (90/360) \times (0.0001)$$
$$= \$25$$

The number of contracts, N, can be found by:

$$N = (\text{Value of Spot Position})/(\text{Face Value of Each Futures Contract})$$
$$= (\$100 \text{ million})/(\$1 \text{ million})$$
$$= 100$$

OR

$$N = (\text{Value of Spot Position})/(\text{Value of Futures Position})$$
$$= (\$100{,}000{,}000)/(\$981{,}750)$$

where

Value of Futures Position $= \$1{,}000{,}000 \times [1 - (0.00315/4)]$
≈ 100 contracts

Barrick is also considering a 12-month loan as an alternative. This approach will result in two additional uncertain cash flows, as follows:

Loan payment initiated	Dec '13 payment (2.295%)	March '14 payment	June '14 payment	Sept '14 payment and principal
9/17/13	12/17/13	3/17/14	6/17/14	9/17/14

b. Describe how Barrick could use a "string of futures contracts" to hedge the 12-month loan, turning the floating-rate debt into fixed-rate. No calculations are needed.

8. Jack Bauer has a liability that
- has a principal balance of $100 million on 30 June 2013,
- accrues interest quarterly starting on 30 June 2013,
- pays interest quarterly,
- has a one-year term to maturity and
- calculates interest due on the basis of 90-day LIBOR.

He wishes to hedge his remaining interest payments against changes in interest rates. He has correctly calculated that he needs to sell (short) 300 Eurodollar futures contracts to accomplish the hedge. He is considering the alternative hedging strategies outlined in the following table.

Contract Month	Initial Position (6/30/13) in 90-Day LIBOR Eurodollar Contracts	
	Strategy A (contracts)	Strategy B (contracts)
September 2013	300	100
December 2013	0	100
March 2014	0	100

a. Explain why strategy B is a more effective hedge than strategy A when the yield curve undergoes an instantaneous nonparallel shift.

b. Discuss an interest rate scenario in which strategy A would be superior to strategy B.

9. In Example 9.4, The Ontario Teachers Pension Fund used Eurodollar futures contracts to hedge interest rate risk. Say the $20,000,000 bond redemption proceeds are to be received in September 2013 rather than in June, and let's say that the manager hedges interest rate risk with September 2013 Eurodollar futures contracts.

a. What is the 90-day LIBOR implied by the September 2013 Eurodollar futures contract?

b. If the interest rate risk is to be hedged with September 2013 Eurodollar futures contracts, how many contracts must be purchased?

c. What gains (or losses) on the September 2013 Eurodollar futures contracts result if, when September rolls around, three-month LIBOR turns out to be 4.5 percent?

10. Our example of the use by a Canadian company of currency call options to hedge a US$1 million receivable was based on a strike price of US$0.9800 for the July call option. The price of that "July 98 call" was 1.96. From Exhibit 9.12 we see that the "July 99 call" had a lower price of 1.69. Calculate the costs and the (conditional) pay-off structure for the hedge with 102 contracts of the "99 June call." Express costs and (conditional) pay-offs in Canadian dollars. What does the difference in cost in constructing the hedge imply for the difference in the (conditional) pay-off structure for the "99" as against the "98"?

11. Our example of the use of currency options by a Canadian company to hedge currency risk involves a US$1 million *receivable* hedged with *call* options. Assume instead that a hedge is required for a

US$1 million *payable* that comes due for a Canadian corporation in June. With the use of the "June Canadian *put* at US$0.9500," calculate the (conditional) pay-off structure for a hedge. What is the cost of the hedge?

12. It is 11 June 2013. The Canadian and US dollars are trading at an exchange rate of 1:1. The US interest rate is 0.50 percent. The Canadian interest rate is 1.00 percent. The volatility of the exchange rate, σ, is 15 percent.

    a. As of that date, apply the currency option pricing model presented in Appendix 9A to compute the price of a Canadian dollar call option with an exercise price (US$/C$) of 1.00 that expires on 20 July 2013.

    b. What is the effect on the option price if the volatility of the exchange rate is 16 percent as opposed to 15 percent?

    c. Assuming that the volatility is 15 percent, what is the effect on the option price if the Canadian interest rate is 5.00 percent as opposed to 4.75?

INTERNET EXERCISE

Online currency futures quotations can be found at www.castletrading.com/historiccharts.htm. Go to this website and the currency with the most trading volume today. Click on the currency name to determine in which contract expiration there is the most trading volume. Is it the near-term contract or a deferred delivery contract?

MINI CASE

The Options Speculator

A speculator is considering the purchase of five three-month Japanese yen call options with a strike price of 96 cents per 100 yen. The premium is 1.35 cents per 100 yen. The spot price is 95.28 cents per 100 yen and the 90-day forward rate is 95.71 cents. The speculator believes the yen will appreciate to $1 per 100 yen over the next three months. As the speculator's assistant, you have been asked to do the following:

1. Diagram the call option.
2. Determine the speculator's profit if the yen appreciates to $1/100 yen.
3. Determine the speculator's profit if the yen appreciates only to the forward rate.
4. Determine the future spot price at which the speculator will only break even.

REFERENCES & SUGGESTED READINGS

Barone-Adesi, Giovanni, and Robert Whaley. "Efficient Analytic Approximation of American Option Values." *Journal of Finance* 42 (1987), pp. 301–20.

Biger, Nahum, and John Hull. "The Valuation of Currency Options." *Financial Management* 12 (1983), pp. 24–28.

Black, Fischer. "The Pricing of Commodity Contracts." *Journal of Financial Economics* 3 (1976), pp. 167–79.

Black, Fischer, and Myron Scholes. "The Pricing of Options and Corporate Liabilities." *Journal of Political Economy* 81 (1973), pp. 637–54.

Bodurtha, James, Jr., and George Courtadon. "Efficiency Tests of the Foreign Currency Options Market." *Journal of Finance* 41 (1986), pp. 151–62.

Cox, John C., Jonathan E. Ingersoll, and Stephen A. Ross. "The Relation between Forward Prices and Futures Prices." *Journal of Financial Economics* 9 (1981), pp. 321–46.

Cox, John C., Stephen A. Ross, and Mark Rubinstein. "Option Pricing: A Simplified Approach." *Journal of Financial Economics* 7 (1979), pp. 229–63.

Garman, Mark, and Steven Kohlhagen. "Foreign Currency Option Values." *Journal of International Money and Finance* 2 (1983), pp. 231–38.

Giddy, I. H. and G. Dufey. "Uses and Abuses of Currency Options." *Journal of Applied Corporate Finance* 8 (3) (1995).

Grabbe, J. Orlin. "The Pricing of Call and Put Options on Foreign Exchange." *Journal of International Money and Finance* 2 (1983), pp. 239–54.

———— *International Financial Markets*, 3rd ed. Upper Saddle River, NJ: Prentice Hall, 1996.

Merton, Robert. "Theory of Rational Option Pricing." *The Bell Journal of Economics and Management Science* 4 (1973), pp. 141–83.

Philadelphia Stock Exchange. *Understanding Foreign Currency Options* and other PHLX information brochures. Philadelphia: Philadelphia Stock Exchange, 2006.

Shastri, Kuldeep, and Kishore Tandon. "Arbitrage Tests of the Efficiency of the Foreign Currency Options Market." *Journal of International Money and Finance* 4 (1985), pp. 455–68.

——— "Valuation of Foreign Currency Options: Some Empirical Tests." *Journal of Financial and Quantitative Analysis* 21 (1986), pp. 145–60.

Appendix 9A

Foreign Currency Option Pricing Model

This chapter focused on the essentials of foreign currency futures and options that a manager must know in order to use these instruments in dealing with foreign exchange risk. Currency options, as we have explained, are market-traded derivative securities.

A major step in modern finance is the development of a framework for *pricing* options. The basic model expresses the price of a foreign currency option in terms of six observable factors:

Spot exchanges rate, S_t
Exercise price, E
Length of time to expiry of the option, T
Interest rate on the currency in which the option is priced, say the US interest rate, $r_\$$
Interest rate in the country of the "other" currency, r_i
Volatility of the exchange rate, σ

Exact European call and put pricing formulas are[1]

$$C_e = S_t e^{-r_i T} N(d_1) - E e^{-r_\$ T} N(d_2) \tag{A9.1}$$

and

$$P_e = E e^{-r_\$ T} N(-d_2) - S_t e^{-r_i T} N(-d_1) \tag{A9.2}$$

Interest rates $r_\$$ and r_i are expressed on an annualized basis and are assumed to be constant over the life of the option, that is until time T, which is expressed as a fraction of a year.

Invoking *interest rate parity* and continuous compounding, we derive an estimate of F_T, the futures price of the foreign exchange.

$$F_T = S_t e^{(r_\$ - r_i)T}$$

This results in simplified expressions for the price of the call and the put:

$$C_e = [F_T N(d_1) - E N(d_2)]e^{-r_\$ T} \tag{A9.3}$$

and

$$P_e = [E N(-d_2) - F_T N(-d_1)]e^{-r_\$ T} \tag{A9.4}$$

where

$$d_1 = \frac{\ln(F_T/E) + 0.5\sigma^2 T}{\sigma \sqrt{T}}$$

---

[1]The European option pricing model was developed by Biger and Hull (1983), Garman and Kohlhagen (1983) and Grabbe (1983). The model is based on the theory of European option pricing developed by Merton (1973) and Black (1976).

and

$$d_2 = d_1 - \sigma \sqrt{T}$$

$N(d)$ denotes the cumulative area under the standard normal density function from $-\infty$ to d_1 (or d_2). σ is the annualized volatility of exchange rate changes, $\ln(S_{t+1}/S_t)$.

Equations A9.3 and A9.4 represent C_e and P_e as functions of only five variables, F_T, E, $r_{\$}$, T and σ. (r_i is subsumed within F_T.)

$N(d)$ can be calculated using the NORMSDIST function of Microsoft Excel.

Equations A9.3 and A9.4 for C_e and P_e are widely used in practice, especially by international banks in trading over-the-counter options.

Example A.1   *Pricing a Canadian Dollar Call Option*

To illustrate the pricing of a currency option, we look at the 11 June 2013 quote on a July Canadian dollar call as examined in Section 9.7. With an exercise price of 98.00(US$/C$), the call option recently traded at 1.96 US cents per Canadian dollar in the contract.

We use the European option pricing model even though the call is an American option. This is frequently done in practice. Prices between the two modes vary very little.[2]

The spot exchange rate on 11 June is 98.14. US and Canadian interest rates of 0.05 and 1.00 percent respectively imply $F(US\$/C\$)$ for July is 98.04. Volatility of the exchange rate, σ, is estimated at 15 percent. T is $39/365 = 0.1068$.

Values of d_1 and d_2 are:

$$d_1 = \frac{\ln(98.14/98) + (0.5 \times 0.15^2 \times 0.1068)}{0.15 \times 0.1068^{0.5}} = 0.0536$$

and

$$d_2 = 0.0536 - (0.15 \times 0.1068^{0.5}) = 0.0046$$

In turn, $N(0.0536) = 0.5214$ and $N(0.0046) = 0.5018$.

We now have everything necessary to compute the price of the July 98 call option on the Canadian dollar:

$$C_e = (98.04 \times 0.5214 - 98 \times 0.5018) \times 2.718^{0.0005 \times 0.1068}$$

$$= 1.942 \text{ US cents per Canadian dollar}$$

The model has done a respectable job of valuing the currency call option. The option price would have been higher, however, had we used a larger estimate of volatility.

---

[2]Barone-Adesi and Whaley (1987) developed an approximate American call option-pricing model that has proven to be quite accurate in valuing American currency call options.

Chapter (10)

Interest Rate and Currency Swaps

CHAPTER OUTLINE

CHAPTER 4 INTRODUCED forward contracts as a vehicle for hedging exchange rate risk. Chapter 9 introduced futures and options contracts on foreign exchange as alternative tools to hedge foreign exchange exposure. These types of instruments seldom have terms longer than a few years, however. Chapter 9 also discussed Eurodollar futures contracts for hedging short-term dollar-denominated interest rate risk. In this chapter, we examine interest rate swaps, both single-currency and cross-currency, which are widely used techniques for hedging long-term interest rate risk and foreign exchange risk.

We begin by distinguishing interest rate swaps from currency swaps followed by data on the global size of the respective swap markets. Then, through a series of illustrations of increasing complexity, we outline the intricate structure of swaps while demonstrating their usefulness for reallocating risk between "counterparties." We explain how to read published "swap quotations" that guide the pricing of over-the-counter swaps. We closely examine the crucial role of the swap bank in serving the complementary objectives of the counterparties, and we demonstrate how the swap bank is compensated for its role.

10.1 TYPES OF SWAPS

In an interest rate swap, two parties called **counterparties** agree to exchange cash flows at periodic intervals. There are two types of interest rate swaps. One is a **single-currency interest rate swap**, a name typically shortened to *interest rate swap*. The other type is a **cross-currency interest rate swap** or simply a *currency swap*.

In the basic ("plain vanilla") *fixed-for-floating rate* interest rate swap, one counterparty exchanges the interest payments of a floating-rate debt obligation for the fixed-rate interest payments of the other counterparty. Both debt obligations are denominated in the same currency. An interest rate swap can better match the respective counterparties' cash inflows and outflows and can result in cost savings. There are many variants of the basic interest rate swap, some of which are discussed below.

Currency Swaps I—The World Bank and IBM are International Financial Innovators

The World Bank ranks among the world's largest borrowers. It borrows in many national capital markets around the world as well as in the Eurobond market. The World Bank then lends money to (usually poorer) nations for development projects.

In the 1970s and early 1980s, the World Bank was a heavy borrower in the deutschemark and the Swiss franc. By 1981, it was near its official borrowing limits in the currencies, but it wanted to borrow more. Many of the World Bank's creditors preferred to service their loans in these European currencies. By coincidence, IBM had a large amount of deutschemark and Swiss franc debt that it had incurred a few years earlier. The proceeds of IBM's borrowings had been converted to dollars for corporate use. IBM had no substantial cash flow in deutschemarks and Swiss francs. Salomon Brothers, the investment bank, saw an opportunity.

Salomon Brothers advised the World Bank to issue Euro*dollar* debt with service payment dates that matched IBM's debt payment schedule. In the novel arrangement, the World Bank agreed to pay the debt service on IBM's deutschemark and Swiss franc debt. Meanwhile IBM, also on the advice of Salomon Brothers, agreed to pay the debt service (interest and principal) on the World Bank's Eurodollar bonds. A few contracts, handshakes all around, and Salomon Brothers had designed the first "currency swap."

Both the World Bank and IBM benefited more through a lower all-in cost (interest expense, transaction costs and service charges) than they would have otherwise. The World Bank benefited by developing an indirect way to obtain debt service cash flow in their preferred currencies without going directly to the German or Swiss capital markets. IBM was happy to be relieved of the need to make periodic (and transactionally risky) currency conversions of dollars for deutschemarks and Swiss francs.

The currency swap market was born.

In a **currency swap**, counterparties exchange debt service obligations denominated in one currency for debt service obligations denominated in another currency. The basic currency swap involves the exchange of *fixed-for-fixed rate* debt service. Currency swaps allow firms to match the currency of their debt-service obligations to the currency of their more fundamental operating cash flows. For instance, while a company may have or had good reason to borrow in, say, euro, the firm's operating earnings may be predominantly in dollars. The mismatch in currencies as far as debt-service obligations are concerned can be addressed through a currency swap. In the process, as we shall see, *both* sides of a currency swap can potentially benefit from interest cost savings to the extent that the currency swap relaxes a constraint on their preferred location for raising capital.

The International Finance in Practice box "Currency Swaps I" discusses the first currency swap.

10.2 SIZE OF THE SWAP MARKET

www.isda.org

The website of the International Swaps and Derivatives Association. This site describes the activities of the ISDA and provides educational information about interest rate and currency swaps, other OTC interest rate and currency derivatives, and risk management activities. Market survey data about the size of the swaps market are also provided.

As the International Finance in Practice box suggests, currency swaps date back no further than the early 1980s. Even so, currency swaps have been around longer than interest rate swaps. Today, however, the interest rate swap market is much the larger of the two.

Exhibit 10.1 indicates the size and rapid growth in the respective swap markets. Market size is measured by **notional principal**, a reference amount of principal for determining interest payments on either side of a swap.

The total global amount of interest rate swaps outstanding increased from $3,065 billion at year-end 1991 to $379 *trillion* by 2012, an astounding average annual growth rate of 26 percent. The notional principal of currency swaps over the same period grew at an average annual rate of 20 percent.

The five most common currencies involved in interest rate and currency swaps are the US dollar, the euro, the Japanese yen, the British pound sterling and the Swiss franc.

A recent survey of foreign exchange activity in Canada carried out by the Bank of Canada indicates robust growth in currency derivatives involving the Canadian dollar. The average growth of the outstanding value of interest rate swaps involving the Canadian dollar is 20 percent per year over the past decade. The Canadian base figure of "daily turnover" in foreign exchange derivative products exceeds $100 billion per day.

EXHIBIT 10.1

Size of Interest
Rate and Currency
Swap Markets: Total
Notional Principal
Outstanding
Amounts in billions
of US Dollars*

Year	Interest Rate Swaps	Currency Swaps
1991	3,065	807
1992	3,851	860
1993	6,177	900
1994	8,816	915
1995	12,811	1,197
1996	19,171	1,560
1997	22,291	1,824
1998	36,262	2,253
1999	43,936	2,444
2000	48,768	3,194
2001	58,897	3,942
2002	79,161	4,509
2003	111,209	6,371
2004	127,570	7,033
2005	145,876	9,543
2006	165,016	12,964
2007	309,588	14,347
2008	309,760	13,322
2009	349,236	16,509
2010	364,377	19,271
2011	402,611	22,791
2012	379,401	24,156

*Notional principal is used only as a reference measure to which interest rates are applied for determining interest payments. In an interest rate swap, principal does not actually change hands.

Source: Bank for International Settlements, *International Banking and Financial Market Developments,* Table 19, various issues.

10.3   THE SWAP BANK

www.bis.org

The website of the Bank
for International
Settlements. Describes
the activities and purpose
of the BIS. Many online
publications about foreign
exchange and OTC
derivatives are available.

A **swap bank** is a generic term to describe a financial institution that facilitates swaps between counterparties. A swap bank can be an international commercial bank, an investment bank, a merchant bank or an independent operator. The swap bank serves as either a **swap broker** or a **swap dealer.** As a broker, the swap bank matches counterparties but does not assume any risk of the swap. The swap broker receives a commission for this service. Today, most swap banks serve as dealers or market makers. As a market maker, the swap bank stands willing to accept either side of a currency swap to then later lay it off or match it with a counterparty. In this capacity, the swap bank assumes a position in the swap and therefore assumes certain risks. The dealer capacity is obviously the more risky. The swap bank receives a portion of the cash flows passed through it to compensate it for bearing this risk.

10.4 INTEREST RATE SWAPS: AN ILLUSTRATION

The basic features of an interest rate swap are remarkably simple. An interest rate swap is a financial arrangement involving two sides, the counterparties, that invariably are large corporations. One side has fixed rate debt but would prefer the debt-service structure (and risks) of floating rate debt. The other side has floating rate debt but would prefer to deal with the steadier debt-service obligations of fixed rate debt. As with any swap or exchange, both sides would be happier with what the other side has.

Since an interest rate swap involves floating rate debt, this aspect of the swap requires a "reference floating interest rate" to determine the floating rate interest payments over the life of the swap. This point will become clear in the illustrations that follow.

In an interest rate swap, the principal amounts of the debts of the counterparties are *not* swapped. Only the obligations for interest payments are exchanged. These periodic transactions are scheduled according to the "re-set dates" of the floating debt, typically every three months.

An interest-rate swap always opens as a zero-outlay transaction for both sides. As with any contract that has derivative features however, the unfolding of future events (such as unanticipated changes in interest rates) may cause the interest rate swap to become more valuable to one side than the other.

The best way to demonstrate the structure and managerial usefulness of interest rate swaps is through an example or two.

Exhibit 10.2 highlights the main features of an interest rate swap and develops the intuition that can then be extended to more complex arrangements. This illustration involves only one currency, the Canadian dollar, with interest rates denominated in the Canadian dollar. We deal with other currencies in due course. For the moment, we can ignore the role of the "swap bank."

Say Manulife of Toronto has arranged to borrow $100 million for three years at a fixed interest rate. Meanwhile, CN of Montreal has arranged to borrow $100 million for three years at a floating rate. To motivate an interest rate swap between CN and Manulife, the starting position is that Manulife has fixed rate debt but prefers floating rate debt, whereas CN has floating rate debt but prefers fixed rate debt.

It is more than mere convenience to specify that both sides, Manulife and CN, are involved with an identical $100 million amount of principal. The principal will *not* be swapped. Likewise, it is more than mere convenience that the terms of the debt outstanding are three years for both Manulife's fixed rate debt and CN's floating rate debt. The swap must have a finite life agreeable to both sides.

We have not explicitly indicated the fixed rate of interest that Manulife pays on its borrowing. Nor have we indicated explicitly the basis of the floating interest rate that CN pays on its debt. Those corporate borrowing costs are not central to the swap. All that is required is that at the outset Manulife has fixed debt and prefers floating, whereas CN has floating debt and prefers fixed.

Let's say Manulife and CN agree to swap their interest payments over the lives of their respective three-year debts. Within the swap, CN becomes the *fixed-rate payer* and Manulife becomes the *floating rate payer*. CN agrees to make payments to Manulife at a fixed rate (compounded semi-annually) of 2.5 percent applied to $100 million. CN's payments

EXHIBIT 10.2

Interest Rate Swap Between Manulife and CN

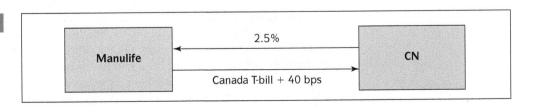

EXHIBIT 10.3

Cash Flows (Millions of Dollars) From Manulife to CN in a $100 Million 3-Year Interest Rate Swap With a Fixed Rate of 2.50 Percent (Compounded Semi-Annually) Paid and Six-Month Canada Treasury Bill Rate (Plus 40 bps) Received

	Six-Month Canada Treasury Bill Rate (+ 40 bps)	Floating Cash Flow Received	Fixed Cash Flow Paid	Net Cash Flow
7 March 2013	1.50			
7 September 2013	1.80	0.75	−1.25	−0.50
7 March 2014	2.10	0.90	−1.25	−0.35
7 September 2014	2.30	1.05	−1.25	−0.20
7 March 2015	2.50	1.15	−1.25	−0.10
7 September 2015	2.70	1.25	−1.25	0
7 March 2016		1.35	−1.25	+0.10

to Manulife are made every six months. For its part, Manulife agrees to pay CN the floating rate cost of borrowing $100 million. Again, these payments will be made every six months. Manulife and CN agree that the floating rate payments are calculated every six months on the basis of the Canada Treasury Bill rate plus 40 basis points (bps).

It is now a relatively simple matter to create a table of payments that will be made from one side to the other over the life of the swap. The three-year swap essentially involves a series of six payments, once every six months, beginning six months from now. The complete set of swapped payments is presented in Exhibit 10.3.

The first exchange of payments occurs on 7 September 2013, six months into the swap. CN pays $1.25 million to Manulife. This is interest on the $100 million principal for six months at 2.5 percent. ($0.5 \times 0.025 \times \$100$ million = $1.25 million.) Manulife pays CN on the $100 million principal at the six-month Canada Treasury bill rate (plus 40 bps) prevailing on the day (7 March 2013) that the swap was initiated. On 7 March 2013, the Canada Treasury bill rate was 1.1 percent (or 110 basis points). The payment from Manulife to CN in September is $0.50 \times (0.0011 + 0.0004) \times \$100$ million = $75,000. There is no uncertainty about the first exchange of payments because it is determined by the Canada Treasury bill rate at the time the swap contract is entered into.

The second exchange of payments is scheduled for 7 March 2014, one year after the initiation of the swap. Again, CN pays $1.25 million to Manulife. Manulife pays CN on the basis of the six-month Canada Treasury bill rate (plus 40 bps) prevailing on 7 September 2013. On that date the Canada Treasury bill rate was 1.8 percent (or 180 basis points). Therefore, on 7 March 2014, Manulife pays CN an amount of $0.5 \times (0.0014 + 0.0004) \times \$100$ million = $90,000.

All told, six exchanges of payments are built into the interest rate swap. The fixed rate payments are straightforward, the same every period. The floating rate payments are calculated using the reference rate of the six-month Canada Treasury bill rate prevailing six months before the payment date. As a practical matter, an interest rate swap is usually structured so that one side pays to the other the *difference* between the two payments. In our example, for the first payment, CN would pay $50,000 to Manulife.

Exhibit 10.3 presents the constituent payments of the swap in detail. The six-month Canada Treasury bill rates beyond March 2013, of course, are *assumed* values for the purpose of the illustration. Indeed, the interest rate risk addressed via the swap, especially for CN, is the uncertainty of the floating rate during the life of the swap. It now seems rather obvious that CN enters the swap with the expectation that floating rates are more likely than not to rise over the next three years. On the other hand, given the structure of (hypothetical) Treasury bill rates we have built into the illustration, if those rates were to unfold in that specific way, it suggests that Manulife entered the interest rate swap with a more benign view of the rise of Treasury bill rates going forward from 2013 to 2015.

The principal amounts on Manulife and CN's original debts are not swapped. In swap jargon, these amounts are referred to as *notional principal*. The role of the notional principal is to serve as the basis for computing interest payments that are swapped. This reinforces the basic point that when two sides enter into an interest rate swap, they bring to the arrangement the same amount of notional principal.

In summary, an interest rate swap is simply an exchange (swap) of fixed rate interest payments for floating rate interest payments over a predetermined time period. Interest rate swaps are a popular tool for locking in a fixed rate when interest rates are low and expected to rise. Similarly, this same product can be used to switch fixed rate debt into floating when interest rates are high and expected to fall.

10.5 ANOTHER INTEREST RATE SWAP ILLUSTRATION: HIGHLIGHTING THE QUALITY SPREAD DIFFERENTIAL AND COSTS

Interest rate swaps, even of the "plain vanilla" sort, are more complex than what we saw with Manulife and CN. Let's now consider the case of a fixed-for-floating rate swap while taking explicit account of costs and benefits to the counterparties as well as to the swap bank.

Bank A is an AAA-rated bank located in the United Kingdom. The bank needs $10,000,000 to finance floating-rate Eurodollar term loans to its clients. It is considering issuing five-year floating-rate notes (FRNs) indexed to LIBOR. Alternatively, the bank could issue five-year fixed-rate Eurodollar bonds at 4 percent. The FRNs make the most sense for Bank A, since it would be using a floating-rate liability to finance a floating-rate asset. In this manner, the bank avoids the interest rate risk associated with a fixed-rate issue. Bank A could end up paying a higher rate than it is receiving on its loans should LIBOR fall substantially.

Company B is a BBB-rated global industrial company. It needs $10,000,000 to finance a capital expenditure with a five-year economic life. Company B can issue five-year fixed-rate bonds at a rate of 5.25 percent in the Eurodollar bond market. Alternatively, it can issue five-year FRNs at LIBOR plus 0.50 percent. The fixed-rate debt makes more sense for Company B because it locks in a financing cost. The FRN alternative could prove unwise should LIBOR increase substantially over the life of the note and could possibly result in the project being unprofitable.

A swap bank familiar with the financing needs of Bank A and Company B has the opportunity to set up a fixed-for-floating interest rate swap that will benefit each counterparty and the swap bank. The key, or necessary condition, giving rise to the swap is the **quality spread differential (QSD)** reflected in borrowing costs facing Bank A and Company B. The quality spread reflects the difference in the credit (or default) risk of Bank A versus Company B. The menu of borrowing costs indicates that Company B is posed greater risk than Bank A.

The QSD is the difference between the default-risk premium differential on the fixed-rate debt and the default-risk premium differential on the floating-rate debt. In general, the former is greater than the latter. The reason is that the yield curve for lower-quality debt tends to be steeper than the yield curve for higher-rated debt because lenders have the option not to renew, or to roll over, short-term debt. Thus, they do not need to be concerned with "locking in" a high default-risk premium. Exhibit 10.4 shows the calculation of the QSD.

EXHIBIT 10.4

Calculation of
Quality Spread
Differential

	Company B	Bank A	Differential
Fixed-rate	5.25%	4.00%	1.25%
Floating-rate	LIBOR + 0.50%	LIBOR	0.50%
			QSD = 0.75%

Given that a QSD exists, it is possible for each counterparty to issue the debt alternative that is *least* advantageous for it (given its financing needs), then swap interest payments. The result, as we shall see, is that each counterparty has its preferred type of interest payment but at a lower all-in cost than it could arrange on its own.

Exhibit 10.5 outlines a possible scenario the swap bank could arrange for the two counterparties. The interest rates used in Exhibit 10.5 refer to the rate paid per annum on the notional principal of $10,000,000.

From Exhibit 10.5, we see that the swap bank instructs Company B to issue FRNs at LIBOR plus 0.50 percent, rather than the more suitable fixed-rate debt at 5.25 percent. Company B passes through to the swap bank 4.50 percent (on the notional principal of $10,000,000) and receives LIBOR in return. In total, Company B pays 4.50 percent (to the swap bank) plus LIBOR + 0.50 percent (to the floating-rate bondholders) and receives LIBOR (from the swap bank) for an **all-in cost** or **AIC** (interest expense, transaction costs and service charges) of 5.00 percent. Thus, through the swap, Company B has converted floating-rate debt into fixed-rate debt at an all-in cost 0.25 percent lower than the 5.25 percent fixed rate it could arrange on its own.

Similarly, Bank A is instructed to issue fixed-rate debt at 4 percent rather than the more suitable FRNs. Bank A passes through to the swap bank LIBOR and receives 4.375 percent in return. In total, Bank A pays 4 percent (to the fixed-rate Eurodollar bondholders) plus LIBOR (to the swap bank) and receives 4.375 percent (from the swap bank) for an all-in cost of LIBOR—0.375 percent. Through the swap, Bank A has converted fixed-rate debt into floating-rate debt at an all-in cost that is 0.375 percent lower than the floating rate of LIBOR it could arrange on its own.

EXHIBIT 10.5

Fixed-for-Floating
Interest Rate Swap*

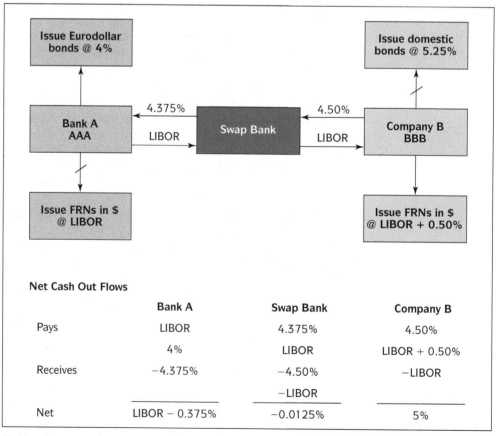

Net Cash Out Flows			
	Bank A	**Swap Bank**	**Company B**
Pays	LIBOR	4.375%	4.50%
	4%	LIBOR	LIBOR + 0.50%
Receives	−4.375%	−4.50%	−LIBOR
		−LIBOR	
Net	LIBOR − 0.375%	−0.0125%	5%

*Debt service expressed as a percentage of $10,000,000 notional value.

The swap bank also benefits because it pays out less than it receives from each counterparty to the other counterparty. The swap bank receives 4.5 percent (from Company B) plus LIBOR (from Bank A) and pays 4.375 percent (to Bank A) and LIBOR (to Company B). The net inflow to the swap bank is 0.125 percent per annum on the notional principal of $10,000,000.

In sum, Bank A has saved 0.375 percent. Company B has saved 0.25 percent. And the swap bank has earned 0.125 percent. This totals 0.75 percent, which equals the QSD. Thus, if a QSD exists, it can be split among the swap parties in a way that lowers all-in borrowing costs for the counterparties and makes money for the swap bank.

In an interest rate swap, the principal sums the two counterparties raise are not exchanged since both counterparties have borrowed in the same currency. The interest payments that are exchanged are based on a notional sum which may not equal the exact amount actually borrowed by each counterparty. Moreover, while Exhibit 10.5 portrays a gross exchange of interest payments based on the notional principal, in practice only the net difference is actually exchanged. For example, Company B would pay to the swap bank the net difference between 4.50 percent and LIBOR on the notional value of $10,000,000.

Unwinding an Interest Rate Swap

Once an interest rate swap is set up, one and/or the other counterparty may later decide to get out of, or sell, the swap. Such moves are common in international corporate finance.

The value of an interest rate swap to a counterparty is the difference in the present values of the payment streams that the counterparty will receive and pay on the notional principal. For example, consider Company B from our illustration. Company B pays fixed 4.50 percent and receives floating LIBOR on a notional principal of $10,000,000. This represents an all-in cost to Company B of 5 percent because it has issued FRNs at LIBOR + 0.50 percent.

Suppose that one year into the swap, fixed rates for BBB-rated issuers have fallen from 5.25 percent to 4 percent.

On any reset date, the present value of a future floating rate obligation in a swap, inclusive of principal, will always be equal to the amount of the notional principal, in this case $10,000,000, regardless of the floating rate.

On the other hand, the present value of Company B's $10,000,000 liability with eight remaining semiannual fixed 4.5 percent coupon payments discounted at the new (lower) fixed rate of 4 percent is $10,183,137 = ($225,000 $\times$ PVIFA$_{2\%,8}$) + ($10,000,000 $\times$ PVIF$_{2\%,8}$).

The value of the swap has turned negative for Company B, the fixed payer. The value of the swap is now $10,000,000 − $10,183,137 = −$183,137.

Thus, Company B should be willing to pay up to $183,137 to get out of, or "sell," the swap and refinance at the new, lower fixed rate (4 percent) that is available.

10.6 INTEREST RATE SWAP QUOTATIONS

The interest rate swap market is one of the largest and most active segments of the global market for debt finance. The swap market allows individual corporate borrowers to structure their debt service obligations to meet their unique cash flow pattern while considering their capacity to deal with interest rate uncertainty. An industrial manufacturing firm, for example, that borrows in order to acquire plant and equipment is likely to prefer fixed rate debt since fixed rates provide a degree of certainty to cash flow planning. On the other hand, for financial institutions such as banks or insurance companies, money is their stock-in-trade. Financial institutions are able to quickly adjust the retail price of the financial products—mortgages, for example—to reflect changes in market interest rates. They are therefore likely to prefer floating-rate debt, confident in their ability to maintain an appropriate profit margin on their (financial) products.

The swap market is predominantly an "over the counter" (OTC) market. A retail customer looking for a swap will approach a swap bank with specific needs in regard to the company's debt position. The swap banks will then tailor the terms of interest rate and currency swaps to customers' needs.

The reference point for an interest rate swap is the "plain vanilla" or "bullet" quote on a simple, well-defined swap of a particular term. Through these quotes, swap banks signal that they stand ready either to receive payments at a specific fixed rate and pay at a floating rate or, to take the opposite stance, to receive payments at a floating rate and pay at a specific fixed rate. Swap banks' bid and ask quotations for interest rate swaps appear daily in the financial press for most major currencies. The quotes are remarkably simple to read.

Exhibit 10.6 presents a typical array of interest rate swap quotations as of mid-2013. At that time, short-term interest rates were extraordinarily low. Major industrial nations—the United States, the United Kingdom and Japan—were pursuing aggressive low-interest-rate policies. The exhibit is constructed to reflect low short-term interest rates together with more typical features of the yield curve in the longer term, especially the normal context in which interest rates rise the longer the term. The cross-country differences in quotations among the six currencies reflect differences observed as of mid-2013. As a practical matter, interest rate swap quotations like those in the exhibit are assembled daily by Bloomberg through a survey of the leading swap banks dealing in Canadian dollar debt, such as TDCapital, ScotiaCapital, RBCDominion and Merrill Lynch (Canada).

EXHIBIT 10.6   Interest Rate Swap Quotations

March 6	Canadian Dollar		United States Dollar		Euro		Pound Sterling		Swiss Franc		Japanese Yen	
	Bid	Ask	Bid	Ask	Bid	Ask	Bid	Ask	Bid	Ask	Bid	Ask
1 year	0.75	0.77	0.33	0.36	0.44	0.48	0.58	0.61	0.10	0.16	0.21	0.27
2 year	0.97	0.99	0.55	0.58	0.64	0.68	0.84	0.88	0.21	0.29	0.25	0.31
3 year	1.37	1.39	0.95	0.98	0.89	0.93	1.13	1.17	0.37	0.45	0.30	0.36
4 year	1.81	1.83	1.39	1.42	1.15	1.19	1.47	1.52	0.59	0.67	0.37	0.43
5 year	2.21	2.23	1.79	1.82	1.40	1.44	1.80	1.85	0.83	0.91	0.45	0.51
6 year	2.56	2.58	2.14	2.17	1.61	1.65	2.07	2.12	1.04	1.12	0.55	0.61
7 year	2.84	2.86	2.42	2.45	1.80	1.84	2.31	2.36	1.22	1.30	0.65	0.71
8 year	3.07	3.09	2.65	2.68	1.96	2.00	2.50	2.55	1.38	1.46	0.76	0.82
9 year	3.25	3.27	2.83	2.86	2.10	2.14	2.66	2.71	1.51	1.59	0.87	0.93
10 year	3.40	3.42	2.98	3.01	2.23	2.27	2.79	2.84	1.63	1.71	0.97	1.03
12 year	3.65	3.67	3.23	3.26	2.43	2.47	2.98	3.05	1.79	1.89	1.16	1.24
15 year	3.89	3.91	3.47	3.50	2.62	2.66	3.16	3.25	1.94	2.04	1.43	1.51
20 year	4.07	4.09	3.65	3.68	2.73	2.77	3.27	3.40	2.03	2.13	1.73	1.81
25 year	4.15	4.17	3.73	3.76	2.74	2.78	3.31	3.44	2.07	2.17	1.87	1.95
30 year	4.20	4.22	3.78	3.81	2.72	2.76	3.31	3.44	2.09	2.19	1.94	2.02

Note: This table is constructed for the purpose of developing the illustration of an interest rate swap. The figures closely reflect the structure of interest rate swap quotations as of mid-2013. With actual quotations, US$ is quoted against three-month LIBOR. Sterling and yen are quoted against semiannual compounded six-month LIBOR. Euro and Swiss franc are quoted against six-month Euribor/LIBOR with the exception of the one-year rate which is quoted against three-month Euribor/LIBOR. Canadian dollar quotes are against Canadian Dollar Offer Rate (CDOR) derived from three-month banker's acceptances.

Consider first the Canadian dollar quotes. The one-year "bid" is 0.75 percent, the one-year "ask" is 0.77. Both figures refer to the fixed interest side of a swap. The bid of 0.75 means that a swap bank will pay 0.75 percent fixed on a one-year swap in which case the bank will receive the floating rate. The one-year Canadian "ask" of 0.77 percent is the rate that swap banks demand in fixed interest in a swap from fixed to floating. The bank will pay the floating rate, again based on a relevant reference short-term floating rate. The Canadian reference floating rate is the three-month **Canadian Dollar Offer Rate (CDOR)** reported daily by Reuters.[1] But, of course, in any over-the-counter swap deal, the swap bank is free to demand its own terms to reflect the actual circumstances (such as credit risk) of the counterparties.

In the other currencies, the bid and ask rates on interest rate swaps are generally "quoted against" three- or six-month LIBOR for the respective currency. From the interest rate swap quotations, it is clear that the swap banks are prepared to construct swaps in a wide range of time, from a few months to 30 years.

The "bullet" quotes in Exhibit 10.6 do not involve any premium for credit risk. Swap banks typically bear some or all of the credit risk of both counterparties to a swap. Swap banks address credit risk for a particular counterparty either through upward adjustments of the ask (fixed) interest rate or to the "X" in CDOR $+ X$ on the floating-rate side.

10.7 CURRENCY SWAPS

Our detailed development of the intuition and structure of interest rate swaps enables us to make a straightforward extension to currency swaps.

Currency swaps allow a cash flow stream in one currency—say, a dollar flow of interest payments—to be swapped into a stream of payments in another currency—say, a flow of payments in euro.

From Exhibit 10.6 we see that a one-year US dollar interest payment can be swapped at 0.33–0.36 while at the same time one-year euro interest payments can be swapped at 0.44–0.48. Putting these two "bid and ask" pairs together, we can determine what a swap bank is prepared to do in a currency swap. A swap bank is prepared to receive fixed US payments at 0.36 percent and simultaneously pay fixed euro at 0.44 percent. In what sort of situation might a firm want to do that?

A typical corporate context for a currency swap arises when a firm can borrow at a favourable rate in one currency while its use for the funds is in another currency. If that firm can find another firm with mirror-image cross-currency borrowing opportunities and needs, the scene is set for a mutually beneficial currency swap. Because of the currency swap market, the chances of striking such a rewarding arrangement are good.

We will illustrate the general structure of a currency swap through an example. One side of the swap is Magna International, the car-parts manufacturer based in Aurora, Ontario.[2] Magna has important manufacturing operations in Steyr, Austria. Our currency swap story begins with Magna looking for the best way to finance a €40 million project in Austria. We will soon see that Magna will be on the "dollar side" of a currency swap, borrowing in dollars while using the funds to invest in euros.

The Magna (Austria) capital expenditure, the purchase of a modern robotic manufacturing system, has an economic life of five years. The cost of the project is €40,000,000. At the current exchange rate of $1.30/€, Magna International could consider raising

[1]In constructing the CDOR, Reuters each day asks a number of dealers to indicate their going rate on three-month Canadian dollar banker's acceptances (BA), a high-grade, very liquid money market instrument. CDOR is an average of BA rates offered by a number of dealers.

[2]Magna is one of the world's largest auto parts suppliers to original equipment manufacturers. Magna designs and manufactures automotive systems and components primarily for original equipment manufacturers (OEMs) of cars and light trucks in three geographical segments—North America, Europe and "Rest of World" (primarily Asia, South America and Africa).

$52,000,000 by issuing five-year dollar-denominated bonds at 6 percent. Magna could then convert the dollars to euros to pay for the robotic system in Austria. Magna (Austria) would then be expected to earn enough on the project to meet the annual dollar debt service and to repay the principal to Magna International in five years. The problem with this situation is that it creates long-term transaction exposure. If the dollar appreciates substantially against the euro over the loan period, it may be difficult for Magna (Austria) to earn enough in euros to service the dollar loan.

An alternative is for Magna International to raise €40,000,000 by issuing euro-denominated bonds. However, since Magna is not well known in the Euromarkets, it will have difficulty borrowing at a favourable rate of interest. Let's say Magna can borrow €40,000,000 for a term of five years at a fixed rate of 5 percent. The current normal borrowing rate for a well-known European firm of equivalent creditworthiness, for example Volkswagen, is 4 percent.

We can now turn to the other side of the currency swap—a firm with international financial opportunities and needs that are the mirror-image opposite of Magna's.

Say Danone—the French food company with global brands such as Delisle and Silhouette yogurts—has plans to expand its North American operations centre in Boucherville, Quebec. Danone needs $52,000,000 to finance a capital expenditure with an economic life of five years. Danone in France could raise €40,000,000 in the Eurobond market at a fixed rate of 4 percent and convert the funds to dollars to finance the expenditure. Transaction exposure is created, however, insofar as the euro could appreciate substantially against the dollar. In this event, Danone's Canadian subsidiary might have difficulty earning enough in dollars to meet the debt service. Although Danone (France) could issue dollar bonds, since the firm is not well known in North American capital markets its borrowing cost would be relatively unattractive, say a fixed rate of 7 percent.

A swap bank familiar with the financing needs of Magna and Danone could arrange a currency swap that would address the double problem of each, that is, the uncomfortable choice of choosing between long-term transaction exposure or borrowing at a disadvantageous rate.

(To keep the illustration uncomplicated and intuitive, we assume the bid and ask swap rates charged by the swap bank are the same; that is, there is no bid-ask spread. This assumption is later relaxed in Exhibit 10.9.)

The swap bank would instruct each parent firm to raise funds in its home capital market where it is well known and has a comparative advantage because of name or brand recognition. Then, the principal sums would be exchanged through the swap bank. Annually, Magna's Austrian subsidiary would remit to Magna International an amount of €1,600,000 in interest (4 percent of €40,000,000) to be passed through the swap bank to Danone (France) to meet the euro debt service. Danone (Canada) would annually remit $3,120,000 in interest (6 percent of $52,000,000) to be passed through to the swap bank to Magna International to meet the dollar debt service. At the debt retirement date, the subsidiaries remit the principal sums to their respective parents to be exchanged through the swap bank in order to pay off the bond issues on either side of the Atlantic. The structure of this currency swap is illustrated in Exhibit 10.7.

Exhibit 10.7 demonstrates the cost savings for each counterparty stemming from their comparative advantage in their respective home capital markets. Magna effectively borrows euros at an AIC of 4 percent through the currency swap instead of the 5 percent that it would have to pay in the Eurobond market. Danone effectively borrows dollars at an AIC of 6 percent through the swap instead of the 7 percent that it would have to pay in the dollar bond market.

The currency swap serves to contractually lock in a series of future foreign exchange rates for the debt service obligations of each counterparty. At inception, the principal sums are exchanged at the current exchange rate of $1.30/€ = $52,000,000/€40,000,000. Each year prior to debt retirement, the swap agreement calls for the counterparties to exchange $3,120,000 of interest on the dollar debt for €1,600,000 of interest on the euro debt; this is a contractual rate of $1.95/€. At the maturity date, a final exchange, including the last interest payments and the

INTERNATIONAL FINANCE *in Practice*

Currency Swaps II—Clever Canadians Circumvent Foreign Content Restrictions

Until recently, Canadians were significantly restricted in the extent to which they could hold foreign (non-Canadian) assets in their portfolios. If more than 30 percent of the value of a Canadian's portfolio was foreign, the Canadian would incur a tax penalty under the Registered Retirement Savings Plan (RRSP) rules. By these rules, Canadians were effectively captive to Canadian securities which, as we have seen, represent only about 2 percent of the world's securities. Canadians were denied the full benefits and good sense of international diversification.

Canadian pension funds and mutual funds, repositories for and managers of the vast bulk of Canadians' savings, saw a way around the RRSP restrictions. The objective was to provide Canadian investors with "exposure" to the returns (and risks) of foreign financial assets. The solution involved currency swaps.

Here is how Canadian investment firms such as Altamira or AIC Mutual Funds created "RRSP-compliant" funds with foreign exposure. The Canadian investment firm would begin by purchasing, say, $10,000,000 in Canadian bonds, an investment that was certainly RRSP-compliant. Next, the investment firm arranged a currency swap into, for example, US funds. With respect to the cross-currency debt-service obligations, whether

the currency swap was fixed-to-fixed or fixed-to-floating was a matter of preference. The key point is that debt-service obligations on a Canadian dollar bond portfolio swapped to foreign currency provides Canadian investors with foreign "exposure" on an interest cash flow stream while still being RRSP-compliant.

RRSP-complaint (foreign) equity portfolios were only a bit more complicated to construct. Here the objective is to have a portfolio that, while invested in Canadian funds, generates returns (and risks) that mimic foreign returns. The solution involves a combination of Canadian bonds (RRSP-compliant) and derivatives (long calls and short puts) on one or more foreign equity indices such as the US S&P 500. The highly leveraged equity-like returns (and risks) on the foreign derivatives, which represent a small fraction of the portfolio relative to the Canadian bonds, are diluted by the relatively stable performance of the Canadian bonds. It is a well-known principle of modern engineering that any risky cash flow stream (such as foreign equities) can be replicated by a combination of bonds and derivatives.

In 2005, Canada's so-called "foreign content rules" were scrapped. While the rules were in place, however, the restrictions provided a strong incentive to Canadian financial institutions to devise ways around them.

re-exchange of the principal sums, takes place: $55,120,000 for €41,600,000. The contractual exchange rate at year 5 is thus $1.325/€. Clearly, the swap locks in foreign exchange rates for each counterparty to meet its debt service obligations over the term of the swap.

The International Finance in Practice Box "Currency Swaps II" illustrates a clever regulation-circumventing use of currency swaps by Canadian mutual fund managers.

EXHIBIT 10.7 $/€ Currency Swap*

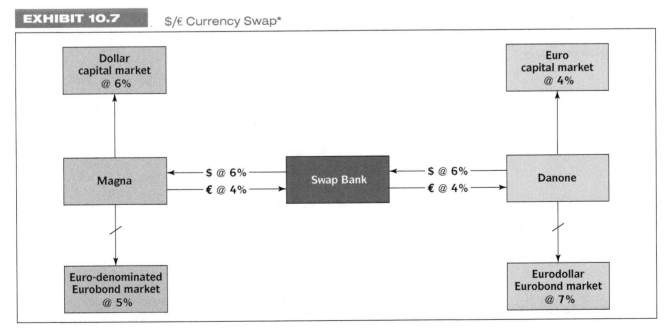

*Debt service in dollars (euros) expressed as a percentage of $52,000,000 (€40,000,000) notional value.

259

10.8 EQUIVALENCY OF CURRENCY SWAP DEBT SERVICE

To continue with our example, at first glance it appears that Danone is not getting as good a deal from the currency swap as Magna. The reasoning is that Danone is borrowing at a rate of 4 percent (€1,600,000 per year) but paying 6 percent ($3,120,000). Magna receives the $3,120,000 and pays €1,600,000. To suggest that Danone is not doing as well as Magna fails to appreciate international parity relationships, as Exhibit 10.8 is designed to show. In short, the exhibit shows that borrowing euros at 4 percent is equivalent to borrowing dollars at 6 percent.

Line 1 of Exhibit 10.8 shows the cash flows of the euro debt in millions. Line 2 shows the cash flows of the dollar debt in millions. The AIC for each cash flow stream is also shown for each currency. Line 3 shows the contractual foreign exchange rates between the two counterparties that are locked in by the swap agreement. Line 4 shows the foreign exchange rate that each counterparty and the market should expect on the basis of covered interest rate parity (IRP) and the forward rate being an unbiased predictor of the expected spot rate, if we can assume that IRP holds between the 4 percent euro rate and the 6 percent dollar rate. This appears reasonable, since these rates are, respectively, the best rates available for each counterparty who is well known in its national market. According to this parity relationship: $S_t(\$/€) = S_0[1.06/1.04]^t$. For example, from the exhibit, the implicit FX rate for year 2 is $\$1.350/€ = \$1.30 \times [1.06/1.04]^2$.

Line 5 shows the equivalent cash flows in euros that have a present value of €40,000,000 at a rate of 6 percent. Without the currency swap, Danone would have to convert dollars into euros to meet the euro debt service. The expected rate at which the conversion takes place in each year is given by the implicit foreign exchange rates in line 4. Line 5 can be viewed as a conversion of the cash flows of line 2 via the implicit exchange rates of line 4. That is, for year one, $3,120,000 has an expected value of €2,350,000 at the expected exchange rate of $1.325/€. For year two, $3,120,000 has an expected value of €2,310,000 at an exchange rate of $1.350/€. Note that the conversion at the implicit exchange rates converts *6 percent cash flows* into *4 percent cash flows*.

The lender of €40,000,000 should be indifferent between receiving the cash flows of line 1 or the cash flows of line 5 from the borrower. From the borrower's standpoint, however, the cash flows of line 1 are free of foreign exchange risk because of the currency swap, whereas the cash flows of line 5 are not. Thus, the borrower prefers the

EXHIBIT 10.8	Equivalency of Currency Swap Cash Flows						
	Time of Cash Flow						
	0	1	2	3	4	5	AIC
1 Euro debt cash flow	40.00	−1.60	−1.60	−1.60	−1.60	−41.60	4%
2 Dollar debt cash flow	52.00	−3.12	−3.12	−3.12	−3.12	−55.12	6%
3 Contractual FX rate	1.30	1.95	1.95	1.95	1.95	1.33	NA
4 Implicit FX rate	1.30	1.33	1.35	1.38	1.40	1.43	NA
5 Indifference euro cash flow	40.00	−2.35	−2.31	−2.27	−2.22	−38.55	4%
6 Indifference dollar cash flow	52.00	−2.12	−2.16	−2.20	−2.24	−59.48	6%

Note: Lines 1 and 5 present alternative cash flows in euros that have present values of €40,000,000 at a 6 percent discount rate. The cash flows in line 1 are free of exchange risk if the swap is undertaken, whereas the implicit cash flows of line 5 are not if the swap is forgone. The certain cash flows are preferable. The uncertain euro cash flows of line 5 are obtained by dividing the dollar cash flows of line 2 by the corresponding implicit FX rate of line 4. Analogously, lines 2 and 6 present alternative cash flows in dollars that have present values of $52,000,000 at an 8 percent discount rate. The cash flows in line 2 are free of exchange risk if the swap is undertaken, whereas the implicit cash flows of line 6 are not if the swap is forgone. The certain cash flows are preferable. The uncertain dollar cash flows of line 6 are obtained by multiplying the euro cash flows of line 1 by the corresponding implicit FX rate of line 4.

certainty of the swap, regardless of the equivalency. Line 6 shows in dollar terms the cash flows based on the implicit foreign exchange rates of line 4 that have a present value of $52,000,000. Line 6 can be viewed as a conversion of the 4 percent cash flows of line 1 into the 6 percent cash flows of line 6 via these expected exchange rates. A lender should be indifferent between these and the cash flow stream of line 2. The borrower will prefer to pay the cash flows of line 2, however, because they are free of foreign exchange risk.

Pricing the Currency Swap

Suppose that a year after the dollar–euro swap was arranged, dollar interest rates decreased from 6 percent to 4.75 percent and euro interest rates decreased from 4 percent to 3 percent. Further assume that because the dollar rate decreased proportionately more than the euro rate, the dollar appreciated versus the euro. Instead of being $1.325/€ as expected, it is $1.310/€. Magna or Danone might be induced to sell their position in the swap to a swap dealer in order to refinance at the new lower rate.

The market value of the dollar debt is $54,318,316; this is the present value of the four remaining coupon payments of $3,120,000 and the principal of $52,000,000 discounted at 4.75 percent. Similarly, the market value of the euro debt at the new rate of 3 percent is €41,486,839. Magna should be willing to buy its interest in the currency swap for $54,318,316 − (€41,486,839 × 1.310) = −$29,444. That is, Magna should be willing to pay $29,444 to give up the stream of dollars it would receive under the swap agreement in return for not having to pay the euro stream. Magna is then free to refinance the $52,000,000 under 6 percent debt at 4.75 percent, and perhaps enter into a new currency swap.

From Danone's perspective, the swap has a value of €41,486,839 − $54,318,316/1.310 = €22,476. Danone should be willing to accept €22,476 to sell the swap, that is, give up the stream of euros in return for not having to pay the dollar stream. Danone is then in a position to refinance the €40,000,000 under 6 percent debt at the new rate of 3 percent. Danone might also enter into a new currency swap.

10.9 FINALLY, A LITTLE MORE REALISM ON CURRENCY SWAPS

We can add realistic detail to our example of a currency swap by recognizing the bid-ask spreads that the swap bank charges for making a market in currency swaps.

To extend our Magna–Danone example, assume that the swap bank quotes five-year dollar interest rate swaps at 6.00–6.15 and euro interest rate swaps at 4.00–4.10 against dollar LIBOR flat. As a practical matter, the swap bank can deal with Magna and Danone separately.

The principal sums raised in the home capital markets by Magna ($52,000,000) and by Danone (€40,000,000) would be sold to the swap bank at the current spot rate of $1.30/€ to obtain the desired currency, €40,000,000 for Magna and $52,000,000 for Danone.

Magna (Austria) annually remits €1,640,000 in interest (4.10 percent of €40,000,000) to Magna International to be passed through to the swap bank. The swap bank in turn annually remits €1,600,000 (4.0 percent of €40,000,000) to Danone in order for it to meet the euro debt service.

Danone (Canada) annually remits $3,198,000 in interest (6.15 percent of $52,000,000) to Danone (France) to be passed through to the swap bank. The swap bank, in turn, annually remits $3,120,000 (6 percent of $52,000,000) to Magna International in order for it to meet the annual dollar debt service.

At the debt retirement date, the subsidiaries, Magna (Austria) and Danone (Canada), remit the principal sums to their respective parents (dollars from Danone (Canada) and euros from Magna (Austria)) in order to pay off the bond issues in the home capital markets.

EXHIBIT 10.9 $/€ Currency Swap with Bid-Ask Spreads*

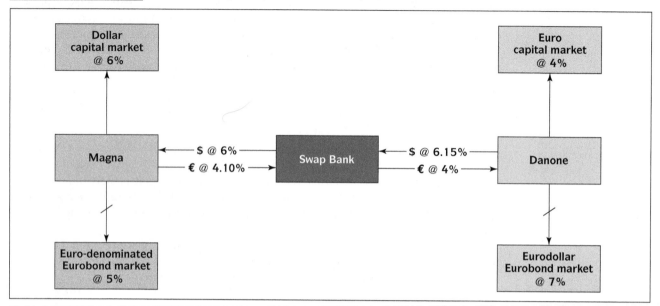

*Debt service in dollars (euros) expressed as a percentage of $52,000,000 (€40,000,000) notional value.

The net result is that Magna International borrows at an AIC of 4.10 percent through the currency swap instead of the 5 percent it would have to pay in the Eurobond market. Danone borrows dollars at an AIC of 6.15 percent through the swap instead of the 7 percent that it would have to pay in the Eurobond (dollar) market. Exhibit 10.9 shows the swap in schematic form.

10.10   VARIATIONS OF BASIC CURRENCY AND INTEREST RATE SWAPS

There are several variants of the basic currency and interest rate swaps we have discussed. Currency swaps, for example, need not involve the swap of fixed-rate debt. *Fixed-for-floating* and *floating-for-floating* currency rate swaps are also frequently arranged. Additionally, *amortizing* currency swaps incorporate an amortization feature in which periodically the amortized portions of the notional principals are re-exchanged. A fixed-for-floating interest rate swap does not require a fixed-rate coupon bond. A variant is a *zero-coupon-for-floating* rate swap, wherein the floating-rate payer makes the standard periodic floating-rate payments over the life of the swap, but the fixed-rate payer makes a single payment at the end of the swap. Another variation is the *floating-for-floating* interest rate swap. In this swap, each side is tied to a different floating rate index (e.g., LIBOR or Treasury bills) for a different frequency of the same index (such as three-month and six-month LIBOR). For a swap to be possible, a QSD must still exist. Additionally, interest rate swaps can be established on an amortizing basis, where the debt service exchanges decrease periodically through time as the hypothetical notional principal is amortized. See the International Finance in Practice box "Eli Lilly and Company: The Case of the Appreciating Yen" for a classic example of a currency swap.

10.11   RISKS OF INTEREST RATE AND CURRENCY SWAPS

A swap dealer confronts a variety of risks. Some of the major ones are discussed here. *Interest rate risk* refers to the risk of interest rates changing unfavourably before the swap bank can lay off to an opposing counterparty the other side of an interest rate swap

Eli Lilly and Company: The Case of the Appreciating Yen

Eli Lilly and Company (Lilly) is an international pharmaceutical company with corporate headquarters in Indianapolis, Indiana. Lilly markets its products worldwide. Being the second-largest pharmaceutical market in the world, Japan represents a particularly significant market for Lilly's products. As sales to Japan grew throughout the 1980s, Lilly became increasingly concerned about the volatility effect on overall sales and earnings performance stemming from fluctuations in the yen exchange rate.

In 1987, the company decided to investigate the possibility of developing a hedging strategy to, in effect, fix in American dollars that portion of its sales to Japan. At the time of consideration, the yen was trading in the mid-¥140/$1 range. Not too many years earlier, the yen was trading in the ¥240–¥270/$1 range. If the yen were to retreat back to those levels, obviously Lilly's sales in terms of dollars would be significantly diminished. It was Lilly's desire, therefore, to fix future sales at current exchange rates, and the way to do that, of course, was to borrow yen, sell the yen for dollars at the current exchange rates and service the yen debt with the future yen sales revenues. The dollars would then be used to meet current corporate requirements, and thus, the hedge would be completed.

The initial thought was for Lilly to incur yen-denominated borrowings and convert the principal into dollars. The future yen sales could then service the newly created yen liability. This idea, however, was not favoured because it would have meant adding new debt to the company's balance sheet. The alternative would be to use the yen liability to replace existing debt. The most targetable long-term debt item in Lilly's capital structure was a $150,000,000, 10.25 percent fixed-rate Eurodollar bond issue with a 1992 maturity date. These bonds were issued primarily to allow Lilly to establish name recognition and access to the European

bond markets. Unfortunately, this debt was noncallable. Had it had a call feature, the decision most likely would have been to allow for the creation of a yen liability in order to retire this higher-cost long-term source of funds.

To accomplish the same result, the financial division at Lilly conceived the idea of a currency swap, which involves no exchange of borrowings. At the current exchange rate of ¥144.1, the $150 million Eurodollar issue had a yen value of ¥21.615 billion. Lilly entertained bids from a select group of investment banks to put together a uniquely structured currency swap arrangement. One of the bids was ultimately selected, and the uniqueness of the arrangement centred around the fact that Lilly would contribute to the investment bank five annual level payments in the amount of ¥4.864 billion each during the remaining five years of the life of the Eurodollar bond issue. In return, Lilly would receive dollars each year equal to the $15,375,000 coupon payments on the bond issue plus the $150,000,000 principal repayment at the end of year 5. The level-contribution and variable-receipt arrangement was unique to the swap market, but essential to Lilly, in that it enabled the hedging of a level stream of future yen receipts. While the swap did not provide a complete hedge of all rate-affected sales revenue, it did eliminate the volatility associated with a significant percentage of those revenues. The other unique aspect of the arrangement was the adjustment for interest rate changes since the inception of the Eurodollar bond offering. Eurodollar rates had fallen from the 10.25 percent range to the 7.8 percent range, and yen rates had fallen similarly. To compensate the investment bank and the opposite party for servicing Lilly's debt at 10.25 percent, Lilly's cost of yen contribution was grossed up to 6.2 percent from the then current yen rate of less than 4 percent. Exhibit 10.10 diagrams this interesting example of a currency swap.

---

entered into with a counterparty. Reconsider the interest rate swap example examined in Section 10.5. In that example, the swap bank earns a spread of 0.125 percent. Company B passes through to the swap bank 4.5% percent (on the notional principal of $10,000,000) and receives LIBOR percent in return. Bank A passes through to the swap bank LIBOR and receives 4.375 percent in return. Suppose the swap bank entered into the position with Company B first. If fixed rates increase substantially, say, by 0.50 percent, Bank A will not be willing to enter into the opposite side of the swap unless it receives, say, 4.875 percent. This would make the swap unprofitable for the swap bank.

Basis risk refers to a situation in which the floating-rates of the two counterparties are not pegged to the same index. Any difference in the indexes is known as the basis. For example, one counterparty could have its FRNs pegged to LIBOR while the other counterparty has its FRNs pegged to the Treasury bill rate. In this event, the indexes are not perfectly positively correlated, and the swap may periodically be unprofitable for the swap bank. This could occur if the Treasury bill rate was substantially larger than LIBOR.

Exchange-rate risk refers to the risk the swap bank faces from fluctuating exchange rates during the time it takes for the bank to lay off a swap it undertakes with one counterparty with an opposing counterparty.

Credit risk, the major risk faced by a swap dealer, refers to the probability that a counterparty will default. The swap bank that stands between the two counterparties is not obligated to the defaulting counterparty, only to the nondefaulting counterparty. There is a single agreement between the swap bank and each counterparty.

Mismatch risk refers to the difficulty of finding an exact opposite match for a swap the bank has agreed to take. The mismatch may be with respect to the size of the principal sums the counterparties need, the maturity dates of the individual debt issues, or the debt service dates. Textbook illustrations typically ignore these real-life problems.

Sovereign risk refers to the probability that a country will impose exchange restrictions on a currency involved in a swap. This may make it costly, or perhaps impossible, for a counterparty to fulfill its obligation to the dealer. In this event, provisions exist for terminating the swap, which results in a loss of revenue for the swap bank.

To facilitate the operation of the swap market, the International Swaps and Derivatives Association (ISDA) has standardized two swap agreements. One is the "Interest Rate and Currency Exchange Agreement" that covers currency swaps, and the other is the "Interest Rate Swap Agreement" that lays out standard terms for dollar-denominated interest rate swaps. The standardized agreements have reduced the time necessary to establish swaps and also provided terms under which swaps can be terminated early by a counterparty.

10.12 IS THE SWAP MARKET EFFICIENT?

The two primary reasons for a counterparty to use a currency swap are to obtain debt financing in the swapped currency at an interest cost reduction brought about through comparative advantages each counterparty has in its national capital market, and/or the benefit of hedging long-run exchange rate exposure. These reasons seem straightforward and difficult to argue with, especially to the extent that name recognition is truly important in raising funds in the international bond market.

The two primary reasons for swapping interest rates are to better match maturities of assets and liabilities and/or to obtain a cost savings via the quality spread differential (QSD). In an efficient market without barriers to capital flows, the cost-savings argument

EXHIBIT 10.10

Eli Lilly's Eurodollar Bond/Yen Swap

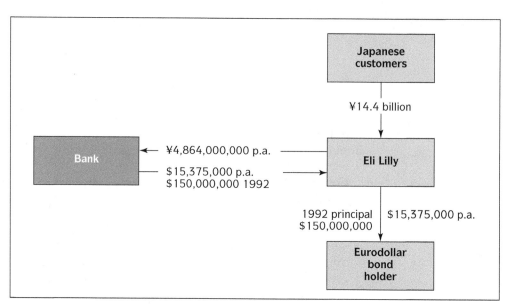

Source: Dale R. Follmer, Manager of Accounting Operations, Eli Lilly and Company.

through a QSD is difficult to accept. It implies that an arbitrage opportunity exists because of some mispricing of the default risk premiums on different types of debt instruments. If the QSD is one of the primary reasons for the existence of interest rate swaps, one would expect arbitrage to eliminate it over time and that the growth of the swap market would decrease. Quite the opposite has happened, as Exhibit 10.1 shows; the volume of interest rate swaps has grown dramatically over the past 20 years. Thus, the arbitrage argument does not seem to have much merit. Indeed, Turnbull (1987) analytically shows that a QSD can exist in an efficient market. Consequently, one must rely on an argument of **market completeness** for the existence and growth of interest rate swaps. That is, all types of debt instruments are not regularly available for all borrowers. Thus, the interest rate swap market assists in tailoring financing to the type desired by a particular borrower. Both counterparties can benefit (as well as the swap dealer) through financing that is more suitable for their asset maturity structures.

10.13 CONCLUDING POINTS ABOUT SWAPS

The growth in financial swaps has been tremendous. They offer counterparties benefits and opportunities that were not previously available. Another feature of swaps is that they are off-book transactions for both the counterparties and the swap bank; that is, they do not appear as assets or liabilities on the balance sheet. The only indication that they exist is through an examination of the footnotes of the financial reports.

Swaps have become an important source of revenue for commercial banks. As swap activity increased, bank regulators became concerned that the potential liability posed by swaps might create capital adequacy problems for banks. Central bankers from the Group of Ten countries and Luxembourg agree to a set of principles, called the Basle Accord, which standardizes bank capital requirements across nations. As discussed in Chapter 6, the accord established guidelines for risk-adjusted capital requirements for off-balance-sheet activities that increase a bank's risk exposure, including swaps.

SUMMARY   This chapter provides a presentation of currency and interest rate swaps. The discussion details how swaps might be used and the risks associated with each.

1. The chapter opens with definitions of an interest rate swap and a currency swap. The basic interest rate swap is a fixed-for-floating rate swap in which one counterparty exchanges the interest payments of a fixed-rate debt obligation for the floating-interest payments of the other counterparty. Both debt obligations are denominated in the same currency. In a currency swap, one counterparty exchanges the debt service obligations of a bond denominated in one currency for the debt service obligations of the other counterparty which are denominated in another currency.

2. *Swap bank* is a generic term to describe a financial institution that facilitates swaps between counterparties. A swap bank serves as either a broker or a dealer. When serving as a broker, the swap bank matches counterparties but does not assume any risk of the swap. When serving as a dealer, the swap bank stands willing to accept either side of a currency swap.

3. An example of a basic interest rate swap is presented in this chapter. A necessary condition for a swap is the existence of a quality spread differential between the default-risk premiums on the fixed-rate and floating-rate interest rates of the two counterparties. There is no exchange of principal sums between the counterparties of an interest rate swap because both debt issues were denominated in the same currency. Interest rate exchanges were based on a notional principal.

4. Pricing an interest rate swap after inception is illustrated. After inception, the value of an interest rate swap to a counterparty should be the difference in the present values of the payment streams the counterparty will receive and pay on the notional principal.

5. A detailed example of a basic currency swap is presented. The debt service obligations of the counterparties in a currency swap are effectively equivalent to one another in cost. Nominal differences can be explained by international parity relationships.

6. Pricing a currency swap after inception is illustrated. After inception, the value of a currency swap to a counterparty is the difference in the present values of the payment stream the counterparty will receive in one currency and pay in the other currency, converted to one or the other currency denominations.

7. In addition to the basic fixed-for-fixed currency swap and fixed-for-floating interest rate swap, many other variants exist. One variant is the amortizing swap which incorporates an amortization of the notional principals. Another variant is a zero-coupon-for-floating rate swap, in which the floating-rate payer makes the standard periodic floating-rate payments over the life of the swap, but the fixed-rate payer makes a single payment at the end of the swap. Another is the floating-for-floating rate swap. In this type of swap, each side is tied to a different floating rate index or a different frequency of the same index.

8. The reasons for the development and growth of the swap market were critically examined. Market completeness explains the existence and growth of interest rate swaps. Interest rate swap markets assist in tailoring financing to the needs of a particular borrower when all types of debt instruments are not regularly available to all borrowers.

QUESTIONS

1. Describe the difference between a swap broker and a swap dealer.

2. What is the necessary condition for a fixed-for-floating interest rate swap to be possible?

3. Discuss the basic motivations for a counterparty to enter into a currency swap.

4. How does the theory of comparative advantage relate to the currency swap market?

5. Discuss the risks confronting interest rate and currency swap dealers.

6. Briefly discuss some variants of the basic interest rate and currency swaps diagrammed in the chapter.

7. If the cost advantage of interest rate swaps would likely be arbitraged away in competitive markets, what other explanations exist to explain the rapid development of the interest rate swap market?

8. Assume you are the swap bank in the Eli Lilly swap discussed in the chapter. Develop an example of how you might lay off the swap to an opposing counterparty.

9. Discuss the motivational difference in the currency swap presented as Exhibit 10.7 and the Eli Lilly and Company swap discussed in the chapter.

10. Assume a currency swap between two counterparties of comparable credit risk; each borrows at the best rate available, and yet the nominal rate of one counterparty is higher than the other. After the initial principal exchange, is the counterparty that is required to make interest payments at the higher nominal rate at a financial disadvantage to the other in the swap agreement? Explain your thinking.

PROBLEMS

1. Develop a different arrangement of interest payments among the counterparties and the swap bank in Exhibit 10.9 that still leaves each counterparty with an all-in cost 0.50 percent below their best rate and the swap bank with a 0.25 percent inflow.

2. Alpha and Beta Companies can borrow at the following rates:

	Alpha	Beta
Moody's credit rating	Aa	Baa
Fixed-rate borrowing cost	5.5%	7.0%
Floating-rate borrowing cost	LIBOR	LIBOR + 1%

a. Calculate the quality spread differential (QSD).

b. Develop an interest rate swap in which both Alpha and Beta have an equal cost savings in their borrowing costs. Assume Alpha desires floating-rate debt and Beta desires fixed-rate debt.

3. Company A is an AAA-rated firm desiring to issue five-year FRNs. It finds that it can issue FRNs at six-month LIBOR + 0.125 percent or at three-month LIBOR + 0.125 percent. Given its asset structure, three-month LIBOR is the preferred index. Company B is an A-rated firm that also desires to issue five-year FRNs. It finds it can issue at six-month LIBOR + 1 percent or at three-month LIBOR + 0.625 percent. Given its asset structure, six-month LIBOR is the preferred index. Assume a notional principal of $15,000,000. Determine the QSD and set up a floating-for-floating rate swap where the swap bank receives 0.125 percent and the two counterparties share the remaining savings equally.

4. Suppose Morgan Guaranty, Ltd. is quoting swap rates as follows: 7.75–8.10 percent annually against six-month dollar LIBOR for dollars and 11.25–11.65 percent annually against six-month dollar LIBOR for British pound sterling. At what rates will Morgan Guaranty enter into a $/£ currency swap?

5. A corporation enters into a five-year interest rate swap with a swap bank in which it agrees to pay the swap bank a fixed rate of 9.75 percent annually on a notional amount of €15,000,000 and receive LIBOR. As of the second reset date, determine the price of the swap from the corporation's viewpoint assuming that the fixed-rate side of the swap has increased to 10.25 percent.

6. Karla Ferris, a fixed income manager at Mangus Capital Management, expects the current positively sloped Treasury yield curve to shift parallel upward.

Ferris owns two $1,000,000 corporate bonds maturing on June 15, 2009, one with a variable rate based on six-month dollar LIBOR and one with a fixed rate. Both yield 50 basis points over comparable Treasury market rates, have very similar credit quality, and pay interest semiannually.

Ferris wished to execute a swap to take advantage of her expectation of a yield curve shift and believes that any difference in credit spread between LIBOR and Treasury market rates will remain constant.

a. Describe a six-month dollar LIBOR-based swap that would allow Ferris to take advantage of her expectation. Discuss, assuming Ferris's expectation is correct, the change in the swap's value and how

that change would affect the value of her portfolio. (No calculations are required to answer part a.)

Instead of the swap described in part a, Ferris would use the following alternative derivative strategy to achieve the same result.

b. Explain, assuming Ferris's expectation is correct, how the following *strategy* achieves the same result in response to the yield curve shift. (No calculations are required to answer part b.)

Settlement Date	Nominal Eurodollar Futures Contract Value
12-15-07	$1,000,000
03-15-08	$1,000,000
06-15-08	$1,000,000
09-15-08	$1,000,000
12-15-08	$1,000,000
03-15-09	$1,000,000

c. Discuss *one* reason why these two derivative strategies provide the same result.

7. Dustin Financial owns a $10-million, 30-year maturity, noncallable corporate bond with a 6.5 percent coupon paid annually. Dustin pays annual LIBOR minus 1 percent on its three-year term time deposits.

Vega Corporation owns an annual-pay LIBOR floater and wants to swap for three years. One-year LIBOR is now 5 percent.

a. Diagram the cash flows between Dustin, Vega, Dustin's depositors, and Dustin's corporate bond. Label the following items:
   • Dustin, Vega, Dustin's depositors, and Dustin's corporate bond
   • Applicable interest rate at each line; specify whether it is floating or fixed
   • Direction of each of the cash flows

Answer part a in the template provided.

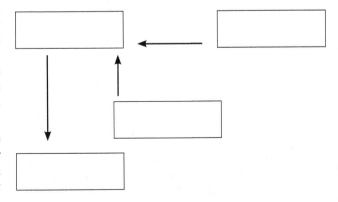

b. i. Calculate the first new swap payment between Dustin and Vega and indicate the direction of the net payment amount.

ii. Identify the net interest rate spread that Dustin expects to earn.

8. [CFA® PROBLEMS] Ashton Bishop is the debt manager for World Telephone, which needs €3.33 billion financing for its operations. Bishop is considering the choice between issuance of debt denominated in

- Euros (€), or
- Dollars, accompanied by a combined interest rate and currency swap

a. Explain *one* risk World would assume by entering into the combined interest rate and currency swap.

Bishop believes that issuing the dollar debt and entering into the swap could lower World's cost of debt by 45 basis points. Immediately after selling the debt issue, World would swap the dollar payments for euro payments throughout the maturity of the debt. She assumes a constant currency exchange rate throughout the tenor of the swap.

Exhibit 1 gives details for the two alternative debt issues. Exhibit 2 provides current information about spot currency exchange rates and the three-year-life euro/dollar currency and interest rate swap.

EXHIBIT 1

World Telephone Debt Details

Characteristic	Euro Currency Debt	Dollar Currency Debt
Par value	€3.33 billion	$3 billion
Term to maturity	3 years	3 years
Fixed interest rate	6.25%	7.75%
Interest payment	Annual	Annual

EXHIBIT 2

Currency Exchange Rate and Swap Information

Spot currency exchange rate	$0.90 per euro ($0.90/€1)
3-year life euro/dollar fixed interest rates	5.80% euro/7.30% dollar

b. Show the notional principal and interest payment cash flows of the combined interest rate and currency swap.

Note: Your response should show both the correct currency ($ or €) and amount for *each* cash flow. Answer part b in the template provided.

Cash Flows of the Swap	Year 0	Year 1	Year 2	Year 3
World pays				
Notional principal				
Interest payment				
World receives				
Notional principal				
Interest payment				

c. State whether World would reduce its borrowing cost by issuing the debt denominated in US dollars, accompanied by the combined interest rate and currency swap. Justify your response with *one* reason.

INTERNET EXERCISE

The website www.finpipe.com/intrateswaps.htm provides a brief description of interest rate swaps. Links at the bottom of the screen lead to other descriptions of derivative products, including currency swaps and other types of swaps that you will find interesting. It is a good idea to bookmark this site for future reference. Use it now to see how well you understand interest rate and currency swaps. If you cannot follow the discussions, go back and reread this chapter.

MINI CASE

The Centralia Corporation's Currency Swap

The Centralia Corporation is a Canadian manufacturer of small kitchen electrical appliances. It has decided to construct a wholly owned manufacturing facility in Zaragoza, Spain, to manufacture microwave ovens for sale to the European Union market. The plant is expected to cost €5,000,000 and to take about one year to complete. The plant is to be financed over its economic life of eight years. The borrowing capacity created by this capital expenditure is $2,000,000; the remainder of the plant will be equity-financed. Centralia is not well known in the Spanish or international bond market; consequently, it would have to pay 7 percent per annum to borrow euros, whereas the normal borrowing rate in the Eurozone for well-known firms of equivalent risk is 5 percent. Centralia could borrow dollars in Canada at a rate of 6 percent.

Study Questions

1. Suppose a European MNC has a mirror-image situation and needs $2,000,000 to finance a capital expenditure in Canada. It finds that it must pay a 7 percent fixed rate for dollars, whereas it can borrow euros at 5 percent. The exchange rate has been forecast to be $1.50/€ in one year. Set up a currency swap that will benefit each counterparty.

2. Suppose that one year after the inception of the currency swap between Centralia and the Spanish MNC, the dollar fixed rate has fallen from 6 to 5 percent and the Eurozone fixed rate for euros has fallen from 5 to 3.5 percent. In both dollars and euros, determine the market value of the swap if the exchange rate is $1.51/€.

REFERENCES & SUGGESTED READINGS

Beidleman, Carl R., ed. *Cross Currency Swaps.* Burr Ridge, IL.: Business One Irwin, 1992.

Price, John A. M., Jules Keller, and Max Neilson. "The Delicate Art of Swaps." *Euromoney* (April 1983), pp. 118–25.

Solnik, Bruno. *International Investments,* 4th ed. Reading, MA.: Addison-Wesley, 2000.

Smith, Clifford W., Charles W. Smithson, and Lee Macdonald Wakeman. "The Evolving Market for Swaps." *Midland Corporate Finance Journal* (Winter 1986), pp. 20–32.

———. "The Market for Interest Rate Swaps." *Financial Management* (Winter 1988), pp. 34–44.

Smithson, Charles W. *Managing Financial Risk,* 3rd ed. Burr Ridge, IL.: Irwin Professional Publishing, 1998.

Turnbull, Stuart M. "Swaps: A Zero Sum Game?" *Financial Management* (Spring 1987), pp. 15–21.

Wall, Larry D., and John J. Pringle. "Alternative Explanations of Interest Rate Swaps: A Theoretical and Empirical Analysis." *Financial Management* (Summer 1989), pp. 59–73.

Chapter (11)

International Portfolio Investment

CHAPTER OUTLINE

INTERNATIONAL PORTFOLIO investment refers to the purchase of financial assets—corporate shares—that have been issued in another country and that typically are denominated in a foreign currency. For instance, when a dentist in Winnipeg buys 100 shares of Disney listed on the New York Stock Exchange, he has made an international portfolio investment. Likewise, when The Ontario Teachers Fund buys 100,000 shares of France Telecom listed on the Paris Bourse, that too is international portfolio investment.

A distinguishing characteristic of international portfolio investment is that investors are interested primarily in the financial return on the (foreign) investment as opposed to, say, management or control of the foreign firms whose shares they buy. The individual's investment is a very small fraction of the total public ownership of the firms whose shares are purchased. Even Ontario Teachers Fund's 100,000 shares of France Telecom would amount to less than one-tenth of 1 percent of the total capitalization of France Telecom. Beyond their rights as shareholders, portfolio investors have no direct control or influence on the foreign firms whose shares they hold—nor do they typically want such influence or control.

International portfolio investment has grown substantially over the past three decades, much of it through large financial institutions, such as mutual funds, pension funds and trust companies. Both institutional and individual investors look more and more to diversify their portfolios with foreign shares.

The rapid growth in international portfolio investment reflects the globalization of financial markets. The impetus for globalized financial markets—or the "international integration" of markets—came from governments of major industrialized nations as they moved to deregulate foreign exchange and capital markets in the 1970s. For instance, in 1979, the United Kingdom dismantled its "investment dollar premium" system which imposed a heavy charge on cross-currency investments. Japan liberalized its foreign exchange markets in 1980, thus allowing its residents, for the first time, to freely invest in foreign securities. The United States and Canada reduced or eliminated taxes that had previously discouraged financial integration. Even some developing countries, for example, Brazil, India, Korea and Mexico, took measures to allow foreigners to invest in their capital

270

markets by offering country funds or by directly listing shares on international stock exchanges. In addition, modern advances in telecommunication and computer technologies have contributed to the globalization of investments by facilitating cross-border transactions and rapid dissemination of information around the world.

In this chapter we examine the opportunities and risks involved in international portfolio investment. We note, in particular, that a prime motive for investing in foreign securities is to reduce risk below what it would otherwise be with a purely domestic portfolio. Canadian corporate equities represent only about 2.5 percent of the publicly traded equities around the world. The other 97.5 percent of shares present substantial and, for the most part, easily accessible opportunities for portfolio diversification. It is somewhat curious, then, to note that Canadians maintain close to 80 percent of their equity holdings in shares of Canadian firms, which suggests that perhaps they may be missing out on offshore opportunities. We will examine this issue of "home bias" in equity investment.

Just before turning to a more technical discussion of the potential rewards and risks of international portfolio investment, we must acknowledge that the topic may not appear immediately to be *managerial*, or at least not for industrial companies. In fact, however, international portfolio investment is central to questions involving the integration of international capital markets which in turn has direct implications for that most important of managerial concerns—the cost of capital. The more that investors, including individual investors but above all large institutional investors, view the world at large as a reliable and safe source of securities to hold in their portfolios, the more the world's capital markets come to behave, in a financial sense, as a global market. Integration refers to the ease with which investors in one country can purchase and hold securities issued in another country.

11.1 PORTFOLIO ARITHMETIC—INTERNATIONAL PERSPECTIVES

Adding foreign securities to a portfolio introduces two important considerations to portfolio management. First, the world beyond one's own borders offers substantial opportunities for portfolio diversification. Second, since foreign securities are denominated in foreign currencies, the portfolio manager must contend with foreign exchange risk.

The main points concerning foreign assets can be illustrated with a simple example. Say a Canadian portfolio manager wants to buy some British equities. He decides to buy 10 Marks & Spencer shares at a price of £10 per share. In order to buy the British shares, he must first purchase £100. Let us say that the exchange rate—dollars per pound—is $1.60. In that case £100 costs $160. When the foreign exchange transaction and the equities purchase are complete, the Canadian portfolio is "long" in both British equity and the British pound. The Canadian dollar value of this foreign investment is positively related to changes in the price of the security and/or the exchange rate.

Let us predict outcomes. By the end of the period, the security has risen to £110. Meanwhile the pound has fallen against the Canadian dollar; by the end of the period £1 is worth $1.45. The end-of-period Canadian dollar value of the shares is $1.45 times £110, or $159.50. This figure can be compared with the original outlay of $160. From the point of view of the Canadian portfolio manager, the 10 percent gain in the pound value of the shares is more than erased by the 8.7 percent fall in the value of the pound. The transactions and the values are summarized in Exhibit 11.1.

The key relationships in holding a foreign-denominated security can be expressed as three rates of return: (1) the return on the security itself (as earned in the foreign currency),

		(1)	(2)	(3)
	Time	Exchange Rate ($/£)	£ Value of Shares	$ Value of Shares (1 × 2)
EXHIBIT 11.1	0	1.60	100	160.00
The Transactions	1	1.45	110	159.50

(2) the return that results from the change in the domestic value of the foreign currency used to finance the investment and (3) the total return which is a composite of the other two. With respect to our example, we have:

Security return in pounds:
$$r_\pounds = (110/100) - 1 = 1.10 - 1$$
$$r_\pounds = 0.10$$

Exchange rate return:
$$r_x = (1.45/1.60) - 1 = 0.906 - 1$$
$$r_x = -0.094$$

Total dollar return:
$$1 + r_\$ = (1 + r_\pounds)(1 + r_x)$$
$$r_\$ = r_\pounds + r_x + r_\pounds r_x$$
$$= 0.10 + (-0.094) + (0.10)(-0.094)$$
$$= -0.0031$$

The fully converted-to-dollar return on an equity investment in a foreign-denominated security depends jointly on the gain or loss on the security together with the gain or loss on the foreign exchange transaction. A more extensive illustration with more conditional outcomes is useful for understanding how the two return-generating factors—the share price in pounds and the exchange rate—interact to create a distribution of conditional returns for the Canadian investor.

In Exhibit 11.2, the first column presents a range of end-of-period values of 10 Marks & Spencer shares expressed in pounds. The initial £100 investment is in the middle of the column. The other cells in the column are plus-or-minus 5, 10, 15 and 20 percent of £100.

Similarly, the top row presents a range of end-of-period exchange rates between the Canadian dollar and the British pound. The values are centred on the initial $1.60 (per £1) with specific values plus-or-minus 5, 10, 15 and 20 percent of $1.60. Values of the exchange rate greater than $1.60 imply that the British pound has become more expensive in terms of the Canadian dollar—the pound has appreciated or the Canadian dollar has depreciated. Conversely, values less than $1.60 imply that the British pound has become less expensive in terms of the Canadian dollar—the pound has depreciated or the Canadian dollar has appreciated.

The cells of the matrix correspond to 81 possible discrete end-of-period pairs of the Marks & Spencer shares and the exchange rate. Each cell reports the (total) percentage return on the investment in Canadian dollars.

Each cell of the matrix presents a possible—or "joint conditional"—return to the Canadian investor that is determined by a change in the share price together with a change in the

| **EXHIBIT 11.2** | Canadian Dollar Gain or Loss on a British Investment: End of Period |

		Conditional Exchange Rates, $/£							
		1.40	1.45	1.50	1.55	1.60	1.65	1.70	1.75	1.80
Conditional Share Values, £	80	−48.0	−44.0	−40.0	−36.0	**−32.0**	−28.0	−24.0	−20.0	−16.0
	85	−41.0	−36.8	−32.5	−28.3	**−24.0**	−19.8	−15.5	−11.3	−7.0
	90	−34.0	−29.5	−25.0	−20.5	**−16.0**	−11.5	−7.0	−2.5	2.0
	95	−27.0	−22.3	−17.5	−12.8	**−8.0**	−3.3	1.5	6.3	11.0
	100	**−20.0**	**−15.0**	**−10.0**	**−5.0**	**0.0**	**5.0**	**10.0**	**15.0**	**20.0**
	105	−13.0	−7.8	−2.5	2.8	**8.0**	13.3	18.5	23.8	29.0
	110	−6.0	−0.5	5.0	10.5	**16.0**	21.5	27.0	32.5	38.0
	115	1.0	6.8	12.5	18.3	**24.0**	29.8	35.5	41.3	47.0
	120	8.0	14.0	20.0	26.0	**32.0**	38.0	44.0	50.0	56.0

exchange rate. When we turn our attention to the risk of a foreign investment, we will see that it is necessary to break up each joint conditional return into its component parts.

The end-of-period price (in pounds) of Marks & Spencer shares determines the return on holding the British security. This return is computed before currency conversion back into Canadian dollars. Of the nine possible—or "conditional"—end-of-period share prices, only one will occur. Each conditional end-of-period share price and hence each conditional return can be assigned a probability of happening. The probability distribution—the conditional values together with their respective probabilities—is a quantitative depiction of the fortunes of the risky shares.

Likewise the end-of-period exchange rate, and hence the return resulting from foreign exchange gain or loss, also has a probability distribution made up of nine conditional values and associated probabilities.

Holding a security denominated in a foreign currency is like holding a "portfolio" consisting of the security itself and the foreign currency. Viewed this way, the risk of a foreign security is determined in light of the variance of the return to the security (in its own currency), the variance of the exchange rate and the covariance between the two sources of return. As with any jointly probable outcome, we compute the risk of the dollar-denominated investment return as its standard deviation:

$$SD(r,\$) = [\text{Var}(r_i) + \text{Var}(r_x) + 2\,\text{Cov}(r_i,r_x)]^{1/2}$$

As a practical matter, the covariance between the return on the shares and the exchange rate, $\text{Cov}(r_i,r_x)$, may generally be assumed to be small, close to zero. In that case, the total risk of the foreign security in our example is

$$SD(r,\$) \approx [\text{Var}(r_i) + \text{Var}(r_x)]^{1/2}$$

International Portfolio Diversification

As long as movements in exchange rates are less than perfectly correlated with the return to a security denominated in the foreign currency, a foreign security may be *less* risky to an offshore investor than to a domestic investor. However, this diversification advantage from holding foreign securities is, in fact, a result of the foreign investor being "exposed" to foreign exchange risk, which essentially means that the portfolio manager is speculating on one or more foreign currencies.

Foreign exchange gains (or losses) aside, international portfolio diversification is the pursuit of an expanded set of investment opportunities—involving assets in different industries, markets and business cycles. In other words, foreign assets are likely to have different return-generating processes, and therefore they offer valuable opportunities for portfolio diversification. Foreign assets expand the efficient set of risky assets; they provide the opportunity for a higher Sharpe ratio. Exhibit 11.3 illustrates the idea.

To illustrate the benefits of international diversification, the diagram compares domestic and international investment opportunities. The curved line *Domestic portfolio risk-return combinations* depicts expected risk-return combinations that are available from investments in exclusively domestic risky assets (domestic equities). The straight line CML$_{\text{DOMESTIC}}$ (for capital market line, domestic) depicts combinations of expected return and risk that are available from optimally diversified domestic equities together with investment in the (domestic) risk-free security. Locally optimal diversification in only domestic assets is identified by the point at which a ray from r_f is tangent to domestic risk-return combinations.

The curved line *International portfolio risk-return combinations* depicts expected risk-return combinations that are available from investments in both domestic and foreign risky assets. The straight line CML$_{\text{INTERNATIONAL}}$ (for capital market line, international) depicts combinations of expected return and risk that are available when one adds the domestic risk-free assets into the international mix of risky assets. Optimal *international* diversification (domestic and foreign assets) is identified by the point at which a ray from r_f is tangent to the international portfolio risk-return combinations.

EXHIBIT 11.3

Expanding the
Efficient Frontier
through International
Investment

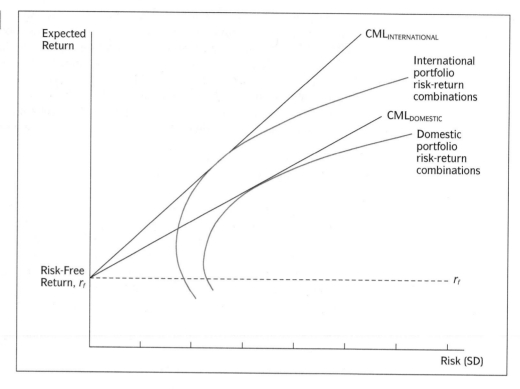

For every point on CML_D there are corresponding points on CML_I that offer the same expected return at lower risk or higher expected return at the same risk.

The **Sharpe performance ratio (SHR)** is defined as "expected return minus the risk-free rate divided by risk." In effect the Sharpe ratio measures the slope of the CML. The higher the CML, the greater is the expected return per unit of risk. The diagram indicates that the Sharpe ratio for internationally diversified portfolios (along CML_I) is higher than for strictly domestic portfolios (along CML_D).

11.2 OPTIMAL INTERNATIONAL PORTFOLIO SELECTION

www.msci.com

Provides an extensive
coverage of world stock
markets, including
historical time series
of major stock market
indexes around the world.

Rational investors select portfolios by considering both risk and expected return. Investors will generally take on additional risk if they are compensated by higher expected return. The analytic challenge is to express both risk and expected return in reasonable and consistent empirical terms. Both expected return and risk, of course, involve a forward-looking (or *ex ante*) perspective. On the other, the data that analysts use to estimate expected returns and risk is backward-looking (or *ex post*) which may appear to violate the most basic premise of capital market efficiency, namely that past information is irrelevant.

Past information on returns, however, is relevant to the extent that it captures verifiably consistent relationships. The best examples of reliable historical information in international investing are the variances of individual national markets—some nations are consistently more volatile than others—and the covariances between pairs of nations. Covariances or, more accurately, correlation coefficients among nations tend to be remarkably stable over time. For example, in subperiods within the past 25 years, the Canadian dollar returns on the S&P TSX (Toronto) and the S&P 500 (New York) have correlation coefficients consistently in the range of 0.50 to 0.75.

As a basis for determining expected return, information on past returns is less reliable. For example, an extraordinarily high return on a country's stock market in one year or even for a couple of years in a row is not a sound basis for *expecting* such returns to continue. Likewise, although negative returns occasionally occur as was the case for stock markets in almost all countries in 2001, 2002, 2008 and 2011, we seldom *expect* returns to be negative. Otherwise no one would hold any of that country's stock. We will see, however, that the crucial source of benefit from international diversification is the less-than-perfect correlation (correlation coefficients less-than-one) that indeed are quite stable and predictable.

Exhibit 11.4 presents annual returns on the major stock exchanges in 11 industrial countries for each year from 1990 to 2012. To report returns as received in Canadian dollars, the data account for the exchange rate between the Canadian dollar and the corresponding currency for each country in each year. For reference, the table also includes the annual return on the MSCI-EAFE.[1]

At a glance, Exhibit 11.4 reveals that to a remarkable degree major international markets move in unison. A rising tide lifts all boats, and conversely. The across-the-board negative returns in 2008 and 2011, for example, reflect the common influence of the 2007 financial crisis, global recession and corresponding stock market retraction.

Over the full 22-year period, the average annual returns on 10 of 11 markets are strongly positive and clustered in a relatively narrow range. Seven of the 10 national indexes have average annual returns between 6 and 10 percent. Japan, at −3 percent, is a negative outlier; Japan was in significant transitional adjustment during the observation period.

A striking message emerges from Exhibit 11.4. Over the past 22 years, from a Canadian investor's perspective, impressive risk-adjusted equity returns were generated right here in Canada. The Sharpe ratio for Canadian investment by Canadian investors, 0.17, dominates all others with the exception of Sweden and Switzerland. These results for Canada would perhaps make one skeptical of the merits of international diversification. That would be unfortunately wrong. Optimal international diversification is a forward-looking strategy. Canada's outperformance of other countries is largely explained by the post-2003 rise in the value of the Canadian dollar against other currencies along with the extraordinary performance of Canada's resource-based companies such as those in oil and gas and minerals. Such events cannot be reasonably predicted to persist.

Let's examine the correlation coefficients among these markets, as we do in Exhibit 11.5. The correlation of Canadian equities returns with returns in foreign markets varies from 0.46 with Switzerland to 0.85 with Sweden. The Canada:United States correlation seems relatively low at 0.53 despite our close economic integration. Canadian and US equities returns (converted to Canadian dollars) began to diverge dramatically in 2002 with a lack of synchronicity that persisted over the past decade. Much of that is explained by the remarkable appreciation of the Canadian dollar throughout this period. In addition, the structures of the Canadian and US economies differ significantly, with Canada being much more resource-based. Other nations that are geographically close and economically similar—such as France, Germany and Italy—tend to have relatively high pair-wise correlations. These three particular countries, of course, have also used a common currency, the euro, since 2000. In contrast, the returns on the Japanese equities markets (even when converted to Canadian dollars) have noticeably low correlation with most other markets around the world.

The average correlation coefficient across all countries, a figure that comes into play if one were to construct an international portfolio on the basis of purely random selection, is 0.70. For a Canadian investor looking abroad, the average correlation coefficient for Canadian (TSX) returns relative to returns in the other 10 countries is even lower at 0.60.

---

[1]The MSCI-EAFE Index (Morgan Stanley Composite Index: Europe, Australasia and the Far East) is a widely recognized benchmark to measure international equity performance. It comprises 21 MSCI country indexes representing developed markets outside the United States and Canada. MSCI includes in its international indexes 85 percent of the free float-adjusted market capitalization in each industry group, within each country. As of June 2013, the MSCI-EAFE Index contained 900 securities with a total market capitalization of over US$11 trillion. The MSCI-EAFE Index is published daily by MSCI and through multiple vendors and in real time every 60 seconds through Reuters and Bloomberg.

EXHIBIT 11.4 Foreign Equity Returns (percent per year, based on conversion to Canadian dollars)

	1990	1991	1992	1993	1994	1995	1996	1997	1998	1999	2000	2001	2002	2003	2004	2005	2006	2007	2008	2009	2010	2011	2012	Average Annual Return	Standard Deviation	Sharpe Ratio
Canada	-14	13	5	29	9	13	27	11	-1	31	6	-14	-14	23	14	20	14	8	-37	34	15	-13	3	8	17	0.17
Australia	-17	39	7	45	-2	14	8	-6	10	13	-8	5	-4	18	21	4	23	8	-46	39	11	-7	9	8	19	0.16
France	-25	22	18	36	-9	3	27	15	53	25	-4	-22	-24	16	12	4	26	-3	-33	6	-10	-23	18	6	22	0.03
Germany	-21	11	3	53	-1	5	20	33	37	13	-10	-20	-36	36	12	6	32	15	-32	11	6	-18	30	8	23	0.14
Hong Kong	7	51	42	127	-25	20	31	-19	8	54	-9	-20	-18	10	7	-4	26	-10	-42	3	-21	-29	6	8	35	0.10
Italy	-29	2	9	57	12	-3	7	42	60	1	0	-26	-14	12	20	3	25	19	-34	26	1	-17	18	8	24	0.13
Japan	-41	1	-15	18	15	2	-7	-29	13	44	-32	-29	-11	11	6	12	2	-20	-21	3	10	-9	1	-3	19	-0.43
Sweden	-25	20	1	71	-6	18	49	13	29	49	-16	-24	-31	27	22	3	33	-13	-41	32	24	-17	15	10	28	0.18
Switzerland	-23	26	37	56	-3	24	18	52	34	-15	10	-19	-15	9	9	10	22	-9	-16	7	6	-9	19	10	22	0.23
U.K.	-10	21	28	33	-2	19	13	27	26	6	-14	-13	-20	7	10	0	24	-11	-40	17	4	-9	9	6	18	0.03
U.S.	-5	32	16	15	7	34	21	30	41	13	-8	-7	-26	4	4	1	12	-13	-28	9	7	0	8	7	17	0.14
MSCI-EAFE	-25	13	-5	39	14	8	4	15	32	18	-12	-12	-23	9	8	14	26	11	-43	32	8	-12	17	6	19	0.05

Source: Rotman Finance Centre, authors' calculations.

EXHIBIT 11.5

Summary Statistics of Returns of 11 Major International Stock Market Indexes (1996–2012, weekly data, annualized)

Correlation Coefficients

	Canada	Australia	France	Germany	Hong Kong	Italy	Japan	Sweden	Switzerland	United Kingdom	United States
Canada	1.00										
Australia	0.78										
France	0.66	0.65									
Germany	0.71	0.65	0.88								
Hong Kong	0.58	0.69	0.68	0.59							
Italy	0.59	0.60	0.83	0.88	0.46						
Japan	0.62	0.54	0.53	0.48	0.44	0.41					
Sweden	0.85	0.77	0.84	0.84	0.75	0.70	0.69				
Switzerland	0.46	0.49	0.75	0.75	0.55	0.78	0.18	0.62			
United Kingdom	0.68	0.74	0.85	0.81	0.67	0.77	0.41	0.80	0.84		
United States	0.53	0.54	0.78	0.68	0.47	0.62	0.38	0.68	0.73	0.88	
MSCI-EAFE	0.80	0.81	0.80	0.87	0.54	0.86	0.64	0.83	0.62	0.80	0.68

Returns converted to Canadian dollar returns at exchange rate prevailing for each country pair in each week.

β is the systematic risk of a country's stock market index (recorded in Canadian dollars) measured against the world stock market index MSCI-World (C$).

$\beta = cov(r_i, r_{MSCI})/var(r_{MSCI})$

The Sharpe Ratio is computed as $(r_i - r_f)/SD_i$ where r_i and SD_i are respectively the mean and standard deviation of returns to the ith market.

The risk-free interest rate, r_f, is 4.0 percent, the average six-month Canadian Treasury bill rate during the sample period 1996–2012.

Source: Rotman Finance Centre, authors' calculations.

EXHIBIT 11.6

Risk Reduction:
Domestic versus
International
Diversification

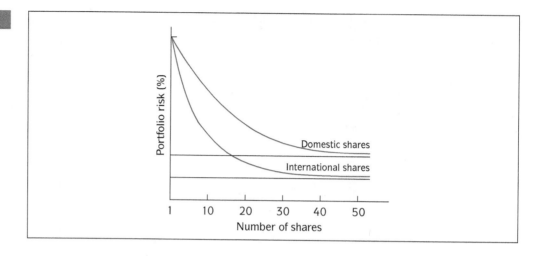

This highlights the basis of the advantage of international investment for portfolio risk reduction. The effect is illustrated in Exhibit 11.6. Since the lower average correlation coefficient across all countries is lower than the average correlation of assets within one country, say Canada, a given degree of risk reduction through diversification is achieved with fewer assets in the international setting.

International Portfolio Design—The Simple Case of 2

We can now usefully go through an example to illustrate the gains generated by international investment versus strictly domestic investment.

To keep the illustration simple and focused on the key source of the gains from international investment, namely diversification effects, we take the perspective of a Canadian investor who is considering buying US stocks to build an internationally diversified portfolio. The investor is already diversified within Canada in her holdings of Canadian equities.

The example involves the following data:

Expected return on Canadian equities (S&P TSX)	$E[r_c]$	11%
Expected return on US equities (S&P 500)	$E[r_{us}]$	11
Standard deviation of returns on Canadian equities	SD_c	17
Standard deviation of returns on US equities	SD_{us}	17
Risk-free interest rate in Canada	$r_{f,c}$	3
Correlation of Canadian returns and US returns	$\rho_{c,u}$	0.53

The expected return on US equities and the associated risk are as converted to Canadian dollar returns. Canadian dollar returns from the foreign investment involve a combination of returns on the equities in US dollars plus associated gains or losses that stem from exchange rate changes (as outlined in Exhibit 11.2). With both Canadian and US returns and risks expressed in Canadian dollar terms, we are able to compare "apples to apples."

To picture the situation, it is convenient to think of the Canadian investor as holding an S&P TSX index fund while considering adding an S&P 500 (NYSE) index fund. The question is, what proportions of the portfolio should be in the S&P TSX and in the S&P 500 in order to maximize the Sharpe ratio?

Sharpe ratio: $SR = (E[r_p] - r_{f,c})/SD_p$

$E[r_p]$ is the expected return on the internationally diversified portfolio in Canadian dollar terms and SD_p is the risk (standard deviation) of those returns.

To introduce data, we will say the Canadian investor's expected return on the S&P TSX and on the S&P 500 are identical at 11 percent. As mentioned, we have no compelling reason to believe that *ex ante* the returns on Canadian and US markets are different.

However, for standard deviations and covariances, we will draw from the actual data in Exhibit 11.4. Potential gain from international diversification as measured by the Sharpe ratio stems from the less-than-perfect correlation between returns on the S&P TSX and on the S&P 500.

Our 0.53 value for the correlation coefficient ($\rho_{c,u}$) is the actual value observed for the period 1996–2012.

The Canadian investor's purely domestic Sharpe ratio is $(11 - 3)/17 = 0.4706$. This is the appropriate reference for observing gains from international diversification.

The domestic and foreign proportions that maximize the Sharpe ratio call for 50 percent of the value of the portfolio to be invested in Canada and 50 percent to be invested in the United States. This optimally diversified portfolio of Canadian and US stocks has an expected return of 11 percent and risk (standard deviation) of 14.9. The Sharpe ratio increases to 0.538, an improvement of more than 14 percent in the risk-return measure. Lower values of the correlation coefficient would call for more investment by Canadian investors in the US (and, of course, *vice versa*) and would create even greater expected improvements in the Sharpe ratio.

A few alternative (nonoptimal) values of the international allocation weights help to illustrate the optimality of the 50:50 split that maximizes the Sharpe ratio.

Weights(%)				
Canada	US	$E[r_P]$	SD_P	Sharpe Ratio
80	20	11	15.7	0.511
70	30	11	15.2	0.525
60	40	11	15.0	0.535
50	**50**	**11**	**14.9**	**0.538**
40	60	11	15.0	0.535
30	70	11	15.2	0.525
20	80	11	15.7	0.511

The gains from international diversification presented here stem entirely from the less-than-perfect correlation in Canadian and US returns as summarized in the correlation coefficient. If Canadian and US returns were perfectly correlated ($\rho_{c,u} = 1.00$) there would be no diversification gains.

International diversification gains through portfolio risk reduction can be sufficiently powerful to offset a differential in expected returns between, say, the S&P TSX and the S&P 500. In our framework, if $E[r_c]$ is 11 and $E[r_{us}]$ is 10 and $\rho_{c,u} = 0.53$, the Canadian investor is still advised to invest in US equities. By investing 40 percent of the portfolio value in the (foreign) S&P 500 and 60 percent domestically in the S&P TSX, the Sharpe ratio increases from 0.471 to 0.508, an 8 percent enhancement over the strictly Canadian portfolio.

Correlation of TSX and NYSE	100% TSX Sharpe Ratio	Optimal Sharpe Ratio	Optimal US Allocation, %	Sharpe Ratio Improvement (%)
0.75	0.471	0.480	25	2
0.50	0.471	0.513	40	9
0.25	0.471	0.560	45	19
0.00	0.471	0.625	47	33

International Diversification—An Extensive Illustration

A more extensive illustration can be useful for understanding the power of international diversification. Let's consider the international strategy of a Canadian investor, either an individual or perhaps a global fund manager, who has decided to invest in stocks in Canada, the United States, Europe, Japan and Brazil. The issue to resolve is how much to invest in each country.

To simplify a bit as we address the problem, we proceed as if an investment in a particular country essentially involves buying a fund that tracks the major stock index of that country. So, for the US for example, the Canadian investor would purchase an S&P 500 index fund. Similarly European returns are represented by an index fund on the German DAX. This approach is not only simple but highly advisable since it represents a reliable and convenient way to achieve in-country diversification.

All returns and risks on foreign investments are converted to Canadian dollar values as explained earlier. To a Canadian investor, part of the return on a foreign investment derives from the foreign currency return on the foreign asset (stock or index fund) while part of the return derives from appreciation or depreciation of the foreign currency relative to the Canadian dollar.

The following data define the international opportunity set:[2]

	Expected Return, %	Risk (SD), %
Canada	20	30
US	19	30
Europe	15	25
Japan	12	25
Brazil	15	35

Correlation Coefficients

	Canada	US	Europe	Japan	Brazil
Canada	1.00				
US	0.64	1.00			
Europe	0.55	0.66	1.00		
Japan	0.24	0.23	0.31	1.00	
Brazil	0.30	0.35	0.25	0.20	1.00

The final piece of information that allows us to compute the country-weights on an optimally diversified international portfolio is the risk-free rate in Canada. We will use the six month Canadian T-bill rate, 4 percent.

With these data, the optimal country-weights are the weights that maximize the Sharpe ratio.[3] The results are:

	Optimal Weight
Canada	0.36
USA	0.21
Europe	0.10
Japan	0.22
Brazil	0.11
	1.00

---

[2]For illustrative purposes, we use somewhat larger values of expected returns and standard deviations than appear in Exhibit 11.5. To enhance the clarity of the graphics in Exhibit 11.7, we apply correlation coefficients that span a broader range than in Exhibit 11.5. Our extensive illustration includes Brazil and average pan-European returns which do not appear in Exhibit 11.5.

[3]The optimal international portfolio is solved by maximizing the Sharpe ratio, $SR = [E(R_p) - R_f]/SD_p$, with respect to the portfolio weights. Refer to Appendix 11B for detailed discussion of the computational methods. With respect to data, professionals are acutely aware of the time-varying nature of securities returns, variances and covariances. Most professionals tend to use their own models to generate expected returns on foreign assets while relying on historical estimates (going back three to five years) to determine country-specific variances and covariances.

An internationally diversified portfolio with these country-weights generates an expected return of 17 percent with a risk (standard deviation) of 21 percent. The expected return and the risk are in Canadian dollar terms.

The benefit of international diversification is observed in the effect on the Sharpe ratio. If a Canadian investor simply held the S&P TSX, the Sharpe ratio would be $(20 - 4)/30 = 0.53$. On the other hand, the optimally diversified international portfolio offers the Canadian investor a Sharpe ratio of $(17 - 4)/21 = 0.61$. With international diversification, the Sharpe ratio is 8 points higher than it is for purely stay-at-home investment. This increase in the Sharpe ratio reflects the extra return per standard deviation (risk) that results from international diversification.

Finally, we can compute the increase in the expected return from international diversification at any Canadian-equivalent risk level. Let's use the standard deviation (SD_C) of the TSX S&P, 30. Then the change in expected return (Δr_c) is found by multiplying the change in the Sharpe ratio times the standard deviation of the strictly Canadian portfolio, that is,

$$\Delta r_c = (SR_{GLOBAL} - SR_{CANADA})SD = (0.61 - 0.53)*30 = 2.4 \text{ percent}$$

At the domestic level of risk, the globally diversified portfolio generates an expected return that is 2.4 percent higher than the expected return on the TSX S&P.

Exhibit 11.7 illustrates the case. The curved line *International risk-return combinations* repeats a similar curve described in detail in Exhibit 11.3. The capital letters C, US, E, J and B depict the country-specific interior risk-return combinations for Canada, the US, Europe, Japan and Brazil.

The benefits of international diversification in terms of an increase in the Sharpe ratio stem from a combination of factors involving differences in expected return and differences in risk (standard deviation) between domestic and foreign investments as well as *all* pairwise covariances of returns among the countries considered. The calculations to determine the optimal amount of investment in various foreign assets are complicated by the fact that returns and risk from foreign investment when expressed in the investor's

EXHIBIT 11.7

Optimal International Diversification

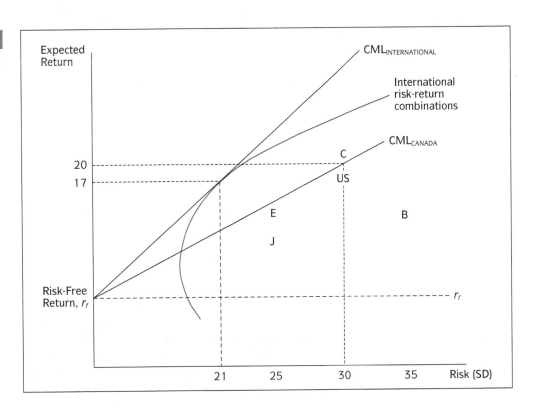

home currency stem from the returns in the foreign currency together with the returns that arise from changes in the exchange rate.

To summarize the effects of these various factors, the optimal proportion of investment in foreign assets in any particular country is greater

1. The greater the expected return on foreign assets (recorded in terms of foreign currency) relative to expected returns on domestic assets.

2. The greater the expected (real) appreciation of foreign currency against the investor's home currency.

3. The lower the risk (standard deviation) of returns on foreign assets (converted to the domestic investor's currency) compared to the risk of domestic investment.

4. The smaller the correlation coefficient between returns on foreign assets (converted to the domestic investor's currency) and returns on domestic assets.

5. The lower the domestic risk-free rate.

Analyses of gains from international portfolio diversification, such as we have presented in this chapter, are generally *ex post* in the sense that the risk-return characteristics are observed from the past. In application of these analytic methods, there is an underlying assumption that historically observed returns, variances and covariances are reasonable estimates of future (or expected) returns, variances and covariances. To the extent that the past is not an accurate representation of the future, the resulting "estimation errors" in the data—when used to construct "optimal" international portfolios—may lead to inefficient (or suboptimal) allocation of funds.

Finally, much of the diversification gain from international investment stems from the less-than-perfect correlation of national industries and national indexes. For instance, Canada's resource industries, of which we have many, generate returns that are substantially different from—and not highly correlated with—returns on, say, industrial sectors in Japan or Italy. Beyond these cross-country industrial differences, however, another element of diversification in international investing stems from exchange rate variance and currency correlations. Since exchange rate movements tend to be random, they tend to dampen the benefits of the more fundamental (country or industrial) diversification. Therefore, the strategy of constructing an international equity portfolio while hedging foreign exchange risk allows the investor to emphasize (or capture the gains from) international industrial diversification while neutralizing exchange rate effects. In Appendix 11A, we outline in technical detail how to hedge exchange rate risk in an international portfolio.

11.3   INTERNATIONAL MUTUAL FUNDS: ACCESS TO THE WORLD

Canadian investors can achieve international diversification quite easily through Canadian international mutual funds that now number well over 1,500. By investing in international mutual funds, Canadian investors can buy the funds in Canadian dollars and likewise receive foreign-source dividends, interest and capital gains in Canadian dollars. The process is simple and convenient. For the Canadian investor, there is nothing "foreign" about the purchase of an international mutual fund beyond the crucial fact that the securities in the fund are foreign. Professional managers establish the international portfolio strategy and they look after diversification and portfolio transactions. Professional managers are in a position to deal with legal, institutional and foreign-exchange matters that could be formidable to the individual investor. The 1,500+ Canadian international mutual funds offer a broad array of portfolios, including country funds and sector funds as well as funds that focus on international growth or value or simply offshore indexes.

An investor adds foreign content to a portfolio with a view to enhancing performance—a combination of higher returns and lower risk. Returns and risk ought to be measured in the investor's home currency. How, then, have Canadian investors fared in their choice between domestic and foreign investments? As always, *ex post* assessment of performance depends on the time period that one looks at. For example, foreign funds served Canadian investors very well in the period 1991–2001 as the Canadian dollar fell steadily against foreign currencies, especially the US dollar. Then, the meltdown of 2001 hit all equities markets hard, which, like the crash of 1987, tends to make comparative *ex post* performance difficult to assess. Finally, in 2003, markets rallied strongly everywhere. Canadian investors and foreign investors in Canada were doubly blessed as the Canadian dollar also strengthened considerably.

Exhibit 11.8 is a two-panel presentation of the risk-return profiles of samples of international mutual funds offered by Canadian financial institutions. The returns are in Canadian dollars and so reflect both the foreign returns on the foreign assets and the exchange rate effect on conversion to Canadian dollars. The risk measure is the conventional three-year standard deviation of daily returns in Canadian dollars. The Sharpe ratio is computed for each fund. The exhibit includes a set of global funds that do not include US equities and a set of funds that consist exclusively of US equities. For comparison, we note the performance of the S&P/TSX index (Toronto).

The two panels, A and B, are presented to firmly establish that, for Canadian investors, changes in the exchange rate have a significant bearing on the relative merits of investing at home or abroad. Sometimes, by the time foreign returns are converted to Canadian dollar returns, exchange rate changes swamp the returns denominated in foreign currency.

The top panel shows performance of mutual funds of foreign equities in 2006–2007. The year 2006 was the one just before the financial crisis; 2007 saw the first dramatic effects of that crisis on equities. In 2006 non-US stocks, especially those in emerging markets, exhibited strong performance. In 2007, stock returns were generally weak across the globe, and especially so in the United States. But for Canadian investors in those foreign assets, the results were even worse because of the sharp appreciation of the Canadian dollar against most other currencies.

Exchange rate changes explain much of the two-year performance (as measured from a Canadian investor's perspective). In 2006, from the beginning of the year until the end, the Canadian dollar was unchanged against the US dollar. In 2007, however, the Canadian dollar appreciated by almost 20 percent, depressing Canadian dollar returns on foreign equities to negative values. The average Canadian investor who limited investments to domestic equities earned 13.48 percent over the two-year period with a handsome Sharpe ratio of 0.86. Foreign funds fared much worse.

The foreign investment story is significantly different in 2011–2012. In 2011, from the Canadian investor's perspective, neither global (non-US) equity funds nor US equity funds did well. Both had negative returns. But investing in Canada was even worse. When things turned around in 2012, Canadian equities continued to fare much worse than either US or non-US foreign equity funds. Unlike the earlier case, explanation for the relative foreign-versus-domestic equities returns for Canadians is not a currency story; exchange rate movements had virtually nothing to do with Canadian relative performance in 2011–2012. Canadian returns were simply much lower than were returns abroad.

In 2008, in this chapter in this book's previous edition, we wrote:

It is clear from Exhibit 11.8 [which is now the upper panel, 11.8A] that the recent performance of Canadian equities was exceptional by world standards, reflecting the combination of positive returns on Canadian securities and the strengthening of the Canadian dollar. Insofar as the Canadian dollar rose substantially more against the US dollar than against non-US currencies, Canadian equities performance is correspondingly stronger against US equities than against non-US equities.

The Canadian performance is, indeed, so strong through the recent (2006–2007) period that to apply this statistical information to an optimal portfolio of assets from the Canadian perspective would result in severe overweighting of Canadian shares. A bright past is seldom

EXHIBIT 11.8

International Mutual Fund Performance: Canadian Dollar Returns, 2006–2007 and 2011–2012

Panel A

	Return, Annualized			Risk (SD)	2006–07 Sharpe Ratio
	2006	**2007**	**2006–07**		
Global Equities (non-US)					
BMO Global Equity	23.09	−2.07	9.79	10.91	0.53
IG AIF International Equity	19.09	−4.92	6.41	10.32	0.23
Manulife Global	16.58	−4.07	5.75	9.77	0.18
RBC International Equity	13.94	−3.20	5.02	10.17	0.10
HSBC Global Equity	17.46	−6.19	4.97	11.21	0.09
Scotia Global	14.76	3.14	8.79	9.79	0.49
TD Global Equity	12.79	−8.02	1.85	7.29	−0.29
Average, Global Equities	**16.82**	**−3.62**	**6.09**	**9.92**	**0.21**
US Equities					
BMO US Equity	11.82	−6.09	2.47	11.03	−0.14
IG AIF US Growth	11.13	2.69	6.83	11.72	0.24
Manulife Core US Fund	11.07	−18.64	−4.94	10.38	−0.86
RBC US Equity	11.59	−1.25	4.97	9.13	0.11
HSBC US Equity	10.99	−11.53	−0.91	9.92	−0.49
Scotia US Growth	8.52	−7.94	−0.05	9.51	−0.43
TD US Equity	10.76	−9.95	−0.13	9.80	−0.42
Average, US Equities	**10.84**	**−7.53**	**1.18**	**10.21**	**−0.28**
S&P TSX 500 (Canada)	**17.26**	**9.83**	**13.48**	**10.99**	**0.86**

Panel B

	Return, Annualized			Risk (SD)	2011–2012 Sharpe Ratio
	2011	**2012**	**2011–2012**		
Global Equities					
BMO Global Equity	−0.02	0.09	0.04	14.28	0.24
IG AIF International Equity	−0.03	0.10	0.04	14.77	0.22
RBC International Equity	−0.12	0.14	0.01	17.34	−0.02
HSBC Global Equity	−0.15	0.09	−0.03	23.02	−0.17
Scotia Global	−0.12	0.12	0.00	16.39	−0.05
TD Global Equity	−0.12	0.12	0.01	17.85	−0.03
Average, Global Equities	**−0.09**	**0.11**	**0.01**	**17.28**	**0.03**
US Equities					
BMO US Equity	0.04	0.08	0.06	13.39	0.41
IG AIF US Growth	−0.05	0.11	0.03	17.69	0.12
RBC US Equity	−0.06	0.07	0.01	14.39	0.00
HSBC US Equity	−0.02	0.07	0.02	14.04	0.09
Scotia US Growth	−0.01	0.05	0.02	12.32	0.06
TD US Equity	0.00	0.13	0.07	18.88	0.34
Average, US Equities	**−0.02**	**0.09**	**0.04**	**15.12**	**0.17**
S&P/TSX Composite	**−0.11**	**0.02**	**−0.04**	**15.49**	**−0.30**

Note: "Risk" is the three-year standard deviation of daily returns. Author's calculations from data provided by the Rotman Finance Centre.

a true indicator of the relative rewards, risks and covariances of the broader international set of assets. The recent (2006–2007) *ex post* data are telling Canadian investors to keep their money at home. Nevertheless, Canadian investors are well advised to capture the *ex ante* diversification benefits that result from holding international assets.

The lower panel of Exhibit 11.8 confirms the wisdom of those words.

Supplementary Material

In addition to international mutual funds, investors may achieve international portfolio diversification "at home" by investing in (1) country funds, (2) American depository receipts (ADRs) or (3) world equity benchmark shares (WEBS), without having to invest directly in foreign stock markets. In the following section, we discuss each of these instruments.

11.4 INTERNATIONAL DIVERSIFICATION THROUGH COUNTRY FUNDS

Country funds are a popular means of international investment. As the name suggests, a country fund invests exclusively in shares of a single country. Using country funds, investors can

1. Speculate in a single foreign market with minimum costs.
2. Construct their own *personal* international portfolios using country funds as building blocks.
3. Diversify into *emerging markets* that are otherwise practically inaccessible.

Many emerging markets such as India, Brazil, China, Russia and Turkey still remain largely segmented. As a result, country funds provide international investors with a practical way of diversifying into these relatively difficult to reach foreign markets.

The majority of country funds have a *closed-end* status. A **closed-end country fund (CECF)** issues a given number of shares that trade on the stock exchange of the host country as if the fund were an individual share by itself. Unlike shares of open-end mutual funds, shares of a closed-end country fund cannot be redeemed at the underlying net asset value set at the home market of the fund. Currently, about 30 countries offer CECFs, a partial list of which is provided in Exhibit 11.9.

Closed-end country funds present a pricing puzzle that intrigues international financial researchers. Research into "asset pricing" attempts to identify factors that explain the rate of return on financial assets, of which closed-end country funds are one particular type. The puzzle is that CECFs often deviate substantially above or below the value of the individual shares that make up the country fund. It is a bit like saying that a bag of groceries sells for more or less than the sum of the prices of the items in the grocery bag. In the following discussion, we summarize the results of a landmark study of CECF pricing. The purpose is to provide an outline of the "puzzle" along with an attempt to disentangle two important effects that influence the pricing of CECFs, which goes some distance toward providing an explanation of the peculiar pricing. The study was carried out on country funds that trade on the New York and American Stock Exchanges. The focus is relevant for Canadian investors as well, since Canadian investors often seek international diversification by buying the readily available CECFs that trade in New York.

Since the share value of a CECF is set on a US stock exchange, it may diverge from the underlying net asset value (NAV) set in the fund's home market. The difference is known as a *premium* if the fund share value exceeds the NAV, or a *discount* in the opposite case. Exhibit 11.9 provides the magnitude of premiums/discounts for a sample of CECFs. The average premium varies a great deal across funds, ranging from 63 percent (for the Korea Fund) to −24 percent (for the Brazil Fund). Like the Korea Fund, the Taiwan and Spain funds commanded large premiums, 38 percent and 22 percent, respectively. Like the Brazil Fund, the Mexico Fund traded at a steep discount, −21 percent on average. It was also observed that the fund premium/discount fluctuates widely over time. For instance, the Taiwan Fund premium varied between −25 percent and 205 percent. Most funds have

EXHIBIT 11.9	US and Home Market Betas of Closed-End Country Funds and Their Net Asset Values (sample period 1985–1991)

Country	Average Fund Premium (%)	Fund Share Value			Net Asset Value		
		β^{US}	β^{HM}	R^2	β^{US}	β^{HM}	R^2
Australia	−14.77	0.62	0.48	0.13	0.25	0.81	0.60
Brazil	−24.72	0.11	0.16	0.02	0.32	0.65	0.60
Canada	−6.29	0.04	0.47	0.03	−0.19	0.29	0.11
Germany	1.80	0.73	0.53	0.11	0.15	0.69	0.40
India	−2.66	0.87	0.26	0.04	−0.27	0.66	0.40
Italy	−12.49	0.89	0.68	0.21	0.13	0.57	0.28
Korea	63.17	1.00	0.63	0.19	0.24	0.76	0.62
Malaysia	−0.36	1.34	0.60	0.24	0.58	0.68	0.79
Mexico	−21.14	0.99	0.53	0.13	0.33	0.75	0.62
Spain	21.57	1.56	0.28	0.14	0.39	0.75	0.65
South Africa	12.16	0.00	0.35	0.13	0.08	0.85	0.59
Switzerland	−7.65	0.79	0.47	0.25	0.33	0.65	0.75
Taiwan	37.89	1.46	0.39	0.26	0.19	0.40	0.13
Thailand	−6.86	1.20	0.44	0.14	0.63	0.85	0.75
United Kingdom	−16.55	1.04	0.62	0.36	0.55	0.73	0.37
Average		0.84	0.46	0.16	0.25	0.67	0.51

Source: E. Chang, C. Eun, and R. Kolodny, "International Diversification through Closed-End Country Funds," *Journal of Banking and Finance* (November 1995). Reprinted with permission of Elsevier Science.

traded at both a premium and a discount since their inception.[4] The behaviour of the fund premium/discount implies that the risk-return characteristics of a CECF can be quite different from those of the underlying NAV.

Cash flows from CECFs are generated by the underlying assets held outside the United States. But CECFs are traded in the US and their US market values often diverge from the NAVs. This "hybrid" nature of CECFs suggests that they may behave partly like US securities and partly like securities of the home market. To investigate this issue, consider the following "two-factor" market model:[5]

$$r_i = \alpha_i + \beta^{US}{}_i\, r_{US} + \beta^{HM}{}_i\, r_{HM} + e_i$$

---

[4] A study by Bonser-Neal, Brauer and Wheatley (1990) suggests that the country fund premium/discount reflects the barriers to direct portfolio investment in the home countries of the funds. They found that whenever these barriers were lowered, the fund premium declined.

[5] The returns to the home market, r_{HM}, is in fact the "residual" obtained from regressing the home market returns on US market returns. Investors who wish to diversify risk internationally will value exposure to the "pure" (or orthogonal) foreign market risk, that is, β_{HM}.

where

r_i = the return on the ith country fund

r_{US} = the return on the US market index proxied by the Standard & Poor's 500 Index

r_{HM} = the return on the home market of the country fund

β^{US}_i = the US beta of the ith country fund, measuring the sensitivity of the fund returns to the US market returns

β^{HM}_i = the home market beta of the ith country fund, measuring the sensitivity of the fund returns to the home market returns

e_i = the residual error term

The equation above is estimated for both the CECFs and their underlying net assets; that is, we run two regressions for each fund. In the first regression, the left-hand side (dependent) variable, r_i, is the return that investors receive on the CECF share itself. In the second regression, the left-hand side variable is the return on the NAV. The estimation results are provided in Exhibit 11.9.

Exhibit 11.9 shows that CECFs tend to have substantially higher US beta values than their underlying NAVs. The average US beta value is 0.84 for CECFs but is only 0.25 for the NAVs. On the other hand, the average home market beta is 0.46 for CECFs, which compares with 0.67 for the NAVs. In the case of Korea, for example, the fund (underlying net assets) has a US beta of 1.00 (0.24) and a home market beta of 0.63 (0.76). In the case of Thailand, the fund (underlying net assets) has a US beta of 1.20 (0.63) and a home market beta of 0.44 (0.85). In other words, CECF returns are substantially more sensitive to the US market factor and less so to the home market factor than their corresponding NAVs. This implies that CECFs behave more like US securities in comparison with the NAVs.[6] However, the majority of CECFs retain significant home market betas, allowing investors to achieve international diversification to a certain extent. Also the coefficients of determination, R^2, tend to be quite low, 0.16 on average, for CECFs. This implies that CECFs are subject to significant *idiosyncratic* (or unique) risks that are related to neither US nor the home market movements.

While CECFs behave more like US securities, they provide investors with the opportunity to achieve international diversification without incurring excessive transaction costs.

We now estimate the potential gains from international diversification using CECFs. Exhibit 11.10 provides the risk-return characteristics of 15 sample funds as well as the US stock market index during the sample period. It also presents the composition of the optimal international portfolio comprising CECFs and, for comparison purposes, the composition of the corresponding optimal portfolio comprising the NAVs.

The optimal portfolio consisting of CECFs dominates the US index in terms of risk-return efficiency; the Sharpe performance measure is 0.233 for the former and 0.320 for the latter. This point can be seen clearly from Exhibit 11.11, which traces out the efficient sets, separately, for CECFs and NAVs.

The figure shows that the NAVs offer superior diversification opportunities compared with the CECFs. Consequently, those who can invest directly in foreign markets without incurring excessive costs are advised to do so. However, for the majority of investors without such opportunities, CECFs still offer a cost-effective way of diversifying internationally. Lastly, note that country funds from emerging markets receive significant weights in the optimal portfolio of CECFs. Specifically, the weight is 12.71 percent for the Brazil Fund, 7.50 percent for the India Fund, and 24.27 percent for the Mexico Fund. These emerging market funds, as a whole, receive about a 45 percent weight in the optimal CECF portfolio. This implies that CECFs from emerging markets can play an important role in expanding the investment opportunity set for international investors.

---

[6]This finding is consistent with the Bailey and Lim (1992) study showing that CECFs act more like American securities than foreign stock market indexes.

| EXHIBIT 11.10 | Summary Statistics of the Weekly Returns for Closed-End Country Funds and Their Net Asset Values and the Compositions of Optimal Portfolios |

Country	Country Fund Share			Net Asset Value			Optimal Portfolio	
	Mean (%)	SD (%)	Correlation with US	Mean (%)	SD (%)	Correlation with US	CECF (Weight)	NAV (Weight)
Australia	0.46	5.64	0.12	0.01	1.78	0.25	0.0033	0.0000
Brazil	0.73	6.31	−0.01	0.29	7.55	−0.02	0.1271	0.0023
Canada	0.14	4.91	−0.31	−0.19	1.98	−0.19	0.0660	0.0000
Germany	0.78	9.70	0.22	0.38	4.67	−0.11	0.0253	0.0000
India	0.36	5.93	0.18	0.15	3.92	−0.21	0.0750	0.0882
Italy	0.44	7.00	0.22	0.39	2.20	0.25	0.0000	0.1044
Korea	−0.37	6.79	0.25	0.00	2.91	0.08	0.0000	0.0000
Malaysia	0.72	7.89	0.35	0.37	3.21	0.29	0.0000	0.0000
Mexico	1.11	6.07	0.50	0.77	2.63	0.24	0.2427	0.6026
Spain	0.39	8.76	0.40	0.03	3.08	0.29	0.0000	0.0000
South Africa	0.43	4.00	−0.13	0.36	5.06	−0.03	0.2993	0.0954
Switzerland	0.27	4.50	0.46	0.20	2.48	0.36	0.0000	0.0000
Taiwan	0.57	7.42	0.31	−0.06	7.95	0.05	0.0000	0.0000
Thailand	0.71	8.42	0.29	0.50	5.14	0.23	0.0000	0.0000
United Kingdom	0.35	4.01	0.44	0.27	4.08	0.23	0.0424	0.0616
U.S. index	0.18	2.06	1.00	0.18	2.06	1.00	0.1189	0.0454

						Total =	1.0000	1.0000
						Mean =	0.58%	0.58%
						SD =	2.49%	1.81%
						SHP =	0.233	0.320

Source: E. Chang, C. Eun, and R. Kolodny, "International Diversification through Closed-End Country Funds," *Journal of Banking and Finance* (October 1995). Reprinted with permission of Elsevier Science.

| EXHIBIT 11.11 | |

Efficient Sets: Country Funds versus Net Assets

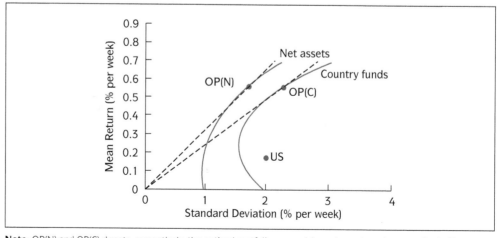

Note: OP(N) and OP(C) denote, respectively, the optimal portfolios comprising net assets and country funds. The efficient sets are illustrated by the dotted lines.

11.5 INTERNATIONAL DIVERSIFICATION WITH ADRS

www.adr.com

This website managed by J. P. Morgan & Co. is a comprehensive source of information on American depository receipts.

Investors can achieve international diversification using American depository receipts (ADRs), as well as country funds. As explained in Chapter 8, ADRs represent receipts for foreign shares held in the American (depository) banks' foreign branches or custodians. Like closed-end country funds, ADRs are traded on US exchanges like domestic US securities. Consequently, investors can save transaction costs and also benefit from speedy and dependable disclosures, settlements, and custody services. The International Finance in Practice box, "Live Here, Invest Abroad," describes the virtues of investing via ADRs.

British and European investors may achieve international diversification at home using global depository receipts (GDRs) which represent ownership claims on those foreign shares that are listed on the London Stock Exchange.

A few studies examined the potential benefits of international diversification with ADRs. Officer and Hoffmeister (1987) found that adding ADRs to a domestic portfolio had substantial risk reduction benefits. Including as few as four ADRs in a representative stock portfolio reduced risk, measured by the standard deviation of returns, by as much as 25 percent without reducing the expected return. They also found that ADRs tend to have very low beta exposure to the US stock market. During the sample period 1973–1983, ADRs were found to have an average US beta of only 0.264.

Wahab and Khandwala (1993) found similar results. They report that when investors held an equally weighted portfolio of seven ADRs and the S&P 500, the annualized standard deviation of daily returns dropped from 30.2 percent (for a purely domestic portfolio) to 17.5 percent. They also reported that most of the nonsystematic risk of the portfolio was eliminated by adding only seven ADRs to the S&P 500. Adding ADRs beyond seven did not reduce the portfolio risk materially, regardless of portfolio weights.

Considering that the majority of ADRs are from such developed countries as Australia, Japan and the United Kingdom, investors have a limited opportunity to diversify into emerging markets using ADRs. However, in a few emerging markets like Mexico, investors can choose from several ADRs. In this situation, investors should consider the relative advantages and disadvantages of ADRs and CECFs as a means of international diversification. Compared with ADRs, CECFs are likely to provide more complete diversification. As shown previously, however, the potential gains from investing in them tend to be reduced by premiums/discounts.

11.6 INTERNATIONAL DIVERSIFICATION WITH WEBS

www.ishares.com

Provides extensive coverage of exchange-traded funds, including WEBS.

In April 1996, the American Stock Exchange (AMEX) introduced a class of securities called **World Equity Benchmark Shares (WEBS)**, designed and managed by Barclays Global Investors. In essence, WEBS are exchange-traded open-end country funds that are designed to closely track foreign stock market indexes. Currently, there are 20 WEBS tracking the Morgan Stanley Capital International (MSCI) indexes for the following individual countries: Australia, Austria, Belgium, Brazil, Canada, France, Germany, Hong Kong, Italy, Japan, Korea, Malaysia, Mexico, the Netherlands, Singapore, Spain, Sweden, Switzerland, Taiwan and the United Kingdom. The AMEX had previously introduced a similar security for the US market, Standard & Poor's Depository Receipts (SPDRs) known as "spiders," designed to track the S&P 500 Index. Using **exchange traded funds (ETFs)** like WEBS and spiders, investors can trade a whole stock market index as if it were a single share. Being open-end funds, WEBS trade at prices that are very close to their net asset values. In addition to single-country index funds, investors can achieve global diversification instantaneously just by holding shares of the S&P Global 100 Index Fund that is also trading on the AMEX with other WEBS.

A study by Khorana, Nelling and Trester (1998) found that WEBS indeed track the underlying MSCI country indexes very closely. For example, the average correlation of

INTERNATIONAL FINANCE *in Practice*

Live Here, Invest Abroad

Global consumers, global investors. Our appetite for products from abroad only begins with French champagne, Swiss chocolate and Japanese televisions. Wise investors are flocking to buy stock in the foreign corporations that make such goods—and not only through the already well-publicized route of mutual funds. They are purchasing shares of individual companies in the form of American depository receipts, or ADRs.

ADRs of about 1,300 foreign firms trade on U.S. stock markets, with one ADR certificate equaling a given number of shares of stock. In 2007, total ADR trading volume on the New York and American exchanges and Nasdaq topped $1.6 trillion, up from $1 trillion in 2005. With an average of 15 new ADRs a month, the trend shows no signs of topping out.

It's easy to comprehend the enthusiasm. Last year, the Bank of New York's ADR Composite Index, which tracks 210 ADRs, chalked up a 35 percent gain. That was far ahead of the 10.1 percent gain in the Standard & Poor's 500-stock index and just slightly below the average 30.2 percent return for international stock funds.

Half a Dozen Winning ADRs

Of the American depository receipts that trade on major U.S. exchanges, the six best performers over the year are listed below.

Company (Country)	Business	Recent Price	12-Month Price Change
Macronix (Taiwan)	Hardware	$16.55	408%
Cambridge Antibody Technology (UK)	Health care	7.80	324
Yukos (Kyrgyzstan)	Energy	12.65	135
Northgate (Canada)	Industrial materials	23.72	110
Embratel Participacoes (Brazil)	Telecommunication	14.80	97
Baidu (China)	Media	76.25	86

Source: Rotman Finance Centre.

---

daily returns between WEBS and the underlying country indexes is 0.97. They also found that the average correlation of WEBS with the S&P 500 Index is quite low, 0.22, which makes WEBS an excellent tool for international risk diversification. For those investors who desire international equity exposure, WEBS may well serve as a major alternative to such traditional tools as international mutual funds, ADRs and closed-end country funds.

11.7 INTERNATIONAL DIVERSIFICATION WITH HEDGE FUNDS

Hedge funds which represent privately pooled investment funds have experienced a phenomenal growth in recent years. This growth of hedge funds has been mainly driven by institutional investors, such as pension plans, endowments and private foundations searching for positive returns regardless of whether markets are rising or falling. Unlike traditional mutual funds that generally depend on "buy and hold" investment strategies, hedge funds may adopt flexible, dynamic trading strategies, often aggressively using leverages, short positions and derivative contracts in order to achieve their investment objectives. These funds may invest in a wide spectrum of securities, such as currencies, domestic and foreign bonds and stocks, commodities, real estate and so forth.

Legally, hedge funds are private investment partnerships. As such, these funds generally do not register as an investment company under securities law and are not subject to any reporting or disclosure requirements. As a result, many hedge funds operate under rather opaque environments. Hedge fund advisors typically receive a management fee, often 1–2 percent of the fund asset value, as compensation, plus a performance fee that can be 20–25 percent of capital appreciation. Investors may not be allowed to liquidate their

"U.S. stocks are increasingly pricey and precarious," explains Mark Coler, publisher of the *Global Portfolio*, an ADR newsletter that compiles brokerage reports but doesn't make its own recommendations. "Many foreign shares still have some big gains ahead as a global economic recovery takes hold."

To buy ADRs, you don't have to dial overseas; all it takes is a quick call to a broker. ADRs are issued by the U.S. banks that hold the underlying foreign shares in custody and are sold in U.S. dollars through brokers, just like stocks.

Watch the News

ADRs open the door to a new world, but staying abreast of currency fluctuations and economic and political developments is a must. When Mexico's top presidential candidate was assassinated last week, for example, the ADR price of Teléfonos de México, the national telephone company, dropped by more than 6 percent overnight.

Many foreign firms, moreover, tell shareholders—including those back home—as little as possible. About 70 percent of foreign companies offering ADRs choose not to file financial statements with the Securities and Exchange Commission. Executive pay, lines of business and insider trading thus remain mysteries, and shareholders rarely get prospectuses or quarterly income reports. As a result, these companies' ADRs trade on the "pink sheets" segment of the over-the-counter market, a realm exempt from the rules of the bigger exchanges.

Big Feet

Prices can be hard to track in that thinly traded part of the market, but that doesn't mean the companies are fly-by-nights or start-ups. Most pink-sheeted ADRs are big-foot entities like Nestlé, Mitsubishi and Deutsche Bank that simply reject the arduous process of conforming to U.S. standards.

For investors who want to learn more, Chicago-based Morningstar Inc. publishes mutual fund reports in *Morningstar American Depository Receipts* (800-876-5005; biweekly). The report probes 700 ADRs, including about 300 pink sheeters and all of the others, with up to 10 years of data, business summaries and market snapshots, as well as a list of the five mutual funds owning the greatest number of a company's shares.

Investors hungry for foreign fare sans stomachache can dine at foreign stock mutual funds. "Overseas funds probably won't see quite as much action this year, but the good ones are still likely to outperform the U.S. market," says Michael Stolper, publisher of the *Mutual Fund Monthly* newsletter.

Copyright, April 4, 1994, *U.S. News & World Report*. (Data up-dated by authors.)

investments during a certain lock-up period. In Canada and the United States, only institutional investors and wealthy individuals are allowed to invest in hedge funds. In many European countries, however, retail investors are also allowed to invest in these funds.

Hedge funds tend to have relatively low correlations with various stock market benchmarks and thus allow investors to diversify their portfolio risk. In addition, they allow investors to access foreign markets that are not easily accessible. For example, J. P. Morgan provides access to the Jayhawk China Fund, a hedge fund investing in Chinese stocks not readily available in conventional markets. Also, hedge funds may allow investors to benefit from certain global macroeconomic events. In fact, many hedge funds are classified as "global/macro" funds. Examples of global/macro funds include such well-known names as George Soros' Quantum Fund, Julian Robertson's Jaguar Fund and Louis Bacon's Moore Global Fund. Hedge funds were active during the British pound crisis of 1992 and Asian financial crisis of 1997. As is well known, George Soros correctly anticipated the withdrawal of the British pound from the European Monetary System (EMS) and bet on the pound depreciation upon the withdrawal. His funds reportedly took a $10 billion short position on the British pound and made about $1 billion dollar profit during September 1992. Soros funds also had short positions in the Thai baht and Malaysian ringgit during the Asian currency crisis of 1997. This touched off a series of acrimonious exchanges between the Malaysian Prime Minister and Mr. Soros on whether hedge funds were responsible for the currency crisis.

While investors may benefit from hedge funds, they need to be aware of the associated risk as well. Hedge funds may make wrong bets based on the incorrect prediction of future events and wrong models. The failure of Long Term Capital Management (LTCM) provides an example of the risk associated with hedge fund investing. John Meriwether, a former fixed income trader at Salomon Brothers, founded LTCM in 1993. Teamed up with a group of veteran Wall Street traders and two Nobel laureates, Myron Scholes and Robert Merton, LTCM enjoyed solid credibility and respectability among the investment community. Using its good name, LTCM pursued highly leveraged fixed-income arbitrage strategies. Among other things, LTCM borrowed heavily and bet on international interest convergence between high- and low-quality debts. For example, LTCM bought Italian government bonds and sold German Bund futures. Initially, LTCM did well, realizing about 40 percent annual returns on equity in the first few years. But following the Asian and Russian currency crises, gradual convergence turned into a dramatic divergence. As a result, LTCM's debts increased and its capital base depleted, eventually leading to its downfall. Investors lost enormous sums of money.

11.8 INTERNATIONAL DIVERSIFICATION WITH SMALL-CAP STOCKS

To the extent that investors diversify internationally, well-known large-cap stocks receive the dominant share of fund allocation. There is a "large-cap" bias as well as a home bias in international investment. These biases are consistent with the proposition that "familiarity breeds investment." Increasingly, however, returns to large-cap stocks or stock market indexes that are dominated by large-cap stocks tend to co-move, mitigating the benefit from international diversification. This point is illustrated in Exhibit 11.12, which plots the average return correlation among 10 major international stock markets. The average correlation among international stock returns fluctuated around 0.37 until the mid-1990s. It has increased steadily since then. The average correlation reached 0.80 in 2008 when the global financial crisis was at its height. The tendency of international correlations to rise has led investors to doubt the benefit of international diversification.

Well-known large-cap stocks that are popular among international investors are likely to be multinational firms with a substantial foreign customer and investor base. In contrast, small-cap firms are likely to be locally oriented with limited international

EXHIBIT 11.12

Average Return Correlation among 10 Major International Stock Markets, 1981–2009[a]

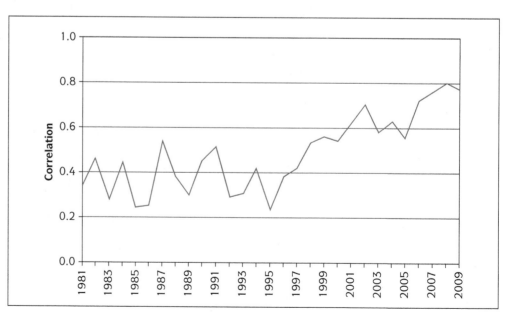

[a]The 10 markets are Australia, Canada, France, Germany, Hong Kong, Italy, Japan, the Netherlands, the United Kingdom and the United States. Weekly stock market index returns, in US dollars, are used to compute the correlations for each year of the study period.
Source: *Datastream.*

exposure. Hence, returns on large-cap stocks tend to be driven by "global factors," whereas returns on small-cap stocks are likely driven by "local factors." This implies that locally oriented small-cap stocks may be the more effective vehicle for international diversification. In a recent study, Eun, Huang and Lai (2008) confirm that this is the case.

Exhibit 11.13, based on the study, presents a summary of risk-return characteristics of large-cap versus small-cap funds of 10 major markets. For each fund, the exhibit presents the annualized mean return of the funds, the standard deviation of return, the Sharpe performance measure and the correlation with the S&P 500. From the last row of the exhibit, we see that small-cap funds on average outperform large-cap funds by 4.5 percent, that is, 21.1 versus 16.6 percent. This confirms the so-called "small-cap premium" observed in most countries with the exception of two, the Netherlands and the United States.

As expected, the standard deviation of returns for small-cap funds (25.3 percent) is on average higher than for large-cap funds (22.3 percent). However, the Sharpe performance measure indicates that small-cap funds outperform their large-cap counterparts on a risk-adjusted basis in every country except for the same two, the Netherlands and the United States. The extra attraction of the international diversification opportunity is that small-cap funds around the globe are less correlated with each other than is the case for large-cap funds. In contrast, large-cap funds tend to have relatively high correlations with each other, reflecting common exposure to global factors.

Small-cap funds are less correlated with the S&P 500 than their large-cap counterparts in each of the 10 countries examined. For instance, the correlation of the Canadian small-cap (large-cap) funds with the S&P 500 is 0.45 (0.71). Thus, small-cap stocks can be an effective vehicle for international diversification.

Against this backdrop, Canadian investment companies offer small-cap international diversification via small-cap international mutual funds, which allow Canadian investors to diversify into foreign small-cap funds with only modest transactions costs. The BMO Global Small Cap Equity Fund is a typical example.

EXHIBIT 11.13   Large- versus Small-Cap Funds: Risk-Return Characteristics

Countries	Large-Cap Funds				Small-Cap Funds			
	Mean	SD	SHP	Cor (US)	Mean	SD	SHP	Cor (US)
Australia	14.9%	25.7%	0.32	0.45	24.9%	33.1%	0.55	0.22
Canada	10.9%	17.9%	0.24	0.71	24.6%	22.5%	0.80	0.45
France	15.3%	21.9%	0.40	0.46	17.2%	21.9%	0.48	0.27
Germany	14.4%	20.1%	0.39	0.41	14.6%	16.5%	0.48	0.19
Hong Kong	22.1%	34.3%	0.45	0.38	27.6%	39.7%	0.53	0.26
Italy	20.0%	27.7%	0.48	0.26	23.2%	27.2%	0.61	0.21
Japan	15.6%	24.2%	0.37	0.22	23.1%	27.8%	0.59	0.13
Netherlands	18.4%	16.2%	0.73	0.61	16.3%	18.4%	0.52	0.20
UK	17.3%	19.1%	0.56	0.54	24.0%	23.7%	0.73	0.31
US	17.4%	15.1%	0.71	0.99	15.9%	21.7%	0.43	0.55
Average	16.6%	22.2%	0.46	0.50	21.1%	25.3%	0.57	0.28

Source: Cheol Eun, Victor Huang, and Sandy Lai, "International Diversification with Large- and Small-Cap Stocks," *Journal of Financial and Quantitative Analysis* 43 (2008), pp. 489–524. Copyright © School of Business Administration, University of Washington 2008. Reproduced with permission.

Going Abroad: The Attractions of Foreign Investment

In general, the attraction of adding foreign securities to a portfolio is in the opportunity for diversification. You find assets abroad that you cannot find at home. To what extent is the foreign selection greater than the domestic? Well, Canada represents 2.5 percent of total world market capitalization. So, 97.5 percent of available assets are in other countries.

Special difficulties and risks arise when dealing in foreign shares and bonds. For one thing, there is the legitimate fear of the unknown. The foundation of good investment decisions is information, and access to dependable and relevant information tends to fade with distance. Then there are the problems associated with dealing in foreign currencies and foreign taxes, as well as foreign rules and regulations. All of this may seem forbidding. The question, as always in investing, is whether the potential gain is worth the effort. It generally is.

Foreign securities substantially expand the number and variety of assets that can be introduced into a portfolio. Consider that there are approximately 4,000 shares listed on the TSE, MSE, and the Canadian Venture Exchange. In comparison, there are 29,000 shares listed on exchanges around the world. So, for every Canadian stock available to a Canadian investor, seven shares are available abroad. The opportunity set expands even further when we bring in foreign bonds.

A portfolio is designed and constructed in view of expected return and risk. The attraction of foreign securities is *not* so much a matter of pursuing higher expected returns, but, rather, it is to achieve fuller diversification. The less-than-perfect correlation of the returns on domestic assets and foreign assets is all that is required to expand the set of return/risk combinations. At every level of expected return, risk is reduced through diversification. This expansion of the "efficient" set allows a portfolio to be designed with higher expected return per unit of risk. The smaller the domestic–foreign correlation, the more attractive are foreign shares in a portfolio.

Returns on foreign shares are less than perfectly correlated with returns on domestic shares for various reasons. Above all, some foreign shares are fundamentally different from anything that is available at home. For instance, Italian shoe companies are uniquely Italian. Even when we consider a foreign share that has a Canadian counterpart, the two are likely to have different price processes that result in diversification opportunities. For example, German banks and Canadian banks have different price responses to similar interest rate changes, not to mention that German and Canadian interest rates are not in perfect sync. As a result, holding Canadian *and* German banks can reduce risk at each level of expected return.

Another potential source of diversification is the exchange rate. A foreign asset is denominated in foreign currency. Even if the asset value is unchanged in terms of its home currency, holding that asset will result in a gain or loss for the Canadian investor if the exchange rate changes relative to the Canadian dollar. If the foreign currency appreciates, the Canadian investor captures a foreign exchange gain; if the foreign currency weakens, the investor incurs a foreign exchange loss.

If all the shares in the world acted in synchrony, international diversification would be a fruitless exercise. If all securities are priced off the same "global index," a phenomenon which itself implies complete capital market integration, the effects of global diversification would then be built into all securities, foreign and domestic alike. An investor might as well stay at home. On the other hand, if capital markets around the world are not fully integrated, then differences among markets can be exploited through foreign investment.

The potential for fruitful, risk-reducing international diversification can be read directly from the correlations of, say, the TSE 300 and comparable indexes in other places, such as the S&P 500 in New York, FTSE in London, the CAC 40 in Paris, the Hang Seng in Hong Kong, and the All Ordinaries in Australia. A correlation coefficient of 1 indicates perfect correlation, and hence no diversification potential, whereas values less than 1 suggest that combining Canadian shares with that index or the shares within it would reduce risk. [See Table 11.1.]

TABLE 11.1	Correlation Coefficients: Canadian Index versus

Indexes in 11 Foreign Countries Monthly Data, 1995 to 2003

Country	Correlation Coefficient
United States	0.82
United Kingdom	0.73
France	0.66
Germany	0.65
Australia	0.61
Mexico	0.60
Hong Kong	0.57
Brazil	0.54
Singapore	0.53
Italy	0.45
Japan	0.37

A number of factors can make investing in foreign securities a bit more onerous than investing at home. High among these are informational problems, such as limited data on firms, differences in accounting and reporting practices, and the lack of performance benchmarks. In addition, some countries impose withholding taxes on interest and dividends paid to foreigners. Other countries, Canada among them, have tax-based impediments to foreign investments, such as the denial of RRSP eligibility beyond a certain limit of foreign investment.

Impediments to foreign investment seem bigger than they really are. For example, foreign transactions costs are not substantially greater than they are for domestic transactions. Taxes paid to foreign governments can usually be credited against the investor's tax at home. Information, especially for the major foreign companies or country indexes, is readily available. However, as discussed below, the foreign play can often be done very effectively through domestic vehicles, such as mutual funds—with professionals attending to information and analysis.

Many well-known foreign securities are readily available through brokers. Major Canadian brokers, including discount brokers, deal in all shares listed on North American exchanges. So, that provides direct access to the American shares and bonds. But what about destinations farther away, say, London, Paris or Tokyo? Again, brokers can make arrangements. With substantial volume in these major exchanges and virtually no restrictions on foreign participation, Canadian brokers are only a few computer key strokes away from placing a direct order.

In addition, shares of major companies from outside of North America are often available in the form of American Depository Receipts (ADRs). The ADR mechanism is simple and convenient. An offshore branch of an American bank purchases shares of a foreign company, say, Volvo in Sweden, and holds the shares in trust in its vault. American operations then issues a depository receipt, a Volvo ADR, which is traded in the United States and beyond. An ADR is a security issued by an American bank in place of the foreign shares that it holds in trust. ADRs represent ownership in a foreign company. The value of the ADR is determined by the value of the underlying shares—a value relationship that is ensured by the fact that an investor can always trade in the ADR for a true share and hence eliminate any price discrepancy through arbitrage. The conveniences that ADRs provide include their denomination in American dollars, dividend flow through, tax management, and the bank's role as the custodian of the shares.

When dealing with direct purchases, the brokers' primary concerns are to do with liquidity and restrictions on trading in foreign markets. These concerns become increasingly serious with respect to more remote and unexplored markets. While Singapore and Rio are now well into the mainstream of global finance, one ought to be more circumspect in the case of, say, Kiev or Accra. Ukrainian or Ghanaian shares are unlikely to be well researched. The markets are thin. Moreover, the currency risk is high. The Canadian investor will encounter substantial difficulty in direct purchases of securities in such remote markets.

In short, direct purchases are generally not the best route to foreign markets. For one thing, the Canadian investor is well advised to *diversify* foreign holdings. That can be especially challenging in terms of gathering information and executing transactions. Fortunately, most of the gain with little of the pain can be captured in other ways, such as through mutual funds with foreign content.

Mutual funds offer individual investors access to a variety of prefabricated portfolios with varying degrees and types of foreign content. For example:

Global funds invest in Canadian and non-Canadian shares.

International funds invest in non-Canadian shares only.

A *regional* fund invests in a specific geographic area, for example, Europe or Asia.

A *country* fund invests in a specific country, for example, the United States or Japan.

A *specialty* fund consists of shares in an industry group, such as telecommunications—with international diversification; for example, Nortel, Nokia, and France Telecom.

At the institutional level, the big players, such as insurance companies and pension funds, mimic foreign exposure—both its rewards and its risks—through derivatives. Through derivatives, the portfolio effects of foreign investment can be achieved through mimicry as opposed to direct purchase of foreign securities. Institutions often favour this approach, as it allows them to satisfy regulatory restrictions and yet have a significant foreign play with minimal capital commitment.

In summary, a world of opportunity beckons the wise investor. Adding foreign securities to the portfolio brings risk-reducing diversification along with a panorama of returns that are unavailable at home. The case for holding foreign securities is all the more compelling when one considers the full extent of most investors' undiversified exposure to the economic and financial idiosyncrasies of Canada. One's human capital and employment, house, tangible assets, pension, and bank account—the bulk of personal wealth—are all "domestic" assets. The investor's securities portfolio is virtually the only way to diversify within the broad portfolio of wealth.

Source: Excerpted fom D.J.S. Brean, "Going Abroad: The Attractions of Foreign Investment," in D.J.S. Brean and John Hull, eds., *International Financial Research, Advisor's Guide Series* (Toronto: RMPublishing, 2000).

11.9   WHY HOME BIAS IN PORTFOLIO HOLDINGS?

As previously documented, investors can potentially benefit a great deal from international diversification. The actual portfolios that investors hold, however, are quite different from those predicted by the theory of international portfolio investment. Various researchers including French and Poterba (1991), Cooper and Kaplanis (1994), Tesar and Werner (1993) and Glassman and Riddick (1993) documented the extent to which portfolio investments are concentrated in domestic equities.

Exhibit 11.14, adapted from S.T. Lau *et al.* (2010), shows the extent of **home bias in portfolio holdings** across a range of countries. Canadian investors, for instance, invested about 29 percent of their funds in domestic equities as of 2009 when the Canadian stock market accounted for 2.1 percent of total world market capitalization value. In other words, Canadian investors hold more than 70 percent of their portfolio in foreign equities. In contrast, U.S. investors invest 87 percent of their holdings at home, which accounts for only 45 percent of global opportunities. Japan exhibits severe home bias, with only 2.5 percent of the value of its investments placed abroad. Relatively speaking, French investors seem to invest more internationally—they put 45 percent of their funds in foreign equities, leaving 55 percent in domestic equities. Considering, however, that the French share in the world market is only 4.1 percent, French investors still display a striking degree of home bias in their portfolio holdings.

This home bias in actual portfolio holdings obviously runs counter to the strong case for international diversification. This points to the following possibilities. First, domestic securities may provide investors with certain extra services, such as hedging against domestic inflation, that foreign securities do not. Second, there may be barriers, formal or informal, to investing in foreign securities that keep investors from realizing gains from international diversification. In what follows, examine possible reasons for the home bias in portfolio holdings.

First, consider the possibility that investors face country-specific inflation risk due to the violations of purchasing power parity and that domestic equities may provide a hedging service against domestic inflation risk. In this case, investors who would like to hedge domestic inflation risk may allocate a disproportionate share of their investment funds to domestic equities, resulting in home bias. This, however, is not a likely scenario. Those investors who are averse to inflation risk are likely to invest in domestic risk-free bonds, rather than domestic equities, which tends to be a poor hedge against inflation. In addition, the study by Cooper and Kaplanis (1994) rules out inflation hedging as a primary cause for home bias.

Second, the observed home bias may reflect institutional and legal restrictions on foreign investments. For example, many countries used to restrict foreigners' ownership share of

EXHIBIT 11.14

The Home Bias in Equity Portfolios: Selected Countries, 1998–2007

Country	Share in the World Market Value (%)	Proportion of Local Equities in Domestic Mutual Funds (%)
Australia	1.70	78.91
Belgium	0.63	17.71
Canada	2.67	28.67
France	4.13	55.48
Germany	3.21	29.35
Japan	9.29	98.50
Sweden	1.00	48.36
United Kingdom	7.64	42.95
United States	44.86	86.88

Source: Adapted from S.T. Lau et al., "The World Price of Home Bias," *Journal of Financial Economics* 97(2) (August 2010), pp. 191–217.

domestic firms. In Finland, foreigners could own at most 30 percent of the shares outstanding of any Finnish firm. In Korea, foreigners' ownership proportion was restricted to 20 percent of any Korean firm. As a result, foreigners had to pay premiums for local shares, which might reduce the gains from investing in those restricted markets. At the same time, some institutional investors may not invest more than a certain fraction of their funds overseas under the so-called *prudent man rule*. For example, Japanese insurance companies and Spanish pension funds may invest at most 30 percent of their funds in foreign securities. These inflow and outflow restrictions may contribute to the home bias in actual portfolio holdings.

Third, extra taxes and transaction/information costs for foreign securities can inhibit cross-border investments, giving rise to home bias. Investors often have to pay withholding taxes on dividends from foreign securities for which they may or may not receive tax credits in their home country. Transaction costs can be higher for foreign securities, partly because many foreign markets are relatively thin and illiquid and partly because investment in foreign securities often involves transactions in foreign exchange markets. Moreover, investors tend not to hold securities which they are not familiar with. To the extent that investors feel familiar with domestic securities, but not with foreign securities, they are going to allocate funds to domestic, but not to foreign, securities. It is even possible that some investors may not be fully aware of the potential gains from international investments. The International Finance in Practice box, "Going Abroad: The Attractions of Foreign Investment" provides a practical guide for individual investors interested in the benefits of international investments.

The observed home bias in asset holdings is likely to reflect a combination of some of the factors mentioned above. Considering the ongoing integration of international financial markets, coupled with the active financial innovations introducing new financial products, such as country funds and international mutual funds, home bias may be substantially mitigated in the near future.

SUMMARY

This chapter discusses the gains from international portfolio diversification, which emerged as a major form of cross-border investment in the 1980s, rivalling foreign direct investment by firms.

1. International portfolio investment (IPI) has been growing rapidly in recent years due to the deregulation of financial markets, and the introduction of such investment vehicles as international mutual funds, country funds and internationally cross-listed shares which allow investors to achieve international diversification without incurring excessive costs.

2. Investors diversify to reduce risk; the extent to which the risk is reduced by diversification depends on the covariances among individual securities making up the portfolio. Since security returns tend to covary much less across countries than within a country, investors can reduce portfolio risk more by diversifying internationally than purely domestically.

3. In a full-fledged risk-return analysis, investors can gain from international diversification in terms of "extra" returns at the "domestic-equivalent" risk level. Empirical evidence indicates that regardless of domicile and the numeraire currency used to measure returns, investors can capture extra returns when they hold their optimal international portfolios.

4. Foreign exchange rate uncertainty contributes to the risk of foreign investment through its own volatility as well as through its covariance with local market returns.

Generally speaking, exchange rates are substantially more volatile than bond market returns but less so than stock market returns. This suggests that investors can enhance their gains from international diversification, especially in the case of bond investment, when they hedge exchange risk using, say, forward contracts.

5. International mutual funds that investors actually held did provide investors with an effective global risk diversification. In addition, the majority outperform the domestic stock market index in terms of the Sharpe performance measure. Closed-end country funds (CECFs) also provide investors with an opportunity to achieve international diversification at home. CECFs, however, were found to behave more like securities in comparison with their underlying net asset values (NAVs).

6. Despite sizable potential gains from international diversification, investors allocate a disproportionate share of their funds to domestic securities, displaying so-called home bias. Home bias is likely to reflect imperfections in the international financial markets, such as excessive transaction/information costs, discriminatory taxes for foreigners and legal/institutional barriers to international investments.

QUESTIONS

1. What factors are responsible for the recent surge in international portfolio investment?

2. Security returns are found to be less correlated across countries than within a country. Why might this be so?

3. Explain the concept of the world beta of a security.

4. Explain the concept of the Sharpe performance ratio.

5. Explain how exchange rate fluctuations affect the return from a foreign market, measured in dollar terms. Discuss the empirical evidence on the effect of exchange rate uncertainty on the risk of foreign investment.

6. Would exchange rate changes always increase the risk of foreign investment? Discuss the conditions under which exchange rate changes may actually reduce the risk of foreign investment.

7. Evaluate a home country's multinational corporations as a tool for international diversification.

8. Discuss the advantages and disadvantages of closed-end country funds (CECFs) relative to American depository receipts (ADRs) as a means of international diversification.

9. Why do you think closed-end country funds often trade at a premium or discount?

10. Why do investors invest the lion's share of their funds in domestic securities?

11. What are the advantages of investing via international mutual funds?

12. Discuss how the advent of the euro might have affected international diversification strategies.

PROBLEMS

1. Suppose you are a euro-based investor who just sold the Microsoft shares that you had bought six months ago. You had invested 10,000 euros to buy Microsoft shares at $120 per share; the exchange rate was $1.50 per euro. You sold the shares at $135 per share and converted the dollar proceeds into euros at the exchange rate of $1.60 per euro. First, determine the profit from this investment in euro terms. Second, compute the rate of return on your investment in euro terms. How much of the return is due to the exchange rate movement?

2. Mr. James K. Silber, an avid international investor, just sold a share of Nestlé, a Swiss firm, for SF5,080. The share was purchased for SF4,600 a year ago. The exchange rate is SF1.60 per dollar now and was SF1.78 per dollar a year ago. Mr. Silber received SF120 as a cash dividend immediately before the share was sold. Compute the rate of return on this investment in terms of dollars.

3. In problem 2, suppose that Mr. Silber sold SF4,600, his principal investment amount, forward at the forward exchange rate of SF1.62 per dollar. How would this affect the dollar rate of return on this Swiss stock investment? In hindsight, should Mr. Silber have sold the Swiss franc amount forward or not? Why, or why not?

4. Japan Life Insurance Company invested $10,000,000 in pure-discount bonds when the exchange rate was 100 yen per dollar. The company liquidated the investment one year later for $10,650,000. The exchange rate turned out to be 120 yen per dollar at the time of liquidation. What rate of return did Japan Life realize on this investment in yen terms?

5. At the start of 2007, the annual interest rate was 6 percent in the United States and 2.8 percent in Japan. The exchange rate was 95 yen per dollar at the time. Mr. Jorus, manager of a Bermuda-based hedge fund, thought that the substantial interest advantage associated with investing in the dollar assets relative to investing in Japan was not likely to be offset by the decline of the dollar against the yen. He thus concluded that it might be a good idea to borrow in Japan and invest in US bonds. At the start of 2007, in fact, he borrowed ¥1,000 million for one year and invested in US bonds. At the end of 2007, the exchange rate became 105 yen per dollar. How much profit did Mr. Jorus make in dollar terms?

6. Consider the following data in dollar terms:

Stock Market	Return (Mean)	Risk (SD)
Canada	1.26% per month	4.43%
United Kingdom	1.23% per month	5.55%

The correlation coefficient between the two markets is 0.58. Suppose that you invest equally, that is, 50 percent in each of the two markets. Determine the expected return and standard deviation risk of the resulting international portfolio.[7] This problem can be solved using the spreadsheet MPTSolver.xls.

7. Suppose you are interested in investing in the stock markets of seven countries—Canada, France, Germany, Japan, Switzerland, the United Kingdom and the United States. Specifically, you would like to solve for the optimal (tangency) portfolio comprising the above seven stock markets. In solving the optimal portfolio, use the input data (i.e., correlation coefficients, means and standard deviations) provided in Exhibit 11.4. The risk-free interest rate is 5 percent. You can take a short position in any stock market. What are the optimal weights for each of the seven stock markets? This problem can be solved using the MPTSolver.xls spreadsheet.

8. **CFA® PROBLEMS** The ERB Trustees have solicited input from three consultants concerning the risks and rewards of an allocation to international equities. Two of them strongly favour such action, while the third consultant commented as follows:

"The risk reduction benefits of international investing have been significantly overstated. Recent studies relating to the cross-country correlation structure of equity returns during different market phases cast serious doubt on the ability of international investing to reduce risk, especially in situations when risk reduction is needed the most."

a. Describe the behaviour of cross-country equity return correlations which the consultant is referring to. Explain how that behaviour may diminish the ability of international investing to reduce risk in the short run.

Assume the consultant's assertion is correct.

b. Explain why it might still be more efficient on a risk/reward basis to invest internationally, rather than only domestically, in the long run.

The ERB Trustees have decided to invest in foreign equity markets and have hired Jacob Hind, a specialist manager, to implement this decision. He has recommended that an unhedged equities position be taken in Japan, providing the following comment and the table data to support his views:

"Appreciation of a foreign currency increases the returns to a Canadian investor. Since appreciation of the yen from 100¥/$ to 98¥/$ is expected, the Japanese stock position should not be hedged."

Market Rates and Hind's Expectations

	Canada	Japan
Spot rate (yen per $)	n.a.	100
Hind's 12-month currency forecast (yen per $)	n.a.	98
1-year Eurocurrency rate (% per annum)	6.00	0.80
Hind's 1-year inflation forecast (% per annum)	3.00	0.50

Assume that the investment horizon is one year and that there are no costs associated with currency hedging.

c. State and justify whether Hind's recommendation (not to hedge) should be followed. Show any calculations.

9. **CFA® PROBLEMS** Rebecca Taylor, an international equity portfolio manager, recognizes that an optimal country allocation strategy combined with an optimal currency strategy should produce optimal portfolio performance. To develop her strategies, Taylor produced the table below, which provides expected return data for the three countries and three currencies that she may invest in. The table contains the information she needs to make market strategy (country allocation) decisions and currency strategy (currency allocation) decisions.

Expected Returns for a Canadian-Based Investor

Country	Local Currency Equity Returns	Exchange Rate Returns	Local Currency Eurodeposit Returns
Japan	7.0%	1.0%	5.0%
United Kingdom	10.5	−3.0	11.0
Canada	8.4	0.0	7.5

a. Prepare a ranking of the three countries in terms of expected equity-market return premiums. Show your calculations.

b. Prepare a ranking of the three countries in terms of expected currency return premiums from the perspective of a Canadian investor. Show your calculations.

---

[7]The mean return on the portfolio is simply the weighted average of the returns on the individual securities that are included in the portfolio. The portfolio variance, on the other hand, can be computed using the following formula:

$$\text{Var}(R_p) = \Sigma_i \Sigma_j x_i x_j \sigma_{ij}$$

where x_i represents an investment weight for the ith security, and σ_{ij} denotes the variances and covariances among individual securities. In the case where the portfolio comprises two securities, its variance is computed as follows:

$$\text{Var}(R_p) = x_1^2 \sigma_1^2 + x_2^2 \sigma_2^2 + 2x_1 x_2 \sigma_{12}$$

The standard deviation, of course, is the square root of the variance. It is also noted that the covariance σ_{ij} is related to the correlation coefficient ρ_{ij} via $\sigma_{ij} = \rho_{ij} \sigma_i \sigma_j$, where σ_i is the standard deviation of returns on the ith security.

c. Explain *one* advantage a portfolio manager obtains, in formulating a global investment strategy, by calculating both expected market premiums and expected currency premiums.

10. The Socrates Aid Foundation is a philanthropic society based in Athens that provides scholarships to Greek students. The foundation has just received a gift of a €20 million portfolio of government bonds denominated in five different currencies, the euro and four others that we will call A, B, C and D.

    The recording currency of the bond portfolio is the euro. Although the portfolio is currently unhedged, the portfolio manager, Patricia Piraeus, is investigating various alternatives to hedge the currency risk to which the portfolio is exposed. The bond portfolio's current allocation and the respective country performance data are given in Exhibits 1 and 2. Historical correlations for the currencies are given in Exhibit 3. Piraeus expects that future returns and correlations will be approximately equal to those given in Exhibits 2 and 3.

    a. Calculate the expected total annual return (euro-based) of the current bond portfolio if Piraeus decides to leave the currency risk unhedged. Show your calculations.

    b. Explain, with respect to currency exposure and forward rates, the circumstances under which Piraeus should use a currency forward contract to hedge the current bond portfolio's exposure to a given currency.

    c. Determine which *one* of the currencies being considered by Piraeus should be the *best* proxy hedge for Country B bonds. Justify your response with *two* reasons.

    Piraeus has been disappointed with the low returns on the current bond portfolio relative to the benchmark— a diversified global bond index—and is exploring general strategies to generate excess returns on the portfolio. She has already considered investing in markets outside the benchmark index.

    d. Identify *two* strategies (other than investing in markets outside the benchmark index) that Piraeus could use to generate excess returns on the current bond portfolio. For each strategy, indicate a potential benefit specific to the current bond portfolio.

EXHIBIT 1			

Socrates Aid Foundation Current Allocation Global Government Bond Portfolio

Country	Allocation (%)	Maturity (years)
Greece	25	5
A	40	5
B	10	10
C	10	5
D	15	10

EXHIBIT 2

Country Performance Data (in local currency)

Country	Cash Return (%)	5-Year Excess Bond Return (%)	10-Year Excess Bond Return (%)	Unhedged Currency Return (%)	Liquidity of 90-Day Currency Forward Contracts
Greece	2.0	1.5	2.0	—	Good
A	1.0	2.0	3.0	−4.0	Good
B	4.0	0.5	1.0	2.0	Fair
C	3.0	1.0	2.0	−2.0	Fair
D	2.6	1.4	2.4	−3.0	Good

	EXHIBIT 3

Historical Currency Correlation Table (2000–2007, weekly observations)

Currency	€ (Greece)	A	B	C	D
€ (Greece)	1.00	−0.77	0.45	−0.57	0.77
A	—	1.00	−0.61	0.56	−0.70
B	—	—	1.00	−0.79	0.88
C	—	—	—	1.00	−0.59
D	—	—	—	—	1.00

INTERNET EXERCISE

1. You would like to invest in the Mexican stock market and consider two alternative ways of investing in Mexico: (i) the Mexican closed-end country fund trading on the New York Stock Exchange and (ii) the WEBS for Mexico trading on the American Stock Exchange. Their websites are

   www.themexicofund.com

   http://us.ishares.com/product_info/fund/overview/EWW.htm

   Study all the relevant information from the websites and evaluate the relative merits and demerits of the two securities for your Mexican investment. Which one would you prefer?

2. You would like to evaluate the performance of the seven major stock markets of the world—Canada, France, Germany, Japan, the Netherlands, the United Kingdom and the United States—for the last five years. In doing so, you want to use the Sharpe ratio, providing a risk-adjusted performance measure. Compute this Sharpe performance measure for each of the seven markets using the data from the following website: www.msci.com. Briefly discuss your findings.

MINI CASE

Solving for the Optimal International Portfolio

Suppose you are a financial advisor, and your client, who is currently investing only in the Canadian stock market, is considering diversifying into the British stock market. At the moment, there are neither particular barriers nor restrictions on investing in the British stock market. Your client would like to know what kind of benefits can be expected from doing so. Using the data provided in problem 6, solve the following problems:

1. Graphically illustrate various combinations of portfolio risk and return that can be generated by investing in the Canadian and British stock markets with different proportions. Two extreme proportions are (a) investing 100 percent in Canada with no position in the British market and (b) investing 100 percent in the British market with no position in the Canadian market.

2. Solve for the optimal international portfolio comprising the Canadian and British markets. Assume that the risk-free interest rate is 0.5 percent per month. Investors can take a short (negative) position in either market. This problem can be solved using the spreadsheet MPTSolver.xls.

3. What is the extra return that Canadian investors can expect to capture at the Canadian-equivalent risk level? Also trace out the efficient set. Appendix 11.B provides an example.

REFERENCES & SUGGESTED READINGS

Adler, Michael, and Bernard Dumas. "International Portfolio Choice and Corporation Finance: A Synthesis." *Journal of Finance* 38 (1983), pp. 925–84.

Bailey, Warren, and J. Lim. "Evaluating the Diversification Benefits of the New Country Funds." *Journal of Portfolio Management* 18 (1992), pp. 74–80.

Bonser-Neal, Catherine, G. Brauer, and S. Wheatley. "International Investment Restrictions and Closed-End Country Fund Prices." *The Journal of Finance*. Volume 45, Issue 2 (June 1990), pp. 523–47.

Cooper, Ian, and Evi Kaplanis. "Home Bias in Equity Portfolios, Inflation Hedging, and International Capital Market Equilibrium." *Review of Financial Studies* 7 (1994), pp. 45–60.

Cumby, R., and J. Glen. "Evaluating the Performance of International Mutual Funds." *Journal of Finance* 45 (1990), pp. 497–521.

Errunza, Vihang, Ked Hogan, and Mao-Wei Hung. "Can the Gains from International Diversification Be Achieved without Trading Abroad?" *Journal of Finance* (1999), pp. 2075–107.

Eun, Cheol, and Bruce Resnick. "Exchange Rate Uncertainty, Forward Contracts and International Portfolio Selection." *Journal of Finance* 43 (1988), pp. 197–215.

Eun, Cheol, Victor Huang, and Sandy Lai, "International Diversification with Large- and Small-Cap Stocks," *Journal of Financial and Quantitative Analysis* 45 (2008), pp. 489–524.

Eun, Cheol, and Bruce Resnick. "International Diversification of Investment Portfolios: U.S. and Japanese Perspectives." *Management Science* 40 (1994), pp. 140–61.

Eun, Cheol, and Bruce Resnick. "International Equity Investments with Selective Hedging Strategies." *Journal of International Financial Markets, Institutions and Money* 7 (1997), pp. 21–42.

Eun, Cheol, Richard Kolodny, and Bruce Resnick. "Performance of U.S.-Based International Mutual Funds." *Journal of Portfolio Management* 17 (1991), pp. 88–94.

French, K., and J. Poterba. "Investor Diversification and International Equity Markets." *American Economic Review* 81 (1991), pp. 222–26.

Glassman, Debra, and Leigh Riddick. "Why Empirical Portfolio Models Fail: Evidence That Model Misspecification Creates Home Asset Bias." Unpublished manuscript, 1993.

Grubel, H. G. "Internationally Diversified Portfolios." *American Economic Review* 58 (1968), pp. 1299–1314.

Jorion, Philippe. "Asset Allocation with Hedged and Unhedged Foreign Stocks and Bonds." *Journal of Portfolio Management* 15 (Summer 1989), pp. 49–54.

Khorana, A., E. Nelling, and J. Trester. "The Emergence of Country Index Funds." *Journal of Portfolio Management* (Summer 1998), pp. 78–84.

Larsen, Glen, Jr., and Bruce Resnick. "Universal Currency Hedging for International Equity Portfolios under Parameter Uncertainty." *International Journal of Business* 4 (1999), pp. 1–17.

Larsen, Glen, Jr., and Bruce Resnick. "The Optimal Construction of Internationally Diversified Equity Portfolios Hedged against Exchange Rate Uncertainty." *European Financial Management* 6 (2000), pp. 479–514.

Longin, Francois, and Bruneo Solnik. "Is the Correlation in International Equity Returns Constant?: 1960–1990." *Journal of International Money and Finance* 14 (1995), pp. 3–26.

Officer, Dennis, and Ronald Hoffmeister. "ADRs: A Substitute for the Real Thing?" *Journal of Portfolio Management* (Winter 1987), pp. 61–65.

Roll, Richard. "The International Crash of 1987." *Financial Analyst Journal* 44 (1988), pp. 19–35.

Sener, T. "Objectives of Hedging and Optimal Hedge Ratios: U.S. vs. Japanese Investors." *Journal of Multinational Financial Management* 8 (1998), pp. 137–53.

Tesar, L., and I. Werner. "Home Bias and High Turnover." Unpublished manuscript, 1993.

Uppal, Raman. "The Economic Determinants of the Home Country Bias in Investors' Portfolios: A Survey." *Journal of International Financial Management and Accounting* 4 (1992), pp. 171–89.

Wahab, Mahmood, and Amit Khandwala. "Why Not Diversify Internationally with ADRs?" *Journal of Portfolio Management* (Winter 1993), pp. 75–82.

Appendix 11A

International Investment with Exchange Risk Hedging

In this appendix, we show how hedging the exchange rate risk in an international portfolio can enhance the risk-return efficiency of an internationally diversified portfolio of financial assets. We begin with return and variance of returns from the point of view of a Canadian dollar investor investing in individual foreign security i:

$$R_{i\$} = (1 + R_i)(1 + e_i) - 1 \tag{11A.1a}$$
$$= R_i + e_i + R_i e_i \tag{11A.1b}$$
$$\approx R_i - e_i \tag{11A.1c}$$

In Equation 11A.1c, we ignore the cross-product term, $R_i e_i$, which is generally small, for discussion purposes. Consequently, the expected return to the Canadian dollar investor from investing in foreign security i can be approximated as

$$\bar{R}_{i\$} \approx \bar{R}_i + \bar{e}_i \tag{11A.2}$$

Also, we can express the variance of dollar returns from the ith foreign security as follows:

$$\text{Var}(R_{i\$}) = \text{Var}(R_i) + \text{Var}(e_i) + 2\text{Cov}(R_i,e_i) \tag{11A.3}$$

Similarly, we can state the covariance between dollar returns from two different foreign securities as follows:

$$\text{Cov}(R_{i\$},R_{j\$}) = \text{Cov}(R_i,R_j) + \text{Cov}(e_i,e_j) + \text{Cov}(R_i,e_j) + \text{Cov}(R_j,e_i) \tag{11A.4}$$

Now, consider a simple exchange risk hedging strategy in which the Canadian dollar investor sells the expected foreign currency proceeds forward. In dollar terms, it amounts to exchanging the "uncertain" dollar return, $(1 + \bar{R}_i)(1 + e_i) - 1$, for the "certain" dollar return, $(1 + \bar{R}_i)(1 + f_i) - 1$, where $f_i = (F_i - S_i)/S_i$ is the forward exchange premium of the currency denominating security i. Although the expected foreign investment proceeds will be converted into Canadian dollars at the known forward exchange rate under this strategy, the unexpected foreign investment proceeds will have to be converted into Canadian dollars at the uncertain future spot exchange rate. The dollar rate of return under the hedging (H) strategy is thus given by

$$R_{i\$H} = [1 + \bar{R}_i](1 + f_i) + [R_i - \bar{R}_i](1 + e_i) - 1 \tag{11A.5a}$$
$$= R_i + f_i + R_i e_i + \bar{R}_i(f_i - e_i) \tag{11A.5b}$$

Since the third and fourth terms of Equation 11A.5b are likely to be small in magnitude, the expected hedged return for the Canadian dollar investor can be approximated as follows:

$$\bar{R}_{i\$H} \approx \bar{R}_i + f_i \tag{11A.6}$$

Recall from the forward expectations parity discussion in Chapter 5 that f_i can be an unbiased estimate of $\bar{e}_i$, that is, $f_i \approx \bar{e}_i$. Comparison of Equations 11A.1c and 11A.6 thus indicates that the expected return to the Canadian dollar investor is approximately the same, whether the investor hedges the exchange rate risk in the investment or remains unhedged.

To the extent that the investor establishes an effective hedge to eliminate exchange rate uncertainty, the $\text{Var}(e_i)$ and $\text{Cov}(R_i, e_i)$ terms in Equation 11A.3 will be close to zero. Similarly, the $\text{Cov}(e_i, e_j)$, $\text{Cov}(R_i, e_j)$ and $\text{Cov}(R_j, e_i)$ terms in Equation 11A.4 will be close to zero. Consequently, given that f_i is a constant, it follows that

$$\text{Var}(R_{i\$H}) < \text{Var}(R_{i\$}), \text{ and}$$
$$\text{Cov}(R_{i\$H}, R_{j\$H}) < \text{Cov}(R_{i\$}, R_{j\$})$$

It thus follows that the risk-return efficiency is likely to be superior if the investor hedges the exchange rate risk when investing internationally.

Appendix 11B

Solving for the Optimal Portfolio

In this appendix we explain how to solve for the optimal weights in a portfolio of two risky securities plus a risk-free asset, R_f. Since investors prefer more wealth to less and are averse to risk, the "optimal" portfolio is found by maximizing the Sharpe ratio (SR_p) of the excess portfolio return to the standard deviation. That is,

$$\text{maxSHP}_p = \max\{[R_p - R_f]/\sigma_p\} \tag{11B.1}$$

where R_p is the expected rate of return on the portfolio and σ_p is the standard deviation of the portfolio returns. The expected portfolio return, R_p, is just the weighted average of the expected returns to individual assets, R_i, included in the portfolio, that is,

$$R_p = \Sigma x_i R_i \tag{11B.2}$$

where x_i denotes the fraction of the value of the portfolio invested in the ith individual asset. This fraction is referred to as the "weight" on asset i. The sum of the weights must be equal to one, that is, $\Sigma_i x_i = 1$.

The portfolio risk, σ_p, is determined by the variances and covariances of individual asset returns as follows:

$$\sigma_p = [\Sigma_i \Sigma_j x_i x_j \sigma_{ij}]^{1/2} \tag{11B.3}$$

where σ_{ij} denotes the covariance of returns to the ith and jth assets. The term inside the brackets is the variance of portfolio return.

Now, let's consider a simple case where the portfolio includes only two risky assets, A and B. In this case, the risk and return of the portfolio are determined as follows:

$$R_p = x_A R_A + x_B R_B \tag{11B.4}$$

$$\sigma_p = [x_A^2 \sigma_A^2 + x_B^2 \sigma_B^2 + 2x_A x_B \sigma_{AB}]^{1/2} \tag{11B.5}$$

To solve for the optimal portfolio of two assets, first substitute Equations 11B.4 and 11B.5 into Equation 11B.1 and then maximize the Sharpe ratio with respect to the portfolio weights (the x-values). The solution takes the following form:

$$x_A = \frac{[R_A - R_f]\sigma_B^2 - [R_B - R_f]\sigma_{AB}}{[R_A - R_f]\sigma_B^2 + [R_B - R_f]\sigma_A^2 - [R_A - R_f + R_B - R_f]\sigma_{AB}}$$

$$x_B = 1 - x_A \tag{11B.6}$$

Example B.1

Suppose you want to construct an international portfolio that combines the Canadian S&P TSX and the MSCI-World index. The MSCI-World index is converted to Canadian dollar returns. Data drawn from annual returns averaged over the past five years along with the respective variances of those returns (based on weekly data) describe the two indexes. We will use this historical data as the basis for our estimates of the forward-looking expected returns and their variances required to solve the problem.

$$R_C = 20 \qquad \sigma_C^2 = 30$$
$$R_W = 18 \qquad \sigma_W^2 = 26$$

The correlation coefficient of the S&P TSX and the MSCI-World returns is

$$\rho_{CW} = 0.60$$

The covariance of the Canadian dollar returns to the S&P TSX and the MSCI-World is

$$\sigma_{CW} = \sigma_C \sigma_W \rho_{CW} = (5.48)(5.10)(0.60) = 16.76$$

Using the risk-free rate of 5 percent, we can substitute the given data into Equation 11B.6 to obtain the optimal portfolio weights:

$$x_C = 0.554$$
$$x_W = 1 - x_C = 1 - 0.554 = 0.446$$

For a Canadian investor, the optimal international portfolio consists of 55.4 percent of the portfolio value invested in the Canadian market and 44.6 percent in the MSCI-world market.

The expected return and risk of the optimal portfolio can be computed as follows:

$$R_{OP} = (0.554)(20) + (0.446)(18) = 19.11 \text{ percent}$$
$$\sigma_{OP} = [(0.554)^2(30) + (0.446)^2(26) + 2(0.554)(0.446)(16.76)]^{1/2}$$
$$= 4.76$$

The Sharpe ratio of the optimal international portfolio is $(19.11 - 5)/4.76 = 2.96$. This compares to $(20 - 5)/5.48 = 2.74$ for the exclusively Canadian (S&P TSX) index.

One can thus compute the extra return from holding the optimal international portfolio at the Canadian domestic-equivalent risk level as follows:

$$\Delta R_C = (\Delta SR) \times (\sigma_C) = (2.96 - 2.74) \times 5.48 = 1.22 \text{ percent per year}$$

To capture the enhanced gains from international diversification while maintaining the risk of the original all-Canadian portfolio ($\sigma_C = 5.48$), the investor would construct a "levered" portfolio. The investor would borrow (at 5 percent) and invest the funds in the S&P TSX and the MSCI-World in the optimal proportions (55.4 and 44.6, respectively). The question is, how much should he borrow?

The risk of the S&P TSX is 5.48 with an expected return of 20 percent. At that level of risk, the enhancement to return through international diversification is 1.22 percent. To determine the borrowing required to construct an internationally diversified portfolio with an expected return of (20 + 1.22) percent, we solve for Φ in the following expression:

$$21.22 = (\Phi \times 5) + [(1 - \Phi) \times 19.11]$$
$$\Phi = -0.0.1495 \approx -0.15$$

By borrowing 15 percent of the value of the portfolio, the investor has an expected return of

$$E[R] = (-0.15 \times 5) + (1.15 \times 19.11) = 21.11$$

The following diagram illustrates the solution.

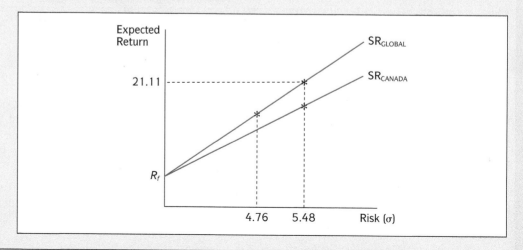

Part 3

Foreign Exchange Exposure and Management

Part Three is composed of three chapters covering the topics of economic, transaction and translation exposure management, respectively.

12 Management of Economic Exposure

Chapter 12 covers economic exposure—that is, the extent to which the value of the firm will be affected by unexpected changes in exchange rates. The chapter provides a way to measure economic exposure, discusses its determinants and presents methods for managing and hedging economic exposure.

13 Management of Transaction Exposure

Chapter 13 covers the management of transaction exposure that arises from contractual obligations denominated in a foreign currency. Several methods for hedging this exposure are compared and contrasted. The chapter also includes a discussion of why an MNC should hedge, a debatable subject in the minds of both academics and practitioners.

14 Management of Translation Exposure

Chapter 14 covers translation exposure or, as it is sometimes called, accounting exposure. Translation exposure refers to the effect that changes in exchange rates will have on the consolidated financial reports of an MNC. The chapter discusses, compares and contrasts the various methods for translating financial statements denominated in foreign currencies and includes a discussion of managing translation exposure using funds adjustment and the pros and cons of using balance sheet and derivatives hedges.

Chapter 12

Management of Economic Exposure

CHAPTER OUTLINE

IN JANUARY 2003, the Canadian dollar exchange rate, that is, the number of Canadian dollars required to buy one US dollar in the spot market, was $1.575. By the end of the year 2003, the Canadian dollar had soared—or the US dollar had plummeted—to $1.300. Throughout the year the Canadian dollar appreciated more than 23 percent against the US dollar. That sharp change in the external value of the Canadian dollar, which was largely unexpected, had serious consequences for many Canadian firms. Some firms, such as those involved in exporting manufactured goods—for instance, automobiles or furniture—experienced a significant drop in their volume and profit on export sales. Other Canadian companies, especially those that import intermediate goods, enjoyed a windfall as their costs of production fell in Canadian dollar terms. Still other Canadian-based companies with foreign-source earnings saw the value of those earnings fall in line with the fall in the value of the US dollar. Toronto-based Four Seasons Hotels, for instance, reported a first-half 2003 net loss of $11 million compared with earnings of $26 million for the comparable period in 2002. The decline in Four Seasons' net earnings was attributed primarily to a foreign exchange loss which, according to the firm, "arose as a result of unprecedented movements in the US and Canadian dollars, British pound, and euro."

While 2003 saw a dramatic rise in the Canadian dollar, appreciation against the US dollar continued in each of the subsequent three years as well. Smaller changes in the "external value" of the Canadian dollar occurred in 2006/07.

	$/US$	US$/$		$/US$	US$/$
January 2003	1.58	0.64	January 2008	1.01	0.99
January 2004	1.30	0.77	January 2009	1.22	0.82
January 2005	1.22	0.82	January 2010	1.04	0.96
January 2006	1.16	0.86	January 2011	0.99	1.01
January 2007	1.17	0.85	January 2012	1.01	0.99

The years 2008–2012 suggest a different Canadian exchange rate environment. Compared to 2003–2007, the more recent time frame—at least based on the January observations—seems to be much less volatile. Well, yes and no. The once-a-year January observations mask extraordinary day-to-day Canadian exchange rate volatility in the period following the global financial crisis. We discussed this in Chapter 5. In the 2001–2007 period, despite the large currency swings, the average daily percentage change in the CDN:USD exchange rate was 1 percent. More recently, however, in the post-financial crisis era (2008 to 2013), the average daily percentage change in the CDN:USD exchange rate was twice as large, 2 percent. That calls for a significant adjustment to the focus of foreign exchange risk management.

In this chapter we explore the implications for financial management of changes in exchange rates in terms of both the wider swings over time, say, years, and the unsettling frothiness of shorter-term volatility.

12.1 EXCHANGE RATE EXPOSURE ILLUSTRATED

Changes in exchange rates affect not only operating cash flows but also the dollar (home currency) values of assets and liabilities. A well-known example from Nova Scotia involves the finance of a bridge between Halifax and Dartmouth. In 1970, the Bridge Commission arranged loans from German and Swiss bankers to build the second of two bridges across the harbour. The loans—in fact, bonds denominated in German marks and Swiss francs—seemed attractive because of the low foreign interest rates. The Bridge Commission saved on interest expense and kept the tolls low. However, the subsequent and protracted drop in the value of the Canadian dollar against the German mark and the Swiss franc wiped out the interest cost advantage and added massively to the annual debt servicing costs. At its peak, the Bridge Commission's debt amounted to $125,000,000, nearly triple the total cost of construction for both harbour bridges.

Another classic illustration of the peril of facing currency exposure comes from Laker Airways, a British firm founded by Sir Freddie Laker, who pioneered the concept of mass-marketed, no-frills, low-fare air travel. Laker borrowed heavily in US dollars to finance acquisitions of aircraft. Meanwhile, the airline derived more than half its revenue in British pounds. As the US dollar appreciated against the British pound (and most other currencies) throughout the first half of the 1980s, the burden of servicing the dollar debts became overwhelming for Laker Airways, forcing it to default.

Effects on profits and corporate value that stem from changes in exchange rates, which are almost always unexpected, create "exchange rate risk." The unexpected nature of the exchange rate changes is crucial in the sense that an *expected* change would be built into the projections of profit and the value of, say, a firm's shares. We might ask, how do we know that the sharp appreciation of the Canadian dollar in 2003 was *unexpected*? The evidence is in the forward exchange rates that reveal traders' and financial institutions' views of what the exchange rate will be over ensuing months. In January 2003, for example, the 180-day forward rate was $1.59. If we consider this forward rate in January to be an informed forecast of what the exchange rate would be in June 2003, the forecast can then be compared with the actual exchange rate in June 2003. It turned out to be $1.37. The forward markets for foreign exchange were certainly not accurately forecasting the Canadian dollar appreciation of 2003.

The preceding examples suggest that exchange rate changes can systematically affect the value of the firm through impacts on operating cash flows as well as the domestic currency values of its assets and liabilities. In a study examining the exposure of firms to currency risk, Jorion (1990) documented that a significant relationship exists between stock returns and the dollar's value. Studies such as those by Choi and Prasad (1995), Simkins and Laux (1996), and Allayannis and Ofek (2001), also document that stock returns are sensitive to exchange rate movements.

Exhibit 12.1, drawn from the Simkins and Laux study, provides estimates of market betas as well as the "forex" betas for a number of industries. The market and forex betas measure the sensitivities of an industry portfolio against the stock market index and the dollar exchange rate index, respectively. As Exhibit 12.1 shows, the forex beta varies greatly across industry lines; it ranges from −1.272 for pharmaceuticals to 1.831 for textiles. A negative (positive) forex beta means that stock returns tend to move down (up) as the dollar appreciates. Out of the 25 industries studied, 10 were found to have significant exposure to exchange rate movements.

A closer look at a couple of cases from Exhibit 12.1 ought to make this form of analysis clear. Keep in mind that the study was done for US-based industries. They focus on the implications of appreciation or depreciation of the US dollar on each of 25 specific industries. Look first at number 10, "furniture," with an estimated forex beta of 1.217. That number suggests that a 1 percent appreciation of the US dollar induces a 1.217 percent

EXHIBIT 12.1

Exchange Rate Exposure of Industry Portfolios[a]

Industry	Market Beta[b]	Forex Beta[c]
1. Aerospace	0.999	0.034
2. Apparel	1.264	0.051
3. Beverage	1.145	−0.437
4. Building materials	1.107	0.604
5. Chemicals	1.074	−0.009
6. Computers, office equipment	0.928	0.248
7. Electronics, electrical equipment	1.202	0.608*
8. Food	1.080	−0.430
9. Forest and paper products	1.117	0.445
10. Furniture	0.901	1.217*
11. Industrial and farm equipment	1.125	0.473
12. Metal products	1.081	−0.440
13. Metals	1.164	0.743*
14. Mining and crude oil	0.310	−0.713
15. Motor vehicles and parts	0.919	1.168*
16. Petroleum refining	0.515	−0.746*
17. Pharmaceuticals	1.124	−1.272*
18. Publishing and printing	1.154	0.567
19. Rubber and plastics	1.357	0.524
20. Science, photo and control equipment	0.975	−0.437*
21. Cosmetics	1.051	0.417
22. Textiles	1.279	1.831*
23. Tobacco	0.898	−0.768*
24. Toys, sporting goods	1.572	−0.660
25. Transportation equipment	**1.613**	**1.524***

[a]The market and forex (foreign exchange) betas are obtained from regressing the industry portfolio (monthly) returns, constructed from the Fortune 500 companies, on the American stock market index returns and the rate of change in the dollar exchange rate index over the sample period 1.1989–12.93.

[b]For every industry portfolio the market beta is statistically significant at the 1 percent level.

[c]The forex beta is significant for some industry portfolios and insignificant for others. Those forex betas that are significant at 10 percent or higher are denoted by (*).

Source: Betty Simkins and Paul Laux, "Derivatives Use and the Exchange Rate Risk of Investing in Large U.S. Corporations," Case Western Reserve University working paper (1996).

increase in returns to the average firm in the US-based furniture industry. By way of explanation, one might surmise that when the US dollar appreciates, imported inputs to the US-based furniture industry, say, wood from Canada or fabrics from Asia, become cheaper for the US-furniture producers. Since most US-produced furniture is sold in the United States, the US-furniture producers' profits and share values rise accordingly.

Now look at number 17, "pharmaceuticals" with a forex beta of −1.272. That forex beta suggests that a 1 percent appreciation of the US dollar induces a 1.272 percent *decrease* in returns to the average firm in the US-based pharmaceutical industry. For the US pharmaceutical industry, exports are a major part of their market and their profit base. The negative relation between the value of the US dollar currency and returns in the pharmaceutical industry could be explained as follows. When the US dollar appreciates against other countries' currencies, US-originating drugs become more expensive in the export market. As a result, export sales decline and profits and values of US pharmaceutical firms fall accordingly.

Empirical indicators of how the returns to the average firm in a specific industry are affected by changes in the exchange rate are a useful first step in understanding economic exposure. A study similar to the one summarized in Exhibit 12.1 looks at exchange rate effects on four major Canadian industries—metal mining, paper and forest products, department stores and transportation.[1] The significant findings, expressed as forex betas, are:

Metal mining	−0.97
Paper and forest products	−0.62
Department stores	0.92
Transportation	1.30

Consider the result for mining. The coefficient of −0.97 indicates that a 1 percent appreciation of the Canadian dollar is associated with approximately a 1 percent decrease in the returns to the average Canadian-based mining company, averaged across such firms as Inco, Falconbridge or Teck Cominco. The logic seems straightforward. The Canadian metal mining industry is export-oriented. An increase in the value of the Canadian dollar raises the cost of Canadian metals to foreigners, in particular if the Canadian metal exports are priced in Canadian dollars. This reduces the competitiveness of Canadian-sourced metals on world markets insofar as other countries—such as Australia, Russia, Mexico or Chile—produce similar products. If Canadian metal exports are priced in a foreign currency, say in US dollars, then a higher Canadian dollar reduces the Canadian dollar unit-value of metal exports. Either way, with Canadian dollar appreciation, Canadian metal producers face an uncomfortable choice: lose international market share or accept a lower Canadian dollar price of Canadian-sourced metals exports. Such factors underlie the negative forex beta for the Canadian metal mining industry.

Of course for some Canadian industries, a stronger Canadian dollar is a value-increasing influence. The Canadian transportation industry is a case in point. The estimated coefficient of 1.30 suggests that a 1 percent increase in the value of the Canadian dollar against other currencies is associated with a 1.3 percent increase in returns to firms in the Canadian transportation industry, such as CN, Air Canada and Canada Steamship Lines. Although the positive coefficient summarizes a large number of influences that stem from Canadian dollar appreciation, one could speculate that the key point is that a stronger Canadian dollar is a direct reflection of a stronger, growing Canadian economy. As the wheels of Canadian industry spin faster, more business and more profit are created for firms in the transportation sector.

[1]Bodnar, Gordon M., "Exchange Rate Exposure and Market Value," *Mastering Risk: The Complete Financial Companion* (London: Pitman Publishing for *The Financial Times*, 1998).

12.2   THREE TYPES OF EXPOSURE

Before we turn to the important issue of how to measure and manage economic exposure, let us briefly discuss different types of exposure. It is conventional to classify foreign currency exposures into three types:

- Economic exposure
- Transaction exposure
- Translation exposure

www.stern.nyu.edu

Provides an overview
of exchange risk
management issues.

Economic exposure is defined as the extent to which the value of the firm is affected by unanticipated changes in exchange rates. Anticipated changes in exchange rates would already be discounted and reflected in the firm's value. Unanticipated changes in exchange rates can have a profound effect on the firm's competitive position and thus on its cash flows and market value.

Transaction exposure, a subject to be discussed in Chapter 13, is defined as the sensitivity of "realized" domestic currency values of the firm's contractual cash flows *denominated* in foreign currencies to unexpected exchange rate changes. Since settlements of these contractual cash flows affect the firm's domestic currency cash flows, transaction exposure is sometimes regarded as a short-term exposure. Transaction exposure arises from fixed-price contracting in a world where exchange rates change randomly.

On the other hand, **translation exposure**, which will be discussed in Chapter 14, refers to the potential that the firm's consolidated financial statements can be affected by changes in exchange rates. Consolidation involves translation of subsidiaries' financial statements from local currencies to the home currency. Consider a Canadian multinational firm that has subsidiaries in the United Kingdom and Japan. Each subsidiary will produce financial statements in local currency. To consolidate financial statements worldwide, the firm must translate the subsidiaries' financial statements in local currencies into the Canadian dollar, the home currency. As we will see later, translation involves many controversial issues. Resultant translation gains and losses represent the accounting system's attempt to measure economic exposure *ex post*. It does not provide a good measure of *ex ante* economic exposure.

In the remainder of this chapter, we focus on how to measure and manage economic exposure.

12.3   HOW TO MEASURE ECONOMIC EXPOSURE

Currency risk refers to random changes in exchange rates. It is not the same as currency exposure, which measures "what is at risk." Under certain conditions, a firm may not face any exposure at all, that is, nothing is at risk even if exchange rates change randomly. Suppose your Canadian company maintains a vacation home for employees in the British countryside and the local price of this property always moves together with the pound price of the Canadian dollar. As a result, whenever the pound depreciates against the dollar, the local currency price of this property goes up by the same proportion. In this case, your company is not exposed to currency risk even if the pound/dollar exchange rate fluctuates randomly. The British asset your company owns has an embedded hedge against exchange risk, rendering the dollar price of the asset *insensitive* to exchange rate changes.

Consider an alternative situation in which the local (pound) price of your company's British asset barely changes. In this case, the dollar value of the asset will be highly *sensitive* to the exchange rate, since the former will change as the latter does. To the extent that the dollar price of the British asset exhibits "sensitivity" to exchange rate movements, your company is exposed to currency risk. Similarly, if your company's operating cash flows are sensitive to exchange rate changes, the company is again exposed to currency risk.

Exposure to currency risk, thus, can be properly measured by the *sensitivities* of (1) the future home currency values of the firm's assets (and liabilities) and (2) the firm's operating cash flows to random changes in exchange rates. The same point is illustrated by Exhibit 12.2;

EXHIBIT 12.2

Channels of
Economic Exposure

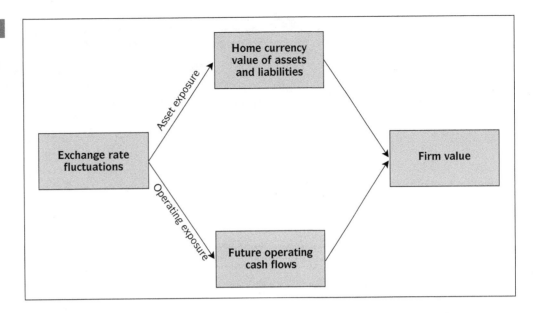

assets include the tangible assets (property, plant and equipment, inventory) as well as financial assets. Let us first discuss the case of asset exposure. For expositional convenience, assume that dollar inflation is nonrandom. Then, from the perspective of the Canadian firm that owns an asset in Britain, the exposure can be measured by the coefficient (b) in regressing the dollar value (P) of the British asset on the dollar/pound exchange rate (S):

$$P = a + bS + e \qquad (12.1)$$

where a is the regression constant and e is the random error term with an expected value of zero. $P = SP^*$, where P^* is the local currency (pound) price of the asset. The regression coefficient b measures the sensitivity of the dollar value of the asset (P) to the exchange rate (S). If the regression coefficient is zero, that is, $b = 0$, the dollar value of the asset is independent of exchange rate movements, implying no exposure. One can say that *exposure is the regression coefficient*. Statistically, the **exposure coefficient,** b, is defined as follows:

$$b = \frac{\text{Cov}(P, S)}{\text{Var}(S)}$$

where $\text{Cov}(P,S)$ is the covariance between the dollar value of the asset and the exchange rate, and $\text{Var}(S)$ is the variance of the exchange rate.

Next, we show how to apply the exposure measurement technique using numerical examples. Suppose that a Canadian firm has an asset in Britain whose local currency price is random. For simplicity, let us assume that there are three possible states of the world, with each state equally likely to occur. The future local currency price of this British asset as well as the future exchange rate will be determined by the realized state of the world. First, consider Case 1, described in Panel A of Exhibit 12.3. Case 1 indicates that the local currency price of the asset (P^*) and the dollar price of the pound (S) are positively correlated so that depreciation (appreciation) of the pound against the dollar is associated with a declining (rising) local currency price of the asset. The dollar price of the asset on the future (liquidation) date can be $2,156, $2,300 or $2,568, depending on the realized state of the world.

When we compute the parameter values for Case 1, we obtain $\text{Cov}(P,S) = 13.73$, $\text{Var}(S) = 0.02/3$, and thus $b = £2,060$. This pound amount, £2,060, represents the sensitivity of the future dollar value of the British asset to random changes in exchange rate. This finding implies that the Canadian firm faces exposure to currency risk. Note that the magnitude of

EXHIBIT 12.3

Measurement of
Currency Exposure

State	Probability	P^*	S	$P\,(= SP^*)$	Parameters
A. Case 1					
1	1/3	£980	$2.20	$2,156	Cov(P,S) = 13.73
2	1/3	£1,000	$2.30	$2,300	Var(S) = 0.02/3
3	1/3	£1,070	$2.40	$2,568	**b = £2,060**
Mean			$2.30	$2,341	
B. Case 2					
1	1/3	£1,000	$2.20	$2,200	Cov(P,S) = 0
2	1/3	£957	$2.30	$2,200	Var(S) = 0.02/3
3	1/3	£917	$2.40	$2,200	**b = 0**
Mean			$2.30	$2,200	
C. Case 3					
1	1/3	£1,000	$2.20	$2,200	Cov(P,S) = 6.67
2	1/3	£1,000	$2.30	$2,300	Var(S) = 0.02/3
3	1/3	£1,000	$2.40	$2,400	**b = £1,000**
Mean			$2.30	$2,300	

the exposure is expressed in British pounds. For illustration, the computations of the parameter values for Case 1 are shown in Exhibit 12.4.

Next, consider Case 2. This case indicates that the local currency value of the asset is clearly negatively correlated with the Canadian dollar price of the British pound. In fact, the effect of exchange rate changes is exactly offset by movements of the local currency price of the asset, rendering the dollar price of the asset totally insensitive to exchange rate changes. The future dollar price of the asset will be uniformly $2,200 across the three states of the world. One, thus, can say that the British asset is effectively

EXHIBIT 12.4

Computations of
Regression
Parameters: Case 1

1. *Computation of Means*

$$\bar{P} = \sum_i q_i P_i = (0.333)(2{,}156 + 2{,}300 + 2{,}568) = 2{,}341$$

$$\bar{S} = \sum_i q_i S_i = (2.20 + 2.30 + 2.40) = 2.30$$

2. *Computation of Variance and Covariance*

$$Var(S) = \sum_i q_i (S_i - \bar{S})^2$$

$$= (0.333)[(2.20 - 2.30)^2 + (2.30 - 2.30)^2 + (2.40 - 2.30)^2]$$

$$= 0.02/3$$

$$Cov(P,S) = \sum_i q_i (P_i - \bar{P})(S_i - \bar{S})$$

$$= (0.333)[(2{,}156 - 2{,}341)(2.20 - 2.30) + (2{,}300 - 2{,}341)(2.30 - 2.30)$$

$$+ (2{,}568 - 2{,}341)(2.40 - 2.30)]$$

$$= 13.73$$

3. *Computation of the Exposure Coefficient*

$$b = Cov(P,S)/Var(S) = 13.73/(0.02/3) = 2{,}060$$

Note: q_i denotes the probability for the ith state.

denominated in terms of the dollar. Although this case is clearly unrealistic, it shows that uncertain exchange rates or exchange risk do not necessarily constitute exchange exposure. Despite the fact that the future exchange rate is uncertain, the Canadian firm has nothing at risk in this case. Since the firm faces no exposure, no hedging is necessary.

We now turn to Case 3, where the local currency price of the asset is fixed at £1,000. In this case, the Canadian firm faces a "contractual" cash flow that is *denominated* in pounds. This case, in fact, represents an example of the special case of economic exposure, transaction exposure. Intuitively, what is at risk is £1,000, that is, the exposure coefficient, *b*, is £1,000. Readers can confirm this by going through the same kind of computation as shown in Exhibit 12.4. Measurement of transaction exposure is, thus, very simple. The exposure coefficient, *b*, is the same as the magnitude of the contractual cash flow fixed in terms of foreign currency.

Once the magnitude of exposure is known, the firm can hedge the exposure simply by selling the exposure forward. In Case 3, where the asset value is fixed in terms of local currency, it is possible to completely eliminate the variability of the future dollar price of the asset by selling £1,000 forward. In Case 1, however, where the local currency price of the asset is random, selling £2,060 forward will not completely eliminate the variability of the future dollar price; there will be a residual variability that is independent of exchange rate changes.

On the basis of regression Equation 12.1, we can decompose the variability of the dollar value of the asset, Var(P), into two separate components: exchange-rate-related and residual. Specifically,

$$\text{Var}(P) = b^2\text{Var}(S) + \text{Var}(e) \tag{12.2}$$

The first term on the right-hand side of the equation, $b^2\text{Var}(S)$, represents the part of the variability of the dollar value of the asset that is related to random changes in the exchange rate, whereas the second term, Var(e), captures the residual part of the dollar value variability that is independent of exchange rate movements.

The consequences of hedging the exposure by forward contracts are illustrated in Exhibit 12.5. Consider Case 1, where the firm faces an exposure coefficient (*b*) of £2,060. If the firm sells £2,060 forward, the dollar proceeds that the firm will receive are given by

$$\$2,060(F - S)$$

where *F* is the forward exchange rate and *S* is the spot rate realized on the maturity date.

EXHIBIT 12.5

Consequences of Hedging Currency Exposure

Future Amounts	State 1	State 2	State 3	Variance
Case 1 (b = £2,060)				
Local currency asset price (P*)	£980	£1,000	£1,070	
Exchange rate (S), $/£	2.20	2.30	2.40	
Dollar value (P = SP*)	$2,156	$2,300	$2,568	29,154
Proceeds from forward contract	$206	0	−$206	
Dollar value of hedged position (HP)	$2,362	$2,300	$2,362	854
Case 3 (b = £1,000)				
Local currency asset price (P*)	£1,000	£1,000	£1,000	
Exchange rate (S), $/£	2.20	2.30	2.40	
Dollar value (P = SP*)	$2,200	$2,300	$2,400	6,667
Proceeds from forward contract	$100	0	−$100	
Dollar value of hedged position (HP)	$2,300	$2,300	$2,300	0

Note: In both cases, the forward exchange rate (F) is assumed to be $2.30/£. Proceeds from the forward contract are computed as $b(F − S). Recall that each of the three states is equally likely to happen, that is, $q_i = 1/3$ for each state.

INTERNATIONAL FINANCE *in Practice*

Firms Feel the Pain of Peso's Plunge

Foreign-exchange traders and investors aren't the only Americans feeling the pain of the two-week plunge in the value of the Mexican peso.

For U.S. companies that are paid in pesos or that own substantial assets in Mexico, the recent 37% decline in the currency's value is a vivid example of just how quickly and substantially changes in the value of foreign currency can affect sales and profits.

And for the hundreds of companies that see Mexico as a ticket for expansion, the peso's fall is another reminder that foreign markets aren't anything like those at home. The Mexican financial crisis forces U.S. companies to "pay attention to the direction of the economy in any country they invest in," says Serge Ratmiroff, senior manager, international services, at Deloitte & Touche in Chicago.

The impact of the peso's fall on those that do business in the Mexican currency is striking. A U.S. company that sold widgets for 345 pesos early last month received about $100. Now, 345 pesos is valued at between $60 and $65. Meanwhile, as the value of the peso declines, prices of U.S. exports will rise, making them less affordable for Mexican buyers.

Ford Motor Co., for instance, said the peso's problems could dent its growth in exports to Mexico next year. Ford sent 27,000 to 28,000 vehicles to Mexico in 1994, up from a few hundred in 1992. It had hoped those sales would double over time with the aid of the North American Free Trade Agreement. But the auto maker's chairman and chief executive officer, Alexander Trotman, noted Tuesday that the cost of Ford autos "in peso terms has gone up enormously." Ford continues to build more than 200,000 vehicles a year in Mexico, but its Mexican output excludes such hot-sellers as the Mustang sports coupe, which is imported from the U.S. While wages should fall at its Mexican plants, at least in dollar terms, a spokesman said the company wouldn't see much gain from that because most of the parts used to assemble cars in Mexico actually are made in the U.S.

Other companies are feeling the impact immediately. Toy maker Mattel Inc. said yesterday that it will take an eight-cent-a-share charge for the fourth quarter because the peso's decline has reduced the value of its Mexican inventory and receivables. The charge means that despite a 35% jump in world-wide sales,

Mattel's record earnings for the year will be on the "conservative" side of analysts' estimates.

Metalclad Corp., a Newport Beach, Calif., company with waste-oil recycling and landfill operations in Mexico, said the peso's plunge may wipe out its hopes for a profitable fiscal third quarter, ending Feb. 28. And Pilgrim's Pride, a Pittsburg, Texas, chicken producer, expects to take a substantial write-down for its first quarter ended Dec. 31, as it marks down its $120 million in assets in Mexico. A spokesman for Goodyear Tire & Rubber Co. in Akron, Ohio, said the company has "seen tire business fall off in Mexico because dealers don't want to sell the product at less than what they bought it for."

For many big U.S. companies, however, the swings are just another day in the currency markets. Mexico is a relatively small international market, though it accounts for about 9% of U.S. exports. Many companies say they do business in dollars or have otherwise hedged against currency changes, and won't feel any immediate financial impact. Further, those who manufacture there should see lower labor costs while some businesses, like trucking and hotels, contend they will benefit from increasing U.S. imports and tourism.

Still, some firms are putting expansion plans on hold and even large companies expect exports to Mexico to fall off this year as Mexican buyers adjust to the higher prices of U.S. goods. After all, that's part of Mexico's goal in letting the peso's value fall in relation to the dollar. "The whole purpose of what they're doing is to try to reduce the level of imports and increase Mexican exports," says Sidney Weintraub of the Center for Strategic and International Studies, a Washington think tank.

A drop in product sales to Mexico would be felt particularly in Texas, which exported about $20.38 billion in goods to its southern neighbor in 1993—nearly half the U.S. exports to Mexico. The state comptroller's office is predicting that exports will grow another 5% to 7% this year, but rise just 3% a year in 1996 and beyond, in part, because currency changes will curtail demand.

Source: Reprinted with permission of *The Wall Street Journal*, January 5, 1995, p. A2. © 1995 Dow Jones & Company, Inc. All rights reserved worldwide.

For each pound sold forward, the firm receives a dollar amount equal to $(F - S)$. In Exhibit 12.5, the forward exchange rate is assumed to be $2.30, which is the same as the expected future spot rate. Thus, if the future spot rate turns out to be $2.20 under state 1, the dollar proceeds from the forward contract will be $206 = 2,060 × ($2.30 − $2.20). Since the dollar value (P) of the asset is $2,156 under state 1, the dollar value of the hedged position (HP) is $2,362 (= $2,156 + $206) under state 1.

As shown in the top part of Exhibit 12.5, the variance of the dollar value of the hedged position is only 854($)^2, whereas that of the unhedged position is 29,154($)^2. This result implies that much of the uncertainty regarding the future dollar value of the asset is associated with exchange rate uncertainty. As a result, once the exchange exposure is hedged, most of the variability of the dollar value of the asset is eliminated. The residual variability of the dollar value of the asset that is independent of exchange rate changes, Var(e), is equal to 854($)^2.

Let us now turn to Case 3 where the local currency price of the asset is fixed. In this case, complete hedging is possible in the specific sense that there will be no residual variability. As shown in the second part of Exhibit 12.5, the future dollar value of the asset, which is totally dependent upon the exchange rate, has a variance of 6,667($)^2. Once the firm hedges the exposure by selling £1,000 forward, the dollar value of the hedged position (HP) becomes nonrandom and is $2,300 across the three states of the world. Since the asset now has a constant dollar value, it is effectively *redenominated* in terms of the Canadian dollar.

12.4 OPERATING EXPOSURE: DEFINITION

While many managers understand the effects of exchange rate changes on the dollar value of their firms' assets and liabilities denominated in foreign currencies, they often do not fully understand the effect of exchange rates on operating cash flows. As the economy becomes increasingly globalized, more firms are subject to international competition. Fluctuating exchange rates can seriously alter the relative competitive positions of such firms in domestic and foreign markets, affecting their operating cash flows.

Unlike the exposure of assets and liabilities (such as accounts payable and receivable, loans denominated in foreign currencies, and so forth) that are listed in accounting statements, the exposure of operating cash flows depends on the effect of exchange rate changes on the firm's competitive position, which is not readily measurable. This difficulty notwithstanding, it is important for the firm to properly manage **operating exposure** as well as **asset exposure**. In many cases, operating exposure may account for a larger portion of the firm's total exposure than contractual exposure. Formally, operating exposure can be defined as the *extent to which the firm's operating cash flows would be affected by changes in exchange rates.*

12.5 ILLUSTRATION OF OPERATING EXPOSURE

Before we discuss what determines operating exposure and how to manage it, it is useful to illustrate the exposure using a simple example. Suppose that a Canadian computer company, Newleaf Technologies of Kanata, Ontario, operates a wholly owned French subsidiary, Calais Computers, that assembles and sells Newleaf computers throughout Europe. Calais Computers imports microprocessors from Intel, at a cost of $512 per unit. At the current exchange rate of $1.60 per euro, each Intel microprocessor costs €320. Calais Computers hires French workers and sources all the other inputs locally. Calais faces a 50 percent income tax rate in the France.

Exhibit 12.6 summarizes projected operations for Calais Computers, assuming that the exchange rate remains unchanged at $1.60 per euro. The company expects to sell 50,000 units of personal computers per year at a selling price of €1,000 per unit. The unit variable cost is €650, which comprises €320 for the imported input and €330 for the locally sourced inputs. Needless to say, the euro price of the imported input will change as the exchange rate changes, which, in turn, can affect the selling price in the European market. Every year, Calais incurs fixed overhead costs of €4 million for rents, property taxes, and the like, regardless of output level. As the exhibit shows, the projected operating cash flow is €7,250,000 per year, which is equivalent to $11,600,000 at the current exchange rate of $1.60 per euro.

EXHIBIT 12.6

Projected
Operations for
Calais Computers
PLC: Benchmark
Case ($1.60/€)

Sales (50,000 units at €1,000/unit)	€50,000,000
Variable costs (50,000 units at €650/unit)ᵃ	32,500,000
Fixed overhead costs	4,000,000
Depreciation allowances	1,000,000
Net profit before tax	€12,500,000
Income tax (at 50%)	6,250,000
Profit after tax	6,250,000
Add back depreciation	1,000,000
Operating cash flow in euros	€ 7,250,000
Operating cash flow in dollars	$11,600,000

ᵃThe unit variable cost, €650, comprises €330 for the locally sourced inputs and €320 for the imported input, which is priced in Canadian dollars, that is, $512. At the exchange rate of $1.60/€ the imported part costs €320.

Now, consider the possible effect of a depreciation of the euro on the projected Canadian dollar operating cash flow of Calais Computers. Assume that the euro depreciates from $1.60 to $1.40 per euro. The dollar operating cash flow changes following a euro depreciation for a couple of reasons:

1. The **competitive effect**: A euro depreciation may affect operating cash flow in euros by altering the firm's competitive position in the marketplace.
2. The **conversion effect**: A given operating cash flow in euros will be converted into a lower dollar amount after the euro depreciation.

To get a feel for how the Canadian dollar operating cash flow may change as the exchange rate changes, consider the following cases with varying degrees of realism:

Case 1:   No variables change, except the price of the imported input.

Case 2:   The selling price as well as the price of the imported input changes, with no other changes.

Case 3:   All the variables change.

In Case 1, illustrated in Exhibit 12.7, the unit variable cost of the imported input rises to €366 (= $512/$1.40) following the euro depreciation, with no other changes. Following the euro depreciation, the total variable costs become €34.8 million, lowering the firm's before-tax profit from €12.5 million (for the benchmark case) to €10.2 million. Considering that the firm faces a 50 percent income tax rate, depreciation of the euro will lower the net operating cash flow from €7.25 million (for the benchmark case) to €6.1 million. In terms of Canadian dollars, Calais's projected net operating cash flow changes from $11.6 million to $8.54 million as the exchange rate changes from $1.60 per euro to $1.40 per euro. Calais may be forced not to raise the euro selling price because it faces a European competitor

EXHIBIT 12.7

Projected
Operations for
Calais Computers
PLC: Case 1
($1.40/€)

Sales (50,000 units at €1,000/unit)	€50,000,000
Variable costs (50,000 units at €696/unit)	34,800,000
Fixed overhead costs	4,000,000
Depreciation allowances	1,000,000
Net profit before tax	€10,200,000
Income tax (at 50%)	5,100,000
Profit after tax	5,100,000
Add back depreciation	1,000,000
Operating cash flow in euros	€ 6,100,000
Operating cash flow in dollars	$ 8,540,000

EXHIBIT 12.8

Projected
Operations for
Calais Computers
PLC: Case 2
($1.40/€)

Sales (50,000 units at €1,143/unit)	€57,150,000
Variable costs (50,000 units at €696/unit)	34,800,000
Fixed overhead costs	4,000,000
Depreciation allowances	1,000,000
Net profit before tax	€17,350,000
Income tax (at 50%)	8,675,000
Profit after tax	8,675,000
Add back depreciation	1,000,000
Operating cash flow in euros	€ 9,675,000
Operating cash flow in dollars	$13,545,000

that manufactures similar products using only locally sourced inputs. An increase in selling price can potentially lead to a decline in unit sales volume. Under this kind of competitive environment, Calais's costs are responsive to exchange rate changes but the selling price is not. This asymmetry makes the firm's operating cash flow sensitive to exchange rate changes, giving rise to operating exposure.

In Case 2, which is analyzed in Exhibit 12.8, the selling price as well as the price of the imported input increases following the euro depreciation. In this case, Calais Computers does not face any serious competition in the European market and faces a highly inelastic demand for its products. Thus, Calais can raise the selling price to €1,143 (to keep the dollar selling price at $1,600 after the euro depreciation) and still maintain the sales volume at 50,000 units. Computations presented in Exhibit 12.8 indicate that the projected operating cash flow actually increases to €9,675,000, which is equivalent to $13,545,000. Compared with the benchmark case, the Canadian dollar operating cash flow is higher when the euro depreciates. This case shows that a euro depreciation need not always lead to a lower dollar operating cash flow.

We now turn to Case 3 where the selling price, sales volume and the prices of both locally sourced and imported inputs change following the euro depreciation. In particular, we assume that both the selling price and the price of locally sourced inputs increase at the rate of 8 percent, reflecting the underlying inflation rate in Europe. As a result, the selling price will be €1,080 per unit and the unit variable cost of locally sourced inputs will be €356. Since the price of the imported input is €366, the combined unit variable cost will be €722. Facing an **elastic demand** for its products, sales volume declines to 40,000 units per year after the price increase. As Exhibit 12.9 shows, Calais's projected operating cash flow is €5.66 million, which is equivalent to $7.924 million. The projected dollar cash flow under Case 3 is lower than that of the benchmark case by $3.676 million.

EXHIBIT 12.9

Projected
Operations for
Calais Computers
PLC: Case 3
($1.40/€)

Sales (40,000 units at €1,080/unit)	€43,200,000
Variable costs (40,000 units at €722/unit)	28,880,000
Fixed overhead costs	4,000,000
Depreciation allowances	1,000,000
Net profit before tax	€ 9,320,000
Income tax (at 50%)	4,660,000
Profit after tax	4,660,000
Add back depreciation	1,000,000
Operating cash flow in euros	€ 5,660,000
Operating cash flow in dollars	$ 7,924,000

EXHIBIT 12.10	Summary of Operating Exposure Effect of Euro Depreciation on Calais Computers			
Variables	Benchmark Case	Case 1	Case 2	Case 3
Exchange rate ($/€)	1.60	1.40	1.40	1.40
Unit variable cost (€)	650	696	696	722
Unit sales price (€)	1,000	1,000	1,143	1,080
Sales volume (units)	50,000	50,000	50,000	40,000
Annual cash flow (€)	7,250,000	6,100,000	9,675,000	5,660,000
Annual cash flow ($)	11,600,000	8,540,000	13,545,000	7,924,000
Four-year present value ($)[a]	33,118,000	24,382,000	38,671,000	22,623,000
Operating gains/losses ($)[b]		−8,736,000	5,553,000	−10,495,000

[a]The discounted present value of dollar cash flows was computed over a four-year period using a 15 percent discount rate. A constant cash flow is assumed for each of four years.

[b]Operating gains or losses represent the present value of change in cash flows, which is due to euro depreciation, from the benchmark case.

Exhibit 12.10 summarizes the projected operating exposure effect of the euro deprecia-tion on Calais Computers. For expositional purposes, it is assumed here that a change in exchange rate will have effects on the firm's operating cash flow for four years. The exhibit provides, among other things, the four-year present values of operating cash flows for each of the three cases as well as for the benchmark case. The proper discount rate for Calais's cash flow is assumed to be 15 percent. The exhibit also shows the operating gains or losses computed as the present value of changes in operating cash flows (over a four-year period) from the benchmark case that are due to the exchange rate change. In Case 3, for instance, the firm expects to experience an operating loss of $10,495,000 due to the euro depreciation.

12.6 DETERMINANTS OF OPERATING EXPOSURE

Unlike contractual (i.e., transaction) exposure, which can readily be determined from the firm's accounting statements, operating exposure cannot be determined in the same man-ner. A firm's operating exposure is determined by (1) the structure of the markets in which the firm sources its inputs, such as labour and materials, and sells its products, and (2) the firm's ability to mitigate the effect of exchange rate changes by adjusting its markets, prod-uct mix and sourcing.

To highlight the importance of market structure in determining operating exposure, con-sider a hypothetical company, Ford Mexicana, a subsidiary of Ford, which imports cars from its US parent and distributes them in Mexico. If the US dollar appreciates against the Mexican peso, Ford Mexicana's costs go up in peso terms. Whether this creates operating exposure for Ford critically depends on the structure of the car market in Mexico. For example, if Ford Mexicana faces competition from Mexican car makers whose peso costs did not rise, it will not be able to raise the peso price of imported Ford cars without risking a major reduction in sales. Facing a highly elastic demand for its products, Ford Mexicana cannot let an **exchange rate pass-through** happen with regard to the peso price. As a result, an appreciation of the dollar will squeeze the profit of Ford Mexicana, subjecting the parent firm to a high degree of operating exposure.

In contrast, consider the case in which Ford Mexicana faces import competition only from other car makers like General Motors and Chrysler, rather than from local producers. Since peso costs of those other imported cars will be affected by a dollar appreciation in the same manner, the competitive position of Ford Mexicana will not be adversely affected. Under this market structure, the dollar appreciation is likely to be reflected in higher peso prices of imported cars pretty quickly. As a result, Ford will be able to better maintain its dollar profit, without being subject to a major operating exposure.

Generally speaking, a firm is subject to high degrees of operating exposure when *either* its cost *or* its price is sensitive to exchange rate changes. On the other hand, when *both* the cost *and* the price are sensitive or insensitive to exchange rate changes, the firm has no major operating exposure.

Given the market structure, however, the extent to which a firm is subject to operating exposure depends on the firm's ability to stabilize cash flows in the face of exchange rate changes. Even if Ford faces competition from local car makers in Mexico, for example, it can reduce exposure by starting to source Mexican parts and materials, which would be cheaper in dollar terms after the dollar appreciation. Ford can even start to produce cars in Mexico by hiring local workers and sourcing local inputs, thereby making peso costs relatively insensitive to changes in the dollar/peso exchange rate. In other words, the firm's flexibility regarding production locations, sourcing and financial hedging strategy is an important determinant of its operating exposure to exchange risk.

Before we discuss how to hedge operating exposure, it is important to recognize that changes in nominal exchange rates may not always affect the firm's competitive position. This is the case when a change in exchange rate is exactly offset by the inflation differential. To show this point, let us again use the example of Ford Mexicana competing against local car makers. Suppose that the annual inflation rate is 4 percent in the United States and 15 percent in Mexico. For simplicity, we assume that car prices appreciate at the same pace as the general domestic inflation rate in both the United States and Mexico. Now, suppose that the dollar appreciates about 11 percent against the peso, offsetting the inflation rate differential between the two countries. This, of course, implies that purchasing power parity is holding.

Under this situation, the peso price of Ford cars appreciates by about 15 percent, which reflects a 4 percent increase in the dollar price of cars and an 11 percent appreciation of the dollar against the peso. Since the peso prices of both Ford and locally produced cars rise by the same 15 percent, the 11 percent appreciation of the dollar will not affect the competitive position of Ford relative to local car makers. Ford, thus, does not have operating exposure.

If, however, the dollar appreciates by more than 11 percent against the peso, Ford cars will become relatively more expensive than locally produced cars, adversely affecting Ford's competitive position. Ford is, thus, exposed to exchange risk. Since purchasing power parity does not hold very well, especially in the short run, exchange rate changes are likely to affect the competitive positions of firms that are sourcing from different locations but selling in the same markets.

Facing exchange rate changes, a firm may choose one of the following three pricing strategies: (1) pass the cost shock fully to its selling prices (complete pass-through), (2) fully absorb the shock to keep its selling prices unaltered (no pass-through) or (3) adopt some combination of the two strategies described above (partial pass-through). Import prices generally do not fully reflect exchange rate changes, exemplifying a partial pass-through.

Yang (1997) investigated exchange rate pass-through in U.S. manufacturing industries during the sample period 1980–1991. Yang found that the pricing behaviour of foreign exporting firms is consistent with partial pass-through.

Exhibit 12.11, from the Yang study, presents pass-through coefficients for different industries; the coefficient would be 1 for complete pass-through and 0 for no pass-through. As can be seen from the exhibit, the pass-through coefficient ranges from 0.0812 for SIC 24 (lumber and wood products) to 0.8843 for SIC 32 (stone, glass, and concrete products). The average coefficient is 0.4205, implying that when the dollar appreciates or depreciates by 1 percent, import prices of foreign products change on average by about 0.42 percent. It is noteworthy that partial pass-through is common but varies a great deal across industries.

EXHIBIT 12.11

Exchange Rate
Pass-Through
Coefficients for US
Manufacturing
Industries

Industry Code (SIC)	Industry	Pass-Through Coefficient
20	Food and kindred products	0.2485
22	Textile mill products	0.3124
23	Apparels	0.1068
24	Lumber and wood products	0.0812
25	Furniture and fixtures	0.3576
28	Chemicals and allied products	0.5312
30	Rubber and plastic products	0.5318
31	Leather products	0.3144
32	Stone, glass, concrete products	0.8843
33	Primary metal industries	0.2123
34	Fabricated metal products	0.3138
35	Machinery, except electrical	0.7559
36	Electrical and electronic machinery	0.3914
37	Transportation equipment	0.3583
38	Measurement instruments	0.7256
39	Miscellaneous manufacturing	0.2765
Average		0.4205

Source: Jiawen Yang, "Exchange Rate Pass-Through in U.S. Manufacturing Industries," *Review of Economics and Statistics* 79 (1997), pp. 95–104.

Import prices are affected relatively little by exchange rate changes in industries with low product differentiation and, thus, high demand elasticities. In contrast, in industries with a high degree of product differentiation and, thus, low demand elasticities, import prices tend to change more following an exchange rate change.

Pass-Through Canadian Evidence

The Canadian evidence on exchange rate pass-through indicates that, on average, pass-through is approximately 25 percent. That is to say, when the Canadian dollar appreciates by 10 percent, import prices in Canadian dollar terms on average tend to fall by about 2.5 percent rather than by a full 10 percent.[2] This average pass-through seems remarkably low. Only 25 percent of a reduction on the cost of imports is passed on to Canadian consumers. If purchasing power parity were to hold, of course, a 10 percent appreciation of the Canadian dollar would imply a 10 percent reduction in the Canadian dollar cost of imports.[3]

---

[2]Stanley W. Kardasz and K. R. Stollery. "Exchange Rate Pass-Through and Its Determinants in Canadian Manufacturing Industries," *Canadian Journal of Economics* Volume 34, Issue 3 (August 2001).

[3]Exchange rate pass-through is defined as the change in domestic prices that results from a change in the exchange rate. This concept is typically measured as the percentage change in the domestic-currency price of an imported good resulting from a 1 percent change in the nominal exchange rate between the exporting and importing countries. This definition has evolved over time to include other types of prices, notably consumer prices.

Averages disguise variance in a more complex reality. The Canadian evidence of pass-through involves 33 industries, each of which exhibits its own degree of exchange rate pass-through. The range is from 0 to 0.70 with a majority clustered around 0.25. The question then turns to the sorts of industries that have high pass-through versus those with low pass-through.

Industries involved in products for which domestically produced goods are close substitutes for imported goods—automobiles for example—tend to have higher pass-through. That is, the foreign producers adjust their (export) prices to match the price in the destination market. Say Kia, the Korean automobile producer, exports cars to Canada at a Korean won price of 10,000,000 or $12,000 at an exchange rate of 833 won/$. If the Canadian dollar depreciates to, say, 800 won/$, Kia would have to raise the Canadian price to $12,500 to maintain the Korean price of 10,000,000 won. Kia may be reluctant to raise the Canadian dollar price for fear of losing market share in Canada to Canadian-produced vehicles. To the extent that Kia reduces the won price to maintain the Canadian dollar price, Kia absorbs the exchange rate change and does not pass it through to the Canadian consumer. If Kia reduced the Korean export price to 9,600,000 won, Kia's pricing strategy would represent zero pass-through.

On the other hand, industries involved in relatively unique products that do not have close substitutes tend to be more insulated from exchange rate changes. Such industries tend to exhibit low exchange rate pass-through. They are under less pressure to "price to the market" in the destination country. Capital equipment exported to Canada from Germany might be an example. Say a German-sourced machine cost €100,000. At an exchange rate of $1.40/€, the machine sells in Canada for $140,000. If the Canadian dollar depreciated to $1.50/€, and if the German exporter simply did not change the euro-price of the product, the machine would sell for $150,000 in Canada. In that case, since the exchange rate depreciation is fully reflected in the Canadian selling price of the imported machine, the German exporter's pricing strategy implies pass-through of 1.

12.7 MANAGING OPERATING EXPOSURE

As the economy becomes increasingly globalized, many firms are engaged in international activities, such as exports, cross-border sourcing, joint ventures with foreign partners, and establishing production and sales affiliates abroad. The cash flows of such firms can be quite sensitive to exchange rate changes. The objective of managing operating exposure is to stabilize cash flows in the face of fluctuating exchange rates.

Since a firm is exposed to exchange risk mainly through the effect of exchange rate changes on its competitive position, it is important to consider exchange exposure management in the context of the firm's long-term strategic planning. For example, in making such strategic decisions as choosing where to locate production facilities, where to purchase materials and components, and where to sell products, the firm should consider the currency effect on its overall future cash flows. Managing operating exposure is, thus, not a short-term tactical issue. The firm can use the following strategies for managing operating exposure:

1. Selecting low-cost production sites
2. Flexible sourcing policy
3. Diversification of the market
4. Product differentiation and R&D efforts
5. Financial hedging

Selecting Low-Cost Production Sites

When the domestic currency is strong or expected to become strong, eroding the competitive position of the firm, it can choose to locate production facilities in a foreign country where costs are low due to either the undervalued currency or underpriced factors of production.

Japanese car makers, including Honda, Nissan and Toyota, have been shifting production to manufacturing facilities in both the United States and Canada in order to mitigate the negative effect of the strong yen on North American sales. German car makers, such as Daimler-Benz and BMW, also decided to establish manufacturing facilities in North America for the same reason. A real-world example is provided by the International Finance in Practice box "Porsche Powers Profit with Currency Plays."

Also, the firm can choose to establish and maintain production facilities in multiple countries to deal with the effect of exchange rate fluctuations. Consider Toyota, which has manufacturing facilities in Canada, the United States and Mexico as well as Japan. Multiple manufacturing sites provide Toyota with a great deal of flexibility regarding where to produce, given the prevailing exchange rates. While the yen appreciated substantially against both the US and Canadian dollars, the Mexican peso depreciated against the North American currencies in recent years. Under this exchange rate development, Toyota chose to increase production in Mexico in order to serve the North American market. Multiple manufacturing sites, however, may prevent the firm from taking advantage of economies of scale, raising its cost of production. The resultant higher cost can partially offset the advantages of maintaining multiple production sites.

Flexible Sourcing Policy

Even if the firm has manufacturing facilities only in the domestic country, it can substantially lessen the effect of exchange rate changes by sourcing from where input costs are low. When the dollar is strong against most major currencies, multinational firms often purchase materials and components from low-cost foreign suppliers.

Facing a strong yen, many Japanese firms adopt the same practice. Japanese manufacturers, especially in the car and consumer electronics industries, depend heavily on parts and intermediate products from such low-cost countries as Thailand, Malaysia and China. The **flexible sourcing policy** need not be confined just to materials and parts. Firms can also hire low-cost guest workers from foreign countries instead of high-cost domestic workers in order to be competitive. For example, Japan Airlines is known to hire foreign crews to stay competitive in international routes in the face of a strong yen.

Diversification of the Market

Another way of dealing with exchange exposure is **diversification of the market**—that is, geographically diversifying the firm's sales pattern. For example, Nova Chemicals Corporation, with global headquarters in Calgary, has markets throughout North America as well as in Europe and Asia for polystyrene and high-performance polymers. Reduced sales in, say, Japan due to a weakening yen would be partially offset by sales to Europe if the euro rose against the Canadian dollar as the yen weakened. Whenever exchange rates in relation to the Canadian dollar are less than perfectly correlated—which is virtually always the case—then geographic diversification of sales has a risk-moderating effect.

It is sometimes argued that the firm can reduce currency exposure by diversifying across different business lines. The idea is that although each individual business may be exposed to exchange risk to some degree, the firm as a whole may not face a significant exposure. However, the firm should not get into new lines of business solely to diversify exchange risk because conglomerate expansion can bring about inefficiency and losses. Expansion into a new business should be justified in its own right.

R&D Efforts and Product Differentiation

Investment in R&D activities can allow the firm to maintain and strengthen its competitive position in the face of adverse exchange rate movements. Successful R&D efforts allow the firm to cut costs and enhance productivity. In addition, R&D efforts can lead to **product differentiation**—the introduction of new and unique products for which competitors offer

Porsche Powers Profit with Currency Plays

The weak dollar is denting many European car makers, but Porsche AG may have found a way of using the ailing buck to rev up its results.

Investment analysts believe sophisticated currency bets—not sports cars like the 911—are turbo-charging Porsche's profits. Goldman Sachs, for one, estimates that as much as 75% of the company's pretax profits—or up to 800 million ($1.07 billion) of the €1.1 billion Porsche reported for the fiscal year that ended July 31—came from skillfully executing currency options. Other analysts say that percentage is too high, but most European auto watchers agree that Porsche probably racks up a big chunk of its operating profit from crafty currency plays.

The company declined to make Chief Financial Officer Holger Haerter available to comment on its foreign-exchange profits. A spokesman, Manfred Ayasse, acknowledges that Porsche's hedging generates a profit and is an important part of its overall strategy. Porsche currency exposure is fully hedged through July 31, 2007, and the auto maker is working to extend its protection well beyond that date, he adds. "Fully hedged" refers to taking currency positions that aim to protect all of a company's earnings from movements in the foreign-exchange market, but currency options and other derivatives can also become profit centers depending on how well a company makes its bets.

Without elaborating, Mr. Ayasse says Goldman's estimate of Porsche's currency earnings is "far too high," and "by far the majority" of Porsche's profits come from selling cars.

Among other analysts, Michael Raab at Sal. Oppenheim & Cie. in Frankfurt and Stephen Cheetham at Sanford C. Bernstein in London believe Porsche is getting 40% to 50% of its pretax profit from hedging.

Porsche's apparent success in turning a profit while weathering the dollar's dips is rare these days, though auto makers have been able to do so in the past. For example, even as its North American unit struggled last year, Daimler-Chrysler AG earned hundreds of millions of euros on currency hedges.

Typically, however, the strong euro makes German cars, French wines or British drugs more expensive for customers who pay in dollars and harms European manufacturers.

Among car makers, Volkswagen AG expects a $1.3 billion loss in North America this year, largely as a result of the euro's strength. Ford Motor Co.'s Jaguar unit has cited the dollar's slide as contributing to its decision this year to cut output by 12%. BMW AG and Daimler Chrysler's Mercedes division have been hurt less because, unlike Porsche and Volkswagen, both operate U.S. plants that export cars in Europe, providing a natural hedge against exchange-rate swings.

At late afternoon in New York yesterday, the dollar was trading at $1.347, near its all-time low, against the euro. (See related article on page C2.)

Pinpointing how much Porsche makes from currency options is difficult, because the family-controlled company reports earnings only twice a year. The company also provides fewer details about its accounting practices than other automakers.

But in its report, Goldman points out that Porsche books hedging profits in the cost-of-materials line in its profit-and-loss statement. The investment bank notes that in fiscal 2002–03 Porsche's raw material costs fell 7%—even though the company built 33% more cars than the year before. Goldman says falling development costs and other savings are "insufficient" to generate such a drop.

Porsche won't describe its hedging technique, but Goldman Sachs believes the car maker essentially bets on a weak dollar, by buying from another party—presumably a bank—an option to exchange dollars for euros at an artificially low exchange rate for the euro—for example, 96 U.S. cents to one euro.

If the dollar's value on the open market falls below that level—to, say, $1.20 for one euro—Porsche gets a hefty cash payout, Goldman writes. Conversely, if the dollar strengthens, the only losses Porsche incurs are the premiums it has paid for buying those options. Although those premiums are high—around 2% annually of the total amount Porsche wants to hedge, or $20 million on hypothetical U.S. revenues of $1 billion—Porsche can afford them, since its profit margins are among the highest in the industry.

Goldman Sachs says Porsche's profit levels are unsustainable. Mr. Cheetham, the Bernstein analyst, agrees. "Hedging is just a short-run thing," he says.

Predicting the dollar's swings is critical for Porsche. It makes its cars entirely in Europe, but generates 40% or 45% of its sales in the U.S. During the late 1980s and early 1990s, Porsche made little effort to shield itself from currency effects, raising prices as often as three times a year in response to a weak dollar. The result: Porsche's U.S. sales slid from 30,000 cars in 1986 to 4,500 in 1992.

Mr. Ayasse acknowledges the company raised its prices too often, but says other car makers "made this error, too." "We don't want to see negative surprises in the forthcoming years," he adds.

Source: Stephen Power, "Porsche Powers Profit with Currency Plays," *The Wall Street Journal* (December 8, 2004), p. C3. Reprinted with permission.

no close substitutes. Since the demand for unique products tends to be highly inelastic (i.e., price-insensitive), the firm would be less exposed to exchange risk. At the same time, the firm can strive to create a perception among consumers that its product is, indeed, different from those offered by competitors. Once the firm's product acquires a unique identity, its demand is less likely to be price sensitive.

Volvo, a Swedish automobile manufacturer, provides a good example here. The company has invested heavily in strengthening safety features of its cars and successfully established its reputation as the producer of safe cars. This reputation, reinforced by a focused marketing campaign, "Volvo for Life," helped the company carve out a niche among safety-minded consumers in highly competitive world automobile markets.

Financial Hedging

While not a substitute for the long-term, **operational hedging** approaches discussed above, **financial hedging** can be used to stabilize the firm's cash flows. For example, the firm can lend or borrow foreign currencies on a long-term basis. Or, the firm can use currency forward or options contracts and roll them over, if necessary. Financial contracts are designed to hedge against nominal, rather than real, changes in exchange rates. Since the firm's competitive position is affected by real changes in exchange rates, financial contracts can at best provide an approximate hedge against the firm's operating exposure. However, if operational hedges, which involve redeployment of resources, are costly or impractical, financial contracts can provide the firm with flexible and economical ways of dealing with exchange exposure.

How Canadian Firms Deal with Economic Exposure

We began this chapter on economic exposure to exchange rate changes by referring to the extraordinary appreciation of the Canadian dollar against all currencies in the world—and especially against the US dollar—in the period from 2003 to 2006. From our perspective, the interesting question is how Canadian firms were affected by this currency appreciation and how, if at all, they adjusted to it. In 2005 the Bank of Canada undertook a comprehensive survey to find answers to these questions.[4]

About one-half of Canadian firms surveyed by the Bank of Canada reported being adversely affected by the appreciation of the Canadian dollar. Roughly one-quarter reported a favourable impact, while the remaining one-quarter said that there was no effect.

The firms most adversely affected tended to be in the manufacturing sector and in primary industries. Those that benefited were largely in retail and wholesale trade and in transportation. Firms least affected by the appreciation were predominantly in the so-called "non-traded sectors"—construction, finance, insurance and real estate and personal services.

The adverse impact of the appreciation stemmed largely from lower profit margins on foreign sales, since many goods are priced in US dollars. In contrast, favourably affected firms generally benefited from lower input costs.

Exhibit 12.12 summarizes the responses to the Bank of Canada's survey. As could be expected, the survey results indicate that Canadian dollar appreciation hurts our export-oriented industries. They suffer a combination of lower export volumes and lower profit margins on those volumes. Import competing industries in Canada are hurt as well but in this case through reduced domestic volumes and lower margins on those volumes.

For those industries that gain from Canadian dollar appreciation, the predominant reason is lower imported-input costs. In addition, imported capital goods (machinery and equipment) becomes cheaper with a higher Canadian dollar. Eleven percent of respondents indicate that the reduction in the Canadian dollar value of their (foreign-denominated) debt is added value to their firm.

---

[4]Jean Mair, "How the Appreciation of the Canadian Dollar Has Affected Canadian Firms: Evidence from the Bank of Canada *Business Outlook Survey*," *Bank of Canada Review* (Autumn) 2005.

EXHIBIT 12.12

Effects on
Canadian Firms
from Canadian
Dollar Appreciation

Effects of Canadian Dollar Appreciation Reported by Firms Adversely Affected	
Effect	**Adversely Affected Firms, %**
Lower profit margins from foreign sales	77
Lower export volumes	24
Lower margins on domestic sales	22
Lower domestic volumes	16
Other effects	12
Effects of Canadian Dollar Appreciation Reported by Firms Favourably Affected	
Effect	**Favourably Affected Firms, %**
Lower input costs	80
Cheaper machinery and equipment	28
Lower Canadian dollar value of liabilities	11
Other	11

Source: Jean Mair, "How the Appreciation of the Canadian Dollar Has Affected Canadian Firms: Evidence from the Bank of Canada *Business Outlook Survey*," *Bank of Canada Review* (Autumn 2005), pp. 19–25.

Exhibit 12.13 summarizes the results of the survey question concerning how Canadian firms adjusted to the higher value of the Canadian dollar. Firms undertook a diverse set of actions in response to the appreciation, including measures to cut costs, to increase productivity, to move certain activities abroad and to reorient their activities toward more profitable products and markets. However, fully one-third of companies that were adversely affected reported no plans to respond. Typically, such firms were affected only moderately by the appreciation or were otherwise enjoying the stronger demand for their products.

Managerial and Strategic Perspectives on Economic Exposure

Most major multinational firms do not attempt to hedge economic exposure. Typically the best one can do is to try to *understand* it.

Economic exposure is a longer-term phenomenon wherein the *value* of a firm's foreign operations—which is ultimately based on costs and revenues in foreign currency—is potentially affected by changes in exchange rates. If exchange rates moved rapidly and smoothly to maintain purchasing power parity, then economic exposure would not be an

EXHIBIT 12.13

Canadian
Corporate
Adjustments to
Canadian Dollar
Appreciation

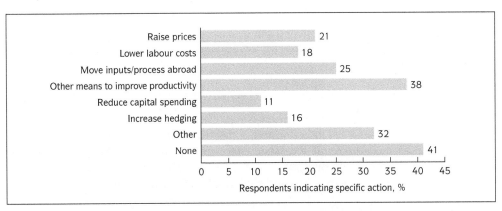

Note: Responses do not sum to 100 because firms may report several actions. "Other" includes measures to introduce new products, to reorient sales strategies and to change the currency of denomination of sales or purchases prices.

Source: Jean Mair, "How Appreciation of the Canadian Dollar Has Affected Canadian Firms: Evidence from the Bank of Canada *Business Outlook Survey*," *Bank of Canada Review* (Autumn 2005).

issue at all. In that case the "international law of one price" would hold and exchange rates would not matter for international industry.

Of course, PPP seldom holds in the short term. In the longer term, the speed of adjustment to PPP can be sporadic because of price rigidities and exchange rate changes that are induced more by capital flows than by relative prices of industrial inputs or product prices. The crux of economic exposure is the risk of protracted deviations from PPP that affect the cost structure and competitive position of a multinational firm.

Hedging the long-term consequences of (real) exchange rate changes is substantially more complicated than hedging either transaction or translation risk. Perhaps the biggest problem in setting up a strategy to hedge economic exposure—if, indeed, a firm was so inclined—is to estimate the longer-term effects of exchange rate fluctuations on the firm's cash flows. Consider, for example, the case of a Canadian firm like BlackBerry, which manufactures smart phones in Canada and sells them in Europe. What is the effect of a shift in the Canadian dollar/euro exchange rate on BlackBerry's long-term profitability?

To answer this question, one must first determine whether the change in the dollar–euro exchange rate is in line with a general change in price levels (in Europe as compared to Canada) such that the inflation-adjusted (real) exchange rate is constant. As mentioned above, if the real exchange rate remains constant, then a nominal exchange rate change is likely to have only a minor impact on BlackBerry's cash flows. However, changes in real exchange rates can have a significant effect on cash flows.

Consider what happens if the Canadian dollar strengthens against the euro, as it did so substantially from 2003 onward. If the euro weakened because of general inflation in Europe (with European inflation being higher than Canadian inflation), then the euro-price of BlackBerrys could rise without BlackBerry losing competitive position to European produced handheld communications devices such as Nokia. In this case, European demand for BlackBerrys would not be affected by the change in the exchange rate. Furthermore, BlackBerry's higher euro revenue and profits would result in an unchanged amount of Canadian profit on BlackBerry's European operations converted at the lower euro.

Contrast this case with the one in which the real exchange rate does change. Let's say that the Canadian dollar appreciates from $1.60/€ to $1.40/€. This exchange rate shift is far greater than what can be explained by the European–Canadian inflation differentials. At the higher real Canadian dollar, *either* Europe-bound BlackBerrys become more expensive for Europeans and fewer will be sold *or*, if BlackBerry does not raise the euro-price of its smart phones, BlackBerry will see its profit margin on European sales shrink. Either way, BlackBerry's cash flows are negatively affected by the exchange rate change.

As these arguments suggest, a major difficulty in assessing the effect of exchange rate shifts on cash flows has to do with predicting the underlying cause of the exchange rate movement. If we cannot predict whether future exchange rate fluctuations are in line with relative price changes, then forward and futures contracts—the standard tools for hedging transactions exposure—are imperfect hedges.

Illustrated **Mini Case**

Exchange Risk Management at Merck[5]

To examine how companies actually manage exchange risk exposure, we choose Merck & Co. Incorporated, a major American pharmaceutical company, and study its approach to overall exchange exposure management. While Merck's actual hedging decision reflects its own particular business situation, the basic framework for dealing with currency exposure can be informative for other firms.

---

[5]This case is adapted from Lewent and Kearney (1990).

Merck & Co. primarily develops, produces and markets health-care pharmaceuticals. As a multinational company that operates in more than 100 countries, Merck had world-wide sales of $6.6 billion in 1989, and it controlled about a 4.7 percent market share worldwide. Merck's major foreign competitors are European firms and emerging Japanese firms. Merck is among the most internationally oriented American pharmaceutical companies, with overseas assets accounting for about 40 percent of the firm's total and with roughly 50 percent of its sales overseas.

As is typical in the pharmaceutical industry, Merck established overseas subsidiaries. These subsidiaries number about 70 and are responsible for finishing imported products and marketing in the local markets of incorporation. Sales are denominated in local currencies, and thus, the company is directly affected by exchange rate fluctuations. Costs are incurred partly in the U.S. dollar for basic manufacturing and research and partly in terms of local currency for finishing, marketing, distribution and so on. Merck found that costs and revenues were not matched in individual currencies mainly because of the concentration of research, manufacturing and headquarters operations in the United States.

To reduce the currency mismatch, Merck first considered the possibility of redeploying resources in order to shift dollar costs to other currencies. The company decided, however, that relocating employees and manufacturing and research sites was not a practical and cost-effective way of dealing with exchange exposure. Having decided that operational hedging was not appropriate, Merck considered the alternative of financial hedging. Merck developed a five-step procedure for financial hedging:

1. Exchange forecasting
2. Assessing strategic plan impact
3. Deciding whether to hedge
4. Selecting the hedging instruments
5. Constructing a hedging program

Step 1: Exchange Forecasting
The first step involves reviewing the likelihood of adverse exchange movements. The treasury staff estimates possible ranges for dollar strength or weakness over the five-year planning horizon. In doing so, the major factors expected to influence exchange rates, such as the US trade deficit, capital flows, the US budget deficit and government policies regarding exchange rates, are considered. Outside forecasters are also polled on the outlook for the dollar over the planning horizon.

Step 2: Assessing Strategic Plan Impact
Once the future exchange rate ranges are estimated, cash flows and earnings are projected and compared under the alternative exchange rate scenarios, such as strong dollar and weak dollar. These projections are made on a five-year cumulative basis, rather than on a year-to-year basis, because cumulative results provide more useful information concerning the magnitude of exchange exposure associated with the company's long-range plan.

Step 3: Deciding Whether to Hedge
In deciding whether to hedge exchange exposure, Merck focused on the objective of maximizing long-term cash flows and on the potential effect of exchange rate movements on the firm's ability to meet its strategic objectives. This focus is ultimately intended to maximize shareholder wealth. Merck decided to hedge for two main reasons. First, the company has a large portion of earnings generated overseas, while a disproportionate share of costs is incurred in dollars. Second, volatile cash flows can adversely affect the firm's ability to implement the strategic plan, especially investments in R&D that form the

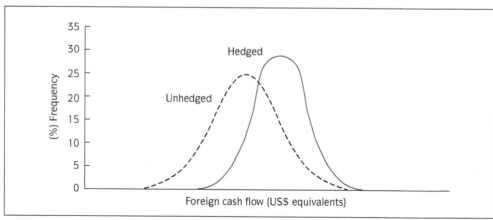

basis for future growth. To succeed in a highly competitive industry, the company needs to make a long-term commitment to a high level of research funding. But the cash flow uncertainty caused by volatile exchange rates makes it difficult to justify a high level of research spending. Management decided to hedge in order to reduce the potential effect of volatile exchange rates on future cash flows.

Step 4: Selecting the Hedging Instruments
The objective was to select the most cost-effective hedging tool that accommodated the company's risk preference. Among various hedging tools, such as forward currency contracts, foreign currency borrowing, and currency options, Merck chose currency options because it was not willing to forgo the potential gains if the dollar depreciated against foreign currencies as it has been doing against major currencies since the mid-1980s. Merck regarded option costs as premiums for the insurance policy designed to preserve its ability to implement the strategic plan.

Step 5: Constructing a Hedging Program
Having selected currency options as the key hedging vehicle, the company still had to formulate an implementation strategy regarding the term of the hedge, the strike price of the currency options, and the percentage of income to be covered. After simulating the outcomes of alternative implementation strategies under various exchange rate scenarios, Merck decided (1) to hedge for a multiyear period using long-dated options contracts, rather than hedge year by year, to protect the firm's strategic cash flows, (2) not to use far out-of-money options to save costs and (3) to hedge only on a partial basis, with the remainder self-insured.

To help formulate the most cost-effective hedging program, Merck developed a computer-based model that simulated the effectiveness of various hedging strategies. Exhibit 12.14 provides an example of simulation results, comparing distributions of hedged and unhedged cash flows. Obviously, the hedged cash flow distribution has a higher mean and a lower standard deviation than the unhedged cash flow distribution. As we will discuss in Chapter 13, hedging may not only reduce risk but also increase cash flows if a reduced risk lowers the firm's cost of capital and tax liabilities. In this scenario, hedging is preferred to no hedging.

EXHIBIT 12.14

Cash Flows Unhedged versus Hedged

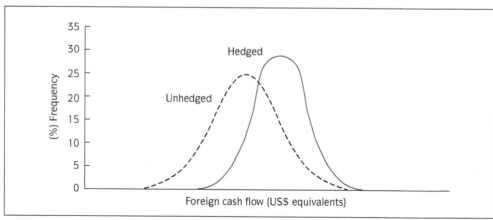

Source: J. Lewent and J. Kearney, "Identifying, Measuring, and Hedging Currency Risk at Merck." Reprinted with permission from the Bank of America *Journal of Applied Corporate Finance* (Winter 1990).

SUMMARY

This chapter discusses how to measure and manage economic exposure to exchange risk. It also examines how companies manage currency risk in the real world.

1. Exchange rate changes can systematically affect the value of the firm by influencing the firm's operating cash flows as well as the domestic currency values of its assets and liabilities.

2. It is conventional to classify foreign currency exposure into three classes: economic exposure, transaction exposure and translation exposure.

3. Economic exposure can be defined as the extent to which the value of the firm is affected by unexpected fluctuations in exchange rates. Transaction exposure is defined as the sensitivity of realized domestic currency values of the firm's contractual cash flows denominated in foreign currencies to unexpected exchange rate shifts. Translation exposure refers to the extend to which the firm's consolidated financial statements are affected by movement in exchange rates.

4. If the firm has an asset in a foreign country, its exposure to currency risk can be measured by the coefficient in regressing the dollar value of the foreign asset on the exchange rate. Once the magnitude of exposure is known, the firm can hedge the exposure simply by selling the exposure forward.

5. Unlike the exposure of assets and liabilities that are listed in accounting statements, operating exposure depends on the effect of random exchange rate shifts on the firm's future cash flows, which are not readily measurable. Despite this difficulty, it is important to properly manage operating exposure, since operating exposure may account for a larger portion of the firm's total exposure than contractual exposure.

6. A firm's operating exposure is determined by (a) the structure of the markets in which the firm sources its inputs and sells its products and (b) the firm's ability to mitigate the effect of exchange rate shifts on its competitive position by adjusting markets, product mix and sourcing.

7. Since a firm is exposed to exchange risk mainly via the effect of exchange rate fluctuations on its competitive position, it is important to consider exchange exposure management in the context of the firm's overall long-term strategic plan. The objective of exposure management is to stabilize cash flow in the face of fluctuating exchange rates.

8. To manage operating exposure, the firm can use various strategies, such as (a) choosing low-cost production sites, (b) maintaining flexible sourcing policy, (c) diversification of the market, (d) product differentiation, and (e) financial hedging using currency options and forward contracts.

QUESTIONS

1. Define economic exposure to exchange risk.

2. Explain the following statement: "Exposure is the regression coefficient."

3. Suppose that your company has an equity position in a French firm. Discuss the condition under which dollar/euro exchange rate uncertainty does not constitute exchange exposure for your company.

4. Explain the competitive and conversion effects of exchange rate shifts on the firm's operating cash flow.

5. Discuss the determinants of operating exposure.

6. Discuss the implications of purchasing power parity for operating exposure.

7. General Motors exports cars to Spain, but the strong dollar against the euro hurts sales of GM cars in Spain. In the Spanish market, GM faces competition from Italian and French car makers, such as Fiat and Renault, whose operating currencies are the euro. What kinds of measures would you recommend so that GM can maintain its market share in Spain?

8. What are the advantages and disadvantages to a firm of financial hedging of its operating exposure compared with operational hedges (such as relocating its manufacturing site)?

9. Discuss the advantages and disadvantages of maintaining multiple manufacturing sites as a hedge against exchange rate exposure.

10. Evaluate the following statement: "A firm can reduce its currency exposure by diversifying across different business lines."

11. Exchange rate uncertainty may not necessarily mean that firms face exchange risk exposure. Explain why this may be the case.

PROBLEMS

1. Suppose that you hold a piece of land in London, England, that you may want to sell in one year. As a Canadian resident, you are concerned with the Canadian dollar value of the land. Assume that if the British economy booms in the future, the land will be worth £2,000, and one British pound will be worth $2.40. If the British economy slows down, on the other hand, the land will be worth less, say, £1,500, but the pound will be stronger, say, $2.50/£. You feel that the British economy will experience a boom with a 60 percent probability and a slowdown with a 40 percent probability.

   a. Estimate your exposure (*b*) to the exchange risk.

   b. Compute the variance of the dollar value of your property that is attributable to exchange rate uncertainty.

   c. Discuss how you can hedge your exchange risk exposure and also examine the consequences of hedging.

2. A Canadian firm holds an asset in France and faces the following scenario:

	State 1	State 2	State 3	State 4
Probability	25%	25%	25%	25%
Spot rate	$1.20/€	$1.10/€	$1.00/€	$0.90/€
P*	€1,500	€1,400	€1,300	€1,200
P	$1,800	$1,540	$1,300	$1,080

   In the above table, *P** is the euro price of the asset held by the Canadian firm and *P* is the dollar price of the asset.

   a. Compute the exchange exposure faced by the firm.

   b. What is the variance of the dollar price of this asset if the firm remains unhedged against this exposure?

   c. If the firm hedges against this exposure using a forward contract, what is the variance of the dollar value of the hedged position?

3. Suppose you are a British venture capitalist holding a major stake in an e-commerce start-up in Ottawa. As a British resident, you are concerned with the pound value of your Canadian equity position. If the Canadian economy booms in the future, your equity stake will be worth $1,000,000, and the exchange rate will be $1.40/£. If the Canadian economy experiences a recession, on the other hand, your Canadian equity stake will be worth $500,000, and the exchange rate will be $1.60/£. You assess that the Canadian economy will experience a boom with a 70 percent probability and a recession with a 30 percent probability.

   a. Estimate your exposure to the exchange risk.

   b. Compute the variance of the pound value of your Canadian equity position that is attributable to the exchange rate uncertainty.

   c. How would you hedge this exposure? If you hedge, what is the variance of the pound value of the hedged position?

4. Viceroy Homes of Port Hope, Ontario, manufactures prefabricated houses. A significant share of Viceroy sales are its exports to the United States. In 2007, Viceroy had exports to the US in the amount of $800 million. Viceroy's pricing policy is to quote all prices, including sales to the US, in Canadian dollars. Once a year, in September, Viceroy releases a catalogue and price list (in Canadian dollars).

   a. What is the nature of the foreign exchange risk that Viceroy faces with respect to the uncertainty of the Canada–US exchange rate? Be specific.

   b. Would you expect Viceroy sales to increase, decrease or remain unchanged in the face of appreciation of the Canadian dollar relative to the US dollar? Explain.

   c. Would you expect Viceroy profits to increase, decrease or remain unchanged in the face of appreciation of the Canadian dollar relative to the US dollar? Explain.

   d. What sorts of marketing and cost information would you require in order to present Viceroy management with a more complete assessment of the firm's foreign exchange risk?

   e. What mechanisms would you recommend to Viceroy to address its foreign exchange risk?

   f. To what extent does Viceroy "pass through" changes in the Canada–US exchange rate to its customers in the US?

INTERNET EXERCISE

Coca-Cola derives about three-quarters of its revenue from overseas markets. It is, thus, highly likely that the company is exposed to currency risks. Investigate the company's exchange risk management policies and practices from its Annual Report (10-K) filed with the US Securities and Exchange Commission (SEC), especially the "Financial Risk Management" section, which are available from the following website: www.edgr.com/

How would you evaluate Coca-Cola's approach to exchange risk management?

MINI CASE

Economic Exposure of Calais Computers PLC

Consider Case 3 of Calais Computers PLC discussed in the chapter. Now, assume that the euro is expected to depreciate to $1.50 from the current level of $1.60 per euro. This implies that the euro cost of the imported part, that is, Intel's microprocessors, is €341 (= $512/$1.50). Other variables, such as the unit sales volume and the European inflation rate, remain the same as in Case 3.

a. Compute the projected annual cash flow in dollars.

b. Compute the projected operating gains/losses over the four-year horizon as the discounted present value of change in cash flows, which is due to the euro depreciation, from the benchmark case presented in Exhibit 12.6.

c. What actions, if any, can Calais take to mitigate the projected operating losses due to the euro depreciation?

REFERENCES & SUGGESTED READINGS

Adler, Michael, and Bernard Dumas. "Exposure to Currency Risk: Definition and Measurement." *Financial Management* (Spring 1984), pp. 41–50.

Allayannis, George, and Eli Ofek. "Exchange Rate Exposure, Hedging, and the Use of Foreign Currency Derivatives." *Journal of International Money and Finance* 20 (2001), pp. 273–96.

Bartov, Eli, and Gordon Bodnar. "Firm Valuation, Earnings Expectations, and the Exchange-Rate Exposure Effect." *Journal of Finance* 49 (1994), pp. 1755–85.

Bodnar, Gordon M. "Exchange Rate Exposure and Market Value." *Mastering Risk: The Complete Financial Companion* (London: Pitman Publishing for *The Financial Times*, 1998).

Choi, Jongmoo, and Anita Prasad. "Exchange Rate Sensitivity and Its Determinants: A Firm and Industry Analysis of U.S. Multinationals." *Financial Management* 23 (1995), pp. 77–88.

Dornbusch, Rudiger. "Exchange Rates and Prices." *American Economic Review* 77 (1987), pp. 93–106.

Dufey, Gunter, and S. L. Srinivasulu. "The Case for Corporate Management of Foreign Exchange Risk." *Financial Management* (Winter 1983), pp. 54–62.

Flood, Eugene, and Donald Lessard. "On the Measurement of Operating Exposure to Exchange Rates: A Conceptual Approach." *Financial Management* 15 (Spring 1986), pp. 25–36.

Glaum, M., M. Brunner, and H. Himmel. "The DAX and the Dollar: The Economic Exchange Rate Exposure of German Corporations." Working paper, Europa-Universitat Viadrina, 1998.

Hekman, Christine R. "Don't Blame Currency Values for Strategic Errors." *Midland Corporate Finance Journal* (Fall 1986), pp. 45–55.

Jorion, Philippe. "The Exchange-Rate Exposure of U.S. Multinationals." *Journal of Business* 63 (1990), pp. 331–45.

Kardasz, Stanley, and K.R. Stollery. "Exchange Rate Pass-Through and Its Determinants in Canadian Manufacturing Industries." *Canadian Journal of Economics* Volume 34, Issue 3 (August).

Lessard, Donald, and S. B. Lightstone. "Volatile Exchange Rates Can Put Operations at Risk." *Harvard Business Review* (July/August 1986), pp. 107–14.

Lewent, Judy, and John Kearney. "Identifying, Measuring and Hedging Currency Risk at Merck." *Journal of Applied Corporate Finance* (Winter 1990), pp. 19–28.

Mair, Jean. "How Appreciation of the Canadian Dollar Has Affected Canadian Firms: Evidence from the Bank of Canada Business Outlook Survey," *Bank of Canada Review* (Autumn, 2005).

Pringle, John, and Robert Connolly. "The Nature and Causes of Foreign Currency Exposure." *Journal of Applied Corporate Finance* (Fall 1993), pp. 61–72.

Simkins, Berry, and Paul Laux. "Derivatives Use and the Exchange Rate Risk of Investing in Large U.S. Corporations." Working paper, Case Western Reserve University, 1996.

Wihlborg, Clas. "Economics of Exposure Management of Foreign Subsidiaries of Multinational Corporations." *Journal of International Business Studies* (Winter 1980), pp. 9–18.

Williamson, Rohan. "Exchange Rate Exposure and Competition: Evidence from the Automotive Industry." *Journal of Financial Economics* 59 (2001), pp. 441–75.

Yang, Jiawen. "Exchange Rate Pass-Through in U.S. Manufacturing Industries." *Review of Economics and Statistics* 79 (1997), pp. 95–104.

 **connect** For more information on the resources available from McGraw-Hill Ryerson, go to www.mcgrawhill.ca/he/solutions.

Chapter (13)

Management of Transaction Exposure

AS DISCUSSED in Chapter 12, **transaction exposure** arises when a firm faces contractual cash flows that are fixed in a foreign currency. For example, suppose that CHC Helicopters of St John's, Newfoundland, a world leader in supply logistics to offshore oil rigs, has billed British Petroleum (BP) for services provided to BP's sites on the North Sea. CHC's invoice is for £1 million, due in three months.[1] When CHC Helicopters receives £1 million three months from now, it will convert these British pounds into Canadian dollars at the spot rate of exchange prevailing at that time. The future spot rate cannot be known in advance. Consequently, in dollar terms, the value of the settlement is uncertain. If the British pound appreciates (depreciates) against the Canadian dollar, the dollar receipt will be higher (lower). The uncertain end-result suggests that if CHC Helicopters does nothing to address this uncertainty, it is effectively speculating on the future course of the exchange rate. It is as if CHC is willing to take a bet that the British pound will appreciate against the Canadian dollar.

Consider another example. Say Mitsubishi of Japan enters into a loan contract with the Swiss bank UBS that calls for payment of SF100 million for principal and interest in one year. To the extent that the yen/Swiss franc exchange rate is uncertain, Mitsubishi does not know how much yen will be required to buy SF100 million spot in one year's time. If the yen appreciates (depreciates) against the Swiss franc, a smaller (larger) yen amount will be needed to retire the SF-denominated loan.

These examples suggest that whenever a firm has foreign-currency-denominated receivables or payables, it is subject to transaction exposure, and the eventual settlements have the potential to affect the firm's cash flow position. Since modern firms are often involved in commercial and financial contracts denominated in foreign currencies, management of transaction exposure has become an important function of international financial management.

Unlike economic exposure, transaction exposure is well defined. Transaction exposure is simply the amount of foreign currency to be received or paid.

---

[1]There may be some question as to why CHC Helicopters would invoice BP in pounds rather than in Canadian dollars. It is quite likely that the original contract was tendered by BP in a global competition that specified that settlement would be in British pounds.

This chapter focuses on alternative ways of hedging transaction exposure using various financial contracts and operational techniques:

Financial contracts:

- Forward hedge
- Money market hedge
- Options hedge
- Swap market hedge

Operational techniques:

- Choice of the invoice currency
- Lead/lag strategy
- Exposure netting

As we proceed to describe and illustrate various ways to address transaction exposure, it is useful to establish another specific business situation that gives rise to exposure. Let us say that Bombardier of Montreal exports commuter aircraft to Austrian Airlines. A payment of €10 million will be received by Bombardier in one year. Money market and foreign exchange rates relevant to the financial contracts that we will examine are:

Canadian interest rate	1.1% per annum
European interest rate	3.0% per annum
Spot exchange rate	$1.31/€
One-year forward exchange rate	$1.27/€

Let us now look at the various techniques for managing Bombardier's transactions exposure involving €10 million to be received one year from now.

13.1 FORWARD HEDGE

http://merage.uci.edu/~jorion/pacnet/case.html

A case study by Prof. Philippe Jorion presents the situation of a company with transaction exposure to the deutschemark/dollar exchange rate.

Perhaps the most direct and popular way of hedging transaction exposure is by currency forward contracts or **forward hedge**. Generally speaking, the firm may sell (buy) its foreign currency receivables (payables) forward to eliminate its exchange risk exposure. In the above example, in order to hedge foreign exchange exposure, Bombardier may simply sell forward its euro receivable, €10 million for delivery in one year, in exchange for a given amount of Canadian dollars. On the maturity date of the contract, Bombardier will deliver €10 million to the bank, which is the counterparty of the contract and, in return, take delivery of $12.7 million ($1.27 × 10 million) regardless of the spot exchange rate that may prevail on the maturity date. Bombardier will, of course, use the €10 million that it will receive from Austrian Airways to fulfill the forward contract. Since Bombardier's euro receivable is exactly offset by the euro payable (created by the forward contract), the company's net euro exposure is zero.

Bombardier is assured of receiving a given dollar amount, $12.7 million, from the counterparty of the forward contract. The dollar proceeds from this European sale will not be affected at all by future changes in the exchange rate. This point is illustrated in Exhibit 13.1. Once Bombardier enters into the forward contract, exchange rate uncertainty becomes irrelevant for Bombardier. Exhibit 13.1 also illustrates how the dollar proceeds from the European sale will be affected by the future spot exchange rate when exchange exposure is not hedged. The exhibit shows that the dollar proceeds under the forward hedge will be higher than those under the unhedged position if the future spot exchange rate turns out to be less than the forward rate, that is, $S < \$1.27/€$, and the opposite will hold if the future spot rate turns out to be higher than the forward rate. In the latter case, Bombardier forgoes an opportunity to benefit from potential euro appreciation.

EXHIBIT 13.1

Dollar Proceeds
from the European
Sale: Forward
Hedge versus
Unhedged Position

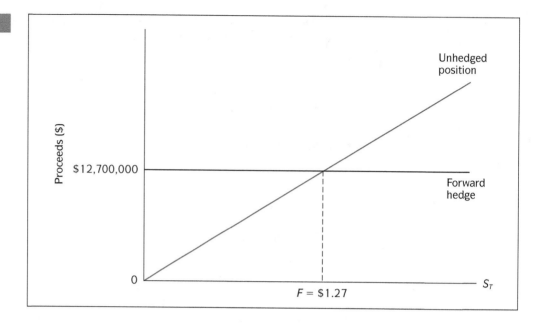

Suppose that on the maturity date of the forward contract, the spot rate turns out to be $1.20/€, which is less than the forward rate, $1.27/€. In this case, Bombardier would have received $12.0 million, rather than $12.7 million, had it not entered into the forward contract. Thus, one can say that Bombardier gained $0.7 million from the forward hedge. Needless to say, Bombardier will not always gain in this manner. If the spot rate is, say, $1.31/€ on the maturity date, then Bombardier could have received $13.1 million by remaining unhedged. Thus, one can say *ex post* that the forward hedge cost Bombardier $0.40 million.

The gains and losses from the forward hedge can be illustrated as in Exhibits 13.2 and 13.3. The gain/loss is computed as follows:

$$\text{Gain} = (F - S_T) \times €10 \text{ million} \tag{13.1}$$

Obviously, the gain is positive if the forward exchange rate is greater than the spot rate on the maturity date, that is, $F > S_T$, and the gain will be negative (i.e., a loss will result) if the opposite holds. As Exhibit 13.3 shows, the firm theoretically can gain as much as $12.7 million should the euro become worthless, which of course is extremely unlikely, whereas there is no limit to possible losses.

EXHIBIT 13.2

Gains/Losses from
Forward Hedge

Spot Exchange Rate on the Maturity Date (S_T)	Receipts from the European Sale		
	Unhedged Position	Forward Hedge	Gains/Losses from Hedge**
1.10	$11,000,000	$12,700,000	$1,700,000
1.20	$12,000,000	$12,700,000	$ 700,000
1.27*	$12,700,000	$12,700,000	$ 0
1.30	$13,000,000	$12,700,000	–$ 300,000
1.40	$14,000,000	$12,700,000	–$1,300,000

*The forward exchange rate (F) is $1.27/€.

**The gains/losses are computed as the proceeds under the forward hedge minus the proceeds from the unhedged position at the various spot exchange rates on the maturity date.

EXHIBIT 13.3

Illustration of Gains
and Losses from
Forward Hedging

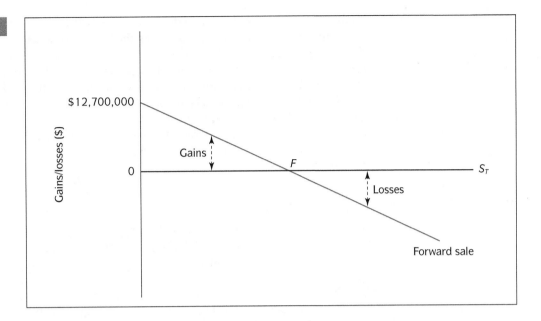

It is important, however, to note that the above analysis is *ex post* in nature and that no one can know for sure what the future spot rate will be beforehand. The firm must decide whether to hedge or not to hedge *ex ante*. To help the firm decide, it is useful to consider the following three alternative scenarios:

1. $\bar{S}_T \approx F$
2. $\bar{S}_T < F$
3. $\bar{S}_T > F$

where $\bar{S}_T$ denotes the firm's expected spot exchange rate for the maturity date.

Under the first scenario, where the firm's expected future spot exchange rate, $\bar{S}_T$, is about the same as the forward rate, F, the "expected" gains or losses are approximately zero. But a forward hedge eliminates exchange exposure. In other words, the firm can eliminate foreign exchange exposure without sacrificing any expected Canadian dollar proceeds from the foreign sale. Under this scenario, the firm would be inclined to hedge as long as it is averse to risk. Note that this scenario becomes valid when the forward exchange rate is an unbiased predictor of the future spot rate.[2]

Under the second scenario, where the firm's expected future spot exchange rate is less than the forward rate, the firm expects a positive gain from its forward hedge. Since the firm expects to increase the Canadian dollar proceeds while eliminating exchange exposure, it would be even more inclined to hedge under this scenario than under the first scenario. The second scenario, however, implies that the firm's management dissents from the market's consensus forecast of the future spot exchange rate as reflected in the forward rate.

Under the third scenario, on the other hand, where the firm's expected future spot exchange rate is more than the forward rate, the firm can eliminate exchange exposure via the forward contract only at the cost of reduced expected Canadian dollar proceeds from the foreign sale. Thus, Bombardier would be less inclined to hedge under this scenario. Despite lower expected Canadian dollar proceeds, however, the firm may still end up hedging. Whether Bombardier actually hedges or not depends on its degree of risk aversion; the more risk-averse the firm is, the more likely it is to hedge. If Bombardier

---

[2]As mentioned in Chapter 5, the forward exchange rate will be an unbiased predictor of the future spot rate if the exchange market is informationally efficient and the risk premium is not significant. Empirical evidence indicates that the risk premium, if it exists, is generally not very significant. Unless the firm has private information that is not reflected in the forward rate, it would have no reason for disagreeing with the forward rate.

decides to hedge, the reduction in the expected Canadian dollar proceeds can be viewed as an "insurance premium" paid for avoiding the hazard of exchange risk.

Bombardier can use a currency futures contract, rather than a forward contract, to hedge. However, a futures contract is less suitable than a forward contract for the purpose of hedging for two reasons. First, unlike forward contracts that are tailor-made to the firm's specific needs, futures contracts are standardized in terms of contract size, delivery date and so forth. In most cases, therefore, the firm can only hedge approximately. Second, due to the marking-to-market property, there are interim cash flows prior to maturity of the futures contract that may have to be invested at uncertain interest rates. As a result, exact hedging again would be difficult.

13.2 MONEY MARKET HEDGE

Transaction exposure can also be hedged by lending and borrowing in the domestic and foreign money markets—that is, **money market hedge**. Generally speaking, the firm may borrow (lend) in foreign currency to hedge its foreign currency receivables (payables), thereby matching its assets and liabilities in the same currency. Again using the same example presented above, Bombardier can eliminate the exchange exposure arising from the European sale by first borrowing in euros, then converting the loan proceeds into Canadian dollars which then can be invested at the dollar interest rate. On the maturity date of the loan, Bombardier will use the euro receivable to pay off the euro loan. Bombardier can borrow a precise euro amount such that the maturity value of this loan is exactly equal to the euro receivable from the European sale. Bombardier's net euro exposure is thus reduced to zero and Bombardier will receive the future maturity value of the dollar investment.

The first step in money market hedging is to determine the amount of euros to borrow. Since the maturity value of borrowing should be the same as the euro receivable, the amount to borrow can be computed as the discounted present value of the euro receivable, that is, €10 million/(1.03) = €9,708,738. When Bombardier borrows €9,708,738, it then has to repay €10 million in one year which is equivalent to its euro receivable. The step-by-step procedure of money market hedging can be illustrated as follows:

Step 1: Borrow €9,708,738 in Europe.

Step 2: Convert €9,708,738 into $12,718,447 at the spot rate of $1.31/€.

Step 3: Invest $12,718,447 in Canadian Treasury bills.

Step 4: Collect €10 million from Austrian Airways and use it to repay the euro loan.

Step 5: Receive the maturity value of the dollar investment, that is, $12,858,350 = $12,718,447(1.011), which is the guaranteed Canadian dollar proceeds from the European sale.

Exhibit 13.4 provides a cash flow analysis of money market hedging. The table shows that the net cash flow is zero at the present time, implying that apart from possible transaction costs the money market hedge is fully self-financing. The table also shows how the 10 million euro receivable is exactly offset by the 10 million euro payable (created by borrowing), leaving a net cash flow of $12,858,350 on the maturity date.[3]

The maturity value of the dollar investment from the money market hedge turns out to be nearly identical to the dollar proceeds from a forward hedge. This result is no coincidence. Rather, it is due to the fact that the interest rate parity (IRP) condition is approximately holding in our example. If the IRP is not holding, the dollar proceeds from a money market hedge will not be the same as those from a forward hedge. As a result, one hedging method will dominate the other. In a competitive and efficient world financial market, however, any deviations from IRP are not likely to persist.

---

[3]In the case where the firm has an account payable denominated in euro, the money market hedge calls for borrowing Canadian dollars, buying euro spot, and investing at the euro interest rate.

EXHIBIT 13.4

Cash Flow Analysis
of a Money Market
Hedge

Transaction	Current Cash Flow	Cash Flow at Maturity
1. Borrow euros	€ 9,708,738	−€10,000,000
2. Buy dollar spot with euros	$12,718,447 −€ 9,708,738	
3. Invest in Canadian TBs	−$12,718,447	$12,858,350
4. Collect euro receivable Net cash flow	0	€10,000,000 $12,858,350

13.3   OPTIONS HEDGE

A shortcoming of both forward and money market hedges is that these methods completely eliminate exchange exposure. Consequently, the firm forgoes the opportunity to benefit from favourable exchange rate changes. To elaborate on this point, let us assume that the spot exchange rate turns out to be $1.40 per euro on the maturity date of the forward contract. In this instance, a forward hedge would cost Bombardier $1.3 million in terms of forgone dollar receipts (see Exhibit 13.2). If Bombardier had, indeed, entered into a forward contract, it would regret doing so. With its euro receivable, Bombardier ideally would like to protect itself only if the euro weakens while retaining the opportunity to benefit from a stronger euro. Currency options provide such a *flexible* "optional" hedge against exchange exposure. Generally speaking, the firm may buy a foreign currency call (put) option to hedge its foreign currency payables (receivables), which is known as an **options hedge**.

To show how the options hedge works, suppose that in the over-the-counter market Bombardier purchased a put option on 10 million euros with an exercise price of $1.27 and a one-year expiration. Assume that the option premium (price) is $0.02 per euro. Bombardier thus pays $200,000 (= $0.02 × 10 million) for the option. This transaction provides Bombardier with the right, but not the obligation, to sell up to €10 million for $1.27/€ regardless of the future spot rate.

Now, assume that the spot exchange rate turns out to be $1.10 on the expiration date. Since Bombardier has the right to sell each euro for $1.27, it will certainly exercise its put option on the euro and convert €10 million into $12.7 million. The main advantage of options hedging is that the firm can decide whether to exercise the option based on the realized spot exchange rate on the expiration date. Recall that Bombardier paid $200,000 upfront for the option. Considering the time value of money, this upfront cost is equivalent to $202,200 (= $200,000 × 1.011) as of the expiration date. This means that under the options hedge, the net dollar proceeds from the European sale become $12,497,800:

$12,497,800 = $12,700,000 − $202,200

Since Bombardier will exercise its put option on the euro if the future spot exchange rate ends up below the exercise rate of $1.27, it is assured of a "minimum" dollar receipt of $12,497,800 from the European sale.

Next, consider an alternative scenario where the euro appreciates against the Canadian dollar. Say the spot rate turns out to be $1.40 per euro on the expiration date. In this event, Bombardier has no reason to exercise the option. It will let the option expire and convert €10 million into $14 million at the spot rate. Subtracting $202,200 for the option cost, the net dollar proceeds become $13,797,800 under the options hedge. As

Managing Currency Exposure: The Perspective of a Bank

Our extensive example of a forward contract illustrates the arrangement from the retail client's perspective. The retail client starts the process by contacting a bank. Once the forward contract is established, the bank has taken on the risk that the client had faced.

Banks, however, are not in the business of taking large speculative positions on foreign currencies. The foreign exchange desk of a bank is there to serve its clients. When a bank makes a forward foreign exchange commitment to a customer, the bank typically tries to quickly neutralize the exposure that it has taken on. This note illustrates how this is done. The setting is a Canadian firm that purchases US dollars six months forward from a Canadian bank.

All forward foreign currency transactions are done by banks. More than 95 percent of all foreign currency transactions are done *within* banks. Thus, banks are foreign exchange *brokers* to the industrial and commercial world. The foreign exchange desks of banks are not in the business of speculating, that is, taking exposed positions on foreign currencies.

A typical transaction that a bank might encounter in dealing with a customer looks like this: Someone phones the bank to enquire about *buying* one million US dollars six months from now. Perhaps it is a Canadian company retiring a US dollar-denominated corporate bond.

The bank's customer wants US$1,000,000 six months forward.

Today, June 1, the six-month *forward* rate is 0.9600. Of course, this is in US dollars per Canadian dollar.

The bank officer at the foreign exchange desk says, "OK, one million December US dollars at 0.9600. That will be 1,041,667 Canadian dollars. Done!"

The customer's problem is solved.

Now, the bank has a problem. The bank is *short* US dollars. The bank must provide US$1,000,000 six months from now. The bank is exposed.

How does the bank manage *its* risk?

Immediately, the bank will reverse its US dollar forward position by an offsetting transaction in the spot market. The bank will immediately *buy* US$1,000,000 spot.

Why wouldn't the bank make an offsetting transaction in the *forward* market—that is, why wouldn't it commit to *buy* US$1,000,000 in December? That is a deceptive question. The bank would if it could. Imagine if the officer at the foreign exchange desk had simultaneous calls from two customers, one looking to *buy* US$1,000,000 in December and one wanting to *sell* the same amount at the same time. Of course, these two offsetting transactions would cancel each other out from the bank's perspective, and the bank would simply—and profitably—capture the bid-ask spread. Pure brokerage.

However, things are seldom that simple. The bank must *manage* its brokerage operations. That is the bank's skill.

The *spot* market is much more liquid and generally presents substantially smaller spreads than the *forward* market. So the bank can more easily and more readily sell US dollars in the *spot* market.

Now, let us say that the *forward* exchange rate (expressed in US dollars per Canadian dollar) is greater than the *spot* exchange rate.

Spot:	0.9550	Now, June
Forward:	0.9600	December

In the back of your mind—but not too far back—you should be asking yourself what this forward premium implies for (1) the expected future spot rate and (2) the US–Canada interest differential. The latter will soon become important.

The bank pays $1,047,120 for US$1,000,000. This is a *spot* transaction.

After the offsetting transaction in the *spot* market (establishing a *long* position in the US dollar to offset the *short* forward position), the remaining net exposure is to the US–Canada interest differential. That is foreign interest rate exposure. The bank can swap that risk away with a US–Canada interest rate swap. The transactional cost of the US–Canada interest rate swap is the cost of insurance for the remaining bit of risk. The swap assures the bank of receiving a flow of Canadian dollar interest despite the fact that it holds US dollars on account.

suggested by these scenarios, the options hedge allows the firm to *limit the downside risk while preserving the upside potential.* The firm, however, has to pay for this flexibility in terms of the option premium. There is rarely a free lunch in finance!

Exhibit 13.5 provides the net Canadian dollar proceeds from the European sale under options hedging for a range of future spot rates. The same results are illustrated in

The bank's three transactions can be illustrated with a simple diagram:

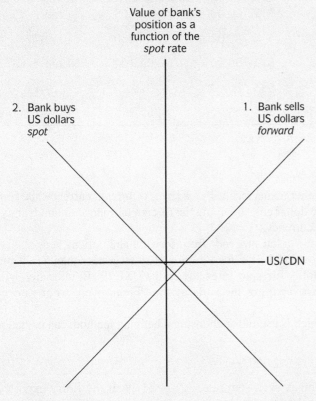

After Steps 1 and 2, that is, after the bank offsets its *forward* short position with a *spot* long, the remaining net exposure is to the US–Canada interest differential for six months. The bank will swap that risk away with a US–Canada interest rate swap.

In the diagram, the intersection of the two axes is the *spot* rate. A little to the right is the *forward* rate. The bank's exposure due to the first transaction is represented by an upward sloping 45-degree line passing through the *forward* rate. Why is the line sloping upward? Well, if the exchange rate (expressed as US$/$) increases, it would take fewer Canadian dollars to buy the requisite US$1,000,000. Unhedged, the bank's value (on the vertical axis) would increase if US$/$ increases, that is, if the Canadian dollar appreciates. The second (offsetting) transaction requires a downward-sloping 45-degree line passing through the *spot* rate. The third transaction, the *swap*, eliminates the exposure associated with the gap between the *spot* and *forward* rates.

Finally, there is another way that the bank could handle its exposure to the exchange rate risk that it incurs in its function as a forward exchange broker.

The key point is that the bank must deliver US$1,000,000 in December, for which it will receive $1,041,667. The $1,041,667 is secure. The issue for the bank is how to structure the future delivery of US$1,000,000 while avoiding exchange rate risk.

Buying US dollars *spot* gets rid of most of the foreign exchange risk. However, buying the full US$1,000,000 may be overkill. The US-interest flow on the securities that the bank purchases with those funds leaves residual exchange rate risk associated with the US-interest that accrues between now and December.

Instead of buying US$1,000,000, the bank could purchase December US discount bonds in the amount of US$1,000,000/(1 + r_{US}/2) where r_{US} is the yield on the discount bonds. In other words, the bank purchases riskless securities today that retire in December with a liquidation value of US$1,000,000.

Say r_{US} equals 1 percent. Then, US$1,000,000/(1 + r_{US}/2) equals US$995,025.

The purchase today of December US discount bonds in the amount of US$995,025 will result in US$1,000,000 in December.

In this way, the bank establishes its own "money market" hedge on its US-forward obligation.

What would determine whether the bank ought to "over-borrow" the full US$1,000,000 and swap the US-interest into Canadian dollars as opposed to buying US$995,025 of December US discount bonds? This type of decision generally turns on considerations such as whether the bank has a substantial swap book that would make it easy (and cheap) to swap US interest into Canadian or whether the bank is heavily involved in the US discount securities market, in which case it may have an operational advantage in that market.

All in all, the difference between the two approaches is likely to be small. The advantage of purchasing US discount bonds is that it is neater and it reduces the bank's capital commitment.

Keep in mind that the bank is essentially operating as a broker in the forward market, and hence it ought to take advantage of any internal administrative efficiencies that it may have in managing its own risk.

Exhibit 13.6, which shows that the options hedge sets a "floor" for the Canadian dollar proceeds. The future Canadian dollar proceeds will be at least $12,497,800 under the options hedge. Bombardier, thus, can be said to have an insurance policy against its exchange risk; the upfront option cost, $200,000, that Bombardier incurred can be regarded as an insurance premium.

EXHIBIT 13.5

Dollar Proceeds
from Options
Hedge

Future Spot Exchange Rate	Exercise Decision	Gross Dollar Proceeds	Option Premium	Net Dollar Proceeds
$1.10	Exercise	$12,700,000	$202,200	$12,497,800
$1.20	Exercise	$12,700,000	$202,200	$12,497,800
$1.27	Neutral	$12,700,000	$202,200	$12,497,800
$1.30	Not exercise	$13,000,000	$202,200	$12,797,800
$1.40	Not exercise	$14,000,000	$202,200	$13,797,800

Note: The exercise exchange rate is $1.27 in this example.

When a firm has a payable rather than a receivable in terms of foreign currency, the firm can set a "ceiling" for the future dollar cost of buying the foreign currency amount by buying a call option on the foreign currency.

Exhibit 13.6 also compares the dollar proceeds from forward and options hedges. The options hedge dominates the forward hedge for future spot rates greater than $1.29 per euro, whereas the opposite holds for spot rates lower than $1.29. Bombardier will be indifferent between the two hedging methods at the "break-even" spot rate of $1.29 per euro.

The break-even spot rate, which is useful for choosing a hedging method, can be determined as follows:

$$\$(10,000,000)S_T - \$202,200 = \$12,700,000$$

Solving for S_T, we obtain the break-even spot rate, $S_T^* = \$1.29$. If the firm's expected future spot rate is greater (less) than the break-even rate, then it would likely prefer the options (forward) hedge.

Unlike a forward contract, which has only one forward rate for a given maturity, there are multiple exercise exchange rates for options contracts. In the preceding discussion, we worked with an option with an exercise price of $1.27. Considering that Bombardier has a euro receivable, it is tempting to think that it would be a good idea for Bombardier to buy a put option with a higher exercise price, thereby increasing the minimum dollar receipt

EXHIBIT 13.6

Dollar Proceeds
from the European
Sale: Option versus
Forward Hedge

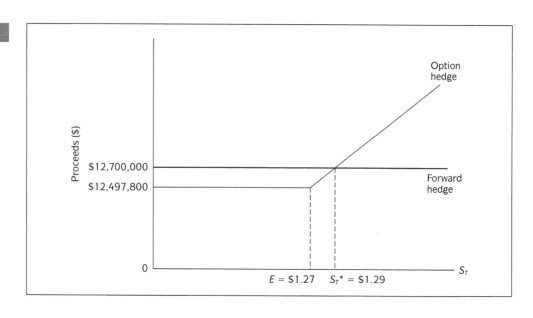

EXHIBIT 13.7	Bombardier's Alternative Hedging Strategies: A Summary	
Strategy	**Transactions**	**Outcomes**
Forward hedge	1. Sell €10,000,000 forward for dollars now. 2. In one year, receive €10,000,000 from the European client and deliver it to the counterparty of the forward contract.	Assured of receiving $12,700,000 in one year; future spot exchange becomes irrelevant.
Money market hedge	1. Borrow €9,708,738 and buy $12,718,447 spot now. 2. In one year, collect €10,000,000 from the European client and pay off the euro loan using the amount.	Assured of receiving $12,718,447 now or $12,858,358 in one year; future spot exchange rate becomes irrelevant.
Options hedge	1. Buy a put option on €10,000,000 for an upfront cost of $200,000. 2. In one year, decide whether to exercise the option upon observing the prevailing spot exchange rate.	Assured of receiving at least $12,497,800 or more if the future spot exchange rate exceeds the exercise exchange rate; Bombardier controls the downside risk while retaining the upside potential.

from the European sale. But it becomes immediately clear that the firm has to pay for it in terms of a higher option premium. Again, there is no free lunch. Choice of the exercise price for the options contract ultimately depends on the extent to which the firm is willing to bear exchange risk. For instance, if the firm's objective is only to avoid very unfavourable exchange rate changes (i.e., a major depreciation of the euro in Bombardier's example), then it should consider buying out-of-money put options with a low exercise price, saving option costs. The three alternative hedging strategies are summarized in Exhibit 13.7.

13.4 CROSS-HEDGING MINOR CURRENCY EXPOSURE

If a firm has receivables or payables in major currencies, such as the US dollar, euro, British pound or Japanese yen, it can easily use forward, money market or options contracts to manage exchange risk exposure. In contrast, if the firm has positions in minor currencies, such as the Korean won, Thai baht or Czech koruna, it may be either very costly or impossible to use financial contracts in these currencies. This is because markets in such currencies are relatively underdeveloped and often highly regulated. Facing this situation, the firm may consider **cross-hedging** techniques to manage minor currency exposure. Cross-hedging involves hedging a position in one asset by taking a position in another asset.

Suppose a Canadian firm has a receivable in Korean won and would like to hedge its won position. If there were a well-functioning forward market in won, the firm would simply sell the won receivable forward. But the firm finds it impossible to do so. However, since the won/Canadian dollar exchange rate is highly correlated with the yen/dollar exchange rate, the Canadian firm may sell a yen amount, which is equivalent to the won receivable, forward against the Canadian dollar thereby cross-hedging its won exposure. Obviously, the effectiveness of this cross-hedging technique depends on the stability and strength of the won/yen correlation.

Aggarwal and Demaskey (1997) find that Japanese yen derivative contracts are effective in cross-hedging exposure to minor Asian currencies such as the Indonesian rupiah, Korean won, Philippine peso and Thai baht. Likewise, euro derivatives can be effective in cross-hedging exposures in Central and East European currencies, such as the Czech koruna, Estonian kroon and Hungarian forint.

Another study, by Benet (1990), suggests that commodity futures contracts may be used effectively to cross-hedge minor currency exposures. Suppose the Canadian dollar price of the Mexican peso is positively correlated to the world oil price. Mexico is a major exporter of oil, accounting for roughly 5 percent of the world market share. Considering this situation, a firm may use oil futures contracts to manage its peso exposure. The firm can sell (buy) oil futures if it has peso receivables (payables). In the same vein, soybean and coffee futures contracts may be used to cross-hedge a Brazilian real exposure. Again, the effectiveness of this cross-hedging technique depends on the strength and stability of the relationship between the exchange rate and the commodity futures prices.

13.5 HEDGING CONTINGENT EXPOSURE

In addition to providing a flexible hedge against exchange exposure, options contracts can also provide an effective hedge against what might be called **contingent exposure**. Contingent exposure refers to a situation in which the firm may or may not be subject to exchange exposure. Let us consider an example from the perspective of an American firm with Canadian dollar transaction exposure. Suppose General Electric (GE) is bidding on a hydroelectric project in Quebec. If the bid is accepted, which will be known in three months, GE is going to receive $100 million to initiate the project. Since GE may or may not face exchange exposure depending on whether its bid will be accepted, it faces a typical contingent exposure situation.[4]

It is difficult to deal with contingent exposure using traditional hedging tools such as forward contracts. Suppose that GE sold $100 million forward to hedge the contingent exposure. If GE's bid is accepted, then GE will have no problem because it will have $100 million to fulfill the forward contract. However, if the bid is rejected, GE now faces an unhedged short position in Canadian dollars. Clearly, a forward contract does not provide a satisfactory hedge against contingent exposure. A "do nothing" policy does not guarantee a satisfactory outcome either. The problem with this policy is that if GE's bid is accepted, the American firm ends up with an unhedged long position in Canadian dollars.

An alternative approach is to buy a three-month put option on $100 million. In this case, there are four possible outcomes:

1. The bid is accepted, and the spot exchange rate turns out to be less than the exercise rate; in this case, GE will simply exercise the put option and convert $100 million at the exercise rate.

2. The bid is accepted, and the spot exchange rate turns out to be greater than the exercise rate; in this case, GE will let the put option expire and convert $100 million at the spot rate.

3. The bid is rejected, and the spot exchange rate turns out to be less than the exercise rate; in this case, although GE does not have Canadian dollars, it will exercise the put option and make a profit.

4. The bid is rejected, and the spot rate turns out to be greater than the exercise rate; in this case, GE will simply let the put option expire.

---

[4]These days, it is not unusual for the exporter to let the importer choose the currency of payment. For example, in the Bombardier case, Bombardier may allow Austrian Airways to pay either $13 million or €10 million. To the extent that Bombardier does not know in advance which currency it is going to receive, it faces a contingent exposure. Given the future spot exchange rate, Austrian Airways will choose to pay with a cheaper currency. In effect, Bombardier provides Austrian Airways with a free option to buy up to $13 million using euros (which is equivalent to an option to sell euros for dollars) at the implicit exercise rate of $1.30/€.

EXHIBIT 13.8

Contingent
Exposure
Management:
The Case of GE
Bidding for a
Quebec Hydro-
electric Project

	Bid Outcome	
Alternative Strategies	**Bid Accepted**	**Bid Rejected**
Do nothing	*An unhedged long position in $100 million*	No exposure
Sell $ forward	No exposure	*An unhedged short position in $100 million*
Buy put option on $[a]	If the future spot rate becomes less than the exercise rate, $(S_T < E)$	
	Convert $100 million at the exercise price	Exercise the option and and make a profit
	If the future spot rate becomes greater than the exercise rate, $(S_T > E)$	
	Let the option expire and convert $100 million at the spot exchange rate	Simply let the option expire

[a]If the future spot rate turns out to be equal to the exercise price, that is, $S_T = E$, GE will be indifferent between (i) exercising the option and (ii) letting the option expire and converting $100 million at the spot rate.

The above scenarios indicate that when the put option is purchased, each outcome is adequately covered; GE will not be left with an unhedged foreign currency position. Again, it is stressed that GE has to pay the option premium upfront. The preceding discussion is summarized in Exhibit 13.8.

13.6 HEDGING RECURRENT EXPOSURE WITH SWAP CONTRACTS

Firms often have to deal with a "sequence" of accounts payable or receivable in terms of a foreign currency. Such recurrent cash flows in a foreign currency can best be hedged using a currency swap contract, which is an agreement to exchange one currency for another at a predetermined exchange rate, that is, the swap rate, on a sequence of future dates. As such, a swap contract is like a portfolio of forward contracts with different maturities. Swaps are very flexible in terms of amount and maturity; the maturity can range from a few months to 20 years.

Suppose that Bombardier is scheduled to deliver an aircraft to Austrian Airways at the beginning of each year for the next five years, starting in 2013. Austrian Airways, in turn, is scheduled to pay €10,000,000 to Bombardier on December 1 of each year for five years, starting in 2013. In this case, Bombardier faces a sequence of exchange risk exposures. Bombardier can hedge this type of exposure with a swap agreement by which Bombardier delivers €10,000,000 to the counterparty of the contract on December 1 of each year for five years and takes delivery of a predetermined dollar amount each year. If the agreed swap exchange rate is $1.30/€, then Bombardier will receive $13 million each year, regardless of the future spot and forward rates. Note, in contrast, that a sequence of five forward contracts would not be priced at a uniform rate, $1.30/€; forward rates differ for different maturities. Moreover, longer-term forward contracts may not be readily available.

13.7 HEDGING THROUGH INVOICE CURRENCY

While financial hedging instruments such as forward contracts, money market hedges and options contracts are well known, **hedging through invoice currency**—an operational technique—has not received much attention. The firm can *shift*, *share* or *diversify* exchange

The LCBO and Foreign Exchange Risk Management

The Liquor Control Board of Ontario (LCBO) is the single largest importer of wines, spirits, and beer in the world. In 2012, the LCBO imported liquor worth more than $1 billion. These imports come from many sources. Wines come from Australia, Chile, France, Italy, the United States and several other warm countries. Ireland, Sweden and the United Kingdom are important providers of spirits. Jamaica sends us strong rum.

The LCBO's foreign exchange exposure creates a complex risk management problem. When the Canadian dollar rises or falls, it does not move to the same degree against all currencies. The LCBO is exposed to risk from a variety of foreign exchange movements.

The LCBO has devised a method to simplify its currency dealings with foreign suppliers of wines and spirits. First, the LCBO makes known to agents that the LCBO deals only in a small number of foreign currencies—primarily the US dollar and the euro. For suppliers from the United States or Europe, this is not an issue. On the other hand, agents for Chilean wine or Swedish vodka must quote prices to the LCBO either in US dollars or euros—or perhaps Canadian dollars. This pushes foreign exchange transactional exposure (between, say, the Swedish krone and the Canadian dollar) on to suppliers of wines and spirits from countries other than the United States or Europe. This is a policy that only a very large importer could sustain.

The second feature of the LCBO's exchange risk management takes the form of "announced exchange rates" for purchases of imported wines and spirits. Again, this arrangement is workable because the LCBO is an important customer for its suppliers. The LCBO announces exchange rates that it will apply in processing invoices in foreign currencies over the subsequent quarter. For example, in July 2012, the LCBO announced that it will process all euro-denominated invoices received in August, September and October at $1.40/€. The LCBO orders a shipment of wine from a French supplier at an invoice price of, say, €100,000 specified at the time of the order. The supplier accepts the LCBO's "offer exchange rate" scheme. Compared with what the French supplier would receive in euro if he were to take payment in Canadian dollars on the spot market at the time of delivery, under the LCBO "offer exchange rate" scheme, a change in the exchange rate between the time of the order and the time of delivery results in a foreign exchange *gain* (recorded in euro) for the exporter if the Canadian dollar appreciates against the euro or a foreign *loss* if the Canadian dollar depreciates.

Finally, during each three-month span of its "announced rates" the LCBO protects itself with forward contracts and foreign exchange options. The policy is to hedge approximately 50 percent of the exposure.

risk by appropriately choosing the currency of invoice. For instance, if Bombardier invoices $13 million rather than €10 million for the sale of the aircraft, then Bombardier does not face exchange exposure. The exchange exposure has not disappeared; it has merely shifted to the European importer. Austrian Airways now has a payable denominated in Canadian dollars.

Instead of shifting the exchange exposure entirely to Austrian Airways, Bombardier can share the exposure with Austrian Airways by, for example, invoicing half the bill in Canadian dollars and half in euros, that is, $6.5 million and €5 million. In this case, Bombardier's exchange exposure is reduced by half. As a practical matter, however, the firm may not be able to use risk sharing as much as it wishes to for fear of losing sales to competitors. Only an exporter with substantial market power can use this approach. In addition, if the currencies of both the exporter and the importer are not suitable for settling international trade, neither party can resort to risk shifting/sharing to deal with exchange exposure. The International Finance in Practice box "The LCBO and Foreign Exchange Risk Management" illustrates how one organization with substantial market power over its suppliers is able to shift foreign exchange risk to the suppliers.

The firm can diversify exchange exposure to some extent by using currency basket units, such as the SDR, as the invoice currency. Often, multinational corporations and sovereign entities were known to float bonds denominated either in the SDR or in the ECU prior to the introduction of the euro. For example, the Egyptian government charges for the use of the Suez Canal using the SDR. Obviously, these currency baskets are used to reduce exchange exposure. As previously noted, the SDR now comprises four individual currencies: the US dollar, the euro, the Japanese yen and the British pound. Because the SDR is a portfolio of currencies, its value is generally more stable than the value of any individual constituent currency. Currency basket units can be a useful hedging tool, especially for long-term exposure for which no forward or options contracts are readily available.

13.8   HEDGING VIA LEAD AND LAG

Another operational technique the firm can use to reduce transaction exposure is leading and lagging foreign currency receipts and payments. To "lead" means to pay or collect early, and to "lag" means to pay or collect late. The firm would like to lead soft-currency receivables and lag hard-currency receivables to avoid the loss from depreciation of the soft currency and benefit from the appreciation of the hard currency. For the same reason, the firm will attempt to lead the hard-currency payables and lag soft-currency payables.

To the extent that the firm can effectively implement a **lead/lag strategy**, the transaction exposure the firm faces can be reduced. However, a word of caution is in order. Suppose, concerned with the likely depreciation of the euro, Bombardier would like Austrian Airways to prepay €10 million. Bombardier's attempt to lead the euro receivable may encounter difficulties. First of all, Austrian Airways would like to lag this payment, which is denominated in the soft currency (the euro), and thus has no incentive to prepay unless Bombardier offers a discount to compensate for the prepayment. This, of course, reduces the benefits of collecting the euro receivable early. Second, pressing Austrian Airways for prepayment can hamper future sales efforts by Bombardier. Third, to the extent that the original invoice price, €10 million, incorporates the expected depreciation of the euro, Bombardier is already partially protected against euro depreciation.

The lead/lag strategy can be employed more effectively to deal with intrafirm payables and receivables, such as material costs, rents, royalties, interest and dividends, among subsidiaries of the same multinational corporation. Since management of various subsidiaries of the same firm are presumably working for the good of the entire firm, the lead/lag strategy can be applied more aggressively.

13.9   EXPOSURE NETTING

In 1984, Lufthansa, a German airline, signed a contract to buy $3 billion worth of aircraft from Bombardier and entered into a forward contract to purchase $1.5 billion forward to hedge against the expected appreciation of the dollar against the German mark. This decision, however, suffered a major flaw: a significant portion of Lufthansa's cash flows was also dollar-denominated. As a result, Lufthansa's net exposure to the exchange risk might not have been significant. Lufthansa had a so-called natural hedge. In 1985, the dollar depreciated substantially against the mark and, as a result, Lufthansa experienced a substantial foreign exchange loss in settling the forward contract. This episode shows that when a firm has both receivables and payables in a given foreign currency, it should hedge only its *net* exposure.

So far, we have discussed exposure management on a currency-by-currency basis. In reality, a typical multinational corporation is likely to have a portfolio of currency positions. For instance, a Canadian firm may have a payable in euros and, at the same time, a receivable in Swiss francs. Considering that the euro and Swiss franc move against the dollar almost in lockstep, the firm can simply wait until both accounts become due and then buy euros spot with Swiss francs. It would be wasteful and unnecessary to buy euros forward and sell Swiss francs forward. In other words, if the firm has a portfolio of currency positions, it makes sense to hedge residual exposure rather than hedge each currency position separately.

If the firm would like to apply **exposure netting** aggressively, it helps to centralize the firm's exchange exposure management function in one location. Many multinational corporations are using a **reinvoice centre**, a financial subsidiary, as a mechanism for

INTERNATIONAL FINANCE *in Practice*

To Hedge or Not to Hedge

"Most value-maximising firms do not hedge." Thus Merton Miller and Christopher Culp, two economists at the University of Chicago, said in an article[1] about Metallgesellschaft, a firm that saw its value plunge after its oil-price hedging strategy came a cropper. Yet the vast majority of firms that use derivatives do so to hedge. Last year's survey of big American non-financial companies by the Wharton School and Chase Manhattan Bank found that, of those firms that used derivatives (about one-third of the sample), some 75% said they did so to hedge commitments. As many as 40% of the derivatives users said they sometimes took a view on the direction of markets, but only 8% admitted to doing so frequently.

To justify speculation, managers ought to have good reason to suppose that they can consistently outwit firms for which playing the financial markets is a core business. Commodity businesses, such as oil or grain companies taking positions on the direction of their related commodity markets, may have such reason, but non-financial firms taking bets on interest rates or foreign-exchange rates almost certainly do not—though some claim to make a profit on it. But why might hedging be wrong?

In the 1950s, Merton Miller and Franco Modigliani, another financial economist, demonstrated that firms make money only if they make good investments—the kind that increase their operating cash flows. Whether those investments are financed through debt, equity or retained earnings is irrelevant. Different methods of financing simply determine how a firm's value is divided between its various sorts of investors (e.g., shareholders or bondholders), not the value itself. This surprising insight helped win each of them a Nobel prize. If they are right, it has crucial implications for hedging. For if methods of financing and the character of financial risks do not matter, managing them is pointless. It cannot add to the firm's value; on the contrary, as derivatives do not come free, using them for hedging might actually lower that value. Moreover, as Messrs. Miller and Modigliani showed, if investors want to

avoid the financial risks attached to holding shares in a firm, they can diversify their portfolio of holdings. Firms need not manage their financial risks; investors can do it for themselves.

In recent years, other academics have challenged the Miller-Modigliani thesis—at least in its pure form—and demonstrated that hedging can sometimes add value. That is because firms may be able to manage certain risks internally in ways that cannot be replicated by outside investors. Some investors may not want, or be able, to hold diversified share portfolios (for instance, if the firm is family-owned). It may be possible to use derivatives to reduce profits in good years and raise them in bad years in order to cut the firm's average tax bill. Hedging can also be used to prevent the firm getting into financial difficulties, or even going bust.

Another view has also been winning converts. According to Kenneth Froot, David Sharfstein and Jeremy Stein, three Boston-based economists, firms should hedge to ensure they always have sufficient cash flow to fund their planned investment programme.[2] Otherwise some potentially profitable investments may be missed because of inefficiencies in the bond and equity markets that prevent the firm raising the funds, or the reluctance of managers to tap these markets when internal cash is tight. Merck, an American pharmaceuticals firm, has helped to pioneer the use of derivatives to ensure that investment plans—particularly in R&D—can always be financed. In a paper explaining the firm's strategy, Judy Lewent and John Kearney observed that "our experience, and that of the [drugs] industry in general, has been that cash-flow and earnings uncertainty caused by exchange-rate volatility leads to a reduction in research spending."[3]

Though apparently simple, such a strategy has some intriguing implications. As Messrs. Froot, Scharfstein and Stein point out, the factors that cause cash flow to fall below expectations may also cut the number of profitable investment opportunities, so lessening the need to hedge. For instance, an oil company's cash flow

centralizing exposure management functions. All the invoices arising from intrafirm transactions are sent to the reinvoice centre where exposure is netted. Once the residual exposure is determined, then foreign exchange experts at the centre determine optimal hedging methods and implement them.

13.10 SHOULD THE FIRM HEDGE?

We have discussed how the firm can hedge exchange exposure if it wishes. We have not discussed whether the firm should try to hedge to begin with. As can be seen from the International Finance in Practice box "To Hedge or Not to Hedge," there hardly exists a consensus on whether the firm should hedge. Some would argue that exchange exposure management at the corporate level is redundant when shareholders can manage the exposure

348

may suffer due to a fall in oil prices. However, that fall in prices also reduces the value of investing in developing new oil fields. With fewer profitable projects to invest in, the firm will need less cash to finance investment.

All about Cash Flow

Rene Stulz, an economist at Ohio State University, sees even more powerful implications.[4] He says that there are only a couple of good reasons why a firm should hedge. One is to cut its tax bills, which is likely to happen only if the firm's profits tend to yo-yo between lower and higher tax bands. The other one is being unable to get cash when it needs it, or facing a serious risk of running short. By this rule, reckons Mr. Stulz, a firm with little debt or with highly-rated debt has no need to hedge, as the risk of it getting into financial trouble is tiny. If he is right, many of America's biggest hedgers—including some of those that have revealed losses on derivatives, such as Procter & Gamble—may be wasting their energies, or worse. By contrast, Mr. Stulz thinks that if a firm is highly geared, hedging can boost its value significantly. Indeed, during the leveraged buy-out craze of the 1980s, when firms were taken over by buying off shareholders and loading up on debt, tough risk-management requirements were standard in any borrowing arrangement.

Messrs. Culp and Miller, of the University of Chicago, take this argument a step further in defending the management of Metallgesellschaft from some of the wilder accusations of recklessness (a matter that is now before the American courts). Instead of analysing the firm's hedging strategy (which involved selling oil for up to ten years ahead and hedging this exposure with futures contracts) in terms of its effectiveness in reducing risk, Messrs. Culp and Miller argue that the company had no need to reduce its risk-exposure because it had no reason to suppose it could not get hold of cash if needed. After all, the mighty Deutsche Bank, as its principal creditor and controlling shareholder, was behind the firm, ensuring that it could not go bust; and, as it turned out, it did not. Rather, the aim of the hedging strategy was to exploit what Metallgesellschaft thought was its superior understanding of the relationship between spot prices and futures prices—risky but not obviously foolish.

Not everyone agrees that firms with little debt should not hedge. Myron Scholes, an economist at Stanford University, reaches the opposite conclusion: firms with little debt could reduce their riskiness by hedging, and so be able to borrow more and rely less on equity. Equity can be expensive compared with debt; it is inherently riskier, offering no guaranteed payout, so investors require a higher average return on it than they do on bonds. Ultimately, through risk-reducing hedging and borrowing, more firms might be able to remain (or become) privately owned, reckons Mr. Scholes. But to do this well, managers will need a very good understanding of the risks to which their firm is exposed, and of opportunities to hedge.

However, the way firms typically use derivatives to reduce the cost of capital is different from that described above. Rather than hedge and borrow more, they substitute for traditional debt a hybrid of bonds and options and/or futures that will pay off in certain circumstances, thus lowering capital costs. This is speculation dressed up as prudence, because if events take an unexpected turn, capital costs go up by at least the cost of the options.

-----

[1]"Hedging in the Theory of Corporate Finance: A Reply to Our Critics." By Christopher Culp and Merton Miller. *Journal of Applied Corporate Finance*; Spring 1995.

[2]"A Framework for Risk Management." By Kenneth Froot, David Scharfstein and Jeremy Stein. *Harvard Business Review*; November 1994.

[3]"Identifying, Measuring and Hedging Currency Risk at Merck." By Judy Lewent and John Kearney. In *The New Corporate Finance*, edited by Donald Chew, McGraw-Hill; 1993.

[4]"Rethinking Risk Management." By Rene Stulz. Ohio State University working paper; 1995.

Source: *The Economist,* February 10, 1996, pp. PS10–12.
© 1996 The Economist Newspaper Group, Inc. Reprinted with permission.

themselves. Others would argue that what matters in the firm valuation is only systematic risk; corporate risk management may only reduce the total risk. These arguments suggest that corporate exposure management would not necessarily add to the value of the firm.

While the above arguments against corporate risk management may be valid in a "perfect" capital market, one can make a case for it based on various market imperfections:

1. *Information asymmetry.* Management knows about the firm's exposure position much better than shareholders. Thus, the management of the firm, not its shareholders, should manage exchange exposure.

2. *Differential transaction costs.* The firm is in a position to acquire low-cost hedges; transaction costs for individual shareholders can be substantial. Also, the firm has hedging tools like the reinvoice centre that are not available to shareholders.

3. *Default costs.* If default costs are significant, corporate hedging would be justifiable because it will reduce the probability of default. Perception of a reduced default risk, in turn, can lead to a better credit rating and lower financing costs.

4. *Progressive corporate taxes.* Under progressive corporate tax rates, stable before-tax earnings lead to lower corporate taxes than volatile earnings with the same average value. This is because under progressive tax rates, the firm pays more taxes in high-earning periods than it saves in low-earning periods.

The last point merits elaboration. Suppose the country's corporate income tax system applies a tax rate of 20 percent to the first $10 million of earnings and a 40 percent rate to earnings exceeding $10 million. Firms thus face a simple progressive tax structure. Now consider an exporting firm that expects to earn $15 million if the dollar depreciates but only $5 million if the dollar appreciates. Assume the dollar may appreciate or depreciate with equal chances. In this case, the firm's expected tax will be $2.5 million:

$$\text{Expected tax} = 0.5[(0.2 \times \$5,000,000) + (0.2 \times \$10,000,000) + (0.4 \times \$5,000,000)]$$
$$= \$2,500,000$$

Now, consider another firm, B, identical to firm A in every respect except that, unlike firm A, firm B aggressively and successfully hedges its risk exposure. As a result, Firm B expects to realize certain earnings of $10,000,000, the same as firm A's expected earnings. Firm B, however, will pay only $2 million as taxes. Obviously, hedging results in a $500,000 tax saving. Exhibit 13.9 illustrates this situation.

While not every firm hedges exchange exposure, many firms do, suggesting that risk management is relevant to maximizing the firm's value. To the extent that shareholders themselves cannot properly manage exchange risk, the firm's managers can do it for them, contributing to the firm's value. Some corporate hedging activities, however, might be motivated by managerial objectives; managers may want to stabilize cash flows so that the risk to their managerial positions can be reduced.

A study by Allayannis and Weston (2001) provides direct evidence on the important issue of whether hedging actually adds to the value of the firm. Specifically, they examine whether firms with currency exposure that use foreign currency derivative contracts, such as currency forward and options, increase their valuation. Firms that face currency risk and

EXHIBIT 13.9

Tax Savings from Hedging Exchange Risk Exposure

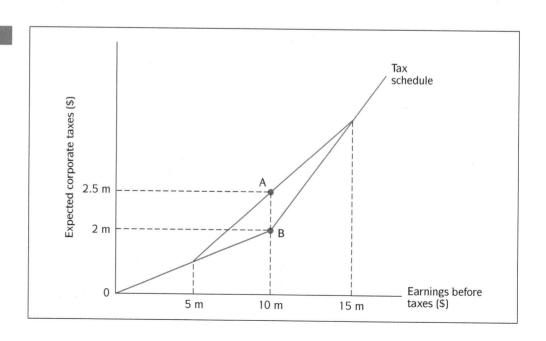

use currency derivatives for hedging have, on average, about 5 percent higher value than firms that do not use derivatives. Firms that have no direct foreign involvement but may be exposed to exchange rate movements via export/import competition enjoy a small hedging valuation premium. Firms that stop hedging experience a decrease in firm valuation compared with those firms that continue to hedge. Overall, the indications are that corporate hedging contributes to firm value.

13.11 WHAT RISK MANAGEMENT PRODUCTS DO FIRMS USE?

Jesswein, Kwok and Folks (1995) document the extent of knowledge and use of foreign exchange risk management products by corporations. On the basis of a survey of Fortune 500 firms, they found that the traditional forward contract is the most popular product. As Exhibit 13.10 shows, about 93 percent of respondents of the survey used forward contracts. This old, traditional instrument has not been supplanted by recent "fancy" innovations. The next commonly used instruments are foreign currency swaps (53 percent) and over-the-counter currency options (49 percent). Such recent innovations as compound options (4 percent) and lookback options (5 percent) are among the least extensively used instruments. These findings indicate that most firms meet their exchange risk management needs with forward, swap and options contracts.

EXHIBIT 13.10

A Survey of Knowledge and Use of Foreign Exchange Risk Management Products[a]

Type of Product	Heard of (awareness)	Used (adoption)
Forward contracts	100.0%	93.1%
Foreign currency swaps	98.8	52.6
Foreign currency futures	98.8	20.1
Exchange-traded currency options	96.4	17.3
Exchange-traded futures options	95.8	8.9
Over-the-counter currency options	93.5	48.8
Cylinder options	91.2	28.7
Synthetic forwards	88.0	22.0
Synthetic options	88.0	18.6
Participating forwards, etc.	83.6	15.8
Forward exchange agreements, etc.	81.7	14.8
Foreign currency warrants	77.7	4.2
Break forwards, etc.	65.3	4.9
Compound options	55.8	3.8
Lookback options, etc.	52.1	5.1
Average across products	84.4%	23.9%

[a]The products are ranked by the percentages of respondents who have heard of products. There are 173 respondents in total.
Source: Kurt Jesswein, Chuck Kwok, and William Folks, Jr., "Corporate Use of Innovative Foreign Exchange Risk Management Products," *Columbia Journal of World Business* (Fall 1995).

The Jesswein et al. survey also shows that the finance/insurance/real estate industry stands out as the most frequent user of exchange risk management products. This finding is not surprising. This industry has more finance experts who are familiar with derivative securities. In addition, this industry handles mainly financial assets, the sort that tend to be exposed to exchange risk. The survey further shows that the corporate use of foreign exchange risk management products is positively related to the firm's degree of international involvement. Again, not a surprise. As a firm becomes more internationalized through cross-border trade and investments, it is likely to handle an increasing amount of foreign currencies, giving rise to a greater demand for exchange risk hedging.

SUMMARY

This chapter shows how to manage risk that arises from business transactions denominated in foreign currencies. It is all about hedging. Various hedging techniques are identified and illustrated.

1. The firm is subject to a transaction exposure when it faces contractual cash flows denominated in foreign currencies. Transaction exposure can be hedged by financial contracts, such as forward, money market and options contracts, as well as by such operational techniques as the choice of invoice currency, lead/lag strategy, and exposure netting.

2. If the firm has a foreign-currency-denominated receivable (payable), it can hedge the exposure by selling (buying) the foreign currency receivable (payable) forward. The firm can *expect* to eliminate the exposure without incurring costs as long as the forward exchange rate is an unbiased predictor of the future spot rate. The firm can achieve equivalent hedging results by lending and borrowing in the domestic and foreign money markets.

3. Unlike forward and money market hedges, currency options provide flexible hedges against exchange exposure. With the options hedge, the firm can limit the downside risk while preserving the upside potential. Currency options also provide the firm with an effective hedge against contingent exposure.

4. The firm can shift, share and diversify exchange exposure by appropriately choosing the invoice currency. Currency basket units, such as the SDR, can be used as an invoice currency to partially hedge long-term exposure for which financial hedges are not readily available.

5. The firm can reduce transaction exposure by leading and lagging foreign currency receipts and payments, especially among its own affiliates.

6. When a firm has a portfolio of foreign currency positions, it makes sense only to hedge the residual exposure rather than hedging each currency position separately. The reinvoice centre can help implement the portfolio approach to exposure management.

7. In a perfect capital market where shareholders can hedge exchange exposure as well as the firm, it is difficult to justify exposure management at the corporate level. In reality, capital markets are far from perfect, and the firm often has advantages over the shareholders in implementing hedging strategies. There thus exists room for corporate exposure management to contribute to the firm value.

QUESTIONS

1. Define *transaction exposure*. How is it different from economic exposure?

2. Discuss and compare hedging transaction exposure using the forward contract versus money market instruments. When do alternative hedging approaches produce the same result?

3. Discuss and compare the costs of hedging by forward contracts and options contracts.

4. What are the advantages of a currency options contract as a hedging tool compared with the forward contract?

5. Suppose your company has purchased a put option on the euro to

manage exchange exposure associated with an account receivable denominated in that currency. In this case, your company can be said to have an "insurance" policy on its receivable. Explain in what sense this is so.

6. Recent surveys of corporate exchange risk management practices

indicate that many firms simply do not hedge. How would you explain this result?

7. Should a firm hedge? Why, or why not?

8. Using an example, discuss the possible effect of hedging on a firm's tax obligations.

9. Explain *contingent exposure* and discuss the advantages of using currency options to manage this type of currency exposure.

10. Explain cross-hedging and discuss the factors determining its effectiveness.

PROBLEMS

The spreadsheet TRNSEXP.xls may be used in solving parts of problems 2, 3, 4, and 6.

1. Celestica of Toronto sold an advanced computer system to the Max Planck Institute in Germany on credit and invoiced €10 million payable in six months. Currently, the six-month forward exchange rate is $1.50/€ and the foreign exchange adviser for Celestica predicts that the spot rate is likely to be $1.42/€ in six months.

   a. What is the expected gain/loss from a forward hedge?

   b. If you were the financial manager of Celestica, would you recommend hedging this euro receivable? Why, or why not?

   c. Suppose the foreign exchange adviser predicts that the future spot rate will be the same as the forward exchange rate quoted today. Would you recommend hedging in this case? Why or why not?

2. BlackBerry of Waterloo purchased computer chips from NEC, a Japanese electronics concern, and was billed ¥250 million payable in three months. Currently, the spot exchange rate is ¥105/$, and the three-month forward rate is ¥100/$. The three-month money market interest rate is 5 percent per annum in Canada and 3 percent per annum in Japan. The management of BlackBerry decided to use a money market hedge to deal with this yen account payable.

   a. Explain the process of a money market hedge and compute the Canadian dollar cost of meeting the yen obligation.

   b. Conduct a cash flow analysis of the money market hedge.

3. You plan to visit Geneva, Switzerland, in three months to attend an international business conference. You expect to incur a total cost of SF5,000 for lodging, meals and transportation during your stay. As of today, the spot exchange rate is $1.10/SF and

the three-month forward rate is $1.13/SF. You can buy the three-month call option on SF with an exercise price of $1.14/SF for the premium of $0.05 per SF. Assume that your expected future spot exchange rate is the same as the forward rate. The three-month interest rate is 6 percent per annum in Canada and 4 percent per annum in Switzerland.

   a. Calculate your expected dollar cost of buying SF5,000 if you choose to hedge by a call option on SF.

   b. Calculate the future dollar cost of meeting this SF obligation if you decide to hedge using a forward contract.

   c. At what future spot exchange rate will you be indifferent between the forward and option market hedges?

   d. Illustrate the future dollar cost of meeting the SF payable against the future spot exchange rate under both the options and forward market hedges.

4. Bombardier just signed a contract to sell aircraft to Air France. Air France will be billed €20 million payable in one year. The current spot exchange rate is $1.50/€ and the one-year forward rate is $1.55/€. The annual interest rate is 5 percent in Canada and 6 percent in France. Bombardier is concerned with the volatile exchange rate between the dollar and the euro and would like to hedge exchange exposure.

   a. It is considering two hedging alternatives: sell the euro proceeds from the sale forward or borrow euros from Crédit Lyonnaise against the euro receivable. Which alternative would you recommend? Why?

   b. Other things being equal, at what forward exchange rate would Bombardier be indifferent between the two hedging methods?

5. Suppose that Kitchener Machinery sold a drilling machine to a Swiss firm and gave the Swiss client a

choice of paying either $10,000 or SF9,000 in three months.

   a. In the example, Kitchener Machinery effectively gave the Swiss client a free option to buy up to $10,000 using Swiss francs. What is the "implied" exercise exchange rate?

   b. If the spot exchange rate turns out to be $1.08/SF, which currency do you think the Swiss client will choose to use for payment? What is the value of this free option for the Swiss client?

   c. What is the best way for Kitchener Machinery to deal with exchange exposure?

6. The Bay of Fundy Cruise Company (BofF) purchased a ship from Mitsubishi Heavy Industry for 500 million yen payable in one year. The current spot rate is ¥100/$, and the one-year forward rate is 110/$. The annual interest rate is 3 percent in Japan and 5 percent in Canada. BofF can also buy a one-year call option on yen at the strike price of $0.01 per yen for a premium of 0.014 cents per yen.

   a. Compute the future dollar costs of meeting this obligation using the money market and forward hedges.

   b. Assuming that the forward exchange rate is the best predictor of the future spot rate, compute the expected future dollar cost of meeting this obligation when the option hedge is used.

   c. At what future spot rate do you think BofF may be indifferent between the option and forward hedge?

7. Airbus sold an A400 aircraft to Air Canada and billed $30 million payable in six months. Airbus is concerned about the euro proceeds from international sales and would like to control exchange risk. The current spot exchange rate is $1.50/€, and the six-month forward exchange rate is $1.575/€. Airbus can buy a six-month put option on Canadian dollars with a strike price of €0.65/$ for a premium of €0.02 per Canadian dollar. Currently, the six-month interest rate is 5 percent in the eurozone and 6 percent in Canada.

   a. Compute the guaranteed euro proceeds from the sale to Air Canada if Airbus decides to hedge using a forward contract.

   b. If Airbus decides to hedge using money market instruments, what action does Airbus need to take? What would be the guaranteed euro proceeds from the sale in this case?

   c. If Airbus decides to hedge using put options on Canadian dollars, what would be the "expected" euro proceeds from the sale? Assume that Airbus regards the current forward exchange rate as an unbiased predictor of the future spot exchange rate.

   d. At what future spot exchange do you think Airbus will be indifferent between the option and money market hedge?

INTERNET EXERCISE

BankWare, an Ottawa-based company specializing in banking-related softwares, exported its software for automated teller machines (ATM) to Oslo Commerce Bank, which is trying to modernize its operation. Facing competition from European software vendors, BankWare decided to bill the sales in the client's currency, Norwegian krone 500,000, payable in one year. Since there are no active forward markets for the Norwegian currency,

BankWare is considering selling a euro or British pound amount forward for cross-hedging purpose. Assess the hedging effectiveness of selling the euro versus pound amount forward to cover the company's exposure to the Norwegian currency. In solving this problem, consult exchange rate data available from the following website: http://fx.sauder.ubc.ca/.

MINI CASE

Barrick's Real Option on Tires

In January 2008, Barrick Gold Corp of Toronto (www.barrick.com) struck an unconventional deal with the Japanese tire manufacturer Yokohama Rubber. Amid a chronic global tire shortage, Barrick locked in its supply of tires with an innovative financial play.

   Barrick agreed to invest—by way of a $35 million loan—in a Yokohama tire-plant expansion. In return,

Yokohama agreed to sell tires to Barrick for the next 10 years at their "direct-from the-manufacturer's price."

   "This is an innovative response to the worldwide tire shortage now facing the mining industry," said Barrick President and CEO Greg Wilkins. "We are providing partial financing for our supplier's plant expansion to secure a supply of high-quality tires for our global mining operations.

In our view, Yokohama produces the finest tires on the market, so we are proud to partner with them as a key tire supplier."

"Direct-from-manufacturer's prices" for mining vehicle tires range from $200 for a pickup truck tire to $60,000 for the largest loader tire. Because of supply shortages, tires often sell on the spot market for many times their retail value. On the open market or in internet auctions, giant tires have sold for as much as $300,000. (The mining trucks that use such giant tires cost $3 million each.)

Tires are a critical part component for mining and one of the largest procurement expenses. For all tire categories, Barrick spent $80 million in 2006. Barrick currently buys about 3,000 giant tires a year. That number was expected to increase to 4,500 by 2012.

Under the agreement with Yokohama, Barrick will purchase approximately 1,300 tires a year beginning in 2009. To meet this demand, Yokohama will expand its plant in Hiroshima. The $50 million (5 billion yen) expansion will be primarily funded by the $35 million loan from Barrick. Yokohama's expansion supports its strategy to expand its share of the global tire market and demonstrates Barrick's partnership approach with suppliers.

In view of strategy and tactics for dealing with transactions risk addressed in this chapter together with our analysis of options in Chapter 9, answer the following questions.

1. Outline how the arrangement addresses Barrick's transactions risks.

2. Describe the "option" character of the deal. Who sells the option? Who buys? What factors determine the value of the option? How would these factors affect the terms of Barrick's $35 million loan to Yokohama?

3. In general terms rather than with precise empirical answers: What are the "pay-off(s)" of the option? What is the exercise price? What is the price of the option?

4. Analyze the international financial aspects of the arrangement and the cost and pay-offs of the option.

REFERENCES & SUGGESTED READINGS

Adler, Michael, and B. Dumas. "Exposure to Currency Risk: Definition and Measurement." *Financial Management* (Spring 1984), pp. 41–50.

Aggarwal, R., and A. Demaskey. "Cross-Hedging Currency Risks in Asian Emerging Markets Using Derivatives in Major Currencies." *Journal of Portfolio Management* (Spring 1997), pp. 88–95.

Allayannis, George, and E. Ofek. "Exchange Rate Exposure, Hedging, and the Use of Foreign Currency Derivatives." *Journal of International Money and Finance* 20 (2001), pp. 273–96.

Allayannis, George, and James Weston. "The Use of Foreign Currency Derivatives and Firm Market Value." *Review of Financial Studies* 14 (2001), pp. 243–76.

Bartov, Eli, and G. Bodnar. "Firm Valuation, Earnings Expectations, and the Exchange-Rate Exposure Effect." *Journal of Finance* 49 (1994), pp. 1755–85.

Benet, B. "Commodity Futures Cross-Hedging of Foreign Exchange Exposure." *Journal of Futures Markets* (Fall 1990), pp. 287–306.

Beidelman, Carl, John Hillary, and James Greenleaf. "Alternatives in Hedging Long-Date Contractual Foreign Exchange Exposure." *Sloan Management Review* (Summer 1983), pp. 45–54.

Bodnar, Gordon M. "Exchange Rate Exposure and Market Value." *Mastering Risk: The Complete Financial Companion* (London: Pitman Publishing for *The Financial Times,* 1998.

Bouakez, Hafedh, and N. Rebei, "Has Exchange Rate Pass-Through Really Declined in Canada?" Bank of Canada working paper 2005–29, October 2005.

Choi, Jongmoo, and A. Prasad. "Exchange Rate Sensitivity and Its Determinants: A Firm and Industry Analysis of U.S. Multinationals." *Financial Management* 23 (1995), pp. 77–88.

Dornbusch, Rudiger, "Exchange Rates and Prices." *American Economic Review* 77 (1987), pp. 93–106.

Dufey, Gunter, and S. Srinivasulu. "The Case for Corporate Management of Foreign Exchange Risk." *Financial Management* (Winter 1983), pp. 54–62.

Giddy, Ian. "The Foreign Exchange Option as a Hedging Tool." *Midland Corporate Finance Journal* (Fall 1983), pp. 32–42.

Hekman, Christine R. "Don't Blame Currency Values for Strategic Errors." *Midland Corporate Finance Journal* (Fall 1986), pp. 45–55.

Jesswein, Kurt, Chuck C. Y. Kwok, and William Folks, Jr. "Corporate Use of Innovative Foreign Exchange Risk Management Products." *Columbia Journal of World Business* (Fall 1995), pp. 70–82.

Jorion, Philippe. "The Exchange-Rate Exposure of U.S. Multinationals." *Journal of Business* 63 (1990), pp. 331–45.

Kardasz, Stanley, and K. R. Stollery. "Exchange Rate Pass-Through and Its Determinants in Canadian Manufacturing Industries." *Canadian Journal of Economics* Volume 34, Issue 3 (August).

Khoury, Sarkis, and K. H. Chan. "Hedging Foreign Exchange Risk: Selecting the Optimal Tool." *Midland Corporate Finance Journal* (Winter 1988), pp. 40–52.

Lessard, Donald, and S. B. Lightstone. "Volatile Exchange Rates Can Put Operations at Risk." *Harvard Business Review* (July/August 1986), pp. 107–14.

Lewent, Judy, and J. Kearney. "Identifying, Measuring and Hedging Currency Risk at Merck." *Journal of Applied Corporate Finance* (Winter 1990), pp. 19–28.

Pringle, John, and R. Connolly. "The Nature and Causes of Foreign Currency Exposure." *Journal of Applied Corporate Finance* (Fall 1993), pp. 61–72.

Smithson, Charles. "A LEGO Approach to Financial Engineering: An Introduction to Forwards, Futures, Swaps and Options." *Midland Corporate Finance Journal* (Winter 1987), pp. 16–28.

Stulz, Rene, and Clifford Smith. "The Determinants of Firms' Hedging Policies." *Journal of Financial and Quantitative Analysis* (December 1985), pp. 391–405.

Williamson, Rohan. "Exchange Rate Exposure and Competition: Evidence from the Automotive Industry." *Journal of Financial Economics* 59 (2001), pp. 441–75.

Yang, Jiawen. "Exchange Rate Pass-Through in U.S. Manufacturing Industries." *Review of Economics and Statistics* 79 (1997), pp. 95–104.

Chapter 14

Management of Translation Exposure

CORPORATE ACCOUNTS—including the income statement, balance sheet, cash flow statement and statement of changes in financial position—present a detailed picture of the firm's financial structure and income flow. The balance sheet is a detailed list of assets and liabilities. It is like is a snapshot. For a moving picture, we have the income statement with its report of revenues and costs and, ultimately, net income. The statement of changes in financial position identifies where the firm's cash comes from and where it goes.

For a strictly domestic firm, the line items in the corporate accounts are expressed in only one currency, for example, in the Canadian dollar for Canadian firms. Changes in the exchange rate obviously have no direct impact on the corporate accounts of a purely domestic firm. However, when a Canadian firm has assets and liabilities as well as revenues, costs and profits abroad, these items are first denominated locally—that is, in the foreign country—in a *foreign* currency. The Canadian parent company of a foreign branch or subsidiary is then required to *translate* the financial values denominated in foreign currency into Canadian dollar values. Changes in the exchange rate result in changes in translated values.

The accounting exercise of translating foreign currency values into values expressed in the home-country currency is referred to as *consolidation*. Consolidation is meant to produce accurate and relevant values of offshore corporate assets, liabilities and operations.

A simple example illustrates the mechanics of foreign currency translation. Toronto-based Four Seasons Hotels and Resorts owns and operates a hotel in Paris on the exquisite Avenue Georges V. The hotel property is valued in euro at €100 million. Four Seasons has arranged a €70 million mortgage on the property, held by Banque Paribas. Net equity is €30 million. Let us say that on December 31, 2013, the $/€ exchange rate is $1.50 = €1. A year later, on December 31, 2014, following a strengthening of the euro against the Canadian dollar, the exchange rate has moved to $1.70 = €1. The table below shows the impact of the change in the exchange rate on the Canadian dollar value of the asset, the liability and the equity.

	Euro	$1.50 = €1	$1.70 = €1	Change ($)
Hotel Property (an asset)	€100 m	$150 m	$170 m	$20 m (+)
Mortgage (a liability)	€ 70 m	$105 m	$119 m	$14 m (−)
Equity	€ 30 m	$ 45 m	$ 51 m	$ 6 m (+)

From the perspective of Four Seasons in Toronto, the Canadian dollar value of the Paris property has risen by $20 million as a result of the appreciation of the euro. This is a gain from the Canadian perspective (hence the plus sign). On the other hand, the Canadian dollar value of the mortgage owed to Banque Paribas has risen by $14 million. This is a loss to Four Seasons (Toronto). Finally, Four Seasons' equity in the Paris hotel has risen by $6 million, which, of course, represents the net gain to Four Seasons (Toronto) as a result of the change in the exchange rate.

These changes in the Canadian dollar values of euro-denominated assets, liabilities and equity illustrate the fundamental principle of translation exposure and the effects of translation. Being long in an asset in a foreign currency—for example, Four Seasons' ownership of the hotel property in Paris—gives rise to a foreign exchange gain when the foreign currency appreciates. On the other hand, a liability—or being "short" a financial asset—such as the mortgage at Paribas, results in a foreign exchange loss if the foreign currency appreciates.

The reverse of these principles is equally true. Being long in an asset in a foreign currency results in a foreign exchange loss when the foreign currency depreciates, that is, when the Canadian dollar appreciates. On the other hand, having a liability—or being "short" a financial asset—results in a foreign exchange gain if the foreign currency depreciates.

The rule of thumb is that an investor always wants to be long in assets denominated in an appreciating foreign currency.

These translation effects of changes in the exchange rate do not affect Four Seasons' Paris-based operations. Nor does it seem reasonable or appropriately conservative, as accountants would want us to be, to "recognize" these foreign exchange gains immediately as part of income for the year. We will return to this point in a moment.

Let us consider some shorter-term balance sheet items and cash flows associated with Four Seasons' hotel operations in Paris. Let us say that Current Assets—cash, inventory, receivables—are €8 million. Current Liabilities are €6 million and over the year the hotel on Georges V generated after-tax income of €12 million. What do we make of these euro numbers as translated into Canadian dollars in the parent's accounts kept in Toronto?

	Euro	$1.50 = €1	$1.70 = €1	Change ($)
Current Assets	€ 8 m	$12 m	$13.6 m	$1.6 m (+)
Current Liabilities	€ 6 m	$ 9 m	$10.2 m	$1.2 m (−)
Net Income	€12 m	$18 m	$20.4 m	$2.4 m (+)

These particular items—Current Assets, Current Liabilities and Net Income—are affected by the appreciation of the euro in a similar fashion to the hotel property, mortgage and equity discussed above. However, Current Assets, Current Liabilities and Net Income are much "closer to cash" than is the case for the hotel, the mortgage or equity. The impact of the appreciation of the euro on the Canadian dollar value on each of these items close to cash is less likely to be reversed by a euro depreciation before they leave the cash cycle. When Four Seasons (Toronto) reports its consolidated worldwide income for 2014 in Canadian dollar terms, foreign exchange gains or losses on near-cash items are more appropriately included in the consolidated "bottom line" figure.

It is less relevant to include foreign exchange gains or losses on longer-term assets and liabilities in Four Seasons' consolidated, translated worldwide income figure for 2014. Consider the hotel property and the mortgage. In view of the substantial random element in foreign exchange rate movements, the rise in the euro against the Canadian dollar in 2014 could well be reversed over subsequent years. If foreign exchange gains and losses on long-lived assets and liabilities are annually (or quarterly) translated and consolidated in the parent company's worldwide net income figure, the random variance of the exchange rate over the life of these long-lived assets or liabilities could introduce substantial year-to-year variance in the net income of the firm.

Professional accounting organizations, which develop and oversee accounting regulations, such as the Canadian Institute of Chartered Accounts (CICA), are acutely aware of the need for accurate and relevant translated accounting statements for the foreign operations of Canadian-based multinational enterprises. They are also aware that random year-over-year variance resulting from foreign exchange rate variance can compromise the accuracy, stability and usefulness of corporate accounts. The CICA in Canada and comparable groups elsewhere, like the Financial Accounting Standards Board (FASB) in the United States, address the issue in similar but not identical ways. We will briefly outline key features of the Canadian approach.

14.1 TRANSLATION METHODS

Foreign Operations

www.cica.ca

The web page of the Canadian Institute of Chartered Accountants.

The *CICA Handbook* Section 1650 contains recommendations on procedure and accounting policy in regard to foreign operations of Canadian companies. Section 1650 begins by defining and categorizing foreign operations. Foreign operations can take the form of a subsidiary, division or branch of a Canadian company or a cooperative joint venture with a foreign company. Foreign operations involve business activities that are made and recorded in a currency other than the Canadian dollar. Foreign operations are divided into two categories:

- An **integrated foreign operation** is financially or operationally interdependent with the Canadian parent company such that exposure to exchange rate changes is similar to the exposure which would exist had the transactions of the foreign operation been undertaken directly by the Canadian parent.

- A **self-sustaining foreign operation** is a foreign operation that is financially and operationally independent of the Canadian company such that the exposure to exchange rate fluctuations is limited to the Canadian company's net investment in the foreign operation.

For purposes of our focus on managerial implications of these distinctions, an offshore branch of a Canadian bank, such as the Bank of Nova Scotia's branch in London, England, is typical of an integrated foreign operation. The London banking operations of the Bank of Nova Scotia require the capital base, the security and information base, the Canadian regulatory structure and the direct and immediate managerial guidance that Canadian headquarters provide. On the other hand, a typical self-sustaining foreign operation is an offshore corporate arrangement that a manufacturing firm, such as Magna International of Aurora, Ontario, has with its subsidiary in Steyr, Austria. Magna (Austria) is financially and operationally independent of the parent Canadian company such that the exposure to exchange rate changes is limited to Magna's net investment in the European operations.

Two Approaches to Translation: Current Rate Method and Temporal Approach

The Canadian approach to foreign currency translation calls for the application of one of two alternative approaches: either the **current rate method** or the **temporal approach**.

The current rate method is widely used around the world today. Under this method, all items in financial statements are translated at the *current* exchange rate with few exceptions. Line items include:

- *Assets and liabilities.* All assets and liabilities are translated at the current rate of exchange, that is, the rate of exchange in effect on the day the balance sheet is prepared.

- *Income statement items.* All items, including depreciation and cost of goods sold, are translated at either the actual exchange rate on the dates that the various revenues, expenses, gains and losses were incurred or at an appropriately weighted average exchange rate for the period.

Four Seasons Hotels and Resorts

The following description of policy objectives and management strategy in regard to foreign exchange risk is taken from the 2006 annual report of Four Seasons Hotels and Resorts, the Canadian-based luxury hotel chain.

Currency Exposure

We have entered into management agreements with respect to hotels throughout the world and accordingly we earn revenue and make investments and advances in many foreign currencies. Our most significant currency is US-dollars, as approximately half of our revenues and assets currently are US-dollar-denominated as are the majority of our investment commitments. However, we incur the majority of our costs in Canadian dollars and our most significant liability (which is related to our convertible senior notes) is a Canadian dollar obligation.

In 2005 we adopted US dollars as our reporting currency. This means that our Canadian dollar consolidated financial statements are translated into US dollars for reporting purposes. Our consolidated statements of operations, consolidated statements of cash provided by operations and consolidated statements of cash flow are translated using the weighted average exchange rates for the period. Assets and liabilities are converted from Canadian dollars into US dollars at the exchange rate applicable at the balance sheet date.

We have not changed our functional currency, which remains Canadian dollars, or the functional currencies of any of our subsidiaries. As a result, while US dollar reporting will minimize currency fluctuations related to the majority of our US dollar management fee revenues, it will not eliminate the impact of foreign currency fluctuations related to our management fees in

other currencies or our general and administrative expenses which are incurred primarily in Canadian dollars. It will also not eliminate foreign currency gains and losses related to unhedged net monetary assets and liability positions. Consequently, our consolidated results will continue to include gains and losses related to foreign currency fluctuations. The impact of foreign currency gains and losses has been material in the past and could continue to be material in the future.

We endeavour to match foreign currency revenues to costs, liabilities and investment commitments to provide a natural hedge against currency fluctuations, although there can be no assurance that these measures will be effective in the management of those risks. We also endeavour to manage our currency exposure through, among other things, the use of foreign exchange forward contracts. As at 31 December 2006 we held $39.1 million in foreign exchange forward contracts for the sale of US dollars into Canadian dollars to meet our operating needs. In addition, certain currencies are subject to exchange controls or are not freely tradable and as a result are relatively illiquid. We attempt to minimize our foreign currency risk by monitoring our cash position, keeping fee receivables current, monitoring the political and economic climate and considering whether to insure convertibility risk in each country in which we manage property. In certain hotels, the foreign currency risks are further mitigated by pricing room rates in US dollars. However, no assurances can be given as to whether our strategies relating to currency exposure will be successful or that foreign exchange fluctuations will not materially adversely affect our business, results of operations and financial condition.

- *Distributions.* Dividends paid are translated at the exchange rate in effect on the date of payment.
- *Equity items.* Common shares and paid-in capital accounts are recorded at historical rates. Year-end retained earnings consist of the original beginning-of-year retained earnings plus or minus any income or loss for the year.

The current rate method has features that are important both for the consistency of international accounting and for corporate financial management. Above all, gains or losses resulting from translation are not included in the calculation of consolidated net income. Instead, they are reported in a separate **reserve account** on the consolidated balance sheet with such a title as **cumulative translation adjustment**. If a foreign subsidiary is later sold or liquidated, gains or losses that have accumulated in this account are reported as one component of the total gain or loss on sale or liquidation. By keeping translation gains and losses separate, the current rate method offers accounting information to management, shareholders and creditors concerning income and performance in foreign operations that is not confounded with nonbusiness gains or losses due to exchange rate changes.

Under the current rate method, gains or losses on translation flow to a reserve account. They do not end up year-to-year in the income statement. As a result, reported earnings do not suffer variance due to foreign exchange translation gains or losses.

The current rate method ensures that relative proportions of individual balance sheet items in the (translated) financial statements of foreign operations are not distorted by foreign exchange gains and losses. Important managerial signals, such as the profit margin, the current ratio or the debt-to-equity ratio for foreign operations, remain as they are in the foreign currency. Perhaps the main shortcoming of the current rate method is that it compromises the accounting convention (called the **conservatism principle**) of recording balance sheet items at historical cost. For example, foreign assets purchased with dollars and then recorded on the subsidiary's statements at their foreign currency historical cost are translated back into dollars at a different rate. Consequently such assets are reported in the consolidated statement (in dollars) at something other than their historical Canadian dollar cost.

Temporal Method

Under the temporal method, specific assets and liabilities are translated at exchange rates that correspond to the time the asset was acquired or the liability was incurred. The temporal method ensures that income-generating assets, such as inventory and net plant and equipment, are restated regularly to reflect their market value. The main tenets of the temporal method are:

- *Monetary assets*, such as cash, marketable securities, accounts receivable and long-term receivables, as well as monetary liabilities, such as current liabilities and long-term debt, are translated at current exchange rates.

- *Nonmonetary assets and liabilities*, such as inventory and fixed assets, are translated at historical exchange rates.

- *Income statement items* are translated at the average exchange rate for the period. Exceptions include the noncash expense of depreciation and cost of goods sold that are directly associated with nonmonetary assets and liabilities; these items are translated at their historical rates.

- *Distributions*. Dividends paid are translated at the exchange rate in effect on the date of payment.

- *Equity items*. Common shares and paid-in capital accounts are recorded at historical rates. Year-end retained earnings consist of the original beginning-of-year retained earnings plus or minus any income or loss for the year, plus or minus any imbalance from translation.

Under the temporal method, gains or losses resulting from translation are carried directly to current consolidated income. Unlike the current rate method, these gains or losses do not go to an equity reserve account. Under the temporal method, then, foreign exchange gains and losses arising from translation introduce volatility of consolidated earnings. However, the volatility is damped to the extent that many items in the temporal approach are translated at their historical rates.

The advantage of the temporal method of translation is that foreign nonmonetary assets are recorded at their original cost in the consolidated statement. This is consistent with the conservative accounting convention of "original cost treatment" of assets as they appear in the accounts of the parent firm. In practice, however, if some foreign accounts are translated at one (historical) foreign exchange rate, while others are translated at different rates, the resulting translated balance sheet will not balance. Hence there is a need for a "plug" to remove what has been called the *dangling debit or credit*. The economic or managerial nature of the gain or loss represented by the "plug" is open to question.

Which Method in Canada: Current Rate or Temporal

The *CICA Handbook* Section 1650 outlines the advantages and disadvantages of both the *current rate method* and the *temporal method* of translation for consolidation. The ultimate objective of translation is to express financial statements of the foreign operation in

EXHIBIT 14.1

Salient Economic
Factors for
Determining the
Reporting Currency

The **reporting currency** is defined as the currency in which the MNC prepares its consolidated financial statements. That currency is usually the currency in which the parent firm keeps its books, which, in turn, is usually the currency of the country in which the parent is located and conducts most of its business.

Cash Flow Indicators
Foreign Currency: Foreign entity's cash flows are primarily in foreign currency, and they do not directly affect the parent firm's cash flows.
Parent's Currency: Foreign entity's cash flows directly affect the parent's cash flows and are readily available for remittance to the parent firm.

Sales Price Indicators
Foreign Currency: Sales prices for the foreign entity's products are generally not responsive on a short-term basis to exchange rate changes but are determined more by local competition.
Parent's Currency: Sales prices for the foreign entity's products are responsive on a short-term basis to exchange rate changes, where sales prices are determined through worldwide competition.

Sales Market Indicators
Foreign Currency: There is an active local sales market for the foreign entity's products.
Parent's Currency: The sales market is primarily located in the parent's country or sales contracts are denominated in the parent's currency.

Expense Indicators
Foreign Currency: Factor of production costs of the foreign entity are primarily local costs.
Parent's Currency: Factor of production costs for the foreign entity are primarily, and on a continuing basis, costs for components obtained from the parent's country.

Financing Indicators
Foreign Currency: Financing of the foreign entity is primarily denominated in the foreign currency and the debt service obligations are normally handled by the foreign entity.
Parent's Currency: Financing of the foreign entity is primarily from the parent, with debt service obligations met by the parent, or the debt service obligations incurred by the foreign entity are primarily made by the parent.

Intercompany Transactions and Arrangements Indicators
Foreign Currency: There is a low volume of intercompany transactions and a minor inter-relationship of operations between the foreign entity and the parent. However, the foreign entity may benefit from competitive advantages of the parent, such as patents or trademarks.
Parent's Currency: There is a large volume of intercompany transactions and an extensive inter-relationship of operations between the foreign entity and the parent. Moreover, if the foreign entity is only a shell company for carrying accounts that could be carried on the parent's books, the functional currency would generally be the parent's currency.

Source: Excerpted from *Foreign Currency Translation, Statement of Financial Accounting Standards No. 52,* Paragraph 42, Financial Accounting Standards Board, Stamford, CT. Used by permission.

Canadian dollars in a manner which best reflects the reporting enterprise's exposure to exchange rate changes. The recommended approach depends on the circumstances.

For *integrated* foreign operations, such as an offshore *branch*, the Canadian parent company's exposure to exchange rate changes is similar to the exposure which would exist had the transactions and activities of the foreign operation been undertaken by the parent company. Therefore, financial statements of foreign operations should be consistent with the measurement of domestic transactions and operations. The translation method that best achieves this objective is the temporal method because it uses the Canadian dollar as the unit of measure.

Exhibit 14.1 identifies various economic consideration to guide the managerial decision as to which currency–domestic-translated-from-foreign or simply foreign–ought to be the reporting currency for a firm's foreign currency operations.

| **EXHIBIT 14.2** | Foreign-Currency Translation Methods Used in Other Major Developed Countries |

JAPAN

Receivables and payables in foreign currencies must be translated into yen at the end of the accounting period. Both translation gains or losses and realized foreign exchange gains or losses are treated as taxable income or loss and flow through earnings. Historical exchange rates that existed at the transaction date are generally used to record revenue, costs, and expenses resulting from foreign currency transactions.

Short-term foreign currency receivables and payables are translated at the prevailing year-end rate. Long-term foreign currency receivables and payables are translated at the historical rate, except in unusual circumstances. Securities, inventories, and fixed assets are translated at the rate in effect when they were acquired (historical rate).

Any change in the method of translating foreign currencies requires prior approval by tax regulators.

GERMANY

As of year-end 1992, a common treatment of foreign-currency translation had not been implemented. All translation methods are, in principle, acceptable.

A broad variety of practices are followed, including the (1) current/noncurrent, (2) monetary/nonmonetary, (3) temporal, (4) closing and (5) current rate methods. Some companies flow translation gains or losses through shareholders' equity, while others flow the impact of foreign currency translation through the profit and loss account.

FRANCE

Many different methods of foreign currency translation are followed.

Group Accounts

Most companies appear to use the closing exchange rate for balance sheet translations (translation gains and losses impact shareholders' equity) and the average exchange rate for the income statement.

Differences between income statement and balance sheet translation gains and losses (if different exchange rates are used) would flow through shareholders' equity.

Individual Accounts

Detailed rules govern foreign currency translation in individual company accounts. These give rise to long-term deferred charges and credits.

Unsettled monetary assets and liabilities denominated in a foreign currency must be restated to their closing value at the balance sheet date. Foreign exchange gains are recorded as long-term deferred credits and released when the account is settled.

Foreign exchange losses result in the following entries: (1) The original account is adjusted and a deferred charge appears on the balance sheet; (2) a balance sheet provision is set up, and the income statement is debited.

Foreign currency translation policies may differ. Some firms only provide against unrealized foreign exchange losses if they exceed unrealized foreign exchange gains. These deferred exchange gains and losses could be offset against each other with the difference applied to the risk provision.

ITALY

Realized Gains and Losses

Income, receipts, and expenditures in foreign currency are translated at the exchange rates that existed on the transaction date. These realized gains and losses flow through the income statement.

Unrealized Gains and Losses

The average exchange rate of the last month of the accounting period is used for foreign currency translation. Items denominated in foreign currency are originally recorded at the exchange rate that existed on the transaction date.

Unrealized foreign currency translation gains and losses flow through a special provision, impacting shareholders' equity.

UNITED KINGDOM

Foreign-currency translation adjustments are disclosed for both individual and group (consolidated) accounts. In cases of consolidation, companies prepare a set of translation accounts for (1) the individual firms within the group and (2) the group as a whole.

Individual Company

Foreign currency transactions are generally translated into the home currency of each company using the average rate method. Nonmonetary assets are not restated.

Currency differences flow through the profit and loss account (separately from ongoing businesses) and are shown as discontinued operations. Exchange rate gains and losses related to foreign currency hedging pass through reserves.

Group Accounts

The average rate/net investment method is commonly used, although the temporal method is also acceptable. Consolidated accounts are prepared in the currency in which the parent company is based.

Investments in the foreign enterprises are represented by the net worth held by the parent. Exchange rate gains or losses that impact the group accounts pass through reserves, with no impact on the group profit and loss account.

Source: © Goldman Sachs.

For *self-sustaining* foreign operations, such as an offshore *subsidiary*, the Canadian parent company's exposure to exchange rate changes is limited to its net investment in the foreign operation. Therefore, accounting for such operations as if they were transacted in Canadian dollars is less relevant than measuring the overall effect of changes in the exchange rate on the net investment in such operations. The financial statements of self-sustaining foreign operation should be expressed in a way that does not change the financial results and relationships of the foreign operation. The translation method that best achieves this objective is the current rate method because it uses the currency of the foreign operation as the unit of measure.

For **foreign currency transactions**, the objective of translation is to express such transactions in a manner that achieves consistency with the accounting treatment for domestic transactions. Since domestic transactions are automatically measured in Canadian dollars, the Canadian dollar is the appropriate unit of measure for foreign currency transactions. Accordingly, the temporal method should be used to translate foreign currency transactions. Methods used in other countries are outlined in Exhibit 14.2.

Illustrated **Mini Case**

Consolidation of Accounts According to the *CICA Handbook* Section 1650: The Maple Corporation

We use a mini case to illustrate consolidating the balance sheet of an MNC according to *CICA Handbook* Section 1650. The basic information in Exhibit 14.3 shows the unconsolidated balance sheets for Maple Corporation, a Canadian parent firm, and its two wholly owned affiliates located in Mexico and Spain. Maple Corp. is a Manitoba-based manufacturer of wooden furniture. The Mexican manufacturing affiliate has been established to serve the Mexican market, which is expected to expand rapidly under NAFTA. Similarly, the Spanish manufacturing affiliate was established to handle demand in the European Union.

EXHIBIT 14.3	Nonconsolidated Balance Sheet for Maple Corporation and Its Mexican and Spanish Affiliates, 31 December 2012 (in 000 currency units)		
	Maple Corp. (parent)	Mexican Affiliate	Spanish Affiliate
Assets			
Cash	$ 950[a]	Ps 6,000	€ 825
Accounts receivable	1,750[a]	9,000	1,045
Inventory	3,000	15,000	1,650
Investment in Mexican affiliate	2,200[b]	—	—
Investment in Spanish affiliate	1,660[c]	—	—
Net fixed assets	9,000	46,000	4,400
Total assets	$18,560	Ps 76,000	€7,920
Liabilities and Net Worth			
Accounts payable	$ 1,800	Ps 10,000	€1,364
Notes payable	2,200	17,000	1,210[d]
Long-term debt	7,110	27,000	3,520
Common shares	3,500	16,000	1,320[c]
Retained earnings	3,950	6,000	506[c]
Total liabilities and net worth	$18,560	Ps 76,000	€7,920

[a]The parent firm is owed Ps3,000,000 by the Mexican affiliate. This sum is included in the parent's accounts receivable as $300,000. The remainder of the parent's (Mexican affiliate's) accounts receivable (payable) are denominated in dollars (pesos).

[b]The Mexican affiliate is wholly owned by the parent firm. It is carried on the parent firm's books at $2,200,000. This represents the sum of the common shares (Ps16,000,000) and retained earnings (Ps6,000,000) on the Mexican affiliate's books, translated at Ps10/$1.

[c]The Spanish affiliate is wholly owned by the parent firm. It is carried on the parent firm's books at $1,660,000. This represents the sum of the common shares (€1,320,000) and the retained earnings (€506,000) on the Spanish affiliate's books, translated at €1.10/$1.

[d]The Spanish affiliate has outstanding notes payable of SF375,000 (÷ SF1.3636/€1 = €275,000) from a Swiss bank. This loan is carried on the Spanish affiliate's books as part of the €1,210,000 = €275,000 + €935,000.

	Maple Corp. (parent)	Mexican Affiliate	Spanish Affiliate	Consolidated Balance Sheet
EXHIBIT 14.4 Consolidated Balance Sheet for Maple Corporation and Its Mexican and Spanish Affiliates, 31 December 2012 (in $000): Pre–Exchange Rate Change				
Assets				
Cash	$ 950	$ 600	$ 750	$ 2,300
Accounts receivable	1,450ª	900	950	3,300
Inventory	3,000	1,500	1,500	6,000
Investment in Mexican affiliate	—ᵇ	—	—	—
Investment in Spanish affiliate	—ᶜ	—	—	—
Net fixed assets	9,000	4,600	4,000	17,600
Total assets				$29,200
Liabilities and Net Worth				
Accounts payable	$ 1,800	$ 700ª	$1,240	$ 3,740
Notes payable	2,200	1,700	1,100ᵈ	5,000
Long-term debt	7,110	2,700	3,200	13,010
Common shares	3,500	—ᵇ	—ᶜ	3,500
Retained earnings	3,950	—ᵇ	—ᶜ	3,950
Total liabilities and net worth				$29,200

ª$1,750,000 − $300,000 (= Ps3,000,000/(Ps10.00/$1.00)) intracompany loan = $1,450,000.
ᵇ,ᶜThe investment in the affiliates cancels with the net worth of the affiliates in the consolidation.
ᵈThe Spanish affiliate owes a Swiss bank SF375,000 (÷ SF1.3636/€1.00 = €275,000). This is carried on the books as part of the €1,210,000 = €275,000 + €935,000. €1,210,000/(€1.10/$1.00) = $1,100,000.

The functional currency of the Mexican affiliate is the peso, and the euro is the functional currency for the Spanish affiliate. The reporting currency is the Canadian dollar. The initial exchange rates assumed in the example are: $1 = Ps10 = €1.10 = SF1.50.

The nonconsolidated balance sheets and the footnotes to the statements indicate that the Mexican affiliate owes the parent firm Ps3,000,000, which is carried on the parent's books as a $300,000 account receivable at the current exchange rate of Ps10.00/$1. The $2,200,000 investment of the parent firm in the Mexican affiliate is the translated amount of Ps22,000,000 of equity on the Mexican affiliate's books. Similarly, the $1,660,000 investment of the parent in the Spanish affiliate is the translated amount of €1,826,000 of equity on the Spanish affiliate's books. The footnotes also show that the Spanish affiliate has a SF375,000 loan outstanding from a Swiss bank, translated at SF1.3636/€1, and carried at €275,000 as part of its €1,210,000 of notes payable.

Exhibit 14.4 shows the process of consolidating the balance sheets for Maple Corp. and its affiliates. Note that *both* intracompany debt *and* investment net out in the consolidation. That is, the Ps3,000,000 owed by the Mexican affiliate to the parent is reflected neither in the consolidated accounts receivable nor in the accounts payable. When this debt is eventually paid, in effect it will be the same as taking money out of one company pocket and putting it into another. In a similar vein, the investment of the parent in each affiliate cancels with the net worth of each affiliate. The parent owns the affiliates and, in turn, the shareholders' investment represents ownership of the parent firm. In this manner, the shareholders own the entire MNC.

The consolidation presented in Exhibit 14.4 is rather simplistic. It is nice and neat from the standpoint that the consolidated balance sheet, in fact, balances. That is, total assets equal total liabilities and net worth. In the example, it is implied that the current exchange rates used are the same as those used when the affiliates were originally established; that is, they have not changed from that time. Thus, the example is not very realistic even though it properly presents the mechanics of the consolidation process under CICA rules. After all, the central purpose of a translation method is to deal in some systematic way with exchange rate *changes*.

EXHIBIT 14.5

Translation Exposure
Report for Maple
Corporation and
Its Mexican and
Spanish Affiliates,
31 December 2012
(in 000 currency
units)

	Mexican Peso	Euro	Swiss Franc
Assets			
Cash	Ps 6,000	€ 825	SF 0
Accounts receivable	9,000	1,045	0
Inventory	15,000	1,650	0
Net fixed assets	46,000	4,400	0
Exposed assets	Ps 76,000	€7,920	SF 0
Liabilities			
Accounts payable	Ps 7,000	€1,364	SF 0
Notes payable	17,000	935	375
Long-term debt	27,000	3,520	0
Exposed liabilities	Ps 51,000	€5,819	SF 375
Net exposure	Ps 25,000	€2,101	(SF375)

To determine the effect that exchange rate changes have on the consolidated balance sheet of an MNC, it is useful to prepare a translation exposure report. A **translation exposure report** shows, for each account that is included in the consolidated balance sheet, the amount of foreign exchange exposure that exists for each foreign currency in which the MNC has exposure. Continuing with our example of Maple Corp. and its affiliates, we know from Exhibit 14.3 that the MNC has foreign exchange exposure from the Mexican peso, euro and Swiss franc. A change in any one of these currency exchange rates versus the reporting currency will affect the consolidated balance sheet if there exists a net translation exposure for that currency.

Exhibit 14.5 presents the translation exposure report for Maple Corp. The report shows, for each exposure currency, the amount of exposed assets and exposed liabilities denominated in that currency and the net difference, or net exposure. For the Mexican peso the net exposure, a positive Ps25,000,000; for the euro, a positive €2,101,000; and for the Swiss franc, a negative SF375,000. A positive net exposure means there are more exposed assets than liabilities and *vice versa* for negative net exposure. When the exchange rate of an exposure currency depreciates against the reporting currency, exposed assets fall in translated value by a greater (smaller) amount than exposed liabilities if there is positive (negative) net exposure. Analogously, when an exposure currency appreciates against the reporting currency, exposed assets increase in translated value by a smaller (greater) amount than exposed liabilities if there is negative (positive) net exposure. Consequently, the consolidation process will not result in a consolidated balance sheet that balances after an exchange rate change.

To show the effect on the consolidation process after an exchange rate change, let us perform the consolidation of the nonconsolidated balance sheets from Exhibit 14.3 once again, assuming this time that exchange rates have changed from $1 = Ps10 = €1.10 = SF1.50 to $1 = Ps10 = €1.1786 = SF1.50. We are assuming that only the euro has changed (depreciated) versus all other currencies in order to keep the example simple so as to better decipher the effect of an exchange rate change.

To get an overview of the effect of the exchange rate change, recall from Exhibit 14.5 that there is a positive net exposure of €2,101,000. This implies that after the 6.67 percent depreciation from €1.1000/$1 to €1.1786/$1, the exposed assets denominated in euros will have fallen in translated value by $127,377 more than the exposed liabilities denominated in euros. This can be calculated as follows:

$$\frac{\text{Net exposure currency } i}{S_{new}(i/\text{reporting})} - \frac{\text{Net exposure currency } i}{S_{old}(i/\text{reporting})}$$

= Reporting currency imbalance.

EXHIBIT 14.6	Consolidated Balance Sheet for Maple Corporation and Its Mexican and Spanish Affiliates, 31 December 2012 (in $000): Post–Exchange Rate Change			
	Maple Corp. (parent)	**Mexican Affiliate**	**Spanish Affiliate**	**Consolidated Balance Sheet**
Assets				
Cash	$ 950	$ 600	$ 700	$ 2,250
Accounts receivable	1,450[a]	900	887	3,237
Inventory	3,000	1,500	1,400	5,900
Investment in Mexican affiliate	—[b]	—	—	—
Investment in Spanish affiliate	—[c]	—	—	—
Net fixed assets	9,000	4,600	3,733	17,333
Total Assets				$28,720
Liabilities and Net Worth				
Accounts payable	$1,800	$ 700[a]	$1,157	$ 3,657
Notes payable	2,200	1,700	1,043[d]	4,943
Long-term debt	7,110	2,700	2,987	12,797
Common shares	3,500	—[b]	—[c]	3,500
Retained earnings	3,950	—[b]	—[c]	3,950
CTA	—	—	—	(127)
Total liabilities and net worth				$28,720

[a]$1,750,000 − $300,000 (= Ps3,000,000/(Ps10/$1)) intracompany loan = $1,450,000.

[b,c]Investment in affiliates cancels with the net worth of the affiliates in the consolidation.

[d]The Spanish affiliate owes a Swiss bank SF375,000 (÷ SF1.2727/€1.00 = €294,649). This is carried on the books, after the exchange rate change, as part of €1,229,649 = €294,649 + €935,000. €1,229,649/(€1.1786/$1) = $1,043,313.

For our example,

$$\frac{€2,101,000}{€1.1786/\$1} - \frac{€2,101,000}{€1.1000/\$1} = -\$127,377$$

In other words, the net translation exposure of €2,101,000 in dollars is currently $1,910,000 when translated at the current exchange rate of €1.1000/$1. A 6.67 percent depreciation of the euro to €1.1786/$1 will result in a translation loss of $127,377 = €2,101,000 ÷ 1.1000 × 0.0667.

Exhibit 14.6 shows the consolidation process and consolidated balance sheet for Maple Corporation and its two foreign affiliates after the depreciation of the euro. Note that the values for the accounts are the same as in Exhibit 14.4 for the parent firm and the Mexican affiliate. However, the values of the accounts of the Spanish affiliate are different because of the exchange rate change. In order for the consolidated balance sheet to now balance, it is necessary to have a "plug" equity account with a balance of −$127,377. This special equity account is referred to as the cumulative translation adjustment account, or CTA account. The balance of this account at any time represents the accumulated total of all past translation adjustments.

The *CICA Handbook* Section 1650 handles the effect of exchange rate changes as an adjustment to equity, rather than as an adjustment to net income, because exchange rate changes have an indirect effect on the net investment that may be realized upon sale or liquidation. Prior to sale or liquidation, that effect is so uncertain and remote as to require that translation adjustments arising currently not be reported as part of operating results.

14.2 MANAGEMENT OF TRANSLATION EXPOSURE

In Chapter 13, we discussed transaction exposure and ways to manage it. It is interesting to note that some items that are a source of transaction exposure are also a source of translation exposure, and some are not. Exhibit 14.7 presents a transaction exposure report for

EXHIBIT 14.7

Transaction Exposure
Report for Maple
Corporation and Its
Mexican and
Spanish Affiliates,
31 December 2012

Affiliate	Amount	Account	Translation Exposure
Parent	Ps3,000,000	Accounts receivable	No
Spanish	SF375,000	Notes payable	Yes

Maple Corp. and its two affiliates. Items that create transaction exposure are receivables or payables that are denominated in a currency other than the currency in which the unit transacts its business, or cash holdings denominated in a foreign currency. From the exhibit, it can be seen that the parent firm has two sources of transaction exposure. The Ps3,000,000 account receivable the parent holds on the Mexican affiliate is also a transaction exposure, but it is not a translation exposure because of the netting of intracompany payable and receivables. The SF375,000 note payable the Spanish affiliate owes the Swiss bank is both a transaction and a translation exposure.

It is generally not possible to eliminate both translation and transaction exposure. In some cases, the elimination of one exposure will also eliminate the other. But in other cases, the elimination of one exposure actually creates the other. Since transaction exposure involves real cash flows, it should be considered the most important of the two. That is, one would not want to create transaction exposure at the expense of minimizing or eliminating translation exposure. As previously noted, the translation process has no direct effect on reporting currency cash flows and will only have a realizable effect on net investment upon the sale or liquidation of the assets.

Maple Corporation and its affiliates can take certain measures to reduce its transaction exposure and to simultaneously reduce its translation exposure. The parent firm can request payment of the Ps3,000,000 owed to it by the Mexican affiliate. The Spanish affiliate has enough cash to pay off the SF375,000 loan to the Swiss bank. If these steps are taken, all transaction exposure for the MNC will be eliminated. Moreover, translation exposure will be reduced. This can be seen from Exhibit 14.8, which presents a revision of Exhibit 14.5, the translation exposure report for Maple Corporation and its affiliates. Exhibit 14.8 shows that there is no longer any translation exposure associated with the Swiss franc. The exhibit shows that the net exposure has been reduced from Ps25,000,000 to Ps22,000,000 for the peso and from €2,101,000 to €1,826,000 for the euro.

Hedging Translation Exposure

Exhibit 14.8 indicates that there is still considerable translation exposure with respect to changes in the exchange rate of the Mexican peso and the euro against the Canadian dollar.

EXHIBIT 14.8

Revised Translation
Exposure
Report for Maple
Corporation and
Its Mexican and
Spanish Affiliates,
31 December 2012
(in 000 currency
units)

	Mexican Peso	Euro	Swiss Franc
Assets			
Cash	Ps 3,000	€ 550	SF0
Accounts receivable	9,000	1,045	0
Inventory	15,000	1,650	0
Net fixed assets	46,000	4,400	0
Exposed assets	Ps 73,000	€7,645	SF0
Liabilities			
Accounts payable	Ps 7,000	€1,364	SF0
Notes payable	17,000	935	0
Long-term debt	27,000	3,520	00
Exposed liabilities	Ps 51,000	€5,819	SF0
Net exposure	Ps 22,000	€1,826	SF0

There are two methods for dealing with this remaining exposure if one feels compelled to attempt to control accounting changes in value of net investment. These methods are a balance sheet hedge or a derivatives hedge.

Balance Sheet Hedge

Note that translation exposure is not entity-specific; rather, it is currency-specific. Its source is a mismatch of net assets and net liabilities denominated in the same currency. A **balance sheet hedge** eliminates the mismatch. Using the euro as an example, Exhibit 14.8 shows that there are €1,826,000 more exposed assets than liabilities. If the Spanish affiliate, or more practically the parent firm or the Mexican affiliate, had €1,826,000 more in liabilities, or less in assets, denominated in euros, there would not be any translation exposure with respect to the euro. A perfect balance sheet hedge would have been created. A change in the €/$ exchange rate would no longer have any effect on the consolidated balance sheet since the change in value of the assets denominated in euros would completely offset the change in value of the liabilities denominated in euros. Nevertheless, if the parent firm or the Mexican affiliate increased its liabilities through, say, euro-denominated borrowings to affect the balance sheet hedge, it would simultaneously be creating transaction exposure in the euro if the new liability could not be covered from euro cash flows generated by the Spanish affiliate.

Derivatives Hedge

According to Exhibit 14.5, we determined that when the net exposure for the euro was €2,101,000, a depreciation from €1.1000/$ to €1.1786/$ would create a loss of shareholders' equity equal to $127,377. According to the revised translation exposure report shown as Exhibit 14.8, the same depreciation in the euro will result in an equity loss of $110,704, still a sizable amount. (The calculation of this amount is left as an exercise for the reader.) Management could use a derivative product, such as a forward contract, to attempt to hedge this potential loss. We use the word "attempt" because as the following example demonstrates, using a **derivatives hedge** to control translation exposure really involves speculation about foreign exchange rate changes.

Example 14.1 *Hedging Translation Exposure with a Forward Contract*

To see how a forward contract can be used to hedge the $110,704 potential translation loss in equity, assume that the forward rate coinciding with the date of the consolidation is €1.1393/$. If the expected spot rate on the consolidation date is forecast to be €1.1786/$, a forward sale of €3,782,468 will "hedge" the risk:

$$\frac{\text{Potential translation loss}}{F(\text{reporting/functional}) - \text{Expected}[S(\text{reporting/functional})]}$$

$$= \text{Forward contract position in functional currency,}$$

$$\frac{\$110,704}{1/(€1.1393/\$) - 1/(€1.1786/\$)} = €3,782,468$$

The purchase of €3,782,468 at the expected spot price will cost $3,209,289. The delivery of €3,782,468 under the forward contract will yield $3,319,993, for a profit of $110,704. If everything goes as expected, the $110,704 profit from the forward hedge will offset the equity loss from the translation adjustment. Note, however, that the hedge will not provide a certain outcome because the size of the forward position is based on the expected future spot rate. Consequently, the forward position taken in euros is actually a speculative position. If the realized spot rate turns out to be less than €1.1393/$, a loss from the forward position will result. Moreover, the hedging procedure violates the hypothesis that the forward rate is an unbiased predictor of the future spot rate.

INTERNATIONAL FINANCE *in Practice*

The Shell Case

Measurement of translation gains and losses is an accounting exercise. It is generally considered to have relatively little managerial significance. Management, as well as investors and creditors, ought to be able to "see through" the effects of translation changes in recorded values. Informed and interested analysts likewise ought to be able to distinguish mere accounting entries from real value-relevant changes in cash flows.

Translation can become more relevant for management when it influences other real processes, such as tax calculations. Whereas a company's tax liability must be determined with regard for generally accepted accounting principles, such principles can be obscured through translation, for example in determining the cost of funds borrowed from foreign sources. A famous tax/accounting case involving Shell Canada is especially interesting in this respect, not least for being very contentious. The Shell Canada case moved through various levels of the courts, ultimately arriving at the Supreme Court of Canada. The Supreme Court decided in favour of Shell. The decision was shaped largely by the judges' view that it was not the Supreme Court's responsibility to disentangle a complex international corporate borrowing arrangement. This note reviews the case.

In 1988, Shell Canada structured an international financing arrangement that resulted in substantial savings of Canadian corporate tax. Shell was able to convert translation losses on foreign borrowing into tax deductions in Canada.

Shell Canada borrowed New Zealand dollars at a time New Zealand was experiencing high inflation and high nominal interest rates. Shell immediately swapped the New Zealand funds for US dollars and simultaneously structured a series of forward contracts to buy back New Zealand funds in order to service and retire the debt over the ensuing five years. When it reported its Canadian tax liability, Shell claimed interest deductions based on the New Zealand interest rate which included a substantial "inflation" component. The inflated New Zealand interest rate resulted in interest deductions that exceeded deductions that would have applied to money borrowed in US or Canadian dollars. In addition, the steadily weakening New Zealand dollar against the US dollar (built into the forward exchange rate) allowed Shell eventually to realize a substantial foreign exchange gain that enjoyed preferential tax treatment in Canada.

When Shell Canada filed its corporate tax return, Revenue Canada disallowed the portion of the interest deduction that represented the difference between the interest rate on the New Zealand debt and the market rate of interest on a comparable dollar loan. In the opinion of the Canadian tax authorities, Shell's borrowing in New Zealand dollars together with the array of forward contracts was a merger of two contracts into one—a borrowing contract and the swap-plus-forward-purchase—which, in effect, created a borrowing of US funds and future obligations to pay interest in US funds. Revenue Canada also treated Shell Canada's foreign exchange gain on the transaction as a gain on income account as opposed to a (tax-preferred) capital gain.

On appeal to the Tax Court of Canada, Shell Canada successfully reversed the assessment. In turn, the Minister of Revenue appealed the Tax Court's decision to the Federal Court of Appeal and won on behalf of Revenue Canada.

Finally, Shell Canada took the case to the Supreme Court on appeal. In June 1999, The Supreme Court allowed the appeal of Shell Canada and dismissed the cross-appeal of the Minister of Revenue. Shell won.

The Shell Case illustrates international tax arbitrage. The deliberations and testimony in the Shell Case accentuate the ambiguity of the translated cost of money borrowed in a foreign currency.

Translation Exposure versus Operating Exposure

As noted, an unhedged depreciation in the euro will result in an equity loss. Such a loss, however, would only be a paper loss. It would not have any direct effect on reporting currency cash flows. Moreover, it would only have a realizable effect on net investment in the MNC if the affiliate's assets were sold or liquidated. However, as was discussed in Chapter 12, the depreciation of the local currency may, under certain circumstances, have a favourable operating effect. A currency depreciation may, for example, allow the affiliate to raise its sales price because the prices of imported competitive goods are now relatively higher. If costs do not rise proportionately and unit demand remains the same, the affiliate would realize an operating profit as a result of the currency depreciation. It is with such substantive issues as these, which result in realizable changes in operating profit, that management should concern itself.

14.3 ANALYSIS OF A CHANGE IN ACCOUNTING FOR TRANSLATION GAINS AND LOSSES

Garlicki et al. (1987) tested a sample of MNCs to determine if there was a change in value when the firms were required to switch their methods for accounting for translation gains and losses. The old US system (FASB 8) called for recognizing translation gain or loss immediately in net income. The replacement system (FASB 52) called for translation gains and losses to be recognized in the cumulative translation adjustment account on the balance sheet. Consequently, the change in the translation process had an effect on reported earnings. "Despite the impact of the change . . . on reported earnings, the actual cash flow of multinationals would not be affected *if managers were not making suboptimal decisions based on accounting rather than economic considerations under Statement 8.* In such circumstances, the mandated switch . . . should not change the value of the firm."

The researchers tested their hypothesis concerning a change in value on the initial exposure draft date and on the date FASB 52 was adopted. They found that there was no significant positive reaction to the change or perceived change in the foreign currency translation process. The results suggest that market agents do not react to cosmetic earnings changes that do not affect value. Other researchers have found similar results when investigating other accounting changes that had only a cosmetic effect on earnings. The results underline the futility of attempting to manage translation gains and losses.

SUMMARY

In this chapter, we discuss the nature and management of translation exposure, that is, the effect that an unanticipated change in exchange rates will have on the consolidated financial reports of an MNC.

1. The four recognized methods for consolidating the financial reports of an MNC include the current/non-current method, the monetary/nonmonetary method, the temporal method and the current rate method.

2. The chapter presents an example comparing and contrasting the four translation methods under the assumptions that the foreign currency had appreciated and depreciated. It is noted that under the current rate method the gain or loss due to translation adjustment does not affect reported cash flows, as it does with the other three translation methods.

3. In implementing the *CICA Handbook* Section 1650, the functional currency of the foreign entity must be translated into the reporting currency in which the consolidated statements are reported. The local currency of a foreign entity may not always be its functional currency. If it is not, the temporal method of translation is used to remeasure the foreign entity's books into the functional currency. The current rate method is used to translate from the functional currency to the reporting currency. In some cases, a foreign entity's functional currency may be the same as the reporting currency, in which case translation is not necessary.

4. Foreign currency translation methods used in other major developed countries were briefly summarized in Exhibit 14.2. As the exhibit shows, a broad variety of methods are used in practice.

5. The chapter presents a mini case illustrating the translation process of the balance sheet of a parent firm with two foreign wholly owned affiliates according to the *CICA Handbook* Section 1650. This is done assuming that the foreign exchange rates had not changed since the inception of the businesses and, again, after an assumed change to more thoroughly show the effects of balance sheet consolidation under the *CICA Handbook* Section 1650. When a net translation exposure exists, a cumulative translation adjustment account is necessary to bring balance to the consolidated balance sheet after an exchange rate change.

6. Two ways to control translation risk are presented in the chapter: a balance sheet hedge and a derivatives "hedge." Since translation exposure does not have an immediate direct effect on operating cash flows, its control is relatively unimportant in comparison to transaction exposure which involves potential real cash flow losses. Since it is generally not possible to eliminate both translation and transaction exposure, it is more logical to effectively manage transaction exposure, even at the expense of translation exposure.

QUESTIONS

1. Explain the difference in the translation process between the current rate method and the temporal method.

2. How are translation gains and losses handled differently according to the current rate method in comparison with the other method, that is, the temporal method?

3. Identify instances under the *CICA Handbook* (Section 1650) when a foreign entity's functional currency would be the same as the parent firm's currency.

4. Describe the remeasurement and translation process under the *CICA Handbook* (Section 1650) of translating into the reporting currency the books of a wholly owned affiliate that keeps its books in the local currency of the country in which it operates, which is different from its functional currency.

5. It is generally not possible to completely eliminate both translation exposure and transaction exposure. In some cases, the elimination of one exposure will also eliminate the other. But in other cases, the elimination of one exposure actually creates the other. Discuss which exposure might be viewed as the most important to effectively manage, if a conflict between controlling both arises. Also, discuss and critique the common methods for controlling translation exposure.

INTERNET EXERCISE

1. The TD Bank is one of Canada's largest banks, and it has large foreign currency exposure. For example, TD has more branches in the United States than it has in Canada. Go to the TD Bank Annual Report for 2012 (www.td.com/investor-relations/ir-homepage/annual-reports/2012/index.jsp) to get a sense of the bank's official views on managing foreign currency risk; they might surprise you.

   Go first to page 61, "Risk Factors and Management: Risk Factors That May Affect Future Results." There you will see that with respect to risks that arise from changes in exchange rates, the TD Bank policy statement is remarkably brief and noncommittal:

   > Currency rate movements in Canada, the U.S., and other jurisdictions in which the TD Bank does business impact the Bank's financial position (as a result of foreign currency translation adjustments) and its future earnings. For example, if the value of the Canadian dollar rises against the U.S. dollar, the Bank's investments and earnings in the U.S. may be negatively affected, and vice versa. Changes in the value of the Canadian dollar relative to the U.S. dollar may also affect the earnings of the Bank's small business, commercial, and corporate clients in Canada.

   In a later section entitled "Bank Specific Risks," the annual report states: "The types of risk to which TD Bank is subject include credit, market (including equity, commodity, foreign exchange, and interest rate), liquidity, operational (including technology),

   reputational, insurance, strategic, regulatory, legal, environmental, capital adequacy and other risks."

   In what sense is foreign exchange risk a "market" risk, a category that includes equity and interest rate risk?

   What do you understand by TD Bank's foreign exchange risk exposure? What sorts of foreign-currency-denominated assets, foreign-currency-denominated liabilities and net foreign currency assets does the bank have? Limit yourself to consideration of TD Bank's US banking operations.

   While TD Bank has substantial assets denominated in US dollars, do you think that TD Bank faces substantial risk as a result of its US operations? Explain.

2. Ford Motor Company manufactures and sells motor vehicles worldwide. Through its worldwide operations, the company is exposed to all types of foreign currency risk. Go to www.ford.com and access Ford's most recent annual report. Scroll through until you find the section "Quantitative and Qualitative Disclosures about Market Risk." In the subsection "Foreign Currency Risk" is a discussion of how Ford uses VAR analysis (see Chapter 6) in evaluating foreign currency exposure for hedging. Ford includes transaction exposure in the analysis but does not include translation exposure. This is consistent with the discussion in this chapter mentioning that the translation process does not have a direct effect on reporting currency cash flows and will only have a realizable effect on net investment upon the sale or liquidation of exposed assets.

MINI CASE

Sundance Sporting Goods, Inc.

Sundance Sporting Goods, Inc. is an American manufacturer of high-quality sporting goods—principally for golf, tennis and racquet sports, and also for lawn sports, such as croquet and badminton—with administrative offices and manufacturing facilities in Chicago. Sundance has two wholly owned manufacturing affiliates, one in Mexico and the other in Canada. The Mexican affiliate is located in Mexico City and services all of Latin America; the Canadian affiliate is in Toronto and serves only Canada. Each affiliate keeps its books in its local currency, which is also the functional currency for the affiliate. The current exchange rates are: US$1 = $1.25 = Ps3.30 = A1 = ¥105 = W800. The nonconsolidated balance sheets for Sundance and its two affiliates appear in the accompanying table.

You joined the International Treasury division of Sundance six months ago after spending the last two years studying for your MBA degree. The corporate treasurer has asked you to prepare a report analyzing all aspects of the translation exposure faced by Sundance as an MNC. She has also asked you to address in your analysis the relationship between the firm's translation exposure and its transaction exposure. After performing a forecast of future spot rates of exchange, you decide that you must do the following before any sensible report can be written:

a. Using the current exchange rates and the nonconsolidated balance sheets for Sundance and its affiliates, prepare a consolidated balance sheet for Sundance.

Nonconsolidated Balance Sheet for Sundance Sporting Goods, Inc. and Its Mexican and Canadian Affiliates, 31 December 2012 (in 000 currency units)

	Sundance, Inc. (parent)	Mexican Affiliate	Canadian Affiliate
Assets			
Cash	US$ 1,500	Ps 1,420	$ 1,200
Accounts receivable	2,500[a]	2,800[e]	1,500[f]
Inventory	5,000	6,200	2,500
Investment in Mexican affiliate	2,400[b]	—	—
Investment in Canadian affiliate	3,600[c]	—	—
Net fixed assets	12,000	11,200	5,600
Total assets	US$27,000	Ps 21,620	$10,800
Liabilities and Net Worth			
Accounts payable	US$ 3,000	Ps 2,500[a]	$ 1,700
Notes payable	4,000[d]	4,200	2,300
Long-term debt	9,000	7,000	2,300
Common shares	5,000	4,500[b]	2,900[c]
Retained earnings	6,000	3,420[b]	1,600[c]
Total liabilities and net worth	US$27,000	Ps 21,620	$10,800

[a]The parent firm is owed Ps1,320,000 by the Mexican affiliate. This sum is included in the parent's accounts receivable as US$400,000, translated at Ps3.30/US$1. The remainder of the parent's (Mexican affiliate's) accounts receivable (payable) are denominated in dollars (pesos).

[b]The Mexican affiliate is wholly owned by the parent firm. It is carried on the parent firm's books at US$2,400,000. This represents the sum of the common shares (Ps4,500,000) and retained earnings (Ps3,420,000) on the Mexican affiliate's books, translated at Ps3.30/US$1.

[c]The Canadian affiliate is wholly owned by the parent firm. It is carried on the parent firm's books at US$3,600,000. This represents the sum of the common shares ($2,900,000) and the retained earnings ($1,600,000) on the Canadian affiliate's books, translated at C$1.25/US$1.

[d]The parent firm has outstanding notes payable of ¥126,000,000 due a Japanese bank. This sum is carried on the parent firm's books as US$1,200,000, translated at ¥105/US$1. Other notes payable are denominated in US dollars.

[e]The Mexican affiliate has sold on account A120,000 of merchandise to an Argentine import house. This sum is carried on the Mexican affiliate's books as Ps396,000, translated at A1/Ps3.30. Other accounts receivable are denominated in Mexican pesos.

[f]The Canadian affiliate has sold on account W192,000,000 of merchandise to a Korean importer. This sum is carried on the Canadian affiliate's books as C$300,000, translated at W800/C$1.25. Other accounts receivable are denominated in Canadian dollars.

b. i. Prepare a translation exposure report for Sundance Sporting Goods, Inc. and its two affiliates.

ii. Using the translation exposure report you have prepared, determine if any reporting currency imbalance will result from the change in exposure currency exchange rates. Your forecast is that exchange rates will change from US$1 = C$1.25 = Ps3.30 = A1 = ¥105 = W800 to US$1 = C$1.30 = Ps3.30 = A1.03 = ¥105 = W800.

c. Prepare a second consolidated balance sheet for the MNC using the exchange rates you expect in the future. Determine how any reporting currency imbalance will affect the new consolidated balance sheet for the MNC.

d. i. Prepare a transaction exposure report for Sundance and its affiliates. Determine if any transaction exposures are also translation exposures.

ii. Investigate what Sundance and its affiliates can do to control its transaction and translation exposures. Determine if any of the translation exposure should be hedged.

REFERENCES & SUGGESTED READINGS

Arpan, J. S., and L. H. Radenbaugh. *International Accounting and Multinational Enterprises,* 2nd ed. New York: Wiley, 1985.

Coopers & Lybrand. *Foreign Currency Translation and Hedging.* New York: Coopers & Lybrand, February 1994.

Financial Accounting Standards Board. *Accounting for the Translation of Foreign Currency Transactions and Foreign Currency Financial Statements, Statement of Financial Accounting Standards No. 8.* Stamford, CT: Financial Accounting Standards Board, October 1975.

Financial Accounting Standards Board. *Foreign Currency Translation, Statement of Financial Accounting Standards No. 52.* Stamford, CT: Financial Accounting Standards Board, December 1981.

Garlicki, T. Dessa, Frank J. Fabozzi, and Robert Fonfeder. "The Impact of Earnings under FASB 52 on Equity Returns." *Financial Management* 16 (1987), pp. 36–44.

Haried, Andrew A., Leroy F. Imdieke, and Ralph E. Smith. *Advanced Accounting,* 6th ed. New York: Wiley, 1994.

Napolitano, Gabrielle. *International Accounting Standards: A Primer.* New York: Goldman, Sachs & Co., November 24, 1993.

connect For more information on the resources available from McGraw-Hill Ryerson, go to www.mcgrawhill.ca/he/solutions.

Part  4

Financial Management of the Multinational Firm

Part Four covers topics on financial management practices for the multinational corporation (MNC).

15 Foreign Direct Investment and Cross-Border Acquisitions

Chapter 15 discusses why multinational corporations (MNCs) make capital expenditures in productive capacity abroad, rather than producing domestically and exporting to foreign markets.

16 International Capital Structure and the Cost of Capital

Chapter 16 deals with the international capital structure and cost of capital of an MNC. We present theory and evidence that the firm's cost of capital is lower when its shares trade internationally and when debt is sourced internationally.

17 International Capital Budgeting

Chapter 17 presents the adjusted present value (APV) framework that is useful for analyzing a capital expenditure in foreign operations.

18 Multinational Cash Management

Chapter 18 covers issues in cash management for the MNC. The chapter shows that if an MNC establishes a centralized cash depository and a multilateral system, the number of foreign cash flow transactions can be reduced, saving money and resulting in better control of cash.

19 International Trade Finance

Chapter 19 provides an introduction to trade finance and countertrade. An example of a typical foreign trade transaction illustrates the three primary documents that are used in trade financing: letter of credit, time draft and bill of lading.

20 International Tax Environment

Chapter 20 opens with a discussion of the theory of taxation. With respect to taxation of foreign-source income, the focus is on Canadian rules and regulations.

21 Corporate Governance around the World

Chapter 21 provides an introduction to issues in corporate governance and discusses how corporate governance structure affects corporate decision making and shareholder security.

Chapter 15

Foreign Direct Investment and Cross-Border Acquisitions

CHAPTER OUTLINE

McCAIN FOODS of tiny Florenceville, New Brunswick, has 55 plants on six continents. One out of every three French fries in the world is produced by McCain. When McCain sets up operations in, say, the United States to wash, slice, freeze, package and distribute French fries throughout the United States, McCain is involved in **foreign direct investment (FDI)**. Foreign direct investment refers to corporate investment when the corporation that makes the investment is foreign-owned. Foreign direct investment is done by multinational enterprise.

Canadian firms have a substantial global presence through foreign direct investment (Exhibit 15.1). Magna International, the diversified global automotive supplier with corporate headquarters in Aurora, Ontario, is an excellent example. Magna International had total sales worldwide of $31 billion on assets of $17 billion in the year 2012, and it employed 118,975 people around the globe.

The Bank of Montreal (BMO) has major retail banking operations in mid-west United States, which BMO conducts through its wholly owned subsidiary, the Harris Bank. Magna also has plants throughout Europe, Asia and Latin America to serve the global automobile industry. The Bata Shoe Company, with headquarters in Batawa, Ontario, has manufacturing plants and retail facilities in 50 countries. The list of examples of foreign direct investment by Canadian firms includes Bell Canada Enterprises, Nortel, Irving Oil, CN, Seagrams and many others.

Canada, of course, is also host to a great deal of foreign direct investment from other countries (Exhibit 15.2). Foreign-owned companies, such as British Petroleum (BP), Coca-Cola, General Foods, General Motors, General Electric, Honda, Nestlé and Weyerhaeuser, have plants and operations throughout Canada.

Foreign direct investment implies a substantial degree of ownership and control of operations in the host country. Honda, for example, with two manufacturing plants in Alliston, Ontario, is 100 percent owned by the parent company in Japan. Honda (Canada) answers to corporate headquarters in Japan.

The benefits from foreign direct investment are economically important. Foreign direct investment generally comes as a package of capital, technology and managerial know-how—in production, marketing, finance, and human resources—as well as patents and trade marks. Inbound FDI brings that package to the host country, adding to productive capital, creating employment and often introducing advanced technology. Outbound FDI, such as Barrick's gold operations in Australia or Peru, reflects the profitable pursuit of investment

EXHIBIT 15.1

Largest Canadian
MNCs, 2012 (millions
of Canadian dollars
and number)

	Industry	Sales	Employees
A. Industrial			
Barrick Gold	Precious metals	14,662	18,400
Magna International	Machinery equipment	30,988	118,975
Bombardier	Aircraft manufacture	17,438	71,500
Imperial Oil	Petroleum	30,448	5,263
Onex	Electronic equipment	28,442	250,000
Encana	Petroleum & gas	5,366	4,193
Celestica	Electronic equipment	6,508	29,000
Husky Energy	Petroleum & gas	23,393	5,178
Suncor Energy	Petroleum	40,361	13,932
Canadian Pacific	Diversified	5,695	14,594
Teck Resources	Integrated mines	11,634	13,500
Agrium Inc.	Chemicals	15,575	14,800
B. Tertiary			
George Weston	Trade	32,751	139,600
Loblaw	Trade	31,712	134,000
BCE	Telecommunications	21,082	55,500
Quebecor	Publishing, printing & media	4,553	16,865
Thomson Reuters	Publishing, printing & media	14,192	59,400
Empire Company	Trade	17,115	47,000
Air Canada	Transport & storage	12,236	24,003
TELUS	Publishing, printing & media	10,927	41,400
Canadian Tire	Trade	11,389	22,525
Hudson's Bay	Trade	n/a	31,700
Sears Canada	Trade	4,478	29,128
CN	Transport & storage	1,024	23,430
TransCanada	Electricity, gas & water	8,274	4,869
Atco	Electricity, gas & water	4,372	9,428
Rogers Communications	Telecommunications	12,540	26,801
		Assets	**Employees**
C. Finance and Insurance			
Royal Bank	Finance	837,585	74,377
Bank of Nova Scotia	Finance	736,361	81,497
Canadian Imperial Bank of Commerce	Finance	392,783	42,595
Toronto-Dominion Bank	Finance	818,482	78,397
Bank of Montreal	Finance	542,265	46,272
SunLife	Insurance	225,782	14,880
Manulife	Insurance	486,056	28,000
Power Corp	Insurance	271,645	30,900
Power Financial Corp	Insurance	268,593	29,300
Great West Life	Insurance	253,718	17,870
National Bank of Canada	Finance	183,796	19,920
Fairfax Financial	Insurance	36,941	11,507
Industrial Alliance	Insurance	41,747	4,314

Source: *UNCTAD: Canada FDI Profile 2012.*

opportunities by Canadian firms. McCain Foods would be severely constrained if it produced and sold French fries only in Canada.

Foreign direct investment is a facet of the globalization of industry. Over the past decade, FDI has grown rapidly, indeed almost twice as fast as international trade. In fact, more than 80 percent of international trade in manufactured goods takes place within multinational enterprise, for example from subsidiary to parent. Much of the enormous

EXHIBIT 15.2	Largest Foreign Investments in Canada 2012		
Company	**Home Country**	**Revenue ($000s)**	**Parent Company**
A. Industrial			
General Motors of Canada	United States	8,300,000	General Motors Co.
Imperial Oil	United States	30,474,000	Exxon Mobil Corp.
Ford Motor of Canada	United States	9,420,225	Ford Motor Co.
Honda Canada	United Kingdom	8,600,000	Honda
Ultramar	United States	11,401,954	Valero Energy
Toyota Canada	Japan	9,900,000	Toyota Motor Corp
IBM Canada	United States	5,746,050	IBM
Hewlett-Packard Canada	United States	4,645,656	Hewlett-Packard
B. Tertiary/Services			
Walmart Canada	United States	23,400,000	Walmart Stores
Costco Wholesale Canada	United States	13,238,056	Costco Wholesale
Direct Energy Marketing	United Kingdom	9,696,626	Centrica
Canada Safeway	United States	6,633,223	Safeway
Home Depot Canada	United States	5,200,000	Home Depot
Sears Canada	United States	4,619,300	Sears, Roebuck & Co.
Cargill	United States	6,653,000	Cargill
Best Buy Canada	United States	5,614,817	Best Buy
Westcoast Energy	United States	3,588,000	Spectra Energy Corp.
Winners Apparel	United States	2,655,950	TJX Cos
Fluor Canada	United States	4,082,097	Fluor
Company	**Home Country**		**Parent Company**
C. Finance and Insurance			
HSBC Bank Canada	United Kingdom		HSBC Holdings
Standard Life of Canada	United Kingdom		Standard Life Oversea Holdings
Aviva Canada	United Kingdom		Aviva
Lloyd's Underwriters (Canada)	United Kingdom		Lloyd's of London

Source: *Financial Post BUSINESS, June 19, 2012.* "FP500: Largest Foreign-controlled Companies" Special to *Financial Post,* June 19, 2012. Material reprinted with the express permission of National Post, a division of Postmedia Network Inc.

back-and-forth trade between Ontario and Michigan in the integrated North American automobile sector is *intrafirm* within Ford, GM and Chrysler.

In this chapter, we investigate why companies decide to undertake FDI as opposed to the alternative of exporting their products and services. We quickly see that in some cases FDI is virtually the only option to penetrate foreign markets. Four Seasons Hotels and Resorts cannot export hotel rooms so it exports the hotel business by setting up hotels abroad. Likewise Barrick goes where the gold is. Like all corporate investment, FDI is motivated by the search for new and expanded markets or by the opportunity to produce more efficiently with the use of foreign resources, such as lower-cost labour.

We will look closely at an increasing popular mode of FDI, namely, **cross-border mergers and acquisitions**. For example, CN, Canada's national railway, acquired Illinois Central and Wisconsin Central Railways as part of CN's strategy to reshape itself from an east–west one-country railway to a continental transportation system. In the financial sector, Manulife of Toronto acquired John Hancock of Boston to form the second–largest life insurance company in North America. Such cross-border mergers and acquisitions reflect corporate strategy along with substantial international financial reorganization.

In the latter part of the chapter, we introduce an investment perspective that is unique to foreign direct investment—*political risk*. Once a corporation establishes facilities in a foreign country, its operations are subject to the "rules of the game" set by the host country.

Political risk ranges from unexpected restrictions on repatriation of foreign earnings to outright confiscation of corporate assets. It is essential to the security and welfare of the corporation to assess and manage political risk effectively. Before we turn to corporate issues, however, let us briefly review global trends in foreign direct investment.

15.1 GLOBAL TRENDS IN FDI

The recent trends in **FDI flows** are presented in Exhibit 15.3 and Exhibit 15.4. FDI flows represent new additions to the existing stock of FDI. During the period 1997–2012, total annual worldwide FDI flows amounted to about $1.137 trillion on average. In the most recent years, the volume of the cross-border flow of direct investment has waned a bit compared to the heady days around 2007.

As can be expected, several developed countries are the dominant sources of FDI *outflows*. The United States, on average, invested about $213 billion per year overseas, closely followed by the United Kingdom, which invested about $113 billion per year. For the United States in 2005, the curious *negative entry* in the outflows line indicates that in that year US-based investors reduced absolutely the stock of US-FDI abroad.

France, Germany and Japan also invest heavily abroad, each exceeding $55 billion per year. After these "big five" come the Netherlands, Spain, Canada, Switzerland and Italy.

The industrial countries account for about 90 percent of the total worldwide FDI outflows during the past decade. This implies that multinational corporations based in these countries have significant comparative advantages in FDI. Examples are perhaps the clearest way to illustrate the importance of the unique industrial advantages that allow foreign direct investors to successfully enter foreign markets. Nestlé of Switzerland, the world's largest food company, brings its brands, production methods and marketing skills to virtually every corner of the globe. Likewise Lafarge, France's building materials giant, has a firm global grip on the production and distribution of a relatively humble product like cement. Calgary-based Agrium, one of the world's largest producers and distributors of fertilizer products and agricultural nutrients (such as nitrogen, potassium and phosphate) has a global-sites map with more pins in the United States and South America than in Canada.

Exhibits 15.3 and 15.4 also show FDI *inflows* by country. During the 1997–2012 period, the United States received the largest annual FDI inflow, $175 billion per year on average, among all countries. The next most popular destinations of FDI flows were China, the United Kingdom, Germany, France, the Netherlands, Canada, Spain and Mexico. These nine countries account for about 45 percent of the total worldwide FDI inflows, suggesting these countries have locational advantages for FDI over other countries. Multinationals are generally drawn on the production side to efficient foreign sites of manufacturing, such as outsourcing to China or Mexico, or on the marketing side to wealthy consumers such as in the United States and Europe.

In contrast to its substantial role as an originating country of FDI outflows, Japan plays a relatively minor role as a host of FDI inflows; Japan received only $6.9 billion worth of FDI, on average, per year during the period 1997–2012. In the modern era, Japan's inflows of FDI peaked in 2008 and by 2013 had dropped peak-to-trough by almost 90 percent. This relatively low inflow of FDI to Japan reflects a variety of legal, economic and cultural barriers to foreign investment in Japan.

FDI flows into China have dramatically increased in recent years. The annual inflow increased from $3.5 billion in 1990 to $124 billion in 2011. By 1993, China had emerged as the second most important host country for FDI, trailing only the United States. Early on in its economic transition, China's low-wage labour was the primary magnet for foreign direct investment, but increasingly the foreign direct investors' strategy is to tap the huge and expanding consumer market within China. Among developing countries, Mexico is another that experienced substantial FDI inflows of about $16 billion on average per year. It is well known that MNCs invest in Mexico, a low-cost country, to serve the North

EXHIBIT 15.3   Foreign Direct Investment—Outflows (Inflows), Billions of US Dollars

	1997	1998	1999	2000	2001	2002	2003	2004	2005	2006	2007	2008	2009	2010	2011	2012	Annual Average
Australia	5.9 / −8.6	2.5 / −6.6	−0.7 / −2.9	−0.8 / −13.1	12.2 / −4.0	7.6 / −14.0	15.6 / −9.7	18.0 / −42.4	−40.9 / 34.5	22.6 / −25.7	24.2 / −22.2	33.6 / −47.0	16.2 / −26.7	27.3 / −35.2	14.3 / −65.3	16.1 / −57.0	11.0 / −21.6
Canada	22.0 / −11.5	26.6 / −16.5	17.2 / −24.7	44.7 / −66.8	36.1 / −27.5	26.4 / −21.0	21.5 / −7.6	43.3 / −1.5	34.1 / −33.8	39.1 / −62.8	64.6 / −116.8	79.3 / −61.6	39.6 / −22.7	34.7 / −29.1	49.8 / −41.3	53.9 / −45.4	39.6 / −36.9
China	2.6 / −44.2	1.6 / −45.5	1.8 / −40.3	0.9 / −40.7	6.9 / −46.9	2.5 / −52.7	0.2 / −53.5	1.8 / −60.6	11.3 / −72.4	21.2 / −72.7	26.5 / −83.5	55.9 / −103.3	56.5 / −95.0	58.8 / −114.7	74.7 / −124.0	84.2 / −121.0	25.5 / −73.2
France	35.6 / −23.2	40.6 / −28.0	126.9 / −46.5	177.4 / −43.3	86.8 / −50.5	49.4 / −48.9	53.1 / −42.5	57.0 / −31.4	115.7 / −63.6	121.4 / −78.1	164.3 / 96.2	155.0 / −64.2	107.1 / −24.2	64.6 / −33.6	59.6 / −38.5	37.2 / −25.1	90.7 / −34.1
Germany	40.3 / −9.6	86.6 / −19.9	108.7 / −56.1	56.6 / −198.3	36.9 / −21.1	8.6 / −36.0	6.2 / −29.2	1.9 / 15.1	45.6 / −32.7	94.7 / −55.1	170.6 / −80.2	72.8 / −8.1	69.6 / −22.5	121.5 / −57.4	52.2 / −48.9	66.9 / −6.6	65.0 / −41.7
Italy	10.2 / −3.7	12.1 / −2.6	6.7 / −6.9	12.3 / −13.4	21.5 / −14.9	17.1 / −14.5	9.1 / −16.4	19.3 / −19.8	39.7 / −20.0	42.1 / −39.2	96.2 / −43.8	67.0 / 10.8	21.3 / −20.1	32.7 / −9.2	53.6 / −34.3	30.4 / −9.6	30.7 / −16.1
Japan	26.0 / −3.2	24.2 / −3.2	22.7 / −12.7	31.6 / −8.3	38.3 / −6.2	32.3 / −9.2	28.8 / −6.3	31.0 / −7.8	45.8 / −2.8	50.3 / 6.5	73.5 / −22.6	128.0 / −24.4	74.7 / −11.9	56.3 / 1.2	107.6 / 1.8	122.6 / −1.7	55.8 / −6.9
Mexico	1.1 / −12.8	1.4 / −10.2	1.5 / −13.2	1.0 / −16.6	4.4 / −26.8	0.9 / −14.7	14.2 / −1.3	18.7 / −4.4	18.1 / −6.2	5.8 / −19.3	8.3 / −31.4	1.2 / −27.9	8.5 / −16.6	15.0 / −21.4	12.1 / −21.5	25.6 / −12.7	8.6 / −16.0
Netherlands	21.5 / −9.4	38.3 / −31.9	57.6 / −41.2	75.6 / −63.9	48.0 / −51.9	34.6 / −25.6	44.2 / −21.7	17.3 / −0.4	119.5 / −43.6	47.1 / −8.0	55.6 / −119.4	68.3 / −4.5	34.5 / −38.6	63.3 / 7.4	40.9 / −17.2	−3.5 / 0.2	47.7 / −29.4
Spain	12.5 / −6.4	18.4 / −11.3	42.1 / −15.8	54.7 / −37.5	33.1 / −28.0	31.5 / −35.9	27.5 / −25.9	60.5 / −24.8	39.8 / −22.3	100.2 / −26.9	137.1 / −64.3	74.7 / −77.0	13.1 / −10.4	37.8 / −39.9	36.6 / −26.6	−4.9 / −27.8	44.7 / −30.0
Sweden	12.6 / −10.9	22.5 / −19.4	21.9 / −60.9	40.6 / −23.2	6.4 / −11.9	10.7 / −11.6	21.1 / −5.0	21.0 / −12.6	25.9 / −13.4	22.0 / −23.2	38.3 / −28.9	30.4 / −46.9	25.9 / −10.0	20.2 / 0.1	28.2 / −9.2	33.4 / −13.7	23.8 / −18.8
Switzerland	16.7 / −4.9	17.4 / −3.7	33.3 / −11.7	44.7 / −19.3	18.2 / −8.9	7.6 / −5.6	15.4 / −16.5	26.8 / −0.8	42.9 / −5.8	69.9 / −26.3	51.0 / −32.4	45.3 / −15.1	26.4 / −28.9	79.3 / −32.6	47.3 / −11.8	44.3 / −3.6	36.7 / −14.2
United Kingdom	63.6 / −37.0	114.2 / −63.1	201.5 / 88.0	233.4 / −118.8	58.9 / −52.6	35.2 / 27.8	62.2 / −16.8	94.9 / −56.2	101.1 / −164.5	86.8 / −147.2	325.4 / −200.0	183.3 / −89.0	39.3 / −76.3	39.5 / −50.6	106.7 / −51.1	71.4 / −62.4	113.6 / −66.9
United States	110.0 / −109.3	132.8 / −193.4	209.4 / −283.4	142.6 / −214.0	124.9 / −159.5	115.3 / −63.9	129.4 / −53.1	222.4 / −122.4	−12.7 / −99.4	221.7 / −236.7	393.5 / −216.0	308.3 / −306.4	287.0 / −143.6	304.4 / −197.9	396.7 / −228.9	328.7 / −167.6	213.4 / −174.7
World	475.1 / −464.3	648.9 / −643.9	1,092.3 / −1,086.8	1,186.8 / −1,388.0	721.5 / −817.6	596.5 / −678.8	561.1 / −557.9	813.1 / −710.8	778.7 / −916.3	1,323.2 / −1,411.0	2,272.0 / −2,002.7	2,005.3 / −1,816.4	1,149.8 / −1,216.5	1,504.9 / −1,408.5	1,678.0 / −1,651.5	1,391.0 / −1,350.9	1,137.4 / −1,132.6

Source: UNCTAD, *World Investment Report*, various issues up to 2013, Annex Table B.1.

EXHIBIT 15.4 FDI Outflows and Inflows Average Annual Flow, 1997–2012, Billions of US Dollars

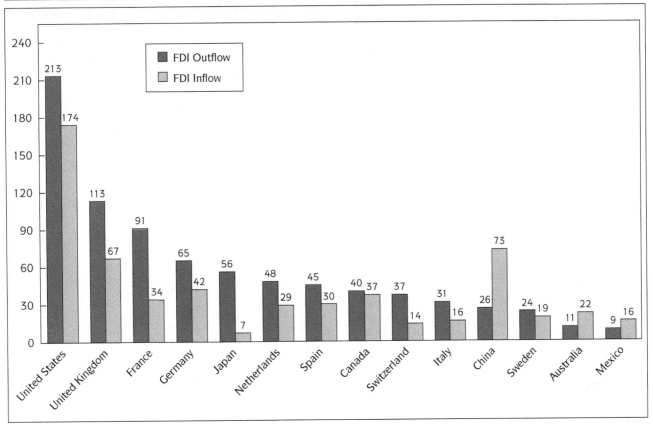

Source: Adapted from UNCTAD, *World Investment Report*, 2012.

American as well as Mexican markets. Similarly in Europe, MNCs invested heavily, $30 billion per year, in Spain where costs of production are relatively low compared with other European countries such as France and Germany. Spain and Ireland are especially attractive countries to non-European based MNCs with an eye to gaining a foothold in the huge single market of the European Union.

Now, let us turn our attention to **FDI stocks**, which are the accumulation of previous FDI flows. The overall cross-border production activities of MNCs are best captured by FDI stocks. Exhibit 15.5 provides a summary of FDI stocks, both *outward* (referred to as "FDI abroad") and *inward* (referred to as "hosted FDI"), by country. The total world-wide FDI stock, which was about $514 billion in 1980, rose to $23.6 trillion in 2012. In the case of Canada, our FDI stock abroad rose by a factor of 31 from $23 billion in 1980 to $715 billion in 2012. Over the past 32 years, Canada's foreign direct investment position has shifted dramatically from the case where we hosted more FDI than we had abroad to the situation today where Canadian FDI abroad exceeds FDI in Canada.

Canada ranks with the United States, the United Kingdom, Germany, Japan, the Netherlands, France and Switzerland as the source of the most outward FDI. For FDI inward stock, on the other hand, the United States, China, the United Kingdom, Germany, France and the Netherlands are the most important hosts. Exhibit 15.6 shows the direction of FDI stocks among the so-called international triad—three major global economic groups, that is, North America, the European Union and Asian group. While our data do not indicate such explicitly, FDI flows and accumulated stocks tend to be concentrated *within* each of these three major economic regions.

EXHIBIT 15.5   Foreign Direct Investment—Outward (Inward) Stocks, Billions of US Dollars

Country	1980	1985	1990	1995	2000	2003	2005	2012
Australia	2 (13)	7 (25)	31 (74)	53 (96)	85 (111)	117 (174)	159 (211)	424 (611)
Canada	**23 (54)**	**43 (65)**	**85 (113)**	**118 (223)**	**238 (212)**	**308 (276)**	**399 (357)**	715 (637)
China	0 0	0 (6)	4 (21)	16 (135)	28 (193)	37 (502)	46 (318)	509 (833)
France	24 (23)	38 (37)	110 (87)	204 (191)	445 (260)	634 (434)	853 (601)	1,497 (1,095)
Germany	43 (37)	60 (37)	152 (111)	258 (193)	542 (272)	623 (545)	697 (503)	1,547 (716)
Italy	7 (9)	17 (19)	60 (60)	97 (64)	180 (121)	239 (174)	293 (220)	565 (366)
Japan	20 (3)	44 (5)	201 (10)	239 (37)	278 (50)	336 (90)	387 (101)	1,055 (205)
Mexico	0 (9)	0 (19)	3 (22)	3 (41)	8 (97)	12 (166)	28 (210)	138 (315)
Netherlands	42 (19)	48 (25)	107 (69)	173 (116)	305 (244)	384 (336)	641 (463)	976 (573)
Spain	1 (5)	5 (9)	16 (66)	36 (109)	168 (156)	208 (230)	381 (368)	627 (635)
Sweden	6 (4)	11 (4)	51 (13)	73 (31)	123 (94)	189 (143)	203 (172)	407 (376)
Switzerland	22 (9)	25 (10)	66 (34)	143 (57)	230 (87)	344 (154)	395 (172)	1,129 (666)
United Kingdom	80 (63)	100 (64)	229 (204)	305 (200)	898 (437)	1,129 (672)	1,238 (817)	1,808 (1,321)
United States	220 (83)	238 (185)	431 (395)	699 (536)	1,316 (1,257)	2,069 (1,554)	2,051 (1,626)	5,191 (3,932)
World FDI Stock	514 (513)	739 (972)	1,791 (1,789)	2,898 (2,992)	6,471 (5,803)	8,197 (8,245)	10,672 (10,130)	23,593 (22,813)

Note: For each country, the upper line reports that country's stock of foreign direct investment abroad while the lower line reports the (foreign-owned) stock of direct investment in that country. The latter are recorded as "negative" since, in the Balance of Payments (Capital Account) they represent a liability to foreigners.

Source: UNCTAD, *World Investment Report*, Annex Table 2, various issues up to 2013.

Exhibit 15.5 shows that in 1980, the stock of FDI in Canada was more than twice the stock of Canadian direct investment abroad. By 2012, the inward and outward stocks of FDI were almost equal. This rapid and remarkable reversal of Canada's FDI position reflects, in part, the aggressive pursuit of offshore investment opportunities by Canadian firms, such as Bombardier, Canfor, Domtar and firms all the way through the industrial alphabet. On the other hand, these figures may also prompt the disturbing suggestion that Canada has become a less attractive destination for foreign capital.

15.2   WHY DO FIRMS INVEST OVERSEAS?

Why do firms locate production overseas rather than exporting from the home country or licensing production to a local firm in the host country? In other words, why do firms seek to extend corporate *control* overseas by forming multinational corporations? Unlike the theory of international trade or the theory of international portfolio investment, we do not have a well-developed, comprehensive theory of FDI. However, several theories shed light on certain aspects of the FDI phenomenon. Most explanations, in one way or another, involve *market imperfections* in product, factor or capital markets as the key motivating forces driving FDI.

In what follows, we discuss some of the key factors that are important in firms' decisions to invest overseas:

- Trade barriers
- Imperfect labour market
- Intangible assets
- Vertical integration
- Product life cycle
- Shareholder diversification services

Trade Barriers

Tariffs, which are essentially taxes on imports imposed by the destination nation, are among the oldest and most obvious restrictions on trade. Rather than paying the tariff on exported goods, foreign companies would often opt to set up production facilities to serve the market protected by tariff. For example, an American company that faced tariffs on goods destined for, say, Canada, would often choose to "jump the tariff wall" by setting up production facilities in Canada. Indeed, Canada has a long history of attracting such foreign direct investment.

When foreign firms produced just for the Canadian market, such firms—say in household durables, such as General Electric (Canada) or Westinghouse (Canada)—were forced into smaller and less efficient production runs in Canada than in the home country. Canada's tariff barriers were recognized long ago as a source of industrial inefficiency in Canada, especially in manufacturing. Canada came to be known as a "branch plant" economy.

A recent example in Canada where tariffs induced FDI involves the automobile sector. A 6 percent tariff on imported finished vehicles from outside of North America was a major reason for Honda and Toyota of Japan to build manufacturing plants in Canada.

Fortunately, over the past 50 years, import tariffs have been cut dramatically. Indeed, for all practical purposes, Canada no longer imposes tariffs on imports, especially on goods from our largest trading partner, the United States. The Free Trade Agreement with the United States followed by the North American Free Trade Agreement (NAFTA), which includes Mexico, set up an agenda to virtually eliminate tariffs among the NAFTA member countries.

The same story applies throughout most of the world. Trade among the 27 member states of the European Union crosses old borders tariff-free.

Tariff barriers have been largely dismantled except in two particularly troublesome areas, agriculture and textiles. The remaining tariffs that affect these sectors, such as US tariffs on sugar or Europe's tariffs on textiles, create serious difficulties for developing nations as they deny markets for the labour-intensive, relatively low-skill production in which developing countries have comparative advantage.

Trade barriers can also arise *naturally* from transportation costs. Such products as mineral ore and cement that are bulky relative to their economic values may not be suitable for exporting because high transportation costs will substantially reduce profit

EXHIBIT 15.6

Labour Costs
around the Globe
(2003, 2007 and
2012)

Country	Average Hourly Cost (US$)		
	2003	2007	2012
Belgium	20.25	25.80	54.77
Sweden	18.41	25.85	49.12
Germany	23.04	27.64	47.38
France	16.70	22.04	47.12
Australia	13.22	17.86	46.28
Canada	**15.70**	**25.94**	**36.56**
Italy	14.51	19.38	36.17
Japan	19.52	22.56	35.71
United States	20.67	25.36	35.53
United Kingdom	15.75	21.84	30.77
Spain	10.94	15.50	28.44
Israel	10.54	12.66	21.42
Korea	7.53	11.15	18.91
Taiwan	5.44	6.12	9.34
Hong Kong	5.47	5.98	6.85
Mexico	1.70	2.60	6.48
Philippines	0.66	1.07	2.01
China	0.60	1.10	1.64
India	0.68	0.97	1.45
Indonesia	0.22	0.27	1.15

Source: US Department of Labor, Labor Statics.

margins. In these cases, FDI can be made in the foreign markets to reduce transportation costs.

Imperfect Labour Market

Samsung, the Korean conglomerate, wanted to build production facilities for its consumer electronics products to serve North American markets. Samsung could have located its production facilities anywhere in North America if the firm was concerned only with circumventing trade barriers imposed by NAFTA. Samsung chose to locate its production facilities in northern Mexico rather than in Canada or the United States mainly because it wanted to take advantage of the lower costs of labour in Mexico.

Labour services in a country can be severely underpriced relative to its productivity because workers are not allowed to freely move across national boundaries to seek higher wages. Among all factor markets, the international labour market is the most imperfect. Severe restrictions in the labour market lead to persistent wage differentials among countries. Exhibit 15.6 provides the hourly labour costs in the manufacturing sector for selected countries in 2003, 2007 and 2012.

For most of the past 50 years, the United States had the highest average hourly manufacturing wage in the world. Exhibit 15.6 indicates that those days are over. The combination of the rise of sophisticated manufacturing and labour productivity in other countries plus the 2004–2007 fall of the US dollar against almost all other currencies has resulted in across-the-board international increases in wage costs measured in US dollars.

When workers are not mobile because of immigration barriers, firms move to the workers in order to benefit from lower-cost labour. This is one of the main reasons MNCs move production to such countries as Mexico, China and India or to Thailand, Malaysia and Indonesia, where labour costs are low relative to worker productivity.

Intangible Assets

Coca-Cola has invested in bottling plants all over the world rather than, say, licensing local firms to produce Coke. Coca-Cola chose FDI as a mode of entry into foreign markets for an obvious reason—it wanted to protect the formula for its famed soft drink. If Coca-Cola licenses a local firm to produce Coke, it has no guarantee that the secrets of the formula will be maintained. Once the formula is leaked to other local firms, they may come up with similar products which would hurt Coca-Cola's sales. In the 1960s, in a famous example, Coca-Cola faced strong pressure from the Indian government to reveal the formula as a condition for continued operations in India; instead, Coca-Cola chose to withdraw from India.[1]

MNCs may undertake overseas investment projects in a foreign country despite the fact that local firms may enjoy inherent advantages. This implies that MNCs have significant advantages over local firms. The basis of the advantages that MNCs hold are generally referred to as their **intangible asset**. Examples include technological, managerial and marketing know-how, superior R&D capabilities and brand power. These intangible assets are often hard to package and sell to foreigners. In addition, the property rights in intangible assets are difficult to establish and protect, especially in foreign countries where legal recourse may not be readily available. As a result, firms may find it more profitable to establish foreign subsidiaries and capture returns directly by *internalizing* transactions in these assets. The **internalization theory** helps explain why MNCs often dominate local firms. Imagine how difficult it would be for a new Canadian firm to outperform L'Oréal, Sony or Microsoft or, conversely, how difficult it is for firms abroad to go head-to-head with McCain, Seagrams or Barrick.

Firms that have intangible assets that are crucial to their brand-image or their unique production processes tend to invest directly in foreign countries in order to use these assets on a larger scale and, at the same time, to avoid misappropriations of intangible assets that may occur while transacting in foreign markets through a market mechanism.

Vertical Integration

Suppose Royal Dutch Shell purchases a significant portion of crude oil for its refinery facilities from a Saudi oil company that owns the oil fields. In this situation, Royal Dutch Shell can experience a number of problems. For example, Royal Dutch Shell, the downstream firm, would like to hold the crude oil price down, whereas the Saudi oil company, an upstream firm, would like to push the price up. If the Saudi company has stronger bargaining power, Royal Dutch Shell may be forced to pay a higher price than it would like to, adversely affecting the firm's profits. As the world's demand for refined oil fluctuates, one of the two firms is likely to bear more risk than the other. The conflict between the upstream and downstream firms can be resolved, however, if the

---

[1]Coca-Cola reentered the Indian market as India gradually liberalized its economy, improving the climate for foreign investments.

UNCTAD's Outward FDI Performance Index

UNCTAD, the United Nations Conference on Trade and Development, has devised a country-specific index of "FDI performance" (see Exhibit 15.7). The Outward FDI Performance Index measures the world share of a country's outward stock of FDI relative to that country's share in world GDP. According to this ranking, several countries from South-East Asia, West Asia and Latin America are among the global leaders.

Some developing economies, including Chile, Hong Kong (China), Malaysia and Singapore, as well as economies in transition—such as Azerbaijan and the Russian Federation—have seen increases in their index values over the past 10 years. The fact that the outward-FDI from these countries grew faster than their respective shares of global GDP may indicate that their enterprises are building ownership advantages rapidly and/or are increasingly choosing to exploit their advantages by establishing operations in foreign locations. Conversely, the values for Bahamas, Brazil, Panama and Taiwan Province of China fell significantly.

The index value for Hong Kong has risen at an exceptionally fast pace, partly reflecting Hong Kong's particular position as a staging post for FDI into China and as a recipient of "round tripping" FDI by Chinese enterprises. For the period 2003–2005, Singapore and Panama also showed disproportionately large outflows of FDI. However, apart from these economies, index values are on average higher for developed than for developing countries. Most of the large developing economies with considerable absolute levels of outward FDI, such as Brazil, China, India and Mexico, are found at the opposite end of the spectrum. The fact that their index values are below 0.5 suggests considerable potential for future expansion of FDI from these economies.

EXHIBIT 15.7		UNCTAD FDI Performance Index

(selected economies, 1993–1995 and 2003–2005 averages, ranked by 2003–2005)

Rank	Economy	1993–1995	2003–2005
1	Hong Kong, China	4.63	9.97
2	Norway	1.40	5.80
3	Luxembourg	—	4.99
4	Switzerland	4.32	4.42
5	Netherlands	4.13	4.22
6	Belgium	—	4.00
7	Singapore	3.61	3.97
8	Panama	5.45	3.36
9	United Kingdom	2.72	2.47
10	Sweden	2.80	2.46
11	Ireland	3.32	2.28
12	Denmark	1.32	1.84
13	Finland	1.20	1.76
14	France	1.33	1.66
15	Iceland	0.24	1.62
16	**Canada**	**1.92**	**1.50**
17	Bahrain	1.84	1.46
18	Germany	1.08	1.41
19	Spain	0.59	1.41
20	Malaysia	1.07	1.39
21	Taiwan	1.68	1.19
22	Australia	1.43	1.12
23	Bahamas	4.12	1.10
24	Azerbaijan	—	1.09
25	Portugal	0.30	1.06
26	Austria	0.48	0.92
27	Chile	0.34	0.76
28	Russian Federation	0.06	0.73
29	Cyprus	0.08	0.73
30	Malta	0.10	0.70
39	United States	0.50	0.50
41	Brazil	0.80	0.42
59	Korea, Republic of	0.18	0.18
62	Mexico	0.11	0.13
67	Turkey	0.09	0.10
71	China	0.26	0.09
88	India	0.01	0.04

Source: UNCTAD.

two firms form a vertically integrated firm. Obviously, if Royal Dutch Shell controls the oil fields, the problems will disappear.

Generally speaking, MNCs undertake FDI in countries where inputs are available in order to secure their supply at a stable price. Furthermore, if MNCs have significant control over the input market, this creates a barrier to entry to the industry. Many MNCs involved in extractive/natural resources industries directly own oil fields, mine deposits and forests for these reasons. Likewise, MNCs in manufacturing and processing often find it profitable to locate facilities near the natural resources in order to save transportation costs. It would be costly to bring bulky bauxite ore to the home country and then extract the aluminum.

Although the majority of vertical FDIs are *backward* in that FDI involves an industry abroad that produces inputs for MNCs, foreign investments can take the form of *forward* vertical FDI when they involve an industry abroad that sells an MNC's outputs. As is well known, North American car makers found it difficult to market their products in Japan. This is partly because most car dealers in Japan have a long and close business relationship with the Japanese car makers and are reluctant to carry foreign imports. To overcome this problem, North American car makers began to build their own network of dealerships in Japan to help sell their cars. This is an example of forward vertical FDI.

Product Life Cycle

It is often obvserved that firms undertake FDI at a particular stage in the life cycle of the products that they initially introduced. Throughout the twentieth century, the majority of new products such as computers, televisions and mass-produced cars, were developed in industrialized nations and first marketed at home. According to **product life-cycle theory**, when firms first introduce new products, they choose to keep production facilities at home, close to customers. In the early stage of the product life cycle, the demand for the new product is relatively insensitive to the price and thus the pioneering firm can charge a relatively high price. At the same time, the firm can continuously improve the product on the basis of feedback from its customers at home.

As demand for the new product develops in foreign countries, the pioneering firm begins to export to those countries. As the foreign demand for the product continues to grow, the pioneering firm, as well as foreign firms, may be induced to start production in foreign countries to serve local markets. As the product becomes standardized and mature, it becomes important to cut the cost of production to stay competitive. A foreign producer operating in a low-cost country has an advantage in world markets. They export. Likewise, the pioneering firm has an incentive to set up operations in the low-cost country. In other words, FDI takes place when the product reaches maturity and cost becomes an important consideration. FDI can, thus, be interpreted as a *defensive* move to maintain the firm's competitive position against its domestic and foreign rivals. The International Finance in Practice box "Linear Sequence in Manufacturing: Singer & Company" provides an interesting historical example supporting the product life-cycle view of FDI.

Product life-cycle theory predicts that over time, most manufactured products, such as laptop computers today, become standardized commodities with production gravitating to the places where they can be manufactured at the lowest cost. The advanced countries that first developed and manufactured the products, often for export, switch to become importers of the product. The dynamic changes in the international trade pattern are illustrated in Exhibit 15.8. The product life-cycle theory is consistent with the locational changes observed for many products. For instance, personal computers were first developed by US firms (such as IBM and Apple Computer) and exported to overseas markets. As PCs became a standardized commodity, however, the wealthier countries became net importers of PCs from producers based in such countries as Japan, Korea and Taiwan.

New products tend to be created in richer, more industrially developed countries because research and development skills and capacity tend to be located in these wealthier nations. Innovation is a knowledge-intensive activity. Production, on the other hand, requires less-sophisticated skill and therefore the producers eventually focus on finding the lowest-cost sites of production, which typically involves locations with relatively low labour costs.

Linear Sequence in Manufacturing: Singer & Company

Singer was one of the first United States–based companies to internationalize its operations. In August 1850, I. M. Singer invented a sewing machine and established I. M. Singer & Company in New York in 1851 to manufacture and sell the machines in the United States. To protect this innovative product, Singer had applied for and obtained domestic and some foreign patents by 1851. Until 1855, the company concentrated on fine-tuning its operations in the domestic market.

The first step towards internationalizing took place in 1855, when Singer & Co. sold its French patent for the single thread machine to a French merchant for a combination of lump-sum payment and royalties. This proved to be a bad experience for Singer as the French merchant was reluctant to pay royalties and handled competitors' products, leading to disputes and discouraging Singer from selling foreign patents to independent businesspersons. By 1856, Singer stopped granting territorial rights to independents in the domestic market due to bad experiences and began establishing its own sales outlets. Independent agents were not providing user instructions to buyers and failed to offer servicing. They were also reluctant to risk their capital by providing instalment payments as well as carrying large inventories.

Learning from its domestic problems, Singer used franchised agents as a mode of entry abroad; they sold and advertised the company's product in a given region. By 1858, Singer had independent businesspersons as foreign agents in Rio de Janeiro and elsewhere. Between September 1860 and May 1861, the company exported 127 machines to agents in Canada, Cuba, Curacao, Germany, Mexico, Peru, Puerto Rico, Uruguay, and Venezuela. Due to its domestic experience, Singer sped up the linear sequence, sometimes simultaneously using both franchised agents and its own sales outlets.

Singer also started extending its policy of establishing sales outlets to foreign markets. By 1861, it had salaried representatives in Glasgow and London. They established additional branches in England, to each of which the machines were sold on commission. By 1862, Singer was facing competition in England from imitators. Foreign sales of Singer machines increased steadily as the company was able to sell machines abroad at prices lower than in the United States because of the undervaluation of the dollar. In 1863, Singer opened a sales office in Hamburg, Germany, and later in Sweden. By 1866, the European demand for Singer machines surpassed supplies and competitors were taking advantage of Singer's inability to supply the machines. After the Civil War, the United States currency appreciated; at the same time, wages in the United States began to rise, increasing manufacturing costs and affecting firms' international competitiveness. As a result, some United States firms started establishing factories abroad.

In 1868, Singer established a small assembly factory in Glasgow, with parts imported from the United States. The venture proved to be successful and, by 1869, Singer decided to import tools from the United States to manufacture all parts in Glasgow. By 1874, partly due to the recession at home, Singer was selling more than half of its output abroad. Then, Singer started replacing locally financed independent agents with salaried-plus-commission agents. By 1879, its London regional headquarters had 26 offices in the United Kingdom and one each in Paris, Madrid, Brussels, Milan, Basel, Capetown, Bombay, and Auckland.

By the 1880s, the company had a strong foreign sales organization, with the London regional headquarters taking the responsibility for sales in Australia, Asia, Africa, the southern part of South America, the United Kingdom, and a large part of the European continent. The Hamburg office was in charge of northern and middle Europe, while the New York office looked after sales in the Caribbean, Mexico, the northern part of South America and Canada. By 1881, the capacity in Singer's three factories in Glasgow was insufficient to meet demand. Therefore, in 1882, Singer established a modern plant in Kilbowie near Glasgow with the latest United States machine tools and with a capacity equivalent to that of its largest factory in the United States. In 1883, Singer set up manufacturing plants in Canada and Australia. Through experience, Singer learned that it could manufacture more cost effectively in Scotland than in the United States for sales in Europe and other markets.

Source: *World Investment Report 1996*, UNCTAD, p. 77.

The life cycle theory was developed in the 1960s when the United States was the unquestioned leader in R&D and product innovations. Increasingly, product innovations are taking place in a broader global arena and new products are introduced simultaneously in many advanced countries. Production facilities may be located in multiple countries from the inception of a new product. The international system of production is becoming too complicated to be explained by a simple version of the product life-cycle theory.

EXHIBIT 15.8

The Product Life
Cycle

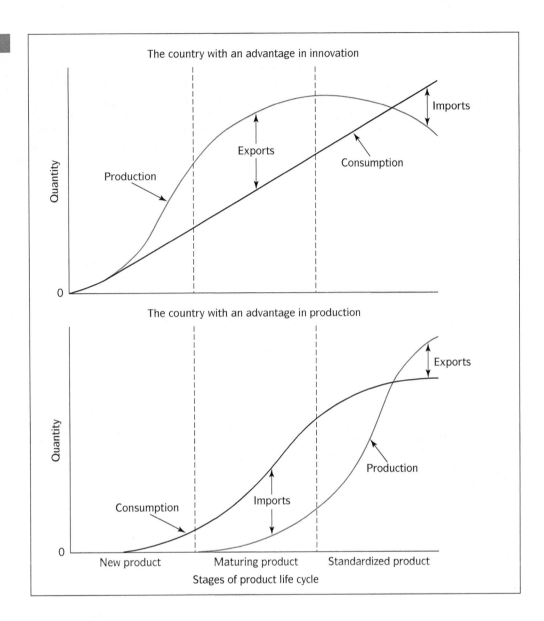

Shareholder Diversification Services

If investors cannot effectively diversify their portfolio holdings internationally because of
barriers to cross-border capital flows, firms may be able to provide their shareholders with
indirect diversification services by making direct investments in foreign countries. When a
firm holds assets in many countries, the firm's cash flows are internationally diversified.
Thus, shareholders of the firm can indirectly benefit from international diversification even
if they are not directly holding foreign shares. Capital market imperfections, thus, may
motivate firms to undertake FDI.

Although shareholders of MNCs may indirectly benefit from corporate international
diversification, it is not clear that firms are motivated to undertake FDI for the purpose of
providing shareholders with diversification services. Considering the fact that many barriers to international portfolio investments have been dismantled in recent years, enabling
investors to diversify internationally by themselves, capital market imperfections as a motivating factor for FDI are likely to become less relevant.

The Exchange Rate and Foreign Direct Investment

Foreign direct investment decisions are distinctly "long-term." In the longer term, exchange rate movements are generally in line with inflation differentials and hence are nominal rather than real. Therefore we ordinarily assume that exchange rate movements are unlikely to have a strong influence on foreign direct investment decisions. In contrast, the following article suggests that the rapid and dramatic rise in the value of the euro against the US and Canadian dollars through 2006–2007 had a significant influence on decisions of European automobile manufacturers as to where they locate their production facilities.

Volkswagen AG will consider building its first plant in North America if the U.S. dollar remains weak against the euro, says its chief executive, Martin Winterkorn.

It would then join a growing number of European carmakers looking to boost manufacturing on this continent to counter the currency exchange disadvantage.

VW, the world's fourth-biggest carmaker, is already planning a second administrative centre near Detroit "to get closer to our customers" in North America, Mr. Winterkorn told German magazine *Focus* in an interview.

"If the dollar exchange rate stays at its present level, we will have to begin thinking about a factory in North America," he said. "In North America, we are actually quite far away from where we want to be."

Several European automakers are weighing whether to establish their first factories in North America or boost production as the euro rises in value. A higher euro makes importing European-made vehicles into North America more expensive than producing locally.

The euro has gained 17% against the U.S. dollar over the past year although the euro is unchanged against the Canadian dollar over the same period.

BMW, whose single largest market is the United States, said in May a weak U.S. dollar and Japanese yen cost it €666 million ($952.1 million) in the last financial year alone. BMW said it would expand output at its factory in Spartanburg, South Carolina, to lower its currency risk.

Magna International, whose Magna Steyr unit assembles vehicles on contract for several automakers in Austria, stands to lose 26 cents to 39 cents in annual per-share earnings from that move as BMW shifts assembly of its next-general X3 SUV from Austria to Spartanburg in 2010. But on the whole it is hoping to benefit from the cross-ocean migration.

Magna Steyr is hunting for a site for its first North American auto assembly plant and has said it expects its key customers to include European carmakers looking to escape the currency-exchange penalty.

"I think that the factors that drove BMW to think about not exporting from Europe is going to drive others to do the same thing," Mark Hogan, president of Magna International, said last month.

Magna is in talks with several automakers about doing assembly work for them in North America, spokeswoman Tracy Fuerst said yesterday. But it still needs to strike a firm contract before selecting a site.

Source: © Financial Post, 2007. "Greenback Depreciation May Drive Volkswagen across the Atlantic," by Nicolas Van Praet. July 10, 2007. Material reprinted with the express permission of National Post, a division of Postmedia Network Inc.

15.3 CROSS-BORDER MERGERS AND ACQUISITIONS

Foreign direct investment can take place either through **greenfield investments**, which involve building new production facilities in a foreign country, or through cross-border mergers and acquisitions which occur when a company in one country buys or merges with a company in another country. In recent years, a growing portion of FDI has taken the form of cross-border mergers and acquisitions, accounting for more than 50 percent of FDI flows in terms of dollar amount.

Canadian firms involved in M&A have made headlines of late. For example:

Inco, a Canadian nickel mining company, is bought by Brazil's CVRD.

Falconbridge of Sudbury, Ontario, is acquired by Swiss-based Xstrata.

Kinder Morgan of Houston bought Vancouver-based utility company Terasen.

Dofasco of Hamilton is purchased by Luxembourg-based Arcelor SA.

Graphics chip maker ATI Technologies of Markham, Ontario, is purchased by Advanced Micro Devices of California.

Fairmont Hotels—which includes the Chateau Frontenac in Ottawa and the Banff Springs Hotel among others—is bought by an investors group led by a Saudi prince.

Intrawest, owner of B.C.'s Whistler resort, is purchased by a New York firm.

Vincor, Canada's largest winemaker, is sold to New York–based Constellation Brands.

Sleeman Breweries of Guelph is acquired by Japan's Sapporo Breweries.

Four Seasons Hotels agrees to a US takeover bid from Cascade Investments and Kingdom Hotels International.

Domtar, the paper-maker based in Montreal, merges with US paper giant Weyerhaeuser.

Norway's Statoil ASA buys Alberta's closely held North American Oil Sands, giving Statoil a foothold in the Canadian oil sands project.

Essar Global of India makes a successful takeover bid for Canada's Algoma Steel.

SSAB of Sweden purchases rolled steel maker IPSCO of Regina.

Dubai Aerospace purchases Standard Aero of Winnipeg.

Cross-border takeovers go the other way, too. Recent major Canadian purchases of foreign firms include:

Manulife took over Boston-based John Hancock Financial.

TD Bank acquired New England's Banknorth.

Thomson Corporation bought Reuters.

Onex of Toronto, together with Goldman Sachs, acquired the aircraft business of Raytheon of the US.

TransCanada Corp. bought ANR Pipeline from the El Paso Corporation of Texas.

Quebec-based drugstore chain Jean Coutu Group acquired 1,549 Eckerd Drugstores from J. C. Penney.

Molson's Brewery merged with US brewer Adolph Coors Co.

Exhibit 15.9 lists major cross-border mergers and acquisitions around the world that were completed in 2012. The rapid increase in cross-border M&A deals can be attributed to the ongoing liberalization of capital markets and the integration of the world economy.

Firms may be motivated to engage in cross-border M&A deals to bolster their competitive positions in the world market by acquiring special assets from other firms or using their own assets on a larger scale. As a mode of FDI entry, cross-border M&As offer two key advantages over greenfield investments: speed and access to proprietary assets. A recent United Nations study aptly discusses why firms choose M&As as a mode of investment.

> Mergers and acquisitions are a popular mode of investment for firms wishing to protect, consolidate and advance their global competitive positions, by selling off divisions that fall outside the scope of their core competence and acquiring strategic assets that enhance their competitiveness. For those firms, "ownership" assets acquired from another firm, such as technical competence, established brand names, and existing supplier networks and distribution systems, can be put to immediate use towards better serving global customers, enhancing profits, expanding market share and increasing corporate competitiveness by employing international production networks more efficiently.[2]

The International Finance in Practice box "DaimlerChrysler: The First Global Car Colossus" provides a real-world example involving the merger deal between Daimler, a German car company, and Chrysler, the third-largest American car maker. As mentioned in the box, the combined company expects to cut costs by as much as $3 billion annually and fill product and geographic gaps. Anticipating the synergistic gains, share prices of both companies rose upon the announcement of a $40.5 billion deal.

---

[2] UNCTAD, *World Investment Report 1996*, p. 7.

EXHIBIT 15.9   Cross-Border M & A (deals with values of over $3 billion completed in 2012)

Rank	Value ($ billion)	Acquired Company	Host Economy[a]	Industry of the Acquired Company	Acquiring Company	Home Economy[a]	Industry of the Acquiring Company	Sares Acquired
1	12.9	International Power PLC	United Kingdom	Electric services	Electrabel SA	Belgium	Electric services	41
2	11.9	Pfizer Nutrition	United States	Dry, condensed, and evaporated dairy products	Nestlé SA	Switzerland	Chocolate and cocoa products	100
3	11.5	Cooper Industries PLC	Ireland	Current-carrying wiring devices	Eaton Corp	United States	Fluid power cylinders and actuators	100
4	8.9	ING Direct USA	United States	Functions related to depository banking	Capital One Financial Corp	United States	National commercial banks	100
5	8.3	Tyco International Ltd	United States	Security systems services	Shareholders	United States	Investors	100
6	6.7	Alliance Boots GmbH	Switzerland	Drug stores and proprietary stores	Walgreen Co	United States	Drug stores and proprietary stores	45
7	6.6	Cequel Communications LLC	United States	Cable and other pay television services	Investor Group	Canada	Investors	100
8	6.1	Viterra Inc	Canada	Crop harvesting, primarily by machine	Glencore International PLC	Switzerland	Metals service centers and offices	100
9	6.0	Actavis Group	Switzerland	Pharmaceutical preparations	Watson Pharmaceuticals Inc	United States	Pharmaceutical preparations	100
10	5.6	Ageas NV	Netherlands	Life insurance	Ageas SA/NV	Belgium	Life insurance	100
11	5.6	BP PLC	United States	Oil and gas field exploration services	Plains Exploration & Production Co	United States	Crude petroleum and natural gas	100
12	5.4	Progress Energy Resources Corp	Canada	Crude petroleum and natural gas	Petronas Carigali Canada Ltd	Canada	Crude petroleum and natural gas	100
13	5.2	De Beers SA	Luxembourg	Miscellaneous nonmetallic minerals, except fuels	Anglo American PLC	United Kingdom	Gold ores	40
14	5.2	OAO "MegaFon"	Russian Federation	Radiotelephone communications	Investor Group	Cyprus	Investors	25
15	5.1	Annington Homes Ltd	United Kingdom	Operators of apartment buildings	Terra Firma Capital Partners Ltd	United Kingdom	Investors	100
16	5.0	NDS Group Ltd	United Kingdom	Prepackaged	Cisco Systems Inc	United States	Computer peripheral equipment	100
17	5.0	Exxon Mobil	Japan	Petroleum and petroleum products wholesalers	TonenGeneral Sekiyu KK	Japan	Petroleum refining	99
18	4.9	Tyco Flow Control	United States	Industrial valves	Pentair Inc	United States	Service industry machines	100
19	4.8	Viviti Technologies Ltd	United States	Computer storage devices	Western Digital Corp	United States	Computer storage devices	100
20	4.8	Petrogal Brasil Ltda	Brazil	Crude petroleum and natural gas	Sinopec International Petroleum Exploration & Production Corp	China	Investors	30
21	4.5	Ariba Inc	United States	Prepackaged	SAP America Inc	United States	Prepackaged	100
22	4.3	Asia Pacific Breweries Ltd	Singapore	Malt beverages	Heineken International BV	Netherlands	Malt beverages	40
23	4.1	Open Grid Europe GmbH	Germany	Natural gas transmission	Investor Group	Canada	Investors	100
24	3.9	Thomas & Betts Corp	United States	Current-carrying wiring devices	ABB Ltd	Switzerland	Switchgear, switchboard equip	100
25	3.9	Denizbank AS	Turkey	Banks	OAO "Sberbank Rossii"	Russian Federation	Banks	100
26	3.8	VimpelCom Ltd	Netherlands	Radiotelephone communications	Altimo Cooperatief UA	Netherlands	Investors	16
27	3.7	Inoxum AG	Germany	Steel works, blast furnaces, and rolling mills	Outokumpu Oyj	Finland	Steel works, blast furnaces, and rolling mills	100

(Continued)

EXHIBIT 15.9 (continued)

Rank	Value ($ billion)	Acquired Company	Host Economy[a]	Industry of the Acquired Company	Acquiring Company	Home Economy[a]	Industry of the Acquiring Company	Shares Acquired
28	3.7	Goodman Global Group Inc	United States	Heating equipment	Daikin Industries Ltd	Japan	Refrigeration and heating equipment	100
29	3.7	Lincare Holdings Inc	United States	Home health care services	Linde AG	Germany	Industrial gases	100
30	3.7	SuccessFactors Inc	United States	Prepackaged	SAP America Inc	United States	Prepackaged	100
31	3.5	Starbev Management Services	Czech Republic	Malt beverages	Molson Coors Brewing Co	United States	Malt beverages	100
32	3.5	Energias de Portugal SA	Portugal	Electric services	China Three Gorges International (Europe) SA	Luxembourg	Investors	21
33	3.5	Korea Exchange Bank	Korea, Republic of	Banks	Hana Financial Group Inc	Korea, Republic of	Banks	51
34	3.5	RBC Bank	United States	National commercial banks	PNC Financial Services Group Inc	United States	National commercial banks	100
35	3.5	Milton Roy Co	United States	Measuring and dispensing pumps	Hamilton Sundstrand Corp SPV	United Kingdom	Investment offices	100
36	3.4	TAM SA	Brazil	Air transportation, scheduled	LAN Airlines SA	Chile	Air transportation, scheduled	100
37	3.4	Koninklijke KPN NV	Netherlands	Telephone communications, except radiotelephone	AMOV Europa BV	Netherlands	Investment offices	23
38	3.3	Quadra FNX Mining Ltd	Canada	Copper ores	KGHM Polska Miedz SA	Poland	Copper ores	100
39	3.3	Roy Hill Holdings Pty Ltd	Australia	Iron ores	Investor Group	Korea, Republic of	Investors	25
40	3.3	OAO "Telekominvest"	Russian Federation	Radiotelephone communications	AF Telecom Holding	Cyprus	Investors	26
41	3.2	Forsakrings AB Skandia	Sweden	Life insurance	Livforsakrings AB Skandia	Sweden	Life insurance	100
42	3.2	JPLSPE Empreendimentos e Participacoes SA	Brazil	Hospital and medical service plans	UnitedHealth Group Inc	United States	Hospital and medical service plans	86
43	3.2	ING Bank of Canada	Canada	Banks	Bank of Nova Scotia	Canada	Security brokers, dealers, and flotation companies	100
44	3.1	Logica PLC	United Kingdom	Prepackaged	CGI Holdings Europe Ltd	United Kingdom	Investors	100
45	3.1	Medicis Pharmaceutical Corp	United States	Pharmaceutical preparations	Valeant Pharmaceuticals International Inc	Canada	Pharmaceutical preparations	100
46	3.0	MGN Gas Networks(UK)Ltd	United Kingdom	Natural gas transmission	Investor Group	Hong Kong, China	Investors	100
47	3.0	Karachaganak Petroleum Operating BV	Kazakhstan	Crude petroleum and natural gas	AO Natsionalnaya Kompaniya "KazMunaiGaz"	Kazakhstan	Crude petroleum and natural gas	10

Source: UNCTAD FDI-TNC-GVC Information System, cross-border M&A database (www.unctad.org/fdistatistics).

[a]The economy where the immediate acquired/immediate acquiring company is located.

Note: As long as the ultimate host economy is different from the ultimate home economy, M&A deals that were undertaken within the same economy are still considered cross-border M&As.

DaimlerChrysler: The First Global Car Colossus

The champagne was on ice at the Dorchester Hotel in London. Earlier in the day on May 6, the board of Chrysler Corp. and the management board of Daimler Benz approved a historic merger, creating a $130 billion automotive colossus known as DaimlerChrysler AG. The chief executives of two of the world's largest auto makers, Chrysler's Robert J. Eaton and Daimler's Jürgen Schrempp, strode across the room and sealed the largest merger in automotive history—and the third-largest deal ever—with a handshake. The mood was electric as the assembled executives prepared to pop the cork on a pact that would send shock waves around the world. "Both men were enormously energized," says a source close to the deal.

And why not? It looks like a marriage made in automotive heaven. In one bold stroke, the pending merger of Daimler and Chrysler dramatically changes the landscape of the global auto industry. By combining forces, Daimler, Germany's biggest industrial concern, and Chrysler, America's No. 3 carmaker, bring a range of hot-selling models and formidable financial muscle under one garage roof. Simply said, DaimlerChrysler is set to transform the way the auto industry operates worldwide.

The megadeal, which was set to be formally announced on May 7, unites two of the world's most profitable auto companies—with combined 1997 net earnings of $4.6 billion. And if ever a merger had the potential for that elusive quality—synergy—this could be the one. Mercedes-Benz passenger cars are synonymous with luxury and sterling engineering. Chrysler is renowned for its low-cost production of trucks, minivans, and sport-utility vehicles. Chrysler is almost wholly domestic, and Mercedes is increasing global sales—albeit within the confines of the luxury-car market. By spreading Chrysler's production expertise to Daimler operations and merging both product-development forces, the new company could cut costs by up to $3 billion annually—including $1.1 billion in purchasing costs, analysts say.

But DaimlerChrysler is about more than cutting costs and filling product and geographic gaps. It's about the emergence of a new category of global carmaker at a critical moment in the industry—when there is plant capacity to build at least 15 million more vehicles each year than will be sold. And overcapacity is expected to balloon to 18.2 million vehicles by 2002

as Asia continues to decline, predicts Standard & Poor's DRI, a division of The McGraw-Hill Companies. Consolidation is inevitable—from about 40 auto companies now, to about 20 in the next century, says DRI analyst Sam Fiorani.

DaimlerChrysler, then, may be the first member of the 21st century 20. "The Mercedes-Chrysler deal sanctions the concept of auto mergers and is a major catalyst for more," says Joseph S. Phillippi, auto analyst for Lehman Brothers Inc. Eaton, in an Apr. 27 interview with *Business Week*, predicted that Western auto makers with the wherewithal would snap up the troubled auto makers of South Korea and Southeast Asia. General Motors Corp., for example, is considering a big stake in Korea's beleaguered Daewoo. In Europe, auto makers such as Volvo, Fiat, PSA (Peugeot/Citröen), and Renault are ripe for takeover.

DaimlerChrysler will have the wherewithal. It will have $130 billion in annual sales and assets totaling $120 billion. It will have factories on four continents.

Indeed, both partners were giants in their own right. So why merge? Top executives at the two companies came to realize that if they continue to go it alone, their companies could survive as strong regional players—but might be forced onto the shoulder in a global industry. "There are world forces at work that are driving consolidation," Eaton said in the April interview. "Two factors are huge: the worldwide excess capacity in autos and the Asian economic crisis."

Eaton and Schrempp hatched their stunning plan in secret meetings over the past nine months in Germany and Detroit. Daimler was represented by Goldman, Sachs & Co. and Deutsche Bank, while CS First Boston represented Chrysler. The estimated $40 billion deal is being financed by a stock swap of two Chrysler shares for every one Daimler share. It will leave Chrysler shareholders with 43% of the combined entity, while Daimler stockholders control 57%, say sources familiar with the deal. That will make DaimlerChrysler a German company for tax and accounting benefits, these sources say.

But the company will have dual headquarters. A source close to Daimler says that Daimler and Chrysler headquarters will remain in Stuttgart and Auburn Hills, Mich., for some time to come. "Can you imagine Daimler leaving Stuttgart? Can you imagine Chrysler leaving Detroit?" It will also have co-CEOs—to start. After

---

Cross-border acquisitions of businesses can be a politically sensitive issue, as most countries prefer local control of domestic firms. As a result, although countries may welcome greenfield investments, as they are viewed as representing new investment and employment opportunities, foreign firms' bids to acquire domestic firms are often resisted and sometimes even resented. Whether or not cross-border acquisitions produce **synergistic gains** and how such gains are divided between acquiring and target firms are, thus, important issues from the perspective of shareholder welfare and public policy. Synergistic gains are obtained when the

three years, however, Eaton is expected to retire, allowing Schrempp to take full control, say sources familiar with the arrangement.

Investors immediately applauded—pushing Chrysler shares up $7^3/_8$ to $48^{13}/_{16}$ on May 6. "Chrysler has the trucks, vans, and SUVs, and Daimler has the luxury cars," says Seth M. Glickenhaus of Glickenhaus & Co., an investment firm that holds 8 million Chrysler shares. "There are enormous synergies in product."

One of the biggest opportunities is for the paired company to plunge into new markets that neither could assay alone. Neither has much of a presence in Latin America or Asia, although Daimler does sell heavy trucks there. Chrysler's inexpensive small cars will give Daimler a vehicle to drive into emerging markets. "With our [upscale] product portfolio, we will never be a mass marketer," says a source close to Daimler. "There are some markets where [Mercedes] will never be able to have an impact."

The first venture of the new merged company likely will be a barebones little car, smaller than Chrysler's subcompact Neon model, to sell in Asia and Latin America. "We would like a sub-Neon vehicle for the international market," says Eaton. "We started looking at projects four years ago, and it's something we're looking at harder now." Ironically, such a car may be powered by engines to be made in Brazil in a joint venture between Chrysler and BMW—Mercedes' archival in Germany. BMW declines to comment on the DaimlerChrysler union.

Indeed, most rivals are too stunned to react. Both Ford and GM declined to comment. On the other hand, many industry watchers immediately questioned whether the enormously divergent cultures of Auburn Hills and Stuttgart won't get in the way of all that synergy. "I can't imagine two more different cultures," says Furman Selz auto analyst Maryann N. Keller.

Chrysler's brushes with bankruptcy forged a culture dedicated to speedy product development, lean operations, and flashy design. Daimler remains a buttoned-down, engineering-driven bureaucracy known for conservatively styled products. "The reaction here is shock, excitement, enthusiasm, and concern," says one Chrysler exec.

Schrempp and Eaton are certainly an odd couple. Eaton, 58, is a Kansas-born engineer who worked his way up the ranks at GM before replacing Lee Iacocca as Chrysler chairman in 1993. His soft-spoken manner belies his reputation as a savvy manager. When he took the job at Chrysler, Motown observers expected that his rival, Robert A. Lutz, would bolt. Yet Eaton and Lutz came together to drive Chrysler to record sales and profits. Lutz, 66, now vice-chairman, is expected to retire soon.

Schrempp, who once trained as an auto mechanic, is also an engineer who climbed the corporate ladder to become CEO in 1995 after 28 years with Daimler. After he won the top post, he forced out his rival for the job, Helmut Werner, who had engineered a turnaround with hot products, like the M-class sport utility vehicles and SLK roadster, and youthful, irreverent marketing.

Can Chrysler and Mercedes live together? It could be tough because they will want to protect their vastly different brands. The Mercedes network "is not the kind of distribution system that Chrysler wants or needs, or even could use," says Keller. Nor is it likely that a Mercedes sedan will one day roll down a Chrysler line. "People buy Mercedes because they think they're made by guys in white coats," says Keller. "That image better not be contaminated by the idea that it's being built by a bunch of guys in Indiana."

So how will Chrysler and Mercedes help each other without losing their identities? Chrysler's slowly improving quality could take a quantum leap forward with help from Daimler engineers. And Daimler's diesel engines, for example, could help Chrysler in its efforts to sell subcompacts and minivans in Europe and elsewhere. Chrysler, for its part, has the industry's best supplier relations, while Daimler still relies on strong-arm techniques to get lower prices from its suppliers. Together, they can save on warehousing and logistics for cars and spare parts in both Europe and the U.S. They also can jointly make internal components like air-conditioning systems and door latches and pool their resources in developing basic technology.

Well before anyone knows if DaimlerChrysler is a success, however, its very existence could reshape the industry. Look for auto makers to scramble for partners to ensure survival as one of the 21st century 20. How that plays out is anybody's guess. "The odd man out here seems to be the Japanese," says Phillippi of Lehman Brothers. "Nissan and Honda in particular have only two legs to stand on: North America and Japan." That won't be enough in this race.

Source: *Business Week*, "DaimlerChrysler: The First Global Car Colossus," by David Bruser. May 18, 1998, pp. 40–43. Used with permission of Bloomberg L. P. Copyright © 2013. All rights reserved.

value of the combined firm is greater than the stand-alone valuations of the individual (acquiring and target) firms.[3] If cross-border acquisitions generate synergistic gains and both the acquiring and target shareholders gain wealth at the same time, one can argue that cross-border acquisitions are mutually beneficial and thus should not be thwarted.

---

[3]Synergistic gains may arise if the combined companies can save on the costs of production, marketing, distribution and R&D and redeploy the combined assets to the highest-value projects.

Synergistic gains may or may not arise from cross-border acquisitions, depending on the motives of the acquiring firms. In general, gains result when the acquirer is motivated to take advantage of the market imperfections mentioned earlier. In other words, firms may decide to acquire foreign firms to take advantage of mispriced factors of production and to cope with trade barriers.

As previously mentioned, imperfections in the market for *intangible assets* can also play a major role in motivating firms to undertake cross-border acquisitions. According to the internalization theory, a firm with intangible assets that have a public good property, such as technical and managerial know-how, may acquire foreign firms as a platform for using its special assets on a larger scale and, at the same time, avoid the misappropriation that may occur while transacting in foreign markets through a market mechanism. Cross-border acquisitions may also be motivated by the acquirer's desire to acquire and internalize the target firm's intangible assets. In this *backward-internalization* case, the acquirer seeks to create wealth by appropriating the rent generated from the economy of scale obtained from using the target's intangible assets on a global basis. The internalization, thus, may proceed *forward* to internalize the acquirer's assets, or *backward* to internalize the target's assets.

Morck and Yeung (1992) investigate the effect of international acquisitions on the share prices. They show that acquiring firms with information-based intangible assets experience a significantly positive share price reaction upon foreign acquisition. This is consistent with the findings of their earlier work (1991) that the market value of the firm is positively related to its multinationality because of the firm's intangible assets, such as R&D capabilities, with public good nature. It is not the multinationality *per se* that contributes to the firm's value. Their empirical findings support the (forward-) internalization theory of FDI.

Eun, Kolodny and Scheraga (1996), on the other hand, directly measure the magnitude of shareholders' gains from cross-border acquisitions using a sample of major foreign acquisitions of US firms that took place during the period 1979–1990. Their findings are summarized in Exhibit 15.10. First, the exhibit shows that target shareholders realized significant wealth gains, $103 million on average, regardless of the nationality of the acquirers. Second, the wealth gains to foreign acquiring shareholders, however, varied greatly across the acquiring countries. Shareholders of British acquirers of US firms experienced significant wealth reduction, −$123 million on average, whereas Japanese shareholders experienced major wealth increases, $228 million on average. Canadian acquisitions of US firms produced modest wealth increases for their shareholders, $15 million, on average.

Third, cross-border acquisitions are generally found to be synergy-generating corporate activities. Shareholders of the "paired" sample of US targets and foreign acquirers experienced positive combined wealth gains, $68 million, on average. Synergistic gains,

| EXHIBIT 15.10 | Average Wealth Gains from Cross-Border Acquisitions: Foreign Acquisitions of American Firms |

Country of Acquirer	Number of Cases	R&D/Sales (%)		Average Wealth Gains (in million US$)		
		Acquirer	Target	Acquirer	Target	Combined
Canada	10	0.21	0.65	14.93	85.59	100.53
Japan	15	5.08	4.81	227.83	170.66	398.49
UK	46	1.11	2.18	−122.91	94.55	−28.36
Other	32	1.63	2.80	−47.46	89.48	42.02
All	103	1.66	2.54	−35.01	103.19	68.18

Source: Reprinted from *Journal of Banking and Finance* 20, C. Eun, R. Kolodny, and C. Scheraga, "Cross-Border Acquisitions and Shareholder Wealth: Tests of the Synergy and Internalization Hypotheses," pp. 1559–1582, ©1996 with kind permission from Elsevier Science-NL, Sara Burgerhartstreet 25, 1055 KV Amsterdam, The Netherlands.

Reebok Laces Up CCM Deal
Venerable brand now U.S. owned Hockey's growth appeals to buyer

The American shoe company named for an African gazelle is now in the hockey business. Reebok International Ltd. announced plans yesterday to acquire Montreal-based hockey equipment manufacturer Hockey Company Holdings Inc. in a deal valued at $436 million. The transaction marks the sale of the last of Canada's leading hockey equipment brands to a big U.S. sporting goods maker and lengthens Reebok's reach into the continent's major sports leagues.

Hockey Co., which makes apparel and equipment under the CCM, Jofa and Koho brands, had sales of $239.9 million last year for a profit of $18.6 million. The deal will give Massachusetts-based Reebok, the second largest U.S. athletic-shoe maker, the long-term rights to supply game jerseys to the NHL's 30 teams, as well as the Canadian Hockey League and American Hockey League. Hockey Co. also makes replica jerseys for sale to the public.

Hockey Co.'s leading investors have agreed to Reebok's cash offer of $21.25 a share. The offer is for $204 million (U.S) plus $125 million assumed debt.

Reebok spokesperson John Frascotti cited hockey's increasing popularity as a reason to get into business.

"At the youth level, college level and professional level, the sport is really an appealing sport because it is captivating to both play and watch," he said. Last year Hockey Co. claimed, in a prospectus filed with Canadian securities officials, that hockey was the second-fastest growing sport in the United States, with 2.2 million participants in 2001.

Analyst Phil Yockey sees the trend, too. "Hockey is bigger than it's ever been," said Yockey, president of When2Trade of St. Louis. "Globally, soccer and hockey are where the growth is. I don't think they're going to expand any more baseball teams or football teams."

Yockey said the deal could bump Reebok's stock 10 per cent over the next year.

But that growth might depend, in part, on the outcome of the NHL's current labour negotiations, which some believe could lead to a players strike or lock-out in the 2004–05 season.

With the announcement yesterday, Reebok appears to be breaking away from Nike, which made its foray into the hockey business 10 years ago when it bought Canstar Sports Inc., maker of Bauer and Cooper skates, for $546 million. The Bauer name dates back to 1930. In June, 2003, when Hockey Co. went public, the company claimed to have a 30 per cent share of the worldwide market for hockey equipment and apparel in 2001, with its closest competitor, Bauer Nike Hockey Inc., at 19 per cent. Hockey Co. also claims that as of late 2002, 99 per cent of NHL players used at least one piece of its gear.

Hockey Co. maintains three manufacturing facilities in the Montreal area, one in Sweden, one in Finland and a U.S. sales and distribution office, and employs 1,300 worldwide, about 1,000 of whom work in Canada. Though he praised Hockey Co.'s management, Frascotti said he did not know if the takeover will affect its operations. "We think they have done a wonderful job in the last four, five years," he said. "We haven't gone down the path of looking for operations synergies in terms of figuring out at this stage how these organizations will dovetail. . . . We have a lot of confidence in the management team at the Hockey Company."

When Nike acquired Canstar, it promised little would change at [the] Montreal-based company, but workforces at Canadian plants have seen cuts. More than 130 employees lost their jobs in January when regular production ceased at the Cambridge hockey stick plant. Ten to 14 employees remain but the plant is expected to fully close at the end of this month. The Mississauga goalie equipment plant and its 33 employees will stop production some time in the fall. And the St. Jerome, Que., plant is expected to lose 118 of its current 220 workers in July.

But Hockey Co. president and CEO Matt O'Toole said he does not expect the proposed takeover by Reebok to result in cuts. "I think one of the exciting things about the acquisition is it's really not based on cost reduction . . . but much more (on) growth opportunities to bring the Reebok brand name into hockey," he said. "It's business as usual for us here."

CCM, the Canadian Cycle and Motor Co., opened its doors in Weston in September 1899. But shortly after, as the bicycle market in Canada declined, CCM started making skates. The CCM Tackaberry (Tacks) hockey skate has been a favourite of hockey players since 1937.

Source: *Toronto Star,* "Reebok Laces Up CCM Deal," by Bill Vlasic. Saturday, April 9, 2004. Reprinted with permission of Torstar Syndication Services.

however, vary a great deal across acquiring countries. Japanese acquisitions generated large combined gains, $398 million, on average, which were shared by target shareholders (43 percent) and acquiring shareholders (57 percent).[4] In contrast, British acquisitions

---

[4]This result is quite different from the findings of studies of domestic acquisitions showing that target shareholders capture the lion's share of synergistic gains.

produced a somewhat negative combined wealth gain, $-\$28$ million, on average, and caused a wealth transfer from acquiring to target shareholders.

Eun et al. argue that the significant gains for Japanese acquirers can be attributed to the successful internalization of the R&D capabilities of their targets which have a much higher R&D intensity, on average, than the targets of acquirers from other countries. Thus, the desire to "backward" internalize the target's intangible assets appears to be an important driving force for Japanese acquisition programs in the United States. This supports the backward-internalization hypothesis.[5] In the case of British acquisitions, the average combined wealth gain was negative, and the acquiring shareholders lost substantial wealth. Thus, it appears that the managers of British firms often undertook negative net present value (NPV) projects when they acquired US firms. It is well known that corporate acquisitions can be driven by managers who pursue growth and diversification at the expense of shareholders' interests. As Jensen (1986) points out, managers may benefit by expanding the firm beyond the size that maximizes shareholder wealth for various reasons.[6]

15.4 POLITICAL RISK AND FDI

In assessing investment opportunities in a foreign country, it is important for a parent firm to consider the risk arising from the fact that investments are located in a foreign country. A sovereign country can take various actions that may adversely affect the interests of MNCs. In this section, we discuss how to measure and manage **political risk**, which refers to the potential losses to the parent firm resulting from adverse political developments in the host country. Political risks range from the outright expropriation of foreign assets to unexpected changes in the tax laws that hurt the profitability of foreign projects.

Political risk that firms face can differ in terms of the incidence as well as the manner in which political events affect them. Depending on the incidence, political risk can be classified into two types:

1. *Macro-risk,* where all foreign operations are affected by adverse political developments in the host country
2. *Micro-risk,* where only selected areas of foreign business operations or particular foreign firms are affected

The collapse of Zimbabwe is an example of macro-risk, whereas the predicament of Enron in India, which we will discuss shortly, is an example of micro-risk.

Depending on the manner in which firms are affected, political risk can be classified into three types:

1. *Transfer risk,* which arises from uncertainty about cross-border flows of capital, payments, know-how, and the like
2. *Operational risk,* which is associated with uncertainty about the host country's policies affecting the local operations of MNCs
3. *Control risk,* which arises from uncertainty about the host country's policy regarding ownership and control of local operations

Examples of transfer risk include the unexpected imposition of capital controls, inbound or outbound, and withholding taxes on dividend and interest payments. Examples of operational risk, on the other hand, include unexpected changes in environmental policies, sourcing/local content requirements, minimum wage law and restriction on access to local

---

[5]Japanese acquirers themselves are highly R&D-intensive. This suggests that Japanese acquisitions of American firms may generate technological synergies and that Japanese firms may be capable of using American target firms' technical know-how.

[6]For example, managers' payments are often positively related to the size of the assets they control, not just profits.

credit facilities. Lastly, examples of control risk include restrictions imposed on the maximum ownership share by foreigners, mandatory transfer of ownership to local firms over a certain period of time (fadeout requirements), and the nationalization of local operations of MNCs.

History is replete with examples of political risk. As Mao Ze-dong took power in China in 1949, his communist government nationalized foreign assets with little compensation. The same happened again when Castro took over Cuba in 1960. Even in a country controlled by a noncommunist government, strong nationalist sentiments can lead to the expropriation of foreign assets. For example, when Gamal Nasser seized power in Egypt in the early 1950s, he nationalized the Suez Canal, which had been controlled by British and French interests. Politically, this move was immensely popular throughout the Arab world. The International Finance in Practice box "Stories Past and Present" provides other historical examples of foreign investments decimated by nationalistic actions of host countries.

As Exhibit 15.11 shows, the frequency of expropriations of foreign-owned assets peaked in the 1970s when as many as 30 countries were involved in expropriations every year. Since then, however, expropriations have dwindled to practically nothing.

This, however, does not mean that political risk is a thing of the past. In 1992, the Enron Development Corporation, a subsidiary of the Houston-based energy company, signed a contract to build the largest-ever power plant in India, requiring a total investment of $2.8 billion. Severe power shortages have been one of the bottlenecks hindering India's economic growth. After Enron had spent nearly $300 million, the project was cancelled by Hindu nationalist politicians in the state of Maharashtra where the plant was to be built. Subsequently, Maharashtra invited Enron to renegotiate its contract. If Enron had agreed to

EXHIBIT 15.11

Frequency of Expropriations of Foreign-Owned Assets

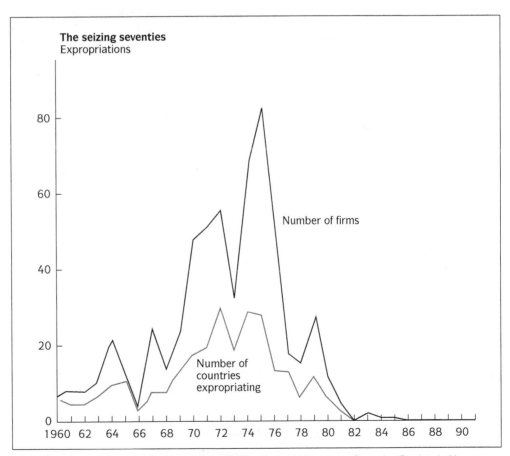

Source: *The Economist,* March 27, 1993, p. 19. ©1993 The Economist Newspaper Group, Inc. Reprinted with permission.

Stories Past and Present

An old story: Brazilian Tramways

The first electric trams in Brazil were built in 1891 by Thomson-Houston Company of Lynn, Massachusetts, which the following year became the General Electric Company. GE went on to build most of the early electric lines in Brazil and throughout Latin America, often retaining ownership. Other players soon entered the field, and, by 1907, a Canadian group had created South America's first great tramway empire, holding most of the lines in Rio de Janeiro and São Paulo as well as an assortment of telephone, gas, and water companies. The Canadians were bitterly and publicly opposed by a powerful Brazilian family, the Guinles, who also sought control of utilities in the major cities. The dispute profoundly affected the attitudes of Brazilians toward foreign-owned tramways. As a result of street riots and large-scale destruction of equipment in the city of Salvador, the Canadians curtailed their expansion efforts and in 1912 consolidated their assets into Brazilian Traction, Light & Power.

American & Foreign Power, the GE affiliate, eventually joined the fray and acquired 333 utilities in Brazil alone, with tramway systems in 13 Brazilian cities. By 1933, however, rising anti-Yankee sentiment led to freezing of tram fares at their 1909 level. A number of small companies shut down. Others switched to closed cars to increase fare collections. These cars were distinctly unpopular with riders because of the heat (and perhaps because of the better fare collection).

Still, on the eve of World War II, North American companies operated roughly two-thirds of Brazil's tramway systems. The lethal combination of parts shortages, increased hydroelectric power costs, and the effect of inflation on fixed fares led companies to cut back on service and, in some cases, to leave the business. In 1947, Brazilian Traction sold its São Paulo system to the municipal transport board, which then

proceeded to raise fares by 250%. Rioting citizens pleaded for the foreigners and low rates. But, by 1950, a new president had vowed to rid Brazil of foreign corporations. AFP and most other foreign investors were quite willing by this point to sell their unprofitable tram systems to the Brazilians. By 1960, only Brazilian Traction's Rio system remained foreign owned; this last holdout went the way of the rest when it was acquired by the state in January 1965.

A recent story: Bangkok Toll Road

To help relieve Bangkok's horrible traffic congestion, a Japanese-led consortium was granted a 30-year concession to build a 12-mile toll road in the city. Just as part of the road was about to be opened in 1993, the Thai Expressway and Rapid Transit Authority (ETA) balked at the 30-baht toll that had been specified in the contract. Hesitating to absorb the proposed 10-baht toll reduction, the private consortium delayed opening the completed sections of road, and it halted further construction when its lenders suspended credit. Claiming to fear riots on the part of frustrated motorists who were angered at being unable to use the expressway, the ETA obtained a court order to force the road open and insisted on reopening negotiations to settle this and a number of other outstanding issues. Kumagai Gumi, the lead investor, reportedly with more than $100 million exposure, and its bankers, with still more at stake, cried foul, publicly accusing the Thai government of nationalizing the project. Eventually, Kumagai sold its 65% interest. And all this occurred in a country that is viewed as being very hospitable to foreign direct investment.

Source: Reprinted by permission of *Harvard Business Review.* From "Is Foreign Infrastructure Still Risky?" by Louis T. Wells and Eric S. Gleason, Sept./Oct. 1995. © 1995 by the President and Fellows of Harvard College; all rights reserved.

renegotiate, it might have had to accept a lower profitability for the project. The lack of an effective means of enforcing contracts in a foreign country is a major source of political risk associated with FDI.

Political risk is not easy to measure. Difficult as it may be, MNCs still have to measure political risk for foreign projects under consideration. Experts in political risk analysis evaluate, often subjectively, a set of key factors such as:

- *The host country's political and government system.* Whether the host country has political and administrative infrastructure that allows for effective and streamlined policy decisions has important implications for political risk. If a country has too many political parties and frequent changes in government (Italy, for example), government policies may be inconsistent and discontinuous, creating political risk.

- *Track records of political parties and their relative strength.* Examination of the ideological orientations and historical track records of political parties reveals a great deal about how they run the economy. If a party has a strong nationalistic ideology and/or socialist beliefs, it may implement policies detrimental to foreign interests. On the other hand, a party that subscribes to a liberal and market-oriented ideology is less likely to take actions to damage the interests of foreign concerns. If the former party is more popular than the latter party and, thus, more likely to win the next general election, MNCs will face more political risk.

- *Integration into the world system.* If a country is politically and economically isolated and segmented from the rest of the world, it would be less willing to observe the rules of the game. North Korea, Iraq, Libya and Cuba are examples. If a country is a member of a major international organization, such as the EU, OECD and WTO, it is more likely to abide by the rules of the game, reducing political risk. In the same vein, since China joined the World Trade Organization (WTO), MNCs operating in China generally face less political risk.

- *The host country's ethnic and religious stability.* As can be seen from recent civil war in Bosnia, domestic peace can be shattered by ethnic and religious conflicts, causing political risk for foreign business. Additional examples are Nigeria, Rwanda, Northern Ireland, Turkey, Israel and Sri Lanka.

- *Regional security.* Real and potential aggression from a neighbouring country is obviously a major source of political risk. Kuwait is a recent example. Such countries as South Korea and Taiwan may potentially face the same risk, depending on the future course of political developments in East Asia. Israel and its Arab neighbours still face this risk as well.

- *Key economic indicators.* Often, political events are triggered by economic situations. Political risk is not entirely independent of economic risk. For example, persistent trade deficits may induce a host country's government to delay or stop interest payments to foreign lenders, erect trade barriers or suspend the convertibility of the local currency, causing major difficulties for MNCs. Severe inequality in income distribution (e.g. in many Latin American countries) and deteriorating living standards (as in Russia after the collapse of the Soviet Union) can cause major political disturbances. Argentina's protracted economic recession and the eventual collapse of the peso–dollar parity led to the freezing of bank deposits, street riots, and three changes of the country's presidency in as many months in 2002.

MNCs may use in-house experts to do the analysis. But often, MNCs use outside experts for professional assessments of political risks in different countries. For example, Morgan Stanley offers in-depth analysis of country/political risks using a variety of data sources, including government and private sector publications, statistics provided by international organizations, newspaper articles and on-site due diligence in countries with government officials and the private sector. Exhibits 15.12 and 15.13 provide such an analysis for two countries, Vietnam and Turkey, both of which became full-fledged democracies in the last decade.

As Exhibit 15.14 shows, *Euromoney* provides country ratings by political risk, credit rating, economic performance and other factors. It also provides the overall country risk ranking based on an opinion poll of economists and political analysts, plus market data and debt figures. **Country risk** is a broader measure of risk than political risk, as the former encompasses political risk, credit risk, and other economic performances. As of 2013, such countries as Switzerland, Norway, Luxembourg and Denmark were considered practically free of political risk. In contrast, such countries as Israel, China, India, Mexico and Brazil were rated as having substantial political risk, while such countries as Argentina, Indonesia, Russia and Bosnia-Herzegovina were rated as among the most politically risky countries. Exhibit 15.14 shows that the ranking of countries by political risk closely coincides with that by overall country risk.

www.euromoney.com/
index.html

Provides data and articles
from *Euromoney*.

EXHIBIT 15.12 Political Risk Analysis: Turkey

Sovereign Rating: Moody's: Ba2; S&P: BB, Outlook: Positive

Political Strengths
- Transition to democracy at the end of 1970s
- Significant liberalization and stabilization by a drive to join European Union

Political Weaknesses
- Instability fuelled by conflict between the army and the civilian government
- Strained relations between religious conservatives and secular modernists

Political & Governance Indicators
- World Bank Ranking—Ease of doing business — 73rd/183
- Freedom House—Political rights and civil liberties — Partly Free
- Transparency International Ranking—Corruption Perception Index — 61st/180
- OECD country risk rating (Scale: 0–7, 0 is least risk, 7 is highest risk) — 4

Economic Strengths
- Key dimensions of economic performance on a par with central and eastern European countries
- Was able to weather the recent global economic crisis
- Debt is highly sought after by foreign investors
- Healthy growth forecast

Economic Weaknesses
- Mounting macroeconomic imbalances and major reliance on foreign financing
- Widening current account deficit, surging credit growth, and building inflation pressures
- High business cycle and currency risk
- Lira a volatile emerging market currency

Economic Indicators
- GDP (US$ bn) — 615
- GDP per capita (US$) — 8,723
- Real GDP growth (15-year average, %) — 3.9
- Fiscal balance (% of GDP) — −5.8
- Public debt (% of GDP) — 45.5
- Foreign direct investment (inflow, US$ bn) — 7.4
- Current account (% of GDP) — −2.3
- External debt (% of GDP) — 44.8
- Foreign reserves (US$ bn) — 108.9

Source: http://www.efic.gov.au; 2009 figures.

At the end of the 1970s, Turkey was under martial law and handicapped by protectionism, triple-digit inflation, and financial crisis. It has since undertaken significant democratization, liberalization, and stabilization by a drive to join the European Union. Trade liberalization introduced by the late president Turgut Ozal in the 1980s helped to open the economy up. On key dimensions of economic performance such as per capita income, business climate, creditworthiness and growth, Turkey is about on a par with other Central and Eastern European countries. The Turkish economy only really began to demonstrate its full potential in the wake of a 2002 IMF-led stabilization program, which helped put in place policies that: sharply reduced inflation from 70 percent per annum to single digits, restored fiscal solvency and unleashed GDP growth of almost 7 percent per annum over 2002–2007. Turkey was able to weather the global financial and economic crises reasonably well, and its economy is forecast to grow by 6½ percent in 2010. Its debt is highly sought after by foreign investors. And despite the lack of an investment-grade sovereign rating (S&P: BB, Fitch: BB+ and Moody's: Ba2), the country's sovereign bond spreads are roughly in line with those of investment-grade emerging markets such as Russia and Brazil (BBB−).

But, for all this progress, significant vulnerabilities remain. Mounting macroeconomic imbalances and a reliance on foreign financing are key economic challenges. The main near-term economic challenges are a widening current account deficit, surging credit growth and building inflation pressures. Turkey also faces a sizable external financing requirement in 2010 on the order of 14 percent of GDP, which makes it vulnerable to domestic and international setbacks. In the political sphere, instability is fuelled by conflict between the army and the civilian government and between religious conservatives and secular modernists. Exporters and investors in Turkey face high business cycle and currency risk; Turkish GDP growth has recently experienced a large bust and rebound and the lira is a volatile emerging market currency.

Let us now turn to the issue of how to manage political risk. First, MNCs can take a conservative approach to foreign investment projects when faced with political risk. When a foreign project is exposed to political risk, the MNC can explicitly incorporate political risk into the capital budgeting process and adjust the project's NPV accordingly. The firm may do so either by reducing expected cash flows or by increasing the cost of capital. The MNC may undertake the foreign project only when the adjusted NPV is positive. It is important here to recognize that political risk may be diversifiable to some extent. Suppose

---

Canada's National Policy Framework concerning FDI

Since 1985, the basic legal framework for foreign investment in Canada is provided by the *Investment Canada Act* which replaced the more restrictive *Foreign Investment Review Act*. As of October 2001, the main features of the national FDI regime include the following:

Admission and establishment: Canada has a formal investment review process. Any investment by a non-Canadian to establish a new enterprise, regardless of size, or to acquire direct control of any existing business with assets of at least $200 million or in an activity that is identified as being "culturally sensitive" must be reported to Investment Canada. Notification is also required when a foreign company plans to acquire indirect control of any existing Canadian business with assets over $50 million. Investment in some activities is covered by special legislation. For example, the banking industry is governed by the *Bank Act*. Amendments to the *Bank Act* in 1992, 1997, and 1999 have facilitated foreign bank operations, and since 1999, foreign banks are permitted to open branches in Canada. The *Broadcast Act* covers foreign investment in radio, television, and broadcasting.

Ownership and control: There are no general ownership and control limitations but some foreign ownership restrictions exist in specific sectors, such as commercial aviation (25 percent foreign ownership), energy and mining (foreign investors cannot be majority owners of uranium mines), telecommunications and fishing (49 percent). There are no overall limitations on foreign ownership with regard to privatization.

Incentives: Canada offers a wide array of incentives at the federal and provincial levels. Municipal governments, however, are prohibited from offering tax incentives. The incentives are designed mainly to encourage research and development and promote regional economies. They are available to any qualifying investor, whether Canadian or foreign. Generally, incentives are not oriented toward the promotion of exports. Incentives may take the form of grants, loans, loan guarantees, venture capital or tax credits.

---

that an MNC has assets in, say, 30 different countries. Since the political risks in different countries may not be positively correlated, the political risk associated with a single country may be diversifiable to some extent. To the extent that political risk is diversifiable, a major adjustment to the NPV may not be necessary. This consideration also suggests that MNCs can use geographic diversification of foreign investments as a means of reducing political risk. Put simply, do not put all your eggs in one basket.

Second, once an MNC decides to undertake a foreign project, it has various options to minimize exposure to political risk. For example, an MNC can form a joint venture with a local company. If the project is partially owned by a local company, the foreign government may be less inclined to expropriate it since that would hurt the local company as well as the MNC. The MNC may also consider forming a consortium of international companies to undertake the foreign project. In this case, the MNC can reduce its exposure to political risk and, at the same time, make expropriation more costly to the host government. Understandably, the host government may not wish to take action that antagonizes many countries at the same time. Alternatively, MNCs can use local debt to finance the foreign project. In this case, the MNC has an option to repudiate its debt if the host government takes action to hurt its interests.

Third, MNCs may purchase insurance against the hazard of political risk. Such insurance policies, which are available in many advanced countries, are especially useful to small firms that are less well equipped to deal with political risk on their own. In Canada, **Export Development Canada (EDC)**, a federally owned organization, offers insurance against (1) the inconvertibility of foreign currencies, (2) expropriation of Canadian-owned assets overseas, (3) destruction of Canadian-owned physical properties due to war, revolution

EXHIBIT 15.13	Political Risk Analysis: Vietnam

Sovereign Rating: Moody's: Ba3; S&P: BB, Outlook: Negative

Political Strengths	**Economic Strengths**

Political Strengths
- Political stability with Communist Party in government since end of the country's civil war in 1975
- The party's communist ideology has become less important over time

Economic Strengths
- Transformation to market-oriented economy since late 1980s
- High GDP growth facilitated by foreign investment
- Well-educated and cheap labour force
- Sizable natural resources and advantageous location

Political Weaknesses
- Inconsistent and evolving regulations
- Unreliable legal system and corruption
- Risk of economic slowdown if more conservative leadership emerges in 2011 national congress

Economic Weaknesses
- Large fiscal and trade deficits and weak banking system
- Plethora of state-owned enterprises and less diversification
- Industry and credit policies favour state-owned enterprises

Political & Governance Indicators
- World Bank Ranking—Ease of doing business — 93rd/183
- Freedom House—Political rights and civil liberties — Not Free
- Transparency International Ranking—Corruption Perception Index — 120th/180
- OECD country risk rating (Scale: 0–7, 0 is least risk, 7 is highest risk) — 5

Economic Indicators
- GDP (US$ bn) — 92
- GDP per capita (US$) — 1,060
- Real GDP growth (15-year average, %) — 7.3
- Fiscal balance (% of GDP) — −9.7
- Public debt (% of GDP) — 55.0
- Foreign direct investment (inflow, US$ bn) — 6.5
- Current account (% of GDP) — −7.8
- External debt (% of GDP) — 36.0
- Foreign reserves (US$ bn) — 14.7

Source: http://www.efic.gov.au ; 2009 figures.

The collapse of the Soviet Union in the late 1980s forced Vietnam to transform from central planning and autarky to market orientation and international reintegration. Overall, this has been very successful. GDP growth has averaged nearly 8 percent a year, with foreign investment a key driver. Per capita income has risen from US$100 in 1990 to over US$1,000 in 2008. Vietnam has a number of attractions for investors and exporters: a large, young and rapidly growing population; a labour force that is relatively well educated and cheap; sizable natural resources; an advantageous location; and a high level of political and social stability. Vigorous policy stimulus and spending helped Vietnam avoid the worst of the global financial crisis. But the authorities are now facing a fiscal deficit topping 10 percent of GDP, accelerating inflation and a weakening banking system. In addition, a large trade deficit is putting strain upon the value of the dong—pegged to the US dollar—and has forced the central bank to run down reserves and devalue by 8 percent. Standard & Poor's views the country's external foreign currency debt as speculative grade with a BB rating and a negative outlook, and Moody's rating for the same is Ba3. Public debt is equivalent to 55 percent of GDP and contingent liabilities—in the banking sector and state-owned enterprises—are large.

The Vietnamese Communist Party (CPV) has been in government since the end of the country's civil war in 1975. The party has a firm grip on power, which ensures a high degree of political stability. Although the party's communist ideology has become less important over time, it led to a plethora of state-owned enterprises, which span most sectors and account for nearly 40 percent of GDP. Foreign investors face a number of challenges, including: inconsistent and evolving regulations, an unreliable legal system, a weak banking system, corruption and industry and credit policies that favour state-owned enterprises.

and other violent political events in foreign countries and (4) loss of business income due to political violence. EDC's primary goal in respect of FDI is to support Canadian private investment in developing countries. Alternatively, MNCs may also purchase tailor-made insurance policies from private insurers, such as Lloyd's of London.

When the political risk faced by an MNC can be fully covered by an insurance contract, the MNC can subtract the insurance premium from the expected cash flows from the project in computing its NVP. The MNC then can use the usual cost of capital, which would be used to evaluate domestic investment projects, in discounting the expected cash flows from foreign projects. Lastly, it is pointed out that many countries have concluded bilateral or

EXHIBIT 15.14   Country Risk Rankings

Rank	Country	Country Risk 100.00	Political Risk 30.00	Economic Performance 30.00	Credit Rating 7.50
1	Norway	94.05	28.01	26.25	7.50
2	Luxembourg	92.35	27.82	24.83	7.50
3	Switzerland	90.65	28.24	22.41	7.50
4	Denmark	88.55	27.55	21.75	7.50
5	Finland	87.81	27.82	20.29	7.50
6	Sweden	86.81	27.91	19.19	7.50
7	Austria	86.50	27.02	19.77	7.50
8	Canada	86.09	28.00	19.41	7.50
9	Netherlands	84.86	27.36	17.81	7.50
10	Australia	84.16	26.74	17.72	7.34
11	Germany	83.84	27.70	16.44	7.50
12	France	83.46	26.42	17.34	7.50
13	United States	82.29	26.84	16.76	7.50
14	Belgium	81.63	26.18	16.22	7.03
15	United Kingdom	81.48	26.05	15.73	7.50
16	Hong Kong	81.32	25.72	17.96	6.72
17	Singapore	80.58	26.18	16.22	7.50
18	New Zealand	80.56	27.32	14.07	7.19
19	Japan	77.83	26.26	15.09	6.56
20	Slovenia	77.17	24.77	16.58	6.56
21	Ireland	77.07	24.38	14.38	6.56
22	Qatar	76.77	22.92	19.41	6.33
23	Malta	76.65	24.76	15.94	5.47
24	Italy	76.57	23.27	15.00	6.09
25	Spain	76.48	24.65	12.12	7.34
32	Taiwan	71.17	24.06	12.98	5.94
35	Korea South	69.01	23.17	13.43	5.31
36	Saudi Arabia	68.09	20.82	13.89	5.94
40	Israel	65.70	20.64	13.60	5.31
43	China	64.75	20.85	15.04	5.63
44	Poland	64.17	23.64	12.93	4.84
50	Mexico	58.34	20.26	11.42	3.91

(Continued)

EXHIBIT 15.14   (continued)

Rank	Country	Country Risk 100.00	Political Risk 30.00	Economic Performance 30.00	Credit Rating 7.50
51	Brazil	58.18	20.27	13.01	3.28
52	India	58.12	19.25	11.62	3.28
53	South Africa	56.89	19.70	10.83	4.38
54	Russia	55.06	18.37	12.08	3.91
59	Turkey	53.33	19.12	10.64	2.34
62	Thailand	52.49	16.45	11.71	4.06
64	Malaysia	52.04	19.97	12.83	4.69
69	Egypt	50.31	15.40	10.87	2.81
70	Indonesia	49.74	16.41	12.66	2.34
74	Kazakhstan	47.90	16.38	10.15	3.44
79	Vietnam	46.52	17.52	7.09	2.03
91	Argentina	41.10	14.24	10.44	0.31
98	Ukraine	39.31	13.49	9.07	0.47
104	Venezuela	37.40	11.38	9.75	1.41
115	Pakistan	34.58	10.45	7.57	0.47
134	Nigeria	31.61	12.67	8.14	1.64
137	Iran	30.87	11.75	11.17	0.00
186	Zimbabwe	6.00	5.03	0.98	0.00

Source: *Euromoney*, March 2010.

multilateral investment protection agreements, effectively eliminating most political risk. As a result, if an MNC invests in a country that signed an investment protection agreement with the MNC's home country, it need not be overly concerned with political risk.

One particular type of political risk that MNCs and investors may face is corruption associated with the abuse of public offices for private benefits. Investors often encounter demands for bribes from politicians and government officials for contracts and smooth bureaucratic processes. If companies refuse to make *grease payments*, they may lose business opportunities or face difficult bureaucratic red tape. If companies pay, on the other hand, they risk violating laws or being embarrassed when the payments are discovered and reported in the media. Corruption can be found anywhere in the world. But it is a much more serious problem in developing and transition economies where the state sector is large, democratic institutions are weak and the press is often muzzled. In 1997, the OECD adopted a treaty to criminalize the bribery of foreign officials by companies. Bribery thus is both morally and legally wrong for companies from most of the developed countries. Another particular risk that companies may face is extortion demands from Mafia-style criminal organizations. For example, the majority of companies in Russia are known to have paid extortion demands. To deal with this kind of situation, it is important for companies to hire people who are familiar with local operating environments, strengthen local support for the company and enhance physical security measures.

SUMMARY

This chapter discusses various issues associated with foreign direct investments (FDI) by MNCs, which play a key role in shaping the nature of the emerging global economy.

1. Firms become *multinational* when they undertake FDI. FDI may involve either the establishment of new production facilities in foreign countries or acquisitions of existing foreign businesses.

2. During the recent five-year period, total annual worldwide FDI flows amounted to about $764 billion on average. The United States is the largest recipient, as well as initiator, of FDI. Besides the United States, the United Kingdom, France, Germany and Japan are the leading sources of FDI outflows, whereas China, the United Kingdom, Germany, France, the Netherlands, Canada, Spain and Mexico are the major destinations for FDI in recent years.

3. Most existing theories of FDI put emphasis on various market imperfections, that is, imperfections in product, factor and capital markets, as the key motivating forces driving FDI.

4. The *internalization* theory of FDI holds that firms that have intangible assets with a public good property tend to invest directly in foreign countries in order to use these assets on a larger scale and, at the same time, avoid the misappropriations that may occur while transacting in foreign markets through a market mechanism.

5. According to the product life-cycle theory, when firms first introduce new products, they choose to produce at home, close to their customers. Once the product becomes standardized and mature, it becomes important to cut production costs to stay competitive. At this stage, firms may set up production facilities in low-cost foreign countries.

6. In recent years, a growing portion of FDI has taken the form of cross-border acquisitions of existing businesses. *Synergistic* gains may arise if the acquirer is motivated to take advantage of various market imperfections.

7. Imperfections in the market for intangible assets, such as R&D capabilities, may play a key role in motivating cross-border acquisitions. The internalization may proceed *forward* to internalize the acquirer's intangible assets or *backward* to internalize the target's intangible assets.

8. In evaluating political risk, experts focus their attention on a set of key factors, such as the host country's political/government system, historical records of political parties and their relative strengths, integration of the host country into the world political/economic system, the host country's ethnic and religious stability, regional security and key economic indicators.

9. In evaluating a foreign investment project, it is important for the MNC to consider the effect of political risk, as a sovereign country can change the *rules of the game*. The MNC may adjust the cost of capital upward or lower the expected cash flows from the foreign project. Or the MNC may purchase insurance policies against the hazard of political risks.

QUESTIONS

1. Recently, many foreign firms from both the developed and the developing countries acquired high-tech American firms. What has motivated these firms to acquire American firms?

2. Japanese MNCs, such as Toyota, Toshiba and Matsushita, made extensive investments in Southeast Asian countries, such as Thailand, Malaysia and Indonesia. What forces are driving Japanese investments in this region?

3. Since NAFTA was established, many Asian firms, especially those from Japan and Korea, have made extensive investments in Mexico. Why do you think these Asian firms decided to build production facilities in Mexico?

4. How would you explain the fact that China emerged as the second most important recipient of FDI after the United States in recent years?

5. Explain the internalization theory of FDI. What are the strengths and weaknesses of the theory?

6. Explain product life-cycle theory of FDI. What are the strengths and weaknesses of the theory?

7. Why do some host countries resist cross-border acquisitions rather than greenfield investments?

8. How would you incorporate political risk into the capital budgeting process of foreign investment projects?

9. Explain and compare forward versus backward internalization.

10. It has been ovserved that the profitability of Canadian FDI in the United States is significantly lower than the profitability of US investments in Canada. What factors might account for this difference?

11. Define *country risk.* How is it different from political risk?

12. What are the advantages and disadvantages of FDI as compared with a licensing agreement with a foreign partner?

13. What operational and financial measures can an MNC take to minimize the political risk associated with a foreign investment project?

14. Study the experience of Enron in India and discuss what we can learn from it for the management of political risk.

15. Discuss different ways political events in a host country may affect local operations of an MNC.

16. What factors would you consider in evaluating the political risk associated with making FDI in a foreign country.

INTERNET EXERCISE

You are hired as a political consultant for General Motors Company, which is considering building automobile plants in three countries: Brazil, China and Poland. Choose a country and analyze the political risk of investing in that country. In doing so, utilize such websites as www.cia.gov/library/publications/the-world-factbook/ or any other relevant internet resources. You may prepare a final report to GM using a format similar to that of Exhibit 15.12.

MINI CASE 1

Inward and Outward FDI—Enhancing the Competitiveness of Countries

Countries may use both inward and outward FDI to upgrade the competitiveness of their indigenous resources and capabilities to facilitate structural change, thereby promoting comparative advantage. In both cases, foreign assets (resources, capabilities, access to markets, patents, trademarks, entrepreneurial skills and institutions) are bought by *strategic asset*–seeking FDI.

The Investment Development Path (IDP) suggests that at low levels of economic development, both imports and inward FDI are likely to be the most favoured means of securing "created" assets. This is obviously one of the quickest ways to gain access to the "competitive advantage" of foreign firms; but unless it is to be a portfolio investment, the purchaser must have some other capabilities to manage the purchased firm effectively. In such cases, outward FDI is being used as a means of *augmenting* existing advantages.

Normally, however, in the early stages of the IDP, countries are likely to obtain created assets through inward FDI. First, these are directed to low/medium knowledge-intensive industries and/or resource-based sectors in which the host countries have or are developing a comparative advantage; later as countries move upwards along their IDPs, FDI is directed to higher technology-intensive sectors, and/or more efficiency-seeking FDI takes place.

Over time, through a variety of spillover effects, inward FDI acts as a competitive spur to domestic firms. Eventually, the most efficient of these will start to penetrate foreign markets (through exports, FDI or contractual agreements). Because of recent technological and communication advances and the pressures of globalization,

this process is accelerating. Sometimes it is aided by governments, as in the Republic of Korea in the 1980s and 1990s, and Malaysia and China today.

The principle of comparative advantage suggests a continuing restructuring of economic activity as countries move upwards along their IDP. Both inward and outward FDI policies play a critical role in guiding or facilitating this process, as do other macroeconomic and micro-management policies.

Many firms engage in a combination of the two types of FDI (asset-exploiting and asset-augmenting). In their development policies, countries may also opt for both inward and outward FDI. Finally, the geography of inward and outward FDI may differ just as much as that of trade. Certain companies might be in a favourable position to exploit or gain new assets via outward FDI, while others might best advance their competitive/comparative advantage by encouraging inward FDI from a different group.

Source: UNCATD, *World Investment Report 2006,* Box IV.2; p. 147.

Discussion Points

Below are readily recognizable names of eight successful multinational enterprises. Four are based in Canada. Four are foreign-owned firms with significant operations in Canada.

Barrick Gold	Honda (Canada)
Bombardier	Merrill Lynch (Canada)
CN Rail	Walmart (Canada)
McCain Foods	Weyerhaeuser Forestry (Canada)

1. For each firm, identify specific intangible assets (patents, command-of-technology, trademarks, networks,

reputation, operating systems etc.) that underlie that firm's success in foreign direct investment.

2. Comment on how unique those specific intangible assets are to each firm and how difficult it might be for potential competitors to replicate these assets.

3. In what ways are the MNCs' respective intangible assets crucial to the success of their foreign direct investments—as the Canadian-based firms seek opportunities abroad and as the foreign-based MNCs come to Canada?

MINI CASE 2

Enron versus Bombay Politicians*

On August 3, 1995, the Maharashtra state government dominated by the nationalist, right-wing Bharatiya Janata Party (BJP), abruptly cancelled Enron's $2.9 billion power project in Dabhol, located south of Bombay, the industrial heartland of India. This came as a huge blow to Rebecca P. Mark, the chair and chief executive of Enron's international power unit, who spearheaded the Houston-based energy giant's international investment drive. Upon the news release, Enron's share price fell immediately by about 10 percent to US$33½. Mark sprang to action to resuscitate the deal with the Maharashtra state, promising concessions. This effort, however, was met with scorn from BJP politicians. Enron's Dabhol debacle cast a serious doubt on the company's aggressive global expansion strategy, involving some $10 billion in projects in power plants and pipelines spanning across Asia, South America, and the Middle East.

Enron became involved in the project in 1992 when the new reformist government of the Congress Party (I), led by Prime Minister Narasimha Rao, was keen on attracting foreign investment in infrastructure. After meeting with the Indian government officials visiting Houston in May, Enron dispatched executives to India to hammer out a "memorandum of understanding" in just 10 days to build a massive 2,015 megawatt Dabhol power complex. New Delhi put the project on a fast track and awarded it to Enron without competitive bidding. Subsequently, the Maharashtra State Electricity Board (MSEB) agreed to buy 90 percent of the power Dabhol would produce. Two other American companies, General Electric (GE) and Bechtel Group, agreed to join Enron as partners for the Dabhol project.

In the process of structuring the deal, Enron made a profound political miscalculation: It did not seriously take into consideration a rising backlash against foreign investments by an opposition coalition led by the BJP.

During the state election campaign in early 1995, the BJP called for a reevaluation of the Enron project. Jay Dubashi, the BJP's economic advisor, said that the BJP would review all foreign investments already in India, and "If it turns out that we have to ask them to go, then we'll ask them to go." Instead of waiting for the election results, Enron rushed to close the deal and began construction, apparently believing that a new government would find it difficult to unwind the deal when construction was already under way. Enron was not very concerned with local political sentiments. Enron fought to keep the contract details confidential, but a successful lawsuit by a Bombay consumer group forced the company to reveal the details: Enron would receive 7.4 cents per kilowatt-hour from MSEB and Enron's rate of return would be 23 percent, far higher than 16 percent over the capital cost that the Indian government guaranteed to

*The depiction of political risk in this mini-case remains relevant despite the subsequent and infamous collapse of Enron and the change in the Indian political scene.

others. Critics cited the disclosure as proof that Enron had exaggerated project costs to begin with and that the deal might have involved corruption.

The BJP won the 1995 election in Maharashtra state and fulfilled its promise. Manohar Joshi, the newly elected Chief Minister of Maharashtra, who campaigned on a pledge to "drive Enron into the sea," promptly cancelled the project, citing inflated project costs and too-high electricity rates. This pledge played well with Indian voters with their visceral distrust of foreign companies since the British colonial era. (It helps to recall that India was first colonized by a foreign company, the British East India Company.) By the time the project was cancelled, Enron had already invested some $200 million. Officials of the Congress Party who championed the Dabhol project in the first place did not come to the rescue of the project. The BJP criticized the Congress Party, rightly or wrongly, for being too corrupt to reform the economy and too cozy with business interests. In an effort to pressure Maharashtra to reverse its decision, Enron "pushed like hell" for the US Energy Department to make a statement in June 1995 to the effect that cancelling the Enron

deal could adversely affect other power projects. The statement only compounded the situation. The BJP politicians immediately criticized the statement as an attempt by Washington to bully India.

After months of nasty exchanges and lawsuits, Enron and Maharashtra negotiators agreed to revive the Dabhol project. The new deal requires that Enron cut the project's cost from $2.9 billion to $2.5 billion, lower the proposed electricity rates and make a state-owned utility a new 30 percent partner of the project. A satisfied Chief Minister Joshi stated: "Maharashtra has gained tremendously by this decision." Enron needed to make a major concession to demonstrate that its global power projects were still on track. The new deal led Enron to withdraw a lawsuit seeking $500 million in damages from Maharashtra for the cancellation of the Dabhol project.

Discussion Points

1. Discuss the chief mistakes that Enron made in India.
2. Discuss what Enron might have done differently to avoid its predicament in India.

REFERENCES & SUGGESTED READINGS

Caves, Richard. *Multinational Enterprise and Economic Analysis.* Cambridge, MA: Harvard University Press, 1982.

Doukas, John, and Nicholas Travlos. "The Effect of Corporate Multinationalism on Shareholders' Wealth: Evidence from International Acquisitions." *Journal of Finance* 43 (1988), pp. 1161–75.

Dunning, John H. "Location and the Multinational Enterprise: A Neglected Factor." *Journal of International Business Studies* 29 (1998), pp. 45–66.

Eun, C., R. Kolodn, and C. Scheraga. "Cross-Border Acquisitions and Shareholder Wealth: Tests of Synergy and Internalization Hypotheses." *Journal of Banking and Finance* 20 (1996), pp. 1559–82.

Harris, Robert, and David Ravenscraft. "The Role of Acquisitions in Foreign Direct Investment: Evidence from the U.S. Stock Market." *Journal of Finance* 46 (1991), pp. 825–44.

Hejazi, Walid. "Canada's FDI Experience: What Kind of Host Are We?" *Policy Options/Options Politiques.* Montreal: The Institute for Research on Public Policy, April 2004.

Hejazi, Walid, and Peter Pauly. "Motivations for FDI and Domestic Capital Formation." *Journal of International Business Studies* 34 (2002), pp. 282–89.

Jensen, Michael. "The Takeover Controversy: Analysis and Evidence." *Midland Corporate Finance Journal* 5 (1986), pp. 1–27.

Kang, Jun-Koo. "The International Market for Corporate Control: Mergers and Acquisitions of U.S. Firms by Japanese Firms." *Journal of Financial Economics* 35 (1993), pp. 345–71.

Lessard, Donald R. "Incorporating Country Risk in the Valuation of Offshore Projects." *Journal of Applied Corporate Finance,* Volume 9, Issue. 3 (1996), pp. 52–63.

Morck, Randall, and Bernard Yeung. "Why Investors Value Multinationality." *Journal of Business* 64 (1991), pp. 165–87.

_____. "Internalization: An Event Study Test." *Journal of International Economics* 33 (1992), pp. 41–56.

Rugman, Alan. "Internalization Is Still a General Theory of Foreign Direct Investment." *Weltwirtschaftliche Archiv* 121 (1985), pp. 570–76.

Rummel, R. J., and David Heenan. "How Multinationals Analyze Political Risk." *Harvard Business Review* 56 (1978), pp. 67–76.

The Transnational Corporations Journal, published in three issues per year by The UN Centre on Transnationals (Geneva) is a rich source of information on foreign direct investment.

UNCTAD (United Nations Conference on Trade and Development). *The World Investment Report* (Geneva), annual.

Vernon, Raymond. "The Product Cycle Hypothesis in a New International Environment." *Oxford Bulletin of Economics and Statistics* 41 (1979), pp. 255–67.

 For more information on the resources available from McGraw-Hill Ryerson, go to www.mcgrawhill.ca/he/solutions.

Chapter (16)

International Capital Structure and the Cost of Capital

CHAPTER OUTLINE

CAPITAL STRUCTURE refers to the right-hand side of the corporate balance sheet. A company's capital structure is a description of how that company is financed—how much debt and how much equity. Corporate decisions on capital structure generally involve adjusting the debt–equity ratio so as minimize the overall cost of capital. Whereas debt tends to be relatively cheap with interest payments that are tax-deductible, equity is generally more costly. However, since a firm cannot raise low-cost debt without having an equity base, the choice of the optimal debt–equity ratio can be a complex problem involving interest and tax rates, business and financial risk, and equity market conditions.

This chapter deals with international aspects of capital structure and the cost of capital. The main theme is that modern corporations look beyond their national borders and outside their domestic financial markets to raise capital. For several substantial reasons discussed in this chapter, going abroad for capital can provide significant benefits in the form of expanded access to capital and lower capital costs. A lower cost of capital enhances corporate value. Furthermore, since the cost of capital is the cut-off or "hurdle rate" in investment decisions, a lower cost of capital can make otherwise unattractive projects attractive.

There is a close connection between the corporate themes of the chapter and the global phenomenon of *capital market integration*. Capital market integration refers to the increasing ease of accessing capital from other countries. As we saw in Chapter 8 on international equity markets and in Chapter 11 on international portfolio investment, corporate bonds and shares of foreign companies are readily accessible to investors virtually anywhere in the world. Impediments and costs to purchasing foreign securities are much less onerous than they once were. When investors and corporations buy or sell securities in other countries, they are part of the process of international capital market integration.

If international capital markets were completely integrated, it would not matter whether firms raised capital from domestic or foreign sources, since the cost of capital would be equalized across countries. Just as a high degree of competition in, say, the market for produce means that you do not have to run all over town to find the best price for lettuce—and so you can confidently shop at your local green grocer—a truly integrated international capital market would reflect global competition for capital, and hence, local capital costs would equal global capital costs. However, barriers to cross-border capital flows including incompatible regulations, costly information and foreign exchange risk can cause segmentation in the markets. If capital markets are segmented to some degree, firms may be able to create value for their shareholders by issuing securities in foreign as well as domestic markets.

Cross-listing a firm's shares on both domestic and foreign stock exchanges is an effective way for a firm to counteract the negative effects of market segmentation. This is essentially "internationalizing" capital structure. Many Canadian firms, including Agrium, Brookfield, CN, Domtar, Nordion and TD Bank, that are listed on the Toronto Stock Exchange are also listed on the New York Stock Exchange or Nasdaq. In all, 74 Canadian firms are listed on the NYSE and 52 on Nasdaq. Large global firms, such as IBM, Sony and British Petroleum are simultaneously listed and traded on the New York, London and Tokyo stock exchanges. By internationalizing its share ownership structure, a firm can potentially increase its share price and lower its cost of capital.

In this chapter, we examine various implications of internationalizing the capital structure for the firm's market value and cost of capital. We look at existing restrictions on foreign ownership of domestic firms and their effects on the corporate cost of capital. We are ultimately concerned with the ability of a multinational corporation (MNC) to obtain capital at the lowest possible cost so that it can profitably expand its capital expenditure program and enhance shareholder wealth. We begin the chapter with a review of cost of capital concepts and basic asset pricing theory.

16.1 COST OF CAPITAL

The **cost of capital** is the minimum rate of return an investment project must generate in order to pay its financing costs. If the return on an investment project is just equal to the cost of capital, undertaking the project will leave the firm's value unaffected. When a firm identifies and undertakes an investment project that generates a return exceeding its cost of capital, the firm's value will increase. It is thus important for a value-maximizing firm to try to lower its cost of capital.

When a firm has both debt and equity in its capital structure, its financing cost can be represented by the **weighted average cost of capital**. It can be computed by weighting the after-tax borrowing cost of the firm and the cost of equity capital using the capital structure ratio as the weight. Specifically,

$$K = (1 - \lambda)K_l + \lambda(1 - \tau)i \qquad\qquad (16.1)$$

where

K = weighted average cost of capital

K_l = cost of equity capital for a levered firm

i = before-tax cost of debt capital (i.e., borrowing)

τ = corporate income tax rate

λ = debt-to-total-market-value ratio

In general, both K_l and i increase as the proportion of debt in the firm's capital structure increases. At the optimal combination of debt and equity financing, however, the weighted average cost of capital (K) will be the lowest. Firms may have an incentive to use debt financing to take advantage of the tax-deductibility of interest payments. In most countries, interest payments are tax-deductible, unlike dividend payments. Debt financing, however, must be balanced against possible bankruptcy costs associated with higher debt. A trade-off between the tax advantage of debt and potential bankruptcy costs is thus a major factor in determining optimal capital structure.

EXHIBIT 16.1

The Firm's
Investment
Decision and the
Cost of Capital

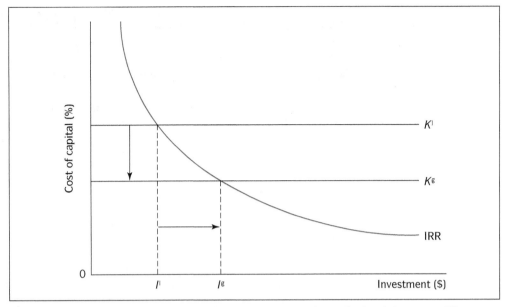

Note: K^l and K^g represent, respectively, the cost of capital under local and international capital structures; IRR represents the internal rate of return on investment projects; I^l and I^g represent the optimal investment outlays under the alternative capital structures.

Optimal capital structure is important since maximizing shareholder wealth implies financing new capital expenditures up to the point where the marginal return on invested capital equals the cost of capital. Policy that lowers the firm's cost of capital will increase profitable capital expenditures that the firm takes on and increase shareholder wealth. Internationalizing the firm's cost of capital is one such policy.

Exhibit 16.1 illustrates this point. The value-maximizing firm would undertake an investment project as long as the internal rate of return on the project exceeded the firm's cost of capital. When investment projects are ranked in descending order of internal rate of return (IRR), the firm faces a negatively sloped IRR schedule as depicted in the exhibit. The firm's optimal capital expenditure is determined at the point where the IRR schedule intersects the cost of capital.

Now, suppose that the firm's cost of capital can be reduced from K^l under the local capital structure to K^g under an internationalized capital structure. The firm can then increase its profitable investment outlay from I^l to I^g, contributing to the firm's value. It is important, however, to note that a reduced cost of capital increases the firm's value not only through increased investments in new projects but also through revaluation of the cash flows from existing projects.

16.2 COST OF CAPITAL IN SEGMENTED VERSUS INTEGRATED MARKETS

The main difficulty in computing the financing cost (K) of a firm is related to the cost of equity capital (K_e). The cost of equity capital is the expected return on the firm's shares that investors require. This return is typically estimated using the **Capital Asset Pricing Model (CAPM)**. The CAPM states that the equilibrium expected rate of return on a share (or more generally any security) is a linear function of the systematic risk inherent in the security. Specifically, the CAPM-determined expected rate of return for the ith security is:

$$\bar{R}_i = R_f + (\bar{R}_M - R_f)\beta_i \tag{16.2}$$

where R_f is the risk-free rate of return and $\bar{R}_M$ is the expected return on the **market portfolio**, the market-value-weighted portfolio of all assets. **Beta**, β_i, is a measure of systematic risk inherent in security *i*. **Systematic risk** is the nondiversifiable market risk of an asset. The CAPM equation shows that the required return of security *i*, $\bar{R}_i$, increases in β_i. The greater the market risk, the greater the required return.

Beta is calculated as $\text{Cov}(R_i, R_M)/\text{Var}(R_M)$, where $\text{Cov}(R_i, R_M)$ is the covariance of returns between security *i* and the market portfolio and $\text{Var}(R_M)$ is the variance of returns of the market portfolio.

Now, suppose that international financial markets are segmented and, as a result, investors can only diversify domestically. In this case, the market portfolio (M) in the CAPM formula would represent the domestic market portfolio, proxied by S&P/TSX in Canada. The relevant risk measure in pricing assets is beta measured against the domestic market portfolio. In segmented capital markets, similar cash flows are likely to be priced differently across countries as they would be viewed as having different systematic risks by investors from different countries.

On the other hand, suppose international financial markets are fully integrated and, consequently, investors can diversify internationally. In this case, the market portfolio in the CAPM ought to be the "world" market portfolio comprising all assets in the world. The relevant risk measure then is beta measured against the world market portfolio. In integrated international financial markets, similar cash flows are priced in the same way everywhere. Investors require, on average, lower expected returns on securities under integration than under segmentation because they can diversify risk more efficiently under integration.

Example 16.1   *A Numerical Illustration*

Suppose the domestic Canadian beta of Barrick, the Toronto-based gold company, is 1.2. This Canadian beta for Barrick is estimated in a regression of the returns on Barrick shares on the returns of the S&P/TSX, the Toronto index. In addition, let us say that the expected return on the S&P/TSX is 12 percent and the Canadian risk-free interest rate, proxied by the Canadian Treasury bill rate, is 4 percent. If Canadian capital markets are segmented from the rest of the world, the expected return on Barrick shares is determined as follows:

$$R_{\text{BAR}}^{\text{CAN}} = R_f^{\text{CAN}} + (R_{\text{TSX}}^{\text{CAN}} - R_f^{\text{CAN}})\beta_{\text{BAR}}^{\text{CAN}}$$

$$= 4 + (12 - 4)1.2 = 13.6$$

In view of the Canadian systematic risk of Barrick, Canadian investors require 13.6 percent return on their investment in Barrick shares.

Suppose now that Canadian capital markets are integrated with the rest of the world. For all practical purposes, it is enough to say that Canadian and US capital markets are integrated. In this situation, American investors can hold Barrick shares. American investors would be concerned with Barrick's beta as estimated in a regression of Barrick shares on the returns of the S&P 500, the New York index. Say this American beta for Barrick is 1.0. Say the expected return on the S&P 500 is 13 percent and the US risk-free interest rate, proxied by the US Treasury bill rate, is 4 percent. Then, the American valuation of Barrick is

$$R_{\text{BAR}}^{\text{US}} = R_f^{\text{US}} + (R_{\text{NYSE}}^{\text{US}} - R_f^{\text{US}})\beta_{\text{BAR}}^{\text{US}}$$

$$= 4 + (13 - 4)1.0 = 13$$

American investors would accept a lower return on Barrick shares than Canadian investors. American investors would bid up the price of Barrick shares.

As a matter of fact, Barrick is listed on both the Toronto Stock Exchange (ABX.TO) and the New York Stock Exchange (ABX) so the "world" perspective is relevant.

Obviously, the integration or segmentation of international financial markets has major implications for determining the cost of capital. While empirical evidence on the issue is less than clear-cut, there are strong indications to the effect that international financial markets are becoming increasingly integrated (Carrieri et al., 2007). In a study examining the integration of the Canadian and US stock markets, Mittoo (1992) found that Canadian shares cross-listed on US exchanges are priced in an integrated market and that segmentation is predominant for those Canadian shares that are not cross-listed.

These studies suggest that international financial markets are certainly not entirely segmented but still are not fully integrated. If international financial markets are less than fully integrated, which is likely to be the case, there can be systematic differences in the cost of capital among countries.

16.3 ADJUSTING THE COST OF EQUITY TO ACCOUNT FOR COUNTRY-SPECIFIC RISK[1]

A typical need to calculate a risk-adjusted cost of equity capital arises when a company, in our case a Canadian company, considers a project in a foreign country. Suppose Agrium, the Calgary-based agricultural fertilizer producer, plans to expand its operations in South America by buying a fertilizer company in Colombia. Although Agrium is confident that it knows its cost of equity in Canadian and US operations, the Colombia venture comes with a unique set of risks. The word "unique" is important since country-specific risks in Colombia could perhaps be diversifiable and relatively inconsequential to a well-diversified foreign firm. How is Agrium to proceed to calculate a cost of equity capital to ultimately fit within the weighted average cost of capital used to value the Colombian operations?

To back up for a moment, there are two different approaches to adjusting project value in the face of country-specific risks of a foreign investment. The analyst either makes a *downward* adjustment to the projected cash flows to account for expected loss that could arise from, for example, expropriation, unexpected tax increases, restricted profit repatriation or disruption due to political events in Colombia, *or* the analyst makes an *upward* adjustment to the discount rate applied to the expected country-specific earnings. In the professional jargon, the first approach is referred to as "adjusting the numerator" while the second is termed "adjusting the denominator" in the valuation calculation. To a close approximation, increasing the discount rate by 1 percent is equivalent to reducing expected annual cash flows by 10 percent. In most industrial investment cases it is easier and more practical to adjust the discount rate (upward) than it is to adjust the expected cash flows (downward).

The following is an *ad hoc* but focused approach to estimating Agrium's cost of equity capital in its proposed Colombian venture. The model takes the basic form

$$R_e = R_f + \beta_i \times \text{EMRP} + \frac{\Phi_1 + \Phi_2 + \Phi_3}{30} \times \text{PRP} \tag{16.3}$$

where

R_e = the cost of equity for Agrium's Colombia project

β_i = the global CAPM beta for Agrium corresponding to its ordinary business risk and optimal capital structure

EMRP = the global equity market risk-premium, for example $R_{\text{MSCI}} - R_f$

Φ_1 = access to capital market score (score 0 to 10 with 0 indicating full access to global capital markets)

[1]This approach to country-specific risk adjustment to the cost of equity draws on Salomon Smith Barney (2002).

Φ_2 = susceptibility of Agrium's Colombian investment to political risk (score 0 to 10 with 0 indicating the least susceptibility to costly political intervention)

Φ_3 = importance of the Colombian investment for Agrium (score 0 to 10 with 0 indicating the investment represents only a small portion of Agrium's global assets)

PRP = unadjusted political risk premium for Colombia

With Φ_1 we measure the extent to which Agrium's access to capital markets in, say, Canada and the US are likely to have fully diversified investors who are primarily concerned about systematic risk captured by CAPM beta and less concerned about diversifiable country-specific risks.

The role of Φ_2 is to take account of the extent to which political risk premium represents potential cash flow loss from expropriation or other such intervention because of the specific industry that Agrium is in.

Finally, Φ_3 captures the degree to which the Colombian investment constitutes a major part of Agrium's global operations.

If the Colombian investment is relatively small, then it is unlikely to significantly increase Agrium's total risk and indeed may reduce it because of diversification. On the other hand, if the Colombian investment represents a major part of Agrium's assets, then political uncertainty in Colombia could significantly affect the firm's risk profile.

Exhibit 16.2 outlines how the foreign-investment risk premium weights, Φ_1, Φ_2 and Φ_3, are applied.

An Illustration with Data

Equation 16.3 is essentially an augmented international CAPM calculation of Agrium's cost of equity capital. Consider the first two items on the right-hand side. The relevant risk-free rate (R_f) plus Agrium's global *beta* times the equity market risk premium, for example $\beta_i (R_{MSCI} - R_f)$ if one were to derive Agrium's *beta* on the basis of the Morgan Stanley World Index, results in Agrium's basic CAPM-determined cost of equity.

The factor augmenting the international CAPM involves Φ_1, Φ_2 and Φ_3 and the unadjusted political risk premium for Colombia. The maximum values of Φ_1, Φ_2 and Φ_3 are

EXHIBIT 16.2

Accounting for Country-Specific Risk

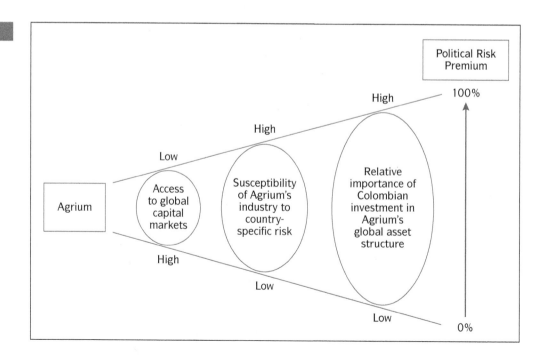

respectively 10, 10 and 10. So, for instance, if each was assigned its maximum value, the ratio $(\Phi_1 + \Phi_2 + \Phi_3)/30$ would equal 1 in which case the full political risk premium for Colombia would be added to Agrium's cost of equity for evaluating the proposed Colombia project. On the other hand, if each of the Φ's was zero, no political risk premium would be assigned to the Colombia project. Values of Φ_1, Φ_2 and Φ_3 that fall between zero and one result in some but not all of the unadjusted political risk premium for Colombia to be added to Agrium's international cost of equity when evaluating the Colombia-specific project.

The final piece of the puzzle is to determine the unadjusted political risk premium for Colombia. The typical method is to turn to country-specific credit ratings published by international credit agencies or professional magazines such as *Institutional Investor* or *Euromoney*.

Institutional Investor has published a survey of country credit ratings in March and September of every year since 1979. The survey gathers responses from approximately 75–100 chief economists at leading institutional banks and money management firms. Ratings are currently available for 179 countries. Respondents rate each country on a scale of 0 to 100, with 100 representing the least chance of default or unanticipated intervention.

Euromoney has published country risk ratings since 1982 with 185 countries now covered. The *Euromoney* ratings are based on nine indicators including political risk (25 percent), country economic performance (25 percent), debt indicators (10 percent), debt in default or rescheduled (10 percent), credit ratings (10 percent), discount of forfeiting, access to bank finance, short-term finance and capital markets (5 percent each).

To illustrate our approach to estimating the risk-adjusted discount rate for Agrium's proposed investment in Colombia, assume the following values for the various components of the model for determining R_e

$$\beta_i = 1.2$$

$$\text{EMRP} = R_{MSCI} - R_f = 12 - 4 = 8 \text{ percent}$$

$\Phi_1 = 2$ (access to capital markets score)

$\Phi_2 = 7$ (susceptibility of Agrium's Colombian investment to political risk)

$\Phi_3 = 4$ (importance of the Colombian investment for Agrium)

$\text{PRP} = 5$ (unadjusted political risk premium for Colombia)

Then

$$R_e = R_f + \beta_i \times \text{EMRP} + \frac{\Phi_1 + \Phi_2 + \Phi_3}{30} \times \text{PRP}$$

$$= 4 + 1.2(12 - 4) + \frac{(2 + 7 + 4)}{30} \times 5$$

$$= 15.8\,\%$$

Agrium's basic (no political risk) CAPM-derived cost of equity is 13.6 percent, a figure that is appropriate for investments in Canada and the United States. For the riskier Colombia project, the political risk-adjusted cost of equity rises to 15.8 percent or 2.2 percentage points higher.

This approach is practical and relatively easy to tailor to the specific circumstances of a company's foreign investment program. Its foundation is the firm's CAPM-determined cost of equity and the consensus unadjusted political risk premium for a particular country. A meaningful political risk premium is generally beyond the scope of an individual company such as Agrium to generate on its own. The company, then, is required to focus only on industry-and-project-specific factors (the Φ's) that it is best positioned to understand and to assign "scores" on a 10-point scale.

16.4   DOES THE COST OF CAPITAL DIFFER ACROSS COUNTRIES?

The cost of capital is likely to vary across countries, due to international differences in the degree of financial integration, quality of corporate governance, macroeconomic conditions, and other factors. In a recent study, Lau, Ng and Zhang (2010) document that the cost of equity capital indeed differs substantially across countries. For example, the estimated cost of capital is relatively low for many developed countries like Japan (7.4 percent), the United States (8.5 percent), the UK (8.9 percent) and Canada (9.5 percent), but quite high for some developing countries like India (13.1 percent), South Africa (14.5 percent) and Brazil (16.8 percent). They report, among other things, that the cost of capital of a country is strongly related to the home bias in portfolio holdings, which reflects the country's degree of financial integration with the rest of the world.

Specifically, Lau et al. first compute the home bias of a country as the difference between the percentage of domestic mutual funds' holdings in domestic securities in a country and that country's weight in the world stock market capitalization. If a country's weight in the world market capitalization is 6 percent and domestic mutual funds collectively invest more than 6 percent of their investment funds in domestic securities, then the country is judged to exhibit a home bias. Lau et al. then compute the so-called "implicit cost of capital" (ICOC) as a proxy for the country's cost of capital. For each firm in a country, they estimate ICOC based on four different models, as implied by the current stock price and earning forecasts, and then take the average of the four estimates. For each country, the value-weighted ICOC estimate of all sample firms in the country is then used as the country's ICOC.[2]

Exhibit 16.3 presents both the degree of home bias and the ICOC for each of the 38 sample countries. Note that the degree of home bias is the percentage of domestic mutual funds' holdings in domestic securities in a country divided by the percentage weight of the country in the world market capitalization and is expressed in natural log. The degree of home bias ranges from 0.70 for the United States to 7.56 for Peru. The United States exhibits the lowest degree of home bias and, at the same time, has the lowest cost of capital (8.5 percent), whereas Peru exhibits the highest degree of home bias and has the second-highest cost of capital (16.5 percent), after Brazil (16.8 percent). The analysis suggests that Canada has the fifth-smallest home bias (2.27 percent) among those countries examined.

Exhibit 16.4 plots the implicit cost of capital and the degree of home bias for different countries, showing that the two variables are positively related to each other. A higher home bias is associated with a higher cost of capital.

When a country exhibits a high degree of home bias, as Peru does, the global risk sharing is hampered, thereby increasing the cost of capital for the country. Based on this finding, Lau et al. suggest that reduced home bias and greater global risk sharing would help reduce the cost of capital. In addition, they report that accounting transparency also helps reduce the cost of capital.

In perfect markets, firms would be indifferent between raising funds abroad or at home. When markets are imperfect, however, international financing can lower the firm's cost of capital. In Chapter 7, for example, we saw that Eurobond financing was typically a less expensive form of debt financing than domestic bond financing. We continue with this line of thinking in this chapter, where we explore ways of lowering the cost of equity capital through internationalizing the firm's ownership structure. Let us first examine the now-classic experience of one firm, Novo Industri, that successfully internationalized its cost of capital by cross-border listings.

---

[2]In computing ICOC, Lau et al. (2010) actually use the method that was previously employed by Hail and Leuz (2006). The basic premise of the ICOC method is that the ICOC is the internal rate of return (IRR) that equates current stock price to the present value of expected future stream of unexpected earnings. Refer to Hail and Leuz (2006) for details of the ICOC method.

EXHIBIT 16.3

The Cost of Capital around the World

Country	World Market-Cap Weight (%)	Domestic Funds Local (%)	Home Bias	Implied Cost of Capital
Argentina	0.16	60.46	6.02	0.133
Australia	1.70	78.91	3.96	0.087
Austria	0.15	22.91	4.91	0.096
Belgium	0.63	17.71	3.31	0.088
Brazil	0.71	100.00	4.95	0.168
Canada	2.67	28.67	2.27	0.095
Chile	0.23	55.31	5.52	0.106
China	1.84	99.40	3.99	0.106
Czech Republic	0.06	58.59	7.08	0.110
Denmark	0.37	23.69	4.11	0.085
Finland	0.55	66.20	4.43	0.111
France	4.13	55.48	2.65	0.089
Germany	3.21	29.35	2.17	0.086
Greece	0.33	91.94	5.63	0.096
Hong Kong	2.08	22.51	2.34	0.101
India	0.71	99.51	4.98	0.131
Ireland	0.26	2.51	2.20	0.103
Italy	1.96	40.76	3.03	0.087
Japan	9.29	98.50	2.36	0.074
Luxembourg	0.12	12.21	4.54	0.077
Malaysia	0.43	99.90	5.44	0.100
Mexico	0.44	77.73	5.19	0.115
Netherlands	1.57	31.18	2.91	0.092
New Zealand	0.09	61.38	6.52	0.093
Norway	0.29	52.27	5.29	0.112
Peru	0.05	89.01	7.56	0.165
Philippines	0.12	99.52	6.71	0.098
Poland	0.12	82.46	6.69	0.119
Portugal	0.18	42.95	5.49	0.089
Singapore	0.51	20.00	3.52	0.100
South Africa	0.80	79.92	4.54	0.145
Spain	2.09	38.89	2.94	0.095
Sweden	1.00	48.36	3.93	0.090

(Continued)

EXHIBIT 16.3

(continued)

Country	World Market-Cap Weight (%)	Domestic Funds Local (%)	Home Bias	Implied Cost of Capital
Switzerland	2.24	21.08	2.17	0.084
Taiwan	1.10	100.00	4.51	0.113
Thailand	0.23	100.00	6.09	0.138
United Kingdom	7.64	42.95	1.71	0.089
United States	44.86	86.88	0.70	0.085

Note: The sample period of the study is 1998 to 2007.

Source: S. T. Lau et al., "The World Price of Home Bias," *Journal of Financial Economics* 97 (2010), pp. 191–217.

EXHIBIT 16.4

Implied Cost of
Capital versus
Home Bias

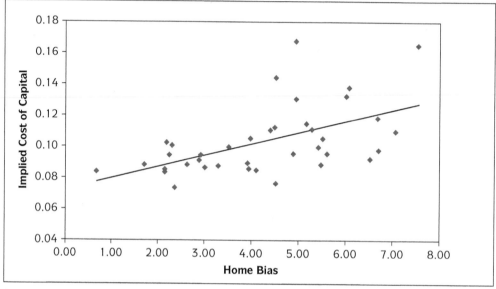

Source: S. T. Lau et al., "The World Price of Home Bias," *Journal of Financial Economics* 97 (2010), pp. 191–217.

Illustrated **Mini Case**

Novo Industri

www.novo.dk

The homepage of Novo
provides basic information
about the company.

Novo Industri A/S is a Danish multinational corporation that controls about 50 percent of the world industrial enzyme market. The company also produces health-care products, including insulin. On 8 July 1981, Novo listed its shares on the New York Stock Exchange, thereby becoming the first Scandinavian company to directly raise equity capital in the United States.

In the late 1970s, Novo management felt that in order to finance the planned future growth of the company, it had to tap into international capital markets. Novo could not expect to raise all the necessary funds exclusively from the Danish stock market, which is relatively small and illiquid. In addition, Novo management felt that the company faced a higher cost of capital than its main competitors, such as Eli Lilly and Miles Lab, because of the segmented nature of the Danish stock market.

Novo thus decided to internationalize its cost of capital in order to gain access to additional sources of capital and, at the same time, lower its cost of capital. Initially, Novo increased the level of financial and technical disclosure, followed by a Eurobond issue and the listing of its shares on the London Stock Exchange in 1978. In pursuing its goals further, Novo management decided to sponsor an American depository receipt (ADR) so that American investors could invest in the company's shares using dollars rather than Danish kroner. Morgan Guarantee issued the ADR shares, which began trading in the over-the-counter (OTC) market in April 1981. On 8 July 1981, Novo sold 1.8 million ADR shares, raising DKr450 million and, at the same time, listed its ADR shares on the New York Stock Exchange. The chronology of these events is provided in Exhibit 16.5.

As can be seen from Exhibit 16.6, Novo's share price reacted very positively to the American listing. Other Danish shares, though, did not experience comparable price increases. The sharp increase in Novo's share price indicates that the stock became fully

EXHIBIT 16.5

Process of Internationalizing the Capital Structure: Novo

1977:	Novo increased the level of its financial and technical disclosure in both Danish and English versions.
	Grieveson, Grant and Co, a British stock brokerage firm, started to follow Novo's shares and issued the first professional security analyst report in English. Novo's share price: DKr200–225.
1978:	Novo raised $20 million by offering convertible Eurobond, underwritten by Morgan Grenfell.
	Novo listed on the London Stock Exchange.
1980 April:	Novo organized a marketing seminar in New York City promoting its share to American investors.
1980 December:	Novo's share price reached DKr600 level; P/E ratio rose to around 16.
1981 April:	Novo ADRs were listed on Nasdaq (5 ADRs = one share). Morgan Guaranty Trust Co. served as the depository bank.
1981 July:	Novo listed on NYSE.
	Novo share price reached DKr1400.
	Foreign ownership increased to over 50 percent of the shares outstanding.
	American institutional investors began to hold Novo shares.

Source: Arthur Stonehill and Kare Dullum, *Internationalizing the Cost of Capital* (New York: John Wiley & Sons, 1982).

EXHIBIT 16.6

Novo B's Share Prices Compared to Stock Market Indexes

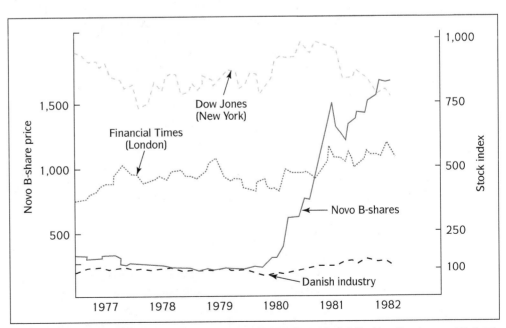

Source: Arthur I. Stonehill and Kare B. Dullum, *Internationalizing the Cost of Capital: The Novo Experience and National Policy Implications* (John Wiley & Sons, 1982), p. 73. Note that Novo A shares are nontradable shares held by the Novo Foundation. Reprinted with permission.

priced internationally upon American listing. This, in turn, implies that the Danish stock market was, indeed, segmented from the rest of the world. From the experiences of Novo, we can derive the following lesson: *Firms operating in a small, segmented domestic capital market can gain access to new capital and lower the cost of capital by listing their shares on large, liquid capital markets, such as the New York and London Stock Exchanges.*

16.5 CROSS-BORDER LISTINGS OF SHARES

www.bnymellon.com/
depositaryreceipts/index.
html

Provides general
information about
depositary receipts.

As we have seen from the case of Novo Industri, firms can potentially benefit from cross-border listings. As a result, cross-border listings of stocks have become quite popular among major corporations. Exhibit 16.7 presents the country-to-country frequency distribution of overseas listings that Sarkissian and Schill (2004) documented in their geographical analysis of cross-listings. As of 1998, their study period, there were 2,251 overseas listings. As can be seen from the bottom of the exhibit, US and UK exchanges are, by far, the most popular hosts of overseas listings, probably reflecting the depth and credibility of these markets. Other important hosting markets are Belgium, France, Germany, Luxembourg, the Netherlands and Switzerland, each hosting more than 100 foreign stocks. Examination of the exhibit suggests that to a certain extent, firms seem to prefer to list in neighbouring markets. Out of the 266 Canadian overseas listings, 211 listings are on US exchanges. New Zealand firms list heavily in Australia and *vice versa*. Similarly, Belgian firms list heavily in the Netherlands and *vice versa*. Sarkissian and Schill interpret this tendency as implying that the same proximity preference that is believed to be responsible for "home bias" in portfolio holdings may also influence firms' choice of overseas listing venues.

Exhibit 16.8 provides a partial list of overseas stocks that are cross-listed on the New York Stock Exchange (NYSE). Many well-known international companies like BHP, Nokia, Siemens, Honda Motor, Telmex, ING, Unilever, BP and Vodafone are all listed and traded on the NYSE. The London Stock Exchange (LSE) is another popular venue for cross-border listings. Exhibit 16.9 provides a list of foreign stocks listed on the LSE. Many companies from the British Commonwealth countries, such as Australia, Canada and India, are listed on the LSE. Reflecting London's traditional position as the centre of European finance, many companies from the continental European countries, such as France, Germany, the Netherlands, Poland and Russia, are also listed on the LSE. In addition, many high-profile US companies, such as Bank of America, Boeing, Dow, Ford, GE, IBM, Pfizer and Verizon, are also cross-listed on the LSE. Many exchanges of the world are now competing for cross-listings and trading volume of international stocks.

Exhibit 16.10 presents a selective list of foreign companies listed on the Toronto Stock Exchange (TSX and TSXV). The striking point about these listings—and they are typical of the broader set of foreign firms that chose to list on the Canadian exchanges—is that they are almost exclusively in natural resources and energy. Toronto is internationally recognized for its expertise in structuring equity issues in mining and extraction, part of the process of achieving the lowest cost of capital for firms in these sectors.

Generally speaking, a company can benefit from cross-border listings of its shares in the following ways:

1. The company can expand its potential investor base, which will lead to a higher stock price and a lower cost of capital.

2. Cross-listing creates a secondary market for the company's shares, which facilitates raising new capital in foreign markets.[3]

---

[3]Chaplinsky and Ramchand (1995) report that, compared with exclusively domestic offerings, global equity offerings enable firms to raise capital at advantageous terms. In addition, they report that the negative stock price reaction that equity issue often elicits is reduced if firms have a foreign tranche in their offer.

EXHIBIT 16.7 Country-to-Country Frequency Distribution of Foreign Listings

Home Country	Australia	Austria	Belgium	Brazil	Canada	Denmark	France	Germany	H. Kong	Ireland	Italy	Japan	Luxem.	Malaysia	Nether.	N. Zealand	Norway	Peru	Singapore	S. Africa	Spain	Sweden	Switz.	UK	US
Argentina				1									3										2	1	12
Australia					4			2				4	1		45				3				2	10	26
Austria			1				2	8							1										
Belgium							7	3					4		7	1							4		1
Brazil													5											1	21
Canada	4		8				6	2				1			4				1	1			8	20	211
Chile																									22
Colombia													3												1
Czech R.																							5		
Denmark															1							1	1	3	3
Finland							1	2														3		2	4
France			11		1			7		1	2	2			7						1	3	5	6	23
Germany		17	7				13				2	9	6		12				1		2	1	26	11	11
Greece													1		1									4	2
H. Kong	3											1				1			9					1	4
Hungary		1											5											4	1
India													48											17	
Indonesia													1											2	4
Ireland																								58	14
Israel			2																					4	59
Italy			2				4	5							1						1				14
Japan		1	5		1		30	52					21		19				6				14	29	28
Korea													12											14	3
Luxem.			5				3	1							2						1	1		6	3
Malaysia												1							1					5	
Mexico																									30
Nether.		4	11				9	20		1	1		6						1			1	12	13	26
N. Zealand	17																								5
Norway					1	1	2								1							2	1	5	6
Peru																									3
Philippines													5						1						1
Poland													1											7	
Portugal								1																	5
Singapore	2												2												1
S. Africa			9				15	5					4										4	40	11

(Continued)

EXHIBIT 16.7 (continued)

Home Country	Australia	Austria	Belgium	Brazil	Canada	Denmark	France	Germany	H. Kong	Ireland	Italy	Japan	Luxem.	Malaysia	Nether.	N. Zealand	Norway	Peru	Singapore	S. Africa	Spain	Sweden	Switz.	UK	US
Spain							4	4				4			1								2	4	5
Sweden		1	1			5	3	3				2					2		2				4	12	12
Switz.		1	1		1	5	10					4			1									1	5
Taiwan												14							1					10	2
Thailand												2							1						
Turkey													1											6	
UK	6		8		4	1	13	10	1	13		8	1	3	12		2		7	1			4		77
US	8		31		27		32	42				23	1		71		3	2				5	67	104	
Venezuela													1												3
Total	40	25	106	1	37	8	148	179	1	13	4	60	150	3	140	45	10	2	34	2	4	17	157	406	659

Source: Sergei Sarkissian and Michael Schill, "The Overseas Listing Decision: New Evidence of Proximity Preference," *Review of Financial Studies* 17 (2004).

EXHIBIT 16.8

Foreign Firms Listed on the New York Stock Exchange (selected)

Country	Firms
Australia	BHP Billiton, James Hardie, Westpac Banking
Brazil	Embraer, Petrobras, Telebras, Unibanco, VALE
Canada	Agrium, Barrick Gold, Canadian Pacific, Cameco Domtar, Fairfax Financial, Mitel, TD Bank
China	China Eastern Airlines, China Life Insurance, Huaneng Power, PetroChina, China Mobile
Finland	Nokia Corp.
France	Alcatel-Lucent, Technicolor, France Telecom, Sanofi-Aventis, Total FinaElf
Germany	Deutsche Bank, SAP, Siemens
India	ICICI Bank, Tata Communications, Wipro
Italy	ENI, Luxottica, Natuzzi, Telecom Italia
Japan	Canon, Honda Motor, Hitachi, Kubota, Kyocera, NTT Docomo, Sony, Panasonic
Korea	Korea Electric Power, Korea Telecom, Pohang Iron & Steel, SK Telecom
Mexico	Cemex, Empresas ICA, Grupo Televisa, Telefonos de Mexico
Netherlands	Aegon, Arcelor Mittal, Reed Elsevier, Unilever, CNH Global, ING
South Africa	ASA, Anglo Gold Ashanti, Sasol
Spain	Banco Santander, Repsol
Switzerland	ABB, Novartis, UBS
United Kingdom	Barclays, BP, BT Group, Diageo, GlaxoSmithKline, Lloyds, Prudential, Royal Bank of Scotland, Vodafone

Source: Datastream.

EXHIBIT 16.9

Foreign Firms Listed
on the London Stock
Exchange (selected)

Country	Firms
Australia	Allied Gold, Medusa Mining, Platinum Australia, Range Resources
Canada	Antrim Energy, Canadian Pacific Railway, Greystar Resources, Ondine Biopharma, Turbo Power Systems, Western Coal
China	Air China, China Petroleum & Chemical, Datang Intl Power Generation, Zhejiang Expressway
Czech Republic	Komercni Banka, Telefonica O2 Czech Republic
Egypt	Commercial Intl Bank, Suez Cement, Telecom Egypt
France	Compagnie de St-Gobain, Groupe Eurotunnel, Total FinaElf
Germany	BASF, Deutsche Bank, Siemens, Volkswagen
India	Lloyd Electric & Engineering, Reliance Infrastructure, State Bank of India, Tata Motors
Ireland	Abbey Plc, Aer Lingus Group Plc, Bank of Ireland, Ryanair Hldgs
Israel	Bank Hapoalim, Dori Media Group, Metal-Tech
Japan	Fujitsu, Nippon Tel & Tel, Sony, Toyota Motor
Korea	Hyundai Motor, LG Electronics, Posco, Samsung Electronics
Netherlands	Aegon, European Assets Trust, New World Resources
Poland	Bank Pekao, Polski Koncern Naftowy Orlen, Telekomunikacja Polska
Russia	Gazprom, Lukoil, Severstal, Rosneft
Taiwan	Acer, Evergreen Marine, Hon Hai Precision Industry
Turkey	Turk Ekonomi Bankasi, Turkiye Petrol Rafinerileri, Uzel Makina Sanayi
United States	Abbott Laboratories, Bank of America, Boeing, Caterpillar, Dow Chemical, Ford Motor, General Electric, IBM, Pfizer, Verizon Communications

Source: London Stock Exchange.

3. Cross-listing can enhance the liquidity of the company's stock.

4. Cross-listing enhances the visibility of the company's name and its products in foreign marketplaces.

5. Cross-listed shares may be used as the "acquisition currency" for taking over foreign companies.

6. Cross-listing may improve the company's corporate governance and transparency.

The last point deserves detailed discussion here. Consider a company domiciled in a country where shareholders' rights are not well protected, and controlling shareholders (e.g., founding families and large shareholders) derive substantial private benefits, such as perks, inflated salaries, bonuses and even thefts, from controlling the company. Once the company cross-lists its shares on the New York Stock Exchange (NYSE), London Stock Exchange (LSE) or other foreign exchanges that impose stringent disclosure and listing requirements, controlling shareholders may not be able to continue to divert company resources to their private benefit. As argued by Doidge, Karolyi and Stulz (2001), in spite of the "inconveniences" associated with a greater public scrutiny and enhanced transparency, controlling shareholders may choose to cross-list the company shares overseas, as it

EXHIBIT 16.10

Foreign Firms Listed
on the Toronto Stock
Exchange, TSX and
TSXV (selected)

Country	Firms
Argentina	Estrella International Energy, Lithium Americas, Minsud Resources
Australia	Aurora Oil & Gas, Azimuth Resources, Chalice Gold, Coalspur Mines, Ivanhoe *and* 30 others
Brazil	MBAC Fertilizer, Rio Novo Gold, Talon Metals, Verde Potash, HRT Participações em Petróleo
China	Bouyan Construction, China Gold, GLG Life, Hanwei Energy, Silvercorp Metals *and* 39 others
Colombia	Ecopetrol, Gran Colombia Gold, Pacific Rubiales Energy, Petrominerales, PetroNova
France	Foraco International, Inovalis Real Estate
Ghana	Geodrill
Nigeria	Oando Energy
South Africa	Delrand Resources, Platinum Group, Rockwell Diamonds, Witwatersrand Gold
United Kingdom	Amara Mining, Anglo-Pacific, Arian Silver, Aureus Mining, Centamin, Gabriel Resources, Serabi Gold *and* 13 others
Tanzania	Orca Exploration Group
United States	Atlantic Power, General Motors, Royal Gold, Silver Bull Resources, Tahoe Resources, Thompson Creek Metals *and* 175 others

Source: Toronto Stock Exchange.

can be ultimately in their best interest to bond themselves to "good behaviour" and to be able to raise funds to undertake profitable investment projects (thereby increasing share prices). This implies that if a foreign company does not need to raise capital, it may choose not to pursue US listings, so that controlling shareholders can continue to extract private benefits from the company. The aforementioned study shows that, other things being equal, those foreign companies listed on US exchanges are valued nearly 17 percent higher, on average, than those that are not, reflecting investors' recognition of the enhanced corporate governance associated with US listings. Since the London Stock Exchange also imposes stringent disclosure and listing requirements, foreign firms cross-listed on the exchange may also experience positive revaluation due to the effect of enhanced corporate governance.[4]

A study by Lang, Lins and Miller (2003) shows that cross-listing can enhance firm value through improving the firm's overall information environments. Specifically, they show that foreign firms that cross-list in US exchanges enjoy greater analyst coverage and increased forecast accuracy for firms' future earnings relative to those firms not cross-listed. They further show that firms that have greater analyst coverage and higher forecasting accuracy have a higher valuation, other things equal. These findings are consistent with these of other studies that cross-listed firms generally enjoy a lower cost of capital and better corporate governance.

---

[4]As Dahya, McConnell and Travlos (2002) point out, the standard of corporate governance has been raised significantly in the United Kingdom since the "Cadbury Committee" issued the *Code of Best Practice* in 1992, recommending that corporate boards include at least three outside directors and that the positions of chairman and CEO be held by different individuals.

Despite these potential benefits, not every company seeks overseas listings because of the costs:

1. It can be costly to meet the disclosure and listing requirements imposed by the foreign exchange and regulatory authorities.
2. Controlling insiders may find it difficult to continue to derive private benefits once the company is cross-listed on foreign exchanges.
3. Once a company's stock is traded in overseas markets, there can be volatility spillover from those markets.
4. Once a company's stock is made available to foreigners, they might acquire a controlling interest and challenge the domestic control of the company.

According to various surveys, disclosure requirements appear to be the most significant barrier to overseas listings. For example, adaptation to US accounting rules, which is required by the US Securities and Exchange Commission (SEC), is found to be the most onerous barrier facing foreign companies that consider NYSE listings. According to a German survey conducted by Glaum and Mandler (1996), one-third of the German sample firms are, in principle, interested in US listings but view the required adaptation of financial statements to the US generally accepted accounting principles (US-GAAP) as a major obstacle. Daimler, a German firm listed on the NYSE, employs US-GAAP as well as German accounting law and publishes two versions of consolidated financial statements with different reported earnings.[5] As can be seen from Exhibit 16.11, the company's net earnings were positive by German accounting rules but negative by American rules in 1993 and 1994. In the light of the costs and benefits of overseas listings, a foreign listing should be viewed as an investment project to be undertaken if it is judged to have a positive net present value (NPV) and thus adds to the firm's value.

EXHIBIT 16.11

Daimler's Net Profit/
Loss (DM bn):
German vs. American
Accounting Rules

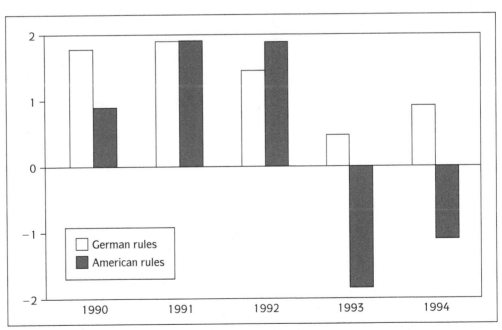

Source: *The Economist,* 20 May 1995.

---

[5]Unlike Canadian and US accounting rules, German accounting rules are driven by tax considerations and creditor protection. For this reason, prudence, not a true and fair view, is the dominant accounting principle. German managers are granted broad discretion in accounting policy, and they try to achieve income smoothing.

In an extensive survey of the academic literature on the corporate decision to cross-list shares, Karolyi (1996) reports, among other things, that (1) the share price reacts favourably to cross-border listings, (2) the total postlisting trading volume increases on average, and, for many issues, home-market trading volume also increases, (3) liquidity of trading in shares improves overall, (4) the stock's exposure to domestic market risk is significantly reduced and is associated with only a small increase in global market risk, (5) cross-border listings resulted in a net reduction in the cost of equity capital of 114 basis points on average and (6) stringent disclosure requirements are the greatest impediment to cross-border listings. A detailed study by Miller (1999) confirms that dual listing can mitigate barriers to international capital flows, resulting in a higher stock price and a lower cost of capital. Considering these findings, cross-border listings of stocks seem to have been, on average, positive NPV projects.

Supplementary Material

16.6   CAPITAL ASSET PRICING UNDER CROSS-LISTINGS

To fully understand the effects of international cross-listings, it is necessary to understand how assets will be priced under the alternative capital market regimes. In this section, we discuss an **International Asset Pricing Model (IAPM)** in a world in which some assets are internationally tradable while others are not. For ease of discussion, we will assume that cross-listed assets are **internationally tradable assets** while all other assets are **internationally nontradable assets**.

It is useful for our purpose to recalibrate the CAPM formula. Noting the definition of beta, the CAPM Equation 16.2 can be restated as

$$\bar{R}_i = R_f + [(\bar{R}_M - R_f)/\text{Var}(R_M)]\text{Cov}(R_i, R_M) \tag{16.4}$$

For our purposes it is best to define $[(\bar{R}_M - R_f)/\text{Var}(R_M)]$ as equal to $A^M M$, where A^M is a **measure of aggregate risk aversion** of all investors and M is the aggregate market value of the market portfolio. With these definitions, Equation 16.4 can be restated as

$$\bar{R}_i = R_f + A^M M \text{Cov}(R_i, R_M) \tag{16.5}$$

Equation 16.4 indicates that, given investors' aggregate risk-aversion measure, the expected rate of return on an asset increases as the asset's covariance with the market portfolio increases.

Before we introduce the IAPM with cross-listing, however, let us first discuss the asset pricing mechanism under complete segmentation and integration as benchmark cases. Suppose that there are two countries in the world, the domestic country and the foreign country. In a **completely segmented capital market** where no assets are internationally tradable, they will be priced according to their respective

country systematic risk. For domestic country assets, the expected asset return is calculated as

$$\bar{R}_i = R_f + A^D D \text{Cov}(R_i, R_D) \tag{16.6}$$

and for foreign country assets, the expected asset return is calculated as:

$$\bar{R}_g = R_f + A^F F \text{Cov}(R_g, R_F) \tag{16.7}$$

where $\bar{R}(\bar{R}_g)$ is the current equilibrium expected return on the ith (gth) domestic (foreign) asset, R_f is the risk-free rate of return that is assumed to be common to both domestic and foreign countries, $A^D(A^F)$ denotes the risk-aversion measure of domestic (foreign) investors, $D(F)$ denotes the aggregate market value of all domestic (foreign) securities, and $\text{Cov}(R_i, R_D)[\text{Cov}(R_g, R_F)]$ denotes the covariance between the future returns on the ith (gth) asset and returns on the **domestic (foreign) country market portfolio**.

By comparison, in **fully integrated world capital markets** where all assets are internationally tradable, each asset will be priced according to the **world systematic risk**. For both domestic and foreign country assets:

$$\bar{R}_i = R_f + A^W W \text{Cov}(R_i, R_W) \tag{16.8}$$

where A^W is the aggregate risk-aversion measure of world investors, W is the aggregate market value of the **world market portfolio** that comprises both the domestic and foreign portfolios, and $\text{Cov}(R_i, R_W)$ denotes the covariance between the future returns of the ith security and the world market portfolio.

As we will see shortly, the asset pricing relationship becomes more complicated in **partially integrated world financial markets** where some assets are internationally tradable (i.e., those that are cross-listed), while others are nontradable.

To tell the conclusion first, internationally tradable assets will be priced *as if* world financial markets were completely integrated. Regardless of the nationality, a tradable asset will be priced solely according to its world systematic risk as described in Equation 16.7. Nontradable assets, on the other hand, will be priced according to a world systematic risk, reflecting the spillover effect generated by the traded assets, as well as a country-specific systematic risk. Due to the **pricing spillover effect**, nontradable assets will *not* be priced as if world financial markets were completely segmented.

For nontradable assets of the domestic country, the pricing relationship is given by

$$\bar{R}_i = R_f + A^W W \text{Cov}^*(R_i, R_W) + \\ A^D D[\text{Cov}(R_i, R_D) - \text{Cov}^*(R_i, R_D)] \qquad (16.9)$$

where $\text{Cov}^*(R_i, R_D)$ is the *indirect* covariance between the future returns on the ith nontradable asset and the domestic country's market portfolio that is induced by tradable assets. Formally,

$$\text{Cov}^*(R_i, R_D) = \sigma_i \sigma_D \rho_{iT} \rho_{TD} \qquad (16.10)$$

Where σ_i and σ_D are, respectively, the standard deviations of returns of the ith asset and the domestic country's market portfolio; ρ_{iT} is the correlation coefficient between the ith nontradable asset and portfolio T of tradable assets, and ρ_{TD} is the correlation coefficient between the returns of portfolio T and the domestic country's market portfolio. Similarly, $\text{Cov}^*(R_i, R_W)$ is the *indirect* covariance between the ith nontradable asset and the world market portfolio. Nontradable assets of the foreign country will be priced in an analogous manner; thus, it is necessary to concentrate only on the pricing of nontradable assets in the domestic country.

Equation 16.9 indicates that nontradable assets are priced according to: (1) the **indirect world systematic risk**, $\text{Cov}^*(R_i, R_W)$, and (2) the *pure* domestic systematic risk, $\text{Cov}(R_i, R_D) - \text{Cov}^*(R_i, R_D)$, which is the domestic systematic risk, net of the part induced by tradable assets. Despite the fact that nontradable assets are traded only within the domestic country, they are priced according to an indirect world systematic risk as well as a country-specific systematic risk. This partial international pricing of nontradable assets is due to the pricing spillover effect generated by tradable assets.

Although nontradable assets are exclusively held by domestic (local) investors, they are priced partially internationally, reflecting the spillover effect generated by tradable assets. As can be inferred from Equation 16.9, nontradable assets will not be subject to the spillover effect and, thus, be priced solely domestically only if they are not correlated at all to tradable assets. This, of course, is not a likely scenario. The pricing model also implies that if the domestic and foreign market portfolios can be exactly replicated using tradable assets, all nontradable as well as tradable assets will be priced fully internationally as if world financial markets were completely integrated.

The IAPM has a few interesting implications. First, international listing (trading) of assets in otherwise segmented markets directly integrates international capital markets by making these assets tradable. Second, firms with nontradable assets essentially get a **free ride** with firms with tradable assets in the sense that the former indirectly benefit from international integration in terms of a lower cost of capital and higher asset prices, without incurring any associated costs. Appendix 16A makes this point clear using numerical simulations.

The asset pricing model with nontraded assets demonstrates that the benefits from partial integration of capital markets can be transmitted to the entire economy through the pricing spillover effect. The pricing spillover effect has an important policy implication: *To maximize the benefits from partial integration of capital markets, a country should choose to internationally cross-list those assets that are most highly correlated with the domestic market portfolio.*

Consistently with the theoretical analyses presented above, many firms have indeed experienced a reduction in the cost of capital when their shares were listed on foreign markets. In their study of foreign shares listed on US stock exchanges, Alexander, Eun and Janakiramanan (1988) found that foreign firms from such countries as Australia and Japan experienced a substantial reduction in the cost of capital. Canadian firms, in contrast, experienced a rather modest reduction in the cost of capital upon US listing, probably because Canadian markets were more integrated with US markets than with other markets when US listing took place.

16.7   THE EFFECT OF FOREIGN EQUITY OWNERSHIP RESTRICTIONS

While companies have incentives to internationalize their ownership structure to lower the cost of capital and increase their market values, they may be concerned, at the same time, with possible loss of corporate control to foreigners. Consequently, governments in both the developed and the developing countries often impose restrictions on the maximum percentage ownership of local firms by foreigners. In such countries as India, Mexico and Thailand, foreigners are

EXHIBIT 16.12

Restrictions on
Equity Ownership
by Foreigners:
Historical Examples

Country	Restrictions on Foreigners
Australia	10% in banks, 20% in broadcasting, and 50% in new mining ventures.
Canada	20% in broadcasting, and 25% in bank/insurance companies.
China	Foreigners are restricted to B shares; only locals are eligible for A shares.
France	Limited to 20%.
India	Limited to 49%.
Indonesia	Limited to 49%.
Mexico	Limited to 49%.
Japan	Maximum of 25–50% for several major firms; acquisition of over 10% of a single firm subject to approval of the Ministry of Finance.
Korea	Limited to 20%.
Malaysia	20% in banks and 30% in natural resources.
Norway	0% in pulp, paper, and mining, 10% in banks, 20% in industrial and oil shares, and 50% in shipping companies.
Spain	0% in defence industries and mass media. Limited to 50% for other firms.
Sweden	20% of voting shares and 40% of total equity capital.
Switzerland	Foreigners can be restricted to bearer shares.
UK	Government retains the veto power over any foreign takeover of British firms.

Source: Various publications of Price Waterhouse.

allowed to purchase no more than 49 percent of the outstanding shares of local firms. These countries want to make sure that foreigners do not acquire majority stakes in local companies. France and Sweden once imposed an even tighter restriction of 20 percent. In Korea, foreigners were allowed to own only 20 percent of the shares of any local firm until recently.

In Switzerland, a local firm can issue two different classes of equity shares, bearer shares and registered shares. Foreigners are often allowed to purchase only bearer shares. In a similar vein, Chinese firms issue A shares and B shares, and foreigners are allowed to hold only B shares. Exhibit 16.12 lists examples of historical restrictions on foreign ownership of local firms for various countries. Obviously, these restrictions are imposed as a means of ensuring domestic control of local firms, especially those considered strategically important to national interests.[6]

Pricing-to-Market Phenomenon

Suppose that foreigners, if allowed, would like to buy 30 percent of a Korean firm, but they are constrained to purchase at most 20 percent due to ownership constraints imposed on foreigners. Because the constraint is effective in limiting desired foreign ownership, foreign and domestic investors may face different market share prices. In other words, shares can exhibit a dual pricing or **pricing-to-market (PTM) phenomenon** due to legal restrictions imposed on foreigners.

---

[6]Stulz and Wasserfallen (1995) suggest a theoretical possibility that firms may impose restrictions on foreigners' equity ownership to maximize their market values. They argue that when domestic and foreign investors have differential demand functions for a firm's shares, the firm can maximize its market value by discriminating between domestic and foreign investors.

Illustrated **Mini Case**

Nestlé

The majority of publicly traded Swiss corporations have up to three classes of common shares: (1) registered shares, (2) voting bearer shares and (3) nonvoting bearer shares. Until recently, foreigners were not allowed to buy registered shares; they were only allowed to buy bearer shares. Registered shares were made available only to Swiss nationals.

In the case of Nestlé, a well-known Swiss multinational corporation that derives more than 95 percent of its revenue from overseas markets, registered shares accounted for about 68 percent of the votes outstanding. This implies that it was practically impossible for foreigners to gain control of the firm. On 17 November 1988, however, Nestlé announced that the firm would lift the ban on foreigners buying registered shares. The announcement was made after the Zurich Stock Exchange closed.

Nestlé's board of directors mentioned two reasons for lifting the ban. First, despite the highly multinational nature of its business activities, Nestlé maintained a highly nationalistic ownership structure. At the same time, Nestlé made high-profile cross-border acquisitions, such as Rowntree (the United Kingdom) and Carnation (the United States). Nestlé's practices, thus, were criticized as unfair and incompatible with free-market principles. The firm needed to remedy this situation. Second, Nestlé realized that the ban against foreigners holding registered shares had the effect of increasing its cost of capital, negatively affecting its competitive position in the world market.

As Exhibit 16.13 illustrates, prior to the lifting of the ban on foreigners, (voting) bearer shares traded at about twice the price of registered shares. The higher price for bearer shares suggests that foreigners desired to hold more than they were allowed to in the absence of ownership restrictions imposed on them. When the ban was lifted, however, prices of the two types of shares immediately converged; the price of bearer shares declined by about 25 percent, whereas that of registered shares increased by about 35 percent. Because registered shares represented about two-thirds of the total number of voting shares, the total market value of Nestlé increased substantially when it fully internationalized its ownership structure. This, of course, means that Nestlé's cost of equity capital declined substantially.

www.nestle.com

The homepage of Nestlé provides basic information about the company.

EXHIBIT 16.13

Price Spread between Bearer and Registered Shares of Nestlé

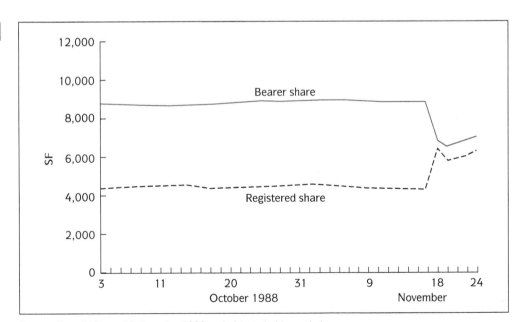

Source: *Financial Times,* 26 November 1988, p. 1. Adapted with permission.

Hietala (1989) documented the PTM phenomenon in the Finnish stock market. Finnish firms used to issue restricted and unrestricted shares, with foreigners allowed to purchase only unrestricted shares. Unrestricted shares accounted for at most 20 percent of the total number of shares of any Finnish firm. Because of this legal restriction, if foreigners desired to hold more than 20 percent of a Finnish firm, dual pricing could result. Indeed, Hietala found that most Finnish firms exhibited the PTM phenomenon, with unrestricted shares trading at roughly a 15–40 percent premium relative to restricted shares. Recently, Finland completely abolished restrictions imposed on foreigners.

Supplementary Material

Asset Pricing under Foreign Ownership Restrictions

In this section, we formally investigate how equilibrium asset prices are determined when foreigners are subject to ownership restrictions on the maximum proportionate ownership of domestic firms. As before, we assume that there are two countries in the world, the domestic country and the foreign country. For simplicity, we assume that the foreign country imposes an ownership constraint on investors from the domestic country but that the domestic country does not impose any constraints on investors from the foreign country. Consequently, domestic country investors are restricted to holding at most a certain percentage of the shares of any foreign firms, whereas foreign country investors are not restricted in any way from investing in the domestic country.

Since we assume that there are no investment restrictions on domestic shares, both domestic and foreign country investors face the same price for the same domestic asset, which equals the perfect capital market price. As far as domestic assets are concerned, the law of one price prevails. For foreign shares, however, the PTM phenomenon applies.

Specifically, domestic country assets will be priced according to Equation 16.8, the fully integrated world capital market's IAPM. Foreign shares will be priced differently, depending upon whether the investor is from the foreign or domestic country. Investors from the domestic country will pay a premium above and beyond the *perfect market price* that would prevail in the absence of restrictions, whereas investors from the foreign country will receive a discount from the perfect market price. This implies that the domestic country investors would require a lower return on foreign country shares than the foreign country investors.

Eun and Janakiramanan (1986) offer the following solutions for the equilibrium rates of return for foreign asset *i* from the domestic and the foreign country investors' perspectives, respectively:

$$\bar{R}_i^d = R_f + A^w W \text{Cov}(R_i, R_w) - (A^w W - \delta A^D D)[\text{Cov}(R_i, R_F) - \text{Cov}(R_i, R_s)] \qquad (16.11)$$

$$\bar{R}_i^f = R_f + A^w W \text{Cov}(R_i, R_w) + [(1 - \delta)A^D D - A^w W] [\text{Cov}(R_i, R_F) - \text{Cov}(R_i, R_S)] \qquad (16.12)$$

where δ represents the fraction of the *i*th foreign firm that domestic country investors as a whole are allowed to own. In the above equations, portfolio S refers to the **substitution portfolio**, which is the portfolio of domestic country assets that is most highly correlated with the foreign market portfolio F. Portfolio S can thus be regarded as the domestic country investors' best *home-made* substitute for the foreign market portfolio F.

According to the above model, the equilibrium rates of return depend critically on (1) the severity of the ownership constraint (δ) and (2) the ability of domestic country investors to replicate the foreign market portfolio using their domestic assets, which is measured by the **pure foreign market risk**, $\text{Cov}(R_i, R_F) - \text{Cov}(R_i, R_S)$. In the special case where portfolio S is a perfect substitute for the foreign market portfolio F, we have $\text{Cov}(R_i, R_F) = \text{Cov}(R_i, R_S)$. In this event, the foreign asset will be priced as if world capital markets are fully integrated from both the domestic and foreign investors' perspectives, even though an ownership constraint is in force. In general, however, domestic country investors will pay premiums for foreign assets (i.e., accept a lower rate of return than the perfect capital market rate) to the extent that they cannot precisely replicate the foreign market portfolio using domestic assets. Foreign country investors, on the other hand, will get a discount (i.e., receive a higher rate than the perfect capital market rate).

Example 16.2 *A Numerical Illustration*

To illustrate the effect of foreign ownership restrictions on the firm's cost of equity capital, we conduct a numerical simulation using the model economy described in Exhibit 16.14.

Exhibit 16.14 provides the standard deviations and correlation matrix of our model economy. Firms D1 to D4 belong to the domestic country and firms F1 to F4 belong to the foreign country. For simplicity, the correlation matrix reflects the stylized fact that asset returns are typically less correlated between countries than within a country; the pairwise correlation is uniformly assumed to be 0.50 within a country and 0.15 between countries. Both domestic and foreign investors are assumed to have the same aggregate risk-aversion measure, and the risk-free rate is assumed to be 9 percent.

Exhibit 16.15 considers the case in which the foreign country imposes a 20-percent ownership constraint ($\delta_F = 20$ percent), whereas the domestic country does not impose any constraint on foreign investors. In this case, domestic country assets are priced as if the capital markets were completely integrated. Foreign country assets, however, are priced to market.

EXHIBIT 16.14   Description of the Model Economy

Firm	Expected Future Share Price ($)	Standard Deviation of Share Price ($)	Correlation Matrix						
			D2	D3	D4	F1	F2	F3	F4
D1	100	16	0.50	0.50	0.50	0.15	0.15	0.15	0.15
D2	100	20		0.50	0.50	0.15	0.15	0.15	0.15
D3	100	24			0.50	0.15	0.15	0.15	0.15
D4	100	28				0.15	0.15	0.15	0.15
F1	100	18					0.50	0.50	0.50
F2	100	22						0.50	0.50
F3	100	26							0.50
F4	100	30							

Note: Firms D1 to D4 are from the domestic country; firms F1 to F4 are from the foreign country. The risk-free interest rate is assumed to be 9 percent. The domestic and foreign country investors are assumed to have the same aggregate (absolute) risk-aversion measure.

EXHIBIT 16.15

International Capital Market Equilibria: The Effect of Foreign Equity Ownership Restrictions

Asset	Complete Segmentation	σ-Constraint		Complete Integration
		$\delta_D = 20\%$ $\delta_F = 20\%$	$\delta_F = 20\%$	
A. Equilibrium Asset Prices ($)[a]				
D1	81.57	83.04/87.45	85.25	85.25
D2	78.53	80.45/86.22	83.34	83.34
D3	75.30	77.75/85.07	81.41	81.41
D4	71.88	74.86/83.82	79.34	79.34
F1	79.19	86.91/81.12	87.86/80.16	84.01
F2	75.87	85.66/78.31	86.87/77.11	81.99
F3	72.34	84.50/75.38	85.92/73.96	79.94
F4	68.62	83.24/72.28	84.90/70.62	77.76
B. Cost of Equity Capital (%)				
D1	22.59	19.15	17.30	17.30
D2	27.34	22.54	19.99	19.99
D3	32.80	26.24	22.84	22.84
D4	39.12	30.46	26.04	26.04
F1	26.28	21.54	22.40	19.03
F2	31.80	25.34	26.48	21.97
F3	38.24	39.96	32.82	25.09
F4	45.73	47.95	38.85	28.60

[a]The two figures indicate the asset prices for domestic/foreign country investors, respectively.

In general, the exhibit shows that the firm's cost of capital tends to be higher under the 20 percent ownership constraint than under complete integration. This implies that restricting foreign equity ownership in a firm will have a negative effect on the firm's cost of equity capital. For comparison purposes, we again provide the results obtained under complete segmentation and integration. Specifically, consider foreign firm F1. The exhibit shows that with the 20 percent ownership constraint, the firm's cost of capital is 22.40 percent, which is computed as a weighted average of the required returns by the domestic and foreign country investors in F1. Note that in the absence of the restriction, the firm's cost of capital would have been substantially lower, 19.03 percent. It is also noteworthy that when the PTM phenomenon prevails, the firm's cost of capital depends on which investors, domestic or foreign, supply capital. The exhibit also provides the case where both the domestic and foreign countries impose restrictions at the 20 percent level, that is, $\delta_D = 20$ percent and $\delta_F = 20$ percent. Interpretation of this case is left to the readers.

16.8   THE FINANCIAL STRUCTURE OF SUBSIDIARIES

A problem faced by financial managers of multinational corporations is how to determine the financial structure of foreign subsidiaries. There are essentially three different approaches to determining the subsidiary's financial structure:

1. Conform to the parent company's norm.
2. Conform to the local norm of the country where the subsidiary operates.
3. Vary judiciously to capitalize on opportunities to lower taxes, reduce financing costs and risks, and take advantage of various market imperfections.

Which approach to take depends largely on the extent to which the parent company is responsible for the subsidiary's financial obligations. When the parent is fully responsible for the subsidiary's obligations, the independent financial structure of the subsidiary is irrelevant; it is the parent's overall financial structure that is relevant. When the parent is legally responsible for the subsidiary's debts, potential creditors examine the parent's overall financial conditions, not the subsidiary's.

When, however, the parent company is willing to let its subsidiary default, or the parent's guarantee of its subsidiary's financial obligations becomes difficult to enforce across national borders, the subsidiary's financial structure becomes relevant. In this case, potential creditors will examine the subsidiary's financial conditions closely to assess default risk. As a result, the subsidiary should choose its own financial structure to reduce default risk and, thus, financing costs.

In reality, the parent company cannot let its subsidiary default on its debts without expecting its worldwide operations to be hampered in one way or another. Default by a subsidiary can deplete the parent's reputational capital, possibly increase its own cost of capital and certainly make it difficult to undertake future projects in the country where default occurred. Various surveys suggest that parent firms of MNCs indeed will not allow their subsidiaries to default regardless of circumstances.

An immediate implication of the parent's legal and moral obligation to honour its subsidiary's debts is that the parent should monitor its subsidiary's financial conditions closely and make sure that the firm's overall financial conditions are not adversely affected by the subsidiary's financial structure. What really matters is the marginal impact that the subsidiary's financial structure may have on the parent's worldwide financial structure. The subsidiary's financial structure should be chosen so that the parent's overall cost of capital can be minimized.

In the light of the above discussion, neither the first nor the second approach to determining the subsidiary's financial structure can be deemed appropriate. The first approach, which calls for replicating the parent's financial structure, is not necessarily consistent with minimizing the parent's overall cost of capital. Suppose the subsidiary can locally borrow at a subsidized interest rate because the host government is eager to attract foreign investments. In this situation, the subsidiary should borrow locally and exploit the lower interest rate, even if this means that the subsidiary's debt ratio will exceed the parent's norm. If deemed necessary, the parent can simply lower its own debt ratio. In other words, the distribution of debt between the parent and the subsidiary can be adjusted to take advantage of the subsidized loans. Also, in a special case where the subsidiary is operating in a country that regulates its financial structure, it would be difficult to replicate the parent's norm even if that were desirable.

The second approach calls for adopting the local financing norm. In essence, the approach is based on "When in Rome, do as the Romans do." By following the local norm, the firm can reduce the chance of being singled out for criticism. This approach makes sense only when the parent is not responsible for the subsidiary's obligations and the subsidiary has to depend on local financing due to, say, segmentation of financial markets. Otherwise, it does not make much sense. Suppose each foreign subsidiary conforms to the local financing norm, which reflects the host country's cultural, economic and institutional environments. Then the parent firm's worldwide financial structure will be determined strictly in a "residual" manner. The overall financial structure so determined is not likely to be the optimal one that minimizes the parent's overall cost of capital. When the host country's norm reflects, for example, the immature nature of local financial markets, a subsidiary of the MNC with ready access to global financial markets should not slavishly follow the local norm. Doing so means that the MNC gives up its advantage in terms of a lower cost of capital.

This brings us to the third approach, which appears to be the most reasonable and consistent with the goal of minimizing the firm's overall cost of capital. The subsidiary should take advantage of subsidized loans as much as possible whenever available. It should also take advantage of tax deductions of interest payments by borrowing more heavily than is implied by the parent's norm when the corporate income tax rate is higher in the host country than in the home country, unless foreign tax credits are useful.

Apart from the tax factor, political risk is another factor that should be considered in choosing the method of financing the subsidiary. Political risk generally favours local financing over the parent's direct financing. The parent company can renounce the subsidiary's local debt in the event that the subsidiary's assets are expropriated. When the subsidiary is financed by local creditors and shareholders, the chance of expropriation itself can be lowered. When a subsidiary is operating in a developing country, financing from such international development agencies as the World Bank and International Finance Corporation will lower political risk. When the choice is between external debt and equity financing, political risk tends to favour the former. This is the case because the host government tolerates repatriation of funds in the form of interest much better than dividends.

To summarize, since the parent company is responsible, legally and/or morally, for its subsidiary's financial obligations, it has to decide the subsidiary's financial structure considering the latter's effect on the parent's overall financial structure. The subsidiary, however, should be allowed to take advantage of any favourable financing opportunities available in the host country because that is consistent with the goal of minimizing the overall cost of capital of the parent. If necessary, the parent can adjust its own financial structure to bring about the optimal overall financial structure.

SUMMARY

In this chapter, we discuss the cost of capital for a multinational firm. Reflecting the trend toward more liberalized and deregulated financial markets, major corporations of the world are internationalizing their capital structure by allowing foreigners to hold their shares and debts.

1. International comparison of the cost of funds indicates that while the costs of funds are converging among major countries in recent years, international financial markets are less than fully integrated. This suggests that firms can increase their market values by judiciously raising capital overseas.

2. When a firm is operating in a segmented capital market, it can reduce the negative effects by cross-listing its shares on foreign stock markets, thereby making the shares internationally tradable.

3. A firm can benefit from international cross-listings in terms of (a) a lower cost of capital and a higher share price and (b) access to new sources of capital.

4. When a firm's shares are cross-listed on foreign exchanges in an otherwise segmented capital market, the shares will be priced according to the world systematic risk as if international capital markets were fully integrated. Internationally nontradable assets will be priced according to a country-specific systematic risk and an indirect world systematic risk, reflecting the pricing spillover effect generated by internationally tradable assets.

5. Although the trend is toward more liberal world financial markets, many countries still maintain restrictions on investment by foreigners, especially the maximum percentage ownership of a local firm by foreigners. Under an ownership constraint, foreign and domestic country investors may face different share prices, resulting in the pricing-to-market (PTM) phenomenon. PTM generally raises the firm's overall cost of capital.

6. The parent company should decide the financing method for its own subsidiary with a view to minimizing the parent's overall cost of capital. To the extent that the parent is responsible for its subsidiary's financial obligations, the subsidiary's own financial structure is irrelevant.

QUESTIONS

1. Suppose that your firm is operating in a segmented capital market. What actions would you recommend to mitigate the negative effects?

2. Explain why and how a firm's cost of capital may decrease when the firm's shares are cross-listed on foreign stock exchanges.

3. Explain the pricing *spillover effect*.

4. In what sense do firms with non-tradable assets get a *free ride* from firms whose securities are internationally tradable?

5. Define and discuss *indirect world systematic risk*.

6. Discuss how the cost of capital is determined in segmented versus integrated capital markets.

7. Suppose there exists a nontradable asset with a perfect positive correlation with a portfolio *T* of tradable assets. How will the nontradable asset be priced?

8. Discuss what factors motivated Novo Industri to seek American listing of its shares. What lessons can be derived from Novo's experiences?

9. Discuss foreign equity ownership restrictions. Why do you think countries impose these restrictions?

10. Explain the *pricing-to-market phenomenon*.

11. Explain how the premium and discount are determined when assets are priced to market. When would the law of one price prevail in international capital markets even if foreign equity ownership restrictions are imposed?

12. Under what conditions will the foreign subsidiary's financial structure become relevant?

13. Under what conditions would you recommend that the foreign subsidiary conform to the local norm of financial structure?

PROBLEMS

1. Given the following information:

Risk Free Rate	2%
Market Risk Premium	9%
Tax Rate	30%
Cost of Debt	8%
Debt to Equity Ratio	1.5

a. If the company has a beta of 1.2, what is the weighted average cost of capital?

b. If the company has a beta of 0.9, what is the weighted average cost of capital?

2. MW Winery is a Canadian-based company that produces wines in the Niagara Peninsula. The company is planning to gradually expand its current production and needs an additional $60 million in total for the expansion. The firm could go to either the Canadian domestic markets or the US capital markets to find the capital it needs, and the schedules are as follows:

New Capital (Mn)	Domestic		US	
	Cost of Equity	Cost of Debt	Cost of Equity	Cost of Debt
0–20	13%	9%	14%	7%
21–40	17%	12%	16%	10%
41–60	22%	15%	24%	19%

Assuming the company is under the following conditions and restriction:

a. It needs to maintain a debt-to-equity ratio of 1:1

b. It is subject to an income tax rate of 30%

c. It could only finance its debt and equity in blocks of $10 million.

Answer the following questions:

d. What is the lowest marginal cost of capital for each increment of $20 million of new capital?

e. If the company only needs $40 million, how should the expansion be financed? And what is the weighted average cost of capital for the expansion?

Answer problems 3–5 based on the stock market data given by the following table:

	Correlation Coefficients				
	Telmex	Mexico	World	SD(%)	$\bar{R}$(%)
Telmex	1.00	0.90	0.60	18	?
Mexico		1.00	0.75	15	14
World			1.00	10	12

This table provides the correlations among Telmex, a telephone/communication company located in Mexico, the Mexican stock market index and the world market index, together with the standard deviations (SD) of returns and the expected returns ($\bar{R}$). The risk-free rate is 5 percent.

3. Compute the domestic country beta of Telmex as well as its world beta. What do these betas measure?

4. Suppose the Mexican stock market is segmented from the rest of the world. Using the CAPM paradigm, estimate the equity cost of capital of Telmex.

5. Suppose now that Telmex has made its shares tradable internationally via cross-listing on the NYSE. Again using the CAPM paradigm, estimate Telmex's equity cost of capital. Discuss the possible effects of international pricing of Telmex shares on the share prices and the firm's investment decisions.

INTERNET EXERCISE

You are the controlling shareholder of Taiwan-based Dragon Semicon, a company with a strong growth potential. In order to fund future growth, you are considering listing the company shares either on the New York or the London stock exchange. Visit the websites of the two exchanges to compare their listing and disclosure requirements for foreign companies.

REFERENCES & SUGGESTED READINGS

Adler, Michael. "The Cost of Capital and Valuation of a Two-Country Firm." *Journal of Finance* 29 (1974), pp. 119–32.

Alexander, Gordon, Cheol Eun, and S. Janakiramanan. "Asset Pricing and Dual Listing on Foreign Capital Markets: A Note." *Journal of Finance* 42 (1987), pp. 151–58.

———. "International Listings and Stock Returns: Some Empirical Evidence." *Journal of Financial and Quantitative Analysis* 23 (1988), pp. 135–51.

Black, Fisher. "International Capital Market Equilibrium with Investment Barriers." *Journal of Financial Economics* 1 (1974), pp. 337–52.

Carrieri, Francesca, V. Erranza, and K. Hogan. "Characterizing World Market Integration through Time." *Journal of Financial and Quantitative Analysis*, Volume 42, Issue 4 (December 2007), pp. 915–40.

Chan, K. C., Andrew Karolyi and Rene Stulz. "Global Financial Markets and the Risk Premium on U.S. Equity." *Journal of Financial Economics* 32 (1992), pp. 137–67.

Chaplinsky, Susan, and Latha Ramchand. "The Rationale for Global Equity Offerings." University of Virginia working paper, 1995.

Cohn, Richard, and John Pringle. "Imperfections in International Financial Markets: Implications for Risk Premia and the Cost of Capital to Firms." *Journal of Finance* 28 (1973), pp. 59–66.

Dahya, J., J. McConnell and N. Travlos. "The Cadbury Committee, Corporate Performance, and Top Management Turnover." *Journal of Finance* 57 (2002), pp. 461–83.

Doidge, Craig, Andrew Karolyi, and Rene Stulz. "Why Are Foreign Firms Listed in the U.S. Worth More?" *Journal of Financial Economics* 71 (2004).

Errunza, Vihang, and Etienne Losq. "International Asset Pricing under Mild Segmentation: Theory and Test." *Journal of Finance* 40 (1985), pp. 105–24.

Eun, Cheol, and S. Janakiramanan. "A Model of International Asset Pricing with a Constraint on the Foreign Equity Ownership." *Journal of Finance* 41 (1986), pp. 897–914.

Foerster, Stephen, and G. A. Karolyi. "The Effects of Market Segmentation and Investor Recognition on Asset Prices: Evidence from Foreign Stocks Listing in the U.S." *Journal of Finance* 54 (1999), pp. 981–1014.

French, K., and J. Poterba. "Investor Diversification and International Equity Markets." *American Economic Review* 81 (1991), pp. 222–26.

Glaum, Martin, and Udo Mandler. "Global Accounting Harmonization from a German Perspective: Bridging the GAAP." Europa-Universität Viadrina working paper, 1996.

Glaum, Martin, and Udo Maudler. "German Managers' Attitudes toward Anglo-American Accounting: Results from an Empirical Study on Global Accounting Harmonization," *The International Journal of Accounting,* Volume 32, Issue 4 (1997), pp. 463–85.

Hail, Luzi, and Christian Leuz. "International Differences in the Cost of Equity Capital: Do Legal Institutions and Securities Regulation Matter?", *Journal of Accounting Research,* Volume 44, Number 3, June 2006, pp. 485–531.

Harvey, Campbell. "The World Price of Covariance Risk." *Journal of Finance* 46 (1991), pp. 111–57.

Hietala, Pekka. "Asset Pricing in Partially Segmented Markets: Evidence from the Finnish Markets." *Journal of Finance* 44 (1989), pp. 697–718.

Jayaraman, N., K. Shastri and K. Tandon. "The Impact of International Cross Listings on Risk and Return: The Evidence from American Depository Receipts." *Journal of Banking and Finance* 17 (1993), pp. 91–103.

Karolyi, G. Andrew. "What Happens to Stocks That List Shares Abroad? A Survey of the Evidence and Its Managerial Implications." *Financial Markets, Institutions and Instruments* 7 (1998),

Lang, Mark, Karl Lins and Darius Miller. "ADRs, Analysts, and Accuracy: Does Cross Listing in the United States Improve a Firm's Information Environment and Increase Market Value?" *Journal of Accounting Research* 41 (2003), pp. 317–45.

Lau, Sie T., Lilian Ng and Bohui Zhang. "The World Price of Home Bias." *Journal of Financial Economics* 97 (2010), pp. 191–217.

Lee, Kwang Chul, and Chuck C. Y. Kwok. "Multinational Corporations vs. Domestic Corporations: International Environmental Factors and Determinants of Capital Structure." *Journal of International Business Studies* 19 (1988), pp. 195–217.

Lessard, D., and A. Shapiro. "Guidelines for Global Financing Choices." *Midland Corporate Finance Journal* 3 (1984), pp. 68–80.

Loderer, Claudio, and Andreas Jacobs. "The Nestlé Crash." *Journal of Financial Economics* 37 (1995), pp. 315–39.

McCauley, Robert, and Steven Zimmer. "Exchange Rates and International Differences in the Cost of Capital." In Y. Amihud and R. Levich (eds.), *Exchange Rates and Corporate Performance.* Burr Ridge, IL: Irwin, 1994, pp. 119–48.

Miller, Darius. "The Market Reaction to International Cross-Listing: Evidence from Depository Receipts." *Journal of Financial Economics* 51 (1999), pp. 103–23.

Mittoo, Usha. "Additional Evidence on Integration in the Canadian Stock Market." *Journal of Finance* 47 (1992), pp. 2035–54.

Salomon Smith Barney. *A Practical Approach to the International Valuation and Capital Allocation Puzzle.* New York, July 2002.

Stapleton, Richard, and Marti Subrahmanyan. "Market Imperfections, Capital Market Equilibrium and Corporation Finance." *Journal of Finance* 32 (1977), pp. 307–21.

Sarkissian, Sergei, and Michael Schill. "The Overseas Listing Decision: New Evidence of Proximity Preference." *Review of Financial Studies* 17 (2004), pp. 769–809.

Stulz, Rene. "On the Effect of Barriers to International Investment." *Journal of Finance* 36 (1981), pp. 923–34.

———. "Pricing Capital Assets in an International Setting: An Introduction." *Journal of International Business Studies* 16 (1985), pp. 55–74.

———. "The Cost of Capital in Internationally Integrated Markets: The Case of Nestlé." *European Financial Management* 1 (1995), pp. 11–22.

———. "Does the Cost of Capital Differ across Countries? An Agency Perspective." *European Financial Management* 2 (1996), pp. 11–22.

Stulz, Rene, and Walter Wasserfallen. "Foreign Equity Investment Restrictions, Capital Flight, and Shareholder Wealth Maximization: Theory and Evidence." *Review of Financial Studies* 8 (1995), pp. 1019–57.

Appendix 16A

Pricing of Nontradable Assets: Numerical Simulations

To further explain the theoretical results presented in the preceding section, we provide a numerical illustration in which we assume a two-country and eight-firm world as described in Exhibit 16.14 to arrive at the equilibrium share prices and expected rates of return, or costs of equity capital, under the alternative structures of international capital markets.

Exhibit 16A.1 presents the equilibrium asset prices and the costs of equity capital for each of the eight firms as computed according to the asset pricing models presented earlier. Cross-listing domestic asset D1 on the foreign exchange in an otherwise segmented market decreases the equilibrium cost of equity capital from 22.59 percent (under segmentation) to 17.30 percent upon cross-listing. Clearly, international trading of the asset leads to a decrease in the cost of capital.

Once asset D1 is cross-listed, it will be priced (at $85.25) to yield the same expected rate of return that it would obtain under complete integration. Moreover, when the domestic asset is cross-listed, other domestic assets, which remain internationally nontradable, also experience a decrease in their costs of equity capital. Take asset D2 for example; the cost of capital falls from 27.34 percent under segmentation to 23.72 percent after cross-listing asset D1. This reflects the spillover effect generated by asset D1 when it becomes internationally tradable.

Exhibit 16A.1 shows that when foreign asset F1 is cross-listed in the domestic country, it will lower its own cost of equity capital as well as that of the other foreign firms. The exhibit shows that when F1 is cross-listed, its cost of equity capital falls from 26.28 percent to 19.03 percent, the same as if capital markets were completely integrated. Moreover, other foreign assets that remain internationally nontradable also experience a decrease in their costs of capital as a result of the spillover effect from the cross-listing of F1.

EXHIBIT 16A.1 International Capital Market Equilibria: The Effect of Cross-Listings	Asset	Complete Segmentation	Cross-Listing Asset D1	Cross-Listing Assets D1 and F1	Complete Integration
	A. Equilibrium Asset Prices ($)				
	D1	81.57	85.25	85.25	85.25
	D2	78.53	80.83	80.37	83.34
	D3	75.30	78.06	77.51	81.41
	D4	71.88	75.10	74.45	79.34
	F1	79.19	78.57	84.01	84.01
	F2	75.87	75.11	78.36	81.99
	F3	72.34	71.45	75.29	79.94
	F4	68.62	67.59	72.02	77.76
	B. Cost of Equity Capital (%)				
	D1	22.59	17.30	17.30	17.30
	D2	27.34	23.72	24.42	19.99
	D3	32.80	28.11	29.02	22.84
	D4	39.12	33.16	34.32	26.04
	F1	26.28	27.28	19.03	19.03
	F2	31.80	33.14	27.62	21.97
	F3	38.24	39.96	30.97	25.09
	F4	45.73	47.95	36.10	28.60

Chapter 17

International Capital Budgeting

CHAPTER OUTLINE

IN THIS BOOK, we take the view that the fundamental goal of the financial manager is shareholder wealth maximization. Shareholder wealth is created when the firm makes an investment that will return more in a present value sense than the investment costs. Perhaps the most important decisions that confront the financial manager are which capital projects to select. By their very nature, capital projects denote investment in capital assets that build the productive capacity of the firm. These investments, which are typically expensive relative to the firm's overall value, determine how efficiently the firm produces the products it intends to sell and, thus, will also determine how profitable the firm will be. In total, capital expenditure decisions determine the competitive position of the firm and the firm's long-run survival. Consequently, a dependable framework for analysis of capital expenditure is important. The generally accepted methodology in modern finance is the **net present value (NPV)** discounted cash flow model.

In Chapter 15, we explored why a multinational corporation (MNC) would make direct investment in another country. In Chapter 16, we discussed the cost of capital for a multinational firm. We saw that a firm that could source funds internationally, rather than just domestically, could have a lower cost of capital than a domestic firm because of its greater opportunities to raise funds. A lower cost of capital means that more capital projects will have a positive net present value to the multinational firm. Our objective in this chapter is to illustrate a proper method for a multinational firm to analyze an investment in a capital project in a foreign land.

Most readers will already be familiar with NPV analysis and its superiority over other capital expenditure evaluation techniques as a tool for maximizing shareholder wealth. Therefore, the chapter begins with only a brief review of the basic NPV capital budgeting framework. Next, the basic NPV framework is extended to an *adjusted present value (APV)* model. APV extends NPV in ways that are especially well suited to analysis of various cash flows that are unique to international expenditures. The chapter concludes with an illustrated mini case showing how to implement the APV decision framework.

17.1 REVIEW OF CAPITAL BUDGETING

The basic net present value (NPV) capital budgeting equation is

$$\text{NPV} = \sum_{t=1}^{T} \frac{\text{CF}_t}{(1 + K)^t} + \frac{\text{TV}_T}{(1 + K)^T} - C_0 \tag{17.1}$$

where

CF_t = expected after-tax cash flow for year t

TV_T = expected after-tax terminal value, including recapture of working capital

C_0 = initial investment

K = weighted-average cost of capital

T = economic life of the capital project in years

The NPV of a capital project is the present value of all cash inflows, including those at the end of the project's life, minus the present value of all cash outflows. The *NPV rule* is to accept a project if NPV ≥ 0 and to reject it if NPV < 0.[1]

For our purposes, it is necessary to expand the NPV equation. First, however, it is beneficial if we discuss annual cash flows. In capital budgeting, our concern is only with the change in the firm's total cash flows that are attributable to the capital expenditure. CF_t represents the **incremental cash flow** change in total firm cash flow for year t resulting from the capital project. Algebraically, CF_t is defined as

$$\text{CF}_t = (R_t - \text{OC}_t - D_t - I_t)(1 - \tau) + D_t + I_t(1 - \tau) \tag{17.2a}$$
$$= \text{NI}_t + D_t + I_t(1 - \tau) \tag{17.2b}$$
$$= (R_t - \text{OC}_t - D_t)(1 - \tau) + D_t \tag{17.2c}$$
$$= \text{NOI}_t(1 - \tau) + D_t \tag{17.2d}$$
$$= (R_t - \text{OC}_t)(1 - \tau) + \tau D_t \tag{17.2e}$$
$$= \text{OCF}_t(1 - \tau) + \tau D_t \tag{17.2f}$$
$$= \text{nominal after-tax incremental cash flow for year } t$$

Equation 17.2a presents a detailed expression for incremental cash flow that is worth learning so that we can easily apply the model. The equation shows that CF_t is the sum of three flows, or that the cash flow from a capital project goes to three different groups. The first term, as Equation 17.2b shows, is expected income, NI_t, which belongs to the equity holders of the firm. Incremental NI_t is calculated as the after-tax, $(1 - \tau)$, change in the firm's sales revenue, R_t, generated from the project minus the corresponding operating costs, OC_t, project depreciation, D_t, and interest expense, I_t. (As we discuss later in the chapter, we are only concerned with the interest expense that is consistent with the firm's optimal capital structure and the borrowing capacity created by the project.) The second term reflects the fact that depreciation is a *non*cash expense, that is, D_t is removed from the calculation of NI_t only for tax purposes.

---

[1]The internal rate of return (IRR), payback method, and the profitability index are three additional methods for analyzing a capital expenditure. The IRR method solves for the discount rate, that is, the project's IRR, that causes the NPV to equal zero. In many situations, a project will have only a single IRR, and the IRR decision rule is to select the project if the IRR $\geq K$. However, under certain circumstances a project will have multiple IRRs, thus causing difficulty in interpreting the simple decision rule if one or more IRRs are less than K. The payback method determines the period of time required for the cumulative cash inflows to "pay back" the initial cash outlay; the shorter the payback period, the more acceptable the project. However, the payback method ignores the time value of money. The profitability index is computed by dividing the present value of cash inflows by the initial outlay; the larger the ratio, the more acceptable the project, However, when dealing with mutually exclusive projects, a conflict may arise between the profitability index and the NPV criterion due to the scale of the investments. If the firm is not under a capital rationing constraint, it is generally agreed that conflicts should be settled in favour of NPV criterion. Overall, the NPV decision rule is considered the superior framework for analyzing a capital budgeting expenditure. See Ross, Westerfield, Jaffe and Roberts (2013), Chapter 6, for an overview of the NPV, IRR, payback and profitability index methods.

It is added back because this cash did not actually flow out of the firm in year t. D_t can be viewed as the recapture in year t of a portion of the original investment, C_0, in the project. The last term represents the firm's after-tax payment of interest to debtholders.

Equation 17.2c provides a computationally simpler formula for calculating CF_t. Since $I_t(1 - \tau)$ is subtracted in determining NI_t in Equation 17.2a and then added back, the two cancel out. The first term in Equation 17.2c represents after-tax net operating income, $NOI_t(1 - \tau)$, as stated in Equation 17.2d.

Equation 17.2e provides an even simpler formula for calculating CF_t. It shows the result from Equation 17.2c of combining the after-tax value of the depreciation expense, $(1 - \tau)D_t$, with the before-tax value of D_t. The result of this combination is the amount τD_t in Equation 17.2e, which represents the tax saving due to D_t being a tax-deductible item. As summarized in Equation 17.2f, the first term in Equation 17.2e represents after-tax operating cash flow, $OCF_t(1 - \tau)$, and the second term denotes the tax savings from the depreciation expense.[2]

17.2   ADJUSTED PRESENT VALUE

To continue our discussion, we need to expand the NPV model. To do this, we substitute Equation 17.2f for CF_t in Equation 17.1, allowing us to restate the NPV formula as

$$NPV = \sum_{t=1}^{T} \frac{OCF_t(1 - \tau)}{(1 + K)^t} + \sum_{t=1}^{T} \frac{\tau D_t}{(1 + K)^t} + \frac{TV_T}{(1 + K)^T} - C_0 \qquad (17.3)$$

Following the well-known Modigliani-Miller approach to valuation, we know the value of a levered firm (V_l)—that is, a firm with debt in its capital structure—is greater than the value of an unlevered firm (V_u), a firm with no debt. The difference in value stems from the tax-deductibility of interest payments on the debt. For perpetual debt at an interest rate (i), the annual tax savings via the tax deduction of interest is (τ_tDebt) where τ is the tax rate. Discounting the flow of annual tax saving at the rate i results in a present value of τDebt.

$$V_l = V_u + \tau\text{Debt} \qquad (17.4a)$$

Assuming the firm is an ongoing concern and the debt the levered firm issued to finance a portion of its productive capacity is perpetual, Equation 17.4a can be expanded as

$$\frac{NOI(1 - \tau)}{K} = \frac{NOI(1 - \tau)}{K_u} + \frac{\tau I}{i} \qquad (17.4b)$$

where i is the levered firm's borrowing rate, $I = i$Debt, and K_u is the cost of equity for an **all-equity**-financed firm.

Recall from Chapter 16 that the weighted average cost of capital can be stated as

$$K = (1 - \lambda)K_l + \lambda i(1 - \tau) \qquad (17.5a)$$

where K_l is the cost of equity for a levered firm, and λ is the optimal debt ratio. K can be stated as[3]

$$K = K_u(1 - \tau\lambda) \qquad (17.5b)$$

Equation 17.2a can be simplified to Equation 17.2d. This recognizes that NOI is independent of the firm's debt–equity ratio which is naturally the case, since NOI is computed *before* deduction of interest payments. From Equation 17.5b, if $\lambda = 0$ (i.e., an all-equity-financed firm), then $K = K_u$ and $I = 0$; thus, in Equation 17.4a $V_l = V_u$. However, if $\lambda > 0$ (i.e., a levered firm), then $K_u > K$ and $I > 0$, thus, $V_l > V_u$. For Equation 17.4b to hold as an equality, it is necessary to add the present value of the tax savings the levered

---

[2]Annual cash flows might also include incremental working capital funds. These are ignored here to simplify the presentation.

[3]To derive Equation 17.5b from Equation 17.5a, note that $K_l = K_u + (1 - \tau)(K_u - i)(\text{Debt}/\text{Equity})$.

firm receives. The value of a levered firm is greater than an equivalent unlevered firm earning the same NOI because the levered firm also has tax savings from the tax deductibility of interest payments to bondholders. The following example clarifies the tax savings to the firm from making interest payments on debt.

Example 17.1 *Tax Savings from Interest Payments*

Exhibit 17.1 provides an example of the tax savings arising from the tax-deductibility of interest payments. The exhibit shows a levered firm and an unlevered firm, each with sales revenue and operating expenses of $100 and $50, respectively. The levered firm has interest expense of $10 and earnings, before taxes of $40, while the unlevered firm enjoys $50 of before-tax earnings, since it does not have any interest expense. The levered firm pays only $16 in taxes as opposed to $20 for the unlevered firm. This leaves $24 for the levered firm's shareholders and $30 for the unlevered firm's shareholders. Nevertheless, the levered firm has a total of $34 (= $24 + $10) of funds available for investors, while the unlevered firm has only $30. The extra $4 comes from the tax savings on the $10 before-tax interest payment.

By direct analogy to the Modigliani-Miller equation for an unlevered firm, we can convert the NPV Equation 17.3 into the **adjusted present value (APV)** model:

$$\text{APV} = \sum_{t=1}^{T} \frac{\text{OCF}_t(1-\tau)}{(1+K_u)^t} + \sum_{t=1}^{T} \frac{\tau D_t}{(1+i)^t} + \sum_{t=1}^{T} \frac{\tau I_t}{(1+i)^t} + \frac{\text{TV}_T}{(1+K_u)^T} - C_0 \quad (17.6)$$

The APV model is a **value-additive approach** to capital budgeting. That is, each cash flow is a source of value to be considered individually. In the APV model, each cash flow is discounted at a rate consistent with the risk inherent in that cash flow. The OCF_t and TV_T are discounted at K_u. The firm would receive these cash flows from a capital project, regardless of whether the firm was levered or unlevered. The tax savings due to interest, τI_t, are discounted at the before-tax borrowing rate, i, as in Equation 17.4b. The tax savings due to depreciation, τD_t, are also discounted at i because they are relatively less risky than operating cash flows if tax laws are not likely to change radically over the economic life of the project.

The APV model is useful for a domestic firm analyzing a domestic capital expenditure. If APV $\geq$ 0, the project should be accepted. If APV $<$ 0, the project should be rejected. Thus, the model is useful for an MNC for analyzing one of its domestic capital expenditures or for a foreign subsidiary of the MNC analyzing a proposed capital expenditure from the subsidiary's viewpoint.

EXHIBIT 17.1		Levered	Unlevered
Comparison of Cash Flows Available to Investors	Revenue	$100	$100
	Operating costs	−50	−50
	Net operating income	50	50
	Interest expense	−10	−0
	Earnings before taxes	40	50
	Taxes @ 0.40	−16	−20
	Net income	24	30
	Cash flow available to investors	$24 + 10 = $34	$ 30

17.3   CAPITAL BUDGETING FROM THE PARENT FIRM'S PERSPECTIVE

The APV model as stated in Equation 17.6 is not useful for the MNC in analyzing a foreign capital expenditure of one of its subsidiaries from the MNC's, or parent's, perspective. In fact, it is possible that a project may have a positive APV from the subsidiary's perspective and a negative APV from the parent's perspective. This could happen, for example, if certain cash flows are blocked by the host country from being legally remitted to the parent or if extra taxes are imposed by the host country on foreign exchange remittances. A higher marginal tax rate in the home country may also cause a project to be unprofitable from the parent's perspective. If we assume that the MNC owns the foreign subsidiary but domestic shareholders own the MNC parent, it is the currency of the parent firm that is important because it is that currency into which the cash flows must be converted to benefit the shareholders whose wealth the MNC is attempting to maximize.

Using the basic structure of the APV model developed in the previous section,

$$\text{APV} = \sum_{t=1}^{T} \frac{S_t \text{OCF}_t (1 - \tau)}{(1 + K_{ud})^t} + \sum_{t=1}^{T} \frac{S_t \tau D_t}{(1 + i_d)^t} + \sum_{t=1}^{T} \frac{S_t \tau I_t}{(1 + i_d)^t} + \frac{S_t \text{TV}_T}{(1 + K_{ud})^T}$$

$$- S_0 C_0 + S_0 \text{RF}_0 + S_0 \text{CL}_0 - \sum_{t=1}^{T} \frac{S_t \text{LP}_t}{(1 + i_d)^t} \tag{17.7}$$

An APV model suitable for an MNC must recognize that foreign cash flows are eventually converted into the currency of the parent. APV is especially well suited to deal with special cash flows of the sort frequently encountered in foreign project analysis. First, cash flows denominated in foreign currency are converted to the currency of the parent at the expected spot rate, S_t, applicable to year t. Second, the discount rates, K_{ud} and i_d, the cost of unlevered equity and the cost of debt, respectively, are identified (by subscript d) as the firm's *domestic* costs of capital. Once cash flows are converted to domestic currency, domestic costs of capital apply. Third, a distinguishing feature of *adjusted present value* is that specific cash flow streams or items are discounted at specific discount rates appropriate to the risk of the stream or item. For example, the net after-tax operating cash flow $S_t \text{OCF}_t(1 - \tau)$ and the terminal value $S_T \text{TV}_T$ are risky cash flows for which it is appropriate to apply K_{ud}. On the other hand, a tax shield from the use of debt, $S_t \tau D_t$, or a concessionary loan, $S_t \tau I_t$, are cash flows for which the cost of borrowing, i_d, is appropriate. Finally, nowhere in the formula for adjusted present value do we see the Canadian tax rate. This reflects the fact that foreign-source income earned from active business by Canadian companies does not incur a Canadian tax liability.

In Equation 17.7, the OCF_t represents only the portion of net operating cash flow available for remittance that, indeed, can be effectively remitted to the parent firm. Cash flows earned in the foreign country that are blocked by the host government from being repatriated do not provide any benefit to the shareholders of the parent firm and, thus, are not relevant to the project valuation analysis. Likewise, cash flows that are repatriated in circuitous ways, such as through transfer price manipulation, are not included here.

As with domestic project analysis, it is important to include only incremental revenues and operating costs in calculating the OCF_t. An example will help illustrate the concept. An MNC may presently have a sales affiliate in a foreign country that is supplied by merchandise produced by the parent or a manufacturing facility in a third country. If a manufacturing facility is put into operation in the foreign country to satisfy local demand, sales may be larger overall than with just a sales affiliate if the foreign subsidiary is better able to assess market demand with its local presence. However, the former manufacturing unit will experience **lost sales** as a result of the new foreign manufacturing facility; that is, the new project has *cannibalized* part of an existing project. Thus, incremental revenue is not the total sales revenue of the new manufacturing facility but, rather, that amount minus the lost sales revenue. However, if the sales would be lost regardless, say, because a competitor who is better able to satisfy local demand is gearing up, then the entire sales revenue of the new foreign manufacturing facility is incremental sales revenue.

Equation 17.7 includes additional terms representing cash flows frequently encountered in foreign projects. The term S_0RF_0 represents the value of accumulated **restricted funds** (of amount RF_0) in the foreign land from existing operations that are freed up by the proposed project. These funds become available only *because* of the proposed project and are therefore available to offset a portion of the initial capital outlay. Examples are funds whose use is restricted by exchange controls or funds on which additional taxes would be due in the parent country if they were remitted. RF_0 equals the difference between the face value of these funds and their present value used in the best alternative. The extended illustration at the end of this chapter will help clarify the meaning of this term.

$$S_0CL_0 - \sum_{t=1}^{T} \frac{S_t LP_t}{(1 + i_d)^t}$$

www.worldbank.org/
guarantees/

This website of the World
Bank provides information
on doing business in the
developing world, includ-
ing information on project
financing.

The above term denotes the present value in the currency of the parent firm of the benefit of below-market-rate borrowing in foreign currency. In certain cases, a **concessionary loan** (of amount CL_0) at a below-market rate of interest may be available to the parent firm if the proposed capital expenditure is made in the foreign land. The host country offers this financing in its foreign currency as a means of attracting economic development and investment that will create employment for its citizens. The benefit to the MNC is the difference between the face value of the concessionary loan converted into the home currency and the present value of the similarly converted concessionary loan payments (LP_t) discounted at the MNC's normal domestic borrowing rate (i_d). The loan payments will yield a present value less than the face amount of the concessionary loan when they are discounted at the higher normal rate. This difference represents a subsidy the host country is willing to extend to the MNC if the investment is made. It should be clear that the present value of the loan payments discounted at the normal borrowing rate represents the size of the loan available from borrowing at the normal borrowing rate with a debt service schedule equivalent to that of the concessionary loan.

Recall that to calculate the firm's weighted-average cost of capital, it is necessary to know the firm's optimal debt ratio. When considering a capital budgeting project, it is never appropriate to think of the project as being financed separately from the way the firm is financed since the project represents a portion of the firm. When the asset base increases because a capital project is undertaken, the firm can handle more debt in its capital structure. That is, the borrowing capacity of the firm is increased because of the project. Nevertheless, the investment and financing decisions are separate. There is an optimal capital structure for the firm; once this is determined, the cost of financing is known and used to determine if a project is acceptable. We do not mean to imply that *each* and every capital project is financed with the optimal portions of debt and equity. Rather, some projects may be financed with all debt or all equity or a suboptimal combination. What is important is that in the long run, the firm does not stray too far from its optimal capital structure so that overall the firm's assets are financed at the lowest cost. Thus, the interest tax shield term $S_t \tau I_t$ in the APV model recognizes the tax shields of the **borrowing capacity** created by the project, *regardless* of how the project is financed. Handling the tax shields in any other way would bias the APV favourably or unfavourably, respectively, if the project were financed by a larger or smaller portion of debt. This is an especially important point in international capital budgeting analysis because of the frequency of large concessionary loans. The benefit of concessionary loans, which are dependent on the parent firm making the investment, is recognized in a separate term.

Generality of the APV Model

APV includes many terms for cash flows frequently encountered in analyzing foreign capital expenditures. However, *all* possible terms are not included in the version presented as Equation 17.7. Nevertheless, the reader should now have the knowledge to incorporate into the basic APV model terms of a more unique nature for specific cash flows encountered in a particular analysis.

For example, there may be tax savings or deferrals that come about because of multinational operations. That is, the MNC may be able to shift revenues or expenses among its affiliates in a way that lowers taxes or be able to combine profits or affiliates from both low- and high-tax environments in a manner that results in lower overall taxes.

Through interaffiliate transfer pricing strategies, licensing arrangements, royalty agreements or other means, the parent firm might be able to repatriate some funds that are meant to be blocked, or restricted, by the host country.[4] These cash flows are the counterpart to the unrestricted funds available for remittance as part of operating cash flows. As with the cash flows arising from tax savings or deferrals, it may be difficult for the firm to accurately estimate the size of these cash flows or their duration. Since these cash flows will exist regardless of how the firm is financed, they should be discounted at the all-equity rate.

One of the major benefits of the APV framework is the ease with which difficult cash flow terms, such as tax savings or deferrals and the repatriation of restricted funds, can be handled. The analyst can first analyze the capital expenditure as if they did not exist. Additional cash flow terms do not need to be explicitly considered unless the APV is negative. If the APV is negative, the analyst can calculate how large the cash flows from other sources need to be to make the APV positive and then estimate whether these other cash inflows will likely be that large.

Estimating the Future Expected Exchange Rate

The financial manager must estimate the future expected exchange rates, S_t, in order to implement the APV framework. Chapter 5 provided a wide variety of methods for estimating exchange rates. One quick and simple way to do this is to rely on purchasing power parity (PPP) and estimate the future expected spot rate for year t as

$$S_t = S_0(1 + \bar{\pi}_d)^t/(1 + \bar{\pi}_f)^t \tag{17.8}$$

where $\bar{\pi}_d$ is the expected long-run annual rate of inflation in the (home) domestic country of the MNC and $\bar{\pi}_f$ is the rate in the foreign land.

As noted in Chapter 5, PPP is not likely to hold precisely in reality. Nevertheless, unless the financial manager suspects that there is some systematic long-run bias in using PPP to estimate S_t that would result in a systematic over- or underestimate of the series of expected exchange rates, then PPP should prove to be an acceptable tool. Alternatively, the analyst may choose to use long-dated forward prices to estimate the future expected spot exchange rates.

Illustrated **Mini Case**

BlackBerry/Europe[5]

BlackBerry, formerly Research in Motion (RIM) of Waterloo, Ontario, is a world leader in mobile communications. The company developed and manufactures the BlackBerry, the stunningly successful wireless handheld communicator with access to e-mail, internet and phone along with organizer features.

BlackBerry has been exporting its smart phones to Europe for several years. European sales are currently 9,600 units a year and have been increasing at a rate of 5 percent. The European marketing manager believes that a manufacturing facility in Europe offers real advantages in production efficiencies. A local presence in Europe is also strategically wise in view of the potential market expansion driven by European enlargement.

---

[4]Chapter 18 covers interaffiliate transfer pricing strategies, licensing arrangements and royalty agreements as methods the parent firm might use to repatriate funds restricted by the host country.

[5]As this edition was in production, Research in Motion officially changed its name to BlackBerry.

BlackBerry is considering establishing a manufacturing and sales operation in Europe, to be based in the high-tech centre of Ulm, in the state of Baden–Württemberg in Germany. Ulm is located about 100 kilometres west of Munich.

The European marketing manager and Canadian production managers have drawn up plans for a wholly owned manufacturing facility in Ulm. A major attraction of locating in Ulm is that the Government of Baden–Württemberg has promised to arrange for a substantial portion of the construction cost to be financed at an attractive so-called *concessionary* interest rate if the plant is built there.

The Executive Committee of BlackBerry has instructed the financial manager and her team to determine if the plan has financial merit. If the manufacturing facility is built, BlackBerry will no longer export units from Canada to Europe.

On its current exports, BlackBerry receives $180 per unit of which $40 represents the contribution margin. Thirty thousand units are forecast to be sold in Europe during the first year of operation. This volume will increase at the rate of 12 percent per year. European sales will be invoiced in euros. When the plant in Ulm begins operation, units will be priced at €110 each. Production cost is estimated to be €80 per unit, which results in a per-unit contribution of €30. Sales price and production costs in Europe are expected to keep pace with European inflation, which is forecast to be 3 percent per annum for the foreseeable future. By comparison, Canadian inflation is forecast to be 2 percent per annum. The current exchange rate is $1.60/€1.

Construction of the manufacturing plant is estimated to cost €5,000,000. Since the capital expenditure on the plant and its equipment provides security in borrowing, we assume that the project expands BlackBerry's borrowing capacity by $4,000,000.

The basic corporate tax rate in Germany is 35 percent. The German tax authorities will allow the plant to be depreciated over an eight-year period. Little, if any, additional investment will be required over that time. The market value of the facility at the end of this period is difficult to estimate, but BlackBerry believes that the plant should still be in good condition and have reasonable market value.

An attractive feature of the proposal is the special financing the German government is willing to arrange. If the plant is built in Ulm, BlackBerry will be eligible to borrow €3,200,000 at a rate of 6 percent per annum. BlackBerry's normal borrowing rate is 8 percent in dollars, and 9 percent in euros. The loan schedule calls for the principal to be repaid in eight equal installments. In dollar terms, BlackBerry estimates its after-tax all-equity cost of capital to be 11 percent.

Here is a summary of the key points in the analysis:

The current exchange rate: $S_0 = \$1.60/€1$

Expected inflation, Europe: $\pi_f = 3$ percent per annum

Expected inflation, Canada: $\pi_d = 2$ percent per annum

The initial cost of the project in Canadian dollars is

$S_0 C_0 = \$1.60 \times €5,000,000 = \$8,000,000$

For simplicity, we assume that PPP holds. Thus, the future path of the nominal exchange rate in Canadian dollars per euro is

$S_t = S_0 (1 + \pi_d)^t/(1 + \pi_f)^t = 1.60 (1.02)^t/(1.03)^t$

The before-tax incremental operating cash flow per unit in the first period of operations $(t = 1)$ is €110 − €80 = €30. The nominal contribution margin on made-in-Europe BlackBerrys in each subsequent year is €30$(1 + \pi_f)^{t-1}$.

Export sales (unit volume) "lost" to the parent in Canada as manufacturing shifts to Europe are 9,600(1.05)^t units for year t.

Contribution margin per unit of "lost" sales in year t equals $40(1 + \pi_d)^{t-1} = \$40(1.02)^{t-1}$.

The German tax rate, τ, is 35 percent.

Terminal value will initially be assumed to be zero.

Straight-line depreciation implies: $D_t = €5,000,000/8$ years $= €625,000$ per year.

EXHIBIT 17.2		Calculation of the Present Value of the After-Tax Operating Cash Flows					
			(a)		(b)	(a + b)	
Year	S_t $\$/€$	European Sales (units)	European Sales (units) × €30 × S_t × $(1.03)^{t-1}$ $\$$	Lost Sales (units)	Lost Sales (units) × \$40 × $(1.02)^{t-1}$ $\$$	OCF_t $\$$	$\frac{OCF_t(1-\tau)}{(1+K_{ud})^t}$ $\$$
1	1.5845	30,000	1,426,019	−10,080	−403,200	1,022,819	598,948
2	1.5691	33,600	1,629,085	−10,584	−431,827	1,197,257	631,619
3	1.5538	37,632	1,861,066	−11,113	−462,487	1,398,579	664,709
4	1.5388	42,148	2,126,082	−11,669	−495,324	1,630,759	698,250
5	1.5238	47,206	2,428,836	−12,252	−530,491	1,898,345	732,274
6	1.5090	52,870	2,774,702	−12,865	−568,156	2,206,546	766,811
7	1.4944	59,215	3,169,820	−13,508	−608,495	2,561,325	801,894
8	1.4799	66,320	3,621,202	−14,184	−651,699	2,969,504	837,555
							5,732,061

BlackBerry's cost of borrowing at the concessionary rate: i_c = 6 percent.

BlackBerry's Canadian dollar cost of borrowing: i_d = 8 percent.

BlackBerry's Canadian dollar cost of unlevered equity: K_{ud} = 11 percent.

The last two items refer to the pre-tax cost of debt and the after-tax cost of (unlevered) equity capital that BlackBerry faces in Canada. Thus, these are relevant "opportunity costs" to be used as discount rates in appropriate places in the APV analysis.

The present value of the expected after-tax operating cash flows from BlackBerry's proposed manufacturing facility in Europe is calculated in Exhibit 17.2. Column (a) presents the annual revenue in dollars from operating the new manufacturing facility. The figures in column (a) are calculated for each year by multiplying the expected quantity of BlackBerrys sold times the initial incremental operating cash flow of €30 per unit. This product is, in turn, multiplied by the European inflation factor of $(1 + \pi_f)^{t-1}$. For example, for year 2, the factor is $(1.03)^{2-1}$, which equals 1.03. Euro sales are then converted to dollars at the expected spot exchange rates.

Column (b) reports annual lost sales revenue in dollars that results from BlackBerry (Canada) no longer selling to Europe. These losses for the parent are calculated by multiplying the estimated quantity of lost sales in units by the contribution margin of \$40 per unit, which is, in turn, multiplied by the Canadian inflation factor $(1 + \pi_c)^{t-1}$. The incremental dollar operating cash flow is the sum of columns (a) and (b). Taking into account the German tax and then discounting at BlackBerry's unlevered discount rate K_{ud} results in a present value of after-tax net operating income flows of \$5,732,061.

The present value of the depreciation tax shield is calculated in Exhibit 17.3. Tax savings on annual straight-line depreciation of €625,000 are converted to dollars at the expected future spot exchange rates and discounted to the present using BlackBerry's Canadian cost of borrowing, 8 percent. The present value of the depreciation tax shield is \$1,932,959.

The present value of the benefit of the concessionary loan is calculated in Exhibits 17.4 and 17.5. In Exhibit 17.4, the aim is to compute the present value of the concessionary loan payments in dollars. Since the annual principal payment on the €3,200,000 concessionary loan is the same each year, interest payments decline as the loan balance

EXHIBIT 17.3

Calculation of the Present Value of the Depreciation Tax Shields

Year	S_t $\$/€$	D_t $€$	$\dfrac{S_t \tau D_t}{(1 + i_d)^t}$ $\$$
1	1.5845	625,000	320,928
2	1.5691	625,000	294,270
3	1.5538	625,000	269,827
4	1.5388	625,000	247,414
5	1.5238	625,000	226,863
6	1.5090	625,000	208,019
7	1.4944	625,000	190,740
8	1.4799	625,000	174,897
			1,932,959

EXHIBIT 17.4

Calculation of the Present Value of the Concessionary Loan Payments

Year	(a) S_t $\$/€$	(b) Principal Payment $€$	(c) $€$	(a) × (b + c) $S_t LP_t$ $\$$	$\dfrac{S_t LP_t}{(1 + i_d)^t}$ $\$$
1	1.5845	400,000	192,000	938,004	868,522
2	1.5691	400,000	168,000	891,239	764,094
3	1.5538	400,000	144,000	845,294	671,022
4	1.5388	400,000	120,000	800,157	588,139
5	1.5238	400,000	96,000	755,817	514,396
6	1.5090	400,000	72,000	712,262	448,846
7	1.4944	400,000	48,000	669,482	390,636
8	1.4799	400,000	24,000	627,465	339,000
		3,200,000			4,584,654

declines. For example, during the first year, interest of €192,000 (= 0.06 × €3,200,000) is paid on the full amount borrowed. During the second year, interest of €168,000 (= 0.06 × (€3,200,000 − €400,000)) is paid on the outstanding balance over year 2. The annual loan payment equals the sum of the annual principal payment and the annual interest charge. The sum of their present values in dollars, converted at the expected spot exchange rates and discounted at BlackBerry's borrowing rate of 8 percent, is $4,584,654. This sum represents the size of the equivalent loan available (in dollars) from borrowing at the normal borrowing rate with a debt service schedule equivalent to that of the concessionary loan.

Exhibit 17.5 concludes the analysis of the concessionary loan. It shows the difference between the dollar value of the concessionary loan and the equivalent dollar loan value calculated in Exhibit 17.4. The difference of $535,346 represents the present value of the benefit of the below market rate financing of the concessionary loan.

EXHIBIT 17.5

Calculation of the
Present Value of
the Benefit from
the Concessionary
Loan

$$S_0 CL_0 - \sum_{t=1}^{T} \frac{S_t LP_t}{(1 + i_d)^t} = (\$1.60 \times 3,200,000) - 4,584,654 = \$535,346$$

The present value of the interest tax shield is calculated in Exhibit 17.6. The interest payments in column (b) of Exhibit 17.6 are drawn from column (c) of Exhibit 17.4. That is, we follow a conservative approach and base the interest tax shield on using the concessionary loan interest rate of 6 percent. The concessionary loan of €3,200,000 represents 64 percent of the project cost of €5,000,000. By comparison, the borrowing capacity created by the project is $4,000,000, which implies an optimal debt ratio λ for the parent firm of 50 percent = $4,000,000/$8,000,000 of the dollar cost of the project. Thus, only 78 percent = (50/64) of the interest payments on the concessionary loan should be used to calculate the interest tax shield. Discounted at BlackBerry's borrowing rate of 8 percent, the present value of the interest tax shield is $287,137.

APV = PV of net operating cash flows (after German tax)

    + PV of depreciation tax shield

    + PV of the benefit for the concessionary loan

    + PV of the interest tax shield

    − Initial cost of the project in Canadian dollars

APV = $5,732,061 + $1,932,959 + $535,346 + $287,137 − $8,000,000

    = $487,502

There appears little doubt that the proposed European manufacturing facility will be a profitable venture for BlackBerry. Had the APV been negative or closer to zero, we would want to consider the present value of the after-tax terminal cash flow. We are quite uncertain as to what this amount might be, and fortunately in this case, we do not have to base a decision on this cash flow, which is difficult at best to forecast.

The European sales affiliate has accumulated €550,000 from past operations which can be used to partially finance the capital expenditure. These accumulated funds were earned under special tax concessions offered during the initial years of the sales operation and were taxed at a rate of 20 percent. If these funds are repatriated to Canada, additional German tax at the 35 percent marginal rate would be owing.

EXHIBIT 17.6

Calculation of the
Present Value of
the Interest Tax
Shield

Year	(a) S_t $/€	(b) I_t €	(c) λ/Project Debt Ratio	(a × b × c × τ) $S_t \times 0.78 \times \tau \times I_t$ $	$\dfrac{S_t \times 0.78 \times \tau \times I_t}{(1 + i_d)^t}$ $
1	1.5845	192,000	0.78	83,184	77,023
2	1.5691	168,000	0.78	72,080	61,797
3	1.5538	144,000	0.78	61,183	48,569
4	1.5388	120,000	0.78	50,491	37,112
5	1.5238	96,000	0.78	40,000	27,224
6	1.5090	72,000	0.78	29,709	18,722
7	1.4944	48,000	0.78	19,614	11,444
8	1.4799	24,000	0.78	9,712	5,247
					287,137

To calculate the amount of the freed-up restricted remittances, it is first necessary to gross up the after-tax value of the €550,000 on which the European sales affiliate has previously paid taxes at the rate of 20 percent. This amount is €687,500 = €550,000/(1.20). The dollar value of this sum at the current spot exchange rate S_0 is $1,100,000 = $1.60(€687,500). If BlackBerry decided not to establish a manufacturing facility in Germany, the €550,000 should be repatriated to the parent firm.

17.4 RISK ADJUSTMENT IN CAPITAL BUDGETING

APV is suitable for analyzing a capital expenditure that has the average riskiness of the firm as a whole. Some projects may be more or less risky than average, however. The *risk-adjusted discount method* is the standard way to handle this situation. This approach requires adjusting the discount rate upward or downward for increases or decreases, respectively, in the systematic risk of the project relative to the firm as a whole. In the APV model presented in Equation 17.7, only the cash flows discounted at K_{ud} incorporate systematic risk; thus, only K_{ud} needs to be adjusted when project risk differs from that of the firm as a whole.[6]

A second way to adjust for risk in the APV framework is the *certainty equivalent method*. This approach extracts the risk premium from the expected cash flows to convert them into equivalent riskless cash flows, which are then discounted at the risk-free rate of interest. This is accomplished by multiplying the risky cash flows by a certainty-equivalent factor that is unity or less. The more risky the cash flow, the smaller the certainty-equivalent factor. In general, cash flows tend to be more risky the further into the future they are expected to be received. We favour the risk-adjusted discount rate method over the certainty-equivalent approach because we find that it is easier to adjust the discount rate than it is to estimate the appropriate certainty-equivalent factors.[7]

17.5 SENSITIVITY ANALYSIS

The way we have approached the analysis of BlackBerry's expansion into Europe results in a point estimate of the APV through using expected values of the relevant cash flows. The expected values of these inputs are what the financial manager expects to obtain given the information at the time the analysis was performed. However, each cash flow has its own probability distribution. Hence, the realized value that may result for a particular cash flow may be different from expected. To examine these possibilities, the financial manager typically performs a sensitivity analysis. In a *sensitivity analysis*, different scenarios are examined by using different exchange rate estimates, inflation rate estimates, and cost and pricing estimates in the calculation of the APV. In essence, the sensitivity analysis allows the financial manager a means to analyze the business risk, economic exposure, exchange rate uncertainty and political risk inherent in the investment. Sensitivity analysis puts financial managers in a position to more fully understand the implications of planned capital expenditures. It also forces them to consider in advance actions that can be taken should an investment not develop as anticipated.

For example, if BlackBerry's European unit sales in the base year are assumed to be 29,000 units, rather than 30,000, the APV of the project falls to $240,693. Or, if the annual rate of growth of European unit sales is assumed to be 11 percent, rather than 12 percent,

---

[6]See Ross, Westerfield, Jaffe and Roberts (2003) for a treatment of capital budgeting using discount rates adjusted for project systematic risk.

[7]Brealey, Myers and Allen (2014), Chapter 9, for a more detailed discussion of the certainty equivalent method of risk adjustment.

the APV of the project falls to $250,494. Perhaps most telling of all is the sensitivity of APV to the "contribution" (selling price minus production costs) in Europe. If the contribution is €28, rather than €30, as a result of either a lower selling price or higher production costs than were assumed in the analysis, the APV falls to −$6,116 in which case the terminal value of the project becomes an important consideration in the accept/reject decision.

17.6   REAL OPTIONS

Throughout this chapter, we have recommended the APV framework for evaluating capital expenditures in real assets, such as when a firm plans to set up production operations abroad. A decision based on APV relies on specific assumptions and forecasts involving revenues, operating costs, discount rates, exchange rates, and the like. When evaluated at appropriate APV discount rates, a project is accepted or rejected on the basis of whether APV is positive or negative. The evaluation exercise assumes that all relevant considerations involving future cash flows have been taken into account. It is often the case, however, that certain crucial, value-enhancing or value-destroying pieces of information are unavailable at the time of analysis or even at the time the project is scheduled to begin. Such information is typically *binary*, that is, one thing or the other will happen, one of which is favourable, and one of which is not. But we do not know which one will unfold.

In this situation, it is often wise to wait. Management has alternative paths—or *options*—that it can take until the new crucial information arrives. Option pricing theory can be useful for evaluating investment opportunities in such cases, for instance, as BlackBerry's plans for Europe. In Chapter 9, we saw that option pricing is widely applied in the case of financial assets, such as foreign exchange. Now, with a little modification, we can apply option pricing theory to option-like situations that involve real projects. These are referred to as **real options**.

The firm is confronted with many possible real options over the life of a capital asset. For example, the firm may have a *timing option* about when to make the investment; it may have a *growth option* to increase the scale of the investment; it may have a *suspension option* to temporarily cease production; and it may have an *abandonment option* to quit the investment early. All of these situations can be evaluated as real options.

In international capital expenditures, the MNC is faced with the political uncertainties of doing business in a foreign host country. For example, a stable political environment for foreign investment may turn unfavourable if a different political party wins power by election—or worse, by political coup. Moreover, an unexpected change in a host country's monetary policy may cause a depreciation in its exchange rate versus the parent firm's home currency, thus adversely affecting the return to the shareholders of the parent firm. These and other political uncertainties make real options analysis ideal for use in evaluating international capital expenditures. Real options analysis, however, should be thought of as an extension of discounted cash flow analysis, not as a replacement of it, as the following example makes clear.

Example 17.2   *Timing Option*

Suppose the sales forecast for the first year of BlackBerry's operations in Europe had been only 28,000 smart phones rather than 30,000. At the lower base year figure for unit sales, the project APV turns out to be −$6,116. The European project would not look promising. It becomes questionable as to whether BlackBerry ought to proceed with the construction of the manufacturing facility in Germany when the APV under carefully chosen assumptions turns out to be negative.

However, suppose there is substantial uncertainty about the future course of the euro exchange rate *vis-à-vis* the Canadian dollar. The doubt hinges on whether the European Central Bank will tighten or loosen monetary policy. An expert advises BlackBerry that a change in European monetary policy would cause the euro to either appreciate to $1.70/€ or depreciate to $1.50/€1.

Under a restrictive European monetary policy and euro appreciation to $1.70/€, the APV of BlackBerry's project drops to a *negative* $239,931. With a more valuable euro, the present value (in Canadian dollars) of operating cash flows, the depreciation tax shield, the interest tax shield and the value of the concessionary loan all become more valuable in Canadian dollar terms but these gains are not sufficient to offset the increased Canadian dollar cost of the initial investment. On the other hand, under looser European monetary policy and euro depreciation to $1.50/€, the APV of BlackBerry's project jumps to an encouraging $227,699.

BlackBerry's project analysts believe the effect of any change in monetary policy will be known in a year's time. Thus, BlackBerry plans to put the project on hold until it learns what the European Central Bank decides to do. In the meantime, BlackBerry can obtain a buy option for a year on the parcel of land that would be its building site. The German landowner has offered to extend to BlackBerry the option to purchase the land in one year's time for a fee of €10,000 or $16,000.

The situation is a classic example in which the **real options framework** is useful in evaluating a capital expenditure. The buy option of €10,000 represents the option premium of the real option to buy the land and launch the project. The initial investment of €5,000,000 represents the exercise price of the option. BlackBerry will only exercise its option if the European Central Bank decides to adopt a looser monetary policy that would result in euro depreciation that gives BlackBerry's project a positive APV of $227,699. The €10,000 seems like a small amount to allow the flexibility to postpone a costly capital expenditure until crucial information is at hand. The following example explicitly values the timing option using the binomial option pricing approach.

Example 17.3 *Valuing BlackBerry's Timing Option*

BlackBerry's timing option can be valued with the use of the binomial option pricing model developed in Chapter 9. We use BlackBerry's 8 percent borrowing cost in Canadian dollars and the 9 percent borrowing cost in euros as our estimates of the domestic and foreign risk-free rates of interest. Depending on the action of the ECB, the euro will either appreciate from $1.60/€ to $1.70/€, or 6.25 percent, or the euro will depreciate by an equal percentage to $1.50/€. Thus, $u = 1.0625$ and $d = 0.9375$. This implies that the risk-neutral probability of a depreciation of the euro is

$$q = \{[(1 + i_d)/(1 + i_f)] - d\}/(u - d)$$
$$= [(1.08/1.09) - 0.9375]/(1.0625 - 0.9375)$$
$$= 0.42$$

The probability of euro depreciation is 0.42.

The option will be exercised if the APV is positive, which occurs if the euro depreciates, and hence the value of the option is

$$C = (0.42 \times \$227,699)/1.08$$
$$= \$88,550$$

Since $88,550 is substantially in excess of the $16,000 cost of the option to purchase the land, BlackBerry is well advised to take advantage of the timing option in order to "buy time" and to wait and see what monetary policy the European Central Bank decides to pursue.

SUMMARY

This chapter begins with a review of the NPV capital budgeting framework. NPV is then expanded into adjusted present value (APV) that is suitable for analyzing capital expenditures by an MNC in a foreign land.

1. NPV is the difference between the present value of project cash inflows and outflows. If NPV ≥ 0 for a capital project, it should be accepted.

2. The annual after-tax cash flow formula was presented in a number of variations. This was necessary to expand the NPV model into the APV model.

3. APV separates the operating cash flows from the cash flows due to financing. Each cash flow is discounted at a rate of discount commensurate with its inherent risk.

4. APV is well suited to an MNC analyzing a foreign capital project. Cash flows were converted into the parent firm's home currency. Additional terms can be added to address cash flows typically encountered in international capital projects.

5. An illustrated mini case showing how to apply the APV model was presented and solved.

QUESTIONS

1. Why is capital budgeting analysis so important to the firm?

2. What is the intuition behind the NPV capital budgeting framework?

3. Discuss what is meant by the *incremental* cash flows of a capital project.

4. Discuss the nature of the equation sequence, Equations 17.2a to 17.2f.

5. What makes the APV capital budgeting framework useful for analyzing foreign capital expenditures?

6. Relate the concept of *lost sales* to the definition of incremental cash flows.

7. What problems can enter into the capital budgeting analysis if project debt is evaluated instead of the *borrowing capacity* created by the project?

8. What is the nature of a *concessionary loan*, and how is it handled in the APV model?

9. What is the intuition of discounting the various cash flows in the APV model at specific discount rates?

10. Why is the market value of the levered firm greater than the market value of an equivalent unlevered firm?

11. Discuss the difference between capital budgeting analysis from the parent firm's perspective as opposed to the project perspective.

12. Define a real option. Discuss the sorts of real options a firm may confront when investing in real projects.

PROBLEMS

1. Beaver! is a Canadian fashion shop with operations abroad. Beaver! has formed a joint venture with a UK firm. Beaver! expects to receive cash dividends from the joint venture over the next several years. The first dividend will be paid one year from now with an amount of £50,000. For the following end-of-year dividend is expected to increase by 10% annually. If the current CAD/GBP exchange rate is 1.58CAD/GBP, and Beaver! has a WACC of 11%, answer the following questions.

   a. What is the present value of the expected dividend stream in CAD if the pound is expected to appreciate 3% a year against the Canadian dollar?

   b. What is the present value of the expected dividend stream if the pound is expected to depreciate 4% a year against the Canadian dollar?

2. Japan also became a fast growth market for Beaver!. Executives at Beaver! know that Japanese buyers prefer goods from their own country. Therefore, the executives are currently considering building a new factory in Japan.

   The initial capital investment would be ¥100,000,000, or $C1,000,000 at a current exchange rate of ¥100 = $C1. The management expects the free cash flow that could be repatriated from Japan to be ¥10,000,000 for the first year with a growth rate of 10% a year for 3 years. The terminal growth rate of the free cash flow is expected to be 3%. At the same time, Beaver!'s financial advisor tells Beaver! that the yen will depreciate for the next 3 years at 5% a year after which the exchange rate will stabilize. Project WACC equals 11%.

   a. Determine whether Beaver! should make such an investment.

   b. Determine whether Beaver! should invest if there is no devaluation of the Japanese yen.

3. Alpha Company plans to establish a subsidiary in Hungary to manufacture and sell fashion wristwatches. Alpha has total assets of $70 million, of which $45 million is equity-financed. The remainder is financed with debt. Alpha considered its current capital structure optimal. The construction cost of the Hungarian facility in forints is estimated at HUF2,400,000,000, of which HUF1,800,000,000 is to be financed at a below-market borrowing rate arranged by the Hungarian government. Alpha wonders what amount of debt it should use in calculating the tax shields on interest payments in its capital budgeting analysis. Can you offer assistance?

4. The current spot exchange rate between the Canadian dollar and the Hungarian forint is HUF150/$1. Long-run inflation in Hungary is estimated at 10 percent annually and 3 percent in Canada. If PPP is expected to hold between the two countries, what spot exchange rate should one forecast five years into the future?

5. Beta Corporation has an optimal debt ratio of 40 percent. Its cost of equity capital is 12 percent and its before-tax borrowing rate is 8 percent. Given a marginal tax rate of 35 percent, calculate (a) the weighted-average cost of capital, and (b) the cost of equity for an equivalent all-equity-financed firm.

6. Suppose that in the illustrated mini case the APV for BlackBerry's German project had been −$60,000. How large would the after-tax terminal value of the project need to be before the APV would be positive and BlackBerry would accept the project?

7. With regard to the BlackBerry case, how would the APV change if

   a. the forecasts of π_d and/or π_f are incorrect?

   b. depreciation cash flows are discounted at K_{ud} instead of i_d?

   c. the host country did not provide the concessionary loan?

INTERNET EXERCISE

Concessionary finance is very important as a source of funds to encourage investment in developing countries. For an example of this, type "concessionary finance Brazil" in your search engine. You should immediately be led to the website of the Brazilian Centre for Enterprise and Development and their recent document on concessionary finance for private foreign investment in infrastructural development. Indeed, many such articles can be found on the Internet by performing a search on the term "concessionary finance."

MINI CASE 1

Dorchester

Dorchester is an old-line confectioner specializing in high-quality chocolates. Through its facilities in the United Kingdom, Dorchester manufactures candies that it sells throughout Western Europe and North America. With its current manufacturing facilities, Dorchester has been unable to supply the North American market with more than 290,000 kilograms of candy per year. This supply has allowed its sales affiliate, located in Halifax, to penetrate the North American market no farther west than Montreal and only as far south as Boston.

Dorchester believes that a separate manufacturing facility located in Windsor, Ontario, would allow it to supply the entire North American market. Dorchester currently estimates initial demand in the North American market at 390,000 kilograms, with growth at a 5 percent annual rate. A separate manufacturing facility would obviously free up the amount currently shipped to the United States and Canada. But Dorchester believes that this is only a short-run problem. It expects that the economic development taking place in Eastern Europe will allow it to sell there the full amount currently shipped to North America within a period of five years.

Dorchester presently realizes £3 per kilogram on its North American exports. Once the Canadian manufacturing facility begins operating, Dorchester expects that it will be able to initially price its product at $7.70 per kilogram. This price would represent an operating profit of $4.40 per kilogram. Both sales price and operating costs are expected to keep track with North American inflation which is running at 3 percent in both Canada and the United States and is expected to remain at that rate. In the United Kingdom, long-run inflation is expected to be in the 4–5 percent range, depending on which economic service one follows. The current spot exchange rate is $1.50/£1. Dorchester explicitly believes PPP to be the best means to forecast future exchange rates.

The manufacturing facility is expected to cost $7,000,000. Dorchester plans to finance this amount by a combination of equity capital and debt. The plant will increase Dorchester's borrowing capacity by £2,000,000, and it plans to borrow only that amount. The city of

Windsor (Ontario) will provide $1,500,000 of debt financing for a period of seven years at 7.75 percent. The principal is to be repaid in equal installments over the life of the loan. At this point, Dorchester is uncertain whether to raise the remaining debt it desires through a domestic bond issue or a Eurodollar bond issue. It believes it can borrow pounds sterling at 10.75 percent per annum and dollars at 9.5 percent. Dorchester estimates its all-equity cost of capital to be 15 percent.

The Canada Revenue Agency will allow Dorchester to depreciate the new facility over a seven-year period.

After that time, the confectionery equipment, which accounts for the bulk of the investment, is expected to have substantial market value.

Dorchester does not expect to receive any special tax concessions. Further, because the corporate tax rates in the two countries are the same—30 percent in the United Kingdom and in Canada—transfer pricing strategies are ruled out.

Should Dorchester build the new manufacturing plant in Canada?

MINI CASE 2

Timmins Gold Mining Company

The Timmins Gold Mining Company is contemplating expanding its operations. To do so it will need to purchase land that its geologists believe is rich in gold. Timmins's management believes that the expansion will allow it to mine and sell an additional 2,000 troy ounces of gold per year. The expansion, including the cost of the land, will cost $500,000. The current price of gold bullion is $275 per ounce and one-year gold futures are trading at $291.50 = $250(1.06). Extraction costs are $225 per ounce. The firm's cost of capital is 10 percent. At the current price of gold, the expansion appears profitable: NPV = ($275 − $225) × 2,000/0.10 − $500,000 =

$500,000. Timmins's management is, however, concerned with the possibility that large sales of gold reserves by Russia and the United Kingdom will drive the price of gold down to $240 for the foreseeable future. On the other hand, management believes there is some possibility that the world will soon return to a gold reserve international monetary system. In the latter event, the price of gold would increase to at least $310 per ounce. The course of the future price of gold bullion should become clear within a year. Timmins can postpone the expansion for a year by buying a purchase option on the land for $25,000. What should Timmins's management do?

REFERENCES & SUGGESTED READINGS

Ang, James S., and Tsong-Yue Lai. "A Simple Rule for Multinational Capital Budgeting." *The Global Finance Journal* 1 (1989), pp. 71–75.

Booth, Lawrence D. "Capital Budgeting Frameworks for the Multinational Corporation." *Journal of International Business Studies* (Fall 1982), pp. 113–23.

Brealey, Richard A., Stewart C. Myers and Franklin Allen, *Principles of Corporate Finance*, 11th ed. New York: McGraw-Hill/Irwin, 2014.

Coy, Peter. "Exploiting Uncertainty: The Real Options Revolution in Decision Making." *Business Week* (June 7, 1999), pp. 118–24.

Endleson, Michael E. "Real Options: Valuing Managerial Flexibility (A)." *Harvard Business School Note* (March 31, 1994).

Holland, John. "Capital Budgeting for International Business: A Framework for Analysis." *Managerial Finance* 16 (1990), pp. 1–6.

Lessard, Donald R. "Evaluating International Projects: An Adjusted Present Value Approach." In Donald R. Lessard

(ed.), *International Financial Management: Theory and Application*, 2nd ed. New York: Wiley, 1985, pp. 570–84.

Luenberger, David G. "Evaluating Real Investment Opportunities." *Investment Science*. New York: Oxford University Press, 1998, pp. 337–43.

Luehrman, Timothy A. "Capital Projects as Real Options: An Introduction." *Harvard Business School Note* (March 22, 1995).

Luehrman, Timothy A. "Investment Opportunities as Real Options: Getting Started on the Numbers." *Harvard Business Review* (July–August 1998), pp. 51–67.

Modigliani, Franco, and Merton H. Miller. "Corporate Income Taxes and the Cost of Capital: A Correction." *American Economic Review* 53 (1963), pp. 433–43.

Ross, Stephen A., W. Westerfield, F. Jaffe and G. Roberts. *Corporate Finance*, 3rd Canadian ed. New York: McGraw-Hill/Ryerson, 2003.

 **For more information on the resources available from McGraw-Hill Ryerson,** go to www.mcgrawhill.ca/he/solutions.

Chapter 18

Multinational Cash Management

CHAPTER OUTLINE

OUR CONCERN in this chapter is the efficient management of cash within a multinational corporation. We focus on the size of cash balances, their currency denominations and where these cash balances are located among the MNC's affiliates. Efficient cash management can reduce the investment in cash balances as well as foreign exchange transaction expenses and it can provide for enhanced return from the firm's holdings in cash and near-cash balances. Efficient cash management can reduce borrowing costs during temporary cash shortages.

The amounts at stake can be huge. By some estimates for large nonfinancial corporations, the amount of cash and near-cash (marketable securities) represents as much as 15 percent of the firms' total assets. Economizing on cash holdings, for example if a firm could reduce cash from 15 to 10 percent of total assets, the effect would be to free up 5 percent of the firm's assets to more productive and profitable use.

18.1   MANAGEMENT OF INTERNATIONAL CASH BALANCES

Cash management refers to how a firm handles its cash. Cash, of course, is synonymous with liquidity. Cash is the lifeblood of corporate operations.

Cash management has features of inventory management. Inventory is useful, but it is also costly. A firm needs inventory of inputs to ensure that production is not disrupted by shortages and, likewise, the firm needs inventory of its own output to ensure that sufficient product is available to meet the uncertainties of sales. But then, excess inventory sitting on the shelves—or cash in the bank—hardly seems to be productive.

Firms hold cash in the form of **transactions balances** to cover scheduled outflows of funds over the cash budgeting cycle. Wages, purchases, rents, interest payments, utilities and taxes are all rather predictable transactional outflows. Correspondingly predictable cash inflows, mostly derived from sales, increase cash on hand. **Precautionary cash balances** are necessary to deal with situations in which cash outflows have been underestimated and/or cash inflows have been overestimated. To be short of cash can lead to the urgent need to borrow, often at punitive rates. Good cash management includes investing excess funds at favourable rates and borrowing at low rates when temporary cash shortages arise.

Many of the skills necessary for effective cash management for firms that operate internationally are the same as for those with only domestic operations. In both cases the managerial objective is to handle cash efficiently while weighing the risks of cash shortages against the cost of holding cash balances.

Treasurers of domestic and international firms alike strive to source funds at the lowest borrowing cost and to place excess funds wherever the greatest return can be earned. Firms with multinational operations, however, regularly deal in more than one currency and hence the cost of foreign exchange transactions is an additional factor in efficient cash management. Moreover, the treasurer of a firm with multinational operations must decide on whether the cash management function should be centralized at corporate headquarters (or elsewhere) or decentralized and handled locally by each affiliate.

In this chapter, we make a strong case for centralized cash management. We begin with an extensive case-based illustration of the development of a centralized cash management system for an MNC. The system includes interaffiliate netting and a centralized cash depository. The benefits of a centralized system are clearly detailed. A second mini case illustrates the challenge of setting intra-firm transfer prices along with the unbundling of services as strategies to reposition cash among affiliates and, under some circumstances, to reduce the MNC's overall income tax liability. The chapter concludes with discussion of moving blocked funds from a host country that has imposed foreign exchange or capital-repatriation restrictions.

Illustrated **Mini Case**

Teltrex's Cash Management System

Teltrex International illustrates the workings of centralized cash management. Teltrex is a multinational firm with headquarters in California's Silicon Valley. It manufactures quartz watches which it markets throughout North America and Europe. In addition to its manufacturing facilities in California, Teltrex has sales affiliates in Canada, Germany and the United Kingdom.

The foundation of a cash management system is the cash budget. The **cash budget** is a plan detailing the time and the size of expected cash receipts and disbursements. Teltrex prepares a cash budget in advance for the fiscal year (updating it periodically as the year progresses), using a weekly time interval as the planning frequency. Exhibit 18.1 presents a payments matrix for one week during the cash budget planning horizon; it summarizes interaffiliate cash receipts and disbursements of Teltrex *and* the receipts from and disbursements to external parties with which Teltrex does business. Exhibit 18.1 is denominated in US dollars, the reporting currency of the parent firm. However, the functional currency of each foreign affiliate is the local currency.

Exhibit 18.1 shows, for example, that the US parent expects to receive the equivalent of $30,000 in Canadian dollars from its Canadian affiliate, the equivalent of $35,000 in euros from its German affiliate, and the equivalent of $60,000 in British pounds sterling from its affiliate in the United Kingdom. In total, it expects to receive $125,000 from interaffiliate transactions. The parent also expects to receive $140,000 directly from external parties, say, from sales in the United States. In total, the parent expects to receive $265,000 in cash during the week. On the disbursements side, the parent expects to make payments in dollars in the amounts of $20,000 to its Canadian affiliate, $10,000 to its German affiliate and $40,000 to its British affiliate. It also expects to make direct disbursements of $120,000 to suppliers for component parts and to cover other operating costs. Analogous cash flows exist for each of the three affiliates.

Exhibit 18.1 shows that the equivalent of $350,000 in interaffiliate cash flows is expected to flow among the parent and its affiliates. Note that no increase in cash in the

| EXHIBIT 18.1 | | | | Cash Receipts and Disbursements Matrix for Teltrex ($000) | | | |

		Disbursements					
Receipts	US	Canada	Germany	UK	External	Total Internal	Total Receipts
US	—	30	35	60	140	125	265
Canada	20	—	10	40	135	70	205
Germany	10	25	—	30	125	65	190
UK	40	30	20	—	130	90	220
External	120	165	50	155	—	—	490[a]
Total internal	70	85	65	130	—	350	—
Total disbursements	190	250	115	285	530[b]	—	1,370[c]

[a]Total cash disbursed by the parent firm and its affiliates to external parties.
[b]Total cash received by the parent firm and its affiliates from external parties.
[c]Balancing check figure.
Note: $350,000 is shifted among the various affiliates; $530,000 − $490,000 = $40,000 = increase in cash balances for Teltrex during the week.

MNC occurs as a result of interaffiliate transactions. Interaffiliate transactions effectively represent taking money out of one pocket of the MNC and putting it into another. However, Teltrex expects to receive the equivalent of $530,000 from external parties and make payments of $490,000 to other external parties. From these external transactions, a net increase of $40,000 in cash among the affiliates is expected during the week.

Netting Systems
Let us first consider the interaffiliate transactions that make up part of Exhibit 18.1. Later, we will examine the transactions Teltrex expects to have with external parties. Exhibit 18.2 presents only the portion of Teltrex's receipts and disbursements matrix from Exhibit 18.1 that concerns interaffiliate cash flows.

Exhibit 18.2 shows the amount that each affiliate is to pay and receive from the other. Without a netting policy, 12 foreign exchange transactions will take place among the four affiliates. In general, if there are N affiliates, there will be a maximum of $N(N − 1)$ transactions; in our case $4(4 − 1) = 12$. Exhibit 18.3 diagrams these 12 transactions.

Exhibit 18.3 indicates that the equivalent of $350,000 in funds flows among the four affiliates in 12 foreign exchange transactions. This represents a needless use of administrative time in arranging the transactions and a waste of corporate funds in making the

| EXHIBIT 18.2 | | | | Teltrex's Interaffiliate Cash Receipts and Disbursements Matrix ($000) | |

		Disbursements				
Receipts	US	Canada	Germany	UK	Total Receipts	Net[a]
US	—	30	35	60	125	55
Canada	20	—	10	40	70	(15)
Germany	10	25	—	30	65	0
UK	40	30	20	—	90	(40)
Total disbursements	70	85	65	130	350	0

[a]Net denotes the difference between total receipts and total disbursements for each affiliate.

EXHIBIT 18.3

Teltrex's
Interaffiliate
Foreign Exchange
Transactions without
Netting ($000)

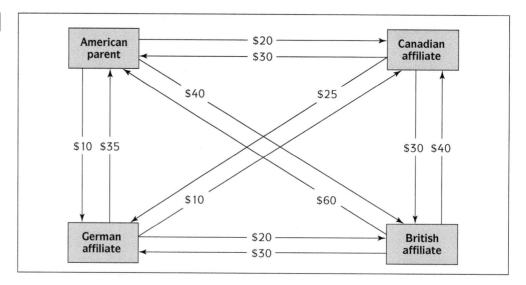

transactions. The cost of transferring funds is in the range of 0.25 percent to 1.5 percent of the transaction; this includes transaction expenses and the opportunity cost of funds tied up in interaffiliate float. If we assume a cost of 0.5 percent, the cost for transferring $350,000 is $1,750 for the week.

The 12 transactions can be reduced at least by half through bilateral netting. Under a **bilateral netting** system, each pair of affiliates determines the net amount due between them, and only the net amount is transferred. For example, the parent and the Canadian affiliate would net the $30,000 and the $20,000 to be received from one another. The result is that only one payment is made; the Canadian affiliate pays the parent an amount equivalent to $10,000. Exhibit 18.4 shows the results of bilateral netting among Teltrex's affiliates.

From Exhibit 18.4, it can be seen that a total of $90,000 flows among the affiliates of Teltrex in six transactions. Bilateral netting can reduce the number of foreign exchange transactions among the affiliates to $N(N - 1)/2$, or less. The equivalent of $260,000 in foreign exchange transactions is eliminated through bilateral netting. At 0.5 percent, the cost of netting interaffiliate foreign exchange transactions is $450, a savings of $1,300 (= $1,750 − $450) over a non-netting system.

EXHIBIT 18.4

Bilateral Netting
of Teltrex's
Interaffiliate
Foreign Exchange
Transactions ($000)

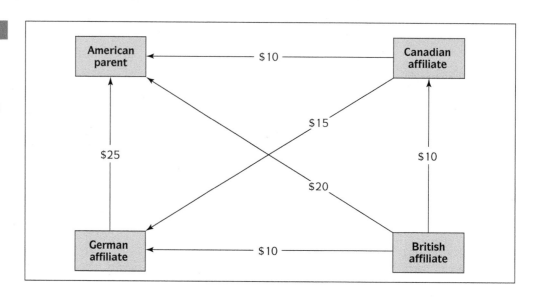

EXHIBIT 18.5

Multilateral
Netting of Teltrex's
Interaffiliate
Foreign Exchange
Transactions ($000)

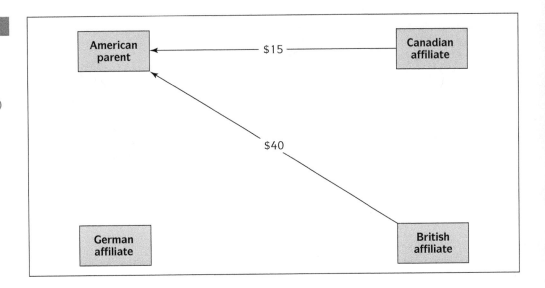

Exhibit 18.2 implies a way to limit interaffiliate transfers to no more than $(N - 1)$ separate foreign exchange transactions. Rather than stop at bilateral netting, the MNC can establish a multilateral netting system. Under a **multilateral netting** system, each affiliate nets all of its interaffiliate receipts against all of its disbursements. It then transfers or receives the balance, respectively, if it is a net payer or receiver. Recall from Exhibit 18.1 that total interaffiliate receipts will always equal total interaffiliate disbursements. Thus, under a multilateral netting system, the net funds to be received by the affiliates will equal the net disbursements to be made by the affiliates.

Exhibit 18.5 illustrates a multilateral netting system for Teltrex. Because the German affiliate's net receipts equal zero, only two foreign exchange transactions are necessary. The Canadian and British affiliates, respectively, pay the equivalent of $15,000 and $40,000 to the parent firm. At 0.5 percent, the cost of transferring $55,000 is only $275 for the week, a savings of $1,475 (= $1,750 − $275) with a multilateral netting system.

Centralized Cash Depository

A multilateral netting system requires a certain degree of administrative structure. At minimum, a netting centre manager must oversee the interaffiliate cash flows from the cash budget. The **netting centre** manager determines the amount of net payments that each affiliate makes or receives. A netting centre does not imply that the MNC has a central cash manager, however. Indeed, the multilateral netting system presented in Exhibit 18.5 suggests that each affiliate has a local cash manager who is responsible for investing excess cash and borrowing when there is a temporary cash shortage.

Exhibit 18.6 presents a modified diagram of multilateral netting for Teltrex with the addition of a centralized depository. Under a centralized cash management system, unless otherwise instructed, all interaffiliate payments will flow through the *central cash depository*.

Exhibit 18.6 shows the Canadian affiliate remits the equivalent of $15,000 to the central depository and the British affiliate remits the equivalent of $40,000. In turn, the central depository remits $55,000 to the parent. One might question the wisdom of this system. It appears as if the foreign exchange transactions have doubled from $55,000 in Exhibit 18.5 to $110,000 in Exhibit 18.6. But that is not the case. The Canadian and British affiliates might be instructed to remit to the central depository in US dollars. Alternatively, the central depository could receive the remittances in Canadian dollars and British pounds sterling and exchange them for US dollars before transferring the funds to the parent.

EXHIBIT 18.6

Multilateral
Netting of Teltrex's
Interaffiliate
Foreign Exchange
Transactions with
a Centralized
Depository ($000)

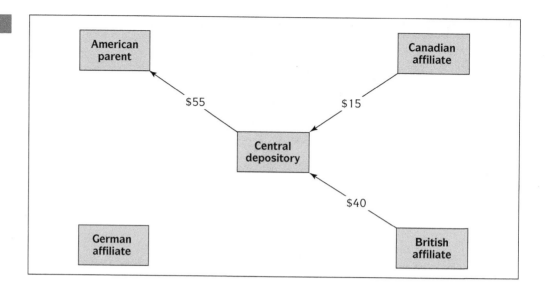

The benefits of a central cash depository derive mainly from the business transactions the affiliates have with external parties. Exhibit 18.7 presents a table showing the net amount of external receipts and disbursements each affiliate of Teltrex is expected to have during the week, as originally presented in Exhibit 18.1.

Exhibit 18.7 shows that the American parent expects net receipts of $20,000 by the end of the week. Analogously, in dollars, the German affiliate expects net receipts of $75,000. The Canadian affiliate expects a cash shortage of $30,000, and the British affiliate expects a cash shortage of $25,000. In total, $40,000 of net receipts are expected for the MNC as a whole.

With a **centralized cash depository**, excess cash is remitted to the central cash pool. Analogously, the central cash manager arranges to cover shortages of cash. The central cash manager has a global view of the MNC's overall cash position and needs. Consequently, there is less chance for *mislocated funds*; that is, there is less chance for funds being denominated in the wrong currency. Moreover, because of his global perspective, the central cash manager will know the best borrowing and investing rates. A centralized system facilitates *funds mobilization* where systemwide cash excesses are invested at advantageous rates and cash shortages are covered by borrowing at favourable rates. Without a centralized cash depository, one affiliate might end up borrowing locally at an unfavourable rate while another is investing temporary surplus funds locally at a disadvantageous rate. Exhibit 18.8 diagrams the cash payments for Teltrex depicted in Exhibit 18.7, showing flows to and from the central cash pool.

Exhibit 18.8 shows that the parent remits $20,000 excess cash from transactions with external parties to the central cash pool and similarly the German affiliate remits the $75,000 it has obtained. Both the Canadian and British affiliates will have their

EXHIBIT 18.7

Expected Net
Cash Receipts and
Disbursements
from Teltrex
Transactions with
External Parties
($000)

Affiliate	Receipts	Disbursements	Net
United States	$140,000	$120,000	$20,000
Canada	135,000	165,000	(30,000)
Germany	125,000	50,000	75,000
United Kingdom	130,000	155,000	(25,000)
			$40,000

EXHIBIT 18.8

Flow of Teltrex's
Net Cash
Receipts from
Transactions with
External Parties
with a Centralized
Depository ($000)

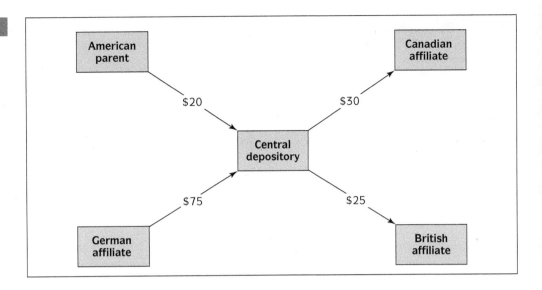

cash shortages of $30,000 and $25,000, respectively, covered by the central pool. In total, a net increase of $40,000 is expected at the central cash depository at the end of the week. The diagram shows that a total of $150,000 of cash is expected to flow to ($95,000) and from ($55,000) the cash depository.

Supplementary Material

18.2 REDUCTION IN PRECAUTIONARY CASH BALANCES

Up to this point, we have handled the multilateral netting of interaffiliate cash flows (Exhibit 18.6) *and* the net receipts of the affiliates from the transactions with external parties (Exhibit 18.8) as two separate sets of cash flows through the central cash depository. While it was easier to develop the concepts in that manner, it is not necessary, practical or efficient to do it that way in practice. Instead, the two sets of net cash flows can be bilaterally netted, with the resulting

net sums going through the central depository. This will further reduce the number, size and expense of foreign exchange transactions for the MNC. Exhibit 18.9 calculates the net amount of funds from Teltrex affiliates to flow through the central depository.

Exhibit 18.9 shows the result of netting the cash receipts that flow through the central cash depository via multilateral netting with the net cash flows that would flow through the

EXHIBIT 18.9

Net Cash Flows
of Teltrex Affiliates
through the Central
Cash Depository
($000)

Affiliate	Net Receipts from Multilateral Netting[a]	Net Excess Cash from Transactions with External Parties[b]	Net Flow[c]
United States	$55,000	$20,000	$35,000
Canada	($15,000)	($30,000)	$15,000
Germany	0	$75,000	($75,000)
United Kingdom	($40,000)	($25,000)	($15,000)
			($40,000)

[a]Net receipt from (payment to) the central depository resulting from multilateral netting, as shown in Exhibit 18.2.

[b]Net excess (shortage) of cash to be remitted to (covered by) the central depository, as shown in Exhibit 18.7.

[c]A positive amount in this column denotes a payment to an affiliate from the central cash depository; a negative amount denotes a payment from the affiliate.

EXHIBIT 18.10

Net Cash Flows of Teltrex Affiliates through the Central Cash Depository after Netting Multilateral Netting Payments and Net Payments from External Transactions ($000)

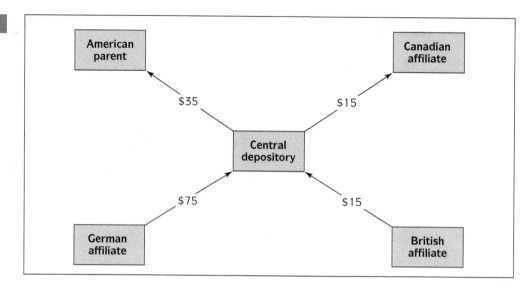

central depository as a result of external transactions. The parent receives a single payment from the cash pool of $35,000 and the Canadian affiliate receives $15,000. The German affiliate remits to the central depository $75,000 and the British affiliate remits $15,000.

In total, the central depository receives $90,000 and disburses $50,000 for an expected net increase in cash of $40,000 for the week. Instead of two separate sets of cash flows totalling $55,000 from the multilateral netting and $150,000 from transactions with external parties, there is only one set of cash flows after the netting totalling $140,000. Thus, there is a saving on foreign exchange transactions of $65,000 for the week. Exhibit 18.10 diagrams the resulting $140,000 of cash flows for Teltrex that are calculated in Exhibit 18.9.

18.3 BILATERAL NETTING OF INTERNAL AND EXTERNAL NET CASH FLOWS

An additional benefit of a centralized cash depository is that the MNC's investment in precautionary cash balances can be reduced without compromising the firm's ability to cover unforeseen expenses. To see how this is accomplished, consider the receipts and disbursements each affiliate of Teltrex expects to make with external parties during the week. Assume, for simplicity, that each affiliate will make *all* its planned payments to external parties before it receives any cash from other external sources. For example, from Exhibit 18.7, the Canadian affiliate expects to pay to external parties the equivalent of $165,000 before it receives any of the expected $135,000 in receipts. Thus, the Canadian affiliate will need a transactions balance of $165,000 to cover expected transactions.

As previously mentioned, a firm keeps a precautionary cash balance to cover unexpected transactions during the budget period. The size of this balance depends on how safe the firm wants to be in its ability to meet unexpected transactions. The larger the precautionary cash balance, the greater the firm's ability to meet unexpected expenses and the lower its risk of financial embarrassment and loss of credit standing. Assume that cash needs are normally distributed and that the cash needs of one affiliate are independent of the others. If Teltrex follows a conservative

policy, it might keep three standard deviations of cash for precautionary purposes in addition to the cash needed to cover expected transactions for the planning period. Thus, the probability that Teltrex would experience a cash shortage is only 0.13 of 1 percent; it will have sufficient cash to cover transactions 99.87 percent of the time.

Under a decentralized cash management system, each affiliate would hold its own transaction balance and precautionary cash. Exhibit 18.11 shows the total cash held for transactions and precautionary purposes by each affiliate and by Teltrex as a whole.

As can be seen from Exhibit 18.11, Teltrex needs the equivalent of $490,000 in cash to cover expected transactions and an additional $615,000 in precautionary balances to cover unexpected expenses, for a total of $1,105,000. A centralized cash management system will greatly reduce the investment in precautionary cash balances. Under a centralized system, the amount of cash held by the MNC is viewed as a portfolio. Each affiliate will continue to hold cash sufficient to cover its expected cash transactions, but the precautionary cash balances are held by the central cash manager at the central cash depository. In the event one of the affiliates experiences a cash shortage, funds would be transferred from precautionary cash held in the central cash pool.

EXHIBIT 18.11

Transaction and
Precautionary Cash
Balances Held
by Each Teltrex
Affiliate under a
Decentralized
Cash Management
System

Affiliate	Expected Transactions (a)	Standard Deviation (b)	Expected Needs plus Precautionary (a + 3b)
United States	$120,000	$50,000	$ 270,000
Canada	165,000	70,000	375,000
Germany	50,000	20,000	110,000
United Kingdom	155,000	65,000	350,000
Total	$490,000		$1,105,000

From portfolio theory, the standard deviation of the portfolio of cash held by the centralized depository for N affiliates is calculated as[1]

$$\text{Portfolio Std. Dev.} = \sqrt{(\text{Std. Dev. Affiliate 1})^2 + \ldots + (\text{Std. Dev. Affiliate } N)^2}$$

For our example,

$$\text{Portfolio Std. Dev.} = \sqrt{(\$50,000)^2 + (\$70,000)^2 + (\$20,000)^2 + (\$65,000)^2}$$

$$= \$109,659$$

Thus, under a centralized system, only $328,977 (= 3 × $109,659) needs to be held for precautionary purposes by Teltrex's central cash manager. A total of $818,977 (= $490,000 + $328,977) is held by Teltrex. The reduction in precautionary cash balances under the centralized system is $286,023 (= $1,105,000 − $818,977), a sum that most likely can be used more profitably elsewhere, rather than standing by as a potential safety net.

18.4 TRANSFER PRICING AND RELATED ISSUES

Within a large business firm with multiple divisions, goods and services are frequently transferred from one division to another. The process brings into question the **transfer price** that should be assigned, for bookkeeping purposes, to the goods or services as they are transferred between divisions. Obviously, the higher the transfer price, the larger will be the profits reported for the transferring division relative to the receiving division. Even within a domestic firm, it is difficult to decide on the transfer price that most accurately reflects the internal transfer of value and is most consistent with managerial incentives. Within an MNC, the decision is further compounded by international income tax considerations that stem from differences in tax rates between the two countries. Capital-repatriation restrictions may also come into play to the extent that "transfer pricing" is a difficult-to-detect means to transfer funds from one place to another.

The following illustrated mini case, which looks at Mintel Products, develops several key strategic considerations in international transfer pricing. In particular, there is a focus on the implications of transfer pricing for the consolidated (or worldwide) after-tax income of Mintel. In simplest terms, if an MNC can use transfer pricing to shift revenues to one of its affiliates in a low-tax country and/or to shift costs to an affiliate in a high-tax country (where tax deductions are more valuable), then the company's overall taxes are reduced and consolidated after-tax income is greater. The size of the tax-saving effect depends on the tax rates, rules and regulations of the countries involved. Therefore, an illustration and discussion of transfer-pricing strategy requires a specific context—above all, the illustration must be presented in the context of a *specific home country's* rates, rules and regulations.

In the following illustrative case, Mintel is based in the United States. Therefore the tax-minimizing benefits from a transfer pricing depend primarily on US rates, rules and

---

[1] The standard deviation formula assumes that interaffiliate cash flows are uncorrelated with one another.

regulations. As we shall see, the benefit to Mintel from transferring reported income from a high-tax country (say, the US) to a low-tax country depends on the *difference* between the tax rates in the two countries. For US-based firms, the US tax authorities include the firm's non-US income in calculating the US tax liability and then the US gives a **foreign tax credit** for the taxes paid to other countries.

For a Canadian-based MNC, the tax rules and regulations concerning foreign source income are somewhat different from the US and therefore the incentives for transfer pricing are likewise different. For all practical purposes, a Canadian-based MNC is not taxed on income that it earns outside of Canada. As a result Canadian-based MNCs have a stronger incentive than comparable US-based MNCs to find low-tax countries in which to operate.

For a Canadian manager, in view of the significant presence of US-owned subsidiaries in Canada as well as the force of competition of US-based companies on Canadian MNCs at home and abroad, it is crucial for Canadian managers to appreciate the transfer pricing strategy—and the potential effects on after-tax profitability that follow from such strategy—from the perspective of US-based MNCs. Subtle differences for the case of a Canadian-based MNC are discussed in Chapter 20. An extensive illustration, "Mintel Products Transfer Pricing Strategy," follows. Immediately following that case, an International Finance in Practice box, "The Sea Change for Tax and Transfer Pricing," outlines the tension between international business, which seeks to minimize global tax, and tax authorities intent on defending the integrity of their corporate tax systems.

Illustrated **Mini Case**

Mintel Products Transfer Pricing Strategy

Low versus High Markup Policy

Mintel Products, Inc. manufactures goods for sale in the United States and overseas. Finished goods are transferred from the parent firm to its wholly owned sales affiliate for overseas retail sale. Mintel's financial manager, Hilary Van Kirk, has decided that the firm's transfer pricing strategy should be reevaluated as part of a routine review of the operations of the sales affiliate. Van Kirk has decided to explore both low and high markup policies. She notes that both the parent firm and the sales affiliate have a 40 percent income tax rate, that the variable production cost of one unit is $1,500, and that the unit retail sales price charged by the sales affiliate to the final customer is $3,000. As a first step in her analysis, Van Kirk prepares Exhibit 18.12. The upper portion of the exhibit presents the analysis of a low markup policy, where the transfer price is set at $2,000. The lower portion of the exhibit analyzes the effect of a high markup policy, where the transfer price is $2,400 per unit.

Van Kirk notes from Exhibit 18.12 that the low markup policy results in larger pre-tax income, income taxes, and net income per unit in the selling country. On the other hand, the high markup policy has the opposite effect, that is, higher taxable income, income taxes and net profit per unit in the manufacturing country. She also notes that because the income tax rates are the same in both countries, the consolidated results are identical, regardless of whether the MNC follows a low or a high transfer pricing scheme.

Exchange Restrictions

Van Kirk wonders if Mintel should be indifferent between the low and high markup policies, since the consolidated results are the same. She reasons, however, that if the distribution country imposes exchange restrictions limiting or blocking the amount of profits that can be repatriated to the manufacturing parent, Mintel would no longer be indifferent between the two markup policies. It obviously would prefer the high markup policy.

EXHIBIT 18.12

Low versus High
Transfer Pricing
Strategy between
Mintel Affiliates with
the Same Income
Tax Rate

	Manufacturing Affiliate	Sales Affiliate	Consolidated Company
Low Markup Policy			
Sales revenue	$2,000	$3,000	$3,000
Cost of goods sold	1,500	2,000	1,500
Gross profit	500	1,000	1,500
Operating expenses	200	200	400
Taxable income	300	800	1,100
Income taxes (40%)	120	320	440
Net income	180	480	660
High Markup Policy			
Sales revenue	$2,400	$3,000	$3,000
Cost of goods sold	1,500	2,400	1,500
Gross profit	900	600	1,500
Operating expenses	200	200	400
Taxable income	700	400	1,100
Income taxes (40%)	280	160	440
Net income	420	240	660

According to Exhibit 18.12, the higher markup allows $240 per unit to be repatriated to the parent that otherwise may have been blocked. This amount represents the $400 higher markup minus the $160 additional taxes paid in the parent country.

Van Kirk notes that the low markup policy is disadvantageous from the host country's perspective. If the transferring affiliate attempts to reposition funds by changing from the low to the high markup policy, the exchange controls have been partially bypassed and there is a loss of tax revenue in the host country. Thus, the host country may take measures to enforce a certain transfer price. She decides that she needs to research how this might be accomplished and also to consider the effect of a difference in income tax rates between the two affiliates.

Differential Income Tax Rates
As a second step, Van Kirk prepares Exhibit 18.13, which examines the low versus the high markup policy when the tax rate in the transferring country is assumed to be 25 percent, or 15 percent less than the tax rate of 40 percent in the receiving country.

Van Kirk notes from Exhibit 18.13 that the consolidated *taxable* income is $1,100 under both markup policies. However, Mintel would no longer be indifferent when there is a differential in the income tax rates. In the absence of governmental restrictions on the transfer price, the MNC would prefer a high markup policy when the tax rate in the parent country is lower than the tax rate in the receiving country. Consolidated net income for Mintel would be $60 [= ($2,000 − $2,400) × (0.25 − 0.40)] per unit greater under the high versus the low markup policy. The high markup policy results in $400 per unit of taxable income being shifted from the receiving country to the transferring country, where it is taxed at a 15 percent lower rate. Consequently, the consolidated income taxes paid by Mintel drop from $395 to $335 per unit.

If the tax rate in the receiving country is lower than in the parent country, it is not clear that a low markup policy should be pursued. Van Kirk recalls that American MNCs are taxed on their worldwide income. Hence, income repatriated to the American parent from a receiving country with a low tax rate would be "grossed up" to its pre-tax amount so that American taxes could be figured. A credit for the taxes paid in the

EXHIBIT 18.13

Low versus High
Transfer Pricing
Strategy between
Mintel Affiliates with
Differential Income
Tax Rates

	Manufacturing Affiliate	Sales Affiliate	Consolidated Company
Low Markup Policy			
Sales revenue	$2,000	$3,000	$3,000
Cost of goods sold	1,500	2,000	1,500
Gross profit	500	1,000	1,500
Operating expenses	200	200	400
Taxable income	300	800	1,100
Income taxes (25%/40%)	75	320	395
Net income	225	480	705
High Markup Policy			
Sales revenue	$2,400	$3,000	$3,000
Cost of goods sold	1,500	2,400	1,500
Gross profit	900	600	1,500
Operating expenses	200	200	400
Taxable income	700	400	1,100
Income taxes (25%/40%)	175	160	335
Net income	525	240	765

receiving country would be given against taxes owed in the United States. Thus, pursuing a low markup policy would not result in a dollar tax savings if net income was to be repatriated. However, if the net income of the foreign subsidiary was to be reinvested in the host country, the low markup policy would result in a tax savings and allow more funds for reinvestment. Nevertheless, this would only be temporary, Van Kirk reasons. At some point, profitable investment opportunities would be exhausted, and the parent firm and its shareholders would desire some return on the investment made—and this means repatriation.

Regulations Affecting Transfer Prices

Van Kirk believes that governmental authorities within a host country would be quite aware of the motives of MNCs to use transfer pricing schemes to move blocked funds or evade tax liabilities. After doing some research, she learns that most countries have regulations controlling transfer prices. In the United States, the US Internal Revenue Code Section 482: Allocation of Income and Deductions among Taxpayers stipulates that the transfer price must reflect an *arm's-length price*, that is, a price the selling affiliate would charge an unrelated customer for the good or service. The Internal Revenue Service (IRS) "may distribute, apportion, or allocate gross income, deductions, credits, or allowances between or among such organizations . . . [if it is] necessary in order to prevent evasion of taxes or clearly to reflect the income of any such organizations. . . ." Moreover, in the event of conflict, the burden of proof lies with the taxpayer to show that the IRS has unreasonably established the transfer price and determined taxable income.

She learns that there are three basic methods prescribed by the IRS, and recognized internationally, for establishing arm's-length prices of tangible goods. The method considered the best is to use a *comparable uncontrolled price* between unrelated firms. While this method seems reasonable and theoretically sound, it is difficult to use in practice because many factors enter into the pricing of goods and services between two business enterprises. The Code allows for some adjustments because differences in the terms of sale, the quantity sold, quality differences, and the date of sale are all factors that can realistically affect the sale price among various customers. Thus, what is a reasonable price for one customer may not be reasonable for another. The next-best method is the *resale price* approach, which can be used if, among other things, there is no comparable uncontrolled sales price. Under this method, the price at which the good is resold by the distribution affiliate is reduced by an amount sufficient to cover overhead costs and a reasonable profit. However, it may be difficult to determine the value added by the distribution affiliate. The third method is the *cost-plus* approach, where an appropriate profit is added to the cost of the manufacturing affiliate. This method assumes that the manufacturing cost is readily accountable. Additionally, a group of methods collectively referred to as *fourth methods* can be applied to approximate arm's-length prices when the three basic methods are not applicable. The fourth methods include those based on financial and economic models and econometric techniques. The comparable uncontrolled price method and fourth methods are used for determining an arm's-length transfer price for intangible goods, whereas cost methods are used for pricing services.

The Organization for Economic Co-operation and Development (OECD) Model Tax Convention sets out the same methods as the IRS Code for use by member countries. Van Kirk concludes that all methods present operational difficulties of some type and are also difficult for the taxing authority to evaluate. Thus, transfer pricing manipulation cannot be completely controlled and the potential exists for manoeuvrability by the MNC to reposition funds or reduce its tax liability.

The International Finance in Practice box "The Sea of Change for Tax and Transfer Pricing" discusses a recent survey by the international accounting firm Ernst & Young.

Import Duties

After some reflection, Van Kirk concludes that import duties are another factor that need to be considered. When a host country imposes an *ad valorem* import duty on goods shipped across its borders from another country, the import tax raises the cost of doing business within the country. An *ad valorem* duty is a percentage tax levied at customs on the assessed value of the imported goods. She reasons that an import tax will affect the transfer pricing strategy an MNC uses, but that, in general, the income tax will have the greatest after-tax effect on consolidated net income. To analyze the effect of an import duty on Mintel, she prepares Exhibit 18.14, which shows the low and high transfer price alternatives presented in Exhibit 18.13 with the imposition of a 5 percent import duty by the receiving country.

Comparison of Exhibits 18.13 and 18.14 shows Van Kirk that under the low markup policy, Mintel would receive $60 less (= $645 − $705) per unit if a 5 percent import duty was imposed by the host country. The $60 represents the after-tax cost of the $100 import duty on the $2,000 per-unit transfer price cost of the good. Mintel would still prefer the high markup policy as before, however, as it results in an increase in net income from $645 to $693 per unit. The difference in the net incomes between the two markup policies is only $48, in comparison with $60 without the 5 percent import tax. The loss of $12 represents the after-tax cost of an additional $20 of import duty per unit when the transfer price is $2,400 instead of $2,000 per unit.

Unbundling Fund Transfers

As Van Kirk knows, host countries are well aware of transfer pricing schemes used by MNCs to evade taxes within country borders or to avoid exchange restrictions. She wonders if there are ways to avoid suspicion from host-country governmental authorities, and the administrative hassle likely to arise from such an inquiry, when the firm is merely trying to repatriate a sufficient amount of funds from a foreign affiliate to make the investment worthwhile. To learn more about transfer pricing strategies and related issues, she decides to attend a one-day seminar on the topic she saw advertised by a professional

EXHIBIT 18.14

Low versus High
Transfer Pricing
Strategy between
Mintel Affiliates with
Differential Income
Tax Rates and a
5 Percent Import
Duty

	Manufacturing Affiliate	Sales Affiliate	Consolidated Company
Low Markup Policy			
Sales revenue	$2,000	$3,000	$3,000
Cost of goods sold	1,500	2,000	1,500
Import duty (5%)	—	100	100
Gross profit	500	900	1,400
Operating expenses	200	200	400
Taxable income	300	700	1,000
Income taxes (25%/40%)	75	280	355
Net income	225	420	645
High Markup Policy			
Sales revenue	$2,400	$3,000	$3,000
Cost of goods sold	1,500	2,400	1,500
Import duty (5%)	—	120	120
Gross profit	900	480	1,380
Operating expenses	200	200	400
Taxable income	700	280	980
Income taxes (25%/40%)	175	112	287
Net income	525	168	693

organization to which she belongs. She hopes it is beneficial, as the registration fee is $500 for the day!

As it turns out, the money was well spent. In addition to making the acquaintance of financial managers from other companies, Van Kirk learned at the conference that an MNC is likely to fare better if, instead of lumping all costs into a single transfer price, the parent firm unbundles the package to recognize the cost of the physical good and each service separately that it provides the affiliate. A detailing of the charges makes it easier, if ever necessary, to present and support to the taxing authority of a host country that each charge is legitimate and can be well substantiated. For instance, in addition to charging for the cost of the physical good, the parent firm could charge a fee for technical training of the affiliate's staff, a share of the cost of worldwide advertising or other corporate overhead, or a royalty or licensing fee as payment for use of well-recognized brand names, technology or patents. The royalty or licensing fee represents remuneration for expense previously incurred by the parent for development or having made the product one that is desirable to own.

As a final step in her analysis, Van Kirk prepares Exhibit 18.15, which reproduces the low versus high markup policy analysis for Mintel with differential income tax rates presented in Exhibit 18.13. In addition, Exhibit 18.15 shows that a $2,000 transfer price and $400 per unit charge for royalties and fees results in the same consolidated net income of $765 as does the high markup policy with a $2,400 transfer price. By comparison, the low markup policy only provides $705 per unit consolidated net income. This is the case, regardless of whether a portion of the $480 net income of the sales affiliate is repatriated to the manufacturing affiliate as a dividend, because the tax rate in the distribution country is higher. As Van Kirk learned at the conference, the strategy of recognizing specific services may be acceptable to the host government, whereas the high markup policy may not, if $2,400 appears to be more than an arm's-length price for the transferred good.

EXHIBIT 18.15

Low versus High
Transfer Pricing
Strategy for Mintel
with Low Transfer
Price and Additional
Royalty Charge with
Differential Income
Tax Rates

	Manufacturing Affiliate	Sales Affiliate	Consolidated Company
Low Markup Policy			
Sales revenue	$2,000	$3,000	$3,000
Cost of goods sold	1,500	2,000	1,500
Gross profit	500	1,000	1,500
Operating expenses	200	200	400
Taxable income	300	800	1,100
Income taxes (25%/40%)	75	320	395
Net income	225	480	705
High Markup Policy			
Sales revenue	$2,400	$3,000	$3,000
Cost of goods sold	1,500	2,400	1,500
Gross profit	900	600	1,500
Operating expenses	200	200	400
Taxable income	700	400	1,100
Income taxes (25%/40%)	175	160	335
Net income	525	240	765
Low Markup Policy and Royalty			
Sales revenue	$2,000	$3,000	$3,000
Royalty and fee income	400	—	—
Cost of goods sold	1,500	2,400	1,500
Gross profit	900	600	1,500
Operating expenses	200	200	400
Taxable income	700	400	1,100
Income taxes (25%/40%)	175	160	335
Net income	525	240	765

Miscellaneous Factors

Transfer pricing strategies may be beneficial when the host country restricts the amount of foreign exchange that can be used for importing specific goods. In this event, a lower transfer price allows a greater quantity of the good to be imported under a quota restriction. This may be a more important consideration than income tax savings, if the imported item is a necessary component needed by an assembly or manufacturing affiliate to continue or expand production.

Transfer prices also have an effect on how divisions of an MNC are perceived locally. A high markup policy leaves little net income to show on the affiliate's books. If the parent firm expects the affiliate to be able to borrow short-term funds locally in the event of a cash shortage, the affiliate may have difficulty doing so with unimpressive financial statements. On the other hand, a low markup policy makes it appear, at least superficially, as if affiliates, rather than the parent firm, are contributing a larger portion to consolidated earnings. To the extent that financial markets are inefficient, or securities analysts do not understand the transfer pricing strategy being used, the market value of the MNC may be lower than is justified.

Obviously, transfer pricing strategies have an effect on international capital expenditure analysis. A very low (high) markup policy makes the APV of a subsidiary's capital expenditure appear more (less) attractive. Consequently, in order to obtain a meaningful analysis,

The Sea of Change for Tax and Transfer Pricing

Transfer pricing continues to be a significant source of controversy between the world's tax authorities and multinational enterprises (MNEs). Since the publication of EY's last transfer pricing survey in 2010, the pace of globalization has increased, and businesses have been working hard to adapt by better managing their cross-border activities. They're struggling to comply with unfamiliar and frequently changing tax and statutory requirements in new markets, examining the tax efficiency of supply chains and administering a vast array of indirect taxes, including value-added taxes (VATs), customs duties and goods and services taxes (GSTs).

At the same time, tax authorities worldwide have stepped up their enforcement, and they are paying special attention to transfer pricing. Transfer pricing has also taken on a bigger profile with non-tax stakeholders who are acutely aware that, according to the OECD, "around 60% of world trade actually takes place within multinational enterprises."[1]

Many companies are facing increasing exposure to new transfer pricing inquiries on a much broader scale. Our *2013 Global Transfer Pricing Survey* of international tax practitioners and C-suite executives in 26 countries confirms that controversy and double taxation are on the rise.

It also confirms that companies around the world are reacting to the new pressures. Most notably, 66% of companies identified "risk management" as their highest priority for transfer pricing in this latest survey, a 32% increase over surveys conducted in 2007 and 2010. Correspondingly, the percentage of companies identifying cash tax or effective tax rate optimization as their highest transfer pricing priority fell by nearly one-third— to 17%—from just three years ago.

We attribute this more cautious posture to three main factors.

1. Controversy on the rise, as transfer pricing deemed "high risk"

First, we have seen a sharp increase in tax controversy around the world in general, and regarding transfer pricing in particular. For instance, 77% of companies surveyed in our *2011–12 Tax Risk and Controversy Survey* said they anticipated managing tax risk and controversy would become more important in the next two years.[2]

Respondents to that survey reported that governments are demanding more disclosure from taxpayers, stiffening economic substance doctrines and, in some countries, imposing criminal sanctions for compliance failures. They also reported more frequent and aggressive audits that were more costly to defend or litigate, as well as more assessments and proposed penalties.

An increased focus on international tax by tax authorities and tax policymakers is reflected in a range of enforcement initiatives and even the proposal of alternatives to the arm's-length standard for transfer pricing.

We are seeing more and more governments expanding their definition of "aggressive tax planning" and contemplating or adopting general anti-avoidance rules that empower their tax authorities to make broad challenges.

In addition, we are seeing tax authorities increasingly assert the existence of a permanent establishment and the triggering of the associated taxing rights.

The *2011–12 Tax Risk and Controversy Survey* found 57% of tax administrators identified transfer pricing as their top risk focus in the next 12 months, while some 40% of companies responding to that survey also identified transfer pricing as their leading risk. Separately, our *2012 Global Transfer Pricing Tax Authority Survey* supported these findings, reporting that 46 of 48 countries surveyed are backing up their concern with additional resources to examine transfer pricing.[3]

EXHIBIT 18.16   Tax Risk Management Increases as a Priority

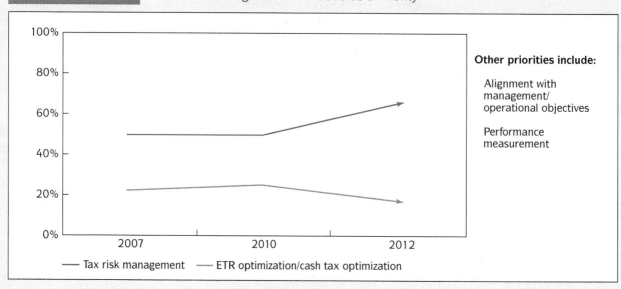

This 2013 Global Transfer Pricing Survey finds plenty of evidence that the authorities' emphasis is having an effect. Respondents report that examinations by revenue authorities have expanded in scope and complexity, while adjustments resulting in penalties are on the rise. Documentation requirements are also being strengthened—the frequency of transfer pricing documentation filed as being deemed adequate on audit declined for MNEs in 22 of the 26 countries covered by our survey. And there has been a significant increase in unresolved reviews and audits compared with previous years. In cases where examinations resulted in adjustments, penalties were imposed 24% of the time, up from 19% in 2010 and 15% in 2007.

2. Rapid-growth markets emerging risks

The rise of compliance activities by tax authorities in some rapid-growth markets is the second reason companies report that risk management is an increased priority for transfer pricing.

The number of respondents to this *2013 Global Transfer Pricing Survey* that reported they were subject to a review of their transfer pricing policies in India, for example, more than doubled in 2012 from 2007. Nearly 30% of parent companies operating in BRIC and African countries now say those are their No. 1 or No. 2 most important areas when it comes to managing transfer pricing.

At the same time, the imposition of penalties by tax authorities in markets such as China, India and Indonesia indicates companies may need to increase their resources and change their focus to deal with transfer pricing matters in those jurisdictions.

The growing assertiveness by rapid-growth markets gives rise to occurrences of double taxation. Nearly 70% of companies answering the survey reported they had experienced double taxation as a result of an adjustment. The number of companies saying they had referred a transfer pricing matter to competent authority in the past three years increased 55% from 2010, the last time we asked the question.

3. Reputational risks

The final factor influencing the shift to prioritizing transfer pricing risk management is the attention paid to transfer pricing by stakeholders who are not tax professionals. Transfer pricing has become a hot topic for journalists, antipoverty and social justice organizations, and political leaders around the world who are challenging international tax rules they feel do not fairly deliver the revenue they were intended to capture.

A broad debate about tax "fairness" playing out worldwide has thrust tax to the top of the C-suite risk agenda. In February 2013, British Prime Minister David Cameron compared "aggressive" tax avoidance by corporations to tax evasion: "The problem with that is that there are some forms of tax avoidance that have become so aggressive that I think there are moral questions we have to answer about whether we want to encourage or allow that sort of behavior."[4]

In the United States, senators Carl Levin (D-MI) and Bernard Sanders (I-VT.) have used similar rhetoric and held public hearings examining how companies treat tax as part of their cross-border activities. Officials in Australia, New Zealand, Canada, as well as South Africa and Zambia have been equally critical of what they perceive to be a high frequency of international tax avoidance by multinational corporations. In June 2013, the G8 responded to the growing concerns with a communiqué expressing support for greater transparency with tax authorities and endorsing the OECD's ongoing work on BEPS.

James Henderson, Chief Executive of global public relations firm Pelham Bell Pottinger, referred to the debate as "the tax spring" in the January 2013 edition of EY's *T Magazine*. "In today's climate of economic austerity, the public expects everyone to do their bit," Henderson wrote. "Expectations about good citizenship are particularly high for well-known and popular consumer brands."[5]

Many of the headlines and activist protests, as well as much of the political rhetoric, betray a lack of technical knowledge about how transfer pricing works. But the coverage has created a number of reputation risk challenges for companies looking to reconcile legally compliant tax positions with public perceptions about them. These concerns are magnified when accusations of tax avoidance are amplified by social media.

The media has focused its coverage heavily on the mobility of intangible assets. That appears to reflect the concern of tax authorities. It also appears to help explain an increase in the percentage of companies predicting intangible property will be their most important area of transfer pricing controversy by 2014.

Interestingly, this survey demonstrates that companies are mainly struggling with the burdens of complying with an increasingly onerous worldwide regulatory framework. The need to consider how the public at large has come to perceive transfer pricing only makes that task more complex.

[1] "OECD Insights," *OECDInsights*, http://oecdinsights.org/2012/03/26/price-fixing/, 18 April 2013 Debate the Issues

[2] "2011-12 Tax risk and controversy survey," Ernst & Young, http://www.ey.com/GL/en/Services/Tax/2011-12-Tax-risk-and-controversy-survey/, 28 April 2013

[3] "2012 global transfer pricing tax authority survey," *T Magazine*, http://tmagazine.ey.com/insights/2012-global-transfer-pricing-tax-authority-survey/, 18 April 2013

[4] "Cameron likens multinationals tax avoidance to illegal evasion." www.Bloomberg.org, http://www.bloomberg.com/news/2013-02-18/cameron-likens-multinationals-tax-avoidance-to-illegal-evasion.html, 23 April 2013

[5] James Henderson. "How to talk about a tax crisis." *T Magazine*. January 2013. http://tmagazine.ey.com/insights/how-talk-tax-crisis/

Source: Ernst & Young, "Navigating the Choppy Waters of International Tax," 2013 Global Transfer Pricing Survey, pp. 3–4. Reprinted with permission of Ernst & Young. http://www.ey.com/GL/en/Services/Tax/2013-Global-Transfer-Pricing-Survey.

arm's-length pricing should be used in the APV analysis to determine after-tax operating income, regardless of the actual transfer price employed. A separate term in the APV analysis can be used to recognize tax savings from transfer pricing strategies. This was the recommended approach detailed in Chapter 17.

18.5 BLOCKED FUNDS

For a variety of reasons, a country may find itself short of foreign currency reserves and thus impose exchange restrictions on its own currency, limiting its conversion into other currencies so as not to further reduce scarce foreign currency reserves. When a country enforces exchange controls, the remittance of profits from a subsidiary firm to its foreign parent is blocked. The blockage may be only temporary or it may be for a considerable period of time. A lengthy blockage is detrimental to an MNC. Without the ability to repatriate profits from a foreign subsidiary, the MNC might as well not even have the investment as returns are not being paid to the shareholders of the MNC.

Prior to making a capital investment in a foreign subsidiary, the parent firm should investigate the potential of future funds blockage. This is part of the capital expenditure analysis outlined in Chapter 17. The APV framework developed in that chapter only considers the expected operating cash flows that are available for repatriation.

Unexpected funds blockage after an investment has been made, however, is a political risk with which the MNC must contend. Thus, the MNC should be familiar with methods for moving blocked funds so as to benefit its shareholders. Several methods for moving blocked funds have already been discussed in this chapter and others. For example, transfer pricing strategies and unbundling services are methods the MNC might be able to use to move otherwise blocked funds. These methods were covered earlier in this chapter. Moreover, in Chapter 13, leading and lagging of payments were discussed primarily as a means of controlling transaction exposure. However, leading and lagging payments may be used as a strategy for repositioning funds within an MNC. Additional strategies that may be useful for moving blocked funds are *export creation* and *direct negotiation*.

Export creation involves using the blocked funds of a subsidiary in the country in which they are blocked to pay for exports that can be used to benefit the parent firm or other affiliates. Thus, instead of using repatriated funds to pay for goods or services that will benefit the MNC, blocked funds are used. Examples include using consulting firms located in the host country where funds are blocked, instead of a firm in the parent country, to provide necessary consulting work that benefits the MNC; transferring personnel from corporate headquarters to the subsidiary offices, where they will be paid in the blocked local currency; using the national airlines of the host country, when possible, for the international travel of all MNC executives, where the reservations and fare payments are made by the subsidiary; and holding business conferences in the host country, instead of elsewhere, where the expenses are paid by the local subsidiary. All of these possibilities not only benefit the MNC, since these goods and services are needed, but also benefit various industries within the host country.

Host countries want to attract foreign industries that benefit their economic development and the technical skills of their people. Thus, foreign investment in industries that produce export goods, such as automobiles or electronic equipment, or in industries that attract tourists, such as resort hotels, is desirable. For the host country, this type of investment provides good employment and training and is also a source, rather than a use, of foreign exchange. The host country should not expect an MNC to make beneficial investment within its borders if it is not likely to receive an appropriate return. Consequently, MNCs in desirable industries may be able to convince the host-country government through direct negotiation that funds blockage is detrimental to all.

SUMMARY

This chapter discusses cash management in the multinational firm. Special attention is given to the topics of multilateral netting and transfer pricing policy. Illustrated case problems are used to show the benefits of centralized cash management and to examine transfer pricing strategies.

1. A multilateral netting system is beneficial in reducing the number of and the expense associated with interaffiliate foreign exchange transactions.

2. A centralized cash pool assists in reducing the problem of mislocated funds and in funds mobilization. A central cash manager has a global view of the most favourable borrowing rates and most advantageous investment rates.

3. A centralized cash management system with a cash pool can reduce the investment the MNC has in precautionary cash balances, saving the firm money.

4. Transfer pricing strategies are a means to reposition funds within an MNC and a possible technique for reducing tax liabilities and removing blocked funds from a host country that has imposed foreign exchange restrictions.

5. Unbundling fund transfers, export creation and direct negotiation are other means for removing blocked funds from a host country that is enforcing foreign exchange restrictions.

QUESTIONS

1. Describe the key factors contributing to effective cash management within a firm. Why is the cash management process more difficult in an MNC?

2. Discuss the pros and cons of an MNC having a centralized cash manager handle all investment and borrowing for all affiliates of the MNC versus each affiliate having a local manager who performs the cash management activities of the affiliate.

3. How might an MNC use transfer pricing strategies? How do import duties affect transfer pricing policies?

4. What are the various means the taxing authority of a country might use to determine if a transfer price is *reasonable?*

5. Discuss how an MNC might attempt to repatriate blocked funds from a host country.

PROBLEMS

1. Affiliate A sells 5,000 units to Affiliate B per year. The marginal income tax rate for Affiliate A is 25 percent and the marginal income tax rate for Affiliate B is 40 percent. The transfer price per unit is currently $2,000, but it can be set at any level between $2,000 and $2,400. Derive a formula to determine how much annual after-tax profits can be increased by selecting the optimal transfer price.

2. Affiliate A sells 5,000 units to Affiliate B per year. The marginal income tax rate for Affiliate A

is 25 percent and the marginal income tax rate for Affiliate B is 40 percent. Additionally, Affiliate B pays a tax-deductible tariff of 5 percent on imported merchandise. The transfer price per unit is currently $2,000, but it can be set at any level between $2,000 and $2,400. Derive (a) a formula to determine the effective marginal tax rate for Affiliate B and (b) a formula to determine how much annual after-tax profits can be increased by selecting the optimal transfer price.

INTERNET EXERCISE

The Transfer Pricing Management Benchmarking Association conducts benchmarking studies to identify the best transfer pricing processes that will improve the overall operations of its members. Go to its website, at

www.tpmba.com, to learn about the objectives of the association and the events it sponsors. You may be interested in receiving its free newsletter.

MINI CASE 1

Efficient Funds Flow at Eastern Trading Company

The Eastern Trading Company of Singapore purchases spices in bulk from around the world, packages them into consumer-size quantities and sells them through sales affiliates in Hong Kong, the United Kingdom and the United States. For a recent month, the payments matrix of interaffiliate cash flows (at right), stated in Singapore dollars, was forecast. Show how Eastern Trading can use multilateral netting to minimize the foreign exchange transactions necessary to settle interaffiliate payments. If foreign exchange transactions cost the company 0.5 percent, what savings result from netting?

Eastern Trading Company Payments Matrix (S$000)

	Disbursements				
Receipts	Singapore	Hong Kong	UK	US	Total Receipts
Singapore	—	40	75	55	170
Hong Kong	8	—	—	22	30
UK	15	—	—	17	32
US	11	25	9	—	45
Total disbursements	34	65	84	94	277

MINI CASE 2

Eastern Trading Company's Optimal Transfer Pricing Strategy

The Eastern Trading Company of Singapore ships prepackaged spices to Hong Kong, the United Kingdom and the United States, where they are resold by sales affiliates. Eastern Trading is concerned with what might happen in Hong Kong now that control has been turned over to China. Eastern Trading has decided that it should reexamine its transfer pricing policy with its Hong Kong affiliate as a means of repositioning funds from Hong Kong to Singapore. The table (at right) shows the present transfer pricing scheme, based on a carton of assorted, prepackaged spices, which is the typical shipment to the Hong Kong sales affiliate. What do you recommend that Eastern Trading should do?

Eastern Trading Company Current Transfer Pricing Policy with Hong Kong Sales Affiliate

	Singapore Parent	Hong Kong Affiliate	Consolidated Company
Sales revenue	S$300	S$500	S$500
Cost of goods sold	200	300	200
Gross profit	100	200	300
Operating expenses	50	50	100
Taxable income	50	150	200
Income taxes (31%/16.5%)	16	25	41
Net income	34	125	159

MINI CASE 3

Eastern Trading Company's New MBA

The Eastern Trading Company of Singapore currently follows a decentralized system of cash management wherein it and its affiliates each maintain their own transaction and precautionary cash balances. Eastern Trading believes that it and its affiliates' cash needs are normally distributed and independent from one another. It is corporate policy to maintain 2.5 standard deviations of cash as precautionary holdings. At this level of safety, there is a 99.37 percent chance that each affiliate will have enough cash holdings to cover transactions.

A new MBA hired by the company claims that the investment in precautionary cash balances is needlessly large and can be reduced substantially if the firm converts

to a centralized cash management system. Use the projected information for the current month, which is presented below, to determine the amount of cash Eastern Trading needs to hold in precautionary balances under its current decentralized system and the level of precautionary cash it would need to hold under a centralized system. Was the new MBA a good hire?

Affiliate	Expected Transactions	One Standard Deviation
Singapore	S$125,000	S$40,000
Hong Kong	60,000	25,000
United Kingdom	95,000	40,000
United States	70,000	35,000

REFERENCES & SUGGESTED READINGS

Allman-Ward, Michele. "Globalization and the Cash/Treasury Manager." *Journal of Cash Management* 12 (1992), pp. 26–34.

Bogusz, Robert J. "The Renaissance of Netting." *Journal of Cash Management* 13 (1993), pp. 10–17.

Brean, Donald J. S., "Financial Dimensions of Transfer Pricing," in Alan M. Rugman and Lorraine Eden, eds., *Multinationals and Transfer Pricing.* New York: St. Martin's Press, 1985.

Burns, Jane O. "Transfer Pricing Decisions in U.S. Multinational Corporations." *Journal of International Business Studies* 11 (1980), pp. 23–39.

Canada Customs and Revenue Agency. *International Transfer Pricing.* Ottawa: Circular 87-2R (1999).

Collins, J. Markham, and Alan W. Frankle. "International Cash Management Practices of Large U.S. Firms." *Journal of Cash Management* 5 (1985), pp. 42–48.

Diewert, W. Erwin. "Transfer Pricing and Economic Efficiency," in Alan M. Rugman and Lorraine Eden, eds., *Multinationals and Transfer Pricing.* New York: St. Martin's Press, 1985.

Griffiths, Susan. "International Pooling—Getting the Story Straight." *Journal of Cash Management* 12 (1992), pp. 5–7.

Pagar, Jill C., and J. Scott Wilkie. *Transfer Pricing Strategy in a Global Economy.* Amsterdam: IBFD Publications, 1993.

Prusa, Thomas J. "An Incentive Compatible Approach to Transfer Pricing." *Journal of International Economics* 28 (1990), pp. 155–72.

Srinivasin, Venkat, and Yong H. Kim. "Payments Netting in International Cash Management: A Network Optimization Approach." *Journal of International Business Studies* 17 (1986), pp. 1–20.

Tang, Roger Y. W. *Transfer Pricing in the 1990s: Tax and Management Perspectives.* Westport, CT: Quorum Books, 1993.

Tax Aspects of Transfer Pricing within Multinational Enterprises: The United States Proposed Regulations. Paris: Organization for Economic Cooperation and Development, 1993.

Chapter 19

International Trade Finance

CANADA IS ONE of the most economically "open" nations in the world. With annual merchandise exports approaching half a trillion dollars and imports of almost the same magnitude, Canada's total trade (the sum of exports and imports) is 80 percent of the size of our GDP—$3.5 billion of trade crosses our borders every day.

Exhibits 19.1 and 19.2 present statistics on Canada's merchandise trade by product category for the years 2006 to 2012 along with the 2012 share in the total for individual product categories. The export numbers show that Canada ships a substantial amount of natural resources such as energy, oil and gas, minerals and forest products to the rest of the world. Our manufactured or processed exports include automobiles, aircraft, metals (aluminum, copper, nickel), chemicals and fertilizers and industrial machinery. Our largest product categories of imports include industrial goods and materials, machinery and equipment (capital goods) and consumer goods. Overall, the technology content of Canada's exports is lower than the technology content of our imports.

Each transaction in trade has a corresponding international financial side. Things must be paid for. In international trade, the buyer and the seller of a product are in different countries, each with its own currency. Ultimately, a foreign exchange transaction ensues.

International trade can be more difficult and riskier than domestic trade. With foreign trade, there is a greater likelihood that the seller of a product (an exporter) may not be familiar with the purchaser (the importer), creating a problem in judging the foreign purchaser's credit risk. If merchandise is shipped abroad and the buyer does not pay, it may prove difficult if not impossible for the exporter to take legal recourse in the foreign country. On the other hand, from the importer's point of view it is risky to make advance payment for goods that might not ever arrive.

This chapter deals with such issues. We begin with an example of a simple yet typical foreign trade transaction. The mechanics of the trade are discussed in a way that reveals how institutional arrangements have developed over time to facilitate international trade in the light of financial risks that we have identified. The three basic documents required in a foreign trade transaction—a letter of credit, a time draft and a bill of lading—are discussed in detail. We explain how a time draft becomes a banker's acceptance, a negotiable money market instrument. Indeed, banker's acceptances are among the most widely circulated forms of short-term (money market) finance in Canada.

The second part of the chapter outlines the role and operational methods of Export Development Canada (EDC), a Crown corporation that provides financing and risk

EXHIBIT 19.1 Canada's Exports of Goods by Product ($ millions)

	2006	2007	2008	2009	2010	2011	2012	Share 2012 (%)
Total Exports	440,365	450,320	483,489	359,754	398,857	446,450	454,376	
Crude oil and bitumen	37,952	41,849	67,449	42,835	51,950	68,804	74,371	16.4
Passenger cars and light trucks	50,196	48,219	36,623	27,108	37,790	39,100	46,704	10.3
Intermediate metal products	36,290	42,864	42,852	28,492	41,003	47,923	42,165	9.3
Industrial machinery, equipment and parts	22,846	23,859	25,690	21,440	20,303	23,091	24,387	5.4
Farm and fishing products	12,603	15,402	20,311	17,355	16,465	18,824	21,335	4.7
Food, beverage and tobacco products	17,332	17,498	18,792	18,307	19,100	20,371	20,518	4.5
Basic chemicals and industrial chemical products	17,767	20,388	21,586	15,791	19,103	22,961	20,250	4.5
Building and packaging materials	26,751	22,697	18,849	14,530	15,263	15,806	17,492	3.8
Tires; motor vehicle engines and motor vehicle parts	22,615	21,872	17,476	12,327	15,657	15,872	16,976	3.7
Refined petroleum energy products	7,701	7,931	11,465	7,247	8,927	10,510	14,205	3.1
Aircraft, aircraft engines and aircraft parts	12,580	14,030	13,572	13,962	12,479	12,211	13,063	2.9
Other electronic and electrical machinery, equipment and parts	15,994	15,519	15,720	12,964	12,172	13,083	12,924	2.8
Pulp and paper stock	17,742	17,070	17,251	12,910	14,120	14,248	12,715	2.8
Special transactions trade	18,032	16,935	16,979	13,941	10,971	11,340	12,254	2.7
Plastic and rubber products	13,550	12,831	12,672	9,636	10,676	10,872	11,936	2.6
Natural gas, natural gas liquids and related products	30,157	30,417	35,514	17,930	17,625	15,588	10,605	2.3
Metal ores and concentrates	5,874	6,867	8,019	6,735	7,038	9,852	9,564	2.1
Non-metallic minerals	5,301	6,181	11,633	6,574	8,822	10,566	9,369	2.1
Cleaning products, appliances, and miscellaneous goods and supplies	8,082	8,181	8,837	8,721	8,865	9,585	8,850	1.9
Other energy products	3,356	3,076	6,356	5,141	6,185	8,177	6,506	1.4
Food and tobacco intermediate products	2,078	2,612	3,931	3,346	4,041	5,441	6,145	1.4
Pharmaceutical and medicinal products	5,501	6,840	6,791	7,600	6,161	5,926	5,600	1.2
Recyclable waste and scrap	3,896	4,314	4,825	3,333	4,327	5,766	5,414	1.2
Communications and audio and video equipment	9,443	9,134	7,648	6,349	5,799	5,444	5,399	1.2
Furniture and fixtures	5,970	5,422	4,790	3,356	3,700	3,876	4,064	0.9
Paper and published products	5,347	5,110	4,842	4,505	4,249	4,053	3,767	0.8
Fabricated metal products	4,264	4,151	3,914	2,924	3,260	3,473	3,643	0.8
Clothing, footwear and textile products	4,703	4,196	3,598	3,133	3,224	3,379	3,551	0.8
Other transportation equipment and parts	2,290	2,374	2,644	2,392	2,040	2,004	2,363	0.5
Medium and heavy trucks, buses and other motor vehicles	6,865	4,383	4,135	2,309	1,556	2,064	2,148	0.5
Computers and computer peripheral equipment	2,040	2,410	2,601	2,423	2,144	2,118	1,983	0.4
Electricity	2,396	3,096	3,788	2,383	2,023	2,032	1,927	0.4
Non-metallic mineral products	2,295	2,159	2,010	1,467	1,408	1,466	1,563	0.3
Logs, pulpwood, and other forestry products	560	436	326	290	414	627	621	0.1

Source: Statistics Canada, Table 228-0059, "Merchandise Imports and Exports, Customs and Balance of Payments Basis for All Countries, North American Product Classification System (NAPCS)."

EXHIBIT 19.2 Canada's Imports of Goods by Product ($ millions)

	2006	2007	2008	2009	2010	2011	2012	Share 2012 (%)
Total Imports	**394,440**	**406,311**	**432,657**	**365,360**	**403,702**	**444,609**	**462,060**	
Industrial machinery, equipment and parts	38,375	37,670	40,881	33,391	36,123	42,388	45,301	9.8
Tires; motor vehicle engines and motor vehicle parts	39,723	39,531	34,284	27,686	33,525	34,699	38,768	8.4
Passenger cars and light trucks	32,016	34,492	32,351	25,482	31,118	31,062	34,093	7.4
Crude oil and crude bitumen	23,053	23,753	32,719	20,247	23,271	28,884	29,762	6.4
Other electronic and electrical machinery, equipment and parts	28,646	26,973	26,774	24,234	25,455	27,186	27,481	5.9
Intermediate metal products	20,343	19,059	20,814	14,940	21,343	26,718	25,421	5.5
Cleaning products, appliances, and miscellaneous goods and supplies	21,486	22,845	24,267	23,260	23,745	23,854	25,151	5.4
Basic chemicals and industrial chemical products	15,905	17,020	17,507	14,577	16,629	20,397	22,288	4.8
Food, beverage and tobacco products	14,723	16,155	17,940	18,670	18,681	20,455	22,118	4.8
Communications and audio and video equipment	10,485	13,164	15,599	14,434	16,310	15,905	17,972	3.9
Building and packaging materials	13,654	13,942	14,890	13,326	14,578	15,818	17,652	3.8
Clothing, footwear and textile products	14,864	15,261	15,823	15,115	15,464	16,692	17,021	3.7
Plastic and rubber products	15,230	14,511	14,776	12,372	14,198	15,523	15,869	3.4
Pharmaceutical and medicinal products	11,606	12,143	12,951	14,754	13,637	13,929	13,602	2.9
Computers and computer peripheral equipment	9,497	9,689	8,480	8,374	9,443	10,320	10,174	2.2
Medium and heavy trucks, buses and other motor vehicles	8,663	7,663	7,073	5,066	7,098	8,466	10,033	2.2
Refined petroleum energy products	5,995	5,985	9,538	5,891	7,328	11,896	9,686	2.1
Metal ores and concentrates	6,321	7,626	8,396	6,221	8,513	10,041	9,495	2.1
Farm and fishing products	6,591	7,161	7,991	8,098	8,185	9,009	9,121	2.0
Aircraft, aircraft engines and aircraft parts	8,756	10,820	11,192	9,945	8,786	8,777	8,978	1.9
Paper and published products	8,723	8,757	9,311	8,844	8,629	8,254	8,199	1.8
Fabricated metal products	7,164	7,147	7,292	6,124	6,642	7,280	7,997	1.7
Special transactions trade	4,785	5,211	6,131	4,758	4,953	5,474	5,939	1.3
Furniture and fixtures	4,900	5,199	5,574	4,860	5,197	5,374	5,809	1.3
Non-metallic mineral products	4,377	4,541	4,754	4,375	4,751	4,819	5,128	1.1
Natural gas, natural gas liquids and related products	3,132	4,123	6,514	4,583	5,112	5,092	3,814	0.8
Other transportation equipment and parts	3,999	4,019	4,490	3,816	3,410	4,235	3,802	0.8
Food and tobacco intermediate products	2,077	2,296	2,840	2,937	2,870	3,123	3,214	0.7
Recyclable waste and scrap	2,745	3,360	4,640	3,614	3,312	3,977	3,205	0.7
Pulp and paper stock	2,943	3,019	3,041	2,657	2,568	2,513	2,548	0.6
Other energy products	1,496	1,246	1,495	1,211	1,265	1,173	1,226	0.3
Non-metallic minerals	605	564	677	513	601	637	668	0.1
Logs, pulpwood, and other forestry products	468	375	321	340	317	270	295	0.1
Electricity	1,097	991	1,332	646	650	370	232	0.1

Source: Statistics Canada, Table 228-0059, "Merchandise Imports and Exports, Customs and Balance of Payments Basis for All Countries," North American Product Classification System (NAPCS).

management services to Canadian exporters and investors in up to 200 markets worldwide. In 2012, EDC's services and deal-structuring programs helped generate $90 billion in transactions for nearly 7,400 Canadian companies. Most of EDC's clients are small and medium-sized businesses. Canadian companies call on EDC services for virtually every world market, although their services can be especially effective in facilitating trade and investment in emerging markets where opportunities are attractive but which also pose high levels of risk. The EDC mandate is to support and develop Canada's export trade and Canadian capacity to engage in that trade and to respond to international business opportunities through trade finance and risk mitigation for Canadian companies.

The chapter closes with a brief discussion of the fascinating world of "countertrade," in which cash-strapped countries pay for imports through arrangements that are strikingly similar to barter.

19.1 A TYPICAL FOREIGN TRADE TRANSACTION

To understand the mechanics, especially the *financial* mechanics, of a typical foreign trade transaction, it is best to use an illustration. Let's say that Black's Photography ("Black's Is Photography") which operates coast-to-coast in Canada, places an order with Zeiss Optical of Germany for a shipment of lenses. The order amounts to €100,000. If Zeiss could have its way, it would prefer to have Black's pay €100,000 *in advance* for the shipment. That would eliminate all credit and foreign exchange risk from Zeiss's point of view. For its part, Black's would prefer to pay for goods in Canadian dollars, say €100,000 times today's €/$ exchange rate, when the goods arrive, thus eliminating Black's foreign exchange risk and the risk of delayed delivery.

The challenge is to structure the international transaction in a way that addresses the legitimate concerns of both sides with respect to the risks they bear. Fortunately for both Black's and Zeiss, they are not the first two parties to have faced this situation. Over the years, an elaborate process has evolved with the participation of banks for handling just this type of foreign commercial transaction. Exhibit 19.3 presents a schematic of the process that is typical in the finance of foreign trade. Working our way through Exhibit 19.3 in a narrative fashion will allow us to understand the mechanics of trade and also the three major documents involved.

Exhibit 19.3 begins with (1) Black's order sent to Zeiss, asking Zeiss to ship the lenses under a letter of credit. If Zeiss agrees, Zeiss will confirm with Black's the price and other terms of sale, including the credit terms. For purposes of the example, we will assume the length of the credit period is 60 days. Black's then (2) applies to its bank in Toronto, say the Royal Bank, for a letter of credit (L/C) for the merchandise ordered, providing the Royal Bank with the terms of the sale.

A **letter of credit (L/C)** is a guarantee from the Royal Bank that it will act on behalf of Black's and pay Zeiss for the merchandise if all relevant documents specified in the L/C are presented according to the terms of the L/C. In essence, the Royal Bank is substituting its creditworthiness for that of Black's. Hence at this point, among all parties to the transaction, the Royal Bank is most at risk. As we shall see, the Royal Bank's compensation for the risk it bears will soon be built into the deal.

At this stage, since Black's commitment to Zeiss is to pay €100,000, the Royal Bank and Black's will make an arrangement to address Black's foreign exchange exposure, perhaps via a 60-day forward contract. This has nothing to do with Zeiss.

The L/C is (3) sent via the Royal Bank to Zeiss's bank in Germany, say Deutsche Bank. Once the L/C is received, Deutsche Bank (4) notifies Zeiss. Zeiss (5) then ships the lenses.

After shipping the lenses, Zeiss (6) presents to Deutsche Bank a (60-day) time draft drawn up according to the instructions in the L/C, the bill of lading, and any other shipping documents that are required, such as the invoice and a packing list. A **time draft** is a written order instructing Black's or its agent, the Royal Bank, to pay the amount

EXHIBIT 19.3 Process of Typical Foreign Trade Transaction

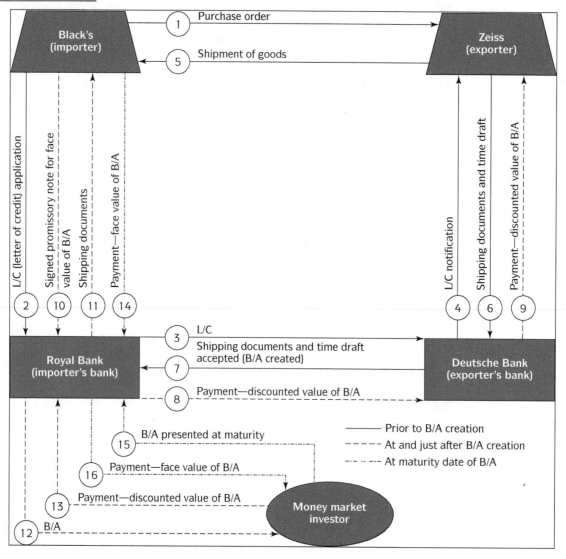

specified on its face on a certain date (i.e., the end of the credit period in a foreign trade transaction). A **bill of lading (B/L)** is a document issued by the common carrier (say Air Canada) specifying that it has received the goods for shipment; it can serve as title to the goods.

Deutsche Bank (7) presents the shipping documents and the time draft to the Royal Bank. After taking title to the goods via the bill of lading, the Royal Bank accepts the time draft, creating at this point a **banker's acceptance (B/A)**, a negotiable money market instrument for which a vibrant secondary market exists in Canada. The Royal Bank charges a B/A commission, referred to as a **stamping fee**, which is typically paid in advance. (In some arrangements where the stamping fee is not paid by the importer in advance, the fee is charged by the bank at the point at which the B/A is given to the exporter, in which case the exporter pays the fee at the time it receives the B/A.) The B/A stamping fee, generally less than 1 percent of the amount of the B/A, is based on the term to maturity of the time draft and the creditworthiness of the importer, Black's.

One of several things can happen with the B/A. The agreement could dictate that the B/A is to be delivered to Zeiss, who would hold it as a receivable for 60 days and then present it for payment to the Royal Bank at maturity. (In this scenario, Zeiss would receive Canadian dollars amounting to €100,000 times the $/€ exchange rate on the 60th day.) Should Zeiss suddenly find it needs funds prior to the maturity date, the B/A can be sold at a discount in the Canadian money market. Since their risks are similar, banker's acceptances trade at rates similar to rates for negotiable bank certificates of deposit. Alternatively, as in Exhibit 19.3, Zeiss could instruct Deutsche Bank to have the B/A (8) discounted by the Royal Bank and (9) be paid that amount. Analogously, the Royal Bank may decide to take back the B/A in order to hold it to maturity as an investment, paying Zeiss the discounted equivalent.

Black's (10) signs a (60-day) promissory note with the Royal Bank for the face value of the banker's acceptance, due on the maturity date of the B/A. In return, the Royal Bank (11) provides Black's with the shipping documents needed to take possession of the lenses from Air Canada.

If the B/A is not held by Zeiss or Deutsche Bank, the Royal Bank may hold it itself for 60 days until maturity at which point it collects the face value from Black's via the promissory note. The Canadian funds (the face value of the B/A) would be exchanged for euro and paid to Deutsche Bank which credits Zeiss's account. Alternatively, as in Exhibit 19.3, the Royal Bank may (12) sell the B/A in the money market to an investor (13) at a discount from face value. At maturity, the Royal Bank (14) collects the face value of the B/A via the promissory note from Black's, the money market investor (15) presents the B/A for payment to the Royal Bank and Royal Bank (16) pays the face value of the B/A to the investor. In the event of default by Black's, the Royal Bank can seek recourse against Black's under Canadian law. B/As usually have maturities ranging from 30 to 180 days; as such, they are only short-term sources of trade financing.

These international financial arrangements are typical and generalize for a wide range of cross-border commercial transactions. The process builds on three pairs of trusted established working relations—between Black's and the Royal Bank, between Zeiss and Deutsche Bank, and between the Royal Bank and Deutsche Bank.

Example 19.1 *Cost Analysis of a Banker's Acceptance*

As mentioned in our discussion of the schematic describing a typical foreign trade transaction, the exporter (Zeiss) may hold the B/A to maturity and collect payment at that time. Alternatively, Zeiss may discount the B/A directly with the Royal Bank or sell it at a discount in the Canadian money market.

We assume that the stamping fee is *not* paid in advance by Black's. In fact, as the following case illustrates, it is possible for Zeiss to capture the benefits of the Canadian banker's acceptance (by virtue of receiving cash earlier than the agreed 60-day term of credit) and so it is reasonable that Zeiss pay the stamping fee.

Suppose the face amount of the B/A is $100,000 and the Royal Bank charges a stamping fee of 1 percent. Since the B/A is for 60 days, Zeiss will receive $99,833 = $100,000 × [1 − (0.01 × 60/360)] if it decides to hold the B/A until maturity. Thus the Royal Bank's commission is $167 = $100,000 − $99,833.

If 60-day B/A rates are 5.25 percent and Zeiss discounts the B/A with the Royal Bank, Zeiss will receive $98,958 = $100,000 × [1 − ((0.01 + 0.0525) × 60/360)]. Thus, as in effect a lender to Zeiss, the Royal Bank receives a discount rate of interest of 6.25 percent = 5.25 + 1.0 percent on its loan. The Royal Bank, of course, reverts to holding the B/A.

At maturity the Royal Bank receives $100,000 from Black's. The bond equivalent yield it receives on its investment (which is figured on the actual number of days in a year instead of a 360-day banker's year) is 6.403 percent, or 0.06403 = [$100,000/$98,958 − 1] × 365/60.

Zeiss pays the stamping fee regardless of whether it discounts the B/A or holds it to maturity; hence, it is not marginal to its decision to discount the B/A. Since this 1 percent cost to Zeiss is known from the outset, it would likely be built into Zeiss's offer price on the lenses to Black's.

The bond equivalent borrowing rate that Zeiss receives from discounting the B/A and taking cash before the 60-day maturity date is 5.38 percent, or $0.0538 = [(\$99,833/\$98,958 - 1) \times 365/60]$. If Zeiss's opportunity cost of capital (borrowing rate in Germany) is greater than 5.38 percent compounded bimonthly (an effective annual rate of 5.5 percent), discounting the B/A makes sense; if not, Zeiss should hold the B/A to maturity.

19.2   EXPORT FINANCE

Our extensive analysis of the finance of a "typical transaction" in international trade involved a Canadian firm importing merchandise from a German exporter. From the Canadian perspective, this represents "import" finance. The banks played a central role, especially the Royal Bank.

We now turn to questions of the international finance of Canadian exports. We will again look at the role of Canadian commercial banks in the process, but we will also deal with the important function of a federal Crown corporation, Export Development Canada.

We begin by outlining widely used commercial arrangements—buyer credits, supplier credits and forfaiting and international leasing. These international financial arrangements conveniently allow exporters to minimize their own direct role in processing international payments, passing such tasks on to banks.

Buyer Credits and Lines of Credit

Buyer credits in export finance are structured in the following way. A Canadian exporter initiates an arrangement whereby a Canadian lender (a commercial bank) extends funds directly to the foreign borrower (the purchaser of Canadian goods) to the borrower's financial specifications. The Canadian bank arranges for the foreign borrower to receive funds that are directly tied to the exported Canadian goods which serve as collateral to the Canadian bank. Buyer credits tend to involve relatively high transaction costs in setting up the international contracts which make smaller deals unattractive.

Buyer credits offered in support of Canadian capital goods and services exports are typically designed to be without recourse to the Canadian exporter. As such, the availability of buyer credit financing for a particular project is dependent upon the creditworthiness of the foreign buyer and the country involved. Buyer credits used to support capital goods and services exports include **direct loans** and allocations under **lines of credit**.

Direct loans are well suited to financing large, distinct capital goods export transactions involving complex international loan agreements. Accordingly, this financing instrument will not normally be relative to the SME market exporter.

A line of credit allocation is often used in support of Canadian capital goods and services exports. In this financing arrangement, a general line of credit is negotiated between a Canadian lender and a foreign bank, which provides umbrella financing for approved exports. The Canadian lender needs only to determine the creditworthiness of an established foreign bank that it relies upon for repayment, while the foreign bank is able to use its local market strength to market the line of credit financing and on-lend the funds to local, creditworthy buyers of Canadian capital goods and services. Line of credit allocations are especially useful for smaller capital goods and services exports with contract values of $50,000 to $5 million.

An example will illustrate the structure of an international buyer credit to finance a Canadian export of capital goods. Linetech Design Company of St. Catharines, Ontario, is one of North America's leading manufacturers of equipment used to paint lines on highways. Let's say that Linetech arranges a sale of two line-painting machines, worth $500,000 each, to the highways department of the State of Maine in the United States. The State of Maine finds the Linetech offer especially attractive since Linetech has conditionally arranged a buyer credit as the means for the State of Maine to finance the purchase. Concurrent with negotiations for the export sale, Linetech approached its banker, TD Canada Trust, with a request to structure a deal. Conveniently, TD Canada Trust has a 100-percent-owned US subsidiary, TDBanknorth with branches in Maine. TD Canada Trust proposes to set up a buyer credit for the State of Maine in the amount of US$900,000 (which at the current exchange rate equals $1,000,000, the cost of the two line-painting machines) with the loan to be extended from the TDBanknorth branch in Portland, Maine. Once all the legal work is complete and the contracts signed, the net result will be that Linetech receives $1,000,000 from TD Canada Trust, the State of Maine receives two highway line-painters, and the TDBanknorth branch in Portland, Maine, extends a US$900,000 loan (buyer credit) to the State on Maine against which the line-painters are collateral. The interest and repayment of the loan flows in the first instance to TDBanknorth and ultimately into the foreign-source income of TD Canada Trust. Any subsequent failure on the part of the State of Maine to meet the terms of the loan becomes an issue for TDBanknorth (and TD Canada Trust) but not for Linetech.

Supplier Credits and Forfaiting

www.tdglobaltrade
finance.com

TD Canada trust online
information about trade
finance.

Supplier credits, sometimes referred to as "note purchase agreements," are international financing arrangements in which a commercial bank provides funds directly to the Canadian exporter, who in turn offers medium-term financing support to its foreign buyer, typically a foreign buyer of capital goods and services. In most cases, supplier credit financing involves a bank purchasing the foreign buyer's promissory note from the Canadian exporter. This use of promissory notes allows the industrial parties—the Canadian exporter and the foreign purchaser—to avoid the costs and time involved in negotiating and securing an international loan agreement. This makes supplier credits particularly attractive to smaller exports where high transaction and financing costs can discourage export sales. Most supplier credits are in the range of $250,000 to $1 million, although transactions of $2–3 million are not uncommon.

www.forfaiting.com

London Forfaiting House,
a global leader in trade
finance.

Note purchase agreement financing involves a bank purchasing promissory notes issued by the foreign buyer to the Canadian exporter. **Forfaiting** is a special case of note-purchase financing. Forfaiting is a type of medium-term trade financing used to finance the sale of capital goods. Forfaiting involves the sale of promissory notes signed by the foreign importer in favour of the Canadian exporter. The *forfait,* usually a bank, buys the notes at a discount for face value from the exporter. In this way, the exporter receives payment for the export and does not have to carry the financing. The forfait does not have recourse against the exporter in the event of default by the importer. Promissory notes are typically structured to extend out in a series over a period of from three to seven years, with a note in the series maturing every six months. Forfaiting is typically done to finance capital goods since the collateral of such valuable physical assets offers comfort to the banks involved. Forfait contracts are usually for amounts of $500,000 or more.

Forfaiting began in Switzerland and Germany in the 1960s and 1970s to meet the need for non-recourse medium-term financing for sales by Western European exporters to Eastern European state-owned buyers. It has now spread throughout most of Western Europe and beyond, taking hold as an alternative source of medium-term fixed-rate financing, especially for exports of capital goods. The mechanism allows exporters to convert medium-term credit sales to cash sales. The global centres for forfait financing are London, Zurich and Frankfurt. In Canada, forfaiting services are offered by the Export Development Corporation (EDC) and the Royal Bank of Canada.

A distinguishing feature of forfaiting is that it is supplier credit financing without recourse to the exporter. In essence, the term "forfaiting" is an English derivative of the French "forfait" which means "to give up the right" of recourse to the endorser of the notes (the exporter in this case). As notes purchased in forfaiting transactions are without recourse to the exporter, they must carry the "avail" of a commercial or state bank that establishes the notes as an unconditional obligation of the availing bank.

Several other features of forfaiting distinguish it from standard note purchase agreements. First, forfaiting provides only fixed-rate financing to the foreign buyer, whereas standardized note purchase agreements can provide either fixed- or floating-rate financing. Second, forfaiting requires a separate promissory note for each "repayment" date of principal and interest set out in the loan amortization schedule. As such, if the export transaction calls for 6 percent fixed-rate, five-year financing with semiannual payments commencing six months after delivery of the capital goods, the exporter must secure 10 promissory notes for forfaiting. Each note is typically the sum of the principal payment due on that date plus interest on the outstanding balance of the loan, although blended principal and interest repayments can also be arranged. The forfaiter then purchases, at a discount, each of the notes from the exporter, having deducted interest due on each note from the point of discounting until the maturity of the note. Finally, forfaiting financing is quoted on a discount rate basis. Since interest is deducted in advance, the discount rate quote results in a higher effective yield to the forfaiter than would an identical interest rate quote. This difference between the discount rate quote and the effective interest rate increases substantially as the financing term lengthens.

Forfait Finance—An Example[1]

In August 1999 Northwestern Turkey, the country's most densely populated region and industrial heartland, was struck by a massive earthquake that measured 7.4 on the Richter scale. Izmit, a city of one million, was near the epicentre. The death toll was over 18,000, with some 44,000 people injured, nearly 300,000 homes and more than 40,000 business buildings either damaged or collapsed. Tens of thousands of the survivors were still living in tents or makeshift housing a year after the tragic earthquakes.

Select Homes, a housing manufacturer in Sacramento, California, got a call. A cement company in Turkey had heard of Select Homes and its housing technology that revolutionized the way structures are built. Select Homes produces insulating concrete forms that crews stack into the shape of the exterior walls of a building. After the forms are fastened with adhesives, reinforced concrete is poured in the mould to produce a foam-concrete sandwich that is water- and termite-proof as well as wind- and earthquake-resistant.

Select Homes agreed to sell a production licence to a Turkish cement company which became a joint-venture partner. Together, the joint venture received a contract from the Turkish Housing Ministry for 52 schools. The joint venture purchased a manufacturing facility from Select Homes for $649,000. The joint venture could not qualify for three-year financing on its own but was able to get a Turkish Development Bank guarantee. Select Homes found a London Forfait House willing to finance the transaction through forfait trade financing. The transaction followed these steps:

1. The commercial contract was signed with the Turkish Housing Ministry.
2. A forfaiting agreement was signed with the London Forfait House.
3. The manufacturing facility was shipped and delivered.
4. The promissory note drafts were delivered to the Forfait House.
5. The drafts were endorsed according to forfaiting agreement along with shipping and trade documents including the invoice.
6. Select Homes was paid the total amount of all drafts less discount.

---

[1]Adapted from an illustration in *Trade and Export Finance Online*, http://tefo.com/products/forfait-financing.php.

7. London Forfait House presented drafts for collection at maturity to the joint venture.

8. The joint venture honoured all drafts as agreed.

International forfaiting is a fast, uncomplicated way for an exporter to extend credit to foreign customers for periods of time typically ranging from six months to five years. The exporter agrees to a schedule of payment of the receivables. Payment schedules are flexible and structured to accommodate the buyer's cash flow.

International Leasing

International leasing provides for the transfer of goods to a foreign buyer without the transfer of title to the goods. In essence, the foreign buyer does not buy the goods at all but rather obtains the use of the goods by agreeing to pay a series of (usually) monthly lease payments. This exchange of goods for a series of payments is not unlike a typical capital goods financing arrangement between a Canadian exporter and a foreign buyer. The primary difference is that the Canadian exporter retains title.

There are two types of leases, namely operating and financial. **Operating leases** involve a true rental agreement where the lessor (the Canadian exporter) provides functional equipment for the use of the lessee (foreign customer). **Financial leases** normally involve the Canadian manufacturer selling the equipment to a lender (leasing house) that then leases the equipment to the foreign lessee for a period that reflects the expected life of the equipment. Ownership of the equipment is usually transferred to the lessee at the end of the term for a nominal sum. An enhancement of the financial lease is the leveraged lease that involves a lender in addition to the lessor.

With leveraged leasing, the lessor provides a portion of the value of the equipment as equity (for instance 25 percent) and finances the remaining portion (75 percent), using the equipment as collateral for the loan.

Cross-border and international leasing both serve as a financial mechanism for Canadian exports of capital equipment. In cross-border leasing, upon finding a foreign customer for its equipment, the manufacturer sells the equipment to a Canadian leasing company that, in turn, leases the equipment to the foreign customer. In contrast, international leasing involves the manufacturer directly exporting the equipment to a leasing company in the foreign customer's country. The leasing arrangement is common in the export of aircraft, urban transportation equipment, ships and vehicle fleets.

19.3 GOVERNMENT FINANCIAL SUPPORT OF EXPORTS

To this point our examples of trade finance—including banker's acceptances, buyer credits, supplier credits, forfaiting and leasing—have been exclusively commercial. These financial arrangements have developed into standard international commercial procedures that typically originate with the initiative of importers and/or exporters working closely with their banks or near-bank institutions such as forfait houses or leasing companies.

Governments of almost all nations, and certainly all industrial nations, have agencies that assist in the finance of exports. Nations view exports as a source of economic growth and industrial development in line with comparative advantage. To the extent that short-to-medium-term finance represents an impediment to exports, or simply if the process of arranging secure finance is difficult for exporters, the government sees a role for itself in addressing these difficulties. When governments have financial resources and expertise that can be useful to exporters, governments are willing to step in.

www.edc.ca

Export Development Canada's Website.

Export Development Canada (EDC) is a federal Crown corporation that provides financing and risk management services to Canadian exporters and investors. The EDC mandate is to support and develop Canada's export trade and Canadian capacity to engage in that trade and to respond to international business opportunities through trade finance and risk mitigation for Canadian companies.

The EDC lends to foreign companies, governments and agencies subject to their creditworthiness. If a foreign customer does not meet all the criteria, the EDC may still be able to lend to them through a local bank. Generally, EDC financing solutions provide one to-ten-year coverage for up to 85 percent of the value of export sale. Time and process vary with the complexity of the sale or loan.

EDC assists companies of all sizes and economic sectors anywhere in Canada. EDC financing is generally available for export contracts covering capital goods, quasi-capital goods, merchandise or certain trade-related services.

EDC offers competitive rates to borrowers based on credit quality, general market conditions and the length of repayment terms being considered. An exposure fee may be charged in connection with export financing consistent with OECD regulations. Below are details of several specific financial programs offered by the EDC.

Export Guarantee Program

Through its **Export Guarantee Program**, EDC encourages Canadian financial institutions to advance pre-shipment loans to Canadian companies exporting goods or services. Pre-shipment financing gives Canadian companies the financial strength to close and fulfill international deals. The Export Guarantee Program can cover up to 75 percent of a bank loan, to a maximum of 100 percent of the direct costs (excluding overhead) associated with contract fulfillment. The Export Guarantee Program is available for export contracts that involve capital, noncapital or knowledge-based business goods and services. The cost of EDC's guarantee includes the bank's interest spread on the loan and a percentage of the bank's setup fees.

Note Purchases

As we have seen, foreign customers may issue promissory notes to Canadian companies as a means to extend payment for goods and services. EDC purchases these promissory notes (with no requirement for security from the customers), thereby reducing the risk of non-payment while increasing the Canadian company's access to cash. Under this program, Canadian companies are able to offer attractive payment terms to foreign customers with reduced risk. In some cases, foreign customers can show promissory notes as extended trade payables in their financial records rather than debt. EDC must be contacted before the contract is signed with the foreign customer to determine whether a **note purchase agreement** is feasible and what arrangement is optimal. The Canadian company is actively involved in negotiation and implementation of the terms and conditions.

Lines of Credit

EDC provides lines of credit to foreign companies that repeatedly buy goods or services from Canadian companies and to foreign banks or intermediaries that on-lend money to buyers of Canadian goods and services.

Factoring

EDC does not directly buy or discount receivables (a process known as **factoring**), but does help Canadian companies establish factoring arrangements with financial institutions. With **EDC accounts receivable insurance (ARI)** in place, banks may be willing to purchase some or all of a company's receivables for cash, knowing they are protected should their customers fail to pay. For example, EDC has an insurance policy with NatExport (the factoring facility of the National Bank of Canada) under which all of the accounts receivable discounted or factored by NatExport are insured. Similar EDC programs are in place with TD CanadaTrust and Banque Paribas.

Security Compliance Loans

Canadian companies shipping to the US may need to enhance their security programs in order to meet the requirements of **C-TPAT**, *The Customs-Trade Partnership against Terrorism*.

www.customs.gov
US Customs Service with
links to C-TPAT.

EDC's **security compliance loan** helps Canadian companies to finance the upgrades required to meet security standards, and helps them qualify to become C-TPAT-compliant. Security enhancements to property, personnel and procedures may be required. EDC provides a term loan for up to $150,000 to finance the costs related to becoming C-TPAT-compliant thereby allowing Canadian firms to compete for US opportunities that may otherwise be disadvantaged by the demands for security clearance. Border clearance times are reduced and goods have access to the fast lanes at the Canada/US border.

Once eligibility and creditworthiness for a Security Compliance Loan has been established, EDC will offer the choice of a fixed or a floating rate of interest. Other than the interest payable quarterly, EDC does not charge any other fee.

Bank Guarantee Program

EDC's Bank Guarantee Program provides cover to Canadian and international banks financing the sale of Canadian exports to customers in developing markets.

When the financed amount is less than $11 million, the EDC guarantees financing for transactions, providing 100 percent cover on 85 percent of the export contract. The bank determines and retains the loan interest rate. The bank's costs include a guarantee fee (OECD minimum premium rate plus a credit risk adjustment factor) and an administration fee of 25 basis points. Both are payable on the financed amount.

When the financed amount is greater than $11 million, the EDC guarantees consensus transactions only. EDC provides 90 or 100 percent cover on 85 percent of the export contract. EDC and the bank jointly determine the loan interest rate, and the bank retains up to LIBOR (the London Interbank Offered Rate) plus 50 basis points from that rate. The bank's costs include a guarantee fee (the OECD minimum premium rate) and an administration fee of 25 basis points. Both are payable on the financed amount.

Governing Agreements and CIRR Rates

Canada and the EDC provide financial services and assistance to Canadian exporters that is consistently benchmarked to commercial alternatives such as borrowing from banks or issuing commercial paper. The EDC is *not* engaged in subsidizing exports. Indeed, Canada complies with international agreements under the World Trade Organization, NAFTA and other official arrangements that explicitly preclude export subsidies. An important pillar of undistorted international trade is an agreement among nations to restrict government-supported export finance programs to those that have transparent reference to commercial interest rates.

www.oecd.org
Paris-based Organization
for Economic Co-
operation and
Development.

Canada is a member of the Organization for Economic Co-operation and Development (OECD). The OECD's *Arrangement on Guidelines for Officially Supported Export Credits* (the "Consensus") provides a regulatory framework for export-assistance from member countries. The **OECD Consensus** promotes competition among exporters based on the quality and price of the goods or services being sold rather than on export credit support. The Consensus governs the administration of *Commercial Interest Reference Rates*—the **CIRRs**—which are updated monthly for each country in the light of the government's cost of borrowing. See Exhibit 19.4 for Canada's rates, and for the rates of United States and Europe.

EXHIBIT 19.4 Consensus Interest Reference Rates for Canada		Rate		
Term		**Canada**	**US**	**Euro**
Less than 5 years		2.25	1.58	1.48
5–8.5 years		2.63	2.20	1.95
More than 8.5 years		2.94	2.71	2.42

Source: Organization for Economic Cooperation and Development (OECD), "Consensus Interest Reference Rates," July 2013.

The CIRRs and corresponding regulations set various conditions on government assistance to exports and exporting industries. In addition to explicit minimum interest rates that agencies such as the EDC must charge for their loans (which differ by length of the loan), the OECD Consensus also stipulates the maximum amount of a loan (relative to the cost of the exported goods), the starting point and the repayment terms. Repayments are made in equal semiannual installments beginning from the starting point of credit defined as final commissioning of the project or final acceptance of goods in accordance with the terms of the commercial export contract.

Canada, along with the other members of the Consensus, signed an agreement providing for the setting of minimum fee levels for officially supported medium- and long-term export credits. This agreement, called the Knaepen Package, came into force in 1999.

www.wto.org

Geneva-based World Trade Organization.

The rates and regulations under the OECD Consensus and Knaepen Package are recognized by the World Trade Organization as relevant references in trade disputes involving subsidized exports when such disputes make their way to the WTO.

19.4   INTRA-FIRM INTERNATIONAL TRADE

All of the trade finance arrangements that we have discussed to this point are structured as if the exporter and the importer (or the seller and the buyer) are at "arm's length" from each other. For example, Black's Photography is not affiliated, except through business, with Zeiss Optical, nor is Linetech of St. Catharines formally associated with the State of Maine. Our examples of import and export finance capture the traditional idea of a company in one country selling products to a company or agency in another country.

In important respects, however, this arm's-length framework is an incomplete representation of international trade. A large and growing amount of international trade flows across borders but within firms. The integrated North American automotive sector is a prime example. General Motors, Ford and Chrysler, with their large assembly operations in Windsor, Oakville and Oshawa, Ontario, are each part of an international supply chain that involves parts delivered from sister subsidiaries around the world. A specific example might involve General Motors US-built engines for Chevrolets and Buicks being shipped to GM (Canada) in Oshawa, at the rate of 500 engines per day. Subsequently, many of GM's finished vehicles are shipped from Canada to the US, with the engines returning to where they originated. The central point for international finance is that GM (Canada) is wholly owned by the General Motors Corporation. Continuous cross-border, intra-firm trade involves a different set of financing considerations than we have seen in our discussion of trade finance. For one thing, there is no market-determined price for US-built GM automobile engines that are "sold" and delivered to the GM assembly operation in Canada.

The global phenomenon of **intra-firm trade** goes hand in hand with foreign direct investment. Modern international firms, especially in manufacturing, relentlessly try to locate low-cost sites of production of inputs to the final product. A Dell notebook computer, for example, may include a chip manufactured in Korea, a monitor from Taiwan, a keyboard from Mexico and assembly in Brazil. The movement of components around the world but within the firm is referred to as a "supply chain." Some components are supplied at "arm's length" (e.g., the chip could be purchased from Samsung) while others are manufactured in Dell subsidiaries. Regardless, once components are purchased by Dell, their subsequent movement within the Dell company but across a border, say partially assembled laptops shipped from Dell (Brazil) to Dell (Canada), represents intra-firm trade.

In Chapter 18 on multinational cash management, we saw how sophisticated internal systems of intra-firm payments enable a firm to minimize foreign exchange risks and transactions costs associated with complex international intra-firm trade.

19.5 COUNTERTRADE

www.countertrade.org

Official site of the American Countertrade Association (ACA). The ACA provides a forum for companies involved in countertrade and a resource for companies exploring the possibilities held by countertrade.

To help protect elephants and rhinos from poachers, the Ugandan government needed 18 helicopters. Unfortunately, it did not have the $25 million needed to cover the cost. In stepped Gary Pacific, the head of countertrade for McDonnell Douglas Helicopters. He helped Uganda set up several local factories that are able to generate hard currency. One was a plant to catch and process Nile perch and another was a factory for making passion-fruit and pineapple concentrate from fresh fruit. Pacific also found foreign buyers for the output of these plants. After 14 months, Uganda had earned enough hard currency to start receiving the helicopters it needed.

Countertrade is an umbrella term used to describe many different types of transactions, each in which the seller provides a buyer with goods or services and promises in return to purchase goods or services from the buyer. Countertrades may or may not involve the use of money. If money is not exchanged, the trade is a type of barter. Regardless, countertrade usually results in a two-way flow of commodities.

Countertrade can be traced back to prehistoric times and has been used throughout history whenever money was scarce. While it is difficult to determine the exact volume of countertrade, the practice is nevertheless widespread. Some estimates put countertrade at only 5 percent of total world trade, whereas other estimates are as high as 40 percent. Moreover, countertrade transactions are not accounted for in official trade statistics. The IMF and the World Bank estimate that as much as half of all international trade transactions are conducted as countertrade.[2] Countertrade occurs when financial crises leave debtor countries without sufficient foreign exchange reserves or bank lines of credit to carry on normal commerce.

Forms of Countertrade

We can identify six fundamental forms of countertrade: barter, clearing arrangement, switch trading, buy-back, counterpurchase and offset. The first three do not involve the use of money; the latter three do.

Barter is the direct exchange of goods between two parties. While money does not exchange hands in a barter transaction, it is common to value the goods each party exchanges in an agreed-upon currency. It is often necessary to place a monetary value on the goods for accounting, taxation and insurance purposes.

Barter is a rather primitive way to do business. It fosters bilateral trade which, in turn, under mercantilist economies and imperialistic policies, fostered a tight system of colonial dependency with protected markets and captive sources of raw materials. Barter flourished until after World War II when the Bretton Woods fixed-exchange-rate system was established to provide for currency convertibility and fostered free trade.

Today, barter transactions are typically one-time exchanges of merchandise that take place when circumstances warrant. Schaffer (1989) describes a modern example of barter that took place between General Electric (GE) and Romania. GE had agreed to sell Romania a turbine generator for cash. The Romanian loan financing subsequently fell through. In order to complete the deal, GE agreed to accept Romanian products which it in turn sold for cash through its trading company.

A *clearing arrangement* (also called *bilateral clearing agreement*) is a form of barter in which the counterparties (governments) contract to purchase a certain amount of goods and services from one another. Both parties set up accounts with each other that are debited whenever one country imports from the other. At the end of an agreed-upon period of time, any account imbalances are settled for hard currency or by the transfer of goods. The clearing arrangement introduces the concept of credit to barter transactions and means that bilateral trade can take place that does not have to be immediately settled. Account balances

---
[2]See Anyane-Ntow and Harvey (1995, p. 47) for this estimate.

Armed Forces Tops in Countertrade List

The Armed Forces of the Philippines (AFP) leads all government agencies in countertrade transactions, accounting for a total of $143.4 million worth from 1989 to August 2004 based on figures provided by the Philippine International Trading Corporation (PITC). Countertrade refers to reciprocal and compensatory agreements involving the purchase of goods or services by the seller from the buyer of this product or arrangements where the seller assists the buyer in reducing the net cost of the purchase through some form of compensatory financing.

The AFP yesterday announced that the Philippines recently benefited from two countertrade transactions by the military. In February last year, the Philippine Army procured $2.1 million worth of Squad Automatic Weapons from FN Herstal of Belgium, with a countertrade commitment of $1.8 million or 85 percent of the contract price.

The program has paved the way for the development of Philippine semi-processed rubber exports worldwide through a financing scheme packaged by Raifeissen Centrobank of Austria, the designated trading partner of FN Herstal under the Countertrade Program of the Philippines.

The assistance has opened doors to new exports markets including Czech Republic, Australia, Italy, Germany, and New Zealand, officials added. The AFP also purchased $7.6 million worth of HF/SSB Transceivers and Manpack Communications equipment from Harris Corp. in December 2003 and February 2004. As a direct beneficiary of the countertrade program, the military received some $6.1 million worth of offset activities.

Under the arrangement Harris Corporation is obligated to an 80 percent offset of some $6.2 million and a 20 percent counterpurchase or $1.5 million. Some of the offset benefits included software upgrades for 324 Manpack Communication units, donation of additional Manpack batteries, donation of one automated test set and spare modules, officials said.

The government countertrade program was established under Executive Order 120, which provides that all government procurements equivalent of $1 million and above have to have a countertrade component of at least 50 percent of the value of the supply contract. In response, the Department of National Defense issued Dept. Circular 4 dated July 20, 2001, requiring countertrade to be part of the AFP's acquisition program for all projects costing more than $1 million.

The AFP is closely followed by the National Food Authority with a total of $136.6 million worth of countertrade transactions. More than $300 million worth of Philippine products have been exported under the Countertrade Program of the Government through its foreign procurement.

Source: Karl Lester M. Yap, *BusinessWorld*, August 17, 2004, p 1.

are periodically determined, and any trade imbalances are settled in an agreed-upon currency. Anyane-Ntow and Harvey (1995) note that clearing arrangements have usually taken place between Third World and Eastern European countries. They also cite the 1994 agreement between China and Saudi Arabia with a $1 billion target as an example.

A *switch trade* involves the purchase by a third party of one country's clearing arrangement imbalance for hard currency which is in turn resold. The second buyer uses the account balance to purchase goods and services from the original clearing arrangement counterparty who had the account imbalance. Anyane-Ntow and Harvey (1995) give the example of a switch trade when the United States exported fertilizers to Pakistan through a Romanian–Pakistani clearing arrangement.

A *buy-back transaction* involves a technology transfer via the sale of a manufacturing plant. As part of the transaction, the seller agrees to purchase a certain portion of the plant output once it is constructed. Money enters into the agreement in two ways. First, the plant buyer borrows hard currency in the capital market to pay the seller for the plant. Second, the plant seller agrees to purchase enough of the plant output over a period of time to enable the buyer to pay back the borrowed funds. A buy-back transaction can be viewed as a form of direct investment in the purchasing country. Examples of buy-back transactions include Japan's agreements with Taiwan, Singapore and Korea to exchange computer chip production equipment for a certain percentage of the output.[3]

A *counterpurchase* is similar to a buy-back transaction but with some notable differences. The two counterparties are usually an Eastern importer and a Western exporter of

---

[3]See Anyane-Ntow and Harvey (1995, p. 48).

technology. The major difference between a buy-back and a counterpurchase transaction is that in the latter, the merchandise the Western seller agrees to purchase is unrelated and has not been produced on the exported equipment. The seller agrees to purchase goods from a list drawn up by the importer at prices set by the importer. Goods on the list are frequently items for which the buyer does not have a ready market. As an example of a counterpurchase, Anyane-Ntow and Harvey (1995) cite the agreement to exchange Italian industrial equipment for Indonesian rubber.

An *offset transaction* can be viewed as a counterpurchase trade agreement involving the aerospace/defence industry. Offset transactions are reciprocal trade agreements between an industrialized country and a country that has defence and/or aerospace industries. Hammond (1990) cites the example of the sale of F-16 jet fighters manufactured by General Dynamics to Turkey and Greece in exchange for olives, hydroelectric power projects, the promotion of tourism and aircraft co-production.

Some Generalizations about Countertrade

Countertrade transactions became prominent in international trade in the 1980s and 1990s. Arguments both for and against countertrade transactions can be made. Hammond (1990) notes that there are both negative and positive incentives for a country to be in favour of countertrade. Negative incentives are those that are forced upon a country or corporation whether or not it desires to engage in countertrade. They include the conservation of cash and hard currency, the improvement of trade imbalances and the maintenance of export prices. Positive reasons from both the country and corporate perspectives include enhanced economic development, increased employment, technology transfer, market expansion, increased profitability, less costly sourcing of supply, reduction of surplus goods from inventory and the development of marketing expertise.

Those against countertrade transactions claim such transactions tamper with the fundamental operation of free markets and therefore resources are used inefficiently. Opponents claim that transaction costs are increased, that multilateral trade is restricted through fostering bilateral trade agreements and that, in general, transactions that do not make use of money represent a step backward in economic development.

Hennart (1989) studied all 1,277 countertrade contracts between 1983 and 1986 that were reported in *Countertrade Outlook*. Of these transactions, 694 were clearing arrangements, 171 barters, 298 counterpurchases, 71 buy-backs and 43 offsets. The countries involved were classified into the World Bank categories of: Developed, Organization of Petroleum Exporting Countries (OPEC) Members, Centrally Planned Economies (CPE), Middle-Income and Low-Income.

Hennart found that each country grouping had a propensity to engage in certain types of countertrade transactions. OPEC, middle-income and low-income countries used more counterpurchases, CPEs more buy-backs and developed and middle-income countries more offsets. Barter was most common between two middle-income countries, between developed and middle-income countries and between middle-income countries and CPEs.

The high frequency of buy-backs among CPEs is consistent with their use as a substitute for foreign direct investment. The reasons that CPEs and low-income countries do not actively engage in offset transactions are two: CPEs are not allowed to purchase Western weapons, and low-income developing countries cannot afford sophisticated weapons systems typically sold via offset transactions. Barter between two middle-income countries (the most frequent) is consistent with the two countries desiring to avoid the repayment of external debt. The absence of barter among the OPEC countries and among the developed countries is consistent with the use of barter to bypass cartels and commodity arrangements.

Whether countertrade transactions are good or bad for the global economy, it appears certain that they will increase in the near future as world trade increases.

SUMMARY

Export and import transactions and trade financing are the main topics discussed in this chapter.

1. Conducting international trade transactions is difficult in comparison with domestic trades. Commercial and political risks enter into the equation, which are not factors in domestic trade. Yet it is important for a country to be competitively strong in international trade in order for its citizens to have the goods and services they need and demand.

2. A typical foreign trade transaction requires three basic documents: letter of credit, time draft and bill of lading. A time draft can become a negotiable money market instrument called a banker's acceptance.

3. Forfaiting, in which a bank purchases at a discount from an importer a series of promissory notes in favour of an exporter, is a medium-term form of trade financing.

4. Export Development Canada provides competitive assistance to Canadian exporters through direct loans to foreign importers, loan guarantees and credit insurance to Canadian exporters.

5. Countertrade transactions are gaining renewed prominence as a means of conducting international trade transactions. There are several types of countertrade transactions, only some of which involve the use of money. In each type, the seller provides the buyer with goods or services in return for a reciprocal promise from the seller to purchase goods or services from the buyer.

QUESTIONS

1. Why is international trade more difficult and risky from the exporter's perspective than domestic trade?

2. What three basic documents are necessary to conduct a typical foreign commerce trade? Briefly discuss the purpose of each.

3. How does a time draft become a banker's acceptance?

4. Discuss the various ways the exporter can receive payment in a foreign trade transaction after the importer's bank accepts the exporter's time draft and it becomes a banker's acceptance.

5. What is a forfaiting transaction?

6. What is the purpose of Export Development Canada?

7. Do you think that a country's government should assist private business in the conduct of international trade through direct loans, loan guarantees and/or credit insurance?

8. Discuss some of the pros and cons of countertrade from the country's perspective and the firm's perspective.

9. What is the difference between a buy-back transaction and a counterpurchase?

PROBLEMS

1. Assume the time from acceptance to maturity on a $2,000,000 banker's acceptance is 90 days. Further assume that the importing bank's acceptance commission is 1.25 percent and that the market rate for 90-day B/As is 7 percent. Determine the amount the exporter will receive if he holds the B/A until maturity and also the amount the exporter will receive if he discounts the B/A with the importer's bank.

2. The time from acceptance to maturity on a $1,000,000 banker's acceptance is 120 days. The importer's bank's acceptance commission is 1.75 percent, and the market rate for 120-day B/As is 5.75 percent. What amount will the exporter receive if he holds the B/A until maturity? If he discounts the B/A with the importer's bank? Also determine the bond equivalent yield the importer's bank will earn from discounting the B/A with the exporter. If the exporter's opportunity cost of capital is 11 percent, should he discount the B/A or hold it to maturity?

INTERNET EXERCISE

The chapter indicated that banker's acceptances were negotiable money market instruments. You might be interested in including B/As in your portfolio. Fiscal Agents Financial Services Group is an investment advisory service specializing in helping investors structure portfolios to meet their needs. Go to www.fiscalagents.com/knowledge/inforeport/ba.shtml to learn what Fiscal Agents has to say about B/As as an investment.

MINI CASE

Manitoba Machine Tools, Inc.

Manitoba Machine Tools is a manufacturer of tool-and-die-making equipment. The company has had an inquiry from a representative of the Kazakhstan government about the terms of sale for a $5,000,000 order of machinery. The sales manager spoke with the Kazakhstan representative, but he is doubtful that the Kazakhstan government will be able to obtain enough hard currency to make the purchase. While the Canadian economy has been growing, Manitoba Machine Tools has not had a very good year. An additional $5,000,000 in sales would definitely help. If something cannot be arranged, the firm will likely be forced to lay off some of its skilled workforce.

Is there a way that you can think of that Manitoba Machine Tools might be able to make the machinery sale to Kazakhstan?

REFERENCES & SUGGESTED READINGS

Amiti, Mary, and David E. Weinstein. "Exports and Financial Shocks." National Bureau of Economic Research Working Paper No. 15556, December 2009.

Anyane-Ntow, Kwabena, and Santhi C. Harvey. "A Countertrade Primer." *Management Accounting* (April 1995), pp. 47–50.

Asmondson, Irena, T. Dorsey, A. Khachatryan, I. Niculcea, and M. Saito. "Trade and Trade Finance in the 2008–09 Financial Crisis." International Monetary Fund Working Paper 11/16, January 2011.

Auboin, Marc. "Restoring Trade Finance during a Period of Financial Crisis: Stock-Taking of Recent Initiatives." WTO Staff Working Paper ERSD-2009-16, December 2009.

Berman, Nicolas, and Jerome Hericourt. "Financial Factors and the Margins of Trade: Evidence from Cross-Country Firm-level Data." *Journal of Development Economics,* November 2010, Vol. 93, No. 2, pp. 206–17.

Chor, Davin, and Kalina Manova. "Off the Cliff and Back? Credit Conditions and International Trade during the Global Financial Crisis." *Journal of International Economics,* 87(1), 2012, pp. 117–33.

Contessi, Silvio, and Francesca de Nicola. "The Role of Financing in International Trade during Good Times and Bad." Federal Reserve Bank of St. Louis *The Regional Economist,* January 2012.

Eaton, Jonathan, Samuel Kortum, Brent Neiman, and John Romalis. "Trade and the Global Recession." NBER Working Paper No. 16666, January 2011.

Hammond, Grant T. *Countertrade, Offsets and Barter in International Political Economy.* New York: St. Martin's Press, 1990.

Hennart, Jean-Francois. "Some Empirical Dimensions of Countertrade." *Journal of International Business Studies* (Second Quarter, 1989), pp. 243–70.

Marin, Dalia, and Monika Schnitzer. "Tying Trade Flows: A Theory of Countertrade with Evidence." *The American Economic Review* 85 (1995), pp. 1047–64.

Manova, Kalina. "Credit Constraints, Equity Market Liberalization and International Trade." *Journal of International Economics,* September 2008, Vol. 76, No. 1, pp. 33–47.

Chapter 20

International Tax Environment

CHAPTER OUTLINE

THIS CHAPTER provides an introduction to the international tax environment that will be useful to multinational firms in their tax planning. While taxation is a complex topic at the domestic level, it is even more so in the international sphere where at least two and sometimes more tax systems interact to determine how much tax a corporation pays. This chapter is, at most, an introduction.

We begin with a discussion of two major objectives of taxation that have special relevance to international corporate taxation: *efficiency*, sometimes called "tax neutrality," and *national treatment*. We then turn to three categories of tax most pertinent to multinational enterprise: the corporate income tax, withholding taxes and value-added tax. This is followed by an outline of how various nations adopt fundamentally different approaches to achieve similar policy objectives. The chapter examines in particular the Canadian way of taxing multinational enterprise versus the American way. As we shall see, the Canadian system is remarkably simple whereas the American method is remarkably complex. We develop an extensive illustration based on the American approach.

Some issues in taxation were introduced earlier in view of specific concerns at hand. For example, Chapter 17 on capital budgeting required basic knowledge of international taxation from the Canadian perspective. Chapter 18 on cash management investigated the role of intra-firm transfer pricing as a means to reduce the overall tax liability of a multinational corporation (MNC).

20.1   THE OBJECTIVES OF TAXATION

Two fundamental policy objectives frame our thinking about the international tax environment: tax neutrality and national treatment.

Tax Neutrality

Tax neutrality is closely allied to economic efficiency. The issue is whether taxes distort investment decisions. Good tax policy does not penalize investment. In the international dimension, a neutral tax is one that does not interfere with international investment decisions, either inbound or outbound. In a world of mobile international capital, tax distortions are the modern counterpart of trade distortions caused by tariffs.

Nations impose tax in a variety of ways, including personal income tax, sales taxes, corporate income tax and value-added tax. International business is primarily concerned with corporate income tax, the tax most likely to distort investment decisions. For instance, if an MNC faces higher tax in one country than in another, then that MNC has an incentive to invest more in the low-tax country and less in the high-tax country. Likewise, as is often the case, when an MNC must choose between investing at home or abroad, it will invest more abroad if the burden of "home" taxation is greater than taxation abroad. Such tax-based bias in favour of foreign investment, we will see, is almost always the case for both Canadian and American firms—but for very different reasons.

The tax authorities recognize that cross-border investment decisions are sensitive to taxation. No nation wants to discourage investment, domestic or otherwise. However, a nation can set only its own tax rules, rates and regulations. Nations deal with joint tax concerns through bilateral tax treaties.

Tax treaties establish that MNCs must comply first with taxation in the host country. A host country *always* has priority to tax companies within its jurisdiction, an international understanding referred to as *national tax sovereignty*. The international question then is how does the home country of a multinational enterprise tax the foreign-source income of the parent companies in that home country? We will turn to that issue in a moment.

National Treatment

The second principle of international taxation is **national treatment**. To abide by national treatment, a nation agrees to tax foreign-owned business in exactly that same way—with the same rules, rates and regulations—as it taxes domestic firms. National treatment is a commitment to no tax discrimination. National treatment combined with national tax sovereignty creates a situation where, in matters of corporate taxation, the host country of an MNC sees no difference between foreign-owned and domestic corporations.

National treatment is enshrined in virtually every bilateral tax treaty as well as in free trade agreements such as the North American Free Trade Agreement (NAFTA).

Since the host country is both entitled and conveniently positioned to tax a foreign-owned firm first and since the host country levies corporate tax according to its own rules, rates and regulations, it is up to the *home country* to extend any special concession to foreign-source corporate income of the MNC that the home country considers to be appropriate. "Concession" usually involves relief of so-called "international double taxation." Relief of double taxation is exclusively the responsibility or prerogative of the home country of the MNC. For example, Canada is responsible for relief of double taxation on the foreign-source earnings of Barrick, CN, Domtar, Quebecor or TD Bank. The United States is responsible for the relief of double taxation of the foreign-source income of General Electric, General Motors, Disney or IBM. Canada and the United States approach this responsibility in fundamentally different ways.

The Canadian versus the American Way of Taxing Multinational Enterprise

Within Canada, all corporations, regardless of ownership, are liable for Canadian corporate tax on their in-Canada income. So, for example, income earned in Canada by Walmart (Canada), which is foreign-owned, is taxed in exactly the same way as Canadian Tire, which is wholly owned by Canadians, is taxed. This reflects Canada's commitment to national treatment. Canada does not discriminate along the lines of nationality of corporate ownership. In our commitment to national treatment, Canada is in line with all modern industrial nations.

International taxation is substantially more complicated—and different among nations—in the case of home (or *residence*) taxation of foreign-source income. We are now referring to how Canada taxes, for instance, the US earnings of CN or how the United States levies tax on income that Walmart earns in Canada. This is the perspective of the home country in regard to taxation of foreign-source corporate income.

When a Canadian-based multinational enterprise—such as Bombardier, McCain Foods or BlackBerry—earns income in, say, the United States or Europe, such foreign-source corporate income is *not* subject to additional tax in Canada. This Canadian approach, known as *exemption*, differs significantly from the way that, say, the United States taxes the foreign-source income of US-based multinationals. We will turn to the United States in a moment, but a brief word on the logic of the Canadian approach is useful.

The rationale for Canada's exemption policy follows directly from Canada's recognition that virtually all countries are committed to national treatment together with the fact that it is not in Canada's interest to penalize outbound foreign direct investment. If Canada were to impose Canadian tax on foreign source earnings of Canadian MNCs after such firms had paid tax abroad, the foreign source earnings would be taxed twice—once by the foreign country and once again by Canada. No modern country wants to penalize outbound foreign direct investment (FDI) in that way.

A fundamental efficiency condition in international taxation, referred to as **capital export neutrality**, is not guaranteed by exempting earnings of Canadian FDI from Canadian taxation. Capital export neutrality calls for corporate income of Canadian corporations to be taxed at the same rate regardless of where in the world the income is earned. With exemption, Canadian MNCs can do themselves a favour by locating in low-tax jurisdictions. This is where Canada is being practical in its international tax affairs. Canada realizes that for almost all countries in which Canadian MNCs have a serious interest, such as the United States, the EU or other OECD nations, these countries have corporate tax rates that are quite similar to Canada. Canada accepts that for all practical purposes, other countries will tax the local income (called *source* income) of Canadian MNCs at approximately the same rate as Canada would tax such income. So Canadian tax authorities leave foreign-source business income alone.

The United States, on the other hand, takes a fundamentally different approach to taxing the foreign-source income of its multinational enterprises. The United States taxes the worldwide income of US-based MNCs. For instance, the United States taxes the Canadian-source income of Walmart. The US Internal Revenue Service requires all US-based MNCs to compute a US tax liability on foreign-source income using US tax rules, rates and regulations. At the same time, the United States also allows a *foreign tax credit* for taxes that US-owned MNCs pay to foreign governments. For instance, taxes that Walmart pays to Ottawa are credited against Walmart's US tax liability.

The American system of taxing foreign-source income of US-based MNCs has another significant feature known as *deferral*. While every US-based MNC must annually compute its US tax liability on foreign-source income using US rules, rates and regulations, it is not liable for the US tax until such income is repatriated to the United States in the form of dividends paid by the foreign subsidiary to the parent firm in the United States. The deferral provision creates a strong incentive for US-based MNCs to leave their earnings abroad; that is, they have an incentive *not* to repatriate. Since, as finance people recognize, a payment delayed is a payment reduced, the deferral provision in effect lowers the effective corporate tax rate on foreign-source earnings of US-based MNCs.

Taxes and Transfer Pricing

The way that a home country taxes the foreign-source income of its MNCs has implications for the effectiveness of transfer pricing as a means to lower taxes. In the Mintel example that we saw in Chapter 18, which takes the vantage point of a US-based MNC, Mintel realizes no tax advantage through transfer pricing. At most, transfer pricing allows Mintel to shift taxable income abroad and thereby delay—but not evade—the eventual US tax liability.

On the other hand, an MNC with its home in Canada can always pursue a potential gain from shifting income out of Canada and into a lower-tax jurisdiction. If a Canadian-based MNC maintains a high margin on transfers to Canada from a subsidiary in, say, low-tax Ireland (or a low margin on transfers from Canada to Ireland), income is shifted from Canada to Ireland. Less tax is paid in Canada, a bit more tax is paid in Ireland and the MNC, as a whole, saves tax.

A well-known example of such arrangements involves Irving Oil, the New Brunswick–based oil company. For many years, Irving imported crude oil from Venezuela destined for the Irving refinery in Saint John. The crude oil shipments from Caracas to Saint John were channelled (in an accounting sense) through an Irving affiliate in Bermuda. By assigning a high transfer price to crude as it was "transferred" from Bermuda to Saint John, profits that would otherwise be reported in Canada were reported in low-tax Bermuda.[1]

Neither the US Internal Revenue Service nor the Canada Revenue Agency takes kindly to international accounting tricks that might cost them tax revenue to which they are otherwise entitled. The tax auditors are vigilant. As a practical matter in how MNCs manage their internal transfer prices, strategies designed to save tax are less likely to involve actual *physically* transferred goods and more likely to involve intangibles such as management fees, royalties and interest on intrafirm loans. This was illustrated in "The Shell Case," the International Finance in Practice box in Chapter 14.

20.2 TYPES OF TAXATION

This section discusses the three basic types of taxation that national governments throughout the world use in generating revenue: income tax, withholding tax and value-added tax.

Income Tax

Many countries in the world obtain a significant portion of their tax revenue from imposing **income tax** on personal and corporate incomes. An income tax is a **direct tax** paid directly by the taxpayer on whom it is levied. The corporate tax is levied on **active income** that results from production by the firm.

One of the best guides detailing corporate income tax regulations in most countries is the PricewaterhouseCoopers annual *Corporate Taxes*: *Worldwide Summaries*. Exhibit 20.1 is derived from the PricewaterhouseCoopers summaries. It lists the normal, standard, or representative upper-end marginal income tax rates for domestic nonfinancial corporations for 125 countries. As the exhibit shows, national tax rates vary from a low of zero percent in such tax-haven countries as Bahrain, Bermuda, the British Virgin Islands and the Cayman Islands to well over 40 percent in some countries. The current Canadian marginal tax rate of 30 percent is positioned pretty well in the middle of the rates assessed by the majority of countries.

Withholding Tax

www.tax.kpmg.net

KPMG International, a global professional advisory firm, manages this website. A useful corporate tax survey that compares tax rates for 68 countries can be downloaded from this site.

www.taxup.com

This website provides tax and accounting information by country.

A **withholding tax** is a common form of tax on international capital income flows such as interest, dividends or royalties. For instance, when interest flows from Country A to Country B because Country A has borrowed from Country B, a withholding tax could be imposed by Country A on those cross-border interest outflows. The tax is required to be "withheld" by the financial institution through which the interest flows, typically a bank in Country A.

Withholding taxes represent a significant source of tax distortion in international finance and a barrier to capital market integration. A withholding tax on, say, interest tends to raise the net-of-tax interest that borrowers in the taxing country must pay, especially if that country is relatively small in terms of international finance. For example, if the "world interest rate" is 10 percent and a country imposes a 20 percent withholding tax on interest paid to foreigners, then foreign lenders will lend to that country only if borrowers pay interest of at least $10/(1 - 0.20) = 12.5$ percent. Since the government of the borrowing country imposes a 20 percent tax on interest paid to foreigners, foreign lenders—focusing on after-tax proceeds—view a *gross* interest rate of 12.5 percent as equal to 10 percent

---

[1]Irving Oil's transfer pricing arrangements prompted Revenue Canada Taxation (as the federal tax agency was then known) to reassess Irving's Canadian tax obligation, substantially raising Irving's Canadian tax bill. Irving challenged the reassessment. The case went all the way to the Supreme Court. The Supreme Court found in favour of Irving Oil.

EXHIBIT 20.1 Corporate Income Tax Rates in Various Countries[a]

Country	Tax Rate	Country	Tax Rate	Country	Tax Rate
Albania	10	Denmark	25	Kyrgyzstan	10	Romania	16
Angola	35	Dominican Republic	25	Latvia	15	Russian Federation	20
Antigua & Barbuda	25	Dominica,		Lao, People's		Rwanda	30
Argentina	35	Commonwealth of	30	Democratic Republic	28	Saint Kitts and Nevis	35
Armenia	20	Ecuador	23	Lebanon	15	Saint Lucia	30
Aruba	28	Egypt	25	Libya	20	Saudi Arabia	20
Australia	30	El Salvador	30	Liechtenstein	12.5	Senegal	25
Austria	25	Equatorial Guinea	35	Lithuania	15	Serbia	10
Azerbaijan	20	Estonia	21	Luxembourg	22.05	Singapore	17
Bahrain	0	Fiji	20	Macau	12	Sint Maarten	34.5
Barbados	25	Finland	24.5	Macedonia	10	Slovak Republic	19
Belarus	24	France	36.1	Madagascar	21	Slovenia	18
Belgium	35.54	Gabon	35	Malawi	30	South Africa	28
Bermuda	0	Georgia	15	Malaysia	25	Spain	30
Bolivia	25	Germany	≦ 33	Malta	35	Sri Lanka	28
Bosnia Herzegovina	10	Ghana	25	Mauritius	15	Swaziland	30
Botswana	22	Gibraltar	10	Mexico	30	Sweden	26.3
Brazil	34	Greece	20	Moldova	12	Switzerland	11.5–24.2
Bulgaria	10	Guatemala	31	Mongolia	25	Syria	28
Cambodia	20	Guyana	40	Montenegro	9	Taiwan	17
Cameroon	38.5	Honduras	25	Morocco	30	Tajikistan	15
Canada	15	Hong Kong	16.5	Mozambique	32	Tanzania	30
Cayman Islands	0	Hungary	19	Namibia	34	Thailand	23
Cape Verde	25	Iceland	20	Netherlands	25	Timor-Leste	10
Caribbean Netherlands	0	India	34.5	New Zealand	28	Trinidad & Tobago	25
Chad	40	Indonesia	25	Nicaragua	30	Tunisia	30
Channel Islands, Guernsey	0	Iraq	15	Nigeria	30	Turkey	20
Channel Islands, Jersey	0	Ireland	12.5	Norway	28	Turkmenistan	8
Chile	17	Isle of Man	0	Oman	12	Uganda	30
China	25	Israel	25	Pakistan	35	Ukraine	21
Colombia	33	Italy	27.5	Panama	27.5	United Arab	
Congo, Democratic		Ivory Coast	25	Papua New Guinea	30	Emirates	≦ 55
Republic of	40	Jamaica	33.33	Paraguay	10	United Kingdom	24
Congo, Republic of	34	Japan	42	Peru	30	United States	35
Costa Rica	30	Jordan	14	Philippines	30	Uruguay	25
Croatia	20	Kazakhstan	20	Poland	19	Uzbekistan	9
Curacao	27.5	Kenya	30	Portugal	25	Venezuela	34
Cyprus	10	Korea	22	Puerto Rico	30	Vietnam	25
Czech Republic	19	Kuwait		Qatar	10	Zimbabwe	25.75

[a]The table lists normal, standard or representative upper-end marginal tax rates for nonfinancial corporations.

Source: PricewaterhouseCoopers, *Corporate Taxes: Worldwide Summaries*, 2012/13, www.pwc.com.

net of the withholding tax, namely 12.5 × (1 − 0.20) = 10. In general, a withholding tax of t_w raises the gross interest rate required from small country borrowers by a factor of $1/(1 - t_w)$ above the "world interest rate." For the corporate borrower, of course, the important interest rate for determining its cost of capital is the gross interest rate, the rate that it must pay to its foreign bondholders.

Most countries negotiate **tax treaties** with one another specifying the withholding tax rates applied to various types of cross-border capital income. Exhibit 20.2 lists the *basic* withholding tax rates that Canada imposes on other countries through its tax treaties with them. For specific types of income, the tax rates may be different from those presented in the exhibit.

It is well established in tax research that borrowing costs of multinational corporations are affected by withholding taxes, especially withholding taxes on interest that discourage MNEs from borrowing from the lowest-cost sources of debt. See Brean (1984). Recently, Canada and the United States took the constructive step of eliminating withholding taxes on cross-border interest payments. The new ruling applies to both arm's-length and non-arm's-length (intra-firm) debt. Furthermore, Canada intends to phase in a reduction to zero of withholding tax rates on arm's-length debt payments to all other treaty countries. With this action, Canada has demonstrated its commitment to removing one of the last serious barriers to international capital market integration.

Withholding tax rates presented in Exhibit 20.2 are for the most part *bilateral* in the sense that Canada and each of the nations represented in the exhibit have negotiated a bilateral tax treaty. Rates within a tax treaty are reciprocally equal. For example, within the Canada–France tax treaty, the rate of withholding tax on interest payments from one country to the other is 10 percent. Canada withholds 10 percent on interest payments paid to France and France withholds 10 percent on interest payments paid to Canada.

Withholding tax rates on dividends are also important for multinational corporations since intra-firm dividends are how MNC subsidiaries repatriate earnings to the parent firm. Exhibit 20.2 in most cases reports two withholding tax rates for cross-border dividends, for example "15 or 25" for Brazil or "5 or 15" for France and most OECD nations. The higher rate applies to individual taxpayers and intracorporate dividends where the ownership share is small, say less than 10 percent, whereas the lower rate applies to international intracorporate dividends paid by a subsidiary to its parent. The rationale for the lower rate on corporate dividends is straightforward: The country from which the dividend is sent has already levied a corporate tax on the income that underlies the dividend.

Value-Added Tax

A **value-added tax (VAT)** is an indirect tax levied on the value added in the production of a good (or service) as it moves through the various stages of production. There are several ways to implement a VAT. The "subtraction method" is frequently followed in practice.

Example 20.1 *Value-Added Tax Calculation*

As an example of the subtraction method of calculating VAT, consider a VAT of 15 percent charged on a consumption good that goes through three stages of production. Suppose that Stage 1 is the sale of raw materials to the manufacturer at a cost of €100 per unit of production. Stage 2 results in a finished good shipped to retailers at a price of €300. Stage 3 is the retail sale to the final consumer at a price of €380.

€100 of value has been added in Stage 1, resulting in a VAT of €15. In Stage 2 the VAT is 15 percent of €300, or €45, with a credit of €15 given against the value added in Stage 1. In Stage 3, an additional VAT of €12 is due on the €80 of value added by the retailer. Since the final consumer pays a price of €380, he effectively pays the total VAT of €57 (= €15 + €30 + €12), which is 15 percent of €380. Obviously, a VAT is the equivalent of imposing a national sales tax.

EXHIBIT 20.2 Canada's Treaty Withholding Tax Rates, 2013

	Dividends	Related-Party Interest[3]	Royalties[4]
Algeria	15	15	0 or 15
Argentina	10 or 15	12.5	3, 5, 10 or 15
Armenia	5 or 15	10	10
Australia N	5 or 15	10	10
Austria	5 or 15	10	0 or 10
Azerbaijan	10 or 15	10	5 or 10
Bangladesh	15	15	10
Barbados	15	15	0 or 10
Belgium	5 or 15	10	0 or 10
Brazil	15 or 25	15	15 or 25
Bulgaria	10 or 15[1]	10	0 or 10[1]
Cameroon	15	15	15
Chile[1]	10 or 15	15	15
China P.R. N [not Hong Kong]	10 or 15	10	10
Colombia, Rep. of	5 or 15	10	10[1]
Croatia	5 or 15	10	10
Cyprus	15	15	0 or 10
Czech Rep.	5 or 15	10	10
Denmark	5 or 15	10	0 or 10
Dominican Rep.	18	18	0 or 18
Ecuador	5 or 15	15	10 or 15[1]
Egypt	15	15	15
Estonia	5 or 15	10	10[1]
Finland	5 or 15	10	0 or 10
France	5 or 15	10	0 or 10
Gabon	15	10	10
Germany	5 or 15	10	0 or 10
Greece	5 or 15	10	0 or 10
Guyana	15	15	10
Hong Kong	25 → [5 or 15]	25 → [10]	25 → [10]
Hungary	5 or 15	10	0 or 10
Iceland	5 or 15	10	0 or 10

	Dividends	Related-Party Interest[3]	Royalties[4]
India	15 or 25	15	10, 15 or 20
Indonesia	10 or 15	10	10
Ireland	5 or 15	10	0 or 10
Israel N	15	15	0 or 15
Italy	5 or 15	10	0, 5 or 10
Ivory Coast	15	15	10
Jamaica	15	15	10
Japan	5 or 15	10	10
Jordan	10 or 15	10	10
Kazakhstan	5 or 15	10	10[1]
Kenya	15 or 25[1]	15	15
Korea (South)	5 or 15	10	10
Kuwait	5 or 15	10	10
Kyrgyzstan	15[1]	15[1]	0 or 10
Latvia	5 or 15	10	10[1]
Lebanon	25 → [5 or 15]	25 → [10]	25 → [5 or 10]
Lithuania	5 or 15	10	10[1]
Luxembourg	5 or 15	10	0 or 10
Madagascar N	25% imposed by Canada		
Malaysia N	15	15	15
Malta	15	15	0 or 10
Mexico	5 or 15	10	0 or 10
Moldova	5 or 15	10	10
Mongolia	5 or 15	10	5 or 10
Morocco	15	15	5 or 10
Namibia	25 → [5 or 15]	25 → [10]	25 → [0 or 10]
Netherlands N	5 or 15	10	0 or 10
New Zealand	15 → [5 or 15]	15 → [10]	15 → [5 or 10]
Nigeria	12.5 or 15	12.5	12.5
Norway	5 or 15	10	0 or 10
Oman	5 or 15	10[1]	0 or 10
Pakistan	15	15	0 or 15
Papua New Guinea	15	10	10

	Dividends	Related-Party Interest[3]	Royalties[4]
Peru[1]	10 or 15	15	15
Philippines	15	15	10
Poland	15 → [5 or 15]	15 → [10]	0 or 10 → [5 or 10]
Portugal	10 or 15	10	10
Romania	5 or 15	10	5 or 10
Russia	10 or 15	10	0 or 10
Senegal	15	15	15
Serbia	25 → [5 or 15]	25 → [10]	25 → [10]
Singapore	15	15	15
Slovak Republic	5 or 15	10	0 or 10
Slovenia	5 or 15	10	10
South Africa	5 or 15	10	6 or 10
Spain N	15	15	0 or 10
Sri Lanka	15	15	0 or 10
Sweden	5 or 15	10	0 or 10
Switzerland	5 or 15	10	0 or 10
Tanzania	20 or 25	15	20
Thailand	15	15	5 or 15
Trinidad and Tobago	5 or 15	10	0 or 10
Tunisia	15	15	0, 15 or 20
Turkey	15 or 20	15	10
Ukraine	5 or 15	10	0 or 10
United Arab Emirates	5 or 15	10	0 or 10
United Kingdom N	5 or 15	10	0 or 10
United States	5 or 15	0[2]	0 or 10
Uzbekistan	5 or 15	10	5 or 10
Venezuela	10 or 15[1]	10	5 or 10
Vietnam	5, 10 or 15	10	7.5 or 10
Zambia	15	15	15
Zimbabwe	10 or 15	15	10

This table summarizes treaty withholding tax rates (%) on payments arising in Canada. Rates in square brackets after an arrow are set out in a protocol, replacement treaty or new treaty that is signed, but not in force. To the left of the arrow are the rates that are being replaced, that is, the rate or rates in the existing treaty or protocol or, if no treaty is in force, the 25 percent rate imposed by Canada. If two or more dividend rates are provided, the lower (lowest two for Vietnam) applies if the recipient is a company that owns or controls a specified interest of the payor.

N: Negotiation or renegotiation of tax treaty or protocol under way, or concluded (but not signed).

1. If the other state (Canada for treaty with Oman) concludes a treaty with another country providing for a lower rate (higher for Kenya), the lower rate (higher for Kenya) will apply in respect of specific payments or with limits, in some cases.

2. For the United States, the nil rate applies subject to the Limitation of Benefits article.

3. Canadian withholding tax does not apply to interest (except for "participating debt interest") paid to arm's-length nonresidents.

4. A nil royalty rate generally applies to
- Copyright royalties and payments for a literary, dramatic, musical or other artistic work (but not royalties for motion picture films or works on film or videotape or other means of reproduction for use in television)
- Royalties for computer software or a patent, or for information concerning industrial, commercial or scientific experience (but not royalties for a rental or franchise agreement)

Source: PricewaterhouseCoopers. *Tax Facts and Figures (Canada)*. 2013. http://www.pwc.com/ca.

Throughout the European Union and Latin America, VAT has become a major source of taxation. Many tax experts prefer a VAT in place of a personal income tax because the latter is a disincentive to work, whereas a VAT discourages consumption. A VAT fosters saving whereas an income tax is a disincentive to save insofar as the returns from savings are taxed. Moreover, tax authorities find that a VAT is easier to collect than income tax. Under VAT, taxpayers at each stage in the production process must obtain documentation from the previous stage that the VAT was paid in order to get the greatest tax credit possible. Of course, some argue that the cost of record keeping under a VAT system imposes an economic hardship on small businesses.

A problem with VAT is that not all countries impose the same VAT tax rate. For example, in Denmark the VAT rate is 25 percent, but in Germany it is only 16 percent. Consequently, consumers who reside in a high-VAT country can purchase goods less expensively by simply shopping across the border in a lower-VAT country. Indeed, *The Wall Street Journal* reports that Danish customers frequently *demand* the lower German VAT rate on their purchases in Denmark! This problem should eventually be resolved, or at least mitigated, in the EU countries through harmonization in VAT rates among member states.

Canada's Goods and Services Tax (GST) is essentially a VAT. An important motive for implementing the GST in 1991 was to establish a tax regime that is "export friendly" insofar as the GST, like VAT, is fully rebated on exports. Canadian exported goods enter the world market free of Canadian tax.

20.3 NATIONAL TAX ENVIRONMENTS

The international tax environment confronting an MNC or an international investor is a function of the tax jurisdictions established by the individual countries in which the MNC does business or in which the investor owns financial assets. There are two fundamental types of tax jurisdiction: the *worldwide* and the *territorial*. Unless some mechanism is established to prevent it, double taxation results if all nations follow both methods simultaneously.

Worldwide Taxation

The **worldwide** or **residential** method of national tax jurisdiction is to tax residents of the country on their worldwide income, no matter in which country it is earned. This is the approach adopted by the US, the UK and Japan. The national tax authority, according to this method, defines its tax jurisdiction over people and businesses. An MNC with many foreign affiliates would be taxed by its home country on its income earned at home and abroad. Obviously, if the host countries of the foreign affiliates of an MNC also tax the income earned within their territorial borders, the possibility of double taxation exists unless there is provision to prevent it.

Territorial Taxation

The **territorial** or **source** method of tax jurisdiction is to tax all income earned within the country by any taxpayer, domestic or foreign. Hence, regardless of the nationality of a taxpayer, if the income is earned within the territorial boundary of a country, it is taxed by that country. The national tax authority, according to this method, declares tax jurisdiction over transactions conducted within its borders. Consequently, local firms and affiliates of foreign MNCs are taxed on the income earned in the *source* country.

Foreign Tax Credits

The Canadian approach to avoiding double taxation is not to tax foreign-source income of Canadian-based MNCs. An alternative method, and the one the United States follows, is to grant to the parent firm **foreign tax credits** against US taxes for taxes paid to foreign tax authorities on foreign-source income. In general, foreign tax credits are categorized as direct or indirect. A *direct* foreign tax credit is computed for direct taxes paid on active foreign-source income of a foreign branch of an American MNC or on the indirect withholding taxes withheld from passive income distributed by the foreign subsidiary to the US parent. For foreign subsidiaries of American MNCs, an *indirect* foreign tax credit is computed for income taxes *deemed paid* by the subsidiary. The deemed-paid tax credit corresponds to the portion of the distribution of earnings available for distribution that were actually distributed. For example, if a wholly owned foreign subsidiary pays out dividends equal to 50 percent of the earnings available for distribution, the deemed-paid tax credit is 50 percent of the foreign income taxes paid by the foreign subsidiary.

In a given tax year, an *overall limitation* applies to foreign tax credits; that is, the maximum total tax credit is limited to the amount of tax that would be due on the foreign-source income if it had been earned in the United States. The maximum tax credit is figured on worldwide foreign-source income; losses in one country can be used to offset profits in another. Excess tax credits for a tax year can be carried back two years and forward five years. Examples of calculating foreign tax credits for American foreign branch and subsidiary operations are provided in the next section. Value-added taxes paid may not be included in determining the amount of the foreign tax credit, but they are, nevertheless, indirectly expensed as part of the cost of a good or service.

20.4   ORGANIZATIONAL STRUCTURES FOR REDUCING TAX LIABILITIES

Countries differ in how they tax foreign-source income of their domestic MNCs. Regardless of the twin objectives of tax neutrality and tax equity, different forms of structuring a multinational organization can result in different tax liabilities for the firm. Thus, it behooves management to be familiar with the different organizational structures that can be useful at various stages in the life cycle of the MNC for reducing tax liabilities.

Branch and Subsidiary Income

A foreign affiliate of a Canadian MNC can be organized as a branch or a subsidiary. A **foreign branch** is not an independently incorporated firm separate from the parent; it is an extension of the parent. Consequently, active or passive foreign-source income earned by the branch is consolidated with the domestic-source income of the parent for determining the Canadian tax liability, regardless of whether or not the foreign-source income has been repatriated to the parent. Canadian banks and other financial institutions typically set up foreign operations in the form of branches—say, for example, the Rome branch of the Bank of Nova Scotia—so that the capital strength (which is so important in banking) of the parent supports the operations of the foreign branches. On the other hand, some Canadian-owned foreign banking operations are set up as subsidiaries, although in such cases the foreign operations are typically large and substantially independent such as BMO's ownership of Harris Bank in Chicago or TD Bank's purchase of Banknorth in the eastern US.

Canadian firms in manufacturing and other nonfinancial industries for the most part set up foreign operations as subsidiaries. A **foreign subsidiary** is an affiliate of the MNC that is independently incorporated in the foreign country, and one in which the Canadian MNC owns at least 10 percent of the voting equity shares. The active business income of foreign subsidiaries can flow back to the Canadian parent firm in the form of dividends declared to be "exempt surplus" in which case it does not bear tax in Canada.

For US-owned MNCs, the tax situation is substantially different. The difference, of course, is important for Canada and Canadians since Canada is host to a large number of subsidiaries of US-based MNCs.

A foreign subsidiary in which the US-MNC owns more than 10 but less than 50 percent of the voting equity is a minority foreign subsidiary or an "uncontrolled foreign corporation." Active and passive foreign-source income derived from a minority foreign subsidiary is taxed in the United States only when remitted to the US parent firm via a dividend (the so-called "deferral principle"). A foreign subsidiary in which the US-based MNC owns more than 50 percent of the voting equity is a "controlled foreign corporation." Active foreign-source income from a controlled foreign corporation is taxed in the United States only as remitted to the US parent, but passive income is taxed in the United States as earned even if it has not been repatriated to the parent. A more detailed discussion on US-controlled foreign corporations is reserved for later in this section.

Example 20.2 *US Foreign Tax Credit Calculations*

Exhibit 20.3 presents examples of calculating the foreign tax credits for both a foreign branch and a wholly owned foreign subsidiary of a US-based MNC in the host countries of Finland and Japan. The examples use the actual domestic marginal income tax rates presented in Exhibit 20.1 and the withholding tax rates presented in Exhibit 20.2. Both Finland and Japan tax foreign branch income at the same rate as domestic taxable income. The examples show the total tax liability for $100 of foreign taxable income when any excess foreign tax credits can be used and when they cannot. As a rule, excess tax credits can be carried back two years and forward five years. The examples assume that *all* after-tax foreign-source income available for remittance is immediately remitted to the parent.

Exhibit 20.3 indicates that when the US-based MNC can use the full excess tax credits, the total tax liability is $35 per $100 of foreign taxable income, or 35 percent, the same amount due on $100 of taxable income earned in the United States. This is true: (1) regardless in which country the foreign affiliate is located; (2) whether the foreign affiliate is established as a branch or a subsidiary; and (3) regardless of the size of the income tax and withholding tax rates. An MNC that consistently generates excess foreign tax credits will never be able to use them in the allowable time. Thus, the more typical situation is that excess foreign tax credits go unused.

When excess tax credits go unused, the foreign tax liability for a branch is greater than the corresponding US tax liability when the foreign income tax rate is greater than the US rate of 35 percent. For a foreign subsidiary, the foreign tax liability is greater than the corresponding US tax liability when: [foreign income tax rate + withholding tax rate − (foreign income tax rate × withholding tax rate)] is greater than the US income tax rate of 35 percent. To illustrate, a foreign subsidiary in Japan for which excess foreign tax credits cannot be used has a total tax liability of: $0.41 + 0.05 - (0.41 \times 0.05) = 0.4395$, or 43.95 percent versus 35 percent in the United States.

This example suggests that the management of a US-based MNC should be aware of the current tax rates levied by various host countries when deciding where to locate foreign affiliate operations. Moreover, the exhibit indicates that there can be a difference in the tax liability due on foreign-source income depending upon the organizational structure selected for the foreign affiliate. Thus, the management of an MNC must be aware of any differences in the taxation of income by a particular host country when deciding whether to organize a foreign operation as a branch or subsidiary. For example, new foreign affiliates frequently experience operating losses in the early years of operation. If this situation is expected, it may be beneficial for a US-based MNC to originally establish overseas operations as a foreign branch of the parent because branch operating losses are consolidated with the parent firm's earnings for tax purposes. Alternatively, when foreign-source income is to be reinvested abroad to expand foreign operations, it may be preferable to organize as a minority foreign subsidiary if the foreign income tax rate is less than the American income tax rate because the tax liability in the United States can be deferred until the subsidiary remits a dividend to the American parent.

EXHIBIT 20.3

Examples of
Calculating US
Foreign Tax
Credits for Branch
and Subsidiary
Operations

	Finland		Japan	
	Branch	**Subsidiary**	**Branch**	**Subsidiary**
Foreign income tax rate	26%	26%	41%	41%
Withholding tax rate	n.a.	10%	n.a.	5%
Taxable income	100.00	100.00	100.00	100.00
Foreign income tax paid	−26.00	−26.00	−41.00	−41.00
Net available for remittance	74.00	74.00	59.00	59.00
Withholding tax[a]	0	−7.40	0	−2.95
Net cash to US parent	74.00	66.60	59.00	56.05
Gross-up: Foreign income tax	26.00	26.00	41.00	41.00
Gross-up: Withholding tax	0	−7.40	0	−2.95
US taxable income	100.00	100.00	100.00	100.00
US income tax at 35%	35.00	35.00	35.00	35.00
Less foreign tax credit:				
Income tax	−26.00	−26.00	−41.00	−41.00
Withholding tax.	0	−7.40	0	−2.95
Net US tax (excess credit)	9.00	1.60	(6.00)	(8.95)
Total tax: Excess credit used	35.00	35.00	35.00	35.00
Total tax: Excess credit not used	35.00	35.00	41.00	43.95

[a]100 percent of the funds available for remittance are assumed to be declared as dividends.

Payments to and from Foreign Affiliates

In Chapter 18, we discussed transfer pricing strategies that may help an American (but not a Canadian) MNC to minimize its global tax liability. Since the discussion there was sufficient, we will only recap the major points in this chapter. Recall that a *transfer price* was the accounting value assigned to a good or service as it was transferred from one affiliate to another. We learned that the higher the transfer price, the larger will be the gross profits of the transferring division relative to the receiving division. Consequently, it is beneficial to follow a high markup policy on transferred goods and services from the parent to a foreign affiliate when the income tax rate in the host country is greater than the tax rate in the parent country because there will be less taxable income remaining in the high-tax host country. However, when the parent country has the higher tax rate, it is not instantly clear that a low markup policy should be pursued. Since American MNCs are taxed on their worldwide income, earnings repatriated to the United States from a low-tax host country would be grossed up to figure the additional tax due in the United States. However, if foreign-source retained earnings were needed for reinvestment in the host country, a low markup policy would result in a tax savings (assuming, of course, that undistributed profits are not highly taxed by the host country).

We also learned from Chapter 18 that governmental authorities are quite aware of transfer pricing schemes used by MNCs to reduce their worldwide tax liability, and most countries have regulations controlling transfer prices. These regulations typically state that the transfer price must reflect an *arm's-length price*, that is, a price the selling affiliate would charge an unrelated customer for the good or service. However, an arm's-length price is frequently difficult to establish and evaluate; thus, there exists a window of opportunity for some manoeuvrability by an MNC to use transfer pricing strategies to reduce its worldwide tax liability.

The International Finance in Practice box "Wake Up and Smell the Coffee" describes a tax-motivated transfer and international royalty arrangement used by the likes of Starbucks, Google and Amazon in Britain to minimize taxes paid in the UK.

Wake Up and Smell the Coffee

"This is an unprecedented commitment," said Kris Engskov, the boss of Starbucks in Britain and Ireland, on December 6th, announcing that the coffee retailer will volunteer to the British taxman around £10m ($16m) a year more in 2013–14 than it is required to pay by law. It is doing so not under any pressure from the authorities, which had not been party to the firm's decision to donate an extra shot of cash to the exchequer, but to please British consumers furious not, as you might expect, at the high price of a latte, but at how little tax the firm pays in their country. "We've heard that loud and clear from our customers," said Mr. Engskov.

Alas, this pioneering effort to transform tax into a marketing expense did not elicit the hoped-for gratitude. On December 8th UK Uncut, a group which campaigns against government austerity and corporate tax avoidance, staged protests at dozens of British Starbucks stores. Campaigners point out that since first opening its doors in Britain in 1998 Starbucks has paid only £8.6m in corporate income taxes there. In testimony last month before a parliamentary committee, Starbucks had said this was because it had made a profit in only one year in Britain, though it also admitted that its British business had made large payments for coffee to a profitable Starbucks subsidiary in Switzerland and large royalty payments to another profitable subsidiary in the Netherlands for use of the brand and intellectual property.

Starbucks is not thought to be using the "Dutch Sandwich" and "Double Irish," even if these sound like items on its menu. They are legal tax-avoidance techniques believed to have been used by, among others, Google, which was also called to testify before Parliament. Most of Google's revenues in Europe are booked in Dublin, then shifted via royalty payments to a Dutch subsidiary, before whatever is left is recognised as profits by a subsidiary in Bermuda, which levies no income tax. Another online giant, Amazon, told parliamentarians that its low British corporate-tax bill—£1.8m in 2011—was due to its British operations merely providing back-office services to its main Europe-wide business, which is based in low-tax Luxembourg.

Although Starbucks denies using tax havens, it admits to having negotiated a secret low rate of tax with the Dutch taxman for its subsidiary in Amsterdam. Worldwide, it says it pays out over 30% of its profits in tax. Many other firms are making extensive use of havens. A study published last year by Action-Aid, an activist charity, said 98 of the firms in the FTSE 100 index have at least one subsidiary in a tax haven. An increasingly popular strategy is to transfer ownership of the multinational's main intellectual property to a subsidiary in a tax haven, then charge other subsidiaries in higher-tax countries for use of it. Data compiled by the OECD, a rich-country think-tank, highlight how many patents are owned by outfits in such unlikely innovation hubs as Barbados, the Cayman Islands and Bermuda.

In many countries, including the US, the UK and Canada, businesses have been lobbying for cuts in marginal corporate-tax rates, even if this means losing a few small loopholes. Their arguments were bolstered by a study in June from the Centre for Business Taxation at Oxford University, which found that the two countries had among the world's highest effective tax rates (i.e., after allowances). Canada's corporate tax rates (federal plus provincial) are somewhat lower.

Now, it seems, the public outrage being whipped up over the most lucrative avoidance strategies may cause politicians to shift their focus from making taxes more business-friendly to shoring up the tax base. George Osborne, Britain's chancellor of the exchequer, has responded to the furor over Starbucks, Google and Amazon by promising to use the country's imminent chairmanship of the G8 club of rich countries to wage war on tax havens. Politicians elsewhere, also facing swelling deficits, may join him in that.

Source: Slightly adapted from *The Economist*, December 15, 2012, p. 66, http://www.economist.com/news/business/21568432-starbuckss-tax-troubles-are-sign-things-come-multinationals-wake-up-and-smell.

Tax Havens

A **tax-haven** country is one that has a low corporate income tax rate and low withholding tax rates on passive income. Some major tax-haven countries, which are suggested by the income tax rates presented in Exhibit 20.1, are the Bahamas, Bahrain, Bermuda and the Cayman Islands.

In Ireland and the Netherlands Antilles, special tax incentives or tax holidays are granted for businesses that develop export markets. In Puerto Rico, certain businesses are granted a reduced flat income tax rate of 7 percent applicable to industrial development income, which, in some areas, may be further reduced to 0 percent. In

Liechtenstein and in many instances in Switzerland, holding companies are exempt from certain income taxes.

Tax havens were once useful as locations for an MNC to establish a wholly owned "paper" foreign subsidiary that, in turn, would own the operating foreign subsidiaries of the MNC. Hence, when the tax rates in the host countries of the operating affiliates were lower than the tax rate in the parent country, dividends could be routed through the tax-haven affiliate for use by the MNC, but the taxes due on them in the parent country could continue to be deferred until a dividend was declared by the tax-haven subsidiary. These days the benefit of a tax-haven subsidiary for MNCs has been greatly reduced by two factors: One is that the present corporate income tax rates in most "home" countries are not especially high in comparison with most non-tax-haven countries, thus eliminating the need for deferral; the second is that the rules governing controlled foreign corporations (the topic to be discussed next) have effectively eliminated the ability to defer passive income in a tax-haven foreign subsidiary.

Canadian corporations, as we have noted, have a strong tax incentive to locate foreign direct investment in countries where corporate tax rates are lower than the tax rate in Canada. The reason is that active business income earned outside Canada can be returned to Canada (as dividends to the Canadian parent) without being subject to any Canadian tax. Therefore, a dollar of *foreign* tax that the Canadian firm avoids by choosing a low-tax country is a dollar that flows directly to the firm's bottom line. It has been observed that Canadian firms are big investors in offshore financial centres (OFCs) such as the Barbados and Ireland. Part of this is tax-driven. Nevertheless, there are interesting real implications for international trade and the success of foreign investment for those Canadian firms that make use of offshore financial centres.

The International Finance in Practice box "On or Off? It's a Matter of Degree" indicates that establishing solid definitions of an offshore financial centre and a tax haven can be a challenge.

Controlled Foreign Corporations

The US *Tax Reform Act* of 1986 created a new type of foreign subsidiary called a controlled foreign corporation. The purpose of the reform was to prevent the tax deferral of certain income in tax haven countries and to raise taxes by reducing the benefit gained by US-based MNCs from foreign tax credits. **A controlled foreign corporation (CFC)** is a foreign subsidiary that has more than 50 percent of its voting equity owned by American shareholders. A US shareholder is any US citizen, resident, partnership, corporation, trust or estate that owns (or indirectly controls) 10 percent or more of the voting equity of the CFC. Thus, six nonaffiliated US shareholders each owning exactly 10 percent of the voting equity would be required for a foreign corporation to be designated a CFC. Alternatively, a wholly owned subsidiary of a US MNC would be a CFC.

The undistributed income of a minority foreign subsidiary of a US MNC is tax-deferred until it is remitted via a dividend. This rule is modified for Subpart F income of CFCs, which is subject to immediate taxation. **Subpart F income** includes income of a type that is relatively easy to transfer between countries and that is subject to a low foreign tax levy. Special rules apply for calculating foreign tax credits for CFCs. Much of the Subpart F income can be classified into four distinct categories or "baskets" of income: passive income, high withholding tax interest, financial services income, and shipping income. The allowable foreign tax credit limit is figured separately for each basket. Operating income of the CFC goes into the overall basket. The result is that high taxes paid in one country on income classified into one basket cannot be used to offset low taxes paid in another country on income classified into a different basket. This procedure results in more excess foreign tax credits, which are unlikely to be completely used.

On or Off? It's a Matter of Degree

What exactly is an offshore financial centre? At its broadest, it is any financial centre that takes in a large chunk of foreign funds—in other words, almost every financial capital in the world. Much of the business conducted in places such as New York, London or Hong Kong is from outside America, Britain or China.

Britain is arguably one of the biggest personal-tax havens in the world. So-called "resident non-domiciles"—people who live in Britain but claim domicile abroad—do not have to pay tax on offshore income. America, for its part, soaks up huge amounts of offshore cash because it takes little of the money held in its banks by non-resident foreigners. Foreigners' bank deposits in America add up to $2.5 trillion, well over twice as much as those in Switzerland.

But as most people understand the term, "OFC" means a smaller jurisdiction where the lion's share of the institutions are controlled by non-residents and many of them are in the financial sector or set up for financial reasons. The volume of business conducted by these financial institutions often far outstrips the needs of the local economy.

When OFCs combine all these attributes with a low- or no-tax regime they are tagged as "tax havens," especially if they also have strict banking-secrecy rules, light supervision and a slack grip on business within their borders. Panama, for instance, still allows bearer shares that can be anonymously owned and traded.

The Financial Stability Forum (FSF), a group that monitors threats to the global financial system, has put together a list of 42 jurisdictions that it defines as OFCs. The OECD in 2000 compiled a narrower list of 35 tax havens. There is a great deal of overlap between the two.

Dividing the world into onshore and offshore financial centres is difficult because "It is a matter of degree, not substance," says one European bank regulator. For example, many people consider Bermuda an OFC, but it is packed with actuaries pricing reinsurance risks. Jersey, where the financial sector accounts for over half of all tax revenues, is home to a sophisticated banking industry, cooperates with other governments on tax matters and requires banks and other licensed institutions to have a "real presence" on the island.

More confusingly, some jurisdictions straddle both categories. One example is Luxembourg, a tiny country sandwiched between Belgium, France and Germany and one of Europe's most important financial centres. A founder-member of the EU, Luxembourg is considered a well-managed, soundly regulated financial centre with real expertise. It is home to more than 2,200 investment funds with almost €1.8 trillion under management. It is also the euro zone's biggest private-banking centre. The financial-services industry contributes a third of Luxembourg's output and, including its indirect contribution (accountants, lawyers and the like), supplies around 40 percent of Luxembourg's tax take.

Luxembourg is sometimes lumped with tax havens because of various scandals involving companies based there, including the notorious BCCI and, more recently, Clearstream. But although Luxembourg got most of the bad press, BCCI was operated out of London and Clearstream is mainly a French affair.

Ireland and Singapore are big in manufacturing but also have thriving financial centres that cater to offshore business. Singapore has strict rules on banking secrecy and does not consider foreign tax evasion a crime. Some people consider Switzerland as a tax haven because of its low tax rates and its fabled banking secrecy.

But onshore economies can be opaque too. A report issued by a government agency in America last April found that few states collect information on the true owners of companies set up within their borders. Delaware and Nevada are particularly lax.

Mr. Owens at the OECD prefers to differentiate between well and poorly regulated financial centres rather than onshore or offshore ones. Well-regulated centres cooperate with foreign tax and other authorities and have sound supervision; poorly regulated ones hide behind secrecy. Low or no taxes on their own, says Mr. Owens, do not constitute a harmful tax practice.

Source: *The Economist*, February 24, 2007, special section p. 7.

SUMMARY

This chapter provides a brief introduction to the international tax environment that confronts MNCs and investors in international financial assets.

1. The twin objectives of taxation are tax neutrality and tax equity. Tax neutrality has its foundations in the principles of economic efficiency and equity. Tax equity is the principle that all similarly situated taxpayers should participate in the cost of operating the government according to the same rules.

2. The three basic types of taxation are income tax, withholding tax, and value-added tax. Corporate income tax rates from many countries were listed and compared. Similarly, the withholding tax rates for certain countries for various types of foreign-source income for which Canada has bilateral tax treaties were listed and compared.

3. Canada, like most countries, taxes foreign-owned forms in Canada in exactly the same way that it taxes domestic firms.

4. Canada, unlike some other countries, notably the United States, does *not* tax the foreign-source active business income of Canadian-based MNCs.

5. Transfer-pricing to shift taxable income away from the home country is potentially more effective for Canadian-based MNCs than for US-based MNCs.

6. The United States, the United Kingdom and Japan tax the worldwide income of their resident MNCs as well as taxing the income of foreign-based (such as Canadian) MNCs within their territorial boundaries. For these countries, double taxation would result unless a mechanism is established to prevent it. The foreign tax credit is a means to eliminate international double taxation.

7. Foreign direct investment carried out through the organizational form of a branch is generally taxed differently by the home country than FDI in the form of a subsidiary.

8. Different forms of organizational structure can affect the tax liability of an MNC. Specifically, there are differences in taxation between branch and subsidiary operations. Transfer pricing strategies, subsidiary operations in tax-haven countries, foreign-controlled corporations and foreign sales corporations were also defined and discussed.

QUESTIONS

1. Discuss the twin objectives of taxation. Define the key words.

2. Compare and contrast the three basic types of taxation that governments levy within their tax jurisdiction.

3. Show how double taxation on a taxpayer might result if all countries were to tax the worldwide income of their residents and the income earned within their territorial boundaries.

4. What methods do taxing authorities use to mitigate the problems of double taxation?

5. The Canadian tax liability on foreign-source income of a Canadian bank depends on whether the foreign (bank) entity is a foreign branch or a subsidiary of the parent Canadian bank. Elaborate on this statement.

PROBLEMS

1. Three production stages are required before a pair of skis produced by Fjord Fabrication can be sold at retail for NOK2,300. Fill in the table at right to show the value added at each stage in the production process and the incremental and total VAT. The Norwegian VAT rate is 24 percent.

Production Stage	Selling Price	Value Added	Incremental VAT
1	NOK450		
2	NOK1,900		
3	NOK2,300		
			Total VAT

INTERNET EXERCISE

The comprehensive website www.taxsites.com provides links to many other websites categorized into the following topics: country-specific sites, IRS Resources, European Union and VAT, Students and Scholars, Tax Associations, Other Resources, Tax Treaties and Governments. For example, go to the Worldwide-Tax section under Other Resources and learn about the history of taxation.

MINI CASE 1

Sigma Corp.'s Location Decision

Sigma Corporation of Boston is contemplating establishing an affiliate operation in the Mediterranean. Two countries under consideration are Spain and Cyprus. Sigma intends to repatriate all after-tax foreign-source income to the United States. At this point, Sigma is not certain whether it would be best to establish the affiliate operation as a branch operation or a wholly owned subsidiary of the parent firm.

In Cyprus, the marginal corporate tax rate is 25 percent. Foreign branch profits are taxed at the same rate. In Spain, corporate income is taxed at 35 percent, the same rate as in the United States. Additionally, foreign branch income in Spain is also taxed at 35 percent. The American withholding tax treaty rates on dividend income are 5 percent with Cyprus and 10 percent with Spain.

The financial manager of Sigma has asked you to help determine where to locate the new affiliate and which organizational structure to establish. The location decision will be largely based on whether the total tax liability would be smallest for a foreign branch or a wholly owned subsidiary in Cyprus or Spain.

MINI CASE 2

Transfer Pricing Cases before the Courts

In Canada, transfer pricing legislation has been in place since 1938, but taxpayers have only recently begun to feel significant pressure to comply. In the 1980s, the Canadian tax authorities strategically focused international audit efforts on specific industries, such as the forestry and pharmaceutical industries, which resulted in a handful of noteworthy transfer pricing appeals. More recent activity shows the Canada Revenue Agency (CRA) working to strengthen overall compliance and enforcement of the transfer pricing rules.

New Cases before the Courts

According to the CRA, the following new cases are now working their way through the Tax Court of Canada:

1. A Canadian company involved in the blueberry business is being challenged on the transfer prices for tangible product involving a related US entity. The amount of the adjustment is $300,000.

2. A Canadian company producing welding guns is being challenged with respect to the prices charged to its related distributor based in Barbados. The amount of the adjustment is $14 million. Interestingly, the taxpayer is arguing that the CRA inappropriately re-characterized the transaction by treating the Barbadian entity as a call centre rather than a distributor.

3. A Canadian company in the pharmaceutical industry is being challenged with respect to the fees charged to its US affiliate for R&D services performed in Canada. The company is being assessed $51 million in transfer pricing adjustments.

4. A Canadian company providing tax return filing services is being challenged with respect to the service fees and interest being charged by its US parent company. The amount of the adjustment is $4.5 million.

For each of these international transfer pricing cases, provide greater detail on a likely structure of corporate transfer pricing arrangements that are being challenged in court by the Canada Revenue Agency.

REFERENCES & SUGGESTED READINGS

Advisory Panel on Canada's System of International Taxation. Final Report: "Enhancing Canada's International Tax Advantage." Ottawa: Department of Finance, December 2008.

Brean, Donald J. S. *International Aspects of Taxation: Canadian Perspectives.* Toronto: Canadian Tax Foundation; Tax Paper No. 75 (1984).

Couzin, Robert. "The End of Transfer Pricing?" (Policy Forum), *Canadian Tax Journal,* (2013) Vol. 61, pp. 159–78.

Harvard Business Review (January 2003), various articles.

Horst, Thomas. "American Taxation of Multinational Firms." *American Economic Review* (July 1977), pp. 376–89.

Kopits, George, ed. *Tax Harmonization in the European Community: Policy Issues and Analysis.* International Monetary Fund Occasional Paper, No. 94, Washington, DC: June 1992.

Metcalf, Gilbert E. "Value-Added Taxation: A Tax Whose Time Has Come?" *Journal of Economic Perspectives* 9 (1995), pp. 121–40.

Mustard, Brian. "Canada's System of International Taxation: A Look Back and a Look Forward," (Policy Forum), *Canadian Tax Journal,* (2013) Vol. 61, pp. 257–70.

OECD. "Transfer Pricing Guidelines for Multinational Enterprise and Tax Administrations." Paris: OECD, 2010.

PricewaterhouseCoopers. *Corporate Taxes: Worldwide Summaries.* New York: John Wiley and Sons, Inc., 2007.

 For more information on the resources available from McGraw-Hill Ryerson, go to www.mcgrawhill.ca/he/solutions.

Chapter 21

Corporate Governance around the World

THE RECENT SPATE of corporate scandals and failures, including Enron, WorldCom and Global Crossing in the United States and Nortel Networks, Hollinger and SNC-Lavalin in Canada, has raised serious questions about the way public corporations are governed around the world. Other well-publicized examples of serious corporate misconduct include Credit Lyonnais of France, Parmalat of Italy, the Daewoo Group of South Korea and HIH, a major insurance group of Australia.

When "self-interested" managers take control of a company, they sometimes engage in actions that are profoundly detrimental to the interests of shareholders and other stakeholders. For example, such managers may give themselves excessive salaries and indulgent perquisites, squander resources for corporate empire building, divert the company's cash and assets for private benefit, engage in cronyism and steal business opportunities from the company. A report in the *Harvard Business Review* (January 2003) describes how executives "treat their companies like ATMs, awarding themselves millions of dollars in corporate perks." In many less developed and transitional countries, corporate governance mechanisms are either weak or virtually nonexistent. In Russia, for example, a weak corporate governance system allows managers to divert assets from newly privatized companies on a large scale.

When managerial self-dealings are excessive and left unchecked, they can have serious negative effects on corporate values and the proper functions of capital markets. In fact, there is a growing consensus around the world that it is vitally important to strengthen **corporate governance** to protect the rights of shareholders, curb managerial excesses and restore confidence in capital markets. *Corporate governance* can be defined as *the economic, legal, and institutional framework in which corporate control and cash flow rights are distributed among shareholders, managers and other stakeholders of the company.* Other stakeholders may include workers, creditors, banks, institutional investors and even the government. As we will see later, corporate governance structure varies a great deal across countries, reflecting divergent cultural, economic, political and legal environments.

21.1 GOVERNANCE OF THE PUBLIC CORPORATION: KEY ISSUES

The *public corporation*, which is jointly owned by a multitude of shareholders protected with limited liability, is a major organizational innovation of vast economic consequence. The majority of global corporations that drive economic growth and innovation worldwide, including Microsoft, General Electric, IBM, Toyota, Danone, British Petroleum, Nokia and BlackBerry, are public corporations rather than private companies. The genius of public corporations stems from their capacity to allow efficient sharing or spreading of risk among many investors who can buy and sell their shares on stock exchanges and let professional managers run the company on behalf of shareholders. This risk-sharing mechanism enables public corporations to raise large amounts of capital at relatively low cost and undertake investment projects that individual entrepreneurs or private investors might eschew because of the costs and/or risks. Public corporations play a pivotal role in generating economic growth worldwide.

However, the public corporation has a key weakness—namely, the conflict of interest between managers and shareholders. The separation of the company's ownership and control, where corporate ownership is highly diffuse, gives rise to possible conflicts between shareholders and managers.

In principle, shareholders elect the board of directors of the company which, in turn, hires managers to run the company in the interests of shareholders. Managers are thus agents working for their principals, that is, shareholders, who are the real owners of the company. In a public company with diffuse ownership, the board of directors is entrusted with the vital tasks of monitoring management and safeguarding the interests of shareholders.

In reality, however, management-friendly insiders often dominate the board of directors, with relatively few outside directors to independently monitor management. In the cases of Enron, Hollinger and similarly dysfunctional companies, the boards of directors grossly failed to safeguard shareholder interests. Furthermore, with diffuse ownership, few shareholders have strong enough incentive to incur the costs of monitoring management themselves when the benefits from such monitoring accrue to all shareholders alike. The benefits are shared, but not the costs. This "free rider" problem discourages shareholder activism. As a result, the interests of managers and shareholders are often allowed to diverge.

With an ineffective and unmotivated board of directors, shareholders are left without effective recourse to control managerial self-dealings. Recognition of this key weakness of the public corporation can be traced at least as far back as Adam Smith's *Wealth of Nations* (1776), which stated:

> The directors of such joint-stocks companies, however, being the managers rather of other people's money than of their own, it cannot well be expected that they should watch over it with the same anxious vigilance with which the partners of a private copartnery frequently watch over their own. . . . Negligence and profusion, therefore, must always prevail, more or less, in the management of the affairs of such a company.

Two hundred years later, Jensen and Meckling (1976) provided a formal analysis of the "agency problem" of the public corporation in their celebrated paper "Theory of the Firm: Managerial Behavior, Agency Costs, and Ownership Structure." The Jensen-Meckling agency theory drew attention to this vitally important corporate finance problem.

Outside the Anglo-American (English speaking) industrial world, diffuse ownership of the company is more the exception than the rule. In Italy for instance, the three largest shareholders control about 60 percent of the shares of most public companies. The average comparable ownership by the three largest shareholders is 54 percent in Hong Kong, 64 percent in Mexico, 48 percent in Germany, 40 percent in India and 51 percent in Israel.[1] These large shareholders (often including founding families of the company) effectively control managers and may run the company for their own interests, expropriating outside shareholders in one way or another. In many countries with concentrated corporate ownership, conflicts of interest are greater between large controlling shareholders and small outside shareholders than between managers and shareholders.

www.oecd.org/daf/
corporate-affairs/
governance/

This site provides an overview of corporate governance in OECD countries.

---

[1] R. La Porta, F. Lopez-de-Silanes, A. Shleifer, and R. Vishny, "Law and Finance," *Journal of Political Economy* 106 (1998), pp. 1113–55.

In a series of influential studies, La Porta, Lopez-de-Silanes, Shleifer and Vishny (LLSV hereafter) document sharp differences among countries with regard to (1) corporate ownership structure, (2) depth and breadth of capital markets, (3) access of firms to external financing and (4) dividend policies. LLSV argue that these differences among countries can be explained largely by how well investors are protected by law from expropriation by the managers and controlling shareholders of firms. LLSV also argue that the degree of legal protection of investors significantly depends on the "legal origin" of countries. Specifically, English common law countries, such as Canada, the United States and the United Kingdom, provide the strongest protection for investors, whereas civil law countries, such as France, Belgium, Italy and Mexico, provide the weakest. We will revisit the issue of law and corporate governance later in the chapter.

Shareholders in different countries may, indeed, face divergent corporate governance systems. However, the central problem in corporate governance remains the same everywhere: *how to best protect outside investors from expropriation by the controlling insiders so that the former can receive fair returns on their investments.* How to deal with this problem has enormous practical implications for shareholder welfare, corporate allocation of resources, corporate financing and valuation, development of capital markets and economic growth. In the rest of this chapter, we discuss the following issues in detail:[2]

- The agency problem
- Remedies for the agency problem
- Law and corporate governance
- Consequences of law
- Corporate governance reform

21.2   THE AGENCY PROBLEM

Suppose that the manager (or entrepreneur) and the investors sign a contract that specifies how the manager will use corporate funds and also how the investment returns will be divided between the manager and the investors. If the two sides can write a **complete contract** that specifies exactly what the manager will do under each of all possible future contingencies, there will be no room for conflict of interest or managerial discretion. Thus, under a complete contract, there will be no **agency problem**. However, it is impossible to foresee all future contingencies and write a complete contract. This means that the manager and the investors must allocate the right (control) to make decisions under those contingencies that are not specifically covered by the contract. Because outside investors may be neither qualified nor interested in making business decisions, the manager often ends up acquiring most of this **residual control right**. Investors supply funds to the company but are not involved in the company's daily decision making. As a result, many public companies come to have "strong managers and weak shareholders."

Having captured residual control rights, management can exercise substantial discretion over the disposition and allocation of investors' capital. Under this situation, the investors are no longer assured of receiving fair returns on their funds. In the contractual view of the firm described above, the agency problem arises from the difficulty that outside investors face in assuring that they actually receive fair returns on their capital.[3]

With the control rights, management may opt to consume exorbitant perquisites. For example, the late Steve Jobs, then CEO of Apple Computer, reportedly had a $90 million company jet at his disposal.[4] Sometimes, the manager simply steals investors' funds. Think of Bernie Madoff.

---

[2]Our discussion here draws on the contributions of Jensen and Meckling (1976), Jensen (1989), La Porta, Lopez-de-Silanes, Shleifer, and Vishny (1997–2002) and Denis and McConnell (2002).

[3]The contractual view of the firm was developed by Coase (1937) and Jensen and Meckling (1976).

[4]*Financial Times* (November 27, 2002), p. 15.

Alternatively, management may use more sophisticated schemes, setting up an independent company and diverting to it the main company's cash and assets through *transfer pricing*. Unscrupulous managers could sell the main company's output to the management-owned "subsidiary" at below-market prices. Some Russian oil companies are known to sell oil to manager-owned trading companies at below market prices and not always bother to collect the bills.[5]

Self-interested managers may also waste funds by undertaking unprofitable projects that benefit themselves but not investors. For example, managers may misallocate funds to take over other companies and overpay for the targets if it serves their private interests. Needless to say, this type of investment will destroy shareholder value. What is more, the same managers may adopt anti-takeover measures for their own company in order to ensure their personal job security and perpetuate private benefits. In the same vein, managers may resist attempts to be replaced even if shareholders' interests will be better served by their dismissal. These **managerial entrenchment** efforts are clear signs of the agency problem.

The agency problem tends to be more serious in companies with "free cash flows." **Free cash flows** represent a firm's internally generated funds in excess of the amount needed to undertake all profitable investment projects, that is, those with positive net present values (NPVs). Free cash flows tend to be high in mature industries with low future growth prospects, such as the steel, chemical, tobacco, paper and textile industries. It is the *fiduciary duty* of managers to return free cash flows to shareholders as dividends. However, managers in these cash-rich and mature industries will be most tempted to waste cash flows to undertake unprofitable projects, destroying shareholders' wealth but possibly benefiting themselves.

There are a few important incentives for managers to retain cash flows. First, cash reserves provide corporate managers with a measure of independence from the capital markets, insulating them from external scrutiny and discipline. This makes life easy for managers. Second, expanding the size of the company via retention of cash tends to have the effect of raising managerial compensation. As is well known, executive compensation depends as much on the size of the company as on its profitability. Third, senior executives can boost their social and political power and prestige by increasing the size of their company. Executives presiding over large companies are likely to enjoy greater social prominence and visibility than those running small companies. Also, the company's size itself can be a way of satisfying the executive ego.

In the face of strong managerial incentives for retaining cash, few effective mechanisms exist to compel managers to disgorge cash flows to shareholders. Jensen cites a revealing example of this widespread problem (1989, p. 66):

> A vivid example is the senior management of Ford Motor Company which sits on nearly $15 billion in cash and marketable securities in an industry with excess capacity. Ford's management has been deliberating about acquiring financial service companies, aerospace companies, or making some other multibillion-dollar diversification move—rather than deliberating about effectively distributing Ford's excess cash to its owners so they can decide how to reinvest it.

He also points out that in the 1980s, many Japanese public companies retained enormous amounts of free cash flow, far exceeding what they needed to finance profitable internal projects. For example, Toyota Motor Company, with a cash hoard of more than $10 billion, was known as the "Toyota Bank." Lacking effective internal control and external monitoring mechanisms, these companies went on an investment binge in the 1980s, engaging in unprofitable acquisitions and diversification moves. Such wasteful corporate spending is, at least in part, responsible for the economic slump that Japan has experienced since the early 1990s.

---

[5]A. Shleifer and R. Vishny, "A Survey of Corporate Governance," *Journal of Finance* 52 (1997).

The preceding examples show that the heart of the agency problem is the conflict of interest between managers and outside investors over the disposition of free cash flows. However, in high-growth industries, such as biotechnology, financial services and pharmaceuticals, where companies' internally generated funds fall short of profitable investment opportunities, managers are less likely to engage in unprofitable projects. After all, managers in these industries need to have a "good reputation" as they must repeatedly come back to capital markets for funding. If managers of a company were suspected of wasting funds for private benefit, external funding for the company would dry up quickly. Managers in industries with growth potential thus have an incentive to serve the interests of outside investors and build a reputation so that they can raise funds for undertaking "good" investment projects.

21.3 REMEDIES FOR THE AGENCY PROBLEM

It is a matter of vital importance for shareholders to control the agency problem; otherwise, they may not be able to get their money back. It is also important for society as a whole to solve the agency problem, since the agency problem leads to waste of scarce resources, hampers capital market functions and retards economic growth. Several governance mechanisms exist to alleviate or remedy the agency problem:

1. Board of directors
2. Incentive contracts
3. Concentrated ownership
4. Debt
5. Overseas share listings
6. Market for corporate control

In the following sections, we discuss the corporate governance role of each of these mechanisms.

Board of Directors

In most countries in the so-called Anglo-corporate tradition, including Canada and the United States as well as the United Kingdom, shareholders have the right to elect the board of directors, which is legally charged with representing the interests of shareholders. If the board of directors remains independent of management, it can serve as an effective mechanism for curbing the agency problem. For example, studies show that the appointment of outside directors is associated with a higher turnover rate of CEOs following poor firm performances, thus curbing managerial entrenchment. In the same vein, in a study of corporate governance in the United Kingdom, Dahya, McConnell and Travlos (2002) report that the board of directors is more likely to appoint an outside CEO after an increase in outsiders' representation on the board. But due to the diffuse ownership structure of the public company, management often gets to choose board members who are likely to be friendly to management. As can be seen from the International Finance in Practice box "When Boards Are All in the Family," an insider-dominated board can be a poor governance mechanism.

The structure and legal charge of corporate boards vary greatly across countries. In Germany, for instance, the corporate board is not legally charged with representing the interests of shareholders. Rather, it is charged with looking after the interests of stakeholders (e.g., workers, creditors and so on) in general, not just shareholders. In Germany, there are two-tier boards consisting of supervisory and management boards. Based on the German *codetermination* system, the law requires that workers be represented on the supervisory board. Likewise, some American companies have labour union representatives on their boards, although it is not legally mandated. In the United Kingdom, the majority of public

INTERNATIONAL FINANCE *in Practice*

When Boards Are All in the Family

There is much talk these days about the need to increase the independence of directors on company boards. That has been obvious for a long time. Indeed, it is fairly easy to spot those boards for which chief executives have handpicked friends or business associates who are not truly independent.

This characteristic is a reliable indicator of whether a chief executive acts as a baronial owner of the company, or as one chosen by—and responsible to—the stakeholders. In fact, one can argue that making boards more independent is the single most important thing we can do in the current reform climate to restore public confidence.

By now it is well documented that boards dominated by their chief executives are prone to trouble. W. R. Grace is a good example. Peter Grace, the company's chief executive, was too powerful. He controlled his board as if the enterprise were his personal fief.

Even though the business was foundering in the late 1990s, the board allowed Mr Grace to negotiate a retirement package that included generous perks—including use of a corporate jet and a company-owned apartment. The directors also sold a subsidiary to Mr Grace's son and bestowed other benefits that they neglected to disclose to shareholders. This nondisclosure was against the law and resulted in an SEC-type enforcement action.

Another example is Apple, whose board I was once asked, briefly, to consider joining. Apart from Steve Jobs, the CEO, the board currently has only four members while Mr Jobs searches for a replacement for his friend Larry Ellison of Oracle, who resigned from Apple's board in September.

That is all to the good, as Mr Ellison attended fewer than half of Apple's board meetings anyway. Bill Campbell, another director, is nominally independent but may not be truly so. Mr Campbell, who chairs the company's audit committee, qualifies as an independent director, because he is not currently connected with Apple. But he formerly worked at Apple and sold his software company, Claris, to Apple.

Another member of Apple's audit committee, Jerome York, is the chief executive of MicroWarehouse, whose Mac Warehouse catalogue was responsible for nearly $150m of Apple's $5.4bn sales in 2001. As a former chief financial officer for International Business Machines and Chrysler Mr York is well qualified but his presence on the all-important audit committee had to be treated as an exceptional circumstance by the Nasdaq market.

Such choices, to my mind, can yield bad judgment. In January 2000, for example, Apple's board awarded Mr Jobs 20m shares, worth $550m if the share price increased 5 per cent over 10 years. They also authorised the company to buy a $90m Gulfstream jet for him. The share price sank, putting Mr Jobs's options under water. So the board granted him 7.5m more shares. At the time of the grant, Apple shares were underperforming other stocks in their industry subclass by 28 per cent.

There is plenty of evidence that public scrutiny and a spotlight can help improve corporate governance. The California Public Employees' Retirement System began pressing underperforming companies to change the composition of their boards in 1993. Calpers drew up a list of corporate governance standards: make independent directors a majority on boards; let these directors meet the chief executive separately three times a year; make boards perform an annual assessment of their own performance, and so on.

A study by Wilshire Associates looked at the performance of 62 companies named by Calpers as poor performers. These companies' stocks underperformed the Standard & Poor's 500 index by an average of 89 per cent in the five years before they were singled out. After the spotlight was shone on them, they outperformed the index by an average of 23 per cent over five years.

This does not, of course, mean all companies will fail without a model board of directors. At Warren Buffett's Berkshire Hathaway, the seven directors include Mr Buffet's wife, his son, his business partner Charlie Munger, a partner at his company's law firm and a co-investor with Berkshire Hathaway in other companies.

Mr Buffett makes a persuasive argument that the best directors may well be those who have the greatest personal economic stake in the company. But the correlation of seduced boards with underperforming or ethically flawed enterprises suggests that independent overseers are much less likely to give into temptation or corruption.

Source: Arthur Levitt, *Financial Times*, November 27, 2002. p. 15. Reprinted with permission.

companies voluntarily abide by the *Code of Best Practice* on corporate governance recommended by the *Cadbury Committee*. The code recommends that there should be at least three outside directors and that the board chairman and the CEO should be different individuals. Apart from outside directors, separation of the chairman and CEO positions can further enhance the independence of the board of directors. In Japan, most corporate boards are insider dominated and are primarily concerned with the welfare of the *keiretsu* to which the company belongs.

Incentive Contracts

As previously discussed, managers capture residual control rights; they have enormous discretion over how the company is run. But they own relatively little of the equity of the company they manage. To the extent that managers do not own equity shares, they do not have cash flow rights. Although managers run the company at their own discretion, they may not significantly benefit from the profit generated from their efforts and expertise. Jensen and Murphy (1990) show that the pay of executives changes only by about $3 per every $1,000 change of shareholder wealth; executive pay is nearly insensitive to changes in shareholder wealth. This situation implies that managers may not be very interested in the maximization of shareholder wealth. This "wedge" between managerial control rights and cash flow rights may exacerbate the agency problem. *When professional managers have small equity positions of their own in a company with diffused ownership, they have both power and a motive to engage in self-dealings.*

Aware of this situation, many companies provide managers with **incentive contracts**, such as shares and share options, in order to reduce this wedge and better align the interests of managers with those of investors. With the grant of shares or share options, managers can be given an incentive to run the company in such a way that enhances shareholder wealth as well as their own. Against this backdrop, incentive contracts for senior executives have become common among public companies in Canada and the United States. As we have seen lately, however, senior executives can abuse incentive contracts by artificially manipulating accounting numbers, sometimes with the connivance of auditors (e.g., Arthur Andersen's involvement with the Enron debacle), or by altering investment policies so as to reap enormous personal benefits. It is thus important for the board of directors to set up an independent compensation committee that can carefully design incentive contracts for executives and diligently monitor their actions.

Concentrated Ownership

An effective way to alleviate the agency problem is to concentrate shareholdings. If one or a few large investors own significant portions of the company, they will have a strong incentive to monitor management. For example, if an investor owns 51 percent of the company, he or she can definitely control the management (e.g., can easily hire or fire managers) and will make sure that shareholders' rights are respected in the conduct of the company's affairs. With **concentrated ownership** and high stakes, the free-rider problem afflicting small, atomistic shareholders dissipates.

In the United States and the United Kingdom, concentrated ownership of a public company is relatively rare. For publicly traded firms on the major American and British exchanges, the largest single owner of shares of any one company seldom holds more than 2 to 3 percent of the shares. While corporate ownership is characterized by widely dispersed share holdings, financial institutions have emerged as the major shareholders.

Canada's corporate structure is characterized by a substantial degree of family ownership, such as the Westons, Thomsons, Beaudoins, Irvings, Aspers or McCains. Firms with strong family ownership either do not publicly trade shares at all or they retain family control through substantial family ownership of traded shares. On the other hand, many large Canadian firms are subsidiaries of multinationals and, as such, are not subject to demanding disclosure requirements.

Elsewhere in the world, however, concentrated ownership is the norm. In Germany, for example, commercial banks, insurance companies, other companies and families often own significant blocks of company shares. Similarly, extensive cross-holdings of equities among *keiretsu* member companies and main banks are commonplace in Japan. In France, cross-holdings and "core" investors are common. In Asia and Latin America, many companies are controlled by founders or their family members. In China, the government is often the controlling shareholder for public companies. Previous studies indicate that concentrated ownership has a positive effect on a company's performance and value. For example, Kang and Shivdasani (1995) report such positive effects for Japan, and Gorton and Schmid (2000) for Germany. This suggests that large shareholders indeed play a significant governance role.

Of particular interest here is the effect of managerial equity holdings. Previous studies suggest a nonlinear relationship between managerial ownership share and firm value and performance. Specifically, as the managerial ownership share increases, firm value may initially increase, since the interests of managers and outside investors become better aligned (thus reducing agency costs). But if the managerial ownership share exceeds a certain point, firm value may actually start to decline as managers become more entrenched. With larger shareholdings, for example, managers may be able to more effectively resist takeover bids and extract larger private benefits at the expense of outside investors. If the managerial ownership share continues to rise, however, the alignment effect may become dominant again. When managers are large shareholders, they do not want to rob themselves. To summarize, there can be an "interim range" of managerial ownership share over which the entrenchment effect is dominant.

This situation is illustrated in Exhibit 21.1, depicting a possible relationship between managerial ownership share and firm value. According to Morck, Shleifer and Vishny (1988), who studied the relationship for Fortune 500 companies, the first turning point (x) is reached at about 5 percent and the second (y) at about 25 percent. This means that the "entrenchment effect" is roughly dominant over the range of managerial ownership between 5 percent and 25 percent, whereas the "alignment effect" is dominant for the ownership shares less than 5 percent and exceeding 25 percent.[6] The relationship between managerial ownership and firm value is likely to vary across countries. For instance, Short and Keasey (1999) find that the inflection point (x) is reached at 12 percent in the United Kingdom, a higher level of managerial ownership than in the United States. They attribute

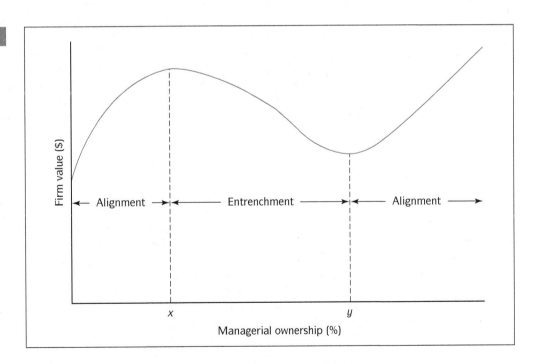

EXHIBIT 21.1

The Alignment versus Entrenchment Effects of Managerial Ownership

---

[6]"Tobin's q" is used to measure firm value. Tobin's q is the ratio of the market value of company assets to the replacement costs of the assets.

this difference to more effective monitoring by British institutional investors and the lesser ability of British managers to resist takeover.

Debt

Although managers have discretion over how much of a dividend to pay to shareholders, debt does not allow such managerial discretion. If managers fail to pay interest and principal to creditors, the company can be forced into bankruptcy and its managers may lose their jobs. Borrowing and the subsequent obligation to make interest payments on time can have a major disciplinary effect on managers, motivating them to curb private perks and wasteful investments and trim bloated organizations. In fact, debt can serve as a substitute for dividends by forcing managers to disgorge free cash flow to outside investors, rather than wasting it. For firms with free cash flows, debt can be a stronger mechanism than stocks for inducing managers to release cash flows to investors.[7]

Excessive debt, however, can create its own problem. In turbulent economic conditions, equity can buffer the company against adversity. Managers can pare down or skip dividend payments until the situation improves. With debt, however, managers do not have such flexibility and the company's survival can be threatened. Excessive debt may also induce the risk-averse managers to forgo profitable but risky investment projects, causing an underinvestment problem. For this reason, debt may not be such a desirable governance mechanism for young companies with few cash reserves or tangible assets. In addition, companies can misuse debt to finance corporate empire building. Daewoo, a Korean *chaebol*, borrowed excessively to finance global expansion until it went into bankruptcy; its debt-to-equity ratio reached 600 percent before bankruptcy.

Overseas Share Listings

Companies based in countries with weak investor protection such as Italy, Korea and Russia can credibly commit to better investor protection by listing their shares in countries with strong investor protection, such as the United States and the United Kingdom. In other words, foreign firms with weak governance mechanisms can opt to outsource a superior corporate governance regime available in the United States via cross-listings. Suppose that Benetton, an Italian clothier, announces its decision to list its shares on the New York Stock Exchange (NYSE).[8] Since the level of shareholder protection afforded by the US Securities Exchange Commission (SEC) and the NYSE is much greater than that provided in Italy, the action will be interpreted as signaling Benetton's commitment to shareholder rights. Then, investors both in Italy and abroad will be more willing to provide capital to the company and value the company shares more. Generally speaking, the beneficial effects from US listings will be greater for firms from countries with weaker governance mechanisms.

Studies confirm the effects of cross-border listings. Specifically, Doidge, Karolyi and Stulz (2004) report that foreign firms listed in the United States are valued more than those from the same countries that are not listed in the United States. They argue that firms listed in the US can take better advantage of growth opportunities and that controlling shareholders cannot extract as many private benefits. It is pointed out, however, that foreign firms in mature industries with limited growth opportunities are not likely to seek US listings, even though these firms face more serious agency problems than firms with growth opportunities that are more likely to seek US listing. In other words, firms with more serious problems are less likely to seek the remedies.

---

[7]Leveraged buyouts (LBOs) can also be viewed as a remedy for the agency problem. LBOs involve managers or buyout partners acquiring controlling interests in public companies, usually financed by heavy borrowing. Concentrated ownership and high level of debt associated with LBOs can be effective in solving the agency problem.

[8]Benetton is listed on the New York Stock Exchange.

Market for Corporate Control

Suppose a company continually performs poorly and all of its internal governance mechanisms fail to correct the problem. This situation may prompt an outsider (another company or investor) to mount a takeover bid. In a hostile takeover attempt, the bidder typically makes a tender offer to the target shareholders at a price substantially exceeding the prevailing share price. The target shareholders thus have an opportunity to sell their shares at a substantial premium. If the bid is successful, the bidder will acquire the control rights of the target and restructure the company. Following a successful takeover, the bidder often replaces the management team, divests some assets or divisions and trims employment to enhance efficiency. If these efforts are successful, the combined market value of the acquirer and target companies will be higher than the sum of stand-alone values of the two companies, reflecting the synergies created. The market for corporate control, if it exists, can have a disciplinary effect on managers and enhance company efficiency.

Hostile takeovers can serve as a drastic governance mechanism of last resort. Under potential threat of takeover, managers cannot take their control of the company for granted. In many countries, however, hostile takeovers are quite rare. This is so partly because of concentrated ownership in these countries and partly because of cultural values and political environments disapproving hostile corporate takeovers. But even in these countries, the incidence of corporate takeovers has been gradually increasing. This is due in part to the spread of equity culture and deregulation of capital markets. In Germany, for instance, takeovers are carried out through transfer of block holdings. In Japan, as in Germany, inter-firm cross-holdings of equities are loosening, creating capital market conditions that are more conducive to takeover activities. To the extent that companies with poor investment opportunities and excess cash initiate takeovers, it is a symptom of, rather than a cure for, the agency problem.

21.4 LAW AND CORPORATE GOVERNANCE

When outside investors entrust funds to the company, they receive certain legally protected rights. Among these are the rights to elect the board of directors, to receive dividends on a pro-rata basis, to participate in shareholders' meetings and to sue the company for expropriation. These rights empower investors to extract fair returns on their funds.

The content of law protecting investors' rights and the quality of law enforcement vary a great deal across countries. According to the studies of La Porta et al., observed differences in international corporate governance systems arise from differences in how well outside investors are protected by law from expropriation by managers and other corporate insiders. The legal protection of investor rights systematically varies depending on the historical origins of national legal systems.

Legal scholars show that the commercial legal systems (for example, company, security, bankruptcy and contract laws) of most countries derive from relatively few **legal origins**:

- English common law
- French civil law
- German civil law
- Scandinavian civil law

The French and German civil laws derived from the Roman law, whereas the Scandinavian countries developed their own civil law tradition that is less derivative of Roman law. The civil law tradition, which is the most influential and widely spread, is based on the comprehensive *codification of legal rules*. In contrast, English common law is formed by the *discrete rulings* of independent judges on specific disputes and *judicial precedent*.

These distinct legal systems, especially **English common law** and **French civil law**, spread around the world through conquest, colonization, voluntary adoption and subtle imitation. The United Kingdom and its former colonies, including Australia, Canada, India, Malaysia, Singapore, South Africa, New Zealand and the United States, have the English common law system. France and the parts of Europe conquered by Napoleon, such as Belgium, the Netherlands, Italy, Portugal and Spain, ended up with the French civil law tradition. Further, many former overseas colonies of France, the Netherlands, Portugal and Spain—such as Algeria, Argentina, Brazil, Chile, Indonesia, Mexico and the Philippines—also ended up with the French civil law system. The German civil law family comprises Germany and the Germanic countries of Europe, such as Austria and Switzerland, and a few East Asian countries, such as Japan, Korea and Taiwan. The Scandinavian civil law family includes the four Nordic countries: Denmark, Finland, Norway and Sweden.

Thus, in most countries, the national legal system did not indigenously develop but rather was transplanted from one of several legal origins. Although national legal systems have evolved and adapted to local conditions, it is still possible to classify them into a few distinct families. Such a classification is provided in Exhibit 21.2. The exhibit also provides the indexes for shareholder rights and rule of law for each country as computed by La Porta et al. (1998).

Exhibit 21.2 shows that the average shareholder rights index is 4.00 for English common law countries, 2.33 for both French and German civil law countries, and 3.00 for Scandinavian civil law countries. Thus, English common law countries tend to offer the strongest protection for investors, French and German civil law countries offer the weakest and Scandinavian civil law countries fall in the middle. The quality of law enforcement as measured by the rule of law index is the highest in Scandinavian and German civil law countries followed by English common law countries; it is lowest in French civil law countries.

Clearly, there is a marked difference in the legal protection of investors between the two most influential legal systems, namely, English common law and French civil law. A logical question is: Why is the English common law system more protective of investors than the French civil law system? According to the prevailing view, the state historically has played a more active role in regulating economic activities and has been less protective of property rights in civil law countries than in common law countries. In England, control of the court passed from the crown to Parliament and property owners in the seventeenth century. English common law thus became more protective of property owners, and this protection was extended to investors over time. This legal tradition in England allows the court to exercise its discretionary judgment or "smell test" over which managerial self-dealings are *unfair* to investors. In France as well as in Germany, parliamentary power was weak, and commercial laws were codified by the state, with the role of the court confined to simply determining whether the codified rules were violated or not. Since managers can be creative enough to expropriate investors without obviously violating the codified rules, investors receive low protection in civil law countries.

Glaesser and Shleifer (2002) offer an intriguing explanation of the English and French legal origins based on the divergent political situations prevailing in the Middle Ages. In France, local feudal lords were powerful and there were incessant wars. Under this turbulent situation, there was a need for the protection of adjudicators from local powers, which can only be provided by the king. France came to adopt a royal judge-inquisitor model based on the *Justinian code* of the Roman Empire in the thirteenth century. According to this model, judges appointed by the king collect evidence, prepare written records and determine the outcome of the case. Understandably, royal judges were mindful of the preferences of the king. The French legal tradition was formalized by the *Code Napoleon*. Napoleon extensively codified legal rules, *bright line rules* in legal terms, and required state-appointed judges to merely apply these rules. In England, in contrast, local lords were less powerful and war was less frequent. In a more peaceful England, which partly reflects the country's geographical isolation, local magnates were mainly afraid of royal power and preferred adjudication by a local jury that was not beholden to

EXHIBIT 21.2

Classification of
Countries by
Legal Origins

Legal Origin	Country	Shareholder Rights Index	Rule of Law Index
English common law	Australia	4	10.00
	Canada	5	10.00
	Hong Kong	5	8.22
	India	5	4.17
	Ireland	4	7.80
	Israel	3	4.82
	Kenya	3	5.42
	Malaysia	4	6.78
	New Zealand	4	10.00
	Nigeria	3	2.73
	Pakistan	5	3.03
	Singapore	4	8.57
	South Africa	5	4.42
	Sri Lanka	3	1.90
	Thailand	2	6.25
	United Kingdom	5	8.57
	United States	5	10.00
	Zimbabwe	3	3.68
	English-origin average	**4.00**	**6.46**
French civil law	Argentina	4	5.35
	Belgium	0	10.00
	Brazil	3	6.32
	Chile	5	7.02
	Colombia	3	2.08
	Ecuador	2	6.67
	Egypt	2	4.17
	France	3	8.98
	Greece	2	6.18
	Indonesia	2	3.98
	Italy	1	8.33
	Jordan	1	4.35
	Mexico	1	5.35
	Netherlands	2	10.00
	Peru	3	2.50
	Philippines	3	2.73
	Portugal	3	8.68
	Spain	4	7.80
	Turkey	2	5.18
	Uruguay	2	5.00
	Venezuela	1	6.37
	French-origin average	**2.33**	**6.05**
German civil law	Austria	2	10.00
	Germany	1	9.23
	Japan	4	8.98
	South Korea	2	5.35
	Switzerland	2	10.00
	Taiwan	3	8.52
	German-origin average	**2.33**	**8.68**
Scandinavian civil law	Denmark	2	10.00
	Finland	3	10.00
	Norway	4	10.00
	Sweden	3	10.00
	Scandinavian-origin average	**3.00**	**10.00**

Note: Shareholder rights index scales from 0 (lowest) to 6 (highest). Rule of law index scales from 0 (lowest) to 10 (highest).

Source: Rafael La Porta, Florencio Lopez-de-Silanes, Andrei Shleifer, Robert W. Vishny, "Law and Finance," *Journal of Political Economy* 106 (1998), pp. 1113–55.

the preferences of the crown and was more knowledgeable about local facts and preferences. Initially, the jury consisted of 12 armed knights who were less likely to be intimidated by local bullies or special pressure groups. After the *Magna Carta* of 1215, local magnates basically paid the crown for the privilege of local, independent adjudication and other rights.

The divergent legal developments in England and France came to have lasting effects on the legal systems of many countries.

21.5 CONSEQUENCES OF LAW

Protection of investors' rights has interesting legal origins. The concept also has major consequences for the pattern of corporate ownership and valuation, the development of capital markets and economic growth. To illustrate, consider two European countries, Italy and the United Kingdom. As shown in Exhibit 21.3, Italy has a French civil law tradition with weak shareholder protection whereas the United Kingdom, with its common law tradition, provides strong investor protection. In Italy (UK), the three largest shareholders own 58 percent (19 percent) of the company, on average. Company ownership is thus highly concentrated in Italy and more diffuse in the United Kingdom. In addition, as of 1999, only 247 companies are listed on the stock exchange in Italy, whereas 2,292 companies are listed in the United Kingdom. In the same year, the stock market capitalization as a proportion of the annual GDP was 71 percent in Italy but 248 percent in the United Kingdom. The stark contrast between the two countries suggests that protection of investors has significant economic consequences. Concentrated ownership can be viewed as a rational response to weak investor protection but it may create a different agency conflict between large controlling shareholders and small outside shareholders. We now discuss some of the issues in detail.

Ownership and Control Pattern

Companies based in countries with weak investor protection may view concentrated ownership as a substitute for legal protection. With concentrated ownership, large shareholders can control and monitor managers effectively and solve the agency problem. La Porta et al. (1998), indeed, found that corporate ownership tends to be more concentrated in countries with weaker investor protection. As can be seen from Exhibit 21.4, the three largest shareholders own 43 percent of companies on average in English common law countries, and 54 percent of companies on average in French civil law countries.

If large shareholders benefit only from pro-rata cash flows, there will be no conflict between large shareholders and small shareholders. What is good for large shareholders should be good for small shareholders as well. Since investors may be able to derive

---

EXHIBIT 21.3

Does Law Matter? Italy versus the United Kingdom

	Italy	UK
Legal origin	French civil law	English common law
Shareholder rights	1 (low)	5 (high)
Ownership by three largest shareholders	58%	19%
Market cap/GDP	71%	248%
Listed shares	247	2,292

Note: Shareholder rights refer to the antidirector rights index as computed by La Porta, Lopez-de-Silanes, Shleifer, and Vishny (1998). Both the ratio of stock market capitalization to GDP and the number of listed shares are as of 1999.
Source: Various studies of La Porta et al. and the CIA's *World Factbook*.

EXHIBIT 21.4 Consequences of Law: Ownership and Capital Markets

Legal Origin	Country	Ownership Concentration	External Cap/ GNP	Domestic Firms/ Population
English common law	Australia	0.28	0.49	63.55
	Canada	0.40	0.39	40.86
	Hong Kong	0.54	1.18	88.16
	India	0.40	0.31	7.79
	Ireland	0.39	0.27	20.00
	Israel	0.51	0.25	127.60
	Kenya	na	na	2.24
	Malaysia	0.54	1.48	25.15
	New Zealand	0.48	0.28	69.00
	Nigeria	0.40	0.27	1.68
	Pakistan	0.37	0.18	5.88
	Singapore	0.49	1.18	80.00
	South Africa	0.52	1.45	16.00
	Sri Lanka	0.60	0.11	11.94
	Thailand	0.47	0.56	6.70
	United Kingdom	0.19	1.00	35.68
	United States	0.20	0.58	30.11
	Zimbabwe	0.55	0.18	5.81
	English-origin average	**0.43**	**0.60**	**35.45**
French civil law	Argentina	0.53	0.07	4.58
	Belgium	0.54	0.17	15.50
	Brazil	0.57	0.18	3.48
	Chile	0.45	0.80	19.92
	Colombia	0.63	0.14	3.13
	Ecuador	na	na	13.18
	Egypt	0.62	0.08	3.48
	France	0.34	0.23	8.05
	Greece	0.67	0.07	21.60
	Indonesia	0.58	0.15	1.15
	Italy	0.58	0.08	3.91
	Jordan	na	na	23.75
	Mexico	0.64	0.22	2.28
	Netherlands	0.39	0.52	21.13
	Peru	0.56	0.40	9.47
	Philippines	0.57	0.10	2.90
	Portugal	0.52	0.08	19.50
	Spain	0.51	0.17	9.71
	Turkey	0.59	0.18	2.93
	Uruguay	na	na	7.00
	Venezuela	0.51	0.08	4.28
	French-origin average	**0.54**	**0.21**	**10.00**
German civil law	Austria	0.58	0.06	13.87
	Germany	0.48	0.13	5.14
	Japan	0.18	0.62	17.78
	South Korea	0.23	0.44	15.88
	Switzerland	0.41	0.62	33.85
	Taiwan	0.18	0.86	14.22
	German-origin average	**0.34**	**0.46**	**16.79**
Scandinavian civil law	Denmark	0.45	0.21	50.40
	Finland	0.37	0.25	13.00
	Norway	0.36	0.22	33.00
	Sweden	0.28	0.51	12.66
	Scandinavian-origin average	**0.37**	**0.30**	**27.26**

Note: Ownership concentration measures the average share ownership by three largest shareholders. External Cap/GNP is the ratio of the stock market capitalization held by minority shareholders (other than three shareholders) to the gross national product. Domestic Firms/Population is the ratio of the number of domestic firms listed in a given country to its population (million).

Source: Various studies of La Porta et al.

private benefits from control, however, they may seek to acquire control rights exceeding cash flow rights. Dominant investors may acquire control through various schemes, such as:

1. Shares with superior voting rights
2. Pyramidal ownership structure
3. Interfirm cross-holdings

Many companies issue shares with differential voting rights, deviating from the one-share, one-vote principle. By accumulating superior voting shares, investors can acquire control rights that exceed cash flow rights. In addition, large shareholders, who are often founders and their families, can use a **pyramidal** structure in which they control a holding company that owns a controlling block of another company, which, in turn, owns controlling interests in yet another company, and so on. Also, cross-holdings of equities among a group of companies, such as *keiretsu* and *chaebols*, can be used to concentrate and leverage voting rights to acquire control. Obviously, a combination of these schemes may also be used to acquire control.

Hutchson Whampoa, the third most valuable public company in Hong Kong, provides an interesting example of pyramidal control structure, as illustrated in Exhibit 21.5. The company is 43.9 percent controlled by another public company, Cheung Kong Holdings, which is the fifth largest publicly traded company in Hong Kong. Cheung Kong Holdings, in turn, is 35 percent controlled by the Li Ka-Shing family. The cash flow rights of the Li family in Hutchson Whampoa are, thus, 15.4 percent ($0.35 \times 0.439 = 0.154$), but the family's control rights in Hutchson Whampoa are 43.9 percent.

In Korea, the ownership structure can be more complicated. Take Samsung Electronics, Korea's most valuable company. Lee Keun-Hee, the chairman of the Samsung *chaebol* and the son of Samsung's founder, controls 8.3 percent of Samsung Electronics directly. In addition, Lee controls 15 percent of Samsung Life, which controls 8.7 percent of Samsung Electronics and 14.1 percent of Cheil Chedang, which controls 3.2 percent of Samsung

EXHIBIT 21.5

Hutchson Whampoa: The Chain of Control

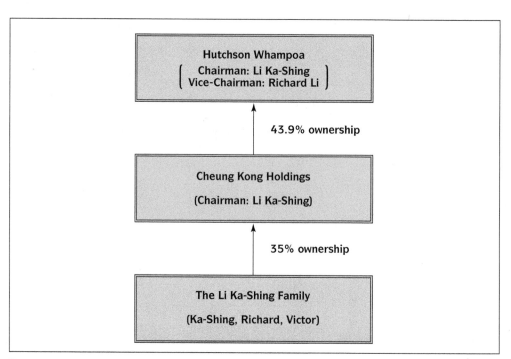

Source: R. La Porta, F. Lopez-de-Silanes, A. Shleifer, and R. Vishny, "Corporate Ownership around the World," *Journal of Finance* 54 (1999), p. 483.

Electronics and 11.5 percent of Samsung Life. This byzantine web of cross-holdings enables Lee to exercise an effective control of Samsung Electronics.[9]

As in Asia, concentrated ownership and a significant wedge between control and cash flow rights are widespread in continental Europe. Exhibit 21.6 illustrates the pyramidal ownership structure for Daimler-Benz, the German company, at the beginning of the 1990s.[10] The company has three major block holders: Deutsche Bank (28 percent), Mercedes-Automobil Holding AG (25 percent), and the Kuwait government (14 percent). The remaining 32.37 percent of shares are widely held. The pyramidal ownership structure illustrated in Exhibit 21.6 makes it possible for large investors to acquire significant control rights with relatively small investments. For example, Robert Bosch GmbH controls 25 percent of Stella Automobil, which, in turn, owns 25 percent of Mercedes-Automobil Holding, which controls 25 percent of Daimler-Benz AG. Robert Bosch can possibly control up to 25 percent of the voting rights of Daimler-Benz AG with only 1.56 percent cash flow rights in the company.

Private Benefits of Control

Once large shareholders acquire control rights exceeding cash flow rights, they may extract **private benefits of control** that are not shared by other shareholders on a pro-rata basis. A few studies document the existence and magnitude of private benefits. Nenova (2001) computed the premium for voting shares relative to nonvoting shares in different countries. The voting premium, defined as the total vote value (value of a vote times the number of votes) as a proportion of the firm's equity market value, is only about 2 percent in the United States and 2.8 percent in Canada. This implies that private benefits of control are not very significant in these countries. In contrast, the voting premium is 23 percent in Brazil, 9.5 percent in Germany, 29 percent in both Italy and Korea and 36 percent in Mexico, suggesting that in these countries, dominant shareholders extract substantial private benefits of control. Unless investors can derive significant private benefits of control, they will not pay substantial premiums for voting shares over nonvoting shares.

Dyck and Zingales (2003), on the other hand, computed "block premium," that is, the difference between the price per share paid for the control block and the exchange price after the announcement of the control transaction, divided by the exchange price after the control transaction. Obviously, control blocks will command premiums only if block holders can extract private benefits of control. Similarly to Nenova's findings, Dyck and Zingales report that during the period 1990–2000, the average block premium was only 1 percent in Canada, the United Kingdom and the United States, and 2 percent in Australia and Finland. The average block premium, however, was much higher in other countries—65 percent in Brazil, 58 percent in the Czech Republic, 27 percent in Israel, 37 percent in Italy, 16 percent in Korea and 34 percent in Mexico. Clearly, large shareholders extract significant private benefits of control in those countries where the rights of minority shareholders are not well protected.

Capital Markets and Valuation

The legal analysis of corporate governance predicts that investor protection promotes the development of external capital markets. When investors are assured of receiving fair returns on their funds, they are willing to pay more for securities. To the extent that this induces companies to seek more funds from outside investors, strong investor protection is

---

[9]Examples here are from R. La Porta et al., "Corporate Ownership around the World," *Journal of Finance* 54 (1999), pp. 471–517.

[10]This example is from Julian Franks and Colin Mayer, "Ownership and Control of German Corporations," *Review of Financial Studies* 14 (2001), pp. 943–77. Note that the ownership structure of Daimler-Benz has been significantly altered since 1990.

EXHIBIT 21.6 Ownership Structure of Daimler-Benz AG, 1990

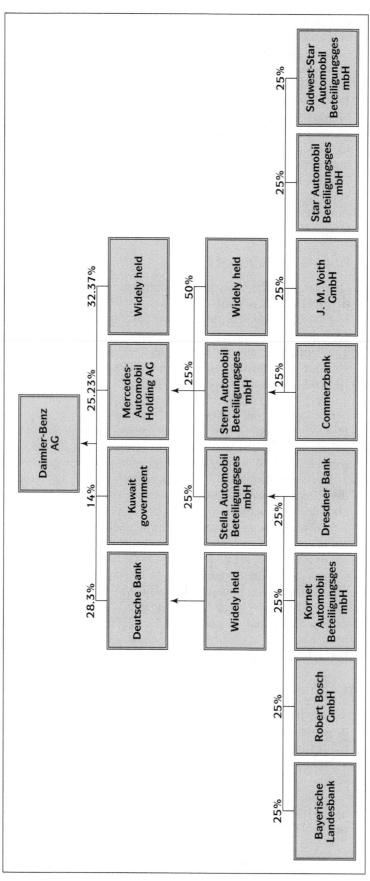

Source: Julian Franks and Colin Mayer, "Ownership and Control of German Corporation," *Review of Financial Studies* 14 (2001), p. 949.

conducive to large capital markets. La Porta et al. (1997) show that countries with strong shareholder protection tend to have more valuable stock markets and more companies listed on stock exchanges per capita than countries with weak protection. Other studies report that higher insider cash flow rights are associated with higher valuation of corporate assets, whereas greater insider control rights are associated with lower valuation of corporate assets. Exhibit 21.4 shows that the stock market capitalization held by minority shareholders (excluding the three largest shareholders) as a proportion to the GNP for the year 1994 is 0.60 in English common law countries and 0.21 in French civil law countries. The exhibit also shows that the number of domestic firms listed on stock exchanges per population (million) is about 35 in English common law countries compared with only 10 in French civil law countries.

Weak investor protection can also be a contributing factor to sharp market declines during a financial crisis. In countries with weak investor protection, insiders may treat outside investors reasonably well as long as business prospects warrant continued external financing. However, once future prospects dim, insiders may start to expropriate the outside investors as the need for external funding dissipates. The accelerated expropriation can induce sharp declines in security prices. Johnson, Boon, Breach and Friedman (2000) report that during the Asian financial crisis of 1997–1998, stock markets declined more in countries with weaker investor protection.

Well-developed financial markets promoted by strong investor protection may stimulate economic growth by making funds readily available for investment at low cost. Long ago, Schumpeter (1934) argued that financial development promotes economic growth. Several studies now document the empirical link between financial development and economic growth, supporting the Schumpeter hypothesis.[11] According to Beck et al. (2000), financial development can contribute to economic growth in three major ways: (1) by enhancing savings; (2) by channelling savings toward real investments in productive capacities, thereby fostering capital accumulation; and (3) by enhancing the efficiency of investment allocation through the monitoring and signalling functions of capital markets.

www.worldbank.org/
privatesector/cg/

This site discusses corporate governance reform.

21.6 CORPORATE GOVERNANCE REFORM

In the wake of the Asian financial crisis of 1997–1998 and the spectacular failure of several major companies, such as Daewoo, Enron and WorldCom, scandal-weary investors around the world are demanding corporate governance reform. The failure of these companies hurts shareholders as well as other stakeholders, including workers, customers and suppliers. Many employees who invested heavily in company shares for their retirement were dealt severe financial blows. It is not just the companies' internal governance mechanisms that failed; auditors, regulators, banks and institutional investors also failed in their respective roles. Failure to reform corporate governance damages investor confidence, stunts the development of capital markets, raises the cost of capital, distorts capital allocation and can even shake confidence in capitalism itself.

Objectives of Reform

During the 1980s when the economies of Germany and Japan were strong performers, the governance systems of these two countries received much attention and admiration. In both Germany and Japan, banks and a few permanent large shareholders play the central role in corporate governance. This "bank-centred" governance system was seen as guiding corporate managers to pursue long-term performance goals and also as effectively supporting companies when they were in financial distress. In contrast, the "market-centred" governance system of the Anglo-American nations was viewed as inducing short-term-oriented

---

[11]Examples include King and Levine (1993), Rajan and Zingales (1998) and Beck, Levine and Loayza (2000).

corporate decisions and being ineffectual in many ways. However, as the US economy and its stock market surged ahead in the 1990s, with Germany and Japan lagging behind, the market-centred governance system replaced the German-Japanese system as a subject of admiration. The market-oriented system seemed the wave of the future. But then, the subsequent slowdown of the US economy and stock market and the shocking corporate scandals again dethroned the market-centred system. It seems fair to say that no country has an optimal system for other countries to emulate.

There is a growing consensus that corporate governance reform should be a matter of global concern. Although some countries face more serious problems than others, existing governance mechanisms have failed to effectively protect outside investors in many countries. What should be the objective of reform? Our discussion in this chapter suggests a simple answer: *Strengthen the protection of outside investors from expropriation by managers and controlling insiders.* Among other things, reform requires (1) strengthening the independence of boards of directors with more outsiders, (2) enhancing the transparency and disclosure standard of financial statements and (3) energizing the regulatory and monitoring functions of securities commissions, such as the Ontario Securities Commission (OSC), the flagship securities commission in Canada, or the Securities and Exchange Commission (SEC) in the United States. In many developing and transition countries, it may be necessary to first modernize the legal framework.

Political Dynamics

From the experiences of many countries, we see that governance reform is easier said than done. First of all, the existing governance system is a product of the historical evolution of the country's economic, legal and political infrastructure. It is not easy to change historical legacies. Second, many parties have vested interests in the current system and they will resist any attempt to change the status quo. For example, Arthur Levitt, chairman of the SEC during much of the 1990s, attempted to reform the accounting industry but was thwarted by lobbyists and advertising. In Levitt's words (*Wall Street Journal*, June 17, 2002, p. C7): "The ferocity of the accounting profession's opposition to our attempt to reform the industry a few years ago is no secret. . . . They will do everything possible to protect their franchise, and will do so with little regard for the public interest." This earlier failure to reform the accounting industry contributed to the breakout of corporate scandals. The former executives of WorldCom were indicted for allegedly orchestrating the largest accounting fraud in history with the help of conniving auditors.[12]

Following the Asian financial crisis, the Korean government led efforts to reform the country's *chaebol* system but met with stiff resistance from the founding families, which were basically afraid of losing their private benefits of control. Nevertheless, reform efforts in Korea were partially successful, partly because the weight and prestige of the government were behind them and partly because public opinion was generally in favour of reform.

To be successful, reformers should understand the political dynamics surrounding governance issues and seek help from the media, public opinion and nongovernmental organizations (NGOs). The role of NGOs and the media can be illustrated by the success of the People's Solidarity for Participatory Democracy (PSPD) in Korea, organized by Hasung Jang of Korea University. The PSPD and Professor Jang used legal pressure and media exposure to create public opinion and shame corporate executives into changing their practices. For example, PSPD successfully challenged the transfer pricing of SK Telecom. Specifically, SK Telecom transferred huge profits to two subsidiaries, Sunkyung Distribution, which is 95 percent owned by SK Group Chairman Choi Jong-Hyun, and Daehan Telecom, fully owned by Choi's son and his son-in-law, thereby expropriating

www.brt.org

This site discusses the principles of corporate governance.

---

[12]*New York Times* (September 2, 2002), p. A16.

outside shareholders of SK Telecom. The PSPD exposed this practice to the media, and the episode was reported in the *Financial Times* as well as local newspapers and television. Facing unfavourable public opinion, SK Telecom finally agreed to stop the practice.[13]

Facing public uproar following the US corporate scandals, politicians took action to remedy the problem. The US Congress passed the **Sarbanes-Oxley** Act in 2002. The major components of the *Act* are:

- *Accounting regulation.* The creation of a public accounting oversight board charged with overseeing the auditing of public companies and restricting the consulting services that auditors can provide to clients
- *Audit committee.* The requirement that the company appoint independent "financial experts" to its audit committee
- *Executive responsibility.* The requirement that the chief executive and finance officers (CEO and CFO) sign off on the company's quarterly and annual financial statements, and that they return any bonuses if fraud causes an overstatement of earnings

The New York Stock Exchange also is currently considering various measures to protect investors. These measures call for, among other things: (1) listed companies to have boards of directors with a majority of independents; (2) the compensation, nominating and audit committees to be entirely composed of independent directors; and (3) the publication of corporate governance guidelines and reporting of annual evaluation of the board and CEO. These measures, if properly implemented, should improve corporate governance.

The Cadbury Code of Best Practice

The United Kingdom was hit by a spate of corporate scandals in the 1980s and early 1990s that resulted in the bankruptcy of such high-profile companies as Ferranti, Colorol Group, BCCI and Maxwell Group. The "scandalous" collapse of these prominent British companies was popularly attributed to their complete corporate control by a single top executive, weak governance mechanisms and the failure of their boards of directors. Against this backdrop, the British government appointed the *Cadbury Committee* in 1991 with the broad mandate to address corporate governance problems in the United Kingdom. Sir Adrian Cadbury, CEO of Cadbury Company, chaired the committee.[14] The work of the committee led to successful governance reform in the United Kingdom.

The Cadbury Committee issued its report, including the *Code of Best Practice* in corporate governance, that recommends (1) boards of directors of public companies include at least three outside (non-executive) directors and (2) the positions of chief executive officer (CEO) and chairman of the board (COB) of these companies be held by two different individuals (boards of directors of most British companies were dominated by insiders, with the positions of CEO and COB often held by the same individuals). Specifically, the code prescribed that

> The board should meet regularly, retain full and effective control over the company and monitor the executive management. There should be a clearly accepted division of responsibilities at the head of a company, which will ensure a balance of power and authority, such that no one individual has unfettered power of decisions. Where the chairman is also the chief executive, it is essential that there should be a strong and independent element on the board, with a recognized senior member. The board should include non-executive directors of significant calibre and number for their views to carry significant weight in the board's decisions.

---

[13]Alexander Dyck and Luigi Zingales, "The Corporate Governance Role of the Media," NBER Working Paper No. 9309 (2002).

[14]For a detailed discussion of the Cadbury Committee and its effect on corporate governance in the United Kingdom, refer to Dahya, McConnell and Travlos (2002).

The **Cadbury Code** has not been written into law, so compliance is voluntary. However, the London Stock Exchange (LSE) now requires each listed company to show whether the company is in compliance with the code and explain why if it is not. This "comply or explain" approach has apparently persuaded many companies to comply rather than explain; currently, 90 percent of all LSE-listed companies have adopted the Cadbury Code. According to a study by Dahya, McConnell and Travlos (2002), the proportion of outside directors rose from 26 percent before the adoption to 47 percent afterward among those companies newly complying with the code. On the other hand, joint CEO/COB positions declined from 37 percent of the companies before the adoption to 15 percent afterward. Even though compliance is voluntary, the Cadbury Code has had a significant impact on the internal governance mechanisms of British companies. The Dahya et al. study further shows that the "negative" relationship between CEO turnover and the company performance became stronger after the introduction of the Cadbury Code. The job security of chief executives has become more sensitive to the company performance, strengthening managerial accountability and weakening its entrenchment.

SUMMARY

In the wake of recurrent financial crises and high-profile corporate scandals, corporate governance has attracted attention worldwide. This chapter provides an overview of corporate governance issues with an emphasis on intercountry differences in governance mechanisms.

1. The public corporation, which is jointly owned by many shareholders with limited liability, is a major organizational innovation with significant economic consequences. The efficient risk-sharing mechanism allows the public corporation to raise large amounts of capital at low cost and profitably undertake many investment projects.

2. The public corporation has a major weakness, the agency problem characterized by conflict of interest between shareholders and managers. Self-interested managers can take actions to promote their own interests at the expense of shareholders. The agency problem tends to be more serious for firms with excessive free cash flows but without growth opportunities.

3. To protect shareholder rights, curb managerial excesses and restore confidence in capital markets, it is important to strengthen corporate governance, defined as the economic, legal and institutional framework in which corporate control and cash flow rights are distributed among shareholders, managers and other stakeholders of the company.

4. The central issue in corporate governance is how best to protect outside investors from expropriation by managers and controlling insiders so that investors can receive fair returns on their funds.

5. The agency problem can be alleviated by various methods, including (a) strengthening the independence of boards of directors, (b) providing managers with incentive contracts, such as shares and share options, to better align the interests of managers with those of shareholders, (c) concentrated ownership so

that large shareholders can control managers, (d) using debt to induce managers to disgorge free cash flows to investors, (e) listing shares in the London or New York stock exchanges where shareholders are better protected and (f) inviting hostile takeover bids if the managers waste funds and expropriate shareholders.

6. Legal protection of investor rights systematically varies across countries depending on the historical origins of the national legal system. English common law countries tend to provide the strongest protection, French civil law countries the weakest. The civil law tradition is based on the comprehensive codification of legal rules, whereas the common law tradition is based on the discrete rulings by independent judges on specific disputes and judicial precedent. The English common law tradition, based on independent judges and local juries, evolved to be more protective of property rights, which were extended to the rights of investors.

7. Protecting the rights of investors has major economic consequences in terms of corporate ownership patterns, the development of capital markets, economic growth, and more. Poor investor protection results in concentrated ownership, excessive private benefits of control, underdeveloped capital markets and slower economic growth.

8. Outside the United States and the United Kingdom, large shareholders, often founding families, tend to control managers and expropriate small outside shareholders. In other words, large, dominant shareholders tend to extract substantial private benefits of control.

9. Corporate governance reform efforts should be focused on how to better protect outside investors from expropriation by controlling insiders. Often, controlling insiders resist reform efforts, as they do not like to lose their private benefits of control. Reformers should understand political dynamics and mobilize public opinion to their cause.

QUESTIONS

1. The majority of major corporations are franchised as public corporations. Discuss the key strength and weakness of the "public corporation." When do you think the public corporation as an organizational form is unsuitable?

2. The public corporation is owned by a multitude of shareholders but run by professional managers. Managers can take self-interested actions at the expense of shareholders. Discuss the conditions under which the so-called agency problem arises.

3. Following corporate scandals and failures in the United States and abroad, there is a growing demand for corporate governance reform. What should be the key objectives of corporate governance reform? What kinds of obstacles can thwart reform efforts?

4. Studies show that the legal protection of shareholder rights varies a great deal across countries. Discuss the possible reasons why the English common law tradition provides the strongest protection of investors and the French civil law tradition the weakest.

5. Explain "the wedge" between control and cash flow rights and discuss its implications for corporate governance.

6. Discuss different ways that dominant investors may establish and maintain control of a company with relatively small investments.

7. The Cadbury Code of Best Practice, adopted in the United Kingdom, led to a successful reform of corporate governance in the country. Explain the key requirements of the code, and discuss how it contributed to the success of reform.

8. Many companies grant shares or share options to managers. Discuss the benefits and possible costs of using this kind of incentive compensation scheme.

9. It has been shown that foreign companies listed on US stock exchanges are valued more than those from the same countries that are not listed in the United States. Explain why US-listed foreign firms are valued more than those that are not. Also explain why not every foreign firm wants to list shares in the United States.

10. Explain "free cash flows." Why do managers like to retain free cash flows instead of distributing them to shareholders? Discuss what mechanisms may be used to solve this problem.

INTERNET EXERCISE

It is often mentioned that the United States has a "market-centred" corporate governance system, whereas Germany has a "bank-centred" system. Review the website of OECD, www.oecd.org/daf/corporate-affairs/governance/ or any other relevant websites and answer the following questions:

(a) Compare and contrast the corporate governance systems of the two countries.
(b) How did the two countries come to have the particular governance systems?
(c) What are the consequences of the different governance systems in the two countries?

MINI CASE

Parmalat: Europe's Enron

Following such high-profile corporate scandals as Enron and WorldCom in the United States, European business executives smugly proclaimed that the same cannot happen on their side of the Atlantic as Europe does not share America's laissez-faire capitalism. Unfortunately, however, they were quickly proven wrong when Parmalat, a jewel of Italian capitalism, collapsed spectacularly as a result of massive accounting frauds.

Parmalat was founded in 1961 as a dairy company. Calisto Tanzi, the founder, transformed Parmalat into a national player by embarking on an aggressive acquisition program in the 1980s when local governments of Italy privatized their municipal dairies. While solidifying its dominant position in the Italian home market, Parmalat aggressively ventured into international markets during the 1990s, establishing operations in 30 countries throughout the Americas, Asia/Pacific, and Southern Africa. To finance its rapid expansion, the company borrowed heavily from international banks and investors. Worldwide sales of Parmalat reached €7.6 billion in 2002 and its aspiration to become the Coca-Cola of milk seemed within reach. However, things began to unravel in 2003.

Parmalat first defaulted on a $185 million debt payment in November 2003, which prompted a scrutiny of the firm's finances. Auditors and regulators soon found out that a $4.9 billion cash reserve supposedly held in a Bank of America account of the Cayman Island subsidiary of Parmalat actually did not exist, and that the total debt of the company was around €16 billion—more than double the amount (€7.2 billion) shown on the balance sheet. Italian investigators subsequently discovered that Parmalat managers simply "invented assets" to cover the company's debts and falsified accounts over a 15-year period. Following the discovery of massive frauds, Parmalat was forced into bankruptcy in December 2003. Calisto Tanzi, founder and former CEO, was arrested on suspicion of fraud,

embezzlement, false accounting and misleading investors. The Parmalat saga represents the largest and most brazen corporate fraud in European history and is widely dubbed Europe's Enron.

Enrico Bondi, a new CEO of Parmalat, filed a $10 billion lawsuit against Citigroup, Bank of America and former auditors Grant Thornton and Deloitte Touche Tohmatsu for sharing responsibility for the company's collapse. He also filed legal actions against UBS of Switzerland and Deutsche Bank for the transactions that allegedly contributed to the collapse of Parmalat. Bondi has alleged that Parmalat's foreign "enablers," including international banks and auditors, were complicit in the frauds. He maintained that they knew about Parmalat's fraudulent finances and helped the company to disguise them in exchange for fat fees. Bondi effectively declared a war on Parmalat's international bankers and creditors.

Discussion Points

1. How was it possible for Parmalat managers to "cook the books" and hide it for so long?

2. Investigate and discuss the role that international banks and auditors might have played in Parmalat's collapse.

3. Study and discuss Italy's corporate governance regime and its role in the failure of Parmalat.

REFERENCES & SUGGESTED READINGS

Beck, T., R. Levine and N. Loayza. "Finance and the Sources of Growth." *Journal of Financial Economics* 58 (2000), pp. 261–300.

Brean, Donald J. S., and C. Kobrak. "Corporate Governance in the Twenty-First Century," in Fratianni, Savona and Kirton, eds., *Corporate, Public and Global Governance.* London: Ashgate (2006).

Claessens, S., S. Djankov and L.H.P. Lang. "The Separation of Ownership and Control in East Asian Corporations." *Journal of Financial Economics* 58 (2000), pp. 81–112.

Coase, Ronald. "The Nature of the Firm." *Economica* 4 (1937), pp. 386–405.

Dahya, Jay, J. McConnell and N. Travlos. "The Cadbury Committee, Corporate Performance, and Top Management Turnover." *Journal of Finance* 57 (2002), pp. 461–83.

Demsetz, H., and K. Lehn. "The Structure of Corporate Ownership: Causes and Consequences." *Journal of Political Economy* 93 (1985), pp. 1155–77.

Denis, D., and J. McConnell. "International Corporate Governance." Working paper (2002).

Doidge, C., A. Karolyi and R. Stulz. "Why Are Foreign Firms Listed in the US Worth More?" *Journal of Financial Economics* 71 (2004), pp. 205–238.

Dyck, A., and L. Zingales. "The Corporate Governance Role of the Media." NBER Working Paper No. 9309 (2002).

———. "Private Benefits of Control: An International Comparison." *Journal of Finance* 58 (2003).

Franks, J. R., and C. Mayer. "Ownership and Control of German Corporations." *Review of Financial Studies* 14 (2001), pp. 943–77.

Glaesser, E., and A. Shleifer. "Legal Origin." *Quarterly Journal of Economics* 117 (2002), pp. 1193–229.

Gorton, G., and F. A. Schmid. "Universal Banking and the Performance of German Firms." *Journal of Financial Economics* 58 (2000), pp. 28–80.

Holstrom, B., and S. N. Kaplan. "Corporate Governance and Merger Activity in the U.S.: Making Sense of the 1980s and 1990s." NBER Working Paper (2001).

Jensen, M. "Eclipse of the Public Corporation." *Harvard Business Review* (1989), pp. 61–74.

Jensen, M., and W. Meckling. "Theory of the Firm: Managerial Behavior, Agency Cost, and Ownership Structure." *Journal of Financial Economics* 3 (1976), pp. 305–60.

Jensen, M., and K. Murphy. "Performance Pay and Top Management Incentives." *Journal of Political Economy* 98 (1990), pp. 225–63.

Johnson, S., P. Boon, A. Breach and E. Friedman. "Corporate Governance in the Asian Financial Crisis." *Journal of Financial Economics* 58 (2000), pp. 141–86.

Johnson, S., R. La Porta, F. Lopez-de-Silanes, and A. Shleifer. "Tunneling." *American Economic Review* 90 (2000), pp. 22–27.

Kang, J., and A. Shivdasani. "Firm Performance, Corporate Governance, and Top Executive Turnover in Japan." *Journal of Financial Economics* 38 (1995), 29–58.

King, R., and R. Levine. "Finance and Growth: Schumpeter Might Be Right." *Quarterly Journal of Economics* 108 (1993), pp. 717–38.

La Porta, R., F. Lopez-de-Silanes, A. Shleifer, and R. Vishny. "Legal Determinants of External Finance." *Journal of Finance* 52 (1997), pp. 1131–50.

———. "Law and Finance." *Journal of Political Economy* 106 (1998), 1113–55.

———. "Corporate Ownership around the World." *Journal of Finance* 54 (1999), pp. 471–517.

———. "Investor Protection and Corporate Governance." *Journal of Financial Economics* 58 (2000), pp. 3–27.

———. "Investor Protection and Corporate Valuation." *Journal of Finance* 57 (2002), pp. 1147–69.

Martin, Roger L. *Fixing the Game: How Runaway Expectations Broke the Economy, and How to Get Back to Reality.* Boston, Massachusetts: Harvard Business Review Press (2011).

Morck, R., A. Shleifer, and R. Vishny. "Management Ownership and Market Valuation: An Empirical Analysis." *Journal of Financial Economics* 20 (1988), pp. 293–315.

Nenova, T., "The Value of Corporate Votes and Control Benefits: A Cross-Country Analysis." Working paper (2001).

Rajan, R., and L. Zingales. "Financial Dependence and Growth." *American Economic Review* 88 (1998), pp. 559–86.

Reese, W. A., Jr., and M. S. Weisbach. "Protection of Minority Shareholder Interests, Cross-Listings in the United States, and Subsequent Equity Offerings." NBER Working Paper (2001).

Shleifer, A., and R. Vishny. "A Survey of Corporate Governance." *Journal of Finance* 52 (1997), pp. 737–83.

Short, H., and K. Keasey. "Managerial Ownership and the Performance of Firms: Evidence from the UK." *Journal of Corporate Finance* 5 (1999), pp. 79–101.

Smith, Adam. *An Inquiry into the Nature and Causes of the Wealth of Nations* (1776).

Schumpeter, J. *The Theory of Economic Development.* Translated by R. Opie. Cambridge, MA: Harvard University Press, 1934.

Stulz, R., and R. Williamson. "Culture, Openness, and Finance." *Journal of Financial Economics* (2003).

Zingales, L. "The Value of the Voting Right: A Study of the Milan Stock Exchange Experience." *Review of Financial Studies* 7 (1994), pp. 125–48.

A

Active Income   Income from production or services provided by an individual or corporation.

Adjusted Present Value (APV)   A present value technique which discounts cash flows at different rates depending on the risk of the cash flows.

Affiliate Bank   A bank with an established relationship with a bank in another country wherein the two banks facilitate trade finance.

Agency Market   A broker takes a client's order from an agent and matches it with another public order.

Agency Problem   The prospect that managers hired as the agents working for shareholders may pursue their own interests at the expense of shareholders, reflecting conflict of interest. Agency problems are especially acute for firms with diffuse share ownership.

All-Equity (Cost of Capital)   The required return on a company's shares in the absence of debt.

All-In Cost (AIC)   All costs of a swap, including interest expense, transaction cost and service charges.

American Depository Receipt (ADR)   A certificate of ownership issued by a bank representing a multiple of foreign shares that are deposited in that bank. ADRs can be traded on organized exchanges or in the over-the-counter (OTC) market.

American Option   An option that can be exercised at any time during the option contract.

American Terms   A foreign exchange quote with the dollar on the top of the ratio, for example $S = \$/£$ or $S(\$/£) = \$1.5000/£$. From the dollar perspective, this is commonly called a "direct quote" (in dollars).

Arbitrage   Zero-risk profits as a result of mispricing of similar assets.

Ask Price   *See* Offer Price.

Asset Exposure   Potential gain or loss in value of assets denominated in a foreign currency due to a change in the exchange rate.

Asymmetric Pay-Off   When buyers and sellers of options face different possible outcomes from uncertain events. The maximum amount the buyer of an option can lose is limited to the amount paid for the option. In contrast, the seller of the option faces potentially greater losses.

B

Balance of Payments   A country's record of international transactions presented in a double-entry bookkeeping form.

Balance of Payments Identity   The Balance of Payments *must* balance. A surplus (deficit) on Current Account equals a corresponding deficit (surplus) on Capital Account.

Balance Sheet Hedge   Intended to reduce translation exposure of a multinational corporation (MNC) by eliminating the mismatch of exposed net assets and exposed net liabilities denominated in the same currency.

Bank Capital Adequacy   Equity capital and other securities a bank holds as reserves against risky assets to reduce the probability of a bank failure.

Banker's Acceptance (B/A)   A negotiable money market instrument for which a secondary market exists, issued by the importer's bank once the bill of lading and time draft are accepted. It is essentially a promise that the bank will pay the draft when it matures.

Basle Accord   An agreement arranged by the Bank for International Settlements to establish a framework to measure bank capital adequacy for banks.

Bearer Bond   A bond with ownership demonstrated through possession of the bond.

Benchmark   A reference rate of interest, such as the yield on a 10-year Government of Canada bond, against which riskier (say, corporate) bonds of the same term to maturity are priced.

Beta   A statistical measure of the systematic risk of a company's shares. Beta is the coefficient on the independent variable "market return" in a regression of returns of a company's shares against the return on the market.

Bid Price   The price at which dealers will buy a financial asset.

Bilateral Netting   A system in which a pair of affiliates determines the net amount due between them and only this amount is transferred.

Bill of Lading (B/L)   In exporting, a document issued by a common carrier specifying that it has received goods for shipment, serves as title to the goods.

Bimetallism   A double standard maintaining free coinage for both gold and silver.

Bond with Equity Warrants   A bond sold with warrants attached that entitle the bond-purchaser to buy shares of equity at a specific price.

Borrowing Capacity   The maximum amount of debt that a firm is willing to take on.

Bought Deal   A deal in which an investment house, acting as underwriter, purchases the entire amount of a security issue.

Brady Bonds   Loans converted into collateralized bonds with a reduced interest rate devised to resolve the international debt crisis in the late 1980s. Named after the US Treasury Secretary Nicholas Brady.

Bretton Woods System   An international monetary system created in 1944 to promote postwar exchange rate stability and coordinate international monetary policies.

BRIC   Brazil, Russia, India, China—four large emerging markets.

Broker   An agent prepared to engage in transactions involving, for example, foreign exchange, on behalf of a client.

Buyer Credits   In export finance, where the exporter arranges for a commercial bank to lend money to the importer.

C

Cadbury Code   The *Code of Best Practice* in corporate governance for British companies, recommending, among other things, at least three outside board directors and having the positions of CEO and board chairman held by two different individuals.

Call   The right but not the obligation to purchase an asset at a specified price within a specified period.

Call Market   Wherein market and limit orders are accumulated and executed at specific intervals during the day.

Call Option   The right but not the obligation to purchase an asset (e.g., a share) for a specified price at a specified price on or before a specified date.

Canadian Dollar Offer Rate (CDOR)   The rate of interest that Canadian banks charge on loans to other Canadian banks or similar financial institutions.

Capital Account   Balance-of-payment entries capturing cross-currency sales and purchases of financial assets, real estate and businesses.

Capital Asset Pricing Model (CAPM) A formal model that relates the expected (or required) rate of return on risky assets to systematic risk.

Capital Export Neutrality The criterion wherein domestic versus international investment is not influenced by tax.

Capital Import Neutrality An international tax arrangement in which the structure of tax does not favour domestic capital over foreign capital or *vice versa*.

Capital Structure The relative amounts of debt and equity used to finance a company.

Cash Budget A plan that details the time and size of expected cash receipts and disbursements.

Cash Management The handling of cash within a firm, such as the investment a firm has in transaction balances, funds tied up in precautionary cash balances, investment of excess funds at the most favourable rate and borrowing at the lowest rate when there is a temporary cash shortage.

Centralized Cash Depository In an MNC, a central cash pool in which excess cash from affiliates is collected and invested or used to cover system-wide cash requirements.

CIRRs Commercial Interest Reference Rates: interest rates published (by the OECD) that define the allowable limits on government provided financial assistance to exporters.

Civil Law A system of law made explicit in Acts (in contrast to common law based on precedents of past judgments).

Clearinghouse An integral part of the institutional structure of financial markets. The Canadian Derivatives Clearing Corporation (CDCC), for example, associated with the Montreal Stock Exchange, is the issuer, clearinghouse, and guarantor of interest rate, equity and index derivative contracts traded on the MSE. LIFFE (International Financial Futures and Options Exchange) in London is a major clearinghouse for foreign exchange derivative contracts.

Client Market In foreign exchange dealings, the market in which clients arrange transactions (in contrast to the interbank market, which exclusively involves banks).

Closed-End Country Fund (CECF) A fund invested exclusively in the securities of one country that issues a given number of shares that are traded on the host country exchange as if it were an individual share.

Commission Fee paid to a broker to carry out a transaction in a financial market.

Comparative Advantage A proposition by David Ricardo to explain the benefits of international trade. If countries specialize production where they produce goods more efficiently and engage in trade, all countries are better off.

Competitive Effect The effect of exchange rate changes on a firm's international competitive position.

Complete Contract A contract that specifies what each party will do under all possible future contingencies.

Completely Segmented Capital Market A situation wherein cross-border capital flows are so restricted that no cross-border capital flows take place.

Concentrated Ownership Ownership of a company's shares by relatively few shareholders.

Concessionary Loan A loan below the market interest rate offered by the host country to an MNC to encourage investment in the host country.

Conservatism Principle An accounting principle whereby assets are valued at the lower of cost or market value.

Contingent Claim A claim, such as a call or a put, whose value depends on the price of something else, for instance the exchange rate.

Contingent Claim Security *See* Derivative Security.

Contingent Exposure The risk due to uncertain situations in which a firm does not know if it will face exchange risk exposure in the future.

Continuous Trading A market in which market and limit orders are executed at any time during business hours.

Contract Size In a futures contract, the number of units of the underlying asset in one contract.

Controlled Foreign Corporation (CFC) A foreign subsidiary in which shareholders own more than 50 percent of voting equity shares.

Conversion Effect The dollar amount converted from a given cash flow from foreign operation affected by exchange rate changes.

Convertible Bond A corporate bond that can be converted to a specific number of the issuing company's shares.

Corporate Governance The economic, legal and institutional framework in which corporate control and cash flow rights are distributed among shareholders, managers and other stakeholders of the company.

Correspondent Banking Relationship A cooperative relationship between banks in two countries to serve the international banking needs of commercial and corporate customers.

Cost of Capital The required rate of return on a risky investment.

Counterparty One of the two parties involved in financial contracts who agree to exchange cash flows on specific terms.

Countertrade Transactions in which parties exchange goods or services. If these transactions do not involve an exchange of money, they are a type of barter.

Country Systematic Risk In banking and investment, the probability that unexpected events in a country influence its ability to repay loans and repatriate dividends. It includes political and credit risk.

Covered Interest Arbitrage (CIA) If interest rate parity (IRP) does not hold, arbitrage profits that can be made without risk.

Cross-Border Acquisition A takeover or outright purchase of a company based in one country by a company based in another country.

Cross-Border Merger A merger of companies from two different countries.

Cross-Currency Interest Rate Swap Typically called a "currency swap." One counterparty exchanges the debt service obligations of a bond denominated in one currency for the debt service obligations of the counterparty denominated in another currency.

Cross-Exchange Rate An exchange rate within a currency pair where neither currency is the US dollar.

Cross-Hedging Hedging a position in one asset by taking a position in another asset.

Cross-Listing Directly listing securities on a foreign financial exchange. Cross-listing requires meeting the listing and disclosure standards of the foreign exchange.

Cross-Rates Exchange rates between pairs of currencies *except the US dollar*. The cross-rate calculation is based on the exchange rates of each of the currencies in the pair to the US dollar.

Crowd Trading An equity trading arrangement in which traders and specialists congregate around a trading post to execute orders.

C-TPAT Customs Trade Partnership against Terrorism; a joint business–government initiative to strengthen border security. The program recognizes that importers rely on supply chain partners (carriers, brokers, warehouse operators and manufacturers) to ensure the integrity of their security practices.

Cumulative Translation Adjustment (CTA) Used in the current rate method of translating foreign currency financial statements, this equity account allows balancing of the balance sheet by accounting for translation gains and losses.

Currency against Currency A foreign exchange transaction in which the US dollar is not involved. Most interbank foreign exchange transactions involve the US dollar on one side of the transaction. "Currency against currency" is an exception in which one non-dollar currency is exchanged for another non-dollar currency, for example, the euro for the Canadian dollar.

Currency Board A fixed exchange rate regime under which local currency is fully backed by the US dollar or another standard currency.

Currency Futures A standardized foreign exchange contract with a future delivery date that is traded on organized exchanges.

Currency Swap A counterparty exchanges debt service obligations of a bond denominated in one currency for debt service obligations of the other counterparty denominated in another currency.

Current Account Balance-of-payments entries for exports and imports of goods and services and cross-border investment income.

Current/Noncurrent Method In foreign currency translation, current assets and liabilities are converted at the current exchange rate while noncurrent assets and liabilities are translated at historical exchange rates.

Current Rate Method In foreign currency translation, balance sheet accounts are translated at the current exchange rate except shareholders' equity, which is translated at the exchange rate on the date of issuance.

D

Daily Price Limit The maximum allowable movement in the price of a security—such as a bond or a share—as specified by the exchange.

Dealer Market A market in which the broker takes the trade through the dealer, who participates in trades as a principal.

Delivery Month The month in which settlement of a futures contract must be completed.

Derivative Claim Synonymous with contingent claim.

Derivative Security A security whose value is contingent upon the value of the underlying security. Examples are futures, forward and options contracts.

Derivatives Hedge A hedge in which derivatives (calls, puts, futures or forwards) are purchased or sold so as to create a distribution of pay-offs that offset foreign exchange exposure.

Direct Loan A loan from one division to another in multinational corporate finance.

Direct Quote A foreign exchange quote expressed in terms of units of domestic currency per one unit of a foreign currency—1.25 Canadian dollars per one US dollar is a direct quote from the Canadian perspective (C$1.25/US$1).

Direct Tax A tax paid directly by the taxpayer on whom the tax is levied.

Discount In respect of foreign exchange, when the forward rate is less than the spot rate.

Diversification of the Market A strategy for managing operating exposure in which a firm diversifies the market for its product. Thus, exchange rate changes in one country may be offset by opposite exchange rate changes in another.

Domestic Country Market Portfolio A broad index, such as the S&P TSX in Toronto, the S&P 500 in New York, the FTSE in London or the Nikkei in Tokyo, that is representative of a diversified portfolio of the equities in the nation.

Draft A written order instructing the importer or his agent to pay the amount specified on its face at a certain date.

Dual-Currency Bond A fixed-rate bond that pays coupon interest in the issue currency but at maturity pays the principal in a currency other than the issue currency.

E

Economic Exposure The possibility that the value of the firm may be affected by unanticipated changes in exchange rates.

EDC Accounts Receivable Insurance (ARI) An arrangement under which Canada's Export Development Corporation insures (for the exporter) accounts receivable owed to the exporter by foreign purchasers.

Edge Act **Bank** Federally chartered subsidiaries of American banks that may engage in the full range of international banking operations.

Efficient Market Hypothesis (EMH) Proposition that financial markets are informationally efficient, i.e., asset prices reflect all the relevant and available information.

Elastic Demand Sensitive demand for a product with respect to its price.

Emerging Market A country experiencing strong economic growth following commitment to reforms that encourage market activity, international trade and investment.

English Common Law Law not contained within specific acts. It is built up by the courts and their judgments. English common law acknowledges the origins of this form of law (in contrast with the French or German civil law) and its use in most English-speaking countries.

Equity-Related Bond A bond with warrants or a bond with a conversion-to-equity provision.

Euro Introduced in 1999, the common currency of the countries of the European Union (EU) that make up the EMU.

Euro Interbank Offered Rate (EURIBOR) The rate at which interbank deposits of the euro are offered by one prime bank to another in countries that make up the European Monetary Union (EMU) as well as prime banks in non-EMU EU countries and major prime banks in non-EU countries.

Euro-Medium-Term Note (euro-MTN) A flexible medium-term debt instrument that is issued and traded outside of Canada and the United States and requires fixed dollar payments. Euro-MTNs are issued directly to the market with maturities of less than five years and are offered continuously rather than all at once like a bond issue.

Eurobank A financial institution that accepts deposits in foreign currencies and makes foreign currency loans.

Eurobond A bond issue denominated in a particular currency but sold in capital markets other than the issuing country.

Eurocommercial Paper Notes with maturities up to 360 days issued by companies in international money markets.

Eurocredit A medium-term loan for large corporate and governmental bodies denominated in European currencies from a syndicate of banks.

Eurocurrency A time deposit of money in an international bank located in a country other than the country that issues the currency.

Euronext A pan-European stock exchange based in Paris with subsidiaries in Belgium, Netherlands, Portugal and the United Kingdom dealing in equities and derivatives markets. The Euronext group also provides clearing and information services.

Euronote The paper associated with short-term (usually less than seven months) commercial borrowings in the Euro-markets.

European Central Bank (ECB) The central bank of the 17 countries that make up the EMU, responsible for maintaining price stability via monetary policy.

European Currency Unit (ECU) A basket currency made up of a weighted average of the currencies of the members of the European Union. The precursor of the euro.

European Monetary System (EMS) A system to establish monetary stability in Europe and promote European economic and political unification.

European Monetary Union (EMU) The monetary union of the EU that irrevocably fixed exchange rates en route to the common euro currency.

European Option An option that can be exercised only at the maturity date of the contract.

European System of Central Banks (ESCB) The monetary arrangement in which the European Central Bank (ECB) in Frankfurt takes overall responsibility for monetary policy in the European Union while the central banks of member states assume the responsibilities of regional banks.

European Terms A foreign exchange quote in which the dollar is on the bottom of the ratio $S = £/\$$ or $S(£/\$) = £0.6548/\$$. From the dollar perspective, this is commonly called an "indirect quote" (in foreign currency) or, less frequently, "currency per \$."

European Union (EU) An economic and political union of 28 member states located primarily in Europe that operates through a system of supranational institutions, such as the European Central Bank, and cooperative governance arrangements.

Exchange Rate Mechanism (ERM) The procedure, prior to the introduction of the euro, by which EMS member countries collectively manage their exchange rates based on a parity grid system, a system of par values between ERM countries.

Exchange Rate Pass-Through The relationship between exchange rate changes and price adjustments of internationally traded goods.

Exchange-Traded A security such as a futures contract that is traded on an exchange.

Exchange-Traded Funds Portfolios of shares and/or bonds that are traded on formal exchanges.

Exercise Price The prespecified price paid or received when an option is exercised.

Expanded Opportunity Set In international portfolio construction, the increase in opportunities to invest in foreign assets.

Export Development Canada (EDC) The Canadian government agency that provides finance on commercial terms to purchasers of Canadian exports.

Export Guarantee Program A program of Export Development Canada that encourages Canadian financial institutions to advance pre-shipment loans to Canadian exporters. The EDC guarantees the loans.

Exposure Coefficient The coefficient obtained from regressing the home currency value of assets on the foreign exchange rate under consideration. This provides a measure of the firm's economic exposure to currency risk.

Exposure Netting Hedging only the net exposure by firms that have both payables and receivables in foreign currencies.

F

Factoring Buying or discounting receivables, typically on export sales.

FDI Flow An aggregate measure of the amount of foreign direct investment that flows into a country (or out of a country) in a given year.

FDI Stock An aggregate measure of the accumulated total amount of foreign direct investment in a country.

Financial Hedging Hedging exchange risk exposure using financial contracts, such as currency forward, futures and options contracts.

Financial Lease A financial arrangement whereby a manufacturer sells equipment to a leasing house (sometimes an affiliate of the manufacturer) that then leases the equipment to the end user.

Fisher Effect Concept that the nominal interest rate is the sum of the real interest rate and the expected inflation rate.

Flexible Sourcing Policy A strategy for managing operating exposure that involves sourcing from areas where input costs are low.

Floating-Rate Note (FRN) Medium-term bonds with coupon payments indexed to a reference rate, such as the three-month LIBOR.

Foreign Bond A bond offered by a foreign borrower to the investors in a national capital market and denominated in that nation's currency. Example: A Canadian company selling yen-denominated bonds in Japan to local investors.

Foreign Branch An overseas affiliate of an MNC that is not independently incorporated but is rather an extension of the parent.

Foreign Branch Bank A branch of a bank of which the owner is foreign. Branches have no corporate independence from the parent bank. If the Royal Bank, based in Toronto, sets up a branch in Bermuda, the parent bank in Canada owns all the assets and is fully responsible for all the liabilities of the Bermuda branch.

Foreign Currency Transaction Any transaction involving an exchange of foreign currencies.

Foreign Direct Investment (FDI) Investment by a multinational corporation in one country that sets up operations in another country; gives the MNC a measure of control.

Foreign Exchange (FX or FOREX) Markets Encompass the conversion of one currency into another, bank deposits of foreign currencies and trading in foreign currency spot, forward, futures, swap and options contracts.

Foreign Exchange Risk The risk of facing uncertain future exchange rates.

Foreign Subsidiary An affiliate of an MNC that is independently incorporated in a foreign country.

Foreign Tax Credits A tax provision wherein a country allows its resident taxpayers credit for foreign taxes paid.

Forfaiting A form of medium-term trade financing used to finance exports in which the exporter sells promissory notes to a bank at a discount, thereby freeing the exporter from carrying the financing.

Forward Exchange Rate The exchange rate on currency specified to involve delivery at a specific date in the future.

Forward Expectations Parity (FEP) Proposition that the forward premium or discount is equal to the expected change in the exchange rate between two currencies.

Forward Hedge A method of hedging exchange risk exposure in which a foreign currency contract is sold or bought forward.

Forward Market A market for trading foreign exchange contracts initiated today but to be settled at a future date.

Forward Premium/Discount The amount over (under) the spot exchange rate for a forward rate expressed as an annualized percent deviation from the spot rate.

Forward Rate A rate of exchange of one currency for another that is agreed today for fulfillment at a specific time in the future.

Forward Rate Agreement (FRA) An interbank contract used to hedge the interest rate risk in mismatched deposits and credits.

Free Cash Flow A firm's internally generated fund in excess of the amount needed to finance all investment projects with positive net present values.

Free Ride Wherein one party takes advantage of a costly process—such as information search—borne by another party.

French Civil Law *See* Civil Law.

Fully Integrated World Capital Markets Global markets without barriers caused by institutional deficiencies, transaction costs or regulations.

Functional Currency For a foreign subsidiary of an MNC, the currency of the primary economic environment in which the entity operates. This is typically the local currency of the country in which the entity conducts most of its business.

Futures Contract A standardized contract to buy or sell an asset, foreign exchange or commodity at a specific time in the future at a specific price.

G

General Agreement on Tariffs and Trade (GATT) A multilateral agreement between member countries to promote international trade. The GATT played a key role in reducing international trade barriers.

Global Bond A bond issued simultaneously in several capital markets around the world.

Gold-Exchange Standard A monetary system in which countries hold most of their reserves in the form of a currency of a particular country. That country is on the gold standard.

Gold Standard A monetary system in which currencies are defined in terms of their gold content. The exchange rate between a pair of currencies is determined by their relative gold contents.

Greenfield Investment A foreign direct investment that takes the form of new plant and equipment and associated operations as opposed to a takeover.

Gresham's Law Under the bimetallic standard, the abundant metal was used as money while the scarce metal was driven out of circulation, based on the fact that the ratio of the two metals was officially fixed.

H

Hedger One who creates offsetting positions in an asset and a derivative security on that asset.

Hedging through Invoice Currency Hedging exchange risk exposure by invoicing in terms of the home currency of the firm.

Home Bias in Portfolio Holdings The tendency of an investor to hold a larger portion of home country securities than is optimal for diversification of risk.

I

In-the-Money A call option, for example, is in-the-money when the price of the option is greater than the exercise price.

Incentive Contract A contract, typically an employment contract or a contract for managerial services, in which the employee (or manager) is rewarded on the basis of measurable performance that is positively related to the value of the firm.

Income Tax A direct tax levied on the active income of an individual or corporation.

Incremental Cash Flow The change in corporate cash flow that results from undertaking a project. Incremental "project" cash flow is generally built up from component changes in cash flows in the project—in revenues, costs, changes in working capital and so on.

Indirect Quote A foreign exchange quote expressed in terms of units of foreign currency per one unit of the domestic currency—US$0.90/C$1 is an indirect quote from the Canadian perspective.

Indirect World Systematic Risk The returns-covariance between a non-tradable asset and the world market portfolio involving tradable assets. Non-tradable assets are priced partly by indirect world systematic risk and partly by domestic systematic risk.

Initial Margin An initial collateral deposit needed to establish an asset position.

Intangible Assets The proprietary assets, such as trademarks, good-will, reputation and patented technology, that are crucial to the commercial uniqueness of a company.

Integrated World Capital Markets A situation in which capital is unrestricted from flowing across international borders and, as a result, interest rates and rates of return on risky assets are determined by global financial market factors and conditions.

Interbank Market The market for loans and for currencies in which only banks are involved. Transactions are in large amounts among highly informed traders.

Interest Rate Parity (IRP) An arbitrage equilibrium condition holding that the interest rate differential between two currencies is equal to the forward premium or discount. Violation of IRP gives rise to profitable arbitrage opportunities.

Internalization Theory A set of propositions that deal with how multinational companies establish "internal markets" for trade among divisions of the company.

International Asset Pricing Model (IAPM) A model of asset valuation that takes account of the investors' opportunity to hold a globally diversified portfolio of assets. In this case, which assumes a high degree of international financial integration, individual assets (company shares) are "priced" in terms of global risks and financial conditions.

International Banking Facility (IBF) Banking operation within domestic American banks that act as foreign banks in the United States and, as such, are not bound by domestic reserve requirements or FDIC insurance requirements. They seek deposits from non-American citizens and can make loans only to foreigners.

International Fisher Effect (IFE) The proposition that the expected change in the spot exchange rate is equal to the difference in the nominal interest rates of the two countries.

International Leasing Provides for the transfer of goods to a foreign buyer without the transfer of title to the goods.

International Monetary System The institutional framework within which international payments are made, movements of capital are accommodated and exchange rates among currencies are determined.

Internationally Nontradable Asset A financial asset that trades only in its home capital market.

Internationally Tradable Asset A financial asset that trades on several exchanges in the world—for example, New York, Toronto, London and Tokyo—and can be readily bought or sold by anyone, anywhere.

Intra-Firm Trade Shipments of intermediate goods between subsidiaries of a multinational enterprise, for example when Magna (Canada) ships auto parts to Magna (Europe) for assembly.

Invisible Trade International trade in services, tourism, intellectual property and other intangibles.

iShares MSCI Exchange-traded securities with value based on the Morgan Stanley Composite Index.

J

J-curve Effect The initial deterioration and eventual improvement of the trade balance following a depreciation of a country's currency.

Jamaica Agreement International monetary agreement in January 1976 by which flexible exchange rates were accepted and gold was abandoned as an international reserve asset.

L

Law of One Price The requirement that similar commodities or securities should be trading at the same or similar prices.

Lead/Lag Strategy Reducing transaction exposure by paying or collecting foreign financial obligations early (lead) or late (lag) depending on whether the currency is hard or soft.

Lead Manager In a syndicate of underwriters of equity or debt, the investment bank that oversees the issuance and organizes the syndicate.

Legal Origin Refers to alternative national or cultural sources from which legal systems are derived; for example, English common law or French civil law.

Letter of Credit (L/C) A guarantee from the importer's bank that it will act on behalf of the importer and pay the exporter for merchandise if all documentation is in order.

Limit Order An order away from the market price that is held until it can be executed at the specified price.

Line of Credit An arrangement whereby a bank extends credit up to a specified amount that the borrower may draw on without further negotiation.

Liquidity The scope for securities to be bought and sold quickly at close to the current quoted price.

London Interbank Offered Rate (LIBOR) The interest rate at which a bank will offer Eurocurrency deposits to another bank in London. LIBOR is the basis for setting Eurocurrency loan rates. The loan rate is determined by adding a risk premium to LIBOR.

Long Holding an asset. In a long position, a rise or fall in the value of an asset is captured or borne by the asset holder.

Lost Sales In capital budgeting, the prospect that a new project—say, to manufacture widgets—will reduce the sale of another of the firm's products—say, gizmos—since widgets and gizmos are substitutes.

Louvre Accord Prompted by the dollar's decline, the G-7 countries in 1987 agreed to (i) cooperate to achieve greater exchange rate stability, and (ii) consult and coordinate their macroeconomic policies.

M

Maastricht Treaty Treaty signed in 1991 that committed to irrevocably fix exchange rates among member countries of the EU by January 1999 and introduce a common European currency to replace national currencies.

Maintenance Margin Collateral needed to maintain an asset position.

Managed-Float System Established by the Louvre Accord in 1987; allowed G-7 countries to jointly intervene in the exchange market to correct over- or undervaluation of currencies.

Managerial Entrenchment The scope for managers of corporations to resist market discipline in respect of self-serving behaviour or managerial ineptitude. Managerial entrenchment reflects relatively weak corporate governance on the part of the shareholders and the Board.

Maple Bond A bond denominated in Canadian dollars issued by a foreign company or government.

Marked-to-Market The process of recording daily price gains and losses in the futures market by the change in the settlement price of the futures contract.

Market Capitalization For a corporation, the market value of its equity plus debt. For a stock market, the total value of all listed equity securities.

Market Completeness The situation in a market where each state of the economy is matched by security payoff.

Market Imperfections Various frictions, such as transaction costs and legal restrictions, that prevent markets from functioning perfectly.

Market Order An order executed at the best price available (market price) when the order is received in the market.

Market Portfolio A broad index, such as the S&P TSX, of corporate share prices in a country.

Maturity Date The date on which a contract—such as a call, a put or a futures contract—expires.

Measure of Aggregate Risk Aversion A statistical index of the degree to which capital markets exhibit a preference to avoid risk (volatility).

Mercantilism The policy of encouraging exports in order to accumulate precious metals such as gold or silver.

Monetary/Nonmonetary Method In dealing with foreign currency translation, the idea that monetary balance sheet accounts, such as accounts receivable, are translated at the current exchange rate, while nonmonetary balance sheet accounts, such as shareholders' equity, are converted at the historical exchange rate.

Money Market Hedge A method of hedging transaction exposure by borrowing and lending in the domestic and foreign money markets.

Multilateral Netting A system in which all affiliates each net their individual interaffiliate receipts against all their disbursements and transfer or receive the balance, respectively, if it is a net payer or receiver.

Multinational Corporation (MNC) A firm that has business activities and interests in multiple countries.

N

National Treatment In matters of taxation, national treatment calls for foreign-owned corporations to be taxed exactly as domestic corporations.

Negotiable Certificate of Deposit (NCD) A negotiable bank time deposit.

Net Present Value (NPV) A capital budgeting method in which the present value of cash outflows is subtracted from the present value of expected future cash inflows to determine the net present value of an investment project.

Netting Centre In multilateral netting, a system that determines the amount of net payments and which affiliates are to make or pay them.

Nontradables Tangibles or intangibles that are typically not traded, such as construction, personal services and domestic infrastructure.

North American Free Trade Agreement (NAFTA) An agreement established in 1994 that includes the United States, Canada and Mexico as members in a free trade area.

Note Purchase Agreements International financing arrangements in which a commercial bank provides funds directly to the exporter who in turn offers medium-term financing support to its foreign buyer, typically a foreign buyer of capital goods. In most cases, this form of supplier credit financing involves a bank purchasing the foreign buyer's promissory note from the exporter.

Notional Principal A reference amount of principal used for determining payments under various derivative contracts.

O

OECD Consensus The arrangement managed by the OECD whereby government agree on interest rates that define the allowable limits on government provided financial assistance to exporters.

Offer Price The price at which a dealer will sell a financial asset.

Offshore Banking Centre A country in which the banking system is organized to allow external accounts beyond the normal economic activity of the country. Their primary function is to seek deposits and grant loans in currencies other than the host country currency.

Open Interest The total number of short or long contracts outstanding for a particular delivery month in the derivative markets.

Operating Exposure The extent to which the firm's operating cash flows are affected by changes in the exchange rate.

Operating Lease A rental agreement where the lessor, say a Canadian exporter, provides equipment to a lessee, say a foreign customer.

Operational Hedging Adjustments to how a firm operates its production to mitigate risk, for example relocating production internationally to get a better currency-match of costs to revenues.

Optimal International Portfolio A portfolio of shares and bonds from around the world that offers the highest ratio of expected return to risk as measured in one (reference) currency, such as the Canadian dollar.

Optimum Currency Area A geographical area suitable for sharing a common currency by virtue of a high degree of factor mobility within the area.

Option A contract giving the owner the right, but not the obligation, to buy or sell a given quantity of an asset at a specified price at some date in the future.

Options Hedge Use of put and call options to limit the downside risk of transaction exposure while preserving the upside potential. The price of such flexibility is the option premium.

Out-of-the-Money A call option, for example, is out-of-the-money when the price of the option is less than the exercise price.

Outright Forward Transaction A forward currency contract with a locked-in exchange rate and delivery date.

Over-the-Counter (OTC) Said of a trading market in which there is no central marketplace, and instead buyers and sellers are linked via a network of telephones, telex machines, computers and automated dealing systems.

P

Par Value The nominal or face value of shares or bonds.

Partially Integrated World Financial Markets The global asset pricing relationship where some financial assets are not traded internationally due to regulatory restrictions, transaction costs or institutional barriers.

Pay-off Structure The possible set of outcomes on an option (for the buyer or seller) as will occur at expiry.

Plaza Accord G-5 agreement in 1985 that depreciation of the dollar is desirable to correct the US trade deficit.

Political Risk Potential losses to the parent firm resulting from adverse political developments in the host country.

Portfolio Investment Cross-border investment in the form of bonds or non-controlling equity. The latter refers, for example, to shares in a foreign company in which case the shareholder holds an insufficient number of shares to control the company, usually defined to be 10 percent or less of the total number of shares outstanding.

Portfolio Risk Diversification Portfolio risk is reduced by investing in securities that do not have strong correlations with one another.

Precautionary Cash Balance Emergency funds a firm maintains in case it has underestimated its transaction cash requirements.

Premium To compensate for risk in equities, a rate of return in excess of the risk-free rate. In option pricing, the amount per share that an option buyer pays to the seller.

Price Convergence The market behaviour wherein futures prices and forward prices (for identical term) converge to be equal.

Price Discovery The process of determining market prices for financial assets and exchange rates through the interaction of buyers and sellers.

Price-Specie-Flow Mechanism Under the gold standard, it is the automatic correction of payment imbalances between countries. This is based on the fact that under the gold standard, the domestic money stock rises or falls as the country experiences inflows or outflows of gold.

Pricing Spillover Effect Company X has operations in a segmented capital market, for example China. Company X's stock is traded internationally via ADR. The pricing of other Chinese stocks can then be partially informed by "spillover" of pricing of Company X stock. Such stocks are priced partially internationally and partially domestically.

Pricing-to-Market (PTM) Phenomenon When an exporter sets the price of an exported product in light of market conditions in the importing country. The exporter tends not to change the foreign currency price following a change in the exchange rate.

Primary Market The market in which new security issues are sold to investors. In bringing new securities to market, investment bankers play a role as either broker or dealer.

Private Benefits of Control Corporate control structured such that the benefits of ownership (influence on corporate decisions or perquisites) are unevenly shared, typically to the advantage of shareholders who hold large share positions and to the detriment of minority shareholders.

Private Placement A security issue transaction wherein the issuer sells it directly to the purchaser, typically an investment bank.

Privatization Act of a country divesting itself of ownership and operation of business ventures by turning them over to the free market system.

Product Differentiation Creating a perception among consumers that a firm's product(s) differ from those offered by competitors, thereby reducing price sensitivity of demand.

Product Life Cycle The view that a manufactured product goes through a cycle that begins with invention and product development in a high-income market for domestic consumption. Foreign demand is met through exports. As export demand increases, production shifts to low-cost foreign sites. As the foreign site of production becomes the low-cost site, the product is exported to the country in which it was first developed.

Prompt Offering Qualification System ("POP") A set of rules and regulations that allow for the rapid issue of new securities. POP requires relevant information regarding the issuing firm to have been previously submitted to the securities exchange.

Publicly Traded Issues Corporate securities traded on stock or bond markets and thereby available to all members of the public.

Purchasing Power Parity (PPP) The proposition that the exchange rate between currencies of two countries should be equal to the ratio of the countries' price levels of a commodity basket.

Put An option to sell an underlying asset at a specified price.

Pyramidal A structure of corporate ownership in which owners of companies that own other companies wield significant corporate control with relatively little capital commitment.

Q

Quality Spread Differential (QSD) The difference between the fixed interest rate spread differential and the floating interest rate spread differential of the debt of two counterparties of different creditworthiness. A positive QSD is a necessary condition for an interest swap to occur that ensures that the swap will be beneficial to both parties.

R

Random Walk Hypothesis A hypothesis that in an efficient market, asset prices change randomly (i.e., independently of historical trends), or follow a "random walk."

Real Exchange Rate Measures the degree of deviation from purchasing power parity (PPP) over a period of time, assuming PPP held at the beginning of the period.

Real Options Framework Option valuation techniques applied to capital budgeting decisions. A real option is the right—but not the obligation—to undertake certain business initiatives such as deferring, abandoning, expanding, staging, or contracting a capital investment project.

Registered Bond A bond whose ownership is demonstrated by associating the buyer's name with the bond in the issuer's records.

Reinvoice Centre A central financial subsidiary of a multinational corporation where intrafirm transaction exposure is netted and the residual exposure is managed.

Reporting Currency The currency in which an MNC prepares its consolidated financial statements. Typically, this is the currency in which the parent firm keeps its books.

Representative Office An office of a bank established in a foreign country for liaison between the head office of the bank and the financial institutions (including banks), companies, commissions, and private and public institutions in the foreign country.

Reserve Account In Balance of Payments accounts, the government's (or central bank's) account in which foreign exchange reserves are recorded.

Residential Taxation *See* Worldwide Taxation.

Residual Control Right The right to make discretionary decisions under contingencies not specifically covered by a contract.

Restricted Funds When a multinational enterprise is restricted from moving money (dividends or capital repatriations) out of a foreign country in which it has an investment.

Retail Market In the market for foreign exchange, the market that serves the needs of individuals and industry (approximately 10 percent of transaction volume, with the rest involving banks and nonbank dealers).

Reversing Trade   A trade in either the futures or forward market that will neutralize a position.

S

Sarbanes-Oxley Act   Law passed by the US Congress in 2002 to strengthen corporate governance; requires the creation of a public accounting oversight board and that the CEO and the CFO sign off the company's financial statements.

Secondary Market   The market in which securities are bought and sold among investors; the original issuer is not involved in such trades. The secondary market provides liquidity and valuation of securities.

Security Compliance Loans   Loans extended by Export Development Canada to help Canadian companies finance upgrades required to meet security standards and to thus become C-TPAT-compliant.

Segmented Capital Market   What occurs when capital is unable to flow across borders because of legal, institutional or technical restrictions, thus preventing cross-border equalization of interest rates and/or an international equilibrium in rates of return on risky assets.

Shareholder Rights   The individual and/or collective legal rights of shareholders in respect of the company whose shares they own. Shareholders generally exercise their rights through the corporate board of directors.

Shareholder Wealth Maximization   An objective of corporate management to guide corporate decisions. Managers maximize shareholder wealth by maximizing the market value of the firm.

Sharpe Performance Ratio (SHR)   A risk-adjusted performance measure for a portfolio that expresses excess return (above the risk-free interest rate) relative to standard deviation of returns.

Shelf Registration   Allows bond issuer to pre-register a securities issue that will occur at a later date.

Short Selling   Selling an asset that you do not own with the intention of buying it back ("covering") at a later date at a lower price. The short seller captures the difference in price.

Single-Currency Interest Rate Swap   Typically called an *interest rate swap*. There are many variants; however, all involve swapping interest payments on debt obligations denominated in the same currency.

Smithsonian Agreement   The December 1971 agreement of the G-10 countries to devalue the US dollar against gold and most major currencies in an attempt to save the Bretton Woods system.

Snake   European version of fixed exchange rate system which appeared as the Bretton Woods system declined.

Source Taxation   *See* Territorial Taxation.

Special Drawing Rights (SDRs)   An artificial international reserve created by the International Monetary Fund (IMF), which is a currency basket currently comprising five major currencies.

Specialist   On exchange markets in the United States, one who makes a market by holding an inventory of the security.

Speculator   One whose sole interest is to make money from changes in prices of financial assets, and whose guide is the rule "Buy low, sell high."

Spot Market   The market in which assets are bought or sold for "on-the-spot" delivery.

Spot Rate   Price at which foreign exchange can be sold or purchased for immediate (within two business days) delivery.

Stamping Fee   Fee charged by securities exchanges for transactions stemming from the issue of securities.

Standardized   Said of a contract, such as a foreign exchange futures contract, that specifies a specific amount of foreign exchange in the contract as well as the time of expiry and various other conditions.

Sterilization of Gold   A process of placing gold in an "inactive" account in the nation's treasury so as to prevent the money-expanding effect of an influx of gold. For example, in the early part of the twentieth century, when monetary systems were on the gold standard, gold pouring into a country would increase the money supply and create inflationary pressures.

Straight Fixed-Rate Bond   Bonds with a specified maturity date that have fixed coupon payments.

Strike   The exercise price of an option.

Strike Price   *See* Exercise Price.

Stripped Bond   A synthetic zero-coupon bond created by an investment bank via selling the rights to a specific coupon payment or the bond principal of a coupon bond, typically a US Treasury bond.

Subpart F Income   Income of US-controlled foreign corporations that is subject to immediate US taxation and includes income that is relatively easy to transfer between countries and subject to a low foreign tax levy.

Subsidiary Bank   A foreign subsidiary of a bank that has legal independence from the parent bank. Harris Bank of Chicago is a subsidiary of the Bank of Montreal; the Bank of Montreal's liability to Harris Bank is limited to BMO's capital in Harris Bank (in contrast to the unlimited liability that a parent bank has with respect to a foreign branch bank).

Supplier Credits   International financing arrangements in which a commercial bank provides funds directly to the exporter, who in turn offers medium-term financing support to its foreign buyer, typically a foreign buyer of capital goods.

Swap Bank   A financial institution that facilitates currency and interest rate swaps between counterparties.

Swap Broker   Matches counterparties but does not assume any risk of the swap; however, the swap broker receives a commission for this service.

Swap Dealer   Makes a market in one or the other side of a currency or interest rate swap.

Swap Transaction   The simultaneous spot sale (purchase) of an asset against a forward purchase (sale) of an approximately equal amount of the asset.

Syndicate   A group of Eurobanks banding together to share the risk of lending Eurocredits.

Synergistic Gains   In a corporate merger or acquisition, the gains that result from enhanced efficiency that arise from the merger or acquisition over and above the simple combining of assets.

Systematic Risk   A measure of the relationship between the returns of an asset (a company's shares, for example) and the return on a broad index of shares. Represented by beta in the Capital Asset Pricing Model.

T

Tax Haven A country that has a low corporate income tax rate and low withholding tax rates on passive income.

Tax Neutrality A principle in taxation, holding that taxation should not have a negative effect on the decision-making process of taxpayers.

Tax Treaty A bilateral agreement between nations that governs matters of taxation of mutual concern.

Technical Analysis A method of predicting the future behaviour of asset prices on the basis of their historical patterns.

Temporal Approach In dealing with foreign currency translation, current and noncurrent monetary accounts as well as accounts carried on the books at current value are converted at the current exchange rate. Accounts carried on the books at historical cost are translated at the historical exchange rate.

Territorial Taxation A method of declaring tax jurisdiction in which all income earned within a country by any taxpayer, domestic or foreign, is taxed.

Time Draft A written order instructing the importer or the importer's bank to pay a specific sum of money on a certain date. Used in import-export trade financing.

Tobin Tax A tax on international financial transactions proposed by economist James Tobin to discourage cross-border financial speculation.

Trade Balance The difference between a nation's credits on traded goods (exports) and its debits (imports).

Transaction Cash Balance Funds designated to cover scheduled outflows during a cash budgeting period.

Transaction Exposure The potential change in the value of financial positions due to changes in the exchange rate between the inception of a contract and the settlement of the contract.

Transfer Price The price assigned, for bookkeeping purposes, to the receiving division within a business for the cost of transferring goods or services from another division.

Translation Exposure The effect of an unanticipated change in the exchange rates on the consolidated financial position of a multinational corporation.

Translation Exposure Report A corporate report that indicates the foreign exchange exposure for each foreign currency in which the multinational corporation has exposure.

Triangular Arbitrage The process of trading one currency for a second currency and subsequently trading this for a third currency. This third currency is then traded back to the first currency. The purpose is to earn arbitrage profit via trading from the second currency to the third.

Triffin Paradox Under the gold-exchange standard, the reserve-currency country should run a balance-of-payments deficit, but this tends to decrease confidence in the reserve currency and undermine the system.

U

Uncovered Interest Rate Parity A parity condition that the difference in interest rates between two countries is equal to the expected change in exchange rate between the countries' currencies.

Underwriters Investment banks that raise capital from investors on behalf of corporations and governments that issue securities (both equity and debt). Underwriting services are typically used during a public offering as a way of distributing a newly issued security to investors.

Underwriting Spread The difference between what underwriters pay an issuing company for its securities and what the underwriters receive from selling the securities in the public offering.

Underwriting Syndicate A temporary group of investment banks and broker-dealers who come together to sell new offerings of equity or debt securities to investors. The syndicate is formed and led by the lead underwriter. An underwriter syndicate is usually formed when an issue is too large for a single firm to handle. The syndicate is compensated by the underwriting spread.

Universal Banks International banks that provide such services as consulting in foreign exchange hedging strategies, interest rate and currency swap financing and international cash management.

V

Value-Added Tax (VAT) A tax levied on the value added in the production of goods and services as they move through various stages of production.

Value-Additive Approach The decomposition of the adjusted present value of a project into additive components.

Value-at-Risk (VaR) An analysis that generates a confidence interval on the probability of maximum loss that can occur during a given period of time.

Variation Margin Margin paid on a daily basis on accounts in foreign exchange futures contracts in order to reduce exposure to risky positions. Variation margin addresses exposure to participants' accumulation of adverse price movements.

W

Weighted Average Cost of Capital (WACC) A corporate discount rate on an investment project that takes account of the mix of finance (debt and equity) used to finance the project. WACC equals the cost of debt times its proportional share in the mix of finance plus the cost of equity times its proportional share in the mix of finance.

Wholesale Market In the market for foreign exchange, the core of the market (close to 90 percent of transaction volume) involving banks and nonbank dealers.

Withholding Tax A tax on dividend or interest flows from one country to another. The tax is levied by the country from which the capital payments originate.

World Beta A measure of the sensitivity of an asset or portfolio to the world market movements. This is a measure of the world systematic risk.

World Equity Benchmark Shares (WEBS) Exchange-traded, open-end country funds designed to closely track national stock market indexes; traded on the American Stock Exchange (AMEX).

World Market Portfolio A concept of a global portfolio represented by an index that comprises all shares in the world. A working approximation is an overall index consisting of all major national stock market indexes weighted by their respective shares of total global market capitalization.

World Systematic Risk A measure of the relationship between the returns of an asset (a company's shares, for example) and the return on a global stock index. Represented by beta in the International Capital Asset Pricing Model.

World Trade Organization (WTO) A permanent international organization created by the Uruguay Round to replace GATT; has power to enforce international trade rules.

Worldwide Taxation A method of declaring national tax jurisdiction in which national residents of the country are taxed on their worldwide income, regardless of which country it is earned in.

Writer The person who "sells" an option.

Z

Zero-Coupon Bond A bond that pays no coupon interest and simply returns the face value at maturity.

Zero-Sum Game A game in which one side gains at the expense of the other. An option, such as a call or a put, is a zero-sum game.

INDEX

A

abandonment option, 452
accounts receivable insurance (ARI), 488
active income, 499
ad valorem duty, 469
adjusted present value (APV)
  certainty equivalent method, 451
  formula, 443
  Modigliani-Miller equation, 442
  other uses, 445–446
  risk-adjusted discount method, 451
Adler, M., 214
Advanta Seeds, 3–4
affiliate bank, 138
agency problem
  board of directors, 516–517
  complete contract, 514
  concentrated ownership, 518–520
  debt, 520
  defined, 514
  free cash flows, 515
  hostile takeover, 521
  incentive contracts, 518
  Jensen-Meckling, 513
  managerial entrenchment, 515
  overseas share listings, 520
  residual control right, 514
  solutions, 516–521
  transfer pricing, 515
Aggarwal, R., 343
AIC, 254
AIG, 156
Allayannis, G., 309, 350
all-in cost, 254
Amazon, 507
American depository receipts (ADRs)
  defined, 209
  foreign investment, 295
  history, 209–210
  international diversification, 289, 290, 291
  issuance/cancellation, 211
  performance research, 212–213
American option, 232
American terms, 83
amortizing currency swaps, 262
Angiotech Pharmaceuticals, 172
Anyane-Ntow, K., 493
Apple, 517
APV. *See* adjusted present value (APV)
arbitrage
  arbitrage transactions, 77
  covered interest arbitrage (CIA), 102–105
  defined, 101
  forward vs. futures market, 226
  purchasing power parity (PPP), 117–119
  triangular arbitrage, 88–90

arbitrage transactions, 77
Argentina's Currency Board Collapse, 2002, 152–153
Armed Forces of the Philippines (AFP), 492
Arm's length price, 468, 506
Arrangement on Guidelines for Officially Supported Export Credits, 489–490
Asian Financial Crisis, 1997, 150–152
Asian Flu, 154
ask price, 84, 183
Asprem, M., 214
asset pricing under foreign ownership restrictions, 432–434
asymmetric pay-off, 232
AT&T, 170
automated trading, 196
Ayasse, Manfred, 325

B

backward internalization, 396
balance of payments
  balance-of-payments identity, 60
  Capital and Financial Account, 57, 58
  Current Account, 57–58
  defined, 56
  gold standard, 32
  national income accounting, 72
  Reserve Account, 57, 58
  trade balance, 62
  trends, 67–69
  United States, 65, 66
balance of payments, Canada
  1982–2012, 66
  accounts balances, 58, 59
  Capital and Financial Account, 62–64
  Current Account, 60–62
  external balance and exchange rate, 64–67
  foreign direct investment (FDI), 63
  J-curve effect, 62, 63
  "openness", 56–57
  portfolio investment, 63–64
  trends, 67–69
balance sheet hedge, 369
balance-of-payments identity, 60. *See also* Balance of Payments
Bangkok Toll Road, 400
bank capital adequacy, 139
Bank for International Settlements (BIS), 74, 139, 149–150
Bank Guarantee Program, 489
Bank of Canada, 68, 77, 80, 159
bank-centred governance, 529
banker's acceptance (BA), 482–484
Barrick Gold Corp., 6, 354–355
barter, 491

Basel II, 140–141, 158
Basel III, 158
basis risk, 263
Basle Accord, 139–141
Bauer, 397
Bear Stearns, 156
bearer bond, 168
Beck, T., 529
Becker, S., 215
Beecroft, Nick, 77
Benchmark Government Bonds, 186–187
Benet, B., 344
Berkshire Hathaway, 517
bid price, 84, 183
bid-ask spread, 84–85, 261–262
Big Bang, 8
big figure, 85
Big Mac index, 110–112
bilateral netting system, 460, 463–465
bill of lading (B/L), 482
bimetallism, 30
BlackBerry case, 446–451
blocked funds, 474
BMW, 390
board of directors, 516–517
bond, 165
Bondi, Enrico, 534
bonds with equity warrants, 172
Boon, P., 529
bought deals, 170
Brady bonds, 149
Brau-Beteiligung AG, 178
Brazilian Sneeze, 154
Brazilian Tramways, 400
Breach, A., 529
break forwards, 351
Brean, D. J. S., 501
Bretton Woods System, 33–36
brokers, 184
Buffet, Warren, 517
bulge bracket, 156
Bulldog bonds, 167
buy-back transaction, 492
buyer credits, 484–485

C

Cadbury Code, 531–532
California Public Employees' Retirement System (CALPERS), 517
call markets, 196
call option, 231–232, 233–236
Campbell, Bill, 517
Canada. *See also* Canadian dollar
  balance of payments. *See* balance of payments, Canada
  capital export neutrality, 497–498
  CME Canadian dollar futures, 223
  concentrated ownership, 518